BREWER'S
DICTIONARY
OF LONDON
PHRASE
& FABLE

For my mother and father, Londoners born and bred

BREWER'S DICTIONARY OF LONDON PHRASE & FABLE

Russ Willey

CHAMBERS
An imprint of Chambers Harrap Publishers Ltd
338 Euston Road, London, NW1 3BH

Chambers Harrap Publishers Ltd is an Hachette UK Company

© Russ Willey under licence to Chambers Harrap Publishers Ltd 2009
This book includes material adapted from Brewer's Dictionary of Phrase and Fable © Chambers Harrap
Publishers Ltd 2009 and Chambers London Gazetteer © Chambers Harrap Publishers Ltd 2006, which
remain © Chambers Harrap Publishers Ltd

Chambers® is a registered trademark of Chambers Harrap Publishers Ltd

This edition published by Chambers Harrap Publishers Ltd 2010
Hardback edition published 2009

The moral rights of the author have been asserted.
Database right Chambers Harrap Publishers (makers).

A CIP catalogue record for this book is available from the British Library.

ISBN 978 0550 100313

www.brewersreference.com
www.chambers.co.uk

Cover designed by Nextbigthing
Text designed by Chambers Harrap Publishers Ltd
Typeset in Kepler Std by Chambers Harrap Publishers Ltd
Printed and bound in Finland, by WS Bookwell Ltd.

CONTENTS

INTRODUCTION

B REWER'S *Dictionary of Phrase & Fable* has run through my life like the Thames through London. Terry Pratchett has averred that *Brewer's* was the first book he ever bought for himself, and it was my first literary purchase too: a tattered copy that I found in a second-hand bookshop in Clevedon, Somerset, while on holiday with my family as a child. When I was in my twenties, a friend and I invented a game we imaginatively called *Brewer's*, which consisted of reading out the definitions from randomly selected entries in the dictionary and challenging one's opponents to guess the headword(s). Half points were given if a clue was requested and there was a slightly complex rule about what to do if you came across one or more of the headwords within the entry you were reading out (contact the undersigned for details). We would occasionally inflict the game on erudite friends gathered in pubs on Upper Street, or in the Island Queen on Noel Road. Over the following years I acquired a further four editions of the dictionary, all new, and it was a highlight of my time at BBC World Service to interview Adrian Room on the occasion of the publication of the 15th edition of *Phrase & Fable*, which he had edited.

It was therefore an honour and a privilege, as they say, to be asked to compile this volume, and thus to combine my passion for London (and for writing about it) with my admiration for Dr Brewer's magnificent compendium.

In compiling a London-specific dictionary of phrase and fable, the most difficult task has been to decide which potential entries to omit. A significant proportion of English proverbs, expressions and catchphrases were coined in London, and many of the language's ancient and modern fables were first told in the city. However, for the most part, only those with a particular link to London are mentioned herein.

Like *Brewer's Dictionary of Phrase & Fable* itself, there is much more to this book than sayings and stories. *Brewer's London* brings together the London-related entries from *Brewer's* and *Brewer's Dictionary of Modern Phrase & Fable* (often with added London detail), abridged geographical information from *Brewer's Britain and Ireland* and *Chambers London Gazetteer*, selected entries from *Chambers Dictionary of Literary Characters* and more than a thousand wholly new articles. In common with recent editions of the parent dictionary, nicknames, phrases from popular culture and terms based on place names feature strongly. There are also articles about well-known districts, buildings, institutions and events, and about celebrated Londoners.

Notwithstanding the emphasis on classical material in his *Dictionary of Phrase & Fable*, Dr Brewer could be surprisingly metrocentric at times, despite his own East Anglian background, often writing little articles on subjects that were likely to be of interest only to Londoners. Almost all the especially obscure London entries have been excised from the present edition of the main dictionary, but many have been reinstated in this volume.

With the exceptions of polari and the vocabulary of the Sloane Ranger, the distinctive language of London has evolved almost entirely among the working classes, from the argots of apprentices and costermongers and the foul-mouthed talk that became inextricably associated with Billingsgate market to the most famous of all: cockney rhyming slang. Few slang dictionaries identify the geographic origin of most terms, but it has been necessary for me to attempt such distinctions. However, much cockney slang had its origins in the native languages of East End immigrants or in the criminal underworld, and then gained wider usage in the armed forces or sometimes among circus workers or theatrical artistes, and spread from there into universal parlance, so the same term, perhaps differently spelt, could appear in a multiplicity of specialist dictionaries.

As this book sets out to be far more than a dictionary of cockney slang, it must necessarily be selective in this area, sometimes arbitrarily so. Thus a particularly colourful coinage may be included, even if it is somewhat obscure, while a more mundane term may not. One online dictionary of rhyming slang (and there are many) allows users to vote on whether they consider a listed term to be 'classic', 'modern' or 'rubbish' – a nice taxonomy. I have included a few allegedly 'rubbish' terms in this book where I believe they would have received very different votes a few decades ago. Except for a handful of the most popular terms, 'modern' rhyming slang is likely to be excluded, because of doubts regarding the authenticity of its cockney origins.

I have endeavoured to make *Brewer's London* as up-to-date as it could possibly be, but this has carried some risks. Given the economic turmoil of 2008–9, and especially its effects on the commercial property market, some of the nicknamed structures mentioned in the book may never be built. The Cheesegrater and the Walkie Talkie look particularly vulnerable, although the Shard of Glass seems almost certain to ascend to its proposed remarkable height.

In the great *Brewer's* tradition, there are numerous entries in this volume that I do not expect readers to actively seek out but that I hope they will come across while browsing and gain from them some unexpected enlightenment or enjoyment. Lest you miss them, allow me to recommend a couple of my own favourites: 'little apples grow quickly please' and 'thirteen houses, fourteen cuckolds and never a house between'.

Russ Willey
May 2009

ACKNOWLEDGEMENTS

Chris Barrett, Lucy Gaster and family, Juliet Haydock, Paul Humphreys, Jo Hutchings, Anna James, Christina Kyriakidou, Kate Lewis, Phil Manning, Kevin McGetrick, Jan Newbigin, Nic Oatridge, Michael Quinion and Andreea Rusu. And special thanks to Andra Lupea for accompanying me on some particularly recherché fact-checking expeditions. Also, sincere thanks to my agent Andrew Lownie, editor Rosie Anderson and everyone at Chambers, especially Camilla Rockwood. In addition, the author is deeply indebted to the compilers of *Brewer's Dictionary of Phrase & Fable*, *Brewer's Dictionary of Modern Phrase & Fable* and *Brewer's Britain and Ireland*, without whom this book would scarcely have been possible.

USING THE DICTIONARY

E NTRIES are arranged in alphabetical order on a letter-by-letter basis. Thus, for example, 'Skylon' appears before 'sky (rocket)', and 'Liberties of the Fleet' appears before 'Liberty of London'. As has always been the case with *Brewer's*, words that are linguistically related are normally grouped together, which means that the entries on 'Going Straight' and 'gone to Pimlico' can be found under the main entry 'go', and 'gateway to the south' is discussed under the main entry 'gate'. However, there are exceptions to this rule, usually in cases where the common root of two headwords may not be immediately obvious to all readers, so that 'rockney', for example, is separated from 'rock'. As is the *Brewer's* way, such separations may occasionally seem a little arbitrary, so readers may sometimes have to look in two places before finding the headword they seek.

Unlike those in *Brewer's Dictionary of Phrase & Fable*, headwords in this volume are set with an initial capital letter only where this is the case in normal contextual usage. Thus, for example, 'Albert' takes an upper-case 'A', whereas 'alderman' does not. Where the same word has different meanings according to whether or not the first letter is capitalized, the pair are separately enumerated, even where they may be etymologically related, as with 'Enfield[1]' (the district and borough) and 'enfield[2]' (the mythical beast).

Words and phrases that appear after a main headword are arranged in *two alphabetical sequences*. The first is made up of those terms that commence with the main word or its root; the second consists of entries in which the main word appears later on in the term (and very often these refer the reader to another part of the *Dictionary*). For example, the sequence at 'Fleet' is:

Fleeter-Streeter
Fleet line
Fleet marriages
Fleet Prison
Fleet Street
Fleet Street dove
Bishop of Fleet Street
Demon Barber of Fleet Street
Liberties of the Fleet

Phrases and expressions appear for the most part under their first word: thus, 'like the two kings of Brentford' comes under 'like'. However, headwords that begin with 'to' – or with the definite or indefinite article – appear under the next word, so that the entry for 'to agree like the clocks of London' will be found under 'agree', and 'The Ladykillers' will be found under 'lady'.

The use of brackets in headwords indicates that the parenthesized word or words are optionally articulated. This device is infrequently employed in Brewer's Dictionary of Phrase and Fable but it crops up much more often in Brewer's London because it is used for most cockney rhyming slang terms, in which the second element is usually dropped, as in 'treacle (tart)'.

To help readers find their way around the *Dictionary*, and to draw their attention to articles that are either directly or tangentially related to one another, a large number of cross-references have been included. These are indicated by the use of SMALL CAPITALS.

ABBREVIATIONS

AD	*Anno Domini* (Year of Our Lord) (= CE, Common Era)
b.	born
BC	before Christ (= BCE, Before Common Era)
Bk	book
c.	*circa* (about)
d.	died
fl.	*floruit* (flourished)
Pt	part
r.	reigned / governed
Rev	Reverend

THE DICTIONARY

abandoned habits A punning tag for the riding costumes worn on ROTTEN ROW in HYDE PARK by the ladies of the demi-monde during the late 19th century. These were women on the fringes of respectable society who were often the lovers of wealthy gentlemen. The demi-monde was, as Dr Brewer put it, 'the society only half acknowledged'.

abbey
Abbey Mills A commercial and industrial district by the River LEA, situated south of STRATFORD High Street and taking its name from watermills belonging to Stratford Langthorne Abbey, a Cistercian monastery founded in 1134 by William de Montfichet. The abbey survived until the dissolution of the monasteries in the 1530s and the area is now best known for its pumping station, a much-admired masterpiece of Victorian public works engineering, nicknamed 'the cathedral of sewage'. Designed by Sir Joseph Bazalgette, the pumps draw sewage from the drains of north London and send it down to the filter-beds at BECKTON. Because it is still in use, the magnificent interior, with its ornate cast iron, is not open to the public.
Abbey National plc A leading banking group, now Spanish-owned and branded simply as Abbey. It was born from the merger of the National Building Society and the Abbey Road and St John's Wood Permanent Building Society. Parent company Santander intends to phase out the Abbey name during 2010.
Abbey Road A primarily residential street running north-westwards out of ST JOHN'S WOOD. Abbey Road was created in 1829 from an existing farm track called Abbey Lane as part of the development of St John's Wood. Its name derived from the nearby presence of KILBURN Priory.
Abbey Road Studios EMI recording studios best known for the Beatles' album that took its name from the address. The record's celebrated cover photograph, with no title or text, was taken on the morning of 8 August 1969 and features the four Beatles, including a shoeless Paul McCartney, on a zebra crossing outside the studios. Occasional public events are held at the studios, which are nowadays especially involved with film scores.

Abbey Wood An affordable dormitory district situated south of THAMESMEAD, which it prefigured. It is named after the ancient woodlands that surround the remains of LESNES ABBEY, founded in 1178.

Abbott's Priory One of several slang terms for the KING'S BENCH PRISON.

Abercrombie Plan The shorthand name for a set of proposals for London's reconstruction and development drawn up towards the end of the Second World War by the architect Patrick Abercrombie (1879–1957). The plan was instrumental in the postwar creation of the GREEN BELT, the conversion of some urban bomb sites into new parks and the development of NEW TOWNS. On balance, history has judged the Abercrombie Plan a success and several foreign cities have followed its example in their planning of recreational spaces.

Abershaw, Jerry A callous but colourful highwayman (1773–95) from KINGSTON UPON THAMES. Abershaw led a gang that operated out of the Bald Faced Stag in PUTNEY VALE, preying on travellers as they crossed open terrain such as WIMBLEDON COMMON and HOUNSLOW HEATH. He was finally apprehended at a pub in SOUTHWARK, but not before he had shot two police officers, killing one. Noted for his vulgar humour, Abershaw used the juice of black cherries to paint pictures of his exploits on the white walls of his cell while awaiting trial. At the age of 22 he was convicted of murder at CROYDON assizes and hanged on KENNINGTON COMMON, where he is said to have gone to the gallows with his chest bared and a flower in his mouth. His body was subsequently taken to the spot now called Jerry's Hill, on PUTNEY HEATH, where it was displayed on a gibbet until the birds had pecked the bones clean.

Abney Park A cemetery in STOKE NEWINGTON, named after a former house on the site owned by Sir Thomas Abney (d.1722), one-time LORD MAYOR OF LONDON. Founded in 1840, it succeeded BUNHILL FIELDS as the centre of Nonconformist burials in London. Among those interred here is William Booth (1829–1912), founder of the Salvation Army. Booth would probably have taken a dim view of the cemetery's use in the 1980s and 1990s as a gay trysting-place.

Abraham

Abraham man or **Abram man** One of a number of beggars in the 16th and 17th centuries who pretended to be maniacs and so gain alms. Genuine inmates of BEDLAM who were not dangerous were occasionally allowed out of the 'Abraham ward', where they were kept, and given the opportunity to beg on the streets. The impostors caught on to the custom and capitalized on it, hence to 'sham Abraham'. *See also* TOM O' BEDLAM.

Abrahamstead A facetious nickname given in the 1970s to HAMPSTEAD (blending the Jewish name Abraham with Hampstead) on the basis of its large Jewish population.

Abraham's willing 'Shilling' in early COCKNEY RHYMING SLANG.

absolute

Absolute Beginners A novel (1959) by Colin MacInnes (1914–76). The second book in the author's 'London Trilogy', the story, the climax of which is the NOTTING HILL race riots of 1958, is narrated by a 19-year-old who is one of the happy-go-lucky generation who are the 'absolute beginners' of the title. The other books in the trilogy are *City of Spades* (1957) and *Mr Love and Justice* (1960). A film version of *Absolute Beginners* (1986) was directed as a musical by Julien Temple.

Absolutely Fabulous A BBC TV sitcom that ran from 1992 to 2005 (with a five-year break in the middle), set mainly in the HOLLAND PARK home of Edina Monsoon, a PR agency boss played by the show's creator, Jennifer Saunders (b.1958). Much of the humour revolved around

Edina's vapidly hedonistic behaviour, especially in the company of her best friend Patsy (Joanna Lumley), and the role-reversed disapproval of her daughter Saffy (Julia Sawalha). Familiarly known as *Ab Fab*, the show popularized SLOANE RANGER vocabulary with its talk of lunching at Quags (Quaglino's) and shopping at HARVEY NICKS.

Acacia Avenue A street name evocative of suburban 'middle England' and its middle-class values. As the acacia flourishes in warm climates, the implication is that the street that bears its name is likely to be in the 'soft' South of England rather than the 'tough' Midlands or North. The *Greater London Street Atlas* (2008) lists eight genuine Acacia Avenues, as well as numerous Acacia Closes, Drives, Gardens, Groves and Roads. Perhaps the most archetypal of these is the Acacia Avenue in RUISLIP.

> Sales of newspapers boomed as the *Daily Mirror* went for the mass working class and the *Daily Express* for Acacia Avenue's Walter Mitty dream of success, sophistication and romance.
> *The Times* (21 January 2000)

according to Miles's boy *See* MILES'S BOY.

Ace Café London's most famous extant motorcyclists' rendezvous. Built on the newly opened NORTH CIRCULAR ROAD in the 1930s, the Ace Café is located near the PARK ROYAL junction, on the ALPERTON/STONEBRIDGE border. It achieved legendary status as a bikers' hangout in the 1950s and 1960s, visited by rock 'n' roll luminaries like Gene Vincent and Billy Fury. The café closed in 1969 but reopened in 2001 after a total refit and holds regular meets for motorcycle (and scooter and classic-car) enthusiasts.

Achilles of England A sobriquet of Arthur Wellesley, 1st Duke of Wellington (1769–1852). Richard Westmacott's massive statue of Achilles (1822) is a tribute to the duke, and was cast from canons captured during his military campaigns. The statue surmounts the Wellington Monument, in the corner of HYDE PARK nearest NO.1 LONDON.

Acol The Standard British system of natural bidding in bridge. The system was devised in the mid-1930s by Jack Marx, S.J. Simon, Harrison Gray and Iain Macleod at the Acol Bridge Club, which operated in the road of that name in

HAMPSTEAD. The system has continued to evolve since its inception.

Acton A large suburb situated between EALING and CHISWICK, now mainly residential but formerly of major industrial significance. First recorded in 1181, Acton's name translates roughly as 'oak farm'. Acton has more tube and rail stations to its name than anywhere else in London: one for each point of the compass, plus Acton Central, Acton Town and Acton Main Line. In 1959 Acton County Grammar School pupils Roger Daltrey, John Entwistle and Pete Townsend formed the Detours band, later to become The Who. Adam Faith, the pop superstar turned actor, grew up on a council estate in Acton Vale.

Acton Green The southernmost part of Acton, bounded by Acton Lane and the tracks of the District line and the North London line. The BATTLE OF TURNHAM GREEN ranged across and beyond Acton Green Common in 1642. Acton Green station (now Chiswick Park) opened in 1879, prompting the rapid completion of the suburbanization process. What survives of the green itself lies at the south-eastern corner of the residential locality and covers 15 acres (6 hectares).

Actors' Church St Paul's, COVENT GARDEN, is so called from its long association with the theatrical profession. The church was completed in 1633, to the design of Inigo JONES. Francis Russell, 4th Earl of Bedford, who commissioned the work, wanted nothing more than a cheap 'barn', as a necessary amenity for his residential development project centred on Covent Garden piazza. Jones famously promised to build him 'the handsomest barn in England'. Little of the original fabric of the building has survived but its appearance remains essentially unchanged. The theatres of Covent Garden brought actors to the parish church from early in its existence and it has become the traditional venue for commemorative services. It is also the base for the PEARLY KINGS AND QUEENS. Memorials in the church are dedicated to numerous illustrious figures from the performing arts, including Charlie Chaplin, Noël Coward and Gracie Fields. The ashes of Dames Ellen Terry and Edith Evans rest in St Paul's.

actresses Thomas Coryate says: 'When I went to a theatre [in Venice] I observed certain things that I never saw before; for I saw women act ... I have heard that it hath sometimes been used in London' (Coryate's *Crudities* (1611)). Female parts on the English stage were always taken by boys until the Restoration. The name of the first English actress is unknown. There are many claimants, but whoever she was she played Desdemona in Shakespeare's *Othello* (1604) at a theatre in CLARE MARKET (8 December 1660).

Adam In the slang of the 19th-century London underworld, a henchman or accomplice.

Adam Adamant The hero of *Adam Adamant Lives!*, a BBC fantasy drama series of the late 1960s. He was an Edwardian adventurer who in 1902 had been encased by his enemies in a block of ice, in a state of suspended animation, and left to posterity. He was thawed out in 1966. He resumes his career as a debonair and resourceful crime-fighter, and much play is made of his bewildered attempts to make sense of SWINGING LONDON. His part was played by Gerald Harper (b.1929).

Adam and Eve 'Believe' in COCKNEY RHYMING SLANG, most often heard in the interrogative expression, 'Would you Adam and Eve it?'

> When the Cockney is surprised and incredulous and says, 'Would you Adam and Eve it?' he slyly spreads his unbelief so as to cast a shadow of doubt on the story of creation in the first book of Genesis.
>
> FRANK BUDGEN: *James Joyce and the Making of 'Ulysses'* (1934)

Adam and the Ants A pop group led by MARYLEBONE-born Stuart Goddard (b.1954), who adopted the name Adam Ant. On their formation in 1977 the band adopted a PUNK ROCK style, which later evolved into a new-wave sound accompanied by a dandified onstage look. The singles 'Stand and Deliver', 'Prince Charming' and 'Goody Two Shoes' were No.1 hits.

Adam brothers Four Scottish architects and builders: John (1721–92), Robert (1728–92), James (1732–94) and William (1738–1822), noted particularly for their elegant neoclassical style. In 1758 Robert Adam set up a London practice, in which James soon became a partner. William, and later John, worked primarily as developers and building contractors. All four brothers co-operated on the over-ambitious ADELPHI scheme, but elsewhere in the capital (and beyond) Robert's solo achievements stand pre-eminent. He designed several grand houses, remodelled others and laid out new streets and squares. Frequently he also decorated the properties' interiors and designed their furniture. His works survive at Apsley House (*see* NO.1 LONDON), KENWOOD HOUSE, OSTERLEY PARK and SYON HOUSE, and in PORTLAND PLACE and FITZROY SQUARE.

Adam's ale An old slang term for water.

Addicks The nickname of CHARLTON ATHLETIC FC. The word almost certainly dates from the earliest years of the club's existence when local fishmonger, and later club vice-president, Arthur Bryan used to provide post-victory suppers of haddock and chips for the players. Allegedly, Bryan would serve the less popular cod in the event of a defeat. The team was soon dubbed 'the Haddocks', which subsequently became corrupted to 'the Addicks'. The club has preferred 'Robins' and 'Valiants' at times in the past but now officially endorses the fishy sobriquet.

Addington A North Downs village lying 2½ miles (4 km) east of SOUTH CROYDON. The name relates to a Saxon landowner and the manor was mentioned in Domesday Book (1086), when it was held by Tezelin, the king's cook. It is said that William the Conqueror presented the manor to Tezelin in gratitude for the pottage called DILLIGROUT that the chef prepared as part of the coronation feast in 1066. Addington Palace, a rather plain mansion built in 1780 with grounds landscaped by CAPABILITY BROWN, was a home of the archbishops of Canterbury in the 19th century. Five archbishops are buried at the Church of St Mary the Blessed Virgin and are remembered in many memorials, decorations and windows around the church. *See also* NEW ADDINGTON

> Note here the ghost-story told me at Addington (evening of Thursday 10th) by the Archbishop of Canterbury: the mere, vague, undetailed faint sketch of it – being all he had been told ...
>
> HENRY JAMES, on the inspiration for *The Turn of the Screw* (1898), in his notebook (12 January 1895)

Adelphi Once a fashionable quarter situated south of the STRAND and east of CHARING CROSS. The name, which comes from the Greek word for 'brothers', strictly referred to Adelphi Terrace, but by extension covered the buildings of the neighbouring streets, all developed by the ADAM BROTHERS between 1768 and 1774. A subterranean network of passages and arched vaults, described as 'a very town' by one writer, led down to the THAMES. The Adelphi was popular with leading figures from artistic and literary circles, and residents have included the actor-manager David GARRICK, the poet Thomas Hood and the writers John Galsworthy and J.M. Barrie. Adelphi Terrace was demolished in 1936 but most of the other streets remain intact, notably the premises of the ROYAL SOCIETY OF ARTS in John Adam Street.

Adelphi dramas The Adelphi Theatre in the STRAND opened in 1806, as the 'Sans Pareil', and changed its name to 'Adelphi' in 1819. In the 1840s it was noted for its 'Adelphi dramas', mostly written by J.B. Buckstone, the best of which were *The Green Bushes* (1845) and *The Flowers of the Forest* (1847).

Adelphi melodramas At the end of the 19th century the Adelphi Theatre became famous for a series of populist plays produced by G.R. Sims, Henry Pettit and Sydney Grundy, e.g. *The Bells of Hazlemere* (1887).

Admiralty The colloquial name for 26 WHITEHALL, built in the mid-1720s on the site of Wallingford House, the former residence of the dukes of Buckingham. It is also known both as the Ripley Building, after its architect Thomas Ripley (*c.*1682–1758), and the Old Admiralty. The building was originally planned as separate apartments for the lords of the Admiralty. It was later converted into offices of the Navy Board and now serves as Cabinet Office accommodation.

Admiralty Arch The imposing structure at the terminal point of the MALL, leading into TRAFALGAR SQUARE and adjoining the Admiralty, in WHITEHALL. It was erected in 1910 as a memorial to Queen Victoria and consists of three identical, deep arches, each with wrought-iron gates, those in the central arch being opened only on ceremonial occasions. Offices in the south wing were occupied by the Ministry of Defence until 1994, while the north wing has two flats, one originally for the use of the First Lord of the Admiralty, the other for the First Sea Lord. *See also the* LONDON NOSE.

Admiralty buildings The collective name for ADMIRALTY ARCH, 26 Whitehall (*see the*

ADMIRALTY), the ADMIRALTY CITADEL and other government offices linked to them.

Admiralty Citadel A windowless and charmless fortress located near the north-west corner of HORSE GUARDS PARADE. It was built in the early part of the Second World War as a bomb-proof naval operations centre. Ivy has been allowed to embrace the citadel to help conceal its ugliness.

> The Admiralty on their own constructed the vast monstrosity which weighs upon the Horse Guards Parade, and the demolition of whose twenty-foot-thick steel and concrete walls will be a problem for future generations when we reach a safer world.
> WINSTON CHURCHILL: *The Second World War*, Volume 2 (1949)

Admiralty could not be more arch, the A catchphrase that was in infrequent use from the mid-20th century, said of something that was mischievous or saucy, and playing on the name of ADMIRALTY ARCH.

Admiralty Screen A centrally arched Doric barrier built across the front of the Admiralty courtyard by Robert ADAM in 1759–61. The screen was adapted in the late 1820s at the request of the Duke of Clarence, when he was Lord High Admiral, to provide easier access for his carriage.

Aesop of England John Gay (1685–1732), poet and playwright. His three-part poem *Trivia, or the Art of Walking the Streets of London* (1716) is filled with witty observations of the city's colourful residents and filthy streets, as well as practical advice for pedestrians. *See also the* BEGGAR'S OPERA.

> Should the big last extend the shoe too wide,
> Each stone will wrench the unwary step aside;
> The sudden turn may stretch the swelling vein,
> The cracking joint unhinge, or ankle sprain;
> And when too short the modish shoes are worn,
> You'll judge the seasons by your shooting corn.
> *Trivia*, I

after

afternoon tea *See* TEA.

after the Lord Mayor's Show An expression nowadays suggesting a sense of anticlimax; formerly a more extreme descent, as from the sublime to the ridiculous. It is a shortening of a COCKNEY catchphrase from the late 19th century: 'after the LORD MAYOR'S SHOW comes the muck-cart.' A more polite version had 'the dust-cart'; a less polite one, 'the shit-cart'. The phrase is much used by sports writers and commentators when a team plays in a cup final one week and against mundane opposition the next.

> Perhaps returning to their domestic leagues after playing on the world's biggest stage has an element of after the Lord Mayor's Show about it and Real Madrid's galaxy of Dream Team stars have certainly suffered a few nightmares.
> *The Daily Telegraph* (31 October 2002)

Agapemone (Greek *agapē*, 'love', and *monē*, 'dwelling') A fanatical sect of men and women, followers of the Rev Henry James Prince (1811–99), curate of Charlynch, Somerset, and his rector Samuel Starky (hence their alternative name of Starkyites). They founded a communal 'abode of love' at Spaxton, Somerset, in 1849, but their licentious conduct led to trouble with authority. In the early 1890s the movement revived in CLAPTON as the Children of the Resurrection under the Rev John Hugh Smyth-Pigott, who proclaimed himself to be Christ. He was unfrocked in 1909.

Agar Town The name of a canalside locality formerly situated east of CAMDEN TOWN, remembered now only in Agar Grove. From 1789 this was the private estate of William Agar of Elm Lodge. In the 1810s Agar fought a desperate battle to prevent the cutting of the REGENT'S CANAL through his property, although his underlying motive may simply have been to maximize the compensation he received. Agar died in 1838 and his widow soon began to grant building leases on part of the estate, while retaining Elm Lodge. Depictions of Agar Town as the worst kind of filthy slum may have been exaggerated but the mainly Irish residents were undeniably poor and conditions were insalubrious. In the mid-1860s the 'town' disappeared beneath the tracks and goods yards that accompanied the opening of the Midland Railway's ST PANCRAS STATION. The displaced inhabitants mostly moved to neighbouring districts like KENTISH TOWN.

Agas map The informal name of *Civitas Londinum*, a panoramic map of the cities of London and WESTMINSTER and part of SOUTHWARK, drawn *c*.1561–71 by an unknown cartographer, formerly thought to be Ralph Agas. Its three-dimensional detail, showing individual houses and representational figures, provides an insight into life in Tudor London. No original copies survive but a facsimile is held in the GUILDHALL library.

agree like the clocks of London, to To disagree.

> It was probably some sarcastic Italian, and, perhaps, horologer, who, to describe the disagreement of persons, proverbed our nation – 'They agree like the clocks of London!'
>
> ISAAC D'ISRAELI: *Curiosities of Literature* (1824)

Agricultural Hall An exhibition centre opened on Liverpool Road, ISLINGTON, in 1862, and renamed the Royal Agricultural Hall in 1884. Built as a new home for the annual SMITHFIELD show, the hall also hosted many of London's other most significant public events, including circuses, grand balls, military tournaments and the inaugural CRUFTS. It was converted into the Business Design Centre in 1986.

Ague Town A nickname for AGAR TOWN, from its reputation for poverty, squalor and ill-health.

> Hordes of dispossessed, ragged Irishmen and farmworkers from decaying villages, living like beasts in wagons on wheels in Ague Town, which Dickens described as 'an English Connemara', were digging the road beds and laying the shining rails made in Bessemer's revolutionary blast furnaces into 'the milk-teeth of the suburb'.
>
> G.W. SHERMAN: *The Pessimism of Thomas Hardy: A Social Study* (1976)

ain't you the one though! A COCKNEY catchphrase of late 19th-century origin, usually employed in lighthearted mockery of one who is perceived to be putting on airs.

airs and graces 'Braces' in COCKNEY RHYMING SLANG, in the sense of what Americans call suspenders. Also 'faces'.

ait or **eyot** A small island, especially one in the THAMES. The two spellings of the word are pronounced identically, as in 'eight'. PLATT'S EYOT, RAVEN'S AIT and CHISWICK EYOT are among those in London's stretch of the river.

Akerman's Hotel One of the dozens of nick-names for NEWGATE PRISON, from the name of a governor in the 1880s.

alacompain 'Rain' in early COCKNEY RHYMING SLANG, long since forgotten. It was presumably a corruption of the French *à la campagne*, 'in the countryside'.

Alan Whickers 'Knickers' (women's underwear) in modern rhyming slang, sometimes shortened to 'Alans', from the broadcaster Alan Whicker (b.1925).

> All right, all right, keep your Alans on!
>
> GUY RITCHIE (writer and director): *Lock, Stock and Two Smoking Barrels* (1998)

An 'Alan Whicker' can also mean a 'nicker': one pound sterling.

> Gawdelpus. An Alan Whicker! Yer goin' off yer head. That's too dear.
>
> JOHN CHAFFEE: *Thinking Critically* (1991)

Albany A block of exclusive flats adjoining Burlington House, PICCADILLY. It was originally built between 1770 and 1774 as a town residence for Lord Melbourne, and named Melbourne House. Shortly afterwards Melbourne exchanged residences with Frederick, Duke of York and Albany, and in 1802 the house was sold to a property speculator, who had it enlarged and converted into bachelor apartments. It attracted distinguished and wealthy residents, who over the centuries have included Lord Palmerston, Lord Byron, William Gladstone, Lord Macaulay (who wrote his *History of England* (1849, 1855) here), Aldous Huxley, Graham Greene, Terence Stamp, Alan Clark and (after the men-only restriction was lifted) Dame Edith Evans. It once enjoyed a social cachet akin to an Edwardian gentlemen's club (E.W. Hornung housed his burglarious toff Raffles here), and it used to be a touchstone of 'U-ness' (upper-class speech) to call it 'Albany' rather than 'the Albany'.

> He enjoyed the intense silence that brooded outside the heavily curtained windows. Here in Albany, Michael was immeasurably aware of the life of London that was surging such a little distance away; but in this modish cloister he felt that the life he was aware of could never be dated, as if indeed he were to emerge into Piccadilly and behold suddenly crinolines and powdered wigs they would not greatly surprise him.
>
> COMPTON MACKENZIE: *Sinister Street* (1913–14)

Albert In a London context, the name is usually a reference to Prince Albert of Saxe-Coburg-Gotha (1819–61), Prince Consort to Queen Victoria.

Albert Bridge One of three THAMES road bridges connecting CHELSEA with BATTERSEA, completed in 1873. Imperfections in the original design have since necessitated two major strengthening projects and a vehicular weight limit. A distinctive notice, also a consequence of the structural vulnerabilities, decrees that 'all troops must break step when marching over this bridge'. The Albert Bridge looks most picturesque at night, when it is illuminated by thousands of light bulbs strung along its suspension cables.

Albert Embankment *See the* EMBANKMENT.

Albert Hall An oval concert hall surmounted by a glass and iron dome, located on KENSINGTON GORE, facing the south side of KENSINGTON GARDENS. The Royal Albert Hall of Arts and Sciences was opened by Queen Victoria in 1871. The hall is best known as the venue for the main events of the PROMS.

Multiples of the auditorium's cubic capacity – which is 3.06 million cubic feet (86,649m³) – are frequently used as media shorthand to convey an impression of volumetric magnitude, as in statements such as: 'Enough garden waste to fill the Albert Hall more than 70 times over is buried in British landfill sites every year.' The measure was immortalized in the Beatles' song 'A Day in the Life' (1967):

Four thousand holes in Blackburn, Lancashire
And though the holes were rather small
They had to count them all
Now they know how many holes it takes to fill
the Albert Hall.

Albert Memorial An ornate and complex structure situated on the southern side of KENSINGTON GARDENS. The monument was designed by Sir George Gilbert Scott (1811–78), with a central gilded statue of Prince Albert by J.H. Foley and Thomas Brock. The prince is sheltered by a towering Gothic canopy and surrounded by statuary commemorating his good works and the glories of civilization, especially those of the British Empire. Construction took almost ten years to complete, as did a restoration project in the 1990s.

Presently the statue of the good, kind, well-meaning gentleman will be placed upon the monumental pedestal – and then what a satire

upon human glory it will be to see ... that long marble array of the world's demi-gods around the base, bracing their shoulders to the genial work and supporting their brother in his high seat. I still feel some lingering discomfort that this princely structure was not built for Shakespeare – but after all, maybe he does not need it as much as the other.

MARK TWAIN: *English Journals* (1872)

Albertopolis An informal name given in the 1850s to the complex of museums, colleges, schools, concert halls and premises for learned societies in SOUTH KENSINGTON that arose in the later part of the 19th century at the behest of Prince Albert, the Prince Consort (1819–61) – who alas did not live to see the realization of his grand vision. The term seems to have lain fallow for many decades, but was used again in the 1990s in the context of an unsuccessful proposal to extend the boundaries of the area.

Meanwhile I regretfully concluded ... that the Brompton of the past was rapidly disappearing, and Albertopolis would flourish in its place. Already a portion of its demesne has been annexed under the title of South Kensington.

GEORGE AUGUSTUS SALA: *Travels in the County of Middlesex* (1861)

Albert Square The centre of activity of BBC Television's EASTENDERS, and a media synonym for the show itself. The square's late 19th-century architecture is based on that of Fassett Square, on the HACKNEY/DALSTON border.

Albert the Good A sobriquet of Prince Albert.

Beyond all titles, and a household name,
Hereafter, thro' all times, Albert the Good.

ALFRED, LORD TENNYSON: *Dedication to Idylls of the King* (1862)

Albert the Great The nickname, given by analogy with Albert the Good, of Albert Chevalier (1861–1923), 'the COSTER's Laureate' and a favourite of the MUSIC HALLS. Among the best known of his COCKNEY songs are 'Knock'd 'em in the Old Kent Road' and 'My Old Dutch' (*see under* DUCHESS).

Royal Albert Dock *See the* ROYAL DOCKS.

alderman In Anglo-Saxon times a nobleman of the highest rank; in the present-day CITY of London, a senior elected officer of the Court of Common Council. The first mention of an alderman of London by name appears in 1111.

Each of the City's 25 wards elects one alderman, nowadays for a term of six years. An alderman automatically becomes a justice of the peace for the City. *See also the* CORPORATION OF LONDON.

Aldermanic Court A meeting of CITY of London aldermen, summoned and presided over by the LORD MAYOR, held on about nine Tuesdays a year in the Aldermen's Court Room in the GUILDHALL.

alderman in chains Formerly a slang term for a roast turkey garnished with sausages. CITY aldermen wore gold chains on ceremonial occasions.

Alderman Lushington is concerned One of several old catchphrases that invoked this city official's name to imply that someone was drunk. Others included 'Lushington is his master' and 'he has been voting for the alderman'. There was a real Alderman Lushington in the 1790s (a merchant tailor, not a brewer) and also a well-known drinking club called the CITY OF LUSHINGTON, which was run by a 'lord mayor' and four 'aldermen'. At around the same time 'lush' became a slang term for alcoholic drink (and later for a drunkard). What is uncertain is which of these came first and whether there was a direct connection between all of them.

> *Beefing*, however, they were, lustily; when, at the turning of the road, I was brought down by a *roller* with a stroke of his long *chiv* over my head. I was bad enough at that time (principally through Alderman Lushington though, I believe.)
>
> ANON: 'The Life, Opinions and Pensile Adventures of John Ketch', *The Metropolitan Magazine*, Volume 14 (1835)

Alderman's Hill A road in PALMERS GREEN. Its name commemorates the CITY alderman Sir William Curtis (*see the* THREE 'R'S), who acquired the local Cullands Grove estate at the end of the 18th century.

Aldersgate One of only two primarily residential wards in the CITY of London (because it includes much of the BARBICAN) and also a former name of Barbican tube station. An aperture in the Roman defences that surrounded the City was added here sometime after the construction of the wall itself, perhaps in the early 4th century. The Aldersgate name, relating to a man named Ealdrēd, probably dates from the late Saxon period. When James I came from Scotland to London in 1603, he entered the City by this gate

and statues of him were erected there, seated on horseback outside the gate and on his throne on the inner side. Aldersgate was demolished in 1761; Thomas More House in the Barbican stands near its site.

Aldersgate Street The street now constitutes the very southernmost end of the A1 and extends just south of the MUSEUM OF LONDON rotunda to meet ST MARTIN'S LE GRAND. By the 1650s the wide road was lined with impressive houses and was described by a contemporary writer as 'resembling an Italian street more than any other in London'. The poet John MILTON resided for much of his adult life in houses on Aldersgate Street and neighbouring streets. There has been a public house on the site of the Lord Raglan, at 61 Aldersgate Street, since SHAKESPEARE's day – indeed, the Bard is said to have been among its regulars. It was rebuilt in the mid-19th century, and renamed then after the Crimean War commander FitzRoy Somerset, first Baron Raglan (1788–1855).

The Man from Aldersgate *See under* MAN.

Aldgate Often regarded as the point where the EAST END meets the CITY of London, Aldgate is now a street running east of LEADENHALL Street, which becomes Aldgate High Street at the junction with the MINORIES. One of the four original entrances to the City, Aldgate was the easternmost gate in the Roman wall, rebuilt in 1606 and then removed in the 1760s to ease traffic congestion. Though it is usually believed to mean 'old gate', the name might be a corruption of 'ale gate', as refreshments were provided here for thirsty travellers. In 1107 the Prior of Aldgate founded the monastery of Holy Trinity just outside the gate. It acquired great wealth and significance but was given by Henry VIII to Sir Thomas Audley at the dissolution of the monasteries (1536–9) and soon dismantled. In 1710 Sir John Cass founded a school here for 90 poor children. Like neighbouring SPITALFIELDS, Aldgate benefited from the economic vitality brought by successive waves of immigrants, notably Huguenots, Irish and Jews, but following destruction by Second World War bombs and 1960s planners, it now consists principally of uninspiring commercial premises encircled by a traffic-clogged one-way system.

The medieval English poet Geoffrey Chaucer resided in apartments above the gate from 1374 to 1386, during which time he wrote several works, including *Troilus and Criseyde*. The poet Edmund Spenser was born locally in 1552 and the philosopher Jeremy Bentham was baptized at St Botolph's Church in 1748.

> Black Bull of Aldgate, may thy horns rot from thy sockets!
> For, jingling threepence, porter's pay, in hungry pockets,
> And thirty times at least beneath thy doorway stepping
> I've waited for this lousy coach that runs to Epping.
>
> ALFRED, LORD TENNYSON: 'Black Bull of Aldgate' (*c*.1837)

Aldgate pump A stone fountain at the junction of FENCHURCH STREET and LEADENHALL STREET. St Michael's well is recorded on the site in King John's time, and a pump is known to have been here at the end of the 16th century. The present structure, with a brass dog's-head spout, dates from 1871. It no longer dispenses water. In the 18th and 19th centuries, the phrase 'a draught on the pump at Aldgate' denoted a forged banknote or fraudulent bill of exchange.

Aldwych A grand crescent breaking away from the STRAND and rejoining it a few hundred yards further on, created by the cutting of Kingsway in 1905 and named Aldwych by the LONDON COUNTY COUNCIL. Although the street is relatively new, it commemorates a site of exceptional importance during the Dark Ages. When the Saxons colonized the London area in the 5th century, after the Romans had departed, they established a riverside market town beyond the CITY walls, calling it Lundenwic. The THAMES was much wider then, and the Strand marks its shoreline. In 886 Alfred the Great captured London from the marauding Danes, refortified the city and moved the trading activities of Lundenwic within it. A century or more later, a Danish community resettled the vicinity of the old market (which is what 'Aldwych' means). Modern Aldwych contains Australia House, India House and Bush House, presently home to the BBC World Service.

Aldwych farces A series of farces by the English playwright Ben Travers (1886–1980) presented at the Aldwych Theatre from the mid-1920s to the early 1930s: *A Cuckoo in the Nest* (1925), *Rookery Nook* (1926), *Plunder* (1928), *A Cup of Kindness* (1929), *A Night Like This* (1931), *Dirty Work* (1932),

and *A Bit of a Test* (1933). They combined absurdly improbable situations, eccentric characters and broad humour with social satire. Most were filmed.

ale silver A rent or tribute formerly paid yearly to the LORD MAYOR OF LONDON by those who sold ale within the CITY.

Alexandra In a London context, the name is usually a reference to Alexandra of Denmark (1844–1925), wife of Edward, Prince of Wales, from 1863 and Queen Consort from 1902 to 1910.

Alexandra Club A women's club established in 1884 in Grosvenor Street, MAYFAIR. Membership was restricted to those eligible to attend 'Her Majesty's Drawing Rooms', which may have been a device for barring divorcées. Unlike the half-dozen other women's clubs of late Victorian London, the Alexandra resolutely excluded men, even as visitors. Short-term residential accommodation was available for members and their accompanying maids. The Alexandra soon gained about 900 members, drawn mostly from the upper echelons of society, but also including professional, literary and theatrical women. It functioned until around 1940.

Alexandra Palace North London's answer to the CRYSTAL PALACE crowns the 313-ft (95m) summit of MUSWELL HILL, west of WOOD GREEN. At the end of the 1850s the Great Northern Railway Company opened Wood Green (now Alexandra Palace) station and the Great Northern Palace Company acquired Tottenham Wood Farm. The latter company opened a pleasure garden and then reused materials from the international exhibition held at SOUTH KENSINGTON in 1862 to build the first Alexandra Palace. Nicknamed 'Ally Pally', the exhibition hall burned down within days of its inauguration in 1873. A new palace opened two years later, with more emphasis on cultural and educational facilities than some of the showier exhibition halls built elsewhere at that time. The BBC transmitted the world's first public television broadcasts from a studio here in 1936. The GREATER LONDON COUNCIL managed the site from 1966 and passed control to the London Borough of HARINGEY in 1980, whereupon half the palace was again ruined by fire. Part of it was restored in 1990 and serves as a minor exhibition and events centre but the rest is still awaiting renovation.

Alexandra Park A hillside public park in the grounds of Alexandra Palace and the late Victorian and Edwardian residential locality to its north. Over the course of its existence the park has had a swimming pool, athletics ground, horse-racing track and dancing and banqueting facilities at Blandford Hall. The hall burned down in 1971 and birch trees now dominate its site.

Alf Garnett *See* GARNETT, ALF.

Alfie A film (1966) based on a play by Bill Naughton (1910–92). Starring Michael Caine as the cheeky COCKNEY misogynist, Alfie, who is permanently on the look-out for more 'birds' to add to his collection of sexual conquests, the film, with its frank confessions to camera, was considered a daring exploration of sexual morals in SWINGING LONDON, and for a time the very title was synonymous with the so-called 'permissive society'. A sequel, *Alfie Darling* (1975), starring Alan Price in the lead role, failed to match the provocative exuberance of its predecessor. Even less notable was the 2004 remake of *Alfie*, starring Jude Law.

Alhambra (Arabic *al-hamrā*, 'the red [house]') A formerly famous theatre and music hall in LEICESTER SQUARE, built in Moorish style. *See also the* PANOPTICON (2).

all

all afloat 'Coat' in early COCKNEY RHYMING SLANG.

all (a) holiday at Peckham A slang expression, now disused – and thankfully so because it seems to have had conflicting meanings. Dr Brewer defined it as 'no appetite, not peckish; a pun on the word peck, as going to Bedfordshire is a pun on the word bed'. His source may have been Jon Bee's *Dictionary of the Turf* (1823). Another definition proposed that it meant to have nothing to eat, despite having an appetite. Others, however, used the phrase to mean 'all over, the business is finished', or to refer to laying one's work or obligations aside for a while. The phrase is said to have been inspired by the popular fairs held at PECKHAM in the 18th and early 19th centuries.

> One might make a long list of Doctors Pedagogic, including poor Oliver Goldsmith, who used to wince and redden with shame and anger when the cant phrase, 'It's all a holiday at Peckham', saluted his ears.
>
> JOHN CORDY JEAFFRESON: *A Book about Doctors* (1860)

All England Lawn Tennis and Croquet Club *See* WIMBLEDON.

all Lombard Street to a China orange Unfeasibly short odds, the wealth of LOMBARD STREET being infinite compared to the value of a China orange (an ordinary sweet orange – they originally came from China). In other words, the thing referred to is virtually certain. The expression appears to date from the early 19th century. Variations on the same theme have included 'all Lombard Street to a Brummagem [Birmingham] sixpence' and 'all Lombard Street to an eggshell'. *See also* LONDON TO A BRICK.

> If you didn't already know … then it's most of Lombard Street to a China Orange you'd never find out.
>
> *The Times* (30 November 1974)

All London Knowledge *See the* KNOWLEDGE.

all right, treacle? *See* TREACLE (TART).

all round St Paul's, not forgetting the trunkmaker's daughter A booksellers' catchphrase, used in the late 18th and early 19th centuries when referring to unsaleable books. The ST PAUL'S area was at that time well known for its bookshops and the 'trunkmaker' was a nickname for the repository of unwanted literature.

Alley, the An old name for Change Alley in the CITY of London, where dealings in the public funds used to take place. Following their expulsion from the ROYAL EXCHANGE in 1698, London's stock dealers began trading in the Alley's many coffee houses, especially JONATHAN'S. The Fire of CORNHILL began here in March 1748, destroying most of the coffee houses; they were subsequently rebuilt.

Alleyn, Edward An Elizabethan and Jacobean actor, entrepreneur and philanthropist (1566–1626). Born in BISHOPSGATE, where his father was a publican, he was a contemporary of SHAKESPEARE and acted in many of Christopher Marlowe's plays. Thomas Nashe compared him with Roscius, the Roman slave who gained his freedom and a great fortune by virtue of his talent on the stage. Alleyn's success enabled him to build a small property empire on BANKSIDE, where he owned two theatres and assorted bear pits, brothels and public houses. He founded DULWICH COLLEGE (1619) and deposited in its library documents relating to his career (including the *Diary* of his business partner Philip Henslowe, whose stepdaughter he married), which give a unique insight into the financial aspects of Elizabethan theatre. On his death he was buried in the college chapel.

Ally Pally The nickname of ALEXANDRA PALACE, originally in its role as the early headquarters of BBC Television. The first transmission was on 26 August 1936 as *Here's Looking at You*, a variety show introduced by Leslie Mitchell, and the nickname followed soon after.

Almack's A gambling club established in PALL MALL in 1762 by William Almack, with the support of regular young gamesters from WHITE'S. In 1764 the club split into two others which became known as BOODLE'S and BROOKS'S. His next venture, also called Almack's, was a suite of assembly rooms in KING STREET, ST JAMES'S, opened in 1765. Success came early and weekly subscription balls, presided over by ladies of the highest rank, were held there during the LONDON SEASON for more than 75 years. To be admitted was regarded as being almost as great a distinction as being presented at court. On Almack's death in 1781 the establishment passed to his niece, Mrs Willis. In 1893 part of the premises was taken over by auctioneers and the rest let as shops. The building was bombed in the Second World War, and in 1949–50 a block of offices known as Almack House was built on the same site.

> From 1762 until his death in 1781 the central figure in the history of London clubs was William Almack, whose origin and career have been inaccurately related by many writers ... [and] handsomely embellished by the statement that Almack's real name was 'M'Caul', and that he had changed it because he found that in England a Scots name prejudiced his business. Almack was in fact almost certainly of Yorkshire origin, and the theory that this was an assumed name is undoubtedly false.
>
> F.H.W. SHEPPARD (general editor): *Survey of London*, Volume 29 (1960)

Almeida

Almeida Street A short street off UPPER STREET, named in commemoration of the Battle of

Almeida (1811) in the Peninsular War. The reading rooms and lecture hall of the Islington Literary and Scientific Institute were built here in 1837 and achieved early fame as the London venue where an Egyptian mummy was first 'unrolled' and publicly displayed. The building later served as a MUSIC HALL, a SALVATION ARMY hostel and a factory for carnival novelties; in 1980 it became home to the ALMEIDA THEATRE.

Almeida Theatre The 325-seat theatre was the brainchild of Pierre Audi (b.1957), who organized a festival of contemporary music here. Since 1990, when the actors Ian McDiarmid and Jonathan Kent took over its artistic direction, followed by Michael Attenborough in 2002, the theatre has attracted leading British and overseas actors, such as Alan Bates, Juliette Binoche, Ralph Fiennes, Ian Holm, Glenda Jackson, Diana Rigg and Kevin Spacey.

almond rocks 'Socks' in COCKNEY RHYMING SLANG; usually rendered as 'almonds'. Almond rocks are a chocolate and nut confection of Indian origin.

Alperton The southernmost part of WEMBLEY. First recorded in 1199, the name may relate to a Saxon landowner or may have meant 'apple farm'. Alperton's transformation from a country village began with the arrival of the GRAND JUNCTION CANAL in 1801. By the latter part of the 19th century Alperton had become the most industrialized village in the Wembley area and 'the smelliest village in Middlesex'. The newly created Wembley urban district council helped to clean up the more noxious factories from 1894. The district was almost fully built up by 1933 but underwent a decline after the Second World War, with a fall in population. From the 1970s, East African Asians, many of Gujarati origin, began to move to Alperton. The new community brought a revival to the shopping parade on Ealing Road, selling a variety of specialist products – especially jewellery, sometimes crafted at home. The locality has been called an 'Asian HATTON GARDEN'.

Alsatia In the 17th and 18th centuries an area between FLEET STREET and the THAMES that was a notorious haunt of thieves, debtors, vagabonds and prostitutes. The name came from Latin for 'Alsace', because that much-disputed territory between France and Germany was famous for harbouring the disaffected. Alsatia encompassed the precincts of the former WHITEFRIARS Monastery, which had a right to grant sanctuary to fugitives until the dissolution of the monasteries (1536–9). Thereafter the area's low-life continued to invoke the privilege and in 1580 Elizabeth I declared Alsatia to be exempt from the jurisdiction of the CITY of London, making it virtually a no-go area for the civil authorities. Its powers of sanctuary were rescinded in 1697 but Alsatia's low character persisted for many decades afterwards. The district is described in Thomas Shadwell's *The* SQUIRE OF ALSATIA (1688), from which Sir Walter Scott borrowed freely when describing this precinct in *The Fortunes of Nigel* (1822), as did Leigh Hunt in *The Town* (1848).

Althea (Greek *althainein*, 'to heal') The 'divine Althea' of Richard Lovelace (1618–58) was Lucy Sacheverell, also called Lucasta by the poet.

> When love with unconfinèd wings
> Hovers within my gates;
> And my divine Althea brings
> To whisper at my grates:
> When I lie tangled in her hair,
> And fettered to her eye;
> The gods, that wanton in the air
> Know no such liberty.
>
> 'To Althea, from Prison' (1649)

Lovelace was imprisoned in the Gatehouse, WESTMINSTER, by the Long Parliament for his Royalist activities. Hence the 'grates' (railings) referred to. Lovelace Green in WELL HALL is named after the poet, who was born in nearby WOOLWICH.

Alton Estate An extensive and historically significant municipal estate situated on ROEHAMPTON's border with RICHMOND PARK. Much of the land hereabouts constituted the grounds of Parkstead, a Palladian villa built in the 1760s for Lord Bessborough and later renamed Manresa House. Parts of its grounds were developed from around 1850 as a high-class suburban estate known as Coombe Park or Roehampton Park. Alton Lodge was an early 19th-century villa on the Kingston Road, occupied by Dr Thomas Hake from around 1854 until 1872. Dr Hake was a cousin of General GORDON of Khartoum and a friend of Dante Gabriel Rossetti. The poet and painter stayed at Alton Lodge in 1872 while recovering from a mental collapse.

In 1951 the architect's department at the LONDON COUNTY COUNCIL selected this area as the site for one of the largest and most radical housing developments ever undertaken in London. The best villas and some of the landscaping were preserved but 130 acres (53 hectares) were otherwise totally cleared to make way for the project. The Scandinavian-inspired Alton East was completed in 1955 and it was followed four years later by the much larger Alton West, which was influenced by the high-rise creations of the Swiss-French architect Le Corbusier. Both stages include a mix of tower blocks, maisonettes and terraced houses, permitting a combination of high population density with extensive open spaces.

always in trouble, like a Drury Lane whore An unsympathetic expression dating from the late 19th century, said of or to someone who wallows in self-pity. It derives from the alleged tendency of these ladies to hyperbolize their woes.

Amen Corner A site at the western end of PATERNOSTER ROW in the CITY, where the clergy of ST PAUL'S Cathedral finished the Paternoster (the Lord's Prayer) on Corpus Christi Day as they went in procession to the cathedral. They began the prayer in Paternoster Row and continued it to the end of the street, and they said Amen at the corner of the Row. On turning down AVE MARIA LANE they began chanting the Hail Mary, then, crossing LUDGATE they entered CREED LANE chanting the Credo. Amen Corner was destroyed in an air raid on 28 December 1940.

American
American Embassy *See* GROSVENOR SQUARE; NINE ELMS CORRIDOR.
American Werewolf in London, An A comic horror film in which an American student murderously stalks the streets of London after being bitten by a Yorkshire werewolf. The film won an Oscar for its special effects make-up and was notable for a scene of havoc and carnage in PICCADILLY CIRCUS.

> Puts you in mind of the days of the old demon barber of Fleet Street, don't it? ... Haven't you heard? Last night ... six of 'em. All in different parts of the city, all mutilated.
>
> JOHN LANDIS (writer and director): *An American Werewolf in London* (1981)

American workhouse A name formerly applied by taxi drivers to the PARK LANE Hotel, because of its popularity with affluent Americans, and hence in general a hotel offering luxurious accommodation.

Amhurst Four *See the* STOKE NEWINGTON EIGHT.

Anacreontic Society A 'wild and jovial' music club established in 1766 at the London COFFEE HOUSE on LUDGATE HILL and named in honour of the Greek lyric poet Anacreon (570–488 BC), who wrote chiefly in praise of love and wine. Originally a select group of bankers and merchants, the society organized concerts that drew hundreds of new members and in 1773 its meetings moved to the great ballroom of the Crown and Anchor tavern in the STRAND. Women were later admitted to the main performances but proved slow to leave at the point in the evening when members liked to begin singing 'improper songs and other vicious compositions'. The ramifications of this issue were a major factor in the society's dissolution in 1794.

'The Anacreontic Song', written by two senior members, Ralph Tomlinson and John Stafford Smith, was rousingly performed at all meetings. It later provided the melody for the US national anthem, 'The Star-Spangled Banner'.

> To Anacreon in Heav'n, where he sat in full glee,
> A few sons of harmony sent a petition,
> That he their inspirer and patron would be;
> When this answer arrived from the jolly old
> Grecian –
> Voice, fiddle, and flute, no longer be mute,
> I'll lend ye my name and inspire ye to boot:
> And besides I'll instruct ye, like me, to entwine
> The myrtle of Venus with Bacchus's vine.

Ancient Deists A society of mystics that met in HOXTON from 1770 to 1790. They believed that they could converse with the dead.

and so to bed The signature phrase of the diarist Samuel PEPYS. He used the precise words about once a month and some variation, such as 'and so home and to bed', about once a week. Yorkshire Television's 1983 production 'Pepys and So to Bed' starred Harry Secombe as Pepys.

> … and there we staid talking and singing,
> and drinking great drafts of claret, and eating
> botargo and bread and butter till 12 at night,

> it being moonshine; and so to bed, very near
> fuddled.
>
> (5 June 1661)

Anerley Now an unfashionable collection of cul-de-sacs located on the south-western side of PENGE. The northern dialect word 'anerly' means 'alone' or 'only', and Anerley House (later called Anerley Lodge) was the first dwelling on this part of what was then Penge Common. The poet Walter de la Mare lived at three houses in the area from 1899 to 1925, including Thornsett Road, where he found himself a next-door neighbour of the plumber Thomas Crapper.

> There was an Old Person of Anerley,
> Whose conduct was strange and unmannerly;
> He rushed down the Strand
> With a Pig in each hand,
> But returned in the evening to Anerley.
>
> EDWARD LEAR: *Book of Nonsense* (1846)

angel

Angel, Edmonton A shopping area situated at the point where the NORTH CIRCULAR ROAD now passes beneath Fore Street. Its full title is Angel Corner, UPPER EDMONTON. Like the better-known Angel, Islington (*see below*), it takes its name from an inn that stood here from at least the 17th century. From the 1860s the Angel became a destination for horse-drawn omnibus services and in the early 20th century for some of London's first motor buses. The North Circular Road was diverted beneath Fore Street via an underpass from 1997, greatly easing the junction's traffic congestion and improving the environment. The shops that presently stand at the Angel are very much a local amenity, with little to attract visitors from further afield.

Angel, Islington A commercial quarter and busy road junction at the southern end of ISLINGTON High Street, best known to non-Londoners for its place on the MONOPOLY board. Goswell Road follows a Saxon route out of the CITY, and the Romans are also believed to have built a road through here. A tavern may have been established as early as the 13th century, with a sign showing the Angel of the Annunciation with the Virgin Mary. However, the first public house that definitely stood here was the Sheepcote in 1614 and the first confirmed use of the Angel name came when this house was rebuilt in 1638. The new structure was a coaching inn with a galleried yard, offering entertainment by groups of travelling actors and players. It was popular with overnight guests who were travelling to the City but did not want to risk highway robbery on the hazardous last stretch of their journey. Following the creation of what became CITY ROAD in 1761 a turnpike was set up at the Angel; it was moved eastward in 1800. The galleried inn was demolished in 1819 and rebuilt in Flemish style at the end of the 19th century. Angel tube station opened in 1901. A branch of the Co-operative Bank has since taken the place of the pub, and the reconstructed tube station is now part of the Angel Square complex. Inspired by the French Revolution, the republican Thomas Paine probably wrote the first part of *The Rights of Man* while staying at the Angel in 1790, although some have suggested that he was at the Old Red Lion.

Angel of Christian Charity See EROS.

Angerstein, John Julius A financier and underwriter of Russian origin (1735–1823). His collection of 38 paintings bought by the nation in 1824 for £57,000, formed the nucleus of the NATIONAL GALLERY.

Angry Brigade An urban guerrilla organization responsible for various acts of terrorism in the late 1960s and early 1970s. Among their London targets were the SCOTLAND YARD computer room at Tintagel House on the Albert EMBANKMENT, the home of employment secretary Robert Carr in HADLEY, a BBC outside broadcast vehicle covering the Miss World competition at the ALBERT HALL, the Ford Motor Company offices in GANTS HILL and several Army offices, banks and foreign embassies. The group also claimed responsibility for other attacks across England, Scotland and the European mainland, made with guns as well as bombs. At the time, the intensity of the bombing campaign exceeded anything seen in London since the Second World War but no one was killed and much of the damage done to property was subject to a news blackout. *See also the* STOKE NEWINGTON EIGHT.

Animal A nickname for any public house bearing a zoological name, but formerly especially for the ELEPHANT AND CASTLE tavern, and also for Elephant and Castle station:

'Third-class Animal' is, or was, quite understood by the railway booking-clerks of the district.

J. REDDING WARE: *Passing English of the Victorian Era* (1908)

Animals in War See THEY HAD NO CHOICE.

Annabel's A famous nightclub located in a BERKELEY SQUARE basement. It was opened in 1963 by Mark Birley and named after his then wife, Lady Annabel Vane-Tempest-Stewart (b.1934), an Anglo-Irish heiress who in 1978 married Sir James Goldsmith. Its heyday was in the 1970s, when Lady Annabel persuaded many of her well-connected friends to become members. Former Annabel's guests have included Princess Anne and Princess Diana, Camilla Parker Bowles, Frank Sinatra, Lord Lucan, President Nixon and Aristotle Onassis. It is said to be the only nightclub the Queen has visited. Shortly before his death in 2007 Birley sold the club to the clothing and leisure industry tycoon Richard Caring, in a deal estimated to have been worth £90 million.

Ant, Adam See ADAM AND THE ANTS.

Antic Hay A novel by Aldous Huxley (1894–1963), published in 1923. The book is a satire on intellectual posturing in London's bohemia in the years after the First World War. The title comes from Christopher Marlowe's *Edward II* (1593), I.i:

My men, like satyrs grazing on the lawns,
Shall with their goat feet dance an antic hay.

'Antic' is an archaic word for 'fantastical' or 'grotesque', while a 'hay' was an old country dance in which the dancers weave in and out of a circle. Thus the title sums up what Huxley thought of the goings-on of his contemporaries.

There are few who would not rather be taken in adultery than in provincialism.

ALDOUS HUXLEY: *Antic Hay*

Antigallican The name of several former London pubs, derived from hostility towards the French around the time of the Napoleonic Wars. The most notable of these was the Antigallican Tavern, an establishment of dubious repute that stood in the now-lost Shire Lane near TEMPLE BAR. The extant Antigallican Hotel in CHARLTON may have been so named by a French émigré landlord who was anxious to demonstrate his loyalty to the Crown.

'apenny

'apenny bumper A halfpenny omnibus ride in late Victorian London.

'apenny dip 'Ship' in old COCKNEY RHYMING SLANG.

'apenny-lot day COSTERMONGERS' slang for a bad day for business, when everything had to be sold off at cut prices.

Apostle's Grove A 19th-century nickname for ST JOHN'S WOOD; as was the Grove of the Evangelist.

apples (and pears) 'Stairs', in one of the oldest and most archetypal examples of COCKNEY RHYMING SLANG. It has been suggested that the coinage was inspired by the tiered arrangement of fruit on a typical London market stall. Because the term is so well known it is increasingly used sarcastically, in mockery of a Londoner or the cockney lingo.

> As the show comes to an end my mum is standing there with a mug of Horlicks, telling me to get up the apples and pears.
>
> ANDY SUMMERS: *One Train Later* (2006)

apprentices From the late Middle Ages the adolescent shop assistants and trainees of London's trades guilds gained a notorious reputation as instigators of trouble. The 'prentices, as they were usually known, were in the habit of going about armed with clubs, ostensibly for the preservation of the peace, but often in practice to quite opposite ends. They were feared and disliked for their drunken rowdiness and for their random attacks on the servants of noblemen and, especially, on the city's many foreign residents. Apprentices played a central role in the events of EVIL MAY DAY. When offenders were imprisoned, notably in BRIDEWELL, their comrades would regularly break in and free them. In the 17th century many apprentices adopted a distinctive, cropped hairstyle that is said to be the origin of the term 'Roundhead' – a supporter of the Parliamentary cause in the Civil War.

> They had an arm ready for any cause that might require their interference, and the cry of 'prentices! prentices! clubs! clubs!' was sufficient to rouse the whole body, and attract them to the spot where their aid might be summoned; and he was bold indeed who ventured to insult one of a body so unanimous in feeling and powerful in retaliation.
>
> HENRY THOMAS: *The Wards of London* (1828)

April (in Paris) *See* ARIS.

Apsley House *See* NO.1 LONDON.

Aq, the The popular nickname of the Royal Aquarium, also known as 'the Tank', which opened in WESTMINSTER in 1876. The edifice was essentially a palace of varieties, with the added attractions of a 'whale tank' in the basement, which never contained more than seals and a manatee, and smaller tanks lining the walls upstairs, which had 'but a beggarly show of fish'. Art exhibitions and concerts were at first staged but these soon gave way to more populist fare, including the performances of ZAZEL, 'the human cannonball'. George Robey made his debut at the Aq, as assistant to a spoof mesmerist, in 1891; he later gained fame as the PRIME MINISTER OF MIRTH. Having become increasingly dingy and disreputable, the Royal Aquarium was demolished in 1903 and was later replaced by CENTRAL HALL.

> Fun that's never slack,
> Eyes brown, blue, and black
> Make one feel in Paradise
> While lounging in the Aq.
>
> T.C. CLAY: 'Lounging in the Aq' (song) (1880)

Arches Court *See* COURT OF ARCHES.

Archway The locality at the southern end of Archway Road, which skirts the eastern side of HIGHGATE Hill. In the early 19th century work had begun on a tunnel under HORNSEY Lane but the roof collapsed, bringing the lane down with it. This forced a change of plan and in 1813 a cutting was dug and a Roman-style viaduct built to carry Hornsey Lane across it. Junction Road was constructed at the same time as a feeder for the new road. However, the viaduct proved too narrow for the volume of traffic and the present Archway Bridge opened in 1900. Archway station was the northern terminus from 1907 to 1939 of what is now the HIGH BARNET branch of the NORTHERN LINE, during which time the station was called Highgate. After this, the Archway name took hold in the area, which had formerly been considered part of UPPER HOLLOWAY. Archway Bridge is known locally as 'suicide bridge'.

Arcos Affair A diplomatic contretemps between Britain and the Soviet Union in 1927. It came about when MI5 suspected that personnel working for the All Russian Cooperative Society (Arcos Ltd), headquartered at 49 MOORGATE, were intelligence officers. A raid was made on Arcos warehouses and offices and alleged evidence of espionage was found, as a result of which diplomatic ties were severed with the USSR, and remained so for two years.

Arding & Hobbs A department store at CLAP-HAM JUNCTION, very often spoken of as 'Arding 'n'obbs'. It opened in 1885, when it was the largest shop of its kind south of the THAMES. Destroyed by fire in 1909, it was rebuilt the following year in Edwardian baroque style, with a cupola and clock. The store is now part of the DEBENHAMS group, which has dropped the Arding & Hobbs identity. However, the original signage remains in place above the main entrance and most locals continue to call the store by its familiar name.

> A Tariff Reformer of my acquaintance said
> genially that he was sure that Mr John Burns set
> fire to Arding and Hobbs at Clapham Junction,
> so that he might cut a fine figure in Battersea.
>
> G.K. CHESTERTON: 'Man in the Cosmos' (1910)

Are You Being Served? A BBC TV sitcom created by Jeremy Lloyd (b.1932) and David Croft (b.1922). It ran for ten series between 1972 and 1985. The show's setting, an old-fashioned WEST END department store named Grace Brothers, was inspired by Lloyd's experience of working at Simpson of PICCADILLY.

aris 'Arse' in the only instance of doubled COCK-NEY RHYMING SLANG in common usage. It derives from the rhyme of 'Aristotle' with 'bottle', as in 'bottle and glass', and the latter's rhyme with 'arse'. The matter is further complicated by the occasional extension to 'April (in Paris)', for 'aris'.

> Aristotle invented logic, saying that since (i)
> every Greek is a person, and (ii) every person
> is mortal: then it follows that (iii) every Greek
> is mortal. Sounds logical. Aris is also cockney
> rhyming slang for the body part many people
> say philosophers talk out of.
>
> *The Guardian* (21 November 2002)

Ark, The

1. A house in SOUTH LAMBETH leased in 1626 by the naturalist John Tradescant the Elder (c.1570–1638) to exhibit 'all things strange and rare' that he had collected on his journeys abroad. His son John Tradescant the Younger (1608–62) travelled further afield and brought back plants and artefacts from America to add to the collection. The Ark, as it became known, was the first museum of its kind in London to open to the public and in 1656 Tradescant the Younger published its inaugural catalogue. On Tradescant's death the Ark was acquired by Elias Ashmole (1617–92), who in 1677 donated its contents to the University of Oxford, as part of the founding collection of the Ashmolean Museum. *See also the* GARDEN MUSEUM.

2. A copper and glass office block located at 201 Talgarth Road, overlooking the HAMMERSMITH flyover. So called for its shape, the Ark was completed in 1992 and internally reconfigured in 2008 to increase the floor area and make it more suitable for letting to multiple tenants rather than a single corporate occupier (or no one at all, as has been the case for much of its existence to date).

Arkley An extended village situated on the far western edge of BARNET. Arkley was first recorded in the 14th century and the name is of uncertain origin. It may refer to a meadow where closed baskets (then called arks) were made from wickers or reeds. Arkley windmill was built in 1806 and survives today in the back garden of a private house. Several houses in Arkley were requisitioned for military purposes in the Second World War, notably the now-demolished Arkley View, which housed the Radio Security Service monitoring operation from 1940. Suspicious broadcasts were transcribed and a despatch rider took them to Bletchley Park in Bucking-hamshire for decoding. The RSS was made up of part-time amateurs, such as the historian Hugh Trevor-Roper (later Lord Dacre), and did such good work here – sometimes decoding messages before they had reached Bletchley Park – that the service was subsequently integrated within the military intelligence communications division MI8.

Arnos Grove A classic station (*see below*) and its immediate vicinity, keeping NEW SOUTHGATE at arm's length from SOUTHGATE. In the 14th century this area was Armholt Wood, and later Arnolds. When the City banker James Colebrook bought the estate in 1719 he built a mansion called Arnolds in Cannon Hill, Southgate. Locals called the estate Arno's and the subsequent owner Sir William Mayne, later Lord Newhaven, adopted this convention by renaming the house and estate Arnos Grove, which is now pronounced as though it never had an apostrophe. From 1777 until 1918 the estate belonged to the Walker brewing family, which increased its landholding to over 300 acres (120 hectares) by buying neighbouring Minchenden. In 1928 Lord Inverforth, who had bought the estate from the last of the Walker brothers, sold the southernmost 44 acres (18 hectares) to Southgate council, the mansion to the North Metropolitan Electricity Supply Company for use as offices, and the rest to builders. North Metropolitan enlarged the mansion and encased it in red brick and is now an upmarket residential care home called Southgate Beaumont. The area north of the park was built up by 1939 as the classy Minchenden estate, with Arnos Grove as its central avenue.

Arnos Grove station A LONDON UNDERGROUND station that opened on the far south side of the Arnos Grove estate in 1932. Designed by Charles Holden (1875–1960), this unassumingly elegant station was for its first year the northern terminus of the PICCADILLY LINE.

> When it opened, the station was truly what German art historians would describe as a *gesamtkunstwerk*, a total and entire work of art … I can't help hoping that this king, queen and all princes of a metro station raises at least one commuter's spirit each day as he or she passes into and out of what remains one of the finest of all 20th-century buildings.
>
> JONATHAN GLANCEY, in *The Guardian* (16 October 2007)

Arsenal FC A north London FOOTBALL club usually regarded as one of the 'big four' of the English game. In 1886 WOOLWICH ARSENAL workers founded Dial Square FC at a meeting in the Prince of Wales public house on Plumstead Common Road. The name was soon changed to Royal Arsenal and the club played its early home games on PLUMSTEAD COMMON. In 1913 St John's College of Divinity leased its sports ground at HIGHBURY to the club. TOTTENHAM HOTSPUR and Orient (now LEYTON ORIENT) objected to the relocation but were overruled. The club's achievements were modest until Yorkshireman Herbert Chapman took over as manager in 1925. A strict disciplinarian and canny businessman, Chapman guided Arsenal to FA Cup victory in 1930 and then to two league championships. To honour

the club's successes, Gillespie Road station was renamed Arsenal in 1932. Highbury stadium was erected during the following few years, to the design of Archibald Leitch, who was responsible for most of the great British stadia built before and after the First World War. The club moved to the newly built EMIRATES STADIUM in nearby DRAYTON PARK in 2006. Highbury's art deco east and west stands have since been converted into an apartment complex called Highbury Square. Nick Hornby's novel *Fever Pitch* (1992) evokes the pains and joys of being a fanatical Arsenal supporter. *See also* GOONERS; GUNNERS.

The Arsenal Stadium Mystery A 1939 detective film directed by Thorold Dickinson (1903–84), in which an opposition player dies by poisoning during a match at HIGHBURY stadium and SCOTLAND YARD is called in to investigate. Several Arsenal players of the time appeared in the film, which was one of the earliest to exploit the British love of football, and one of the very few such productions to have been critically acclaimed, despite its low budget.

> It's a slight, B-movie murder mystery, more of a 'quota quickie', so it's not really fair to compare it to the English Hitchcocks. But it's a lot of fun … Dickinson strikes me as a very confident director here, willing to play with the material, to have fun with it.
>
> MARTIN SCORSESE, interviewed in *Sight & Sound* (November 2003)

Artful Dodger The nickname of Jack Dawkins in Charles DICKENS's *Oliver Twist* (1838). A leading member of FAGIN's den of child pickpockets, he is 'as roystering and swaggering a young gentleman as ever stood four feet six, or something less'. He introduces OLIVER TWIST to Fagin but is later convicted of theft and sentenced to transportation. In COCKNEY RHYMING SLANG an 'artful dodger' is a lodger.

Arthur Daley *See* DALEY, ARTHUR.

Art on the Underground *See* PLATFORM FOR ART.

Arup, Ove Nyquist A civil engineer (1895–1988) born in Newcastle upon Tyne, of Danish parentage, he studied philosophy and engineering in Denmark before moving to London in 1923. He became increasingly concerned with the solution of structural problems in Modernist architecture, working with the TECTON partnership on the Highpoint flats (1936–8) in HIGHGATE and the spiral reinforced concrete ramps of the penguin pool at LONDON ZOO (1934). In 1946 he founded the design and engineering consultancy now called Arup.

as

as black as Newgate's knocker Very dark, in colour or character. The simile draws on NEWGATE PRISON's notoriety as a place of death.

> He's just another bloody-minded old upperclass bugger with a heart as black as Newgate's knocker.
> JAMES HAWES: *Speak for England* (2005)

as bold as brass Impudent or immodest. The expression is first recorded in the 1780s, but it is part of a wider association of brass with 'effrontery' that goes back at least to the mid-16th century, and it is unlikely that there is any foundation in the claimed link with the lawyer and politician Brass Crosby (1725–93), who became embroiled in a row with the House of Commons regarding the right of CITY printers to publish reports of Parliamentary debates – a right that Crosby upheld but MPs considered a breach of privilege. In 1771, while he was LORD MAYOR OF LONDON, Crosby freed the printer of the *Evening Post*, who had been arrested by a House of Commons messenger, and had the messenger arrested instead. For this he was remanded to the TOWER OF LONDON. The City rose up in protest, Crosby was freed after six weeks and Parliamentary reports were thenceforth published freely.

as common as cat-shit and twice as nasty A COCKNEY catchphrase dating from around 1920, elaborating on the standard British colloquialism 'as common as muck'.

as common as Ratcliff Highway Formerly said of someone of low class and character, as were the inhabitants of RATCLIFF.

> Another, that had been as common as Ratcliff Highway, would neither lead nor drive; and stood humming and hawing a good while, pretending she had forgot her night-clothes, and such fooleries …
> FRANCISCO DE QUEVEDO: *Works*, Volume 1, 'Vision of the Last Judgment' (1627) (translated by Roger L'Estrange, 1767)

as dirty as Old Brentford at Christmas From early times, BRENTFORD was one of the busiest

market towns in MIDDLESEX and notorious for its muddiness, which was at its worst in midwinter.

> The roads are consumed deep; I'm as dirty as Old Brentford at Christmas.
> GEORGE FARQUHAR: *The Beaux' Stratagem*, II, ii (1707)

as lame as St Giles' Cripplegate The expression combines a pun on the name CRIPPLEGATE with a reference to the Athenian saint to whom its parish church was dedicated; St Giles is the patron saint of the lame.

> This proverb … in common discourse, is spoken rather merrily than mournfully, of such who, for some slight hurt, lag behind; and sometimes is applied to those who, out of laziness, counterfeit infirmity.
> W. CAREW HAZLITT: *English Proverbs and Proverbial Phrases* (1869)

The term was also sometimes used of a lame excuse.

as old as Aldgate A less common equivalent of AS OLD AS PAUL'S.

as old as Paul's (steeple) or **St Paul's** The reference was to the earlier incarnation of ST PAUL'S Cathedral, which dated from the late 11th century and burned down in the GREAT FIRE OF LONDON.

as queer as a clockwork orange According to Anthony Burgess (1917–93), the phrase was at first said of anything that was 'queer to the limit of queerness' and later came to be especially used in reference to homosexual men. Burgess reported that he first heard the phrase in a London pub in 1945. The thought that something as natural as an orange might conceal mechanical workings inspired the title of his dystopian novel *A Clockwork Orange* (1962), filmed (in and around London) by Stanley Kubrick in 1971. In *Why Not Catch 21?: The Stories Behind the Titles* (2007), Gary Dexter questions whether the phrase really did have a prior existence, citing a lack of supporting evidence and conflicting statements the author made on the subject. Dexter proposes that Burgess may have misheard a reference to a Terry's chocolate orange but perhaps liked what he had misheard and did not subsequently want to admit 'the drab mercantile origins of his title'. However, the slang lexicographer Eric Partridge averred that the phrase was indeed used in east London (and possibly also the Royal Navy) before the publication of *A Clockwork Orange*.

as sure as the devil is in London A provincial saying casting aspersions on the virtue of Londoners. The proverb also crossed the Atlantic.

> 'Ay!' says the [Somerset] landlord, 'we have a saying here in our country that 'tis as sure as the devil is in London, and if he was not there they could not be so wicked as they be.'
>
> HENRY FIELDING, in *The Covent Garden Journal* (23 April 1752)

as the bell clinks, so the fool thinks or **as the fool thinks, so the bell clinks** A foolish person believes what he desires. The tale says that when Dick WHITTINGTON ran away from his master, and had got as far as HIGHGATE Hill, he was hungry, tired and wished to return. The bells of ST MARY-LE-BOW began to ring, and Whittington fancied they said: 'Turn again, Whittington, lord mayor of London.' The bells clinked in response to the boy's thoughts.

Ascot races 'Braces' in COCKNEY RHYMING SLANG. The term was usually reduced to 'Ascots' but is now largely redundant.

Ashburton Grove *See the* EMIRATES STADIUM.

Ashes, The The mythical prize contended for in the cricket test matches between England and Australia. When England was beaten at the OVAL in 1882 a mock obituary of English cricket appeared in the *Sporting Times*:

> In Affectionate Remembrance of English Cricket Which died at the Oval on 29th August, 1882. Deeply lamented by a large circle of sorrowing friends and acquaintances.
> R.I.P.
> N.B. – The body will be cremated and the ashes taken to Australia.

The ashes of a burnt cricket stump were subsequently placed in an urn and given to the English team when it next won.

Asia Minor A snide nickname applied to BELGRAVIA in the mid-19th century, on account of the large number of wealthy Jews who lived there. By the mid-1880s it had transferred to BAYSWATER and KENSINGTON, favoured areas for retired military and administrative professionals with south Asian experience. Indian fruits and vegetables were sold in the local shops. The nickname had largely died out by the time of the First World War.

ask cheeks near Cunnyborough! An expression used from the mid-18th to the mid-19th century by 'low London females' when declining to answer a question.

> ... the repartee of a St Giles's fair one, who bids you ask her backside.
>
> FRANCIS GROSE: *A Classical Dictionary of the Vulgar Tongue* (1785)

Astley's The popular name for an enterprising and much patronized place of entertainment from 1770 to 1862, opened and developed by Philip Astley (1742–1814). After service as a Sergeant-Major in the Dragoons under General Eliott during the Seven Years' War, Astley, with his charger Gibraltar, opened a theatre with an unroofed circus at LAMBETH in 1770 for equestrian displays. Eventually called the Royal Grove Theatre, it was burned down in 1794 and rebuilt as the Royal Amphitheatre, when it was patronized by the Prince of Wales and the Duke of York, among other notables. It grew in repute as a centre for equestrian and circus entertainment under Astley's pioneering management. He was the best horse-tamer of his day. Astley's was destroyed again by fire in 1803 but was reopened in 1804. Astley was eventually succeeded by his son who died seven years after his father, when the venture passed into other hands. *See also* SADLER'S WELLS.

> But many other 'cunning tricks' ... have been performed by dogs a few years ago, at Sadler's Wells, and afterwards at Astley's, to the great amusement of the polite spectators.
>
> JOSEPH STRUTT: *Sports and Pastimes*, Book 3 (1801)

Athenaeum This leading intellectual club was founded in 1824 in the apartments of the ROYAL SOCIETY at SOMERSET HOUSE. It was originally known as The Society, but changed its name on moving to its present premises in PALL MALL in 1830. The literary review called *The Athenaeum* was founded by James Silk Buckingham in 1828 and was incorporated with *The Nation* in 1921, which merged with the *New Statesman* in 1931.

Athenian Stuart The sobriquet of the archaeologist and designer James Stuart (1713–88). Born in humble circumstances in CREED LANE, he elevated himself through his talent as an artist and went on to play a central role in the development of the neoclassical style. As an architect, he is probably best known for his contribution to the design of SPENCER HOUSE.

at sixes and sevens *See under* SIX.

Augusta (from Latin *augustus*, from *augēre*, 'to increase', 'to honour') A name given to many Roman provincial towns, from the honorific title accorded to Roman emperors, first held by Caesar Augustus (r.*c*.31 BC–AD 14). LONDINIUM was renamed Augusta some time in the early 4th century as a mark of mutual respect between the settlement and the emperor.

Aunt Sally A game in which sticks or cudgels are thrown at a figure of an old woman's head mounted on a pole, the object being to hit its nose, or break the pipe stuck in its mouth. The original Aunt Sally was a black-faced doll, popular in early 19th-century London. Its face was used as a shop-sign by second-hand clothes dealers. The doll in turn came from Black Sal, a character in Pierce Egan's *Life in London* (1821). 'Aunt Sally' is now a term for anyone or anything that is an object of ridicule or a target of abuse.

Ave Maria Lane A street in the City, running northwards from LUDGATE HILL. The name probably alluded to the processional chanting of Ave Maria (Hail Mary), or alternatively to writers of religious texts working in the vicinity. In the Middle Ages the clergy of ST PAUL'S Cathedral went in procession to the cathedral reciting the Lord's Prayer. They began it in PATERNOSTER ROW, and on turning down Ave Maria Lane they began chanting the Hail Mary. The street was very badly damaged in an air raid on 28 December 1940. *See also* AMEN CORNER.

Avengers, The A British television series screened from 1961 to 1968 in a blend of the chic, the sexy, the violent and the self-mocking. The hero, elegant secret agent John Steed, with BOWLER HAT and UMBRELLA, was played by Patrick Macnee, while his female, leather-clad,

judo-practising sidekick was first Cathy Gale, played by Honor Blackman, then Emma PEEL (Diana Rigg), and finally Tara King (Linda Thorson). Most *Avengers* episodes were filmed at studios in Borehamwood, Hertfordshire, and at external locations in that vicinity, including several in STANMORE and ARKLEY. In 1976 Macnee returned in *The New Avengers* with Joanna Lumley. A Hollywood film version (1998) did not sparkle.

Avenue, The A group of 15 artists' and sculptors' studios situated at 76 FULHAM ROAD from the late 19th century. Alfred Gilbert created EROS for PICCADILLY CIRCUS at No.8 in 1893, and John Singer Sargent worked here for 20 years, lending his studio to James Whistler for a while in 1896.

Avery Hill A Victorian mansion, park and mid-20th-century housing estate, situated east of ELTHAM. A map of 1805 calls the area Pollcat End. It is possible that the present name refers to an aviary that may have existed here in the early 19th century. John Thomas North, 'the NITRATE KING', built Avery Hill House in 1891. He died only five years after the house was completed and the LONDON COUNTY COUNCIL then acquired the building and its 86 acres (35 hectares) of grounds, which in 1903 were opened to the public as Avery Hill Park. In 1906 Avery Hill House became the nucleus of Avery Hill College of Education, which has since been subsumed into the University of GREENWICH. The campus is situated on either side of Avery Hill Park. The library, once the great hall of North's mansion, is a listed building, as is the adjacent glass-domed winter garden. A 'student village' includes the Dome, a purpose-built venue with capacity for a thousand.

Azuriel The fairy who owned what we call HOLLAND PARK. King Oberon gave him his daughter KENNA in marriage when he drove Albion from his empire. Albion invaded KENSINGTON, the territory of King Oberon, but was slain in battle by Azuriel.

B

babbling (brook) 'Crook' in COCKNEY RHYM-ING SLANG. Evolutionary terms such as 'babbler' and 'on the babble' are occasionally heard.

Babes in the Wood An ITV sitcom that ran for two seasons in 1998–9. The show revolved around three women who shared a flat in ST JOHN'S WOOD.

Babylon Benjamin Disraeli called London 'a modern Babylon' in his novel *Tancred* (1847), but he was not the first to thus employ the epithet. The pseudonymous Harry Hawthorn entitled his haphazard survey of the city 'A Visit to Babylon' in 1829.

> In return for their complimentary kindness, what have we done to the Southrons? Heathen'd their metropolis the Modern Babylon! No, England! 'thou can'st not say I did it.' 'Twas done by 'Moody Madness, laughing wild – amidst severest woe.' We never nicknamed London, it being 'a thing so majestical'.
>
> 'Edinburgh Election', *Blackwood's Edinburgh Magazine* (June 1831)

To Rastafarians and some other Caribbeans 'Babylon' is a name synonymous with captivity and has accordingly been applied to Britain generally and London specifically, and also to their institutions, the police, etc. Franco Rosso's 1980 film *Babylon* centres on the lives of a group of black youngsters living in south London.

Bach, Johann Christian *See the* LONDON BACH.

back-slang A form of slang that consists in pronouncing a word near enough backwards. It was formerly much used by 'flash' COCKNEYS, thieves and especially by London's tens of thousands of COSTERMONGERS. The vocabulary was handed down from one generation to another so that younger costers often did not know the origin of the words that they used every day. Back-slang terminology mainly consists of words for coins, vegetables, fruit, police court terms and other aspects of everyday life for market traders. Thus 'cool' is look, 'dunop' a pound, 'elrig' a girl, 'eno' one, 'genitraf' a farthing, 'nam' a man, 'namow' a woman, 'nig' gin, 'rape' a pear, 'shif' fish, 'slop' a policeman, 'storrac' carrots, 'spinsrap' parsnips, 'tenip' a pint, 'yennep' a penny and 'yob' a boy. This last expression has passed into everyday speech. In some cases a combination of poor education, deliberate garbling and folk etymology led to the creation of back-slang words that bore only a passing resemblance to the right-way-round original: 'shilling' for example, became 'generalise', or 'gen' for short. A halfpenny was a 'flatch yennep', often abbreviated to 'flatch'. One reason the language died out was that the police and other outsiders learnt to understand it and in the mid-19th century COCKNEY RHYM-ING SLANG began to take its place.

bacon
bacon and eggs 'Legs' in COCKNEY RHYMING SLANG. Alternatives include SCOTCHES.
bacon-and-egg tie A nickname for the assertive red-and-yellow-striped tie worn by members of the MARYLEBONE CRICKET CLUB.

> A broad-minded understanding of why players might be tempted by the riches on offer did not seem to be high on the agenda of the bacon-and-egg-tie brigade at Lord's; the first loyalty of cricketers was to their country.
>
> *The Independent on Sunday* (13 July 2008)

Bacon Tom One of the many aliases of a foolhardy burglar whose real name was probably Thomas Mason. In 1613 he and two accomplices 'broke burglariously into the King's dwelling-house called WHITEHALL' and stole an extraordinary quantity of curtains and bedding, including such items as 'the whole toppe and vallance of a Bed of Cloth of Silver worth twenty pounds', according to the OLD BAILEY trial transcript. The accomplices escaped but Bacon Tom was tried, found guilty and sentenced to hang at TYBURN.

Badger's Hole Now absorbed within SHIRLEY, this was an enclave that evolved on squatted land in the mid-18th century. A hamlet of weatherboarded cottages followed in the 19th century, centred around the junction of Oaks Road and Upper Shirley Road.

bad hat A rascal or good-for-nothing. One circumstantial account of the origin of the expression, given in Charles Mackay's *Memoirs of Extraordinary Public Delusions* (1841), traces it to an election in the borough of SOUTHWARK around 1838. One of the candidates was a hatter, and whenever he spotted substandard headgear among his audience he would cry out: 'What a shocking bad hat you've got! Call at my warehouse and you shall have a new one.' On the day of the election his opponents encouraged the crowd to shout him down by calling out repeatedly: 'What a shocking bad hat!' Another version has the originator as the Duke of Wellington, who on his first visit to the Peers' Gallery of the House of Commons remarked, on looking down on the members of the Reform Parliament: 'I never saw so many shocking bad hats in my life!' The phrase caught on, soon losing its 'shocking', and remained in popular use until the middle of the 20th century.

bagman or **Leadenhaller** One who dealt in bag-foxes, which were regularly traded at LEADENHALL MARKET. From the late 18th until the mid-19th century, foxes were brought in (mainly from France) to overcome the scarcity created by the destruction of foxes by gamekeepers and farmers. The fox was released from the bag at the time of the hunt.

Bag of Nails A public house located at 6 Buckingham Palace Road, VICTORIA, licensed in 1775 as the Devil and Bag o' Nails. The name probably derives from a tradesman's sign, that of an ironmonger, although some lexicographers accept the story that it is a corruption of 'Bacchanals'. The pub was rebuilt in 1838.

> He squints like a bag of nails; i.e. his eyes are
> directed as many ways as the points of a bag of

nails. The old Bag of Nails at Pimlico; originally the Bacchanals.

FRANCIS GROSE, HEWSON CLARKE and GEORGE CRUIKSHANK: *Lexicon Balatronicum* (1811)

Bailey, the The colloquial short form of the OLD BAILEY, familiarized by RUMPOLE OF THE BAILEY.

Baitul Futuh An imposing mosque built by London's Ahmadiyya Muslim community on the site of a former Express Dairies bottling plant in south MORDEN. Inaugurated in 2003, the mosque cost £5.5 million and can accommodate up to 10,000 worshippers. Ancillary parts of the structure are built around the fabric of the dairy and the old chimney was cleverly converted into a minaret, allowing a taller structure than would otherwise have been permitted.

Bakerloo

Bakerloo line A LONDON UNDERGROUND line running north-westwards from the ELEPHANT AND CASTLE to Harrow & Wealdstone, coloured brown on the map. It opened in 1906 as the Baker Street & Waterloo Railway. Its present name, said to have been coined by 'Quex' (G.H.F. Nichols) of the *Evening News*, was at first considered a vulgar contraction but was so widely used that it soon gained formal acknowledgement. Over the course of its existence the Bakerloo line has been extended, shortened and extended again, while the STANMORE branch, originally part of the METROPOLITAN LINE, has been integrated into the JUBILEE LINE.

Bakerloo syndrome An alternative name for the form of sexual deviance more commonly known as frotteurism, whereby an individual gains arousal from rubbing up against others in crowded environments.

Baker Street A commercial thoroughfare extending north from PORTMAN SQUARE to the south-western edge of REGENT'S PARK. The street is named after Sir Edward Baker (1763–1825), who assisted the Portman family in the development of their estate here. Baker Street gained one of the first LONDON UNDERGROUND stations when the short stretch from PADDINGTON to FARRINGDON Street opened in 1863. The actress Sarah Siddons and the politician and prime minister William Pitt the Younger lived in Baker Street, but its most famous resident is the fictional detective Sherlock HOLMES, who was supposed to have lodged at 221B, an address that did not actually exist at that time. Most Sherlockian scholars advocate No.31 as the likely real address (assuming Conan Doyle ever had a specific location in mind), while a minority prefer 111. The headquarters of the ABBEY ROAD Building Society (later the Abbey National, and now Abbey) occupied the site of 221B Baker Street from 1932 until 2002, during which time the company answered thousands of letters addressed to the great detective. The Sherlock Holmes Museum now deals with the correspondence – and claims the precious address, although it is really at 239 Baker Street. Gerry Rafferty's ballad 'Baker Street' was first a hit in 1978:

> Winding your way down on Baker Street,
> Light in your head and dead on your feet.
> Well, another crazy day, you'll drink the night away
> And forget about everything.

Baker Street Bazaar A grand emporium that in the 19th century sold everything from horses to musical and mechanical automata. MADAME TUSSAUDS waxworks gained its first permanent home here in 1835, moving to MARYLEBONE ROAD in 1884. The Royal SMITHFIELD Club held its annual cattle show here at the bazaar from 1839 to 1861, after which the show relocated to the AGRICULTURAL HALL in ISLINGTON.

Baker Street irregulars A fictional band of young street urchins, led by a lad called Wiggins, employed by Sherlock HOLMES to search for clues, lost articles, etc. The name was adopted by a society of Sherlockian enthusiasts, founded in 1933.

> 'It is the unofficial force – the Baker Street irregulars.' As he spoke, there came a swift pattering of naked feet upon the stairs, a clatter of high voices, and in rushed a dozen dirty and ragged little street Arabs.
>
> ARTHUR CONAN DOYLE: *The Sign of Four* (1890)

Balaam A 'citizen of sober fame' who lived near the MONUMENT in Alexander Pope's *Moral Essays*, Epistle iii (1731). While poor he was 'religious, punctual, and frugal'; but when he became rich and got knighted he seldom went to church, became a courtier, 'took a bribe from France' and was hanged for treason. Balaam was partly based on Thomas Pitt (1653–1726), EAST INDIA merchant, owner of the Pitt Diamond and grandfather of the 1st Earl of Chatham.

Balcombe Street A residential street in MARYLEBONE, running southwards into MARYLEBONE ROAD. When it was originally laid out in the late 1820s it was called Milton Street. The change of name dates from 1886, but it is not known what occasioned it.

Balcombe Street siege In December 1975 four IRA gunmen (Joseph O'Connell, Harry Duggan, Eddie Butler and Hugh Doherty) held a husband and wife hostage at No.22B following a botched attack at a MAYFAIR restaurant. Police surrounded the building, and after six days the men surrendered and gave up the hostages unharmed.

bale of hay It is often claimed that London taxi drivers are, in theory, compelled by an archaic law to carry a bale of hay in their vehicles at all times. Others say the law in question was repealed, but not until 1976. Alternative versions assert that it is a Public Carriage Office licensing requirement that there be sufficient room for such a bale beside the driver or in the boot. In fact, the driver of a horse-drawn cab was merely obliged, if and when he fed his animal in the street, to do so 'only with corn out of a bag, or with hay which he shall hold or deliver with his hands'. This stipulation, from the London Hackney Carriage Act (1831), aimed to prevent feed remnants being scattered all over the highway and was indeed repealed in 1976. Cab drivers are also said to retain the legal right to urinate in public against the rear offside wheel of their vehicles but this too has no basis in fact. Nevertheless, all this misinformation continues to be propagated on the internet, where it can be found on dozens of websites of the 'world's dumbest laws' variety. The Law Commission attempted to debunk the hay myth on its own website in 2006:

> … any taxi driver who travels around accompanied by a bale of hay does so purely for his own amusement and not in compliance with any legal requirement.

Balham A south London suburb situated between TOOTING and CLAPHAM. Baelgenham, which probably means 'smooth or rounded enclosure', was established around the 8th century, when woodland still covered much of the area. Over the past few decades Balham has become increasingly popular as a more afford-able residential alternative to Clapham, though it was once described as 'the ugliest and most abominable of London's unpleasing suburbs' by *Swallows and Amazons* author Arthur Ransome, who stayed here briefly. *See also* GATEWAY TO THE SOUTH.

Balham Group Originally a subsection of the British Communist Party, its foundation in the early 1930s marked the beginning of the British Trotskyist movement. The group's members were soon expelled from the BCP, which they had ac-cused of slavishly following Stalinist orthodoxy.

ball (of chalk) 'Walk' in COCKNEY RHYMING SLANG, usually heard – when heard at all – in the phrase 'to go for a ball'. The term (alternatively rendered as 'ball and chalk') can occasionally mean 'talk', but 'RABBIT (AND PORK)' is usually preferred for that purpose.

Ballad of Peckham Rye, The A novel (1960) by Muriel Spark. It creates a curious picture of the London underworld, with the odd suggestion of necromancy.

Balls Pond Road An unprepossessing road on the eastern edge of the London Borough of ISLINGTON, leading into HACKNEY. Ball's Pond (which survived until the early 19th century) was named after John Ball, who owned a lively tavern that stood near present-day Bingham Street. The pond was used for a 'sport' of the time in which dogs hunt a duck whose wings have been pinioned, its only means of escape being to dive to the bottom of a pond (whence arises the pub name 'Dog and Duck'). A certain suggestiveness about its name made the Balls Pond Road a favourite of 20th-century comedians wanting a cheap 'COCKNEY culture' laugh.

Baltic, the The familiar name of the Baltic Mercantile and Shipping Exchange in the CITY of London, which was founded in the 18th cen-tury. It originated from meetings, at the Baltic COFFEE HOUSE, of merchants concerned with the Baltic trade, and it is now at ST MARY AXE as a commodity and freight-chartering market (its grandiose early 20th-century headquarters there were destroyed by an IRA bomb in 1992, but it has acquired replacement premises in the same street). Membership largely consists

of ship-owners, shipbrokers and merchants. *See also the* GHERKIN; LLOYD'S.

Bandy Leg Walk A thoroughfare that formerly ran along the western side of the BOROUGH, in SOUTHWARK. The name probably reflected the high incidence of rickets in the area. By a curious coincidence, one William Ricketts lived on Bandy Leg Walk in the 1750s, before he was imprisoned for debt. The lane was the birthplace of the watercolourist Thomas Girtin (1775–1802), of whom J.M.W. Turner is supposed to have said: 'Had Tom Girtin lived, I should have starved.' Great Guildford Street and a small section of SOUTHWARK BRIDGE ROAD follow Bandy Leg Walk's route today.

> He buys his boots in Crooked Lane, and his stockings in Bandy-legged Walk; his legs grew in the night, therefore could not see to grow straight: jeering sayings of men with crooked legs.
>
> FRANCIS GROSE, HEWSON CLARKE and GEORGE CRUIKSHANK: *Lexicon Balatronicum* (1811)

bang
bang through the elephant Very drunk, or thoroughly dissipated, in low London slang of the late 19th and early 20th centuries.

bang to rights A justifiable arrest, often where the culprit is caught red-handed. This widely used expression originated in the London crim-inal underworld around 1930 and soon entered the EAST END vernacular. By the 1950s it was understood throughout the UK.

> *Bang to Rights: An Account of Prison Life*
> FRANK NORMAN (book title) (1958)

bang up to the elephant A 19th-century slang term meaning 'excellent', 'perfect'. The reference may have been to the ELEPHANT AND CASTLE tavern.

> 'I'll be right as a trivet in a minute or two, Officer.'
> 'But not quite bang up to the elephant, eh?'
> THOMAS BERTRAM COSTAIN: *The Tontine* (1955)

Banglatown BRICK LANE and its immediate vicinity. The name was invented by the area's restaurateurs in an attempt to imitate the suc-cess of CHINATOWN and has been endorsed by TOWER HAMLETS council.

Bank A LONDON UNDERGROUND and DOCKLANDS

LIGHT RAILWAY station located at the heart of the SQUARE MILE, serving the BANK OF ENGLAND and other nearby financial institutions, such as the ROYAL EXCHANGE and the STOCK EXCHANGE. The present Bank station is an amalgamation of City station, which operated the 'DRAIN' service to Waterloo from 1898, and Bank, which was opened by the City and South London Railway Company in 1900 and became the eastern terminus of the Central London Railway later that year. The station has been nicknamed 'the worm' for its twisting network of pedestrian tunnels interconnecting its platforms and those at MONUMENT.

Bank of England The central bank of the United Kingdom, located at the heart of the SQUARE MILE that constitutes London's prime financial district. The Bank of England began in 1694 as a commercial operation providing funds for a war against France. At first the bank operated out of Mercers' Hall and then Grocers' Hall before acquiring its governor's mansion on THREADNEEDLE STREET as the site for its own premises in 1734. Gradually it became the dominant issuer of notes and the chosen bank of most departments of state, but it was not until the 19th century that the Bank of England fully acquired its present national role. Nowadays, the bank's primary responsibilities are setting interest rates, issuing banknotes and striving to maintain a stable financial system. The Bank of England Museum traces the institution's history and displays a collection of ingots, coins and banknotes.

Banker Chapel Ho An obscure and convoluted nickname for WHITECHAPEL, current around the turn of the 20th century. It represents an anglicization of the cod Italian *bianca capella* 'white chapel' plus the Italianate ending -o.

Bankruptcy Avenue or **Row** A mid-19th-century nickname for WESTBOURNE GROVE, derived from the vainly ambitious attempts of several entrepreneurs to create a 'BOND STREET of west London' here. Eventually, William WHITELEY succeeded.

Bankside A revived riverside cultural destination, situated on the south side of the THAMES between BLACKFRIARS Bridge and SOUTHWARK Bridge. This part of the Southwark riverside has had a remarkably consistent history as a place of often bawdy entertainment. As it fell outside the CITY's jurisdiction, it was free to permit practices outlawed elsewhere and its theatres and brothels consequently flourished in the late Middle Ages. Bankside suffered like other riverside areas from German bombing in the Second World War and from postwar industrial decline but recent years have seen an upturn in its fortunes; it is now best known for the GLOBE and TATE MODERN.

Bankside lady or **wench** A prostitute. The term was in use from the 15th century to the 17th.

Banks's horse A horse called Marocco, belonging to one Banks about the end of Queen Elizabeth I's reign, and trained to do all manner of tricks. One of its exploits is said to have been the ascent of ST PAUL'S steeple. A favourite story of the time is of an apprentice who called his master to see the spectacle. 'Away, you fool,' said the shopkeeper, 'why need I go to see a horse on the top when I can see so many horses at the bottom!' The horse is mentioned by Sir Walter Raleigh, Gayton, Kenelm Digby, Ben Jonson and others.

Banksy The pseudonym of an anonymous 'guerrilla' artist who has specialized in witty images stenciled in public places, especially in London. Works that he has produced for sale have attracted numerous celebrity collectors and achieved auction prices in excess of £250,000. In July 2008 the *Daily Mail* claimed to have 'unmasked' Banksy, revealing him to be 'a former public schoolboy from middle-class suburbia', born in Bristol in 1973.

> Rival graffitists ... tease him about his supposed origins: 'Go back to Bristol, boy', someone has written beside his work on a wall in Clerkenwell, London.
>
> *The Guardian* (5 July 2007)

Banqueting House
1. The only surviving part of WHITEHALL PALACE, completed in 1622, with paintings by Peter Paul Rubens installed in the ceiling in 1636. Designed in the Palladian style by Inigo JONES, it was the venue for state functions, plays and masques laid on for Charles I (r.1625–49) and was later the scene of his execution. After the fire that destroyed the rest of the palace in 1698, it served as a chapel until 1890. Nowadays it is open to visitors and available for function hire.
2. A rambling old house that stood near what

is now Stratford Place, off OXFORD STREET. The LORD MAYOR and CORPORATION OF LONDON regularly dined there after hunting in the adjacent countryside or viewing a hanging at TYBURN. The house was demolished in 1736, the same year in which a site was chosen for the construction of the MANSION HOUSE, where mayoral functions were held afterwards.

banter A noun meaning 'mock impoliteness' or 'lighthearted raillery' and a verb meaning to dispense or exchange that kind of pleasantry. Its earliest recorded usage was by Samuel Pepys in 1667. The word is of unknown derivation but in the *Apology to his Tale of a Tub* (1710), Jonathan Swift says of it:

> This polite word of theirs was first borrowed from the bullies in White Friars; then fell among the footmen; and at last retired to the pedants, by whom it is applied as properly to the production of wit as if I should apply it to Sir Isaac Newton's mathematics; but if this bantering, as they call it, be so despisable a thing, whence comes it to pass they have such a perpetual itch toward it themselves?

Banting diet William Banting (1797–1878) was a KENSINGTON cabinetmaker and royal undertaker who made the Duke of Wellington's coffin. Suffering from acute obesity, he consulted a physician who recommended a high-protein, low-carbohydrate regime that helped him shed 50lb (23kg) in little more than a year. Banting propounded the diet in his privately published *Letter on Corpulence* (1864), which proceeded to run through several editions. The ensuing publicity led to the coinage of words such as 'Bantingize' and 'Bantingism' and even the mock-verb 'to bant'. Banting's method was remarkably similar to the modern Atkins diet; at the time he was derided as a charlatan by much of the medical profession. A popular song of the day ended thus:

> If you don't follow Banting,
> You won't much longer get about,
> If you continue thus so stout,
> You'll fall a victim to the gout,
> You really must try Banting.

barber (ultimately from Latin *barba*, 'beard') A person who cuts men's hair and shaves or trims beards; a hairdresser. Originally barbers also practised dentistry and surgery. The Company of Barber Surgeons in London was first incorporated in 1461, and in 1540 it became the Company of Barbers and Surgeons, limited (other than in its proper functions) to drawing teeth. In 1745 it was renamed the Worshipful Company of Barbers and is still one of the London LIVERY COMPANIES. Barber-Surgeons' Hall is in Monkwell Square, Wood Street.

Demon Barber of Fleet Street *See under* DEMON.

Greenwich barbers *See under* GREENWICH.

Barbican Originally a defensive structure atop the CITY walls (pulled down in 1267), then a street and now a housing estate in the northwest corner of the City of London. In the 19th century the Barbican was a warren of factories, warehouses, markets and shops, but much of it was razed by fire in 1902 and the remainder was devastated in the BLITZ. In 1956 housing minister Duncan Sandys recommended the creation of a model postwar neighbourhood with schools, shops and amenities as well as homes. The architects Chamberlin, Powell and Bon were appointed to design the complex, which included the tallest residential blocks in Britain; with 43 storeys, these were only recently eclipsed by Manchester's Beetham Tower. The first of 2,000 flats were completed in the early 1960s. The Barbican's rain-stained, hammered concrete slabs detract from its aesthetic appeal but it has achieved grade II listed building status by virtue of its distinctive character.

Barbican Centre The term 'Barbican Centre' is often used of the entire Barbican development, but strictly refers only to its arts complex. The centre was built between 1971 and 1982 at a cost of £153 million. Its buildings are on ten floors, the lowest being well below sea level. It is the main home of the LONDON SYMPHONY ORCHESTRA.

bard

Bard of Barking Billy Bragg (b.1957), a singer/songwriter and political activist who was born and bred in Barking but subsequently relocated to Dorset. BARKING AND DAGENHAM council named a cul-de-sac in his honour in 1999.

> From The Stones' Richmond roots to punk's Bromley contingent, the bard of Barking to Britpop, kids have to do it for themselves in the 'burbs.
>
> *Time Out* (6 December 2006)

Bard of Twickenham Alexander Pope (1688–1744), who lived there for 25 years in a house he called 'my TUSCULUM'. Contemporaries sometimes called him the 'Wasp of Twickenham' because of his acerbic wit and defective social skills, which may have been understandable in someone who was only four foot six in (1.3m) tall and in constant pain from curvature of the spine.

Baretti case, the Giuseppe Baretti (1719–89) was an Italian literary critic and lexicographer who spent much of his life in London. On 6 October 1769, in the HAYMARKET, he stabbed and killed a prostitute's pimp. Tried for murder at the OLD BAILEY, he pleaded self-defence and was acquitted. *The Gentleman's Magazine* suggested that only a foreigner would have got off and his nationality did indeed help to explain why he was carrying a knife, as continental restaurants at that time expected customers to bring their own. However, Baretti seems to have benefited more from the character witnesses he was able to call at his trial, who included Joshua Reynolds, Dr JOHNSON, Edmund Burke, David GARRICK and Oliver Goldsmith.

> Q. Look at this knife. (He takes it in his hand.)
> Mr Garrick. I cannot say I ever saw one with a silver sheaf [sic] before. I had one, but I have lost mine. Mrs Garrick has one now, with a steel blade, and gold.
> Q. When you travel abroad, do you carry such knives as this?
> Mr Garrick. Yes, or we should have no victuals.
>
> *Old Bailey Proceedings*, trial transcript (18 October 1769)

Bar Italia A compact Italian café located at 22 FRITH STREET, established in 1949. Travel guides have called it 'a cornerstone of Soho nightlife' and 'the queen of café culture in Soho'.

> You can't go home and go to bed
> Because it hasn't worn off yet,
> And now it's morning.
> There's only one place we can go,
> It's around the corner in Soho,
> Where other broken people go.
>
> PULP: 'Bar Italia' (song) (1995)

In January 1926 John Logie Baird (1888–1946) demonstrated his 'televisor' to members of the ROYAL INSTITUTION in his laboratory above what is now the Bar Italia.

Barking A former fishing port and now a major east London centre, situated south of ILFORD and east of the River RODING. Evidence of Roman occupation has been discovered here and Barking was one of the earliest Saxon settlements east of London, established on a habitable site near navigable water. St Erkenwald founded Barking Abbey in 666 and William the Conqueror used it as a temporary headquarters while the TOWER OF LONDON was being constructed. The abbey escaped the first wave of religious suppression in 1536 but was dissolved in 1539. St Margaret's Church, where Captain Cook was married in 1762, and the abbey ruins are now a designated preservation area. Following a long period as one of the worst regarded parts of outer London, Barking has recently begun to attract the attentions of property developers with upmarket pretensions.

> Barking is in many ways a symbol of what the Thames Gateway is intended to achieve – a deprived area with vast swathes of derelict industrial land, which is ripe for regeneration and renewal.
>
> *The Daily Telegraph* (27 March 2008)

Barking was the childhood home of the footballers Bobby Moore, Trevor Brooking and John Terry, England rugby stalwart Jason Leonard and the BARD OF BARKING, Billy Bragg.

Barking and Dagenham, London Borough of An OUTER LONDON borough comprising almost exactly the area formerly occupied by the individual municipal boroughs of the same names. Barking and Dagenham has the largest proportion of pensioners and is the most solidly working class of all London boroughs. It lacks the young graduate element that increasingly leavens even the poorest parts of inner London, while failing to attract the upwardly mobile types who have brought some wealth to neighbouring HAVERING and, across the river, BEXLEY. The borough is particularly known for its output of footballers and football managers, especially those who came to prominence in the 1960s. Barking and Dagenham's coat of arms includes elements representing Barking Abbey, the THAMES, fishing, industry and the patron saints of the parish of DAGENHAM. The civic motto is *Dei gratia probemur rebus* – 'by the grace of God let us be judged by our deeds'.

Barking Creek The tidal part of the River

RODING, which enters the THAMES 1½ miles (2.5 km) south of Barking. It flows through a bleak landscape of sewage plants and gasworks.

Barkingside An interwar suburb situated at the south-western corner of FAIRLOP Plain. The name was first recorded in 1538 and derives from its location on the BARKING side of HAINAULT Forest, at the boundary of the old parish.

Battle of Barking Creek *See under* BATTLE.

like the ladies of Barking Creek *See under* LIKE.

one stop short of Barking *See under* ONE.

Barkstead's treasure A hoard of ill-gotten gold said to have been buried in the vaults of the TOWER OF LONDON by John Barkstead, lieutenant of the Tower from 1652 to 1659 and a zealous Cromwellian. Barkstead was believed to have cruelly extracted much of the money from prisoners held in the Tower during the Protectorate. He fled the country at the Restoration but was caught in Holland, brought back to London and hanged at TYBURN in 1662. Samuel PEPYS was among those who searched in vain for the treasure.

Barley, Nathan *See* NATHAN BARLEY.

Barnaby Rudge This novel by Charles DICKENS, published in 1841, centres round the GORDON RIOTS of 1780, and he drew upon the memories of survivors of those times. Barnaby is simple-minded but good-natured, with a fantastic appearance. Always accompanied by his raven, Grip, he wanders about the countryside and gets swept up with the anti-Catholic rioters in their destructive acts.

Barnaby (Rudge) 'Judge' in COCKNEY RHYMING SLANG. 'Inky smudge', 'chocolate fudge' and 'vanilla fudge' are lesser-used alternatives.

Barnardo's A charity founded in 1867 by the Dublin-born philanthropist of Spanish ancestry, Thomas John Barnardo (1845–1905). His title of Doctor was strictly speaking honorary, as he had no medical qualifications. A clerk by profession, he converted to Christianity in 1862, and after a spell of preaching in the Dublin slums went to London (1866) to study medicine with the aim of becoming a medical missionary. Instead, he founded, while still a student, the East End Mission for destitute children in STEPNEY (1867). Barnado went on to establish a number of homes in GREATER LONDON, including in 1873 the village home for girls in the grounds of Mossford Lodge, BARKINGSIDE, which was leased to him rent-free as a wedding present. Six hundred girls were soon accommodated in 30 buildings. The village closed in 1986 as part of the charity's plan to disengage itself from running children's homes. Barnardo's is the largest child-care charity working in the UK and is headquartered on Tanners Lane, Barkingside. *See also the* RAGGED SCHOOL MUSEUM.

Barnard's Inn One of the old INNS OF CHANCERY, situated on the south side of HOLBORN and once known as Mackworth's Inn, because Dean Mackworth of Lincoln (d.1454) lived there. Its present name is from the man, one Barnard, who subsequently owned the inn. *See also* WISEACRES' HALL.

Barn Elms Now the collective name for the eastern part of the BARNES peninsula, Barn Elms was originally the manor house of Barnes. A villa nearby was the meeting place for the KIT-CAT CLUB in the early 18th century. The home farm where William Cobbett (1763–1835) practised experimental agriculture in the late 1820s disappeared under Barn Elms reservoirs in the 1890s. Cobbett probably wrote much of his campaigning treatise *Rural Rides* (1830) while based there. From 1894 until 1939 the RANELAGH Club was based at the old manor house, providing sporting facilities comparable with those at HURLINGHAM. The clubhouse was damaged by fire in 1954 and subsequently demolished. Barn Elms' Victorian reservoirs, which became redundant after the inauguration of the Thames Water Ring Main in the mid-1990s, have been spectacularly transformed into the LONDON WETLAND CENTRE.

barner 'A roaring blade, a fast man of North London', according to J. Redding Ware's *Passing English of the Victorian Era* (1908). Such a character would have been a regular at HIGHBURY BARN.

Barnes A classy riverside settlement situated to the north-west of PUTNEY. Domesday Book had the first authenticated appearance of the name, which was the site of the barns that stored grain for the manor of MORTLAKE. The novelist and dramatist Henry Fielding lived briefly at

Milbourne House in the mid-18th century before leaving for southern Europe in a vain attempt to improve his failing health. Barnes is nowadays a popular place of residence for established figures in the arts and media.

Barnet An elongated and elevated suburb situated 5 miles (8 km) west of ENFIELD and 11 miles (18 km) from the centre of London. The name was first recorded around 1070 and derives either from a corruption of 'burnt', indicating the clearance of former woodland, or from *bergnet*, an Old English word describing an area with a little hill. The variant form 'Barnetley' was in use for several centuries, the affix signifying a clearing. EAST BARNET may have been the earliest part of the district to be permanently inhabited and a church stood here by 1140. However, a more significant settlement soon evolved on the higher ground to the north-west following the establishment of a market by the abbey of St Albans. From the 14th century the new centre was known as Chipping Barnet (Barnet market). *See also* BATTLE OF BARNET; HIGH BARNET.

Barnet, London Borough of An OUTER LONDON borough formed in 1965 by merging the municipal boroughs of FINCHLEY and HENDON and the urban districts of Barnet, EAST BARNET and FRIERN BARNET. If the councillors of the largest constituent part had had their way, the new borough would have been called Hendon. The borough's coat of arms includes swords and roses that refer to the BATTLE OF BARNET and a two-bladed airscrew that recalls Hendon's role in the early history of aviation. The civic motto is *unitas efficit ministerium* – 'unity effects service'.

Barnet comb-out The nickname for a policy pursued by Barnet council in the late 1920s, when several of the town's many pubs were closed in a bid to reduce public drunkenness. The tag punned on the COCKNEY RHYMING SLANG meaning of 'Barnet' (*see below*).

Barnet (Fair) 'Hair', of the head-grown variety, in COCKNEY RHYMING SLANG, especially in reference to its styling. The fair was first held in 1588; the term has been in use since the mid-19th century. Barnet was a remote country town at that time but its fair was a magnet for the itinerant London traders who played a significant role in the creation of the rhyming slang vocabulary. In the USA the rhyme has been adapted as 'Bonny Fair' and in Australia as 'Barney Fair', although

neither is much heard anymore. In London the term is so well known that it has occasionally been re-rhymed with Alf GARNETT, further confusing the uninitiated.

> You look in the mirror at the hairdressers and your barnet looks like a turkey's nest.
> MALCOLM STACEY: *Winning Ways* (1999)

Barnsbury A fusion of older terraces and squares and modern council blocks in north-west ISLINGTON. The 13th-century Berners family gave their name to a large manor, of which present-day Barnsbury covers just a small part. From the 1830s rows of narrow-fronted terraces filled much of the locality. Beginning in the late 1960s some of the most run-down parts were demolished and the council and Barnsbury Housing Association built new homes. The latter also restored some older properties. Around this time the pendulum began to swing back in favour of city dwelling and a phase of GENTRIFICATION reversed Barnsbury's protracted decline. Young professionals flocked in and the district became known for its 'liberal intelligentsia', including numerous writers and journalists, as well as Tony Blair before he became prime minister in 1997.

Barnwell, George The subject of a 17th-century ballad in *Percy's Reliques* (1765), which formed the basis of George Lillo's tragedy *The London Merchant, or the History of George Barnwell*. Performed at the THEATRE ROYAL, DRURY LANE (1731), the play is regarded as reflecting the increasing middle-class tastes of the changing London audiences. Characters moralize along such lines as 'business, the youth's best preservative from ill, as idleness his worst of snares' (II, iv), apparently without irony. The play's eponymous protagonist is a London APPRENTICE who falls in with Sarah Millwood, a licentious resident of SHOREDITCH, to whom he gives £200 of his master's money in return for her favours. He next robs his uncle, a rich grazier, and beats out his brains. In the ballad the uncle dwelt in Ludlow, Shropshire, but Lillo moves this action nearer London; by tradition, the setting is identified as CAMBERWELL. Having spent the money, Sarah turns him out. Each informs against the other and both are hanged.

> Sarah Millwood: I would have my conquest complete, like those of the Spaniards in the New

World, who first plundered the natives of all the wealth they had, and then condemned the wretches to the mines for life, to work for more.

GEORGE LILLO: *The London Merchant*, I, ii (12th edition, 1763)

Barons Court A made-up name for the compact residential locality situated between HAMMERSMITH and WEST KENSINGTON. Hammersmith (or Margravine) Cemetery was consecrated in 1869 and soon afterwards Major Sir William Palliser (1830–82) built the first suburban houses to its east. Palliser was the inventor of armour-piercing projectiles known as Palliser shot, while his wife was famous as the model for Sir John Millais's portrait *Charlie is my Darling* (1864). The Barons Court name was probably Palliser's playful allusion to nearby EARLS COURT; there is no evidence of any specific baron having lived here. Barons Court station did not open until 1905, 30 years after the construction of the line. Mohandas Gandhi (1869–1948), the architect of Indian independence, lived at 20 Barons Court Road while studying law at UNIVERSITY COLLEGE LONDON.

barrow
barrow boy A street trader with wares displayed on a barrow; a COSTERMONGER. *See also* GET OFF ME BARRER!
Barrow Poets A group of poets founded in 1951 with the aim of selling their books of verse from street barrows in London during the FESTIVAL OF BRITAIN. When refused a licence for outdoor trading they turned to poetry readings in pubs and other places of public entertainment. By 1969 they had become sufficiently accepted to give a lunchtime reading in WESTMINSTER ABBEY and had official approval to sell from their barrows in the Queen Elizabeth Hall on the SOUTH BANK.

Bartholomew
Bartholomew baby A derisive term for a young woman dressed up in a tawdry manner, like the dolls that were sold at BARTHOLOMEW FAIR.
Bartholomew Fair A fair opened annually at SMITHFIELD on St Bartholomew's Day (24 August) from 1133 to 1752. After the reform of the calendar it began on 3 September. It was removed to ISLINGTON in 1840 and was last held in 1855 (*see* CALEDONIAN MARKET). It was one of the great national fairs, with a variety of amusements and entertainments, and long held its place as a

centre of London life. The Puritans failed to suppress it. Ben Jonson's *Bartholomew Fair*, a comedy of manners, was first acted in 1614.

> Here's that will challenge all the fairs,
> Come buy my nuts and damsons and Burgamy pears!
> Here's the Woman of Babylon, the Devil and the Pope.
> And here's the little girl just going on the rope!
> Here's Dives and Lazarus, and the World's Creation;
> Here's the Tall Dutchwoman, the like's not in the nation.
> Here is the booths where the high Dutch maid is,
> Here are the bears that dance like any ladies;
> Tat, tat, tat, tat, says little penny trumpet;
> Here's Jacob Hall, that does so jump it, jump it;
> Sound trumpet, sound, for silver spoon and fork.
> Come, here's your dainty pig and pork!

Wit and Drollery (1682)

Bartholomew pig A pig roasted and sold piping hot at BARTHOLOMEW FAIR. The tempting manner in which the meat was displayed was a cause of great annoyance to the Puritans. Ben Jonson made much of the subject in *Bartholomew Fair* (1614). His character Zeal-of-the-Land Busy calls a Bartholomew pig 'a spice of idolatry' but falls prey to temptation. Pregnant women believed that eating Bartholomew pig would help them deliver a healthy male child. The term was also used in reference to a very fat person. Doll Tearsheet calls Falstaff:

> Thou whoreson little tidy Bartholomew boar-pig.

SHAKESPEARE: *Henry IV, Part 2*, II, iv (*c*.1597)

Bart's or **Barts** The name, originally a colloquial abbreviation but latterly an official designation, given to St Bartholomew's Hospital in SMITHFIELD. The priory church of St Bartholomew the Great and an adjoining hospital were established in 1123 by Rahere, who is sometimes described as a court jester but was 'more of a priest than a fool', as Rudyard Kipling put it. Both institutions survive today, though nothing remains of the hospital's original building and only a little of the church's. The artist William HOGARTH was christened at St Bartholomew's Church in 1697.

Bassishaw A compact CITY of London ward centred on Basinghall Street. The names of the ward and that street are both corruptions of

Bassingehawe, as it was earliest recorded, an enclosure belonging in the 12th century to the Basing family. The ward encompasses the GUILD-HALL and four LIVERY HALLS.

Bastille A slang term for the house of correction at COLD BATH FIELDS, often abbreviated to the Steel. The term was also applied to some of the early PEABODY BUILDINGS, which had forbidding exteriors and spartan interiors, owing to the attitude of the trust's commissioners rather than any conditions laid down by George Peabody.

Battersea An increasingly upmarket district that nevertheless retains many council-built flats, situated on the south bank of the THAMES, north-east of WANDSWORTH. It is one of the oldest recorded place names in the London area. A late 7th-century charter makes reference to 'Badrices ege', the island of a man called Badric. Industries were later established on reclaimed marshland beside the Thames, including a shot foundry, a whiting (whitewash) works and a brewhouse at NINE ELMS. The original, wooden BATTERSEA BRIDGE, crossing the Thames to CHELSEA, was erected in 1772; the present-day bridge replaced it in 1890. Battersea council was a famously progressive body, in 1906 gaining the first British-born black councillor, John Richard Archer. In 1913 Archer was elected mayor, another first. Battersea's somewhat depressing reputation for inner-city grime and run-down housing was to some extent abated in the 1980s, when renovators and yuppifiers began to move in. (Pundits began to refer to Batt-er-sia (stress on the 'er'), a mangling of the name supposedly engaged in by the area's new wealthy inhabitants in order to distance it as far as possible from its traditional reputation.) Former residents include the author G.K. Chesterton and the artist-craftsman Eric Gill. *See also* SWONE-ONE.

Battersea Bridge A road bridge linking Battersea and CHELSEA. The present structure opened in 1890, replacing a wooden bridge that was the subject of several paintings by James McNeill Whistler (1834–1903), including *Nocturne: Blue and Gold* (*c.*1872–5), which hangs in TATE BRITAIN.

Battersea bundles The form in which Battersea's widely prized asparagus was sold, in the time up to the 1830s when the district's main occupation was market gardening.

Battersea'd An 18th-century slang term de-noting that one's penis had been treated for venereal disease. The underlying allusion is to the curative herbs that grew in the market gardens of Battersea.

Battersea Dogs' Home Britain's most famous animal refuge, sandwiched between two railway lines just off Battersea Park Road. It was founded in HOLLOWAY in 1860 by Mary Tealby, and she moved the home to Battersea in 1871. It has become a minor British institution (notably since the Prince of Wales conferred his royal seal of approval on it in 1879), and has provided generations of aspirant dog-owners with a new pet. The home nowadays also cares for abandoned cats and is officially called Battersea Dogs & Cats Home.

Battersea Dogs' Home here! A facetious way to answer the telephone. The catchphrase was first recorded in the 1950s among Army personnel and subsequently spread into civilian usage, especially when answering internal office calls. By the 1970s it was dying out.

Battersea enamel A description of various types of small articles (e.g. candlesticks, needle cases) ornamented with decorative enamel, as produced in a workshop at York House, Battersea, from the 1740s to 1756. Several similar local businesses were equally short lived.

Battersea Park A feature-filled public park occupying 200 acres (80 hectares) of the Thames riverside between Battersea and NINE ELMS. This was formerly Battersea Fields, an isolated spot that became popular as a duelling ground in the early 19th century; in 1829 the Duke of Wellington, then the prime minister, and the Earl of Winchelsea confronted each other here but no blood was spilt. Battersea Park was laid out from 1846 and officially opened by Queen Victoria in 1858. In 1951 the FESTIVAL OF BRITAIN gardens were laid out in the park, and the site was subsequently occupied by Battersea funfair. The park's riverfront is now embellished by a Buddhist peace pagoda, erected in 1985. Creative works mentioning the park include Petula Clark's 1954 single 'Meet Me in Battersea Park' and the 2001 books *After Battersea Park*, by Jonathan Bennett, and *The Battersea Park Road to Enlightenment*, by Isabel Losada.

Battersea power station A former coal-fired power station located on the south bank of the River Thames, at NINE ELMS, just to the east of CHELSEA Bridge. Designed by Sir Giles Gilbert

Scott, it opened in 1937. It is actually two power stations, the second of which was not built until 1953, when the third and fourth chimneys were added. Following a progressive run-down the power station closed in 1983 and has since been the subject of a succession of abortive redevelopment plans. The present owners hope to have the building put to an array of new uses, including 'green' power generation, by around 2020.

Battersea Shield A unique Celtic ovoid bronze shield with 27 settings of red enamel, recovered from the THAMES near BATTERSEA BRIDGE.

Battersea Tangle An old nickname for the vicinity of Queenstown (formerly Queen's) Road, because of the network of railway lines here.

early Battersea See under EARLY.

go to Battersea to be cut for the simples See under GO.

battle

Battle Bridge The former identity of the district now called KING'S CROSS. In the Middle Ages it was Bradford Bridge, from a 'broad ford' across the upper part of the FLEET river. The corruption of the name to Battle Bridge was not recorded until 1625, and was associated with (perhaps the source of) the legend that BOUDICCA fought a battle with the Romans here. The story was later embellished by the claim that the warrior queen lies buried beneath a platform of KING'S CROSS STATION.

Battlebridge Basin A wharf on the REGENT'S CANAL, north-east of KING'S CROSS STATION. It is the home of the LONDON CANAL MUSEUM.

Battle Bridge Lane A short thoroughfare off TOOLEY STREET, commemorating the site of a bridge across a THAMES inlet built by the abbot of Battle, Sussex, whose medieval London residence stood nearby.

battle (cruiser) 'Boozer' in COCKNEY RHYMING SLANG, in the sense of a public house.

Battle of Barking Creek The sardonic nickname for a 'friendly fire' incident on the third day of the Second World War. Because of mistaken identification by a ground station, a Spitfire from RAF HORNCHURCH shot down two Hurricanes from RAF North Weald. One pilot survived but the other, Montague Hulton-Harrop, was killed. His was the first death of a British fighter pilot in the war and the Hurricanes were the first aircraft to be downed by a Spitfire. The 'battle' took place some distance from BARKING CREEK but the sound of the name (and perhaps the creek's notoriety for sewage pollution) may have appealed to wartime airmen's black sense of humour.

Battle of Barnet The decisive conflict in the Wars of the Roses, in which Edward IV and the Yorkists slew the Earl of Warwick, the Kingmaker, and vanquished Henry VI. It took place on HADLEY GREEN on a foggy Easter Sunday in 1471.

Battle of Brentford

1. One of a series of conflicts between English forces led by Edmund II and the Danes under King Cnut. It probably took place in the summer of 1016. Edmund won this battle but lost the war.

2. A Civil War attack of 12 November 1642 in which Prince Rupert's Royalists stormed and plundered BRENTFORD. The severity of the pillage helped the Parliamentarians rally additional support at the BATTLE OF TURNHAM GREEN on the following day.

Battle of Brighton A gangland encounter at Brighton Racecourse in 1936 when the Sabini brothers of CLERKENWELL (in league with the police) outwitted and defeated their rivals, the HOXTON Gang. The incident provided material for Graham Greene's *Brighton Rock* (1938).

Battle of Cable Street An influential and folkloric clash (4 October 1936), in which local residents and their supporters turned back a march through the heart of the Jewish EAST END by the British Union of Fascists, led by Sir Oswald Mosley (1896–1980). The anti-fascists assembled at Gardiner's Corner, the GATEWAY TO THE EAST END, and, on learning that the march was to be routed along CABLE STREET, rushed to set up barricades there. After a violent confrontation lasting several hours the police told Mosley that the march could not proceed.

Battle of Crayford A brutal confrontation that took place in the valley of the River CRAY, probably in AD 457. If the *Anglo-Saxon Chronicle* is to be believed, 4,000 men were slain and the battle played a decisive role in the formation of the kingdom of England, with the Germanic army of the semi-legendary Hengist driving Prince Vortimer's Britons out of Kent and back to London.

Battle of George Green See WANSTONIA.

Battle of Grunwick A 1977 industrial dispute that centred on the right of a CRICKLEWOOD photo processing company's predominantly Asian, female workforce to join a trade union.

Battle of Highbury The nickname of a so-called friendly football match between England and Italy at HIGHBURY STADIUM on 14 November 1934, which England won 3–2. The name alludes to the behaviour of the Italian team, who, promised exemption from military service if they won, resorted to physical confrontation, leaving a number of England players injured and provoking retaliation.

Battle of London A name occasionally given to an abortive attempt by a posse of Londoners to resist the invading forces of William the Conqueror in 1066.

Battle of London Bridge A semi-legendary battle (*c.*1014) between the Anglo-Saxon forces of Ethelred the Unready (*c.*968–1016) and the Danish fleet of Sweyn Forkbeard (*c.*960–1014). Ethelred was supported by a Norwegian army led by Olaf II (995–1030), and his role is remembered in the dedication of St Olave's Church (*see* ST GHASTLY GRIM), in Hart Street, a western extension of CRUTCHED FRIARS. LONDON BRIDGE is said to have been pulled down during the battle, either by the Danes or by Londoners themselves as a defensive strategy. The event is cited as a possible source of the nursery rhyme 'London Bridge is Falling Down', especially as a similar poem commemorates the battle:

London Bridge is broken down,
Gold is won, and bright renown.
Shields resounding,
War-horns sounding,
Hild is shouting in the din!
Arrows singing,
Mail-coats ringing,
Odin makes our Olaf win!

OTTAR SVARTE, quoted in SNORRI STURLUSON:
Heimskringla (*c.*1225) (translated by Samuel Laing, 1844)

Battle of Mr Smith's club A gang fight in CATFORD in March 1966 that brought about the downfall of south London's most powerful criminal gang, the Richardsons, and led to the revenge killing of George Cornell by the KRAY TWINS.

Battle of Stepney *See the* SIEGE OF SIDNEY STREET.

Battle of Surbiton A rarely used name for a minor skirmish that took place at the tail end of the English Civil War, on 6 July 1648. The Duke of Buckingham and his brother Lord Francis Villiers led a band of local men in a foolhardy Royalist advance on London. Parliamentarian troops from Windsor routed the Royalists near SURBITON COMMON, killing Francis Villiers.

Battle of the Nile 'Tile', meaning a hat, in very early COCKNEY RHYMING SLANG.

Battle of Turnham Green An influential Civil War standoff that took place on TURNHAM GREEN – which was then very much larger than it is today – on 13 November 1642. Confronted by a Parliamentarian force of about 24,000 men, and following some indecisive skirmishes, the smaller Royalist army withdrew, forfeiting its best chance to take London.

Baynard's Castle *See* CASTLE BAYNARD.

Bayswater An enclave of hotels and high-class housing lying north of KENSINGTON GARDENS. Bayswater began as a hamlet located close to present-day LANCASTER GATE but the name now covers a wide area stretching west to NOTTING HILL, north as far as WESTBOURNE GREEN and east to Paddington – or even beyond, to MARBLE ARCH. In 1380 this was Bayard's Watering Place. The water was provided by the stream later known as the WESTBOURNE, while a bayard was a bay (chestnut) horse, though some suggest the name may have come from a man called Baynard, possibly the one who built CASTLE BAYNARD. Artists and writers came here in the early 19th century, when the district was still semi-rural, but were soon succeeded by more conventional members of the upper classes. Greeks and Jews also settled here, establishing their own places of worship on Moscow Road and St Petersburgh Place respectively. Since the 1980s Bayswater has been the focus of a wave of settlement by Middle Eastern expatriates, who patronize the shops and services on QUEENSWAY and EDGWARE ROAD. *See also* ASIA MINOR.

Bayswater captain A former term for a 'dry land sailor'. Also, in slang usage from around 1880 to 1910, a man who scraped a living in good society by scrounging. The idea was evidently of someone who lived in cheapish lodgings in Bayswater, within easy reach of the WEST END.

Baze, the A nickname for BAYSWATER Road in the era of street prostitution (before the 1959 Street Offences Act). It was a major pick-up point, but distinctly down-market from MAYFAIR and PICCADILLY.

Beach, the A nickname for the middle part

of the FULHAM ROAD (near to the Chelsea and Westminster Hospital), in the vicinity of the now-lost village of Little CHELSEA, which was once an area of heathland and nurseries. The modern tag derives from the supposedly Mediterranean feel of this stretch of the road, which has a pleasing mix of pubs and eateries, independent shops and galleries, and a six-screen cinema.

Beam River A minor river flowing into the THAMES at DAGENHAM. It was earlier called the Mark Dyke ('boundary ditch' – between Dagenham and HAVERING), an identity that is recalled at nearby Mardyke Farm. The river's present name is a back-formation from Beam Bridge, a crossing that originally consisted of a single beam of wood. The part of the river that flows through ROMFORD is called the River Rom.

beau

Beau Brummell The sobriquet of George Bryan Brummell (1778–1840), a notorious dandy and personal friend of the Prince REGENT, later George IV. At the height of his social standing, Brummell was the most influential figure of the day in matters of style but he fell out with the prince and in 1816 fled to France to escape his creditors. He died of syphilis in a charitable asylum in Caen.

> I could have repeated numberless specimens of his droll turns in conversation; one only occurs to me at the moment: 'Come to Brighton, my dear fellow,' he said to the present Lord Liverpool, then Cecil Jenkinson, 'let us be off tomorrow; we'll eat currant-tart, and live in chintz and salt-water.'
>
> WILLIAM JESSE: *The Life of George Brummell, Esq.*, Volume 2 (1844)

Beau of Leadenhall Street *See* DIRTY DICK'S.

Beauchamp Place A street in BROMPTON, running between Brompton Road and PONT STREET. Until 1885 it was called Grove Place. It is full of breathtakingly expensive boutiques for the wives and daughters of the ultra-rich and equally expensive restaurants for the delectation of ladies-who-lunch.

Beck A stream flowing through BECKENHAM to the River RAVENSBOURNE, via the Pool River. The stream takes its name from the place, rather than the other way around, as might be supposed.

Beck, Harry *See the* LONDON UNDERGROUND MAP.

Beckenham BROMLEY's little sister lies 2 miles (3 km) to its west. The name is generally held to derive from Beohha, a Saxon farmer. In 1969 David Bowie founded the Beckenham Arts Lab at a pub on the High Street while living in Foxgrove Road.

Beckton The former home of the world's biggest gasworks and now a DOCKLANDS development area, situated west of BARKING CREEK and north of the Royal Albert Dock (*see the* ROYAL DOCKS). In 1870 the Gas, Light and Coke Company established its London base here. Housing was built for the workers and the whole 400-acre (160-hectare) site was named Beckton after the governor of the company, Simon Adams Beck. At its peak, Beckton supplied gas to over four million Londoners, as well as manufacturing by-products such as creosote, fertilizers, inks and dyes. It was not until the switch to natural gas in the 1960s that the works were scaled down. During its dereliction, the old gasworks site was often used as a film and television location, most notably for the Vietnam scenes in Stanley Kubrick's *Full Metal Jacket* (1987) and for James Bond's disposal of Blofeld down a chimney in *For Your Eyes Only* (1981).

Becontree A gargantuan council estate covering 4 square miles (10 sq km) of former fields, heath and parkland north of DAGENHAM. Begun in 1921, Becontree was the flagship of the London County Council's COTTAGE ESTATE housebuilding programme and was intended to accommodate 100,000 people. Many of the first residents came from LIMEHOUSE, where a slum clearance programme was under way at the time. By the 1930s Becontree had grown larger than many provincial cities. With the trends towards smaller families and more people living alone, Becontree's population is now much smaller than originally envisaged.

> Some insight into the novelty of this [electric lighting in council houses] at the time is conveyed by the warning given to tenants on the Becontree estate not to wash the bulbs by dunking them in water.
>
> ALISON RAVETZ with RICHARD TURKINGTON: *The Place of Home: English Domestic Environments, 1914–2000* (2005)

Beddington A very varied district situated between CARSHALTON and the WADDON area of CROYDON. The name is associated with a Saxon landowner. During the 14th century Sir Nicholas Carew acquired a large estate and built a moated and fortified mansion. Succeeding Carews laid out magnificent gardens where the first English oranges were grown in the 17th century, rebuilt the house in the early 18th century and then sold the estate in 1859 to clear gambling debts. The house is now called Carew Manor and is used as a school for children with moderate learning difficulties. Neighbouring WALLINGTON grew at Beddington's expense in the late 19th century and it was not until after the First World War that rapid suburbanization began.

Beddington Corner An assortment of industry, terraced housing and wilderness lying on the east side of the River WANDLE, south of MITCHAM COMMON. Although the name is used to denote the junction of Goat Road, Carshalton Road and London Road, its origin lies in its former location at the north-west corner of Beddington parish.

Beddington Zero Energy Development *See* BEDZED.

Bedfont A bipartite business and residential district situated south of HEATHROW AIRPORT; West Bedfont lies just outside the GREATER LONDON boundary; East Bedfont is in the London Borough of HOUNSLOW. Finds of Roman coins indicate the possible presence of a Roman villa, and the Saxons built a church here. The manor of East Bedfont was first recorded in the 11th century and parts of St Mary's Church date from around 1150. Until relatively recently, East Bedfont remained a charming backwater, with cottages and tall trees surrounding the green and pond, and some outlying timber-framed buildings that may be 500 years old. However, expansion towards FELTHAM altered its character in the second half of the 20th century, as have industrial estates, a 'technopark' and the Bedfont Lakes country park.

Bedfont peacocks In front of St Mary's south porch are two ancient yew trees, trimmed into the shape of a pair of peacocks. The topiary, which may date from 1704, is said to represent two vain young women, possibly sisters, who used to show off their finery by the church gate, to the irritation of humbler worshippers. Thomas Hood wrote a long poem on the subject, which ends thus:

> And where two haughty maidens used to be,
> In pride of plume, where plumy Death hath trod,
> Trailing their gorgeous velvets wantonly,
> Most unmeet pall, over the holy sod;
> There, gentle stranger, thou may'st only see
> Two sombre Peacocks. – Age, with sapient nod
> Marking the spot, still tarries to declare
> How they once lived, and wherefore they are there.

'The Two Peacocks of Bedfont' (1822)

Bedford

Bedford College A former college of London University, founded in 1849 as a women's college. It took its name from the original site in BEDFORD SQUARE. Between 1909 and 1985 it was located in REGENT'S PARK. It was then amalgamated with Royal Holloway College in Surrey, at first becoming the Royal Holloway and Bedford New College. Now Royal Holloway, UNIVERSITY OF LONDON, it retains a small London base in GOWER STREET, used as a venue for teaching and postgraduate activities.

Bedford Estate An area of land in BLOOMSBURY, owned by the dukes of Bedford. Their original land-holding, granted to the 1st Earl of Bedford in 1552 for services to the Crown, was in COVENT GARDEN, but this was sold in 1914. The Bloomsbury territory came into the family by inheritance in 1723. Many of the streets and squares in the area perpetuate the family's name (Russell), the names of its subsidiary titles, the names of its relatives and the name of its Bedfordshire seat, Woburn Abbey: GOWER STREET, Malet Street, RUSSELL SQUARE, Tavistock Square, Torrington Place, Woburn Place and so on.

Bedford Park An influential 'new model suburb' created after 1875 in the south-east corner of ACTON by the speculator Jonathan Carr. The name comes from Bedford House, a Georgian villa in the grounds of which Bedford Park was laid out. The house itself was named after the man who built it, in the 1790s, 'John Bedford' (an assumed name – he was originally John Tubbs). Prompted by the arrival of the Metropolitan Railway at TURNHAM GREEN, Carr bought 24 acres (10 hectares) of land with the intention of building a settlement that would be affordable yet stylish. Unlike many of the more austere Victorian 'model' communities, Bedford Park had an inn, a club and an art school as well as the customary church. The area suffered a decline during the postwar years, and delays in granting statutory protection allowed several houses to be demolished and replaced by blocks of flats in the early 1960s. Preservation groups have since prevented any further destruction and Bedford Park is once again highly popular with the middle classes. W.B. Yeats lived in Bedford Park for most of the 1880s and 1890s, and wrote 'The Lake Isle of Innisfree' at 3 Blenheim Road. Camille Pissarro's painting of *Bath Road in Bedford Park* (1897) is in the Ashmolean Museum, Oxford.

Bedford Square The only complete Georgian square left in BLOOMSBURY, it was until the 1980s synonymous with book publishing, as many publishers had offices here.

Bedknobs and Broomsticks A 1971 Disney movie set in London during the BLITZ. The musical fantasy starred the POPLAR-born actress Angela Lansbury.

Bedlam (form of 'bethlem', a contraction of 'Bethlehem') The priory of St Mary of Bethlehem outside BISHOPSGATE was founded in 1247 and began to receive lunatics in 1377. It was given to the CITY of London as a hospital for lunatics by Henry VIII in 1547. In 1675 it was transferred to MOORFIELDS and became one of the sights of London, where for a few pence anyone might gaze at the poor wretches and bait them. It was a place for assignations and one of the disgraces of 17th-century London. 'Bedlam' became a generic name for a lunatic asylum or madhouse, and hence a place of hubbub and confusion. In 1815 Bethlem Royal Hospital moved to LAMBETH and in 1930 to MONKS ORCHARD. *See also* ABRAHAM MAN.

Bedlamite A madman, a fool, an inmate of Bedlam.

Tom o' Bedlam *See under* TOM.

Bednall Green *See* BETHNAL GREEN; *the* BLIND BEGGAR OF BEDNALL GREEN.

bedsit jungle One might expect this term to have been applied to many parts of London but its usage seems to have been restricted to EARLS COURT.

BedZED A 'carbon neutral' community dubbed 'the UK's largest eco-village' when it was built on the 3½-acre (1.5-hectare) site of an old sewage

works lying between London Road and BEDDINGTON Lane in HACKBRIDGE, in the London Borough of SUTTON. The Beddington Zero Energy Development, completed in 2001, is a PEABODY project in association with the BioRegional Development Group, actively supported by Sutton council. Its cutting-edge architecture addresses environmental, social and economic needs and employs various methods of reducing energy, water and car use.

beef

Beefeater Gin The only major brand of LONDON GIN still made in the capital. The company's founder, pharmacist James Burrough, began producing gin in CHELSEA in 1863. The distillery moved to LAMBETH in 1908 and then in 1958 to its present home, the former Haywards pickle factory in Montford Place, KENNINGTON.

Beefeaters The popular name of the Yeoman Warders of the TOWER OF LONDON, a detachment of the Yeomen of the Guard, created by Henry VII in 1485 and still the ceremonial royal bodyguard. The two corps of yeomen wear an almost identical Tudor uniform, distinguished only by the cross belts worn from the left shoulder by the Yeomen of the Guard. For everyday duties, Beefeaters wear a red and dark blue undress uniform. The literal meaning is 'eaters of beef', and the word does not derive from the (allegedly) French *buffetier*, as was once popularly supposed.

> Those goodly juments of the guard would fight
> (As they eat beef) after six stone a day;
> WILLIAM CARTWRIGHT: *The Ordinary* (c.1635)

Beefsteak Club The original CLUB, frequented by wits, where refreshment was limited to steaks and beer or wine, was established in London in 1709, with a gridiron as its badge. In 1735 the Sublime Society of Steaks was inaugurated when Lord Peterborough supped with John Rich, manager of the Covent Garden Theatre (now the ROYAL OPERA HOUSE). His lordship was so delighted with the steak provided that he proposed to repeat the entertainment every Saturday. The Sublime Society continued to meet there until a fire in 1808, when it moved to other premises. The 'Steaks' included many famous actors until its cessation in 1867. The modern Beefsteak Club was founded in 1876.

Bees A nickname for both BARNET and BRENT-

FORD football clubs, from the first letter of their names.

bees (and honey) 'Money' in COCKNEY RHYMING SLANG.

Beggar's Opera, The A popular ballad opera by John Gay, first staged in 1728. Produced by John Rich (*see* BEEFSTEAK CLUB), it was said to have made 'Gay rich and Rich gay'. The hero is a highwayman, Macheath, and it centres on NEWGATE PRISON. The beggar of the title has only a speaking role. *The Beggar's Opera* was both seminal and successful because it broke with the Italian *opera seria* that dominated the London musical scene at that time. The music was made up of traditional ballads and popular tunes of the day arranged by the German composer Johann Pepusch (1667–1752) and its topical satire featured (thinly disguised) Londoners such as Jack WILD, on whom the character Peachum was modelled. In the 20th century, Bertolt Brecht adapted the drama for his *Threepenny Opera*.

Beirut-on-Thames *See* LONDONISTAN.

Belfast, HMS *See* HMS BELFAST.

Belgravia Probably London's most desirable address, Belgravia is a Georgian estate of terraces, crescents and squares situated between KNIGHTSBRIDGE and VICTORIA. Development began here in the late 18th century, prompted by the rebuilding of Buckingham House (now BUCKINGHAM PALACE). The new district was centred on Belgrave Square, named after the GROSVENOR family's Belgrave estate (which was originally called Merdegrave). As well as providing residences of the very highest quality, Belgravia is home to several embassies; the earliest to locate here was the Austrian Embassy, in the 19th century. Chopin gave his first London recital at 99 Eaton Place in 1848.
Belgravian (A person) of or from Belgravia: 'That ineffable Belgravian, Lady Galbraith', *Athenaeum* (1891).

Belin or **Belinus** A mythical British king who ruled in the early 4th century BC. Among his many achievements he rebuilt the CITY of London, founded the TOWER OF LONDON and built ERMINE STREET and WATLING STREET. BILLINGSGATE is said (equally fictitiously) to be named in his honour. Geoffrey of Monmouth's *Historia Regum Britanniae* (*History of the Kings*

*of Britain, c.*1136) is the primary source of the legend.

> However Belinus after a while returning home,
> the rest of his days rul'd in Peace, Wealth, and
> Honour above all his Predecessors; building
> some Cities ... beautifying others, as Trinovant,
> with a Gate, a Haven, and a Tower, on the
> Thames, retaining yet his Name; on the top
> whereof his Ashes are said to have been laid up
> in a Golden Urn.
>
> JOHN MILTON: *History of Britain* (1670)

bell

Bell and Horns The nickname of the CABMEN'S SHELTER at Thurloe Place, SOUTH KENSINGTON, from an inn that stood nearby from the 18th century until 1915, on the site now occupied by a mansion block called Empire House. Other nicknamed shelters have included the Nursery End, near LORD'S, and the Junior Turf Club, on PICCADILLY. The latter was said to derive from an invading clientele of aristocratic champagne drinkers in the 1920s.

bellman Latterly an alternative term for a town crier, a bellman was originally a night watchman whose duty was to keep a lookout for fires. An act of Parliament introduced the practice to London in 1556 and the first recorded bellman began patrolling the ward of CORDWAINER in the following January. Bellmen became a distinctive feature of the city in the 17th century, parading the streets at night and calling out the hours. In his *Book of Days* (1864), Robert Chambers mentions the sheets of 'insufferable' verse given by bellmen to householders in their district at Christmas, in the expectation of a gratuity. Chambers quotes the bellman of HOLBORN thus:

> Time, Master, calls your bellman to his task,
> To see your doors and windows are all fast,
> And that no villainy or foul crime be done
> To you or yours in absence of the sun.
> If any base lurker I do meet,
> In private alley or in open street,
> You shall have warning by my timely call,
> And so God bless you and give rest to all.
>
> ISAAC RAGG (1684)

belle

Belle Isle, La An ironic nickname for AGAR TOWN.
Belle Sauvage, La The site on the north side of LUDGATE HILL, occupied by the publishing house

of Cassell from 1852 until 11 May 1941, when the whole area was demolished in an air raid. The name is an alteration of 'Savage's Bell Inn' and the French form appears to have been first used by Joseph Addison (1672–1719) in *The Spectator* (No.82). There seems to have been an inn on the site from about the 14th century, originally called the Bell on the Hope, the 'Hope' or 'Hoop' being the garlanded ivy bush. From its position just outside Ludgate, its yard became a rendezvous for bear-baiting, play acting and the like, and from the 17th until the mid-19th century it was a departure point for coaches. The inn licence was not renewed after 1857. *La Belle Sauvage* translates from French as 'the beautiful wild girl', and a representation of her (as a half-kneel skin-clad Pocahontas with bow and arrows) was originally Cassell's colophon (a printer's or publisher's house device).

> Tom had never been in London, and would have liked to have stopped at the Belle Savage, where they had been put down by the Star, just at dusk, that he might have gone roving about those endless, mysterious, gas-lit streets ...
>
> THOMAS HUGHES: *Tom Brown's Schooldays* (1857)

Belmarsh London's most secure prison, located in south-west THAMESMEAD. Planned from 1982 and built on 77 acres (31 hectares) of the disused WOOLWICH ARSENAL site, HMP Belmarsh opened in 1991. It holds around 900 inmates and acts as both a local jail for south-east Londoners and a remand centre for high-risk prisoners, who are held in a separate mini-prison with its own perimeter and enhanced surveillance. To improve security and reduce the amount of staff time spent escorting prisoners to court, a magistrates' court and a Crown court were constructed between the prison and Western Way, and are linked to the prison via a tunnel. In recent years the detention of terrorist suspects without trial has led civil rights campaigners to brand the prison 'Britain's own Guantanamo Bay'. The notorious convict Charles Bronson held three other prisoners hostage at Belmarsh in 1996, fruitlessly demanding a helicopter to Cuba, an axe, submachine guns, a cheese sandwich and an ice cream. Other high-profile inmates have included the train robber Ronnie Biggs and former Conservative ministers Jeffrey Archer and Jonathan Aitken.

> The guard dogs bark, the barbed wire glints,

> As russet dawn unveils each day
> To towers of steel and walls of flint
> Weathered and worn to drabness grey.
>
> JONATHAN AITKEN: 'A Ballad from Belmarsh Gaol' (published in *The Spectator*, 26 June 1999)

Belsize Park A (relatively) poor man's HAMPSTEAD, situated to its south-east. The sub-manor of Belsize was first recorded in the early 14th century and Belsize House in 1496. The name derives from Bel-assis, meaning 'beautifully situated'. Belsize Park has always attracted artists, writers and entertainers. The artist Robert Bevan (1865–1925) lived locally and painted several views of the neighbourhood, including *A Street Scene in Belsize Park* (1917), which shows the influence of his acquaintance Paul Gauguin. Other residents have included the composer Frederick Delius, authors Jerome K. Jerome, Nicholas Monsarrat and Agatha Christie, actors Sadie Frost, Jude Law, Hugh Laurie, Kate Winslet and Helena Bonham-Carter, film director Tim Burton and comedians David Baddiel and Frank Skinner. *See also the* WELSH AMBASSADOR.

Belvedere A diverse industrial and residential district on land rising from the THAMES northwest of ERITH. From the mid-17th century three substantial villas were successively erected beside a crossroads at Blinks Hill on Lessness Heath. The last of these was named Belvedere House, from the Italian meaning 'beautiful view'. Built in the 1770s, the house became home to a series of peers and knights, culminating with the philanthropist and reformer Sir Culling Eardley (1805–63). In the mid-19th century several factors combined to render the area ripe for profitable growth: the establishment of industries beside the Thames, the arrival of the North Kent Railway, and Eardley's willingness to develop his estate with housing for the middle classes. Meanwhile, the riverside hamlet of Picardy became Lower Belvedere, a settlement of terraced cottages for workers at the nearby factories and wharves. On Eardley's death the estate was broken up and his house became a seamen's mission. It was demolished in 1959.

bencher A senior member of one of the four INNS OF COURT.

bend
  Bend Or The nickname of Hugh Richard Gros-

venor, 2nd Duke of Westminster (1879–1958). It derived from the 'bend or' – that is to say, the golden diagonal band – in the GROSVENOR coat of arms. Bend Or was also the name of a racehorse owned by his father, the 1st Duke of Westminster, which won the Derby in 1880.

bendy buses The colloquial name for the articulated single-decker buses introduced to London in 2003, in part as a replacement for the ROUTEMASTER. The buses proved unpopular with many Londoners for the amount of road space they took up, and their consequent tendency to block junctions. They also had a relatively poor safety record and higher fare evasion. In his successful mayoral election campaign of 2008, Boris Johnson (*see* BO-JO) pledged to eliminate the vehicles.

> The Mayor today hit back at critics of his plan to scrap bendy buses by vowing to implement a 'timetable of doom' that will see the last one disappear from London's streets by 2015. On a BBC Radio London phone-in, Boris Johnson said the first bendy buses would be removed next year.
> *Evening Standard* (23 September 2008)

Benet Fink *See* ST BENET FINK.

Bennet's Hill A twisting street branching northward from CASTLE BAYNARD Street in the CITY of London. In the 13th century it was Haggen Lane, 'the lane of the hags', from an unkind opinion of its older female residents. The hill takes its present name from the church of St Benet Paul's Wharf, rebuilt by Christopher WREN after the GREAT FIRE OF LONDON, and from 1879 the City's Welsh church. The church closed in July 2008 as a result of underuse. The architect Inigo JONES is buried here.

Bentley Priory A mansion built in 1766 on the site of the Augustinian priory in STANMORE, and remodelled in the 1790s by Sir John SOANE for the eccentric John James Hamilton (1756–1818), later 1st Marquess of Abercorn. Queen Adelaide, widow of William IV, died at Bentley Priory in 1849. In the 1880s Frederick Gordon converted the mansion into a sumptuous but not very successful hotel, and established a railway company that built a line to Stanmore. The Air Ministry bought Bentley Priory in 1925 and it became the Royal Air Force's Fighter Command Headquarters during the Second World War. RAF Bentley

Priory closed in 2008, when it was acquired by property developers who have agreed to create space for a Battle of Britain museum in the historic rooms of the mansion, and part-fund its running costs.

berk A mild insult, approximating to 'fool', derived from the COCKNEY RHYMING SLANG 'Berkeley Hunt', meaning 'cunt'. The alternative 'Berkshire Hunt' seems to have come much later. Contrary to the usual British pronunciation of 'Berkeley' and 'Berkshire', 'berk' is pronounced to rhyme with 'lurk', and as a consequence is sometimes erroneously spelt 'burk'. *See also* CHARLIE (HUNT).

> Now, I am not a very competent rider, and the nag I was given to ride stood nearly eighteen hands. He knew from the moment he saw me that 'here was a berk', and he devised all sorts of ways to unseat me at rehearsals.
> HARRY SECOMBE: *Strawberries and Cheam* (1996)

Berkeley

Berkeley Dress Show A dinner and fashion show held annually in aid of charity, at which selected young women from wealthy families model outfits created by well-known couturiers. Since the 1950s the event has constituted a curtain-raiser to what remains of the LONDON SEASON.

Berkeley Hunt *See* BERK.

Berkeley Square An aristocratic quadrangle in central MAYFAIR that once rivalled GROSVENOR SQUARE as the most fashionable spot in the WEST END. Berkeley House was built on the north side of PICCADILLY in the 1660s for John Berkeley, 1st Baron Berkeley of Stratton, with grounds stretching far into Mayfair. The house was sold in 1696 with the stipulation that its grounds be preserved, thus setting aside the space that became the square. After the demolition of Berkeley House in 1733, exceptionally grand properties were built on three sides of the very oblong 'square'. The square was home to the writer Horace Walpole, the statesmen George Canning and Winston Churchill and the general Lord Clive. No.50 was the subject of persistent and lurid ghost stories in the latter part of the 19th century. John Balderston's twice-filmed 1929 play *Berkeley Square* is an early time-travel romance. Berkeley Square's fame comes above all from the wartime song *A Nightingale Sang in*

Berkeley Square, recorded by Vera Lynn, Glenn Miller, Frank Sinatra and countless others.

> That certain night, the night we met,
> There was magic abroad in the air,
> There were angels dining at the Ritz,
> And a nightingale sang in Berkeley Square.
>
> ERIC MASCHWITZ and MANNING SHERWIN (1940)

Bermondsey A densely developed district occupying a broad swathe of inner south-east London between TOWER BRIDGE and the OLD KENT ROAD. Bermondsey's Old English name meant 'Beornmund's island' and points to its genesis on habitable ground amid the marshes. Bermondsey's plentiful supply of water and strong links with the CITY of London favoured the growth of its leather industry, with tannery pits dotting the area. Thomas Keyse's discovery of a spa in 1770 created a fashionable resort but its popularity was short-lived, the spa closing in 1804. The area suffered greatly in the Second World War and postwar rebuilding did not treat it kindly. Industries such as leather died away but the Leather Market and the neighbouring Exchange were saved from demolition in 1993 and converted into workspaces. The regeneration of the warehouses to the east of Tower Bridge at Shad Thames has brought the Design Museum and other attractions. Hundreds of bric-à-brac stalls operate at the Friday morning antiques market in Bermondsey Square, formally the New CALEDONIAN MARKET. There are also warehouse-based antiques dealers in Bermondsey Street and Tower Bridge Road.

Bermondsey banger 19th-century slang for:

> ... a society leader among the South London tanneries, who must ... be prepared to hold his own and fight at all times for his social belt ...
>
> J. REDDING WARE: *Passing English of the Victorian Era* (1908)

Banger in this context is both one who 'bangs' his fellows about physically and one who makes a 'bang' in society.

Bermondsey Horror A criminal sensation of 1849, in which husband and wife Frederick and Marie Manning murdered the latter's wealthy lover, Patrick O'Connor, after inviting him to dinner at their house in Miniver Place, Bermondsey. They buried his body under the floorboards, stole valuables from his MILE END home and fled separately. Frederick was arrested in Jersey and Marie in Edinburgh and the pair were tried and convicted at the OLD BAILEY and hanged at Horsemonger Lane gaol, NEWINGTON. Marie Manning's decision to wear black satin to the scaffold is said to have dealt a fatal blow to the fabric's popularity, hence the title of Albert Borowitz's study of the case, *The Woman Who Murdered Black Satin: The Bermondsey Horror* (1981). Charles DICKENS and Herman Melville were among those present at the execution. Dickens partly modelled Mademoiselle Hortense in *Bleak House* (1852–3) on the Swiss-born Marie.

Bermondsey tank *See* STOMPIE.

Bermudas A 17th- and 18th-century slang name for certain no-go areas where criminals hid themselves away and the authorities were not inclined to pursue them. It was applied in particular to the lanes and passageways running near DRURY LANE, and to parts of SOUTHWARK (*see the* MINT). It was inspired by the use of the Bermuda islands, in the Atlantic, as a bolt hole to which certain well-connected debtors had fled to avoid their creditors.

> Engine, when did you see
> My cousin Ever-ill? Keeps he still your quarter
> I' the Bermudas?
>
> BEN JONSON: *The Devil is an Ass,* II, i (1616)

Berseys *See* HUMMINGBIRD.

Bertram Mills At one time Britain's best-known circus, founded by Bertram Mills (1873–1938), owner of a PADDINGTON coach-building firm, after a bet with a friend that he could put on a better show than that currently available at OLYMPIA. From 1920 his circus was the regular Christmas show at Olympia, and from 1929 it toured annually in a big top. It was continued after his death by his two sons, Cyril and Bernard, and held its final season in the winter of 1966.

Berwick Street A market street in central SOHO, laid out in the late 17th century. The market operates from Monday to Saturday, selling mainly fruit and vegetables, flowers and fabric, but in recent years the street has lost many of its small traders, both market stalls and specialist shops.

> Think of this location as the modern day Abbey Road. It's where, in 1995, Oasis photographed

the cover of *(What's the Story) Morning Glory?*, one of the seminal CDs of the age.

JASON COCHRAN: *Pauline Frommer's London* (2007)

best side towards London *See to* TURN THE BEST SIDE TO LONDON.

Bethnal Green One of the most archetypal EAST END neighbourhoods, situated immediately north of WHITECHAPEL and STEPNEY. It was recorded as Blithehale in the 13th century, when a hamlet began to grow around the site of the present TUBE station. During the 18th century Bethnal Green developed into one of the first manufacturing districts in the East End, gaining fame for its chair-making and silk-weaving. During the following century it became London's poorest quarter, described by Karl Marx as a 'notorious district' because of its child labour. A sundial in Vallance Road recreation gardens marks the spot where William Booth began his outdoor preaching, before going on to found the SALVATION ARMY in 1878. Like SPITALFIELDS to the west, Bethnal Green has long been a first home for new waves of immigrants, from Huguenot weavers in the 18th century to the South Asian community of today. Over a third of Bethnal Green's residents are Bangladeshis. *See also the* BLIND BEGGAR OF BEDNALL GREEN; FORT VALLANCE.

Bethnal Green in the Sun A facetious nickname for the Spanish seaside resort of Marbella, which is situated on the Costa del Sol. The coastline as a whole was dubbed the 'Costa del Crime' in the 1960s and 1970s, when a significant proportion of the local population seemed to consist of British criminals fleeing justice (abetted by the lack of an Anglo-Spanish extradition treaty). The Bethnal Green fraternity evidently homed in on Marbella.

Betsey, the The informal name of the Betsey Trotwood, a Victorian public house on FARRINGDON ROAD. Formerly the Butcher's Arms, from its proximity to SMITHFIELD, it takes its present name from the eccentric great-aunt and benefactor of DAVID COPPERFIELD. The pub hosts a variety of (mostly musical) fringe arts events in a small upstairs room and even smaller cellar.

Better 'ole, A *See the* OLD BILL.

Between the Commons An estate agents' term for the pricey area between WANDSWORTH

and CLAPHAM Commons, with Broomwood Road as the central axis. Rapid growth in the value of houses, especially in the 1990s, eroded the area's former diversity in favour of upper middle-class homogeneity.

Beulah Spa A former pleasure garden in NORWOOD, opened in 1831 and focused on the springs that form the source of the River EFFRA, with a maze and gardens laid out by Decimus Burton. Michael Faraday analysed the water and endorsed its quality. Johann Strauss the Elder and his orchestra performed there twice in 1838. For a while the spa drew coachloads of visitors, but the appeal faded in less than two decades. In Charles DICKENS's *Sketches by Boz* (1836) it is remarked that 'the Gordian knot was all very well in its way ... so is the maze at Beulah Spa'. Burton's Tivoli Lodge (originally Rustic Lodge) is the sole surviving structure, at the entrance to a recreation ground on Spa Hill.

> This party to the Beulah Spa is a bright idea of my own; and I expect, by means of it, to gain two important points: first to ascertain, beyond a doubt, that Sydney loves me – and me alone; and next, to drive him into a leetle bit of a corner, and make him tell me so.
>
> CHARLES DANCE: *The Beulah Spa: A Burletta, in Two Acts* (1833)

Bevis Marks A short section of street in the CITY of London, just south of HOUNDSDITCH. It was earlier 'Buries marks', a lane forming the boundary (mark) of land belonging to the abbey of Bury St Edmunds. The intrusion of the letter 'v' seems to have come about as the result of transcription errors in medieval manuscripts.

Bevis Marks Synagogue Opened in 1701 to serve the City's Spanish and Portuguese Jewish community, this is the oldest synagogue in Britain and one of the best-preserved houses of worship of its period still in use.

Bexley The district of Bexley lies on the eastern side of the borough of the same name. Its Old English name, Byxlea, is theorized to have denoted a settlement in a box wood clearing – but some experts disagree, arguing that box trees would have been unlikely to flourish on this terrain. After Bexley station opened in 1866 the town and outlying villages like Coldblow and Bridgen began to expand. Extensive suburbanization took place in the 1920s and 1930s, a process accelerated by the electrification of the railway. The former Conservative prime minister Edward Heath served as Member of Parliament for Bexley (ultimately OLD BEXLEY and SIDCUP) from 1950 to 2001.

Bexley, London Borough of An OUTER LONDON borough formed in 1965 by merging the urban district of CRAYFORD, the northern part of the urban district of CHISLEHURST and SIDCUP and the municipal boroughs of Bexley and ERITH. Almost half the places in the borough have names beginning with the letter B, including a continuous string that commences on the western edge at Blackfen and runs through Blendon, Bridgen, BEXLEYHEATH and Barnehurst, ending on the Kent border at Barnes Cray. The civic heraldry incorporates devices proclaiming Bexley's rural, industrial and riverine characteristics, and a white horse standing on a turreted gateway, which represents the connection with Kent. The borough motto is 'boldly and rightly', a translation of Crayford's *fortiter et recte*.

Bexleyheath The commercial centre of the London Borough of BEXLEY and a densely built-up suburb. Its Upton locality was a medieval hamlet and the Crook Log public house is said to date from 1605 but the present-day town centre had nothing but a lone tree and an old windmill until the early 19th century. Upton was still rural when William Morris and Philip Webb built RED HOUSE in 1859–60. Bexleyheath is classified as a 'metropolitan centre' by the THAMES GATEWAY London Partnership and is a target for further commercial development. In 19th-century COCKNEY RHYMING SLANG Bexleyheath, or Bexley Heath, stood for 'teeth'.

Biba A fashion label that evolved from a mail order business through a succession of trendy boutiques into an opulent department store on KENSINGTON HIGH STREET. It was founded in 1964 by the Polish designer Barbara Hulanicki (b.1936), with her SURBITON-born husband Stephen Fitz-Simon (1937–97). Despite the nostalgic styling of many Hulanicki creations, the Biba look became one of the focal emblems of SWINGING LONDON. The department store, formerly the home of Derry and Toms, closed in 1975 and the Biba label was sold.

big

Big Bang The major modernization of the STOCK EXCHANGE that took place on 27 October 1986. The distinction between stockjobber and stockbroker was abolished, and operations became fully computerized. The aim was to maintain London's position as a leading international financial centre.

Big Ben The great bell in the Clock Tower of the PALACE OF WESTMINSTER, so called after Sir Benjamin Hall, who was Chief Commissioner of Works when it was cast in 1856. The first casting, weighing more than 15 tons, developed serious cracks when being tested in Palace Yard. It was broken up and taken to WHITECHAPEL bell foundry, where it was recast at a weight of about 13 tons and installed in October 1858. This also developed a crack, because of an oversized hammer and an excess of tin in the alloy, but with adjustments it was able to continue in use. There are also four quarter bells whose weight varies between about 4 tons and 1 ton. The clock and tower as a whole are now generally known as 'Big Ben', except to those of a pedantic turn of mind, especially tour guides. *See also the* WESTMINSTER CHIMES.

Big L The nickname of 'Wonderful' Radio London, a pirate radio station that operated from a ship anchored off the ESSEX coast between December 1964 and August 1967. Big L's DJs included John Peel (1939–2004), Tommy Vance (1941–2005) and Kenny Everett (1944–95).

Big Sam The sobriquet of Samuel McDonald (c.1762–1802) of Lairg, in Sutherland. Also known as the Scottish Hercules, he was appointed lodge porter at CARLTON HOUSE by the future George IV. Some accounts suggest that he stood eight foot (2.44m) tall, others that he was a mere six foot ten (2.08m). Bizarrely, he is said to have had a profitable sideline as a female impersonator, advertised as 'the remarkably tall woman'. The NATIONAL PORTRAIT GALLERY has an etching of Big Sam in more conventional dress, executed in 1796 by John Kay.

Big Smoke *See the* SMOKE.

Biggin Hill Now a crowded residential district, situated 2 miles (3 km) south-east of NEW ADDINGTON. It probably takes its name from a hilltop 'bigging' or habitation. Biggin Hill occupies an important place in British history as a military airfield, familiarly known as 'Biggin-on-the-Bump' or simply 'Biggin'. In the Second World War it became a Spitfire station and was attacked a dozen times during the Battle of Britain. Offensive missions flew from here after the pressure for defensive action was relieved. The airfield was downgraded to non-operational status in 1958 and the Royal Air Force finally left in 1992. The North Camp plays host to a Battle of Britain open day every summer, as part of the Biggin Hill International Air Fair. When CROYDON AIRPORT closed, most of the operators who had not already made the move came to Biggin Hill, which is now the most popular light aviation centre south of London, with a collection of thriving light aircraft clubs. A new passenger terminal handles executive charter flights and occasional scheduled diversions.

bill

Bill, the The police force, or its officers. The term is probably a shortening of 'OLD BILL'. It was adopted as the title of a television series set in and around Sun Hill police station, first screened in 1984 and still running. The show is filmed at studios in MERTON and at locations all around London. However, Canley, the fictional borough in which most of the action takes place, seems to be based on TOWER HAMLETS.

> 'What?!' screamed DCI Morrell, understandably appalled. 'You're telling me there may be *two* serial killers out there and we have no idea where they are?!' If ever one sentence ever summed up Sun Hill, it is surely this one.
>
> JIM SHELLEY in *The Guardian* (3 December 2005)

bill of mortality Historically, an official return of births and deaths in the London area (hence 'within the bills of mortality', within the London district for which such returns were made).

Billingsgate A CITY of London ward bounded by the THAMES, Lovat Lane, FENCHURCH STREET, Mark Lane and Sugar Quay. The name is presumed to derive from one Billing (or something similar), a Saxon landowner, rather than the legendary king BELIN. It probably began as a Roman watergate on the Thames and was used by the Saxons as a small port for general cargo, later specializing in fish. *See also the* BOSS OF BILLINGSGATE.

Billingsgate language or **billingsgate** Coarse and vulgar speech, laced with obscenities, of the kind traditionally used by Billingsgate fishwives.

Billingsgate Market A wholesale fish market formerly located in the CITY of London ward of

the same name and now based in DOCKLANDS. An Act of Parliament of 1699 established 'a free and open market for all sorts of fish whatsoever'. Sales were made in wooden sheds until the construction in 1850 of the first trading hall, which was replaced by a larger structure in 1877. This building survives today on Lower Thames Street. With the widening of that road in the late 1960s, trading at Billingsgate became increasingly impractical and the market transferred to a renovated warehouse at the WEST INDIA DOCKS in 1982. Each year since the move the LORD MAYOR OF LONDON has presented the nominal rent to the mayor of TOWER HAMLETS in the form of a gift of fish, which is then distributed to old people's homes in the borough.

Billingsgate pheasant A red herring or a bloater.

Billionaires' Boulevard A revaluation of MILLIONAIRES' ROW.

Billy

Billy Barlow Formerly a generic term for a street clown, from an EAST END character of that name, well known for his witty and droll behaviour in the first half of the 19th century. He died in WHITECHAPEL workhouse.

Billy Williams' Cabbage Patch The English Rugby Football Union's ground at TWICKENHAM, the headquarters of the game, also known as Twickers. It is popularly so called after William (Billy) Williams (1860–1951), who discovered the site and who persisted until it was acquired for rugby in 1907. The latter part of the name refers to the ground's former use as a market garden. The first match played here, on 2 October 1909, was between HARLEQUINS and Richmond, and the first international was England v. Wales the following year. The nearby Railway Tavern changed its name to the Cabbage Patch in 1959 when England and Wales played Scotland and Ireland in a centenary match. The ground is now also the site of the World Rugby Museum, and tours of the stadium are held six days a week, except when a match or event is taking place.

> Billy Williams's cabbage patch has never staged a more momentous game than this afternoon's match between England and the All Blacks.
>
> *The Times* (9 October 1999)

Binkie The regular first name, perhaps originally a childhood nickname, adopted by Hugh (originally Hughes) Beaumont (1908–73), managing director of the theatre group H.M. Tennant and an influential force in WEST END theatre. He was always known thus in theatrical circles.

bin lid 'Quid' (pound sterling) in COCKNEY RHYMING SLANG. *See also* SAUCEPAN LID.

Biogrope An affectionate nickname for the Biograph cinema in VICTORIA, from its postwar popularity as a rendezvous for gay men. The cinema was demolished in 1983 and replaced by a hotel.

> When the Met [police] responded [to a rise in 'cottaging'] by increasing their surveillance of urinals, men appear to have moved towards the Biograph's relative safety. Kenneth Williams clearly expected to find sex in 1952, visiting 'in the hope of traditional entertainment' and complaining bitterly after finding it 'terribly desolate'.
>
> MATT HOULBROOK: *Queer London: Perils and Pleasures in the Sexual Metropolis, 1918–1957* (2005)

Birchington Hunt An old alternative for Berkeley Hunt (*see* BERK) in COCKNEY RHYMING SLANG. The term was infrequently used and there was no real hunt of that name. Nor was there a Burlington Hunt, another rare alternative.

Birchin Lane A short street connecting CORNHILL and LOMBARD STREET. First recorded in the late 12th century, the name is probably a corruption of Middle English words meaning 'beard shaver lane'. It was once famous for all sorts of apparel and references to second-hand clothes in Birchin Lane were common in Elizabethan books.

> Passing through Birchin Lane amidst a camp-royal of hose and doublets, I took ... occasion to slip into a captain's suit – a valiant buff doublet stuffed with points and pair of velvet slops scored thick with lace.
>
> THOMAS MIDDLETON: *The Black Book* (1604)

In the mid-18th century the lane's Pennsylvania coffee house was a meeting place for Americans staying in London. Benjamin Franklin used the café as his mailing address until he began to suspect that 'some scoundrel' was reading, and perhaps forging, his correspondence. In jocular parlance, to be sent to Birchin Lane was to be flogged.

bird (lime) 'Time' in COCKNEY RHYMING SLANG, used almost exclusively nowadays, but not originally, in the sense of serving time in jail.

> When you're in my job you soon get to realise that there are several ways of doing bird. But the only sensible way is to do it the easy way. That is, to take all they can give you and swallow it ... Do your bird and make the most of it, I always said.
>
> BILLY HILL: *Boss of Britain's Underworld* (1955)

Birdcage Walk A street running along the south side of ST JAMES'S PARK. Wellington Barracks are at its western end. The name derives from a former aviary in St James's Park known as 'The Bird Cage', originally created by James I in the early 17th century and later enlarged by his grandson Charles II.

Birkbeck College A constituent college of the UNIVERSITY OF LONDON, named after George Birkbeck (1776–1841), who was the founder and first president of the London Mechanics' Institution (1824), later the Birkbeck Institution.

biscuits (and cheese) 'Knees' in COCKNEY RHYMING SLANG.

bishop An obsolete meaning of the verb 'to bishop' was to murder by drowning, from the name of a man who drowned at least two boys and one woman in BETHNAL GREEN and sold the bodies to surgeons for dissection (*see the* LONDON BURKERS).

Bishop of Fleet Street A nickname given to Hannen Swaffer (1879–1962) by his fellow journalists because of his pronouncements on public morality and his sombre, stylized mode of attire.

Bishop of Hell The sobriquet of Dr John Gaynam (or Gainham), a 'lusty, jolly man' who was said to have conducted 36,000 FLEET MARRIAGES between 1709 and 1740.

Bishops Avenue, The An ultra-exclusive road running from the northern tip of HAMPSTEAD HEATH to EAST FINCHLEY. The name derives from the bishops of London, who owned a large hunting park in the area during the late Middle Ages. This is probably the most 'desirable' address outside central London, for those who like ostentatious displays of wealth. One compact palace, Toprak Mansion, sold for £50 million in 2008 and was accordingly dubbed Top Whack Mansion by the press. The entertainer Gracie Fields used to live on the Bishops Avenue; 12 luxury apartments now occupy the site of her house.

> I ask if most of the homes are as empty as they look. 'Yes,' he [estate agent Richard Humphreys] says. 'These are the wealthiest people in the world – Indians, Russians, Nigerians, Saudis – so the majority [of properties] are just lived in by staff and the owners are here two or three weeks a year. Some families never even move in.'
>
> ALISON BEARD in the *Financial Times* (22 June 2007)

Bishopsgate A former Roman road running north from GRACECHURCH STREET to NORTON FOLGATE. The gate in the CITY wall was called *Porta Episcopi* in Domesday Book, and this was anglicized as Bishopsgate by the 12th century. It is said that the name refers to St Erkenwald, who was bishop of London for eleven years in the late 7th century. Houses began to appear on both sides of the gate in the 13th century and by the 16th century the whole road was lined with buildings, including the merchants' residences of CROSBY PLACE and Gresham House and the churches of St Botolph, St Helen and St Ethelburga. Like many of the gates in the City wall, Bishopsgate was demolished in 1761. Continuous rebuilding has left nothing of the medieval street except for the core fabric of the surviving churches. From the 1960s a succession of office blocks and towers has made Bishopsgate one of the City's most unashamedly commercial thoroughfares. At its northern end the BROADGATE complex borders the street's west side. The NATWEST TOWER was completed on the site of the former Gresham House in 1981, when it was Britain's tallest building.

Bishopsgate Institute A charitable foundation and library that opened at 230 Bishopsgate in 1895. Charles Harrison Townsend (1851–1928) designed an imposing little castle as its home, which it still occupies today.

black

Black Books

1. The records of the principal activities of the Honourable Society of LINCOLN'S INN, from 1422 to the present day. Originally, the Black Book of Lincoln's Inn was a memoranda book of the inn's business in which everything deemed worthy of preservation was written. Until 1641 these books contained more or less full transcripts of annual

accounts rendered by the treasurer, PENSIONER and steward. No separate record of admissions to the society was kept until 1573, of admissions to chambers until 1614, and calls to the bar were entered only in the Black Book up to 1767. The Black Book is now the major minute series of the governing Council of Benchers.

2. A Channel 4 sitcom that ran for three seasons between 2000 and 2004, created by Dylan Moran (b.1971), in which he played Bernard Black, the misanthropic owner of a BLOOMSBURY bookshop.

Black Borough A contemporary urban slang term for the London Borough of SOUTHWARK. For the rationale, *see* BLUE BOROUGH.

black cab The colloquial name for a London licensed taxi of whatever colour, as opposed to a private hire vehicle, which is known (in London and elsewhere) as a minicab. Unlike minicabs, black cabs may be hailed on the street and their drivers must be proficient in the KNOWLEDGE. No law or regulation has ever stated that a London taxi must be black but this was the only standard colour available for many of the earliest models and few drivers were willing to pay the significant premium for a custom colour. Not until the late 1970s did the manufacturer of the FX4 begin to offer a wider range of colours. *See also* BALE OF HAY.

Black Cab Sessions An ongoing contemporary entertainment format in which musicians hail a black cab, take a short ride and are recorded performing a song while travelling. The sessions are made available on the internet and in some cases rebroadcast on television. Participants have included Brian Wilson, Badly Drawn Boy and the Kooks.

> It's the smallest, quickest and hippest gig in town and takes place in the back of a London black cab …
>
> *The Observer* (2 March 2008)

Black Friars The Dominican friars, from their black mantle. The Order in England was dissolved by Henry VIII in 1538. The district of BLACKFRIARS is on the site of the former Dominican monastery.

Black Friday Among the most notable days so called are 6 December 1745, the day on which the news arrived in London that Bonnie Prince Charlie, the Young Pretender, had reached Derby, and 11 May 1866, when the failure of the London bankers Overend, Gurney & Company caused widespread panic.

blackguard An old-fashioned term for a 'contemptible scoundrel'. Its origin is uncertain but Francis Grose provided the following explanation for the variant definition as 'a shabby, mean fellow' in his *Classical Dictionary of the Vulgar Tongue* (1785):

> A term said to be derived from a number of
> dirty, tattered roguish boys, who attended at the
> Horse Guards, and Parade, in St. James's Park,
> to black the boots and shoes of the soldiers, or
> to do any other dirty offices. These, from their
> constant attendance about the time of guard
> mounting, were nicknamed the black guards.

Black Lubyanka A nickname for the Daily Express building in FLEET STREET, while the newspaper was in residence there, modelled on the name of the former KGB headquarters in Moscow. Opened in 1932, the Express building is an art deco classic, with a cinema-style foyer and external black Vitrolite cladding with chromium strips.

Black Mary's Hole A lane that ran near present-day EXMOUTH MARKET, in CLERKENWELL. The lane probably took its name from a well, which was in turn said to have been named after Mary Woolaston, a black woman who lived there during the reign of Charles II. However, numerous other derivations have been proposed, including the dedication of the well to the Virgin Mary, depicted as the 'Black Madonna'. The famous outlaw Jack SHEPPARD frequented an alehouse at Black Mary's Hole, the Fox at Bay. 'Black Mary's Hole' is also the title of an old English dance tune, better known as 'Black Mary's Hornpipe'.

> A Voyage to Lethe; By Capt. Samuel Cock;
> Sometime Commander of the Good Ship
> the Charming Sally. Dedicated to the Right
> Worshipful Adam Cock, Esq; Of Black-Mary's
> Hole; Coney-Skin Merchant
>
> (Title and dedication of an anonymously authored
> pornographic narrative) (1741)

Black Preacher, the The unimaginative London sobriquet – although its very simplicity hints at his pioneering status – of John Marrant, an African-American Methodist minister and talented musician who travelled to England in 1785 and was ordained at Bath into the sect known as the Countess of Huntingdon's Connexion. Returning to North America, he ministered in Nova Scotia and Boston. In March 1790 he came to London, where he at first lived and preached in the EAST END. He soon moved to ALDERSGATE, preaching at the Huntingdonian chapel in Church Street (now Gaskin Street), ISLINGTON. Marrant died in April 1791, at the age of 35, and was buried in the chapel's graveyard. His early death has been attributed to war wounds, the hard life of an itinerant minister and smallpox. Marrant is regarded as a figure of historic significance in Canada and in the USA, where the *Black History Review* has called him 'America's first black preacher'.

Black Saturday The first day of the BLITZ: 7 September 1940.

Black Sea The nickname of a former lake at the northern end of WANDSWORTH COMMON A mid-19th-century wind-pump, part of which survives today, used to extract rainwater from the nearby railway cutting and deposit it in this picturesque lake with islands. The lake was drained in the 1870s and a park was laid out with formal walks and greenery for the benefit of the area's new residents.

as black as Newgate's knocker *See under* AS.

Blackfriars A historic religious and theatrical site located at the eastern end of Victoria EMBANKMENT, now dominated by a railway terminus and a gyratory traffic system. In 1224 the BLACK FRIARS established a priory on the east side of SHOE LANE and moved to what is now the east side of New Bridge Street in 1278. The Dominican Order established more than 50 priories but this was probably the most important and it was the site of early parliamentary conclaves. Unlike some other religious buildings, the priory did not survive the Dissolution to serve a different purpose. It was already reduced to a pile of rubble when the actor James Burbage acquired much of the site to build the Blackfriars Theatre in 1596. William SHAKESPEARE was later involved in the enterprise and bought a house in nearby Ireland Yard. The theatre closed in the Civil War and was demolished in 1655. Playhouse Yard marks its site.

Blackfriars! Underworld slang, in use between approximately 1830 and 1914, meaning 'beware!' or 'look out!'.

Blackfriars Bridge A road bridge built in 1769, using funds generated from rents on the houses and shops of LONDON BRIDGE. Structural problems caused by water scouring necessitated its replacement exactly a century later. Blackfriars Railway Bridge has also been built twice; the piers of the original still protrude from the water. Early on 18 June 1982 the body of Italian financier Roberto Calvi was found hanged under Blackfriars Bridge, his pockets stuffed with bricks and stones. Calvi, dubbed 'God's banker' because of his ties to the Vatican's bank, IOR, had been seeking help for his failing Banco Ambrosiano after escaping house arrest in Italy. Five men were eventually tried in Italy for Calvi's murder, but were found not guilty in 2007.

Blackheath A pretty village and common, separated from GREENWICH PARK by SHOOTERS HILL Road. The followers of Wat Tyler in 1381 and Jack CADE in 1450 assembled on the heath, which got its name either from the colour of the soil or from its bleakness. Here also Londoners welcomed Henry V after Agincourt in 1415 and Charles II met the army on his way to London in 1660. Blackheath was in the hands of the earls (originally barons) of Dartmouth from 1673. The first street to be completed was the prosperous Dartmouth Row in the 1690s. The present charm and popularity of Blackheath village owe much to the survival of properties dating from the late 18th and early 19th centuries, including Montpelier Row and the Paragon, a unique crescent of seven pairs of houses linked by colonnades, designed by Michael Searles.

Blackheath has a proud sporting history. It is the site of the first golf course in England, supposedly laid out by James I at the beginning of the 17th century (*see also* ELTHAM PALACE), and Blackheath was one of the founder members of the Rugby Football Union. The Blackheath Harriers Athletics Club moved south to HAYES[1] in 1927.

Blackheath Park A late Georgian and early Victorian private estate, situated south-east of Blackheath village, bordering KIDBROOKE. The philosopher John Stuart Mill (1806–73) lived at 113 Blackheath Park for 20 years and wrote *On Liberty* (1859) and *Utilitarianism* (1863) there.

Blackwall A historic riverside district situated east of POPLAR. The name probably derives from the embankment built to prevent tidal inundation, although there is a legend that Alfred the Great (r.871–899) had a weir constructed nearby to strand invading Danish ships that had

sailed up the River LEA. Blackwall had a proud maritime tradition and both Sir Walter Raleigh and Admiral Lord Nelson are said to have had homes in the area. The first colonists of Virginia sailed from Blackwall in 1606, and later the East India Docks attracted a thriving international trade. Until recently, Blackwall had a declining residential population and a high level of social deprivation, but luxury riverside apartments began to be built from the late 1980s onwards.

Blackwall frigates A colloquial name for a class of ship that sailed between London and the East Indies and Antipodes in the middle decades of the 19th century. The first and last of these frigates were built at Blackwall, but others were built elsewhere in Britain, and in India. Blackwall frigates were noted for their speed and comfort.

Blackwall Tunnel A road tunnel under the THAMES, between Blackwall in the north and the GREENWICH peninsula in the south. The original (now the northbound) tunnel was built in 1891–7 by Sir Alexander Binnie. It is 4,412 feet (1,345m) long. The southbound tunnel was completed in 1967. In both directions this is a notorious traffic congestion point.

In 20th-century rhyming slang, Blackwall Tunnel denoted a ship's funnel. It is also employed in figurative references to a big mouth or some other gaping orifice, such as a cocaine addict's nostrils.

> There's the dude with a mouth like the Blackwall Tunnel
> With a thick ginger mullet and a voice like a funnel
>
> KELVIN MACKENZIE: 'TalkSport Rap', quoted in *The Independent* (13 June 2005)

blade of light *See the* WOBBLY BRIDGE.

Blake, Sexton A detective hero of boys' stories, in many ways an equivalent of Sherlock HOLMES. He first appeared in Hal Meredith's story 'The Missing Millionaire', published in *Harmsworth's Halfpenny Marvel* in 1893. He later transferred to another Harmsworth magazine, the *Union Jack*, and it was there that he made his name. He has a boy assistant called Tinker and a landlady called Mrs Bardell, a 'treasure' in the best domestic tradition. Like Holmes, he has rooms in BAKER STREET, from which he sallies forth to solve all kinds of mysteries. Unlike Holmes, however, he uses brawn more than brain. His adventures have been written by around 200 different authors.

In COCKNEY RHYMING SLANG 'Sexton Blake', or 'sexton', can signify 'cake', a 'fake' or, in the world of film and television, a 'take'.

Blanchappleton A former manor situated in the vicinity of Mark Lane and FENCHURCH STREET. First recorded in 1177 as Blanchesapel-tuna, the name was at various times corrupted to Blind Chapel and Blanch Chaplin. In 1462 the Common Council ordered basket-makers, gold wire-drawers and other foreign craftsmen to reside only in this quarter. Foreigners' houses in Blanchappleton were attacked on EVIL MAY DAY and a gallows was subsequently set up there. It was probably not used but may have served to deter prospective aggressors thereafter.

blanket fair An alternative name for the earliest FROST FAIRS, especially the event of 1683/4, which was the first to take place on a grand scale. The term derived from the cuboid tents, made out of bedclothes strung between poles, which were set up on the frozen THAMES.

> Try these hard times how to abate the price;
> Tell her how cheap were damsels on the ice.
> 'Mongst City wives, and daughters that came there,
> How far a guinea went at Blanket Fair.
>
> JOHN WILMOT, EARL OF ROCHESTER: prologue to *Valentinian* (1685)

Bleeding Heart Yard A cul-de-sac leading off Greville Street, near HATTON GARDEN. The name derives from an old inn sign, the Bleeding Heart of Our Lady, which depicted the heart of the Virgin Mary pierced through by swords. However, the sanguinary imagery has inspired several colourful legends, which Charles DICKENS summarizes in *Little Dorrit* (1855–7). One tale has it that a lovelorn young lady, imprisoned in her bedchamber by her cruel father, pined away at her window, murmuring 'bleeding heart, bleeding heart, bleeding away' as she expired. The goriest fable suggests that sometime in the early 17th century the much-wooed Elizabeth Hatton was murdered here by the Spanish ambassador – whom she had jilted – and was found at dawn with her heart still pumping blood onto the cobblestones. Another angle on this story, this time featuring Sir Christopher and Lady Alice

Hatton and the Devil, was set to verse by Richard Barham in his *Ingoldsby Legends*:

> Of poor Lady Hatton, it's needless to say,
> No traces have ever been found to this day,
> Or the terrible dancer who whisk'd her away;
> But out in the court-yard – and just in that part
> Where the pump stands – lay bleeding a *large human heart* ...
>
> 'The House-Warming!!' (1840)

Blessing of Throats A Roman Catholic ceremony conducted annually at St Etheldreda's Church, ELY PLACE. St Etheldreda is patron saint of throat ailments but the blessing is specifically associated with St Blaise, a 4th-century Armenian bishop who legendarily saved the life of a boy who had a fishbone stuck in his throat and was in danger of choking to death. The service takes place on St Blaise's Day, 3 February.

blimey *See* GORBLIMEY.

blind
blind beak of Bow Street or the **blind magistrate** A nickname for Sir John Fielding (1722–80), BOW STREET magistrate and brother of the novelist Henry Fielding. Blinded in his youth, he was reputed to know countless thieves by their voices. He was instrumental in the evolution of the BOW STREET RUNNERS into London's first true police force.
Blind Beggar of Bednall Green, The An old ballad included in *Percy's Reliques* (1765); the subject of a play by Chettle and Day (1600) and another by Sheridan Knowles (1834). Also known as 'Bessee the Beggar's Daughter of Bednall Green', the ballad may have been written in the reign of Elizabeth I, though it was subsequently much revised. The beautiful Bessee had four suitors – a knight, a gentleman of fortune, a London merchant and the innkeeper's son at the Queen's Arms in ROMFORD. She told them that they must obtain the permission of her father, the poor blind beggar of BETHNAL GREEN, whereupon they all slunk off except the knight. The beggar consented and gave her a dowry of £3,000 in gold, and £100 to buy her wedding gown. According to Percy's version, the beggar explained to the guests at the wedding feast that he was Henry, son of Sir Simon de Montfort. The Blind Beggar public house (*see the* TARDIS) takes its name from the ballad. Elizabeth Frink's

bronze statue of the *Blind Beggar and His Dog* (1957) adorns the locality's Cranbrook estate.

> As swift as the wind to ride they were seen,
> Until they came near unto Bednall Green,
> And as the knight lighted most courteously,
> They fought against him for pretty Bessee.

Blitz, the The name (an abbreviation of the German 'Blitzkrieg') given to the intensive German air raids on London during the Second World War. The bombardment was initiated by Hitler in retaliation for RAF attacks on Berlin and began on 7 September 1940, when 450 people were killed by a raid over the EAST END. The raids continued almost nightly until 10 May 1941, by which time the death toll in London had exceeded 15,000. Londoners were not the only ones to suffer, and most of Britain's major cities were bombed. A second Blitz took place in 1944–5, with raids on south-east England by V–1 and V–2 weapons.

Blondin One of the best-known acrobats of all time, born at St Omer, France, in 1824, and dying at NORTHFIELDS, near EALING, in 1897. His real name was Jean-François Gravelet and his adopted name came from his tutor in the art, Jean Ravel Blondin. His greatest feat was in 1859, when he crossed the Niagara Falls on a tightrope, embroidering the performance by repeating it blindfold, wheeling a barrow, twirling an umbrella and carrying his manager on his back. He made a fortune by this act and soon after settled in London, where he gave performances until old age forced him to retire. In 1861 he turned somersaults on stilts at the CRYSTAL PALACE, on a rope stretched 170 feet (52m) above the ground. Blondin lived at Northfields from 1886 in a villa he called Niagara House. The house was demolished in the early 1930s and part of its grounds became what is now Blondin Park.

blood

Blood, 'Captain' Thomas A colourful Irish adventurer (*c.*1618–80). In the late 1660s he lived at an apothecary's shop in ROMFORD under an assumed name. His most famous exploit was the attempt, disguised as a clergyman, to steal the CROWN JEWELS from the TOWER OF LONDON in May 1671. After nearly murdering the keeper of the jewels, he succeeded in taking the crown, while one of his associates bore away the orb. He

was pursued, captured and imprisoned, but later pardoned by Charles II.

blood or beer! A jocular challenge to either fight or buy a round of drinks, from the early 20th century.

Bloody Sunday London's Bloody Sunday was 13 November 1887, when a TRAFALGAR SQUARE protest meeting that mixed Irish nationalism with general socialist discontent boiled over into a riot in WESTMINSTER. The Footguards and Life Guards were called in and at least two protestors died.

Bloody Tower Built as the Garden Tower, this addition to the TOWER OF LONDON dates from the reign of Richard II (1377–99). It had won its present name by 1597 from the belief that it witnessed the murder of the PRINCES IN THE TOWER. It subsequently housed such famous prisoners as Sir Walter Raleigh, Archbishop Laud and JUDGE JEFFREYS.

Bloomsbury London's principal academic quarter, noted for its fine squares; COVENT GARDEN lies to the south and EUSTON to the north. From the 13th century this was the manor of Blemund'sbury, probably named after one William Blemund, whose family originated from Blémont in France. Thomas Wriothesley, 4th Earl of Southampton (1607–67), laid out BLOOMSBURY SQUARE in 1661 as a kind of forecourt to his mansion, Southampton House, and the Duke of Montagu built Montagu House on Great Russell Street in 1679. The latter mansion soon burned down but was quickly rebuilt. A succession of high-class developments progressed westwards and northwards over the course of the 18th century to form the present grid of handsome streets and squares, of which the finest is BEDFORD SQUARE and the largest is RUSSELL SQUARE. Following the death of Sir Hans SLOANE, the government acquired his collection of antiquities for the nation and bought Montagu House, which opened to the public as the BRITISH MUSEUM in 1759.

Bloomsbury Burglars, The A knockabout MUSIC HALL sketch performed in the early years of the 20th century by the COCKNEY comedian Lew Lake (1874–1939) and his company. It was adapted into both a film and a stage play.

Bloomsbury Gang A Whig party faction that appeared in July 1765, led by the 4th Duke of

Bedford. Large portions of Bloomsbury are part of the Bedford Estate.

Bloomsbury Group A school of socially aware men and women of letters (also sometimes termed the Bloomsbury Set) active in the early part of the 20th century, of whom the best known was Virginia Woolf. The group first came together in 1904, meeting at the Gordon Square home of Clive and Vanessa Bell. Other prominent members included Roger Fry, E.M. Forster, Lytton Strachey, Duncan Grant, David Garnett, Dora Carrington and John Maynard Keynes. They saw themselves as advocates of a new, rational, civilized society, and several of them had Cambridge links. They had many critics, though, who thought them dilettante and elitist.

Bloomsburyite A usually derogatory name for a member or supporter of the BLOOMSBURY GROUP.

Bloomsbury Publishing plc A publishing house set up in 1986 by Liz Calder and Nigel Newton, specializing mainly in fiction and reference. Its coup in securing the Harry POTTER books (1997–2007) made it the envy of other British publishers. Its original offices were in BLOOMSBURY SQUARE.

Bloomsbury Square London's oldest residential square, laid out in 1661 and just predating ST JAMES'S SQUARE. However, its houses are now mostly Georgian and none of the original buildings survives. The central garden, until 1950 the preserve of paying key-holders, was re-landscaped in 2003 to reflect elements of Humphry Repton's 1806 layout.

blow

blow a raspberry, to *See* RASPBERRY.

Blowbladder Street A former name for what is now the easternmost part of NEWGATE Street. It was so called because bladders used to be sold there, which were inflated and hung on display in shop windows.

> ... his stomach was like Craven Street; his chest like the trunk maker's in the corner of St Paul's Churchyard; the calf of his leg like Leadenhall Market; his pulse like the Green Market in Covent Garden; his neck like Tyburn; and his gait like Newgate; his navel like Fleet Street; and his lungs and his bladder were like Blowbladder Street: everything about him seemed metamorphosed;

> ANDREW ERSKINE: letter to James Boswell (16 February 1762)

Blow-Up or **Blowup** A controversial and influential film (1966) directed by Michelangelo Antonioni, depicting both the glamorous and seedy sides of SWINGING LONDON. David Hemmings plays a photographer who comes to believe that he has unintentionally taken pictures of a murder (in Maryon Park, CHARLTON).

Blow-Up Bridge A nickname for Macclesfield Bridge, which carries Avenue Road over the REGENT'S CANAL to the Outer Circle of REGENT'S PARK. The formal name derives from the Earl of Macclesfield, who was the first chairman of the canal company. On 10 October 1874 a barge carrying five tons of gunpowder and two or three barrels of benzol exploded underneath the bridge, for reasons never fully understood. The bridge was destroyed and three crewmen and a horse died. The most badly damaged house in the vicinity was the Pompeian-style home of the painter Lawrence Alma-Tadema. The bridge was rebuilt using the pre-existing cast iron columns, which were rotated to even out the wear from tow-ropes; thus the pillars now have grooves worn into them on both the canal side and the towpath side.

Blucher A term applied in the late 19th century to an 'outsider' taxicab that was not permitted to enter the London railway termini. It indicates that the reputation of Field Marshal von Blücher (1742–1819), as the leader of Prussian forces which did not come to the aid of their British allies at the Battle of WATERLOO (1815) until there was little left to be done, was still very much alive. Taxis allowed to enter the stations were called Wellingtons.

blue

Blue, the A long-established nickname for Southwark Park Road market in BERMONDSEY, and the square in which this daily local market is held. The name probably derives from the nearby Blue Anchor public house and is sometimes applied to the whole of central Bermondsey.

> As I stood with my comrades in our local marketplace, The Blue, on that Saturday morning ... I was very moved by the number of ordinary Bermondsey people who spontaneously came up to shake my hand ...

> PETER TATCHELL: *The Battle for Bermondsey* (1983)

Blue Book The colloquial name for the *Guide to Learning the Knowledge of London*, issued by the Public Carriage Office to prospective BLACK CAB drivers. Learning all the 320 routes (known as 'runs') in the Blue Book ensures that the applicant for a GREEN BADGE has acquired a thorough KNOWLEDGE of all roads, places of interest and important landmarks within a 6-mile (9.5-km) radius of CHARING CROSS. There is also a suburban Blue Book for would-be holders of the YELLOW BADGE, who are not permitted to ply for hire in central London.

Blue Borough or **Blu Borough** A contemporary urban slang term for the London Borough of LEWISHAM, from the vivid shade of cyan used for much of its street furniture, from signage to litter bins. Such items are the most visible indicator that one has crossed into or out of this southeast London borough and, given the significance of 'territory' within some cultural groups, can thus be a matter of considerable import. By the same token, black and green respectively define neighbouring SOUTHWARK and GREENWICH, although municipal colour co-ordination in these boroughs is less single-minded than in Lewisham.

> So she grew up with her auntie and uncle, who she calls mum and dad, in 'blue borough' – Lewisham, where the rubbish bins are blue (Greenwich is 'green borough' because of its green bins; black-binned Southwark is 'black borough').
>
> PATRICK BARKHAM, in *The Guardian* (4 November 2008)

Bluecoat School Christ's Hospital is so called because the boys there wear a long blue coat with clerical bands and saffron-coloured socks. It was founded in NEWGATE in 1552, but moved to Horsham, West Sussex, in 1902. There were other charity schools so named.

blue devil An early nickname for an officer of the METROPOLITAN POLICE. The term was at first far more commonly used than affectionate alternatives such as 'BOBBY', reflecting widespread initial hostility to what was seen as an oppressive force, especially among the working classes. *See also* RAW LOBSTER.

blue men The colloquial name of *Walls and Trumpets* (2006), an exterior art installation at Maya House in BOROUGH High Street, by the Israeli sculptress Ofra Zimbalista (b.1939). The work consists of three aluminium body casts of naked musicians, painted a vivid blue and mounted at vertical intervals on the facade.

blue plaque A blue ceramic plaque set into the facade of a building (or its former site) in London where a famous person lived, giving the relevant dates and details. The first was placed by the LONDON COUNTY COUNCIL in 1903 on the house Holly Lodge, KENSINGTON, in which Thomas Macaulay died. In recent decades plaques have commemorated events as well as lives. One, set on a railway bridge at Grove Road in BOW in 1988, reads: 'The first Flying Bomb on London fell here, 13 June 1944.' The plaque was later stolen and subsequently replaced.

Blues The official nickname of CHELSEA FC, from the colour of the team's home strip. The club's original nickname, the Pensioners, was formally banished by Ted Drake (1912–95), as part of a programme of modernization that he instigated soon after becoming manager in May 1952. At the same time he removed the image of a CHELSEA PENSIONER from the club crest.

Blues and Royals *See* HORSE GUARDS; HOUSEHOLD TROOPS.

blue stocking A now disparaging nickname for a scholarly or intellectual woman. In 1400 a society of men and women was formed in Venice, distinguished by the colour of their stockings and called *della calza*. A similar society appeared in Paris in 1590 and was the rage among lady *savants*. The name is derived directly from such a society, founded *c.*1750 by Elizabeth Montagu (1720–1800), so nicknamed from the fact that a prominent member, Benjamin Stillingfleet (1702–71), wore blue worsted stockings in place of the usual black silk. The last of the clique was Miss Monckton, afterwards Countess of Cork, who died in 1840. Mrs Montagu is also said to have deliberately adopted the badge of the French *Bas bleu* club.

Boar's Head Tavern An inn immortalized by SHAKESPEARE and Prince Hal, and formerly standing in EASTCHEAP. It was destroyed in the GREAT FIRE OF LONDON, but was rebuilt. Annual Shakespeare dinners were held there until 1784. It was demolished in 1831. Washington Irving has an essay, 'The Boar's Head Tavern, Eastcheap', in his *Sketch Book* (1819–20). Gustav Holst's opera based on Shakespeare's characters is called *At the Boar's Head* (1925).

boat

Boat Race The Oxford and Cambridge Boat Race is an annual rowing competition between two teams of students, held on the THAMES on a Sunday (formerly a Saturday) near Easter. The idea came from Charles Merivale and Charles Wordsworth, students at Cambridge and Oxford respectively, who had been at HARROW SCHOOL together. On 12 March 1829 Cambridge sent a challenge to Oxford, and since then the loser of the previous year's race has challenged the opposition to a re-match. The first race was held at Henley-on-Thames, after which the event moved to WESTMINSTER. PUTNEY BRIDGE has been the starting point for the Boat Race since 1845. It is the best-known event in the rowing calendar, and was in many ways the inspiration for the modern sport. The 4¼-mile (6.8-km) slog to MORTLAKE is usually over in less than 20 minutes. Up to 250,000 spectators watch the race from the banks of the river and in recent years the television audience has exceeded seven million in Britain and 100 million worldwide.

> ... [the] event caught the imagination of ordinary Londoners who had no chance of going to a university, nor even knew where Oxford and Cambridge were. Children especially took vociferous sides in a contest that had apparently no connection with their lives at all.
>
> STEVE ROUD: *London Lore* (2008)

boat (race) 'Face' in COCKNEY RHYMING SLANG. Much more enduring than the alternative 'Chevy Chase'.

boat sails on Tuesday, the According to Berrey and Van den Bark's *American Thesaurus of Slang* (1942) this was 'a stock remark by London managers when an American act fails upon its first performance'. It was not much heard after the decline of the London MUSIC HALLS and the advent of transatlantic air travel.

bobby A policeman, from Sir Robert Peel, home secretary, who established the Metropolitan Police in 1829. However, various municipal officials, notably beadles, tended to be nicknamed 'Bobby' before the creation of the police force. *See also* BLUE DEVIL; PEELER.

Bo-Jo or **BoJo** One of the many nicknames for Alexander Boris de Pfeffel Johnson (b.1964), who was elected MAYOR OF LONDON in 2008. It echoes American nicknames such as Flo-Jo, for the athlete Florence Griffith-Joyner, but with a hint of Bozo the Clown.

> Clown Boris Johnson has been chosen as Conservative candidate for London mayor. But BoJo won't win.
>
> PAUL ROUTLEDGE, in the *Daily Mirror* (28 September 2007)

Most of Johnson's other sobriquets relate to miscellaneous aspects of his appearance and character. The 'blond moptop' and the 'Eton mess' refer to his overgrown thatch, with the latter punning on a dish traditionally served at his old school. 'Bozza' comes in a series of such nicknames for colourful politicians, notably 'Hezza', for that other long-blond-haired Tory, Michael Heseltine. 'Boris the Menace' alludes to his tendency towards misbehaviour of various kinds. It derives from the *Beano* comic character Dennis the Menace, whom Johnson has described as his 'cartoon hero'. 'Bonking Boris' arose from allegations in 2004 that he had had a three-year affair with the former deputy-editor of *The Spectator*, Petronella Wyatt. Johnson dismissed the allegations as a 'pyramid of piffle'. He went on: 'I haven't had an affair with Petronella. It's balderdash. It's all completely untrue and ludicrous conjecture.' When it turned out that it was, *au contraire*, all completely true, he was sacked from his post as shadow arts minister by Conservative Party leader Michael Howard – not because of the affair, insisted Howard, but because of the false denial.

Bolan tree A sycamore located on Queens Ride, in BARNES. The rock star Marc Bolan (1947–77) died when the car in which he was a passenger hit the tree, which is now the site of a shrine to his memory.

Boleyn Ground The proper name for the home ground of WEST HAM UNITED FC, although UPTON PARK is much more widely used. GREEN STREET House was built in the mid-16th century and later became known as Boleyn Castle. There is no evidence for the tradition that Anne Boleyn lived at the house but Richard Breame, the estate's owner and a servant of Henry VIII, may have boasted that the king courted his future bride there. Green Street House was used as a Roman Catholic school from 1869, when the owners demolished its gateway and began to develop the land facing the street. In the early

20th century the house became a maternity home and was then leased by West Ham United, which built a stadium in the grounds. Green Street House was allowed to deteriorate and was demolished in 1955.

Boltons, The A pair of facing crescents, which, together with neighbouring roads (e.g. Little Boltons), form a fashionable residential area in SOUTH KENSINGTON. The name derives from the Bolton family, which held land in the area from at least the mid-16th century until the mid-19th century, when it was sold for building. George Godwin, editor of *The Builder* magazine, laid out the crescents and built the first homes, and the church of St Mary, WEST BROMPTON. Several of the Boltons' mansions approach the palatial, although many have now been adapted to commercial or institutional use. Past residents include the lyricist W.S. Gilbert, the singer Jenny Lind and the film star Douglas Fairbanks, Jnr. Across the Old Brompton Road, the children's writer Beatrix Potter (1866–1943) lived at 2 Bolton Gardens from her birth until her marriage in 1913, when she moved to the Lake District.

Bomber Harris The apt nickname of Marshal of the RAF Sir Arthur Harris, Bt (1892–1984), commander-in-chief of Bomber Command in the Second World War and advocate of strategic bombing. Partly as a response to the BLITZ, he directed a huge bombing offensive in the form of relentless nightly attacks on German cities and manufacturing centres, ports and railways. In 1992 demonstrators marred the unveiling by the Queen Mother of a statue to Harris at ST CLEMENT DANES.

bona drag 'Good clothes', in POLARI, which was the slang of London's gay underworld, especially in the 1950s. *Bona Drag* was the title of an album by the singer/songwriter Morrissey, released in 1990.

Bond

Bond, Thomas A wealthy financier (d.1685) who helped restore Charles II to the throne in 1660. His 1658 motto 'the world is not enough' appears on the dust cover of Ian Fleming's novel *On Her Majesty's Secret Service* (1963), in which James Bond comments that 'it is an excellent motto which I shall certainly adopt'. In 1999 it was used as the title of the 19th Bond film. The words

themselves are a translation of *Non suffcit orbis*, the Latin tag end of a cynical line in Juvenal's *Satires* (2nd century AD), about Alexander the Great: *Unus Pellaeo juveni non suffcit orbis* (For a young fellow from Pella a single world was not enough.) Juvenal in turn derived the phrase from the poet Lucan, who put the words in the mouth of Julius Caesar in a passage in his *Civil War* (1st century AD) in which Caesar quells a mutiny in the ranks. Sir Thomas thus gave his namesake James a classical pedigree of a sort.

Bond Street London's most expensive street for retailers, according to recent research on land values, running north from PICCADILLY to OXFORD STREET through the eastern part of MAYFAIR. Bond Street was begun in 1686 and its name honours Sir Thomas Bond (*see above*). New Bond Street, added in two stages, reached Oxford Street in the 1720s. Almost from its creation Bond Street has been a fashionable address. Among the 18th-century lodgers and residents who helped popularize it were the writers Jonathan Swift, Edward Gibbon, Laurence Sterne and James Boswell, the statesman Lord Chatham (William Pitt the Elder), the poet James Thomson and Admiral Lord Nelson. By the end of that century the street was lined with tailors, jewellers, chemists, perfumers, and purveyors of every kind of superior foodstuff. In Regency times BEAU BRUMMELL reigned supreme among all the dandies, making the reputation of his tailor, Weston, in Old Bond Street. Every variety of merchant in search of a smart address wanted to set up shop here. Samuel Chappell, the music publisher, arrived in 1811. Asprey's, the jewellers, moved to New Bond Street from Mitcham in the 1830s. In 1873 Richard Benson and William Hedges began making cigarettes at 13 Old Bond Street. In 1891 the Northumbrian ladies' outfitter Fenwick's opened its London branch in New Bond Street. Art galleries and auctioneers fitted in splendidly amidst the goldsmiths and silversmiths, culminating in the arrival of Sotheby's at its present location in 1917. Bond Street continues to attract the most prestigious names, especially in contemporary couture.

Bond Street loungers In the late 18th and early 19th centuries, men who took equal pleasure in adorning themselves and in surveying the titled ladies who promenaded in the afternoons. Georgian Bond Street was not just the best place to shop, it was the best place to be *seen* shopping.

Bonkers, Sid and Doris A stereotypical pair of 'nobodies' caricatured in *Private Eye* magazine in the 1960s and 1970s, and still mentioned from time to time as constituting the entire crowd at the home games of (the non-existent) Neasden FC. Their names have been invoked (usually parenthetically, following the magazine's style) outside *Private Eye* in mockery of something that enjoys little support.

> The reappearance of the card catalogue might please Nicholson Baker and his fans (Sid and Doris Bonkers) but would be greeted by groans from our users and those with the wretched task of filing cards in it.
>
> MICHAEL GORMAN: *Our Own Selves: More Meditations for Librarians* (2005)

bonnets so blue 'Irish stew' in early COCKNEY RHYMING SLANG.

Boodle's A CLUB founded in PALL MALL in 1762 as an offshoot from ALMACK'S and at first known as the Savoir Faire. By 1764 it had come under the management of Edward Boodle, and soon adopted his name. In 1783 it moved to its present premises in ST JAMES'S STREET. The majority of the club's members were traditionally country gentlemen in London on business, selected on the basis of mutual compatibility rather than their social rank or political affiliation. Past members include Pitt the Elder and Pitt the Younger, Edward Gibbon, William Wilberforce, BEAU BRUMMELL, the Duke of Wellington. The author Ian Fleming joined in 1944 and in his James Bond stories he modelled M's club, Blades, primarily on Boodle's.

> Lord Goring: Oh! I am not at all romantic. I am not old enough. I leave romance to my seniors.
> Sir Robert Chiltern: Lord Goring is the result of Boodle's Club, Mrs Cheveley.
> Mrs Cheveley: He reflects every credit on the institution.
>
> OSCAR WILDE: *An Ideal Husband*, I (1895)

Booth

Booth, Charles A successful Liverpool businessman and a pioneering social researcher and philanthropist (1840–1916). He moved to London in 1875 with his wife Mary, niece of the historian Thomas Babington Macaulay. Despite the demands of business and a busy social life, Booth found time to take a concerned interest in the extreme poverty that affected much of Victorian London. He began by analysing census returns but, finding them inadequate for his purposes, set out to examine conditions on the ground, assisted by a team of social investigators, including his wife and her cousin Beatrice Potter (later Webb). Booth often lodged for several weeks at a time with working-class Londoners and he and his investigators walked the streets of every district, accompanied by local policemen. The results of his enquiries were published in 17 volumes as *Life and Labour of the People in London* (1889–1903). The study included detailed street maps of London that were colour-coded to show levels of wealth and poverty, ranging from yellow for 'upper-middle and upper classes, wealthy' to black for 'lowest class, vicious, semi-criminal'. These maps, together with the published text and the investigators' notebooks, have proved invaluable to social researchers of succeeding generations, as well as influencing sociological methods. Booth served on several public bodies, including royal commissions on the aged poor and on the poor law. He was made a privy counsellor and a fellow of the ROYAL SOCIETY.

Booth, William *See the* SALVATION ARMY.

booze-shunter An accomplished drinker of beer.

> The booze-shunter moves the beer, or 'booze', from the pot into his visceral arrangements. The term was started by the S.W.R. [South Western Railway] porters and guards, who use the larger public houses in the neighbourhood of the terminus in the Waterloo Road.
>
> J. REDDING WARE: *Passing English of the Victorian Era* (1908)

boracic (lint) *See* BRASSIC.

Boris Island *See* HEATHROW-ON-SEA.

born

born in Stepney Babies born at sea to English parents were formerly (but incorrectly) said to belong to the parish of STEPNEY. The tradition seems to have arisen from the practice of forwarding such children's baptismal certificates to the rector of St Dunstan and All Saints, the parish church of Stepney. In the 18th century, most London-registered ships sailed from docks in that parish, which then took in much of east London's riverside. The certificates often stated 'born in Stepney'. By an extension of the misunderstanding, a belief later arose that a destitute person who had been born at sea could claim financial support from the parish of Stepney and the right of abode there. Until the early 19th century magistrates in various provincial towns would attempt to send such paupers to Stepney but the parish promptly returned them and on at least one occasion took legal action against the ignorant official.

born on the steps of Newgate Formerly said of someone of doubtful parentage.

born within (the) sound of Bow bells Said of a true COCKNEY. The church of ST MARY-LE-BOW, in CHEAPSIDE, has long had one of the most celebrated bell-peals in London, especially when marking special occasions such as Christmas Eve. John Dun, mercer, in 1472 gave two tenements to maintain the ringing of Bow bell every night at nine o'clock, to direct travellers on the road to town. In 1520 William Copland gave a bigger bell for 'sounding a retreat from work.' It is said that the sound of these bells, which seemed to say 'Turn again, Whittington, lord mayor of London', encouraged the young Dick WHITTINGTON to return to the CITY and try his luck again. An air raid destroyed the bells and the interior of the church in 1941. On 20 December 1961 the restored bells rang out to mark the start of the church's rebuilding; one of the bell-ringers that day was HRH Prince Philip, Duke of Edinburgh.

The first recorded connection of Bow bells with cockneys is in Samuel Rowlands's *The Letting of Humours Blood in the Head-Vaine*, Satire IV (1600):

> I scorne ... To let a Bowe-bell Cockney put me downe.

Fynes Morison elaborated on the pejorative association in his *Itinerary* (1617):

> All within the sound of Bow Bell are in reproch called cochnies, and eaters of buttered tostes.

Because of the massive expansion of the metropolis since the 17th century, the depopulation of the City itself and the increase in noise pollution, few who consider themselves true cockneys can nowadays claim to have been born within the sound of Bow bells.

Borough SOUTHWARK's historic commercial centre, noted especially for its inns and as the former site of the MARSHALSEA gaol. The name recalls the presence of a defensive 'burgh' protecting LONDON BRIDGE. In the *Pickwick Papers* (1836–7), Charles Dickens described the Borough as home to 'several ancient inns; great rambling queer old places with galleries and passages'. The most illustrious of these was the TABARD, from which the pilgrims of *The Canterbury Tales* began their journey. The White Hart Inn was the headquarters of Jack CADE during his revolt of 1450 against Henry VI. The GEORGE INN is the only survivor from the days when the Borough's coaching inns thrived on their position serving the route from London to the south coast, and when St Margaret's Hill, now part of Borough High Street, formed a wealthy enclave amidst the surrounding poverty of Southwark.

Borough market A covered food market of medieval origin that has traded at its present site for 250 years. In response to declining business, the wholesale market has expanded into retail, focusing on the 'foodie' consumer, with an emphasis on organic and speciality farmers' produce.

Boro-onions A comical COCKNEY re-interpretation of Boro(ugh)nians, used to designate denizens of the Borough in the early 19th century. The name clearly played on the vegetables sold at its famous market.

Borough Usurer *See the* SOUTHWARK USURER.

Boss of Billingsgate Some sort of post, probably a drinking fountain, that formerly stood at BILLINGSGATE. One source suggests that the boss (or bosse) bore an image of BELIN, another that it was shaped like a pot-bellied man. It was a tradition that fish porters would ask passers-by to kiss the boss and, if they refused, they were bumped against it. One meaning of 'boss' was a water conduit running out of an ornamental standpipe, while a 'buss' was a playful kiss; the practice may have arisen from the congruence of the two words. The boss was said by some to have been erected by Dick WHITTINGTON or his executors. It was the subject of a comic ballad, entitled 'The Marriage of London Stone and the Boss of Billingsgate' (1521), and a play by John Day and others (1603), which has not survived.

Bostall Heath An expansive area of former common land situated north of EAST WICKHAM and BEXLEYHEATH. The developed part is often known simply as Bostall, a name that probably derives from Old English *borg-steall*, 'a secure place', since it provided refuge from the regular flooding of the lower-lying land nearer the THAMES. The commoners resisted attempts by landowners Queen's College, Oxford, to enclose and develop the heath in the 1880s. The college had appointed a local solicitor and builder, whose homes were trashed during riotous scenes, and the authorities drafted in 200 extra police and called out the fire brigade to hose down the mob.

Boston Manor A Jacobean mansion located on the HANWELL/BRENTFORD border. The house was built in 1623 for Lady Mary Reade in preparation for her marriage to Sir Edward Spencer of Althorp. A merchant banker, James Clitherow, bought the house in 1670 and immediately set about enlarging it and adding some ornamentation. Another James Clitherow and his wife Jane entertained William IV and Queen Adelaide to dinner here in 1834. The Clitherow family remained at Boston Manor until 1923, when most of the grounds were sold for housebuilding and HOUNSLOW council bought the house. Although its exterior is dour, some of the rooms and furnishings are splendid, especially the elaborate state drawing room on the first floor. The walls are hung with paintings from the borough's art collection.

Boswell

Boswell, James *See* JOHNSON, SAMUEL.
Boswell, Urania The queen of Kent's Gypsies, who lived near FARNBOROUGH. When she died in 1933 a crowd of 15,000 turned out to watch her funeral procession. Also known as Gypsy Lee, she is buried in St Giles' churchyard.

bottle

bottle (and glass) 'Arse' in COCKNEY RHYMING SLANG. There may have been some link with the term 'on the bottle', which formerly connoted male prostitution. *See also* ARIS.
Bottle Conjuror, the The subject of one of London's most extraordinary manifestations of mass gullibility. In January 1749 an advertisement in the London papers declared that an unnamed performer would be appearing at the Little Theatre in the HAYMARKET (predecessor of the THEATRE ROYAL), where he would take a walking stick from a member of the audience and thereon play 'the music of every instrument now in use', after which he would jump into a quart wine bottle and sing while inside it. Various acts

of spiritualism were promised afterwards. Ten thousand people were said to have thronged the Haymarket in an attempt to witness the spectacle, and the theatre was crowded with members of the nobility and the gentry. The charlatan failed to appear and a riot began, allegedly incited by Prince William, Duke of Cumberland, during which most of the theatre's fixtures and fittings were torn out and thrown onto a bonfire in the street. The hoax was later said to have been cooked up by two aristocrats for a bet.
bottle of spruce 'Deuce', meaning two pence, in early COCKNEY RHYMING SLANG.

Boudicca (Celtic, 'victor') The British warrior queen, wife of Prasutagus, king of the Iceni, a people inhabiting what is now Norfolk and Suffolk. On her husband's death (AD 60) the Romans seized the territory of the Iceni. The widow was scourged for her opposition and her two daughters raped. Boudicca raised a revolt of the Iceni and Trinovantes and burned Camulodunum (Colchester), LONDINIUM and Verulamium (St Albans). According to most sources, when finally routed by the Roman governor Suetonius Paulinus, she took poison. As 'Boadicea', she is the subject of poems by William Cowper and Tennyson. One legend has it that she is buried beneath a platform at KING'S CROSS STATION. A tumulus near PARLIAMENT HILL was also said to be her burial place, but when it was excavated in 1894 little was found except signs that it had already been dug out before. It is said that, if confirmation had been found, Thomas Thornycroft's statue of the queen in her chariot would have been erected at that spot, instead of its present site at WESTMINSTER BRIDGE. *See also* BATTLE BRIDGE; HONOR OAK; PECKHAM RYE.

Boulton and Park Ernest Boulton and William Frederick Park, two young men who were arrested on leaving the STRAND Theatre on the evening of 28 April 1870, when they were dressed as women. They were tried for conspiracy to commit sodomy but the jury found them not guilty. The notoriety of the case gave rise to the term 'B and P', in reference to an effeminate man, later corrupted to 'beanpea'.

bovver A COCKNEY pronunciation of the word 'bother', heard from the late 1960s to the early 1980s in the context of skinheads wearing 'bovver boots', and more recently in 'Am I bovvered?', the catchphrase of Lauren Cooper, a creation of the comic actress Catherine Tate (b.1968). Notwithstanding the London origin of the pronunciation, 'bovver boys' were a nationwide phenomenon and the setting for the Lauren sketches seemed more like a NEW TOWN than the capital.

Bow A socially and geographically unfocused residential district situated between MILE END and the River LEA. Around 1100, Henry I's wife Matilda commissioned the construction of a bridge across the river, allegedly after she had fallen in during an attempted crossing. The bridge's innovative arched shape was the source of the early name for the hamlet that grew up here: Stratford Bow. Chaucer, in the prologue to *The Canterbury Tales* (*c*.1387), says of the Prioress:

> Frenssh she spak ful faire and fetisly [elegantly]
> After the scole of Stratford atte Bowe,
> For Frenssh of Parys was to hir unknowe.

The suggestion is that the Prioress spoke French with the anglicized accent she had learned in her convent, the Benedictine nunnery of St Leonard, Bromley. Along with Stratford Langthorne on the opposite bank and Bromley to the south (now usually called BROMLEY-BY-BOW), Bow became an early centre for trade and industry, notably milling, baking and cloth-dying. By the 17th century it was the most important settlement between STEPNEY and the Lea, and wealthy gentlemen kept country homes here until they were driven away by industrial and suburban expansion and by the relocation here of the MAY FAIR.

bow (and arrow) 'Sparrow' in COCKNEY RHYMING SLANG.

Bow bells *See* BORN WITHIN (THE) SOUND OF BOW BELLS.

Bow Cemetery *See* TOWER HAMLETS CEMETERY.

Bow Church
1. The familiar name of the church of ST MARY-LE-BOW.
2. A DOCKLANDS LIGHT RAILWAY station named after St Mary's Church, which stands at the eastern end of Bow Road. St Mary's was established as a chapel of ease to STEPNEY in 1311; parts of the present building date from that time and from the late 15th century. It became the parish church of BOW in 1719.

Bow Creek The tidal part of the River LEA.

Bow selector A sobriquet of Dylan Mills (b.1985), a rap musician who performs under the name Dizzee Rascal. The nickname puns on his place of birth and the term 'bo selector' (or 'selecta'), a now-hackneyed expression of approval of a DJ's choice of dance music. Mills was an early exponent of the genre of urban music known as GRIME but subsequently evolved his own distinctive and commercially successful style.

Bow Street A street running between LONG ACRE in the north and Wellington Street in the south, just to the east of COVENT GARDEN. It was built between 1633 and 1677 and derives its name from its layout: it runs in a curving line, in the shape of a bow. It was originally an elegant residential street (Dr JOHNSON lodged here for a while), but gradually THEATRELAND encroached (the first Covent Garden Theatre opened here in 1732, on the site of what is now the ROYAL OPERA HOUSE) and by the beginning of the 19th century it had become notorious for its brothels. In 1740 the Bow Street magistrates' office was opened, from which the BOW STREET RUNNERS operated. It stood on the site of what later became Bow Street Magistrates' Court, where the Metropolitan Chief Magistrate sat. The court closed in 2006. *See also* CHINA STREET.

Bow Street Runner A member of a London police force based in Bow Street in the late 18th and early 19th centuries. They had their origins in an irregular force set up in the middle of the 18th century by the Bow Street magistrate, novelist and barrister Henry Fielding (1707–54) to supplement the less than adequate parish constabularies of the time. By the early 19th century, when the term 'Bow Street Runner' is first recorded, they had been placed on a more regular footing, with a uniform of a blue dress-coat, brass buttons and, for some, a bright red waistcoat (hence their nickname, REDBREASTS). They were disbanded in 1839, having been rendered redundant by the new METROPOLITAN POLICE. *See also* BOBBY; PEELER.

Bow ware A type of blue-and-white porcelain originally made in the mid-18th century at the Bow China Manufactory in STRATFORD. The name perhaps refers to early experiments in the technique carried out at Bow. In 1775 manufacture was moved to Derby.

Bower, the One of the many slang terms for NEWGATE PRISON.

bowler hat A hard felt hat, said to have been introduced by the Norfolk landowner William Coke in 1850. Because he found his tall riding hat frequently swept off by overhanging branches, he asked LOCK & CO., the well-known hatters of ST JAMES'S, to design him a hat with a lower crown. The first 'Coke' or bowler may have been made from felt supplied by Thomas and William Bowler. However, according to another account, the name comes from the hatter who designed it, John Bowler. The three-piece pinstripe suit, briefcase, bowler hat and furled UMBRELLA comprised the ensemble traditionally sported by the typical CITY businessman and the hat retains a symbolic significance in this regard.

> If you can protect the people in bowler hats in the banking industry, why can't you support the workers in hard hats in manufacturing and service industries?
>
> BOB CROW, interviewed on *Newsnight* (29 January 2009)

boy

boy Jones, the An apothecary's errand-boy who in 1841 made a habit of sneaking into the queen's private apartments in BUCKINGHAM PALACE. He was twice found hiding close to the royal bedchamber and was another time apprehended en route. His sole aim seemed to be the achievement of notoriety, in which he succeeded. Lady Sandwich suggested that 'he must undoubtedly be a descendant of *In-I-go* Jones, the architect'.

Boy Scouts A popular youth movement started by General Sir Robert Baden-Powell (later Lord Baden-Powell of Gilwell) in 1908. He laid out the basic tenets in the handbook *Scouting for Boys*, which he had begun to write in a cottage beside the windmill on WIMBLEDON COMMON. GILWELL PARK has been the worldwide centre of the movement since 1919.

Golden Boy of Pye Corner *See under* GOLDEN.

Panyer Boy *See the* PANYER STONE.

Brahms (and Liszt) 'Pissed' in COCKNEY RHYMING SLANG, in the sense of being inebriated. The term is more often heard in full than in abbreviated form.

> Harold: He's throwing the annual Christmas dinner down the church hall and he said he would be delighted to see you there, providing
> ...
> Albert: Providing what?

> Harold: Providing you do not get Brahms and Liszt.
>
> RAY GALTON and ALAN SIMPSON (screenwriters): *Steptoe and Son*, 'The Party' (TV comedy) (1973)

Brandy Nan Queen Anne, who was partial to brandy. On her statue in ST PAUL'S churchyard a wit once wrote:

> Brandy Nan, Brandy Nan, left in the lurch,
> Her face to the gin-shop, her back to the church.

A 'gin palace' used to stand at the south-west corner of St Paul's churchyard.

brassic 'Skint' (i.e. broke, penniless) in COCKNEY RHYMING SLANG, via a contraction of 'boracic lint' – formerly a commonplace antiseptic dressing for wounds and infections. The term is nowadays understood far beyond London.

> They were brassic but not desperate. A dress with tags still attached, in the original bag with the receipt, was the answer.
>
> HOLLY YANEZ and SHIRLEY YANEZ: *Looking For Harvey Weinstein* (2004)

brass tacks The term is said by some, but by no means all, lexicographers to have begun as COCKNEY RHYMING SLANG for 'facts'. It now means (and perhaps always meant) 'basics', as in 'to get down to brass tacks'.

bread

bread (and honey) 'Money' in COCKNEY RHYMING SLANG. However, the internationally understood synonymity of 'bread' and 'money' probably does not derive from this rhyme; it is more likely to be of American origin.

Bread Street A CITY of London street and the ward extending westwards from it. Like many streets in the CHEAPSIDE vicinity, it takes its name from the trade carried on there in the Middle Ages. Bread Street was the birthplace of two poets, John Donne (1572–1631) and John Milton (1608–74) and was the site of the MERMAID TAVERN. The ward excludes ST PAUL'S Cathedral, which falls within CASTLE BAYNARD, but takes in PATERNOSTER SQUARE.

Breakspear Chapel An alternative name for the north chapel that forms part of St Mary's Church, HAREFIELD. It derives from the family of Nicholas Breakspear, the only English pope. Nicholas himself grew up in Hertfordshire and was Pope Adrian IV from 1154 to 1159. The family name makes several other appearances in this far north-western corner of GREATER LONDON; for example in Breakspear Road and Breakspear Crematorium.

Breathing A glass and steel sculpture mounted on the roof of the new wing of BROADCASTING HOUSE. Created by Jaume Plensa (b.1955), it is intended as a memorial to international news staff who were murdered or lost their lives in acts of war while working on behalf of the BBC. *Breathing* glows during the hours of darkness and projects a vertical beam of light between 10 and 10.30pm each night. UN secretary-general Ban Ki-moon unveiled the work in June 2008.

Brent A river rising in south Hertfordshire (where it is known as the Dollis Brook) and flowing 20 miles (32 km) southward through the boroughs of BARNET, Brent, EALING and HOUNSLOW to reach the THAMES at BRENTFORD. Along its course it has been dammed to form the WELSH HARP reservoir (also known as Brent reservoir). The name is of Celtic origin, meaning 'high, holy one', from Old Celtic *brigantia*; also the name of a goddess (perhaps reflecting a cult of river-worship in prehistoric times).

> Gentle Brent, I used to know you
> Wandering Wembley-wards at will,
> Now what change your waters show you
> In the meadowlands you fill!
> Recollect the elm-trees misty
> And the footpaths climbing twisty
> Under cedar-shaded palings,
> Low laburnum-leaned-on railings,
> Out of Northolt on and upward to the heights of
> Harrow hill.
>
> JOHN BETJEMAN: 'Middlesex' (1954)

Brent, London Borough of An OUTER LONDON borough formed in 1965 by the merger of WEMBLEY (which had by then incorporated KINGSBURY) and WILLESDEN. It is one of the most ethnically diverse boroughs in Europe and has claimed the greatest linguistic diversity in Britain, with over 70 languages spoken. Brent's civic heraldry combines elements from the arms of its two constituent boroughs, with wavy allusions to the river that formerly separated them. The civic motto is 'forward together'.

Brent Cross A road junction and the retail centre named after it, situated beside the River Brent in south HENDON. The shopping mall,

with its JOHN LEWIS and Fenwick department stores, opened in 1976 with a fully enclosed and air-conditioned format and a late-opening policy that were novel in Britain at that time. Brent Cross was extended and refurbished in 1997 and now contains 110 retail outlets. In 2008 the centre's owners tabled a proposal for further expansion in the direction of CRICKLEWOOD: an ambitious retail and residential scheme that may not be completed until 2030.

Brentford A centre of industry and commerce since the Middle Ages, situated 2 miles (3 km) west of CHISWICK. There is no direct evidence to support the legends that Julius Caesar crossed the Thames or fought a battle here in 54 BC. With its good river and road connections, Brentford developed early as a trading place and was granted the right to hold markets and fairs in 1306. Brentford grew in importance as a coaching stop and market town during the 17th century, with shops, inns, warehouses and dwellings, surrounded by orchards and market gardens. MIDDLESEX county court sessions were held here and, later, parliamentary elections – leading to erroneous claims that it was the county town. The GREAT WEST ROAD (A4) opened in 1925, precipitating a new wave of industrial development. The area's visitor attractions include Waterman's Arts Centre, the MUSICAL MUSEUM and the KEW BRIDGE STEAM MUSEUM. *See also the* BUTTS.

James Boswell, in his *Life of Samuel Johnson* (1791), records a competitive conversation between his subject and Adam Smith. The Scottish economist extolled the charms of Glasgow at some length. The great lexicographer responded with: 'Pray, Sir, have you ever seen Brentford?'

Brentford FC A now-professional FOOTBALL club founded in 1889 by members of the town's rowing club who wanted to pursue a winter sport (a vote of eight to five decided it would be association rather than rugby football). The club moved to its present ground at GRIFFIN Park in 1904.

Brentford Trilogy, The A loosely connected series of eight humorous books by Robert Rankin (b.1949), published between 1981 and 2005.

as dirty as Old Brentford at Christmas *See under* AS.

Battle of Brentford *See under* BATTLE.

face like the Red Lion of Brentford, a *See under* FACE.

like the two kings of Brentford *See under* LIKE.

brick

Brick Lane

1. A market street in SPITALFIELDS, running south from SHOREDITCH towards ALDGATE East and noted for its Bangladeshi community and south Asian cuisine. Its name derives from the making of bricks and tiles in the immediate area since the 16th century; and was first recorded in 1542. Joseph Truman established a brewery here in the late 17th century and built some houses to its south that also survive. A market began to operate in the 18th century and Brick Lane became a 'high street' for London's Russian and Polish Jews from the late 19th century. In the early 1970s, immigrants from Bangladesh began to settle here and the first 'Indian' restaurant opened in 1974. Brick Lane now has the largest concentration of curry houses on one street in the country and a cultural community centred on the old Truman brewery, which has been converted into studios for artists, musicians and fashion designers. The annual Brick Lane Festival began in 1997 and attracts tens of thousands of visitors with its global mix of food, history and culture.

2. A novel (2003) by Monica Ali, telling the story of Nazneen, a teenage girl who moves from a Bangladeshi village to an EAST END tower block following her arranged marriage. She finds an escape from her domestic constraints in a relationship with a young political activist. The book was filmed in 2007.

bricks and mortar 'Daughter' in COCKNEY RHYMING SLANG.

London to a brick *See under* LONDON.

Brides in the Bath A series of murders committed by George Joseph Smith (1872–1915), who was born in BETHNAL GREEN. Smith drowned three women soon after bigamously marrying them, each time under a false name, in Herne Bay, Kent; Blackpool, Lancashire; and at 14 Bismarck Road, now Waterlow Road, in HIGHGATE. Found guilty at the OLD BAILEY of the first of these crimes, he was hanged at Maidstone Prison.

Bridewell Formerly a royal palace built over the holy well of St Bride, near the mouth of the FLEET river. After the Reformation Edward VI made it a penitentiary for unruly APPRENTICES and vagrants. It was demolished in 1863, although much of the palace had already been destroyed in the GREAT FIRE OF LONDON. The original Bridewell gave its name to a generic term for a house of correction or a prison.

> At my first entrance it seemed to me rather a Prince's Palace than a House of Correction, till gazing round me, I saw in a large room a parcel of ill-looking mortals stripped to their shirts like haymakers, pounding a pernicious weed … From thence we turned to the women's apartment … like so many slaves they were under the care and direction of an overseer who walked about with a very flexible weapon of offence to correct such hempen journeywomen as were unhappily troubled with the spirit of idleness.
>
> NED WARD: *The London Spy* (1698)

Bridewell Theatre A small theatre situated on Bride Lane, off FLEET STREET. Its owner, the St Bride Foundation, also runs an adjoining printing and graphic arts library.

Bridge

1. A CITY of London ward encompassing a compact area on the north side of LONDON BRIDGE. Bridge possesses an unexceptional cluster of commercial establishments, together with the MONUMENT, Fishmongers' LIVERY HALL and St Magnus the Martyr Church.

2. In a footballing context and preceded by the definite article, the term is usually a short form of STAMFORD BRIDGE.

Bridge House Estates A body established in 1282 to maintain LONDON BRIDGE, named after its headquarters, a house that lay on the south side of the bridge, in SOUTHWARK. It derives its income from a property portfolio and is nowadays responsible for all five CITY bridges. Its considerable surplus income is distributed via a charitable grant-making arm, the City Bridge Trust, to a wide range of projects benefiting the inhabitants of GREATER LONDON.

Bridge Mark or **Bridge House Mark** A graphic device identifying the BRIDGE HOUSE ESTATES and the bridges for which that body is responsible, probably designed by the surveyor William Leybourn (1626–1716). It consists of a circle over a saltire, or letter X, with the lower points of the X joined to form a base and the circle surmounted by a cross pattée. It is said to be emblematic of the martyrdom of St George;

Leybourn may have adapted his design from one that originated in SOUTHWARK's parish of St George the Martyr. Also known as the Southwark Cross, the mark was employed by the former East Surrey Regiment and incorporated into the arms of the Metropolitan Borough of Southwark in 1902. It does not appear in the arms of the borough's expanded successor, the London Borough of Southwark.

Bridge of Sighs WATERLOO BRIDGE was given this nickname, from the Venetian original, when suicides (especially those of women) were frequent here.

One more unfortunate,
Weary of breath,
Rashly importunate,
Gone to her death!

THOMAS HOOD: 'The Bridge of Sighs' (1844)

Bridget Jones See under JONES.

Brighton The Sussex coastal town has been nicknamed 'London-by-the Sea' since its patronage by the Prince REGENT, who first spent a holiday here in 1782, and especially after the opening of the London and Brighton Railway in 1841. The town was also known as 'Dr Brighton', from its popularity as a health resort.

Brighton Belle A luxury train consisting of Pullman carriages which ran between London VICTORIA and Brighton. The service began in 1934 (succeeding the previous 'Southern Belle', which started in 1908) and its journey time was 55 minutes. Its economic viability was ebbing fast in the 1960s, and British Railways often announced its demise. Supporters, loath to lose its traditional charms (such as kipper breakfasts in the dining car), campaigned to save it. They succeeded for a while, aided no doubt by the influence of such regular users as Lord Olivier, but the service was finally withdrawn in 1972.

Brighton Run An annual rally for veteran cars from HYDE PARK to the promenade at Brighton in Sussex, a distance of 53 miles (85 km). It is held on the first Sunday in November and commemorates the so-called 'Emancipation Run' made by 33 motorists between the two towns on 14 November 1896, the day of the repeal of the Locomotive Act of 1865, limiting the speed of steam carriages to 4 mph (6.5 kph) in the country and 2 mph (3 kph) in the town, and raising it to

14 mph (22.5 kph). The run is commemorated in the 1953 film *Genevieve*.

Brink's-Mat robbery A robbery that took place in November 1983 when a gang stole gold bars worth £26 million, belonging to Johnson Matthey, a firm of dealers in precious metals, from the Brink's-Mat security warehouse at HEATHROW AIRPORT. It was Britain's biggest robbery at the time. The confession of a corrupt security guard gave police their first lead in an investigation which lasted almost ten years and resulted in charges against some 30 people.

Bristol (City) 'Titty' in COCKNEY RHYMING SLANG, generally employed in the plural. Other football teams with 'City' in their name have also been used to the same effect, as well as DICKENS's *A Tale of Two Cities*. There is evidence that 'Manchester Cities' came first, but 'Bristols' now predominates. A recent variation on the same theme has been 'Bristol and West' for 'chest', from the former building society. *See also* THREEPENNY BITS.

You're at the movies, right? By your side is a very tasty young lady you've had your eye on for weeks. Tonight's your big chance. You've got your arm round her, within striking distance of her Bristols. This. Could. Be. It.

PETER MAYLE: *Hotel Pastis: A novel of Provence* (1993)

Britain

Britain's Bourse or **Burse** The name given by James I to the New Exchange when it was built on the south side of the STRAND in 1609, in place of the stables of Durham House. It was modelled on the ROYAL EXCHANGE and sought to draw some business away from that institution. Although it failed in that aim – and the 'bourse' tag never caught on – the exchange's milliners and seamstresses attracted the cream of fashionable society after the Reformation. Samuel PEPYS records several visits there with his wife. The exchange was demolished in 1737 and replaced by eleven houses, one of which later became home to Coutts' Bank. *See also the* WHITE MILLINER.

Little Britain See under LITTLE.

Britart Painting, sculpture, etc. of the late 20th and early 21st centuries produced by a coterie of young, London-based artists, many of whom attended GOLDSMITHS. Notable exponents have included Damien Hirst, Tracey Emin, Rachael

Whiteread, Sam Taylor-Wood, Sarah Lucas, Ron Mueck and the Chapman brothers (Jake and Dinos). Britart came to public notice in the early 1990s, thanks in large part to a series of exhibitions at the SAATCHI GALLERY.

British

British Charlottenburg IMPERIAL COLLEGE was so dubbed at the time of its creation in 1907, because the project was in part modelled on the example set by Royal Technical College of Charlottenburg, now the Technical University of Berlin. German technological advancement was seen as a threat to Britain's commercial and military interests; improved scientific and technical education was considered an important element of the response.

British Film Institute Established in 1933, the BFI seeks to promote understanding and appreciation of Britain's film and television heritage and culture. The institute runs the BFI Southbank, formerly the the National Film Theatre, and the nearby IMAX cinema.

British Library The British national library, formed in 1973 from the BRITISH MUSEUM library. Its services are based on collections that include over 14 million books, 920,000 journal and newspaper titles, 58 million patents and 3 million sound recordings. It opened in new premises at ST PANCRAS, designed by Colin St John Wilson, in 1998. In front of the library is a large piazza, with a bronze statue of Isaac Newton and an amphitheatre that is occasionally used for outdoor events.

British Museum This famous institution began in Montagu House, Great Russell Street, BLOOMSBURY. It resulted from an Act of 1753, and its first collections were purchased from the proceeds of a public lottery. The museum extended the collection with a wealth of books, artefacts, relics and classical sculptures, via donations, government purchases and trophies from imperial expansion and military victories, including the ROSETTA STONE and the Parthenon sculptures known as the ELGIN MARBLES. By 1820 the museum had entirely outgrown its accommodation and Sir Robert Smirke was appointed to design new buildings. Construction began in 1823 and a series of new wings enlarged, and then replaced, Montagu House over a period of three decades. A reading room followed, and new galleries and wings have continued to expand

the British Museum ever since. With around five million visitors a year the British Museum is rivalled only by the NATIONAL GALLERY, TATE MODERN and the LONDON EYE as London's most popular attraction.

British Samson *See the* STRONG MAN OF ISLINGTON.

Brixton The beacon of south London's black community, Brixton lies east of CLAPHAM and north of STREATHAM. Brixton was 'Brixiges stan' when it was first recorded in 1062, and later Brixistan, which means 'the stone of Brixi'. The stone probably stood on Brixton Hill and marked a meeting place for the hundred court, which administered the medieval district of which Brixton was the capital; Brixi was a short form of Beorhtsige, a popular Saxon name meaning 'bright victory'. Brixton Road became a shopping centre in the late 19th century, with a street market on Atlantic Road. As a result of bomb damage, slum clearance and the end of 99-year leases, much of Brixton was rebuilt from the middle of the 20th century, a period that saw the early arrival here of migrants from the Caribbean, partly because LAMBETH council was more welcoming than others. In recent years, Brixton has become known for the relatively free availability of drugs on its streets, especially cannabis, and has been the subject of experiments in 'tolerant' law enforcement. Meanwhile, legitimate trades in exotic fruits, vegetables and fish, specialist record shops and entertainment palaces such as the Ritzy cinema, Fridge nightclub and Academy live music venue have made Brixton south London's liveliest shopping and leisure centre.

With its almost iconic cultural status, Brixton makes frequent appearances in works of music and literature, including The CLASH's 'Guns of Brixton' (1979), local author Alex Wheatle's books, such as *Brixton Rock* (1999) and *East of Acre Lane* (2001), and Nicholas Wright's play *Vincent in Brixton* (2002), which takes artist Vincent van Gogh's 1873 stay in Hackford Road as the inspiration for a fictional love story.

Brixton briefcase A synonym for a ghettoblaster, from the days when the latter term was in vogue.

Brixton riots A series of civil disturbances caused by the poor economic and housing conditions experienced by many of Brixton's black residents, combined with what were perceived as racist policing tactics. The first and most serious riot took place in 1981, when hundreds of buildings and cars were damaged in what was London's largest civil disturbance of the century. Less serious riots followed in 1985 and 1995, again sparked by policing incidents. Some black Londoners object to the term 'Brixton riots', preferring to see the events of 1981 as a righteous uprising.

Broadcasting House The BBC's main site in central London, situated at the southern end of PORTLAND PLACE. Designed by George Val Myer (1883–1959), the elliptical art deco building was constructed in 1932 of ferro-concrete, faced, aptly for its address, with Portland stone. Eric Gill (1882–1940) produced carvings for the interior and, for the exterior, four groups of sculptures featuring Ariel, who, as the invisible spirit of the air, was deemed an appropriate personification of broadcasting. The building is presently being refurbished and extended. When the project is completed in 2012 Broadcasting House will provide production and broadcast facilities for BBC Audio and Music, News, and the World Service (which will move here from Bush House, ALDWYCH), and will be the hub of the BBC's national and international live output. *See also* BREATHING.

Broadgate An 'office city', rivalling the BAR-BICAN as the CITY of London's biggest building project since the GREAT FIRE OF LONDON. The scheme was first mooted by British Rail in the mid-1970s as a means of funding the rebuilding of LIVERPOOL STREET STATION. It eventually got under way a decade later in the wake of the boom that followed stock market deregulation. British Rail sold the site of Broad Street station and the hinterland of Liverpool Street to a joint venture by developers Rosehaugh and Stanhope Properties. Broad Street station closed in 1986, with its services transferring to Liverpool Street, and the first two new buildings opened in the same year. ARUP Associates – later joined by Skidmore, Owings and Merrill – were responsible for the brutalist modernist architecture, mainly clad in pink granite. The social focus of the complex is Broadgate Arena, which is encircled by tiers of shops, bars and restaurants.

Broadwater Farm An ill-famed but much improved housing estate in west TOTTENHAM.

The original Broadwater Farm covered 119 acres (48 hectares) of the huge Downhills estate, which had been in existence since the mid-15th century and by 1728 included Broadwater Farm. Completed in 1973 the Broadwater Farm estate consists of 12 concrete-panelled blocks of flats, most of which have four to six storeys, originally with a deck access system of pedestrianized walkways. By 1976 the design faults, lack of amenities and fear of crime on the estate resulted in more than half of those on the council's housing waiting list refusing accommodation on the estate and there was a long list of transfer requests from existing tenants. During the ten years from 1993, comprehensive improvements were carried out to make the estate a more humane place to live. Disused shops have been replaced by smart new homes and overhead walkways have been dismantled.

Broadwater Farm riot An episode of severe civil unrest that took place on and around the Broadwater Farm estate in October 1985. The riot was sparked by the death of a black woman, Cynthia Jarrett, in a police raid on her house. PC Keith Blakelock was hacked to death and three men were convicted of his killing. The so-called TOTTENHAM THREE were acquitted by the Court of Appeal in 1991 and no one has since been charged in connection with the murder, despite continuing police investigations.

Broadway A street in WESTMINSTER, running north from VICTORIA STREET towards ST JAMES'S PARK. Its most important buildings are New SCOTLAND YARD and 55 Broadway, the monumental art deco headquarters of LONDON UNDERGROUND, designed by Charles Holden. From 1924 to 1966, 54 Broadway was the operational base of the security service, MI6.

Brockley A pleasing Victorian suburb situated south of NEW CROSS and west of LEWISHAM. The name was first recorded in the early 1180s and probably meant 'woodland clearing belonging to a man named Broca'. Alternatively, the 'brock' element could have indicated the presence of badgers or a brook. A village evolved in the vicinity of the Brockley Jack public house during the 18th century, expanding rapidly with the arrival of the railways in the late 19th century. Brockley has been home to music hall performer Marie Lloyd (*see the* QUEEN OF THE MUSIC HALL), humorist Spike Milligan (who joined the Young

Communist League of Brockley), the writer Edgar Wallace and his fictional detective Mr J.G. Reeder.

Brock's benefit A superannuated expression denoting a spectacular firework display, or metaphorically any spectacularly pyrotechnic display. It commemorates the annual firework display held at the CRYSTAL PALACE from 1865 to 1936, which was organized by the firework manufacturers C.T. Brock.

Brockwell Park One of south London's best-known amenities and a popular venue for summer events, situated between TULSE HILL and BRIXTON. A house called Brockalle was in existence by 1563, near the present junction of Norwood Road and Rosendale Road. John Blades, a CITY glass manufacturer, demolished the old house and built Brockwell Hall on the hilltop in 1811–13. LAMBETH council and the LONDON COUNTY COUNCIL acquired Brockwell Hall and its grounds following the death of Blades's grandson and opened Brockwell Park in 1892.

Bromley A major commercial centre and focal point of outer south-east London, located 9 miles (14.5 km) from CHARING CROSS in the upper valley of the River RAVENSBOURNE. It was 'Bromleag' in 862, from Old English *brōm lēah*, 'the heath where broom grows'. An Anglo-Saxon settlement developed around the site now occupied by the market square and Gilbert Glanville, Bishop of Rochester, built a palace nearby in 1185. The bishop's successors encouraged pilgrims to visit St Blaise's well, which was fed by a spring whose waters tasted of iron. In 1205 King John granted a charter to the town's market, which specialized in the wool trade. Bromley flourished as a spa town after the rediscovery of the St Blaise's well in 1754. A new episcopal palace was constructed in 1775, surrounded by a moat. The last bishop of Rochester to be based at Bromley Palace moved away in 1845. Bromley Palace was converted into a teacher training college in the 1930s and now forms the core of Bromley Civic Centre. Bromley's rivalry with CROYDON and KINGSTON as south London's leading shopping destination has been undermined in recent years by competition from the Bluewater centre in Kent.

The writer H.G. Wells was born in 1866 over a shop at 47 High Street. The author Hanif Kureishi grew up here in the 1960s and later mocked Bromley in *The* BUDDHA OF SUBURBIA.

Bromley, London Borough of An OUTER LONDON borough formed in 1965 by merging the municipal boroughs of BECKENHAM and BROMLEY with the urban districts of CHISLEHURST, ORPINGTON, PENGE and the southern part of SIDCUP. This is the largest London borough in area, with, consequently, the greatest length of roads. In 1994 the British government chose to use the cost of living in Bromley as the basis for calculating overseas allowances for its diplomats; this was seen by some as proof that Bromley was the most average place in the country. The borough does align closely with the national breakdowns for household composition, marital status and even religious faith – although it has relatively few Muslims and Sikhs. However, it scores more highly on indicators of affluence such as levels of employment and owner occupation. The borough's coat of arms avoids the usual technique of integrating elements from the heraldry of its constituent parts. The shield has acorns on a green background, symbolizing its country villages, supported by a CITY of London DRAGON and a Kentish white horse. The civic motto is less original: *servire populo* means 'to serve the people'.

Bromley-by-Bow A historic EAST END district situated between BOW and POPLAR. 'Bromley' is a corruption of Old English *bræmbel lēah*, 'woodland clearing with brambles', and the extended name avoids confusion with its southeast London namesake. It was earlier known as Bromley St Leonard, after the Benedictine priory of St Leonard, once the oldest religious house in east London. After the dissolution of the monasteries (1536–9), the manor was granted to Sir Ralph Sadleir, principal secretary of state to Henry VIII. A hunting lodge that stood on what is now St Leonard's Street was said to have been built by James I. Later known as the Old Palace, the building was split into two residences in 1750. The replacement of the palace by a school in 1894 caused an outcry and played a pivotal role in promoting future (often unsuccessful) attempts to preserve east London's heritage. The interior of the state room was salvaged and can be seen at the VICTORIA AND ALBERT MUSEUM.

The political economist David Ricardo, the son of a Dutch Jewish stockbroker, grew up in Bromley St Leonard in the late 18th century.

Bromley-by-Bows 'Toes' in COCKNEY RHYMING SLANG.

Bromley Contingent A 1970s faction of punk fashionistas and early followers of the SEX PISTOLS, most of whom came from the south-east corner of London. The original line-up of Siouxsie and the Banshees emerged from the contingent, as did Billy Idol. *See also* PUNK ROCK.

Brompton A prosperous quarter centred on Brompton Road, which runs south-westward from KNIGHTSBRIDGE station. Brompton (farmstead where broom grows) was first recorded in 1294. The marshy ground was drained in the 16th century and converted into fruit gardens. During Victoria's reign Brompton became a fashionable district in which to live and its reputation for healthy air attracted a number of private hospices. The Royal Brompton Hospital, now on Sydney Street, opened in 1842 as the Hospital for Consumption and Diseases of the Chest. It now specializes in heart and lung surgery. Brompton's identity as a locality has been almost wholly erased by the more prestigious names of CHELSEA, Knightsbridge and SOUTH KENSINGTON.

Brompton bicycle A folding bicycle conceived in 1975 by Andrew Ritchie when he was living in a flat overlooking BROMPTON ORATORY. Full-scale production eventually began in the late 1980s at a factory in BRENTFORD, where the company is still based.

Brompton Boilers Frequently abbreviated to 'the boilers', this was a nickname coined by George Godwin, editor of *The Builder* magazine, for the three adjacent galleries of the SOUTH KENSINGTON Museum, which opened in 1857 on what is now part of the site of the VICTORIA AND ALBERT MUSEUM. The utilitarian building was designed by a firm of engineers, with a cast iron frame, arched rooflines and corrugated iron cladding, erected under the supervision of Sir William Cubitt. It was intended to be a temporary structure and the absence of glazing was a response to problems of overheating that had been experienced in the CRYSTAL PALACE. At the suggestion of Prince Albert it was subsequently painted with green and white stripes to make it look less industrial. Much of the structure was removed to BETHNAL GREEN in 1872 and encased in red brick. It is now the MUSEUM OF CHILDHOOD.

Brompton Cemetery A burial ground located in WEST BROMPTON, founded in 1836 and opened in 1840 as the West of London and Westminster Cemetery. It has a formal layout, with a central chapel based on St Peter's Basilica in Rome. The cemetery was compulsorily purchased from the private owners in 1852 by the General Board of Health, becoming the first and only London cemetery under government control. Around 200,000 people have been buried here, including eleven holders of the Victoria Cross, 3,000 CHELSEA PENSIONERS, the suffragette leader Emmeline Pankhurst, and Richard Tauber, the singer and operetta composer. In 1997 the Sioux Indian chief Long Wolf was reburied in South Dakota, having been interred at Brompton in 1892. The children's writer Beatrix Potter often walked in the cemetery and seems to have found the names for many of her characters on the gravestones here.

Brompton cocktail A powerful painkiller and sedative consisting of vodka or other liquor laced with morphine and sometimes also with cocaine. The preparation is used to relieve pain caused by cancer and is said to be named after Brompton Hospital, where it was first applied to this end.

Brompton Oratory The colloquial name of the London Oratory, a group of Italianate buildings on the Brompton Road. It is the home of the London congregation of the Oratorians, a branch of the Roman Catholic faith established at Rome by St Philip Neri (1515–95). The London Oratory was founded in 1849 by Frederick William Faber (1814–63), on the instructions of Cardinal Newman, in a house in what is now William IV Street, CHARING CROSS, and moved to Brompton in 1854. The Church of the Immaculate Heart of Mary was consecrated in 1884.

> Up those stone steps I climb,
> Hail this joyful day's return.
> Into its great shadowed vault I go,
> Hail the Pentecostal morn.
>
> NICK CAVE: 'Brompton Oratory' (song by Nick Cave and the Bad Seeds) (1997)

Brompton stock *Matthiola incana*, a large, usually red and biennial, flower that takes its name from Brompton Park nursery, which was established in 1681 on land where the VICTORIA AND ALBERT MUSEUM now stands.

Bromstead A thinly veiled BROMLEY in *The*

New Machiavelli (1911), by H.G. Wells, in which he draws on his own boyhood experiences of life in outer south-east London. Elsewhere in the book the author mixes real place names, such as PENGE and WEST WICKHAM, with other artifices, like Beckington for BECKENHAM and the River Ravensbrook for the RAVENSBOURNE. Wells presumably chose to rename Bromley because he wanted to disparage its headlong suburbanization at great length:

> The roads came, – horribly; the houses followed. They seemed to rise in the night. People moved into them as soon as the roofs were on, mostly workmen and their young wives, and already in a year some of these raw houses stood empty again from defaulting tenants, with windows broken and wood-work warping and rotting. The Ravensbrook became a dump for old iron, rusty cans, abandoned boots and the like ...

Brondesbury An upmarket residential district in north KILBURN, set on a ridge that runs from HAMPSTEAD to HARLESDEN, dividing the surroundings into two drainage areas. This was 'the manor of a man called Brand', first recorded as Bronnesburie in 1254. Brand may have been a canon of St Paul's Cathedral.

Brondesbury Tapes, The An album of home-made recordings by Giles, Giles and Fripp, a forerunner of the progressive rock band King Crimson. The tracks were laid down in 1968 but only released in 2001.

Brook An elegant serif typeface designed in 1903 by Lucien and Esther Pissarro for their woodcutting venture, the Eragny Press. It was named after the house in which they lived, which in turn was named after STAMFORD BROOK.

Brook Green HAMMERSMITH's sought-after north-eastern corner, taking its name from a narrow, wedge-shaped green that was traversed by a brook running south from SHEPHERD'S BUSH. This section of the brook was called the Black Bull ditch, after an inn that it passed. Almshouses were built on the south side of the green in 1629. With the aim of saving girls 'from the deluge of vice', Mrs Francis Carpue established a school in 1760 that later evolved to become St Mary's Roman Catholic College. Caterers J. Lyons expanded their Cadby Hall factory to take over the buildings of St Mary's College in 1925, paying enough to enable the college to buy magnificent premises at STRAWBERRY HILL. Brook Green was home to the Victorian actor Sir Henry Irving.

Brook Green Suite, The A suite for strings, consisting of a prelude, air, and dance, composed by Gustav Holst for the junior orchestra of ST PAUL'S GIRLS' SCHOOL, Brook Green. Holst was the school's director of music from 1905 until his death in 1934.

Brook Street A MAYFAIR street running westwards from the south-west corner of Hanover Square to the north-east corner of GROSVENOR SQUARE. West of Grosvenor Square, Upper Brook Street extends to PARK LANE. The street takes its name from the TYBURN brook. 23 Brook Street was the home of the rock legend Jimi Hendrix (1942–70); the composer George Frideric Handel (1685–1759) lived next door at No.25. Both residents are commemorated by BLUE PLAQUES.

Brook Street Bureau An employment agency founded in Brook Street in 1946 by Margery Hurst (1913–89). The agency went on to establish a national network of branches, with an emphasis on the London area. It was famous in the 1970s and 80s for its TUBE CARD advertising, often featuring just the legs of two 'temps', who were discussing the agency's merits. The company's memorable slogan was 'Brook Street Bureau got big by bothering'.

Brooks's This Liberal and social CLUB was originally a gambling club, previously ALMACK'S. Little is known of the man who gave the club its name and built its present premises in ST JAMES'S STREET. He was to have been a wine merchant and moneylender and to have died in poverty, perhaps because not all gambling debts were repaid. Brooks's acquired the former reputation of WHITE'S for the high stakes laid by its members, leading the fashion for hazard and faro in the late 18th century. Notable early members included David GARRICK, Horace Walpole, Edward Gibbon and R.B. Sheridan. The Whig statesman Charles James Fox was a patron, as was the Prince REGENT. The younger Pitt was a member at one time but subsequently withdrew to White's. It later became a leading Whig club.

> From liberal Brooks, whose speculative skill,
> Is hasty credit, and a distant bill;
> Who, nursed in clubs, disdains a vulgar trade,
> Exults to trust, and blushes to be paid!
> RICHARD TICKELL: 'Epistle from the Honourable Charles

Fox, Partridge-Shooting, to the Honourable John Townshend, Cruising' (1779)

brothers

Brothers, Richard *See* NEPHEW OF THE ALMIGHTY.

Brothers' Steps *See the* FIELD OF THE FORTY FOOTSTEPS.

brown

Brown, Capability Lancelot Brown (1715–83), landscape gardener and architect, who was patronized by most of the rich men of taste. He set their great country houses in a surround of parkland and informal pastoral charm. He was given this nickname because he habitually assured prospective employers that their land held 'great capabilities'. In the London area he landscaped SYON PARK and the grounds of ADDINGTON Palace, HAMPTON COURT PALACE, WIMBLEDON PARK, the former Richmond Lodge (now part of KEW GARDENS) and at least a dozen others. He died in Hertford Street, MAYFAIR.

brown Bess 'Yes' in early COCKNEY RHYMING SLANG, from the name of a flintlock musket with a browned barrel.

brown bread 'Dead' in COCKNEY RHYMING SLANG.

As it was, he got hit by a taxi trying to cross Curtain Road ... And that was it: brown bread before he hit the kerb.

HUGO BLICK: *The Last Word Monologues*, 'A Bit of Private Business' (TV drama) (2008)

brown Joe 'No' in early COCKNEY RHYMING SLANG.

Bruce Castle

Bruce Castle A grand and ancient house, but hardly a castle, situated in central TOTTENHAM. The Bruce family built Tottenham manor house here in the mid-13th century but Edward I sequestered their property after Robert the Bruce rebelled and became king of Scotland in 1306. The house was rebuilt in 1514 on a scale that would befit visits from Henry VIII and Elizabeth I. The house was known as 'The Lordship' until the late 17th century, when it was remodelled and named Bruce Castle. In 1827 the Hill family acquired Bruce Castle and converted it into a school. For its first six years the school's headmaster was Rowland Hill, who later devised the basis of the modern postal service. After the school's closure in 1891, the local board bought Bruce Castle and opened the grounds as a public park in the following year. The house is now a museum of local history, with a special collection devoted to the postal service. Bruce Castle is glorified in John Abraham Heraud's lengthy poem 'Tottenham' (1835):

Lovely is moonlight to the poet's eye,
That in a tide of beauty bathes the skies,
Filling the balmy air with purity,
Silent and lone, and on the greensward dies –
But when on ye her heavenly slumber lies,
Towers of Brus! 'tis more than lovely then.–
For such sublime associations rise,
That to young fancy's visionary ken,
'Tis like a maniac's dream – fitful and still again.

Brunel University A technology-oriented university, named in honour of the engineer Isambard Kingdom Brunel (1806–59). It evolved from Acton Technical College, which, in the late 1950s, created a new unit called Brunel College of Technology. In 1966 the college became a university and built a new main campus in UXBRIDGE, closing its ACTON site in 1971. The university subsequently absorbed Shoreditch College of Education and the West London Institute of Higher Education.

Brush Strokes A BBC TV sitcom about an amorous painter and decorator, written by John Esmonde (1937–2008) and Bob Larbey (b.1934). The show ran for five series between 1986 and 1991. MOTSPUR PARK provided the backdrop.

Brutus, Brute or **Brut** (Latin, 'heavy', 'stupid') In the mythological history of Britain the first king and legendary progenitor of the British people. As is the way with mythology, more than one variation of his story exists, but the usual version is that Brutus was the son of Silvius, who was the son of Ascanius, whose father was the Trojan hero Aeneas. Brutus would have lived some time around the 12th century BC. He accidentally killed his father while hunting and fled Troy, eventually taking refuge in Britain. Brutus gave the name TROYNOVANT (New Troy) to the city that he founded and which is now called London. The legend first appears in the 9th-century *Historia Brittonum* and was rewritten by Geoffrey of Monmouth in his *Historia Regum Britanniae* (c.1136). Brutus is said to have reigned for 24 years; on his death he was buried at TOWER HILL and his son Locrinus succeeded him. *See also* GOG AND MAGOG.

Brylcreem Boy The MIDDLESEX and England cricketer and ARSENAL footballer Denis Compton (1918–97), who became one of the first British sportsmen to capitalize on his appeal by appearing in advertisements, in his case for the hair preparation Brylcreem.

BT Tower A telecommunications tower located at 60 CLEVELAND STREET, FITZROVIA. It was built for what was then the General Post Office, under the direction of the Ministry of Public Building and Works' architect Eric Bedford (1909–2001). Construction began in June 1961 and the tower became operational on 8 October 1965, opening to the public in May 1966, with an observation area and a revolving restaurant on the 34th floor. An IRA bomb exploded at the top of the tower in 1971 but it was another ten years before public access was completely withdrawn. The tower is 571 feet (174m) tall – 620 feet (189m) to the top of its highest mast – and was the UK's tallest building from its topping out until 1980. At various times it has also been known as the GPO Tower, the Post Office Tower and Telecom Tower. Several of the microwave antennae on the tower are now defunct but cannot be removed because of the building's listed status, granted in 2003.

bubble

bubble (and squeak) 'Greek' in COCKNEY RHYMING SLANG, usually referring to a person of that nationality. The singer/songwriter George Michael (born Georgios Panayiotou, 1963) was occasionally called 'the bubble with the stubble'. Bubble and squeak is a pan-fried dish made from potatoes and cabbage, and/or other leftovers from a roast dinner. Infrequent alternative meanings include 'leak', 'beak' (magistrate) and 'week'.

bubble (bath) 'Laugh' in COCKNEY RHYMING SLANG, generally in the noun sense of someone or something that is fun. It is perhaps most often heard in the sarcastically rhetorical expression, 'are you having a bubble?'

> Hard done by? A less than ideal world you live in? You're having a bubble, Frank [Lampard], as they say in your native East London.
> RICHARD OLDROYD, at www.clarets-mad.co.uk (2 July 2007)

I'm Forever Blowing Bubbles See under I.

Buck

Buck House A facetious nickname for BUCK-

INGHAM PALACE, first recorded in 1922 and nowadays widely used. The degrading of 'palace' to 'house' is lightheartedly vulgar, although Buckingham Palace actually was Buckingham House originally. The term is said to be used within the royal family itself.

> It is customary to see Prince Harry cradling a pint glass. So to see him, as we did last week, with a pint-sized African orphan was good news. The Buck House spin doctors must have been delighted by the coverage.
> *The Sunday Times* 30 April 2006

Buck's Club A MAYFAIR gentlemen's CLUB founded in 1919 by Captain Herbert Buckmaster, the first husband of the actress Gladys Cooper. In its early days, when P.G. Wodehouse was a member, the club was noted for its relative informality and youthfulness.

Buck's fizz A simple cocktail consisting of champagne (or sparkling white wine) and orange juice, invented in 1921 by Pat McGarry, bartender at Buck's Club.

Bucket of Blood An old nickname for the LAMB AND FLAG, a pub in Rose Street, COVENT GARDEN, said to derive from its former practice of hosting bare-knuckle fights. The building dates from the late 17th or early 18th century and was first recorded as licensed premises in 1772, when it was the Cooper's Arms. It became the Lamb and Flag in 1833. *See also the* ROSE ALLEY AMBUSCADE.

Buckingham Palace A royal palace located at the western end of the MALL. It was built in 1703 (to the design of William Winde) for the Duke of Buckingham and Normanby, and was originally called Buckingham House. George III bought it in 1762, and had it virtually rebuilt on a much grander scale by John Nash. Since the middle of the 19th century it has been used (with varying degrees of enthusiasm) by British monarchs as their official London residence. The ceremony of CHANGING THE GUARD in the palace forecourt is an essential stop on the London tourist route. In 1993 the palace's State Rooms were first opened to the visiting public, for the summer months.

Unauthorized visitors to the palace or its grounds have included the BOY JONES, Michael Fagan (who broke into the Queen's bedroom in 1982), an American paraglider and activists for 'Fathers for Justice'. Arthur Furguson (1883–1938), a conman who specialized in selling bits of London to gullible Americans, once secured a down-payment of £30,000 on Buckingham Palace.

Buckingham Palace garden party A formal party held by the sovereign in the extensive grounds to the rear of Buckingham Palace. Such events have been held since the 1860s, when Queen Victoria instituted what were known as 'breakfasts' (though they took place in the afternoon). Nowadays the Queen hosts at least three garden parties at the palace every summer, and in most years gives an additional party to honour a large national organization celebrating a special anniversary. Approximately 8,000 invited guests attend each party, which takes place between 4 and 6pm.

> The 'secret garden of the crown', as it has been called, will tend to elevate *who* you know above *what* you know, with the Buckingham Palace garden party as the coveted social prize.
>
> CHARLES HAMPDEN-TURNER: *Gentlemen & Tradesmen* (1983)

Bucklersbury A CITY street running south-west from POULTRY and now cut through by Queen Victoria Street. The original Bucklersbury was a medieval tenement – 'Buckerels' manor house' – home of the important and influential Buckerel family of the early Middle Ages. Sir Thomas More lived in Bucklersbury at the beginning of the 16th century. It was in those days noted for its apothecaries and herbalists, and Shakespeare makes Falstaff say:

> I cannot cog [flatter], and say thou art this and that, like a many of these lisping hawthorn buds, that come like women in men's apparel, and smell like Bucklersbury in simple-time [time of harvesting medicinal herbs].
>
> *The Merry Wives of Windsor*, III, iii (1598)

Buddha of Suburbia, The A novel (1990) by the BROMLEY-born writer Hanif Kureishi (b.1954) about racial attitudes in south-east London. The Buddha of the title is the narrator's Indian father, who precipitates a round of sexual musical chairs by leaving his English wife and setting up home with another Englishwoman, at whose parties he gains a reputation as a guru. Karim, the novel's bisexual narrator, becomes an actor, goes to New York, but yearns for London, to which he eventually returns, full of hope for a

less complicated future. A television adaptation (1993) caused controversy for its alleged sexual explicitness.

budge bachelors A company of men clothed in long gowns lined with budge (lambskin fur) who used to accompany the LORD MAYOR OF LONDON at his inauguration.

Bugsby's Marsh An old name for the Green-wich Marshes. Bugsby may have been the commander of a prison hulk that was once moored here, but it has also been suggested that the word is a corruption of 'boggarty', which meant 'haunted by sprites or spirits'. The methane gases of the marshes could have conjured up such manifestations. The stretch of the THAMES between BLACKWALL Reach and WOOLWICH Reach, below Blackwall Point, is called Bugsby's Reach. *See also* GREENWICH PENINSULA.

bull

bull and (a) cow 'Row' (noisy squabble) in COCKNEY RHYMING SLANG.

bullseye An early internal name for the graphic device that Transport for London now calls the 'roundel'. When the device first appeared on underground station signage in 1908 it consisted of white type on a blue bar with a solid red circle behind. In 1919 Edward Johnston replaced the solid circle with a circular frame and changed the typeface to his own JOHNSTON SANS. Thenceforth the design became the corporate symbol for the underground and it has changed remarkably little since then. Following the creation of LONDON TRANSPORT it was adapted for bus stop signage and, with varying colours of circle, is now used across all the areas for which Transport for London has responsibility. For example, the London Overground network uses an orange circle while Tramlink's is green. The blue bar is common to all the most important roundels except that of London Buses, which has both a red bar and circle.

Bull's-eye An ill-treated dog belonging to the villainous Bill SIKES in Charles DICKENS's *Oliver Twist* (1838).

Old Bull and Bush *See under* OLD.

bullock's horn 'Pawn' in COCKNEY RHYMING SLANG, often reduced to 'bullock'. The term was in fairly common usage from the mid-19th to the mid-20th century.

bummaree A former name for a dealer at BILLINGSGATE market or a self-employed porter at SMITHFIELD market. The word is of uncertain origin. It has been suggested that it could be an alteration of French bonne marée, 'good fresh seafish'. A 1960 episode of TV's *Dixon of Dock Green* probed the mystery of 'The Vanishing Bummaree'.

> One man assured me it was a French name; another that it was Dutch. A fishmonger, to whom I was indebted for information, told me he thought that the bummaree was originally a bum-boat man, who purchased of the wind-bound smacks at Gravesend or the Nore, and sent the fish up rapidly to the market by land.'
>
> HENRY MAYHEW: *London Labour and the London Poor*, Volume 1 (1851)

'Bumper' Harris See HARRIS, WILLIAM 'BUMPER'.

bun
Bun House, The See the WIDOW'S SON.
Chelsea bun See under CHELSEA.

Bunhill Fields The CITY of London's oldest surviving graveyard, located at the southern end of CITY ROAD, and now lying within the London Borough of ISLINGTON. Bunhill Fields, which is a corruption of Bone Hill Fields, had been associated with interments since Saxon times and became a Quaker burial ground in 1665, the year of the GREAT PLAGUE. It was popular with Dissenters of various denominations because the ground was unconsecrated. John Bunyan, William Blake and Daniel DEFOE are buried here, but their memorials do not mark the precise sites of the graves as there has been so much disarrangement. By the 1800s the graveyard had become so overcrowded as to constitute a health hazard, although it was not closed until 1863. ABNEY PARK had by then become London's first choice for Nonconformist burials. The CORPORATION OF LONDON then took over Bunhill's maintenance and part of it was laid out as a garden in 1960.

bunny 'Talk' in Cockney rhyming slang, via RABBIT (AND PORK).
Bunny girl A nightclub hostess whose somewhat skimpy costume included a fluffy,

rabbit-like tail and a head-dress with long ears, like those of a rabbit. They were introduced by Hugh Hefner and Victor Lownes in the Playboy Club at 45 PARK LANE in 1966. Thousands of young women applied for the £34-a-week job, which involved wearing the cruelly boned costume, serving drinks with a special 'Bunny dip', retaining a fixed smile for hours on end and keeping the fluffy tail fluffy. Miscreants were made to stand in a corner facing the wall. The name apparently derived from the notion that the girls provided male clients with an evening's chase.

Bunsen burner 'Earner' in COCKNEY RHYMING SLANG. This is a confusing coinage, since its abbreviation to 'bunce' simply picks up on an existing word meaning 'profit' or 'gain' that was in use before the invention of the item of laboratory equipment.

Burcharbro Road A residential street in WEST HEATH (1), in the London Borough of BEXLEY. It was laid out in the 1890s and gains its curious name from its builders, Burrowes, Charlesworth and Brodie, who also developed neighbouring Pinewood Road.

Burdon's Hotel A nickname for the former WHITECROSS STREET Prison, from the name of a sometime governor.

Burgh House The grandest surviving property in HAMPSTEAD's NEW END, built in 1703 for the Sewells, a Quaker family, and later named Burgh House after its tenth owner, the wealthy clergyman Allatson Burgh. Saved from conversion to offices in 1979, Burgh House is now home to the Hampstead Museum, which has a local history collection and watercolours from the Helen Allingham collection.

Burlington
Burlington Arcade A classy shopping arcade, connecting PICCADILLY with Burlington Gardens. It was the creation, in 1819, of Lord George Cavendish (1754–1834) of BURLINGTON HOUSE. It is said that he conceived the innovative covered format out of a desire to prevent Regency rowdies from throwing oyster shells into his garden. Cavendish recruited beadles, frock-coated guards wearing gold braided top hats, from his family regiment the 10th Hussars to enforce a strict code of behaviour that included no whistling,

singing, playing of musical instruments, running, carrying of large parcels or opening of umbrellas and no babies' prams. Beadles still patrol the arcade today.

Burlington Bertie A would-be elegant 'man about town' or 'masher', personified by Vesta Tilley (*see the* LONDON IDOL) in a popular song of this name by Harry B. Norris (1900). The song below is a parody, written by William Hargreaves for his wife, the male impersonator Ella Shields.

> I'm Burlington Bertie:
> I rise at ten thirty
> And saunter along
> Like a toff;
> I walk down the Strand
> With my gloves on my hand,
> And I walk down again
> With them off.
>
> 'Burlington Bertie from Bow' (1915)

In the vernacular of the turf, 'Burlington Bertie' can signify odds of 100/30.

Burlington House A magnificent PICCADILLY mansion completed in 1668 for Richard Boyle, 1st Earl of Burlington (1612–98), and subsequently much altered. The government purchased Burlington House in 1854, allotting new wings to a group of learned institutions that became known as the COURTYARD SOCIETIES and the main building to the ROYAL ACADEMY in 1867.

burnt

burnt cinder 'Window' in COCKNEY RHYMING SLANG. Like many terms in the argot it relies on 'proper' cockney pronunciation to work as a perfect rhyme.

Burnt Oak A disadvantaged locality in southern EDGWARE, dominated by the LONDON COUNTY COUNCIL's Watling estate, built between 1924 and 1930 (*see* LITTLE MOSCOW).

Burton (-on-Trent) 'Rent' in COCKNEY RHYMING SLANG. There is no connection with the phrase 'to go for a Burton', which is of military origin, except that the latter may also derive from the Midlands town – or more specifically its ale. *Compare* STOKE-ON-TRENT.

bushel (and peck) 'Neck' in COCKNEY RHYMING SLANG, from the imperial units of dry volume.

Bushy Park The second-largest but least-known of the eight royal parks of London, situated between TEDDINGTON and the THAMES at HAMPTON COURT. The park was created in the early 16th century to provide a hunting ground for Hampton Court. Sir Christopher WREN created Chestnut Avenue as a formal approach to Hampton Court Palace, with the Arethusa, or Diana, fountain as its centrepiece. In 1900 Queen Victoria gave Bushy House to the Commission of Works for the establishment of the NATIONAL PHYSICAL LABORATORY. George V gave permission for Upper Lodge to become a home for Canadian convalescents during the First World War, and in the Second World War the park became the site of Camp Griffiss, which General Dwight Eisenhower made the centre for planning the 1944 D-Day invasion. The park has few facilities but an abundance of pastoral scenery, including woodland gardens. *See also* COBBLER'S WAY.

In 19th-century slang, a man who was poor was said to be at Bushy Park, or 'in the park'. For obvious reasons, the term has also been used to refer to female pubic hair. To 'take a turn in Bushy Park' was to have sex. In COCKNEY RHYMING SLANG, 'Bushy Park' used to mean a lark, usually in the sense of having fun, rather than the bird.

Business Design Centre *See the* AGRICULTURAL HALL.

busker A person who makes money by singing, dancing, acting and the like in a public place, typically by a theatre queue or in a passage of the LONDON UNDERGROUND. The word may come from French *busquer*, 'to seek'. In 2003 an officially regulated busking scheme was set up for TUBE stations, with prospective performers auditioned and, if successful, granted licences to busk at delineated pitches at prearranged times.

butcher's (hook) 'Look' in COCKNEY RHYMING SLANG, usually in the context of taking a look (a butchers) at something. The expression is widely employed conversationally but its printed usage is largely restricted to bad puns.

> Take a butchers at the dodginesses of Old Bill,
> Aristotle's orchestra are living on the pill.
>
> GINGER BAKER: 'What a Bringdown' (song by Cream) (1969)

Butler's Wharf *See* DESIGN MUSEUM; SHAD THAMES.

butterboy A BLACK CAB driver who has passed the KNOWLEDGE within the previous year or two, implying that such a person is still 'but a boy'.

Butterworth charity or **dole** A ceremony introduced at the priory church of St BARTHOLOMEW the Great, SMITHFIELD, around the time of the GREAT FIRE OF LONDON, in which 21 sixpences were given to as many poor widows on Good Friday. Each coin was placed upon a tombstone and the widow knelt to pick it up. At some point, hot cross buns also began to be distributed to widows and children. The tradition fell into disuse but was revived in 1887 by Joshua Butterworth. Nowadays the largesse consists only of buns, given to all who congregate in the churchyard before the Good Friday service.

butts London formerly had many open spaces called 'the butts', originally used for archery practice and often subsequently as places of general recreation. Artillery Place in WESTMINSTER was one such site. The only London places that still retain the name are the locality of NEWINGTON BUTTS and a square in BRENTFORD. The latter was commandeered for archery practice on the instructions of Henry VIII and in the late 1680s the landlord of the Red Lion inn began to build houses at the Butts that survive today as an unexpectedly glorious enclave.

C

cab A contraction of 'cabriolet', a small one-horse carriage, from French *cabriole*, 'goat-like leap'. The reference is to the lightness of the carriage, which seemed to 'caper' by comparison with its lumbering predecessors. Cabs were introduced into London in the early 19th century. *See also* BLACK CAB.

cabmen's shelters Green-painted roadside sheds surviving at 13 locations in central London. Sir George Armstrong established the Cabmen's Shelter Fund in 1875 to provide HACKNEY carriage drivers with a refuge where they could get a hot meal and a cup of tea, but strictly no alcohol. Similar facilities had previously been introduced in Edinburgh and Birmingham. Sixty-one such structures were erected in the capital, many individually endowed by a local philanthropist, who would also benefit from the improved availability of cabs, and more sober drivers. Depending largely on the area in which they were located, the quality of the establishment could range from sordid to almost luxurious. Many of the shelters had nicknames (*see* BELL AND HORNS). Most shelters nowadays open only from breakfast to lunchtime and enforce a 'cabbies only' rule at the tables inside; several also provide a takeaway service from a window.

A visitor to the WESTBOURNE GROVE shelter in September 1888, calling himself 'Dr J. Duncan', was said to have confessed to the JACK THE RIPPER murders. The explorer Sir Ernest Shackleton was a regular at the HYDE PARK CORNER shelter, while the artist John Singer Sargent used the one near the RITZ. In the 1890s bohemian poets like Ernest Dowson treated their local shelters as a second home.

> They [young poets] used them as night-clubs, and retired to them at four o'clock in the morning for eggs-and-bacon. Not because they wanted eggs-and-bacon at four o'clock in the morning, but because the bourgeois did not eat eggs-and-bacon in cabmen's shelters at four o'clock in the morning.
> THOMAS BURKE: *London in My Time* (1934)

Cable Street A road in SHADWELL, running to the north of and parallel to RATCLIFF HIGHWAY, from just east of the TOWER OF LONDON to LIMEHOUSE BASIN. The name probably derives from the manufacture of ships' cables here; there was a rope-walk running alongside the road from the early 18th century. *See also the* BATTLE OF CABLE STREET.

cad In the 1830s the word became a colloquial term for the conductor of one of London's newly introduced omnibuses, almost certainly as an abbreviation of 'cadet'. The better-known meaning – a scoundrel or BLACKGUARD – arose separately later, probably at Oxford University.

> 'Twas on that verdant spot [Kennington Common] we met – nor can I ever forget the majestic courtesy of Mrs Chuff, as she remembered having had the pleasure of seeing me at Mrs Perkins's – nor the glance of scorn which she threw at an unfortunate gentleman who was preaching an exceedingly desultory discourse to a sceptical audience of omnibus-cads and nurse-maids, on a tub, as we passed by.
> W.M. THACKERAY: *The Book of Snobs* (1848)

Cade, Jack The leader of the Kentish insurrection of 1450, he was also known as John Mortimer. He marched on London, encamped on BLACKHEATH, and demanded redress of grievances from Henry VI (r.1422–61, 1470–1). After crossing LONDON BRIDGE, Cade is said to have struck LONDON STONE with his sword and declared himself LORD MAYOR. He held London for two days, after which a promise of pardon sowed dissension among the insurgents; they dispersed, and a price was set upon Cade's head. He attempted to reach the coast but was killed near Heathfield, East Sussex. The revolt forms an interlude to the main action of Shakespeare's *Henry VI, Part 2* (early 1590s), in which Cade represents a dangerous English spirit of vicious, foolhardy and heroic anarchy.

Jack Cade's Cave A nickname for the BLACK-HEATH Caverns, near Point Hill. Probably former chalk mines, the chambers were the scene of various revels in the 19th century. They were sealed up in 1946.

Caesar's Camp A name given to various locations where Julius Caesar's troops are said to have camped following the Roman invasion of Britain in 55 BC. One is in the southern part of WIMBLEDON COMMON, and is now occupied by the 6th, 7th, 10th and 11th holes of Royal Wimbledon Golf Club. Another is on KESTON COMMON; its site was once an ancient British encampment.

Café Royal The REGENT STREET restaurant developed from that opened in Glasshouse Street in 1865 by the Parisian wine merchant, Daniel Nicolas Thévenon. It offered the then-rare prospect of French haute cuisine in the heart of London. From the 1890s to the 1920s it was a famous and fashionable meeting place for writers and artists, among them Walter Sickert, Augustus John, Aubrey Beardsley and Max Beerbohm. Oscar Wilde dined here in 1892 with the Marquess of Queensberry and his son Lord Alfred Douglas. On another occasion at the café, Wilde's friend Frank Harris found him extolling the physical charms of Olympic athletes in ancient Greece to two 'extremely suspect' COCKNEY youths.

Cain and Abel 'Table' in somewhat outdated COCKNEY RHYMING SLANG.

cake is getting thin, the A COCKNEY expression used in the first half of the 20th century to suggest that one's funds were running low. 'Cake' has long been a slang term for money.

Caledonian
Caledonian Market Originally a general market that grew up beside the Metropolitan Cattle Market in ISLINGTON in the second half of the 19th century. It took its name from the CALEDONIAN ROAD, to which it was adjacent. In the early 20th century, as the concept of 'antiques' took hold, it grew enormously in size: bargain-hunters sifted the junk for elusive masterpieces, fences

moved stolen goods around, and the so-called 'Caledonian Silver Kings' enriched themselves. It was closed during the Second World War, and never returned to its original site. A legacy of the original survives, however, in the New Caledonian Market, an antiques market held on Friday mornings in BERMONDSEY Square. *See also the* THIEVES' MARKET.

Caledonian Road A characterful north–south route running through the western edge of ISLINGTON. In 1826 a company was formed to build a road from KING'S CROSS to HOLLOWAY ROAD. Originally named Chalk Road, the route ran through the open COPENHAGEN FIELDS for most of its length. In 1861 it was renamed Caledonian Road, after the Royal Caledonian Asylum, founded in 1815, which had moved to Copenhagen Fields in 1827. The asylum cared for 'the children of soldiers, sailors and mariners, natives of Scotland, who have died or been disabled in the service of their country; and the children of indigent Scotch parents residing in London, not entitled to parochial relief'. PENTONVILLE PRISON was built on land to the south of the asylum in 1842.

Cally Road A widely used colloquialism for the CALEDONIAN ROAD. Similarly, the CALEDONIAN MARKET was known as the Cally Market.

> I walk out the door and back onto the Cally Road. We walk fast, trying to be inconspicuous, heads slightly down.
>
> J.J. CONNOLLY: *Layer Cake* (2000)

Calves' Head Club Instituted in ridicule of Charles I, and apparently first mentioned in a tract (*Harleian Miscellany*) of 1703 by Benjamin Bridgwater, stating that it first met in 1693. The club was said to have held its last meeting in 1734, at a tavern in Suffolk Street, off PALL MALL East. The annual banquet took place on 30 January, the anniversary of the king's execution, and according to *The Secret History of the Calves' Head Club, or the Republicans Unmasked*, attributed to Ned Ward:

> The bill of fare was a large dish of calves' heads, dressed several ways, by which they represented the king and his friends who had suffered in his cause; a large pike with a small one in its mouth, as an emblem of tyranny; a large cod's head by which they intended to represent the person of

the king singly; a boar's head with an apple in its mouth, to represent the king as bestial, ...

After the banquet the diners burned a copy of the *Eikon Basilike*, the book supposedly written by Charles, and drank a toast from a calf's skull filled with wine to 'those worthy patriots who killed the tyrant'.

Camberwell A socially mixed Victorian suburb situated west of PECKHAM. Camberwell was first recorded in Domesday Book but its name is of uncertain origin. The village was of some medieval significance and St Giles was the mother church of a parish that took in DULWICH and Peckham. High-class terraced houses were built in the 1820s and 1830s, but by the mid-19th century terraces of much smaller dwellings covered much of the district. In 2009 local historian John Chaple discovered the original Camber Well beneath the back garden of a house in south-east Camberwell.

Camberwell Beauty A velvety chocolate-brown butterfly (*Nymphalis antiopa*), rarely seen because it migrates each year from Scandinavia. The name comes from its first recorded sighting, on Coldharbour Lane in 1748. *Camberwell Beauty* is also the title of a V.S. Pritchett story and of the humorist Jenny Eclair's debut novel.

Camberwell carrot A name given to a large marijuana cigarette in Bruce Robinson's cult film *Withnail and I* (1986):

'I': It's impossible to use twelve papers on one joint.
Danny: It's impossible to roll a Camberwell carrot with anything less.
Withnail: Who says it's a Camberwell carrot?
Danny: I do. I invented it in Camberwell and it looks like a carrot.

Camberwell College of Arts The Free Library and Art Gallery moved from BATTERSEA to Camberwell in 1887 and over the following decade the philanthropist John Passmore Edwards funded new buildings that became the South London Gallery and the Camberwell School of Art, now Camberwell College of Arts, part of the UNIVERSITY OF THE ARTS LONDON. Its alumni include the designers and TV presenters Jeff Banks and Laurence Llewelyn-Bowen, the artists R.B. Kitaj, Tom Phillips, Howard Hodgkin and Maggi Hambling, the musicians Humphrey Lyttelton

and Syd Barrett, the film director Mike Leigh and the actor Tim Roth.

Cambridge Circus
1. A traffic intersection at the junction of CHARING CROSS ROAD with SHAFTESBURY AVENUE. The circus was named in honour of the Duke of Cambridge, who performed the official opening of Charing Cross Road in 1887. Cambridge Circus lies at the heart of London's THEATRELAND. *See also the* CIRCUS.
2. A comedy revue produced and performed in 1963 at the Lyric Theatre, SHAFTESBURY AVENUE, and later on New York's Broadway, by members of Cambridge University's Footlights society. The show brought together future comic luminaries Tim Brooke-Taylor, Graham Chapman, John Cleese, Bill Oddie and others, and spawned the long-running BBC radio comedy series, *I'm Sorry, I'll Read That Again*.

Camden The town and the borough take their name from Charles Pratt, 1st Baron Camden from 1765 and 1st Earl Camden from 1786, whose family owned the KENTISH TOWN estate in the 18th and 19th centuries. Pratt was a man of many titles, including Viscount Bayham, but the Camden tag related to his CHISLEHURST property, Camden Place.

Camden, London Borough of An INNER LONDON borough comprising the former metropolitan boroughs of HAMPSTEAD, HOLBORN and ST PANCRAS. Camden's coat of arms is modelled on Holborn's and features the cross of St George and three scallops of the Russell family, dukes of Bedford, with supporters from the arms of LINCOLN'S INN and GRAY'S INN. The crest is surmounted by an elephant, taken from the heraldry of Charles Pratt, 1st Earl Camden. The civic motto is the familiar Latin dictum *non sibi sed toti*, 'not for oneself but for all'.

Camden market(s) London's largest and busiest market began in 1974 in the former Dingwall's packing-case factory at Camden Lock and gained a Sunday licence two years later. The market has since spread to fill every available open space nearby and includes an increasing range of covered sites. The emphasis is on youth-oriented clothing but there are also hundreds of stalls devoted to handicrafts, artwork, music and food. There are predictions that visitor numbers could reach an astonishing 40 million a year. Government statisticians report that Xscape leisure complex in Milton Keynes is Britain's most visited free attraction – but that is only because they do not measure Camden market's hordes.

Camden Passage A short, narrow street running alongside UPPER STREET, just to the north of the ANGEL, ISLINGTON. Like CAMDEN TOWN, it takes its name from the Earls Camden. It is famous for its antique shops and also hosts a weekly book market.

Camden Town A lively commercial destination situated 1 mile (1.6 km) north of EUSTON. An Act of Parliament of 1788 authorized Charles Pratt to develop the land to the east of what is now Camden High Street. George Dance the Younger devised a plan for a neoclassical estate, but the parsimonious Pratt chose a less ambitious option. In 1822 Camden Town became the first London home of Charles DICKENS, when he was ten years old and the district was still surrounded by fields. The now-demolished house, at 16 Bayham Street, was probably the model for Bob Cratchit's home in *A Christmas Carol* (1843). In the mid-1830s the Euston–Birmingham railway brought the noise and dirt of sidings and goods yards and Camden Town's still new gentlemen's residences were subdivided into lodgings for Irish and Italian immigrants. Camden at that time has been described as the 'tradesmen's entrance to the capital'. Shops and places of entertainment later flanked the High Street, including the Camden Theatre, now a nightclub. Municipal housing replaced some bomb sites and run-down streets after the Second World War, when a Greek-Cypriot community took root. In the 1960s Camden Town began to regain popularity with the middle classes, who refurbished dilapidated properties. From the mid-1990s Camden Town gained a reputation as London's prime centre for alternative nightlife.

Camden Town Group An alliance of post-Impressionist artists, founded in 1911 by Walter Sickert (1860–1942), who had painted many of his nude studies in drab boarding-house rooms in Camden Town. In the group's first show he included two such paintings, *Camden Town Murder Series No. 1* and *No. 2*, although the link with any recent murder was more for publicity than for actuality. A fine example of the school is C.W.R. Nevinson's (1889–1946) grim yet romantic view of *The Towpath, Camden Town, by Night* (*c.*1912), in the Ashmolean Museum, Oxford.

Other members of the group were Robert Bevan (1865–1925), Harold Gilman (1876–1919), Charles Ginner (1878–1952), Spencer Gore (1878–1914), Augustus John (1878–1961) and Wyndham Lewis (1882–1957). They had no real identity of style although most shared Sickert's liking for everyday subjects. In 1913 they merged with others to form the larger and more disparate LONDON GROUP.

Camlet Moat A large oblong moat that surrounds the site of a long-demolished house on what is now the northern edge of Trent Park (*see* ENFIELD CHASE). The house was at some time called, or nicknamed, Camelot Castle, hence the corrupted name of the moat, which has prompted a sprinkling of Arthurian mythology to attach itself to the place. It is said to have belonged to the family of Geoffrey de Mandeville (1092–1144), the unpopular 1st Earl of Essex, whose ghost purportedly haunts the island to this day.

> It is my purpose to ride an easy pace through
> the forest, and to linger a while by Camlet
> Moat – he knows the place; and if he be aught
> but an Alsatian bully will think it fitter for some
> purposes than the park.
> WALTER SCOTT: *The Fortunes of Nigel* (1822)

camp it up, to To draw attention to oneself by ostentatious parading or overacting in a camp manner. The origin of camp in its application to homosexuality or effeminacy is uncertain, but the reference is not likely to be to soldiers who in the 19th century clandestinely served as male prostitutes while camped out in REGENT'S PARK, as is sometimes suggested.

Canada
Canada Dock See CANADA WATER (*below*).
Canada Square See CANARY WHARF.
Canada Water A former dock and now a regeneration zone in ROTHERHITHE. Canada Dock was constructed in 1876 as the first major scheme of the Surrey Commercial Docks Company, an amalgamation of former rivals, and took its name from its specialization in Anglo-Canadian trade. In 1926 two neighbouring timber ponds were replaced by Quebec Dock. In the early 1980s, following the progressive closure of the SURREY DOCKS and their reinvention as SURREY QUAYS, most of Canada Dock and all of Quebec Dock were filled in and replaced by shopping and leisure amenities and Associated Newspapers' Harmsworth Quays printing works. The

remaining northern portion of Canada Dock was reduced in depth and reeds were planted to encourage waterfowl. Canada Water station opened in 1999, providing an interchange between the EAST LONDON LINE and the newly built JUBILEE LINE extension. Regeneration of the area continues to the present day.

Canary Wharf A commercial estate occupying much of the former WEST INDIA DOCKS in the north-west corner of the ISLE OF DOGS. The original Canary Wharf was constructed in 1937 for unloading and storing fruit from the Canary Islands (coincidentally, a name indirectly derived from Latin *Canaria insula*, meaning 'isle of dogs'). The West India Docks closed in the late 1960s but it was not until 1987 that the LONDON DOCKLANDS DEVELOPMENT CORPORATION signed an agreement for the site's redevelopment with the Canadian firm Olympia and York, which created a masterplan for the site based on its previous successful projects in Toronto and at Battery Park City in Manhattan. Canary Wharf was laid out as four neighbourhoods, each grouped around a public space and Cesar Pelli's art deco-influenced tower at One Canada Square was completed in 1990.The rest of the first phase was completed two years later, at a time of plunging commercial property values. The developer went into administration, leaving more than half the office space unlet and aggravating the doubts of potential tenants. As the market recovered a refinancing deal created a new consortium that included Olympia and York's owner, Paul Reichmann. The consortium bought Canary Wharf back from the administrators and completed the second phase in 1997. The JUBILEE LINE extension, which had been delayed by the absence of promised funding from the developers, was completed in 1999. As a result of its eventual success, Canary Wharf has gone on to consume the neighbouring HERON QUAYS, which had initially been planned on a much more modest scale. The opening of Jubilee Place boosted Canary Wharf's role as a shopping centre in 2004 and in March of that year the Songbird consortium acquired two-thirds of the share capital in the Canary Wharf Group plc for about £1.1 billion. Many of the banks, including HSBC, have offices in Canary Wharf and preliminary work has started on the Isle of Dogs CROSSRAIL station, which will be sited here.

Candlewick A CITY of London ward, of compact proportions even by the standards of the SQUARE MILE, centred on the eastern part of CANNON STREET. Candlewick and Cannon Street both derive their names from the candlewrights who made and sold candles here in the late Middle Ages.

> Oh, how I long to be transported to the dear regions of Grosvenor Square – far – far from the dull districts of Aldersgate, Cheap, Candlewick, and Farringdon Without and Within!
>
> GEORGE COLMAN and DAVID GARRICK: *The Clandestine Marriage*, I, ii (1766)

Canley, London Borough of *See the* BILL.

Canning

Canning, Elizabeth A servant girl who in 1753 claimed to have been kidnapped and taken to a 'house of ill fame' in ENFIELD WASH, where she was confined in a hay loft for almost a month before making her escape. Despite inconsistencies in Canning's story, the alleged abductors were tried and convicted. Within a fortnight of the trial's conclusion a key witness retracted her evidence and Canning was later tried for perjury, while a mob rioted outside the OLD BAILEY. The jury, with seeming reluctance, found her guilty and she was transported to New England, where she was said to have married advantageously. Dozens of pamphlets were written about the case, such was its notoriety, by authors as diverse as Henry Fielding (in support of Canning) and the royal portrait painter Allan Ramsay.

> Suppose the company to be talking of a German war, or Elizabeth Canning, he would begin thus: 'I'll tell you something to that purpose, that I fancy will make you laugh.'
>
> OLIVER GOLDSMITH: *The Life of Richard Nash* (1762)

Canning Town A solidly working-class district, though increasingly shorn of its industrial base, situated north of the Royal Victoria Dock (*see the* ROYAL DOCKS) and east of the River LEA. The settlement was originally called Hallsville and probably took its modern name from George Canning, briefly prime minister in 1827, or his son Charles Canning, first viceroy of India from 1858 until his death in 1862. Others suggest that the name came from a mid-19th-century factory, possibly a cannery, but historians have failed to trace its identity. The docks brought about significant immigration and Canning Town had the largest black population in London by 1920. The area was heavily damaged in the BLITZ, leading to the construction of numerous council tower blocks after the war. The grim surroundings seem frequently to have inspired humour in the residents; the comic actors Reg Varney, Marty Feldman and Windsor Davies all grew up in Canning Town.

> The only way to understand the poor is to be poor ... No less reliable witness exists than the bishop who boasts that he is more at home in Canning Town than at Fulham Palace, or the 'social worker' who specializes in slums.
>
> E.T. RAYMOND: *Uncensored Celebrities* (1919)

Cannon Street One of the CITY of London's longest streets, linking the MONUMENT to ST PAUL'S CHURCHYARD. Cannon Street traces the route of the ancient riverside track that ran alongside the THAMES towards the STRAND. It was first recorded in 1183 as Candelewrithstret, the street of the candlewrights. The City ward of CANDLEWICK derives its name from the same source. Cannon Street used to stretch only as far west as WALBROOK. It took its present form in the mid-1850s, when a path was cleared through a network of small lanes south-east of St Paul's and the whole route was widened. *See also* LONDON STONE.

Cannon Street station The station and its accompanying bridge over the THAMES opened in 1866. It was the CITY terminus of the South Eastern Railway, which had originally run into LONDON BRIDGE STATION. Its massive single-span train shed was a familiar feature of the north bank of the Thames until, following severe wartime bomb damage, it was removed in the late 1950s. British Rail reconstructed the bridge in 1981 and an office block was built over the station later in the same decade. The station serves Kent and south-east London. The corresponding LONDON UNDERGROUND station, on the DISTRICT and CIRCLE lines, opened in 1884. *See also the* STEELYARD.

Canonbury A Georgian and early Victorian suburb in east ISLINGTON, fringed by postwar council estates. Canonbury, the 'manor of the canons' of St BARTHOLOMEW's Priory in SMITHFIELD, was first recorded in 1373. Canonbury House was in existence by this date and stood isolated here for almost four centuries. The house underwent a

succession of alterations and partial demolitions, of which the lasting results are the 16th-century tower (now a Masonic research centre) and an east range that survives as part of Canonbury Place. In the early 17th century the scientist and philosopher Sir Francis Bacon spent the last ten years of his life at Canonbury House and the writers Oliver Goldsmith and Washington Irving later lodged in the tower. By 1730 the Canonbury Tavern had been built to the north-east of the house, later drawing crowds to its tea gardens. In the late 18th century the stockbroker John Dawes began to erect villas around what remained of the house, including a new Canonbury House in 1795. The writer Evelyn Waugh lived in Canonbury Square in the late 1920s, as did George Orwell in 1945, the year that saw the publication of *Animal Farm* – and the birth of film director Alan Parker in Canonbury. The poet Louis Mac-Neice lived on Canonbury Park South between 1947 and 1952.

> The salubrity of the air, and the proximity of the metropolis, renders Canonbury a very desirable place of residence, and in the summer season, the Tower building, which is seven stories high, is let out as a lodging-house.
>
> E.W. BRAYLEY: *Londiniana: Or, Reminiscences of the British Metropolis* (1828)

canonical five A term frequently applied to the five murders (or the five victims thereof) that almost all authorities ascribe to JACK THE RIPPER, distinguishing them from at least six other attacks for which he may or may not have been responsible.

Canons A palatial mansion built *c*.1718 at what is now CANONS PARK for James Brydges (1673–1744), afterwards the 1st Duke of Chandos. The name derived from the former landowners, the canons of the Priory of St Bartholomew the Great, West SMITHFIELD, who were granted 6 acres (2.5 hectares) of land here in 1331. Brydges was the most ostentatious figure of his day and he went to great lengths to infuse every aspect of life at Canons with the utmost grandeur. He had an orchestra accompany his meals and hired Handel as the house's resident composer.

> Having such a composer was an instance of real magnificence ... such as no prince or potentate on earth could at that time pretend to ...
>
> JOHN MAINWARING: *Memoirs of the Life of the Late George Frideric Handel* (1760)

The mansion survived for less than 30 years before a much smaller substitute took its place, built mainly with materials reclaimed from the demolition of its predecessor. Other parts of the original mansion were sold as architectural salvage and the original colonnade now stands in front of the NATIONAL GALLERY. The house was bought by the North London Collegiate School in 1929.

Canons Park A METROLAND dormitory suburb situated between STANMORE and EDGWARE, especially popular with north London's Jewish community.

Capability Brown *See under* BROWN.

Capel

Capel Court A lane that, until 1973, led to the STOCK EXCHANGE, and where dealers congregated to do business. Hence, formerly, a name for the Stock Exchange itself, and hence also 'Capel Courtier', a humorous term for a stockbroker. It is so called from Sir William Capel, twice LORD MAYOR OF LONDON in the early 16th century, who had a mansion or inn here. In between his two mayoral stints he spent two years in prison for refusing to pay a fine imposed for alleged negligence while in office.

Capel Manor London's only specialist college of horticulture and countryside studies, situated on Bullsmoor Lane, Bulls Cross, in the London Borough of ENFIELD. It occupies the site of an ancient manor established in the late 13th century, and takes its present name from Sir William Capel (*see* CAPEL COURT), who acquired the manor in 1486. The existing manor house was built in the 1750s. The college was established in 1968 in an attempt to bring life back into the derelict buildings and restore the gardens, which now have 30 richly planted acres (12 hectares) and 50 themed gardens open to the public, with the accent on the educational and the informative.

Capital Radio London's first commercial
music radio station. The station first went on air in 1973, splitting into separate AM and FM services in 1989. Capital is presently based in LEICESTER SQUARE but has spent most of its life to date at EUSTON TOWER. Capital was acquired in 2008 by Global Radio, a private London-based company that also owns Heart and LBC.

> There's a tower in the heart of London
> With a radio station right at the top
> They don't make the city beat
> They're making all the action stop.
>
> JOE STRUMMER and MICK JONES: 'Capital Radio' (song by the Clash) (1977)

Cardboard City A grimly descriptive nick-
name for an area near WATERLOO STATION on the SOUTH BANK, in particular its concrete undercroft, neighbouring railway arches and 'Bull Ring' subway, which in the 1980s became the home of the homeless, who devised makeshift residences in discarded cardboard cases and other packing materials. The term came to apply to similar 'cities' elsewhere.

Caretaker, The A play (1960) by Harold Pinter
(1930–2008), first performed at the Arts Theatre, Great Newport Street, in April 1960. It concerns the disruption that ensues when two brothers befriend Davies, a rascally tramp played on stage and in the film version (1964) by Donald Pleasence, and provide him with shelter in the room they share in west London. The title refers to the post of caretaker that the brothers independently offer Davies, who rewards them by trying to drive them apart. The play is littered with precise references to the geography of London.

> Then there is Davies's elusive identity,
> constructed partly through a series of located
> incidents: the tin of tobacco which was knocked
> off on the Great West Road, the sole of his shoe
> which came off on the North Circular just past
> Hendon, and, famously, Sidcup, where he left
> his papers.
>
> PETER RABY: *The Cambridge Companion to Harold Pinter* (2001)

Carey Street A street located to the north of
the Law Courts in the STRAND, named after Nicholas Carey, who had a house in the area in the 17th century. It was once the location of the Bankruptcy Division of the Supreme Court, and in early 20th-century colloquial English to be 'in Carey Street' was to be bankrupt, or at least very short of money. *See also* QUEER STREET.

> It was really rather absurd for a man in Mr
> Chardle's position with a nice little family
> business to his name and no worries, to take his
> step from a man like Mr Broster, who might find
> himself in Carey Street at any moment.
>
> NORMAN COLLINS: *Trinity Town* (1936)

Carlton

Carlton Club The oldest, most elite, and most important of all Conservative clubs. The Carlton Club was founded in 1832 and three years later moved to larger premises in PALL MALL. Following the destruction of that building in the Second World War, the club relocated to its present home at 69 ST JAMES'S STREET. A famous meeting at the club in 1922 resulted in the Tories' withdrawal from the coalition government, and precipitated a general election in which Lloyd George suffered a crushing defeat. Conservative MP Ann Widdecombe became the first female member in 2008.

Carlton Hotel A luxurious hotel that stood on the corner of PALL MALL and the HAYMARKET. Just as its construction was nearing completion in 1897, César RITZ and Auguste Escoffier were controversially sacked from their jobs as manager and head chef of the SAVOY and were persuaded to come to the Carlton, where they bolstered their reputations at the pinnacle of their professions. The hotel was irreparably damaged during the BLITZ and was eventually replaced by New Zealand House in 1961.

Ho Chi Minh (1890–1969) worked at the Carlton around the time of the First World War and a much-told but dubious story suggests that the future leader of the Vietnamese revolution had a one-night stand there with the saucy American actress Mae West (1893–1980).

Carlton House A palatial mansion that stood on the north side of the MALL. It was rebuilt from an existing house for Henry Boyle, 1st Baron Carleton (1669–1725), shortly after 1700. Frederick, Prince of Wales, bought the house in 1732 and it was granted to his grandson, George, later Prince Regent, in 1783. George remodelled, decorated and furnished Carlton House with excellent taste and at great expense but he moved out on his ascent to the throne as George IV in 1820. The house was demolished a few years later, to be replaced by CARLTON HOUSE TERRACE.

Carlton House desk A much-reproduced style of bureau designed for the Prince Regent's home, perhaps by Thomas Sheraton (1751–1806) or George Hepplewhite (c.1727–86). Its most distinctive feature is the curvature of the upper drawers around the writing surface.

Carlton House Terrace A pair of terraces, each of nine sumptuous houses, planned by John Nash (1752–1835) to replace CARLTON HOUSE and completed in 1832. Former residents have included three prime ministers and more than a hundred members of the British and European nobility. Carlton House Terrace is presently home to several important institutions, notably the ROYAL SOCIETY and the Institute of Contemporary Arts.

poor man's Carlton See under POOR.

Carmelites A mendicant order of friars of 12th-century origin, taking its name from Mount Carmel and with a mythical history associating the order with the prophet Elijah. They are also called WHITE FRIARS from the white mantle worn over a brown habit. One of their houses, founded on the south side of FLEET STREET in 1241, gave its name to the district called WHITEFRIARS or ALSATIA, which was long a sanctuary.

Carnaby Street A pedestrianized thoroughfare running parallel with the middle part of REGENT STREET, to its west. The street was laid out in the 1680s and the first property known to have stood here was Karnaby House, built by bricklayer Richard Tyler. The house may have been named after the village of Carnaby in Yorkshire. By the mid-19th century most of the street was given over to trades of various kinds and a number of the premises were subsequently converted to sweatshops working for the gentlemen's outfitters in nearby SAVILE ROW. In the 1950s some of these tailors began to produce more distinctive garments for direct sale, including suits for the smartly dressed Mods of the early 1960s. Off-the-peg fashion retailers soon joined the party and within a few years Carnaby Street and its immediate neighbours had become world-famous for their trendy unisex boutiques. At the height of SWINGING LONDON only the KING'S ROAD offered serious competition. Slow decline set in at the end of the 1960s, with periodic attempts to reverse it. The street was garishly refurbished by the council in 1973, and during the 1990s local traders attempted to 'reposition' the area as West Soho, with very limited success. The latest idea, promoted by landowners Shaftesbury plc, is simply to brand it 'Carnaby'. The street has taken a turn for the better lately, and offers an increasingly eclectic selection of clothes and accessories amid a dwindling proportion of gimmicky tat.

They seek him here, they seek him there,
In Regent Street and Leicester Square.

Everywhere the Carnabetian army marches on,
Each one an dedicated follower of fashion.

RAY DAVIES: 'Dedicated Follower of Fashion' (song by the Kinks) (1966)

carnival In modern London, the word (used without the definite article, and generally with an upper-case 'C') usually refers to the NOTTING HILL CARNIVAL.

Clive Phillip, who runs a clutch of performing bands, agreed. 'Carnival is being taken away from the community.'

The Guardian (9 August 2003)

The word originally related to pre-Lenten festivities, especially their culmination on Shrove Tuesday, which often took a disorderly turn in London, ending in riots almost every other year in the first half of the 17th century.

Carpenter, John *See* LIBER ALBUS.

carpet (bag) Three months in prison in COCKNEY RHYMING SLANG, from the rhyme with 'drag'. 'Drag' is an obsolete word for vehicular crime, dating from the time when vehicles were wagons or carts, and the standard sentence for robberies of this kind was three months in gaol.

carry

Carry On films A long-running series of British film comedies that began with *Carry On Sergeant* in 1958. Their humour was mostly unsubtle or even 'blue', but they won a loyal following and still have their devotees, despite (or perhaps owing to) their complete lack of political correctness. There were 31 in the sequence, all with titles beginning *Carry On*, such as *Carry On Cabby* (1963) and *Carry On up the Khyber* (1968) – see KHYBER (PASS) for the latter's double meaning. Regular members of the cast included the Londoners Kenneth Williams, Barbara Windsor, Bernard Bresslaw and Charles Hawtrey, and the adopted COCKNEY, Sid James. The series proper ended in 1978.

Carry on, London! The sign-off line of the BBC radio chat show *In Town Tonight*, which ran for over 1,000 editions between 1933 and 1960, with simultaneous television broadcasts in the mid-1950s. At the beginning of each programme an announcer would stop 'the mighty roar of London's traffic', which would be permitted to continue when the show was over. It attracted an audience of 20 million at its peak and featured interviews with celebrities who were 'in town tonight', often playing venues like the LONDON PALLADIUM, as well as 'ordinary' Londoners, such as a one-man band, a female chimney sweep and PEARLY KINGS AND QUEENS. *See also the* KNIGHTSBRIDGE MARCH.

I actually thought it was coming from Piccadilly in London – the noise of the traffic and all of a sudden this deep voice saying 'Stop!' and, as a child, I thought a policeman stopped all the traffic to do the show and that London came to a complete standstill.

BRUCE FORSYTH, in *The Archive Hour*, 'In Town Last Night' (radio documentary) (2003)

Carshalton A suburb situated east of SUTTON that began life as a 'farmstead by a river source, where watercress grows', or so its name suggests. Around 1707 Sir John Fellows, subsequently the sub-governor of the ill-fated South Sea Company, employed Charles Bridgeman to landscape the grounds of Carshalton House. A water tower with a delft-tiled plunge bath and a folly called The Hermitage survive.

Cart Marking A ceremony held annually in summer in the GUILDHALL yard. It has its origins in the arrangement by which the Worshipful Company of Carmen inspected and licensed carts to ply for hire in the CITY, and marked them accordingly. Around 40 vehicles of all vintages and types take part in the ceremony, which is followed by a drive-past.

Case is Altered, The This sign hangs outside public houses at EASTCOTE and HARROW WEALD in outer north-west London. It may be an corruption of Casa Alta (Spanish 'High House'), which was said to be adopted as a name when soldiers of the 57th Foot returned to MIDDLESEX after the Peninsular War.

Castelnau An urban village centred on the road of the same name, which leads from BARNES to HAMMERSMITH Bridge. When Major Charles Lestock Boileau built his home here he called it Castelnau House after his family's former estate of Castelnau de la Garde, near Nîmes in France; Boileau's family were Huguenots who had fled to England to escape religious persecution and settled in MORTLAKE. Castelnau House was demolished in the early 1960s and replaced by a public library.

Castle Baynard An irregularly shaped CITY ward, diverging north-westwards and north-eastwards from BLACKFRIARS. Its dominant edifice is ST PAUL'S Cathedral. The ward is named after a castle built by one Baynard, a Norman who came to England with William the Conqueror. It is said that Henry Stafford, 2nd Duke of Buckingham, offered the crown to Richard, Duke of Gloucester, afterwards Richard III, in the court of the castle in 1483. The palatial fortress was rebuilt several times before its final destruction in the GREAT FIRE OF LONDON.

> If you thrive well, bring them to Baynard's
> Castle;
> Where you shall find me well accompanied
> With reverend fathers and well-learned bishops.
>
> SHAKESPEARE: *Richard III*, III, v (*c*.1592)

casualty boy A boy who hired himself out as a COSTERMONGER's assistant, on a casual basis.

cat

cat and mouse 'House' in COCKNEY RHYMING SLANG, but 'rat and mouse' is heard more often.

cats' tails all hot Formerly a stock COCKNEY response to someone who said 'what?', especially if they did so repeatedly. It derived from an extended version chanted by children: 'What? What? Go to pot, cats' tails all hot, you're an ass and I'm not.' 'Ass' was used in the equine sense.

Catford A much-redeveloped town centre surrounded by late Victorian and Edwardian housing, situated on the River RAVENSBOURNE south of LEWISHAM. Perhaps surprisingly, the name is not some arcane corruption, but probably does mean that wild cats used to frequent the ford that is now the site of Catford Bridge, although an alternative explanation is that 'the cat' was a local landowner's nickname.

cathedral

cathedral of sewage A nickname for ABBEY MILLS pumping station.

cathedral of world Methodism The nickname of a small chapel on CITY ROAD, founded in 1777 by John Wesley (*see the* MAN FROM ALDERSGATE). He lived, preached, died and was buried within the confines of the little complex of buildings that now serves as an active memorial to his work. Wesley's house and a museum of Methodism are the chapel's neighbours.

Cato Street A small street running south-eastwards from Crawford Place in MARYLEBONE, named after the Roman statesman Cato (234–149 BC), who was the first important Latin prose author.

Cato Street Conspiracy A plot by Arthur Thistlewood (1770–1820) and his associates to murder Castlereagh and other members of the cabinet while they were dining with the Earl of Harrowby (23 February 1820), set fire to London, seize the BANK OF ENGLAND and MANSION HOUSE and form a provisional government. The conspirators met in a loft in Cato Street, where some were arrested following a tip-off to the police from one of the conspirators. Thistlewood and others escaped, but he was caught the following morning. Five, including Thistlewood, were hanged, and five others transported for life.

cauldron of sedition The nickname of the old Founders' Hall, which was situated in Founders' Court, LOTHBURY. It was noted for its political meetings; the controversial CITY politician Robert Waithman (1764–1833) made his first speech here in 1792, at a fiery gathering that was raided by the constabulary on the orders of the LORD MAYOR. Waithman was himself elected lord mayor in 1823 and was afterwards returned to parliament five times for the City.

Cavendish Square A garden square in southern MARYLEBONE, at the eastern end of WIGMORE STREET. It was laid out from 1717 by Edward Harley, 2nd Earl of Oxford (1689–1741), who had married into the Cavendish family of Newcastle-upon-Tyne. The north side was soon acquired by the megalomaniac 'grand' Duke of Chandos, who fruitlessly planned to acquire all the land between there and what is now CANONS Park, so that he could ride to his country mansion through his own estate. Around the mid-19th century Cavendish Square became a prestigious location for physicians' consulting rooms and the subsequent evolution of HARLEY STREET in that vein derives from its proximity to the square.

Cave of the Golden Calf A bohemian nightclub located in a Heddon Street basement, off REGENT STREET, founded in 1912 by Frida Strindberg (1872–1943), second wife of the Swedish dramatist August Strindberg. It was modelled on the cabaret clubs of Zurich and Vienna and became a rendezvous for the intelligentsia and the plain hedonistic. Eric Gill, Jacob Epstein and members of the CAMDEN TOWN GROUP provided the interior decorations. The establishment, which has been called 'Britain's first modern nightclub', closed early in 1914.

Caxton, William The father of English printing, who was born c.1422 in Kent and learnt his printing in Cologne and Bruges. He set up shop at the sign of the Red Pole in the shadow of WESTMINSTER ABBEY in about 1476 and died in 1491, by which time he had printed about a hundred books. He was a printer, publisher, retailer and translator.

C-Charge A short form of 'CONGESTION CHARGE'.

Cecil

Cecil Court A pedestrianized thoroughfare running between the southern ends of CHARING CROSS ROAD and St Martin's Lane. The court was laid out in the late 17th century and takes its name from the Cecil family of Hatfield House, Hertfordshire, who used to own the land here. The present-day architecture dates mostly from the alley's reconstruction in 1894. By the outbreak of the First World War booksellers had begun to open shops here and Cecil Court soon became renowned for its specialists in old books, maps, prints and other antiquities, a reputation that it retains today. See also FLICKER ALLEY.

Cecil Sharp House London's centre for traditional folk music, at 2 REGENT'S PARK Road. Built in 1930, it is home to the Vaughan Williams Memorial Library, a national archive dedicated to the preservation of English folk music and dance. Born in DENMARK HILL, Cecil Sharp (1859–1924) was a pioneering collector of this genre of music; he founded the English Folk Dance and Song Society in 1911.

Celery A laconic bawdy ditty chanted by some supporters of CHELSEA FC. Its popularity led a small minority to begin throwing sticks of celery onto the pitch during games; the club clamped down hard on the practice.

> Chelsea have banned celery from Stamford Bridge and ordered fans to stop throwing it during matches after the Football Association launched an investigation into instances of salad tossing at their recent matches.
>
> *The Guardian* (16 March 2007)

Celestial Bed See the TEMPLE OF HEALTH.

cenotaph (Greek *kenotáphion*, from *kenós*, 'empty', and *taphos*, 'tomb') A monument raised to the memory of a person or persons buried elsewhere. By far the most noteworthy nationally in Britain is the Cenotaph in WHITEHALL, designed by Sir Edwin Lutyens (1869–1944), which was dedicated on 11 November 1920 to those who fell in the First World War. The Remembrance Service has since been adapted to commemorate the fallen of the Second World War and later conflicts; it takes place at 11am on the Sunday nearest to 11 November each year. An exact replica of the Whitehall Cenotaph stands in Victoria Park, London, Ontario.

central

Central Criminal Court See the OLD BAILEY.

Central Hall A monumental memorial hall built at Storey's Gate, WESTMINSTER, on the west of PARLIAMENT SQUARE, by the Wesleyan Methodist Church and opened in 1912. The building contains a conference and exhibition centre, a concert hall, an art gallery, a Methodist church and a public café. It hosted the inaugural General Assembly of the United Nations in 1946.

Central line A LONDON UNDERGROUND line running from West RUISLIP and EALING Broadway, eastwards through central London and then curving north-eastwards to Epping. A loop line branches off at LEYTONSTONE, runs through HAINAULT and rejoins the main line at WOODFORD. The Central line is coloured red on the map. The first part of the Central London Railway opened in 1900 between CORNHILL (now BANK) and SHEPHERD'S BUSH, and was an immediate success, partly because of the flat fare that prompted the press to nickname it the TWOPENNY TUBE. Following a series of extensions, the line reached its maximum length soon after the Second World War. A shuttle service between the ESSEX towns of Epping and Ongar closed in 1994.

Central Saint Martins A college of art and design, now one of five schools that make up the UNIVERSITY OF THE ARTS LONDON. It was formed in 1989 as a merger of St Martin's School of Art, founded in 1854, and the Central School of Arts and Crafts, founded in 1896. Its buildings are mostly located in and around HOLBORN. The alumni of its constituent schools include the artists Lucian Freud (who also attended GOLDSMITHS) and Frank Auerbach, and fashion designers John Galliano, Alexander McQueen and Stella McCartney. The amalgamated institution is widely known simply as St Martins.

> Just five years out of St Martins and he's covered a football pitch in Berlin with hexagonal black and white football leather. On the centre spot sits a ball. The ball is made of mud and grass. And that's it.
> DAVID THEWLIS: *The Late Hector Kipling* (2007)

centre

Centre 42 An organization of writers, painters, composers, actors and others set up in 1961 by the playwright Arnold Wesker (b.1932) to promote festivals of the arts, exhibitions of craft work and other activities designed for working people. It had trade union support and took its name from the numerical position it held on the agenda of a trade union meeting that solicited greater union involvement in artistic work. Its base was the building that became the ROUND-HOUSE. Wesker disbanded Centre 42 in 1970.

Centrepoint A charity for the homeless founded in 1969 by Kenneth Leech (b.1939), assistant priest at St Anne's, SOHO. Concerned about the number of young people sleeping rough in the WEST END, he and a group of local volunteers opened up the basement of St Anne's House as a temporary night shelter. Now based near ALDGATE, the charity runs accommodation units and support services throughout London and has expanded its remit to include northeast England. HRH Prince William became Centrepoint's patron in 2005.

Centre Point A massive and (at one time) controversial 36-storey office block overlooking ST GILES CIRCUS, at the northern end of CHARING CROSS ROAD, on the corner with New Oxford Street. It was built by the developer Harry Hyams (b.1928) in 1963–7 to the designs of Richard Seifert and Partners. Because of an economic downturn much of it remained empty for several years, with Hyams content to benefit from the escalation in its capital value while he paid no rates. The structure thus gained a reputation as a monument to the evils of capitalism and a hundred squatters occupied it in 1974. Now a grade II listed building, Centre Point's tenants include the Confederation of British Industry.

ceremony

Ceremony of the Keys The oldest and best-known ceremonial tradition of the TOWER OF LONDON. Every evening just before 10pm, the Chief Yeoman Warder, with military escort, locks the outer gates of the Tower. As he tries to return to the inner ward, he is challenged at the BLOODY TOWER by a sentry. Having identified the keys as those of the sovereign and been saluted by the Tower Guard, the Chief then gives them to the Governor for the night.

Ceremony of the Lilies and Roses An annual event at the TOWER OF LONDON, in which the provosts of Eton College and King's College, Cambridge, lay their college emblems of lilies and roses respectively on the spot where Henry VI, founder of both institutions, is said to have been murdered on 21 May 1471.

chalfonts 'Piles' (haemorrhoids) in COCKNEY RHYMING SLANG, from Chalfont St Giles, a village in Buckinghamshire. Alternatives include 'FARMER GILES', 'SEVEN DIALS' and more recently 'X-Files'.

Chalk Farm A north-western extension of CAMDEN TOWN. Its name comes not from the nature of the soil but from Lower Chalcots Farm, which extended across much of what is now PRIMROSE HILL. 'Chalcots' derived in turn from Old English *caldicote*, meaning cold cottage(s). In the 17th century Lower Chalcots farmhouse became a public house, with gardens and an assembly room offering entertainment to field walkers. The present-day commercial premises of Chalk Farm Road include antique and bric à brac shops and MARINE ICES.

Chalk (Farm) 'Arm' in COCKNEY RHYMING SLANG, in use from the mid-19th to the early 20th century.

Chamber of Horrors See MADAME TUSSAUD'S.

champion

Champion of England or **King's** or **Queen's Champion** A person whose office it was to ride up WESTMINSTER HALL on a Coronation Day and challenge anyone who disputed the right of succession. The office was established by William the Conqueror. The custom of the challenge was last observed at the coronation of George IV in 1821, since when the Champion has borne the sovereign's standard at the coronation and, at the coronations of George VI (1937) and Elizabeth (1953), the Union flag instead.

Championship Vinyl The hard-to-find HOLLO-WAY record shop belonging to Rob Fleming, the protagonist of Nick Hornby's novel *High Fidelity* (1995). The film version was set in Chicago but the store's name stayed the same. Championship Vinyl cropped up again in Hornby's next novel *About a Boy* (1998).

Chancery One of the three divisions of the High Court of Justice. It is mainly concerned with equity, bankruptcy and probate business, and it is presided over by the Chancellor of the High Court. The word is shortened from chancellery.

chancery hold A grip in wrestling or boxing in which one's opponent's head is firmly held under one's arm. The term derives from the mid-19th-century pugilistic expression 'to get a man's head into Chancery', a reference to a legal entrapment from which it was difficult to extricate oneself.

> Red secured a chancery hold and dragged his wailing and remonstrating friend to Buck, who frowned with displeasure.
>
> CLARENCE E. MULFORD: *Hopalong Cassidy's Rustler Round-Up* (1906)

Chancery Lane A focal thoroughfare for the London legal profession, running between FLEET STREET and High HOLBORN. Soon after the middle of the 12th century the KNIGHTS TEMPLAR created New Street as a route between their old headquarters in Holborn and their 'New Temple'. In 1377 Edward III gifted the DOMUS CONVERSO-RUM to the Keeper of the Rolls of the Court of Chancery (later MASTER OF THE ROLLS) and by the early 15th century the road was becoming known as Chancery Lane. The Inns of Chancery ceased to serve an educational role after the Civil War and thereafter functioned as professional clubs. With the steady rise of the legal profession from the latter part of the 18th century, solicitors took premises here, as did suppliers such as wig makers, strongbox makers, law stationers and booksellers. The Inns of Chancery closed one by one and some of their buildings were replaced by government institutions with legal connections, such as the Public Record Office and the Patent Office, both of which have since moved to more spacious accommodation elsewhere. The Law Society of England and Wales is headquartered

at 113 Chancery Lane and the office of the Official Solicitor to the Supreme Court is at No.81.

> Long Chanc'ry-lane retentive rolls the sound And courts to courts return it round and round;
>
> ALEXANDER POPE: *The Dunciad*, I (1728)

Inns of Chancery *See under* INN.

Changing (of) the Guard or Guard Mounting

A complex ceremonial exchange of the Queen's Guard in the forecourt of BUCK-INGHAM PALACE, accompanied by the music of a Guards band. It is held daily at 11.30am from May to July, and on alternate days throughout the rest of the year. The ceremony is sometimes curtailed in very inclement weather. A similar daily handover of the Queen's Life Guard takes place at HORSE GUARDS PARADE.

chapel

Chapel Market A thriving but threatened street market, located off the southern end of Liverpool Road, near the ANGEL, ISLINGTON. Townhouses with rear gardens were built along what was then Chapel Street late in the 18th century. The essayist Charles Lamb lived at two houses in the street at different times in the late 1790s. To the annoyance of the well-heeled residents, costermongers began to sell their wares along the street and by the 1860s a fully fledged and relatively reputable market was in operation. Official designation as a street market came in 1879. By the 1890s Chapel Street had one of the two largest markets in the CLERKENWELL and Islington areas, divided about equally between food and non-food stalls. The council renamed the street Chapel Market in 1936. Despite its continuing popularity, Chapel Market is vulnerable to a future change of use owing to the high value of land in Islington.

Chapel of the Rolls Formerly the Chapel of the House of the Converts, or DOMUS CONVERSORUM, in CHANCERY LANE. The name derived from the practice of keeping parchment documents in rolls for convenience of storage at the chapel while it remained a place of worship. Most of the documents were transferred in 1856 to the adjoining and newly built Public Record Office, which has since moved to KEW and become part of the National Archives. *See also the* MASTER OF THE ROLLS.

Chapel on the Green The nickname of COL-LINS'S MUSIC HALL.

Chapel Royal Now a church and chapel owing allegiance directly to the sovereign, but originally a body of priests and singers that would follow the monarch around the country to whichever palace was in favour at the time. In the 17th century the ecclesiastical household came to rest at WHITEHALL and ST JAMES'S palaces, and then exclusively at the latter after Whitehall burned down in 1698. The two main buildings now designated Chapels Royal are both in the St James's Palace complex: the Chapel Royal itself and the Queen's Chapel. *See also* ST PETER AD VINCULA; SAVOY CHAPEL.

Chaplin, Charlie *See the* LITTLE TRAMP.

Chapter House An octagonal building at WESTMINSTER ABBEY, noted for its magnificent windows, sculptures and vaulted ceiling. It served as a meeting place for the abbey's monks and other dignitaries, and also regularly for Parliament between 1377 and 1547. The present structure was completed in 1253; its predecessor, which was probably round, was built in the 1050s. An oak door that opens into the Chapter House has been identified as the oldest in Britain. The door was reused from the original building and was said to have been covered in the skin of a sacrilegious felon who was flogged to death in the Middle Ages. However, fragments of hide found on the door have been tested and identified as having belonged to a cow.

Charing Cross The geographical centre of London, located at the western end of the STRAND. The medieval village of Charing probably took its name from Old English *cerring*, 'a turn', referring either to the bend in the THAMES or in the westward road from the CITY. Edward I placed a wooden cross here in 1290 to mark the final resting point of his wife's funeral procession on its way to WESTMINSTER; it was later replaced by a monument sculpted from Caen stone and raised on marble steps (*see* ELEANOR CROSSES). As the point of entry into WHITEHALL, Charing Cross was for centuries the scene of rebellious confrontations and subsequently of hangings and beheadings. The royal mews and great offices of state stood on the Westminster side of Charing Cross, while slums lay to the north and east. Nowadays, in addition to an unexciting cross-section of offices, shops, pubs and eateries, the Charing Cross locality is noted for its dealers

in stamps and coins. *See also the* SINKING OF QUEEN ELEANOR.

> Fleet-street has a very animated appearance; but I think the full tide of human existence is at Charing-Cross.
>
> SAMUEL JOHNSON: (1775) in James Boswell's *The Life of Samuel Johnson* (1791)

Charing (Cross) 'Horse' in COCKNEY RHYMING SLANG. The rhyme depends on proper cockney pronunciation of the words 'cross' and 'horse' as something like 'crawce' and 'awce'. Julian Franklyn, in his *Dictionary of Rhyming Slang* (1960), says that the term was applied by COSTERMONGERS to their draught animals but never used for racehorses.

Charing Cross Hospital A major teaching hospital, opened in 1818 as the West London Infirmary and Dispensary, and originally situated to the north-west of what became TRAFALGAR SQUARE. It gained its present name in 1827. In a lecture at the hospital in 1906 Ivan Pavlov described experiments in which he had conditioned dogs to salivate at the sound of a bell. Charing Cross Hospital moved to its present site on Fulham Palace Road, HAMMERSMITH, in 1973.

Charing Cross Road A street famed for its bookshops, running north from TRAFALGAR SQUARE to ST GILES CIRCUS. Crown Street and Castle Street formerly followed this route and their improvement was primarily a slum clearance and road-widening project, replacing St Martin's Lane as the area's principal northbound thoroughfare. Despite suggestions that the new street should be named Alexandra Avenue or Nelson Avenue, it was opened in 1887 as Charing Cross Road, a choice apparently preferred by the local inhabitants. Even before the road's creation booksellers had operated in the southern part of the area and after FOYLE'S moved to the northern part in 1906 the trade began to spread along its full length. Recent rent rises have forced away some specialists but many remain, while big-name book superstores also deem it essential to have a presence here.

84, Charing Cross Road (1970) is the story of the US writer Helene Hanff's 20-year correspondence with Frank Doel, of the antiquarian booksellers Marks and Company, at that address, which is now the site of a bar. The book has been adapted for the stage and screen.

Charing Cross station A terminus for trains

from south-east England, opened in 1864. It was built at the western end of the STRAND on the site of the former Hungerford Market. The railway bridge leading to it across the THAMES is generally known as HUNGERFORD BRIDGE, but it is also called Charing Cross Bridge. The station was designed by the engineer John Hawkshaw and its Renaissance-style hotel facing the Strand is the work of Edward Middleton Barry. Barry also designed a replica of Eleanor's cross, sculpted by Thomas Earp, which was placed in the station's forecourt (*see* ELEANOR CROSSES). Phileas Fogg left from Charing Cross station on his journey in Jules Verne's *Around the World in Eighty Days* (1873). The original Charing Cross underground station, on the DISTRICT and CIRCLE lines, opened in 1870, but in 1976 was renamed EMBANKMENT. Three years later TRAFALGAR SQUARE underground station, on the BAKERLOO and NORTHERN lines, was renamed Charing Cross.

chariots of fire A nickname given to BENDY BUSES following a spate of fires during their first few months on London's roads. The fleet was temporarily withdrawn from service while modifications were carried out to eliminate the cause.

Charlie

Charlie Brown's roundabout The official name for the junction of the A406 NORTH CIRCULAR ROAD, A1400 Southend Road and A113 Chigwell Road, in WOODFORD. The Roundabout public house stood here until 1972, when junction 4 of the M11 was added to the intersection. The pub was colloquially known as Charlie Brown's, after its landlord, Charlie Brown junior, son of the UNCROWNED KING OF LIMEHOUSE.

Charlie (Hunt) or **Charley (Hunt)** 'Cunt' in COCKNEY RHYMING SLANG, originally in either the literal or the metaphorical sense. Some lexicographers do not accept that this is the derivation of the word 'Charlie' in its meaning of a fool but its evolution is fairly well documented and parallels that of 'BERK'. The term was first recorded around 1890 and its short form progressively entered common usage. By the 1940s many of its users seem to have been unaware of its origin. It is most often heard in the expressions 'a right Charlie' or 'a proper Charlie'. The uncertainty surrounding the etymology is compounded by the later invention of 'Charlie

Ronce', meaning 'ponce'. *See also* GRUMBLE (AND GRUNT).

Charlies or **Charleys** The old night watch, before the police force was organized in 1829. The name may derive from Charles I, under whom London's watch system was reorganized in 1640.

Charlotte Street The best-known thoroughfare in FITZROVIA, noted for its concentration of media companies and restaurants. The street was probably named after Queen Charlotte (1744–1818), queen consort of George III.

Charlton A residential and industrial district situated between GREENWICH and WOOLWICH. First recorded in Domesday Book, the name means 'homestead belonging to the churls'. Churls constituted the lowest rank of freemen in medieval English society. From 50 BC to AD 250, a large Romano-British settlement occupied the ridge to the north of what is now CHARLTON VILLAGE. A Saxon village later grew up to the south-west, and St Luke's Church was in existence by the 11th century. Following the construction of the palatial CHARLTON HOUSE in the early 17th century, the village grew slowly until the arrival of the railway half a mile (800m) to the north in 1847, when industry began to fill the riverside at what became known as New Charlton. The Maryon Wilson family gave Charlton sandpits in Hanging Wood to the LONDON COUNTY COUNCIL in 1891; one pit became the nucleus of Maryon Park, while another became the VALLEY, home to CHARLTON ATHLETIC FC. Maryon Wilson Park was created across Thorntree Road from Maryon Park in 1926. Maryon Park attained cult significance in 1966 as the key location for Michelangelo Antonioni's film BLOW-UP, starring David Hemmings.

Charlton Athletic FC A south-east London FOOTBALL club founded by a group of teenagers on East Street (now Eastmoor Street) in 1905. The club turned professional and moved to the VALLEY in 1920. Its most consistently successful period came in the years immediately before and after the Second World War, including victory in the FA Cup final of 1947. From a low point in the mid-1980s, when attendances at home games dropped to around 5,000, the ADDICKS have since built a fan base extending across outer south-east London and into Kent.

Charlton House A grand redbrick house built

for Sir Adam Newton, tutor to Prince Henry, the elder son of James I. The house was completed in 1612, the year the prince died. Newton died in 1629. From 1767 the manor and the house belonged to the Maryon Wilsons, the family that later tried to develop HAMPSTEAD HEATH. In 1879 they enclosed the green in front of Charlton House and added it to their grounds. In 1925 the Metropolitan Borough of GREENWICH bought Charlton House and opened the grounds as a public park. From 1930 the council and private developers jointly built the Hornfair and Thornhill estates in the former grounds of Charlton House. The house is now a community centre and events venue.

Charlton Village The old centre of Charlton, as opposed to the much larger and newer suburb that has since engulfed it. St Luke's Church was first mentioned in 1077, when it lay at the centre of an extensive parish. The White Swan inn was built in 1889, while the Bugle Horn was formed from three late 17th-century cottages. Despite the modernization of some premises, the village retains much of its charm. Spencer Perceval, the only British prime minister to have been assassinated, is buried in St Luke's churchyard. The poet Walter de la Mare was born in the village in 1873.

charper A POLARI word meaning to seek or search, probably corrupted from Italian *cercare*.

Charterhouse A former Carthusian monastery situated in north-east SMITHFIELD. The word evolved from French *maison Chartreuse*, 'Carthusian house', influenced by the English word 'house'. It was founded by Sir Walter de Manny in 1371 and dissolved by Henry VIII in 1537. The Carthusians were vociferous opponents of the Dissolution and 17 monks and lay brothers were martyred. Charterhouse afterwards became the residence of successive members of the nobility, who progressively renewed its gloriously rambling buildings. In the year of his death, Thomas Sutton (1532–1611, *see* CROESUS) acquired Howard House, as it was by then called, from the Earl of Suffolk and made provision for the establishment of a hospital for pensioners and a school for boys there. The author W.M. Thackeray attended the school in the 1820s. Charterhouse School moved to Godalming, Surrey, in 1872 and the London site is now entirely occupied by Sutton's Hospital

in Charterhouse, a home for elderly gentlemen known as Brothers.

chase

Chase, The A 120-acre (48.5-hectare) nature reserve in east DAGENHAM. From the 1920s until the early 1970s this was a gravel quarry, providing construction materials for the expansion of east London. Many of the exhausted pits were filled with rubble but others were simply abandoned, allowing wetlands and grasslands to form. Much of the terrain is stony and prone to winter flooding, but the Chase harbours numerous animals and plants unusual in an urban setting. In 1986 BARKING AND DAGENHAM council asked the London Wildlife Trust to take over management of the Chase and to develop it as a recreational and educational resource for the community.

Enfield Chase *See under* ENFIELD.

Chatham House The home, at 10 ST JAMES'S SQUARE, of the Royal Institute of International Affairs, an independent, non-profit institution for the debate and analysis of global issues, founded in 1920.

Chatham House prize An award made annually to the statesperson deemed by Chatham House members to have made the most significant contribution to the improvement of international relations in the previous year. Her Majesty the Queen presented the inaugural prize to Ukrainian president Viktor Yushchenko (b.1954) in 2005.

Chatham House rule Often mistakenly called 'rules', there is just one, namely:

> When a meeting, or part thereof, is held under the Chatham House rule, participants are free to use the information received, but neither the identity nor the affiliation of the speaker(s), nor that of any other participant, may be revealed.

The rule was devised in 1927 and refined in 1992 and 2002, and is invoked to encourage openness and the sharing of information.

Chattertonia Material related to the short life and few works of the poet Thomas Chatterton, much of which is held in the BRITISH MUSEUM. Chatterton came to London from Bristol in April 1770. In August of the same year, unable to make a living from his writing and facing starvation, he committed suicide by swallowing arsenic in his attic room in Brooke Street, HOLBORN. He was 17 years old. Chatterton was buried in the graveyard attached to SHOE LANE workhouse. His biographer, John Dix, reported that the body was later disinterred and reburied in Bristol by the poet's uncle, but this is generally viewed as a fabrication. TATE BRITAIN has Henry Wallis's painting of the boy on his deathbed.

> I thought of Chatterton, the marvellous Boy,
> The sleepless Soul that perished in his pride;
> Of him who walked in glory and in joy
> Following his plough, along the mountain-side:
> By our own spirits are we deified:
> We poets in our youth begin in gladness;
> But thereof come in the end despondency and madness.
>
> WILLIAM WORDSWORTH: *Poems, in Two Volumes*, 'Resolution and Independence' (1807)

chav A materialistic British working-class youth with a fondness for fashionable but often tasteless clothes and ostentatious jewellery. The term, which is first recorded in 1998, is unisex, but a female of the species can also be a 'chavette'. It probably comes from the old POLARI word 'chavy', meaning 'child', which in turn goes back to Romany *chavi*, but other derivations have been suggested. In an online poll conducted in 2008 by the website Chav Towns (www.chav-towns.co.uk), CROYDON was named the 'Chaviest Town in England'.

Cheam A favoured interwar suburb with some impressive older houses and cottages, situated west of SUTTON. The name may be a corruption of two words meaning 'village by the tree stumps'. By the 14th century Cheam had been split into east and west manors, each of which had its own village. East Cheam (later known as Lower Cheam) was the larger of the pair. From the 14th to the 16th century Cheam was known for its potteries, which specialized in making jugs. Whitehall was built on Malden Road around 1500 and is GREATER LONDON's finest remaining example of a medieval hall house (a house in which the main living area was not open to the roof). The house was later extended and weatherboarded and is now open to the public.

Holborn for wealth and Cheam for health
See under HOLBORN.

Cheap A CITY of London ward centred on CHEAPSIDE. Away from the retailers of Cheapside itself the ward is mainly occupied by business premises, notably those of investment banks, and the halls of several LIVERY COMPANIES, which include Goldsmiths' Hall, Mercers' Hall, Sadlers' Hall and Wax Chandlers' Hall.

Cheapside The CITY of London's main shopping street for the past millennium, running eastward from ST PAUL'S towards BANK. It takes its name from 'chepe', a Saxon word for a market. The street connected the north-east corner of St Paul's churchyard with the main City settlement to its east and its alignment was dictated by a convenient bridging point across the (now subterranean) River WALBROOK. The Church of ST MARY-LE-BOW stood here by 1091, when it was seriously damaged in a storm. Market buildings were constructed from the late 12th century, with low roofs that later formed viewing platforms for tournaments. Cheapside became the centre of the jewellery trade, where most London goldsmiths sold their wares, but it was destroyed in the Great Fire of 1666. It took some time for Cheapside to recover from the economic effects of the fire but in 1775 a visitor observed that with its 'many thousands of candles ... the street looks as if it were illuminated for some festivity', although this was just for everyday trade. From the late 19th century, and especially before and after the Second World War, most of the street was rebuilt with office buildings, many of which have recently been replaced. Conventional retailers on Cheapside are nowadays outnumbered by services providers for City workers, such as opticians, building societies and mobile phone stores.

Cheapside clock The timepiece that surmounted Sir John Bennett's clock shop in Cheapside, with figures of GOG AND MAGOG that struck the quarter-hours. When the shop closed in 1931, motor manufacturer Henry Ford acquired both the building and the clock and shipped them to Dearborn, Michigan, where they were reconstructed as part of the Greenfield Village visitor attraction.

Cheapside hoard A notable collection of early 17th-century jewellery discovered in 1912 by workmen at the junction of Cheapside and Friday Street.

Cheapside is the best garden A saying dating from Cheapside's time as London's central market, suggesting that the sensible way to come by the best produce is not to grow it oneself but to buy it. 'COVENT GARDEN' was later substituted for 'Cheapside'.

he came at it by way of Cheapside An expression formerly used with reference to an item obtained for little or nothing, punning on the 'cheap side'.

Cheesegrater A nickname for the Leadenhall Building, an office tower planned for 122 LEADENHALL STREET. Work on the project was suspended in 2008, owing to the state of the commercial property market. The tag derives from the building's wedge-shaped profile and was coined by the website Skyscrapernews. com.

Chelsea A fashionable quarter for nearly half a millennium, Chelsea lies on the north bank of the THAMES between PIMLICO and FULHAM. Speculation on the origin of its name has settled on something between a chalk wharf and a gravel bank. It was farmland from the time of Domesday Book until the early 1520s, when Sir Thomas More built Beaufort House. Henry VIII developed a liking for Chelsea during his visits to More (whom he later had executed), and bought a manor house here, but found it too small and built a new one in what is now CHEYNE WALK. This started a trend, and a succession of grand retreats appeared over the following 200 years, with a supporting village of working people growing up on the riverbank. Several eminent literary and scientific figures lived in Chelsea in the 17th century, but their fine houses have all disappeared. Perhaps the greatest was Shaftesbury House, which stood from 1635 to 1856, spending its latter years as the parish workhouse. During the 18th century Chelsea's proximity to WESTMINSTER was the downfall of its palaces and gardens. Lodges and townhouses replaced them and the modern street plan was laid out. The poorer inhabitants were pushed westward to the WORLD'S END district, which was the subject of slum clearance and municipal building of flats in the mid-20th century.

Chelsea has been particularly popular with the world of arts and letters, and famous residents have included the writers Charles Kingsley, Oscar Wilde and Bram Stoker, the composer and actor Noël Coward and the artist David Hockney. *See also the* SAGE OF CHELSEA.

Chelsea Arts Club A club founded in the 1890s as a meeting place for the many artists who, at that period, lived in Chelsea (among the founder members were James Whistler, Walter Sickert,

Philip Wilson Steer and Frank Brangwyn). It moved to its present premises in Old Church Street in 1902. It sponsored the Chelsea Arts Ball, an annual knees-up for the *jeunesse dorée*, latterly held in the ALBERT HALL. The ball became so rowdy that it was discontinued after 1959, but it was revived in the 1980s.

Chelsea boots A name given in the 1960s to elastic-sided ankle-high boots for men. Hitherto such footwear would have been worn only by septuagenarian survivors of the Victorian age, but SWINGING LONDON declared it sophisticated and fashionable, and signalled its approval by naming it after the with-it borough.

Chelsea bun A type of square sweet currant-bun made from a sheet of yeast dough that has been rolled up into a coil. It was originally made at the Chelsea Bun House, a bakery that opened near SLOANE SQUARE in the late 17th or early 18th century.

Chelsea College of Art and Design Now a constituent college of the UNIVERSITY OF THE ARTS LONDON, it began as a faculty of the South-Western Polytechnic (later Chelsea Polytechnic), which opened in 1895. A new, semi-autonomous Chelsea School of Art was effectively formed in 1964 after amalgamation with The Polytechnic School of Art, previously a faculty of the POLYTECHNIC in REGENT STREET. The institution adopted its present name in 1986 and consolidated its activities on a single site at MILLBANK, next to TATE BRITAIN, in 2005.

Chelsea Drugstore An ultra-stylish venue when it opened at the corner of Royal Avenue and the KING'S ROAD in 1968, with a bar, restaurant, discotheque, pharmacy and boutiques arranged over three floors. It was modelled on Le Drugstore on the Boulevard Saint-Germain in Paris. The Chelsea Drugstore survived only three years in its original incarnation, mainly because of complaints from outraged neighbours.

> I went down to the Chelsea Drugstore
> To get your prescription filled
> I was standing in line with Mister Jimmy
> And man, did he look pretty ill.
>
> MICK JAGGER and KEITH RICHARDS: 'You Can't Always Get What You Want' (song by the Rolling Stones) (1969)

Chelsea FC A west London FOOTBALL club founded in 1905 by the building contractor Henry Augustus 'Gus' Mears (1873–1912), who had earlier acquired an existing sports ground and a neighbouring market garden at STAMFORD BRIDGE, with the aim of creating London's premier footballing venue. He first attempted to persuade FULHAM FC to move in, but when they declined he decided to establish his own team to occupy the premises. Mears considered the names 'Kensington' and 'London' for the new club, before settling on 'Chelsea'. For most of the 20th century the club experienced more failures than successes, but performed strongly enough in the early 1990s to becoming a founding member of the Premier League. The Russian businessman Roman Abramovich (b.1966) bought the club in 2003, and immediately spent almost £100 million on new players; Chelsea has since become one of the most formidable football clubs in Europe. *See also the* BLUES.

Chelsea Flower Show An annual summer display organized by the Royal Horticultural Society in the grounds of the CHELSEA ROYAL HOSPITAL since 1913. The exhibits range from prize vegetables to whole gardens, all housed on the 11 acres (4.5 hectares) of lawn. Opening night is a major occasion, attended by members of the royal family and other celebrities. The event lasts five days and at the end of the final day remaining exhibits are sold to the public.

Chelsea girl A generic term in 1960s SWINGING LONDON for a young woman who shopped on the KING'S ROAD, wore clothes by Mary QUANT and aspired to look like TWIGGY.

Chelsea Green An estate agents' name for the south-eastern purlieus of SOUTH KENSINGTON, to the north of the KING'S ROAD. The patch of grass called Chelsea Green, on Cale Street, is the last remaining section of the original Chelsea Common.

Chelsea Hospital (or College) to a sentry box An old betting expression meaning an absolute certainty. *See also* ALL LOMBARD STREET TO A CHINA ORANGE.

The facetious Jerry Noon remarked that it was 'Chelsea Hospital to a sentry-box' on Jones.

HENRY DOWNES MILES: *Pugilistica: The History of British Boxing*, Volume 3 (1906)

Chelsea Pensioner The popular name for an inmate of the CHELSEA ROYAL HOSPITAL. The Pensioners' scarlet summer uniforms (they wear dark blue in winter) remain a head-turning feature of London's streets when their wearers venture forth.

Chelsea Physic Garden A garden, originally for the cultivation of medicinal plants, established in Chelsea by the Apothecaries' Society in 1676. The first cedar trees in England were planted here (in 1683), and the first English greenhouse was built here in the same decade.

Chelsea porcelain, **china** or **ware** A type of porcelain ware made at the Chelsea Porcelain Works. This was founded in about 1745 and continued until 1784, when all its operations were removed to Derby. Different periods of production are distinguished by the name of the mark then applied: Triangle (the earliest), for example, and Red Anchor. The most familiar of the factory's output are its figurines.

Chelsea Royal Hospital A habitation for old or disabled soldiers, founded in Chelsea by Charles II at the instigation of Sir Stephen Fox, the Paymaster General of the Forces (the story that royal mistress Nell GWYN had a hand in its foundation seems to be apocryphal). Building began in 1682, to designs by Sir Christopher WREN, and it was opened in 1692. Its inmates (who since March 2009 have included women) are known as CHELSEA PENSIONERS. The CHELSEA FLOWER SHOW is held in the hospital's grounds.

Chelsea set The nickname for a postwar clique of socially well-connected figures, some from the world of arts and letters, who featured prominently in the gossip columns of the time.

Chelsea smile A slang term, dating from the 1970s, for a knife slash that runs from the corner of the mouth up and across the cheek. It is so named for allegedly being inflicted on rival fans by the more violent supporters of CHELSEA FC.

Chelsea tractor A derisive early 21st-century nickname for fuel-inefficient 4×4 off-road vehicles, designed for rough terrain, as used by the CHELSEA SET and 'yummy mummies' (or their nannies/au pairs) for doing the shopping, taking their children to school (hence an alternative designation, 'mum trucks'), driving to lunch, etc. In 2004 the then London Mayor Ken Livingstone described their drivers as 'complete idiots'.

Chelski A nickname for CHELSEA FC, popular with the media and supporters of opposition teams, dating from the club's takeover by the Russian billionaire Roman Abramovich in 2003.

Chelsfield The south-eastern part of ORPINGTON, and a completely separate locality from CHELSFIELD VILLAGE. In 1868 the South

Eastern Railway's 'new main line' opened between CHISLEHURST and Tonbridge, Kent, and Chelsfield station was built in what was then open countryside. From the mid-1920s a new and exclusive settlement evolved here, and this has become a popular place of residence for south Londoners who have 'done well', especially in fields such as sport and self-employed trades. **Chelsfield Village** The original heart of Chelsfield, situated almost a mile (1.6 km) to the east of its station. The Church of St Martin of Tours is of early Norman origin, and was altered and enlarged in the 13th century. The Five Bells public house takes its name from the unusual number of bells that the church used to have. The present Court Lodge and its farm have stood near the church since at least the 18th century; in Kent, manor houses were often called 'court lodge' because manorial courts were held there. In 1928 the ORPINGTON bypass divided the church and Court Lodge from the village itself, where Victorian farm labourers' cottages have been altered and gentrified, although many properties retain their rustic charm. The novelist Miss Read (born Dora Shafe, 1913) moved from HITHER GREEN to Chelsfield at the age of 7. Her *Fairacre* books, although set in the Cotswolds, were based on her childhood experiences in the village, at its school and in the surrounding countryside. Miss Read's autobiographical *Time Remembered* (1986) portrays Chelsfield and its inhabitants in the 1920s.

Cheshire Cheese, Ye Olde An ancient inn and chop house located at the corner of Wine Office Court and FLEET STREET, rebuilt after the GREAT FIRE OF LONDON and seemingly little changed since then. Its cellars are said to date from the 13th century. It was famously the haunt of James Boswell and Dr JOHNSON. Dryden, Pope, Goldsmith, Voltaire, Thackeray and DICKENS also drank here. In the early 1890s it was the meeting place of the Rhymers' Club, a group of poets that included Ernest Dowson and W.B. Yeats. G.K. Chesterton and Hilaire Belloc were Cheshire Cheese regulars in the early 20th century.

Chessex A blend of CHELSEA and Essex. A notional location of the early 2000s, now probably past its sell-by date. Its female inhabitants were Chessex girls: fashionable neo-SLOANE RANGERS who affect some of the flashy glamour of their downmarket sisters Essex girls, such as short denim skirts and white high heels. Victoria Beckham was apparently a key style icon for Chessex girls, and the actress and model Liz Hurley was the genre's archetype.

Chessington A heavily developed mid-20th-century suburb occupying most of the tongue of the Royal Borough of KINGSTON that protrudes south beyond HOOK. Cisendone – 'the hill of a man named Cissa' – was mentioned in Domesday Book and St Mary's Church appears in Merton Priory records of 1174. Chessington Hall was built in the early 16th century and from the 1750s it was home to the playwright Samuel Crisp. The novelist Fanny Burney was a frequent guest at the hall and wrote part of her second novel, *Cecilia*, in the summerhouse during the early 1780s. Chessington Hall was rebuilt in 1832 and St Mary's Church was restored in 1854. RAF Chessington was a barrage balloon centre for the defence of London, used throughout the Second World War; it was subsequently converted to military medical use. After the war the council built 400 homes in the grounds of Chessington Hall in the 1950s. The hall itself survived a little longer but was demolished in 1965. Having spent its latter days as a US air force base, RAF Chessington was sold by the Ministry of Defence and housing was built on the site in the mid-1990s.

Chessington World of Adventures GREATER LONDON's only full-scale theme park has evolved out of Chessington Zoo, which opened in 1931 in the 65-acre (26-hectare) grounds of Burnt Stub, a 19th-century house built on the site of a predecessor that had been burnt down to a stub by Parliamentarians during the Civil War. Burnt Stub is now Hocus Pocus Hall. The park is divided into themed areas, with rides, fairground attractions and wild animals, and is OUTER LONDON's most popular paid-for visitor attraction, drawing 1.5 million fun-seekers a year.

Chevy Chase or **Chivy Chase** 'Face' in COCKNEY RHYMING SLANG, but 'BOAT (RACE)' is usually preferred nowadays. The term derives from the medieval *Ballad of Chevy Chase*, which was also responsible for the name of an American comic actor.

Cheyne Walk A celebrated creative hotbed located on CHELSEA's THAMES embankment south of the mid-section of the KING'S ROAD. A Buckinghamshire gentleman, Charles Cheyne, who had got rich by marrying into the Cavendish family and later became Viscount Newhaven, bought the manor of Chelsea on an instalment plan between 1657 and 1661. The riverside walk that later took his name was already well endowed with inns, coffee houses and some grand houses by that time and more building leases were granted by Cheyne's son after he inherited the manor in 1698. The resulting street is of great architectural merit – most of the properties are listed buildings, right down to their garden walls and railings and the phone box by Albert Bridge – but it is most famous for the dazzling array of talented individuals that has lived and worked here. The list includes Thomas More, Hilaire Belloc, George Eliot, Elizabeth Gaskell, Dante Gabriel Rossetti, Philip Wilson Steer, the Brunels, Sylvia Pankhurst, Mick Jagger and Keith Richards. The artist J.M.W. Turner died in Cheyne Walk. Henry Fielding, Tobias Smollett, William Holman Hunt and James Whistler lived around the corner in Lawrence Street. The Cheyne Row house and garden of the 'SAGE OF CHELSEA', the Victorian writer and historian Thomas Carlyle, is now owned by the National Trust. Turner's house was damaged during the Second World War and the LONDON COUNTY COUNCIL afterwards rebuilt it to look as it had before.

Chi Chi A giant panda (1957–72) purchased in 1958 by LONDON ZOO, where she soon became a star attraction. Chi Chi was loaned to Moscow Zoo for eight months in 1966 in a vain attempt to persuade her to breed. A reciprocal visit from her potential partner was also unsuccessful but the exchanges marked a new era of international zoological co-operation at a time when cold war politics made it controversial.

Chicken Soup with Barley A play (1958) by the British playwright Arnold Wesker (b.1932) about the lives and communist politics of the Kahns, an EAST END Jewish family, over the two decades from 1936. The first part of a trilogy, completed by *Roots* (1959) and *I'm Talking About Jerusalem* (1960), in which the central theme is that of caring, the play owed its title to the chicken soup young Ada Kahn is brought by a kind neighbour when she is ill.

child

Child of the Marshalsea A sobriquet of Amy Dorrit, the eponymous protagonist of Charles DICKENS's *Little Dorrit* (1855–7). Born in the MARSHALSEA debtors' prison, she is the daughter of William Dorrit, imprisoned for 25 years, who proudly enjoys the title of 'the Father of the Marshalsea'.

> At thirteen years old, the Child of the Marshalsea presented herself to the dancing-master, with a little bag in her hand, and preferred her humble petition. 'If you please, I was born here, sir.'
>
> *Little Dorrit*, 'The Child of the Marshalsea'

Children of God A sect of adventists founded in BATTERSEA in 1870 by Mary Anne Girling (1827–86), a farmer's daughter. They went on to become the New Forest Shakers but the movement petered out after Mrs Girling's death.

china

china (plate) 'Mate' in COCKNEY RHYMING SLANG. The term is most often employed in the endearment 'my old china'; 'my' is usually pronounced and often spelt 'me', as in this example:

> The Queen Mum threw the empty bottle on to the floor and it smashed. 'You'll have to, me old china,' she said, and stood back, pointing to Madge's body lying half under the table.
>
> MICHAEL DE LARRABEITI: *The Borribles: Across the Dark Metropolis* (2005)

China Street A 19th-century nickname for BOW STREET, perhaps alluding to its proximity to COVENT GARDEN, then a market, where 'China oranges' would have been plentiful.

Chinatown Once a term applied to LIMEHOUSE, Chinatown now identifies the compact neighbourhood around Gerrard Street and Lisle Street, north of LEICESTER SQUARE. The Chinese call Gerrard Street *Tong Yan Kai*, 'Chinese street'. A handful of Chinese restaurants were established in SOHO during the Second World War, when they became popular with soldiers who had acquired a taste for the food abroad. Later, Chinese entrepreneurs began to buy up and convert the rundown properties south of SHAFTESBURY AVENUE. This coincided with an influx of agricultural workers from Hong Kong, who had been forced out of their traditional occupations by changes in the world rice markets. Many found work in the catering trade, often living nearby in tied accommodation, and a variety of other businesses sprang up to serve the new population. Increasing prosperity allowed most members of the community to reside further afield but Chinatown's role as a trading zone is stronger than ever, catering to the Chinese population from all over south-east England. There are oriental arches at each end of Gerrard Street, the street signs are bilingual (as are the notices in the bookmakers) and the telephone kiosks are miniature pagodas. WESTMINSTER council has pedestrianized Gerrard Street and parts of Macclesfield Street and Newport Place. Since 1973, the Chinese New Year has been celebrated on the Sunday closest to the New Year with lion dances and other festivities; the date of the New Year usually falls between mid-January and mid-February, varying because it depends on the phases of the moon.

Chingford A former urban district, now merged with WALTHAMSTOW, which lies to its south, to form the London Borough of WALTHAM FOREST. The name may be derived from words meaning 'ford of the stump-dwellers', a reference to houses built on poles to keep them clear of the marshy ground, but others have suggested that 'ching' is a corruption of 'shingle'. Either way, the early riverside settlement was probably located in modern South Chingford. Patches of EPPING FOREST were being cleared by the 12th century, afterwards becoming the sites of Chingford's disconnected hamlets. These were isolated by the River LEA and the forest and lacked public transport until the railway was extended here from Walthamstow in 1873. Even then suburban development proceeded slowly and Chingford was not built up with the same dense layout that characterized many late Victorian street plans. The builders nevertheless exploited their sites aggressively, demolishing the few older houses that the district possessed at that time. Today the only undeveloped areas are Chingford Plain, which has a public golf course, and Pole Hill, once owned by Lawrence of Arabia.

Chingford Green The modern heart of Chingford, located south-west of the station. In the early 1840s a local grandee, the Rev Robert Boothby Heathcote, commissioned Lewis Vulliamy (1791–1871) to design the Church of St Peter and St Paul, which replaced CHINGFORD MOUNT's All Saints as the parish church.

Chingford Hatch The south-eastern part of Chingford. A hatch was a gate, probably used here to prevent cattle from straying from their pasture on the edge of EPPING FOREST, and the locality is sometimes referred to simply as 'the Hatch'. Although a small village had evolved by the late 18th century, it was not until the early 20th century that radial expansion from CHINGFORD GREEN reached this far.

Chingford Mount The commanding height of Chingford, located on its western side. The parish church of All Saints was founded here in the 12th century and some of the early stonework survives in the present structure, together with additions from the following three centuries. The ABNEY PARK Cemetery Company established Chingford Mount Cemetery in 1884, on Old Church Road. The KRAY TWINS and other members of that family are buried at the cemetery.

Chingford Skinhead or **Strangler** A media nickname for Norman (now Lord) Tebbit (b.1931 in PONDERS END), the right-wing populist Europhobe MP for Chingford from 1974 until his elevation to the peerage in 1992. He is known for his abrasive manner and robust invective and was a leading figure in the cabinets of Margaret Thatcher in the 1980s. He famously told the unemployed to get on their bikes to find work, as his own father had done in the Great Depression.

Chipping Barnet See BARNET.

Chiselbury A fictitious public school invented by Frank Muir and Denis Norden, of which 'Professor' Jimmy Edwards was headmaster in the television sitcom *Whack-O!* (1956–60). The name may have been inspired by CHISLEHURST.

Chislehurst A pretty suburb situated southwest of SIDCUP, with an old village centre and common, and plenty of greenery and 19th-century cottages. First recorded in 974 as a patch of stony woodland, a settlement had developed around the Scadbury estate by the mid-13th century. Camden Place, now a golf clubhouse, is named after William Camden, the Elizabethan antiquary who lived in Chislehurst from 1609 until his death in 1623. Lord Chief Justice Charles Pratt lived here and took the title of Camden when he was made a baron in 1765, subsequently bestowing the name on north London's CAMDEN TOWN. When Napoleon III and his family were expelled from France in 1871 after the country's defeat in the Franco-Prussian War, the imperial family moved to Camden Place. Napoleon died in 1873 and was buried at the Roman Catholic church in Chislehurst until the Empress Eugenie removed his body to Farnborough, Hampshire. Around this time, the 'new' end of Chislehurst began to develop near the railway station, which opened in 1865. The town became suburbanized between the wars and merged with Sidcup in 1934 to form a larger urban district. Sir Malcolm Campbell (1885–1949), who set land and water speed records, was born in Chislehurst and was buried next to his parents at St Nicholas Church.

Chislehurst Caves A disused chalk mine with several miles of passageways split into three sections, colourfully named Saxon, Druid and Roman, although evidence of such early usage is flimsy. The caves were last worked in the 1850s. When the railway reached Chislehurst the caves became a tourist attraction. They were used for military purposes in wartime, for mushroom farming between the wars and have represented a thaesium mine on the planet Solos for an episode of *Dr Who*. During the 1960s, Status Quo, Jimi Hendrix and Pink Floyd all performed here. In 1974 Led Zeppelin launched their Swan Song label with a party in the caves.

Chiswick A west London suburb filling the THAMES peninsula between HAMMERSMITH and BRENTFORD. The name means 'cheese farm' and was in use by 1000. Chiswick came into being as a Thames-side fishing village, clustered around the church of St Nicholas by 1181. The present church dates from the 15th century, but was mostly rebuilt in 1884. The 16th-century Walpole House is the grandest of Chiswick Mall's villas, though much altered, and illustrates the stature of the village's residents at that time. By the late Middle Ages, Chiswick encompassed the neighbouring villages of Little Sutton, TURNHAM GREEN and STRAND ON THE GREEN, across the peninsula. BEDFORD PARK set a new standard for suburban housing after 1875, by which time Turnham Green had become the commercial heart of Chiswick. The latter area is now synonymous with Chiswick for many Londoners, and is popular for its restaurants, cafés and specialist shops. Chiswick's riverfront and Strand on the Green are the least changed parts of this mini-conurbation, the former still grand, the latter hanging on to quaintness.

Erin Pizzey founded the world's first refuge for battered women in Chiswick in 1971. Linoleum and Cherry Blossom shoe polish were created in Chiswick. Chiswick's appeal to the literary community is reflected in its role in several novels, including William Thackeray's *Vanity Fair* (1848) and John Fowles's *A Maggot* (1985).

Chiswick Eyot A narrow AIT lying close to the Chiswick bank of the THAMES. It is about 275 yards (250m) long. It is best known for the annual name-checks it receives from television and radio commentators on the BOAT RACE, which passes the island in its latter stages.

Chiswick House A major example of a Palladian villa, built 1725–9, and subsequently inherited by the dukes of Devonshire. Of modest proportions by aristocratic standards, its splendid decor and ornate ceilings have been faithfully restored by English Heritage. As well as being a showcase of Palladian symmetry, Chiswick House was the place of expiry of two celebrated political figures: Charles James Fox (in 1806) and prime minister George Canning (in 1827).

Chiswick Records An independent record label of some distinction during the PUNK ROCK era. Its most notable signing was the Damned.

Cholmeleian A pupil or former pupil of HIGHGATE SCHOOL, after Sir Roger Cholmeley, who founded the school in 1565.

chovey COSTERMONGERS' slang for a shop, especially a travelling shop. A lock-up chovey was a covered cart. The owner was a man-chovey or Ann-chovey. A crocus-chovey was a pharmacy.

church

Church Army A Church of England evangelical body founded in 1882 by BRIXTON-born Wilson Carlile (1847–1942), when he was a curate at the church of St Mary Abbots, KENSINGTON. It began its work among the poor of London on somewhat similar lines to those of the SALVATION ARMY. In 1905 the Church Army opened its first headquarters building at 55 Bryanston Street, MARBLE ARCH. It has been based at SIDCUP since 2002.

Church End A place name that arose in several parts of the London area when the vicinity of the parish church did not lie at the geographical or commercial centre of a village or nascent town. In particular, the name took root in FINCHLEY, WILLESDEN, HENDON, WALTHAMSTOW and WOODFORD. By what must be pure coincidence, the church in each of these places was called St Mary's. At Finchley a new road helped make the parish's East End (now EAST FINCHLEY) the principal settlement by the 16th century. In Willesden a competing focus of activity grew up at WILLESDEN GREEN, as later did another, at a point between the green and the church that became known as Chapel End. Brent Street became Hendon's commercial hub in the 19th century, relegating Church End to peripheral status. The rise of HOE STREET had the same effect on Walthamstow's Church End, preserving the charm of the locality now better known as WALTHAMSTOW VILLAGE. Woodford was – and to a lesser degree still is – a disparate collection of hamlets and its St Mary's church lay on their southern side.

Waterloo churches *See under* WATERLOO.

Circle line An elongated circuit on the LONDON UNDERGROUND system, coloured yellow on the map. The Circle line connects the central parts of the METROPOLITAN and DISTRICT lines and has no unique stations of its own. The loop has been in existence since 1884. *See also the* LASSO LINE.

circus

Circus, the A nickname for MI6, aka the Secret Intelligence Service, allegedly from CAMBRIDGE CIRCUS, although the organization's headquarters were actually at BROADWAY from 1924 to 1966. The similarity between 'Circus' and 'Service' may have further prompted the name, which was made familiar to the public by the novels of John Le Carré such as *The Honourable Schoolboy* (1977).

Bertram Mills' Circus *See* MILLS, BERTRAM

cispontine (Latin, 'on this side of the bridges') In London, north of the THAMES. This arcane word was occasionally employed to distinguish the theatres of the WEST END from their TRANSPONTINE counterparts.

cit Formerly a slang shortening of 'citizen', usually of London, often used contemptuously of tradesmen and the like, as opposed to gentlemen.

It is not by his liveliness of imagery, his pungency of periods, or his fertility of allusion, that he detains the cits of London, and the boors of Middlesex.

SAMUEL JOHNSON: 'Thoughts on the Late Transactions Respecting Falkland's Islands' (1771)

Citizen Smith The first in a long line of BBC TV sitcoms created by the BALHAM-born writer John Sullivan (b.1946). The protagonist was Walter 'Wolfie' Smith, played by Robert Lindsay, a would-be revolutionary who assembled around himself a handful of misfits known as the TOOTING Popular Front. Smith was wont to utter pithy slogans and catchphrases, such as 'power to the people', 'freedom for Tooting' and 'come the revolution, you'll be first against the wall: bop-bop-bop!' Unlike many such productions, location filming actually took place in the area in which the show was set. *Citizen Smith* first aired from 1977 to 1980.

city

City, the A shorthand way of referring to the CITY OF LONDON, and particularly to the more easterly portion of it, centred on the BANK OF ENGLAND, which concerns itself mainly with business and finance. The usage can be traced back to the early 17th century – a record of House of Commons business in 1621, for instance, notes the comment:

Though money be wanting in the country yet is it in the City ... They of the Citty to lay the riches downe.

The 'City' pages of a newspaper (presided over by the 'City' editor) are where share prices and financial stories and comment are to be found. The City gent, with his inevitable accoutrements – BOWLER hat, pinstripe trousers, tightly furled UMBRELLA – was a familiar sight on the streets of London in the early and middle years of the 20th century, but the more relaxed sartorial conventions of recent times have done away with his uniform, while aggressive trading practices and their consequences have largely done the same to his gentlemanly reputation.

The City empty on a July evening,
All the jam-packed commuters gone, and all
The Wren and Hawksmoor spires and steeples shining
In a honeyed light ...

DONALD DAVIE: 'To Londoners' (1982)

City Airport *See* LONDON CITY AIRPORT.

City & Guilds The City & Guilds of London Institute for the Advancement of Technical Education was established in 1878, following a meeting of 16 of the City of London's LIVERY COMPANIES and the CORPORATION OF LONDON.

The institute set up an art school (*see below*) in KENNINGTON and a technical college in FINSBURY, which subsequently moved to a larger site in SOUTH KENSINGTON. The technical college became part of the Imperial College of Science and Technology, now IMPERIAL COLLEGE LONDON, on its foundation in 1907, while the parent institute continued to promote technical education on a national basis, with a system of qualifying examinations. City & Guilds nowadays offers around 500 qualifications in 28 industry areas and has become the UK's leading vocational awarding body. It also has a presence in almost 100 other countries, with primary overseas hubs in Singapore and Johannesburg.

> Her mother received a City & Guilds qualification for hairdressing. Her father got his City & Guilds certificate for bartending. And yesterday President Mary McAleese received her own award from the vocational education and training body.
>
> *Irish Times* (23 January 2008)

City & Guilds of London Art School A small college teaching the history and the traditional skills of art and craft practice. Since its inception in 1879 it has occupied the same terrace of six 18th-century houses in KENNINGTON.

City Bridge Trust See the BRIDGE HOUSE ESTATES.

City College An old ironic name for NEWGATE PRISON.

City Hall The home of the MAYOR OF LONDON and the LONDON ASSEMBLY, together comprising the GREATER LONDON AUTHORITY. Designed by Norman Foster and completed in 2002, City Hall is situated on the south bank of the THAMES, opposite the TOWER OF LONDON. *See also* EGG, THE (GLASS).

City Lit London's largest adult education centre, founded in 1919 as the City Literary Institute. The institute began by leasing four classrooms at a teacher training college in Greystoke Place, FETTER LANE, acquiring its own home in what is now Stukeley Street, HOLBORN, in 1928. City Lit moved to its present headquarters in Keeley Street, off DRURY LANE, in 2005. Around 25,000 adult learners participate in evening, daytime and weekend courses each year. Among the most popular subjects are photography, massage, creative writing, jewellery, pottery, counselling, web design and acting.

city of cities An immodest nickname occasionally applied to London, but also to other major centres, including Jerusalem, Istanbul, Rome, Paris, New York and more recently Sydney, Australia.

City of London The City extends from CHANCERY LANE in the west to Mansell Street and Middlesex Street (PETTICOAT LANE) in the east. It is bounded by the THAMES to the south and at its northernmost extremity it stops just short of OLD STREET. The Romans appear to have decided to make LONDINIUM their capital soon after invading Britain in AD 43 and built a defensive wall that encompassed 330 acres (134 hectares) on its completion in the 3rd century. With the departure of the Romans early in the 5th century, the Saxons established their main trading settlement in the vicinity of the ALDWYCH and the City fell into decline. The construction of 'old' ST PAUL'S Cathedral in 604 was the first sign of renewed growth and by the 9th century prosperity had returned, with CHEAPSIDE becoming London's high street. Although the Normans made WESTMINSTER their seat of government, William the Conqueror built a castle that later became the TOWER OF LONDON at the south-east corner of the City. Richard I allowed Londoners to choose their own mayor and the GUILDHALL was constructed in the early 15th century as a form of parliament for representatives from the City's merchant guilds. The establishment of the ROYAL EXCHANGE in 1570 consolidated London's role as a leading international trading centre. The BANK OF ENGLAND was founded in 1694 and evolved into the official custodian of the nation's currency over the course of the following century. Other great financial institutions also assumed their modern form during this period, including the insurance brokers LLOYD'S OF LONDON and the main clearing banks. The MANSION HOUSE, the official residence of the LORD MAYOR OF LONDON, was completed in 1752. Britain was relatively unaffected by the wars that blighted Europe for more than two decades from 1792, allowing London to assume an unrivalled position as the mercantile centre of a growing empire. Together with other improvements in transport and increasingly affordable fares, the construction of railways of the mid-19th century stimulated a suburban building boom that allowed an exodus of residents. The destruction wreaked in the BLITZ resulted in the clearance of most of the surviving dwellings and workshops, although the subsequent construction of the BARBICAN brought the return of a residential and cultural aspect. From the late 1980s the regeneration of DOCKLANDS posed the most serious threat to the City's vitality since the Romans left. The CORPORATION OF LONDON reacted by relaxing some of its strict planning controls, improving streetscapes and embarking on a worldwide promotional drive. Despite the loss of some major corporations, construction of new floorspace recovered – most visibly in the form of the GHERKIN – and the City's daytime population remains massive; more than a quarter of a million people commute into the City every day.

City of London Cemetery A cemetery in MANOR PARK. It was founded (in 1856) and is administered by the City of London. It is the largest municipal cemetery in Europe.

City of London Corporation *see the* CORPORATION OF LONDON.

City of London School for Boys A public school in BLACKFRIARS, founded in 1837.

City of London School for Girls A public school in the BARBICAN, founded in 1894.

City of London Theatre A Victorian theatre that specialized in 'domestic and temperance melodrama'. It opened on NORTON FOLGATE in 1837 and closed in 1868.

City of Lushington A convivial club for members of the theatrical profession that met until 1895 at the Harp Tavern on Russell Street, COVENT GARDEN. It was founded some time in the 18th century, perhaps as early as the 1740s but more likely several decades later. The name was probably inspired by the slang word 'lush', meaning 'liquor', although some have suggested that the club came first, or was at least responsible for the later meaning of 'lush': one who is over-fond of drinking. 'Lushington' itself became a slang term for a drunkard in the 19th century. The club's organizing committee consisted of a lord mayor and four aldermen, who represented the 'wards' of Juniper (gin), Poverty, Lunacy and Suicide. A decision in 1822 to restrict membership to actors led stagehands and others to found what became the ROYAL ANTEDILUVIAN ORDER OF BUFFALOES. *See also* ALDERMAN LUSHINGTON IS CONCERNED.

City Road Timber merchant and sawmill pioneer Charles Dingley (d.1769) devised his scheme for a new route linking the CITY of London with the ANGEL, ISLINGTON in the mid-1750s. The road developed as a series of individual sections, which were eventually unified as the City Road in the 1860s.

City Road African A late 19th- and early 20th-century euphemism for a prostitute. It may have reflected the perceived exoticism of the CITY ROAD for those who normally looked for prostitutes in the WEST END.

City Road Basin An arm of the REGENT'S CANAL where timber was once unloaded for finishing in the locality. This area began to be regenerated in the late 1980s.

City sherry An ironic Victorian term for the cheapest sort of ale, which was generally of a muddy consistency.

> The East London people have a modified mistrust of those living amongst them who get their living in the City, especially of the great body of exclusive clerks, whose general poverty they satirise in many ways, of which this is one.
>
> J. REDDING WARE: *Passing English of the Victorian Era* (1908)

City University London A higher-education institution that has close links with the CITY of London, and the incumbent LORD MAYOR as its chancellor, but is actually based just to the north, in Northampton Square, ISLINGTON. Its earliest form of existence was as the Northampton Institute, a local college established in 1894 to promote 'the industrial skill, general knowledge, health and well-being of young men and women belonging to the poorer classes'. In 1966 the college became a university, which in 2008 had 23,835 students from 156 countries.

Civitas Londinum *See the* AGAS MAP.

Clapham A stylish, socially and ethnically mixed neighbourhood situated south-east of BATTERSEA. The name derives from Old English words *cloppa* ('rocks' or 'hills') and *ham* ('a homestead' or 'enclosed pasture'), and was first recorded around 880 in the *Anglo-Saxon Chronicle*. By the 12th century St Paul's Church was the focus of a small village and in the latter part of the 17th century numerous Londoners settled here after plagues and fire ravaged the CITY. The diarist Samuel PEPYS retired to Clapham and died in a house overlooking the common in 1703. Grand houses and terraces filled the Old Town and encircled the common during the 18th century and a new church, Holy Trinity, was built on CLAPHAM COMMON in 1776. In the latter part of the 19th century trains and horse-drawn trams made Clapham accessible to clerks and artisans and its status declined as the population grew. Developers demolished and replaced most of the largest houses. The extension of the City and South London Railway to Clapham Road (now Clapham North station) and Clapham Common in 1900 cemented the change in character. Clapham South station opened in 1926. Following extensive damage during the Second World War, large parts of Clapham were redeveloped in the 1950s and 1960s, mostly with council housing, but many properties survive from the 18th and early 19th centuries.

Clapham Common One of south London's most important open spaces, the common juts into south BATTERSEA from the western side of Clapham. From the time of Domesday Book this has been uncultivated land, split between the manors of Battersea and Clapham. In 1716 tensions over grazing rights erupted into a turf war when Battersea parishioners dug a boundary ditch bisecting the common. Clapham parishioners promptly filled it in. By the mid-18th century the common's edges had become a popular place to build one's country retreat, especially on the north side. Mount Pond had been formed by the extraction of gravel. The American scientist and statesman Benjamin Franklin conducted experiments in pouring oil on troubled water on the pond in 1768. Until the mid-18th century the common remained an important amenity for ordinary people, providing firewood and water as well as pasture for livestock, and even a place to string out a washing line between two trees, but these practices began to die out with the construction of more villas and institutions, especially private girls' schools. Sports clubs established themselves here, including Clapham Golf Club and Clapham Rovers Football Club. In 1877 the METROPOLITAN BOARD OF WORKS acquired Clapham Common from the lords of the manors, relocating a bandstand here from SOUTH KENSINGTON in 1890. A group of houses replaced a grove of chestnut trees behind the Windmill Inn in the 1890s but the common's integrity has otherwise been preserved. Clapham Common now has dozens of pitches for almost every kind of outdoor sport and is a regular venue for fairs,

rallies and concerts. The common's role as an after-dark rendezvous for gay men attracted widespread coverage in 1998 when the secretary of state for Wales, Ron Davies, resigned following an incident here.

Clapham Junction A station, complex railway intersection and shopping area situated in southwest BATTERSEA. When a railway halt opened here in 1846, it was named after the best known of the few buildings on the Old Portsmouth Road, the Falcon Inn. With the multiplication in the number of lines traversing south Battersea, the station was rebuilt in 1863 as Clapham Junction; the choice of name probably resulting from the greater cachet of Clapham as a smart suburb. From the outset Clapham Junction provided links to VICTORIA and WATERLOO stations in London and to most towns in southern England. From the 1880s, cheaper fares made rail travel affordable to labourers and artisans, helping to change the social profile of the neighbourhood. The Falcon was rebuilt as a hotel and the ARDING AND HOBBS department store (now part of the Debenhams group) opened on the opposite corner of the crossroads. Its present appearance dates from 1910. After a very brief period in 2005, when it claimed to be Europe's busiest railway station, Clapham Junction has now reverted to the surer boast that it is Britain's busiest. The station has 16 active platforms and its own retail precinct.

Clapham Sect The name given by the Rev Sydney Smith to a group of evangelicals with common social and political interests, most of whom lived in Clapham in the late 18th and early 19th centuries. William Wilberforce the abolitionist was their leader. Henry Thornton the banker, Zachary Macaulay, John Venn and James Stephen were among his close associates. Its members were 'Claphamites' or, to their derisive opponents, 'the Saints'.

Clapton The north-eastern quadrant of the London Borough of HACKNEY, consisting of Upper Clapton, Lower Clapton, Clapton Park and the Millfields and Springfield Park areas. The name was first recorded in 1339 as Clopton, which meant 'farmstead on a hill'. Clapton's grandest mansion was Brooke House, formerly King's Place. Said to have been a residence of Henry VIII and later home to earls and barons, the house became a lunatic asylum in 1760. It was demolished after the Second World War, having suffered irreparable bomb damage. Many of Clapton's Georgian and Victorian buildings have been supplanted by public housing, either as part of slum clearance programmes or because they were allegedly too large for 20th-century living. Clapton stadium was the home of Clapton (now LEYTON) Orient. Later a dog track, the stadium had given way to housing by 1980.

Clare Market A maze of lanes in CLEMENT'S INN Fields that were used as a food market, named after former landowners the earls of Clare, Nottinghamshire. The market was noted for its cheap cuts of meat and the poverty of its customers. The lanes were destroyed during the creation of KINGSWAY and the ALDWYCH at the beginning of the 20th century. In *Old and New London* (Volume 3, 1878) Walter Thornbury retells the legend of a young man from the country, bearing a black bag, who started one winter night from Portugal Street to get into the STRAND, and wandered round ever after, constantly returning to his starting-point.

> On foggy nights his form may be descried in
> Clare Market. Anyhow, no one has yet heard
> that he ever reached the Strand.

Clarence House A royal residence attached to ST JAMES'S PALACE. It was built in 1825–7 by John Nash for Prince William Henry, Duke of Clarence, who lived there as William IV from 1830 until 1837. Clarence House was the London home of Princess Elizabeth and the Duke of Edinburgh following their marriage in 1947 and of the Queen Mother from 1953 until her death in 2002. It is now the official London residence of the Prince of Wales, the Duchess of Cornwall and Princes William and Harry.

Claridge's The MAYFAIR hotel, associated with the rich and the royal, has its origins in a small hotel in BROOK STREET, which was bought in the mid-19th century by William Claridge, a butler in a royal household. In 1855 he acquired the neighbouring Mivart's Hotel, and this, in rebuilt and extended form, was the physical building from which sprang the present grand edifice.

Clash, The A rock quartet formed in LADBROKE GROVE in 1976. The Clash were pioneers of PUNK ROCK but their music soon evolved to shrug off the confines of the genre and their lyrics were

perhaps the most political of any highly successful band. Many of their songs, mostly composed by lead guitarist Mick Jones (b.1955) and vocalist and rhythm guitarist Joe Strummer (1952–2002), concerned aspects of life in London. Among these were 'CAPITAL RADIO' and 'London's Burning' (both 1977), '(White Man) In Hammersmith Palais' (1978), and 'LONDON CALLING' and the Paul Simonon composition 'The Guns of Brixton' (both 1979).

Clean Air Act *See the* GREAT SMOG.

clearing house An institution which 'clears' or cancels the amounts owed between banks (as a result of various cheques drawn on their accounts) so that only one sum need be paid by one bank to another. LOMBARD STREET was the home of the English clearing house from about 1770 to 1994, at first operating out of the Five Bells tavern and then in a purpose-built centre from 1833.
clearing house of the world The SQUARE MILE, in former times. Nowadays it shares the role with New York and Tokyo. Other serious rivals include Shanghai, Mumbai and Frankfurt.

> Provided that the City of London remains, as
> it is at present, the clearing house of the world,
> any other nation may be its workshop.
>
> JOSEPH CHAMBERLAIN: speech at the Guildhall (19 January 1904)

Clement's Inn A former INN OF CHANCERY, attached to the INNER TEMPLE. It lay in the parish of ST CLEMENT DANES, from which it took its name. The inn was demolished in the early 1880s. SHAKESPEARE made two of his comic characters belong to Clement's Inn: Sir John Falstaff and Justice Shallow.

> I do remember him at Clement's Inn, like a man
> made after supper of a cheese-paring. [Falstaff
> of Shallow]
>
> *Henry IV, Part 2*, III, ii (*c.*1597)

Cleopatra's Needle A granite monolith shipped from Egypt and erected opposite Victoria EMBANKMENT Gardens in 1878. This had been hewn around 1475 BC and carved with the names of gods and pharaohs, with Cleopatra's name added later. At 68½ feet (21m) in height, it is Britain's tallest obelisk cut from a single block of stone. George Vulliamy bracketed the needle with bronze sphinxes in 1880. It is said that they were supposed to face inwards but the workmen mounted them the wrong way round; however, stories of a similar kind are told about other such installations.

> Ye giant shades of Ra and Tum,
> Ye ghosts of gods Egyptian,
> If murmurs of our planet come
> To exiles in the precincts wan
> Where, fetish or Olympian,
> To help or harm no more ye list,
> Look down, if look ye may, and scan
> This monument in London mist!
>
> ANDREW LANG: 'Ballade of Cleopatra's Needle' (1880)

Clerkenwell A former monastic settlement located between KING'S CROSS and the CITY of London. Around 1140 Jordan de Briset and his wife donated land for a priory for the KNIGHTS HOSPITALLER, dedicated to St John, and the nunnery of St Mary. The sisters of the convent drew their water from a well that became known as the clerks' well because City students performed an annual miracle play close by. The nunnery's buildings were also demolished after the Dissolution but the clerks' well can still be seen through the window of an office block on Farringdon Lane. Parts of St John's Priory have survived and a revived 'venerable order' (of which the health care organization St John Ambulance is an offshoot) later returned to St John's Gate, where it maintains its headquarters and a museum. From medieval times Clerkenwell attracted edge-of-City trades like jewellery, lock-making, printing, bookbinding, and the making and repair of clocks and watches – and there are still practitioners of several of these crafts here today. When many larger firms closed or moved out to suburban industrial estates, they left behind factories and warehouses that have now been converted for 'loft-style living'.

Clerkenwell had a murky side too, and the House of Detention, formerly an underground prison, and the Old Sessions House (see X'S HALL) survive from its period as a den of thieves and receivers, pickpockets and coiners. In the 19th century the district was said to have the highest murder rate in London. George Gissing depicted the underbelly of Clerkenwell in his novel *The Nether World* (1889).

Clerkenwell Explosion An explosive incident on Friday 13 December 1867, the result of a Fenian attempt to free one of their number from the House of Detention, using 548 lb (247kg) of gunpowder. The explosive blew a huge hole in the prison wall, and killed six and maimed and injured others living in nearby tenements in Corporation Road. As with Irish Republican attacks on the British capital more than a century later, it caused outrage and panic. It has been claimed that the pejorative term 'Mick' for an Irishman came into currency following the public hanging at NEWGATE on 26 May 1868 of the Fenian Michael Barrett (the last such in Britain) for his supposed role in the incident.

Clerkenwell Tales, The A story of medieval murder and religious intrigue (2003) by Peter Ackroyd, narrated by characters borrowed from Chaucer's *The Canterbury Tales*.

Cleveland Street A predominantly commercial thoroughfare in FITZROVIA, built between 1745 and 1770 on land owned by Charles Fitzroy, Duke of Southampton, son of the Duchess of Cleveland. The PRE-RAPHAELITE BROTHERHOOD grew out of a studio-sharing arrangement at 7 Cleveland Street. The street is nowadays best known as the address of the BT TOWER.

Cleveland Street scandal A society scandal of 1889, when a male brothel was discovered operating in Cleveland Street. The brothel came to light when police investigating a theft at a post and telegraph office came across a teenage delivery boy with 18 shillings in his pocket – a larger amount than someone in his position might be expected to carry. When questioned, the boy revealed that he and others had been moonlighting as rent boys from 19 Cleveland Street. It soon emerged that several highly placed men, including Lord Arthur Somerset (supervisor of the Prince of Wales's stables) and the Earl of EUSTON, were clients of the Cleveland Street operation. There were rumours that the Duke of Clarence, Prince Albert Victor ('Eddy'), the eldest son of the Prince of Wales, was another client.

Clifford's Inn The oldest of the INNS OF CHANCERY, attached to the INNER TEMPLE. Located off FLEET STREET, the inn was first let to law students in 1344 by Isabel, the widow of Robert de Clifford. After the GREAT FIRE OF LONDON the FIRE JUDGES sat here to settle land ownership disputes. The writers Virginia and Leonard Woolf moved into No.13 Clifford's Inn soon after their marriage in 1912. Except for a gatehouse, the buildings of the inn were demolished in 1934 and replaced by an office block. *See also the* HERMIT OF CLIFFORD'S INN; KENTISH MESS.

Climthorpe *See the* FALL AND RISE OF REGINALD PERRIN; POETS' CORNER (2).

clink A slang word for a prison, derived from the Clink gaol on SOUTHWARK'S BANKSIDE, destroyed in the GORDON RIOTS of 1780. The prison itself may have been so called because its gates clinked shut on the prisoner, or from the sound of prisoners' chains or warders' keys. In the Middle Ages the surrounding area was the London estate of the bishops of Winchester, which was called the Liberty of the Clink. As well as Winchester House, the bishops' palace, the area had a healthy population of inns, brothels and places of entertainment, and, like other LIBERTIES, it was inhabited by every kind of rogue and vagabond.

clinker A denizen of the Liberty of the Clink.

Clio Joseph Addison (1672–1719) adopted the name of the Greek muse as a pseudonym, and many of his papers in *The Spectator* are signed by one of the four letters in this word, allegedly the initial letters of the places where they were written: CHELSEA, London, ISLINGTON or the Office.

clip

clip joint A night club or place of entertainment where patrons are lured by the false promise of a live show or sexual services from 'hostesses' and then grossly overcharged or 'clipped'. The word alludes to the former practice of clipping gold and silver coins before passing them on. Such premises are generally unlicensed and often provide imitations of alcoholic drinks. SOHO has historically had a notorious reputation for such establishments but very few remain nowadays.

> I met her in a club down in old Soho
> Where you drink champagne and it tastes just
> like cherry cola
>
> RAY DAVIES: 'Lola' (song by the Kinks) (1970)

clippies Bus conductresses in London and other large cities first gained this nickname in the Second World War when they took over the clipping of tickets from male conductors.

Clissold Park A much-loved 55-acre (22.5-hectare) park located in north-west STOKE NEWINGTON. The METROPOLITAN BOARD OF WORKS bought the former home of the Rev Augustus Clissold in 1887 and laid out its grounds as a park. Joseph Beck and John Runtz were leading proponents of the purchase and the park's twin lakes were named Beckmere and Runtzmere in their honour. Ernest Raymond's *We, The Accused* (1935) was described by John Betjeman as 'the greatest London novel … murder and autumnal mists in Clissold Park', though George Orwell thought it clumsy and long-winded.

clobber Originally clothes, especially stylish clothes, and later, ones accoutrements generally. The term probably spread into general usage from the EAST END Jewish tailoring trade, where 'clobbering' was the renovation of worn-out garments.

> 'Get ready, I'll pop home and get some clobber together …'
> 'He'll put on his *evening* duffel coat,' Russell commented.
>
> MAURICE GRAN and LAURENCE MARKS: *Holding the Fort* (1982)

clock The tale about ST PAUL'S clock striking 13 is given in Mackenzie Walcott's *Memorials of Westminster* (1849), and refers to John Hatfield, a soldier of William III's reign who died in 1770, aged 102. Accused before a court martial of falling asleep on duty on Windsor Terrace, he asserted in proof of his innocence that he heard St Paul's strike 13. His statement was confirmed by several witnesses.

Another incident is related concerning BIG BEN. On the morning of Thursday, 14 March 1861, 'the inhabitants of WESTMINSTER were roused by repeated strokes of the new great bell, and most persons supposed it was for the death of a member of the royal family. It proved, however, to be due to some derangement of the clock, for at four and five o'clock ten and twelve strokes were struck instead of the proper number.' Within 24 hours of this the Duchess of Kent (Queen Victoria's mother) was declared to be dying, and early on 16 March she was dead.

clockwork orange *See* AS QUEER AS A CLOCKWORK ORANGE.

Clowns' Service A church service held annually in memory of the 'King of Clowns' and 'Michelangelo of Buffoonery', Joseph Grimaldi (1778–1837). Born in CLARE MARKET, of Anglo-Italian parentage, Grimaldi performed hundreds of times in Christmas pantomimes at the THEATRE ROYAL, DRURY LANE, where his stylistic innovations did much to define the art of modern clowning. A BLUE PLAQUE marks the house in EXMOUTH MARKET where he lived for ten years. He died in poverty after prolonged ill-heath and was buried at the church of St James, PENTONVILLE. An annual memorial service began there in 1946 and ten years later moved to Holy Trinity, DALSTON, where it is still held on the first Sunday in February, with many costumed clowns in attendance.

club[1] In London, the club has played an important part in social life. John Aubrey (1626–97) says 'we now used the word clubbe for a sodality in a taverne'. Some of the earliest clubs were political, such as the ROTA, the OCTOBER, the GREEN RIBBON and the eccentric CALVES' HEAD CLUB. Clubs came into vogue in the reign of Queen Anne (1702–14) as is evidenced by *Tatler* and *The Spectator*. Samuel JOHNSON's Ivy Lane Club (1749) and the Literary Club (1764), which he founded with Sir Joshua Reynolds, set a new standard in social clubs where like-minded men of culture could meet and converse. The latter included Edmund Burke, David GARRICK, Oliver Goldsmith and James Boswell among its members. For many years clubs met in taverns and COFFEE HOUSES and did not begin to occupy their own premises until the Regency (1811–20). Very soon many new clubs sprang up, with some, such as CROCKFORD'S, being solely gaming houses. The first exclusive modern ladies' club was the ALEXANDRA (1883), to which no man was allowed admittance. Among the principal London clubs still flourishing in the early 21st century (with the dates of their foundation) are the following:

Army and Navy: 1837	Lansdowne: 1934
ATHENAEUM: 1824	National Liberal: 1882
BEEFSTEAK: 1876	Pratt's: 1841
BOODLE'S: 1762	Reform: 1836
BROOKS'S: 1764	Savage: 1857
BUCK'S: 1919	Savile: 1868
CARLTON: 1832	Travellers': 1819
GARRICK: 1831	WHITE'S: 1693
GROUCHO: 1985	

Some well-known clubs have merged. In 1976 the Guards Club moved to the home of the Cavalry Club to form the Cavalry and Guards Club. The United Service Club and the Royal Aero Club merged with the Naval and Military in 1976,

retaining the name of the latter (*see* IN AND OUT). Others have closed.

Among the well-known clubs associated with sport are:

MCC: 1787	Royal Automobile: 1897
ROEHAMPTON: 1901	Turf: 1868

clubland Originally, a collective term for the gentlemen's clubs of the WEST END, concentrated mainly in ST JAMES'S STREET and PALL MALL.

> He was only a junior minister at the Ministry of Information and was presumably only relating Whitehall or Clubland gossip.
>
> DAVID REYNOLDS: *Lord Lothian and Anglo-American Relations, 1939–1940* (1983)

club[2] The definitive weapon of choice of London APPRENTICES, carried over the shoulder and employed both to instigate trouble and to separate combatants. The cry 'clubs!' often went up when a brawl broke out.

> Clubs, clubs! these lovers will not keep the peace.
>
> SHAKESPEARE: *Titus Andronicus*, II, i (*c.*1593)

Coade stone An artificial stone of great durability and firmness of outline, much used from the 1770s until the 1830s for statues and ornamentations for buildings (keystone masks, friezes, vases, etc.). It was made from a kind of frost-resistant terracotta and was produced in Mrs Eleanor Coade's factory at LAMBETH (later the firm of Coade and Sealy). The SOUTH BANK LION is an example of its use. The secret of its manufacture has been lost.

coat and badge 'Cadge' in COCKNEY RHYMING SLANG. *See* DOGGETT'S COAT AND BADGE.

cobbler

cobblers 'Balls' in COCKNEY RHYMING SLANG, almost certainly via a contraction of 'cobblers' awls'. An awl is a sharp-pointed hand tool for making holes in leather. Like the word 'balls' itself, 'cobblers' is employed both to mean 'testicles' and as an emphatic expression of disbelief. In common with other well-established rhymes for vulgarities, it is considered less offensive than the word it signifies, and many users are not even aware of the link. It is heard throughout much of the English-speaking world, notably in South Africa.

> People in Britain think 'oh all this money that

could have been spent on hospitals'. That is a load of cobblers. There was no resource loss to the economy in the longer term.

LORD LAMONT, interviewed in *The Guardian* (16 September 2001)

Cobbler's Way The earls of Halifax beautified BUSHY PARK in the early 18th century but also enclosed it with a wall. A footpath named Cobbler's Way recalls Timothy Bennet's successful campaign in the early 1750s to regain access for the public; the HAMPTON WICK shoemaker was so pleased with his achievement that he wrote a play on the subject.

Cochran revues The impresario Charles Blake Cochran (1872–1951) started his career in the United States but back in England soon became famous for his intimate revues, beginning with *Odds and Ends* (1914) at the Ambassadors Theatre. In 1918 he began a remarkable run of revues at the London Pavilion, including Noël Coward's *On With the Dance* (1925) and *This Year of Grace* (1928). The former was the first to star Cochran's famous 'Young Ladies'. His revues were distinctive from those of the Edwardian era in that they relied more on witty dialogue than on dress and dancing.

cock

cock and hen 'Ten' in COCKNEY RHYMING SLANG.

cock-er-nee A jocular spelling of 'COCKNEY', exaggeratedly imitating the way in which working-class Londoners supposedly articulate the word.

What gives the Dickensian-era grammar an absurd feel is the desperately arcane vocabulary, where words from 'bagatelle' to 'trachea' gleam amidst the cock-er-nee syntax like big, shiny badges of the intellect.

TIM BLACK, at www.spiked-online.com (January 2009)

Cock Lane A short street connecting SNOW HILL and GILTSPUR STREET in SMITHFIELD. The name was first recorded around 1200, and probably signified a lane where fighting cocks were reared and/or sold. In the late Middle Ages Cock Lane was the only place north of the THAMES where brothels – or 'stews' – were legally sanctioned. William Langland's *Vision of Piers Plowman* (late 14th century) contains a reference to one 'Clarisse of Cokkes lone'.

Cock Lane ghost Probably London's most notorious spectral hoax. In 1762 mysterious knockings were heard at 33 Cock Lane, which William Parsons, the owner, said came from the ghost of his sister-in-law, Fanny Kent, who had recently died of smallpox. Parsons, with the hope of blackmail, wished people to think that she had been poisoned by her husband. All London was agog with the story. Royalty and the nobility made up parties to go to Cock Lane to hear the ghost. Dr JOHNSON and other learned people investigated the alleged phenomena. Eventually it was found that the knockings were made by Parsons' 11-year-old daughter rapping on a board that she took into her bed. Parsons was condemned to the pillory, but was said to have been treated kindly there by sympathetic locals who may have still believed there was something in the story. *See also the* STOCKWELL GHOST.

cock linnet 'Minute' in COCKNEY RHYMING SLANG, in the sense of the period of time. Also, former EAST END slang for a 'dapper boy'. The male linnet (*Carduelis cannabina*) was formerly prized as a caged bird because of its sweet singing voice and it features in one of the most famous of all cockney MUSIC HALL songs:

My old man said, 'Follow the van,
Don't dilly-dally on the way!'
Off went the cart with the home packed in it,
I walked behind with me old cock linnet.

CHARLES COLLINS and FRED W. LEIGH: 'Don't Dilly-Dally on the Way' (1919)

Cock of Westminster The sobriquet of Richard Castell (*alias* Casteller, d.1554), from his habit of beginning his labours by 4 o'clock every morning. Castell was a humble shoemaker but through hard work and frugal living he amassed sufficient savings to acquire land and buildings in WESTMINSTER that provided an income of £44 a year. With the consent of his wife – 'who survived him and was a virtuous good woman', according to John Stow – he bequeathed the Westminster properties to Christ's Hospital (*see the* BLUECOAT SCHOOL). In subsequent years they greatly increased in value and beneficially contributed to the institution's finances in the latter part of the 16th century.

Cockaigne An imaginary land of idleness and luxury, famous in medieval European folklore. London has been so called, with punning reference to COCKNEY, but contrary to past supposition there is no etymological connection between the two words. Edward Elgar's boisterous concert overture 'Cockaigne' is subtitled 'In London Town'. It was first performed in 1901 and was intended to be an evocation of Edwardian London.

Cockfosters 'A metropolitan blend of open spaces, excellent facilities and easy commuting', according to a recent property developer's blurb, located at the northern end of the PICCADILLY LINE. In the 16th century this was the 'cock forester's estate', 'cock' meaning head or chief. A LINCOLN'S INN barrister owned a house called Cockfosters in 1613 and a small group of cottages and houses had formed by 1754. The estate of Trent Park, now a MIDDLESEX UNIVERSITY campus, was created when ENFIELD CHASE was enclosed and Cockfosters found itself standing near the main gate. Consequently, its growth from the end of the 18th century (when the Cock Inn was established) was in many ways as a service village for the Trent Park estate. After the Piccadilly line arrived in 1933 Cockfosters was quickly built up south of the station and spread west to meet NEW BARNET. When housebuilding resumed after the Second World War it was constrained by the new GREEN BELT regulations, so suburban expansion came to an abrupt halt north of the station.

Osbert Sitwell, the poet and short-story writer, was educated at Ludgrove School, which he loathed. John Betjeman, poet laureate from 1972 until his death in 1984, taught at Heddon Court School from April 1929 to July 1930. He later recalled this period in his poem 'Cricket Master'.

cockney or **Cockney** A Londoner, especially one BORN WITHIN (THE) SOUND OF BOW BELLS. Adjectivally, the word can mean 'pertaining to London, or Londoners, especially working-class Londoners'. The term is primarily associated with those who speak with the characteristic London dialect or accent, with its rhyming slang, dropped 'h', substitution of a glottal stop for a 't', pronunciation of 'th' as 'f' or 'v' and many distinctive vowel sounds. The derivation of the word 'cockney' continues to provoke debate. In Middle English, *cokeney* meant both a 'cock's egg' (a small, malformed egg; hence, loosely, some kind of oddity) and a pampered, 'cockered' child (later also said of an effeminate man, and later still of a 'soft' townsperson, typically a Londoner, in contrast to those who made their living from

the land). The latter meaning is the accepted origin of 'cockney' and was thought by some to have derived from the former. However, modern lexicographers have tended to disconnect the two medieval meanings, and there is a growing consensus that no link exists between cockneys and cocks' eggs. Other discredited explanations include an association with COCKAIGNE and a convoluted story about a Londoner who visits the country and hears a horse 'laugh', whereupon he is told that the correct word is 'neigh'; soon afterwards a cock crows and he shows off his new-found learning by remarking, 'did you hear that cock neigh?' Although this tale is much told in old books, it is doubtful whether anyone has ever believed that the incident took place, let alone that it could be the true derivation of the word 'cockney'. *See also* ESTUARY ENGLISH; MOCKNEY.

Cockney College An early nickname bestowed by the Tory press upon London University, now UNIVERSITY COLLEGE LONDON, because it aimed to extend the availability of higher education beyond the upper classes, who at that time dominated the intake of Oxford and Cambridge universities.

cockneydom or **cockneyland** The domain of cockneys.

> People who have moved along the railway lines to Leyton and Walthamstow have themselves repudiated Cockneydom and are anxious ... to dissociate from the East End.
>
> ROBERT BARLTROP and JIM WOLVERIDGE: *The Muvver Tongue* (1980)

cockneyess A rarely used term for a female Londoner, mostly employed with jocular intent.

> Her step even was that of a lady, having neither the mincing tread of a Paris grisette, a manner that sometimes ascends even to the bourgeoise, the march of a cockneyess, nor the tiptoe swing of a belle ...
>
> JAMES FENIMORE COOPER: *Home as Found* (1838)

cockneyfy To imbue with cockney qualities; to exert a London influence. Said especially in the context of accents, culture or landscape, and often used derogatorily, almost as a synonym for 'vulgarize'. William Cobbett and Henry James were among the authors to regret the 'cockneyfication' of much of southern England.

> As the member of Blur chary of selling records, guitarist Graham Coxon became their

conscience. Admirably, this halted Damon Albarn's cockneyfication, but it also meant the career nadir that was Beetlebum.

The Guardian (3 August 2001)

cockneyism A cockney idiom or characteristic.

cockney mafia A derogatory nickname invented in 2008 by supporters of Newcastle United FC for the club's senior management of the time, notably the owner Mike Ashley and director of football Dennis Wise. Pictures of fans holding up a large 'cockney mafia out' banner at a home game were widely reproduced in the media. Ashley and Wise originate from Buckinghamshire and KENSINGTON respectively, prompting debate about how far the definition of the word 'cockney' could be stretched.

cockney paradise The term was applied to numerous leisure resorts during the Victorian era. These included EPPING FOREST, several spas and tea gardens on the fringes of the metropolis and, after the coming of the railways, the seaside playgrounds of Southend and BRIGHTON. In other contexts, 'cockney paradise' can refer to London itself, or an idealized version of it. William Morris used the term dismissively to describe the utopian world evoked by Edward Bellamy in his novel *Looking Backward* (1888). Bellamy's vision was set in Boston, Massachusetts; for Morris 'cockney' simply meant 'pretentiously vulgar'.

Cockney Rejects A PUNK ROCK band with EAST END connections, formed in 1979. They were at the forefront of the aggressively proletarian sub-genre known as 'Oi!' and had a minor hit in 1980 with a characteristically rough version of I'M FOREVER BLOWING BUBBLES, the anthem of WEST HAM UNITED FC.

cockney rhyming slang An argot in which various everyday words – mostly nouns – are replaced by a rhyming phrase. The rhyming part of the phrase is then usually dropped, making it difficult for the uninitiated to determine the meaning. For example, in probably the best-known instance, 'apples' equates to 'stairs' because the latter rhymes with 'apples and pears'. The names or nicknames of former celebrities have been employed in the same way, especially where the person has a distinctive first name. Thus to be 'on one's tod' is to be alone, or on one's own, from the late 19th-century jockey Tod Sloan. Several terms depend on distinctively cockney pronunciation to work as a perfect rhyme, such as 'corned beef' (shortened to corns) for 'teeth' or 'burnt cinder' for 'window'. The language evolved among street traders in the mid-19th century (perhaps specifically the mid-1840s, in the vicinity of SEVEN DIALS) and grew in popularity as a successor to BACK-SLANG, which was widely used by London's thousands of COSTERMONGERS. Recorded examples of early usage are rare, as it was almost exclusively an oral tradition, and it remains much more common in speech than in print.

It is often said that cockney rhyming slang was a thieves' language, which aimed to befuddle any policeman or other outsider who might overhear a conspiratorial conversation but this is doubtful as the vocabulary was quickly acquired by local BOBBIES and others with a need to know. Nevertheless, part of its appeal was undoubtedly the sense of exclusive community that it fostered among its speakers. High-profile cockney comedians gave it new life in the late 1930s, as did military usage during the Second World War. Rhyming slang long ago spread beyond London; Glaswegians and Liverpudlians have numerous terms of their own, while vocabularies have also developed in other English-speaking countries, especially Australia, where cockneys may have taken their slang as early as the gold rush of the 1850s. However, it is most entrenched in London and, while dozens of cockney rhyming slang terms have entered the wider English language, hundreds more remain understood only by Londoners. Fresh coinages seem to appear almost daily but the latest additions are more likely to be the invention of students rather than cockneys and frequently involve references to alcoholic beverages. Stella Artois lager, for example, has been rhymed with Cinderella, Nelson Mandela, Uri Geller and several other characters. The drug-taking fraternity also possesses an extensive rhyming slang vocabulary.

Cockney School A nickname given by John Gibson Lockhart (1794–1854) to a supposed school of writers belonging to London, including Leigh Hunt, William Hazlitt, Percy Bysshe Shelley and John Keats. Writing in *Blackwood's Edinburgh Magazine*, Lockhart poured scorn on the 'cockneys' for what he perceived as their 'low birth and low habits' (Shelley excepted), their vulgarity and liberalism, and the kind of rhymes the poets used in their verse, which smacked too much of everyday life instead of the classic purity preferred by the critics. Lockhart's brutal hostility to the Cockney School led in February 1821 to the arrangement of a duel in CHALK FARM between John Scott, editor of the *London Magazine*, and Jonathan Henry Christie, representative of *Blackwood's*, in which Scott was mortally wounded. Christie and his second were tried for murder and acquitted.

> If I may be permitted to have the honour of christening it, it may be henceforth referred to by the designation of the 'Cockney School'.
>
> JOHN LOCKHART: in *Blackwood's Edinburgh Magazine* (October 1817)

Cockney-shire London.
cockney's luxury Breakfast in bed and defecation in a chamber-pot. A slang term occasionally heard between the late 19th century and the 1950s.
cockney sparrow See SPARROW.
Crafty Cockney See the CRAFTY COCKNEY.
king of cockneys See under KING.

cocoa
Cocoa Tree A coffee and chocolate house that stood in PALL MALL in the early 18th century. It was frequented almost exclusively by Tories and later evolved into a gaming house and club.
(coffee and) cocoa 'Say so' in COCKNEY RHYMING SLANG, in a rare example of abbreviation to the last rather than first word of the full term. It is frequently heard in the emphatic expression 'I should cocoa!' and very often used in an ironic or sarcastic context.

> My heart was full of righteous indignation and my head was full of empty spaces. Accordingly, I protested. No dice, I said, not on, get away, I should cocoa ... absolutely not.
>
> ROBERT MCLIAM WILSON: *Ripley Bogle* (1989)

coffee
(coffee and) cocoa See under COCOA.
coffee house The first coffee house in London was opened *c.*1652 by the ex-servant of an importer of Turkish produce. It stood in St Michael's Alley, CORNHILL. Similar establishments soon sprang up all across the CITY, becoming centres for social and political gossip and meeting places for the wits and literary figures of the day, who ignored the assertion in 'The Women's Petition against Coffee' (1674) that the drink made men 'as unfruitful as the deserts whence that unhappy

berry is said to be brought'. *See also* BALTIC; CLUB; DON SALTERO'S; LLOYD'S; TOM'S; WHITE'S.

> For men and Christians to turn Turks, and think
> To excuse the crime, because 'tis in their drink!
> Pure English apes! ye may, for aught I know,
> Would it but mode – learn to eat spiders too.
>
> ANON: 'A cup of Coffee, or Coffee in its colours' (1663)

Cokey Stokey A little-used nickname for STOKE NEWINGTON. It puns on the HOKEY-COKEY dance and the locality's reputation for the usage of cocaine, among other drugs. In some contexts the nickname specifically refers to Stoke Newington police station, which was the centre of a drugs-related corruption scandal in the early 1990s. Several officers were convicted of trafficking, planting evidence and perverting the course of justice and the local drugs squad was disbanded.

Cold Bath Fields or **Coldbath Fields** A district of CLERKENWELL so called from the cold baths established there in 1697 for the cure of rheumatism, convulsions and other nervous disorders. The fields were renowned for the prison that was opened there in 1794 and closed in 1877. With accommodation for 1,800 inmates, it was the largest British jail of its time. Leigh Hunt's brother, John, was an inmate from 1813 to 1815, for his part in an article ridiculing the Prince REGENT. The Post Office acquired the disused prison, rebuilding it as MOUNT PLEASANT sorting office. Cold Bath Fields was the site of a protest meeting in 1833 at which a policeman was stabbed to death, yet the inquest jury returned a verdict of justifiable homicide.

Coleman Street A CITY of London street and a ward encompassing MOORGATE and its hinterland. The street was probably so called for its charcoal burners and gave its name to the ward around 1224. The parish church of St Stephen was destroyed in the BLITZ and not rebuilt. The ward has very few residential properties but is among the City's most crowded with businesses, bars and restaurants.

Coleville An informal name given in the later part of the 19th century to the complex of museums, colleges, schools, concert halls and premises for learned societies in SOUTH KENSINGTON that arose at that time at the behest of Prince ALBERT, the Prince Consort. It honours

Sir Henry Cole (1808–82), the art expert and administrator who implemented much of Albert's plan and who became the first director of the VICTORIA AND ALBERT MUSEUM. *See also* ALBERTOPOLIS.

Colindale A commercial zone strung out along the A5 south of EDGWARE. The name probably derives from 16th-century residents, the Colinn family. The settlement took root at the end of the 19th century, near the older but now-lost hamlet of Colindeep. On Colindale Avenue is the Health Protection Agency's Centre for Infections, formerly the Central Public Health Laboratory, the national base for infectious disease surveillance and specialist microbiology and epidemiology. Prompted by his acquaintance with the station as an airman at Hendon, T.E. Lawrence ('Lawrence of Arabia') adopted the pseudonym 'Colin Dale' when writing reviews for *The Spectator*.

Coliseum A capacious WEST END theatre on St Martin's Lane, designed by Frank Matcham (1854–1920) and opened in 1904. From 1968 it was the home of the SADLER'S WELLS Opera Company and then of its successor, ENGLISH NATIONAL OPERA. The building's most instantly recognizable external feature is the globe with which it is surmounted; this used to revolve, but WESTMINSTER council put a stop to such frivolity.

Coliseum of west London A nickname given to the Empire Theatre, SHEPHERD'S BUSH, in its early years, on account of its relative grandeur in a mainly poor area. Opened in 1903 as a MUSIC HALL, the theatre later belonged to the BBC and is now a live music venue.

college In old slang a prison was known as a college, and the prisoners as collegiates. NEWGATE was 'City College' or 'New College' and to take one's final degree at New College was to be hanged. The KING'S BENCH PRISON was 'King's College' and so on.

college cove A prisoner warder, especially one at NEWGATE.

The college cove has numbered him, and if he is knocked down he'll be twisted; the turnkey of Newgate has told the judge how many times the prisoner has been tried before, and therefore if he is found guilty, he certainly will be hanged.

FRANCIS GROSE, HEWSON CLARKE and
GEORGE CRUIKSHANK: *Lexicon Balatronicum* (1811)

College Green A small grassy open space in front of WESTMINSTER ABBEY, favoured by television journalists for conducting interviews with politicians. The name derives from the abbey's formal designation, the Collegiate Church of St Peter in Westminster.

collier In the vicinity of medieval London, and in the context of its place names, a collier was a charcoal burner, not a coal miner, making his living from the forests that once covered great swathes of what is now OUTER LONDON. *See also* GRIM, THE COLLYER OF CROYDONE.

Collier Row The northernmost extent of ROMFORD's mini-conurbation. Colliers were active here in the 15th and 16th centuries, working in the forest that then filled most of the manor of Gobions, also known as Uphavering. Until the opening of the Eastern Avenue in 1925, Collier Row remained a rural village, surrounded by fields of clover and hay. The improved access to London, combined with the outward growth of Romford, was the impetus for a major programme of speculative construction that lasted until after the outbreak of the Second World War.

Colliers Wood A former industrial village hemmed in by MERTON and TOOTING GRAVENEY. The name was first recorded in 1632. By the early 19th century, mills beside the River WANDLE were switching from grinding corn to printing textiles, an industry that soon employed the bulk of the local labour force. Housing began to fill the area from the 1870s and builders squeezed in a last few pebble-dashed and mock-Tudor properties after the LONDON UNDERGROUND system was extended here in 1926.

Collins's Music Hall An enlarged public house on ISLINGTON GREEN that began to operate as a MUSIC HALL in 1863. It was the creation of the entertainer 'Sam Collins', who by day was a chimney sweep named Samuel Vagg (1825–65). The hall was rebuilt in 1897 as the Collins Theatre of Varieties (later the Islington Hippodrome). Most of the theatre was destroyed by fire in 1958 and a Waterstone's bookshop now occupies its site. A new mixed-use development with an underground auditorium named Collins Theatre was expected to open nearby in 2010, but aspects of the project have been beset by delays.

Colney Hatch A recently transformed residential locality situated south of FRIERN BARNET, formerly famous for its enormous mental hospital. Colney Hatch was a hamlet in 1409 and the hatch may have been a gate providing access to Hollick Wood. In 1831 Colney Hatch had 33 inhabited houses but the hamlet was soon to be overwhelmed when it was chosen as the site for the new Middlesex County Lunatic Asylum. Built in 1851 in the style of an Italian monastery, Colney Hatch asylum had its own gasworks, shoemakers, brewery, bakery and farm and became the best-known institution of its kind in the London area. It was the largest mental hospital in Europe and at one time housed 3,000 patients. The asylum was renamed Friern Hospital in 1937. It closed in 1993 and a flock of developers descended on the site, now renamed Princess Park Manor. The main building has been converted into hundreds of luxury flats and many more big detached houses have been built in the grounds.

Colney (Hatch) 'Match' in old COCKNEY RHYMING SLANG, in the sense of the incendiary implement.

Colney Hatch for you! A catchphrase employed from the late 19th century to light-heartedly suggest that the addressee was mad. Variations on the theme could still be heard long after the former 'lunatic asylum' changed its name to Friern Hospital in 1937.

Colosseum An exhibition hall at REGENT'S PARK designed by Decimus Burton (1800–81) and completed in 1829 (although it opened earlier, owing to financial pressures). Its main attraction was a PANORAMA of London seen from the top of ST PAUL'S Cathedral, which filled nearly an acre (4,000 sq m) of canvas. The Colosseum was demolished in 1875 and replaced by Cambridge Gate.

Columbia Road A horticultural market area in BETHNAL GREEN. There has been a market in what is now Columbia Road almost since Bethnal Green came into existence and in 1869 the philanthropist Baroness Burdett-Coutts initiated the construction of a grand edifice, not unlike ST PANCRAS STATION in appearance, to house the purveyors of affordable fresh food to the people of the EAST END. The project was not a success and traders soon returned to their less-regulated street pitches, which the local residents preferred. The Columbia Market building was subsequently put to a variety of uses,

including cabinet-making workshops for Jewish immigrants. The magnificent Gothic fantasy was demolished in 1958. The presence of a strong Jewish community enabled the market to obtain a Sunday licence, as was the case for PETTICOAT LANE, and as Sunday trading became established the weekday market died out. From as early as 1927 various influences pushed Columbia Road towards a specialization in flowers and plants, which has continued to the present day.

Comical House A nickname for Stone House, which was the first significant building in the St Johns area of LEWISHAM. The name derived from the floridly church-like style employed by the architect George Gibson, who built the place for his own use in 1773. The building has recently been restored.

Commercial Road An EAST END highway connecting WHITECHAPEL with LIMEHOUSE and comprising the westernmost section of the A13. During the 19th century this important road had the distinction of bearing the heaviest volume of traffic of any thoroughfare in the world. It was made in 1803 to provide a direct link between the CITY and the new docks at BLACKWALL. Then came the EAST INDIA DOCK Road and, a few years later, the Barking Road. The completion of an iron bridge over the River LEA also made the Commercial Road into the main route between London and Tilbury.

common

common as cat-shit and twice as nasty, as *See under* AS.

common as Ratcliff Highway, as *See under* AS.

Common Serjeant A circuit judge of the Central Criminal Court (the OLD BAILEY) who has particular duties within the CITY of London, as assistant to the Recorder.

Commonwealth Institute From 1958, the successor to the IMPERIAL INSTITUTE. In 1962 the institute moved to a new building on KENSINGTON HIGH STREET, on the edge of HOLLAND PARK. That building closed in 2002 and the institute now functions solely as an educational charity, based at New Zealand House, in the HAYMARKET.

Conan (Doyle) 'Boil' in COCKNEY RHYMING SLANG, usually employed in the sense of a skin inflammation, and sometimes rendered as a 'Sir Arthur'. Arthur Conan Doyle is best known as the author of the Sherlock HOLMES stories.

condom *Chambers* and other reputable dictionaries agree that the origin of the word is unknown, but some have attributed it to a Colonel Cundum, who is said to have first advanced the idea of using the dried gut of a sheep to prevent infection. In *A Classical Dictionary of the Vulgar Tongue* (1785) Francis Grose tells of the items' early preparation and sale by 'a matron by the name of Phillips, at the Green Canister, in Half Moon Street in the Strand'. She made a fortune from the business and retired, but when 'the town was not well served by her successors' she returned to her occupation in 1776 'out of a patriotic zeal for the public welfare'.

congestion charge A charge levied on drivers using their vehicles in a particular urban area within prescribed times, with the aim of deterring them from entering the area and thus reducing traffic congestion and pollution. The term is first recorded as long ago as 1965, but it did not become widely known until MAYOR OF LONDON Ken Livingstone (*see* RED KEN) introduced such a scheme in central London in 2003. Vehicle registration numbers are checked via remote cameras and matched with the list of charge-payers for that day and those who have omitted to pay are liable to a fine. The initial fee was £5 and revenues were reinvested in London's public transport system. The scheme succeeded in its main aims but net income fell below expectations, primarily because of unexpectedly high operating costs; the charge rose to £8 in 2005. Taxis and minicabs, emergency services vehicles, disabled drivers and alternative energy vehicles are exempt from the charge and those living within or on the border of the zone are eligible for a substantial discount. Livingstone extended the charging zone westwards in 2007; a move subsequently reversed by his successor as mayor Boris Johnson (*see* BO-JO).

Congregational Memorial Hall A tall Gothic structure that formerly stood at 14 FARRINGDON Street. After the FLEET PRISON was pulled down in 1846, railway lines filled much of the site. The remainder was taken by the Congregational Memorial Hall and Library, which was built 'in connection with the bicen-

tenary commemoration of the ejection of the Nonconforming Ministers of the established Church in 1662'. A meeting of trade unionists and socialists founded the Labour Party at the memorial hall on 27 February 1900 and the General Strike was co-ordinated from here in 1926. The hall was replaced in 1972 by Caroone House, a concrete and glass block that became British Telecom offices. This was said to be the base from which international phone calls were tapped in liaison with government security agents. The library of Congregational literature that had been held at the site subsequently merged with DR WILLIAMS'S LIBRARY. Caroone House was demolished in 2004 and has been replaced by Ludgate West.

Congreve

Congreve rocket A rocket for use in war invented in 1804 by Sir William Congreve (1772–1828) at the Royal Laboratories in WOOLWICH and manufactured at his works at MILL MEADS. Congreve rockets were used in the Napoleonic Wars and the Anglo-American War of 1812. The 'red glare' of these rockets at the Battle of Fort McHenry is referred to in the US national anthem.

> But vaccination certainly has been
> A kind antithesis to Congreve's rockets.
>
> LORD BYRON: *Don Juan*, Canto 1 (1819–24)

Congreves Predecessors of the LUCIFER MATCH, said to have been invented by Sir William Congreve (*see above*) but more likely by the inventor John Walker (*c.*1781–1859). The splints were dipped in sulphur then tipped with chlorate of potash paste, in which gum was substituted for sugar, then a small quantity of sulphide of antimony was added. The match was ignited by being pulled smartly through a strip of folded sandpaper.

Congreve's plug The nickname for a prototype fire sprinkler designed by Sir William Congreve for use in theatres. In the event of fire, it would propel a jet of water into every box in the house. He installed the device in a model of the THEATRE ROYAL, DRURY LANE (which was always burning down), and patented the invention in 1812 but full-scale implementation did not prove practical.

> Again should it burst in a blaze,
> In vain would they ply Congreve's plug,

For nought could extinguish the rays
From the glance of divine Lady Mugg.

w. SPENCER: 'The Beautiful Incendiary' (1812)

CO19 The specialist firearm command branch of the METROPOLITAN POLICE. Formerly known as SO19, the branch is part of the Met's central operations directorate. CO19 is subdivided into armed response vehicle teams, tactical support teams, which specialize in support and intelligence operations, and teams of specialist firearms officers who deal with sieges and hostage rescues. Other branches with armed officers and similar codenames include CO6, responsible for diplomatic protection, and CO18, which patrols HEATHROW and LONDON CITY airports.

ITV will follow the Metropolitan Police's secretive CO19 squad, Britain's largest firearms division, in a hard-hitting new documentary series which will air in the late autumn.

Broadcast (9 July 2008)

Constable's Dues A ceremony of the TOWER OF LONDON, recalling a past perquisite of the office of Constable of the Tower. Every large Royal Navy ship that visits the PORT OF LONDON delivers a barrel of rum to the Governor of the Tower on Tower Green. Such an event usually takes place about once a year.

constitution
Constitution Arch *See* WELLINGTON ARCH.
Constitution Hill A pleasant tree-lined road that runs up a slight incline from BUCKINGHAM PALACE to HYDE PARK CORNER. It separates the palace gardens from GREEN PARK. The initial reference (perhaps from the 17th century) was probably to some aspect of law or government, its import now lost. It has been linked with the 'constitutionals' or health-giving walks Charles II reportedly took here, but this is likely to be a later folk etymology, especially as the term 'constitutional' in this sense is not recorded before the mid-19th century. It was the scene of three attempts on the life of Queen Victoria (in 1840, 1842 and 1849), and in 1850 Sir Robert Peel was fatally injured there after being thrown from his horse by the wicket gate into Green Park after calling at the palace.

Container City A commercial development at Trinity Buoy Wharf, in LEAMOUTH, consisting of brightly painted, irregularly stacked shipping containers that have been fitted out as studios and offices. Most of the occupants are from the arts and creative industries. The name is jocular, as the scale of the project is more akin to that of a hamlet than a city.

Coombe A verdant residential locality situated north of NEW MALDEN. There is evidence of a Bronze Age camp at Coombe Warren and the Romans also settled here. Coombe provided well-water for HAMPTON COURT in the 16th century; the connecting pipeline still exists. In the mid-19th century the locality became popular with fashionable London society as a semi-rural retreat and numerous substantial houses were built. Coombe also has important architectural achievements from the mid-20th century: E. Maxwell Fry's Miramonte, in Warren Rise, and a group of Sunspan houses by the Canadian architect Wells Coates in Woodlands Avenue. The Australian soprano Dame Nellie Melba (1861–1931) lived for a while at Coombe House, on Beverley Lane.

Copenhagen Fields A former open space west of ISLINGTON that took its name from Copenhagen House, the Danish ambassador's residence in the 17th century. In the late 18th century the fields became a popular venue for radical demonstrations, drawing crowds of more than 100,000. Copenhagen House was demolished in 1852, when the market for live animals transferred here from SMITHFIELD. Much of the site is now occupied by council-built housing.

Copperfield, David *See* DAVID COPPERFIELD.

Corbets Tey A commuter village located south of UPMINSTER, to which it is now connected by suburban development. As 'Corbinstye' was first recorded in 1461 there is certainly no truth in the story that Elizabeth I said to her servant 'Corbet, stay and ask the name of this place', and when told that it had no name decreed that it be called after her first words. Somewhat more likely is that Corbin was the landowner and Tey comes from Old English *tye*, 'an enclosure'.

cor blimey *See* GORBLIMEY.

Cordwainer A CITY of London ward centred on Bow Lane. A cordwainer was a worker in Cordovan leather, usually a shoemaker, and the area was a centre for this trade from the 13th century.

Today the ward is noted for its concentration of shops and licensed premises.

Cornhill A street at the highest point in the CITY of London. The name, suggesting the early presence of a cornmarket, was first recorded c.1100. Cornhill leads eastwards from the ROYAL EXCHANGE to the junction of BISHOPSGATE and GRACECHURCH STREET, and is nowadays lined mainly with the 19th- and 20th-century offices of financial institutions. It was said to have been notorious for shops selling 'much stolen gear' in the 15th century. London's first COFFEE HOUSE opened in St Michael's Alley, Cornhill, c.1652. The poet Thomas Gray (1716–71) was born in Cornhill, and the literary periodical *The Cornhill Magazine* was first published here in 1860, under the editorship of William Makepeace Thackeray. Cornhill is also a City of London ward.

Cornhill devils or the **three devils of St Peter** Three fiendish terracotta figures, two large and one small, glaring down from the upper reaches of numbers 54 and 55 Cornhill. They are said to have been placed there following a dispute over planning permission with the neighbouring church of St Peter upon Cornhill in the late 19th century.

corns (and bunions) 'Onions' in COCKNEY RHYMING SLANG. 'Corns' may alternatively and occasionally mean 'teeth', from a cockney rhyme with 'corned beef'.

corporation
Corporation of London The traditional semi-formal name for the Mayor and Commonalty and Citizens of the City of London, also known as the City of London Corporation, which is the CITY's overarching governing body. This consists of the LORD MAYOR OF LONDON, and the City's ALDERMEN and 'Common Councilmen'. In 2006 the corporation declared a preference for it to be known as the 'City of London' on a day-to-day basis and the 'City of London Corporation' only when a distinction needs to be made 'from the financial City or the topographical City'.
Corporation of Trinity House See TRINITY HOUSE.

corridors of power A collective term for the ministries in WHITEHALL with their top-ranking civil servants. The phrase was popularized (but not invented) by C.P. Snow in his novel *Home-*

comings (1956) and gained wide acceptance. He later used it for the title of the novel *Corridors of Power* (1964).

coster A commonplace abbreviation for COSTERMONGER.
Coster Comedienne See KATE (CARNEY).
costermonger A now rare term for a street vendor of fruit, vegetables and the like. It derives from 'costard', a large ribbed apple, and 'monger', a dealer or trader (Old English *mangian*, 'to trade'), as in ironmonger or fishmonger. The word came to be particularly associated with London 'barrow boys' and COCKNEY dealers. See *also* PEARLY KINGS AND QUEENS.
costermongering A facetious term for making alterations to orchestral or choral music, especially that of the great composers. It derives from the tendency of the conductor Sir Michael Costa (1808–84) to take such liberties, notably with the works of Handel. From 1830 Costa conducted at the King's Theatre (from 1837 Her Majesty's Theatre) in the HAYMARKET and in 1847 he established the Royal Italian Opera at the Covent Garden Theatre (now the ROYAL OPERA HOUSE). He conducted the inaugural concerts at the CRYSTAL PALACE in 1851 and the ALBERT HALL in 1871. His home at 59 Eccleston Square is marked by a BLUE PLAQUE.
Costers' Carnival A 19th-century nickname for BARNET Fair.
Coster's Laureate See ALBERT THE GREAT.

cottage Originally a POLARI term for a public lavatory, the word has now passed into the wider language in the context of the use of such a place for homosexual encounters.
cottage estates A series of housing estates built by the LONDON COUNTY COUNCIL before and after the First World War. The homes were mostly small, but the surroundings were considerably greener and healthier than those the new residents had formerly endured.
Cottagers The traditional nickname for FULHAM FC, derived from CRAVEN COTTAGE, the ground at which the club has played for more than a hundred years. Because of the word's other meaning, which is associated with homosexual acts in public lavatories, the club has promoted the alternative 'Whites' in recent years, in reference to the main colour of the team's home strip. However, fans and the media still tend to prefer the more distinctive term.

The most specious [conclusion] … is that the Cottagers' success proves that, far from being split into mini-divisions based primarily on income, the league is actually becoming more egalitarian.

The Independent on Sunday (18 January 2009)

cotton A term used by KNOWLEDGE BOYS for the most direct route, obtained by pulling a thread taut between two points on a map and following that line as closely as possible on the ground. To take such a route is to be 'on the cotton'.

Cotton, Dot An anchor character in the BBC TV soap opera EASTENDERS, played by June Brown (b.1927). A gossipy launderette manageress, she is sustained by her Christian faith and a chain-smoking habit. She became Dot Branning upon remarrying in 2002. 'Dot Cotton' can mean 'rotten' in modern rhyming slang.

Cotton's Wharf Fire *See the* TOOLEY STREET FIRE.

Johnny Cotton *See* JOHNNY.

Cottonian Library A rich library of state papers and other manuscripts founded by the antiquary Sir Robert Bruce Cotton (1571–1631) and augmented by his son and grandson. It was secured for the nation in 1700 and transferred first to Essex House, in the STRAND, and then to Ashburnham House, WESTMINSTER, in 1730. A disastrous fire in 1731 destroyed or ruinously damaged over a hundred volumes of irreplaceable manuscripts. The King's librarian, Dr Richard Bentley, famously escaped the inferno clutching the *Codex Alexandrinus* under his arm. The remainder of the library (some 800 volumes) was moved to WESTMINSTER SCHOOL and then lodged in the BRITISH MUSEUM as one of its foundation collections. The Cotton Collection, which includes the *Lindisfarne Gospels* and the unique manuscript of *Beowulf* (still showing signs of fire damage), is now held in the BRITISH LIBRARY.

One apartment [of Robert Southey's] was appropriated to old and disfigured books. These were carefully covered with cotton by the ladies of the house, who indulged their taste, their criticism, or their humour in their selection of the colours and patterns; enveloping a Quaker's book in drab and so on. This room was jocosely called the Cottonian Library.

W.S. AUSTIN and JOHN RALPH: *The Lives of the Poets Laureate* (1853)

Coulsdon A comfortable 20th-century suburb located south-west of PURLEY. In the 19th century the village of Coulsdon consisted of a small group of houses clustered around the village green of what is now Old Coulsdon. Primarily because of the growth in popularity of BRIGHTON, the country track that passed through Smitham Bottom was upgraded to a turnpike road in 1808. A railway station, now called Coulsdon South, opened in 1889. Village residents continued to refer to the developing area as Smitham Bottom until the opening of Coulsdon post office here and the creation of the parish of St Andrew's, Coulsdon, in 1906. The 'new' Coulsdon began to grow in earnest after the First World War.

In 1776 Coulsdon Cricket Club played in the first-ever match to use three stumps. However, the game was staged at their opponents' ground in Chertsey, SURREY, not on the green at Coulsdon.

County Hall An imposing but not beautiful complex of buildings and courtyards situated beside the THAMES in north LAMBETH, between WESTMINSTER BRIDGE and the LONDON EYE. Designed in neo-baroque style by Ralph Knott (1878–1929), the central section was opened by George V and Queen Mary in 1922. Improvement works continued for many years afterwards, and north and south wings were added in 1939. County Hall was the headquarters of the LONDON COUNTY COUNCIL and then of its successor the GREATER LONDON COUNCIL until the latter's dissolution in 1986. Most of the complex has since been converted to hotel accommodation, with a variety of leisure amenities filling the lower levels, including an art gallery and the London Aquarium.

court

Court of Arches or **Arches Court** The ecclesiastical court for the province of Canterbury, held in the church of ST MARY-LE-BOW (*Sancta Maria de Arcubus*, St Mary of the Arches), CHEAPSIDE. Its principal role is the ceremonial confirmation of the election of bishops.

Court of Fire Judges *See* FIRE JUDGES.

Court of St James's The British court to which foreign ambassadors are officially accredited. After the burning of WHITEHALL in 1697, ST JAMES'S PALACE came to be used for state ceremonies, hence the Court of St James's. Since the accession of Queen Victoria in 1837 the monarch has lived at BUCKINGHAM PALACE but St James's Palace remains the 'senior palace of the sovereign'.

Courtyard Societies Five learned societies sharing the wings of BURLINGTON HOUSE. They are the Geological Society, the Linnean Society of London, the Royal Astronomical Society, the Royal Society of Chemistry and the Society of Antiquaries of London.

Central Criminal Court *See the* OLD BAILEY.

Royal Courts of Justice *See under* ROYAL.

Coverley, Sir Roger de A member of an imaginary club in *The Spectator*, 'who lived in SOHO SQUARE when he was in town'. He was supposed to write for *The Spectator*, but was essentially portrayed by Joseph Addison.

Crack Nut Sunday On the Sunday before Michaelmas Day in a scattering of English churches in times past, each parishioner would bring a bag of nuts to church and sitting cracking and munching them during the performance of the divine service. The custom seems to have been most religiously observed in KINGSTON UPON THAMES, where it may have had some connection with the festivities surrounding the election of the corporation officers on Michaelmas Day. Making as much noise as possible seems to have been part of the fun; the clergy stamped out the practice around the end of the 18th century.

> ... it is on record that the noise caused by the cracking was often so loud and so powerful as to oblige the minister to break off for a time his reading or sermon until silence was restored.
>
> EDWARD WALFORD: *Greater London: A Narrative of Its History, Its People, and Its Places*: Volume 2 (1884)

Crafty Cockney

1. The professional sobriquet of Eric Bristow, the world's leading darts player in the 1980s. Born at HACKNEY Hospital in 1957, Bristow played darts with an ebullience that helped build the game's television appeal from the mid-1970s. It was around this time that he began styling himself the Crafty Cockney, after acquiring a branded shirt from a bar of that name in Santa Monica, California. Bristow won the world championship five times between 1980 and 1986. He established a darts pub called The Crafty Cockney after leaving London for Stoke-on-Trent, a move that Bristow's protégé Phil 'The Power' Taylor com-

pared with 'Jesus relocating from the Holy Land to Milton Keynes'.

2. Chris Jackson, the Crafty Cockney, was a character played by Paul Whitehouse in the BBC TV comedy sketch series *The Fast Show*, first broadcast in the mid-1990s. His distinguishing characteristic was a propensity to 'nick anything'.

Craven Cottage Originally a *cottage orné* built in 1780 on the west side of the FULHAM peninsula as a country retreat for William Craven, 6th Baron Craven (1738–91). The cottage burned down in 1888 and FULHAM FC established a permanent home on its site in 1896, 17 years after the club's foundation. In recent times plans for the club to radically rebuild the stadium, or possibly to move elsewhere, have come to nothing and Craven Cottage is likely to remain in roughly its present form for the foreseeable future.

From 1980 until 1984 Craven Cottage was also home to Fulham Rugby League Club. Fulham RLFC played at other London stadia from 1984, eventually mutating into HARLEQUINS Rugby League.

Cray A river that rises in ORPINGTON and flows north through several settlements to which it has given its name, joining the River Darent 1½ miles (2.5 km) before the latter enters the THAMES. Its name, which is of Celtic origin, meant 'fresh' or 'clean'.

Crayford The principal industrial zone in the London Borough of BEXLEY, straddling the River CRAY and the former Roman road of WATLING STREET, between BEXLEYHEATH and Dartford, Kent. Crayford was probably the site of the Roman settlement of Noviomagus, although other authorities place it at WEST WICKHAM. The presence of the freely flowing river brought thirsty industries such as tanning, while barges were built at Crayford Creek. Huguenot refugees established the first calico bleaching works in the late 17th century, and later printed silk here. Machine guns and other armaments were manufactured north of Crayford Road, first by Hiram Maxim and from the end of the 19th century by Vickers, which also built some early flying machines. The company employed more than 14,000 workers during the First World War. Vickers left Crayford in 1969 and its place was taken by distributors and small-scale manufacturers. *See also the* BATTLE OF CRAYFORD.

Crazy Gang The lunatic lot so named first formed in 1932 for a performance of the revue *Crazy Month* at the LONDON PALLADIUM. It consisted of three pairs of already famous comics: Flanagan and Allen, otherwise Bud Flanagan (Robert Wintrop, originally Reuben Weintrop) (1896–1968) and Chesney Allen (1894–1982); Nervo and Knox, viz. Jimmy Nervo (James Henry Holloway) (1897–1975) and Teddy Knox (1896–1974); and the Scots pair Naughton and Gold, i.e. Charlie Naughton (1887–1976) and Jimmy Gold (James McGonigal) (1886–1967). 'Monsewer' Eddie Gray (1898–1969) often appeared with them, but was never more than a semi-detached member of the gang. They remained together until 1960. The name Crazy Gang was applied in the 1980s and 1990s to the players of WIMBLEDON FC, for their vigorous style of play and antics both on and off the football field.

cream

cream crackered 'Knackered' in COCKNEY RHYMING SLANG, meaning worn out following exertion.

> Joanna: I am totally cream crackered. Anybody mind if I hit the sack? ... (*They all say goodnight. She goes.*)
> Felicia: Uh, excuse me, what is cream crackered?
> Lance: Cream crackered, knackered. Er, bushed, beat.
> Felicia: Oh ...
> Amy: Cockney rhyming slang, that right?
> Lance: That's right.
> Felicia: Joanna's a cockney?
> Lance: No. People of her class sometimes use the slang. They find the incongruity what they call 'a bit of a wheeze', apparently.
> DOUG LUCIE: *Grace*, i (1993)

cream ice Jacks Street vendors of ice creams in the late 19th century. They were more likely to be Giacomos than Johns.

Creed Lane A street running southwards from LUDGATE HILL. In the Middle Ages the clergy of ST PAUL'S Cathedral went in procession to the cathedral reciting prayers. They began in PATERNOSTER ROW, and on reaching Creed Lane they began chanting the Creed. Before the 16th century the street was known as Spurrier Row, from a 'row (of houses) occupied by spur-makers'.

Cremorne Gardens Famous pleasure gardens, opened in 1845 to rival VAUXHALL GARDENS on the land of CHELSEA Farm, the former property of Thomas Dawson, Viscount Cremorne. They were a popular venue for fêtes and entertainments, but their clientele degenerated and they were closed in 1877 after many local complaints. Lots Road power station, on the left bank of the THAMES near BATTERSEA BRIDGE, later occupied much of the site. In 1982 Kensington & Chelsea council opened a small park on Lots Road called Cremorne Gardens. *See also* ROSHERVILLE GARDENS.

Cresswell, Madam A notorious bawd and procuress who flourished between about 1670 and 1684 and who was much patronized by Restoration courtiers and politicians. She wintered in CLERKENWELL and kept house in CAMBERWELL in the summer. 'Old Mother Cresswell' was not married, although Sir Thomas Player went by the nickname of Sir Thomas Cresswell. In her old age she became religiously inclined and bequeathed £10 for a funeral sermon, in which nothing ill should be said of her. Sir Walter Scott attributes the sermon to the Duke of Buckingham:

> 'Why,' said the Duke, 'I had caused the little Quodling to go through his oration thus – That whatever evil reports had passed current during the lifetime of the worthy matron whom they had restored to dust that day, malice itself could not deny that she was born well, married well, lived well, and died well; since she was born in Shadwell, married to Cresswell, lived in Camberwell, and died in Bridewell.'
> *Peveril of the Peak* (1823)

Cricklewood A changing and ethnically diverse district situated to the north-west of BRONDESBURY. Its name derives from Middle English words meaning an irregularly shaped wood. The aircraft manufacturer Handley Page began production in Cricklewood in 1912 and inaugurated London to Paris flights from Cricklewood aerodrome in 1919. The following year saw the first-ever fatalities on a scheduled passenger flight, when an aircraft crashed into a house by the aerodrome. In the same year Frank Smith produced the first batch of his potato crisps in two garages behind the Crown public house. Bentley cars were built in Cricklewood from 1919 to 1931. During the Second World War, Handley Page manufactured Halifax bombers at Cricklewood. The Dubreq company produced the seminal Stylophone electronic organ here in the 1960s and 1970s. The district's residential population evolved over the second half of the 20th century with successive waves of settlement by Irish, Caribbean and Asian communities. Cricklewood is presently undergoing massive regeneration, as brownfield sites fill with thousands of mixed-tenure homes, offices and leisure facilities.

Cricklewood Twelve In October 1974 police raided a 'soundclash' at the Carib Club on Cricklewood Broadway and subsequently charged a dozen men with affray, possession of offensive weapons and assault on police. All the defendants were acquitted; nine at the first trial, one after a retrial and two on appeal.

Cries of London

1. A light-hearted consort song by Orlando Gibbons (1583–1625) consisting of a montage of London pedlars' street cries. Other composers later produced similar works based on Gibbons's theme.

2. Various sets of images reproduced initially as prints, and later also on playing cards, decorative plates, etc., depicting London street traders and captioned with their typical patter. The first such series was *The Cryes of the City of London* (1687), by Marcellus Laroon the Elder (1653–1702). As well as being reprinted many times, Laroon's etchings were pirated, modified, parodied (including by HOGARTH) and imitated, in styles ranging from coarse caricature to sentimental realism.

Crippen, Dr Hawley Harvey An American homeopathic doctor (1862–1910), who in 1900 relocated to England with his second wife, Cora Turner. In 1905 the couple moved in at 39 Hilldrop Crescent, HOLLOWAY. Dr Crippen had practised as a dentist and a purveyor of patent medicines; his wife was a MUSIC HALL singer. Cuckolded by the assertive, flirtatious Cora, Crippen turned to his young secretary, Ethel le Neve, and the two became lovers. Crippen poisoned his wife, cut up her body and buried her remains in the cellar. Finding himself under police suspicion, he boarded a steamer bound for Canada, accompanied by Ethel disguised as a boy. The ship's captain noticed that the pair behaved in an unusually affectionate manner and sent a message to London, in the first use of wireless telegraphy for such a purpose. Chief Inspector Dew of SCOTLAND YARD took a faster ship and intercepted them as they docked in Quebec. Both were tried for murder; Le Neve was acquitted but Crippen was found guilty, and hanged at PENTONVILLE PRISON. In recent years forensic scientists have cast doubt on aspects of his conviction.

> Nearly a century later, research appears to show that the evidence which sent Crippen to the gallows was mistaken: the human remains discovered under his London house could not be those of Cora.
>
> *The Guardian* (17 October 2007)

Cripplegate The CITY of London's most populous ward, taking in the eastern and central parts of the BARBICAN. Cripplegate was the northern entrance to the Roman fort, erected around AD 120, and stood at what is now the corner of Wood Street and St Alphage Gardens. The name probably derives from Old English *crypel-geat*; a low arched gate through which one could only creep. An alternative possibility is that it was a corruption of *crepel*, a burrow, indicating that the passageway was a kind of underpass. The Church of St Giles, patron saint of cripples, was built in 1090, probably on the site of a Saxon predecessor, and rebuilt in 1545 after a fire. There is evidence that William SHAKESPEARE was a parish resident in the late 1590s. Oliver Cromwell was married in St Giles' Church and the poet John MILTON is buried here. The writer Daniel DEFOE was born in Cripplegate ward in 1660. The Cripplegate entrance was reconstructed at least twice and demolished in 1761. By this time, the formerly wealthy ward of Cripplegate had gone downhill and religious dissidents and journalists had come to live here, the latter notably in GRUB STREET. Cripplegate was damaged beyond recognition by the Second World War bombing and the church needed comprehensive restoration. Most of the area was rebuilt with the massive concrete blocks of the Barbican, where the first homes were completed in the early 1960s. The remainder of the ward has been filled with office towers.

Cripplegate 'vampire' A tall tale derived from a memorial in St Giles' Church to Constance Whitney (1611–28), said to feature a representation of a lady in a shroud rising from her coffin. This has been interpreted to refer to an unidentified young woman who was buried while in a trance and released from her entombment by an unscrupulous sexton who opened the coffin to steal a valuable ring from her finger. She rose up, the sexton fled in terror and she went on to live a long life and bear several children. The legend was further embellished to suggest that the woman in question was Constance herself. The story has gained new currency in modern times, having been repeated in several semi-scholarly works by 'vampirologists', including Bob Curran's *Encyclopedia of the Undead* (2006).

lame as St Giles' Cripplegate, as *See under* AS.

Crocker's Folly A public house situated on Aberdeen Place, MAIDA VALE. When Frank Crocker built the Crown Hotel (1898) and decorated its interior exceptionally ornately, he did so in the mistaken belief that the planned Great Central Railway would terminate nearby. The terminus was instead constructed at MARYLEBONE, the business failed and he threw himself to his death from a third-floor window, or so legend has it. Crocker's Folly doubled as the New York Writer's Club for the 1981 film *Reds*.

Crockford's Originally an exclusive gambling club established at 50 ST JAMES'S STREET in 1828 by William Crockford (1775–1844), the son of a fishmonger. It attracted the cream of Regency society and fortunes were staked there. Crockford became a millionaire before he retired in 1840. Crockford's closed down in about 1848 in consequence of a change in the gaming laws. A new Crockford's opened at 21 Hertford Street in 1928, essentially as a bridge club, subsequently moving to sumptuous premises at CARLTON HOUSE TERRACE. Crockfords (now sans apostrophe) is presently located at 30 Curzon Street, MAYFAIR. The Betting and Gaming Act of 1960, permitting the revival of games of chance, enabled it to acquire a leading position, with chemin de fer as its main game.

Croesus A nickname for Thomas Sutton (1532–1611), from the proverbially wealthy king of Lydia. Sutton got rich from the discovery of coal on his estate in Newcastle-upon-Tyne, augmented his income by working as a senior government official and by marrying a wealthy widow, and then made an even larger fortune as England's leading moneylender. He founded Sutton's Hospital in CHARTERHOUSE, and SUTTON HOUSE in

HOMERTON takes its name from him, although he did not live there.

Croft

Croft, Henry *See* PEARLY KINGS AND QUEENS.

Croft, Lara The feisty, busty heroine of the *Tomb Raider* computer game series, created in 1996. In the manner of her kind she has a fantasy 'biography', which records that she was born in WIMBLEDON, the daughter of Lord Henshingley Croft, attended Wimbledon High School for Girls, Gordonstoun and a Swiss finishing school, and went out into the world with the occupation of 'adventurer'.

Crosby Place A mansion built on BISHOPSGATE in the 1460s for John Crosby (d.1475), a CITY of London sheriff and grocer, later an alderman and a knight. In order to rescue it from proposed demolition in 1910, the surviving great hall of Crosby Place was taken down and reassembled in CHEYNE WALK. At first used as the dining hall of the British Federation of University Women, it is now a private residence. SHAKESPEARE was familiar with Crosby Place and used it as the setting for Gloucester's plotting in *Richard III* (c.1592).

> The hall was ... the main feature of the edifice; indeed, it often gave name to the whole structure, and great cost and labour seem to have been bestowed upon it.
>
> EDWARD BLACKBURN: *An Architectural and Historical Account of Crosby Place, London* (1834)

Cross, the A short form of CHARING CROSS HOSPITAL.

Crossness Located at the northern tip of the ERITH marshes, Crossness is now an outpost of THAMESMEAD but this was an isolated spot when Victorian engineers chose it as the site for one of their characteristically grand public engineering projects. Sewage pollution had become a serious health hazard in London by the early 19th century and the GREAT STINK OF LONDON finally persuaded Parliament to act. Joseph Bazalgette and his colleagues devised and built a network of sewers that carried the city's waste water to two huge pumping and filtration stations on either side of the Thames, east of the metropolitan conurbation. At Crossness, four massive engines pumped effluent into a reservoir that held 25 million gallons. Opened by Prince ALBERT in 1865, the building was designed in ornate Romanesque style in gault brick, ornamented inside with painted ironwork. The old engines were decommissioned at the end of the 1950s and Thames Water now uses modern technology elsewhere on the site to process the effluent. Since 1985 the Crossness Engine Trust has rescued the Victorian machinery from rust and vandalism.

Crossrail A major new east-west railway project for London and beyond, the central section of which will connect LIVERPOOL STREET and PADDINGTON stations via a new tunnel. The cost is estimated at £16 billion and the line may open in 2017.

> An Act to make provision for a railway transport system running from Maidenhead, in the County of Berkshire, and Heathrow Airport, in the London Borough of Hillingdon, through central London to Shenfield, in the County of Essex, and Abbey Wood, in the London Borough of Greenwich; and for connected purposes.
>
> Crossrail Act (22 July 2008)

crouch

Crouch End A fashionable Victorian suburb centred around a confluence of routes southwest of HORNSEY. The name is of Middle English origin, an 'end' being an outlying place, while a 'crouch' was a cross, which may have been placed here as a boundary post between two manors. During the late 18th century the village took shape as a congregation of labourers' cottages, though there were grander houses in the vicinity – two of which were later acquired by the Booths, the gin distilling family. The Hornsey enclosure award of 1813 prompted a gradual programme of housebuilding that accelerated rapidly after the opening of CROUCH HILL and Crouch End stations in the late 1860s. The latter is now closed and its disused line has become the Parkland Walk that traverses the district. A remarkable number of 1960s pop stars went on to buy homes in Crouch End and the area has acquired quasi-cult status among mid-ranking media personalities. Despite its outward gentility, Crouch End – according to Stephen King's short story of that name (1980) – conceals a gateway to a nightmarish parallel dimension behind its 'elderly brick houses like sleepy dowagers'. Local folklore associates the area with Bob Dylan, who

reputedly waited patiently in the suburban front room of a local resident coincidentally named 'Dave', under the mistaken impression that the house belonged to rock musician Dave Stewart, owner of a Crouch End recording studio.

Crouch Hill The hill is part of the Northern Heights that extend eastward from HAMPSTEAD and HIGHGATE, while the road of that name links Stroud Green with CROUCH END. The farmland here was sprinkled with superior villas in the first half of the 19th century, of which a couple survive in altered form.

Crouch, Jonathan *See the* DEVIL'S GAP.

Crown Jewels The crown and regalia worn by the monarch at CORONATIONS and certain other important occasions, such as the State Opening of Parliament. The priceless gems include the First and Second Stars of Africa, as the largest and third largest diamonds in the world are known, and the Koh-i-Noor, the oldest known major diamond, and they are on public display in the Jewel House at the TOWER OF LONDON.

Croydon The dominant commercial centre of outer London, situated 12 miles (19 km) due south of ST PAUL'S Cathedral. Croydon may have been settled by the Romans as a staging post on the road from the south coast to London – its position at the head of the River Wandle just north of a gap in the North Downs makes it a natural choice – but it was the Saxons who named it 'saffron valley'. Croydon was part of the archbishop of Canterbury's estates from Saxon times and six archbishops were buried in the church between 1583 and 1757. The archbishops' 1,000-year-old residence survives on Old Palace Road, as do Archbishop Whitgift's 16th-century almshouses on George Street. The Croydon Corporation Act of 1956 marked the start of a new era, with its drive to draw businesses from central London creating around six million square feet (557,000 square metres) of office space. What had seemed pioneering in the 1960s was already looking tired and ugly by the 1980s and Croydon's character became the subject of metropolitan disdain. The borough council has since been co-ordinating the wholesale redevelopment of the business, retail and leisure district and innovations in recent years have included the Clocktower arts centre, the Tramlink network and the Centrale shopping centre, with much more to come.

The town centre itself is run down and badly organised ... As a result, plans are in place to bulldoze much of the old architecture and replace it with new state-of-the-art developments. 'We are knocking it down and starting again for the 21st century,' says Emma Peters, executive director of planning, regeneration and conservation at Croydon council.

Financial Times (21 February 2009)

Croydon, London Borough of An OUTER LONDON borough formed in 1965 by merging Croydon county borough with the urban districts of COULSDON and PURLEY. It is London's most populous borough. Croydon's coat of arms draws heavily on religious references, with elements borrowed from the arms of Archbishop Whitgift, Chertsey Abbey (former owners of Coulsdon) and Hyde Abbey (which owned SANDERSTEAD). The civic motto is *ad summa nitamur* – 'let us strive for perfection'.

Croydon Airport London's principal airport between the wars and a fighter station during the BATTLE OF BRITAIN, Croydon opened in 1920 and closed in 1959. Airport House, the former terminal building, is now a business centre.

Croydon facelift A slang expression of the early 21st century for hair that is scraped back so tightly into a ponytail that it pulls back the skin on the wearer's cheekbones – a style supposedly favoured by some young women in Croydon. *See also* CHAV.

Slip on those gold bracelets, and embrace that Croydon facelift hairdo. Let's have no more of this unkind discrimination against the chav underclass, say MPs.

The Sunday Times (3 July 2005)

Croydon's Bishops Avenue A nickname for the exclusive enclave of SHIRLEY Hills, borrowed from the BISHOPS AVENUE on the other side of London. Its main residential road is coincidentally named Bishops Walk. Houses backing onto one of the two golf courses fetch prices in the millions.

Grim, the Collyer of Croydone *See under* GRIM.

No.1 Croydon *See the* 50P BUILDING (*under* FIFTY).

Crufts The world's largest dog show, founded by Charles Cruft (1852–1938) in 1891. His interest in dogs arose largely from his apprenticeship in 1876 to James Spratt, who had recently started a 'dog cake' business in HOLBORN. In 1886 Cruft managed the Allied Terrier Club Show at the Royal Aquarium (*see the* AQ), and organized the first dog show in his own name at Islington's AGRICULTURAL HALL in 1891. Three years after his death the show was taken over by the Kennel Club, which put on its first event at OLYMPIA in 1948. Crufts moved to EARLS COURT in 1979 and left London for Birmingham's National Exhibition Centre in 1991.

crust (of bread) 'Head' in COCKNEY RHYMING SLANG, especially heard in the expression 'to be off one's crust'. 'LOAF (OF BREAD)' is a closely related alternative.

They stop me from groovin', they bang on me wall,
They're doing me crust in, it's no good at all.

STEVE MARRIOTT and RONNIE LANE: 'Lazy Sunday' (song by the Small Faces) (1968)

Crutched Friars A street lying in the shadow of FENCHURCH STREET STATION. The mendicant order of the *Fratres Cruciferi* – Crutched Friars or Friars of the Holy Cross – arrived in England from Italy in 1244. Their name derived from the wooden staffs surmounted by a cross that they carried (later replaced by a small silver cross) and from the crosses of red cloth on their habits. The friars established a house in the street that now bears their name *c*.1298. Their order was suppressed by Pope Alexander VII in 1656.

Crystal Palace One of the glories of the Victorian era. The huge building was designed entirely of glass and iron by Joseph Paxton (1801–65), a former head gardener to the Duke of Devonshire at Chatsworth House, Derbyshire, to house the GREAT EXHIBITION of 1851. The massive iron and glass structure, which had been nicknamed the 'Crystal Palace' by *Punch* magazine, was originally erected in HYDE PARK but moved to SYDENHAM in 1854 with some alterations, including the addition of two towers, and was used as an exhibition, entertainment and recreational centre. The new 200-acre (80-hectare) park that surrounded it contained a magnificent series of fountains; the two largest basins have since been transformed to accommodate the athletics stadium and the sports centre. Water flowed through the fountains into a grand lake, which is now devoted to boating and fishing. Benjamin Waterhouse Hawkins, the draughtsman Darwin had employed on the voyage of the *Beagle*, constructed 29 life-size replicas of extinct animals, under the guidance of Professor Richard Owen, the man who invented the word 'dinosaur'. The park quickly became a sporting venue. It has been home to the Crystal Palace Athletics Club since 1868. Later, the cricketer W.G. Grace founded both the London County Cricket Club and the Crystal Palace Bowling Club (the bowlers using one of the carpeted long galleries of the palace). The Crystal Palace held every kind of national exhibition, including the world's first air show. In 1911 the palace hosted the Festival of Empire, held in honour of George V's coronation. After the First World War, during which it served as a naval barracks, it became the original home of the IMPERIAL WAR MUSEUM. The Crystal Palace was destroyed by fire on 30 November 1936 – an event so momentous that special trains were laid on for sightseers and more than a million people are said to have watched the blaze.

Crystal Palace FC Palace workers founded the club in 1905. The Glaziers, as they were formerly nicknamed, moved to nearby SELHURST PARK in 1924. *See also* EAGLES; GLAD ALL OVER.

Cubitt

Cubitt, Thomas The greatest London builder and developer of his time (1788–1855), nicknamed the Emperor of the Building Trade. His major creation, backed by his patron the Duke of WESTMINSTER, was BELGRAVIA. He also enlarged BUCKINGHAM PALACE for Queen Victoria. Cubitt left one of the longest wills in history, dividing up his million pound fortune.

> In his sphere of life, with the immense business he had in hand, he is a real national loss. A better, kindhearted or more simple, unassuming man never breathed. We feel we owe much to him for the way in which he carried out everything.
>
> QUEEN VICTORIA: *journal* (24 December 1855)

Cubitt Artists A cultural and educational organization founded in 1991 and taking its name from its early base in Cubitt Street, KING'S CROSS. The group's gallery and studios are now located at 8 Angel Mews, ISLINGTON.

Cubittopolis A colloquial name applied in the middle of the 19th century to that area around

Warwick and Eccleston Squares laid out by Thomas Cubitt, and hence broadly to PIMLICO.

Cubitt Town The south-eastern quadrant of the ISLE OF DOGS. During the 1840s most of the land here was acquired by William Cubitt (1791–1863), brother of Thomas Cubitt and LORD MAYOR OF LONDON in 1860/1. Cubitt commissioned a number of builders to erect wharves, mills and other dock-related industries along the riverbank and terraces of three-storey houses inland. The largest of the contractors built 181 houses and shops and three pubs, but many others were responsible for just a handful of properties each. By the early 1850s the whole area had taken the name Cubitt Town, even those parts not developed by the man himself. The township was well regarded for the neatness of the houses, the width of the roads and the absence of squalor and overcrowding. Nearly all of the original properties were subsequently replaced with council housing.

Cuckold's Point A promontory on the south bank of the THAMES in ROTHERHITHE. It marks the eastern extremity of the POOL OF LONDON. It was named from the setting up here in 1562 of a pair of cuckold's horns on a maypole (a cuckold – a man whose wife had been unfaithful – was traditionally represented as having horns on his head). As well as being a generalized warning to husbands, this may have had some connection with the Horn Fair at nearby CHARLTON, to which ferry-borne revellers may well have come via the landing place at Cuckold's Point Stairs. Local legend says that a miller was granted an estate in the vicinity by King John as compensation for having his wife seduced by the king.

> On the left hand lies Ratcliffe, a considerable suburb: on the opposite shore is fixed a long pole with ram's-horns upon it, the intention of which was vulgarly said to be a reflection upon wilful and contented cuckolds.
>
> PAUL HENTZNER: *Travels in England* (1598)

currant

currant bun 'Sun' in COCKNEY RHYMING SLANG, not usually abbreviated. Julian Franklyn, in his *Dictionary of Rhyming Slang* (1960), points out that at the time of the term's coinage the London sun always appeared as a reddish-brown disc, because of the city's polluted air. *The Sun* newspaper has also adopted the term, and registered the URL www.currantbun.com, although it no longer makes use of it.

Currant-Jelly Hall A nickname for EARLS COURT Lodge when it was the home of the BERKELEY SQUARE confectioner James Gunter (1731–1819). The derisive tag was apparently coined by Lord Albemarle's children, who lived nearby. A YWCA hostel in its latter days, the house was demolished in 1973. Successive generations of Gunters amassed an extensive property portfolio in the area and many local street names derive from the family's connections with places elsewhere in England, especially Yorkshire.

Cursitors The 24 junior clerks who, from the 1520s, wrote out in court hand the formal common form (de cursu) CHANCERY writs. The growth of printed forms led to their abolition in 1835.

Cursitor Street A street branching eastwards off CHANCERY LANE, named after the Cursitors, whose office stood on the corner.

customer is always right, the A general rule of retail tacitly adopted by most shops and stores from the turn of the 20th century, and explicitly stated by Harry Gordon Selfridge, founder in 1909 of SELFRIDGES department store. A year or two earlier the Swiss hotelier César RITZ was quoted as saying, *'Le client n'a jamais tort'* ('The customer is never wrong'), which amounts to the same thing. It has been said that Selfridge first heard the phrase while on a buying expedition in Asia. He has also been credited with inventing the line 'business as usual' and first publicizing the countdown of SHOPPING DAYS TO CHRISTMAS.

Custom House

1. From 1275 the building at which duties were levied on foreign goods brought to London by river. In 1385 a new Custom House was erected at the present site, immediately east of BILLINGSGATE, and this has since been wholly rebuilt four times. In the late 19th century it generated annual income for the government of around £20 million: half the import duties levied in the whole of Great Britain. The building is nowadays a base for HM Revenue and Customs' investigation and intelligence unit.

2. A locality and DOCKLANDS LIGHT RAILWAY station in CANNING TOWN, named after a building properly called the Dock Directors' Access Centre, which was refurbished in 1995 and then demolished soon afterwards to make way for the EXCEL exhibition and conference centre.

cut and cover A method of tunnel construction in which a deep trench is dug and then roofed over. Much of the early work on the LONDON UNDERGROUND system was done in this way, especially on the lines now called the DISTRICT, METROPOLITAN, CIRCLE, HAMMERSMITH AND CITY and EAST LONDON. The term TUBE was originally coined in contradistinction – as a nickname for the lines that were constructed by boring – although it is now used to encompass the entire network, including the sections that run above ground.

Cutpurse, Moll The familiar name of Mary Frith (*c.*1585–1660), a woman of masculine vigour who often dressed as a man. In 1611 she was sentenced to do public penance by the COURT OF ARCHES for parading about FLEET STREET and the STRAND in male costume. She was a notorious thief and once attacked General Fairfax on HOUNSLOW HEATH, for which she was sent to NEWGATE PRISON. She escaped by bribery and finally died of dropsy. Middleton and Dekker's comedy *The Roaring Girl* (*c.*1611) is based on her exploits.

Cutty Sark A famous tea clipper built in Dumbarton, Scotland, in 1869. The *Cutty Sark* has a 152-foot (46.5m) main mast and boasted a top speed of 17 knots. The ship made record-breaking voyages bringing tea from China and wool from Australia back to Britain. The ship's name, the inspiration for its figurehead, comes from a Scottish legend, retold by Robert Burns, of Tam O'Shanter's admiration for a graceful young witch who wore a 'cutty sark', a dialect term for a short petticoat or short-tailed shirt. At one stage in the ship's career a short shirt emblem was flown at the mainmast. Burns's poem was illustrated on the carvings round the ship's bows, but the figurehead was of a woman in flowing garments with outstretched arm. The accompanying 'witches' round the bows were naked. The ship was placed in a dry dock at GREENWICH in 1957 after featuring as a showpiece at the FESTIVAL OF BRITAIN. A recent restoration programme was set back by a serious fire in 2007.

Her cutty sark, o' Paisley harn [coarse linen],
That while a lassie she had worn,

In longitude tho' sorely scanty,

It was her best, and she was vauntie [proud].

'Tam O'Shanter' (1791)

Cyprus A rebuilt urban hamlet located northeast of the Royal Albert Dock (*see the* ROYAL DOCKS). The name dates from 1878, when Britain leased the Mediterranean island from Turkey. Also known as New Beckton, this tiny settlement with its shops and services was a 'self-supporting community', entirely owned by the PORT OF LONDON AUTHORITY, providing homes for workers at BECKTON gasworks and the docks. In the 1970s Cyprus became the site of the LONDON DOCKLANDS DEVELOPMENT CORPORATION's first sponsored housing project; the rapid sale of the properties prompted the LDDC to release further land for residential building and drew more developers to DOCKLANDS. *See also the* UNIVERSITY OF EAST LONDON.

D

Dagenham A working-class stronghold situated beside the THAMES marshes east of BARKING. The name was first recorded around 687 and refers to the homestead of a man called Dæcca. In 1205 Dagenham was large enough to have a chaplain and the parish church of St Peter and St Paul was probably built at a similar time. After 1921 the village was rapidly hemmed in to the south by industrial development on Dagenham Marshes – notably in the form of the Ford Motor Company's factory – and then to the north by the huge BECONTREE estate. After the Second World War the council began to pull down decaying buildings and by the early 1970s almost every vestige of the old village had been replaced by municipal housing. The parish church, vicarage and Cross Keys public house are now the only ancient structures. The England football manager Alf Ramsey, comedian and actor Dudley Moore (*see the* DAGENHAM DIALOGUES) and singer Sandie Shaw all grew up in Dagenham.

Dagenham Breach Now an industrial lagoon but originally a local beauty spot, created in the early 18th century by the THAMES's irrepressible habit of breaching flood defences. When first formed it covered almost 1,000 acres (400 hectares) but after many years of repair work it was reduced to a lake of one-twentieth that area. It is now being gradually filled in to provide more space for industrial development.

Dagenham Dave Different songs of the same name by The Stranglers (1977) and Morrissey (1995). The former was about a Mancunian friend of the band, so nicknamed because he had once worked at Ford's Dagenham car plant. Morrissey's concerned a stereotypical male working-class resident of the district:

I love Karen, I love Sharon on the
windowscreen,
With never the need to fight or to question a
single thing.

Dagenham dialogues A series of sketches written and performed by Peter Cook (1937–95) and Dudley Moore (1935–2002) in their BBC TV comedy series *Not Only ... But Also* (1965–70). The conversational exchanges between 'Pete', a delusional know-all, and 'Dud', his credulous foil, were delivered in deadpan style despite the often surreal subject matter. The scripts were collected in book form as *Dud and Pete: The Dagenham Dialogues* (1971).

Pete: I was just about to drop off, when
suddenly, 'tap, tap, tap' at the bloody window
pane – I looked out – you know who it was?
Dud: Who?
Pete: Bloody Greta Garbo!

Dagenham Dock An industrial and bulk storage district built on Dagenham Marshes, south of the A13. The old docks were constructed in 1887 around DAGENHAM BREACH. HMS *Thunderer*, the last warship built on the Thames, was completed at the docks in 1911 and took part in the Battle of Jutland five years later. In the late 1920s the Ford Motor Company built its massive car factory here. For British drivers, Dagenham's name became synonymous with Ford cars but the plant closed in 2001, although the site continues to be used for diesel engine production and as a distribution depot. Dagenham Dock is presently undergoing extensive regeneration as part of the THAMES GATEWAY masterplan.

Dagenham Girl Pipers An all-female Scots-style pipe band formed by the Rev J.W. Graves at Dagenham Congregational Church in Osborne Square between the two world wars to provide wholesome recreation for the young womanhood of the district. Its profile is not as high as it was in its heyday in the 1930s and 1940s, when it entertained the troops and went on world tours, but it is still very much in existence.

More recently, Madge has tended to lunge at Royalty, in the hope of being manhandled by a bodyguard. The other day she even lunged at the Dagenham Girl Pipers in the hope of being manhandled by a woman, poor wretch.

DAME EDNA EVERAGE: *My Gorgeous Life: The Life, the Loves, the Legend* (1989)

'Dagenham girls' is also used (very infrequently) to signify 'windscreen wipers' in modern rhyming slang.

Dagenham Idol A wooden figure dug out of the marshes in 1922. Possibly from the Bronze Age, the idol may have been buried as a talisman to help crops grow.

Dagenham Yanks The nickname given in the middle decades of the 20th century to homecoming Irishmen who had worked at Ford's Dagenham plant. Many had previously been employed at the company's Marina works in Cork. The Dagenham Yanks were noted for their flashy attire, modelled on the American style.

In his youth, Tel [Terry Venables] probably came into contact with the Dagenham Yanks, the wild men from Cork who travelled to Essex to make their fortune and came home to throw the cash around, speaking with a strange, estuary twang. They sounded like Tel.

Irish Independent (28 October 2007)

dagger In the arms of the CITY of London the dagger supposedly commemorates Sir William Walworth's dagger, with which he slew Wat Tyler in 1381. Before this time the cognizance of the City was the sword of St Paul. The inscription below Sir William's statue in Fishmongers' Hall announced:

Brave Walworth Knyght Lord Mayor that slew
Rebellious Tyler in his alarmes –
The king therefore did give in lieu
The Dagger to the Cytyes armes.

Dagger Ale A strong ale first brewed in the 16th century at a HOLBORN inn bearing the sign of a dagger.

My lawyer's clerk I lighted on last night
In Holborn, at the Dagger ...

BEN JONSON: *The Alchemist*, I, i (1610)

Daggers

1. The nickname of Dagenham and Redbridge FC.

2. A nickname supposedly awarded to prime minister Margaret Thatcher by unsympathetic members of her own cabinet, said not to have been inspired by her 'looking daggers' at them,

but as an abbreviation of 'DAGENHAM' – Dagenham being three stops on (on the DISTRICT LINE) from BARKING (as in 'barking mad'). *See also* ONE STOP SHORT OF BARKING.

daisy roots 'Boots' in COCKNEY RHYMING SLANG, sometimes abbreviated to 'daisies'. The term has been in use since the mid-19th century.

At Dunkirk our mob were still pick-outable on account of them still shining up their daisy-roots and working in a quick shave, even on the retreat.

GERALD KERSH: *They Die with Their Boots Clean* (1942)

Daley, Arthur A shady second-hand car dealer who was the main character in the television comedy-drama series MINDER (1979–94). He was played by George Cole. His constantly punctured self-importance endeared him to the public, and his catchphrases (notably 'HER INDOORS', 'a nice little earner' and 'the world is your lobster') were widely copied.

Dally the Tall *See* DOLLY THE TALL.

Dalston KINGSLAND and Dalston are twin localities situated on the western side of HACKNEY, but the latter name is commonly applied to the whole district. First recorded in 1294, the settlement began life as Deorlof's farm. Holy Trinity Church, on Beechwood Road, is the 'clown's church' where the great Joey Grimaldi is honoured with a painting, a stained-glass window and a special prayer at the annual CLOWNS' SERVICE on the first Sunday in February each year. Ridley Road market has nearly 200 pitches, and an emphasis on world foods.

Don't go back to Dalston
And no, don't go up the junction
Don't go round the houses
Just come back to me.

JOHNNY BORRELL: 'Don't Go Back to Dalston' (song by Razorlight) (2004)

dance

Dance of St Paul's A painting on the wall of a cloister that lay within the precinct of the old ST PAUL'S Cathedral. It was paid for by John Carpenter, town clerk of London (*see* LIBER ALBUS), and depicted a 'Dance of Death', an allegorical representation of Death leading people to the grave in order of social precedence, accompanied by translations of French verses by John Lydgate (*c.*1370–1451). The cloister was pulled down by Edward Seymour, 1st Duke of Somerset, in the reign of Edward VI (r.1547–53), and the materials employed in the erection of his own palace in the STRAND. The painting was lost and, contrary to an oft-repeated rumour, there is no copy in the LAMBETH PALACE library. *See also* PARDON CHURCHYARD.

dance the Paddington frisk, to *See* PADDINGTON FAIR DAY.

dance the Tyburn jig, to Slang at the turn of the 19th century for 'to be hanged'.

Dancing Chancellor Sir Christopher Hatton (1540–91) was so called because he first attracted Elizabeth I's notice by his graceful dancing in a masque at court. He was lord chancellor from 1587 until his death and was a major sponsor of Sir Francis Drake's round-the-world voyage. Drake renamed his flagship in honour of his patron, whose family crest featured a GOLDEN HIND. *See also* HATTON GARDEN.

> His bushy beard and shoestrings green,
> His high-crowned hat and satin doublet,
> Moved the stout heart of England's queen,
> Though Pope and Spaniard could not trouble it.
>
> THOMAS GRAY: *A Long Story* (1750)

Dandies' Club A nickname – prompted by an affectionate remark of Lord Byron's – for Watier's, a gentlemen's club that operated at 81 PICCADILLY from 1807 to 1819. The institution took its proper name from Jean-Baptiste Watier, chef to the Prince REGENT, and its original purpose was to provide more adventurous cuisine than did its more straight-laced rivals such as BROOKS'S. However, high-stakes gambling soon took over as the club's main attraction, notably at the card game Macao. BEAU BRUMMELL was life president and Watier's attracted most of the leading fops and beaux of London society before ending its days with a reputation as a haven for BLACKGUARDS.

> It was a superb assemblage of gamesters and fops – knaves and fools; and it is difficult to say which element predominated.
>
> GRACE AND PHILIP WHARTON: *The Wits and Beaux of Society* (1861)

Danson Park A historic parkland site and surrounding suburban development, situated west of BEXLEYHEATH and south of WELLING.

It was first recorded as 'Dansington' in 1294. The 18th-century mansion at its heart was designed by Robert Taylor, architect of the BANK OF ENGLAND. The grade I listed building has recently been restored by its leaseholder, English Heritage.

Darby

Darby and Joan An elderly, loving, harmonious couple. The names belong to a ballad, possibly written by Henry Woodfall, first published in *The Gentleman's Magazine* in 1735. The characters are said to be John Darby, printer, of BARTHOLOMEW Close, SMITHFIELD, who died in 1730, and his wife Joan, described as: 'chaste as a picture cut in alabaster. You might sooner move a Scythian rock than shoot fire into her bosom'. Another account, however, locates the couple in the West Riding of Yorkshire.

Darby Kelly 'Belly' in COCKNEY RHYMING SLANG, from a traditional folk song about three generations of one family who were all military drummers and all named Darby Kelly. The term can be abbreviated to 'Darby' or 'Darby Kell'.

> Boiled beef and carrots,
> That's the stuff for your Darby Kell,
> Makes you fit and keeps you well.
>
> CHARLES COLLINS and FRED MURRAY: 'Boiled Beef and Carrots' (song) (1909)

Darby's fair Nineteenth-century London slang for the day on which a prisoner was moved from one jail to another (often NEWGATE) for trial. Darbies were handcuffs.

Darkplace Hospital The setting for the Channel 4 comedy *Garth Marenghi's Darkplace* (2004), the creation of Matthew Holness and Richard Ayoade. Although only one series was commissioned, this retro-horror and sci-fi spoof subsequently acquired minor cult status. The sinister hospital was located over the very gates of hell itself, in ROMFORD.

Dartmouth Park A group of well-built Victorian estates in south HIGHGATE. Dartmouth Park Hill was originally part of the oldest road in Highgate, a mucky track through thick forest that later became part of the manor and parish boundaries. The earls of Dartmouth acquired much of the land here in the 18th century. In the 1870s the Dartmouth family began to develop its estate and few gaps remained by the end of the century. Dartmouth Park Lodge became a gatehouse for Waterlow Park when it opened in 1891.

Darwin

Darwin, Charles *See* DOWNE.
Darwin Centre *See the* NATURAL HISTORY MUSEUM.

Dave The protagonist of Will Self's novel *The Book of Dave* (2006), subtitled *A Revelation of the Recent Past and the Distant Future.* Dave Rudman is a disgruntled BLACK CAB driver who records his misogynistic ramblings in a book, which he then buries. Five hundred years after Dave's death the book is found by the islanders of Ham, an unflooded part of what was HAMPSTEAD HEATH, and it becomes the sacred text of their new religion, the central gospel of which is called the KNOWLEDGE. (For the 'Dave' urban myth concerning Bob Dylan, *see* CROUCH END.)
Dave Clark Five *See the* TOTTENHAM SOUND.

David Copperfield Charles DICKENS's most autobiographical novel, first published in instalments (1849–50). The story is David's 'written memory' of his confrontation with life. A spoiled infant, his domestic idyll is cut short by his hated new stepfather, Mr Edward Murdstone. His various hardships, from working in the warehouse of Murdstone and Grinby, in BLACK-FRIARS, to attending Salem House, a school near BLACKHEATH, to the death of his first wife, Dora Spenlow, are followed by his happy second marriage to Agnes Wickfield. The events all play crucial roles in his passage from innocence to a painful apprehension of the world, and a comfortable but reflective middle age as a famous author.

Dawley A little-used name for an industrial and commercial zone in HAYES (London Borough of HILLINGDON), situated south of the GRAND UNION CANAL. The statesman and writer Henry St John, Viscount Bolingbroke, acquired the 17th-century Dawley House in 1725 and substantially rebuilt it; Dryden, Pope, Swift and Voltaire were among his visitors there. In 1755, Henry, Earl of Uxbridge, added the manor to his extensive landholdings in the district and built a mile-long wall around Dawley House to keep out smallpox. Dawley House was demolished in 1776 and its once-beautiful gardens became brickfields. The Gramophone Company (later EMI) moved its headquarters to Blyth Road in 1911 and opened a factory and recording studio there. It is said that the company bought all the chickens in the neighbourhood to prevent their cackling being picked up by the recording apparatus. After a peak in its activity in the early 1960s, when the company owned 150 acres (60 hectares) of land and employed 14,000 staff, EMI progressively withdrew from Dawley, relocating its offices, closing the factory, spinning off its central research laboratories and selling the site to a Far Eastern fund in 1999.

Day A once-controversial sculpture (1929) by Jacob Epstein (1880–1959) on the exterior of 55 BROADWAY. The building is graced by ten reliefs, none of which was much appreciated at the time of its construction, including Epstein's companion piece to *Day, Night*, and works by Eric Gill and Henry Moore. However, public and press opprobrium centred on *Day* for its portrayal of a father and his naked son and, in particular, for the proportions of the boy's phallus. Frank Pick, the MAN WHO BUILT LONDON TRANSPORT and commissioned the work, stood by Epstein and threatened to resign rather than remove the sculpture but Epstein deflected the criticism by ascending the building one night and reducing the length of the offending appendage by 1½ inches (3.8 cm).

Daylight Saving Time The system of advancing British clocks by an hour during the summer months was devised in PETTS WOOD by the London property developer William Willett (1856–1915). As he rode through the locality early one morning he noticed how few people seemed to be up and about, despite the bright sunshine outside. He published a pamphlet entitled 'The Waste of Daylight' (1907) and gained some parliamentary support for his proposal. However, it was not implemented until 1916, when wartime pressures made the case for energy saving more compelling. Willett is commemorated by a memorial sundial that stands in a corner of the surviving woodland of Petts Wood.

Dead! And never called me 'mother' *See* GONE! AND NEVER CALLED ME 'MOTHER' (*under* GO).

dean (Late Latin *decanus*, 'one set over ten') The ecclesiastical dignitary who presides over the chapter of a cathedral or collegiate church, this having formerly consisted of ten canons. In the more recent foundations decanal functions are carried out by a provost. The bishop of London is an ex officio 'Dean of the Province of Canterbury' and summons the bishops of the Southern Province to meet in Convocation under a mandate from the archbishop of Canterbury.

Dean of the Arches The judge presiding over the COURT OF ARCHES, held at ST MARY-LE-BOW church.

Dean's Guinea *See the* GREAZE.

Deans of Peculiars Once numerous and including those of collegiate churches such as WESTMINSTER. *See also* PECULIARS.

De Beauvoir Town A contrasting community of council tower blocks and early Victorian villas in west DALSTON, separated from HOXTON by the GRAND UNION CANAL. Richard Benyon de Beauvoir laid out the estate in the 1840s and its civilized proportions made it popular with wealthy commuters to the nearby CITY. In the 1960s HACKNEY council demolished nearly a third of the original estate to build low- and high-rise flats. Since then, designation as a conservation area and a vigorous local campaign have made the most of what remains. *See also the* MOLE MAN.

Debenhams A department store group that evolved from Thomas Clark's draper's shop in WIGMORE STREET, which was established in 1778. William Debenham (1794–1863) became a partner in the business in 1813. The company opened stores throughout Britain and then internationally, and acquired the businesses of several competitors. Following a series of name changes, the group became Debenhams Ltd in 1905. It merged with Marshall and Snelgrove of OXFORD STREET in 1919. Debenhams presently owns 13 stores in GREATER LONDON, including the former ARDING & HOBBS.

> Towards the end of George III's long reign, William Debenham and Thomas Clark had to take account of the dandyism, affected manners, and extravagant clothes of a peacock society peopled by such as 'Beau' Brummell, Mrs Fitzherbert, and Lady Hertford, the Prince Regent's favourite.
>
> MAURICE CORINA: *Fine Silks and Oak Counters: Debenhams, 1778–1978* (1978)

Deck, the A 19th-century slang term for SEVEN

DIALS. A denizen of that district was called a Decker.

Decomposition Row Society slang for ROTTEN ROW in the 1860s.

Dee, Dr John Dee (1527–1608), mathematician, alchemist and astrologer, was patronized by Queen Elizabeth I, but eventually died a pauper at MORTLAKE, where he was buried. He was one of the most inventive scholars of his day, writing 79 treatises on a variety of subjects. In 1563 he published the controversial *Monas Hieroglyphia* on the mystic science of numerology. It was written in his own code and only those in his confidence were able to decipher the text. Dee's magic crystal, through which he claimed to have been granted interviews with angels, is now in the BRITISH MUSEUM.

deerstalker A soft cloth cap with peaks in front and behind and ear flaps that are often joined at the top. It is so called as traditionally worn by sportsmen stalking deer. It is popularly regarded as an essential part of the habiliment of Sherlock HOLMES, an association mostly due to his illustrators and in particular to the *Strand* artist Sidney Paget (1860–1908).

> But the iconic image of Holmes in deerstalker and inverness cape, a calabash clutched in his lips, owes little to Conan Doyle, who never mentions either the cape or the deerstalker by name – the closest references to the latter are to a 'close-fitting cloth cap' in 'The Boscombe Valley Mystery' and an 'ear-flapped travelling cap' in 'Silver Blaze' ...
>
> THOMAS M. LEITCH: *Film Adaptation and Its Discontents* (2007)

Defoe, Daniel A campaigning Londoner, writer and adventurer (*c.*1660–1731). Born in STOKE NEWINGTON, the son of a butcher, he set up in the hosiery trade here in 1683. In Queen Anne's reign he ran into trouble with his famous satire *The Shortest Way with the Dissenters* (1702), which eventually cost him a ruinous fine, the pillory and imprisonment in NEWGATE PRISON. After his release, he founded a newspaper, *The Review* (1704–13), which aimed at being an organ of commercial interests, but also expressed opinions on political and domestic topics, and included the feature the 'Scandal Club', anticipating such magazines as *Tatler* and *The Spectator*. He turned to writing fiction after 1714, and in 1719–20, at the age of nearly 60, published his best-known book, *Robinson Crusoe*. His other major fictions include *Journal of the Plague Year* (1722) and *Moll Flanders* (1722), his most vivid and still one of the best tales of low life. A writer of astonishing versatility, he published more than 250 works in all, among them *Augusta Triumphans, or the Way to make London the Most Flourishing City in the Universe* (1728). He was buried in BUNHILL FIELDS, where an obelisk was erected in his memory in 1870.

Del Boy The informal name of Derek Trotter, protagonist of the long-running BBC TV sitcom ONLY FOOLS AND HORSES. The DEPTFORD-born market trader popularized terms such as 'cushty', 'plonker' and 'lovely jubbly', as well as the three-wheeled Reliant Regal van. Del Boy was played by David Jason.

Délivrance, La *See the* NAKED LADY.

Dell, The A gently sloping bowl in HORNCHURCH that was a popular setting for wrestling matches and other sporting events, especially in the 18th century, and possessed one of the best-known cockpits in the London area. The Dell lay to the south-west of St Andrew's Church, in the Mill Field, which was possibly the site of the town's monastery and is now a recreation ground. In 1795 'Gentleman' John Jackson defeated the 'WHITECHAPEL WHIRLWIND' Daniel Mendoza in a famous fight at the Dell. Jackson's ungentlemanly technique included holding Mendoza by his hair while punching his head with his other hand. Boxers have rarely worn their hair long since.

Demon Barber of Fleet Street The nickname of Sweeney Todd, the legendary FLEET STREET barber who regularly murdered his customers. His Grand Guignol act involved slitting the punter's throat with a razor while he was sitting in the barber's chair, and then disposing of the body via a trapdoor into a cellar, where it was dismembered and transferred by a secret tunnel to a nearby bakery to be made into pies or sausages. He first achieved celebrity as the central character of *The String of Pearls*, an anonymously authored serial published between November 1846 and March 1847 in the *People's Periodical and Family Library*, which was immediately adapted into a play by George

Dibdin Pitt (1799–1855). The character has since featured in numerous other dramatic treatments, including the melodramatic film *Sweeney Todd, the Demon Barber of Fleet Street* (1936), with Tod Slaughter in the named part, and most notably, recently, Stephen Sondheim's much elaborated musical of the same name (1979). Sondheim's musical was adapted for the cinema in 2007 by Tim Burton, starring Johnny Depp as Todd and Helena Bonham Carter as the pie-making Mrs Lovett. The story seems to have no basis in fact, despite the insistence to the contrary of some London tour guides.

> This notion of Todd as an actual historical character makes the tale more horrible … But there is no account of Todd's surely remarkable trial and execution in official records, and thus no real evidence that he ever existed.
>
> LOUISE WELSH, in *The Guardian* (19 January 2008)

dene hole or **denehole** An ancient excavation found in chalk downland in the vicinity of the THAMES estuary, consisting of a deep shaft which widens at the bottom into one or more rooms. They were once thought to be the work of Vikings, used for hiding plunder, and their name may be an alteration of 'Dane hole'. Another theory suggested that the holes were underground Druidic temples. However, they were probably dug to extract good quality chalk to use as fertilizer. One of the largest surviving groups of dene holes is at Cavey's Spring, near BEXLEY.

Denmark

Denmark Hill A street in south CAMBERWELL, connecting with HERNE HILL at its southern end. Originally Camberwell's High Street, it was renamed in honour of Queen Anne's husband, Prince George of Denmark (1653–1708), who had a residence here. In 1842 the writer John Ruskin moved into a detached house on the hill and stayed here for almost three decades. It has been claimed that the sport of roller hockey, now especially popular in the USA and southern Europe, was invented at Denmark Hill's Lava rink in 1885. In 1913 King's College Hospital relocated to new premises in Denmark Hill and established a separate school of medicine here. The Maudsley Hospital opened in 1923 as a LONDON COUNTY COUNCIL HOSPITAL for the early treatment of acute mental illness; it is now part of the KING'S COLLEGE campus. King's College added a dental hospital and teaching school in the late 1960s. The SALVATION ARMY's William Booth College, on Champion Park, was built in 1929 by Sir Giles Gilbert Scott. Its monumental style is reminiscent of Scott's BANKSIDE power station, now TATE MODERN.

Denmark Street A short street connecting ST GILES High Street with CHARING CROSS ROAD. From the 1920s musicians made the street a focus for their off-stage activities and in the 1950s and 60s it became London's 'Tin Pan Alley', home to numerous publishers of sheet music. Jimi Hendrix and the Beatles, the KINKS and ROLLING STONES were among the artists to use its recording studios early in their careers, while Bob Marley is said to have bought his first guitar here. Denmark Street is still renowned for its specialist music shops.

> Down the way from the Tottenham Court Road
> Just round the corner from old Soho
> There's a place where the publishers go
> If you don't know which way to go
> Just open your ears and follow your nose
> 'Cos the street is shakin' from the tapping of toes
>
> RAY DAVIES: 'Denmark Street' (song by the Kinks) (1970)

Deptford A historic THAMES-side settlement, situated west of GREENWICH. Its name was first recorded in 1293 and is a corruption of 'deep ford'. Henry VIII founded a naval dockyard here in 1513 and within a century Deptford had become one of the country's leading ports and a major industrial suburb. Many of the greatest figures of 16th- and 17th-century English history had associations with Deptford. In 1577 Francis Drake sailed from Deptford via Plymouth on his three-year circumnavigation of the globe, claiming a portion of present-day California for Elizabeth I; on his return, Drake was knighted by the Queen after she had dined aboard the GOLDEN HIND at Deptford. In 1593 the dramatist Christopher Marlowe was killed here, reputedly in a tavern brawl. The diarist John Evelyn came to Deptford in 1652 to live at Sayes Court, a house belonging to his wife's family, which he rented to Peter the Great of Russia in 1698 during the Tsar's visit to learn the art of shipbuilding. Evelyn discovered woodcarver and sculptor Grinling Gibbons toiling in a lowly Deptford workshop and introduced him to Christopher WREN; Gibbons went on to become a master carver under five British sovereigns. Another illustrious diarist,

Samuel PEPYS, worked in Deptford as an admiralty official. From the closure of the dockyard in 1869 and of the cattle market that replaced it in 1913, through Second World War bombing and postwar industrial decline, Deptford has suffered a long and damaging period of deterioration but it is now the focus of extensive regenerative building, both commercial and residential.

Deptford Fun City An ironically titled record label that launched the bands Squeeze and Alternative TV in 1977. The seminal punk fanzine *Sniffin' Glue* flourished in Deptford around the same time.

Deptford pink *Dianthus armeria*, a protected species of wildflower with diamond-shaped deep pink petals, similar in appearance to Sweet William. The plant was given its English name by the 17th-century herbalist and apothecary Thomas Johnson, possibly in a case of mistaken identity, as he may in fact have been describing maiden pink (*Dianthus deltoides*).

Derby

Derby ale and London beer The best of both worlds. The two cities had the foremost reputations for the respective brews.

Epsom Derby *See* EPSOM RACES.

Design Museum

Design Museum A museum of modern design founded in 1989 at SHAD THAMES. The brainchild of Sir Terence Conran (b.1931), it occupies the main building of the former Butler's Wharf complex. The museum is devoted to all forms of contemporary design, including architecture, fashion, graphics and consumer and industrial products. It also hosts a programme of temporary exhibitions covering a broad range of design disciplines.

Desmond

Desmond (Hackett) 'Jacket' in COCKNEY RHYMING SLANG. Desmond Hackett was a renowned sports reporter for the *Daily Express* from the 1950s onwards, specializing in football. More recently, 'Desmond' has come to signify (usually among non-cockneys) a lower second-class honours degree, from the homophone of 'two-two' and 'Tutu', in a reference to the South African cleric; while 'tennis (racket)' has been used for 'jacket'.

Desmond's A Channel 4 sitcom created by Trix Worrell (b.1960) that ran for six seasons between 1989 and 1994. The show was set in a PECKHAM barber's shop owned by Desmond Ambrose, played by Norman Beaton. *Desmond's* has been the most successful British TV comedy to feature an overwhelmingly black cast.

devil

devil among the tailors, the Formerly said when a slanging match was in progress. The phrase is also the name of a game in which a top (the 'devil') is spun among a number of wooden men (the 'tailors') with the aim of knocking down as many as possible. The phrase is said to have originated from a fracas made at a benefit performance *c.*1830 for the actor William Dowton (1764–1851). The piece was a burlesque called *The Tailors: a Tragedy for Warm Weather*, and the row was made outside the HAYMARKET Theatre by a large crowd of tailors, who considered the play a slur on their trade.

Devil's Acre A 'universally depraved' ROOKERY that lay in the vicinity of Old Pye Street and Great Peter Street, behind WESTMINSTER ABBEY. It was probably of late medieval origin and was permitted to survive well into the 19th century despite its proximity to the abbey and the seat of British government. Andrew Walker, a Scottish gardener, opened London's first RAGGED SCHOOL here in 1839, in an old stable. One reason for the construction of VICTORIA STREET in the middle of the 19th century was to try to eradicate the Devil's Acre, but many inhabitants simply moved a short distance to the south. Most were rehoused in PEABODY BUILDINGS in the 1870s. Gustave Doré depicted the slum in an evocative etching shortly before its disappearance, with accompanying text by Blanchard Jerrold:

> The Solemn and Venerable is at the elbow of the sordid and the woe-begone. By the noble Abbey is the ignoble Devil's Acre, hideous where it lies now in the sunlight.
>
> *London: A Pilgrimage* (1872)

Devil's Gap An archway and attached tenement that stood on the west side of LINCOLN'S INN FIELDS until 1756. The last permanent resident of the tenement, around a century earlier, was Jonathan Crouch, a lawyer and money lender. Crouch had a reputation for ruthlessness in his financial dealings but he over-reached himself in an effort to secure a rich and youthful heiress as a wife for his son. He was said to have died at Devil's Gap in a struggle with Richard Mainwaring, a rival for the young lady's hand.

> The cold sweat of a mortal terror oozed from every pore of the attorney's body as he fought, tore, wrestled with frenzied but unavailing strength to wrench himself from the hold of his ferocious foe. The portion of wood-work which supported him for a while snapped short; he toppled over, and, locked in each other's death-clutch, Richard Mainwaring and Jonathan Crouch shot through the void, and were dashed with tremendous violence upon the flinty pavement beneath.
>
> WATERS: *Traditions of London: Historical and Legendary* (1859)

Devil's Lane An old nickname for Tollington Lane in HOLLOWAY, derived from the highwayman Claude Duval, who frequented this vicinity until his execution in 1669. Tollington manor house, also known as the Lower Place, stood beside the road to HORNSEY on a site later occupied by a pub called the Devil's House and now filled by Kinloch Street. The pub functioned until at least 1811, latterly under a more wholesome name.

Devil's Own A nickname said to have been given to the INNS OF COURT and BLOOMSBURY Volunteers, later renamed the Inns of Court Rifles (afterwards a Territorial unit) by George III (r.1760–1820) when he found that the regiment consisted mainly of lawyers.

Devil's Plat or **Plot** The land on which PERIVALE mill is said to have stood in the early 17th century. According to legend, the mill was then owned by one Abel Reed, who was the only man in Perivale not to believe in the powers of witchcraft possessed by his neighbour. After an unseemly row between the pair she cursed him and a year later he was crushed by his own millstones. The witch also died, when she ventured into the mill to discover her enemy's fate, missed her footing and fell. The mill lay vacant for a long while after, and when it was reoccupied by an old miser he too soon died. Simon Coston, an orphaned youth who found his body, went missing after fleeing the mill screaming in terror that he had seen a ghost. He reappeared many years later as a wealthy squire, and built himself a fine house on what is now Costons Lane, GREENFORD. Coston eventually revealed that the miser had died in the act of counting his money, and that his terrified disappearance had been a subterfuge to allow him to leave town with the cash. Coston himself seems to have survived to a ripe old age but his ghost reputedly haunted the vicinity long after his house had burnt to the ground in a mysterious fire.

> He [Coston] is said to have lost his wife by the plague, and suffered other misfortunes, though originally so rich that it is now averred his riding horses 'were shod with silver'.
>
> JOHN ALLEN BROWN: *The Chronicles of Greenford Parva* (1890)

Devil's Tavern *See the* PROSPECT OF WHITBY.
Devil Tavern *See* GO TO THE DEVIL; *the* KING OF SKINKERS.
as sure as the devil is in London *See under* AS.
Cornhill devils *See under* CORNHILL.
go to the devil *See under* GO.

Diagon Alley London's main thoroughfare of wizardry in the Harry POTTER books by J.K. Rowling. The name is a respelling of 'diagonally'. Diagon Alley is located off CHARING CROSS ROAD but is hidden from human ('muggle') eyes. The alley has Gringotts Bank, the offices of the *Daily Prophet* newspaper, Ollivander's wand emporium and other specialists in wizarding supplies. Retailers of darker magical merchandise operate in neighbouring KNOCKTURN ALLEY. Diagon Alley scenes in the Harry Potter films were shot in LEADENHALL MARKET, while Australia House, in the STRAND, stood in for Gringotts Bank.

dial The face. *See also* DUCH(ESS OF FIFE).
Dial M for Murder An Alfred Hitchcock film (1954), in which a call to the MAIDA VALE telephone number MAI 3499 is the signal for a killing at the fictional 61A Charrington Gardens. The movie was based on Frederick Knott's play, which was televised by the BBC and staged at the WESTMINSTER Theatre in 1952. Later that year the play transferred to New York's Broadway, where the heroine's name was changed to Margot, lest the audience fail to appreciate that the 'M' in the title was a reference to the Maida Vale telephone exchange.
Dials, the A short form of SEVEN DIALS.

diamond geezer London slang of the late 20th century for a thoroughly excellent, reliable chap, the salt of the earth. The term is now mostly used tongue in cheek. One of London's most-read blogs goes by the name (diamondgeezer.blogspot.com).

Diana, Princess of Wales, Memorial Fountain *See* PRINCESS DIANA MEMORIAL FOUNTAIN.

Dickens, Charles London's greatest writer of prose, Charles Dickens (1812–70) was born in Landport, then a suburb of Portsmouth. In 1822 the family moved to CAMDEN TOWN, and a year later to GOWER STREET North, but his father was arrested for debt in 1824 and sent to the MARSHALSEA PRISON with his whole family, apart from Charles, who was sent to work in a blacking factory at HUNGERFORD MARKET. On his father's release the family moved to SOMERS TOWN, and Charles went back to school, an academy in the Hampstead Road, for three or four years, after which he worked for a solicitor as an office boy (1827). Meanwhile, his father had obtained a post as reporter for the *Morning Herald*, and Charles decided also to attempt the profession of journalism. He taught himself shorthand and visited the BRITISH MUSEUM daily to supplement some of the shortcomings of his reading. It was not until 1835 that he obtained permanent employment on the staff of a London paper as a reporter, and in this capacity he was sent around the country. Meanwhile, in December 1833, the *Monthly Magazine* published a sketch 'Dinner at Poplar Walk', under the pen-name 'Boz', which was the nickname of Charles's younger brother. The *Sketches by Boz* were collected and published early in 1836. In the last week of March that year the first number of the *Pickwick Papers* appeared; three days afterwards he married Catherine, the daughter of his friend George Hogarth, editor of the *Evening Chronicle*. She bore him seven sons and three daughters between 1837 and 1852, three of whom predeceased their father. They were separated in 1858. In fulfilment of publishers' engagements he produced *Oliver Twist* (1838), which appeared in *Bentley's Miscellany*; *Nicholas Nickleby* (1838–9); and *Master Humphrey's Clock*, a serial miscellany which resolved itself into the two stories, *The Old Curiosity Shop* (1840–1) and *Barnaby Rudge* (1841). From then on a great part of Dickens's life was spent abroad, though he continued to make London a focus of many of his stories, most notably in *A Christmas Carol* (1843), *David Copperfield* (1849–50), *Bleak House* (1852–3), *Little Dorrit* (1855–7) and *Great Expectations* (1860–1). Dickens died suddenly at Gadshill, Kent, and was buried in WESTMINSTER ABBEY.

What an amazing place London was to me when I saw it in the distance, and how I believed all the adventures of all my favourite heroes to be constantly enacting and re-enacting there, and how I vaguely made it out in my own mind to be fuller of wonders and wickedness than all the cities of the earth, I need not stop here to relate.

David Copperfield

Dickens House Museum A collection of Dickensiana exhibited at 48 Doughty Street, HOLBORN, a house occupied by Dickens and his family between April 1837 and December 1839. The house came under threat of demolition in 1923, but was saved by the Dickens Fellowship (founded in 1902), which raised the mortgage and bought the freehold.

dicky

dicky bird 'Word' in COCKNEY RHYMING SLANG. The term is not abbreviated, primarily because this could lead to confusion with 'dicky dirt' (*see below*). It is generally used in negative contexts, such as the expression 'I haven't heard a dicky bird [about something or from someone]'.

George: Well? Did he say anything?
Yvonne: Not a dicky bird. I held his hand. He groaned a bit and pulled it away and seemed to want to be alone.

JEAN COCTEAU: *Les Parents Terribles*, I, ix (1938) (translated by Jeremy Sams, 1994)

dicky dirt 'Shirt' in COCKNEY RHYMING SLANG. Also spelt 'dickey' or 'dickie'.

didn't ought 'Port' (wine) in COCKNEY RHYMING SLANG of the late 19th and early 20th centuries. The term was a play on the words of those who 'didn't ought' to have a tipple, but did.

Diehards The nickname of the former MIDDLESEX Regiment. At the Battle of Albuera (1811), the 57th Foot, later the 1st Battalion Middlesex Regiment, and ultimately part of the Princess of Wales's Royal Regiment, had three-quarters of the officers and men either killed or wounded. Colonel Inglis was badly wounded, but refused to be moved; instead he lay where he had fallen crying: 'Die hard, 57th, die hard.' This was the first recorded use of the now-familiar term.

diesel alley REDBRIDGE has been so called, because so many BLACK CAB drivers choose to live here.

Dilettanti Society A CLUB founded in 1732 by a group of aristocrats with an interest in classical Greece and Rome. The society convened at various hostelries, including the King's Arms in PALL MALL and the Thatched House Tavern in ST JAMES'S STREET. The Dilettanti combined a high-minded appreciation of the arts with a spirited enjoyment of good food and wine, with some silly ribaldry and rituals thrown in. Politically, they echoed the civilizations they admired by leaning towards democratic principles. They later became more scholarly than baccanalian and published some important academic studies in the early 19th century.

A famous double portrait by Sir Joshua Reynolds shows members of the Dilettanti Society sipping away while making rude gestures about vaginas while holding up gemstones from classical antiquity and admiring painted Greco-Roman vases.

JUDITH HARRIS, in the *California Literary Review* (30 November 2008)

dilligrout A mess of pottage that in former times was offered to the British monarch on the day of his or her coronation by the lord of the manor of ADDINGTON, as their service to the Crown in return for the lordship. The word seems to be a much altered form of Anglo-French *del girunt* or *geroun*, changed to accommodate obsolete English *grout*, 'porridge'. This is first recorded in the early 14th century, but it is not known where it came from or what it originally literally meant. More recently, 'dilligrout' was a password required by the Fat Lady for granting admission into the Gryffindor common room in the Harry POTTER books.

The lord of the manor of Addington holds it by the tenure of presenting a dish of 'dilligrout', or 'maupygernon', to the king at his coronation. When George IV's long-delayed hour of glory revived all such obsoletisms, this obscure and delicate dish was duly offered; it was found to consist of an herb-pudding boiled in a pig's caul: 'and wasn't that a dainty dish to set before a king?'

MARTIN F. TUPPER, in *Sharpe's London Magazine*, Volume 8 (1849)

Dilly, the PICCADILLY or PICCADILLY CIRCUS. The term was especially popular among male homosexual prostitutes and their clients in the

1950s and 60s, when Piccadilly Circus was their prime London meeting place.

> Me, I'm just a Dilly boy
> Fresh-flower-pressed Piccadilly boy
> Hands on hips, pout on lips
>
> P. DOHERTY and C. BARAT: 'Dilly Boys' (song by the Libertines) (2004)

dine with Duke Humphrey, to To go dinnerless; to have no dinner to go to. The GOOD DUKE HUMPHREY was renowned for his hospitality. On his death it was reported that a monument would be erected to him in ST PAUL'S, but he was buried in St Albans. The tomb of Sir John Beauchamp (d.1358), on the south side of the nave of old St Paul's, was popularly supposed to be that of the duke, and when the promenaders left for dinner, the poor stay-behinds who had no dinner to go to or who feared arrest for debt if they left the precincts, used to say, when asked by the revellers if they were going, that they would 'dine with Duke Humphrey' that day.

The expression was at one time quite common, as was the similar one 'To sup with Sir Thomas Gresham', the Exchange (predecessor of the ROYAL EXCHANGE) built by Sir Thomas being a common lounging-place.

> Though little coin thy purseless pocket line,
> Yet with great company thou art taken up;
> For often with Duke Humphrey thou dost dine,
> And often with Sir Thomas Gresham sup.
>
> ROBERT HAYMAN: *Quodlibets*, 'Epigram on a Loafer' (1628)

Diogenes Club A fictional PALL MALL club named after the cynical Greek philosopher. No member was permitted to take the least notice of any other one, nor to speak at all, except in the Strangers' Room. The Diogenes Club was the haunt of Sherlock HOLMES's brother Mycroft.

> There are many men in London, you know, who, some from shyness, some from misanthropy, have no wish for the company of their fellows. Yet they are not averse to comfortable chairs and the latest periodicals. It is for the convenience of these that the Diogenes Club was started, and it now contains the most unsociable and unclubbable men in town.
>
> ARTHUR CONAN DOYLE: 'The Greek Interpreter' (1893)

Diorama (Greek *dia*, 'through', and *orama*, 'vision') An exhibition mounted at Park Square East, REGENT'S PARK from 1823, in the style of a similar show that had opened a year earlier in Paris. A pair of very large *trompe-l'œil* artworks, executed in materials of varying opacity and partly back-lit, were viewed by 200 spectators occupying seats that revolved around the circular hall. The scenes, mostly featuring architectural subjects and Alpine panoramas by Louis Daguerre (1787–1851) and Charles Bouton (1781–1853), were changed two or three times a year. The Diorama closed in 1851 and the building was converted into a Baptist chapel, later becoming artists' studios and a gallery.

> The views at the Diorama are again changed, and France and Switzerland are once more placed before our eyes without our encountering the nausea of crossing the Channel, the roguery of continental innkeepers, and all the other innumerable and indescribable miseries of foreign travel.
>
> *The Times* (22 April 1830)

dirty

Dirty Den The nickname of Dennis Watts, a character in the BBC television soap opera EASTENDERS. Watts, played by Leslie Grantham, was the landlord of the Queen Victoria pub, and became a nationally known villain for his serial womanizing. In 1989 he was apparently murdered by a hitman, but made a miraculous reappearance in the programme in 2003. Alas, his second coming was shortlived, for he was murdered again in 2005 and is now officially dead.

Dirty Dick's A tavern in BISHOPSGATE, the interior of which used to be festooned with cobwebs and grimed with dirt until environmental health inspectors demanded a clean-up in the early 1980s. The name was taken from the once famous Dirty Warehouse in LEADENHALL Street, owned by Nathaniel Bentley (*c.*1735–1809). He was brought up in easy circumstances and became known as the Beau of Leadenhall Street, but suddenly his mode of life altered completely to one of miserly squalor and he came to be called 'Dirty Dick'. His hardware store became famous for its dirt and decay, which increased with the years, and after his death some of its contents were bought by the tavern keeper to attract custom. His change from a man of fashion to one of slovenliness was reputedly the consequence of a broken engagement.

Fine dames from their carriages, noble and fair,
Have entered his shop – less to buy than to stare;
And have afterwards said, though the dirt was
so frightful,
The Dirty Man's manners were truly delightful.

WILLIAM ALLINGHAM: 'The Dirty Old Man: A Lay of
Leadenhall' (1854)

dirty dozen A sequence of twelve streets in
SOHO used by BLACK CAB drivers as a short cut
between REGENT STREET and CHARING CROSS
ROAD.

Dirty Gertie An alternative nickname for the
statue better known as the NAKED LADY.

Dirty Shirt Club The former Parthenon Club
in Regent Street.

... so called from the great unwashed who
congregate there.

JOHN CAMDEN HOTTEN: *A Dictionary of Modern Slang,
Cant, and Vulgar Words* (1859)

Dirty Square Mile A former nickname for
SOHO, contrasting it with the more respectable
original SQUARE MILE.

District line A LONDON UNDERGROUND line
that runs west-south-westwards from UPMIN-
STER to EARLS COURT, where branches diverge
to terminate at EDGWARE ROAD, Kensington
OLYMPIA, EALING Broadway, RICHMOND and
WIMBLEDON. The line is coloured green on the
map. Its first section opened in 1868 between
SOUTH KENSINGTON and WESTMINSTER. Extensions to HOUNSLOW and UXBRIDGE were later
transferred to the PICCADILLY LINE.

They're a ravenous horde – and they all came on
board at Sloane Square and South Kensington
stations.
And bound on that journey, you find your
attorney (who started that morning from Devon);

W. S. GILBERT: *Iolanthe*, 'The Lord Chancellor's song'
(1882)

Ditch, the An abbreviated East London nickname in the late 19th century for the district of
SHOREDITCH (whence also the joint name Ditch
and Chapel for Shoreditch and WHITECHAPEL)
and for the street called HOUNDSDITCH.

Dixon of Dock Green *See* DOCK GREEN.

do

do bird, to *See* BIRD (LIME).
do me a lemon *See* LEMON (FLAVOUR).
don't be a sinner, be a winner The mantra

of Philip Howard (b.1954), sometimes known
as 'megaphone man', who around 1994 began
haranguing WEST END shoppers with anti-
consumerist, pro-faith messages. In 2006 he was
served with an anti-social behaviour order,
banning him from amplified preaching in the vicinity of OXFORD CIRCUS. He subsequently made
appearances elsewhere and sometimes quietly
distributed tracts at his old *locus standi*.

Last summer he was cleared of harassment,
and, satisfied, told journalists: 'This proves
once and for all that Satan won't win.' He's a
London landmark, a red-faced Big Ben or shouty
Nelson's Column.

The Guardian (5 May 2006)

Don't Dilly-Dally on the Way *See* COCK LIN-
NET.

Don't Have Any More, Mrs Moore A cockney
MUSIC HALL classic (1926), written by Harry
Castling and James Walsh, in which Mrs Moore
is by turns advised to stop producing children,
drinking gin and marrying men with short
lifespans. The HOLBORN-born entertainer Lily
Morris (1882–1952) made the song a famous part
of her repertoire.

Don't have any more, Mrs Moore. Is Peter
Ackroyd a cockney mystic or one of our greatest
scholars? A visionary or bombast?

New Statesman (headline) (4 November 2002)

don't turn that side to London A provincial
catchphrase from the late 19th and early 20th
centuries. It was first used in the world of
commerce when discussing an inferior piece
of merchandise; the implication being that the
item, or one aspect of it, would not satisfy demanding metropolitan customers. Later it was
mockingly said to and of another person. *See also*
TURN THE BEST SIDE TO LONDON.

do you know Mrs Kelly? *See* YOU MUST KNOW
MRS KELLY?

dock

dockers' tanner The name popularly given to
the demand made by striking London dockers
for a minimum wage of sixpence an hour during
their successful strike of 1889.

Dock Green A fictional METROPOLITAN PO-
LICE district in DOCKLANDS, the setting of the
long-running BBC television drama series *Dixon
of Dock Green* (1955–76), created by Ted Willis.
It starred Jack Warner as the firm but kindly

PC George Dixon, whose greeting 'evening, all' became a catchphrase of the time.

Docklands The area covered by the former ports of London, originally 'Dockland', a term invented by journalists at the beginning of the 20th century. Docklands extends from TOWER BRIDGE to BECKTON on the north side of the THAMES, and from LONDON BRIDGE to ROTHERHITHE on the south. Often, however, the term is nowadays used in specific reference to the vicinity of CANARY WHARF. Waterfront development began at WAPPING and St Katharine's in the Middle Ages and progressively extended eastward and across the river as Britain's role as a trading nation increased. From the beginning of the 19th century inland docks were constructed to improve handling capacity and provide greater security from theft. Shipbuilding was concentrated on the ISLE OF DOGS. Speculative builders crammed cheap housing for dockworkers into networks of narrow streets in districts like CANNING TOWN and POPLAR.

The London docks were ravaged by bombing in the Second World War and never fully recovered afterwards. The use of containers and the increased size of ocean-going vessels progressively rendered the facilities redundant from the 1960s and the last docks closed in 1981. In that year, the LONDON DOCKLANDS DEVELOPMENT CORPORATION was established to find new uses for the derelict sites. On the south side of the Thames, the SURREY DOCKS were mostly filled in and covered by housing. In the north, most of LONDON DOCK was also filled in but other large docks were preserved for their aesthetic value or for new purposes. ST KATHARINE DOCKS became a marina, while the ROYAL DOCKS were used for watersports. North of the Royal Albert Dock a new town was built at Beckton. Commercial development was more tentative at first, partly owing to the precarious state of the economy at that time. The LDDC invested in infrastructural improvements, notably in the form of the DOCKLANDS LIGHT RAILWAY, and LONDON CITY AIRPORT opened in 1987. With the eventual success of the Manhattan-style project at Canary Wharf, financial companies relocated to Docklands in droves, causing consternation to the CORPORATION OF LONDON, which consequently relaxed some of its planning restrictions in the SQUARE MILE.

Docklands Light Railway A railway built 1984–7 eastwards from the CITY of London to the tip of the ISLE OF DOGS in the south and STRATFORD in the north. Later extensions took the line to BECKTON and (crossing under the Thames) to LEWISHAM and WOOLWICH ARSENAL. It is underground in the City, but carried on a viaduct for much of the rest of its length. It was built essentially as a quick fix for the transportation problems of the rapidly developing Docklands area, which it was hoped would attract businesses from the centre of London and in which it has succeeded.

doctor

Doctors' Commons The colloquial name for the College of Advocates and Doctors of Law, formerly situated near ST PAUL'S Cathedral. From 1572 it housed the ecclesiastical and Admiralty courts, and the name arose from the fact that the doctors had to dine there four days in each term. The college ceased to function in the mid-19th century, and the buildings were demolished in 1867.

> On the whole, I would recommend you to take to Doctors' Commons kindly, David. They plume themselves on their gentility there, I can tell you, if that's any satisfaction.
> DICKENS: *David Copperfield* (1849–50)

Doctor Williams's Library Britain's pre-eminent library of Dissenting theological literature. The library first opened in CRIPPLEGATE in 1729, funded by the will of Dr Daniel Williams, the leading London Nonconformist minister of his day. Since 1890 it has been based at 14 Gordon Square in BLOOMSBURY. Nowadays the building also houses the library that was held at the CONGREGATIONAL MEMORIAL HALL.

dog

dog (and bone) 'Telephone' in COCKNEY RHYMING SLANG.

> 'Ere now, don't get yer knickers in a twist. I only taped them yesterday. Got on the dog and bone and called you right away, I did.
> F. PAUL WILSON: *Infernal* (2006)

Dog-Woman The heroine of Jeanette Winterson's fantastical novel *Sexing the Cherry* (1989). A truly Rabelaisian character, she cannot remember her own name and so is called Dog-Woman because of the dozens of dogs she keeps in her shack beside the River THAMES. Phenomenally strong (able to send an elephant flying into the air and stop a rifle bullet in her cleavage), it is her love for her son Jordan, a love that she finds hard to show, that sustains her.

I am his Highness' dog at Kew *See under* I.

Doggett's Coat and Badge The prize given in an annual rowing match for amateur WATER-MEN (of either sex), held on a Friday in late July under the auspices of the Fishmongers' Company. It is so called from Thomas Doggett (*c*.1670–1721), an Irish comic actor of DRURY LANE, who conceived the idea to commemorate the first anniversary of the accession of George I to the throne. It is rowed with the incoming tide (formerly against it) from Swan Steps at LONDON BRIDGE to Cadogan Pier at CHELSEA, a distance of 4½ miles (7.2 km). The silver badge and coat of scarlet livery are presented to the winner in a colourful ceremony at Watermen's Hall. 'Doggett' and 'coat and badge' both mean 'cadge' in arcane COCKNEY RHYMING SLANG. In his *Dictionary of Rhyming Slang* (1960), Julian Franklyn speculates, perhaps wildly, that the coinage may date back to the time of professional watermen, when 'holders of the Doggett Coat and Badge could charge higher fares than those without'.

doily, **doyly** or **doyley** A small ornamental mat of lace or lace-like paper, laid on or under cake plates and the like. In the 17th century the word denoted a kind of woollen material, so that John Dryden, in *The Kind Keeper* (IV, i (1678)), speaks of 'Doily Petticoats', and Joseph Addison in No.102 of *The Guardian* (1713) writes of his 'Doily suit'. The Doyleys, from which the material was named, were linen drapers in the STRAND from the time of Queen Anne (r.1702–14) until 1850. Doilies are now regarded as rather 'genteel'.

> Beg pardon, I'm soiling the doileys
> With afternoon tea-cakes and scones.
>
> JOHN BETJEMAN: 'How to get on in Society' (1954)

doll

Doll, Tiddy *See* TIDDY DOLL.

Doll the Pippin Woman An apple seller who was said to have met a nasty end at a FROST FAIR of uncertain date. As she carried her heavy basket from booth to booth, the frozen THAMES cracked beneath her; she fell awkwardly into the water and a shard of ice severed her head from her body. John Gay (*see the* AESOP OF ENGLAND)

made light of the tragedy in the second of his books of TRIVIA (1716):

> The crackling crystal yields, she smiles, she dies;
> Her head, chopped off, from her lost shoulders flies;
> 'Pippins,' she cried, but Death her voice confounds;
> And pip, pip, pip, along the ice resounds.

Dollis Hill A multi-ethnic residential district situated between NEASDEN and CRICKLEWOOD, at one time known as Dollar's Hill. The name may be of 16th-century origin, and connected with a family called Dalley. Surprisingly, the etymology of nearby Dollis Brook may not be the same, although the spellings have converged owing to their physical and orthographic proximity. Most of Dollis Hill's undulating meadows were obliterated by suburban housebuilding before and after the First World War. In 1934 the Post Office engineering research station opened in Brook Road. Two war cabinet meetings were held in the bomb-proofed basement of an outbuilding there, and the wartime prime minister Winston Churchill briefly retained a flat at nearby Neville's Court. The research station was the British base of the 'innocent' in Ian McEwan's 1990 novel of that name. *See also* GLADSTONE PARK.

dolly

Dolly's Chop House An establishment that formerly stood in Queen's Head Passage, off PATERNOSTER ROW, named after its celebrated 18th-century cook. The quality of Dolly's freshly grilled meat drew all the major literary figures of that time. The NATIONAL PORTRAIT GALLERY has James Smith's etching of Dolly, looking grumpy.

> I take this opportunity to send you the history of this day, which has been remarkably full of adventures; and you will own I give you them like a beef-steak at Dolly's, hot and hot, without ceremony and parade ...
>
> TOBIAS SMOLLETT: *The Expedition of Humphry Clinker* (1771)

Dolly the Tall or **Dally the Tall** The nickname of Grace Elliott (*c*.1754–1823), derived from her maiden name, Dalrymple, and her uncommon (but unspecified) height. She embarked on a series of intimate liaisons with some of the leading figures of the day, possibly including the Prince of Wales, prompting her husband, the prince's physician, to pursue a divorce. One of her lovers, the Marquess of Cholmondeley, twice commissioned Thomas Gainsborough to paint her portrait.

My Lady Scandalous: The Amazing Life and Outrageous Times of Grace Dalrymple Elliott, Royal Courtesan
JO MANNING (book title) (2005)

dome

Dome, The A huge shallow dome built to house the Millennium Experience exhibition in 2000. It was erected on a tract of previously derelict land on the GREENWICH PENINSULA as the largest structure of its kind ever built – over half a mile (in fact, almost exactly one kilometre) in circumference. It was divided into 14 exhibition zones, each sponsored by a well-known company. The Dome was opened by Queen Elizabeth II on 31 December 1999, but it disappointed many of its visitors who endured long waits to see poorly explained or even malfunctioning exhibits. It closed on 1 January 2001, having made a heavy financial loss. The Dome has since reopened as a multi-purpose leisure attraction, immodestly rebranded the O2 by the telecommunications company that sponsors it. At its centre is a concert venue that can also serve as a sports arena; it will host both the gymnastics and basketball finals at the 2012 OLYMPIC GAMES.

Dome of Discovery An aluminium cupola erected on the SOUTH BANK for the FESTIVAL OF BRITAIN. Designed by Ralph Tubbs (1912–96), the low, round pavilion contained a series of galleries on the theme of 'discovery', including a planetarium (reached by an 'escalator to outer space') a Polar Theatre (complete with huskies) and a life-sized replica of Captain Cook's *Endeavour*. At 356 feet (111m) in diameter, it was the largest such structure in the world at the time. The press derided the dome (and the whole festival) as a waste of public money and the incoming Conservative government of 1952 overrode objections from its admirers and ensured that it was quickly dismantled.

Tragically, it was demolished by vengeful politicians ... if the dome had lasted longer than a mere 11 months, and if its lessons had been accessible to later generations of architects, then it would no doubt now be regarded as one of the seminal buildings of postwar Britain.
DAN CRUICKSHANK, in the *Architectural Review* (January 1995)

Domus Conversorum or **the House of the Converts** Founded on New Street (now CHANCERY LANE) in 1232 by Henry III, this was England's principal house of indoctrination, where Jews who had been coerced into renouncing their faith were interned away from their community and instructed in the Christian religion. The conversorum was fully active for around a century, thereafter undergoing a protracted decline. The building was demolished in 1717 to make room for the new house of the MASTER OF THE ROLLS, who retained the title of Keeper of the House of Converts until 1873. *See also the* CHAPEL OF THE ROLLS.

don

Dons The nickname of the former WIMBLEDON FC, now Milton Keynes Dons, and of the club's NORBITON-based successor, AFC Wimbledon.

Don Saltero's The nickname of Salter's, a barber's shop, COFFEE HOUSE and museum that stood at 18 CHEYNE WALK for most of the 18th century. It was established by James Salter (d.*c*.1728), a former servant of Sir Hans SLOANE. Salter opened his first barber's shop and coffee house in Cheyne Walk in the mid-1690s and moved to No.18 in 1718. He later added a collection of curios, which began with cast-offs donated by Sloane. Don Saltero's, as everyone called the place, was a favoured haunt of the leading literary figures of CHELSEA.

His reputation as a mixer of punch was very high; he could also shave, bleed, draw teeth, and play a little on the fiddle, and every year he added stranger oddities to his queer mimic museum, from which he probably got as much amusement as his many visitors.
WALTER H. GODFREY: *The Survey of London*, Volume 2 (1909)

donah or **donna** A COSTER's wife or sweetheart.

And writing of the coster, pleasant memories cling to Kate Carney's love ditty:
Liza, you are my donah,
You are my little peach.
Meet me round at the fish shop,
An' I'll buy yer a penn'orth of each.
ERNEST SHORT and ARTHUR COMPTON-RICKETT: *Ring Up the Curtain* (1938)

donkey

donkey in one's throat, to have a An old

COCKNEY equivalent of having a frog in one's throat.

donkey shay *See* SHAY.

Donmar Warehouse The venue of this name, now known for its innovative theatrical productions, opened in 1961 in a banana-ripening warehouse at 41 Earlham Street, COVENT GARDEN. It was at first a private rehearsal studio for the London Festival Ballet, known simply as the Warehouse. 'Donmar' was then added from the names of its original purchasers, Donald Albery (1914– 88) and his friend Margot Fonteyn (1919–91), the ballet dancer. Albery was the son of Bronson Albery (1881–1971), who gave his name to the Albery Theatre, and stepgrandson of Charles Wyndham (1837–1919), after whom Wyndham's Theatre is named.

don't *See under* DO.

Doolittle, Eliza In George Bernard SHAW'S PYGMALION (1913) and the stage musical and film MY FAIR LADY (1956; 1964), the howling, prudish, tenacious Eliza is an 18-year-old flower girl whom the phoneticist Professor Henry Higgins discovers one rainswept evening sheltering in the portico of St Paul's, COVENT GARDEN.

> The note taker: How do you come to be up so far east? You were born in Lisson Grove.
> Liza: [appalled] Oh, what harm is there in my leaving Lisson Grove? It wasn't fit for a pig to live in; and I had to pay four-and-six a week. [In tears] Oh, boo–hoo–oo–.
>
> *Pygmalion*, I

Dorchester, The A luxurious hotel on PARK LANE, haunt of film stars and Arab princes. It occupies the site of Dorchester House, built in 1751 and thus named following its acquisition by Joseph Damer (1718–98), who was made 1st Earl of Dorchester in 1792. Renamed Hertford House by the 3rd Marquis of Hertford, it was rebuilt in 1869 for Robert Stayner Holford (1808–92) in the style of a Renaissance palace. That building was dismantled in 1929, re-erected in Scotland and later sold to an American, Paul Knight, who transported its stairway to Texas. Among its innovative specifications were floors and ceilings lined with compressed seaweed for improved soundproofing.

Doris Day 'Gay' in modern rhyming slang,

possibly influenced by the actress's status as something of a gay icon in her latter years.

Double Deckers A gang of seven London children who appeared in the TV series *Here Come the Double Deckers* (1970–1), an Anglo-American production broadcast in the UK on BBC One. The Double Deckers' hideout was an old RT bus (the forerunner of the ROUTEMASTER) in an EAST END scrapyard on the fictional Water Works Road. Most of the location shooting took place in south Hertfordshire.

dove

Dove, The A public house on Upper Mall, HAMMERSMITH. Formerly a COFFEE HOUSE, the building dates from the early 18th century. Its second bar is reputedly Britain's smallest, with less than 33 square feet (3 sq m) of floor space. The poet James Thomson (1700–48) was a regular customer and may have written the words to *Rule Britannia* (1740) here.

Fleet Street dove *See under* FLEET STREET.

Dowgate A CITY of London ward encompassing a handful of streets either side of CANNON STREET STATION. The original Dowgate was a watergate that lay near the mouth of the WALBROOK. First recorded in 1151, the name probably meant 'gate frequented by doves'.

down

Down and Out in Paris and London An early and part-autobiographical narrative (1933) by George Orwell, in retreat from his Etonian and imperial background, concerning life at the bottom of the social scale in these two cities.

Down at the Old Bull and Bush *See under* OLD.

Down House *See* DOWNE.

Down Syndrome or **Down's Syndrome** A chromosomal disorder named after John Langdon Down (1828–96), who first described the physical and mental features associated with the condition. In 1868 Langdon Down founded Normansfield Hospital in South TEDDINGTON, where he carried out groundbreaking work on the diagnosis and treatment of learning disabilities. The hospital closed in 1997.

down train The train away from London or the local centre, as distinct from the up train, which goes to it. The down platform is similar.

Downe A country village located 3 miles (5 km)

south-west of ORPINGTON. The name was first recorded in 1283 and derives from Old English *dūn*, 'a hill'. It is claimed that the Post Office encouraged its spelling with an 'e' to avoid confusion with County Down in Ulster. On Luxted Road, Petleys was built in the early 18th century and became a home of the Wedgwood pottery family. In 1842 Josiah Wedgwood's daughter Emma came to live at Down House, a former parsonage at the southern end of the village, with her husband Charles Darwin (1809–82). The great scientist took a daily stroll around a circuit of the grounds known as the 'sand walk', set up a laboratory in a brick hut and cultivated orchids in the greenhouse. Darwin lived at Down House until his death and he wrote all his most important works here, including *On the Origin of Species by Means of Natural Selection* (1859). Down House became a Darwin museum in 1929 and was acquired by English Heritage in 1996.

Downe Bank A wood located to the south-east of Down House and known to Charles Darwin as Orchis Bank. Now a Kent Wildlife Trust property, it is rich in orchids and provides one of Britain's best displays of bluebells in spring.

Downham

Downham A COTTAGE ESTATE, also referred to as a 'garden city', situated midway between CATFORD and BROMLEY. It is named after William Hayes Fisher, first Baron Downham, chairman of the LONDON COUNTY COUNCIL until his death in 1920. From 1924 to 1930 the LCC built this huge estate of 6,000 homes on former farmland, part of which had been a popular walking spot known as Seven Fields. Road names were taken from old field names and, for no recorded reason, from Devon resorts and Arthurian legend. A further 1,000 homes were added in north Downham in 1937. Most of the tenants were relocated from decaying inner-city areas on the south side of the THAMES, such as BERMONDSEY, DEPTFORD and ROTHERHITHE. A population of more than 30,000 materialized where there had been a handful just a few years before. The Downham Tavern used to have a place in the *Guinness Book of Records* as Britain's largest pub. Built by the LCC in 1930, it could accommodate 1,000 customers.

Downing

Downing, George An Irish-born soldier and diplomat (*c*.1623–84). He fought for Parliament and later undertook several diplomatic missions for Cromwell, including that of ambassador to the Hague, where he associated with the Royalist exiles so that at the Restoration he continued as ambassador and received other offices, as well as a baronetcy (1663). DOWNING STREET is named after him.

Downing Street A cul-de-sac leading westwards off WHITEHALL. There was probably a road here in medieval times, but Downing Street as we now know it was the creation of Sir George Downing (*see above*). The brick terraced houses he had built around 1680 continued to attract a good class of tenant in the following century: James Boswell lodged here in 1762, Tobias Smollett tried to start up a surgeon's practice here in 1774, and in 1732 No.10 was acquired by the Crown. That house has been the official residence and office of the British prime minister ever since. Meetings of the British cabinet are usually held here. Behind its familiar facade and shiny black door it has undergone considerable expansion and reconstruction over the two-and-a-half centuries since its first occupant, Sir Robert Walpole, moved in. The south side of Downing Street was completely replaced with Sir George Gilbert Scott's Government Offices (now housing the Foreign Office) in the late 1860s, and on the north side only two houses apart from No.10 remain: No.11, home of the chancellor of the exchequer, and No.12, which is occupied by the government chief whip. The entrance to the street via Whitehall was closed off with high-security metal gates in 1989, to guard against terrorist attack (on 7 February 1991 the IRA mounted a mortar attack on No.10 from a nearby van). Since at least the late 18th century, 'Downing Street' (or more specifically No.10) has been used as a metonym for the British prime minister (or those who speak or spin on his or her behalf) or for the British government in general.

Downing Street Declaration An agreement between the British and Irish governments, formulated in 1993 and intended as the basis of a peace initiative in Northern Ireland. The declaration was issued from 10 Downing Street.

D'Oyly Carte

D'Oyly Carte An opera company specializing in the works of Gilbert and Sullivan. The company staged its first performance in 1875, and two years later assumed the name of its founder, the impresario Richard D'Oyly Carte (1844–1901). The success of the operas enabled him to build both the SAVOY Theatre, as the company's home, and in 1889 the Savoy Hotel. With the expiry of the Gilbert and Sullivan copyright in 1961, and in a climate of changing musical tastes and withdrawn subsidies, the company went into a decline; it has not staged a production since 2003.

doyly or **doyley** *See* DOILY.

dragon Since the early 17th century a pair of dragons has supported the crest of the City of London in its coat of arms; and in the latter part of the 19th century ornamental boundary markers were erected at ponts of entry into the CITY, each surmounted by a dragon clutching the heraldic shield. The creatures' introduction seems to have derived from the legend of St George, whose cross has been a City emblem since at least the early 14th century, and may have been specifically linked to a popular misconception that a fan-like object bearing the cross on an earlier crest was a dragon's wing. The City dragon is often incorrectly called a GRIFFIN, or gryphon, even in some official literature. This especially applies to the statue at TEMPLE BAR. It is not clear how the confusion arose but the misnomer has become so entrenched that some authorities consider it to have earned a degree of legitimacy. *See also* LOUSY ST LUKE'S.

Dragon Awards Prizes given annually by the LORD MAYOR OF LONDON in a number of categories, each recognizing corporate community involvement across GREATER LONDON. Winners receive a dragon statuette at a ceremony held in October. The awards were introduced in 1987.

Drain, the A nickname for the Waterloo and City line on the LONDON UNDERGROUND, opened in 1898. It is coloured turquoise on the map. The line runs between WATERLOO STATION and BANK, with no intervening stations. The designation, at first derogatory but latterly almost affectionate, dates from the 1920s and refers to the deep and dingy route. Before its transfer to LONDON UNDERGROUND in 1994 it was the only TUBE line run by British Rail.

Drake, Francis *See* GOLDEN HIND.

Drayton Park A residential and light industrial area centred on the street of that name on the western side of HIGHBURY. This is now a multi-ethnic community, with significant Turkish and Bengali minorities, and nearly 30 different languages are spoken at Drayton Park primary school. John Lydon, formerly Johnny Rotten of the SEX PISTOLS, was born in Benwell Road in 1956, a street that he considers to be part of FINSBURY PARK. Former prime minister Tony Blair lived in Stavordale Road from 1976 until 1982, when he moved to BARNSBURY. *See also* EMIRATES STADIUM.

Dreadnought The first ship of this name was in use in the reign of Elizabeth I (1558–1603). The Seamen's Hospital at GREENWICH was known as the Dreadnought Hospital, taking its name from the seventh *Dreadnought*, which was first in action in 1809, and from 1857 was anchored off Greenwich as a seamen's hospital. The ship was broken up in 1875. The hospital building is now the University of Greenwich's Dreadnought Library. The tradition of special hospital care for seafarers is maintained at the Dreadnought Unit of ST THOMAS' HOSPITAL.

drink at Freeman's Quay, to An obsolete expression signifying drinking at someone else's expense. It is said that, at one time, all porters and carmen calling at Freeman's Quay, near LONDON BRIDGE, had a pot of beer given them, gratis, but this explanation was probably invented to fit an already obvious allusion.

Drones Club A fictional MAYFAIR club created by the author P.G. Wodehouse (1881–1975). It was named after the male of the honey bee which does no work but lives on the labour of the worker bees, hence a sluggard, an idler, a parasite. Bertie WOOSTER was among several Wodehouse characters who belonged to the club.

> In the heart of London's clubland there stands
> a tall and grimly forbidding edifice known
> to taxi-drivers and the elegant young men
> who frequent its precincts as the Drones
> Club. Yet its somewhat austere exterior belies
> the atmosphere of cheerful optimism and
> bonhomie that prevails within. For here it is
> that young gallants of Mayfair forgather for the
> pre-luncheon bracer and to touch lightly on the
> topics of the day.
>
> P.G. WODEHOUSE: *Eggs, Beans, and Crumpets* (1940)

druid

Druid, the The pen name of Henry Hall Dixon, a lawyer turned sports journalist who published several books in the 1850s and 60s. His success enabled him to buy two adjoining houses in KENSINGTON Square.

Druids' Hall A house in TURNAGAIN LANE that belonged to the Ancient Order of Druids – a quasi-Masonic society – and was occasionally let for meetings, lectures and dancing. In the early 1850s its dances attracted the 'frequent congregation of certain persons for immoral practices'. The scandal came to light in 1854, when two men dressed in women's clothes were arrested and charged with 'conducting themselves in a manner to excite others to commit an unnatural offence'.

> Inspector Teague said, '... I exclaimed, "That is a man," upon which he turned round and ran back immediately to the Druids' Hall. I returned and took Campbell into custody and observing Challis, whom I have frequently seen there before, behaving with two men as if he were a common prostitute, I took charge of him also.'
>
> *The Times* (27 July 1854)

Drury Lane A historic COVENT GARDEN thoroughfare, representing the eastern edge of London's THEATRELAND. Until the construction of KINGSWAY in 1905, this was the principal route from High HOLBORN to the STRAND, which it used to join at a point near ST CLEMENT DANES Church. The road was described as 'old' when it was first recorded in 1199 and went under several names, including the Via de Aldewych and Fortescu Lane. Its present name derives from Drury House, built in the mid-16th century for Sir William Drury. By 1650 gentlemen's houses lined both sides of the lane and the first THEATRE ROYAL was established in 1663. Nell GWYN began selling oranges in Drury Lane around this time and soon made her first appearance on the theatre's stage. By this time the neighbourhood was acquiring a reputation for crime, disorder and prostitution. Drury Lane's impoverished conditions persisted until the late 19th century, when its squalid courts were cleared and replaced by model dwellings and commercial properties.

Drury Lane was the name of an amateur sleuth created by Ellery Queen in the 1930s. Lane was a Shakespearean actor, retired through deafness, who turned his keen intellect to solving 'tragedies' that had baffled the police.

Druriolanus A late 19th-century nickname for the THEATRE ROYAL, Drury Lane, originally coined as its telegraphic address (blending Drury and Shakespeare's Coriolanus) by the theatre's celebrated manager Augustus Harris (1852–96). The name was also applied to Harris himself.

Drury Lane ague Venereal disease, also known as COVENT GARDEN ague.

Drury Lane vestal A euphemism from the mid-18th to the early 19th centuries for the prostitutes who then frequented Drury Lane ('vestal' facetiously from the idea of a Roman vestal virgin).

always in trouble, like a Drury Lane whore *See under* ALWAYS.

Sweet Nell of Old Drury *See* Nell GWYN.

dubstep A genre of urban electronic music that developed at the turn of the millennium in south London, with assistance from SHOREDITCH and SOHO. Dubstep incorporates aspects of forerunners such as drum 'n' bass, garage and techno, often adding a dark edge. It is related to another London genre, GRIME, but the latter is more vocal.

> A new sound is infiltrating nightclubs across the world. From humble beginnings in Croydon, its combination of heavy bass, minimal Detroit pulses and sombre rhythms has struck a chord with electronica fans.
>
> *The Independent*, 'Dubstep: Straight outta Croydon' (28 July 2006)

duchess

Duch(ess of Fife) or **dutch** 'Wife' in COCKNEY RHYMING SLANG, especially said in the late 19th and early 20th centuries of the wife of a COSTERMONGER.

> There ain't a lady livin' in the land
> As I'd swop for my dear old Dutch!
>
> ALBERT CHEVALIER: 'My Old Dutch' (song) (1893)

In Chevalier's song the original reference is to 'my old Dutch clock', whose dial (i.e. face) reminded him of his wife. However, the rhyming slang predates the song.

Duchess of Jermyn Street A nickname for Rosa Lewis (1867–1952), a LEYTON-born former scullery maid who owned and ran the Cavendish Hotel in the first half of the 20th century. She was famed for her cooking and her open-minded hospitality. Lewis had earlier worked in several aristocratic homes and was said to have once chased the 10-year-old Winston Churchill out of her kitchen, yelling 'Hop it, copper knob.'

The television series *The Duchess of Duke Street* (1976–7) was loosely based on her story.

> Edward [VII] was an ardent patron of the hotel, which had a private entrance around the corner for merry monarchs and squires on the spree; as Prince of Wales he reputedly bankrolled his blonde, blue-eyed friend when she bought the Cavendish in 1902. 'One king leads to another,' she used to say.
>
> *Time Magazine*, 'Requiem for Rosa's' (29 June 1962)

duck

duck and dive, to To use one's ingenuity to escape from an undesirable or difficult situation. The metaphor may come from a boxer's agile attempts to avoid his opponent's blows, although the expression has also been explained as COCKNEY RHYMING SLANG for 'skive'.

duck's arse In addition to being a colloquialism for a tufted hairstyle and being called upon to signify tightness, usually of the miserly kind, 'duck's arse' has also been used as COCKNEY RHYMING SLANG for a 'GRASS', in the sense of a police informer.

Duel Day A day of celebration held annually at KING'S COLLEGE LONDON on the anniversary of a duel fought on 21 March 1829 between the Duke of Wellington and George Finch-Hatton, 10th Earl of Winchilsea. Wellington helped establish King's as a university college in the tradition of the Church of England, but his simultaneous support for Catholic emancipation prompted uproar in reactionary circles, accompanied by the withdrawal of many promises of financial support. Winchilsea challenged the duke to a duel on Battersea Fields (now BATTERSEA PARK), in which neither man was hurt, quite possibly by agreement in advance. In addition to events nowadays held at King's College itself on Duel Day, alumni around the world are encouraged to mark the occasion in some vaguely appropriate way.

duke

Duke Combe William Combe (1741–1823), also called Count Combe, author of *The Tour of Dr Syntax*, etc., was so called from the splendour of his dress, the profusion of his table and the magnificence of his deportment, in the days of his prosperity. Having spent all his money he turned author, but passed much of his life in the KING'S BENCH PRISON. He died at LAMBETH.

Duke Humphrey's Tower *See* GOOD DUKE HUMPHREY.

duke of Shoreditch The fictitious title was said to have been created by Henry VIII when a SHOREDITCH resident named Barlow won an archery match held at Windsor. Although the king's intentions were light-hearted, London's finest archers thereafter competed very seriously for the title at an annual contest. Similar honours were afterwards invented for winners of less prestigious competitions, such as the marquis of Hogsden (HOXTON) and the earl of PANCRIDGE (ST PANCRAS).

Duke of York's Column or **the York Column** A prominent London landmark situated at the top of Waterloo Steps (also known as the Duke of York's Steps), which lead from the MALL through CARLTON HOUSE TERRACE into Waterloo Place. It was completed in 1833 in memory of Frederick, Duke of York, George III's second son, who died in 1827. Every member of the British Army was docked one day's pay to finance its construction. The column is of the Tuscan order, designed by Benjamin Wyatt, and is made of Aberdeen granite, surmounted by a statue of the duke by Sir Richard Westmacott. It contains a winding staircase to the platform and is 138 feet (42m) high to the top of the statue.

> … some years ago the jumping down from the top and being smashed on the broad stones at its base was a fashionable mode of committing suicide. It's a pity that none of the poor wretches ever thought of over throwing and jumping down with the statue of the Duke of York, for it stands ridiculously high, and the impression it makes on that bad eminence is by no means agreeable.
>
> MAX SCHLESINGER: *Saunterings in and about London* (1853)

Dukery, the An old name for the Duchess of Bedford's Walk, which leads from CAMPDEN HILL towards HOLLAND HOUSE. The lane was formerly flanked by several homes of the nobility, including the mansions of the dukes of Argyll and Rutland, the Dowager Duchess of Bedford and Lords Airlie and Macaulay.

Duke's Meadows Open space to the south of GROVE PARK in CHISWICK, named after former landowner the Duke of Devonshire. Part of the meadows was acquired by the Cherry Blossom shoe-polish company in the 1920s for a packaging plant and an employees' sports ground. The rest was preserved by the council after schemes for a gasworks and a power station were dropped. Nowadays the meadows are awash with sports facilities – for tennis, athletics, cricket and more – as well as with bases for rowing and sailing on the THAMES.

Dulwich An expanded village situated 5 miles (8 km) south of the CITY of London, hemmed in by more prosaic neighbours that have traded on its prestige. First recorded as Dilwihs in a charter signed by King Edgar in AD 967, the name derives from Old English words 'dile wisc', meaning 'dill meadow'. Despite its close historical links with CAMBERWELL, to the north-west, Dulwich has remained distinct and has long been more exclusive.

Dulwich College A school founded in 1619 by the actor Edward ALLEYN (1566–1626) as the College of God's Gift, originally consisting of alm-shouses and a school for under-privileged boys. Most of the college buildings were erected in the late 1860s, financed by the sale of land to the South Eastern and Chatham Railway Company. Alleyn's School and James Allen's Girls' School are spin-offs from the college, and are located on opposite sides of East Dulwich Grove. Literary figures educated at the schools have included Raymond Chandler and P.G. Wodehouse at Dulwich College, C.S. Forester and V.S. Pritchett at Alleyn's School and Anita Brookner at James Allen's Girls' School. Wodehouse fictionalized Dulwich as VALLEY FIELDS.

Dulwich Park An open space formed in 1890 from the fields of Dulwich Court Farm and its neighbours.

Dulwich Picture Gallery The oldest public art gallery in England. It was founded when Sir Francis Bourgeois (1753–1811) bequeathed his collection of old masters. A work of art in itself, the gallery was designed by Sir John SOANE in 1812 and has paintings by Rubens, Rembrandt, Van Dyck and Gainsborough.

Dulwich Village A picturesque hamlet situated north of DULWICH COLLEGE. From the early 18th century, and especially after the mid-1760s, the college allowed wealthy Londoners – often the parents of pupils – to build substantial houses that would maintain their value, and that of the estate. A number of these remain, and only a few have been converted to flats or for other

purposes. The college subsequently permitted more homes to be built, of a progressively more affordable character, but nevertheless kept the numbers down and the standards up. Some of the village's cottage shops have been converted into homes. In the 20th century, building mostly took the form of pastiche replacements of Georgian properties.

dumbbell An aspect of the KNOWLEDGE, whereby prospective BLACK CAB drivers must be able to identify important places along any given route (known as a 'run') and within a quarter-mile (400m) radius of the beginning and end of that route.

Dunkirk House The nickname of Clarendon House, a palatial PICCADILLY mansion built around 1664 for Edward Hyde, 1st Earl of Clarendon. The tag derived from a popular belief that, as Charles II's lord chancellor, Clarendon had taken a commission from Louis XIV when Dunkirk was sold to the French. The assumption was almost certainly unfounded but Clarendon soon afterwards fell from the king's grace and was impeached by the House of Commons in 1667, after which he fled to France. The house was demolished in 1683.

> From Dunkirk House there lately ran away
> A traitor whom you are desired to slay ...
> This hopeful blade being conscious of his crimes,
> And smelling how the current of the times
> Ran cross, forsakes his palace and the town
> Like some presaging rat ere th' house fall down.
> anonymous ballad (1667)

dust

dust ho! One of the most familiar street cries of old London. 'Dust' not only connoted ashes and dirt but all manner of household and organic waste, hence the continuing use of the term 'dustman' for a refuse collector. The dustmen would sift and sort the material they removed, and with a combination of diligence and luck could sometimes turn a good profit. *See also* CRIES OF LONDON.

Dusthole or **Dust Hole**
1. A slum area of WOOLWICH from the late 19th century to its clearance in the 1950s. The Dusthole was squeezed between the dockyard and the Arsenal, and encompassed Hog Lane, Sow Alley, Cock Yard, Pig Court and Cow Yard, all of which have been erased from the map.

Many of the residents were of Irish origin. Charles BOOTH visited the area in May 1900, noting: 'The male inhabitants are bullies [pimps], dock and waterside labourers, costers, hawkers and tramps. The women are prostitutes.' Booth compared the Dusthole to the FENIAN BARRACKS in BROMLEY-BY-BOW, while the police constable who accompanied him likened it to NOTTING DALE. The Waterfront leisure centre now occupies most of the Dusthole's site.

2. A nickname in the mid-19th century (especially among actors) for the Queen's Theatre, TOTTENHAM COURT ROAD. In addition to its dirtiness, inadequate ventilation and the absence of a urinal anywhere in the building, it was noted for its low prices and high melodrama. Originally and later the Scala, its final incarnation was demolished in 1972.

Golden Dustman *See under* GOLDEN.

E

eagle

Eagle, The

1. A CITY ROAD tavern that replaced the Shepherd and Shepherdess ale house and tea garden, at the corner of what is now Shepherdess Walk, around 1745. A new Eagle tavern, combined with a 'Grecian theatre', was built in the 1820s. Marie Lloyd (*see the* QUEEN OF THE MUSIC HALL) started work here as a waitress, at the age of 15. *See also* POP GOES THE WEASEL.

2. A public house on FARRINGDON ROAD, near EXMOUTH MARKET. In 1991 its owners Mike Belben and David Eyre introduced the term 'gastropub' to describe the Eagle's mix of traditional pub decor and uncomplicated modern cuisine. The word and the concept were widely copied and the presence of such an establishment is now the hallmark of any locality with aspirations to coolness. Blackboard menus, open-plan kitchens and stripped floorboards are *de rigueur*; sawdust is optional.

> The Eagle's renown as birthplace of the modern gastropub movement seems to have resulted in an influx of tourists. Aside from the nearby Holiday Inn, this stretch of Farringdon Road is a curious destination for travellers, though they won't find a finer view of an NCP carpark anywhere in London.
>
> GUY DIMOND and CATH PHILLIPS (editors): *Time Out Eating & Drinking Guide* (2008)

3. A pub and restaurant on Hollybush Hill in SNARESBROOK. The present building dates from the 18th century; it is the oldest inn in the WANSTEAD area. As the Spread Eagle, its predecessor's importance in the late 17th and early 18th centuries as a coaching inn on the London–Newmarket road was the principal factor in the development of a settlement here. The Eagle has given its name to the large pond across the road, formerly Snares Pond.

Eagles The present-day nickname of CRYSTAL PALACE FC, promulgated in the mid-1970s following the introduction of a new crest that relegated the formerly dominant image of the glass exhibition hall to secondary, stylized status and added a red and white football surmounted by a blue eagle – later redrawn to look more eagle-like. The redesign was said to have been influenced by the emblem of the Portuguese club Benfica, which is also nicknamed the Eagles (*as águias*) and uses the bird as a symbol of 'independence, authority and nobility'. Crystal Palace had formerly been known as the Glaziers.

Ealing The 'queen of the suburbs', situated west of ACTON and 8 miles (13 km) from central London. Ealing has been occupied since the Iron Age but the name is derived from Old English *Gillingas*, which meant 'the settlement of Gilla's people' and was first recorded in the 7th century. The early village grew up around St Mary's Church, while another hamlet evolved to the north, at Haven Green. Until the late 18th century these nuclei were surrounded by open countryside, bisected by a road running east to west that subsequently became Uxbridge Road and the Broadway. The coming of the railways brought rapid suburban expansion and from just 4,000 a century earlier, Ealing's population had increased to 105,000 by 1901, the year that it became the first MIDDLESEX borough to receive a charter and elect a mayor. Ealing was the birthplace of the writers T.H. Huxley, Nevil Shute and Frank Richards, the creator of Billy Bunter.

Ealing, London Borough of An OUTER LONDON borough formed in 1965 by merging the municipal boroughs of ACTON, Ealing and SOUTHALL. Its coat of arms is dominated by an oak tree, which had featured in the heraldry of the boroughs of both Acton and Ealing and was the origin of Acton's name. The civic motto is 'progress with unity'.

Ealing comedies Comedy films produced by

the EALING STUDIOS from the late 1940s. They typically feature a downtrodden group rebelling against authority and are regarded as quintessentially 'English'. Among several productions with a strong London flavour were *Passport to Pimlico* (1948), in which, following the discovery of an ancient treaty, Pimlico is found to belong to Burgundy, and cocks a snook at England; *The Lavender Hill Mob* (1951), centring on a timid clerk who plans and executes a bullion robbery; and *The Ladykillers* (1955), in which a gang of robbers take refuge in a little old lady's house, but end up falling victim to her guilelessness.

Ealing Studios Established in 1902, Ealing Studios was acquired in the early 1930s by Basil Dean, the owner of Associated Talking Pictures, with Michael Balcon joining as head of production in 1938. In the 1940s and 1950s the film studios became famous for the EALING COMEDIES. The company's fortunes began to fail in the 1950s, when tastes were changing, and after releasing *The Ladykillers* it sold its studios to the BBC. Film stages and offices were subsequently rented out for independent productions, while the BBC made television classics of its own here, like STEPTOE AND SON. An independent partnership bought the studios in 2000 and its recent productions include a remake of *St Trinian's* (2007) and several TV series.

Earls Court A busy residential district located in south-west KENSINGTON. From the time of Domesday Book this was the site of the manor house of the earls of Oxford, who were lords of the manor of Kensington. From the early 17th century they were superseded in this role by the earls of Warwick and Holland. The manor house lay to the east of what is now Earls Court Road, where a hamlet subsequently evolved. Nowadays, the district has a highly transient population, especially of Antipodeans, and relatively few children or old people. The largest ethnic minority is classified as 'Chinese or other ethnic group', which consists primarily of the area's Arabic community.

Earls Court exhibition halls The open ground to the west of Earls Court station was used for fairs and exhibitions from 1887 and impressive buildings were constructed in the 1890s by Imre Kiralfy, who went on to create the WHITE CITY. Kiralfy's fairground included a big wheel that was two-thirds the height of the present LONDON EYE but had a greater passenger capacity. It was later removed to Blackpool, Lancashire. The first Earls Court exhibition hall, now best known for staging the Ideal Home Show and big-name rock concerts, opened in 1937. A second hall was added in 1991.

Earlsfield A late Victorian and Edwardian residential locality in south-east WANDSWORTH, on the eastern slope of the WANDLE Valley. In 1868 Robert Davis bought Elm Lodge on Allfarthing Lane and added a new house, which he called Earlsfield because Earl was his wife's maiden name. Davis bought another 59 acres (24 hectares) of land in 1876 and began to lay out Earlsfield Road. Earlsfield station opened in 1884, and the following year the British Land Company bought the lower part of Davis's estate and rapidly developed it. Earlsfield House was rebuilt as a school in 1908, later serving as a children's home and then a boys' remand hostel. It closed in 1981 and was converted into flats. In 1999 the writer Louis de Bernières, an Earlsfield resident at the time, portrayed the locality in *Sunday Morning at the Centre of the Earth*, a radio play in the style of Dylan Thomas's *Under Milk Wood. See also the* MAYOR OF GARRATT.

Earls Park The fictitious football club that featured in the ITV melodrama *Footballers' Wives* (2002–6). The mundanity of the coinage – an apparent west London portmanteau of EARLS COURT and QUEENS PARK – belied plots so lurid that no less a moral arbiter than the archbishop of Canterbury was moved to deplore their content. Earls Park's home games were filmed at SELHURST PARK.

early Battersea A snide colloquialism of the 1970s denoting vulgar, tasteless decor (BATTERSEA had not yet started to up and come).

Eartha (Kitt) 'Shit' (usually in the literal sense, rather than as an expletive) in modern rhyming slang, from the US singer and actress (1927–2008). The actor Brad Pitt's name is similarly taken in vain. As the quotation indicates, the depth of these terms' London roots is open to question.

> My credulity is strained a bit more when I am asked to accept that a cockney-sparrer stevedore will chirp to his mate, 'I'm going for an Eartha' (Eartha Kitt – shit) or 'for a Brad' ...
> BEVIS HILLIER, in *The Spectator* (14 December 2002)

east

East Acton One of the less prestigious corners of ACTON, bordering WORMWOOD SCRUBS and WHITE CITY. In 1654 a goldsmith named John Perryn settled here, subsequently bequeathing his estate to the Worshipful Company of Goldsmiths. Over the following centuries the Goldsmiths' Company acquired additional land, put up 20 almshouses, promoted the building of a station (now Acton Central) and – after several failed attempts – instigated East Acton's suburbanization in the 1920s, following the construction of the WESTERN AVENUE. Several streets were named after eminent goldsmiths such as Martyn Bowes (1496/7–1566) and Thomas Vyner (1588–1665).

Like NEASDEN and CHEAM, something about East Acton's character has made it a butt of anti-suburban humour. In George and Weedon Grossmith's *Diary of a Nobody* (1892), Mr POOTER regrets visiting such an out-of-the-way place to attend the East Acton Volunteer Ball. A 1955 *Goon Show* lamented the dearth of earthquakes in East Acton. And in the BBC comedy programme SYKES (1972–9), Eric Sykes and Hattie Jacques played a bumbling brother and long-suffering sister who lived at the fictional 24 Sebastopol Terrace, East Acton.

East Barnet A medieval village grew up around what is now the junction of East Barnet Road, Cat Hill and Church Hill Road but East Barnet's name is now used as an umbrella term encompassing NEW BARNET and Oakleigh Park. St Mary's Church is of 12th-century origin, at the latest, and although much altered it is still recognizably Norman. St Mary's was the mother church of BARNET and the entire modern district can be said to have evolved out of East Barnet.

East Cheam *See* CHEAM; RAILWAY CUTTINGS.

East End A 19th-century term, still in frequent usage, for the district lying immediately east of the CITY of London. There is no agreed definition of the East End's extent, but it corresponds roughly with the modern borough of TOWER HAMLETS. From the late Middle Ages housing and industry spread here from two directions: outward from the City and northward from the riverside at ST KATHARINE's and WAPPING. By the early 17th century, despite privy council bans, some of the inner suburbs were already densely built-up. Noxious trades like soap boiling and tanning were concentrated here, because the prevailing wind blew the odours away from the City. But the wind was blowing from the east during the GREAT FIRE OF LONDON, so the narrow streets and tumbledown tenements escaped destruction and grew ever more crowded. Huguenot weavers began to settle in SPITALFIELDS, the first of a succession of immigrant communities that helped make the East End the most economically vital part of the capital. Jewish immigrants later arrived in large numbers, often working in the garment trade. The creation of inland docks in the 19th century brought a flood of casual labourers in search of employment and London's first CHINATOWN evolved in LIMEHOUSE. Child labour was especially rife in BETHNAL GREEN, and WHITECHAPEL gained the most notorious reputation of all through the crimes of JACK THE RIPPER in 1888. During the BLITZ the area suffered worse bombing than any other part of London. After the war, massive municipal schemes decanted EAST ENDERS into ranks of tower blocks, breaking up the traditional patterns of life. Many residents left for the new suburbs of outer London, while industries also moved away or closed down. Commonwealth immigrants, especially from what is now Bangladesh, added another dimension to the ethnic mix, most noticeably on BRICK LANE. DOCKLANDS regeneration has transformed the riverside since the early 1990s but elsewhere many parts of the East End retain some of the highest levels of deprivation in the country.

East Ender A native or inhabitant of the EAST END. The term was often formerly spelt as a single word. Although it is much used in the media, locals are likelier to think of themselves as residents of a more specific locality, such as WHITECHAPEL or BETHNAL GREEN, than as generic 'East Enders'.

EastEnders A BBC soap opera launched in 1985 and soon challenging and even bettering the veteran *Coronation Street* in viewing figures. As its title implies, it is set in the East End of London, in the (fictitious) borough of WALFORD, and centres on ALBERT SQUARE and its Queen Victoria pub, originally run by Den Watts and his wife Angie. A major theme of the series has been the love triangle, and an early story line involved the seduction of a schoolgirl by the lecherous DIRTY DEN. The episode in which Den gave Angie divorce papers for Christmas was watched by a record 30 million viewers. The soap's success has been largely due to its bold treatment of 'tough' issues such as rape, prostitution, unemployment, HIV infection, abortion and homosexuality. Despite the show's pervasive air of misery it retains a high audience share and consistently outperforms its rivals at award ceremonies.

East Finchley A distinctly different community from its parent district, which lies across the NORTH CIRCULAR ROAD to the north-west. As early as the 14th century a chain of little hamlets took root beside HORNSEY Park on the newly created Great North Road (as it later became), and were collectively known as East End. By the 1850s East End was the most populous part of FINCHLEY, crammed with tenements and terraced houses. Conditions were often insanitary and East Finchley (as it became) gained a reputation for drunkenness, godlessness and a lack of moral restraint. Extensive bomb damage during the Second World War prompted the council to radically remodel the district afterwards. East Finchley residents have included comedian and actor Peter Sellers, musicians Vivian Stanshall and Feargal Sharkey, and US chat-show host Jerry Springer, who was born in Chandos Road.

East Ham A densely built-up former borough situated 1 mile (1.6 km) west of BARKING. The Old English word *hamm* indicated an area of dry land bounded by marshes or rivers. The manor of Hammarsh and the riverside marshes belonged to WESTMINSTER ABBEY from at least the time of the Norman Conquest. St Mary Magdalene Church was built around 1130, and it is believed that the site was earlier used for burials. The church's original apse, chancel and nave have all survived, making this one of London's least modified medieval churches. By the late 12th century documents were distinguishing Ham's eastern and western parts. WEST HAM slowly grew but East Ham remained an agricultural backwater until the late 19th century, with a weekly cattle market, potato farms and market gardens noted for their onions, especially pickling onions. Between 1891 and 1911 the population of the borough (as it became in 1904) quadrupled to around 133,000. The present-day population is primarily Asian, mostly of Indian origin but with large Pakistani and Bangladeshi communities as well. East Ham was the birthplace of the singer Vera Lynn (b.1917).

East India A DOCKLANDS LIGHT RAILWAY station in eastern BLACKWALL, providing access,

via a footbridge, to the complex of offices that has replaced the EAST INDIA DOCKS.

East India Company A joint-stock company established in 1600 by merchants trading with the islands of the East Indies and, after 1640, primarily with India. The Honourable East India Company imported vast quantities of Chinese TEA to Britain in the 18th century, funding much of the business by illegal trade in opium. Based in LEADENHALL STREET, the company has been called 'the world's first multinational' and was primarily responsible for maintaining colonial power in India until the British government took direct control of the sub-continent in 1858.

East India Docks In 1803 the success of the newly opened WEST INDIA DOCKS prompted the EAST INDIA COMPANY to promote a similar scheme in eastern BLACKWALL. Construction took three years and filled a 60-acre (24-hectare) site. Brunswick Dock, which had opened in 1790, became the export dock, with an entrance basin to its east and a larger import dock to its north. At the same time East India Dock Road was built as a branch of the COMMERCIAL ROAD, providing a link with the CITY of London. The docks had already begun to decline when they suffered tremendous damage during the BLITZ. The export dock never reopened, while the import dock was repaired but containerization and other changing circumstances rendered it increasingly obsolete and it was gradually filled in from the late 1960s. Only the entrance basin and sections of the dock wall now remain and most of the site has been built up with apartment complexes and granite-faced office blocks in the characteristic DOCKLANDS style, with newly created water features and streets named after eastern herbs and spices. TOWER HAMLETS town hall stands on Clove Crescent.

East London The eastern part of GREATER LONDON, to the east of the TOWER OF LONDON and to the north of the River THAMES. The designation has no clear eastern frontier: it certainly reaches as far as BARKING CREEK, but thereafter, as E-coded POSTAL DISTRICTS give way to what was formerly ESSEX, it seems less and less the *mot juste*. It conjures up many of the same images as the EAST END, but does not bear the same weight of folkloric baggage.

East London line A former line on the LONDON UNDERGROUND system that ran from SHOREDITCH southwards via the THAMES TUN-

NEL to NEW CROSS and NEW CROSS GATE. It had its beginnings in the late 1860s as the East London Railway. In the early 1930s, with the advent of the London Passenger Transport Board, it was absorbed into the METROPOLITAN LINE, but in the 1980s it resumed its own individual identity, coloured orange on the map. The entire East London line closed in 2007 to enable the construction of significant extensions in both directions, which will create new termini at HIGHBURY AND ISLINGTON in the north and West CROYDON in the south, with a spur to CRYSTAL PALACE. Existing overground lines are being adapted for much of the route and the work is due for completion in 2011. When the East London line reopens it will be designated part of the LONDON OVERGROUND network. A branch line from SURREY QUAYS to CLAPHAM JUNCTION is also proposed.

east of the griffin East of TEMPLE BAR, i.e. in the CITY of London. The term derives from the persistent misidentification of the City's DRAGON.

> If something unexpected did not happen, it
> meant another visit to a little office he knew
> too well in the City, the master of which, more
> than civil if you met him on a racecourse, … was
> quite a different person and much less easy to
> deal with east of the Griffin.
>
> ALFRED WATSON: *Racecourse and Covert Side* (1883)

East 17 A boy band formed in 1992, taking its name from WALTHAMSTOW's POSTAL DISTRICT. The band's first album, *Walthamstow* (1993), was a No.1 hit.

East Sheen A socially advantaged locality situated south of MORTLAKE and east of RICHMOND, which was originally called Sheen (or Shene). First recorded in 1247, East Sheen became a separate manor from Mortlake around 1500. The 17th-century Temple Grove was the manor house of East Sheen and Westhall and took its name from the Temple family, later the viscounts Palmerston, who owned it until 1805. East Sheen was later home to the Whig prime minister Earl Grey (1764–1845). Sir Tim Berners-Lee, inventor of the world-wide web, was born in East Sheen in 1955. The last home of the rock star Marc Bolan (1947–77) was 142 Upper Richmond Road West, a large Victorian house surrounded by a high brick wall and foliage. It was only a short distance

from here that Bolan met his death on BARNES Common (*see the* BOLAN TREE).

East Wickham A former medieval manor that became part of suburban north WELLING between the wars. 'Wikam' was first mentioned in 1240 and the reference almost certainly indicated a homestead associated with an earlier *vicus*, a Romano-British settlement that probably stood on WATLING STREET. 'Estwycham' was recorded in 1284, the prefix distinguishing the hamlet from WEST WICKHAM, which lies 9 miles (14.5 km) to the south-west. The farmhouse at East Wickham Farm has a facade dating from 1843 but its timbers are much older. The musician Kate Bush (b.1958) grew up at the farm and continued living there with her family after her early success.

University of East London See under UNIVERSITY.

Eastbury Manor House A National Trust property managed by BARKING AND DAGENHAM council as an arts, heritage and community resource. This grade I listed mansion was built for an Essex merchant during the reign of Elizabeth I. In the early 17th century the house attracted wealthy Catholic families who could practise their religion there in relative safety from persecution, and some GUNPOWDER PLOT mythology has therefore become attached to it.

Eastcheap A now-truncated CITY street extending eastwards for 250 yards (230m) from MONUMENT underground station. Its name means 'east market', and it was so called to distinguish it from West Cheap, now CHEAPSIDE. From the late Middle Ages the street was lined with butchers' shops, none of which remain. Until 1831 it was the site of the BOAR'S HEAD TAVERN.

Eastcote A METROLAND suburb born from a medieval village located east of RUISLIP. The name, which dates from the 13th century or earlier, means 'eastern cottages'; Ruislip at one time had a Southcote and a Westcote as well.

EastEnders *See under* EAST.

Eaton Square A 'square' (actually a very elongated oblong) in BELGRAVIA, to the west of VICTORIA STATION. It was built in the 1820s as part of the development of the Grosvenor estate, the property of the dukes of Westminster. Eaton Hall in Cheshire is the dukes' country seat. Its reputation for extreme exclusivity is sustained by the prices its grand houses fetch. Residents have included Stanley Baldwin, Laurence Olivier and Vivien Leigh, Andrew Lloyd Webber and Margaret Thatcher, and the Bellamys in ITV's UPSTAIRS, DOWNSTAIRS (1971–5) lived just round the corner in Eaton Place. Nowadays, though, you are just as likely to find an ambassador here as a lord (the Belgian Embassy is in Eaton Square, for example, as is the Bolivian Consulate).

> Then Petra flashed by in a wink.
> It looked like Eaton Square – but pink.
>
> SIR CHARLES JOHNSTON: 'Air Travel in Arabia', from *Poems and Journeys* (1979)

ebberman or **hebberman** An old name for a fisherman on the THAMES below LONDON BRIDGE. He was so called because he usually fished at ebb tide.

> Item, That no such Person, being a Hebberman, shall within the Bounds or Limits aforesaid, fish for Smelts between Good Friday and the four and twentieth Day of August yearly ...
>
> JOHN STRYPE: *A Survey of the Cities of London and Westminster*, By-Laws for Fishermen (1720)

Ebury A half-recalled Saxon manor that once stretched from present-day OXFORD STREET southward to the THAMES. In the 16th century Ebury Farm covered 430 acres (174 hectares) and its farmhouse stood on the site of the modern VICTORIA coach station. The estate was regularly leased by the Crown to court favourites until James I sold the freehold in 1623. A Temple barrister, Hugh Audley, purchased the marshy manor and it descended in 1666 to his grandniece Mary Davies, then one year old. Eleven years later Mary married Sir Thomas Grosvenor of Eaton in Cheshire. Their union was not a happy one: she went mad and he died young. But the Grosvenor family profitably developed the land and, as BELGRAVIA came into existence and grew, the Ebury name dropped out of widespread usage. It is remembered today primarily in the context of street names. WESTMINSTER council applies the name Ebury Village to a group of roads lying west of Victoria and has designated it an area of archaeological importance. Mozart composed his first symphony when staying in Ebury Street in 1764. Ebury Street residents have included Ian Fleming, Noël Coward, Thomas Wolfe, Vita Sackville-West, and George Moore, who wrote *Conversations in Ebury Street* in 1924.

Edgware A middle-class suburb with a strongly Jewish character, situated 3 miles (5 km) northwest of HENDON and straddling the course of the former WATLING STREET. The name meant 'Ecgi's weir' and was first recorded in an Anglo-Saxon charter of around 975 but was omitted from Domesday Book. Ecgi probably constructed his weir on what is now the Edgware Brook either to trap fish or to irrigate his field. The area was almost entirely built up between the wars, notably by the property developer George Cross, who later recalled:

> ... moulding that slice of the suburbs of London in any way I pleased; planning roads as I would; naming them as I fancied.
>
> quoted in JOHN RICHARDSON: *London & Its People* (1995)

Some ancient buildings survive on the west side of High Street Edgware, including the 17th-century White Hart Hotel (now the Change of Hart), but many more have been lost through road widening. As well as its very large Jewish population, Edgware has significant Hindu and Muslim minorities, mainly of Indian origin. Agatha Christie created the character Lord Edgware in a 1933 Hercule Poirot story.

Edgware Road A faintly Parisian-style boulevard with a strongly Middle Eastern flavour, running north-westwards from MARBLE ARCH to MAIDA VALE. Although there is another section of the A5 with the same name further north, it is the street separating PADDINGTON from MARYLEBONE that is usually meant by 'the Edgware Road'. Writing around 1596, Ben Jonson mentioned in *A Tale of a Tub* a Red Lion inn that probably stood on the Edgware Road. In 1863 the road gained one of London's original underground stations on the inaugural line that ran between Paddington and FARRINGDON. Since the 1970s, the Edgware Road has become a focus for London's Arabic population, as has QUEENSWAY, its counterpart on the other side of BAYSWATER. The process may have begun with the tendency for wealthy Middle Eastern visitors to stay in hotels here and on nearby PARK LANE, which led to the establishment of shops and restaurants dedicated to serving them. This in turn encouraged Arabic migrants, especially Lebanese, to settle in the area.

Edmonton An overly built-up former borough, situated north of TOTTENHAM. It was first recorded in Domesday Book, as 'Adelmetone', which was a farmstead belonging to a man named Ēadhelm. Edmonton became a desirable residential neighbourhood in the late 18th century but this did not last and by 1800 the gentry were moving out to SOUTHGATE. It fell further as exploitative builders covered the central area with cheap housing in the latter decades of the 19th century. The council built a number of tower blocks in the 1960s and 1970s and many of these properties have recently been refurbished or replaced, notably as part of the redevelopment of the focal Edmonton Green locality. Edmonton gave its name to the Hudson's Bay Company's Edmonton House in Alberta, Canada, in 1785 and thence to the settlement that grew up around it, which is now far larger than its progenitor. The entertainer Bruce Forsyth (b.1928) was born in Edmonton. Charles Lamb (1775–1834) died after falling on his face in Edmonton High Street. *See also the* MERRY DEVIL OF EDMONTON.

> It was in the centre of the above vicinities, at 'Edmonton so gay', the rendezvous of Shakespeare's merry devil, that I profiled, three-quartered, full-faced, and buttoned up the retired embroidered weavers, their crummy wives, and tightly-laced daughters. Ay, those were the days!
>
> JOHN THOMAS SMITH: *A Book for a Rainy Day* (1861)

Edric of Streone A traitorous Saxon lord (*fl.*1001–17) who, according to legend, murdered Edmund II in 1016, or commissioned others to do the deed. Edric was known to be in cahoots with King Cnut but had gained Edmund's confidence by pretending to have switched sides. Cnut had promised Edric that he would reward him by raising him above all others in London, but he distrusted a schemer who would kill his own king and chose to fulfil his pledge by having Edric beheaded and ordering that his head be mounted on a spike atop the highest turret in London. His body was thrown into the THAMES or, some say, cast into the HOUNDSDITCH, where it was left to rot with the dead dogs.

> ... the Danish earl stepped forward, and cut down Edric with his battle-axe: the carcass of the wretch was thrown into the Thames; and the ghastly head, spiked upon the highest gate

of London, announced to the people that the felon had now paid the penalty of his misdeeds.
>
> SIR FRANCIS PALGRAVE: *History of the Anglo-Saxons* (1876)

'E Dunno Where 'E Are See JACK JONES.

eek 'Face' in POLARI. It is an abbreviation of 'ecaf', which, like several other words in the polari lexicon, is BACK-SLANG.

eel

Eel Pie Island Originally called Twickenham AIT, this is the largest island in London's stretch of the THAMES, lying between TWICKENHAM and the HAM Riverside Lands. It is rumoured to have been the site of a monastery and much later was used as a 'courting ground' by Henry VIII. In the 18th century it attracted day-trippers, who came to picnic or fish here, and to enjoy the renowned pies that were made with locally caught eels. Although this is the most obvious explanation of the name, another story suggests that a royal mistress who had a house on the island called it *Île de Paix*, 'island of peace'.

In the late 1950s and 1960s Eel Pie Island became famous for its noisy jazz club, where the ROLLING STONES, The Who, Pink Floyd and Genesis all played gigs early in their careers. The island has even been called 'the place where the Sixties began'. Subsequently the Eel Pie Island Hotel became something of a hippie commune, to the disapproval of straight-laced locals. It was destroyed by fire in 1971. In 1996 a boatyard and 60 neighbouring artists' studios also burnt down. An appeal brought donations from the local community in Twickenham as well as from famous rock stars, but only limited rebuilding has taken place.

eels, jellied See JELLIED EELS.

Effra A now subterranean stream, rising in NORWOOD and entering the THAMES as a sewer outflow near NINE ELMS. The origin of its name is uncertain; however, a 7th-century document recording the bounds of what are now BATTERSEA and WANDSWORTH notes a *hēah yfer* – a high bank or ridge – near its mouth, and there may be a connection.

Effy or **Eff** Familiar names for the Earl of Effingham, and later the Effingham Theatre, a saloon theatre that stood in WHITECHAPEL Road from 1834. It was rebuilt in 1867, and twice again thereafter, operating under a variety of identities that included the New East London Theatre, the Jewish Theatre, the Wonderland (which gained fame as a boxing venue) and the Rivoli Cinema, which was destroyed in the Second World War.

Egg, the (Glass) A nickname for CITY HALL. Its skewed oval shape – intended to maximize energy efficiency – has also drawn comparisons with a fencing mask, a car headlamp, Darth Vader's helmet and a pile of saucepans falling over. Former mayor Ken Livingstone (*see* RED KEN) once likened it to a 'glass testicle', while his successor Boris Johnson (*see* BO-JO) is said to call it 'the Onion'. Yet another nickname is the Leaning Tower of Pizzas.

Eiffel (Tower) 'Shower' in COCKNEY RHYMING SLANG.

eighteen pence 'Sense' in COCKNEY RHYMING SLANG.

> 'You mean to stand there, you lop sided muggins, you,' he says, sarky as you like, 'letting me shout my guts out while I got a guest in the manor? Ain't you got no eighteen pence, you sloppy old cheesecake, you?'
>
> RICHARD LLEWELLYN: *None But the Lonely Heart* (1943)

Eisenhower Platz A sardonic nickname, on the model of German square names (e.g. Alexanderplatz in Berlin), given during the Second World War variously to GROSVENOR SQUARE, which was then largely taken up by the headquarters of the American forces in Europe, commanded by General Eisenhower, and to SHEPHERD MARKET, formerly well known for its prostitutes, whose services were extensively employed by US troops in London.

Eleanor crosses The crosses erected by Edward I (r.1272–1307) to commemorate his first wife Eleanor of Castile, who died at Harby in Nottinghamshire in 1290. She was buried in WESTMINSTER ABBEY and crosses were set up at each of the 12 places where her body rested on its journey southwards: Lincoln, Grantham, Stamford, Geddington, Hardingstone (now part of Northampton), Stony Stratford, Woburn, Dunstable, St Albans, Waltham (now Waltham Cross), West Cheap (CHEAPSIDE) and Charing (now CHARING CROSS). Only those at Geddington, Hardingstone and Waltham Cross survive. The cross at Charing, which stood just to the

south of what is now TRAFALGAR SQUARE, was demolished in 1647 and much of its stone was used to pave WHITEHALL. An equestrian statue of Charles I was erected in its place in 1675 and now marks the exact point from which all distances from London are measured. The present Gothic cross in the courtyard of CHARING CROSS STATION was designed by Edward Middleton Barry and erected in 1865.

electric

Electric Avenue A shopping street in BRIXTON, named for the incandescent lighting that was a pioneering development in British retailing at the time of its introduction.

> We're gonna rock down to Electric Avenue
> And then we'll take it higher
>
> EDDY GRANT: 'Electric Avenue' (song) (1983)

Electric Cinema A picture house that opened on PORTOBELLO ROAD in 1910. It rivals EAST FINCHLEY'S PHOENIX as the capital's oldest working cinema and possesses a similarly classic interior.

elementary, my dear Watson The most famous words that Sherlock HOLMES never uttered in the stories by Arthur Conan Doyle. He came closest in 'The Adventure of the Crooked Man' (1893):

> 'I have the advantage of knowing your habits, my dear Watson,' said he. 'When your round is a short one you walk, and when it is a long one you use a hansom. As I perceive that your boots, although used, are by no means dirty, I cannot doubt that you are at present busy enough to justify the hansom.'
> 'Excellent!' I cried.
> 'Elementary,' said he.

Although it has not been confirmed, the precise phrase is said to have been spoken on the stage by William Gillette (1853–1937), in one of his famous portrayals of the BAKER STREET sleuth, and this may have prompted P.G. Wodehouse to put the words into the mouth of his character Psmith in *Psmith Journalist* (1915). The first documented use of the phrase by Holmes himself came in the closing scene of the film *The Return of Sherlock Holmes* (1929):

> Watson: Amazing, Holmes.
> Holmes: Elementary, my dear Watson, elementary.
>
> BASIL DEAN and GARRETT FORT (screenwriters)

elephant

Elephant and Castle A busy road junction and its improving vicinity, situated in (and better known than) NEWINGTON, and often simply called 'the Elephant'. In 1641 John Flaxman set up a blacksmith's forge on an island site here to take advantage of the passing horse-drawn traffic. Around 1760 the smithy was converted to a tavern that displayed a sign of an elephant and castle. There is almost certainly no truth in the widely held belief that the name is a corruption of *Infanta de Castilla*, 'the princess of Castile'. The more likely connection is with the old heraldic symbol of an elephant with a castellated tower on its back, which was especially used by the Cutlers' Company to indicate the use of ivory in knife handles. The tavern became a coaching halt and thus gave its name to the junction. Following its devastation during the Second World War, the area was clumsily redeveloped from the late 1950s with offices, academic buildings, housing estates and the Elephant and Castle shopping centre – a pioneer in its time but subsequently much derided. A £1.5 billion regeneration programme is presently under way, which will wholly remodel the area with new homes, shops and cultural and leisure facilities.

Elephant Man The nickname given to Joseph Carey Merrick (1862–90), a gravely disfigured person who was a professional 'freak' before he became a permanent patient of the London Hospital in WHITECHAPEL. His childhood was normal until about the age of 5, when he began to show signs of the strange disorder that altered his whole appearance. His head became enormous, some 3 feet (90 cm) in circumference, with big bags of spongy brown skin hanging from the back of his head and across his face. His jaws were deformed, so that he could barely eat or talk, his right arm was discoloured and grotesque, and he was so lame that he could walk only with a stick. His disorder was long thought to be neurofibromatosis, but research in the late 1980s concluded that he had suffered from the extremely rare disease known as the Proteus syndrome. He died of accidental suffocation in hospital at the age of 27.

David Lynch's acclaimed black-and-white film *The Elephant Man* (1980), starring John Hurt, was based on Merrick's story.

elephant's (trunk) 'Drunk' in COCKNEY RHYMING SLANG.

Elfin Oak A tall, thick tree stump situated next to the children's playground on the north side of KENSINGTON GARDENS. It was brought here from RICHMOND PARK in 1928 and decorated with carvings of fairytale creatures by the children's book illustrator Ivor Innes. It has since been restored several times, notably with the help of the comedian Spike Milligan, and is now protected by a cage. The oak was awarded grade II listed status in 1997.

> Eight hundred years ago, when Stephen was King of England, this tree began to grow, in a great forest, where now is Richmond Park. And when it had grown for hundreds of years, and become huge and gnarled and knotty, the Little People began to inhabit it.
>
> ELSIE INNES: *The Elfin Oak of Kensington Gardens* (1930)

Elgin Marbles The 7th Earl of Elgin (1766–1841) was envoy to the Sublime Porte (the Ottoman Court at Constantinople) from 1799 to 1803, when Greece was still under Turkish control, and noticed that many of the classical sculptures at Athens were suffering from neglect and depredations. At his own expense he made a collection of statuary and sculpture, including the frieze from the Parthenon and works of Phidias, and shipped them to England. He sold the 'Elgin Marbles' to the BRITISH MUSEUM in 1816 for £36,000, a good deal less than they had cost him. The Greek government has frequently requested that the Marbles be returned. Their official title in the British Museum is the 'Parthenon Marbles'.

Elia A *nom de plume* used by Charles Lamb (1775–1834), under which a series of essays appeared. The first of these, in the *London Magazine* (1820), was a description of the South Sea House, headquarters of the EAST INDIA COMPANY, with which he associated the name of Elia, an Italian clerk, a 'gay light-hearted foreigner', who was a fellow employee.

Eliot, George The pseudonym of Mary Ann or Marian Evans (1819–80). Her first novel appearing under this name was *Scenes of Clerical Life* (1858). She also wrote *Adam Bede* (1859), *The Mill on the Floss* (1860), *Silas Marner* (1861), *Middlemarch* (1871–2) and other novels. She lived with George Henry Lewes from 1854 until his death in 1878, basing her pen name on that of her lover, and married her 'second' husband John Walter

Cross as Mary Ann Evans Lewes. Though her stories were usually set in the provinces, Eliot spent most of her adult life in London; her many addresses included RICHMOND, EAST SHEEN, SOUTHFIELDS, REGENT'S PARK, and CHEYNE WALK, where she died. She was buried in HIGHGATE CEMETERY.

Eliza A novel (1900) by Barry Pain (1864-1928), in which he pokes fun at the suburban home life of an upwardly mobile near-gentleman and his tolerant wife. It was followed by *Eliza's Husband* (1903), *Eliza Getting On* (1911), *Exit Eliza* (1912) and *Eliza's Son* (1913). BBC Radio 4 serialized the stories from 2005 to 2008.

Eliza Doolittle *See* DOOLITTLE, ELIZA; MY FAIR LADY; PYGMALION.

outside, Eliza! *See under* OUTSIDE.

Ellenborough Lodge One of the many nicknames for the KING'S BENCH PRISON. Sir Edward Law, 1st Baron Ellenborough, was lord chief justice of the King's Bench from 1802 to 1818. The spiked beams fixed atop the prison's wall were called Lord Ellenborough's teeth.

Elms, The The site in SMITHFIELD of judicial burnings and hangings in the late Middle Ages. William 'Braveheart' Wallace was put to death at the Elms in 1305.

Elmstead Woods A diminutive and leafy locality situated between SUNDRIDGE and CHISLEHURST. The name was first recorded in 1320 as Elmsted, 'the place where elm trees grow', and the wood was Elmystediswood in 1392. This was part of the bishop of Rochester's estate and used to provide timber for shipbuilding. The surviving part of Elmstead Wood has paths that are part of the Green Chain Walk that stretches across south-east London and the trees are mainly oak, sweet chestnut and hornbeam. Just beside the station is Elmstead Pit, formerly called Rock Pit, a small site with a nationally important exposure of the geological strata known as Blackheath Beds – marine deposits that were built up approximately 50 million years ago. They are rich in fossils and have yielded fish scales and shark fins.

Eltham A sprawling south-east London suburb, occupying most of the area between BLACKHEATH and SIDCUP. Eltham was first recorded in Domesday Book and its name could relate to a man called Elta, or to Old English *elfitu*, 'a swan'. The High Street gained some characterful premises in the latter part of the 18th century, of which a few survive, notably the Greyhound and Rising Sun inns. The district was progressively covered with housing during the 50 years from the mid-1880s. In 1993 black schoolboy Stephen Lawrence was murdered in a notorious racist attack for which no one was ever convicted.

Eltham Palace Plantagenet kings chose Eltham as a place of rest en route to and from France and converted the manor house into a moated palace in the 14th century. In the 1470s Edward IV added a great hall for royal banquets. For reasons not known, Eltham was particularly popular as a place for the royal families to spend Christmas. The Tudor monarchs preferred GREENWICH and Eltham Palace declined in the 16th century and was ransacked in the Civil War. The trees of the palace's three parks, Great Park, Middle Park, and Horn Park, were cut down and used for shipbuilding. After the Restoration the vintner and influential financier Sir John Shaw leased the Great Park and built Eltham Lodge in 1664. He did not attempt to rescue the palace and the great hall became a barn. The park is now Royal Blackheath Golf Course (*see* BLACKHEATH) and the lodge is its clubhouse. During the 1930s Sir Stephen Courtauld leased the site of Eltham Palace, repaired the great hall and built a new house for himself and his wife Virginia, with lavish art deco interiors. The buildings were magnificently restored by English Heritage in the 1990s and opened to the public. The Flemish artist Sir Anthony Van Dyck spent one or more summers at Eltham Palace in the 1630s and painted several of his greatest works here.

Eltham Park A primarily Edwardian estate situated in the north-east of Eltham, built between 1900 and 1914 by Cameron Corbett, the kingpin of London's suburban housebuilding programme at that time. Corbett was a teetotaller so no public houses were provided; to this day a covenant prohibits the use of any premises for the sale of alcoholic beverages. When an off-licence eventually opened, it was situated on the bridge over the railway, not on Corbett's land. The comedian Bob Hope (1903–2003) was born in Craigton Road. The family migrated to America when he was 4 years old, settling in Cleveland, Ohio.

Ely Place An episcopal mansion, also known as Ely Palace or Ely House, and now the name of the sedate, gated cul-de-sac that occupies its former site, just east of HATTON GARDEN. The house was the London residence of 41 bishops of Ely, Cambridgeshire, from 1290 to 1772, after which the crumbling edifice was pulled down. The surviving church of St Etheldreda was built as their private chapel, and is said to be the oldest Roman Catholic church in England. SHAKESPEARE made Ely House the scene of events in *Richard III* (*c.*1592) and *Richard II* (*c.*1595), including John of Gaunt's 'scepter'd isle' speech from his deathbed. Ye Olde Mitre public house stands in Ely Court, which links Ely Place and Hatton Garden; the present 18th-century building replaced the original tavern built in 1546 by Bishop Goodrich of Ely. *See also the* BLESSING OF THROATS; STRAWBERRY FAYRE.

Embankment Usually a shorthand term for Victoria Embankment, which runs from WESTMINSTER to BLACKFRIARS, but sometimes also encompassing Albert Embankment, on the south bank of the THAMES, and Chelsea Embankment, all created as part of the same project. Parliament first approved a land reclamation scheme on the Thames mudflats in 1846. Although it would have benefits in improving the flow of the Thames and releasing land for building, a vital objective was to permit the creation of an efficient network of sewers beneath the new streets that would skirt the Thames. Progress was painfully slow at first and an exasperated Thomas CUBITT built a section of wall himself so that he could complete the development of PIMLICO. Two factors eventually drove the project forward: the establishment of the METROPOLITAN BOARD OF WORKS in 1855 and the GREAT STINK of 1858. Joseph Bazalgette, the hero of Victorian sanitation, was appointed to oversee the project. Victoria Embankment opened in 1870, as did Embankment station on a section of line that was half buried in the newly reclaimed riverbank. Subsoil excavated during the construction of the line was reused to fill in behind the river wall, while topsoil for Victoria Embankment Gardens was dredged from BARKING CREEK.

> The fear of the sack like a maggot in his heart. How it eats at them, that secret fear! Especially on winter days, when they hear the menace of the wind. Winter, the sack, the workhouse, the Embankment benches!
>
> GEORGE ORWELL: *Keep the Aspidistra Flying* (1936)

Emerson Park A pricey residential district situated north-east of HORNCHURCH. In 1895 William Carter of Parkstone in Dorset bought 20 acres (8 hectares) of Nelmes Manor and Lee Garden Manor to build 'country villas for city gentlemen'. Carter put up a wide variety of dwellings, from bungalows to family houses with accommodation for servants, and named the estate after his eldest son, Emerson. Other developers added their own estates, such as Haynes Park and Great and Little Nelmes, but the original name has come to apply to the whole neighbourhood. It is now completely built over, with cul-de-sacs jutting into what were once the gardens of larger properties.

Emirates Stadium The home of ARSENAL FC since 2006, named in a 15-year sponsorship deal with a Dubai-based airline. During its construction the stadium was known by the name of the road that it erased: Ashburton Grove, in DRAYTON PARK. With a 60,000 sell-out crowd at almost every match, the Emirates has brought the club significant additional revenue, but the enormous construction cost may nevertheless detrimentally affect Arsenal's financial position for many years to come.

Emperor of the Building Trade The sobriquet of Thomas CUBITT.

Empire A theatre built on the north side of LEICESTER SQUARE in 1884, rebuilt as a cinema in 1928 and given a new interior in 1962. The cinema nowadays has five screens; the main auditorium is one of the WEST END's finest.

> Dear Leicester Square, the Empire glowing,
> Two seats to spare and Garbo showing,
>
> HAROLD PURCELL and GEORGE POSFORD: 'The London I Love' (song) (1941)

Empire Promenade A once famous feature of the former Empire Theatre, LEICESTER SQUARE. This open space behind the dress circle was a regular parade of the 'ladies of the town'. In 1894 Mrs Ormiston Chant of the LONDON COUNTY COUNCIL directed a purity campaign against the MUSIC HALLS and sought to effect the closure of the Empire Promenade and its adjoining bars. This led to the erection of canvas screens between them, but these were soon demolished by a riotous crowd, a prominent member being the young Winston Churchill. Brick partitions were subsequently built.

empty plinth *See the* FOURTH PLINTH.

end

End, The A nightclub formerly located in West Central Street, ST GILES'S. Established in 1995, it quickly achieved cult status among London's more musically aware clubgoers. The End closed in January 2009.

'Enders An abbreviation of EASTENDERS.

ends or **endz** An urban slang term for a neighbourhood, directly analogous with the American 'hood'. The word is always used in what looks like the plural, but mostly with a singular sense, and is popular with the capital's working-class teenagers, especially those from minority ethnic groups. Through the phenomenon known as 'dialect levelling', usage of the term has rapidly spread throughout urban England but it originated among the black community of inner London. *See also* JAFAIKAN.

> The words you use are important. One of the ways you know which ends people are from is by the words they use and the way they use them. In south London, buff means big, but in west London it means nice. It's little things like that. The differences are small but important. If you stray into the wrong area, you end up dead.
>
> gang member interviewed in *The Independent on Sunday* (18 February 2007)

Enfield[1] An extensive and diverse district centred on ENFIELD TOWN and encompassing a broad belt of localities such as Southbury, WORLD'S END, GRANGE PARK, GORDON HILL and Bullsmoor. The protected status of ENFIELD CHASE and the inhospitable nature of marshland by the Lea discouraged the early growth of outlying hamlets but the town itself flourished. As the railway companies thrust four fingers of lines into the district from the mid-19th century, the discrete villages began to grow together, coalescing in the early 20th century. In recent years Enfield has begun to present a more cosmopolitan aspect than many other districts on the fringes of GREATER LONDON, and is attracting unmarried young professionals as well as families, although the absence of a LONDON UNDERGROUND line is a deterrent for some. Former Enfield residents include civil engineer Joseph Bazalgette and Isaac D'Israeli, father of prime minister and novelist Benjamin Disraeli and a literary talent in his own right.

Enfield, London Borough of An OUTER LONDON borough that until 1965 was a municipal borough of MIDDLESEX. While most London boroughs are distinctly elongated in shape, Enfield is almost a perfect square by comparison; its main divergence from regularity being a jaggedness to its western edge to take in HADLEY WOOD but exclude EAST BARNET. The principal charge of the borough's coat of arms is an enfield (*see below*). The civic motto is 'by industry ever stronger'.

Enfield Chase A great swathe of woodland that extended from BARNET to present-day Enfield. It was a favourite royal hunting ground (and supposedly a hideaway for Dick TURPIN) until it was deforested in the 18th century. The country park of Trent Park is now all that remains, and the name Enfield Chase has become associated with the locality around the station, half a mile (800m) west of Enfield's centre. The astronomer John Hadley was born in 1682 at Enfield Chase. He became a Fellow of the Royal Society in 1716 and built the first Gregorian reflector telescope in 1721.

Enfield Highway A relatively poor part of north-east Enfield, with Enfield College to its south. Known from 1572 as Cocksmiths End, the present name dates from the mid-18th century and derives from the hamlet's situation in the parish of Enfield on the main road from London to Hertford. Workers from the nearby ROYAL SMALL ARMS FACTORY set up what became the Enfield Highway Co-operative Society in 1872. The society opened branches across Hertfordshire and later built local housing for workers.

Enfield Island Village A 'flagship' development of 'regional significance', according to the government, built from 1997 to 2003 by Fairview New Homes on a 100-acre (40-hectare) flood plain lying between the River LEA and the Cattlegate Flood Relief Channel. The site was formerly occupied by the ROYAL SMALL ARMS FACTORY; some original buildings have been retained.

Enfield Lock A redeveloped former industrial zone located on the banks of the River LEA and the River Lee Navigation channel in the far north-east of Enfield. A lock and a watermill operated here from medieval times and the mill may have been used for making gunpowder in the mid-17th century. The present lock and a surveyor's house were constructed on the Enfield cut of the Lea Navigation in the early 1790s.

Enfield rifle *See the* ROYAL SMALL ARMS FACTORY.

Enfield Town A market town turned suburban centre, situated towards the western side of the wider Enfield district, 9 miles (14.5 km) due north of the CITY of London. During the 18th century, fine houses dotted the surrounding fields and the path facing the Chase to the west became known as Gentleman's Row. The Rev John Ryland opened a school on Nags Head Road which at one point included the poet John Keats amongst its pupils. Most of the town's older buildings were demolished at the end of the 19th century and the centre began to take on its present streetscape. Of the properties that survive, the finest group is the collection of Georgian and early Victorian houses in Gentleman's Row.

Enfield Wash A part of north-east Enfield commonly known as Horsepoolstones until the 18th century, although the present name was first recorded in 1675. A 'wash' was a place that regularly flooded, in this case because of the overflow from Maiden's Brook. ERMINE STREET, the Roman road that ran through here, probably crossed the brook via a ford. The old folk tune 'Enfield Wash' is still popular at country dances. *See also* CANNING, ELIZABETH.

enfield² A mythological beast that has been claimed to represent a mix of creatures that once frequented ENFIELD CHASE. Enfields are said to have protected the bodies of chieftains who had fallen in battle so that they could afterwards be accorded a ceremonial burial, and in this context are primarily associated with the Kelly and O'Kelly families of Ireland. Depictions vary but the beast is usually shown with the head of a fox, the chest of a hound (or, rarely, an elephant), the breast feathers and foreclaws of an eagle, the abdomen of a lion (or wolf) and the hindquarters and tail of a wolf. A horse's mane has also featured in some representations. An enfield appears on the coat of arms of the London Borough of ENFIELD and on the crests and badges of several clubs and institutions in the borough.

English

English Bastille A nickname applied both to NEWGATE PRISON and MILLBANK PENITENTIARY. The house of correction at COLD BATH FIELDS was also known as the Bastille, or the Steel.

English National Opera An opera company (abbreviation: ENO) based at the London CO-LISEUM in St Martin's Lane. It specializes in producing operas sung in English, a practice it has maintained from its previous incarnation, the SADLER'S WELLS Opera Company, from which it metamorphosed in 1974.

English Stage Company A theatre company founded in 1956 by George Devine to present new drama and encourage young playwrights, and based at the Royal Court Theatre in SLOANE SQUARE. In its early years it was particularly associated with the so-called 'kitchen-sink drama' of such writers as John Osborne and Arnold Wesker.

Epping Forest A tract of woodland and open grass covering almost 6,000 acres (24 sq km) to the south-west of Epping. It includes the largest hornbeam forest in England. Most of it is in Essex, but there is also a small corner in the London Borough of WALTHAM FOREST (which was the forest's original name). It is a remnant of the vast primeval forest that once stretched all the way from the THAMES to the Wash. In medieval times, when it was a royal hunting ground, it had shrunk considerably, but still extended as far south as LEYTONSTONE and WANSTEAD. Enclosure and other vicissitudes brought it to its present size by the middle of the 19th century, by which time royal huntsmen had long since lost interest in it (although herds of deer still remain). In 1878 ownership of the forest was made over to the CORPORATION OF LONDON, which opened it to the public as a place of recreation. East Londoners have flocked here to walk and picnic ever since.

Epsom races Epsom lies just beyond the southern border of GREATER LONDON (which has no racecourse of its own) and its horse races have long drawn thousands of Londoners. Since 1780 the high point of the season has been Derby Day, named after Edward Smith Stanley, the 12th Earl of Derby, who owned the OAKS estate at nearby Little Woodcote, now part of the London Borough of SUTTON. 'Epsom races' formerly meant 'braces', or occasionally 'faces', in COCKNEY RHYMING SLANG.

Erith A fast-growing THAMES GATEWAY district situated east of BELVEDERE. The name Earhyth, which means 'muddy landing place', was first recorded in the 7th century when lands here were granted to the bishop of the East Saxons. Henry VIII established a naval storehouse at the end of West Street in 1512. The town briefly flourished as a summer resort in the mid-19th century after the opening of a steamboat pier, a hotel and the station. Riverside gardens were laid out, with a maze and arboretum. At the same time, the docks brought industrial growth, which accelerated over the second half of the century, when Erith's population increased tenfold. In the first half of the 20th century the manufacture of armaments and cables was the dominant industry. As a consequence of its military significance, Erith was the target of heavy bombing during the Second World War and was radically redeveloped afterwards. Alexander Selkirk, the real-life inspiration for Daniel DEFOE's Robinson Crusoe, arrived back at Erith in 1711 after being rescued from his desert island. He is remembered in the names of Friday Road and Crusoe Road.

Ermine Street A Roman road running from London to York, built AD 43–50. The name was probably first applied to a stretch of the road near Arrington in Cambridgeshire, and later generalized to the whole road. The notion that the road was named after Arminius, the Germanic hero who routed Augustus's Roman legions in the Teutoburg Forest in Germany in AD 9, is completely fallacious. Instead, Arrington and Ermine Street both derive their names from 'the people of a man called Earn(a)'. Exiting London via what is now BISHOPSGATE, the road led northwards through SHOREDITCH, STOKE NEWINGTON, TOTTENHAM and EDMONTON towards Royston in Hertfordshire.

Eros The popular name for the statue of a winged archer, located in the centre of PICCADILLY CIRCUS, which was actually intended to represent the angel of Christian charity. A memorial to the 7th Earl of Shaftesbury, it is the work of Sir Alfred Gilbert (1854–1934) and was unveiled in 1893.

Erotic Gherkin *See the* GHERKIN.

Essex The county bordering London to the east, north of the THAMES. A large part of south-west Essex was absorbed into GREATER LONDON following the latter's creation in 1965. Most of the districts in the London boroughs of BARKING AND DAGENHAM, REDBRIDGE and HAVERING retain an Essex postal address, an anomaly that has perpetuated a crisis of geographical identity for some residents. Similar situations pertain in the London parts of other HOME COUNTIES.

Essex lion A 17th- to 19th-century slang term for a calf; Essex was a major source of cattle for the London meat markets. It was also used, especially by Kentishmen, as a contemptuous name for an Essex person.

Essex Man A type of socially ungraced and culturally deprived Conservative voter, typically a self-made businessman or tradesman, who lives in Essex or the boroughs of OUTER LONDON that were formerly part of Essex (especially HAVERING), and who in the late 1980s worshipped the consumer-oriented gospel of Thatcherism. He is likely to speak with an ESTUARY ENGLISH accent. The specific link with Essex is that the south and south-west of the county had been the recipient of a wave of working-class immigrants from EAST LONDON after the Second World War. Hitherto solid Labour voters, in the 1980s they discovered en masse the joys of unfettered capitalism. The term itself suggests an anthropological label such as Neanderthal Man (*see also* SELSDON MAN). The coining of the expression is generally attributed to the late 'left-wing' Conservative MP Julian Critchley, although the claim to authorship is contested by the journalist Simon Heffer. But whoever thought of the name, the species was definitively described in an unsigned profile headed 'Mrs Thatcher's bruiser' that appeared in *The Sunday Telegraph* for 7 October 1990:

> He [Essex Man] is discovered in his original state and in the greatest abundance in the triangle between Brentwood, Southend and the Dagenham Marshes.

Essex Road A street running north-eastwards from ISLINGTON GREEN in the direction of STOKE NEWINGTON. The route may be of Roman origin and was certainly well established by the Middle Ages. The road has gone by a variety of names for part or all of its length, including Seveney Street, Lower Street and Lower Road. Essex Road nowadays possesses a diverse set of commercial premises, from dirt-cheap discount stores to exclusive little French bistros and quirky antiques emporiums. The more interesting establishments tend to lie near Islington Green but these are spreading further along the road with Islington's ever-growing desirability.

Establishment, The An ironically named club founded in 1961 by Peter Cook (1937–95) and Nicholas Luard (1937–2004). Based at 18 Greek Street, SOHO, the Establishment became a hot-bed of the anti-establishment satire boom of that era. It closed in 1964.

estuary English or **estuarine** A type of English accent identified as spreading out from London to the area of the THAMES estuary, and then well beyond, and containing a blend of received (standard) pronunciation and that of COCKNEY or London speech. The term was coined in October 1984 by the linguist David Rosewarne in an article in the *Times Educational Supplement*, in which he suggested that it represented a continuation of the long process by which London pronunciation has influenced the speech patterns of the nation. The accent is regarded as typical of a supposedly growing classless society. *See also* MOCKNEY.

> In contrast with Eliza Doolittle, who had to re-engineer her accent to become socially acceptable, the prime minister [Tony Blair] descended into estuary English in an attempt to reach out to the masses.
>
> *The Sunday Times* (7 June 1998)

Eurostar The high-speed passenger service provided by the railways of Belgium, Britain and France to link London with Paris, Brussels and other cities via the Channel Tunnel. The service first operated in 1994 from WATERLOO and switched to ST PANCRAS in 2007. A non-stop journey to Paris Nord takes about two hours 15 minutes. Eurostar carried a record 9.1 million passengers in 2008.

Euston A compact locality north of BLOOMSBURY, taking its name from EUSTON SQUARE and best known for its main-line railway terminus.

Euston Arch A former Doric gateway, or pro-pylaeum, that constituted the centrepiece of a grand entrance to EUSTON STATION, designed by Philip Hardwick (1792–1870). Euston Arch, as it became known, was demolished by British Rail in the mid-1960s as part of the rebuilding of the station and its surroundings, an act of corporate vandalism that infuriated urban conservationists. The majority of the broken-up structure was used to plug a large hole in the bed of the Prescott Channel, a canal that runs into the River LEA, and the Euston Arch Trust hopes that the landmark might yet be salvaged and reconstructed.

> Last year it was announced there is to be another redevelopment of Euston, in 2012. This

creates a real chance that the arch could return from its watery grave.

The Daily Telegraph (16 August 2008)

Euston Road Present-day Euston Road began life in the 1750s as part of the NEW ROAD, which served as the original 'north circular', taking traffic away from built-up London. Until the end of the 18th century the road marked the outer edge of the metropolis in the same way that the M25 does today.

Euston Road School A name coined in 1938 by the art writer Clive Bell for a group of British painters centred round the School of Drawing and Painting that opened in a studio at 12 Fitzroy Street in 1937, soon transferring to nearby 316 Euston Road. Founding members were William Coldstream (1908–87), Victor Pasmore (1908–98) and Claude Rogers (1907–79). They advocated a move away from modernist styles to a more straightforward naturalism and laid stress on the training of observation in the teaching of art. *See also* FITZROVIA.

Euston Square A former residential rectangle now fused with the extended forecourt of Euston main-line station. Euston Square's name is little used except in the context of the TUBE station, which lies to the west on the corner of GOWER STREET. In the 1810s the northward expansion of BLOOMSBURY crossed the NEW ROAD with the creation of Euston Square, named after the country seat of the 2nd Duke of Grafton at Euston Hall in north Suffolk. The scheme was more of a road-widening project than the creation of a true square: a strip of garden was laid out on the north side of the New Road, with houses around it and on the south side of the main road. Gower Street station opened on the world's first underground railway in 1863 and was renamed Euston Square in 1909. The houses disappeared from the square long ago and the vicinity is now filled with a mixture of 20th- and 21st-century commercial and institutional premises. A garden of sorts remains, but it is split in half by a bus lane that passes between stone lodges from the Victorian entrance to Euston station.

Euston station Opened by the London and Birmingham Railway Company in July 1837, this was London's second railway terminus after LONDON BRIDGE. The engineer in charge of the project was Robert Stephenson, son of the railway pioneer George Stephenson. Philip Hardwick designed the station buildings (*see also* EUSTON ARCH) and his son added a great hall in 1849 as the boardroom of the railway company, which had by then become the London and North Western. In the mid-1960s the station was completely rebuilt in conjunction with the electrification of the west coast main line. At the same time, the entrance structures and adjacent buildings were demolished to make way for a commercial development. Completed in 1978, the complex has half a million square feet of office space, including the headquarters of what is now Network Rail. Most of the Euston complex now belongs to Sydney and London Properties, which is acting as the project manager of the Euston Estate Partnership, a group that has ambitious plans to redevelop both the station and the neighbouring SOMERS TOWN area.

Euston Tower A 36-storey office block built in 1970 near the corner of Hampstead Road and Euston Road. CAPITAL RADIO operated for more than 20 years at Euston Tower following the station's inception in 1973.

Evans Music-and-Supper Rooms In the 19th century one of the best-known resorts of London night life, at 43 King Street, COVENT GARDEN. The premises, which were used by the National Sporting Club, were opened in 1773 as a family hotel, and in the 1830s they were occupied by the Star Dinner and Coffee Room, which was much frequented by the nobility. The name Evans Music-and-Supper Rooms, by which the premises were known until their closure in 1880, derives from W.C. Evans, a member of the chorus of the Covent Garden Theatre, who was a former owner. He made it the most famous song-and-supper room in London, giving entertainment of the 'blue' variety and allowing his patrons to outdo each other in dirty songs. John Greenmore ('Paddy Green') took over in 1844 and added a splendid new hall with a platform at one end. All the performers were male, and women were admitted only if they gave their names and addresses and even then were obliged to watch from behind a screen. The standard of entertainment under Green was outstanding, and Evans Music-and-Supper Rooms can be regarded as the precursor of the MUSIC HALL. The Prince of Wales (afterwards Edward VII) was a frequent visitor.

evening

evening, all *See* DOCK GREEN.

Evening Standard The leading newspaper dedicated to the London region, founded in 1827 as the *Standard*. It became the *Evening Standard* in 1860. Over the course of its existence the *Standard* (as it is still usually known) has absorbed several rivals, including the PALL MALL GAZETTE, *St James Gazette* and *Evening News*, and seen off many others. In January 2009, faced with a seemingly irreversible decline in sales and advertising revenues, long-standing owners the Daily Mail and General Trust sold the *Standard* to the Russian oligarch Alexander Lebedev for a nominal sum. The newspaper has been distributed free of charge since October 2009. *See also* STAR, NEWS AND STANDARD.

Everyman London's oldest repertory cinema, in Holly Bush Vale, HAMPSTEAD. It opened on Boxing Day 1933 in the former Everyman Theatre here, established in 1919 and named after Ben Jonson's comedy *Every Man in His Humour* (1598). The cinema's programme includes classic films, new releases and live screenings of major international arts events.

Evil May Day or **Ill May Day** An anti-alien riot of 1517 and its gruesome aftermath. Stirred up by the rabble-rousing speeches of John Lincoln, official surveyor of goods bought and sold by foreigners, and by a xenophobic Easter sermon given by the canon of the priory of St Mary Spital (*see* SPITALFIELDS), London APPRENTICES and others began a series of physical attacks on foreign merchants and craftsmen. The trouble culminated late on the eve of May Day, when a mob of around a thousand assembled. Over the course of the night, despite the pleas of Thomas More, then under-sheriff of London, they broke into prisons to free comrades who had been arrested during the first wave of violence, and ransacked the homes of merchants from Picardy, Flanders, northern Italy and the Baltic states. Henry VIII came down hard on the troublemakers, decreeing that they be charged not with riot but treason. Hundreds were later pardoned but at least 13 were hanged. John Lincoln was hanged, drawn and quartered. Anthony Munday's play *Sir Thomas More* begins with a dramatization of the events of Evil May Day. A group of writers reworked the play a few years later, partly in an unsuccessful attempt to get it past the censor. Most scholars now believe that William SHAKESPEARE was one of the rewriters.

Then fire the houses, that, the Mayor being busy

About the quenching of them, we may escape;
Burn down their kennels: let us straight away,
Lest this day prove to us an ill May Day.

ANTHONY MUNDAY et al: *Sir Thomas More*, II, ii
(*c*.1594–1604)

ExCeL A capacious conference and exhibition centre that opened in 2000 on a 100-acre (40-hectare) site north of the Royal Victoria Dock (*see the* ROYAL DOCKS). It will host numerous OLYMPIC and Paralympic events in 2012.

Execution Dock The site of a riverside gallows in WAPPING, in use from the 15th century to 1830. Pirates and other civilians who committed capital crimes at sea were tried by the High Court of Admiralty and, if found guilty, taken to Execution Dock to be hanged. Until around the end of the 18th century, the corpses were then chained to a stake at low water mark and left there until three tides had washed over them. The bodies of the more notorious pirates were gibbeted at visible spots downriver. The most famous victim of the gallows was Captain KIDD, who was hanged for piracy in 1701. A pub bearing his name overlooks the site nowadays.

Exeter

Exeter Change Properly called the Exeter Exchange, this was a three-floor indoor market built in 1676 in the STRAND, on the site of the London home of the earls of Exeter. In its latter years much of the building was occupied by a menagerie, which evolved into a full-scale zoo, with all the big cats, polar bears, jackals, kangaroos, vultures, a boa constrictor and an elephant, which ran amok in 1826 and was brutally put down. These and many more exotic creatures were all kept in extremely confined conditions. It is said, unreliably, that the price of admission would be waived for those willing to offer their cat or dog for consumption by the carnivores. On the sale of the building in 1828, to permit the widening of the Strand, the animals were transferred to the newly created Surrey Zoological Gardens, in KENNINGTON.

Exeter Hall A public hall that opened in the STRAND in 1831, filling much of the site of EXETER CHANGE. It was largely used for the MAY MEETINGS of religious and philanthropic organizations. Their influence on colonial policy and in humanitarian causes was considerable, especially in the 1830s, and is generally known as 'the Exeter Hall influence'. The hall was acquired by the YMCA in 1880 and demolished in 1907, to be replaced by the Strand Palace Hotel.

Mr David has since had a 'serious call',
He never drinks ale, wine, or spirits, at all,
And they say he is going to Exeter Hall
To make a grand speech, and to preach and to teach
People that 'they can't brew their malt liquor too small'.

R.H. BARHAM: *Ingoldsby Legends*, 'Look At The Clock!:
Patty Morgan the Milkmaid's Story' (1840)

Exhibition Road A road in KNIGHTSBRIDGE and SOUTH KENSINGTON, running southwards from HYDE PARK to the eastern end of Old BROMPTON Road, at South Kensington underground station. It was so named because the land on which the surrounding cultural complex was built was bought with the profit from the GREAT EXHIBITION, held nearby in 1851. The name was chosen by the moving spirit of the site's development, Prince Albert. It contains the SCIENCE MUSEUM and the South Kensington campus of IMPERIAL COLLEGE LONDON. The NATURAL HISTORY MUSEUM and the VICTORIA AND ALBERT MUSEUM both have frontages on the road. By 2012 Exhibition Road will have been transformed into an open space in which some vehicles are permitted but pedestrians have priority.

Exmouth Market A revitalized street in north CLERKENWELL, named from the Exmouth Arms public house. It is notable for its concentration of cafés and restaurants, which spread their tables across the pedestrianized roadway. The street market that nowadays operates on Fridays and Saturdays specializes in gourmet foods and bears no resemblance to its rough-and-ready predecessor of a few years ago.

Exmouth Market is as close as London gets to the pavement cafés of continental Europe.

R. DEREK WETZEL (editor): *Let's Go London* (2007)

Exon One of the four officers in command of the Yeomen of the Guard (*see* BEEFEATERS), who are exempt from regimental duties. The word is an anglicized pronunciation of French *exempt*, a former title of a junior officer who commanded in the absence of his superiors and who was exempt from ordinary duty.

eyot *See* AIT.

Fabric Perhaps London's best-regarded large nightclub, converted from a former SMITHFIELD cold store in 1999.

> It's said that when the owners power up the underfoot subwoofer, lights dim in London's East End.
>
> DARWIN PORTER and DANFORTH PRINCE: *Frommer's Portable London* (2008)

face like the Red Lion of Brentford, a An old way of saying 'a very red face', perhaps one caused by years of heavy drinking. Given the popularity of that pub name it is uncertain why BRENTFORD's should have been chosen for this expression.

> Perhaps this saying was first made use of when the sign was new painted, or that the breed of red lions were not so numerous as at present.
>
> FRANCIS GROSE: *A Provincial Glossary* (1787)

Fagin The leader of a den of child pickpockets, based near FIELD LANE, and receiver of stolen goods for Bill SIKES in Charles DICKENS's *Oliver Twist* (1838). He is 'a very old shrivelled Jew, whose villainous-looking and repulsive face was obscured by a quantity of matted red hair'. He is bribed by Edward Leeford (known as 'Monks') to make Oliver Twist a thief, but fails. He instigates the murder of Nancy by Sikes, but is betrayed by Noah Claypole and convicted of complicity in her death. He spends a terrifying few days in the condemned cell before being hanged. Fagin is said to have been modelled on Isaac 'Ikey' Solomons (c.1785–1850), a notorious London receiver of the 1820s, who was sentenced to 14 years' transportation for picking pockets.

Fairfield Halls CROYDON's leading cultural and entertainment centre. Opened in 1962, the Fairfield Halls consist of an 1,800-seat concert hall, the 750-seat Ashcroft Theatre and the 500-seat, multi-purpose Arnham Gallery. Fairfield hosts popular and classical music concerts, wrestling, comedy, pantomime and ballet. The rock bands Nice, Soft Machine and Caravan have all released live albums recorded at the Fairfield Halls, as did the pop group Bucks Fizz.

Fairlop A semi-rural hamlet situated south-west of HAINAULT, primarily given over to recreation grounds and playing fields. Fairlop Plain was used as an aircraft base during the Second World War, but plans to create a civil airport were abandoned in 1953. ILFORD council then bought the site from the CORPORATION OF LONDON, and profited from the extraction of over a million cubic yards of gravel. The resultant hole was subsequently filled with refuse and has been landscaped to create Fairlop Waters golf course and country park. There is a nature reserve, an activity centre, and water sports and angling on Fairlop Lake. Plans to create Greater London's only horse-racing course on green-belt land at Fairlop Waters were rejected in 2002.

Fairlop Fair An annual 'beanfeast' that took place beneath the FAIRLOP OAK on the first Friday in July. The fair was begun c.1725 by Daniel Day, a WAPPING man who owned land in Fairlop. At first held solely for Day's employees, the fair later drew thousands. Despite the death of Day in 1767 and the oak in 1820, the event continued until 1853. The 'Fairlop Fair Song' is a traditional ballad that records the custom of riding through the fair while seated in boats:

> Let music sound as the boat goes round,
> If we tumble on the ground, we'll be merry, I'll be bound;
> We will booze it away, dull care we will defy,
> And be happy on the first Friday in July.

Fairlop oak A magnificent old tree that boasted a trunk with a circumference of 36 feet (11m). Damaged by all the fires that had been lit beneath it at FAIRLOP FAIR, the oak blew down in 1820. A 'new Fairlop oak' was planted at the centre of FULWELL CROSS roundabout as part of the FESTIVAL OF BRITAIN celebrations in 1951. *See also* MI-KRAULISKEY GAV.

Fairport Convention An electric folk band formed in 1967 and named after a house in FORTIS GREEN at which they convened for rehearsals.

Fairwater A fictional London suburb that provided the setting for the ITV sitcom *Bless Me, Father*, starring Arthur Lowe as the priest of the Roman Catholic parish of St Jude's. The show was set in 1950 and was first broadcast from 1978 to 1981.

Fairway *See* FX4.

Fall and Rise of Reginald Perrin, The
A popular and inventive BBC TV sitcom that ran for three series in the late 1970s, written by David Nobbs (b.1935) and starring Leonard Rossiter (1926–84). Perrin lives in the fictional south London suburb of Climthorpe, commuting from NORBITON station to his unsatisfying sales job at Sunshine Desserts, where he never arrives on time. Confronted by a mid-life crisis he finds increasingly unlikely ways to escape the monotony of his existence. The BBC revived the show in 2009, with Martin Clunes in the title role.

Twenty-two minutes late, escaped puma, Chessington North.

Series 2, epsiode 7 (1977)

Fanny on the Hill A public house in EAST WICKHAM, and the informal designation of the neighbouring open space. The name is said to derive from a barmaid at an earlier hostelry who would shine a lamp to tell Dick TURPIN when the coast was clear. However, the original Fanny is more likely to have been Anne Muirhead, who ran the White Horse beerhouse for about 20 years in the mid-19th century.

fantabulosa A POLARI word of approbation, meaning something like 'excellent' or 'wonderful'. Like several other terms in the polari lexicon it was created simply by taking the stem of an existing word (or in this case a blend of the words 'fantastic' and 'fabulous') and adding an Italian- or Spanish-sounding suffix. *Kenneth Williams: Fantabulosa!* was a 2006 BBC TV dramatization of the diaries of the troubled comic genius.

Far Cry from Kensington, A A novel (1988) by Muriel Spark; it is essentially a fictionalized autobiographical account of her days in the bed-sitter world of 1950s London and her beginnings as a writer.

Farm, the A nickname for BROADWATER FARM.

farmer An old nickname for a CITY of London ALDERMAN.

farmer Giles 'Piles' (haemorrhoids) in COCKNEY RHYMING SLANG, as an alternative to CHALFONTS. It derives from the generic term for a stereotypical figure of an English farmer.

Farnborough A suburban village situated on the edge of larch woods and open country, at the south-western extremity of ORPINGTON's sprawl. The name referred to a small hill, overgrown with ferns. The manor of Farnborough belonged to the Duchy of Lancaster 'from the first erection of it', as Edward Hasted put it in his *History of Kent* (1797). In 1639 a great storm destroyed the Church of St Giles the Abbot, which had to be rebuilt from scratch. In 1845 BROMLEY's board of guardians built at Locksbottom a union workhouse that subsequently evolved into Farnborough Hospital. The pretty village began to succumb to suburban development following the First World War, causing the fragmentation of the area's long-established Gypsy community (*see* BOSWELL, URANIA). After the Second World War the area north of the High Street filled with housing, but GREEN-BELT legislation prevented building further south.

Farringdon A historic LONDON UNDERGROUND station and its immediate environs, situated in south CLERKENWELL. Farringdon's name defines only a compact quarter because there are other well-known localities close by, such as SMITHFIELD and HATTON GARDEN. The CITY ward of the same name covers a much wider area. Documents of the late 13th century record William de Farindon (whose name is spelt several ways, sometimes within the space of a single paragraph), who was a goldsmith and a City of London ALDERMAN. This area lay well away from the heart of medieval London and remained isolated until the FLEET river was covered in 1737 and Farringdon Street was constructed over it. Shoddy housing went up on SAFFRON HILL and the neighbourhood became seriously overcrowded. The arrival of London's first underground railway brought disruption in 1863, when Farringdon Street station opened. The station was relocated to its present position two years later when the line was extended to MOORGATE and its spacious interior survives from that time. In recent years the Farringdon area has gained new residential accommodation, mainly well-appointed apartments for City business people, and a variety of bars and nightclubs.

Farringdon Road Work to extend Farringdon Street (*see above*) began in the early 1840s. Originally called Victoria Street, and later Farringdon Road, the new thoroughfare pushed very slowly north towards KING'S CROSS over the following two decades, cutting through the SAFFRON HILL slums; 1,600 homes were demolished and *The Times* estimated that 16,000 residents were displaced. Warehouses, type foundries and other commercial and industrial premises were built along Farringdon Road in the 1860s and 1870s and a miscellaneous market began to operate, which at first specialized in watercress and much later in second-hand books. Some of the road's earliest buildings survive, mixed in with a largely unattractive set of office blocks from the latter part of the 20th century. *The Guardian* newspaper moved its headquarters to Farringdon Road in 1976. A newsroom, visitor centre and archive opened in 2002 in a converted Victorian bonded warehouse. Farringdon Road's public houses include the BETSEY and the EAGLE (2).

farthing bundles A tradition introduced at the Fern Street Settlement, BROMLEY-BY-BOW, in 1907 by Clara Grant, headmistress of Devons School. Bundles of toys or trinkets were sold for a farthing to children small enough to pass under an archway inscribed: 'Enter now ye children small, None can come who are too tall.' Queen Mary visited the settlement and afterwards regularly sent her old greetings cards to be reused in the 'bundles'. Following the withdrawal of farthings in 1960 the recipients paid a halfpenny each for their gift. The Fern Street Settlement is still in existence, running a day centre for pensioners and providing other assistance in the community, such as giving presents to children at Christmas, but without any ceremony resembling that of the farthing bundles.

This 'nominal payment' was a deliberate policy

by Clara who believed that 'paying' gave those receiving them, however young, a feeling of self-respect, and even the right to complain if the items were not up to standard!

GARY HAINES, in the *East London Advertiser* (11 August 2008)

Fatal Vespers On 26 October 1623 a congregation of some 300 had assembled in an upper room in the residence of the French ambassador, at BLACKFRIARS, to hear Father Drury, a Jesuit, preach. The flooring gave way, and Drury with another priest and about a hundred of the congregation were killed. This accident was attributed to God's judgement against the Jesuits.

Fat Boy of Peckham The sobriquet of Johnny Trunley or Trundley (b.*c.*1899), who at the age of 5 weighed 11 stones (70 kg) and was put on display as a freak at fairs, MUSIC HALLS, etc. was regularly invoked in the middle years of the 20th century when giving a dire warning of the dangers of obesity.

father

Father, Dear Father An ITV sitcom that ran for seven seasons between 1968 and 1973. The show starred Patrick Cargill as Patrick Glover, a divorced writer of spy novels, and Ann Holloway and Natasha Pyne as his trendy daughters. The three shared a luxurious HAMPSTEAD home in the fictional Hillsdown Avenue. Numerous luminaries of British comedy made guest appearances.

Father of Scientific Surgery The sobriquet of John Hunter (1728–93), a brilliant but temperamental anatomist and surgeon who sought to emphasize the relationship between structure and function in the human body (and in the bodies of all kinds of living creatures), thus providing an analytical basis for surgical practice. He assembled a vast collection of instructive specimens and preparations at his house in LEICESTER SQUARE, which he arranged into a teaching museum (*see the* HUNTERIAN MUSEUM). Hunter died after suffering a fit during an argument at St George's Hospital, HYDE PARK CORNER (since relocated to TOOTING), over the acceptance of students for training.

Father Thames A male personification of the River THAMES, which has become its modern quasi-tutelary deity. He appears in the works of Dryden and Pope and their contemporary

Matthew Green, but was chiefly popularized by Thomas Gray, who apostrophizes him in his *Ode on a Distant Prospect of Eton College* (1747):

Say, Father Thames, for thou hast seen
Full many a sprightly race
Disporting on thy margent green
The paths of pleasure trace,
Who foremost now delight to cleave
With pliant arm thy glassy wave?

He appears in less fragrant guise in periodicals of the mid-19th century, the time of the GREAT STINK OF LONDON, when the Thames was more sewer than river. A particularly famous cartoon in *Punch* (21 July 1855), entitled 'Faraday giving his card to Father Thames', portrays the noisome old man arising slimily from the depths with an old kettle atop his trident.

High in the hills, down in the dales,
Whatever the end may be,
Old Father Thames keeps rolling along,
Down to the mighty sea.

R. WALLACE and B. O'HOGAN: 'Old Father Thames Keeps Rolling Along' (1933)

Fawkes, Guy The Roman Catholic convert (1570–1606) who was one of the conspirators in the GUNPOWDER PLOT. His experience as a soldier and his reputation as a cool schemer won him the actual execution of the plan, but he was caught in the vault under the House of Lords on 4 November 1605, the plot having been betrayed to the government. Under fearful torture he disclosed the names of his fellow conspirators, but by then they had already been killed or apprehended. He was executed before the old PALACE OF WESTMINSTER on 31 January 1606.

Feltham A sprawling suburban development located just inside GREATER LONDON's south-western border, to the west of HANWORTH, with which it has a close historical association. A Saxon hamlet by the 8th century, its name means 'a settlement in a field'. Agriculture remained the main occupation until the 1920s, after which unconstrained urbanization began. By the late 20th century, Feltham had become a run-down district, despite its convenience for HEATHROW AIRPORT. A recent regeneration programme has injected more than £100 million of private and public sector money into a large number of improvement schemes. Freddie Mercury, legendary frontman of the rock group Queen, spent his

teenage years in Feltham after his family moved here from Zanzibar in 1964.

female Howard, the Elizabeth Fry (1780–1845), the philanthropist and prison reformer, so called after John Howard (1726–90), her famous predecessor in this field. Born in Norfolk to a family of wealthy bankers, she spent most of her adult life in EAST LONDON, residing in FOREST GATE and EAST HAM and keeping a holiday cottage at DAGENHAM BREACH.

Fenchurch Street An office-filled street curving south-westwards from ALDGATE, with a shipping-related past and one of London's most commuter-oriented railway stations. The Romans built several municipal structures at the western end of the street in the first and second centuries AD, including a military storehouse. The present name was first recorded in 1283 as Fancherchestrate and probably referred to a street by a church in a marsh. Alternatively, the first part could have come from *faenum*, 'hay', indicating the presence of a haymarket. The church was presumably All Hallows Staining, which stood in Mark Lane. In the late 18th century the EAST INDIA COMPANY built bonded warehouses on Fenchurch Street. The names of some of the street's present-day buildings indicate its mercantile connections: Black Sea and Baltic House, the Marine Engineers' Memorial Building and the offices of Lloyd's Register of Shipping. On its completion in 1957 the 14-storey Fountain House became Britain's first office tower block.

Fenchurch Street station A main-line railway terminus primarily serving office workers arriving from south ESSEX. The station opened in 1841 as the CITY terminus of the London and Blackwall Railway and for many decades London's docks were its raison d'être. In *London River* (1921), H.M. Tomlinson describes:

… a cobbled forecourt, tame pigeons, cabs, a brick front topped by a clock-face: Fenchurch Street Station. Beyond its dingy platforms, the metal track which contracts into the murk is the road to China … It is the beginning of Dockland.

With the disappearance of the docks, Fenchurch Street station is now heavily devoted to commuter traffic. Over 83 per cent of passenger arrivals at Fenchurch Street station take place during the morning peak period. Season tickets account for three-quarters of its passenger revenue.

> There is no station like Fenchurch Street on the road to Tilbury. Conrad could tell you where every husky earringed fellow with a blue, white-spotted handkerchief under his arm was going to ... It most impressed the writer that in the station barber's shop was a placard that read: Teeth scaled two shillings, extractions sixpence ... To come home from the great waters to that!
>
> FORD MADOX FORD: *Joseph Conrad: A Personal Remembrance* (1924)

Fenian Barracks A 19th-century nickname for part of BOW Common, on account of its Irish inhabitants, who were said by the police to be not human but 'wild beasts'. This historically poor quarter, situated south-east of MILE END, was industrialized when factories moved towards the River LEA from districts such as WHITECHAPEL, and the Great Central Gas Company built gasworks to supply the CITY of London. In 1883 Andrew Mearns observed, 'Out of 2,290 persons living in consecutive houses at Bow Common, only 88 adults and 47 children ever attend [a place of worship]', a situation that he blamed on the conditions in which they lived. There has been much slum clearance since.

> ... streets between Gale Street and Furze Street are the worst in the district, worse than almost any district in London. Three policemen wounded there last week. This block sends more policemen to hospital than any other in London.
>
> CHARLES BOOTH: notebook (31 May 1897)

Fenn Street Gang, The *See* PLEASE SIR!

Fern Street Settlement *See* FARTHING BUNDLES.

Ferrier A large, multicultural housing estate in south KIDBROOKE, and 'one of the most deprived neighbourhoods in England' according to the council that is now overseeing its eradication. In 1970 the London Borough of GREENWICH was handed the land occupied by the former RAF depot near Kidbrooke station and immediately began construction of the houses, maisonettes and tower blocks of the Ferrier estate. The subsequent deterioration of the estate, both structurally and socially, became a casebook example of urban decay. At the end of the 20th century the Ferrier estate was the focus of high-profile initiatives to make it a better place to live but in a subsequent admission of defeat Greenwich council earmarked the estate for demolition and replacement. The total cost of the project, which has been part-funded by the sale of council-owned land, will approach £1 billion, making this one of the largest such schemes ever undertaken in London.

Festival of Britain This grand, government-sponsored celebration was staged on an area of derelict ground on the SOUTH BANK in 1951, ostensibly to mark the centenary of the GREAT EXHIBITION of 1851. In reality it was a morale-boosting exercise, a gesture of faith in a brighter future for Britain after the deprivations of the Second World War and the years of austerity that followed. Three of its most striking structures were the DOME OF DISCOVERY, the world's largest dome at the time; the SKYLON; and the ROYAL FESTIVAL HALL, the only permanent building and now one of London's main concert venues.

> We believe in the right to strike,
> But now we've bloody well got to like
> Our own dear Festival of Britain.
>
> NOËL COWARD: *The Lyric Revue*, 'Don't Make Fun of the Fair' (1951)

Fetter Lane A road linking FLEET STREET with HOLBORN (an extension, New Fetter Lane, branches off eastwards to Holborn Circus). The aspersions implicit in its name ('lane frequented by impostors or cheats', from Middle English *faitour*, 'impostor', 'cheat') were probably cast not on the lawyers who have operated in this area since the Middle Ages, nor on the preachers who frequented the lane in the 17th century, still less on the journalists who have been more recent denizens (although Maxwell House, Robert Maxwell's headquarters when proprietor of *The Mirror*, was at the top of New Fetter Lane), but on the local vagrants and beggars of medieval times, who specialized in feigning illness in order to elicit sympathy and money.

Fever Pitch A popular sociological study (1992) by Nick Hornby (b.1957), subtitled 'A Story of Football and Obsession'. It charts the author's personal relationship with the game as a fan (from the age of 10) of ARSENAL FC. The title has obvious punning connotations. A film version (1996), directed by David Evans and starring Colin Firth, presented the original as a romantic comedy. An Americanized version (2005) concerned actor Ben Fallon's character's obsession with the Boston Red Sox.

field

Field Lane A notorious thoroughfare that formerly extended northward from the foot of Holborn Hill. Once known as a centre for the resale of stolen pocket handkerchiefs, the slum was erased in the mid-19th century during the creation of FARRINGDON ROAD. The former Field Lane RAGGED SCHOOL has evolved into a Christian charity and housing association named Field Lane, still based near its point of origin. *See also* MOTHER CLAP'S MOLLY HOUSE.

> It is a commercial colony of itself: the emporium of petty larceny: visited at early morning and setting-in of dusk by silent merchants, who traffic in dark back parlours and go as strangely as they come.
>
> DICKENS: *Oliver Twist* (1838)

Field Lane duck An old colloquialism for a baked sheep's head, or sometimes a bullock's heart.

Field of the Forty Footsteps or **the Brothers' Steps** The land at the back of the BRITISH MUSEUM, near the extreme north-east of the present Montague Street. The tradition is that at the time of the Duke of Monmouth's Rebellion (1685), two brothers fought each other here over a girl with whom they were both in love until both were killed, and for several years 40 of their footprints remained on the field. No grass would grow there nor upon the bank where the young woman sat to watch the fight. The site was built over in about 1800.

Fieldway *See* NEW ADDINGTON.

fifty

Fifty New Churches An objective deemed appropriate for the London area given the enormous growth in its population in the decades after the GREAT FIRE OF LONDON. Established by Act of Parliament in 1711, the Commissioners for Building Fifty New Churches (also known as the Queen Anne Commission) fell well short of their target, funding the construction of eleven new churches and the reconstruction of another two, and subsidizing work on five more. However, they set high architectural and construction standards, and some of London's finest early 18th-century churches stand as testimony to their achievements. These include St John's, SMITH SQUARE, Christ Church, SPITALFIELDS, and St George's, HANOVER SQUARE.

50p building A nickname for the office tower properly called No.1 Croydon, previously the NLA Tower, which is located near East CROYDON station. Completed in 1970, its 24 multangular storeys bear a vague resemblance to a stack of alternately arranged fifty pence coins. It was earlier nicknamed the 'wedding cake' and the 'threepenny bit building'. For some while considered an eyesore, the building has come to be regarded more fondly, especially since a clean-up in 2006.

> French president Nicolas Sarkozy has revealed he is planning to take inspiration from such wonders as the Whitgift Centre and the NLA Tower – more affectionately known by locals as the 50p building – for the future of Paris.
>
> *Croydon Guardian* (8 September 2008)

Finchley A famously conservative residential district, situated north of HAMPSTEAD GARDEN SUBURB. The hamlet of Finchley took root at Gravel Hill in the 12th century and St Mary's Church had been built by 1274. From the mid-14th century, when much of the area was part of Bibbesworth Manor, the Great North Road (as it later became) attracted commerce away to what is now EAST FINCHLEY, and the old village became a woodland backwater known as CHURCH END. Residential development eventually took off after the introduction of tram services in 1905 and the area was almost entirely built up by 1920. The comic actor Terry-Thomas (1911–90), the Kent and England wicketkeeper Godfrey Evans (1920–99) and the singer George Michael (b.1963; original name Georgios Panayiotou) were born in Finchley. In the latter part of the 20th century Finchley was best known nationally as the constituency of Margaret Thatcher, prime minister from 1979 to 1990. She represented the seat from her parliamentary debut in 1959 until her retirement from the House of Commons at the 1992 general election. Finchley provided less controversial heroes in the four Pevensie children, saviours of Narnia in C.S. Lewis's stories.

> Peter Pevensie: I think you've made a mistake. We're not heroes!
>
> Susan Pevensie: We're from Finchley.
>
> *The Chronicles of Narnia: The Lion, the Witch and the Wardrobe* (film) (2005)

Finchley Road A long, curving highway running from ST JOHN'S WOOD to Finchley, and specifically that part of it in the vicinity of Finchley Road tube station, in south-west HAMPSTEAD. Finchley Road sliced through the demesne of FROGNAL in the late 1820s but a number of legalities prevented its commercial exploitation for several decades. Finchley Road station (now Finchley Road and Frognal) opened on the Hampstead Junction Railway in 1860. The Metropolitan Railway built a separate station in 1879 when the line was extended to WILLESDEN GREEN. An ice skating rink opened in 1880 and the first shops appeared shortly afterwards. Within another decade the road had a string of houses, some of which were soon converted to shops at street level. Today the stretch of road between the two stations is a lively strip of shops, bars and places of entertainment, dominated by the O2 Centre. Together with Kilburn High Road and Camden Town, Finchley Road is one of the London Borough of CAMDEN's three designated zones for 24-hour party licences.

The novelist Wilkie Collins and the artist John Everett Millais, walking from Hanover Terrace, REGENT'S PARK, to Millais's studio in GOWER STREET one evening in the late 1850s, encountered what Millais's biography (by his son J.G. Millais, 1899) described as 'a young and very beautiful woman dressed in flowing white robes that shone in the moonlight. She seemed to float rather than run in their direction, and, on coming up to the ... young men, she paused for a moment in an attitude of supplication and terror.' The incident provided Collins with the inspiration for the revelatory scene that takes place on the Finchley Road in his 'sensation novel' *The Woman in White* (1860):

> There, in the middle of the broad, bright high-road ... stood the figure of a solitary Woman, dressed from head to foot in white garments, her face bent in grave enquiry on mine, her hand pointing to the dark cloud over London, as I faced her.

Long Walk to Finchley, The *See under* LONG.
March to Finchley, The *See under* MARCH.

fine and dandy 'Brandy' in COCKNEY RHYMING SLANG.

Fingersmith A novel (2002) by Sarah Waters (b.1966), televised by the BBC in 2005. Set in Victorian London, notably Lant Street in the BOROUGH, it concerns the entanglements of a trio of con artists and their mark. The term 'fingersmith' has been applied to practitioners of various dexterous skills, including midwives and pianists, but in the context of this story it means a petty thief.

Fings Ain't Wot They Used T'Be A musical (1959) with a score and lyrics by Lionel Bart (1930–99) and book by Frank Norman (1930–80) about the gamblers and prostitutes who inhabit low-life London. The success of the title song, which reflects the changes that overtake the lives of all the main characters, was enough to establish it as a popular catchphrase.

> Somebody said it was *Guys and Dolls* with its flies undone, but what it finally was was a play with songs, not a plotted musical.
> LIONEL BART, quoted in MARK STEYN: *Broadway Babies Say Goodnight: Musicals Then and Now* (2000)

Finsbury A now indistinct area situated immediately north and north-west of the CITY of London. First recorded in the 13th century, the manor covered a swathe of the boggy moor that lay beyond the City wall. By the 15th century a manor house stood at what is now the corner of Finsbury Pavement and Chiswell Street. Houses and places of entertainment were built as the marshes were drained. Finsbury Square and Finsbury Circus were laid out in the late 18th and early 19th centuries as the nuclei of a high-class suburb that never achieved its full potential and subsequently converted to commercial use. The metropolitan borough of Finsbury was formed in 1901 from the CLERKENWELL parishes of St James and St John. Many of the borough's civic and public buildings lay in the vicinity of Rosebery Avenue and Finsbury's name thus came to be primarily associated with this neighbourhood. The borough was merged into ISLINGTON in 1965 and has begun to fade from memory. Some Clerkenwell estate agents still refer to properties in the Rosebery Avenue area as being 'in the heart of Finsbury' but most people now associate the name with the park that was created for the constituency's residents 3 miles (5 km) to the north.

> You swear like a comfit-makers wife ...
> And givest such sarcenet surety for thy oaths,
> As if thou never walk'st further than Finsbury.

Swear me, Kate, like a lady as thou art,
A good mouth-filling Oath.

SHAKESPEARE: *Henry IV, Part 1*, III, i (c.1596)

Finsbury Park A 115-acre (47-hectare) public park and its multi-ethnic neighbourhood, situated north of HIGHBURY. The park was created from a surviving corner of HORNSEY Wood in the 1860s for the welfare of the residents of the parliamentary constituency of Finsbury, an overcrowded inner-city area that had no sizeable green spaces of its own. The constituency and the park lay at opposite ends of ISLINGTON parish and its trustees were instrumental in persuading the METROPOLITAN BOARD OF WORKS to finance the project. The opening of the park came at a time when the neighbouring area was filling with two- and three-storey terraced housing for the middle classes. Many houses failed to find buyers of the intended means and were soon subdivided into single-floor flats; they have stayed that way ever since. The park is now the responsibility of HARINGEY council, which has recently restored it to something approaching its Victorian glory in a lottery-funded scheme. It has a small lake, plenty of trees and extensive sports facilities, and is often used for major events and concerts.

Finsbury Park Astoria Edward A. Stone's art deco cinema opened in 1930, with an ornate interior that creates the impression of a Moorish settlement at night. The Astoria (later called the Rainbow) subsequently became a noted live-music venue, and hosted the Beatles' Christmas shows in 1963. It is presently home to the Universal Church of the Kingdom of God.

Finsbury Park mosque The commonly used name for the North London Central Mosque. It was at the centre of controversy in the early 21st century as an alleged base for Muslim extremists, attracted by the preaching of one of its imams, Sheikh Abu Hamza. The mosque was closed for over a year but reopened in 2005 under a more mainstream regime.

fire

Fire Judges or **Fire Court Judges** The 22 judges appointed to settle the land disputes after the GREAT FIRE OF LONDON. They sat in the hall at CLIFFORD'S INN. Full-length portraits of the Fire Judges by John Michael Wright were the first works of art ever commissioned by the CITY of London. Of those that survive, two now hang in the GUILDHALL ART GALLERY and another two in the main hall of the ROYAL COURTS OF JUSTICE.

Fire of London See the GREAT FIRE OF LONDON.

firm An organized gang of criminals or football HOOLIGANS, such as the (fictional) GREEN STREET ELITE.

Firsdon A 'virtual' London district created as the basis for the UK's first fully realistic bus simulator, designed to help trainee drivers get to grips with the vicissitudes of the capital's roads. The name derived from the project's co-sponsors, bus operator First and Transport for London. Introduced in 2005 at WILLESDEN JUNCTION bus depot, the American-made simulator provided detailed, co-ordinated graphics through the windscreen and rear-view mirrors to give the look and feel of a real bus journey. Unpredictable pedestrians, cyclists and traffic contributed to the authenticity. Firsdon bus station was based on WALTHAMSTOW's and the bus depot was a close replica of the one at WESTBOURNE PARK. The two tube stations were generically designed but bore a resemblance to CAMDEN TOWN. People involved in the project gave their names to buildings and streets, which included Livingstone Drive.

> Firsdon was just like any other suburb, full of privet, Tarmac and shopping parades, with the difference that would-be bus drivers could carom about the place presenting no danger to pedestrians or any other road users.
>
> WILL SELF, in *The Independent* (17 December 2005)

First Night of the Proms The first evening of the annual Promenade Concerts at the ALBERT HALL in July, an eagerly awaited event for many concert-goers. The music chosen varies from year to year, and thus lacks the predictability of the pieces at the LAST NIGHT OF THE PROMS. *See also the* PROMS.

firty-free fousand fevvers on a frush *See* FORTY FOUSAND FEVVERS ON A FRUSH.

fisher

Fisher FC A non-league FOOTBALL club that has its roots in a team founded in 1908 and named in honour of John Fisher, Bishop of Rochester (c.1469–1535), who was canonized in 1935. Nowadays known as the Fish, the club's earlier nickname – the Martyrs – derived from the saint's beheading at TOWER HILL, after he had preached against Henry VIII's divorce from Catherine of Aragon.

fisherman's (daughter) 'Water' in COCKNEY RHYMING SLANG, usually in the sense of a drink of water, although not in this example, which makes heavy use of phonetic spelling:

> Yhus, movin' aht, are yeh? Norra bed flat. I sees
> yeh got the fisherman's daughter laid on an'
> all – where 'e's a-goin' teh, they 'ave teh go down
> two flights er apples and pears: still – do fer 'em
> fer a star' off!
>
> JULIAN FRANKLYN: *This Gutter Life* (1934)

Fisher's Folly A large and beautiful house in BISHOPSGATE, with pleasure gardens, bowling green and hothouses, built by Jasper Fisher, one of the six clerks of CHANCERY. Elizabeth I slept there. Also nicknamed Mount Fisher, it was acquired in 1625 by the Earl of Devonshire, and its site is now occupied by Devonshire Square. An old half-rhyme linked Fisher with three other Londoners who built ostentatious houses that were above their station and their means:

> Kirbie's castle and Megse's glory
> Spinola's pleasure and Fisher's folly.

Fish Harvest Festival *See* HARVEST OF THE SEA FESTIVAL.

Fitzjohn's Avenue 'One of the noblest streets in the world', according to the American magazine *Harpers* in 1883, this was formerly a track running southwards from HAMPSTEAD towards ST JOHN'S WOOD, via Shepherd's Well, a spring that was the main source of the TYBURN stream. Several prominent figures attempted in vain to prevent development here in the early 1870s, notably the philanthropist Octavia Hill, whose fund-raising campaign reportedly came within £1,000 of achieving its target. But in 1875 the Maryon Wilson family, lords of the manor of Hampstead, sold 50 acres (20 hectares) for development and named the old footpath Fitzjohn's Avenue after their estate at Great Canfield, Essex. 'Stately dwellings' were built in Queen Anne style with spacious grounds, and the avenue was lined with pink chestnuts, later replaced with plane trees. The project was an immediate success, proving especially popular with artists. Many of the properties

have subsequently been subdivided, some into bed and breakfast accommodation, but the locality retains a prestigious reputation. Stella Gibbons wrote *Cold Comfort Farm* (1932) at 76 Fitzjohn's Avenue.

> I went up to town on an invitation from some
> artistic people in Fitzjohn's Avenue: one of the
> girls was a Newnham chum. They took me to
> the National Gallery.
>
> GEORGE BERNARD SHAW: *Mrs Warren's Profession*, I (1893)

Fitzrovia The present-day name for the area between GREAT PORTLAND STREET and GOWER STREET. The district was first developed by Charles Fitzroy, lord of the manor of Tottenhall from 1757. Fitzroy built for the upper classes, but they soon migrated south-westwards to BELGRAVIA and MAYFAIR, forcing subdivision of the aristocratic houses into workshops, studios and rooms to let. Immigrants from France and other European countries replaced them and helped establish the district as a centre for the furniture trade by the end of the 18th century. Chippendale was among the craftsmen who set up shop here. The artist John Constable maintained a local residence, although he spent most of his time in HAMPSTEAD. In the years before the Second World War, Augustus John and Dylan Thomas helped earn Fitzrovia a Bohemian reputation. John is credited with coining the name 'Fitzrovia' in honour of his favourite hostelry, the Fitzroy Tavern. Greeks and Italians brought new vitality to the area after the Second World War, followed later by Nepalese and Bengalis, but the area's originally jocular name began to fade from use, except by estate agents. Residents later revived it and their pressure resulted in the inclusion of Fitzrovia on Ordnance Survey maps from 1994. Property developers have attempted to rebrand Fitzrovia as NOHO in recent years, thankfully with little success.

> After leaving school he emigrated into what he
> calls Fitzrovia – a world of outsiders, down-
> and-outs, drunks, sensualists, homosexuals and
> eccentrics.
>
> *Times Literary Supplement* (10 January 1958)

Fitzrovian A denizen of Fitzrovia.

Fitzroy Square A small but elegant Georgian square situated at the northern end of Fitzrovia. The east and south sides of the square were designed by Robert ADAM in 1794 and survive in their original form, in Portland stone. The Georgian Group, an architectural preservationist society, is based at 6 Fitzroy Square.

Fitzroy Street A northward continuation of CHARLOTTE STREET, first developed in the late 18th century. The artist James McNeill Whistler took a studio in Fitzroy Street in 1896. George Bernard SHAW lived with his mother at 37 Fitzroy Street in the early 1880s and then in FITZROY SQUARE from 1887 until his marriage in 1898. The former address was the London base of the writer – and founder of Scientology – L. Ron Hubbard in the 1950s. The house now contains an exhibition of Hubbard's life and work.

Fitzroy Street Group An artists' group formed in 1907 by Walter Sickert (1860–1942) and friends, based in rented studios at 19 Fitzroy Street. In 1911 an enlarged and more formal in-carnation of the group reassembled in CAMDEN TOWN.

five kings It is said that in 1363, in a rare period of peace, five kings dined at a lavish banquet in the CITY of London. Their identity is disputed but the most common version of the story suggests they were the kings of England, France, Scotland, Denmark and Cyprus. Their host was the master vintner Henry Picard, leading financier of Edward III and one of the NINE WORTHIES OF LONDON. To this day the ceremonial toast of Picard's LIVERY COMPANY is, 'The Vintners' Company, may it flourish root and branch for ever with Five and the Master', accompanied by five cheers.

flash

flash boy A confident and overdressed working-class youth of the late 19th and early 20th centuries. Some flash boys were honest but raffish COSTERMONGERS; others operated on the fringes of the law and were the forerunners of the 'wide boys' of the mid-20th century. Their fondness for pearl buttons inspired Henry Croft to create an outfit that began the tradition of the PEARLY KINGS AND QUEENS. 'Flash girls' were similarly flamboyant and roguish characters.

flash house A low drinking den and lodging house where criminal plans were laid and stolen goods fenced. In the early 19th century London was said to have more than 200 flash houses, which were often also used as brothels. The Common Lodging House Act (1851) gave the police powers to inspect such places and close them if they failed to meet basic standards of decency and cleanliness. The legislation greatly reduced the number of flash houses but in the process made many poor people homeless.

> Now to the flash-house is my way,
> He may work but I will spree,
> And damned the farthing I shall pay,
> Unless where all are flash like me.
>
> ANTHONY MAHON: *London as it Was and Is*, 'The Night Rambler' (1841)

flash mob or **flashmob** A phenomenon of the early 21st century consisting of a crowd that suddenly assembles in a place, engages briefly in a co-ordinated and apparently gratuitous activity (e.g. a pillow fight) and then as suddenly disperses. The term was probably inspired by the use of 'flash' to characterize something sudden and overwhelming (as in 'flash flood'). Britain's first flash mob gathered soon after 6.30pm on 7 August 2003 in a furniture store on Tottenham Street, off TOTTENHAM COURT ROAD, and con-versed without using words containing the letter 'o'. In October 2004 BBC3 staged 'Flashmob – the Opera' at PADDINGTON STATION. London's largest flash mob to date congregated at VICTORIA STATION in April 2007, when 4,000 people took part in a 'silent disco', dancing to music on their portable media players.

flat-cap A nickname, in the latter part of the 16th century and in the 17th century, for a London citizen or APPRENTICE. Round flat caps were the height of fashion during the reign of Henry VIII (1509–47) but soon became 'last year's thing'. However, many Londoners continued to wear them and the nickname mocked them for doing so. The flat cap retains some London asso-ciations, via older EAST ENDERS and BLACK CAB drivers, but is nowadays more likely to be stere-otypically linked with the north of England.

flea's jump, a It has been estimated that if a man, in proportion to his weight, could jump as high as a flea, he could clear ST PAUL'S Cathedral, 365ft (111.3m) high.

Fleet A river that rises on HAMPSTEAD HEATH and flows 9 miles (14 km) south-eastwards into the THAMES beneath BLACKFRIARS BRIDGE. The name, from Old English *fleot*, 'stream', 'inlet', 'creek', was originally applied only to the lower, navigable part of the river, as far upstream as

HOLBORN, where it was a tidal inlet, but in due course it came to stand for the whole. Navigable it may have been in theory, but in practice it was already by the early Middle Ages a noisome sewer, with human and animal excrement being complemented by the effluvia of trades conducted on its banks (it was commonly termed the Fleet ditch). Various attempts were made to cleanse it, but eventually the authorities gave up, and between the 1730s and the 1760s the lower reaches of the river were covered over (the upper part followed suit in the 19th century). The final part of its course can be followed along FARRINGDON ROAD and New Bridge Street to the Thames. It still functions as a storm drain.

Fleeter-Streeter A creature identified by J.S. Farmer and W.E. Henley in *Slang and Its Analogues* (1890) as 'a journalist of the baser sort, a spunging prophet (i.e. racing tipster); a sharking dramatic critic; a spicy paragraphist; and so on'. They go on to particularize the sort of English he wrote, Fleet-Streetese: 'the so-called English, written to sell by the Fleeter-Streeter, a mixture of sesquipedalians and slang, of phrases worn threadbare and phrases sprung from the kennel; of bad grammar and worse manners ... which is impossible outside of FLEET STREET, but which in Fleet Street commands a price, and enables not a few to live'.

Fleet line The name given in the 1960s to the planned new LONDON UNDERGROUND line that, when it eventually opened in 1979, was called the JUBILEE LINE. Part of the original proposed route ran beneath FLEET STREET. Fleet line signage had already been manufactured when the decision was made in 1977 to change the name in honour of the Queen's silver jubilee. Anti-monarchists of the time campaigned for the retention of the original name, wearing Fleet line badges emblazoned with the slogan 'Don't Jubilee've it'.

Fleet marriages Ceremonies performed, clandestinely and without a licence, originally in the chapel of the FLEET PRISON (the Fleet Chapel) and later in any convenient nearby house or tavern. The first such marriage on record took place in 1613. They were generally performed by so-called Fleet parsons, clergymen imprisoned in the Fleet, and were recorded in documents known as Fleet books or Fleet registers. They were declared illegal in 1753, a step which led to the popularity of Scotland's Gretna Green as a destination for eloping couples.

Fleet Prison A prison on the east bank of the Fleet river, just to the north of the foot of LUDGATE HILL, said to have been built shortly after the Norman Conquest and closed in 1842. In the Middle Ages it mostly incarcerated those condemned by the STAR CHAMBER, but after that was abolished in 1640 it served mainly as a debtors' prison, which was the source of its later notoriety. The prison was destroyed in the GREAT FIRE OF LONDON (1666), rebuilt and again burnt during the GORDON RIOTS of 1780, and immediately rebuilt again. It was finally demolished in 1846 and part of the site was later taken for the CONGREGATIONAL MEMORIAL HALL. DICKENS vividly describes the miseries and indignities of the Fleet Prison's inmates in the section of the *Pickwick Papers* (1836–7) where Mr Pickwick is detained in 'the Fleet' (as it was generally termed) following his unfortunate misunderstanding with Mrs Bardell:

> Most of our readers will remember that, until within a very few years past, there was a kind of iron cage in the wall of the Fleet Prison, within which was posted some man of hungry looks, who, from time to time, rattled a money-box, and explained, in a mournful voice 'Pray, remember the poor debtors; pray, remember the poor debtors.'

Fleet Street The former home of London's newspaper industry; its name is still used as a generic term for the national press. The street originally emerged from the western edge of the CITY of London, crossed the FLEET river via a small island at present-day LUDGATE CIRCUS and led to WESTMINSTER via the STRAND. Fleet Street's association with printing began in 1500 with pioneer Wynkyn de Worde, who produced nearly 800 books from his offices near SHOE LANE. The printing industry flourished here over the next 200 years but it was not until the beginning of 18th century that the first daily newspapers were published. Fleet Street at this time was a frantically busy part of the connecting route between the twin centres of London. It has been called 'a double street' because there was as much going on in its alleys and passageways as on Fleet Street itself. Protruding signboards were mounted above every doorway; one of these fell down in 1718 and killed four people, including the king's jeweller. By the early 19th century Fleet Street's newspapers had achieved massive circulations among both the working and middle classes. Publications ranged from scandal sheets like *John Bull*, through William Cobbett's polemical *Political Register* to *The Times*, which increased its size to eight pages in 1827. *The Daily Telegraph* arrived late on the scene in 1855 but soon outsold *The Times*. The press drove out most of Fleet Street's other businesses, especially after regional newspapers like the *Yorkshire Post* and *Manchester Guardian* began to open London offices here. In the first half of the 20th century the number of national newspapers halved from its peak of around two dozen, while several of the survivors built imposing printing works, of which the finest is the art deco Daily Express building of 1932, clad in black Vitrolite, with a cinema-style foyer. All the major newspapers relocated their offices and printing works during the 1980s. News agency REUTERS remained until 2005. Nowadays the street mixes management consultants and investment specialists with shops and takeaways at street level to serve office workers.

The man must have a rare recipe for melancholy, who can be dull in Fleet Street.

CHARLES LAMB: letter to Thomas Manning (15 February 1802)

Fleet Street dove A 19th-century euphemism for a prostitute (at that time FLEET STREET was good working territory for them). An alternative was Fleet Street houri (a houri was originally one of the virginal female attendants in the Muslim paradise, but the suggestion of *whore* was no doubt not accidental).

Bishop of Fleet Street *See under* BISHOP.
Demon Barber of Fleet Street *See under* DEMON.
Liberties of the Fleet *See under* LIBERTY.

Flicker Alley An old nickname for CECIL COURT, from the film distributors and promoters who based themselves here in the very earliest days of moving pictures. Much of the industry later decamped to WARDOUR STREET.

floating academy A nickname for the HULKS, in the same vein as the use of the word COLLEGE in the nicknames of prisons on land. The hulks were also called Campbell's academy, from the name of the first director.

flying

flying fornicator A facetious nickname applied in the early years of the 20th century to the last express train of the night from London to a provincial town, on which it was luridly supposed that most seats were taken up by necking couples. The last trains both to and from Oxford were especially notorious in this regard.

Flying Pieman of Holborn Hill The sobriquet of one Peter Stokes, who in the early 19th century made a good living by selling hot plum puddings at a penny a slice. He was known for his scrupulous mode of attire and for the rapidity of his lunchtime circuit around FETTER LANE, THAVIES INN, HATTON GARDEN and ELY PLACE. Apparently, his heart lay with painting but he resorted to selling baked goods in order to keep his family.

In his right hand he held a small circular tray or board, just large enough to receive an appetite-provoking pudding, about three inches thick … A broad blunt spatula, brilliantly bright, which he carried in his left hand, enabled him to dispense his sweets without ever touching them. His countenance was open and agreeable, expressive of intellect and moral excellence.

ALEPH (WILLIAM HARVEY): *London Scenes and London People* (1863)

Flying Scotsman Locomotive No.4472 of this name was built in 1923 for the London and North-Eastern Railway. It was soon breaking new ground, and on 1 May 1928 made the first non-stop express run from London to Edinburgh in eight hours and three minutes. Its moment of glory came on 30 November 1934, when on a test run between London and Leeds it reached a speed of 100 mph (160 kph). The name *Flying Scotsman* had been in use for the service itself since 1862.

Flying Squad A police detachment able to proceed rapidly to the scene of a crime such as a robbery. In the METROPOLITAN POLICE, the Flying Squad became the best-known department of SCOTLAND YARD. It was set up in 1918 to patrol dangerous areas of London and in 1920 acquired two motor vans to help in the task. These brought it the name of Flying Squad. The department was reorganized in 1978 as the Central Robbery Squad, but its old name is still in use. *See also the* SWEENEY.

Macavity's a Mystery Cat: he's called the Hidden Paw –

For he's the master criminal who can defy the Law.

He's the bafflement of Scotland Yard, the Flying Squad's despair:

For when they reach the scene of the crime – Macavity's not there!

T.S. ELIOT: *Old Possum's Book of Practical Cats*, 'Macavity: The Mystery Cat' (1939)

folly

Folly Ditch A noisome channel that surrounded much of JACOB'S ISLAND in BERMONDSEY. It took its name from Hickman's Folly, a street that lay just south of the island. DICKENS made the ditch the scene of Bill SIKES's death in *Oliver Twist* (1838). In perhaps his most vicious attack, in November 1845, SPRING-HEELED JACK was said to have flung a young prostitute into the Folly Ditch, where she drowned.

Folly on the Thames A 'floating musical summerhouse' moored between SOMERSET HOUSE and the SAVOY during the 17th century. According to Edward Hatton's *New View of London* (1708), it descended from being a place of royal entertainment to a 'confused scene of folly, madness and debauchery'.

Fonthill Road A street in FINSBURY PARK that developed a rag-trade speciality in the 1960s and now has a Saturday market and daily shops specializing in cut-price 'designer' clothing.

fool

Fool on the Hill, The A song about isolation by the Beatles, credited to John Lennon and Paul McCartney (but mostly by McCartney) and released in Britain in November 1967. It has been claimed that McCartney was inspired to write the song following a perplexing encounter with a stranger on PRIMROSE HILL.

fool will not part with his bauble for the Tower of London, a An ancient proverb, coined before 1500, when the TOWER was the storehouse of the nation's wealth.

There the silver, the mint of money; and there the brass and iron to defend it, the armoury and storehouse of ordnance; yet fools so dote on their darling fancies, that they prize them above all this treasure.

THOMAS FULLER: *The History of the Worthies of England* (1662)

football The game has been played in London for centuries, although in its early form it consisted of little more than gangs of youths running wild through the streets, kicking one or more balls as they went and tackling each other rugby-style. A royal proclamation of 1314 decreed:

Forasmuch as there is great noise in the city caused by hustling over large balls, from which many evils may arise, which God forbid, we command and forbid on behalf of the King, on pain of imprisonment, such game to be used in the city in future.

This had little effect and Elizabeth I vainly tried again in 1572:

No foteball player be used or suffered within the City of London and the liberties thereof upon pain of imprisonment.

Eventually, the game moved from the streets to playing fields and by the early 19th century numerous amateur clubs were in existence in London (and elsewhere), each consisting of several teams that played each other under their own rules. At that time the discrepancies between different clubs' rules prevented the formation of a wider league. Present-day association football took recognizable shape with the establishment of the Football Association at a series of meetings held in 1863 at the Freemason's Tavern in COVENT GARDEN, where, after the withdrawal of dissenting rugby advocates, the basic laws of the game were agreed. The first match under these rules, a goalless draw, was played between BARNES and RICHMOND at MORTLAKE on 19 December 1863. London's oldest professional football club is FULHAM FC, which is usually considered to have been founded, in amateur form, in 1879. LEYTON ORIENT, TOTTENHAM HOTSPUR, QUEENS PARK RANGERS, ARSENAL, MILLWALL, BARNET and BRENTFORD began playing in the 1880s (mostly under variant identities from their present ones) and WEST HAM UNITED in 1895. CHARLTON ATHLETIC, CHELSEA and CRYSTAL PALACE are relative newcomers, all established in 1905. The Football Association was based at LANCASTER GATE for over 70 years; it relocated to SOHO SQUARE in 2000 and then to WEMBLEY STADIUM in 2009.

Footballers' Wives *See* EARLS PARK.

Foots Cray A commercial and residential area in south-east SIDCUP. Domesday Book recorded the landowner as Godwin Fot, who possessed a farm, four cottages and a mill and gave his name to the manor. Conveniently located where the Maidstone road crossed the River CRAY, the village grew steadily over the following centuries. Around 1754, Bouchier Cleeve commissioned the building of Foots Cray Place, a Palladian mansion where he built up a noteworthy collection of art. In 1822 the house was acquired by the chancellor of the exchequer, Sir Nicholas Vansittart, later Lord Bexley. The Vansittart family retained a substantial landholding in the area for the next century but the house burned down in 1949. The arrival of the Sidcup bypass brought businesses here from the 1930s, and the centre of Foots Cray is now dominated by the industrial and commercial premises.

forest

Forest Gate A multicultural district, with no single ethnic group constituting a majority, situated east of STRATFORD. Here was an entrance to EPPING FOREST, of which the nearby WANSTEAD FLATS are still considered a part. Dr John Fothergill established the extensive Ham House estate (as it was later called) from the early 1760s, filling the house and its gardens with 3,400 species of tropical plants. The estate was broken up and sold to developers in 1852. During the remainder of the century an expanding network of rail and tram services drew day-trippers to Wanstead Flats and the Eagle and Child tea gardens became a popular resort. Forest Gate School must have seemed cursed in the last quarter of the 19th century when more than 40 pupils died in three separate incidents. On Boxing Day in 1966 Jimi Hendrix wrote (it is said) and then performed *Purple Haze* at the Ace of Spades Club on Woodgrange Road; during demolition of the building for construction of the Channel Tunnel rail link a purple ceiling was uncovered behind a more modern one. Bodybuilder Arnold Schwarzenegger, later to become governor of California, arrived in Forest Gate in the same year as Hendrix, and stayed for over two years, sleeping on the couch at Wag and Dianne Bennett's house in Romford Road and training at the gym that they ran.

Forest Hill Highly fashionable in the Victorian era, SYDENHAM's northern neighbour has recently begun to show signs of gentrification after a long period of decline. Until the late 18th century it was simply called 'the Forest', and was almost entirely uninhabited. The original 'Forest Hill', now Honor Oak Road, was a grand avenue of well-proportioned merchants' houses built in the 1780s and its name was the developer's invention. In the 1850s the erection nearby of the CRYSTAL PALACE put a seal on the popularity of Forest Hill and most of the neighbouring localities. Among the many notable figures who moved here were the TEA merchants Frederick Horniman and the Tetley family. Horniman established the museum and gardens in London Road that bear his name and later gave them to the public. The notorious art forger Tom Keating (1917–84) was born into 'a large and poverty-stricken household in Forest Hill'. He gained fame during the 1970s and early 1980s for allegedly producing up to 2,500 forgeries.

Fortis Green A leafy locality situated between MUSWELL HILL and EAST FINCHLEY. What became Fortis Green Road was just a track across HORNSEY Common until the early 19th century. Fortis Green now consists of a mixture of late Victorian and early 20th-century semi-detached houses, with a few grand villas in the shady corners. *See also* FAIRPORT CONVENTION; *the* KINKS.

Fortnum & Mason A quality grocery store in PICCADILLY founded in 1707 by William Fortnum, a footman in the household of Queen Anne, together with his grocer friend, Hugh Mason. Mr Fortnum had already been selling candles at cut price to the household staff, and the two men's first commercial venture was little more than a stall in a Piccadilly doorway. A grocer's shop was then opened, and remained in the hands of both men's families until about 1800, since when neither a Fortnum nor a Mason has been connected with the business. In 1964 the store's then owner, W. Garfield Weston, commissioned the installation of an ornate clock two floors above the main entrance, incorporating effigies of Messrs Fortnum and Mason that emerge on the hour.

Fortnum–Mason line A jocular name for the imaginary geographical line that marks off the supposed 'lush' south of England from the 'lean' north and that thus pinpoints the north–south divide or separates the south from all parts of the country NORTH OF WATFORD. The phrase adopts the name of the store as a pun on the Mason–Dixon line that is the boundary between Maryland and Pennsylvania in the United States.

Fort Vallance The name given by the KRAY TWINS, London's most notorious postwar criminals, to their house at 178 Vallance Road, BETHNAL GREEN. It was the home in which they grew up and the headquarters from which they later ran their gangland operation, storing a fearsome armoury of weapons under the floorboards. TOWER HAMLETS council compulsorily purchased the terraced row in 1966 and demolished it. A housing association property now occupies the site.

> Yesterday, I also recalled a long-ago
> conversation in Fort Vallance ... Violet served
> us tea and cakes on her best china. Her twins
> became sentimental about neighbours and said
> they believed in God.
>
> CAL MCCRYSTAL, in *The Independent* (12 October 2000)

forty

forty fousand fevvers on a frush A catchphrase serving as a litmus test of the traditional COCKNEY pronunciation of 'th' as 'f' or 'v'. With full phonetic spelling, 'thousand' must be rendered something like 'fahzn'. The phrase probably originated in the 1920s and has several numerical variations, of which the most popular is 'firty-free fousand fevvers on a frush', which is why 'feathers' can signify a score of 33 in darts. Other versions refer to a 'frush's froat', sometimes with no reduction in the feather count.

> Bells in ev'ry steeple
> Rang out to tell the people,
> London's mighty proud today,
> Another Cockney's learned to say:
> Forty fahsend fevvers on a frush.
>
> PAUL BOYLE and EDDIE CARROLL: 'Forty Fahsend Fevvers on a Frush' (song by Billy Cotton and his Band) (1951)

Forty Hall A minor stately home, situated on the north side of ENFIELD, taking its name from an Old English word meaning a patch of higher ground in a marsh. John Tiptoft, Earl of Worcester, is said to have built Elsing (or Elsynge) Hall on Forty Hill in the 1460s. Sir Thomas Lovell, speaker of the House of Commons and chancellor of the exchequer from 1485, lived here from 1492 and hosted frequent royal visits. It is said that Sir Walter Raleigh laid his cloak across a puddle at Elsing so that Elizabeth I might cross without getting her feet wet, but

other localities also lay claim to this legend. The house was demolished around 1660 and its site was lost until excavations 300 years later. Forty Hall was built to the south-west of Elsing for Sir Nicholas Raynton in 1636 and heavily modified around 1708. Raynton was a haberdasher and LORD MAYOR OF LONDON in 1632. Enfield council acquired the Forty Hall estate in 1951.

Forty Years On This oft-quoted phrase forms the opening of the Harrow Football Song, the first four lines of which are given below. It is also the HARROW SCHOOL song. The words by Edward Bowen were set to music by his colleague John Farmer, who was director of music at Harrow from 1862 to 1885.

> Forty years on, when afar and asunder
> Parted are those who are singing today,
> When you look back and forgetfully wonder
> What you were like in your words and your play.
>
> 'Forty Years On' (published 1886)

Alan Bennett's play *Forty Years On* (1968) satirizes English public schools.

Field of the Forty Footsteps See under FIELD.

four

four-by-two 'Jew' in COCKNEY RHYMING SLANG, from the well-known timber format.

Four Day Johnny The nickname of Detective Chief Superintendent John Du Rose, who headed SCOTLAND YARD's murder squad in the mid-1960s, from the speed with which he brought killers to justice. However, he was unable to solve one of his most famous cases, that of JACK THE STRIPPER. Du Rose's autobiography, *Murder Was My Business*, was published in 1971.

4.50 from Paddington A detective novel (1957) by Agatha Christie (1890–1976), featuring her spinster sleuth Jane Marple. From the 4.50 train from PADDINGTON STATION, Elspeth sees a man strangling a woman in a compartment in another train that is running alongside hers. Then the other train draws away. A disappointing film version, *Murder She Said* (1961), directed by George Pollock, was not even saved by a gallantly British Margaret Rutherford as Miss Marple.

fourpenny one A hit or blow, especially one with the fist. The reference may be to the four knuckles. Some authorities derive the phrase from COCKNEY RHYMING SLANG, in which 'fourpenny bit' means 'hit'.

Four Per Cent Industrial Dwellings Company A housing charity established in 1885 by

Nathan Mayer ROTHSCHILD (1840–1915) and other prominent figures in the Anglo-Jewish establishment. Its purpose was to provide 'the industrial classes with commodious and healthy dwellings at a minimum rent'. Funds to build the dwellings were raised by issuing shares to investors, who were guaranteed a four per cent return. With its early focus on the EAST END, the company's tenants were primarily poor Jews, who made up much of the area's population at that time. Renamed the Industrial Dwellings Society in 1952, it is now a registered housing association and retains close links with the Jewish community. *See also* ROTHSCHILD BUILDINGS.

fourth plinth A rectangular pedestal in the north-west part of TRAFALGAR SQUARE, built in 1841 and originally intended for an equestrian statue of William IV. In the absence at first of sufficient funds and later of agreement on a worthy occupant, the plinth remained empty for more than a century and a half. Since 1999 it has been the platform for a series of contemporary artworks, commissioned from leading artists and displayed for a year or so each. The choice of works is nowadays led by the Fourth Plinth Commissioning Group, a panel of specialist advisers to the MAYOR OF LONDON. The long-term future of the plinth is the subject of continuing debate.

> After all, who can name the other figures in Trafalgar Square? There are two Indian generals who have sunk into total obscurity and George IV, who is remembered for a rather scandalous divorce. We want to commemorate our period.
> SIR JOHN MORTIMER, quoted in *The Independent* (13 May 2000)

Foyle's A name synonymous with bookshops and formerly with literary lunches and eccentric work practices. The store of W. & G. Foyle Ltd in CHARING CROSS ROAD arose from the textbook-selling business set up by the brothers William and Gilbert Foyle in 1903, which was relocated to the store's present site in 1906. Their initial stock was second-hand, but they added new books in 1912. In 1930 William's daughter, Christina Foyle (1911–99), inaugurated monthly literary luncheons, held at GROSVENOR HOUSE, to enable the reading public to meet distinguished writers and artists. She held the reins as managing director until her death, running the business traditionally and ignoring advances in

retailing such as credit cards, labour unions, electronic tills and computerized billing even into the 1990s, after which the store's trading practices were overhauled. Foyle's nowadays has additional branches on the SOUTH BANK, at WESTFIELD and within SELFRIDGES and ST PANCRAS STATION.

Fraffly According to the writer Alistair Morrison (1911–98), the brand of English spoken in the WEST END, humorous examples of which are provided in *Fraffly Well Spoken* (1968) and *Fraffly Suite* (1969), under the supposed authorship of a Professor Afferbeck Lauder. Both volumes present comic dialogues in which upper-class English speech is spelled out phonetically to demonstrate its drawling absurdities. Thus 'York air scissors good as mine' translates as 'Your guess is as good as mine', 'Egg-wetter gree' as 'I quite agree' and 'Rilleh quettex trod nerreh!' as 'Really quite extraordinary!'.

Fred

Fred Karno's army A humorous nickname applied to the new British Army raised during the First World War, in allusion to Fred Karno, the popular comedian and producer of stage burlesques, whose real name was Frederick John Westcott (1866–1941). Fred Karno's company was a household name at the time through its high-spirited and eccentric performances. The name is also applied derisively to other nondescript bodies. Karno himself adopted his stage name when he and two gymnast colleagues found work (while standing at POVERTY CORNER) filling in for an act at the Metropolitan Music Hall in EDGWARE ROAD called 'The Three Carnos'. His agent, Richard Warner, suggested they change the 'C' to a more distinctive 'K'. *See also the* FUN FACTORY.

Fred's FORTNUM & MASON, in the vernacular of the SLOANE RANGER.

Freeborn John The nickname of John Lilburne (*c.*1614–57), who became the unofficial leader of the LEVELLERS. His mother was a courtier and he is said to have been born in the servants' quarters at the palace of Placentia in GREENWICH. During the course of his campaigning he was incarcerated in the FLEET PRISON, NEWGATE PRISON and the TOWER OF LONDON and was whipped from the Fleet to WESTMINSTER. His refusal to take the oath when he appeared before the STAR

CHAMBER influenced the subsequent enshrinement of the right against self-incrimination, both in English law and in the fifth amendment of the United States constitution. Lilburne was twice acquitted of treason, but Oliver Cromwell had him re-imprisoned, fearing that he would take advantage of his popularity to stir up more trouble. Lilburne died at home in ELTHAM, while on parole.

Freedom Pass A card allowing older and eligible disabled people who live in a London borough to travel free on London's public transport network. The pass is paid for by the borough in which its holder lives. Similar schemes have been introduced elsewhere.

> Currently I am enjoying my Freedom Pass, as we call it in the Smoke. I feel calmer when the bus stops in traffic now or the wrong kind of frost gets on the points.
>
> MICHAEL WHITE, in *The Guardian* (30 November 2005)

Freemasonry A secret society that has existed for many centuries and that professes to trace its origins to the building of the Temple of Solomon. In medieval times stonemasons banded together with their secret signs, passwords and tests. Freemasonry in its modern form, as a body with no trade connections, began to flourish in the 17th century. The antiquarian Elias Ashmole (1617–92, *see the* ARK) was initiated in 1646 and Sir Christopher Wren was a member. The first Grand Lodge of England was founded at the GOOSE AND GRIDIRON alehouse in 1717 and took under its aegis the many small lodges in the provinces. From this Grand Lodge of England derive all Masonic lodges throughout the world.

Freezywater Also spelt as two words, Freezywater is a lacklustre residential locality stuck out on a limb in the north-east corner of ENFIELD, south of the M25. Freezywater Farm was recorded here in 1768, taking its name from a local pond, so called because of its bleak and exposed situation. The pond was lost when sewage works were built on Ramney Marsh.

French House, The A public house formerly called the York Minster, located on Dean Street in SOHO. The pub was run by Victor and then Gaston Berlemont, father and son, from 1914 to 1989, and was popularly known as 'the French', although the Berlemonts were Belgian. During the Second World War it became a meeting place for members of the Free French movement, and General de Gaulle is said to have written his 'à tous les Français' declaration in the upstairs restaurant. In its heyday 'the French' attracted writers and artists; drinkers here have included Brendan Behan, Stephen Spender, Dylan Thomas, Salvador Dali and Francis Bacon.

> We knew it was over when instead of it [the York Minster] being known as 'The French' it changed its name to The French House. When they brand their own mythos, it's time to move on.
>
> MICHAEL BYWATER, in *The Independent* (7 July 2007)

Freud, Sigmund The father of modern psychoanalysis (1856–1939). He spent almost all his adult life in Vienna but, following the rise of Nazism in Austria, his wealthy friend Princess Marie Bonaparte helped the family to flee to London in June 1938, when Freud was 82 years old. They settled in the FROGNAL locality of south-west HAMPSTEAD, at 20 Maresfield Gardens, where Freud continued to write and see patients for 13 months. However, he was suffering increasingly unbearable pain from the effects of long-term oral cancer and in September 1939 he prevailed upon his friend and fellow refugee Dr Max Schur to assist his suicide with an overdose of morphine. Freud was cremated at GOLDERS GREEN crematorium, where his ashes are kept on display in a Greek urn. Freud's daughter Anna (1895–1982), the founder of child psychoanalysis in the UK, continued to live and work at Maresfield Gardens until her death. The house is now a museum and research centre. Visitors can see the library and study, which contain the great man's personal collection of antiquities and books as well as his psychoanalytic couch.

Friar Tuck 'Fuck' in COCKNEY RHYMING SLANG, taking the name of Robin Hood's merry cleric in vain. Unlike most rhyming slang, it is seldom abbreviated and so does little to conceal its true meaning. Consequently, 'Friar Tuck' has never gained the euphemistic popularity of words such as 'BERK' and 'COBBLERS'. This example is from a novel set in 1912:

> 'Nothing they do in here is of any perishing use,' said Kelly in a hoarse whisper. 'I don't give a Friar Tuck for anything they do in here.'
>
> PENELOPE FITZGERALD: *The Gate of Angels* (1990)

Friday

Friday Club An information association of progressive artists founded in 1905 by the painter and designer Vanessa Bell, its members initially meeting on Fridays at her home, 46 Gordon Square. For some years there was a strong BLOOMSBURY GROUP presence and exhibitions were held until 1922.

Friday Hill A hill located north of CHINGFORD HATCH. It had previously been Jackatt Hill and its present name derives from John Friday, who was living here in 1467. A story that Friday Hill was inhabited by snakes and toads that spat fire was probably put about to keep away intruders.

Friday Hill House A Tudor-style manor house built in 1839 by Lewis Vulliamy (1791–1871) for the Rev Robert Boothby Heathcote. Some of the original panelling, fireplaces and other features from the house it replaced were reused, and survive today. The grounds remained the last un-developed tranche of CHINGFORD until the death of Louisa Heathcote in 1940 at the age of 86.

Friday Hill plane A particularly impressive LONDON PLANE that has been selected as one of the GREAT TREES OF LONDON. Its grandeur is enhanced by the height of its location.

Friday Street A short street extending south-wards from CANNON STREET, first recorded in the 12th century. Its name may derive from the former presence of a weekly market, quite probably for fish.

Friern Barnet A medieval parish enveloped by a series of late Victorian suburban estates, situated between NEW SOUTHGATE and NORTH FINCHLEY. From around 1274 this was 'Frerenbar-net', because this corner of BARNET was owned by the friars of St John's Priory, CLERKENWELL (*see also the* KNIGHTS HOSPITALLER). At the beginning of the 19th century this was still an entirely rural area but total transformation came with the construction of the Middlesex County Lunatic Asylum at COLNEY HATCH in 1851, which cut off the main village from easy access to London. After a period of quiet isolation, speculative builders laid out several estates from the 1880s onwards.

frighten the horses, to To alarm people. The words are attributed to Mrs Patrick Campbell (1865–1940) in Daphne Fielding's *The Duchess of Jermyn Street* (1964):

'It doesn't matter what you do in the bedroom as long as you don't do it in the street and frighten the horses.'

frockney A MOCKNEY accent affected by some London fashion designers and stylists and their models.

Frockney designers still call you darling, but it's pronounced 'darlin'' as in 'Awrigh' darlin'?'

The Independent (25 May 1997)

frog (and toad) 'Road' in COCKNEY RHYMING SLANG. Although familiar to most Londoners, the term is not widely used. Like APPLES (AND PEARS), it is nowadays most often employed facetiously.

Firebrand Pearly Shop Steward, Stanley Jobbins, told members of the PK&Q Union, that it was 'Down the frog and toad brothers and sisters!' at a mass meeting held on London's famous Lambeth Walk.

www.thespoof.com (22 November 2006)

Frognal A pleasant locality and leafy street meandering between HAMPSTEAD and WEST HAMPSTEAD. Perhaps unexpectedly, the name does signify that this was once a nook frequen-ted by frogs. Frognal was recorded in the early 15th century as a 'customary tenement', an estate held on condition that the customs of the manor (of Hampstead) were adhered to, which involved performing certain tasks and making various payments. During the 17th and 18th centuries Frognal gained a reputation for the 'salubrity of its air and soil' and grew from a single house and farm to a collection of cottages and mansions, many of which adopted the Frognal name. These included Frognal Hall, Frognal Grove, Frognal Priory and, in 1806, Frognal Park – possibly the grandest of them all. The creation of the FINCHLEY ROAD rendered southern Frognal ripe for development, but a number of legalities pre-vented its exploitation until the 1870s, when the road called Frognal was extended southwards. The illustrator Kate Greenaway (1846–1901) lived at 39 Frognal from 1886 until her death. During the latter part of the Second World War, General de Gaulle lived at Frognal House, directing the efforts of the Free French forces.

frost fairs A series of impromptu events held on the frozen THAMES during exceptionally cold winters. Ice would begin to pile up around the numerous bulky piers of old LONDON BRIDGE and then spread upstream. FOOTBALL and other games were played on the river in December 1564 and refreshment booths were set up during the great frost of January 1608. From early December 1683 to 5 February 1684 a tented 'city' flourished, with entrepreneurs offering every conceivable kind of fairground attraction, from bull-baiting to ox-roasting, while HACKNEY coaches plied the Thames from WESTMINSTER to the STRAND. Printers set up presses on the ice and ran off personalized souvenir certificates, including one for Charles II shortly before his death. Almost anything that could be bought on land was also sold on the Thames, usually at an inflated price. Subsequent fairs followed a similar pattern, notably in the winters of 1715/16, 1739/40 and 1788/9. The last of the frost fairs was held at the beginning of February 1814, when a makeshift mall, nicknamed 'City Road', extended along the Thames. WATERMEN compensated for the loss of their regular livelihood by breaking up the ice at the shoreline except at regulated safe access points, at which they set up toll booths. Near BLACKFRIARS BRIDGE, however, a plumber carrying a load of lead crashed through the ice to his death. Several factors combined to prevent the river ever again freezing to a viable depth, of which the most locally significant were the replacement of medieval London Bridge and the construction of embankments that reduced the river's breadth, quickening its flow through London. Meanwhile, at a global level, the 'Little Ice Age' was coming to an end.

> Whereas, you, J. Frost, have by force and
> violence taken possession of the River Thames,
> I hereby give you warning to quit immediately.
> – A. Thaw.
>
> handbill printed and sold on the ice (1814)

Fryent Country Park A 254-acre (103-hectare) park filling much of north KINGSBURY. Like FRIERN BARNET, the name derives from its early ownership by the friars St John's Priory, CLERKENWELL (*see also the* KNIGHTS HOSPITALLER). An original part of the ancient parish of Kingsbury, the Fryent estate was taken over by ST PAUL'S Cathedral in 1543 and remained in agricultural use until the 20th century. The park retains an ancient hedgerow system, farm ponds

and hay meadow grasslands, as well as extensive woodland.

Fulham A primarily late Victorian district occupying a wide THAMES peninsula opposite WANDSWORTH. The Bishop of London acquired the manor of Fulham in 704 and Danish invaders landed here in 879. A fishing village grew up in the vicinity of the present PUTNEY BRIDGE station and Fulham High Street was in existence by 1391, when it was called Burystrete. Medieval villages grew up at three distinct locations in Fulham in addition to the thriving old town: Parsons Green, Walham Green and North End. Over the course of the 19th century industry filled the former marshland of Sands End and elsewhere terraces of suburban housing rolled out across the former market gardens and gentlemen's estates from the 1870s. Much of Fulham's new housing was built for the lower middle classes but by the 1920s large parts of the district had become wholly working class in character, a transformation that has been almost completely reversed since GENTRIFICATION began in the 1960s. The deserted industrial wasteland by the Thames at Sands End has provided the principal zone of opportunity for large-scale developers, beginning with Chelsea Harbour in the 1980s.

> Fulham in the 1930s was a dismal district ... It
> was full of pubs, convents, second-hand clothes
> shops, bagwash laundries and pawnbrokers.
> Everything seemed very broken down.
>
> JOHN OSBORNE: *A Better Class of Person* (1981)

Fulham has been the scene of two high-profile unsolved murders in recent decades. In July 1986 estate agent Suzy Lamplugh went missing after leaving her Stevenage Road office; neither her body nor her presumed killer was ever found. In April 1999 television presenter Jill Dando was shot dead on her doorstep in Gowan Avenue. Local man Barry George was convicted of her murder but cleared on appeal in 2008.

Fulham Broadway A short stretch of the FULHAM ROAD east of its junction with the North End Road, constituting the commercial heart of modern Fulham. The locality was known as Walham Green until the late 19th century, when a flurry of commercial and residential development erased the old green and the former village's character. Walham Green station was renamed Fulham Broadway in 1952.

Fulham FC London's oldest professional FOOT-

BALL club, founded in amateur form in 1879. It plays its home games at a ground known as CRAVEN COTTAGE on the bank of the Thames (a familiar sight to followers of the BOAT RACE, and source of the team's old nickname, the Cottagers). The present Duke of WESTMINSTER once had a trial with the club. It was bought in 1997 by the controversial Egyptian entrepreneur, and owner of department store HARRODS, Mohamed Fayed.

Fulham Palace A country retreat of the bishops of London from at least the 11th century, situated in the south-western part of the Fulham peninsula. The earliest of the surviving buildings date from around 1480. The palace became the bishop's main residence in the 18th century, a role that lasted until 1975. The palace and its grounds are nowadays open to the public.

Fulham Road A fashionable street extending 2½ miles (4 km) south-westwards from BROMPTON Cross to the grounds of FULHAM PALACE. The 'way from Fulham to London' was first mentioned in 1372 and became a functional highway in 1410, when the bishop of London caused STAMFORD BRIDGE to be built across Counters Creek, connecting CHELSEA and Fulham. Open fields bordered much of the road on both sides until the mid-18th century, when speculative builders began to put up clumps of smart houses between the farms. From the late 19th century larger shops and places of entertainment appeared. In 1911 Michelin opened a delightfully ornate tyre-fitting garage at 81 Fulham Road, now a restaurant. Fulham Road became fashionable in the 1960s, particularly at the Brompton end. Terence Conran opened the first Habitat store at 77 Fulham Road in 1964. Art galleries, antique dealers, jewellers and fashion houses later moved here from increasingly unaffordable MAYFAIR.

> Servants ... belong to that ... class of people whose public and private lives have no connection with each other ... Publicly and privately their set-ups are as different as Fulham Road and Grosvenor Square.
>
> D. FROME: *The By-Pass Murder* (1932)

fulhams Underworld slang from the 16th to the late 18th centuries for loaded dice (i.e. weighted on one side so that the thrower can determine how they will fall). The word was also written as *fullams*, and it is not certain that there was originally any connection with Fulham the place

– although Fulham was once a noted resort of 'sharpers'.

Fulham stoneware Hard ceramic ware, typically brown-glazed, of a type made at Fulham Pottery from 1672.

Fulham virgin An ironic 19th-century euphemism for a prostitute. The name may have been inspired by the proximity of CREMORNE GARDENS, a 19th-century pleasure garden on the border of Fulham and Chelsea, which developed a reputation as 'a nursery of every kind of vice' (in the words of one contemporary Baptist minister).

Fulwell A residential and amenity district situated just north of HAMPTON HILL. The Fulwell name was first recorded in the 15th century and is probably a corruption of 'foul well'.

Fulwell Park The former home of the last king of Portugal. Fulwell Lodge, as it was at first called, was built beside the River Crane sometime before 1623. In 1910 Manoel II of Portugal (1889–1932) was overthrown in a republican revolution. He fled first to Gibraltar and then to England, settling with his new wife Auguste at Fulwell Park, from where he continued to strive for reconciliation with Portugal's new government. Manoel died at Fulwell Park in 1932 without an heir and received a state funeral in Lisbon. Afterwards, Auguste returned to her native Germany, where she created a new Fulwell Park. The couple's house was demolished and the grounds were built over.

Fu Manchu The Chinese master villain who is head of the dreaded 'Si-Fan' secret society. He was the creation of Sax Rohmer (Arthur Sarsfield Ward) in a series of stories that ran in the *Story-Teller Magazine* from 1912. Ward claimed that the character was modelled on a Chinese man of unusual appearance whom he had glimpsed on LIMEHOUSE Causeway one foggy night in 1911. The stories were soon collected to form bestselling novels such as *The Mystery of Dr Fu Manchu* (1913). Fu operates internationally, his ultimate aim apparently being to gain mastery of the world, but his evil plans are constantly foiled by the doughty Englishman Dennis Nayland Smith.

Fu Manchu's adventures were later transferred to the screen, and he became established as the 'Yellow Peril incarnate', a familiar racial stereotype. Less serious portrayals have included that of Peter Sellers in *The Fiendish Plot of Dr Fu Manchu* (1980), in which Sellers also played Nayland Smith, and Nicolas Cage, in a cameo within the two-segment film *Grindhouse* (2007).

fun

Fun Factory From 1901 the operational headquarters, props store and rehearsal space for the troupe of MUSIC HALL entertainers managed by the acrobat-turned-impresario Fred Karno (*see* FRED KARNO'S ARMY). It consisted of three knocked-together houses in Vaughan Road, CAMBERWELL.

Funniest Man on Earth The sobriquet of Dan Leno (1860–1904), born George Galvin, in SOMERS TOWN. He was an acrobat, champion clog-dancer, character vocalist and master of physical mimicry. His quick-change act was the hit of the London MUSIC HALLS from the late 1880s and his pantomime dame roles were equally popular on DRURY LANE.

> Leno's ambiguous comic vision was of a
> recalcitrant physical world inhabited by
> unreliable people.

SARAH STANTON and MARTIN BANHAM: *Cambridge Paperback Guide to Theatre* (1996)

Furzedown A residential locality situated between TOOTING and STREATHAM, in the southernmost extremity of the London Borough of WANDSWORTH. The name is of relatively recent origin, dating perhaps from the 17th century, and refers to the gorse that grew here. Furzedown House was built in 1794 and was enlarged and endowed with a conservatory and a single-storey entrance lodge in the early 1860s. The house was saved from demolition by the LONDON COUNTY COUNCIL, which converted it into a teacher training college in 1915; it is now part of Graveney School.

FX4 The best known of the various alphanumeric designations for the 'classic' London taxi. The FX4 replaced the original Austin FX3 (the FX and FX2 were both prototypes) in 1958 and more than 75,000 were produced over the following 40 years. The FX4, in its ultimate incarnation as the Fairway, was succeeded by the TX series, which has presently reached the TX4. *See also* BLACK CAB.

G

gaff *The Chambers Dictionary* defines a 'gaff' as 'one's private accommodation', adding that the term was originally used in the context of 'the site of a burglary'. The word may be of Romany origin. A gaff was also a cheap public entertainment or a low-class MUSIC HALL, often called 'penny gaff' from the price of admission. Such theatres were common in Victorian times on the Surrey side of the THAMES (*see* TRANSPONTINE THEATRES).

Gaiety Girl One of the beauty chorus for which the Old Gaiety Theatre in the STRAND was famous in the 1890s and Edwardian days. Several of them married into the peerage.

galley-foist or **gally-foist** A small square-rigged ship that served as an escort for the new LORD MAYOR OF LONDON when he was carried along the THAMES to take his oath at WESTMINSTER each year. Highly decorated and full of noise from trumpets, drums, muskets, fireworks and cannon, it formed the spectacular centrepiece of the LORD MAYOR'S SHOW. The term was also used as a mocking reference to a vessel (or, figuratively, a person) of diminutive size or armament, or to a floridly painted or bedizened woman.

> Rogues, hell-hounds, Stentors, out of my doors, you sons of noise and tumult, begot on an ill May-day, or when the gally-foist is afloat to Westminster!
>
> BEN JONSON: *Epicene, or The Silent Woman*, VI, ii (1609)

Gallions Reach The stretch of the THAMES between WOOLWICH and BARKING CREEK. Gallions Point, at the entrance to the King George V Dock, is 9 nautical miles (17 km) below LONDON BRIDGE. The Galyons were a 14th-century family who owned property on the shoreline. The DOCKLANDS LIGHT RAILWAY station of the same name is located to the north-west of its prede-

cessor, 'Gallions', a ship-to-rail transfer point that opened in 1880 on the PORT OF LONDON Authority's railway. On the opposite bank of the Thames, Gallions Reach urban village is a recently built housing estate within the new town of THAMESMEAD.

Gallows Corner A major road junction and its immediate surroundings, situated to the north-east of GIDEA PARK. Here the Eastern Avenue splits into the Colchester Road (A12) and the Southend Arterial Road (A127). For several centuries this was an isolated country crossroads on the edge of Romford (or Harold's Wood) Common. Criminals sentenced to death at the court of quarter sessions for the Liberty of HAVERING were executed here in the 16th and 17th centuries, as were some prisoners convicted at Chelmsford. The gallows ceased to be used sometime in the 18th century and was taken down after 1815. Gallows Corner is now dominated by light industry, car dealerships and shed-style retail outlets.

Game On A three-series BBC TV comedy show (1995–8). Like most 20-something London sitcoms, the setting was a flatshare, this time in BATTERSEA. The title referred to the likelihood of sexual activity, a key theme of the show's humour.

gammon rasher 'Smasher' in COCKNEY RHYMING SLANG, from the days when the word it signifies was in common usage.

Gamp, Sarah (Sairey) A fat old nurse, midwife and layer-out of the dead in Charles DICKENS's *Martin Chuzzlewit* (1844). Although 'it was difficult to enjoy her society without becoming conscious of a smell of spirits', she pretends to be abstemious: 'Leave the bottle on the chimley-piece and don't ask me to take none, but let me put my lips to it when I am so dispoged.' She is characterized by idiosyncratic COCKNEY pronunciation and bizarre sayings, an ever-present UMBRELLA and an imaginary friend named Mrs Harris, whom she uses as an authority for her own fabrications.

Gangmoor *See the* VALE OF HEALTH.

Gangs of London A video game (2006) published by Sony for its PSP console. It was heavily advertised in London and sold well, despite mixed reviews. *Gangs of London* incorporates numerous different 'missions' within its story mode, as well as separate mini-games set in a London pub and including darts and skittles. The five playable gangs are of Jamaican, south Asian, Russian, Chinese and COCKNEY origin. The game also features a 'KNOWLEDGE' mode for would-be taxi drivers.

> A computer game, in which players take roles as members of an ethnic-minority crime group competing for supremacy in London's underworld, glamorises gang culture and gun violence, according to campaigners.
>
> *The Daily Telegraph* (19 March 2006)

Gants Hill A compact commercial and residential district centred on a transport hub 2 miles (3 km) north of ILFORD. Its name relates to medieval landowners the Le Gant family, who originated from the Belgian city of Ghent. Gants Hill has a substantial Jewish population, with synagogues and Jewish community centres and schools across the area.

garden

Garden, the *See* COVENT GARDEN; HATTON GARDEN.

garden estate A housing estate laid out in the same way as a GARDEN SUBURB but on a smaller scale. HANGER HILL is an example.

Garden Museum A horticultural museum established in 1977 (as the Museum of Garden History) in the deconsecrated parish church of St Mary-at-Lambeth, which stands beside LAMBETH PALACE. The creation of the museum was prompted by the discovery in the churchyard of the tomb of the 17th-century plant hunters the Tradescants (*see the* ARK (1)) and a garden has been planted with species that they grew.

garden party *See* BUCKINGHAM PALACE GARDEN PARTY.

garden suburb A name applied to certain model suburbs in which housing density is relatively low and natural landscaping takes precedence. Mature trees are retained, as are the pre-existing contours of the land, often with roads curving along them rather than cutting through them. HAMPSTEAD GARDEN SUBURB is the best-known example and probably the most successful. Many other London suburbs were laid out on the same principles from the late 19th century onwards, sometimes by co-partnership groups but more often by enlightened speculative developers.

Gardiner's Corner *See the* GATEWAY TO THE EAST END; HARRODS OF THE EAST.

Garlick

Garlick or **Garlic, Jimmy** The nickname of a mummified man found during excavations at St James Garlickhythe in the mid-19th century. Jimmy may have died in the 1670s and been temporarily embalmed while the church was being rebuilt after the GREAT FIRE OF LONDON. *See also* GARLICKHYTHE.

Garlick Hill A short street extending towards the THAMES south of MANSION HOUSE underground station. The name was first mentioned in the early 16th century and either indicates that garlic was traded here or simply that the hill led down to GARLICKHYTHE.

Garlickhythe A former dock, located near QUEENHITHE. First recorded in 1281, the name suggests that this was an import dock for garlic, which was highly prized for its medicinal qualities in the Middle Ages. The church of St James Garlickhythe is of medieval origin. Rebuilt in 1683, it is known as WREN'S LANTERN.

Garnett, Alf The working-class Londoner played by Warren Mitchell in the television series *Till Death Us Do Part* (1964–74). The show was the creation of Johnny Speight (1920–98), who was born in CANNING TOWN. Garnett is an archetypal royalist and racist, and his forthright pronouncements had the unusual effect of simultaneously endearing him to the viewing public, who may have secretly agreed with his views, yet alienating him from them because of his bigoted attitude and his bad language. His appearance in a sequel, *In Sickness and in Health* (1985–6), seemed much less shocking.

Garratt *See the* MAYOR OF GARRATT.

Garrick

Garrick, David London's most illustrious actor and theatre manager since Edward ALLEYN. Born in Hereford in 1717 and raised in Lichfield, where he briefly attended Samuel JOHNSON's academy, Garrick came to London at the age of 20. After an unsuccessful venture as a vintner, he graduated from amateur to professional dramatics and very quickly won acclaim for his naturalistic style. From 1747 to 1776 he managed the THEATRE ROYAL, DRURY LANE. On his death in 1779 he was buried in WESTMINSTER ABBEY's POETS' CORNER.

Garrick Club The club was founded in 1831 by the Duke of Sussex for actors, painters, writers and similarly creative and artistic individuals. It was named after the actor, whose portrait by Zoffany hangs here. Today its members are mainly lawyers, writers and publishers. It has consistently voted against the admission of women. The club is situated at 15 Garrick Street, COVENT GARDEN.

Garrick of the Clowns A nickname of Joey Grimaldi (*see the* CLOWNS' SERVICE).

Garrick's Ait A narrow Thames AIT with around two dozen wooden bungalows that are mostly used as second homes. Like much of the land in the HAMPTON area, it was once the property of David Garrick.

Garrick's Temple to Shakespeare A small octagonal temple situated by the riverside in HAMPTON. It was built in 1756 for David Garrick in honour of his idol, with grounds landscaped by Capability BROWN. Garrick commissioned a statue of SHAKESPEARE, by Louis-François Roubiliac (1702–62), which he bequeathed to the BRITISH MUSEUM on his death. A replica was installed in the temple.

Garrick's Villa The actor's HAMPTON home from 1754 until his death. The villa dates from around 1500 but has been radically remodelled on several occasions, notably by Robert ADAM. Now divided into nine flats, the building was badly damaged by fire in 2008.

Garrick Theatre A playhouse on CHARING CROSS ROAD, built by the architects Walter Emden and C.J. Phipps with the financial backing of the dramatist W.S. Gilbert. It opened in 1889.

Garth Marenghi's Darkplace *See* DARK-PLACE HOSPITAL.

Gastronomic Symposium of All Nations

A restaurant complex that operated in 1851 at Gore House, KENSINGTON GORE, on the site now occupied by the ALBERT HALL. The venture was the brainchild of Alexis Soyer (1810–58), the former chef of the REFORM CLUB, who sought to imaginatively satisfy the hunger of the crowds visiting the GREAT EXHIBITION. He flamboyantly transformed the house itself and added a Baronial Banqueting Hall and Pavilion of All Nations in the grounds. The Symposium was popular, but not popular enough to cover its enormous costs, and it did not last the life of the exhibition.

> It was a mad year, and all kinds of wild and desperate speculations were entered into. Not one so wild, so desperate, so mad as the Symposium.
>
> GEORGE AUGUSTUS SALA: *Travels in the County of Middlesex* (1861)

gasworks The PALACE OF WESTMINSTER in the parlance of BLACK CAB drivers, not from its external appearance but from the hot air generated inside.

gate

gates of Rome 'Home' in COCKNEY RHYMING SLANG.

Gateway to the Continent *See* VICTORIA STATION.

gateway to the East End An old nickname for the junction also known as Gardiner's Corner, in ALDGATE. The GREATER LONDON COUNCIL's creation of a one-way system in the early 1980s wiped out the former character of the 'gateway', which was once a popular rendezvous for courting couples. This was the place where tens of thousands of EAST ENDERS rallied before the BATTLE OF CABLE STREET. *See also the* HARRODS OF THE EAST.

gateway to the south BALHAM was so dubbed in a mock-travelogue written by Frank Muir and Denis Norden, and memorably performed by an American-accented Peter Sellers in 1958, in which this verse appears:

> Broad-bosomed, bold, becalmed, benign,
> Lies Bal-ham, four-square on the Northern line;
> Matched by no marvel save in Eastern scene,
> A rose-red city, half as gold as green.

Gateway to the South is also the title of a 1996 album by Cajun rock band the Balham Alligators.

gawdelpus A contraction of 'God help us', with appropriate COCKNEY pronunciation. Originally (and still) an exclamation, the word was later used as a noun, in reference to a useless, exasperating or woebegone person.

gazetted Posted in the LONDON GAZETTE as having received some official appointment, service promotion or the like, or on being declared bankrupt.

gedoudovit (or various other spellings) A COCKNEY contraction of 'get out of it', employed as a dismissive ejaculation. The aggressively shouted 'word' opens the Libertines' 2002 single 'Up the Bracket', a song of criminality on the CALLY ROAD and Vallance Road (*see* FORT VALLANCE).

Geffrye Museum In 1685 the wealthy Cornish merchant Sir Robert Geffrye (1613–1703), a former LORD MAYOR OF LONDON, donated land on KINGSLAND Road, SHOREDITCH, for almshouses and these were completed in 1715 by the Ironmongers' Company. By the early 20th century, Shoreditch had become an overcrowded and insanitary quarter, and the company decided to sell the almshouses and build new ones in MOTTINGHAM, then a more salubrious locality. The old buildings became a museum of domestic interiors, which now has collections of furniture, textiles, paintings and decorative arts, displayed in a series of period rooms.

General The dominant name in London buses from the late 1850s to the 1930s. In 1855 the Paris-registered Compagnie Générale des Omnibus de Londres began acquiring and amalgamating London bus companies, exploiting the opportunity created by competition from the railways, which was making business less profitable for smaller operators. As the London General Omnibus Company it created the first comprehensive network of London buses, with Thomas Tilling's TIMES BUSES as its only serious rival. The company introduced motor buses in 1902 and withdrew its last horse-drawn service in 1911. In the following year the business was acquired by the Underground Group, which continued using the General name until the creation of LONDON TRANSPORT in 1933. A present-day operator of London buses has revived the London General identity.

General Post Office *See* ST MARTIN'S LE GRAND.
Thief-Taker General *See under* THIEF.

gentrification The process by which a decayed urban area, especially in inner London, is made newly desirable, and thus increasingly unaffordable to its longer-established inhabitants. The term has been ascribed to the Marxist urban geographer Ruth Glass, who used it in an article of 1964, but it did not become generally familiar until the early 1970s, when the professional middle classes began to buy homes in traditional working-class areas. Their aim was to restore and renovate the properties to suit their tastes, and this in turn led to a change in character of the area as a whole, so that shops went upmarket and pubs and cafés became bistros or wine bars. Often, significant numbers of working-class people remained in the gentrified districts, continuing to rent council or housing association properties, but relatively few businesses targeted their custom because of their inferior spending power, so their presence was masked. ISLINGTON (and specifically the BARNSBURY locality) is often identified as the first part of London to have undergone widespread gentrification.

> The 'gentrification' of Barnsbury is legendary and had regrettable social consequences. But it showed beyond question that redevelopment of overcrowded housing was not the only option.
> GRAHAM TOWERS: *Shelter is Not Enough* (2000)

In areas with vacant commercial premises, a two-stage transformation was sometimes observed, whereby artists and other creative types would first set up studios in disused Victorian warehouses and the like, making a run-down quarter more fashionable. Property developers would subsequently buy them out and convert the buildings into luxury apartment blocks.

Geoffrey (Chaucer) 'Saucer' in COCKNEY RHYMING SLANG.

George

George & Mildred An ITV sitcom that ran for five seasons in 1976–9. The show was a spin-off from MAN ABOUT THE HOUSE. The eponymous couple, played by Brian Murphy and Yootha Joyce, lived in HAMPTON WICK, a place name doubtless chosen for its COCKNEY RHYMING SLANG connotation.

George Davis is innocent A slogan that

appeared across London – especially EAST LONDON – and beyond in the mid-1970s. George Davis (b.1941) had been sentenced to 20 years' imprisonment for his part in an armed payroll robbery in ILFORD in April 1974, but his friends and family insisted he was a victim of mistaken identity (or of a police fit-up) and launched a high-profile campaign on his behalf that included several headline-grabbing publicity stunts as well as the graffiti daubing. The slogan (or the variants 'G. Davis is innocent', 'Free George Davis' and 'George Davis is innocent OK') was painted on scores of walls, TUBE trains and bridges, and a handful of surviving examples can still be seen today. He was released in May 1976 after the home secretary, Roy Jenkins, accepted that his conviction had been unsafe. However, 18 months later, Davis was caught red-handed in the commission of an armed bank robbery in the HOLLOWAY ROAD and sentenced to 15 years.

> Everything they want to pin on you,
> Everything you say and do,
> Looking through their photofits,
> See your face and your face fits.
>
> JIMMY PURSEY and DAVE PARSONS: 'George Davis Is Innocent' (song by Sham 69) (1978)

George Inn London's only surviving galleried coaching inn, situated in a cobbled courtyard off BOROUGH High Street. It was rebuilt in 1676, after fire had destroyed most of SOUTHWARK. The inn used to consist of two parts, on either side of the courtyard, but the Great Northern Railway Company demolished the northern half in the 1870s. At the same time the eastern stables were taken for an extension to GUY'S HOSPITAL. The National Trust acquired the George in 1937.

Georgium sidus A jocular 19th-century nickname for south London. Georgium sidus 'the Georgian planet' (Latin *sidus*, 'star') was the original name given by its discoverer, Sir William Herschel (1738–1822), to the planet now known as Uranus, in honour of George III: Uranus was then the furthest known planet from Earth and thus from 'civilization'.

St George in the East See *under* SAINT.
St George's Fields See *under* SAINT.

German (band) 'Hand' in COCKNEY RHYMING SLANG, usually heard in the plural. German bands provided a great deal of public entertainment in late 19th- and early 20th-century London, especially in the EAST END. They played in the street, often outside public houses, and were hired to perform at weddings and other functions organized by the then-populous German community. The entertainment form came to a sudden end with the outbreak of the First World War but the rhyming slang term lived on. Other kinds of bands, both musical (such as jazz) and non-musical (such as ivory), are occasionally invoked to the same end.

> Go wash your German bands, your boat race too,
> Comb your Barnet Fair, we got a lot to do.
>
> QUINCY JONES and DON BLACK: 'Get A Bloomin' Move On!' (song from the film *The Italian Job*) (1969)

Gerrard Street See CHINATOWN.

Gert and Daisy The pair of COCKNEY gossips were created as a comic duo for BBC radio in the 1930s by the sisters Elsie and Doris Waters. They became national institutions in the Second World War to the extent that Lord Haw-Haw, in a broadcast from Germany, declared: 'The good folk of Grimsby should not expect Gert and Daisy to protect them from attacks by the Luftwaffe.' Doris Waters died in 1978, her sister in 1990.

gertcha *The Chambers Dictionary* defines this word as encapsulating several related admonitions: 'get away (along, off) with you!', 'come off it!', 'clear off!', 'get out of that (or there)!'. It probably originated as a corrupted contraction of the first or last of these. Formerly uttered and understood only in London, and with its usage in terminal decline, 'gertcha' was briefly given a new and national lease of life by the ROCKNEY duo Chas & Dave (Charles Hodges and David Peacock) when their single of that name entered the top 20 of the British charts in June 1979.

> He says it every time that he gets mad,
> A regular caution is my old dad.
> Rub the old man up the wrong way,
> Bet your life you'll hear him say:
> Gertcha, cowson, gertcha.

The song was adapted for use in an award-winning commercial for Courage Best Bitter, set in an EAST END pub.

Gertie (Gitana) 'Banana' in old-fashioned COCKNEY RHYMING SLANG. Gertrude Astbury was an early 20th-century MUSIC HALL singer from Longport, now part of Stoke-on-Trent, who adopted the stage name Gitana on account of her supposed Gypsy origins. Nicknamed the Staffordshire Cinderella, her signature song was Nellie Dean, later the title of a musical in which she starred. The Nellie Dean public house on Dean Street, SOHO, was named in Gertie Gitana's honour. As her fame faded, the 60s pop singer Wayne Fontana briefly took her place in the cockney fruiterer's lexicon.

Gesta Grayorum *See the* PRINCE OF PURPOOLE.

get

Getaway, The A video game (2002) published by Sony for its PlayStation 2 console. It was one of the first action-adventure games to allow players to freely roam a realistic three-dimensional environment, in this case central London, re-created from thousands of photographs. Like the later GANGS OF LONDON, the Getaway featured ethnically based crews of gangsters and an old-style family of COCKNEY criminals, in this case the BETHNAL GREEN Mob.

get away closer! Obsolete COCKNEY (originally COSTERMONGERS') slang, jokily encouraging the attentions of an admirer. Nowadays psychotherapists use the term (without the exclamation mark) to describe the 'push-pull' behaviour of individuals with certain types of borderline personality disorder.

get Chelsea, to An archaic term for obtaining the benefit of that hospital.

get inside and pull the blinds down! A contemptuous remark of the late 19th and early 20th centuries. It was addressed especially to bad horsemen.

> When I go out riding, the vulgar little boys
> about shout out 'Get inside, and pull the blinds
> down!' It makes me so wild, Mr Harkaway, to be
> chaffed before ma and Bobby and Thomasina.
>
> BRACEBRIDGE HEMYNG: *Jack Harkaway at Oxford* (1900)

get off (or out) at Clapham Junction, to To practise *coitus interruptus* (as a form of birth control). The basis of the euphemistic metaphor is leaving a train just before it arrives at a terminus (CLAPHAM JUNCTION is the last major station before VICTORIA and WATERLOO).

get off me barrer! A throwaway line delivered at the end of cockney MUSIC HALL songs and used as a catchphrase. It derived from COSTERMONGERS' talk. The phrase could be used almost meaninglessly, to signify nothing more than 'I am

a cockney', or to suggest something like 'come off it!' – as in this elevated example:

> Nature, babies, dogs are *so* lovable, because they
> can't answer back. The primrose, alas! couldn't
> pipe up and say: Hey! Bill! Get off the barrow!
>
> D.H. LAWRENCE: 'Love Was Once a Little Boy' (1925)

get on someone's wick, to To annoy them. The final word may derive from COCKNEY RHYMING SLANG: *see* HAMPTON (WICK).

Get Stuffed A long-established company based at 105 ESSEX ROAD, ISLINGTON, dealing with all aspects of taxidermy.

> It's my new favourite shop. It's musty, creepy
> and deeply sinister. It smells of death.
> Everywhere cold, dead eyes stare out from
> corners; impending antlers protrude from
> walls; and the unsettling stiffness of rigormortis
> weighs heavy on the air.
>
> MICHAEL WYLIE-HARRIS, in *The Times* (13 April 2007)

get your trousers on, you're nicked A line written by Ian Kennedy Martin (b.1936) and delivered by John Thaw (1942–2002), playing Detective Inspector Jack Regan, in 'Regan', an ITV *Armchair Cinema* episode broadcast in 1974. The choice of words epitomized the production's supposedly realistic portrayal of a rough, tough London policeman who contrasted sharply with the benign characters that had formerly populated most TV crime dramas. The show's broadly favourable reception led to the creation of a spin-off series: *The* SWEENEY.

> Some [real-life policemen], it is alleged, even
> tried to emulate Regan's tough-guy persona.
> (Cue mental picture of coppers in Frinton
> charging into villain's home crying: 'Get your
> trousers on, you're nicked!')
>
> *New Statesman* (26 March 2001)

Gherkin The popular nickname given to a glass-clad office tower shaped like a portly bullet, erected in ST MARY AXE in the CITY of London in 2003 to the design of Norman Foster on a site previously occupied by the BALTIC. The Gherkin was the first building in the SQUARE MILE to break the 600-ft (200m) barrier since TOWER 42 (the NatWest Tower) in 1979. It is officially named simply by its address, 30 St Mary Axe, and is also known as the Swiss Re Tower (after the Swiss Reinsurance Company, which commissioned it). After initial scepticism it has become one of the City's most appreciated landmarks.

The dean and chapter of St Paul's Cathedral are objecting to Lord Foster's proposed giant glass tower in the City of London – on the grounds that the tower dubbed the 'erotic gherkin' invited odious comparison with the cathedral's dome, and damaged its iconic status.

The Guardian (18 February 2000)

Ghosts' Promenade A nickname given to Church Hill Road in EAST BARNET. Spectral sightings have included knights on horseback, headless hounds and wandering noblemen. The root cause of these manifestations is said to be the denial of a Christian burial to the unpopular local landowner Geoffrey de Mandeville in 1144. The 18th-century prophetess Joanna Southcott, also known as 'Satan's mistress', apparently used to sit under an oak tree in what is now Oak Hill Park, which burst into flames on a clear day in the early 1930s. *See also* CAMLET MOAT.

giddy little kipper In the 1880s this was a COCKNEY catchphrase signifying approval (or mock approval) of another's stylish attire, especially clothes a man had put on for a special occasion. 'Giddy young whelk' was an alternative. As with many such coinages it spread to the provinces before fading from most memories, at least with its original meaning. However, 'giddy kipper' hung on in the north of England – especially Lancashire – where it came to be associated with the conventional sense of the word 'giddy': overexcited or dizzy. 'Giddy as a kipper' is also increasingly heard.

Gidea Park An expanded GARDEN SUBURB situated just to the north-east of ROMFORD. At its inception in 1910 this was one of the most imaginative examples of enlightened town planning devised for Londoners who wanted to escape to the country. The name may derive from Old English 'ged' and 'ea', meaning 'pike water', but it could simply mean giddy, or foolish. This would have been a reference to the outlandish architecture of the first Gidea Hall, which stood from the 13th century until 1718. Lady Jane Grey is said to have received tuition there. Its wooded park extended over 150 acres (60 hectares) and its gardens grew vines, melons and oranges. After the opening of the station in 1910, an idealistic Arts and Crafts project named Romford Garden Suburb began here, with designs that won an architects' competition. The homes were well built, light and airy, and constructed in a variety of individual styles on the land attached to Gidea Hall. The retention of several features from the original estate – the orangery, lime walk, ponds and a bathing temple – added a cachet to the marketing prospectus. The suburb's role as a refuge for EAST ENDERS was illustrated by Charles KRAY, who once commented that if he had moved his family here, his twin sons might never have gone to the bad. Gidea Park was the boyhood home of Noel Edmonds (b.1948), now best known as the host of Channel 4's *Deal or No Deal*. The pop group Gidea Park had two minor hits in the early 1970s.

Gilpin, John The protagonist of William Cowper's comic ballad 'The Diverting History of John Gilpin' (published anonymously in 1782 and under Cowper's name in 1785), which tells the story of a Londoner whose runaway horse carries him 10 miles (16 km) past the Bell, at EDMONTON, where he is supposed to be having his wedding anniversary dinner.

> At Edmonton his loving wife
> From the balcony spied
> Her tender husband, wondering much
> To see how he did ride.
> Stop, stop, John Gilpin! – Here's the house –
> They all at once did cry,
> The dinner waits, and we are tired:
> Said Gilpin – So am I!

The poem helped make the Bell so famous that more than one establishment laid claim to the name, and at one time Edmonton had an Old Bell and an Oldest Bell. Today it has a Gilpin's Bell, occupying a former motorcycle shop. The character of John Gilpin is said to represent William Beyer (1693–1791), a noted linen draper at the junction of CHEAPSIDE and PATERNOSTER ROW. It was Lady Austen, widow of Sir Robert Austen and Cowper's neighbour at Olney, Buckinghamshire, who told him the story to divert him from his melancholy. The marriage adventure of Commodore Trunnion in Tobias Smollett's *Peregrine Pickle* (1751) is very similar to that of Gilpin's wedding anniversary.

Giltspur Street A street in SMITHFIELD, first recorded with this name in the mid-16th century. It seems likely to derive from the earlier presence of spurriers, whose wares were in demand for the medieval jousting tournaments held at

Smithfield and CHEAPSIDE. Gilt spurs were also buckled to a man's heels as part of the ceremony of making him a knight. Later, Giltspur Street became known for its Compter, a prison that mostly housed debtors. It had separate sections for men and women and functioned from 1791 to 1854.

Gilwell Park With Sewardstone and Sewardstonebury, between which it lies, this is the only corner of the extended metropolis that is not part of a London borough but falls within a London POSTAL DISTRICT (E4). Henry VIII built a hunting lodge here for his son Edward, which he later granted to Sir Edward Denny of Waltham Abbey. The lodge was rebuilt in the late 18th century as the White House, with landscaped gardens adorned by a stone balustrade from old LONDON BRIDGE. The extravagance helped to bankrupt its owner and the Crown seized the property in 1812 and sold it at auction. The house had fallen into dereliction when W.F. de Bois Maclaren bought it in 1919 for £10,000 and presented it to the Scout Association. Gilwell Park now consists entirely of Scout facilities, both administrative offices and adventure sites. Around 40,000 people attend the centre each year. The founder of the Scout Association, Robert Baden-Powell, was created Lord Baden-Powell of Gilwell in 1929.

Gimme Gimme Gimme A BBC TV sitcom that ran for three seasons in 1999–2001. Written by Jonathan Harvey (b.1968), the show starred Kathy Burke and James Dreyfus as unconventional and somewhat objectionable flatmates living at 69 Paradise Passage, KENTISH TOWN.

Gin Lane The title of a print by William HOGARTH (1697–1764), published in 1751 alongside a contrasting image of cheerful contentment entitled 'Beer Street'. During the first half of the 18th century the consumption of cheap gin reached epidemic proportions in London, with consequent increases in crime, ill-health and mortality. By 1750 Londoners were drinking an average of 2 pints (1.1 litres) of gin per person per week. In the following year Parliament at last found a way to turn the tide with the passage of the TIPPLING ACT, which also paved the way for the evolution of the far superior spirit known as LONDON GIN. 'Gin Lane' depicted a larger-than-life scene in ST GILES, with squalor, madness and

death all around; only the pawnbroker flourishes, while a sozzled and syphilitic woman allows an infant to fall from her arms and another shares a tipple with her baby. Hogarth's friend, the Rev James Townley, supplied three accompanying verses, of which the last runs:

Damned cup! that on the vitals preys,
That liquid fire contains,
Which madness to the heart conveys,
And rolls it thro' the veins.

Gipsy or Gypsy

Gipsy Hill A collection of Victorian villas and terraced houses situated north-west of CRYSTAL PALACE, noted for its fine views across London. During the 17th and 18th centuries, the so-called NORWOOD GIPSIES lived in the area and gave it its present name. The area changed rapidly after Gipsy Hill station opened in 1856. Christ Church was consecrated in 1867 and gained its statuesque tower in 1889. Blocks of flats were built between the world wars, and more have since replaced some of the largest houses. However, most of the Victorian and Edwardian properties have survived, although often in subdivided form. The remarkable Annie Besant (1847–1933), theosophist, socialist, orator and Indian nationalist, lived at 39 Colby Road from 1874 to 1893.

Gipsy's warning 'Morning' in outdated COCKNEY RHYMING SLANG.

Norwood Gipsies *See under* NORWOOD.

Giro the Nazi dog The pet terrier (not an alsatian, as some have claimed) of the German ambassador to the COURT OF ST JAMES'S in 1932–6, Leopold von Hoesch, who was in fact said to have disliked the Nazis. When Giro was accidentally electrocuted in February 1934, Hoesch had his remains buried in the gardens of CARLTON HOUSE TERRACE, part of which was home to the German Embassy until the outbreak of the Second World War. The 'Nazi dog' appellation has been popularized in the context of Giro's diminutive tombstone, which has lately become a destination for those seeking out London's most obscure and offbeat sights. The dog's memorial reads, 'Ein treuer Begleiter!' (A faithful companion). The grave is located behind railings near the DUKE OF YORK'S COLUMN.

He was given a full Nazi burial and his grave lies in what was once the front garden to No.9, now a small space between the Duke of York steps and a garage ramp ... This is London's sole Nazi memorial, situated somewhat inappropriately in an area filled with monuments to heroes of the British empire.

The Times (21 August 2005)

given away with a pound of tea A late Victorian COCKNEY catchphrase that filtered out to the provinces and then weakened during the first half of the 20th century. It derived from a promotional device common among tea dealers of offering a 'gift with purchase', such as a vase, clock or framed print. The phrase was at first used disparagingly of cheap-looking acquisitions, and later wherever it could be made to fit.

They said they wouldn't have me if I was given away with a pound of tea. Told me to go home and not be an old silly.

G.B. SHAW: *Augustus Does His Bit* (1916)

Glad All Over A hit single by the Dave Clark Five, released in November 1963. The song has become the anthem of CRYSTAL PALACE FC. The club's squad recorded a cover version in 1990, when they were FA Cup runners-up. The south Londoners' use of the song is somewhat ironic, given the Dave Clark Five's association with the TOTTENHAM SOUND.

The song resounds with the enduring traces of postwar social change in this part of suburban London. In this sense *Glad All Over* resonates with the experience of class mobility, improvements in council housing and 1960s affluence which affected this district and the families from which Palace fans are drawn.

LES BACK, TIM CRABBE and JOHN SOLOMOS: *The Changing Face of Football* (2001)

Gladstone Park A 96-acre (39-hectare) public park, created in 1901 and dominating the district of DOLLIS HILL. The park was once the grounds of Dollis Hill House, built in the early 19th century and visited frequently by William Gladstone (prime minister four times between 1868 and 1894) when it was owned by Lord Aberdeen (prime minister 1852–5). The US author Mark Twain spent the summer at Dollis Hill House in 1900, writing home:

From the house you can see little but spacious stretches of hay-fields and green turf ... Yet the

massed, brick blocks of London are reachable in three minutes on a horse.

The house was badly damaged by fire in 1996 and more than a decade passed before funding was secured for its restoration. The neighbouring walled garden is kept in immaculate condition with flower displays changed three times a year, while the stable block hosts art exhibitions.

Glasgow (Ranger) 'Stranger' in COCKNEY RHYMING SLANG, in the sense of an outsider, from the colloquial name for Rangers FC. Queens Park Ranger is also used (*see* QUEENS PARK RANGERS FC).

GLC *See* GREATER LONDON COUNCIL.

globe
Globe Theatre The first theatre of this name on BANKSIDE was a round wooden edifice built in 1598 and named after its sign, which showed Hercules with the world on his shoulders. Many of SHAKESPEARE's plays were performed here, the first being *Henry V* (1598), with its reference to 'this wooden O'. In 1613, during a performance of *Henry VIII* (1612), two cannons set the thatch alight and the building was burnt to the ground. It was speedily rebuilt and reopened in 1614, but was closed in 1642 by the Puritans and demolished two years later. In 1970 the US actor Sam Wanamaker (1919–93) founded, and heavily funded, a trust that aimed to build a near replica of the playhouse, based on scholarly guesswork regarding its original appearance. The new Globe opened for its first full season in 1997, near the site of its namesake.

Another theatre of the name opened in SHAFTESBURY AVENUE in 1906, originally as the Hicks Theatre. It became the Globe in 1909 but in 1994 was renamed the Gielgud Theatre in honour of the 90th birthday of the actor Sir John Gielgud (1904–2000).

Globe Town A collection of council-built properties located near the western end of ROMAN ROAD, east of BETHNAL GREEN. A track running north from STEPNEY was called Theven Lane in the Middle Ages, from the Old English plural of 'thief'. By the early 18th century it had been renamed Globe Lane, and later Globe Road, probably after a local inn. In the 1790s land on the Eastfields estate was developed by a consortium of builders and the scheme had become known as Globe Town by 1808. As a result of

TOWER HAMLETS' short-lived division of the borough into seven 'neighbourhoods' in the 1980s, Globe Town is the best branded locality in London, with stylish steel spheres mounted on brick columns or arches at every point of access.

Gloomy Dean The nickname of W.R. Inge (1860–1954), dean of ST PAUL'S Cathedral from 1911 to 1934. The sobriquet sprang from his resistance to current trends and his forcefully expressed doubts regarding political and social reforms that most saw as beneficial.

Glorious Goodwood The five days of the Goodwood Festival, held at the end of July on the estate of this name near Chichester, West Sussex, traditionally marking the end of the LONDON SEASON.

Gloucester Road A commercial street and hotel zone running northward from SOUTH KENSINGTON towards KENSINGTON GARDENS. From the early 17th century this was Hogs Moor or Hogsmire Lane and it was the site of an unsuccessful pleasure garden in the late 18th century. George III's sister-in-law Maria, Duchess of Gloucester (1736–1807), built herself a house on the lane late in her life. The house was later known as Gloucester Lodge and the politician George Canning, briefly prime minister in 1827, lived here for a while. Much of the surrounding area was built up in the second quarter of the 19th century and its underground station opened in 1868, originally as BROMPTON (Gloucester Road). Over the course of the 20th century numerous terraced houses on Gloucester Road were converted into hotels. In a more recent trend, big-name hoteliers have bought up whole groups of these establishments and united them under a single fascia. The author J.M. Barrie lived at 133 Gloucester Road between 1895 and 1902, the period in which he conceived the story of *Peter Pan. See also* PLATFORM FOR ART.

GMT

1. *See* GREENWICH MEAN TIME.

2. An acronym for the Goldsmiths Music Tavern in NEW CROSS. Something of an underground venue in the late 1990s and early 2000s, the Goldsmiths has since been sanitized.

go

go and eat coke A dismissive catchphrase that evolved in the London slums around 1870. By the outbreak of the First World War it was more likely to be encountered in a Billy Bunter story.

go by the Marylebone stage, to *See the* MARYLEBONE STAGE.

Going Straight A one-season BBC TV sitcom (1978), spun off from the popular series *Porridge*. Written by Dick Clement and Ian La Frenais (both b.1937), the show starred Ronnie Barker as Norman 'Fletch' Fletcher, newly released from prison and returning home to MUSWELL HILL.

> Man with fist in mouth cannot no longer give
> lip! Muswell Hill proverb.
>
> *Going Straight,* 'Going to be Alright' (1978)

Gone! And never called me 'mother' A misquotation from Mrs Henry Wood's sensationalist novel *East Lynne* (1861). These precise words are said to have been uttered in one of the stage adaptations, although they do not appear in the best-known version, by T.A. Palmer (1874). *East Lynne* was much performed at the TRANSPONTINE THEATRES of late Victorian London and the line – also rendered with 'dead' in place of 'gone' – became something of a catchphrase, used derogatorily to encapsulate the melodramatic repertoire typically on offer at those playhouses. Later it was employed in other contexts, especially among soldiers in the First World War.

gone to Pimlico A piece of 19th-century slang meaning 'ruined', 'smashed beyond repair', alluding to the reputation of PIMLICO as a home of 'fallen women'.

go to Abney Park, to From the late 19th century into the 1920s, a colloquial euphemism for 'to die'. *See also* ABNEY PARK.

go to Battersea to be cut for the simples or **to get your simples cut** 'Simples' were medicinal herbs, formerly grown at BATTERSEA; the suggestion to a young man that he might be harvested by an apothecary was to say that he was a simpleton.

go to Peckham, to An old and little-used expression meaning to go to dinner, derived from a pun on the south-east London suburb and the word 'peck', as in 'peckish'.

go to Romford to be new-bottomed *See to* RIDE TO ROMFORD.

go to the Devil Go to ruin. In the 17th century wits used to make a play on the applicability of the phrase to the Devil Tavern, TEMPLE BAR, a favoured rendezvous among lawyers and writers.

The sign showed St Dunstan pulling the Devil's nose. *See also the* KING OF SKINKERS.

> Bloodhound: As you come by Temple Bar make a step to the Devil.
> Tim: To the Devil, father?
> Sim: My master means the sign of the Devil, and he cannot hurt you, fool; there's a saint holds him by the nose.
> WILLIAM ROWLEY: *A Match at Midnight*, I, i (1633)

godless institution of Gower Street

An early nickname for London University, now UNIVERSITY COLLEGE LONDON, because it was founded to provide an alternative to the Anglican-dominated colleges of Oxford and Cambridge. Students of all beliefs were allowed entry and no religious subjects were taught.

Gog and Magog Legendary guardians of the CITY of London. Gog and Magog feature in the folklore of a bewildering variety of national cultures, and in the holy writings of several religious faiths, in which they take sharply differing forms. However, in the story preferred by the LORD MAYOR OF LONDON, they were a pair of giants (alternatively called Gogmagog and Corineus), the sole survivors of a monstrous brood, the offspring of demons and the 33 infamous daughters of the Roman emperor Diocletian, who murdered their husbands. They were taken prisoner by BRUTUS and made to serve as guardians (or porters) at the royal palace that stood on the site of the GUILDHALL. Statues of the pair that had stood at the Guildhall from at least the early 15th century were destroyed in the GREAT FIRE and have since been thrice replaced. Wicker effigies of Gog and Magog were traditionally carried in the procession at the LORD MAYOR'S SHOW and after a long absence these were reinstated from 2006 onwards, with new giants created by the Company of Basketmakers and drawn by the Society of Young Freemen.

golden

Golden Arrow A famous Pullman express train service from London to Paris, with a ferry crossing from Dover to Calais. On the French side of the English Channel the train had the equivalent name, *Flèche d'Or*. A train had been leaving VICTORIA STATION at 11am daily for many years on this route before the name was adopted in 1929. The service was withdrawn in 1972. The name itself comes from folklore, in which the Golden Arrow was the one sought by a pair of lovers in the land of their dreams. The legend is alluded to in the title and story of Mary Webb's early novel *The Golden Arrow* (1916). The name is fitting for a train that takes passengers to Paris, the 'City of Lovers'.

Golden Boy of Pye Corner A gilded statue of a naked, and somewhat chubby, little boy, situated at the corner of GILTSPUR STREET and COCK LANE, in SMITHFIELD. This is the spot where buildings were blown up to halt the GREAT FIRE OF LONDON and the inscription beneath the boy blames the fire on the sin of gluttony. The statue was set into the wall of the Fortune of War, a public house frequented by body snatchers in the 1820s (*see the* LONDON BURKERS). The pub was demolished in 1910 and the CITY & GUILDS building now occupies the site.

Golden Cross An inn that features prominently in Charles DICKENS's *Pickwick Papers* (1836–7) and *David Copperfield* (1849–50). A succession of coaching inns bearing this name stood at CHARING CROSS in the 18th and 19th centuries. The Gothic structure that Dickens described was torn down *c*.1827 to make way for TRAFALGAR SQUARE and a new Golden Cross was then built facing CHARING CROSS STATION. Golden Cross House now occupies its site, at the corner of the STRAND and Duncannon Street.

Golden Dustman A nickname of Nicodemus 'Noddy' Boffin in Charles DICKENS's *Our Mutual Friend* (1865). He is made rich by the bequest of his late employer, a miserly dust-contractor.

> The minion of fortune and the worm of the hour, or in less cutting language, Nicodemus Boffin, Esquire, the Golden Dustman, had become as much at home in his eminently aristocratic family mansion as he was likely ever to be.

Golden Hind or **Hinde** The famous ship in which Francis Drake made his voyage of circumnavigation (1577–80). Originally called the *Pelican*, it was renamed the *Golden Hind* at Port St Julian, near the entrance to the Straits of Magellan, in 1578. The change of name honoured Drake's sponsor, Sir Christopher HATTON, whose family crest featured a golden hind. Drake was knighted by Elizabeth I on 4 April 1581, after she had dined aboard the *Golden Hind* at DEPTFORD. A replica of the galleon has been berthed at ST MARY OVERIE Dock since 1996. The *Golden Hind* was also the name of an express train service from London to Plymouth, the latter city being that from which Drake set sail.

Golden Lane A street located on the border of the CITY of London and the London Borough of ISLINGTON. To its west lies the CORPORATION OF LONDON's Golden Lane estate. Nowadays a most unremarkable thoroughfare, it was formerly a main artery of the ROOKERY of ST LUKE'S, with more than a dozen cramped alleyways like Hotwater Court and Cowheel Alley branching off it. Most of the slum buildings were demolished in the early 20th century and the BLITZ completed the job.

> Its thieves are the most desperate and daring in the world; it is rich in examples of that even more dangerous scoundrel, the 'rough'. Annually it yields its crop of coiners and smashers; it is the recognised head-quarters of beggars and cadgers … It is the 'slummiest' of slums.
>
> JAMES GREENWOOD: *In Strange Company* (1874)

Golden Mile The enduring nickname for a stretch of the GREAT WEST ROAD in BRENTFORD, which was lined with impressive art deco factories between the two world wars, built for the likes of Smith's crisps and Maclean's toothpaste. Many of the factories have since been torn down – although a few gems remain – and manufacturing has been replaced by multinational headquarters, media and production operations and some large-scale retail units. The greatest loss was the Firestone factory, which was demolished by owners Trafalgar House just before it was due to gain listed status in 1980. The best survivors include the former Pyrene fire extinguishers and Coty cosmetics factories, both now office buildings, and the Gillette building, which is awaiting redevelopment.

Golden Shears A trophy awarded by the Merchant Taylors' Company (*see* LIVERY COMPANIES) to the winner of a biennial competition for tailoring students and apprentices.

Golden Square A square in south-west SOHO, described by DICKENS in *Nicholas Nickelby* (1839) as 'not exactly in anybody's way, to or from anywhere', which remains true today. Golden Square has undergone several changes of character since it was built up with houses for the gentry in the early 18th century. After descending to the status of an itinerants' quarter, filled with cheap hotels and boarding houses, it was then colonized by solicitors, architects and engineers,

and in the late 19th century became the London centre of the woollen and worsted trade, with warehouses supplying the nearby tailors of SAVILE ROW. Media companies have been the predominant occupants since the mid-20th century. The square is said by some to have taken its name from the first builder there; however, there seems to be some truth in a more colourful explanation:

> It was originally called Gelding Square, from the sign of a neighbouring inn; but the inhabitants, indignant at the vulgarity of the name, changed it to the present.
>
> THOMAS PENNANT: *Some Account of London* (1813)

golden syrup A kind of pale treacle first manufactured in 1883 by Abram Lyle (1820–91) at his sugar refinery at PLAISTOW Wharf, formerly an oil storage facility. The product was initially sold only to employees and local customers, under the brand name 'Goldie'. Its success prompted Lyle to begin distributing tinned golden syrup more widely from 1885. *See also the* SUGAR MILE.

Golders Green Created by American property developers at the beginning of the 20th century, Golders Green is situated to the north-west of HAMPSTEAD HEATH and the name probably derives from a 14th-century resident called Godyere. After the First World War a large number of Jewish families began moving into the area's new housing from the crowded EAST END, and synagogues were built to serve the community. Immigrant Jews fleeing Nazi persecution augmented the settlement during the 1930s. The visible signs of Golders Green's Jewish character are presently diminishing as new ethnic minorities, especially Korean and Japanese, move in.

Golders Green Crematorium The London Cremation Society opened London's first crematorium on Hoop Lane in 1902. It is the resting place of the ashes of many famous people, including Stanley Baldwin, Neville Chamberlain, T.S. Eliot, Sigmund FREUD, Sir Henry Irving, Rudyard Kipling, Anna Pavlova, George Bernard SHAW, Bram Stoker, MARIE STOPES and Ralph Vaughan Williams.

Golders Green Hippodrome A MUSIC HALL built in 1913 to meet the entertainment needs of the rapidly growing new suburb. It subsequently served as a theatre and, from the 1960s, as a BBC radio and television recording studio and concert hall. Despite the opposition of groups such as the Save London's Theatres Campaign, the Hippodrome was sold in 2007 to the El-Shaddai International Christian Centre for use as the charismatic church's London headquarters.

Goldfinger, Ernő A Hungarian-born Marxist architect (1902–87) who settled in London in 1934 after marrying the Crosse & Blackwell heiress, Ursula Blackwell. Goldfinger designed several public buildings and high-rise housing blocks across the capital, culminating with the iconic TRELLICK TOWER in KENSAL TOWN. He built a terrace of three modernist houses in Willow Road, HAMPSTEAD and lived in the middle one, which is now a National Trust property. When the author Ian Fleming named a James Bond villain after the notoriously humourless architect, Goldfinger began an action for damages. Fleming threatened to change the name to Goldprick, and the dispute was settled out of court.

Goldhawk Road Running west from SHEPHERD'S BUSH Green to STAMFORD BROOK, and becoming increasingly upmarket as it progresses westwards, this highway takes its name from a family that lived here in the 15th century. There is a market by the TUBE station, which specializes in fabrics. Simon Bent's play *Goldhawk Road*, described by the *Evening Standard* as 'scathingly funny' and 'wickedly misanthropic', premiered at the nearby Bush Theatre in 1997.

Goldsmiths A college of the UNIVERSITY OF LONDON, based in NEW CROSS and specializing in the visual arts and other creative subjects. It began in 1891 as the Goldsmiths' Technical and Recreative Institute, founded by the Goldsmiths' Company as a local education centre for working people. The University of London acquired the institute and re-established it as Goldsmiths' College in 1904. Since 1989 Goldsmiths (as it now styles itself) has been a full college of the university. Among the college's alumni are the fashion designers Mary QUANT and Vivienne Westwood, the dub poet Linton Kwesi Johnson, the musician Damon Albarn, and the artists Lucian Freud, Bridget Riley and most of the major figures of the BRITART movement.

gold watch 'Scotch' (whisky) in COCKNEY RHYMING SLANG.

golem (Yiddish, from Hebrew *gōlem*, 'shapeless mass') In Jewish legend, a human figure formed from clay that can be supernaturally endowed with life. They were supposedly used as servants by rabbis. Peter Ackroyd reintroduced the concept of the golem in his novel *Dan Leno and the Limehouse Golem* (1994), about a series of mysterious murders in 19th-century EAST LONDON. *See also the* FUNNIEST MAN ON EARTH.

gone *See* GO.

good

Good Duke Humphrey Humphrey, Duke of Gloucester (1391–1447), youngest son of Henry IV. Dr Brewer suggested that he was called 'good', not for his philanthropy, but from his devotion to the Roman Catholic Church. Others, however, have noted his patronage of men of letters and generous donation of books to what became the Bodleian Library at Oxford. When Humphrey inherited the manor of GREENWICH he built a mansion that became the royal palace of Placentia and a tower in GREENWICH PARK that was later replaced by GREENWICH OBSERVATORY. *See also to* DINE WITH DUKE HUMPHREY.

> What though the common people favour him,
> Calling him 'Humphrey, the good Duke of Gloucester',
> Clapping their hands and crying with loud voice,
> 'Jesu maintain your royal excellence!'
> With, 'God preserve the good Duke Humphrey!'
> I fear me, lords, for all this flattering gloss,
> He will be found a dangerous protector.
> SHAKESPEARE: *Henry VI, Part 2*, I, i (early 1590s)

Good Life, The An enduringly popular BBC TV sitcom that first ran from 1975 to 1978. Created by John Esmonde (1937–2008) and Bob Larbey (b.1934), the show depicted a middle-class SURBITON couple, Tom and Barbara Good, and their efforts to go 'back to the land', growing their own food, keeping animals and making their own tools and equipment. Inevitably, the enterprise creates friction with their next-door neighbours, Jerry and Margo Leadbetter. The series owed much to its topicality, its clever scripts and its first-rate acting and casting, with Richard Briers and Felicity Kendal as the Goods and Paul Eddington and Penelope Keith as the Leadbetters. Exterior scenes were filmed in Kewferry Road, NORTHWOOD.

Goodluck Hope *See* LEAMOUTH.

good manners to except the lord mayor of London An old reproof to those whose words suggested that they thought themselves better than the rest.

Goodge Street Like nearby WARREN STREET, Goodge Street's name is associated more with the TUBE station than the thoroughfare, which runs westwards off TOTTENHAM COURT ROAD and soon becomes Mortimer Street. John Goodge obtained Crab Tree Field by marriage in 1718 and his sons developed the land in the 1740s. During the Second World War the government built a deep shelter linked to Goodge Street station, part of which was made available to General Eisenhower as his operational headquarters for D-Day. After the war the army used the shelter as a transit centre until it was damaged by fire in 1956. In the mid-1960s some of Goodge Street's cafés gained a reputation as hang-outs where illicit substances might be obtained. Donovan's 'Sunny Goodge Street' (1965) was one of the first pop songs to include an explicit reference to drug-taking.

> On the firefly platform on sunny Goodge Street
> A violent hash-smoker shook a chocolate
> machine
> Involved in an eating scene.

Goodmayes A multiracial satellite of eastern ILFORD, separated from the BECONTREE estate by Goodmayes Park. Tradition has it that the name derives from John Godemay, a 14th-century landowner, but local historian Peter Foley has argued that Godemay took his name from the place, not the other way around. Citing another local name, Mayfield, Foley suggests a link to the herbaceous plant madder, cultivated for dyeing in pre-industrial times. Like neighbouring SEVEN KINGS, this area was farmland until the end of the 19th century when Cameron Corbett (later Baron Rowallen) built the Mayfield estate south of the railway line. Corbett's Scottish origin shows in the names of many of the streets.

Gooners Supporters of ARSENAL FC, from a mock-northern pronunciation of the team's nickname, the GUNNERS. In 2007 the club filed an application to register 'Gooner' as a trademark, probably to inhibit the sale of unofficial merchandise rather than with an intention to actively promote the name. Many fans expressed their annoyance and the application was withdrawn a year later.

goose
Goose and Gridiron A public house sign, probably in ridicule of the Swan and Harp, a popular sign for the early music houses (*see* MUSIC HALL), but properly the coat of arms of the Company of Musicians, i.e. Azure, a swan with wings expanded argent, within double tressure [the gridiron] flory counterflory.

ST PAUL'S Freemason's Lodge (*see* FREEMASONRY) assembled at the Goose and Gridiron in London House Yard. Sir Christopher Wren presented the lodge with three carved mahogany candlesticks, and the trowel and mallet that he used in laying the cathedral's first stone. Wren was elected Grand Master of the order in 1688. The first Grand Lodge of England was founded at the Goose and Gridiron in 1717. The tavern and the yard in which it stood were demolished in the mid-1890s.

goose's (neck) 'Cheque' in COCKNEY RHYMING SLANG.

gorblimey A COCKNEY contraction of 'God blind me', employed to express surprise, often shortened to 'blimey'. First seen in print in the late 19th century, the word 'gorblimey' came to symbolize the rough-and-ready cockney archetype, gaining an adjectival sense that signified coarseness or vulgarity. In the First World War a gorblimey hat was a peaked cap that had been softened by removing the wire frame, worn in a rakish manner and in defiance of dress regulations. Gorblimey trousers were in similar style and are best remembered from their mention in Lonnie Donegan's hit single 'My Old Man's a Dustman' (1960) (*see the* KING OF SKIFFLE).

> And here I was already, swaggering about in a
> gorblimey hat and a yellow collar and more or
> less keeping my end up among a crowd of other
> temporary gents and some who weren't even
> temporary.
>
> GEORGE ORWELL: *Coming Up for Air* (1939)

Gordon
Gordon (and Gotch) 'Wristwatch' in old COCKNEY RHYMING SLANG, from the distributor of British publications to Australia, New Zealand, South Africa and Canada, founded in 1853. In his *Dictionary of Rhyming Slang* (1960), Julian Franklyn expressed his mystification that the term was

widely used by 'people who do not know, even, that books and periodicals are exported, much less that Gordon & Gotch are the firm who do it'. The company is now part of an Australian communications group.

Gordon Bennett! An exclamation of exasperation or surprise. It comes either from the name of James Gordon Bennett (1795–1872), founding editor of the *New York Herald*, or from that of his similarly named son (1841–1918). Given the COCKNEY pronunciation of 'God' as 'Gawd', Mr Bennett's name was originally invoked by those wishing, at the last moment, to avoid giving blasphemous offence.

Gordon Hill A street and station situated in a pleasant corner of north-west ENFIELD. This was part of the virgin territory of ENFIELD CHASE until its enclosure and division in the late 1770s, when much of the land was acquired by Trinity College, Cambridge. Only one house of note stood here at that time, which was the home of Lord George Gordon, who later became notorious as the instigator of the GORDON RIOTS. In the late 1850s the North London Society bought Gordon House, demolished it and laid out streets, but the area maintained a semi-rural aspect until the 1930s.

Gordon Riots An anti-Catholic uprising that took place in London in early June 1780. It occurred after Lord George Gordon (1751–93), leader of the Protestant Association, had failed in his attempt to have clauses in the 1778 Catholic Relief Act (removing restrictions on the activities of priests) repealed. Gordon led tens of thousands of Protestant demonstrators in a march on Parliament that turned into five days of destructive riots that were eventually put down by the army. Hundreds of rioters were killed and Gordon was charged with treason, but acquitted. He later converted to Judaism. Charles DICKENS made the riots the backdrop of his novel *Barnaby Rudge* (1841):

> But forty thousand men of this our island in
> the wave (exclusive of women and children)
> rivet their eyes and thoughts on Lord George
> Gordon; and every day, from the rising up of the
> sun to the going down of the same, pray for his
> health and vigour.

gorgeous

Gorgeous George Originally, the nickname of the US wrestler George Raymond Wagner (1915–63), who was noted for his flamboyant appearance. It was subsequently applied, with a degree of irony, to the dapper and controversial MP George Galloway (b.1954), who represented Labour until expelled from the party for his extreme criticism of the invasion of Iraq in 2003 by US and UK forces. In 2005 he was elected MP for BETHNAL GREEN and BOW on an antiwar platform.

Gorgeous Gussie The nickname of the US tennis star Gertrude Moran (b.1923), whose lace-trimmed panties caused a sensation on the courts of WIMBLEDON in 1949. They were designed for her by the Wimbledon fashion expert Teddy Tinling.

Gospel Oak A socially polarized locality known to some as 'Hampstead Bottom', situated between KENTISH TOWN and HAMPSTEAD. Gospel Oak's name derives from a tree under which a host of legendary figures are said to have preached, including St Augustine, Edward the Confessor, John Wesley and even St Paul. The tree marked the boundary between the parishes of Hampstead and ST PANCRAS. It vanished sometime in the mid-19th century; the uncertainty as to when exactly this occurred corresponds with the mythological nature of its history. Much of the district was rebuilt with low-rise council flats in the 1960s and 1970s. Surviving Victorian parts of the locality, such as Oak Village, have subsequently been gentrified. Comedian, television presenter and local resident Michael Palin (b.1943) has planted a new gospel oak at Lismore Circus 'pocket park'.

> A week of idleness, the salty winds
> Play in her greying hair; the summer sun
> Puts back her freckles so that Alfred Brown
> Remembers courting days in Gospel Oak
> And takes her to the Flannel Dance tonight.
> JOHN BETJEMAN: 'Beside the Seaside' (1948)

Gower Street An elegantly sombre BLOOMSBURY street connecting BEDFORD SQUARE and EUSTON ROAD, with a northern extension continuing to Hampstead Road. The street was built from the 1780s and retains one of London's longest sets of unbroken Georgian terraces. Critics decried its ugliness and the landowners of the BEDFORD ESTATE later added some stuccoed entrances to relieve the brown-bricked gloom. During Gower Street's development, a square was proposed near the northern end but the land was taken instead for what became UNIVERSITY COLLEGE LONDON (UCL). UNIVERSITY COLLEGE HOSPITAL opened on the west side of Gower Street in 1834, bringing surgeons and doctors to the residences nearby. Gower Street's edifying museums make it a miniature SOUTH KENSINGTON. UCL's Petrie Museum and Grant Museum house respectively Egyptian archaeology and natural history collections. Gower Street residents have included Charles Darwin, who afterwards moved to the country village of DOWNE, the engineer Richard Trevithick and the Italian patriot Giuseppe Mazzini.

Gower Street dialect A type of 19th-century student slang, also known as 'medical (or hospital) Greek'. The 'dialect' was based mainly on what are now called spoonerisms, such as 'poking a smipe' for 'smoking a pipe' and a 'stint of pout' for a 'pint of stout'.

grace

grace and favour residence A property belonging to the Crown and granted to a notable person, usually a senior member of the cabinet, as free accommodation. The best-known such residences are numbers 10 and 11 DOWNING STREET. Others in London include No.1 Carlton Gardens, three apartments in Admiralty House and the apartments of the lord chancellor and the speaker of the House of Commons in the PALACE OF WESTMINSTER.

> 'The whole principle of grace and favour homes for cabinet ministers or others ought to be reviewed,' says one senior Labour MP. 'If you are already given an allowance for living in London and you also have a grace and favour home, that is something I think most Labour MPs find objectionable.'
>
> *The Independent* (10 July 2006)

Grace Brothers See ARE YOU BEING SERVED?

Gracechurch Street A continuation of BISH-OPSGATE, extending in a southerly direction towards the MONUMENT. An 11th-century charter mentions *Gerschereche* – 'grass church' – which may have been either St Benet Gracechurch or All Hallows, neither of which survives. The church may have had a turf roof or have stood in a grassy plot, or been so called from the presence of a nearby haymarket. Now, as ever, the street is

home to a cross-section of unexciting commercial premises.

> Some London streets seem determined never to distinguish themselves. No medieval scuffle has ever occurred in them; no celebrated church hoards its monuments; no City hall cherishes its relics there; no celebrated person has honoured it by birth or death. Gracechurch Street is one of these unambitious streets.
>
> WALTER THORNBURY: *Old and New London*, Volume 3 (1878)

Grahame Park *See the* ROYAL AIR FORCE MUSEUM.

grand

Grand Junction Canal The first major canal to link London with the Midlands. Begun in 1793, it was built southwards from existing connections in Northamptonshire towards the THAMES at BRENTFORD, but before its completion a branch was constructed from Bull's Bridge, near HAYES (now in the London Borough of HILLINGDON), to PADDINGTON, where PRAED STREET commemorates the company's first chairman, William Praed.

grand strut A nickname applied in the 19th century to various promenades frequented by the upper echelons of London society, namely BOND STREET and the Broad Walk and ROTTEN ROW in HYDE PARK.

Grand Union Canal A name given in 1929 to a system of canals formed by amalgamating the GRAND JUNCTION CANAL, the REGENT'S CANAL, and the Warwick and Birmingham, the Warwick and Knapton and the Birmingham and Warwick Junction Canals. In combination, they provide a canal link between London and Birmingham, via Watford, Milton Keynes and Warwick.

Grande Dame of Park Lane A nickname for GROSVENOR HOUSE.

grange

Grange Hill A pioneering children's soap opera (1978–2008), set in the (fictional) comprehensive school of the title. Originally to have been called 'Grange Park', the name was changed because there were several schools of that name in London. The scripts were deliberately vague about the setting but various (often unintentional) visual clues placed Grange Hill in north-west London. Schools in KINGSBURY, WILLESDEN

GREEN and BARONS COURT were used for location shooting during the show's first seven years, after which filming moved to the BBC's Elstree studios and finally to Liverpool. Plot lines included a teenage boy's heroin addiction and a teenage girl's pregnancy, and the regular scenes of hair-pulling and shoplifting outraged many. The producers countered criticism, however, by claiming that the tales were cautionary ones.

Grange Park A 'self-contained orchard city', as the local newspaper extravagantly described it in 1908, situated beside Salmon's Brook in north WINCHMORE HILL. The Old Park estate, north of Green Dragon Lane, occupied the area for centuries, possibly from the time of Domesday Book. The present Old Park House dates from 1735. In 1911 Bush Hill Park Golf Club took over the land surrounding the mansion, which is now its clubhouse. The remaining parkland was built on and marketed as the Old Park Grange estate, with Grange Park station opening in 1910.

Granita meeting The legendary dinner at the Granita restaurant in UPPER STREET, ISLINGTON, in May 1994, at which Tony Blair and Gordon Brown, following the sudden death of John Smith, reputedly resolved which of them should become the leader of the Labour Party. It is said that Brown agreed to support Blair for the leadership on condition that Blair would stand down after two terms. When Blair announced in October 2004 (while Brown was out of the country) that he would run for a third term as prime minister, Brown was reported as saying: 'There is nothing that you could say to me now that I could ever believe.' Blair has always denied that any deal was brokered, while Brown has to date refused to comment. The choice of the Granita, a fashionable 'Cal-Ital' restaurant redolent of rocket and ciabatta, heralded to many the flavour of Blair's New Labour, far removed from the beer and sandwiches of the party's traditional roots in working men's clubs. In 2003 Channel 4 screened a drama about the pact entitled *The Deal*, written by Peter Morgan and directed by Stephen Frears.

> Those suspicious of the recent outbreak of love between Blair and Brown [in the run-up to the 2005 election] may enjoy noting that Granita, the trendy, minimalist restaurant where their original, untrustworthy deal was hatched, is now a Tex-Mex establishment called Desperados.
>
> JACK WINKLER: letter to *The Guardian* (25 April 2005)

grass In criminal slang 'to grass' is to inform, perhaps from COCKNEY RHYMING SLANG 'grasshopper', which was once a familiar term for 'copper'. The particular reference may have been to a plain-clothes officer who 'hopped' from one criminal haunt to another with the aim of gathering intelligence. Alternatively, 'grasshopper' may have been rhymed with 'shopper', in the sense of a criminal who 'shops' his associates.

grasshopper The grasshoppers on London signboards of goldsmiths, bankers and others commemorated the badge of Sir Thomas Gresham (*c*.1519–79), founder of the ROYAL EXCHANGE, a building that is adorned by several grasshoppers, notably the gilded one that sits atop its weathervane. A legend has evolved that Gresham, or one of his forebears, was an abandoned child, found lying half-dead in a Norfolk meadow by a passer-by whose attention was drawn in the infant's direction by the chirruping of a noisy grasshopper. However, the family's use of a grasshopper on its crest was simply a rebus, a heraldic play on the word 'grass', as the surname came from the Norfolk estate Gresham, a name that in turn derived from an Old English form of the words 'grass ham'.

Gray's Inn One of London's leading INNS OF COURT since the 15th century, situated north of CHANCERY LANE, in HOLBORN. The 12th-century manor house that stood on this site belonged to Sir Reginald de Grey, Chief Justice of Chester and Constable and Sheriff of Nottingham, created Baron Grey de Wilton in 1295. He died in 1308 and some time in the following 50 to 60 years a learned society of lawyers based itself at the manor house. The present central hall dates from 1558. Around 1600 Sir Francis Bacon (1561–1626) laid out the inn's gardens with a network of pathways called 'walks', which were a novelty at the time. The library, containing some 30,000 volumes and manuscripts, was destroyed in an air raid in May 1941. The hall, too, was very badly damaged but was afterwards restored. *See also the* PRINCE OF PURPOOLE.

Gray's Inn Road A historic street running north-north-west from CHANCERY LANE station to KING'S CROSS. Gray's Inn itself is at the southern end of the road, on the west side. During the 1680s Robert Rossington pulled down most of the properties in what was then Gray's Inn Lane and replaced them with plain, four-storey terraced houses. The one surviving example of Rossington's development is at 55 Gray's Inn Road. The Calthorpe estate, built around 1820, was the first housing project of Thomas CUBITT. More recent structures of note include the ITN building, created in 1991 by Sir Norman Foster, and the UCL Centre for Auditory Research, which opened in 2005 next to the Royal National Throat, Nose and Ear Hospital.

great

Great Bed of Ware A four-poster bed 11 feet (3.3m) square and capable of holding 12 people. It dates from the late 16th century and was formerly at the Saracen's Head Inn, Ware, Hertfordshire, but in 1931 it passed to the VICTORIA AND ALBERT MUSEUM.

> Although the sheet were big enough for the bed of Ware in England.
>
> SHAKESPEARE: *Twelfth Night*, III, ii (1599)

Great Bottle Hoax *See the* BOTTLE CONJUROR.

Great Cham of Literature An epithet applied to Samuel JOHNSON (1709–84) by Tobias Smollett. 'Cham' is an old form of *khan*, a contraction of Turkish *khāqān*, 'ruler'.

Great Exhibition The Great Exhibition of the Works of Industry of All Nations was held in HYDE PARK from May to October 1851. Prince ALBERT inspired and helped to organize the event, for which the CRYSTAL PALACE was constructed. Despite a gloss of internationalism, in reality it symbolized Britain's mid-19th-century industrial supremacy. There were over 13,000 exhibitors in the four classes: raw materials, machinery, manufacturers and fine arts. It was a conspicuous success and the profits were mainly used for educational foundations at SOUTH KENSINGTON. Its centenary was celebrated on the SOUTH BANK by the FESTIVAL OF BRITAIN, in 1951.

Great Fire of London The fire that broke out in the early hours of Sunday, 2 September 1666 at the bakehouse of Robert Farryner (or Farriner) in Pudding Lane, Thames Street. Aided by high winds it spread from the TOWER OF LONDON to TEMPLE BAR and from the THAMES to SMITHFIELD. ST PAUL'S Cathedral and 87 other churches were destroyed and 13,200 houses. In five days the fire covered 373 acres (151 hectares) within the CITY walls and 63 acres (25 ha) without. Only six deaths were attributed to the fire, however, although more may have gone unrecorded. It was not the reason for the disappearance of the GREAT PLAGUE, as was often believed, since most of the slum quarters escaped. The fire was halted by blowing up houses at Pye Corner, Smithfield (*see the* GOLDEN BOY OF PYE CORNER). A Frenchman, Robert Hubert, unconvincingly confessed to setting fire to the bakehouse and was hanged at TYBURN. In fact, despite Farryner's insistence to the contrary, the cause was almost certainly accidental. The medieval street plan was retained in the City's reconstruction but brick and stone were used for the replacement buildings, rather than wood. Christopher Wren was commissioned to rebuild the City's churches, including St Paul's Cathedral. The MONUMENT was built to commemorate the fire.

> It quickly grew powerful enough to despise the use of buckets, and was too advantageously seated among narrow streets to be assaulted by engines: it was therefore proposed to the Lord Mayor [Sir Thomas Bludworth], who came before three o'clock, to pull down some houses to prevent its spreading; but he, with a pish, answering, that 'a woman might piss it out', neglected that prudent advice, and was not long undeceived of his foolish confidence …
>
> EDWARD WEDLAKE BRAYLEY, quoting 'a contemporary writer', in *Londiniana* (1829)

Great Fire of Tooley Street *See the* TOOLEY STREET FIRE.

Great Frost The term has been applied to several exceptionally cold winters but the frost that lasted from Christmas 1739 to mid-February 1740 was said to have been of a 'severity beyond precedent'. Vessels were sunk in the THAMES by ice or by high winds that dashed them against each other. Many destitute labourers were admitted to the workhouse, subsequently resulting in increased poor rates. Rare birds were observed for the first time searching for food in the London markets. Londoners' sole consolation was a lengthy FROST FAIR.

Great Globe A domed, circular building that occupied the centre of LEICESTER SQUARE from 1851 to 1862. The creation of James Wyld (1812–87), the structure contained a spherical map of the world, 65 feet (20m) in diameter, encircled by exhibition rooms at different heights. A model of the Crimea was added during the war in that region (1854–6), drawing large crowds. The condition in which the area was left after the attraction's closure prompted the improvement works that helped make the square's gardens what they are today.

> On its removal literally a wreck was left behind … Squalid vegetation, mangy cats, and almost equally mangy street-boys took possession of the enclosure, which by degrees became the common dust-heap of the neighbourhood.
>
> CHARLES DICKENS JR.: *Dickens's Dictionary of London* (1879)

Great Harry The name popularly given to the famous warship *Henry Grâce à Dieu* built at ERITH and launched in 1514. With a displacement of about 1,000 tons, the vessel had five masts and 21 guns as well as a multitude of small pieces.

Great House of Easement, A lavatory block built at HAMPTON COURT PALACE for Henry VIII. It could seat 28.

Great London Beer Flood A tragic industrial accident that took place on 17 October 1814 at Meux's brewery on Bainbridge Street, just behind the corner of TOTTENHAM COURT ROAD and what is now New Oxford Street. A huge vat burst open and disgorged 3,530 barrels of PORTER, causing two adjacent vats to rupture as well. A tidal wave of more than 300,000 gallons (almost 1.4 million litres) of beer erupted into the neighbouring streets, knocking down buildings and flooding cellars, many of which were inhabited. Eight people drowned. It has been claimed that a ninth victim died of alcoholic poisoning but this may be a colourful elaboration. The brewery was repaired and production continued for more than another century. It was demolished in 1922 and the Dominion Theatre now occupies much of its former site.

> Many of the cellars on the south side of Russell Street are completely inundated with beer; and in some houses the inhabitants had to save themselves from drowning by mounting their highest pieces of furniture.
>
> *The Times* (19 October 1814)

Great Marlborough Street A street leading eastwards off REGENT STREET, named in honour of John Churchill, 1st Duke of Marlborough (1650–1722). It was built at the beginning of the 18th century. It is probably best known as the home of LIBERTY OF LONDON and for its former

magistrates' court, which closed in 1999 and has since been converted into a hotel. Marlboro cigarettes take their name from the street, which in the late 19th century was the site of the Philip Morris company's factory.

Great North Road A name in use since at least the 19th century for a major road leading from London northwards, passing through HOLLOWAY, HIGHGATE and BARNET on its eventual way to York. The route was already established by the 12th century, as an alternative to the much older ERMINE STREET, which left London further east. At its southern end it is today designated the A1; from FINCHLEY to Welwyn Garden City it is the A1000, and from there to Edinburgh it reverts to the A1. The parts that actually bear the name 'Great North Road' now are a short section at the southern end of the A1000, between ARCHWAY Road and FORTIS GREEN, and the A1000 from Barnet northwards.

Great Ormond Street A street in BLOOMSBURY, running approximately east-west to the east of RUSSELL SQUARE. It was laid out at the end of the 17th century and probably named in honour of James Butler, 1st Duke of Ormonde, Royalist commander in the Irish campaigns of the Civil War. It is most famous for, and now virtually synonymous with, the Hospital for Sick Children, England's premier paediatric hospital, founded in 1851.

Great Piazza Coffee House A flourishing COFFEE HOUSE at the north-east angle of the COVENT GARDEN piazza opened in 1756, previously (1754–6) known as Macklin's. It was here in 1809 that Richard Brinsley Sheridan watched the fire at the THEATRE ROYAL, DRURY LANE, saying: 'A man may surely be allowed to take a glass of wine at his own fireside.' It became a hotel in 1840 and was pulled down to make way for the Floral Hall in 1865.

Great Plague The last occurrence (1665–6) of the bubonic plague, which had frequently erupted in various localities since the Black Death but less disastrously. Outbreaks were particularly bad in London in 1603, 1625 and 1636, doubtless due to growing congestion. The outbreak of 1625 was known as the Great Plague until it was overshadowed by that of 1665. Deaths in London are estimated at *c.*100,000, but the LORD MAYOR remained at his post. *See also the* GREAT FIRE OF LONDON.

Great Portland Street A commercial thoroughfare extending from OXFORD STREET to the eastern end of MARYLEBONE ROAD, where Great Portland Street station is located. Like many streets in the vicinity, its name was a product of the marriage of estate owner Margaret Cavendish Harley to the 2nd Duke of Portland. The car showrooms for which the street was once renowned have been driven away by fashion wholesalers and office furnishers, although it remains home to the Retail Motor Industry Federation. On his visits to London in the 1820s and 1830s, the composer Felix Mendelssohn stayed in Great Portland Street at the home of a German iron merchant. Among the writers who lived here were James Boswell and Leigh Hunt. H.G. Wells was well acquainted with the area; it is the setting for events in both *The Invisible Man* and his lesser-known story *The Crystal Egg* (both 1897).

> I had taken a room in London, a large
> unfurnished room in a big ill-managed lodging-
> house in a slum near Great Portland Street.
>
> *The Invisible Man*

Great Room The designation of an especially grand and capacious room at several landmark buildings in London, which include MARBLE HILL HOUSE, GROSVENOR HOUSE, Christie's saleroom in KING STREET, ST JAMES'S, and the headquarters of the ROYAL SOCIETY OF ARTS.

Great Scotland Yard *See* SCOTLAND YARD.

Great Smog A smoke-filled fog that shrouded London from Friday to Tuesday, 5–9 December 1952. Pollution rose to more than five times the level of a typical SMOG in modern Beijing and on the Saturday and Sunday London's entire transport system virtually ground to a halt. At SADLER'S WELLS a performance of *La Traviata* had to be abandoned after the first act because the smog was so thick inside the theatre. In one four-hour period the air-conditioning filters at the NATIONAL GALLERY clogged at 54 times their normal rate. The Great Smog precipitated an estimated 4,000 early deaths and resulted in the passage of the City of London (Various Powers) Act (1954) and the Clean Air Act (1956), which banned the emission of black smoke and accelerated the introduction of smokeless fuels.

> The advances in environmental legislation, as in
> smoke control technology, were more rapid in
> the postwar years, but all these changes paled

before those catalysed by 'The Great Smog' of 1952.

PETER BRIMBLECOMBE: *The Big Smoke: A History of Air Pollution in London Since Medieval Times* (1987)

Great Stink of London The turning point, in the summer of 1858, in the long gestation period of plans to improve sanitation in Victorian London. The authorities had known for many years that existing drainage arrangements were unable to cope with the quantity of effluent produced by the capital's rapidly growing population. However, they were deterred from taking action by the potential cost of constructing a sophisticated sewerage system and by the inability of rival engineers to agree on the form such a system should take. Matters reached a head in June 1858, when the hottest summer on record turned the THAMES into a turbid cesspool. The stench was so bad that sheets soaked with chloride of lime had to be hung in the windows of the PALACE OF WESTMINSTER and MPs vacated the parts of the building that overlooked the river. Parliament acted swiftly to grant the METROPOLITAN BOARD OF WORKS the power and money it needed to cleanse the city, and the engineer Joseph Bazalgette (1819–91) was appointed to oversee the project.

> The widespread belief that cholera, and other
> fatal diseases, were caused by foul smells also
> helps to account for the panic that afflicted the
> Houses of Parliament as the 'Great Stink' was
> borne in through the windows of the Palace of
> Westminster in the summer of 1858.

STEPHEN HALLIDAY: *The Great Stink of London* (1999)

Great Storm A media nickname for the ferocious winds that battered the south-east of England on the night of 15–16 October 1987. The onslaught caused considerable destruction, uprooting some 15 million trees and inflicting costly ecological damage. At KEW GARDENS the storm destroyed 500 trees and damaged 1,000 others, including some rare specimens. The death toll of 18 was relatively low but insurance losses to property amounted to some £800 million.

Great Thames Disaster *See the* PRINCESS ALICE.

Great Trees of London A scheme that aims to identify and publicize the capital's finest arboreal assets, such as the TREE OF HEAVEN in RAVENSCOURT PARK, the modern FAIRLOP OAK, the FRIDAY HILL PLANE and two trees in the grounds of CHARLTON HOUSE. It is managed by the charity Trees for Cities, an organization founded in 1993 as Trees for London. Members of the public are regularly invited to nominate additional trees for consideration by a panel of judges.

Great Wen An opprobrious nickname for London, viewed as a festering, crowded, over-populated excrescence injurious to the nation on which it feeds. The literal meaning of a 'wen' is a sebaceous cyst. The general metaphorical application of the word to a sprawling city dates from at least the 1780s, and was enthusiastically taken up by the polemical writer William Cobbett (1763–1835). It was he who established the particular application to London:

> But what is to be the fate of the great wen of
> all? The monster, called ... 'the metropolis of the
> empire'?
>
> WILLIAM COBBETT: *Rural Rides* (1830)

Great West Aerodrome The forerunner of HEATHROW AIRPORT, owned between the wars by the aircraft manufacturer Fairey. It became a bomber base late in the Second World War.

Great West Road A name, on the model of the GREAT NORTH ROAD, given to a main arterial road leading from London to the West Country, and in particular to the stretch of the A4 through BRENTFORD (*see the* GOLDEN MILE) to HOUNS-LOW. It opened in 1925 and was extended back to HAMMERSMITH around 1950. J.B. Priestley likened a drive along the Great West Road to a vista of California and in its early days the unprecedent-edly wide straight stretches of concrete proved irresistibly tempting to adventurous motorists, and it became more of a lethal speedway than a public highway:

> And now they had passed Gunnersbury, and
> had turned up to the right, and were ripping up
> the wide, smooth, deserted spaces of the Great
> West Road. ... Gee! – it was like a racing track –
> no wonder he put on speed. It was like being in
> an aeroplane!
>
> PATRICK HAMILTON: *The Siege of Pleasure* (1932)

Greater London The county that contains London. 'London' was originally just the CITY of London, encircled and circumscribed by its wall, but in the Middle Ages it was already outgrowing this straitjacket. By SHAKESPEARE's time the City had taken over the jurisdiction of SOUTHWARK, and its tentacles were advancing towards WEST-MINSTER. Elizabeth I issued a proclamation in 1580 vainly attempting to prevent the further

expansion of London. By slow accretion, sur-rounding villages and hamlets were swallowed up, and almost imperceptibly the scope of the name 'London' widened. The notion of an entity called 'Greater London' seems to have emerged in the 1880s, first with specific reference to the area covered by the London police (consisting of the METROPOLITAN POLICE and the City Police), and then somewhat more loosely applied to the area covered by the County of London (cre-ated 1888). For town planners considering the future scope and structure of London, the name 'Greater London' was an attractive option – and it was officially adopted in the 20th century for census and other purposes, and most signifi-cantly for the GREATER LONDON COUNCIL in 1965. *See also* INNER LONDON.

> Some name, then, for these city-regions,
> these town aggregates, is wanted ... What of
> 'Conurbations'? ... For our first conurbation the
> name of Greater London is ... dominant.
>
> PATRICK GEDDES: *Cities in Evolution* (1915)

Greater London Authority The eventual successor to the GREATER LONDON COUNCIL (*see below*), the Greater London Authority was established in 2000. CITY HALL became its head-quarters on its completion in 2002. The GLA consists of the MAYOR OF LONDON, who runs it, and the LONDON ASSEMBLY, which holds the mayor to account. The GLA does not, of itself, perform any function. Its powers are the mayor's powers, subject to the scrutiny of the London Assembly.

Greater London Council From 1965, the successor authority to the LONDON COUNTY COUNCIL with jurisdiction over 32 London bor-oughs:

BARKING AND DAGENHAM	HOUNSLOW
BARNET	ISLINGTON
BEXLEY	KENSINGTON AND
BRENT	CHELSEA
BROMLEY	KINGSTON UPON THAMES
CAMDEN	LAMBETH
CROYDON	LEWISHAM
EALING	MERTON
ENFIELD	NEWHAM
GREENWICH	REDBRIDGE
HACKNEY	RICHMOND UPON THAMES
HAMMERSMITH AND	SOUTHWARK
FULHAM	SUTTON
HARINGEY	TOWER HAMLETS
HARROW	WALTHAM FOREST
HAVERING	WANDSWORTH
HILLINGDON	WESTMINSTER

Kensington and Chelsea, and Kingston upon Thames are royal boroughs. The borough of Westminster is a city in its own right. In almost all respects, the CITY of London remained independent of the GLC. The new territorial entity swallowed up most of MIDDLESEX together with parts of Hertfordshire, ESSEX, Kent and Surrey. It did not, however, cover quite all of the 'Greater London conurbation' (for example, Epsom and Ewell were not included, and neither were Potters Bar and Watford). The GLC was abolished in 1986 and most of its powers were devolved to the boroughs, while the London Residuary Body disposed of the council's assets.

Greater London Plan *See the* ABERCROMBIE PLAN.

Greaze A one-minute game played every Shrove Tuesday at WESTMINSTER SCHOOL since 1753. The head cook tosses a large pancake over a high bar and selected pupils scramble to grab the largest part. The Dean of Westminster presents the winner with a gold sovereign, known as the Dean's Guinea. However, the pancake is inedible, for in modern times it is made from Polyfilla and horsehair.

Grecian Coffee House A COFFEE HOUSE in Devereux Court, STRAND, possibly named after one Constantine, a Greek who opened one in Essex Buildings in 1681; but the first written record (1709) of the Grecian dates from the reign of Anne. It is mentioned by Steele in *Tatler* and by Addison in *The Spectator*. There was also a Grecian Coffee House in King Street, COVENT GARDEN in 1673, and it was possibly older than that in Devereux Court, which closed in 1843.

Greek Street A street in SOHO, running roughly north–south between SOHO SQUARE and SHAFTESBURY AVENUE. It takes its name from the Greek Orthodox refugees from Turkish rule that gathered here in the late 17th century. The reputation of the street shot up when Josiah Wedgwood moved his pottery showroom here in 1774. Amongst its present-day delights are the restaurants the Gay Hussar (purveyor of Hungarian cuisine since 1953 and a favourite of Labour politicians) and L'Escargot, and it is also home to the Coach and Horses pub, where the inebriated *Spectator* columnist Jeffrey Bernard was a fixture in the latter part of the 20th century (*see* JEFFREY BERNARD IS UNWELL).

green

Green, Stanley *See the* PROTEIN MAN.

Green Badge The badge issued to BLACK CAB drivers who have passed the 'All London KNOWLEDGE' examination. Unlike holders of the YELLOW BADGE, Green Badge drivers are licensed to work anywhere in the GREATER LONDON area.

green belt A stretch of country around a large urban area that has been scheduled for comparative preservation and where building development is restricted. At the end of the Second World War the ABERCROMBIE PLAN proposed the encirclement of GREATER LONDON by a 'green girdle', as it was at first called, which would limit the conurbation's expansion and provide recreational space for the city's inhabitants. Major new housebuilding projects were instead located at arm's length from the capital, in NEW TOWNS. The scheme was largely successful and, for the most part, aided by the vigilance of conservationist campaigners, London's green belt has not since been violated.

Green, Berry and Hill Three servants of the consort of Charles II, Catherine of Braganza (1638–1705), whose residence was SOMERSET HOUSE. Robert Green, cushion-man of the queen's chapel; Lawrence Hill, servant to the treasurer of the chapel; and Henry Berry, porter at Somerset House, were in February 1679 found guilty of the murder of Sir Edmund Berry Godfrey, who had been found dead in a ditch near PRIMROSE HILL the previous October, five weeks after being warned by Titus Oates of the POPISH PLOT. His body and clothes had unexplained marks, he had been strangled and then thrust through with his own sword and, despite the muddy conditions, his shoes were clean. Londoners feared a Catholic conspiracy and Green, Berry and Hill were convicted and hanged on the flimsy evidence of informers. The place where the body was found was later called Barrow Hill but prior to the murder it had been known as Greenberry (or Greenbury) Hill.

> This has been noted as the strangest known coincidence; but it seems to me much more than that – a kind of macabre joke perpetrated by Prance [a tortured informer] as an implicit appeal to posterity. If he had to name someone for the Greenbury Hill murder, why not Green, Berry and Hill?

> HUGH ROSS WILLIAMSON: *Who Was the Man in the Iron Mask?: And Other Historical Mysteries* (2002)

Green Borough A contemporary urban slang term for the London Borough of GREENWICH. For the rationale, *see* BLUE BOROUGH.

Green Lanes One of London's longest stretches of road with a single name, and formerly the 'spinal cord' of Cypriot London, as the magazine *New Society* put it in 1981. This was part of an ancient route that led from London's SHOREDITCH through ENFIELD to Hertford, and may have been in use from the 2nd century AD. The road connected a series of greens, most of which have since been lost, even in name. Over the first half of the 20th century the HARRINGAY part of Green Lanes declined in social status and many houses were subdivided, making property affordable to Turkish immigrants who arrived from Cyprus from the late 1950s onwards. A snowball effect strengthened the community here and the eastern Mediterranean ambience of the shops and cafés later drew Greek Cypriots too. Despite the intercommunal tensions and occasional violence of their native island, the two communities lived here in harmony. Many Greek Cypriots have since moved further north, although some continue to operate or work in businesses here. The Turkish Cypriots have increasingly been joined by compatriots from mainland Turkey, and more recently by Kurds and Bulgarians. Other south-eastern European minorities represented on Green Lanes include Kosovans and Albanians.

Green Midget Café A fictional eatery in BROMLEY that was the setting for the Monty Python 'Spam' sketch (1970), in which that brand of tinned meat formed part (usually multiple parts) of every dish on the menu, and the word was repeated again and again, and sung by a Viking chorus. These Vikings were said by a contributing historian to have sailed from Trondheim and to have achieved a great victory at the Green Midget Café. The use of the word 'spam' to refer to junk email and other unsolicited online messages derives from this sketch.

Green Park The smallest of the central London royal parks, situated east of HYDE PARK CORNER, in the apex of PICCADILLY and CONSTITUTION HILL. Charles II enclosed the park with a brick wall in 1667, stocked it with deer and provided a ranger's house. The park was known at that time as Upper St James's Park but was commonly called Green Park by the mid-18th century. The grass was kept verdant by the TYBURN river, which ran below the surface. Green Park has always been plainer than its more illustrious ST JAMES'S neighbour, although temporary 'temples' were built to mark the end of the Austrian War of Succession and the first 100 years of the Hanoverian dynasty. When George III acquired Buckingham House (*see* BUCKINGHAM PALACE) the part of the park south of Constitution Hill was taken as the royal garden. It was further reduced in size by the construction of three mansions on the east side of Queen's Walk. Green Park was officially opened to the public in 1826. The Ranger's Lodge was demolished by 1855. Twentieth-century modifications included the planting of hedgerows and some further attrition of the park's borders through road widening.

green parrots A nickname for three purpose-built motor launches introduced by the Thames Police in the mid-1960s, from the distinctive colour of the vessels' fibreglass hulls. The last of the green parrots was retired from police service in 2003.

Green Ribbon A short-lived Whig club founded *c.*1675 as the King's Head Club, after the tavern in CHANCERY LANE where it met. The name was changed to the Green Ribbon Club about 1679 from the bow of green ribbon that its members wore in their hats. Changes in the political climate made membership increasingly risky and by 1688 the club had petered out.

Green Street A major shopping street and cultural centre for the community of UPTON PARK, occupying the borderland between EAST HAM and WEST HAM. Queens Market moved to its present location on Green Street in the 1960s and its traders now specialize in textiles, clothes and a range of exotic and everyday foods.

Green Street Elite The name of a FIRM of aggressive supporters of WEST HAM UNITED FC in the film *Green Street* (2005), which starred Elijah Wood (b.1981). It was released in the USA as *Hooligans* and later renamed *Green Street Hooligans*. The film was made at THREE MILLS STUDIOS, with location shooting in the vicinity. It was poorly received at home, especially for its questionable EAST END authenticity, but seemed to strike some sort of chord with international audiences.

Green Street Green A former village now located at the tip of suburban London, south of ORPINGTON. The village was part of the manor of CHELSFIELD and was first recorded in the 1290s as Grenestrete. The name may carry more meaning than its simple appearance suggests: 'street' often indicated an Anglo-Saxon hamlet that stood on a former Roman road and the greenness of the street could indicate that it had fallen into disuse and become overgrown. The village green that gave Green Street its present name was not recorded until the 18th century. Although it seems an unusual name, there is another Green Street Green not far away, in the borough of Dartford, Kent. 'Green Street Green' was a minor hit single for the New Vaudeville Band in 1967.

Greenford A relatively affordable residential area situated to the north-west of EALING. First recorded in 845, Greenford's name derives from a crossing of the River BRENT. The little farming hamlet had both a windmill and a watermill by the 17th century, and it is said that a survey carried out during the plague years found that Greenford was one of the three healthiest places in the country, with its inhabitants surviving much longer than the national average. The 1930s saw the peak period of housebuilding in Greenford, mostly small and medium-sized semi-detached houses.

Greenford Green The industrial part of Greenford, lying north of the station, now undergoing regeneration. The chemist William Perkin (1838–1907) established the world's first commercial dye plant here in 1857. J. Lyons & Co. (*see* LYONS' CORNER HOUSES) opened its factory at Greenford Green in 1921. TEA and coffee were processed and packed here, followed later by a range of grocery and confectionery lines. Ice cream was manufactured at the neighbouring Bridge Park factory from 1954. Lyons' parent company, Allied Domecq, closed the operation at Greenford Green in 2002.

greengages 'Wages' in COCKNEY RHYMING SLANG. The term is not widely used; nor is the alternative 'rock of ages'. 'Greengage' in the singular has been used in the theatrical world to mean 'the stage'.

Greenhill The north-central part of HARROW, and an important shopping area. The name was first recorded in 1334. With its convenient location between Harrow's first two stations, Greenhill grew rapidly from the 1880s, with shops

beginning to line Greenhill Lane, which was renamed Station Road. Sopers (now DEBENHAMS) became the borough's first department store in 1914, by which time Greenhill was part of a continuous ribbon of development stretching north to HEADSTONE and HARROW WEALD.

Greenland Dock The largest remaining dock in south London, situated east of SURREY QUAYS station. It was excavated in 1696 and originally named Howland Great Wet Dock after the family that owned the land. By the mid-18th century it had become a base for Arctic whalers and was renamed Greenland Dock. During the 19th century Greenland Dock handled trade in Scandinavian and Baltic timber and Canadian grain, cheese and bacon. The dock was enlarged in 1904 and closed in 1969, along with the rest of the SURREY DOCKS. The LONDON DOCKLANDS DEVELOPMENT CORPORATION commissioned a plan for mixed developments of squares and streets, which were built between 1984 and 1990. The smaller South Dock now serves as a marina.

Greenwich A world heritage site located on the south shore of the THAMES, opposite the ISLE OF DOGS. The name means 'green trading place or harbour' and it was first recorded in 964. It is likely that the Romans established some kind of settlement but little of the town's history is recorded until 1012, when the Danish fleet moored here and Archbishop Alphege was brutally murdered. Henry V's brother Humphrey, Duke of Gloucester, inherited land at Greenwich in 1427 and built himself a riverside house named Bella Court. After the duke's death Margaret of Anjou, wife of Henry VI, enlarged the house and renamed it Placentia, or 'pleasant place'. Henry VII made the new palace even grander and it became a favourite royal resort. Henry VIII was born here in 1491 and made further elaborate improvements to Placentia. Both his daughters, Mary I and Elizabeth I, were born at the palace and Elizabeth I spent much time there. James I presented the palace and GREENWICH PARK to his wife, Queen Anne, who commissioned Inigo JONES to design a neighbouring house. Anne died before the Queen's House was completed and, on its eventual completion in 1635, Charles I gave it to his queen, Henrietta Maria. The Queen's House became the core of the NATIONAL MARITIME MUSEUM in 1937. Greenwich is the permanent resting place for the world's last tea clipper, the CUTTY SARK.

Greenwich, London Borough of A London borough formed in 1965 by merging the former metropolitan boroughs of Greenwich and WOOLWICH (the part south of the THAMES). The new borough lay within the old LONDON COUNTY COUNCIL boundary, and thus by definition constituted an INNER LONDON borough at the time of its creation. However, it has since been reallocated to OUTER LONDON for official statistical purposes. The borough's coat of arms features 'an Hour Glass proper between two Estoiles Azure and in base three Cannon Barrels erect palewise proper'. The hour glass and stars recognize the achievements of GREENWICH OBSERVATORY, while the cannon barrels represent the WOOLWICH ARSENAL.

Greenwich barber An 18th- and 19th-century slang term applied to the people who obtained and sold sand from the Greenwich sandpits. The underlying metaphor is of the sellers 'shaving' the sand for their product.

Greenwich goose Slang from the 18th- and 19th-centuries for a pensioner of Greenwich Royal Naval Hospital.

Greenwich Hospital The Royal Hospital for Seamen was originally intended as a new palace for Charles II, to replace Placentia, which had suffered from being used as a biscuit factory and prisoner-of-war camp during the Commonwealth. However, by the time the building was nearing readiness, William and Mary were on the throne and they chose to live at HAMPTON COURT instead. The first pensioners arrived at the hospital in 1705. The hospital closed in 1869 and the Royal Naval College moved here from Portsmouth four years later. The college buildings are now divided between the University of Greenwich and Trinity College of Music. *See also the* PAINTED HALL.

Greenwich Mean Time or **Greenwich Time** The local time for the 0° meridian that passes through Greenwich. It is the standard time for Britain and a former basis for determining the time in most other countries of the world. In 1928 Greenwich Mean Time was officially redesignated Universal Time, which has since been refined as Coordinated Universal Time.

Greenwich Meridian The meridian passing through the GREENWICH OBSERVATORY, officially designated as 0°. In former times most countries treated their own capital as the point through which the zero degree of longitude passed, but at an international conference held in Washington DC in 1884 it was agreed that everyone would henceforth recognize Greenwich's as the prime meridian, from which degrees to East and West would be measured. The line is now marked at the observatory by a brass rail set into the ground.

Greenwich Millennium Village *See under* MILLENNIUM.

Greenwich Observatory Flamsteed House was built in 1676 on the highest ground in the park as the home of the Royal Observatory. The observatory's greatest achievement was to devise the conventions of the GREENWICH MERIDIAN and GREENWICH MEAN TIME. The Royal Observatory is now part of the NATIONAL MARITIME MUSEUM. A redevelopment project, completed in 2007, has added a new planetarium, astronomy and time galleries and an education centre.

Greenwich Park A royal park covering 183 undulating acres (74 hectares) of south-east Greenwich. Henry VI enclosed the park in 1433 and deer were introduced by Henry VIII, who was born at Greenwich. In the early 17th century James I had a wall built around the park and its gardens were laid out in the French style. Some of the trees planted at that time remain today and the formal layout remained virtually unchanged for 200 years. The Ranger's House, as it is now known, was built at the BLACKHEATH end of the park at the end of the 17th century and enlarged by the fourth Earl of Chesterfield, who acquired it as a retreat in 1748. The house has a gallery of Tudor portraits from the collection of the earls of Suffolk. Greenwich Park was fully opened to the public in 1830 but a biannual fair was abolished in 1857 because of rowdiness. The park will host equestrian events and the modern pentathlon during the 2012 OLYMPIC GAMES.

Greenwich Peninsula A tongue-shaped 285-acre (115-hectare) regeneration site jutting into the THAMES north-east of maritime Greenwich. Because it regularly flooded at high tide the peninsula remained desolate marshland until it was embanked and drained at the beginning of the 19th century. The newly reclaimed land was used first for grazing and then by industry, especially of the noxious kind, and from the 1880s, the East Greenwich gasworks filled the lion's share of the peninsula, with workers' housing and associated

amenities. The opening of the BLACKWALL TUN-
NEL in 1897 reduced the peninsula's isolation.
Industry declined after the Second World War
and a series of closures led to the demolition
of almost everything that had been built here.
Much of the peninsula lay derelict until the late
1990s, when the DOME, North Greenwich station
and the MILLENNIUM VILLAGE brought a revival.
The regeneration of the peninsula is a continuing
project, creating office complexes, hotels, leisure
facilities and thousands of new homes. *See also*
BUGSBY'S MARSH.

Greenwich Time Signal *See the* PIPS.

Greenwich Tunnel A pedestrian tunnel opened
at the beginning of the 20th century between
Greenwich and the ISLE OF DOGS, to replace a
former ferry.

Treaty of Greenwich *See under* TREATY.

Woolwich (and Greenwich) *See under* WOOL-
WICH.

Gregory (Peck) 'Neck' in COCKNEY RHYMING
SLANG, from the US actor (1916–2003). His name
is most often put to use in exhortations such as
'get that down your Gregory', with reference to
food or (especially) drink.

> Soon every *Minder* aficionado knew that 'getting
> a Ruby down your Gregory' meant going out for
> an Indian meal ...
>
> DICK FIDDY, in the *Encyclopedia of Television* (edited by
> HORACE NEWCOMB) (2004)

The term has also been used to mean 'cheque'
and, in plural form, 'specs' (spectacles).

Grenadier, The A public house located on
Wilton Row, BELGRAVIA. It was once the officers'
mess for the Grenadier Guards and is said to be
haunted by the ghost of an army officer who died
after he was flogged for cheating at cards.

Grendel's Gate The original identity, first
recorded *c.*975, of what is now Barnet Gate, a
western satellite of BARNET. Grendel was the
monster slain by Beowulf, the eponymous hero
of the Old English epic poem, and it has been
suggested that the use of such a portentous
name may indicate that this was a place of some
significance in Saxon times. The gate, however,
merely prevented cattle from straying onto
Barnet Common.

griffin (Old French *grifon*, from Latin *gryphus*,
from Greek *grups*, from *grupos*, 'hooked') A

mythical monster, also called griffon or gryphon,
fabled to be the offspring of the lion and the
eagle. Its legs and all its body from the shoulders
to the head are those of an eagle, while the
rest of its body is that of a lion. It symbolizes
courage, strength and swiftness. The griffin was
the emblem of the London Passenger Transport
Board and featured in the coat of arms of the
former borough of SOUTHALL because London
buses were manufactured there. VAUXHALL cars
and vans are badged with a griffin because it
was the heraldic device of Falkes de Bréauté,
whose hall gave its name to the London district
in which the company was founded. It is now
headquartered at Griffin House, Luton, Bedfordshire. The griffin is also the symbol of Fuller's,
the brewer of LONDON PRIDE and other beers.
The company is based at the Griffin Brewery in
CHISWICK. Its former ownership of the land on
which BRENTFORD FC's stadium was built led to
that ground being called Griffin Park. The griffins
supporting the arms of the London Borough of
RICHMOND UPON THAMES are derived from the
heraldry of the earls Spencer, lords of the manor
of MORTLAKE. *See also* DRAGON.

east of the griffin *See under* EAST.

Grim An old byname of Odin, the Scandinavian
god called Woden by the Anglo-Saxons, who was
popularly linked with the Devil.

Grim's Dyke or **Grimsdyke**

1. The remains of a long ditch and bank that can
still be seen in parts of HARROW WEALD, PINNER
and STANMORE. It dates from the 5th century or
earlier and may have been a defensive barrier or
a political or hunting boundary. Its name suggests that Anglo-Saxon settlers thought Woden
made it. There are other Grim's Dykes elsewhere
in the country.

2. An 'Olde English' style country residence
and its fine woodland gardens, situated in Old
Redding, HARROW WEALD. Built by Richard
Norman Shaw in 1872 and named after the
nearby earthwork, it was once the home of the
dramatist and librettist W.S. Gilbert (1836–1911).
It is now a hotel.

Grim, the Collyer of Croydone A comic play
performed before Elizabeth I in 1577. Charcoal
burning was once the dominant industry of
CROYDON; its workers were called colliers. The
character may have been identified with the

Devil because of his blackened clothes and features.

Grimaldi, Joseph *See the* CLOWNS' SERVICE.

grime A style of urban music that evolved in EAST LONDON at the beginning of the 21st century. The sound combines elements of American hip-hop, Jamaican dance hall and British garage and drum 'n' bass, driving along at around 130–140 beats per minute, which is very fast. Some of the leading early exponents of grime have already deserted the genre, leaving its future vigour uncertain. *See also* DUBSTEP.

> Grime emerged from the rave culture of the
> late nineteen-nineties, and will sound to
> most Americans like hip-hop ... with English
> accents and really fast raps ... The grime
> artist Americans know best is Dizzee Rascal,
> a twenty-year old from Bow, a working-class
> neighborhood in East London, where many
> grime artists live.
> *The New Yorker* (21 March 2005)

Grimmauld Place A fictional London street in the Harry POTTER stories by J.K. Rowling. No.12 is a magical house, home to the Black family of wizards and headquarters of the Order of the Phoenix. Other residents of the street are not aware of the existence of No.12, which faces the 'small and shabby' Grimmauld Square. Grimmauld Place is situated a 20-minute walk from KING'S CROSS STATION, probably somewhere in the boroughs of ISLINGTON or CAMDEN.

Grosvenor The family that developed BELGRAVIA and MAYFAIR. In 1677, at the age of 21, Sir Thomas Grosvenor of Eaton in Cheshire married the 12-year-old Mary Davies. In doing so he gained possession of EBURY Manor, which stretched from the THAMES at what is now PIMLICO to the western end of modern OXFORD STREET. Their son Richard laid out GROSVENOR SQUARE, and his grandson began the development of Belgravia a century later. The present-day Duke of Westminster is the heir to the Grosvenor estates.

Grosvenor House A 420-room luxury hotel on PARK LANE, at the corner of Upper Grosvenor Street. Its smaller predecessor of the same name (earlier Gloucester House) was built in 1730 and became home to successive members of the royal family and illustrious aristocrats, including the Grosvenors themselves for most of the 19th century. The National Trust was founded at a meeting in Grosvenor House in 1895. The house was demolished in 1927 and replaced by the present eight-storey building, which is perhaps best known for hosting a variety of prestigious events, including awards ceremonies in its cavernous banqueting hall and an annual art and antiques fair.

Grosvenor Square One of London's grandest squares, located in north-west MAYFAIR, formerly home to the cream of English society and now better known for its American associations. In July 1725 the *Daily Journal* reported that 'Sir Richard Grosvenor ... is now building a Square called Grosvenor Square, which for its largeness and beauty will by far exceed any yet made in and about London'. Its stately terraces and then private central garden made the development an immediate success. John Adams established the first American mission to the COURT OF ST JAMES'S here in 1765. Rebuilding in the late 18th and early 19th centuries served only to enhance the square's reputation. Subsequent reconstruction has been less elegant but equally prestigious and hotels and offices have been introduced in place of private residences. During the Second World War American military officials operated from several buildings in the area, notably 20 Grosvenor Square, which is still used by the US Navy. The US Embassy filled the western side of the square in 1960 and statues of presidents Franklin D. Roosevelt and Dwight D. Eisenhower are among several memorials erected to honour American leaders and war heroes. On 27 October 1968 the square was the scene of serious rioting, led by Tariq Ali, who brought 5,000 demonstrators from an anti-Vietnam-War rally in HYDE PARK in a breakaway group to the US Embassy. Opponents of the war continued to make their case there into the 1970s, and not inappropriately Grosvenor Squares became a rhyming slang name for that essential bit of 1970s gear, flared trousers ('flares'). Traffic can no longer circulate the square, following the cordoning-off of the west side (outside the embassy) after the New York terrorist attacks of 11 September 2001. It was the focal point of a two-minute silence in the week after that event, when hundreds of people filed into the square to sign a book of remembrance.

Groucho Club A SOHO club founded in 1985 for writers and publishers. Its membership progressively expanded to include those working generally in the arts and media. The name alludes to the celebrated remark by the comedian Groucho Marx (1890–1977) that he would never join any club that would have him as a member. The club is located at 45 Dean Street.

Group, the or **the London Group** A poets' forum that convened for weekly readings and discussions from 1955 to 1965. The Group was founded by Philip Hobsbaum (1932–2005), who had earlier organized similar meetings in Cambridge and later did the same in Belfast and Glasgow. They met first at Hobsbaum's basement flat in STOCKWELL and subsequently in CHELSEA under the chairmanship of Edward Lucie-Smith. Others associated with the Group included Peter Porter, Martin Bell, Peter Redgrove, George MacBeth and Fleur Adcock. Ted Hughes attended occasionally. Hobsbaum and Lucie-Smith edited the defining collection of members' work, *A Group Anthology*, in 1963.

grove

Grove Family, The *See* NEIGHBOURS TO THE NATION.

Grove Park (London Borough of HOUNSLOW) The south-western part of the CHISWICK peninsula, consisting of a popular residential quarter and the extensive sports grounds of DUKE'S MEADOWS. Soap-makers Dan and Charles Mason began to produce Cherry Blossom boot polish at their factory in Burlington Lane in 1906. Bernard Montgomery (1887–1976), later Field Marshal Viscount Montgomery of Alamein, lived on Bolton Road as a teenager.

Grove Park (London Borough of LEWISHAM) A mixed settlement of council and private housing, separated by the railway line from the DOWNHAM estate to the south-west. Edith Nesbit (1858–1924), author of *The Railway Children* and a founder member of the Fabian Society, lived in Grove Park from 1894 to 1899.

Grub Street The former name of a street in the MOORGATE area, now called MILTON STREET. It was originally tenanted by makers of bows, bows strings, arrows and everything archery-related. The street next became associated with small publishing houses and print shops, frequently churning out anonymous and scurrilous pamphlets, and by the late 17th century with hack writers and versifiers, to such a degree of notoriety that Grub Street's name became synonymous with poor standards of composition and accuracy. The expression 'Grub Street' is on record as having been used by writers of the time (including Andrew Marvell and Thomas Shadwell) as a metonym for impecunious penny-a-liners and (in the contemporary idiom) quill-drivers. Quite possibly it was these unflattering connotations that led the residents to insist on the change of name in 1829.

Grub Street hermit Henry Welby (*c*.1552–1636) of Gedney, Lincolnshire, who became a recluse in Grub Street at the age of 40, having resolved to live alone after suffering a pistol attack from his younger brother. He was never seen outside his house and died at the age of 84. He lived abstemiously and was attended by an elderly servant maid, spending his means on the sick and the poor. He had been a student at St John's College, Cambridge, and seems to have spent his time reading.

grumble (and grunt) 'Cunt' in COCKNEY RHYMING SLANG. The term is employed by a minority of men to characterize a sexually available woman or the act of coitus. It may date from around the time of the First World War.

> 'A bit of grumble and grunt,' I was told, 'only costs two francs.' Puzzled, I asked what that meant. 'Cor blimey, lad. Didn't you learn anything at all where you come from?' They thought me a proper mug. Fancy a lad like me, and a Cockney at that, not knowing what that meant …
>
> BERT CHANEY, quoted in MICHAEL MOYNIHAN: *People at War, 1914–18* (1973)

The alternative 'struggle and grunt' is sometimes heard. Although it may more authentically evoke copulation, a disadvantage is that its abbreviation could lead to confusion with 'struggle and strife', which can mean 'wife' (although 'TROUBLE (AND STRIFE)' is much more common). 'Grumble and grunt' is rarely used in the vituperative sense of its rhyming equivalent. If that purpose is intended, the names of certain celebrities are usually called upon, such as the motor racing driver James Hunt (1947–93) or more recently the singer/songwriter James Blunt (b.1974).

gryphon *See* GRIFFIN.

Guard Mounting *See* CHANGING (OF) THE GUARD.

Guildhall The CITY's town hall, situated on Gresham Street. According to legend, BRUTUS erected his palace on this spot and the Romans certainly built an amphitheatre here, significant remains of which may have survived long enough to prompt the choice of this site for the first Guildhall, probably in the early 12th century. The present Guildhall was built between 1411 and 1440; it is the City's only secular stone structure dating from before the GREAT FIRE OF LONDON. Its medieval Great Hall is the third largest civic hall in England and is the meeting place for the City's Court of Common Council.

Guildhall Art Gallery A public gallery established in 1885 to display the CORPORATION OF LONDON's collection of works of art. The original gallery was destroyed in the BLITZ; the present building opened in 1999, adjacent to the Guildhall. The building also houses the remains of the Roman amphitheatre, discovered here in 1987.

Guildhall Library The first library at the Guildhall was founded in the 1420s under the terms of the will of Richard WHITTINGTON. It is now a major public reference library, specializing in the history of London.

Guildhall School of Music & Drama Britain's first municipal music college and now one of Europe's leading conservatoires. The Guildhall School of Music opened in 1880, teaching 62 students in a disused warehouse. Full-time tuition began in 1920 and, following the addition of departments of speech, voice and acting, the school adopted its present name in 1935. It moved to its present site in the BARBICAN in 1977 and presently has more than 800 full-time music and drama students.

guilds *See* LIVERY COMPANIES.

Gunga Din An enduringly familiar fictional name from a single five-stanza poem. Gunga Din is the 'regimental bhisti' or loyal water-carrier in Kipling's poem named after him in *Barrack-Room Ballads* (1892). The COCKNEY verses tell how he is killed while tending a wounded English soldier.

Though I've belted you an' flayed you,

By the livin' Gawd that made you,

You're a better man than I am, Gunga Din!

RUDYARD KIPLING: 'Gunga Din' (1892)

Gunners The official nickname of ARSENAL FC, derived from its origins as a works team of the Royal Arsenal munitions manufactory at WOOLWICH, and from the presence of a cannon on the club crest.

Gunnersbury A locality in west CHISWICK and one of the few places in London to have been named after a woman: Gunnhildr, whose manor this was. There is no evidence for the suggestion that she was a niece of King Cnut but she may have had Danish blood. Gunnersbury station (originally Brentford Road) was rebuilt in 1966 with an 18-storey office block above, now occupied by the British Standards Institution (BSI). The Russian Orthodox Cathedral stands on Harvard Road, just south of the station. It was built in 1998 in the traditional 'Pskov' style, with an onion-shaped dome painted in blue with gold stars. Gunnersbury is the name of one of the principal characters in Patrick Neate's novel *The London Pigeon Wars* (2003).

Gunnersbury Mela *See* MELA.

Gunnersbury Park A large park focused on a pair of mansions to the north-west of CHISWICK. Gunnersbury House was a Palladian mansion built in the mid-17th century for Sir John Maynard, the king's principal SERJEANT-AT-LAW. Princess Amelia, daughter of George II, made the villa her summer residence from 1762 to 1786. The estate was sold in 1800 and the house was demolished and replaced by Gunnersbury Park and Gunnersbury House, later called the Large Mansion and the Small Mansion. Gunnersbury Park was acquired and then enlarged by the banker Nathan Mayer ROTHSCHILD in 1835, shortly before his death. His grandson Leopold de Rothschild bought the Small Mansion in 1889 and put it to use as a guest house for visitors to Gunnersbury Park, who included Edward VII. After Leopold's death in 1917 the estate was split up. Part was sold for building, while the local boroughs bought the mansions and 186 acres (75 hectares) of parkland. The Large Mansion is home to Gunnersbury Park Museum, which displays Ealing and Hounslow's local history collections. The Small Mansion is an arts centre.

Gunnersbury Triangle A 6-acre (2.5-hectare) nature reserve on Bollo Lane, situated between railway lines. It has birch and willow woodland with an attractive pond, marsh and meadow, but not much in the way of rare species.

Gunpowder Plot A plan to destroy James I and Parliament at the opening of the latter on 5 November 1605, as a prelude to a Roman Catholic rising. Barrels of powder were stored in a vault under the House of Lords and Guy FAWKES was to fire the train. Tresham, one of the plotters, warned his Catholic relative, Lord Monteagle, who revealed the plot to the authorities. The cellars were searched, and Guy Fawkes was captured. The ceremony of searching the vaults of Parliament prior to the annual opening takes place as a result of this plot.

Gutter Lane A small street running northwards from CHEAPSIDE; the site of Saddlers' Hall. The name was first recorded around 1185 as Godrun Lane, the lane of a woman called Guthrún, which had become corrupted to its present form by the 15th century. The lane was an early place of residence for the City's goldbeaters. 'Gutter Lane' was formerly a slang term for the throat, a pun on Latin *guttur*, 'throat', as in 'guttural'. The ancient saying 'anything goes (or 'all goeth') down Gutter Lane' was applied to drunks and gluttons.

Guy's Hospital A teaching hospital located at Great Maze Pond, SOUTHWARK, founded in 1721 by Thomas Guy (*c.*1645-1724), MP, bible publisher and retailer, stock speculator and governor of ST THOMAS' HOSPITAL. He amassed an immense fortune in 1720 by speculations in South Sea Stock and gave £238,295 to found and endow the hospital. As Guy's expanded from its original 60 beds for incurables into a major hospital, it retained close links with St Thomas', particularly through the joint medical school that the hospitals shared. The schools separated in 1825 and were reunited as the United Medical and Dental Schools in 1982. In July 2004 Guy's and St Thomas' combined to form one of the UK's first NHS foundation trusts.

Gwyn, **Gwynn** or **Gwynne, Nell** A popular actress and mistress of Charles II, Nell (Eleanor) Gwyn (1651–87) first became known when selling oranges at the THEATRE ROYAL, DRURY LANE. In 1665 she appeared as Cydaria in Dryden's *The Indian Emperour*. An illiterate child of the back streets, she was winsome, sprightly and good company. 'Pretty, witty Nell's' first protector was Lord Buckhurst, but the transfer of her affections to Charles II was genuine – and enthusiastically reciprocated:

> I'll wholly abandon all public affairs,
> And pass all my time with buffoons and with players,
> And saunter to Nelly when I should be at prayers.
>
> ANON, possibly ANDREW MARVELL: 'The King's Vows' (1670)

Her cheerful humour was the stuff of legend; when a mob attacked her coach, under the mistaken impression that its occupant was Louise de Kérouaille, the king's French, Roman Catholic mistress, she is said to have flung open the window and declared insouciantly: 'Pray, good people, be civil, I am the *Protestant* whore!' She had two sons by the king, the elder becoming Duke of St Albans, and the younger, James, Lord Beauclerk. She finally left the stage in 1682, and on his deathbed Charles, according to Gilbert Burnet, said to his brother James: 'Let not poor Nelly starve.' James II fulfilled the request. She was buried in ST MARTIN-IN-THE-FIELDS and the funeral sermon was given by Thomas Tenison, later archbishop of Canterbury.

H

hack The word is short for HACKNEY[2], a horse let out for hire, and hence came to apply to a person whose services are for hire, especially a literary drudge or mediocre journalist. Oliver Goldsmith, who well knew from experience what such a life was, wrote this epitaph on Edward Purdon:

> Here lies poor Ned Purdon, from misery freed,
> Who long was a bookseller's hack:
> He led such a damnable life in this world,
> I don't think he'll wish to come back.

'Epitaph on Edward Purdon' (1774)

See also GRUB STREET.

Hackbridge An area of declining industry and increasing housing, situated beside the River WANDLE in north BEDDINGTON. The name was first recorded around 1235 and probably derives from the Old English words *haca brycg*, meaning 'the bridge at the hook-shaped piece of land'. As was the case along most of the Wandle, mills flourished from the Middle Ages, latterly specializing in tanning and the manufacture of parchment. The Quaker banker and philanthropist Samuel Gurney built (or rebuilt) a house called Culvers and bred black swans on the river until his death in 1856. The crash of his bank ten years later led to the piecemeal sale of the estate. Industry began to appear around 1910; the Mullard radio works was established in the late 1920s. BEDZED eco-village was completed in 2001 on part of the site of Beddington sewage works. Less innovative new housing has been filling other brownfield sites in the area.

Hackney[1] A multicultural, multiracial, multilingual and multi-social district, situated 3 miles (5 km) north-east of ST PAUL'S. Hackney probably takes its name from Haca, a Danish nobleman, and *ey*, an island, for the River LEA and its tributaries once dissected the area. The village had a church by 1275, when wealthy Londoners were already beginning to build country retreats here.

In the 16th and 17th centuries the large, rambling houses of Hackney's aristocrats became a distinctive feature of the landscape. Samuel PEPYS paid several visits to Hackney:

> With my wife only to take ayre, it being very warm and pleasant, to Bowe and Old Ford; and thence to Hackney. There light and played at shuffle board, eat cream and good cherries; and so with good refreshment home.

diary (11 June 1664)

By the 18th century Hackney's wealth, which remained remarkable, no longer derived from the presence of noblemen but from merchants, including Huguenots and Jews. Church Street (now the northern part of Mare Street) was lined with shops and houses by the 1720s, which spread outwards over the next century, while the formerly separate hamlet of Mare Street expanded to meet it. The quality of building declined after the arrival of the railway in the 1850s, and by the end of the 19th century Hackney was looking increasingly like part of the EAST END. Early in the following century the LONDON COUNTY COUNCIL built flats in LONDON FIELDS and on Mare Street, initiating a process that would change the face of Hackney over the following decades. More recently, private building has increased and pockets of Hackney have become gentrified where Victorian streets have survived. Afro-Caribbeans began to replace Jews as the predominant minority from the 1960s and were later joined by immigrants from Africa, south Asia and the eastern Mediterranean.

Hackney, London Borough of An INNER LONDON borough, created in 1965 from the former metropolitan boroughs of Hackney, STOKE NEWINGTON and SHOREDITCH. Hackney does not have a civic motto and did not get around to creating a new coat of arms until four years after the borough had been enlarged. The central feature is a Maltese cross – a reference to the

KNIGHTS TEMPLAR – while two oak trees represent Stoke Newington and three bells symbolize St Leonard's Church, Shoreditch.

Hackney Downs Formerly common land, now a park and playing fields with neighbouring social housing bordering SHACKLEWELL and Lower CLAPTON. From the 1930s, municipal and philanthropic schemes erased many of the early streets. The largest project was the Greater London Council's Nightingale estate, completed in 1972, with tower blocks of up to 21 storeys. Most of that estate has been rebuilt on a more human scale since the mid-1990s. The playwrights Harold Pinter and Steven Berkoff both went to Hackney Downs School, though neither of them much enjoyed the experience. *See also* NAVVIES' ISLAND.

Hackney Empire A theatre (formerly a MUSIC HALL) on Mare Street in Hackney, built to the design of Frank Matcham and opened in 1901. It was extensively refurbished at the beginning of the 21st century.

> No more the Hackney Empire
> Shall find us in its stalls
> When on the limelit crooner
> The thankful curtain falls,
> And soft electric lamplight
> Reveals the gilded walls.
>
> JOHN BETJEMAN: 'The Cockney Amorist' (*c*.1954)

Hackney Marsh The largest recreation ground in London and the second largest common after HAMPSTEAD HEATH, situated on the banks of the River LEA, east of CLAPTON. Hackney Marsh (frequently called Hackney Marshes) covers 336 fairly featureless acres (136 hectares) and has cricket, hockey and rugby pitches and a wildlife and conservation area. Kite-flying is popular but the marsh is best known for its FOOTBALL pitches, and especially for the scores of Sunday league games played here. Dubbed 'the spiritual home of parks football', Hackney Marsh is said to have the largest concentration of football pitches in Europe, although their number has been reduced in recent years. In a 1997 television commercial for Nike, since voted one of the 20 best-ever adverts by viewers, Sunday league footballers on Hackney Marsh were joined by professionals Eric Cantona, Ian Wright, Robbie Fowler and David Seaman.

> Wiv a ladder and some glasses
> You could see to 'Ackney Marshes,
> If it wasn't for the 'ouses in between.
>
> EDGAR BATEMAN and GEORGE LE BRUNN: 'If it Wasn't for the 'Ouses in Between' (song) (1894)

Hackney Wick A run-down industrial area, now divided from the rest of HACKNEY by the East Cross Route (A12). A 'wick' often signified an outlying dairy farm and the 'ferm of Wyk' was recorded in the 13th century. Mid-19th-century industrial growth contributed to social decline in Hackney Wick, which was described in 1879 as a district of 6,000 people who had sunk to the lowest depths, and it became notorious for its jerry-built housing. The parish church of St Mary of Eton with St Augustine was founded in 1880 by Eton College, which wanted to perform charitable work in a poor part of London.

Hackney (Wick) 'Prick' (penis) in COCKNEY RHYMING SLANG. Ray Puxley, in *Britslang* (2002), comments: 'Given Hackney's location in East London, it's a puzzle as to why this is of secondary usage to the widely used "Hampton Wick".' However, Hackney's very familiarity may explain this, since the place name has many other associations, from carriages to clichés. 'Hampton', by contrast, means only one thing to most cockneys.

hackney² Originally (14th century) the name given to a class of medium-sized horses, distinguishing them from warhorses. They were used for riding, and later the name was applied to a horse let out for hire, hence hackney carriage. It was long believed that the word derived from Old French *haquenée*, 'a trotting horse' or, by some definitions, 'an ambling nag'. However, it now seems that so famed was Hackney as a provider of pasture for horses that the French borrowed the word from the English place sometime after the Norman Conquest. A hackney cab is an official term for a taxi. *See also* HACK.

hackneyed expression, a One that is well worn or over used. The allusion is to a weak, hired horse, as originally raised at HACKNEY.

Hadley A loosely scattered picturesque village, also known as Monken Hadley, situated to the north-east of BARNET. The name was first recorded as Hadlegh in 1248 and was formerly thought to mean 'a high place' but is probably derived from the Old English forms of 'heath' and 'lea'. The missionary and African explorer Dr David Livingstone stayed at what is now Livingstone Cottage in 1857–8. Comedian Spike Milligan lived for many years at Monkenhurst, which was built in 1881 on the Crescent and which he saved from demolition. Father and son authors Kingsley and Martin Amis lived at Lemmons, formerly Gladsmuir House, and poet laureate Cecil Day Lewis died there during a visit in 1972.

Hadley Highstone In 1741 Sir Jeremy Sambrook erected an obelisk to the north of Hadley's village green, supposedly at the site where the Earl of Warwick had fallen in the BATTLE OF BARNET, and cottages and inns formed a group here that became known as Hadley Highstone. The monument was relocated a century later, but there is no evidence of the authenticity of either its original or present position.

Hadley Wood A settlement separated by Monken Hadley Common from Hadley itself, which lies to the south-west. In 1885 local farmer Charles Jack subsidized the construction of a station on the Great Northern Railway and began to build substantial houses around it, although only a few had been completed by the time of his death eleven years later. The new estate was to have been called Beech Hill Park, but when the station was opened as Hadley Wood the shorter name stuck. Hadley Wood now has nearly a thousand homes, many of which are highly valued, especially the grander properties on the south side, which are popular with minor celebrities and footballers. Marguerite Radclyffe-Hall, author of the taboo-breaking lesbian novel *The Well of Loneliness* (1928), moved to 67 Camlet Way in 1918 with her lover Una, Lady Trowbridge. The couple quit the 'modern, pretentious and very ugly house' after two years, tired of the suburban monotony and the distance from London.

Hainault A 20th-century urban creation situated in the north-east corner of the London Borough of REDBRIDGE, 3 miles (5 km) east of WOODFORD. The name comes from Old English *higne holt*, meaning 'a wood belonging to a monastic community', in this case the Abbey of BARKING. Hainault Forest once covered a swathe of the countryside hereabouts but was savagely cleared in 1851, with 2,000 acres (800 hectares) of oaks felled in six weeks. Hainault served as an airfield during the First World War but reverted to farmland thereafter. In the 1930s the LONDON COUNTY COUNCIL laid out extensive municipal housing to the north of the existing settlement. To the east are Hainault industrial estate, the

Redbridge Cycling Centre and what remains of Hainault Forest, which is now a country park with woodland, meadows, plains and a public golf course.

Hainault loop A branch of the CENTRAL LINE. It diverges at LEYTONSTONE, runs through Hainault and rejoins the main line at WOODFORD.

half

half-inch 'Pinch', meaning to steal, in COCKNEY RHYMING SLANG. The term is widely used, unabbreviated.

> I'd have to repay 'em if it got half-inched right out of my yard. I'll have to tell the foreman. He's getting forgetful these days.
>
> TERRY PRATCHETT: *The Truth* (2000)

Half Moon Street A short street branching northward from PICCADILLY into MAYFAIR. Half Moon Street was the home of Bertie WOOSTER, and gave its name to a book by Paul Theroux (1984), which contained the short story 'Doctor Slaughter', on which the 1986 film *Half Moon Street* was based, starring Michael Caine and Sigourney Weaver. *Half Moon Street* is also the title of a detective novel (2000) by Anne Perry, which is set in Victorian London.

halfpenny *See* 'APENNY.

hallmark The official mark stamped on gold, silver and platinum articles after they have been assayed, so called because the assaying or testing and stamping was done at the Goldsmiths' Hall. Since 1999 the compulsory elements have been a sponsor's (or maker's) mark, usually in the form of initials enclosed within a shield outline; a millesimal fineness (or purity) mark, indicating the number of parts per thousand of pure metal in the alloy; and an assay office mark, which in London is a leopard's head. Also known as the King's mark, the leopard's head is supposedly taken from the arms of Edward I, who in 1300 enacted the first law defining metallic standards. The normal UK hallmark provided by Assay Office London includes a traditional fineness mark and date letter in addition to the compulsory marks.

Ham An extended village situated to the west of RICHMOND PARK, across the THAMES from TWICKENHAM. The name was first recorded around 1150 and derives from Old English *hamm*, which here meant 'land in a river bend'. Henry V acquired the manor of Hamme Upkyngeston in

1415, bringing the village into a closer relationship with the royal estate at RICHMOND UPON THAMES. Ham House was built in 1610 for Sir Thomas Vavasour, knight marshal to James I. It was the meeting place of the original 'Cabal', Charles II's leading advisers between 1667 and 1673. Sports grounds and playing fields now surround the house, which belongs to the National Trust. Other large houses appeared in the 18th century, and many of these survive today. The character of the village changed radically from the late 1950s as a result of both municipal and private projects. Some of the smaller schemes were imaginative, especially those designed by Eric Lyons (1912–1980).

Ham and High The colloquial name in north London for the *Hampstead and Highgate Express*, which was founded at HAMPSTEAD in 1860. It is one of the capital's best regarded local newspapers.

Ham Common An area of open common land in the south-eastern part of HAM, contiguous with RICHMOND PARK to the east.

Hamlet of Stepney Green, The A play

(1958) by Bernard Kops (b.1926), an EAST ENDER of Dutch-Jewish parentage. An optimistic reworking of SHAKESPEARE's *Hamlet*, the play was first staged at the Theatre Royal, STRATFORD East.

Hamleys A REGENT STREET toy store, variously claimed to be the world's oldest, largest and best known. Cornishman William Hamley opened Noah's Ark, a toy shop on High HOLBORN, in 1760. The venture flourished and descended through several generations of the Hamley family, with a flagship store opening on Regent Street in 1881. The company went into liquidation in 1931 and was rescued by its largest individual creditor, Lines Brothers, which closed all the subsidiary branches. In 1981 Hamleys moved to its present location at 188-196 Regent Street, where merchandise is displayed on seven floors. The group nowadays has outlets at ST PANCRAS STATION and HEATHROW AIRPORT, within regional department stores and airports, and overseas.

Hammer A nickname given by the *Scottish Daily Express* to Sir David McNee (b.1925), Commissioner of the METROPOLITAN POLICE from 1977 to 1982, for his tough approach to law and order when a senior detective in Glasgow. The name

alludes to the historical 'Hammer of the Scots', otherwise Edward I of England (1272–1307).

Hammer Films In financial terms one of the most successful companies in the history of the British cinema. A successor to the failed Hammer Productions, Hammer Films was founded in WARDOUR STREET in 1947 by Will Hammer (real name William Hinds) and Sir James Carreras, who began churning out 'quota quickies' at MARYLEBONE Studios. The company first won fame in 1956 when it launched a cycle of low-budget horror movies that quickly captured wide markets in Britain and the United States. It emphasized blood and gore in vivid colour, and revived such figures from the US cinema as Frankenstein and Dracula. It then expanded into other genres such as science fiction, psychological thrillers and costume dramas. In 1980 it produced an anthology of spine-chilling 'shockers' for television under the title Hammer House of Horror. The name is a byword for any 'grim' situation, literal or metaphorical.

Hammers The official nickname of WEST HAM UNITED FC, derived from the pair of shipbuilder's hammers on its badge, a reference to the club's original incarnation as Thames Ironworks FC.

Hammersmith A strategically significant commercial and cultural centre located on the north bank of the THAMES 1½ miles (2.5 km) west of KENSINGTON. The name was first recorded in 1294 and probably refers to the presence of a hammer smithy or forge. A foreshore of gravel, rather than the more common marsh, made Hammersmith a healthy retreat for jaded Londoners from the Middle Ages onwards. Catherine of Braganza, queen consort of Charles II, came to live on Upper Mall in 1687 after she was widowed, and several fine villas were later built by the river here. Much of Hammersmith's architectural heritage was lost in the middle decades of the 20th century as the district became increasingly urbanized, but some important examples have survived. Hammersmith has three noteworthy entertainment venues: the Apollo, a former cinema that now hosts major rock gigs; the Riverside Studios, which comprises studio theatres, a cinema and an art gallery; and the Lyric, a 19th-century auditorium and a studio theatre encased in concrete. *See also* KELMSCOTT.

Hammersmith and City line A component

of the LONDON UNDERGROUND system, coloured pink on the map. It runs between Hammersmith in the west and BARKING in the east, via MOORGATE and LIVERPOOL STREET (an early south-westward extension to RICHMOND was closed in 1906). It began operation in 1863. It was always represented (on maps of the system, for instance) as being part of the METROPOLITAN LINE, but although to the east of BAKER STREET it runs mainly on Metropolitan (and DISTRICT LINE) tracks it has always been essentially a separate operation, and this was recognized in 1990 with its official designation as 'Hammersmith and City'.

Hammersmith and Fulham, London Borough of An OUTER LONDON borough created in 1965 from the two metropolitan boroughs of those names. Until 1979 it was called the London Borough of Hammersmith. The central feature of the borough's cluttered coat of arms is a pair of hammers interlaced with a horseshoe – a reference to Hammersmith's name. Fulham is accorded episcopal references and a ship representing the Danish landing here in 879. The civic motto is *spectemur agendo*, which means 'let us be judged by our deeds'.

Hammersmith Bridge A suspension bridge crossing the THAMES between Hammersmith and BARNES. It is a notable way-point on the annual Oxford and Cambridge BOAT RACE. Designed by Sir Joseph Bazalgette, it was built in 1887. It replaced an earlier suspension bridge, the first (1827) to be built in London.

Hammersmith Broadway One of London's busiest traffic junctions, flanked by several prestigious office blocks, a bus and tube interchange and a shopping mall.

Hammersmith flyover An overpass carrying the GREAT WEST ROAD above HAMMERSMITH BROADWAY. Dubbed 'the gateway to west London', it was built in 1961. It is overlooked by the landmark office building, the ARK(2).

Hammersmith nude murders See JACK THE STRIPPER.

Hammersmith Palais A colloquial name for the 'Palais de Danse', a dance hall in the Shepherd's Bush Road that opened in 1919. It was the first venue in Britain to present jazz, and caused something of a scandal when it allowed those who arrived unaccompanied to hire a dance partner for sixpence. The palais helped create a fashion for mass dancing to big bands, which

reached a peak in the Second World War and survived into the rock 'n' roll era, later becoming a significant venue for reggae, PUNK ROCK and Brit-Asian music. It was immortalized in The CLASH song '(White Man) In Hammersmith Palais' in 1978. The palais closed its doors for the final time in 2007.

Hammersmith Socialist Choir See KELMSCOTT HOUSE.

Hampden clubs A series of clubs centred on the Hampden Club, set up in 1812 at the Thatched House Tavern, ST JAMES'S STREET, by the veteran agitator Major Cartwright (1740–1824). The aim was to agitate for reform of Parliament and the extension of the franchise to all payers of direct taxes, although some years later the clubs became more democratic, extending membership to all willing to pay a subscription of a penny a week. Each club was technically a separate organization in order to evade the existing law that forbade societies with affiliated branches. The name is derived from the parliamentarian John Hampden (1594–1643).

Hampstead A stratospherically expensive hillside and heathside settlement, situated 3 miles (5 km) due north of PADDINGTON. The name Hemstede was first recorded in 959 and simply means 'homestead'. The letter 'p' did not intrude until the mid-13th century. Hampstead began to develop as a fashionable spa in the 1790s, drawing both visitors and wealthy residents to the south-west edge of HAMPSTEAD HEATH. Fenton House, on Windmill Hill, is the oldest surviving example of a merchant's house from this period and is now the property of the National Trust. The spa became a place of debauchery, lewdness and drunken revelry and was closed. The same thing happened again when an attempt was made to revive it. However, these events did not prevent Hampstead's rapid growth 'from a little country village to a city', as Daniel Defoe put it in 1724. From the 1860s Hampstead underwent its most rapid phase of growth as luxurious detached houses were built on newly created streets. In the middle decades of the 20th century Hampstead became known for its free-thinking elite (*see the* HAMPSTEAD SET) but corporate executives have since almost entirely supplanted liberal intellectuals.

The poet John Keats lodged in the eastern half of what is now the Keats House Museum in

1818–19. The Admiral's House on Admirals Walk is said to have inspired the one in Mary POPPINS and was the home of George Gilbert Scott, architect of ST PANCRAS STATION. TATE BRITAIN has Constable's painting of the house. The novelist John Galsworthy lived next door.

Hampstead Bottom *See* GOSPEL OAK.

Hampstead donkeys Nineteenth-century slang for body lice.

Hampstead Garden Suburb The most architecturally successful of London's planned suburbs, situated to the north-west of HAMPSTEAD HEATH. Faced with the impending arrival of the underground railway at GOLDERS GREEN, Dame Henrietta Barnett set up the Hampstead Garden Suburb Trust in 1906 and with the support of her influential contacts and the LONDON COUNTY COUNCIL acquired the freehold on 243 acres (98 hectares) of Eton College's land at Wylde's Farm. The suburb was planned and built in several phases, beginning with an 'artisans' quarter' extending to the east side of the Finchley Road at Temple Fortune. A central square was laid out at the suburb's highest point, with churches and communal buildings. Nearer the extension to Hampstead Heath (which Dame Henrietta had earlier successfully campaigned to create) grander houses were built to help generate revenue for the whole scheme. The trust acquired additional parcels of land before the First World War and these were mostly developed after the war by co-partners, who built commercially but had to follow strict guidelines. Raymond Unwin (1863–1940) became the suburb's principal architect after the dismissal of the Italianate-inclined Edwin Lutyens, but many other practices played a part and all worked to the same harmonious ends. A vernacular Arts and Crafts style permeated the earlier phases, giving way to neo-Georgian when profit became the primary motivation.

The artist William Ratcliffe (1870–1955), a fringe member of the CAMDEN TOWN GROUP, lived here and his painting of the suburb hangs at TATE BRITAIN.

Hampstead Heath North London's finest open space, situated on high ground north-east of the settlement of Hampstead. It was first recorded as 'a certain heath' in 1312 and as Hampstead Heath in 1543. The moorland landscape and varied habitat of the heath were created by a sandy ridge overlying a belt of clay, which formed springs and consequent muddy hollows, especially where sand and gravel had been extracted. A policy of 'judicious neglect' of most of these diggings has helped create the picturesque terrain of the modern era. From the 18th century the heath became a popular place for Londoners to take a walk in the fresh country air. In the latter part of the 19th century the railway brought day-trippers and revellers by the thousands – sometimes tens of thousands on bank holidays. By an Act of 1871 the heath was preserved forever and sand and gravel extraction was prohibited. Subsequent additions of farmland and parkland have quadrupled the heath's size, with part of the grounds of KENWOOD forming the most recent extension in the 1920s. Hampstead Heath's larger ponds were originally created as reservoirs (*see* HIGHGATE PONDS).

The heath's joys as a place of perambulation for the working classes were captured in Albert Chevalier's MUSIC HALL song "'Appy 'Ampstead" in the 1890s. Hampstead Heath has also been immortalized as COCKNEY RHYMING SLANG for 'teeth' – usually in the shortened form Hampsteads, occasionally in the even further abbreviated hamps.

> Foxes are out on the Heath;
> They sniff the air like knives.
> A hawk turns slowly over Highgate, waiting.
> This is the hidden life of London. Wild.
>
> AL ALVAREZ: 'Mourning and Melancholia' (1968)

Hampstead Heath Lido *See* PARLIAMENT HILL LIDO.

Hampstead Heath sailor A jocular term for a landlubber or a very poor sailor – i.e. someone who is sick before the ship leaves port. The 'joke' is that, apart from a few bathing pools, the heath is dry land.

Hampstead Ponds *See* HIGHGATE PONDS.

Hampstead Set A term originally applied in the 1950s to a group of supporters of Hugh Gaitskell (1906–63), leader of the Labour Party (1955–63). The group, opposed by Aneurin Bevan and his followers, lived, like Gaitskell, in Hampstead. It included Anthony Crosland, Denis Healey, Douglas Jay, Roy Jenkins and Frank Pakenham (Lord Longford). Subsequently, journalists used the term more generally and collectively for liberal and/or left-leaning intellectuals living in and around Hampstead, such as the playwright Harold Pinter (1930–2008) and his wife the historical biographer Antonia Fraser (b.1932), who had been involved in political causes, such as Charter 88, and who were deemed a subset of the chattering classes.

Hampton A settlement by a bend in the river (which is what its name means) in the south-west corner of the London Borough of RICHMOND UPON THAMES. The name is used both for the Thames-side locality west of BUSHY PARK and for the broader district. The 1852 Metropolitan Water Act prohibited the London water companies from taking water from below the tidal reach of the river and the consequent building of a waterworks here was to change Hampton radically. Pumping stations, reservoirs, filter beds and associated buildings were constructed along the river, altering the appearance of the area and employing a large number of people in addition to the labour needed to build the works. The levels of GARRICK'S AIT and PLATT'S EYOT were raised by the depositing on them of soil excavated during the construction of further filter beds in the last years of the 19th century. The pump houses of the riverside waterworks are no longer in use but are listed buildings.

Hampton Court A residential district on the southwestern edge of London, on the River THAMES, partly in the London Borough of RICH-MOND UPON THAMES (which contains the palace and its grounds) and partly in Surrey. It is dominated by its royal palace; the transfer of its name to the area was consolidated by the opening of Hampton Court railway station in 1849. The French Impressionist Alfred Sisley (1839–99) was the greatest artist to have worked prolifically in the Hampton Court area. In a series of works painted in 1874, Sisley depicted the riverside, a regatta, the bridge across the Thames (from the side and below) and *The Road from Hampton Court*.

Hampton Court Conference A conference held in January 1604 at HAMPTON COURT PALACE by James I and the High Church party with some of the Puritans in the Church of England. The High Church bishops would make no concessions of importance and their most valuable decision was to sanction a new translation of the Bible, which would become the Authorized Version of 1611.

Hampton Court Palace A royal palace and gardens, set in a loop of the Thames, south of BUSHY PARK and TEDDINGTON. By 1066 Hampton manor existed as an important agricultural estate with royal connections. The KNIGHTS HOSPITALLER acquired it in 1236 and in 1338 the manor buildings consisted of a chamber block, hall, garden and church. It was leased to Sir Giles Daubeney in 1494. He built a kitchen next to the hall, which survives as the Great Kitchen, and a courtyard and gatehouse. Cardinal Wolsey took the lease from 1514 and extended the existing buildings with a second courtyard of lodgings, Base Court and the Great Gatehouse. He also added a gallery for viewing the garden, constructed a grand chapel and introduced lavish suites for the king and queen. Henry VIII regularly used Hampton Court and by 1528 had made it his own. He commissioned a series of improvements, including new apartments for himself (Bayne Tower) and his queen, bowling alleys, tennis courts, a hunting park and gardens. The buildings changed little until the reign of William III and Mary II (from 1689), who commissioned Sir Christopher Wren to remodel the palace. New apartments were built, overlooking a new privy garden, and the maze was planted. The full court was at Hampton Palace for the last time in 1737. The palace was opened to the public in 1838 and went through a period of restoration. In 1986 a fire destroyed some of the king's apartments; repairing the damage took six years. Hampton Court gardens attract over one million visitors a year and a flower show is held every July.

It was at Hampton Court that the theft of a lock of Belinda's hair took place, which forms the centrepiece of Alexander Pope's *The Rape of the Lock* (1712):

Close by those meads, for ever crown'd with flow'rs,
Where Thames with pride surveys his rising tow'rs,
There stands a structure of majestic frame,
Which from the neighb'ring Hampton takes its name.
Here Britain's statesmen oft the fall foredoom
Of foreign tyrants, and of nymphs at home;
Here thou, Great ANNA! whom three realms obey,
Dost sometimes counsel take – and sometimes Tea ...
For ever curs'd be this detested day,
Which snatched my best, my fav'rite curl away!

Happy! ah ten times happy had I been,
If Hampton-Court these eyes had never seen!

Hampton Court Park The southern part of the palace grounds, also known as the Home Park. The northern part is BUSHY PARK. Hampton Court Park is dominated by the Long Water, an ornamental canal flanked by lime trees imported from Holland by William III. It was in this park that the unfortunate William suffered the fall that resulted in his death, when his horse stumbled on a molehill (*see the* LITTLE GENTLEMAN IN VELVET).

Hampton Hill The popular north-eastern corner of Hampton, bordering TEDDINGTON and FULWELL, with terraces of thriving specialist shops and restaurants. There is no detectable hill here; merely slightly higher ground that may once have lain above the THAMES flood plain. Hampton Hill was the birthplace in 1947 of the astrophysicist and Queen guitarist Brian May. He was educated at Hampton School.

Hampton Wick An annexe of TEDDINGTON, separated from the rest of Hampton by BUSHY PARK. Among the many meanings of the word, a 'wick' could signify a harbour or trading place, and this landing point beside the THAMES is likely to have been used to supply provisions for the original manor house of Hampton, which evolved into Hampton Court Palace. The construction of the wooden KINGSTON Bridge in 1219 added to the significance of the location, yet it remained an undistinguished hamlet for several centuries. A few cottages survive at Hampton Wick from the early 18th century, but these do not seem to include The Hovel, which the Irish writer Richard Steele (1672 –1729) either rented or built for himself in 1707.

Hampton (Wick) 'Prick' (the male member) in COCKNEY RHYMING SLANG. The name-pun Hugh Jampton has often been heard, including in an episode of *The Goon Show*; BBC managers prevented the character from reappearing when they realized what was meant.

Hancock's Half Hour A classic radio and television comedy series (1954–60), written by Ray Galton (b.1930) and Alan Simpson (b.1929) and starring the popular actor Tony Hancock (1924–68), famous for his lugubrious buffoonishness. His gradual decline, alcoholism and suicide added, in hindsight, a note of genuine poignancy to his finely judged roles, one of the most memorable being that of a timorous blood donor. Hancock's fictitious address, 23 Railways Cuttings, East CHEAM, was equally savoured by his fans. Alan Simpson has said that he chose the locality because of its posh connotations and then 'killed it' with the (fictional) street name.

Handel in the Strand A piece of music (1911) by Percy Grainger, originally written for piano and cello. Grainger said of his piece: 'the music seemed to reflect both Handel and English musical comedy … as if jovial old Handel were careening down the STRAND to the strains of modern English popular music.'

hanger An Old English word for a wood lying on the side of a hill or bank.

Hanger Hill A GARDEN ESTATE in north EALING, laid out between 1928 and 1936. Consisting of short terraces of houses and three-storey blocks of flats, all in mock-Tudor style, the development is characterized by lovely gardens and vistas. The locality is especially popular with Japanese families.

Hanger Lane A highway connecting ALPERTON's Ealing Road with Gunnersbury Avenue in EALING. The WESTERN AVENUE crossed Hanger Lane in 1930 and the CENTRAL LINE station opened at the junction in 1947. The 'gyratory' roundabout here was regarded as an innovative traffic management system on its introduction but it remains one of London's most notorious blackspots – almost a byword for queues and delays.

Hanging Judge The nickname of George Jeffreys, 1st Baron Jeffreys of Wem (1645–89), an able but ruthless man who studied law at the INNER TEMPLE and rose through the ranks of the CITY judiciary at a young age. James II made him lord chancellor in 1685. Jeffreys sentenced hundreds to death but was also said to have been willing to pardon those who were sufficiently wealthy to bribe him handsomely. Following the Glorious Revolution of 1688 he tried to flee abroad on a coal-ship. Tradition has it that he disguised himself as a sailor and awaited the boat's departure while drinking in the Red Cow, a WAPPING pub now called the Town of Ramsgate. There he was recognized by a scrivener who had once come up before him. An angry mob detained him and he was imprisoned in the TOWER OF LONDON, where he died a few months later, probably of kidney disease.

Hangover Square A thriller (1941) by Patrick Hamilton (1904–62), subtitled 'A Story of Darkest Earl's Court'. A schizophrenic haunts the streets and public houses in an almost perpetual hangover, obsessed, in his lost periods, with murdering the woman he loves. The title puns on HANOVER SQUARE.

Hankins's folly An early nickname for Sandy Road, which lies on the western side of Hampstead's WEST HEATH(2), from Thomas Hankins, surveyor of the highways.

Hanover Square A square in north-east MAYFAIR with a large central garden. Named in honour of George I (r.1714–27), the Elector of Hanover, it was laid out in the late 1710s. Soon afterwards, St George's Church was built to the south of the square as one of London's planned FIFTY NEW CHURCHES. It became the capital's most fashionable venue for society weddings.

> O could I as Harlequin frisk,
> And thou be my Columbine fair,
> My wand should with one magic whisk
> Transport us to Hanover Square.
>
> W. SPENCER: 'The Beautiful Incendiary' (1812)

hansom A light two-wheeled cab, popular in London before the introduction of taxicabs early in the 20th century. It was invented in 1834 by Joseph Aloysius Hansom (1803–83). The original vehicle had two large wheels with sunk axle trees and a seat for the driver beside the passenger. The size of the wheels was subsequently reduced and the driver placed in a dicky, an exposed seat at the rear.

Hans Town A grand 18th-century suburb, centred on SLOANE STREET. In the 1770s the outward spread of London led FULHAM architect Henry Holland to spot an opportunity south of KNIGHTSBRIDGE. He acquired building rights from the Earl of Cadogan, who had come into possession of the land through his marriage to one of Hans SLOANE's daughters. Spacious three-storey terraced houses were erected along the west side of Sloane Street and in Hans Place, then around SLOANE SQUARE, and finally in Cadogan Place in 1790. Holland built himself a mansion called Sloane Place in the south-west-

ern part of his 'town', with grounds landscaped by Capability BROWN. Cadogan Square replaced this when R. Norman Shaw and other architects redeveloped Hans Town a century later, after criticism of the district's bland and uniform architecture prompted the Cadogan estate to commission new designs. Each house was given its own distinctive detailing, further enhancing the prestige of the locality. Most of the buildings from the second phase survive today but the locality is no longer referred to as Hans Town.

Hanwell A west London suburb connected with EALING to its east via Uxbridge Road. The name probably refers to a stream (*weille*) frequented by cocks (*hana*). St Mary's Church was in existence by the 12th century but has since been rebuilt three times. The merchant and travel writer Jonas Hanway (1712–86) is buried in the crypt of the church (*see* UMBRELLA). Isambard Kingdom Brunel built the Wharncliffe Viaduct for the Great Western Railway and Hanwell station opened two years later. An oft-repeated story has it that Queen Victoria used to halt the royal train on the viaduct so that she could admire the view towards St Mary's. Only a few more homes were built following the creation of this early link to London and the main increase in Hanwell's population derived from the construction in 1856 of the Central London District School. In the 1930s the LONDON COUNTY COUNCIL built the Cuckoo estate on the site of the school, but its imposing main building survives as Hanwell community centre. In the 1960s this centre provided rehearsal rooms for rock bands Uriah Heep and Deep Purple. Much of the album *Deep Purple in Rock* was composed here in 1969.

Hanworth An amorphous area of untidy housing, mixed up with gravel pits and a few factories, lying just inside the GREATER LONDON border, to the east of FELTHAM. Hanworth House (also sometimes called Hanworth Castle or Palace) was the hunting lodge of Hanworth Park, which Henry VIII granted to Anne Boleyn for life. As Anne's life turned out to be shorter than expected, Henry later settled the property on his last wife, Catherine Parr. Princess Elizabeth (later Elizabeth I) came to live at Hanworth at the age of 15. Hanworth House was destroyed by fire in 1797 and a new house was built, but demolished three-quarters of a century later. From 1917 until the opening of HEATHROW AIRPORT, aircraft were built and tested in Hanworth Park, which is now public open space. What had survived of the old village of Hanworth was mostly sacrificed to the construction of the M3 feeder road (the A316) in 1973.

Harefield A large village situated in the far north-western corner of GREATER LONDON. The name was first recorded in Domesday Book and was usually written as 'Herefeld' in the Middle Ages – possibly a reference to a field used by Danish invaders, *here* being an Old English word for an army. St Mary's Church is of 13th-century origin and is noted for its wealth of monuments. The 18th and 19th centuries saw the growth of several estates on which country houses were built, including Belhammonds, also known as Harefield Park, which later formed the core of Harefield Hospital. During the Second World War, wounded Australian and New Zealand troops were brought to the hospital for treatment and many of those who died there are buried in St Mary's churchyard. Since its first heart transplant in 1980 the hospital has had a distinguished history of ground-breaking surgery.

Haringey, London Borough of A GREATER LONDON borough made up of the former municipal boroughs of HORNSEY, TOTTENHAM and WOOD GREEN. The historical variant spelling was used to distinguish the borough from the constituent district of HARRINGAY, but this has perhaps brought more confusion than clarity. The new borough lay outside the old LONDON COUNTY COUNCIL boundary, and thus by definition constituted an OUTER LONDON borough at the time of its creation in 1965. However, it has since been reallocated to INNER LONDON for official statistical purposes. The borough's coat of arms was freshly devised at the time of its creation and does not combine elements from the heraldry of its constituent predecessors. The dominant feature is an arrangement of eight lightning bolts emanating from a central point, celebrating the role of ALEXANDRA PALACE in the history of television broadcasting and figuratively representing action and dynamism.

Harleian Robert Harley, Earl of Oxford (1661–1724), and his son Edward, the 2nd Earl (1689–1741) – *see* HARLEY STREET – were great collectors of manuscripts, scarce tracts and the like. In 1742 the widow of the 2nd Earl sold his

prints and printed books to Thomas Osborne, the GRAY'S INN bookseller, for £13,000 (considerably less than the cost of their binding alone), and in 1753 the manuscript books, charters and rolls were purchased at the bargain price of £10,000 for the BRITISH LIBRARY (then part of the BRITISH MUSEUM), where the Harleian Manuscripts are among its most valuable literary and historical possessions. The *Harleian Miscellany* (ten volumes, first published 1744–6 in eight volumes) contains reprints of nearly 700 tracts, mostly of the 16th and 17th centuries. Since 1870 the Harleian Society has published numerous volumes of Registers, Herald's Visitations and Pedigrees.

Harlequins The shared identity of rugby union and rugby league football clubs based in TWICKENHAM. The Harlequin Football Club gained its present name in 1870, following a brief inaugural existence as Hampstead FC, during which some members broke away to form WASPS. In 1906 Harlequins moved to the new national stadium at Twickenham. From 1963 the team trained on a nearby pitch that later became its permanent home and is now called the Twickenham STOOP. In 1980 FULHAM FC launched a rugby league offshoot that was subsequently reincarnated as London Crusaders and then London Broncos, moving home several times. Since October 2005 the club has been called Harlequins Rugby League, and shares the Twickenham Stoop with its rugby union sister.

Harlesden Variously called 'the West Bronx of London' and 'Jamaica Town', Harlesden is situated south of WILLESDEN and has the capital's highest proportion of residents of Caribbean descent. From the late 1950s immigration from the West Indies began to alter the district's character and as early as 1968 the Curzon Crescent estate had a Caribbean majority. The suddenness of this change, and a degree of civic neglect, caused social problems at first but in time led to the creation of one of London's most culturally effervescent communities. From the 1970s Harlesden became increasingly renowned for its live music, record shops, pirate radio stations and Caribbean food shops and restaurants. Since the 1990s regeneration projects have improved the High Street and the council-built estates, while GENTRIFICATION has begun in the terraced houses. The reggae artist Delroy Washington (b.1952) worked in a Harlesden record shop and members of rock band Aswad grew up in the vicinity. *See also* STONEBRIDGE.

> The promised land (or at least a land not monopolised by any others) for that one group [first generation Caribbean migrants] turned out to be the streets of Harlesden in south Brent.
>
> BETHAN THOMAS and DANIEL DORLING: *Identity in Britain: A Cradle-to-Grave Atlas* (2007)

Harley Street London's premier address for private doctors, Harley Street runs north from CAVENDISH SQUARE to REGENT'S PARK. From around 1719 Edward Harley, later the 2nd Earl of Oxford, began to develop the Cavendish family estate, but Harley Street itself was not completed until 1770. Its architecture was widely scorned for its dullness but the sumptuous interiors, some by the ADAM BROTHERS, attracted the upper echelons of society, including Lady Nelson, the artist J.M.W. Turner and the statesman William Gladstone. Foreign ambassadors chose the street for its quietness and the quality of its accommodation, and families from the country rented houses here during the LONDON SEASON. In Elizabeth Gaskell's *North and South* (1855), the heroine Margaret Hale lives in 'comfort and luxury' with her cousin Edith Shaw at 96 Harley Street. Charles Dickens made the street home to the obscenely wealthy Mr Merdle in *Little Dorrit* (1855–7). Around the time these works were published, Cavendish Square became a prestigious location for physicians' consulting rooms and doctors began to colonize the southern end of Harley Street in order to be near the square. It was not until later in the century that the street acquired a cachet of its own, whereupon spacious rooms were subdivided into consulting suites, and large brass plaques were mounted on front doors because professional restrictions prevented other forms of advertising. By the 1920s the street had almost completely filled up with doctors and Brunswick Place was renamed Upper Harley Street to provide additional capacity. Harley Street lost some of its practices after the creation of the National Health Service, but it remains synonymous with expensive consultancy, including newer forms of treatment such as cosmetic surgery.

Harlington A medieval manor and village transformed by later transportation projects, situated south of HAYES[2]. The Church of St Peter and St Paul was in existence by 1086, when the manor house stood nearby. The church's Norman south door is said to be the best in outer London. During the 19th century the intensity of brickmaking and gravel-working in north Harlington was so great that much of the land was lowered by several feet. The part of the parish that lay south of the Bath Road was taken by the air ministry in 1945 for the creation of what became HEATHROW AIRPORT. The construction of the M4 motorway in the 1960s divided Harlington into two quite distinct halves. The area north of the motorway is now entirely filled with housing, while the old centre to the south has been protected from over-development, although much of the village had already lost its original character as a consequence of the airport's expansion.

Harmondsworth A HEATHROW satellite village located south of WEST DRAYTON. Evidence has been found here of Iron Age huts and 6th-century Saxon dwellings. In 1069 William the Conqueror gave the parish church and the manor to the Benedictine Abbey of Holy Trinity, Rouen, later known as St Catherine's. The manor was appropriated in 1391 to Winchester College, which commissioned the construction of an aisled, timber-framed barn for the manor farm. Completed in 1427, it was the last in a series of vast medieval barns built on this site and survives today as the second longest in England. The Grange and Harmondsworth Hall were among the grandest of the homes built in the 17th century and both remain in existence, the former as offices and the latter as a hotel, with an 18th-century brick front. The development of Heathrow Airport since 1945 has erased all former traces of the parish south of the Bath Road but the old village centre is now both a conservation area and an archaeological priority area. However, part of the village will disappear beneath the airport's third runway if it is built as authorized by the government in 2009.

Harmonious Blacksmith, The The name given, after his death, to the air and variations in Handel's fifth harpsichord suite (1720). An ingenious but baseless fabrication ascribed its origin to the hammering at his forge of a blacksmith,

William Powell (*c.*1702–80), said to have inspired Handel to compose this air when he was sheltering from the rain there one day. Powell's grave at LITTLE STANMORE, was originally surrounded by a wooden rail on one side of which was painted: 'Sacred to the memory of William Powell, the Harmonious Blacksmith, died Feb. 27, 1780, aged about 78', and on the other: 'He was Parish Clerk at this Church many years, and during the Time the Immortal Handel resided much at Canons with the Duke of Chandos.' In 1868 this was replaced by a stone bearing, in a sunk medallion, a hammer, anvil, laurel leaf and a bar of music, with a modified inscription to the effect that: 'He was parish clerk during the time the immortal Handel was organist of this church.' *See also* CANONS.

Harold

Harold Hill A postwar 'new style suburb' in the north-east corner of GREATER LONDON, just inside the M25, earmarked for development as part of the ABERCROMBIE PLAN. Two neighbourhood units with a total of 8,200 dwellings were created, with an industrial zone in the south-west corner. In the opposite corner, on the edge of the GREEN BELT, higher value homes were built as part of a plan to house a wider variety of tenants than was usual with council estates.

Harold Wood A Victorian railway township, now much enlarged and rebuilt, situated just over 2 miles (3 km) north and a little to the east of HORNCHURCH. Harold's Wood was a large forest stretching some way to the north-west of the present district. Although King Harold once owned the estate there is no evidence that he ever visited it. After the trees were cut down in the 15th and 16th centuries the land became known as Harold's Wood (or Romford) Common. The district of Harold Wood grew up on the site of Gubbins Farm following the opening of the station in the late 1860s. However, development was very slow and Harold Wood's rural character did not finally vanish until after the First World War.

Harringay A compact locality situated north of FINSBURY PARK and consisting mostly of rigidly gridded streets of terraced houses. Harringay's name comes from the same root as its parent borough, HARINGEY, as does that of its neighbour, HORNSEY. All are corruptions of Old English *Haringes hecg*, which probably meant a hedged enclosure belonging to a man named Hæring. Although Hornsey can lay claim to being the site of the original enclosure, Harringay House was built in this locality in the 1790s for Edward Grey, a London linen draper, who accumulated an estate of 192 acres (78 hectares) by the 1820s. When Grey died in 1838 the estate was broken up and sold and the house was later demolished. In 1927 the Greyhound Racing Association built Harringay Park, a stadium that later hosted speedway events as well as dog races. The Harringay Boxing and Ice Skating Arena opened on a neighbouring site in 1936, and was famously used for prayer meetings by the Christian evangelist Billy Graham until its closure in 1958. The greyhound stadium closed in 1987 and the two sites are now occupied by a retail park. Harringay was the focus of London's Cypriot community for much of the late 20th century and many of its specialist shops still line the Grand Parade section of GREEN LANES. *See also the* LADDER.

Harris

Harris, Bomber *See* BOMBER HARRIS

Harris's List of Covent Garden Ladies A directory of London's more upmarket prostitutes, published annually between 1757 and 1795. In addition to providing names and addresses, the list contained little biographies of the ladies, sometimes of a moderately witty nature. It was the creation of the Irish-born poet, actor and playwright Samuel Derrick (1724–1769), who got the idea from Jack Harris – the self-styled 'Pimp General to the People of England' – when they were both in NEWGATE PRISON for debt. Harris had previously circulated a handwritten guide of the same kind and Derrick paid him a commission for the use of his name. After Derrick's death the list was continued by others, but in a more banal style. It is believed to have sold around 250,000 copies over the course of its existence.

Harris, William 'Bumper' A one-legged man who in October 1911 was paid to spend one or more days riding the first escalators on the LONDON UNDERGROUND system to allay travellers' fears of the new technology. That, at least, is the story, which has been widely repeated in print and on the internet. However, the London Transport Museum says that Harris, a tunnelling engineer who lost his leg in a workplace accident, did take a ride on the first escalator (at EARLS COURT station) to prove its safety but was never employed to do so repeatedly. He continued to work as an engineer and in 1913 was presented with an ornamental walking stick made from an ancient oak tree found during excavation work for the installation of escalators at CHARING CROSS STATION, in recognition of his role as clerk of works on that project.

Harrods A vast department store in BROMPTON Road, which arose from a small grocer's shop opened there in 1849 by Henry Charles Harrod (1811–85), an EASTCHEAP tea merchant who had married a butcher's daughter. It had become one of London's leading stores by the turn of the century, when it was rebuilt in its present grand style. A hundred years on it was still striving to live up to its old slogan: 'Everything, for everyone, everywhere.' (Its telegraphic address was 'Everything Harrods London'.) The commodious food halls are effectively a superior supermarket, stocking all one could conceivably wish to buy for the table. It is currently owned by the investment arm of Qatar's sovereign wealth fund.

Harrods of the East The nickname of Gardiner's, a departmental clothing store that stood opposite the junction of WHITECHAPEL High Street and Commercial Street until the early 1970s. The intersection is still known informally as Gardiner's Corner. However, the original Harrods of the East was really Harrods itself; the founder of the KNIGHTSBRIDGE emporium set up his first shop on CABLE STREET in 1835.

Harrovian (A pupil) of HARROW SCHOOL. The term, first recorded in the mid-19th century, is based on a modern Latinization of Harrow as *Harrovia*. It is most commonly preceded by the adjective 'Old', denoting former pupils of the school.

Harrow An extensive suburban district that grew outwards from HARROW-ON-THE-HILL after the coming of the railways. Harrow lies 11 miles (18 km) north-west of central London. First recorded in the 8th century, the name derives from the Old English *hearg*, a pagan shrine. The first Harrow station (now Harrow and Wealdstone) opened in 1837, bringing early growth to GREENHILL and WEALDSTONE. Later in the century housing began to fan out into the newly invented localities of West Harrow and North Harrow. New stations opened all around Harrow in the early 20th century and the town expanded

further in all directions except eastwards, with development reaching a crescendo between the world wars. Changes to the built environment in recent decades have been relatively minor compared with the shift in the ethnic mix of the population; around a quarter of all residents can trace their origins to the Indian subcontinent.

Harrow, London Borough of On the creation of the GREATER LONDON COUNCIL in 1965, Harrow was the only borough to replicate the unchanged boundaries of a single former district. The new borough kept the same coat of arms as its predecessor, with references to the hill, the school, Handel, writers and the GREEN BELT. Unusually, the arms' supporters are not rampant beasts but Hygeia (the Greek goddess of health) and a Benedictine monk. The former represents the borough's claim to an excellent record of public health, while the latter is a reference to the former ecclesiastical ownership of numerous properties in the area. The civic motto is *salus populi suprema lex* – 'the welfare of the people shall be the highest law'.

Harrow drive A cricket term that seems originally, in the mid-19th century, to have been applied to an off-drive, presumably thought of as a specialism of Harrovian batsmen. Well before the close of the century, however, those inclined to poke fun at the school's pretensions were using it to denote a botched or edged drive, and by the middle of the 20th century it was firmly attached to a stroke that sends the ball accidentally off the inside edge of the bat past the leg stump.

Harrow-on-the-Hill The southern part of central Harrow and one of London's most authentic-looking villages. Alternatively spelt in unhyphenated form, and later known briefly as Harrow Town, Harrow-on-the-Hill was the site of the original hamlet in the early 7th century. The hill rises to 408 feet (124m) above sea level and was crowned by St Mary's Church from the 11th century. In the Middle Ages the church was one of the most important in Middlesex and was a PECULIAR of the archbishop of Canterbury. A market was established in 1226. With its little shops, tearooms and pubs, the village has changed little since the late 19th century, which has led to accusations of faux-nostalgia but the effect is delightful nonetheless. Lower down the slopes of the hill, modern commercial premises have inevitably intruded but HARROW SCHOOL's extensive grounds have preserved the open space to the east.

> Then Harrow-on-the-Hill's a rocky island
> And Harrow churchyard full of sailors' graves
> And the constant click and kissing of the trolley buses hissing
> Is the level to the Wealdstone turned to waves.
>
> JOHN BETJEMAN: *A Few Late Chrysanthemums*, 'Harrow-on-the-Hill' (1954)

Harrow Rail Disaster A railway accident that took place in Harrow and Wealdstone station at 8.18 on the morning of 8 October 1952. An overnight express sleeper travelling from Perth to EUSTON overshot signals at Harrow and ploughed into a stationary local train waiting in the station. Shortly afterwards a northbound express from Euston ran into the wreckage, causing carnage in a station crowded with rush-hour commuters. In all, 122 people were killed and 150 injured. The Harrow Rail Disaster is second only to the Gretna Green Rail Disaster of 1915 in terms of casualties.

Harrow Road London has several Harrow Roads, but the best known is the stretch of the A404 running from MARYLEBONE to HARLESDEN. In *The Growth of St Marylebone and Paddington* (1990), Jack Whitehead calls it a typical English road that 'wandered from village green to village green, skirting the corners of large estates, avoiding ponds which have now been filled in for centuries, turning and looping for no apparent reason'. Harrow Road was entirely built up in the latter decades of the 19th century, but there has been much piecemeal replacement since then.

> ... in a room on the Harrow Road, the traffic muffled by a plastic sheet, the facing ziggurats with their satellite dishes and tea-towels out to dry,
> a lengthwise Brazilian flag curtaining one window ...
>
> MICHAEL HOFMANN: *Selected Poems*, 'Litany' (2008)

Harrow School A boy's school in HARROW-ON-THE-HILL, paired in the public mind with Eton College, in Berkshire, as the most prototypical of public schools. John Lyon, a local farmer, founded the school in 1572, under a charter granted by Elizabeth I. On the completion of the schoolhouse in 1615 just one pupil was on the roll. Properties in the village were taken over as boarding houses for the pupils from the late 17th century but Harrow remained just one of many local grammar schools until it achieved a leap in its popularity early in the 19th century. The school buildings were doubled in size in 1821, a chapel was added in 1839 and numerous other buildings and purpose-built boarding houses followed. Its old boys include several British prime ministers (Robert Peel, Lord Palmerston, Stanley Baldwin, Winston Churchill) and one Indian one (Jawaharlal Nehru), and such literary figures as Richard Sheridan, Lord Byron, Anthony Trollope, Terence Rattigan and John Mortimer. Its pupils wear distinctive straw hats. It is famous for its school songs, of which the most familiar is 'FORTY YEARS ON'. The game of squash is thought to have originated here.

> Victorian and Edwardian slang persisted; 'tosh' (bath); 'eccer' (exercise/sport); 'groize' (hard worker) still greeted bemused new boys in the 1970s, even if many of the richer seams of local dialect had gone.
>
> CHRISTOPHER TYERMAN: *A History of Harrow School* (2000)

Harrow Weald An elongated residential area situated west of STANMORE, simply called the Weald for most of its history. The London merchant Sir Edward Waldo acquired the manor of Marlpits in the 1680s and created Waldo's Farm from the part of the manor that lay in Harrow Weald. From 1759 the common was steadily enclosed and had been reduced to 685 acres (277 hectares) in 1817. During the 19th century several grand houses were built on the enclosed land, among them the home of Thomas Blackwell, who formed a food company with Edmund Crosse of nearby Clamp Hill. Harrow Weald Park was a mansion occupied by the gaming club owner Henry Crockford until his death in 1844 and was rebuilt in 1870 in sumptuous Victorian Gothic style, looking something like an Oxford college. When Harrow council later destroyed the mansion, retirement homes were built on part of the site, although most of its woodland survives. A rambling house called GRIM'S DYKE was the work of the architect R. Norman Shaw in the early 1870s, and its 'Old English' style influenced the appearance of several other properties in the area.

Harry

Harry Potter *See under* POTTER.

Harry Randall 'Candle' or 'handle' in COCKNEY RHYMING SLANG, from the HOLBORN-born MUSIC

HALL performer (1860–1932) who became famous for his pantomime dame roles.

Harry Tate 'Late' or 'state' (i.e. of agitation) in mid-20th-century COCKNEY RHYMING SLANG. The allusion is to the Scottish MUSIC HALL artiste Harry Tate, born Ronald MacDonald Hutchison (1873–1940), who popularized the catchphrase 'HOW'S YOUR FATHER?' Other rhyming applications of his name were 'mate', especially in the sense of a first officer in the merchant navy, 'plate' and 'eight'.

Harry Wragg 'Fag' (cigarette) in COCKNEY RHYMING SLANG. Harry Wragg (1902–85) was a successful jockey from the 1920s to 1940s and later a trainer. He was punningly nicknamed the Head Waiter, because he would habitually wait until the last possible moment before taking the lead in a race.

harvest

Harvest Festival A day in late September or early October set aside by the Church of England to thank God for the harvest. Although the festival is generally celebrated with more enthusiasm in country parishes, it is a focal occasion for London's PEARLY KINGS AND QUEENS. The pearlies hold services at the churches of ST MARY-LE-BOW (preceded by a parade from the GUILDHALL), St Paul's, COVENT GARDEN (*see the* ACTORS' CHURCH) and ST MARTIN-IN-THE-FIELDS.

Harvest of the Sea Festival A service held annually at St Mary-at-Hill Church, Lovat Lane, in the CITY ward of BILLINGSGATE. The produce offered consists entirely of fish, which is placed on display in the church's narthex.

Harvey

Harvey Nicks or **Nics** The colloquial name for the fashion store Harvey Nichols. Benjamin Harvey opened a linen shop in KNIGHTSBRIDGE in 1813 and passed the business on to his daughter on condition that she went into partnership with Colonel Nichols, adding luxury goods to the store's range. Harvey Nicks later became famous for its cosmetic hall and even more famous in the 1990s for its frequent mentions in ABSOLUTELY FABULOUS. The flagship store remains in Knightsbridge but in 1996 the company opened a branch in Leeds and it now has a presence in several regional and overseas cities. The company also owns a restaurant at the OXO TOWER.

Harvey's sauce A fish sauce invented in the 1760s by Peter Harvey, the landlord of the Black Dog Inn, East BEDFONT, and much admired by the epicures of the day. Harvey resisted all offers to reveal the secret ingredients but, when his sister married a London grocer in 1776, he gave them the recipe as a wedding present. The couple set up a company to market the sauce, which was acquired by Crosse and Blackwell in 1920. The recipe for Harvey's sauce is no longer a secret; directions can be found on several websites.

> Two Harveys had an equal wish,
> To shine in different stations:
> The first invented sauce for fish,
> The second – *Meditations*.
> Each had its pungent powers applied
> To aid the dead and dying:
> That relishes a *sole* when fried,
> This saves a *soul* from frying.
>
> JAMES SMITH: 'Grimm's Ghost' (*c*.1823)

has your mother sold her mangle? An all-purpose catchphrase that flourished briefly in early Victorian London. Although many working-class women of the time truly 'subsisted in an honourable manner by the exercise of a mangle', as Thackeray put it in *Vanity Fair* (1848), the phrase seems to have originated as deliberate nonsense, at least after the first time the enquiry was ever made in seriousness. Its popularity declined as rapidly as it had grown; people simply tired of saying and hearing it.

> Why so pensive, Peri-maiden?
> Pearly tears bedim thine eyes!
> Sure thine heart is overladen,
> When each breath is fraught with sighs.
> Say, hath care life's heaven clouded,
> Which hope's stars were wont to spangle?
> What hath all thy gladness shrouded? –
> *Has your mother sold her mangle?*
>
> Punch, 'Songs for the Sentimental' (17 July 1841)

Hatchards London's oldest bookshop, founded on PICCADILLY in 1797 by John Hatchard (1768–1849), a Tory and evangelical Christian whose beliefs were reflected in the books he sold. In 1801 the store moved a few doors along the street to its present address, 187 Piccadilly, next to FORTNUM & MASON. The institution now known as the Royal Horticultural Society was formed at a meeting held in a room above the shop in 1804. The premises were rebuilt in 1909, retaining the look of the original shopfront.

Although it preserves its distinct identity, Hatchards is now part of Waterstone's, which is in turn a division of the HMV Group.

> But what was she dreaming as she looked into Hatchards' shop window? What was she trying to recover? What image of white dawn in the country, as she read in the book spread open:
> Fear no more the heat o' the sun
> Nor the furious winter's rages.
>
> VIRGINIA WOOLF: *Mrs Dalloway* (1925)

Hatch End The northern tip of the PINNER district. Hatch End's name was first recorded in 1448, although the mention around 1300 of the surname de la Hacche indicates that the settlement may have been in existence even earlier. The hatch (gate) would have given access to Pinner Park, which belonged to the archbishops of Canterbury. In addition to HARROW Arts Centre and an eclectic range of shops, Hatch End is regarded as the restaurant capital of the borough. The novelist Ivy Compton-Burnett (1884–1969) was born in Hatch End. Her father, a homeopathic doctor, moved the family to the Sussex coast in 1891 to give his children the benefit of sea air.

Hatches Bottom *See the* VALE OF HEALTH.

Hatton Garden London's prime jewellery quarter, located just north of HOLBORN Circus. Hatton Garden takes its name from Sir Christopher Hatton, the DANCING CHANCELLOR, who acquired the property from the Bishops of Ely. From an early role as a cutting centre for Indian diamonds, Hatton Garden developed a trade in gold and platinum during the 19th century. The exploitation of South Africa's Kimberley diamond field brought a further increase in trade from the 1870s. 'The Garden' now has around 300 jewellery businesses, including 50 retailers.

Haunted Reach GALLIONS REACH was sometimes so called in the years following the PRINCESS ALICE disaster of 1878.

have
have a bubble (bath), to *See* BUBBLE (BATH).
have a word with yourself A suggestion to someone that he or she is being foolish about a certain matter and should reconsider. This contemporary colloquialism is not exclusive to London but it carries COCKNEY connotations

and is often articulated with the 'h' dropped from 'have'. The essence of the advice is of course nothing new; compare, for example, Pierce Egan's 'whisper into your own ear', quoted under QUARTER FLASH AND THREE PARTS FOOLISH.

> That said, Karin, unsurprisingly, was found guilty. As Frank Butcher used to say to recalcitrant youths in EastEnders: 'You want to have a word with yourself, you do, Karin.'
>
> STUART JEFFRIES, in *The Guardian* (22 May 1999)

have it (away) on one's toes, to To run away or make a quick exit, often in the context of avoiding detection or apprehension.

> Del Boy: Gone?
> Grandad: Packed his rucksack and had it away on his toes!
> Del Boy: What do you mean gone? Where's he gone?
>
> JOHN SULLIVAN: *Only Fools and Horses*, 'Big Brother' (pilot episode for TV series) (1981)

have you seen the Shah? A catchphrase that originated in London and soon spread nationwide, prompted by the Shah of Persia's ostentatious state visit in 1873. The public was enthralled and amused to see the potentate wearing a gold-embroidered coat studded with diamonds, emeralds and rubies, with his scimitar sheathed in a diamond-encrusted scabbard. More than one popular song celebrated the visit, although the Shah was said to have been bad for the entertainment business because crowds followed him everywhere instead of going to the theatre or MUSIC HALL. The second edition of Dr Brewer's *Dictionary of Phrase and Fable* (1896) defined the catchphrase as 'a query implying a hoax, popular with street arabs' but it was used with many other implications, and indeed with none at all.

> Have you seen the Shah, boys, have you seen the Shah?
> With five-pound notes, he lines his coats, which is pecul*iah*!
> From head to waist, with Paris paste, he twinkles like a St*ah*!
> You don't know what it is to be the Shah.
>
> BRACEY VANE: 'Have You Seen the Shah?' (song) (1873)

Havens The informal name of the Sexual Assault Referral Centres set up as a joint initiative of the METROPOLITAN POLICE and the Department of Health to provide care and assistance to victims of rape and sexual assault. There are Havens at KING'S COLLEGE Hospital, the Royal London Hospital and St Mary's Hospital, PADDINGTON. *See also* SAPPHIRE.

Havering Despite the fable that the name is a corruption of I HAVE A RING, it probably derives from a landowner called Hæfer.

Havering, London Borough of An OUTER LONDON borough formed in 1965 by merging the municipal borough of ROMFORD with the urban district of HORNCHURCH. The other main population centres are UPMINSTER, RAINHAM and the mainly council-built district of HAROLD HILL. Havering is London's second largest borough in area, corresponding approximately with the ancient Liberty of Havering and is shaped roughly like a chevron pointing eastwards into ESSEX. The topography ranges from desolate THAMES-side marshes to wooded hills and meadows in the north. More new homes have been built in Havering over recent years than in any other part of London except DOCKLANDS. The borough's coat of arms contains references to the towers of the former royal residence at HAVERING-ATTE-BOWER, the bull's horns of Hornchurch and the sails of Upminster windmill. The central feature is 'a Gem Ring Or set with a Ruby proper', a reference to the I HAVE A RING fable. The civic motto is 'liberty'.

Havering-atte-Bower An extended village standing on high ground 3 miles (5 km) north of ROMFORD. It is said that in the mid-11th century Edward the Confessor built a hunting lodge here, often referred to as a small palace or 'bower'. A succession of royal associations came to an end during the Commonwealth when the house fell into decay and it was demolished early in the 18th century. Bower House was built nearby in 1729, perhaps using some of the old stones. This house was later enlarged and is now owned by the Ford Motor Company, which holds management training sessions and dealer presentations here. The present village is by no means unspoilt but retains sufficient older elements to give it some character, including weatherboarded cottages facing the green, which still contains stocks and a whipping post, and there are glorious views over ESSEX meadowland.

Havering Riverside A new name for the borough's THAMES-side marshland. The mudflats were used for grazing sheep from the Middle Ages and parts came under the plough as drainage was steadily improved. Vegetables were grown for the London market, especially with the coming of faster communications in the 19th century. Later in that century industries were established along parts of the riverside, and many of these continue to operate, although a large swathe of marshes east of RAINHAM Creek and stretching into ESSEX has been preserved, primarily as habitat for birds. Brownfield sites are likely to be redeveloped over the next two decades as part of the borough's role in the THAMES GATEWAY regeneration scheme.

Haverstock Hill A former artists' retreat, now a stretch of the A502 linking CHALK FARM with BELSIZE PARK. First recorded in Rocque's map of 1745, the name probably refers to a place where oats were grown and seems to have originally designated the whole slope rather than the road itself, which was then called Hampstead Road or London Road. Until the building of an orphanage, almshouses and a church in the mid-19th century, the hamlet of Haverstock Hill consisted of just the Load of Hay tavern (rebuilt in 1863) and a few cottages lying below the corner of England's Lane. An early resident was the writer Richard Steele (1672–1729) , co-founder of both *Tatler* and *The Spectator*. Artists' studios replaced the cottages in 1872. George Clausen's *A Spring Morning, Haverstock Hill* (1881) is considered a definitive image of Victorian Britain. The painting hangs in Bury's municipal art gallery.

Hawcubites Street bullies in the reign of Queen Anne (1702–14) who molested and ill-treated the old WATERMEN, women and children who chanced to be in the streets after sunset. The succession of these London pests after the Restoration was: the Muns, the TITYRE-TUS, the Hectors, the Nickers, then the Hawcubites (1711–14), and worst of all the MOHOCKS. The name is probably a combination of 'Mohawk' and 'Jacobite'.

From Mohock and from Hawcubite,
Good Lord deliver me,
Who wander through the streets at night,
Committing cruelty.
They slash our sons with bloody knives,
And on our daughters fall;
And if they murder not our wives,
We have good luck withal.

JOHN GAY: 'A Wonderful Prophecy' (1712)

hay *See* BALE OF HAY for the myth about London taxis.

Hay Country, the A name by which the area around WOODFORD and CHINGFORD was known at the end of the 19th century. By the early 1920s almost all the pasture had been sacrificed to suburban development.

Hay's Wharf A dock established in 1651 on the SOUTHWARK riverside by Alexander Hay, the proprietor of a brewhouse in TOOLEY STREET. His family retained an interest in the development for almost 200 years. By the late 19th century the much enlarged wharf was the principal handler of London's TEA and dairy produce imports. With the decline of London's docks after the Second World War, Hay's Wharf fell into disuse and in the late 1980s the main warehouse was reconstructed behind the existing brick facade as a stylish shopping mall named Hay's Galleria, with offices above. A high, glass-roofed atrium has replaced the old central dock. *See also* LONDON BRIDGE CITY.

Hayes¹ (London Borough of BROMLEY) An elongated suburb extending almost 1½ miles (2.5 km) southwards from BROMLEY. First mentioned in 1177, the name probably meant 'rough ground covered with brushwood'. Hayes Place was in existence by the 15th century and was rebuilt in the 1750s. From 1754 until 1785, Hayes Place was a country seat of the Pitt family, leading figures of British imperial statesmanship. William Pitt the Younger, prime minister 1783–1801 and 1804–6, was born at the house in 1759. His father, William Pitt the Elder, 1st Earl of Chatham and prime minister 1766–8, died here in 1778.

Hayes² (London Borough of HILLINGDON) A 20th-century agglomeration (and obliteration) of former medieval hamlets, centred 2 miles (3 km) west of SOUTHALL, from which it is separated by the River Crane and the PADDINGTON branch of the GRAND UNION CANAL. The name has the same derivation as Hayes in BROMLEY and was first mentioned in the 8th century, when land here was granted to the archbishops of Canterbury. During the first half of the 20th century, Hayes became one of west London's prime industrial locations, and rows of terraced houses were built for the factory workers. Growth was especially rapid between the wars, when private and municipal estates filled most of the former farmland. The hamlet of Botwell became the main shopping area, but lost its identity within Hayes Town. George Orwell, who lived and taught here in 1932 and 1933, once described Hayes as:

> ... one of the most god-forsaken places I have ever struck. The population seems to be entirely made up of clerks who frequent tin-roofed chapels on Sundays and for the rest bolt themselves within doors.

He fictionalized it as West Bletchley in his novel *Coming Up for Air* (1939).

Haymarket A WEST END street extending from the east side of PICCADILLY CIRCUS south to PALL MALL. Hay and straw were sold here from Elizabethan times until 1830, by which time two important theatres were already well established. Her Majesty's Theatre (as it became) and the THEATRE ROYAL, Haymarket, are both still in existence, in rebuilt forms. In the 18th and 19th centuries the Haymarket and its side streets were notorious for their prostitutes, who congregated there on a scale almost unimaginable today:

> Anyone who has visited London will certainly have been to the Haymarket at night. In the vicinity of this area thousands of prostitutes throng certain streets ... Mixing with this crowd is an uncomfortable experience, so motley is it in make-up, with old women, and young beauties before whom you would stop in awe. In all the world, you will not find a more beautiful type of woman than in England. The streets swarm with women who fill the pavements and even the roadway, searching for prey and falling upon the first-comer with shameless cynicism. Curses, quarrels, calls and the timid advances of the as yet young and shy beauties fill the air.
>
> FYODOR DOSTOYEVSKY: *Winter Notes on Summer Impressions* (1863)

he

he is only fit for Ruffians' Hall *See* RUFFIANS' HALL.

he may whet his knife on the threshold of the Fleet He is free of debt. The reference is to the FLEET PRISON.

> The proverb is appliable to those who never owed ought; or else, having run into debt, have crept out of it; so that now they may defy danger and arrests; yea, may *triumphare in hostico,*

laugh in the face of the Serjeants. Surely the threshold of the Fleet, so used, setteth a good edge on the knife, and a better on the wearer thereof, actuating him with a spirit free from all engagements.

THOMAS FULLER: *The History of the Worthies of England* (1662)

he must take (him) a house in Turnagain Lane A very old way of suggesting that someone should mend his ways.

When anyone took to wrong courses, which threatened his destruction, it was usual to say 'he must take a house in Turnagain Lane'.

DAVID HUGHSON: *London*, Volume 3 (1806)

Headquarters The nickname of a workhouse in Gordon Road, PECKHAM, created in the 1850s from a former nunnery and run by CAMBERWELL board of guardians. Destitute men would walk from all over England to seek a bed there as it had a favourable reputation for ease of access and could accommodate more than a thousand. Later renamed the Camberwell reception centre and then the Camberwell resettlement unit, it closed in 1985. Most of the buildings were demolished, while a remaining part became a long-lasting squat. In the opening scene of the film BLOW-UP (1966), Thomas (played by David Hemmings) is seen emerging from the reception centre.

Headstone The northern part of HARROW, bordering PINNER to the west. The settlement was Hegeton in the early 14th century, probably 'the farmstead enclosed by a hedge'. After the First World War private builders filled most of central Headstone's surviving gaps but HENDON council saved HEADSTONE MANOR and part of its grounds.

Headstone Manor The only surviving example of a medieval aisled hall in outer London. Built in the 1310s, it was the principal MIDDLESEX residence of the archbishops of Canterbury from 1307 until 1546. The house was remodelled in the 1630s, given an extra wing in the 1650s and further altered in 1762. However, it was subsequently used simply as a farmhouse and was allowed to deteriorate. Headstone Manor is slowly being restored, as funds permit. In the grounds of the house, two 16th-century barns and an 18th-century granary nowadays comprise Harrow Museum.

Healtheries The nickname of the pioneering International Health Exhibition, held in SOUTH KENSINGTON in 1884. As well as the predictable emphasis on improved sanitation, plentiful exercise and nutritious eating, the exhibition placed great stress on the benefits of more 'hygienic' modes of dress. Dr Gustav JAEGER's 'rational' underwear for ladies became especially popular after a successful showing at the Healtheries.

Heathens Denizens of BLACKHEATH were often facetiously so called in the past. Most of Blackheath's illustrious sports teams have been nicknamed the Heathens, including the rugby, hockey and athletics clubs.

Blackheath crossed over with a goal to love ... The Oxonians ... got two goals, while the Heathens were unable to score.

Pall Mall Gazette (16 November 1891)

Heathrow Formerly a row of houses at the western edge of HOUNSLOW HEATH. Although Heathrow made a relatively late appearance as a hamlet – its presence was not recorded until 1453 – the area was rich in archaeological treasures, with evidence of Bronze Age farming and the only Iron Age temple colonnade in England. The construction of HEATHROW AIRPORT obliterated the settlement, together with the prehistoric sites and the neighbouring hamlets of Perry Oaks and King's Arbour.

Heathrow Airport The world's busiest international airport, situated on the western edge of GREATER LONDON, south of the M4 and M25 motorways' intersection. Aviation began here in 1930 and the government requisitioned the site as a bomber airfield shortly before the end of the Second World War. This seems to have been a ploy to sidestep public objections to Heathrow's intended commercial use when the war was over. The first departure, in January 1946, was a British South American Airways flight for Buenos Aires. The terminal buildings at the centre of the airport site were constructed between 1955 and 1968, when a cargo site was added to the south, with a linking tunnel. Terminal 4 was completed in 1986 and Terminal 5 opened amid disorganized scenes in 2008 (*see* T5). In January 2009 the government authorized the construction of a third runway, together with a sixth terminal that will erase the village of SIPSON. However, the completion of this project is subject to numerous political and judicial uncertainties.

Heathrow held a long-running fascination for the author J.G. Ballard. Much of the action in his early shocker *Crash* (1973) takes place on the highways and sliproads surrounding the airport, while *Millennium People* (2003) opens with a terrorist bomb attack here.

> ... a beached sky-city, half space station and half shanty town.
>
> J.G. BALLARD: *Millennium People*

Heathrow-on-Sea The nickname of a proposed new airport for London, to be sited on an artificial island, or pair of islands, north-east of the Isle of Sheppey, in the THAMES estuary. An alternative nickname, 'Boris Island', alludes to the idea's principal advocate, Boris Johnson (*see* BO-JO). Many commentators believe that the scheme will never proceed.

Heaven A renowned nightclub located on Villiers Street, under the railway arches of CHARING CROSS STATION, catering to a predominantly gay clientele. Earlier the venue was the Global Village, a progressive rock club. From its inception in 1979 Heaven was a pioneer in the emergence of the gay entertainment scene into the mainstream of WEST END nightlife.

heaven between two hells A nickname for Holy Trinity Church, KNIGHTSBRIDGE, because its neighbours on each side were public houses. In fact, the pubs were perfectly respectable establishments and one of the landlords was a well-regarded churchwarden. Holy Trinity was demolished in 1904.

hebberman *See* EBBERMAN.

hell

Hell and Chancery are always open A saying first recorded in Thomas Fuller's *Gnomologia* (1732), suggesting that there is little to choose between lawyers and the Devil. *See also* CHANCERY.

Hellgate: London A fantasy role-playing computer game developed in 2007 by the now-defunct Flagship Studios. The game is set in 2038, when the RAVENS OF THE TOWER have departed and an apocalypse has ensued. Survivors seek sanctuary in the tunnels of the LONDON UNDERGROUND, banding together in factions such as the Templar, a secret society preserving the rites of the KNIGHTS TEMPLAR.

hello

hello hello hello *See* NOW THEN, WHAT'S ALL THIS?

Hello Kitty An excessively cute cartoon cat created in 1974 by the Sanrio company of Japan. Her 'real' name is Kitty White. Of Anglo-Japanese pedigree, she was born in an unnamed London suburb 12 miles (20 km) from the city centre, where she continues to live with her family and, oddly, her pet cat. It is estimated that Hello Kitty's image has adorned more than 50,000 different items of merchandise marketed in 60 countries. In 2008 the Japanese government chose Hello Kitty to be the nation's tourism ambassador to China and a Hello Kitty musical opened in Beijing at the start of a three-year, four-country tour.

> She was made partly English because when she was first drawn, the Japanese rarely travelled abroad; foreign, especially English, associations, were particularly popular.
>
> *The Independent* (21 May 2008)

Helter Skelter A nickname for the Pinnacle (also known as Bishopsgate Tower), a spiralling office tower under construction at Crosby Court, BISHOPSGATE. If built to its planned height of 945 feet (288m), it will be the tallest building in the SQUARE MILE. The developers hope to complete the scheme in the first half of 2012.

Hendon A socially graduated residential district situated 3 miles (5 km) north-west of HAMPSTEAD. Its name (which means 'at the high down') was first recorded in 959. Modern Hendon took shape during the late 19th century as the hamlets around the main-line station, Brent Street and CHURCH END began to coalesce. Hendon Central station opened when the LONDON UNDERGROUND extension to EDGWARE was completed in 1923. Shortly afterwards came the construction of the arterial roads that criss-cross the district, bringing industry and new housing, especially along the NORTH CIRCULAR. In 1931 Hendon was Britain's most populous urban district. During the late 1950s and early 1960s the council pulled down and rebuilt much of the housing stock, preserving the social gradient that begins in the disadvantaged lowlands of West Hendon and rises to the comfortable undulations of Holders Hill. Hendon has the principal campus of MIDDLESEX UNIVERSITY.

Hendon Aerodrome *See the* ROYAL AIR FORCE MUSEUM.

Hendon Police College The original and still the informal name for the METROPOLITAN POLICE training school, founded in 1934, when it took over the buildings of Hendon Country Club, Hendon Aerodrome's clubhouse, in COLINDALE. The college was renamed the Peel Centre when it was rebuilt in 1974.

Henman Hill An informal name bestowed by tennis journalists on a grassy bank at the All England Tennis Club at WIMBLEDON. It is properly called Aorangi Terrace, after Aorangi Park, the ground of London New Zealand RFC, which leased the site from 1966 to 1981. It was from this terrace that those (mainly female) fans of Britain's No.1 tennis player Tim Henman (b.1974), who found themselves without tickets for the show courts, were able to watch the progress of their boyish hero on a large screen. The perennially hopeful Henman, a fine grass-court player but of often limited effectiveness on other surfaces, reached the Wimbledon quarter finals eight times and the semi-finals four times between 1996 and 2005. Since the meteoric rise of Andy Murray (b.1987) there have been attempts to rename the hill 'Murray Mount' or something similar, but the old name seems likely to stick for a while yet.

Hercules and his load The sign of the GLOBE THEATRE showing Hercules carrying the globe upon his shoulders. SHAKESPEARE alludes to it in *Hamlet* (II, ii (1600)):

> Hamlet: Do the boys carry it away?
> Rosencrantz: Ay, that they do, my lord; Hercules and his load too.

Here Come the Double Deckers *See the* DOUBLE DECKERS.

her indoors A person's wife, especially when regarded as taking charge or 'wearing the trousers'. The expression was popularized by the television series MINDER (1979–94), in which the leading character, Arthur DALEY, regularly refers to his wife (who never appears on screen) by this name. The phrase is sometimes spelt ''er indoors' to suggest a COCKNEY tone.

hermit
Hermit of Clifford's Inn George Dyer (1755–

1841), a WAPPING-born writer who occupied chambers at CLIFFORD'S INN for nearly 50 years, surviving on academic HACK work. His literary criticism influenced the Romantic poets of the time, although his own verse was mediocre. Dyer was a close friend of Charles Lamb, who affectionately mocked him in his ELIA essays. He was said to have been accident prone, without a sense of humour and willing to believe any story told to him, as a result of which many stories were. Late in his life he received and accepted a marriage proposal from a Mrs Mather, whose third husband, a solicitor, had just died in the chambers opposite his.

Hermit of Grub Street *See the* GRUB STREET HERMIT.

Queen's Square Hermit *See under* QUEEN.

Herne Hill Young professionals' territory, situated between BRIXTON and DULWICH. The area was part of the medieval manor of Milkwell, and the first mention of Herne Hill did not appear until 1789. The name may derive from a prominent Dulwich family or it may mean 'hill by a nook of land'. Protective landowners restricted development here to a few homes for the wealthy and early in the late 18th century the hill was dotted with grand houses in a largely rural setting. From the second half of the 19th century speculative developers moved in and the streets between Railton Road and Dulwich Road, which are now known as POETS' CORNER, were laid out on the eastern half of Effra Farm in 1855. Rapid change began with the opening in 1862 of Herne Hill station on the London, Chatham and Dover railway line and over the following 50 years terraced streets filled the grounds of Herne Hill's lost mansions.

Herne Hill Velodrome A large cycle track located on Burbage Road. It opened in 1891 and is the last remaining venue from the 1948 OLYMPIC GAMES that is still in active use. The multiple Olympic gold medallist Bradley Wiggins (b.1980) began cycling here at the age of 12.

Heron Quays Originally an 8-acre (3.2-hectare) quay but now extended by a further 3 acres (1.2 ha) to connect with CANARY WHARF at its eastern end. Narrower than the other quays of the WEST INDIA DOCKS, it formerly separated the Export and South Docks and was mostly occupied by offices and stores rather than warehouses. There was a herring shed on the quayside from around

1840, but never any trade in herons or with a place of that name.

Heston A multicultural and multi-use district lying west of OSTERLEY PARK and north of HOUNSLOW, between the M4 and the GREAT WEST ROAD, and best known for its motorway service station. On the western edge of the locality, Heston Airport was operational from 1929 to 1946 and streets that have since been built here have names that commemorate famous aviators. It was at Heston in 1938 that prime minister Neville Chamberlain landed after signing the Munich Agreement with Adolf Hitler. Jimmy Page, guitarist with the rock group Led Zeppelin, was born in Heston in 1944. The chef Heston Blumenthal (b.1966) once joked that his parents had named him in honour of Heston service station, a story that several august publications took seriously.

HGS HAMPSTEAD GARDEN SUBURB, also known as 'the Burb'.

Hicks' Hall *See* X'S HALL.

hide In feudal England the term denoted the amount of land that was sufficient to support a family, usually varying between 60 and 120 acres (24–49 hectares) according to the locality or quality of the land. A hide of good land was smaller than one of poorer quality. It was long used as the basis for assessing taxes. The name represents Old English *hīgid*, related to *hīw*, 'family', 'household', and ultimately to Latin *civis*, 'citizen'. It was often spelt 'hyde' in place names, such as the Hyde, in HENDON, NORTH HYDE, and HYDE PARK.

high

High Barnet Modern maps usually treat High Barnet as the area north of Wood Street, and Chipping Barnet as the part to the south and south-east, but history does not recognize this distinction and nor does the local population. High Barnet made its first appearance as an alternative name for Chipping Barnet, or indeed for plain BARNET, in the late 16th century. Rising to 425 feet (130m) above sea level, Barnet occupies an elevated position by London standards and it was popularly said to be the highest spot on the Great North Road between London and York. Another claim that there is no higher point along a direct line east to Russia's Ural mountains

is not true. The High Barnet name failed to catch on until adopted by the Great Northern Railway Company for the station it opened here in 1872. The name was retained when the station joined the LONDON UNDERGROUND network in 1940 and was consequently used to identify the newly suburbanized town, which some distinguished from the parish of Chipping Barnet.

High Street Ken *See* KENSINGTON HIGH STREET.

Highbury Famous as the former home of ARSENAL FC, for which it is still a metonym, Highbury is an elongated settlement in north ISLINGTON, extending from CANONBURY to FINSBURY PARK. In 1770 John Dawes, a stockbroker, began to acquire land, erecting a Highbury House for himself and granting building leases for the first suburban homes. From the 1820s to the 1870s a succession of developers constructed rows of villas throughout Highbury – often adding the word 'Park' to the name of their little estate to convey an impression of quasi-rural grandeur. The clock tower at Highbury Quadrant was erected in celebration of Queen Victoria's diamond jubilee in 1897. A number of early villas have survived, most of which have been subdivided.

Highbury and Islington station A main-line and LONDON UNDERGROUND interchange situated at HIGHBURY CORNER. The station opened in 1872, when it looked much more imposing than it does now. It is served by NORTH LONDON LINE and VICTORIA LINE trains and by suburban overground trains running into MOORGATE.

Highbury Barn A public house located near the southern end of the road called Highbury Park. Originally the barn of Highbury manor farm, it was converted into a dairy and then into a tea and ale house in 1740. Oliver Goldsmith later wrote of the pleasant time he had spent here. In 1885 the present Highbury Barn opened, replacing the old tavern and pleasure gardens, which had become a scene of disreputable activities. *See also* BARNER.

Highbury Corner A busy roundabout situated at the tips of the Highbury, central ISLINGTON, CANONBURY and HOLLOWAY districts. UPPER STREET and HOLLOWAY ROAD are among the many roads that converge here. Islington council aspires to improve the messy look of the junction, which has been called the borough's 'most used, least loved public space'. The immediate vicinity is best known for HIGHBURY AND ISLINGTON STATION, the Hen and Chickens pub and theatre, Highbury Corner magistrates' court and the Union Chapel, a Congregational church that also serves as a popular venue for live music.

Highbury Fields A park in southern Highbury. The fields belonged to the KNIGHTS HOSPITALLER and their manor house was burned down by Wat Tyler's rebels in the Peasants' Revolt of 1381. Refugees from the GREAT FIRE OF LONDON camped out here. By the end of the 18th century the constricted fields were encircled by imposing terraces of houses. The surviving open space was saved for the public in 1885.

Highbury Square The address of the redeveloped former home of ARSENAL FC, now converted into an apartment complex called the Stadium.

Highgate A much-extended village standing on high ground north-east of HAMPSTEAD HEATH. Highgate took root around a village green peppered with ponds and elm trees, at the top of a 426-foot (130m) hill on the edge of the Bishop of London's estate. It was the bishop who erected a tollgate here sometime before 1354, when Highgate's name was first recorded. Later in the same century Dick WHITTINGTON is supposed to have sat upon a milestone on Highgate Hill and, inspired by the distant sound of the bells of ST MARY-LE-BOW, turned again to find fame and fortune in London. A replica stone marks the alleged spot, surmounted by a 1964 statue of Whittington's cat. From the late 17th century to the end of the 18th century Highgate filled with smart houses for CITY folk. Many of the properties survive, and so does the demographic profile. Highgate's most important 20th-century buildings are Highpoint One and Two, designed in the 1930s by Berthold Lubetkin (*see* TECTON) for Sigmund Gestetner, the copier king. *See also* SWEARING ON THE HORNS.

Highgate Cemetery Opened in 1839, it is now divided into the West (original) Cemetery and the East Cemetery (1854), separated by Swains Lane. Highgate has a number of famous occupants: notably Karl Marx, but also including Charles DICKENS, George ELIOT, Michael Faraday, Christina Rossetti, Elizabeth Siddal (wife of Dante Gabriel Rossetti, who had her clandestinely exhumed in 1869 so that he could retrieve his manuscript poems buried with her), Herbert Spencer and Mrs Henry Wood. Funerals still take place and more recent interments include Sir Ralph Richardson, Sir Michael Redgrave, and Dr Y.D. Dadoo, first chairman of the African National Congress. With its memorials, mausoleums and catacombs, the cemetery is much loved by those of a gothic inclination.

Highgate Ponds or **Hampstead (Heath) Ponds** A series of ponds constructed on the eastern side of HAMPSTEAD HEATH as reservoirs to harness the supply of the FLEET river. The water was never of very good quality and was primarily used for industrial purposes. The ponds were later used for bathing, fishing and model boating.

Highgate resin Another name for copalite, the ochre-coloured ancient fossil resin found in the London clay of Highgate Hill.

Highgate School A co-educational independent school in North Road, Highgate, founded in 1565 as a grammar school for boys. Its former pupils include the cricketer Phil Tufnell, the composers John Rutter and John Tavener and the poets Gerard Manley Hopkins and (at Highgate Junior School) John Betjeman. Another poet, T.S. Eliot, briefly taught French and Latin at the Junior School during the First World War.

Highgate Wood An extensively wooded park on the east side of ARCHWAY Road, run (like HAMPSTEAD HEATH) by the CORPORATION OF LONDON, which took it over from the bishops of London in 1886.

Highway, the *See* RATCLIFF HIGHWAY.

Highwood Hill The northern corner of MILL HILL, formerly known simply as Highwood. It was first identified separately from its parent manor of HENDON in the 14th century and was a fashionable country retreat during the 17th and 18th centuries. The diarist and traveller Celia Fiennes (1662–1741) lived at Highwood Ash from 1713 to 1737. Highwood House was bought in 1825 by Sir Stamford Raffles (1781–1826), the founder of Singapore and the London Zoological Society. He lived here for only a year before he died but Lady Raffles stayed on until her own death in 1858. The adjacent Hendon Park estate was the 140-acre (57-hectare) property of William Wilberforce (1759–1833), the anti-slavery campaigner. To the south, Holcombe House was built for a City glove merchant in 1778. Herbert (later Cardinal) Vaughan bought the villa in 1866 and started a Catholic missionary college here. The school soon outgrew the premises so Vaughan built St Joseph's College, which lies to the south-west. Holcombe House then became home to a sisterhood of Franciscan nuns, who also soon moved to larger, purpose-built premises: the neighbouring St Mary's Abbey. When Holcombe House came back on the market in 1977 it was acquired for the Missionary Institute London, which in turn sold it to a developer in 2007. St Mary's Abbey has been converted into a luxury apartment complex called Highwoods, while the Franciscan sisters have moved into a new lodge next door.

Hillingdon A much-extended village, plentifully endowed with open spaces, situated midway between HAYES[2] and UXBRIDGE. Once occupying a clearing in the dense woodland that covered the area, its name probably referred to 'the hill of a man called Hilda', although others have construed it as 'the fort on a hill' and cited dubious stories of a battle in which the Mercians defeated the West Saxons. Numerous gentlemen's residences were built in the southern part of the parish and of the present-day survivors the most impressive are Cedar House and Hillingdon Court. After the First World War private developers began to expand the village into a commuter suburb, although many open spaces were retained as playing fields and recreation grounds. The strength of Uxbridge as a commercial centre has prevented the old village from acting as a focus for the wider suburb, which has had the benefit of preserving some of its charm.

Hillingdon, London Borough of An OUTER LONDON borough formed in 1965 by merging the municipal borough of UXBRIDGE with the urban districts of HAYES[2] and HARLINGTON, YIEWSLEY and WEST DRAYTON, and RUISLIP-NORTHWOOD. Hillingdon has the third largest area of the London boroughs, corresponding roughly with the ancient Elthorne Hundred. Around half the borough is of rural character, while the GRAND UNION CANAL constitutes the major industrial axis. Most of the prime office accommodation is located in the vicinity of HEATHROW AIRPORT. Since 1977 the borough's headquarters have been at the civic centre in Uxbridge – a structure praised by the Prince of Wales as an encouraging development in public building design. The

borough's intricate coat of arms includes brushwood, an eagle, the north star, a fleur-de-lys, a cog-wheel, a Tudor rose and two ears of rye, 'slipped' (i.e. with the stalk visible). The last of these elements is a pun on the name of Ruislip. Hillingdon's motto is 'forward'.

Hillman (Hunter) 'Punter' (customer) in COCKNEY RHYMING SLANG, from the Rootes Group car of the 1960s and 70s.

hippodrome
Golders Green Hippodrome See under GOLDERS GREEN.
Islington Hippodrome See COLLINS'S MUSIC HALL.
London Hippodrome See the TALK OF THE TOWN.

His Return to London A distinctly pro-London (and anti-West Country) poem by Robert Herrick (1591–1674), celebrating rapturously the poet's return to the capital in 1647 following his removal from a rural living in Devon:

> From the dull confines of the drooping West,
> To see the day spring from the pregnant East,
> Ravished in spirit, I come, nay more, I fly
> To thee, blest place of my nativity! ...
> London my home is: though by a hard fate sent
> Into a long and irksome banishment;
> Yet since called back; henceforward let me be,
> O native country, repossessed by thee!
> For, rather than I'll to the West return,
> I'll beg of thee first here to have mine urn.

hit and miss or **hit or miss** 'Kiss' in COCKNEY RHYMING SLANG. Neither form of the term is in common usage.

Hither Green A dormitory suburb situated east of CATFORD. In medieval times this was the location of the important hamlet of Romborough, but it seems likely that the whole population – and the place's very identity – was wiped out by the Black Death. The present name was coined in the 18th century to distinguish the new settlement, which was nearer to LEWISHAM parish church, from Further Green, on Verdant Lane.

HMS Belfast A Royal Navy cruiser, commissioned in 1939. During the Second World War it took part in the Battle of the North Cape and in the Normandy landings. Since 1971 it has been moored on the THAMES near TOWER BRIDGE and is open to the public. The guns in both the ship's turrets are trained and elevated onto the LONDON GATEWAY(2) motorway service station, some 12½ miles (20 km) distant.

Hobson's (choice) 'Voice' in COCKNEY RHYMING SLANG. In a non-cockney sense the term means 'no choice at all' and originated in Cambridge.

Hockley-in-the-Hole A well-known resort in former days for bear-baiting, bull-baiting and prize-fighting, in what was then a squalid locality near CLERKENWELL Green. It was closed about 1730. Mrs Peachum in John Gay's BEGGAR'S OPERA, says, 'You should go to Hockley-in-the-Hole ... to learn valour'.

Hodge Dr JOHNSON's favourite cat, a much-indulged companion in the late 1760s and early 1770s. 'Hodge' is an alteration of 'Roger', and was used as a familiar and condescending name for a farm labourer or peasant, a country clown or rustic, in the 16th century. In the *Life of Samuel Johnson* (1791) James Boswell records the lexicographer's insistence that Hodge was 'a very fine cat indeed', after he had initially appeared to offend the animal by suggesting that he had had other cats he had liked better. Jon Bickley's bronze statue of Hodge (1997) stands outside Johnson's house in Gough Square, off FLEET STREET.

> The general conduct if we trace
> Of our articulating race,
> Hodge's example we shall find
> A keen reproof of human kind.
>
> PERCIVAL STOCKDALE: 'An Elegy on the Death of Dr Johnson's Favourite Cat' (1778)

Hogarth

Hogarth, William London's greatest 18th-century artist (1697–1764). He was born in Bartholomew Close, SMITHFIELD, and apprenticed at the age of 16 to a silver-plate engraver. Within a few years he had gone into business on his own, at first engraving book plates, but soon producing portraits, satirical prints and vividly populated visual narratives of London life, in which he frequently mixed the comical with the grotesque, most famously in *A* RAKE'S PROGRESS (1733–5) and *Marriage à la Mode* (1743–5). His many other important works included *Industry and Idleness* (1747), *The* MARCH TO

FINCHLEY (1749–50) and GIN LANE (1751). In 1753 he published *The Analysis of Beauty*, an illustrated manuscript in which he combined aesthetic theory with practical advice for artists.

Hogarth Press A publishing venture begun in 1917 by Leonard and Virginia Woolf at Hogarth House, their home in Paradise Road, RICHMOND. Based from 1921 in BLOOMSBURY, the Hogarth Press published books by members of the BLOOMSBURY GROUP, translations of Russian classics and some pioneering works on psychoanalysis, notably FREUD's. From 1946 it operated as a division of Chatto & Windus.

Hogarth Roundabout A busy road junction and somewhat flimsy flyover located just east of HOGARTH'S HOUSE. Here the A316 diverges from the A4 GREAT WEST ROAD. Fuller's GRIFFIN brewery stands just east of the roundabout.

Hogarth's House William Hogarth's 'little country box by the Thames', in which he spent most of each summer from 1749 until his death. Built around 1700, it is situated immediately north of the grounds of CHISWICK HOUSE. Hogarth's House is now a museum of his life and a gallery of his work. The artist's tomb, with a poetic epitaph by his friend David GARRICK, lies a short distance to the east of the house in St Nicholas' churchyard.

Hokey-cokey A light-hearted COCKNEY dance, popular during the 1940s, with a song and tune of this name to go with it. It was also known as the 'Cokey-Cokey', especially in the version written by Jimmy Kennedy in 1945 and recorded by Billy Cotton and his Band, among others.

> You put your left foot in,
> You put your left foot out,
> In, out, in, out, shake it all about,
> You do the Hokey-cokey
> And you turn around,
> That's what it's all about.

Holborn A former metropolitan borough and an office-dominated street running eastward from the north-east corner of COVENT GARDEN towards SMITHFIELD. An early settlement evolved on the edge of the city beside a 'hole bourne' or stream in a hollow. The stream became known as the FLEET and was later covered by Farringdon Street and FARRINGDON ROAD. The road now called Holborn, which becomes High Holborn west of GRAY'S INN ROAD, was in existence as

Holeburnestreete by 1249. Holborn developed as a medieval suburb of the City, with houses that steadily grew in impressiveness. Several lawyers' colleges were established, some later evolving into barristers' colonies while others withered and died. STAPLE INN was among the departed but its 16th-century timber-framed frontage remains. GRAY'S INN to the north of the street and LINCOLN'S INN to the south have prospered and expanded. From 1863 houses in the east of Holborn were demolished for the construction of Holborn Viaduct, which was opened by Queen Victoria in 1869. From that time until the present day Holborn has been progressively redeveloped with hefty office blocks. The six-way junction at Holborn Circus became the site of the offices and printing works of the Mirror newspaper group, now replaced by SAINSBURY's headquarters.

Holborn Bars Originally, posts and rails marking the western boundary of the city, opposite STAPLE INN, later replaced by granite obelisks. Also the name of the terracotta fortress built for the Prudential Assurance Company by Sir Alfred Waterhouse and his son Paul over the last quarter of the 19th century.

Holborn Empire A former MUSIC HALL in High Holborn, opened in 1857 and rebuilt by Frank Matcham at the beginning of the 20th century. The biggest stars of the time appeared here. It was badly damaged by bombing in the Second World War, and demolished in 1960.

Holborn for wealth and Cheam for health Said to have been the words of John Williams, Dean of Westminster, on appointing his friend John Hacket to the rectories of both St Andrew's, Holborn, and St Dunstan's, CHEAM, in 1624.

ride backwards up Holborn hill, to See under RIDE.

hole in the wall The informal term for a cash dispenser, or automated teller machine (ATM), in the outside wall of a building. The comic actor Reg Varney (see ON THE BUSES) unveiled the world's first electronic ATM at Barclay's Church Street branch in ENFIELD TOWN on 27 June 1967.

Holland Park An attractive public park and highly fashionable residential quarter situated south of NOTTING HILL and north of KENSINGTON HIGH STREET. In 1607 chancellor of the exchequer Sir Walter Cope built the nucleus of Kensington House. On his death in 1614 the property passed to his son-in-law Henry Rich, 1st Earl of Holland,

who greatly enlarged what became Holland House before his execution in 1649. Henry Fox, a wily character who later became paymaster general, leased the house from 1726 and acquired the freehold around 1770, by which time he had become the first Baron Holland, though he was no relation of Henry Rich. By the 1850s Holland House had fallen into a state of disrepair and Fox's grandson was forced to sell some land to raise funds for its renovation. Over a period of several decades a series of separate schemes encircled Holland House and its attenuated grounds. Sweeping STUCCOED terraces constitute the most visible theme but some streets have mews cottages or red-brick mansions. Holland House took a direct hit by a bomb in 1941 and was reduced to a shell in the late 1950s. The grounds were opened to the public and an open-air theatre was set up at the rear of the ruined house. The fictional 34 Claremont Avenue in Holland Park was Edina's home in Jennifer Saunders' television comedy series ABSOLUTELY FABULOUS.

Holland Park Circle A group of artists and architects led by Frederic, Lord Leighton (1830–96), classical painter and president of the ROYAL ACADEMY from 1878 until his death. The circle met at Leighton House, which was built in 1879 and survives as a palatial collection of Victorian art.

Opera Holland Park See under OPERA.

Holloway A linear residential settlement bordering the road of the same name (see below), stretching north-westwards away from ISLINGTON. From the 14th century, the 'hollow way' began to lend its name to the scattered collection of dwellings along its length, dislodging the older manorial identity of Tollington. The district was wholly built up in the latter part of the 19th century, mostly with terraced houses – some of which were of substandard construction, but with a few streets of detached and semi-detached houses set well back from the commercial hubbub of Holloway Road itself. From the early 20th century the borough and county councils knocked down houses and put up blocks of flats with increasing zeal until they were persuaded to desist in the 1970s. Nick Hornby made the district a setting for his novels *High Fidelity* (1995), which was transposed to

Chicago for the film version, and *About a Boy* (1998).

> Chris and Paul Weitz, who made the 2002 movie of Mr Hornby's second novel, 'About a Boy', didn't even bother to change the locale. They set the film in the north London neighborhood of Holloway, which is to Mr Hornby roughly what Wessex was to Thomas Hardy.
>
> *New York Times* (9 April 2005)

From the mid-19th century to the 1920s, Holloway was a slang term for the vagina, playing on 'hollow way'.

Holloway cheesecake A famous delicacy in the 18th century, produced on the farms and sold at local taverns, notably the Half Moon, and by street traders in the CITY.

Holloway Prison A prison in Camden Road, Lower Holloway, opened in 1852 on a site that had previously been set aside for the burial of cholera victims. The prison became exclusively a women's jail around 1903; among its earliest female residents were Emmeline Pankhurst and some of her fellow suffragettes, in 1906. In 1970 it was demolished and completely rebuilt.

Holloway Road A major north London thoroughfare (part of the A1), running north-westward from HIGHBURY Corner to ARCHWAY. The road was in existence by the 11th century and was known as the 'hollow way' (the road in a hollow) by the early 14th century, when it had become the main route from the CITY of London to the north. In the 17th century Holloway Road was notorious for its highwaymen but it became safer as houses began to connect the three hamlets along its length. The construction of Archway Road brought an end to the area's rural character in the 1820s. Holloway Road underground station opened in 1906 where the hamlet of Ring Cross had stood. The road was the first home of the Campaign for Nuclear Disarmament on its foundation in 1954, and of the National Youth Theatre – housed in the former People's Picture Palace – two years later. In the early 1960s record producer Joe Meek created a string of hits at his home-cum-studio at 304 Holloway Road, including the Tornados' *Telstar* (1962).

Hollow Pond or **Ponds** A linked series of waterlogged gravel pits in WHIPPS CROSS. The pond is designated a site of special scientific interest and serves as a boating lake in summer.

Holmes, Sherlock The most famous figure in detective fiction, the creation of Sir Arthur Conan Doyle (1859–1930). His solutions of crime and mysteries were related in a series of 60 stories that mainly appeared in the *Strand Magazine* between 1891 and 1927. The character was based on Dr Joseph Bell of the Edinburgh Infirmary, whose methods of deduction suggested a system that Holmes developed into a science: the observation of the minutest details and apparently insignificant circumstances scientifically interpreted. Dr Watson, Holmes's friend and assistant, was a skit on Doyle himself, and BAKER STREET acquired lasting fame through his writings. The US actor William Gillette (1853–1937) was the first to play Holmes on the stage and his portrayal did much to influence public perception of the detective's appearance and mannerisms and the way in which he was depicted in subsequent adaptations. Other actors to have played Holmes include Basil Rathbone (all media), John Gielgud (radio), Jeremy Brett (TV) and Robert Downey Jr. (film).

> How often have I said to you that when you have eliminated the impossible, whatever remains, however improbable, must be the truth?
>
> SIR ARTHUR CONAN DOYLE: *The Sign of Four* (1890)

Holmesian Pertaining to Sherlock Holmes.

> Holmesian inference says that we know that this is what happened only if there is no other explanation consistent with the evidence.
>
> ALEXANDER BIRD, in *Oxford Studies in Epistemology*, Volume 1, 'Abstract Knowledge and Holmesian inference' (2005)

Holophusikon or **Holophusicon** (Greek, 'whole of nature') A museum at Leicester House, LEICESTER SQUARE, opened by Sir Ashton Lever (1729–88) in 1773. The collection included ethnographic material, natural objects and various curiosities. The project caught the public imagination but failed to turn a profit and Lever sold the collection by lottery. His successor fared little better with the enterprise and it closed in 1806.

Holwood House A mansion situated near KESTON, built on a modest scale in the early 17th century and progressively extended. William Pitt the Younger, (1759–1806) acquired the house in 1784 and he employed the services of Sir John SOANE to remodel and enlarge it further, while Humphry Repton improved the grounds. Holwood House became an important meeting place for political figures of the time and has been called 'the original Chequers', in a reference to the prime minister's official country retreat. The hollow trunk of the 'Wilberforce Oak' stands where William Wilberforce gave notice to Pitt that he had resolved to raise the question of the slave trade in the House of Commons. A commemorative stone bench is inscribed with a pertinent extract from Wilberforce's diary. Holwood House was rebuilt in 1826 by Decimus Burton after its predecessor had burnt down.

holy

holy friar 'Liar' in COCKNEY RHYMING SLANG. Modern alternatives include 'Dunlop tyre' and 'deep fat fryer'.

holy ghost 'Toast' in COCKNEY RHYMING SLANG, or the starting post or winning post in a horse race.

Holy Land Ironic 19th-century slang for the area around ST GILES, including SEVEN DIALS, which at the time was the site of a notorious criminal slum. An alternative nickname was Palestine in London.

home

Home Circuit The assize circuit that had London at its centre, around which judges from the ROYAL COURTS OF JUSTICE would tour to try serious cases, including offences for which they could impose the death penalty on those found guilty. The arrival of the assize judge was often accompanied by a solemn ceremony. The counties in the circuit were repeatedly changed but never included London itself, or MIDDLESEX, and most often encompassed Hertfordshire, ESSEX, Kent, SURREY and Sussex. The Courts of Assize were abolished in 1972.

home counties The counties surrounding London. These were originally Kent, SURREY, ESSEX, and MIDDLESEX, but now Buckinghamshire, Berkshire, Hertfordshire and Sussex are often included. The term probably derived from the HOME CIRCUIT.

> He was aware, that in the home counties near London, where straw was dear, this might not be the case, but in country towns, at a distance from the metropolis, the case was widely different.

> *The Parliamentary Register*, quoting General John Burgoyne (26 March 1781)

Homerton A crowded part of east-central HACKNEY, dominated by council-built flats. By the early 17th century more than a dozen lords and knights had houses here, including the governors of Jersey and Guernsey. Some of these property owners were only occasional visitors to Homerton but Edward la Zouche, 11th Baron Zouche (1556–1625), cultivated a physic garden here and extended it to other plots before his death. In the mid-18th century building began to spread well beyond the High Street. Berger's paint factory opened in 1780 and workers' cottages were built nearby. This was the start of a process of industrialization and urbanization that steadily drove the gentry away. *See also* SUTTON HOUSE.

Hong Kong Garden A hit single (1978) by Siouxsie and the Banshees. The song was inspired by, although the lyrics do not concern, a Chinese restaurant of that name in CHISLEHURST High Street, which was a regular haunt of members of the BROMLEY CONTINGENT.

Honor Oak A primarily working-class neighbourhood occupying high ground north of FOREST HILL. One Tree Hill has been claimed as the site of BOUDICCA's defeat by the Roman general Suetonius Paulinus, but this almost certainly occurred in the south Midlands. On May Day 1602 Elizabeth I is said to have picnicked beneath the hill's crowning tree. The story is of doubtful authenticity and it is even less likely that the queen got drunk and knighted the oak, as has been claimed. It is more probable that the tree marked the boundary of a group of manors known as the Honour of LEWISHAM. St Augustine's Church was built in 1873 and the Honor oak was destroyed by a lightning strike around the same time. In 1896 a private golf club enclosed One Tree Hill, prompting an 'agitation' lasting several years, which was said to have drawn up to 100,000 demonstrators. CAMBERWELL council eventually bought the hill for £6,000 and opened it to the public in 1905, when a new oak tree was planted at the summit. The slopes of the hill are nowadays wildly wooded and the park is one the hidden gems of south London.

Honor Oak Park The eastern part of HONOR OAK. Despite misconceptions to the contrary, Honor Oak Park was not the name of an open space; the affix was the invention of Victorian property developers. Several sites in the area have been redeveloped in recent decades, most interestingly at Segal Close, to the south-east, and Walter's Way, to the west. These are both named after Walter Segal (1907–85), who pioneered low-cost low-skill construction methods ideally suited to self-build projects. LEWISHAM council supported the schemes, which served as a model that has since been adopted by several other English councils.

honourable

Honourable Artillery Company (HAC) The oldest surviving British Army unit, having been founded by Henry VIII, in 1537, as the Guild of St George. In Tudor and Stuart days the officers for the TRAINBANDS of London were supplied by the HAC, in whose ranks John Milton, Christopher Wren and Samuel PEPYS served at one time or another.

The HAC is not part of the regular army but is the senior regiment of the Territorial Army Volunteer Reserves. It maintains a headquarters in the CITY ROAD, and has four squadrons and a gun troop. It also provides the Company of Pikemen and Musketeers and has the right to march through the CITY of London with fixed bayonets.

In 1638 Robert Keayne, a member of the London company, founded the Ancient and Honourable Artillery Company of Boston, Massachusetts, which is the oldest military unit in the USA.

Honourable East India Company See the EAST INDIA COMPANY.

Hook A suburb filling the area between CHESSINGTON and SURBITON. The name probably refers to a hook-shaped spur of land, although the 12th-century presence of John Hog, a mill owner later known as John del Hoc, has prompted some alternative etymological theories. Late in the 19th century Hook became caught up in the rapid expansion of Surbiton as a railway suburb, a process that reached its apogee after the opening of the KINGSTON bypass in 1927. The children's author Enid Blyton (1897–1968) honed her craft while working as a nursery governess at Southernhay, 207 Hook Road. After the success of her first book she quit to take up writing full-time. The house has since been converted to flats and doctors' surgeries.

hooligan A violent or lawless young person. The term dates from the 19th century and may derive from the Irish surname Houlihan, alluding to a particular family, said by some to have lived in SOUTHWARK. Others have mentioned a 'Hooley's gang' in ISLINGTON. Another possible source is a cheeky character named Larry Hoolagan in Thomas Rodwell's play *More Blunders Than One* or *The Irish Valet*, first performed at the ADELPHI Theatre in the STRAND in 1824. Alternatively, Rodwell may have made use of a name that had already acquired appropriate connotations.

> Hoolagan: There's only one thing I should like, now, before you go.
> Old Melbourne: And pray what's that?
> Hoolagan: To knock your ugly old jaws about; and if you an't [sic] off with a hop, skip and a jump, by the powers, I'll be after doing it, too.
> *More Blunders Than One*, I, ii

Hoops A nickname of QUEENS PARK RANGERS FC, from the players' horizontally striped shirts, which changed from green and white to blue and white in 1926. In recent years the club has enhanced the nickname to 'Superhoops', with no particular justification. Many fans prefer 'the Rs', with or without an apostrophe.

Hoover Building The architectural highpoint of the WESTERN AVENUE, in PERIVALE, this art deco factory by New York architects Wallis Gilbert and Partners was completed in 1933. It closed in 1982 and reopened ten years later, magnificently restored, with the rear of the building converted into a TESCO superstore.

> Five miles out of London on the Western Avenue,
> Must have been a wonder when it was brand new.
> I'm talking about the splendour of the Hoover factory,
> I know that you'd agree if you had seen it too.
> ELVIS COSTELLO: 'Hoover Factory' (song) (1976)

Hornchurch A primarily interwar suburb situated to the south-east of ROMFORD. Henry II founded a hospice here in 1159, which by 1222 had become known as the *Monasterium Cornutum* or Monastery of the Horns, possibly a reference to the local leather currying industry, which had either a bull's or a stag's head with horns as its guild sign. Leather remained at the heart of Hornchurch's commercial life until the 19th century, with shoemakers, tanners and dealers in animal skins. During the 1920s and 1930s the whole of Hornchurch became a dormitory suburb; its population increasing threefold during this period. The Queen's Theatre moved from a converted cinema to purpose-built premises on Billet Lane in 1975, and has become one of outer London's most successful arts venues. Across the road is Fairkytes, a Georgian house that is now Hornchurch Arts Centre. Hornchurch Country Park occupies much of the former airfield of RAF Hornchurch, which was an important base for Spitfires during the Battle of Britain. To the south, brownfield sites on the Hornchurch Marshes are earmarked for development as part of HAVERING RIVERSIDE.

Horniman Museum A cultural and natural history museum in FOREST HILL, founded by the TEA merchant Frederick John Horniman (1835–1906), who began collecting items from around the world in the 1860s and first exhibited them in part of the family house. The museum moved to its present purpose-built home on London Road in 1901. Its speciality is the display of artefacts from other cultures and there is a particular emphasis on music. The Horniman is one of London's most visited attractions, largely because it draws so many school parties.

Hornsey A late Victorian and Edwardian residential district situated between ALEXANDRA PARK and CROUCH END. The name was recorded as Haringeie in 1201 and had been corrupted to Harynsey two centuries later (*see also* HARRINGAY). By the 18th century Hornsey was a sizeable village where Londoners were building country retreats. With parks in most directions, the district had the country's lowest death rate in the early 20th century and was nicknamed 'healthy Hornsey'. In 1952 Colin Chapman founded the sports car manufacturing firm Lotus Engineering at 7 Tottenham Lane, in converted stables behind the Railway Arms.

Horny and Shallow A nickname for Corney & Barrow, playing on the supposed character of its clientele. Now a chain of wine bars serving the SQUARE MILE and CANARY WHARF, the business began as a wine shop in Old Broad Street, founded in 1780 by Edward Bland Corney. His son Thomas introduced his cousin Robert Barrow to the business in 1838. A division of the company continues to operate as a wine merchant, to which the nickname does not apply.

Horse Guards The British cavalry regiment (formally the Royal Horse Guards, informally the Blues) that in 1969 was amalgamated with the 1st Royal Dragoons to become the Blues and Royals. Their headquarters in WHITEHALL is properly named Horse Guards but is often called 'the Horse Guards building' to distinguish the structure from the former regiment. The building's mounted guards make it a popular spot for photo opportunities. *See also* HOUSEHOLD TROOPS.

Horse Guards Parade A parade ground situated between WHITEHALL and ST JAMES'S PARK. The TROOPING THE COLOUR ceremony takes place here on the sovereign's official birthday. Beach volleyball will be played on Horse Guards Parade at the 2012 OLYMPIC GAMES, when a temporary arena will be built for 15,000 spectators.

Horselydown The largely forgotten identity of the vicinity of the south side of TOWER BRIDGE. The name almost certainly arose simply because horses were kept on the 'down', which was relatively high ground surrounded by marshland. However, some have associated the area with the pagan practice of horse worship, while an improbable legend suggests that King John's horse fell down here (Horselydown: 'horse lay down') when he was making a hurried escape from the house of a miller, who had returned to find his wife and the king engaged in an amorous encounter (*see also* CUCKOLD'S POINT). Dock-related trades dominated Horselydown from the late Middle Ages. Thomas Guy (1644–1724), who founded GUY'S HOSPITAL, was the son of a Horselydown lighterman and coal dealer. Charles Dibdin's song 'Poll of Horselydown' (1807) told the story of a Captain Oakum, who was so distracted by the local beauty that he laid himself open to various misfortunes.

Horseman's Sunday An annual ceremony introduced in 1968 as part of a campaign to retain the stables in HYDE PARK at a time when they were threatened with closure. At noon on the penultimate Sunday in September, the vicar of St John's Hyde Park leads a cavalcade of more than a hundred horses and riders to the church. The horses gather on the forecourt of the church for a blessing, followed by a ride-past and a presentation of rosettes. From its political beginnings the event has evolved into a carnival-like celebration of riding in central London.

Horsenden Hill Among the largest tracts of open space in north-west London, Horsenden Hill and its neighbouring golf courses separate the industry of PERIVALE and GREENFORD from the suburban streets of SUDBURY. Horsenden Hill was acquired by EALING council in 1938 as part of its GREEN-BELT scheme and the park was extended by the acquisition of neighbouring charity-owned land in 1942. The hill has been described as a 'miniature HAMPSTEAD HEATH' and its summit offers one of the most panoramic views in London.

Hosegate *See* NATHAN BARLEY.

hospital (Medieval Latin *hospitale*, from Latin *hospitalis*, a derivative of *hospes*, 'guest') The word was originally applied to a hospice or hostel for the reception of pilgrims. It later denoted a charitable institution for the aged and infirm (as in GREENWICH HOSPITAL, CHELSEA ROYAL HOSPITAL), then charitable institutions for the education of children (as in Christ's Hospital, *see the* BLUECOAT SCHOOL) and finally the present institutions for treatment of the sick and injured. 'Hospital', 'hospice', 'hostel' and 'hotel' are all related words. *See also* SPITALFIELDS.

Hospitallers *See the* KNIGHTS HOSPITALLER.

Hospital Sunday The Sunday nearest St Luke's Day (18 October), when churches have special collections for hospitals. The practice began in London in 1873.

Hot and Cold Corner A nickname given to the corner of KENSINGTON GORE where the Royal Geographical Society is located. The nickname was inspired by the adjacent statues of David Livingstone and Sir Ernest Shackleton, who made their names in the Tropics and the Antarctic respectively.

Houndsditch A poor relation among the CITY's commercial thoroughfares, extending south-eastward from BISHOPSGATE's junction with LIVERPOOL STREET to ALDGATE. The name was first recorded in 1275. Seemingly obvious explanations for the meaning of place names often turn out to be fallacious, but Houndsditch genuinely seems to have been a trench, once forming part of the moat of LONDON WALL, where 'dead dogges were there laid or cast', as John Stow put it in his *Survey of London* (1598). Several canine skeletons were unearthed here in 1989, probably dating from Roman times. During the Middle Ages Houndsditch became the centre of the bellfounding industry. When demand declined following the Dissolution (1536–9) the metalworkers turned to the manufacture of guns and cannons. The ditch was filled in by the end of the 16th century, when second-hand clothes began to be sold here. For most of the 20th century the Jewish-owned Houndsditch Warehouse was a landmark local clothing business but it has since been replaced by one of the many austere office blocks that now line the street. *See also* EDRIC OF STREONE.

Houndsditch murders *See the* SIEGE OF SIDNEY STREET.

Hounslow A major commercial and residential district situated east of HEATHROW AIRPORT. Hounslow was first mentioned in Domesday Book and the name is a corruption of Old English words meaning 'hound's mound'. The mound may have been a burial tumulus but is not known whether the 'hound' element referred to the animal or a man of that name. A friary was established around 1200 and at the time of the dissolution of the monasteries it was the richest Trinitarian house in England. The friary's chapel subsequently evolved into Holy Trinity Church. By 1635 Hounslow had already acquired significance as a coaching halt, conveniently located just before the Bath and Staines roads diverged across HOUNSLOW HEATH. Although the village barely extended beyond the High Street, there were over a hundred residents and at least five inns, some of which had been in existence for more than a century. In the 18th and early 19th centuries Hounslow was the first stop outside of London for nearly all the westbound coaches; in 1833 over 200 coaches passed through every day. From the 1960s large numbers of Asian immigrants began to settle in the area, at first because it was close to their point of arrival at Heathrow Airport, and then as a result of a snowball effect.

Hounslow, London Borough of An OUTER LONDON borough formed in 1965 by merging the municipal boroughs of HESTON and ISLEWORTH and BRENTFORD and CHISWICK with the urban district of FELTHAM. It is one of the most irregularly shaped boroughs, looking a little like Britain tipped clockwise. Hounslow's coat of arms has references to HEATHROW AIRPORT and Feltham's former sword mill, together with a punning image of a hunting hound on a patch of heath-grass. The civic motto is *juncti progrediamur*, which means 'let us go forward jointly'.

Hounslow Harriers A fictional women's football team in the film *Bend It Like Beckham* (2002). Protagonist Jesminder 'Jess' Kaur Bhamra (played by Parminder Nagra) wears the Harriers' No.7 shirt, the same number David Beckham wore for Manchester United and England.

Hounslow Heath A large park situated to the east of the River Crane in south-west Hounslow, including a public golf course and nurseries. The removal of tree cover on the 'Warren of Staines' from the early 13th century created the bleakest terrain in MIDDLESEX, eventually stretching from BRENTFORD to beyond the western boundary of modern London. Rudimentary agricultural usage developed after Henry VIII divided the land among 14 parishes in 1546. On several occasions great armies were mustered here, including those of Oliver Cromwell and James II. In the 17th century the heath covered 25 square miles (65 sq km) and was peppered with gibbets, erected for the punishment of its notorious highwaymen. By the start of the 19th century it still encompassed around 5,000 acres (20 sq km) but a combination of enclosure and the exercise of squatters' rights rapidly diminished it.

> Hounslow Heath ... is a sample of all that is bad in soil and villainous in look. Yet this is now enclosed, and what they call 'cultivated'. Here is a fresh robbery of villages, hamlets and farm and labourers' buildings and abodes!
>
> WILLIAM COBBETT: *Rural Rides* (1830)

Sand and gravel mining began in the mid-19th century, wreaking further damage on the natural environment, which has since been largely restored. In 1919 Hounslow Heath became the site of the LONDON TERMINAL AERODROME, the country's first civil airport.

House An artwork by Rachel Whiteread (b.1963), commissioned in 1993 by the public art agency Artangel, in association with Beck's beer. It was a concrete and plaster cast of the interior of the last remaining house of a late 19th-century terrace, installed in situ at 193 Grove Road, near the corner of ROMAN ROAD in BOW. The work helped Whiteread win the 1993 Turner Prize but was unpopular with many local residents. At the insistence of the neighbourhood council, *House* was demolished in January 1994.

> Eric Flounders, leader of Bow neighbourhood committee, said: 'This structure is a little entertainment for the gallery-going classes of Hampstead ... It's all very well for them, but what people who live in tower blocks in Tower Hamlets want is parkland.'
>
> *The Guardian* (25 November 1993)

House, the A familiar name for the House of Commons, the House of Lords and the ROYAL OPERA HOUSE among the most familiar institutions (a 1995 BBC television documentary about the Royal Opera House was titled *The House*). CITY dealers used to refer to the STOCK EXCHANGE as 'the House'. The House is also the formal name of the home of the ROYAL SOCIETY OF ARTS, at 8 John Adam Street, STRAND.

House of the Converts See DOMUS CONVERSORUM.

House of St Barnabas A charity for the homeless, located at the corner of GREEK STREET and SOHO SQUARE. The organization was established as the House of Charity in 1846 and moved to its present address in 1862. It became the House of St Barnabas-in-Soho in 1961, following the restoration of the imposing Georgian building, which has recently been converted from a hostel for homeless women to a training and 'personal development' centre for London's homeless people and those in crisis. *See also the* PENNY CHUTE.

Houses of Parliament See *the* PALACE OF WESTMINSTER.

Household Troops Those troops whose special duty it is to attend the sovereign. They consist of the Household Cavalry, comprising the two regiments of the Life Guards and the Blues and Royals (*see* HORSE GUARDS), and the Guards Division (formerly Brigade of Guards), consisting of the five Foot Guards regiments of the Grenadier, Coldstream, Scots, Irish and Welsh Guards. The proper collective name for these seven regiments is the Household Division (until 1968 Household Brigade), and the title 'Household Troops' properly applies to the Household Division together with the King's TROOP Royal Horse Artillery.

Howard, Philip *See* DON'T BE A SINNER, BE A WINNER.

Howell, James *See* WELSH AMBASSADOR, HIS EXCELLENCY THE.

how's your father? An all-purpose catch-phrase that evolved in the London MUSIC HALLS in the early 20th century. Its pioneer was Harry Tate (1873–1940), who told gags in which he asked the question as a way of changing from an awkward subject. The phrase was much employed by cocky subalterns during the First World War:

> 'Then this heartiness – this Harry Tate-iness, if I may call it so, the inevitable "How's your Father" joke is merely – er ...'
>
> 'Swank!' I said.
>
> DENIS GARSTIN: *The Shilling Soldiers* (1918)

Without the question mark, it became a stand-in for a missing word or name, in the same vein as 'whatsit' or 'thingummybob'. Later still, it became specifically associated with various forms of mild misbehaviour, usually sexual activity:

> Your bloody stable girls told him I'd had a bit of how's-your-father with Angela effing Brickell.
>
> DICK FRANCIS: *Longshot* (1990)

Hoxton A formerly working-class district in north-west SHOREDITCH, now fashionable with members of London's media and 'dotcom' indus-tries. The creation of Hoxton Square and Charles Square in the late 17th century failed to spark an inrush of wealthy homebuyers. Instead, Hoxton's open spaces retained their market gardens and gained hospitals, schools and public houses and a community of religious dissenters, including the ANCIENT DEISTS. Among the professional men who later settled here was James Parkinson of Hoxton Square. His *Essay on Shaking Palsy* (1815) identified the disease that now bears his name. Hoxton Fields had disappeared beneath Hoxton New Town by 1850. Hoxton was home to the renowned Britannia Theatre, a music hall that DICKENS compared with Milan's La Scala. Built in 1858 it became one of Victorian London's greatest palaces of entertainment. Converted to a cinema in 1923, it was demolished after war-time bomb damage. Hoxton Hall, a saloon-style MUSIC HALL built in 1863, survives and is used for community arts and education purposes. The poet and playwright Ben Jonson killed fellow actor Gabriel Spencer in a duel on Hoxton Fields in 1598, evading a death sentence because he could read from the Latin Bible.

Hoxton fin A men's hairstyle consisting of a gelled crest running from front to back across the middle of the head, briefly fashionable at the beginning of the 21st century. Such a style was sported for a time – and its popularity boos-ted – by the footballer and fashion icon David Beckham (b.1975).

HP Sauce A commercial brand of sauce first made in the 1870s. The initials that form its name are traditionally supposed to stand for 'Houses of Parliament', a picture of which appears on the label. However, the name was adopted by the Midland Vinegar Company, its original manu-facturers, from that of another firm's product, 'Garton's H.P. Sauce', and it was thus ready-made, whatever the letters themselves might have actually meant.

Hulks Old dismasted men-of-war anchored in the THAMES, mostly in the vicinity of WOOLWICH, and used as prison ships, first established as a 'temporary expedient' in 1778 and remaining until 1857. An impression of the Hulks is given by DICKENS in the opening chapters of *Great Expectations* (1860–1).

hummingbird A nickname of London's first self-propelled taxi, deriving from the buzzing noise made by its battery-powered motor. In-troduced in 1897, the vehicles were also called Berseys, after Walter C. Bersey, the young man-ager of the London Electrical Cab Company. The hummingbirds did not see out the century, owing to their unreliability, a proneness to accidents and resistance from the horse-drawn cab trade.

Hunchfront of Lime Grove A somewhat unappealing nickname given to the generously endowed starlet known as Sabrina (b.1936 as plain Norma Sykes), who appeared silently but decoratively on Arthur Askey's television show *Before Your Very Eyes*, made at the LIME GROVE Studios in the early 1950s.

Hungerford

Hungerford Bridge A railway bridge across the THAMES, carrying tracks to and from CHARING CROSS STATION on the north bank. It was built in 1864, to the design of Sir John Hawkshaw, replacing the original Hungerford Suspension Bridge, a footbridge designed by Isambard Kingdom Brunel. At the end of the 20th century the bridge was refurbished, the somewhat makeshift footbridge on its downstream side was removed and a pair of new footbridges, known as the Golden Jubilee Bridges (so named to mark the Golden Jubilee of Queen Elizabeth II), were built on each side. They were opened in 2002. Hungerford Bridge is also known as Charing Cross Bridge.

> I wouldn't want you to walk across Hungerford
> Bridge,
> Especially at twilight;
> Looking through the bolts and the girders
> Into the water below:
> You'll never find your answer there.
>
> ELVIS COSTELLO: 'London's Brilliant Parade' (song) (1994)

Hungerford Market A market set up in 1682 by Sir Edward Hungerford. It was rebuilt in 1833 as a two-storey emporium, which was demolished in 1860 to make way for CHARING CROSS STATION.

Hunterian Relating to or associated with the surgeon John Hunter (*see the* FATHER OF SCIENTIFIC SURGERY), to his anatomical collection, nucleus of the HUNTERIAN MUSEUM, or to the annual Hunterian Oration, organized by the HUNTERIAN SOCIETY.

Hunterian Museum A scientific museum based at the headquarters of the Royal College of Surgeons, in LINCOLN'S INN FIELDS. It has evolved from John Hunter's teaching museum in LEICESTER SQUARE, the contents of which were purchased by the government in 1799 and given to the Company of Surgeons. By the end of the 19th century the museum contained nearly 65,000 specimens covering anatomy and pathology; zoology; palaeontology; archaeology and anthropology. The college was bombed in 1941 but a large part of the collection survived and the highlights are today exhibited in a series of stylish galleries, revamped in 2004. They include human and animal anatomy and pathology specimens, wax teaching models, surgical and dental instruments, paintings, drawings and sculpture.

Hunterian Society A learned society founded in 1819 with the aim of honouring the FATHER OF SCIENTIFIC SURGERY and convivially supporting the pursuit of medical knowledge. Its lectures and debates generally accompany a dinner at the headquarters of the Medical Society of London, in Chandos Street, MARYLEBONE.

Hurlingham An exclusive residential locality occupying the southern tip of the FULHAM peninsula east of PUTNEY BRIDGE station. First recorded in 1489 as Hurlyngholefeld, a name of uncertain origin, this was simply a field of very little consequence until the construction of Hurlingham House (*see the* HURLINGHAM CLUB). Streets to the north of Hurlingham Road were laid out from the early 1880s and to the southwest later in the decade.

Hurlingham Club A famous sporting club based at Hurlingham House, which was built for Dr William Cadogan in 1760. The house was significantly enlarged in two subsequent stages but its original core remains. It later became home to the Duke of Wellington's elder brother and to several governors of the BANK OF ENGLAND. A pigeon shooting club was established at the house in 1869 and the club soon introduced the new sport of polo, becoming the headquarters of the British game. Polo ceased to be played at Hurlingham in 1939 and the Hurlingham Polo Association is now based in Oxfordshire. Nowadays, Hurlingham has facilities for tennis, croquet, cricket, bowls, squash, gymnastics and swimming. The founding sport returned temporarily in June 2009, when Hurlingham hosted the inaugural tournament of the World Polo Series, a television-friendly event with several variations on the traditional rules.

The athletics stadium at Hurlingham was used to film scenes in the Oscar-winning film *Chariots of Fire* (1981).

Hurlothrumbo A popular burlesque, which in 1729 had an extraordinary run at the HAYMARKET Theatre (predecessor of the THEATRE ROYAL). So great was its popularity that a club called the Hurlo-Thrumbo Society was formed. The author was Samuel Johnson (1691–1773), an eccentric Manchester dancing master, who put this motto on the title page:

> Ye sons of fire, read my Hurlo-Thrumbo,
> Turn it betwixt your finger and your thumbo,
> And being quite undone, be quite struck dumbo.

hustings A word originating from Old Norse *hústhing*, from *hús*, 'house', and *thing*, 'assembly'. Hence the assembly of a king, earl or chief, and its subsequent application to open-air meetings connected with parliamentary elections. In many towns the hustings court transacted some legal business, particularly that of the CITY of London, which still exists and is presided over by the lord mayor and sheriffs, although shorn of most of its former powers. The use of the word for the platform on which nominations of parliamentary candidates were made (until the passing of the Ballot Act of 1872) derives from its first application to the platform in the GUILDHALL on which the London court was held. A realistic impression of the old hustings at a parliamentary election is given by DICKENS in the *Pickwick Papers* (1836–7).

Hyde Park Central London's largest open space, situated west of MAYFAIR and north of KNIGHTSBRIDGE. When Henry VIII acquired the land as one of his many hunting grounds, the park was almost twice its present size and included what is now KENSINGTON GARDENS. In the early 1630s Charles I opened the park to the public without any of the public pressure that usually presaged acts of royal generosity. After the king's execution the park was seized by the state but citizens continued to use it as a pleasure resort. Hyde Park has a long tradition of hosting national celebrations, often on the occasion of royal birthdays or military victories; the most magnificent event of all was the GREAT EXHIBITION of 1851. Political meetings have been permitted in Hyde Park since the late 1860s and the park is now London's usual venue for protest rallies that are too large to fit into TRAFALGAR SQUARE. In 1930 George LANSBURY established an open-air lido, which is available for swimming throughout July and August. The PRINCESS DIANA MEMORIAL FOUNTAIN is an oval water chute, opened in 2004 but often closed since for maintenance or due to adverse weather conditions. The park is best known for the SERPENTINE and its wide-open spaces but there are gardens and dells too, and plentiful sports facilities. Boating and rollerblading are among the most popular informal activities. *See also the* RING; ROTTEN ROW; SPEAKERS' CORNER.

In former times 'Hyde Park' was used as COCKNEY RHYMING SLANG for 'nark', i.e. an informer.

Hyde Park Barracks *See* KNIGHTSBRIDGE BARRACKS.

Hyde Park Corner A traffic roundabout said to be 'London's most vital junction' and its hotel-filled vicinity, located at the south-east corner of Hyde Park. When the park first came into existence all the land here was part of it. Hyde Park Corner Lodge and the Lanesborough Hotel (formerly St George's Hospital, which relocated to TOOTING in 1980) both date from the 1820s. In 1952 the words 'Hyde Park Corner' were used as code within the royal household to communicate the death of George VI. *See also* NO.1 LONDON *and* WELLINGTON ARCH.

Hyde Park orator A dismissive term for a loquacious tubthumper of the sort who likes to give the world the benefit of his or her opinions at SPEAKERS' CORNER.

Hyde Park railings Late 19th-century slang for a breast of mutton, alluding to the rib bones' resemblance to the park's fencing, which replaced the old brick walls in 1828.

I

I am his Highness' dog at Kew; Pray tell me sir, whose dog are you? Frederick Louis, Prince of Wales (1707–51), had a dog given him by Alexander Pope, the BARD OF TWICKENHAM, and these words are said to have been engraved on his collar. They are sometimes quoted with reference to an overbearing, bumptious person.

I Am the Only Running Footman *See* RUNNING FOOTMEN.

I had that _____ in the back of my cab The London taxi driver's stereotypical prelude to an anecdote about a celebrity fare. The word 'that' gives the phrase its distinctive ring, and serves to imply 'you will know which person of that name I mean'. In the film *Shakespeare in Love* (1998) a Thames WATERMAN says to the Bard, 'I had that Christopher Marlowe in my boat once'.

> No art is pointless. I had that Immanuel Kant in the back of my cab the other day and he told me that the meaning of art was that it had no function.
>
> CHARLES SAATCHI, interviewed in *The Times* (28 February 2009)

I have a ring According to legend, Edward the Confessor (*c.*1003–66) was once approached near his bower in what is now HAVERING by a beggar asking for alms, to which he replied, 'I have no money, but I *have a ring*', which he handed over, and that is how Havering got its name. The same beggar is later supposed to have met some pilgrims and passed the ring to them, saying: 'Give this to your king, and tell him that within six months he shall die.' And this apparently came to pass. In one version of the story, the beggar identifies himself to the pilgrims as John the Evangelist. The ring in question retains a central position on the London Borough of Havering's coat of arms as a result of the tale.

I have dined as well as my lord mayor of London I may not have eaten sumptuously but I am perfectly satisfied with what I have had.

I heard it from Miles's boy *See* MILES'S BOY.

I'll give you my mother for a maid A catchphrase heard in fashionable London circles between the 1680s and 1740s. Since one's mother could not be a maid (a virgin) the expression was used to convey unlikelihood. Aphra Behn, in her play *The Younger Brother* (published posthumously, 1696), has Sir Morgan Blunder say, 'if ever you catch me at your damn'd clubs again, I'll give you my mother for a maid'.

I'm Forever Blowing Bubbles The club song of WEST HAM UNITED FC and probably the most famous English team anthem after Liverpool's 'You'll Never Walk Alone'. The song was a MUSIC HALL favourite in the 1920s, a time when Pears soap was advertised using John Millais's 'Bubbles' painting (1886). Billy Murray, a youth who played for a local school team and tried out for West Ham, bore a remarkable resemblance to the boy in the painting and his headmaster accordingly encouraged supporters to sing 'I'm Forever Blowing Bubbles' at school matches. The headmaster was a friend of West Ham trainer (and later manager) Charlie Paynter, who introduced the song to his club's fans. The lyric's pessimistic tone marks it out from most football anthems.

> I'm forever blowing bubbles, pretty bubbles in the air.
> They fly so high, they reach the sky,
> And like my dreams they fade and die.
> Fortune's always hiding, I've looked everywhere,
> I'm forever blowing bubbles, pretty bubbles in the air.
>
> JOHN KELLETTE and JAAN KENBROVIN (version usually sung by West Ham fans) (1918)

I'm free! A famous catchphrase from the sitcom ARE YOU BEING SERVED? It was regularly trilled by the camp menswear assistant Mr Humphries, played by John Inman (1935–2007).

I'm with the Woolwich A slogan for the WOOL-WICH Building Society, used from the mid-1970s in a memorable advertising campaign and briefly a popular catchphrase. The Woolwich is now the mortgage arm of Barclays Bank.

> I am not really a panto fan. They remind me of washed-up British comedians yelling, 'Are you with me?'; to which you were expected to yell back, 'No, I'm with the Woolwich.'
>
> *New Zealand Listener* (22–28 December 2007)

I should cocoa! *See under* COCOA.

I suppose 'Nose' in COCKNEY RHYMING SLANG. Alternatives include 'fireman's hose', 'Tokyo Rose' and 'Irish rose'.

ice cream

ice cream (freezer) 'Geezer' in COCKNEY RHYMING SLANG. Alternative terms for a geezer include 'Julius (Caesar)' and 'lemon (squeezer)'. *See also* DIAMOND GEEZER.

ice cream Jacks *See* CREAM ICE JACKS.

Ickenham A genteel residential suburb situated between UXBRIDGE and RUISLIP. The estate was first recorded in Domesday Book as Ticeham, 'the farmstead of a man called Ticca'. St Giles' Church was in existence by the mid-13th century and the oldest part of the present building dates from the 1330s. Three substantial homes built from the 16th century onwards survive today: the modest manor house; Sir Edward Wright's ostentatious Swakeleys House, completed in 1638; and the mid-18th century Ickenham Hall, to which the Compass Theatre and Arts Centre is now attached. Charlotte Gell established almshouses, which were built in 1857 on land she had donated, and bequeathed funds for the construction of the canopied village pump, which was installed in 1866. The opening of a halt on the Metropolitan Railway in 1905 failed at first to alter the character of the village but the sale of most of the Swakeleys estate in 1922 hastened Ickenham's entry into METROLAND. In the 1960s a proposal to build a national exhibition centre on Ickenham Marsh met with local opposition and the scheme went instead to Birmingham. Swakeleys House was restored and converted to offices in the early 1980s. Only the very centre of the old village remains well preserved, although on the outskirts there are three moated sites that are scheduled ancient monuments.

Ideal Home Show An exhibition of the latest home comforts and improvement ideas, held annually at EARLS COURT. The popular show, famous for its spectacular displays, including a full-size house of the future, evolved from the exhibition first held in 1908 by the *Daily Mail* as an advertising gimmick.

idlest man in London Oscar Wilde's description of Lord Arthur Goring, a character in his play *An Ideal Husband* (1895). The best friend of Sir Robert Chiltern, Lord Goring is in many respects a portrait of Wilde himself. A bachelor, he is 34 ('but always says he is younger'), and appears to be merely a social butterfly given to delivering witty epigrams on literature, politics, fashion and society: 'Other people are quite dreadful. The only possible society is oneself.' Being misunderstood as shallow, he reasons, 'gives him a post of vantage'.

ILEA *See the* INNER LONDON EDUCATION AUTHORITY.

Ilford A strategic commercial centre, arguably the most important in outer east London, situated north of BARKING. The name is a corruption of 'Hyleford', 'Hyle' being an old name for the River RODING, and meaning 'trickling brook'. In the first or second century BC an encampment or market existed to the south of the present town centre at a site called Uphall, which covered approximately 48 acres (19 hectares). Adeliza (or Adelicia), Abbess of Barking, founded a hospital around 1145, with a chapel that stands today on Ilford Hill. The original medieval settlement of Ilford may have been established on the opposite bank of the Roding, at what is now LITTLE ILFORD, but the eastern village soon grew larger, and was known as Ilford Magna by 1254, and later by the English form of Great Ilford. The mansion at VALENTINES PARK is an impressive but lonely survivor from the grand houses that were built in the 17th and 18th centuries. From 1879 Alfred Harman's Britannia Works made photographic materials and later changed its name to Ilford Ltd. The Kenneth More Theatre was built in 1974 and is regarded as the borough's premier cultural venue. The town centre's shopping facilities have been extensive redeveloped since 1990.

Ill May Day *See* EVIL MAY DAY.

Illustrated London News A pictorial

newspaper founded in 1842 by Herbert Ingram (1811–60), a Nottingham-born bookseller and printer. He endowed the paper with a relatively liberal political stance and an avoidance of sensationalism. The ILN was especially noted for its informative overseas coverage, provided by artistically talented correspondents who had been despatched to far-flung places hitherto unknown to many readers. Sales reached a peak of 310,000 copies in 1863 (with the issue covering the marriage of the Prince of Wales, the future Edward VII, to Princess Alexandra of Denmark), a circulation far exceeding any daily newspaper of the time. Woodcut illustrations were used until the 1880s, when half-tone printing was introduced. The newspaper, later a colour magazine, was published weekly until 1971, then progressively less frequently. After 1990 only occasional souvenir editions appeared. The parent company continues in existence, primarily as a picture archive and a publisher of magazines for corporate customers.

Immensikoff *See the* SHOREDITCH TOFF.

imperial

Imperial College London A science-based educational institution formed in 1907 by amalgamating the Royal School of Mines, the Royal College of Science and the CITY & GUILDS College. A year after its foundation it became a college of the UNIVERSITY OF LONDON. A series of mergers with medical colleges, beginning with St Mary's Hospital Medical School, resulted in the creation in 1997 of the Imperial College School of Medicine, one of Europe's largest such institutions. In 2007 Imperial withdrew from the University of London, becoming an independent university in its own right. It has four faculties – business, engineering, medicine and natural sciences – and seven London campuses, of which the largest is at SOUTH KENSINGTON.

Imperial Gas Light and Coke Company *See* IMPERIAL WHARF.

Imperial Institute A research institution founded in 1887, when construction of its imposing premises began on EXHIBITION ROAD, in SOUTH KENSINGTON. Its education-oriented successor is the COMMONWEALTH INSTITUTE. Imperial College took over the institute's buildings when it vacated them in 1962, but considered them unsuitable for modern needs and demolished

them. Disgruntled conservationists were appeased by the retention of the Collcutt Tower as a free-standing campanile, now renamed the Queen's Tower.

Imperial Wharf 'London's premier riverside development', according to its creators, situated in the Sands End district of FULHAM and separated by the railway line from Chelsea Harbour. In 1824 the Imperial Gas Light and Coke Company acquired the Sandford manor house estate and began producing gas here in 1829. By the middle of the 19th century Imperial was London's leading gas company and a merger in 1876 created the even larger Gas Light and Coke Company. Further growth between the wars forced Macfarlane Lang's Imperial Biscuit Works to leave Townmead Road for a cleaner site. With the advent of North Sea gas in the 1970s the gasworks closed down and car breakers later occupied much of the site. At the turn of the 21st century property developers St George began to build an extensive estate of luxury apartment blocks and townhouses, with shops, cafés, restaurants and a park. The scheme also includes provision for affordable housing.

in

In and Out The nickname of the Naval and Military Club since the days of HANSOM cabs. To avoid confusion among the various service clubs of that time, the cabbies bestowed nicknames on them, and the 'In' and 'Out' directions on the posts of the respective gateways suggested the name 'In and Out'. In 1998 the Club moved from its long-standing base at 94 PICCADILLY, the former home of Lord Palmerston, to new premises in ST JAMES'S SQUARE. *See also* CLUB.

In Town Tonight *See* CARRY ON, LONDON!; *the* KNIGHTSBRIDGE MARCH.

Industrial Dwellings Society *See the* FOUR PER CENT INDUSTRIAL DWELLINGS COMPANY.

inn The use of this word in the context of London legal institutions derives from its early sense of a dwelling place, specifically a house of residence for students.

Inns of Chancery Former places of residence and study for legal apprentices, probably so called because many of the students trained as clerks in the CHANCERY, although the inns had no direct link with the lord chancellor's office. From the 15th century, by which time there were ten such inns, they evolved into solicitors' colleges, and 'preparatory schools' for the INNS OF COURT. All the Inns of Chancery lay close by the Inns of Court and each gradually attached itself to one in particular, which would provide teachers and exercise a degree of supervision. Later, their educational role declined and they became social associations for members of the legal professions, before expiring over the course of the 19th century. A few buildings of the Inns of Chancery have survived, mostly functioning nowadays as offices.

Inns of Court The four voluntary societies in London that have the exclusive right of calling to the English bar. They are the INNER TEMPLE, the MIDDLE TEMPLE, LINCOLN'S INN and GRAY'S INN. Each is governed by a board of benchers.

inner

Inner Circle

1. The early term for what later became known as the CIRCLE LINE.

2. A road encompassing the central area of REGENT'S PARK. Unlike the park's Outer Circle it really is circular. *See also* QUEEN MARY'S GARDENS.

Inner London As a general term, 'inner London' merely denotes the central, most profoundly urban part of the capital, in contrast with OUTER LONDON, with its connotations of suburbia. In the context of London government, however, it has a specific application. When the GREATER LONDON COUNCIL was set up in 1965, 12 boroughs, plus the CITY of London, were designated as constituting 'Inner London'. They were:

CAMDEN	LAMBETH
GREENWICH	LEWISHAM
HACKNEY	SOUTHWARK
HAMMERSMITH	TOWER HAMLETS
ISLINGTON	WANDSWORTH
KENSINGTON AND	WESTMINSTER
CHELSEA	

Subsequently, compilers of official statistics introduced a revised definition of Inner London that excluded Greenwich and included HARINGEY and NEWHAM.

Inner London Education Authority A branch of the GREATER LONDON COUNCIL set up at the time of the latter's creation in 1965. It perpetuated the LONDON COUNTY COUNCIL's responsibility for the schools and colleges of central London, while delegating control over education in OUTER LONDON to the constituent boroughs. Despite being a constant target of the right-wing press for its allegedly excessive expenditure, bureaucracy and political correctness, the ILEA survived the death of the GLC in 1986, but was itself abolished in 1990, responsibility for education passing to the individual boroughs.

Inner Temple One of the four INNS OF COURT, built on the site of the former headquarters of the KNIGHTS TEMPLAR. The Inner Temple was first distinguished from the MIDDLE TEMPLE in a manuscript yearbook of 1388. Growing membership in the 16th century brought the construction of new buildings, many of which were lost in later fires and the BLITZ. The best preserved chambers buildings of the Inner Temple are in King's Bench Walk, a 17th-century terrace. The hall, treasury office, benchers' rooms and library were all reconstructed after the Second World War. *See also* PEGASUS; TEMPLE.

innit A representation of a casual British pronunciation of 'isn't it', usually as a tag question (as in 'Cold, innit?'). The form dates from the 1950s, though the pronunciation it represents is no doubt of far greater antiquity. Grammatically it emulated its full form in referring back specifically to the subject of the preceding sentence (as in 'That's nice, isn't it?'), but in the latter part of the 20th century, in the street slang of London, it broadened out into an all-purpose tag, rather like French *n'est-ce pas?* (as in 'I've got a lot of work on, innit?').

inspector

Inspector Knacker of the Yard The all-purpose fictitious policeman of the magazine *Private Eye*. The inspector has made appearances in other media too, sometimes when the intention is to imply plodding, or even bungling, conduct but often simply as a generic SCOTLAND YARD officer.

> The French authorities ring up Inspector Knacker of the Yard and say, 'Will you arrest this man? We promise that we will get you the papers within 48 hours.' The inspector arrests the man, the French authorities fail to get the papers there within 48 hours and the man has to be discharged.
>
> LORD GOODHART, in *Lords Hansard* (18 June 2003)

Inspector Sands A codename used in public address announcements made in stations on the LONDON UNDERGROUND and other rail networks to alert staff to a possible emergency, usually when a fire alarm has been triggered. The most common form of the message is: 'Would Inspector Sands please report to the operations room immediately.' The intention is to avoid causing panic, although the subterfuge is increasingly a matter of public knowledge. 'Inspector Sands' or 'Mr Sands' are called upon in similar situations in theatres, sports stadia and other public places. The choice of name probably derives from the former use of buckets of sand to douse fires.

> With the exception of having a crafty fag and setting off a fire alarm, it all went rather smoothly. I did find it funny that the people in the [Upton Park] stadium knew what the 'Inspector Sands' announcement meant, and did nothing but quietly laugh at it.
>
> TOM REYNOLDS: *Blood, Sweat, and Tea: Real-Life Adventures in an Inner-City Ambulance* (2008)

Institute of Contemporary Arts An artistic and cultural centre, founded in 1947 by a collective of artists, poets and writers. In 1968 the ICA moved to its present home at 12 CARLTON HOUSE TERRACE, where it presently consists of two galleries, two cinemas, a theatre, a bookshop, a bar and café and private function rooms. Its programme covers visual arts, music, cinema, talks and educational events.

ipsal dixal A 19th-century COCKNEY corruption of *ipse dixit*, Latin for 'he himself said it', used in reference to an uncorroborated assertion.

iron

iron (hoof) 'Poof' in COCKNEY RHYMING SLANG, in the sense of the derogatory term for a gay man, not on any account to be confused with the IRONS.

Irons A nickname for WEST HAM UNITED FC. It derives from the club's original incarnation as Thames Ironworks FC and the presence of a pair of iron hammers on its crest.

island

Island, The A familiar term for EEL PIE ISLAND, especially among the musicians who performed at its jazz club in the late 1950s and early 60s.

Island Gardens *See* SCRAP IRON PARK.

Isle of Dogs An 800-acre (325-hectare) tongue of land jutting into the THAMES opposite DEPTFORD and GREENWICH, made into a virtual island by the creation of the WEST INDIA DOCKS in

1802. The name, however, was in use by the early 16th century and its origin is not known. The most popular story is that Henry VIII kennelled his hunting dogs here, which is credible since GREENWICH Palace was just across the river, but there is no proof of this. The first attempts at draining what was then called STEPNEY Marsh took place in the 12th century but several centuries elapsed before reliable protection from flooding allowed the development of riverside docks and industry. Over the course of the 19th century wharves, factories and workers' housing progressively occupied the whole island. Large-scale municipal housebuilding projects brought many EAST ENDERS here after each of the world wars. Dock-related activity dominated the Isle of Dogs until the 1970s, when labour relations problems and the increasing size of cargo ships led to the growth of Tilbury and the coastal ports at the expense of London's docks. West India and MILLWALL Docks closed in 1980 and the following year their ownership passed from the PORT OF LONDON AUTHORITY to the LONDON DOCKLANDS DEVELOPMENT CORPORATION. The northern part of the Isle of Dogs has since flourished beyond all early expectations, while the south has become an uneasy fusion of typical East End terraces and upmarket waterfront apartments.

> The river sweats
> Oil and tar
> The barges drift
> With the turning tide
> Red sails
> Wide
> To leeward, swing on the heavy spar.
> The barges wash
> Drifting logs
> Down Greenwich reach
> Past the Isle of Dogs.
>
> T.S. ELIOT: *The Waste Land* (1922)

Isleworth A riverside town of ancient origin, situated east of HOUNSLOW. A copy of an Anglo-Saxon charter indicates that this was Gislheresuuyrth in 677 – 'the enclosed settlement of a man called Gīslehere'. The 'G' was not dropped from the name until the mid-13th century, by which time Isleworth had evolved into a village on a manorial estate. Following the dissolution of the monasteries (1536–9), the increasing private ownership of land led to the development of Isleworth as a wealthy residential area. Rebuilding during the 18th century created the locality now known as Old Isleworth. Isleworth is the home of the massively redeveloped West Middlesex University Hospital and – on the OSTERLEY border – of Sky TV.

Isleworth Ait An unspoilt island in the THAMES, located off Old Isleworth at the mouth of the River Crane. In the 17th century there were four aits here but their dividing channels have since silted up and the island still floods regularly. It was formerly part of the Duke of Northumberland's SYON PARK estate. Isleworth Ait is now a nature reserve managed by the London Wildlife Trust. Public access is discouraged.

Islington A gentrified inner London suburb, though still with a large working-class community, situated 1½ miles (2.5 km) north of ST PAUL'S Cathedral. Islington was Gislandune in the year 1000, the 'hill of a man called Gīsla'. It was a staging post on the route north from London and the ANGEL takes its name from an inn on the turnpike road. By the late 18th century tens of thousands of oxen and hundreds of thousands of sheep were passing along Islington High Street every year – and fattened up in the surrounding fields – on their way to SMITHFIELD. By that time Islington was developing rapidly as a residential suburb, with elegant Georgian and Victorian squares proliferating in BARNSBURY and CANONBURY, while UPPER STREET and Lower Street (now ESSEX ROAD) became busy shopping centres. From the late 1950s the process of GENTRIFICATION began, bringing the middle classes back to restored and revived squares and terraces. The flourishing of the CAMDEN PASSAGE antiques market was a sign of changing times, as Upper Street in particular became a golden mile of smart shops and chic restaurants.

The writer Joe Orton lived in Noel Road from 1959 until his murder in 1967 by his partner Kenneth Halliwell. The pair were imprisoned in 1962 for stealing and defacing Islington library books. Reproductions of the defaced and doctored book jackets are now part of the Joe Orton collection held by the borough's local history centre.

Islington, London Borough of An INNER LONDON borough, created in 1965 by merging the metropolitan boroughs of Islington and FINSBURY. It is London's smallest borough and the third most densely populated. Islington's coat of arms incorporates elements from the

arms of Dick WHITTINGTON, the Order of St John of Jerusalem (*see the* KNIGHTS HOSPITALLER), the Berners family of BARNSBURY and Thomas Sutton (*see* CROESUS), who founded CHARTERHOUSE. An arrow recalls the former practice of archery on the open fields here. The civic motto is 'we serve'.

Islington Green A small park located at the apex of UPPER STREET and ESSEX ROAD. The two roads were Islington's principal thoroughfares from medieval times and the triangle of land at their junction formed an early focus. Funfairs are regularly set up on the green. The Screen on the Green is a well-established independent cinema, programming a mix of art-house and mainstream films. *See also* COLLINS'S MUSIC HALL.

Islington Man or **Person** A middle-class socially aware person of left-wing views, regarded as typical of Islington as a district or borough. This is a usage that is more jibe than compliment.

> Just as Essex Man ... represented the 1980s, Islington Man – more properly Islington Person – may turn out to be the most potent composite of the late 1990s.
>
> *Independent on Sunday* (17 July 1994)

Islington martyrs Five Protestants who were burned to death in 1557. They were among a group that had assembled at the Saracen's Head to celebrate the Communion, under the pretext of attending a play. Another 27 Protestant worshippers were arrested a year later in a field just outside Islington, of whom 13 were put to death, according to John Foxe's *Book of Martyrs* (1563).

Strong Man of Islington *See under* STRONG.

Isokon A London-based design practice led by the engineer Jack Pritchard and the Canadian architect Wells Coates, deriving its name from its principles of isometric construction. During the 1930s the firm created modernist buildings and commissioned furniture designs to suit them. It is now best known for the Lawn Road Flats in HAMPSTEAD, frequently called the Isokon building. Among the early tenants of the block were the Bauhaus architect Walter Gropius, the constructivist artist László Moholy-Nagy and the authors Nicholas Monsarrat and Agatha Christie, who said it looked like 'a giant ocean liner that ought to have had a couple of funnels'. The flats are grade I listed and have recently been restored to a pristine state after a period of dereliction.

it

it's all (a) holiday at Peckham *See under* ALL.

it's got a back to it A disused COCKNEY expression meaning 'I'm lending this to you not giving it', playing on 'I want it back'.

> A hint to repay a loan: 'its gAW tuh bEHk tiOO wit.' (It's got a back to it.)
>
> LEWIS HERMAN and MARGUERITE S. HERMAN: *Foreign Dialects: A Manual for Actors, Directors, and Writers* (1943)

(it) stands to reason, dunnit? *See under* STAND.

it's the poor what gets the blame A traditional COCKNEY expression of lamentation, taken from a MUSIC HALL song that dates from the late 19th or early 20th century. The song's title is rendered either as 'It's the Same the Whole World Over' or 'She Was Poor but She Was Honest'. A 1930 version by Bob Weston and Bert Lee was regularly performed by the comic entertainer Billy Bennett (1887–1942). The lyric exists in varying forms, and has been lewdly adapted for drinking songs, but the gist is always of a country girl who is seduced and abandoned by a wicked squire. Fleeing to London, she receives similar treatment from gentlemen in positions of authority. Finally she throws herself from a bridge into the THAMES at midnight. In one version she drowns but in others she is rescued and rises to her feet to repeat the chorus:

> It's the same the whole world over,
> It's the poor what gets the blame.
> It's the rich what gets the pleasure [or 'gravy'],
> Ain't it all a blooming [or 'bleeding'] shame?

Italia Conti A theatre arts training school founded in 1911 by the eponymous actress (1873–1946) and nowadays offering courses at all levels. Its main base is in Goswell Road, on the northern edge of the CITY of London. The school's alumni include Noël Coward, Naomi Campbell, Leslie

Phillips, Martine McCutcheon and Steve Marriott, of the Small Faces (*see* ITCHYCOO PARK).

Italian

Italian Boy *See the* LONDON BURKERS.

Italian Hill *See* LITTLE ITALY.

Itchycoo Park A song by the EAST LONDON group the Small Faces that reached No.3 in the British singles chart in 1967. The inspirational park has not been conclusively identified, largely because of conflicting remarks later made by the band's members. LITTLE ILFORD Park is named most often by geo-musicologists but others have proposed VALENTINES PARK, WEST HAM Park and WANSTEAD FLATS. The 'itchycoo' nickname could have derived from the presence of biting insects or stinging flora. Alternatively, the song may have been about Oxford – the lyric mentions 'dreaming spires' – or entirely drug-induced, with no connection to any real park, in east London or beyond.

Ivy, The Probably London's best-known 'celebrity restaurant', located on West Street, COVENT GARDEN. It began life in 1917 as an Italian café favoured by the theatrical community; and its present name is said to have derived from a remark made by Alice Delysia (1889–1979) when owner Abel Glandellini apologized for building works. Quoting a popular song of the time, the actress said: 'Don't worry, we will cling to you like the ivy.' The restaurant is now part of a group that includes Le Caprice, Scott's and J. Sheekey. The menu is described as 'modern eclectic', and ranges from burgers and Welsh rarebit to beluga and sevruga caviar. Only the well-connected are able to get a peak-time table without booking weeks in advance.

> There are London restaurants where having a well-known name secures you a table at short notice – and then there's the Ivy.
>
> WILL SELF, in *The Sunday Times* (16 December 2007)

J

J. Arthur (Rank) 'Wank' in COCKNEY RHYMING SLANG – or occasionally 'bank' (when the 'J' is more likely to be omitted). The same potential for confusion exists with the alternative 'Armitage (Shanks)' and 'Tommy (tank)', but not 'Sherman (tank)' or 'SEPTIC (TANK)', which both mean 'yank' (an American). John Arthur Rank, 1st Baron Rank (1888–1972), was a devout Methodist who inherited his father's flour milling business and used some of his wealth to found a film-making company that had the primary aim of promoting family values.

> But the most embarrassing films were the Emmanuelle ones! The lads would be having a fine time being daft, and we would be surrounded by pervs, who I'm sure were having a J. Arthur under their coats.
>
> forum post at www.empireonline.com (21 February 2009)

J. Lyons & Co. *See* LYONS' CORNER HOUSES.

J. Sainsbury *See* SAINSBURY'S.

Jack

Jack Adams's parish CLERKENWELL, in 18th-century slang. A Jack Adams was a fool.

Jack Cade *See* CADE, JACK.

Jackers *See the* JUMP.

Jack Jones To be on one's Jack Jones is to be alone; on one's own. This imperfect piece of COCKNEY RHYMING SLANG appears to derive from the MUSIC HALL song "'E Dunno Where 'E Are' (early 1890s), written by Fred Eplett and made famous by Gus Elen. The lyric concerns one Jack Jones, a former COVENT GARDEN market porter who has come into some money and now considers himself above his old workmates. He reads the *Telegraph* instead of the *Star*, calls his mother 'ma' instead of 'muvver' and stands alone at the bar drinking Scotch and soda. However, modern usage of the term rarely implies aloofness on the part of the person alone; more often

it is close to the opposite – he or she may feel abandoned. For example, 'You lot went off and left me on my Jack Jones!'

> And why you all over there on your Jack Jones?
> You need to let me get behind your backbone.
>
> D. MILLS and C. HARRIS: 'Dance wiv Me' (song by Dizzee Rascal feat. Calvin Harris and Chrome) (2008)

Jack's (alive) 'Five' in COCKNEY RHYMING SLANG, usually in the context of five pounds sterling.

Jack Straw's Castle A weatherboarded structure on WEST HEATH(2) Road in HAMPSTEAD, named after the hero of the Peasants' Revolt (1381), who is said to have addressed crowds from a haywagon here. A coaching inn stood on the site from 1721 but was wrecked by a Second World War bomb and rebuilt in the early 1960s. The pub has since been converted to private flats. The Hampstead-educated poet Thom Gunn published a collection of verse entitled *Jack Straw's Castle* in 1976.

Jack the Hat The nickname of John McVitie, from his habit of never being seen in public without a TRILBY hat, which he probably wore to disguise his baldness. McVitie was a small-time criminal who got on the wrong side of the KRAY TWINS and was killed by them in October 1967. Although the body was never found, the police assembled sufficient evidence to charge the twins with his murder. After the longest murder hearing in British criminal history, they were found guilty in March 1969 and each sentenced to life imprisonment.

Jack the Ripper The name adopted by an unknown killer who murdered at least five prostitutes in WHITECHAPEL in 1888 and mutilated ('ripped') their bodies. The victims included Mary Ann Nichols, Annie Chapman, Elizabeth Stride, Catherine Eddowes and Mary Kelly. Early theories that the killer was a 'gentleman' of some kind (an insane doctor and a cricket-playing lawyer have been proposed) are almost certainly wide of the mark. A recent suggestion is that the murders were planned by a group of high-ranking Freemasons (see FREEMASONRY), including Sir William Gull, the royal physician, their motive being to suppress scandals involving Prince Albert Victor, Duke of Clarence (1846–92), elder son of the then Prince of Wales (later Edward VII); and the US crime-writer Patricia Cornwell has put forward a case (not altogether convincing) for the painter Walter Sickert (1860–1942) being the Ripper. Yet another theory is that the murderer was the Duke of Clarence himself, but a more likely candidate is J.K. Stephen, the duke's lover.

In COCKNEY RHYMING SLANG, 'Jack the Rippers' can be 'kippers', 'strippers' or 'slippers'.

Jack the Stripper The nickname of an unknown man who killed six west London prostitutes in 1963–4 in a spree sometimes called the 'HAMMERSMITH nude murders'. In each case he strangled the woman, smashed out several of her teeth and removed her clothes. Some authorities have named a total of eight victims, beginning in 1959. Detective Chief Superintendent John Du Rose (*see* FOUR DAY JOHNNY) later claimed to have identified the killer but said that he had committed suicide before a case could be mounted against him. Several crime writers have since advanced their own theories, variously naming a senior police officer, a security guard, a Welsh child-murderer who moved to London on his release from jail and even a former world light-heavyweight boxing champion.

Spring-Heeled Jack *See under* SPRING.

Jacko Macacco or **Jackey Macauco** An Italian-bred monkey that gained fame for its dog-fighting exploits at the WESTMINSTER PIT in the early 1820s. Jacko won 14 bouts but a contest with a bull terrier named 'Puss' proved fatal to both animals.

Jackson

Jackson Pollocks 'Bollocks' in modern rhyming slang, often rendered as 'Jacksons'. Like 'bollocks' itself, the term can be used literally to refer to the testicles or figuratively in an emphatically dismissive sense. Jackson Pollock (1912–56) was an American painter; a pioneer of abstract expressionism. The use of his name in this way may not be unrelated to the difficulty that some

have experienced in appreciating the merit of his work.

Jackson's Lane A Victorian road in north-east HIGHGATE, located just south-west of Highgate station. It acquired its name from Joseph B. Jackson, an early 19th-century resident of a house called Hillside. Jackson's Lane previously crossed Archway Road and continued as a footpath, but this eastern part was renamed Shepherd's Hill when it was built up with some very pricey homes in the 1880s. In 1893 a site on the corner of Archway Road was obtained for the construction of Highgate Wesleyan Methodist Church, which eventually opened in 1905 with an adjacent hall and Sunday school that had almost as great a capacity as the church. The church operated a counselling centre in the 1960s but it closed in 1976, since when it has been converted into a theatre, while the adapted hall offers a wide range of arts classes, courses and activities.

Jacob

Jacob's (cream crackers) 'Knackers' (testicles) in modern rhyming slang. Not a term in frequent usage, unlike 'CREAM CRACKERED'.

Jacob's Island An artificial island beside the THAMES and the mouth of the now-hidden River NECKINGER in BERMONDSEY, created *c.*1670 by the cutting of a series of tidal channels that later became stagnant ditches. The island lay east of St Saviour's Dock and south of Bermondsey Wall. Unlike the slums and ROOKERIES on the outskirts of the CITY and the WEST END, Jacob's Island was unknown to most Londoners, yet it was perhaps the filthiest and most disease-ridden of all. Most of the slum was erased in the mid-19th century; however, the Jacob's Island name is still used by the residents' association for the upmarket apartment blocks that nowadays occupy the site. *See also* FOLLY DITCH.

Jaeger This premium clothing brand owes its name to the German hygienist and naturalist Gustav Jaeger (1832–1917), who was convinced that it was healthier for people to wear clothes made of wool, from animals, than of cotton and linen, from plants. The first shop to sell this type of clothing opened in Fore Street, in the CITY, in 1884. George Bernard SHAW regularly wore a Jaeger suit. *See also the* HEALTHERIES.

Jafaikan or **Jafaican** A media term for the inner-city dialect that combines standard English with the vocabulary and accents of various immigrant communities. The word is a blend of 'fake Jamaican'. Language scholars prefer the term 'multicultural London English'. Although Jamaican patois is the main contributor, elements are drawn from the linguistic cultures of Bangladesh, India, West Africa, South America and the Middle East. Jafaikan is not exclusive to London but it has advanced furthest in the capital, where COCKNEY slang and pronunciation is added to the mix. It has been suggested that the dialect is affecting the traditional cockney accent, with the clipping of previously elongated vowels and the diminution of the glottal stop. Jafaikan may also partially be ousting the earlier media demon, ESTUARY ENGLISH. Those putting a positive spin on the phenomenon argue that it is helping to forge a common identity among formerly disparate ethnic groups.

> Safe, man. You lookin buff in dem low batties. Dey's sick, man. Me? I'm just jammin wid me bruds. Dis my yard, innit? Is nang, you get me? No? What ends you from then? If this language sounds familiar, the chances are you're from inner-city London, where a new multicultural dialect is emerging.
> *The Guardian* (12 April 2006)

Jago, the A fictionalized version of a 19th-century slum, bounded by SHOREDITCH High Street and Hackney Road to the north and SPITALFIELDS to the south, known in real life as 'the Nichol'. Inhabited by some 6,000 people, its portrayal in the novel *A Child of the Jago* (1896) by Arthur Morrison (1863–1945) brought the area's appalling conditions to public notice, and it was credited as a major influence on the decision to clear the slums. The Boundary estate was erected in its place, in blocks radiating outwards from Arnold Circus.

jam

jam jar 'Car' in COCKNEY RHYMING SLANG.

> Let's park the old jam jar back there, nearer where we made that first turn. There was a bit more traffic there. Little red motor like this stands out a bit round 'ere.
> JACQUELINE WINSPEAR: *Messenger of Truth* (2006)

jam tart *See* TREACLE (TART).

jarvey An old name for the driver of a HACKNEY coach, and also for the vehicle itself. It is a

diminutive of Jarvis, a personal name that may have been chosen for the purpose because of its similarity to Gervase, a saint whose emblem was a whip (with which he was said to have been beaten to death). Another story suggested that coachmen adopted the name in honour of one of their number who was hanged.

> 'Look alive, then!' interrupted the active Mr Page, as he sprang into a coach the door of which he hastily opened himself; and the constables having tumbled in after him, he exclaimed, 'Edgware Road – and a guinea for the jarvey if he catches up the other vehicle.'
> GEORGE W.M. REYNOLDS: *The Mysteries of the Court of London* (1849)

Javelin The planned express train service from ST PANCRAS to the site of the 2012 OLYMPIC GAMES.

Jeffrey Bernard is Unwell A play (1989) by Keith Waterhouse (b.1929) in which an alcoholic journalist recalls his past career in FLEET STREET. Jeffrey Bernard (1932–97) was a real Fleet Street journalist famed for his ill-health as much as for the dissolute ways that so grievously affected his health. He was a fixture of the Coach and Horses public house, in GREEK STREET, SOHO. The play's title refers to the announcement that regularly appeared in the place of his *Spectator* column when he was 'indisposed'.

Jeffreys, Judge George *See the* HANGING JUDGE.

jellied eels A traditional dish of the EAST END, historically sold from street stalls and in PIE AND MASH shops. It consists of fresh eel slices, boiled in herbs and vinegar and served in a spiced jelly made from their exceptionally fatty stewing juices. The eels were formerly caught in the THAMES estuary, making them cheap and readily available, but supplies are nowadays more likely to come from eel farms in the Netherlands or Northern Ireland. A handful of cafés still specialize in the dish, mostly in the vicinity of East End markets, but consumption is in seemingly irreversible long-term decline. The best-known surviving street vendor is Tubby Isaacs, a business established in 1919 and usually based at the corner of Goulston Street and Whitechapel High Street. Celebrity jellied eel fans have included the actors Laurence Olivier and Vivien Leigh and the footballer David Beckham.

> Mick Jenrick had been in the [wholesale] eel business for 36 years when I talked to him in 2000 ... 'Six years ago, I was selling 2,200 dishes of jellied eels a week, and now I'm selling half that. In another six years, it'll be half again as few.'
>
> RICHARD SCHWEID: *Consider the Eel* (2002)

'Jellied eels' can mean 'wheels', i.e. a vehicle, in modern rhyming slang.

Jermyn Street A high-class thoroughfare running parallel with and to the south of PIC-CADILLY, particularly noted for gentlemen's tailoring. Originally, this was to have been the north part of a 'little town' planned around ST JAMES'S SQUARE by Henry Jermyn, the Earl of St Albans, who leased the land from the Crown in the 1660s. Sir Isaac Newton lived here from 1697 until 1709, when he left for CHELSEA. Newton stayed first at No.88, which was built soon after 1675 on land leased from the earl, and still survives. In 1700 he moved next door to No.87, which is no longer standing. William Blake was baptized at St James's, the Wren church on the corner of Church Place, once the most fashionable church in London. The poet Thomas Gray and the author Sir Walter Scott both lodged in the street. Thomas Wall (1846–1930), purveyor of the sausages that (along with ice cream) bear his and his father's (identical) name, was born in Jermyn Street.

> Your habit of referring to distinguished writers by their Christian names, as if they were personal friends, really irritates me. It makes you sound like an occasional essayist in a middlebrow weekly rather than a trader in fine wines with a whiff of Jermyn Street about him.
>
> WILLIAM DONALDSON: *I'm Leaving You Simon, You Disgust Me* (2003)

Duchess of Jermyn Street *See under* DUCH-ESS.

Jerry's Hill *See* ABERSHAW, JERRY.

Jerusalem
Jerusalem Chamber This chamber adjoins the south tower of the west front of WESTMINSTER ABBEY and probably owes its name to the tapestries hung on its walls depicting scenes of Jerusalem. Henry IV died here on 20 March 1413.

The WESTMINSTER ASSEMBLY (1643–9), which drew up the Calvinistic WESTMINSTER CONFESSION, met in the Jerusalem Chamber, as did the compilers of the Revised Version of the Bible.

Jerusalem Tavern The name of a succession of CLERKENWELL inns since perhaps the 14th century, derived from the nearby Priory of St John of Jerusalem (*see the* KNIGHTS HOSPITALLER). The tavern's most renowned location was at St John's Gate, where it hosted a Freemason's lodge (*see* FREEMASONRY) in the 18th century. Its present address is 55 Britton Street, which was built as a merchant's house in 1720 and later served as a clockmaker's workshop.

Jerwood
Jerwood Foundation A philanthropic organization based in FITZROY SQUARE (*see under* FITZROVIA), devoted primarily to funding arts-related capital projects. It was established in 1977 by John Jerwood, a pearl dealer who began his career in HATTON GARDEN. London projects supported by the foundation include the LONDON SYMPHONY'S ORCHESTRA's Jerwood Hall at LOUSY ST LUKE'S, the Jerwood Pod at the YOUNG VIC, the Jerwood Gallery at the NATURAL HISTORY MUSEUM and the Jerwood Space, which consists of rehearsal studios, a gallery and meeting rooms on Union Street, SOUTHWARK.

Jerwood Theatres The upstairs and downstairs auditoriums of the ROYAL COURT THEATRE.

Jerwood Vanbrugh Theatre *See* RADA.

Jewel Tower One of only two buildings of the original PALACE OF WESTMINSTER to survive the fire of 1834, it is situated on Abingdon Street, just south-east of WESTMINSTER ABBEY. The Jewel Tower, or King's Privy Wardrobe, was built *c.*1365 to safeguard Edward III's treasures. It was home to the Weights and Measures Office between 1869 and 1938. The tower now houses a small museum of the history of Parliament and of imperial weights and measures.

Jewish Quarter The term is no longer used, but once applied to the area on the eastern edge of the CITY of London, around BEVIS MARKS and Creechurch Lane, where Jewish merchants established themselves after Cromwell permitted Jewish resettlement in 1656. From this small quarter Jewish colonization spread slowly outwards into the EAST END. *See also* SPITALFIELDS *and* WHITECHAPEL.

Jimmy (Riddle) 'Piddle' in COCKNEY RHYMING SLANG, meaning to urinate. Unlike most of the personal names used in rhyming slang, the term does not seem to derive from a real-life individual.

> Your John – and there's a nice fella, if ever I saw one – he told me he found you asleep when he came back from taking a Jimmy Riddle. Is that so?
>
> H.R.F. KEATING: *A Detective at Death's Door* (2004)

Joanna 'Piano', in an uncomplicated piece of slang based on the COCKNEY rhyme of the two words' second and third syllables. It was first used in the mid-19th century.

> Stanley was the first to go to the old Joanna, and when Edie's boys produced their ukuleles, everything was set for a really nice sing-song.
>
> ANGUS WILSON: *The Wrong Set and Other Stories*, 'Union Reunion' (1949)

Job's pound One of the many nicknames for BRIDEWELL Prison.

Jodrell (Bank) 'Wank' in COCKNEY RHYMING SLANG, from the Cheshire-based observatory specializing in radio astronomy. This is not a widely used term, which is perhaps surprising since it has the advantage over alternatives like 'J. ARTHUR' that its meaning cannot be confused with 'bank', because it would defeat the purpose of cockney slang for the final word not to differ from the one it represents in rhyme.

Joe (Goss) 'Boss' in rhyming slang, but possibly not of COCKNEY origin. Born in Northampton, Joe Goss (1837–85) became a middleweight and later heavyweight boxer, winning bare-knuckle titles in both London and the USA.

John

John Bell & Croyden London's most prestigious pharmacy, formed in 1908 by the merger of John Bell & Company, founded in 1798, and Croyden & Company, established by one of Bell's former assistants, Charles Croyden, in 1832. The combined business moved to its present location at 50–54 WIGMORE STREET in 1912. It was acquired by the Lloyds Pharmacy group in 1992 but continues to be managed as an autonomous operation.

> I had to perform 'Shout' and I had this terrible cold so Marion whisked me off to the chemist, John Bell & Croyden on Wigmore Street. It was so posh I thought it was like something from a movie. I remember all these big glass medical bottles, painted gold on the inside, with crowns and lions on them. Wow!
>
> LULU, interviewed in *The Independent* (20 May 2002)

John Company The Honourable EAST INDIA COMPANY. It is said that 'John' is an alteration of 'Hon', but it is possible that the name is allied to the familiar John Bull.

John Gilpin, The Diverting History of See GILPIN, JOHN.

John Lewis A national chain of department stores with four branches in GREATER LONDON. John Lewis opened his first shop selling ribbons and haberdashery in 1864, on OXFORD STREET, progressively branching out into new lines. His son John Spedan Lewis (1885–1963) took an active part in the business from an early age but his radical ideas on staff remuneration, welfare and participation brought the two into conflict. Spedan withdrew from any involvement in the Oxford Street business in return for total control at PETER JONES, which his father had acquired in 1905 and where he successfully introduced a consultative system of management. Father and son were eventually reconciled and, on the former's death in 1928, John Spedan Lewis gained sole ownership of the business. Within a year he had established the John Lewis Partnership, the profits of which were distributed among the staff, thenceforth known as 'Partners'. By the outbreak of the Second World War the Oxford Street business had grown to fill a pair of department stores, but these were destroyed by fire after being hit by an oil bomb in 1940 and rebuilt in the present form in the late 1950s. John Lewis became an anchor store of the BRENT CROSS shopping centre when it opened in 1976 and subsequently challenged the dominance of Bentalls in KINGSTON UPON THAMES. The John Lewis Partnership is headquartered in VICTORIA STREET.

John Lewis list The colloquial name for the Additional Costs Claims Guide, a list of typical prices for home furnishings and electrical goods that was used by House of Commons validations clerks to determine whether an expenditure claim was reasonable. MPs were able to spend up to £23,000 a year on such items. Following a media-driven outcry, the system was reformed in July 2008, but without satisfying all its critics.

> Shadow leader of the House Theresa May accused the Government of replacing the 'John Lewis list' with an 'Ikea list'.
>
> *The Independent* (16 July 2008)

John o' London's Weekly A lower-middlebrow literary magazine published between 1919 and 1954. It took its title from the pen-name of its original editor, Wilfred Whitten (d.1942).

St John's Wood *See under* SAINT.

Johnny

Johnny or **Johnnie** The name has been employed in numerous COCKNEY RHYMING SLANG terms, including Johnny Cotton for 'rotten', Johnny Horner for 'corner' and Johnny Skinner for 'dinner'. Most of the characters so invoked have been fictitious. The terms have rarely been abbreviated because of the potential for confusion with each other, as well as with alternative meanings of the first name in a variety of slang contexts.

Four Day Johnny *See under* FOUR.

Johnson

Johnson, Boris *See* BO-JO.

Johnson, Dr Samuel The quintessential Londoner of the 18th century (1709–84), he also uttered the most famous verdict on the city: 'When a man is tired of London, he is tired of life; for there is in London all that life can afford' (20 September 1777). Born in Lichfield, Staffordshire, Johnson came to London in 1737 and scraped a living as a journalist. In 1755 he published his pioneering *Dictionary of the English Language*, the fruit of nine years' labour, for which he was later awarded a government pension. He first met James Boswell (1740–95) in 1763 and their talkative friendship resulted in *The Life of Samuel Johnson* (1791), a ground-breaking work of biography that has done much to make Johnson one of the most quoted writers in the English language after SHAKESPEARE. His home in Gough Square, off FLEET STREET, has been restored to its original condition, with a collection of period furniture, prints and portraits. A memorial to his cat HODGE stands outside.

> Sir, if you wish to have a just notion of the magnitude of this city, you must not be satisfied with seeing its great streets and squares, but must survey the innumerable little lanes and courts. It is not in the showy evolutions of

buildings, but in the multiplicity of human habitations which are crowded together, that the wonderful immensity of London consists.

> (5 July 1763) quoted in *The Life of Samuel Johnson*

Johnston Sans The distinctive sans-serif typeface used on LONDON UNDERGROUND signage and publicity material for more than 90 years. Edward Johnston (1872–1944) created the font – which was originally called 'Underground' – for the Underground Group in 1916 and it was subsequently transferred to LONDON TRANSPORT and then to that organization's successor, Transport for London. For most purposes, TfL presently uses a slightly modified version called New Johnston Medium. The font is easy to read, suitable for a wide variety of uses and authoritative without being excessively formal. Among its most recognizable characteristics are the perfectly circular letter 'O' and the use of a diamond shape in punctuation marks and above the lower-case 'i' and 'j'.

Jolly Sailor The original identity of NORWOOD Junction station. The Jolly Sailor public house backed onto the Croydon Canal in the early 19th century, and was popular with day-trippers who came to fish, take a summertime jaunt on a canal barge or ice skate in winter. When the canal closed in 1836, most of its bed was filled in and the alignment was appropriated by the London and Croydon Railway Company. With the opening of the line from West Croydon to LONDON BRIDGE in 1839, a station was built here and named Jolly Sailor in honour of its neighbour. The route to East Croydon and on to BRIGHTON opened two years later and the station was renamed Norwood Junction after the two lines' operating companies merged in 1846.

Jonathan's A noted COFFEE HOUSE in Change Alley, described in *Tatler* as the general mart of stockjobbers. In 1773 those brokers who used Jonathan's moved to premises in Sweeting's Alley, which came to be known as the STOCK EXCHANGE coffee house. In 1801 they raised capital to build the Stock Exchange in CAPEL COURT.

Jones

Jones, Bridget The independent, unattached woman in her thirties who recounts the ups and (mostly) downs of her life in the humorous fictional *Bridget Jones's Diary* (1996) by Helen

Fielding, in which she lives in HOLLAND PARK and counts her *faux pas*, calories, cigarettes, glasses of Chardonnay, weight and other obsessions. She is shallow and neurotic, but also endearingly amusing in her manic enthusiasms and petulant disappointments. Her name became shorthand for any female relationship-obsessed thirty-something of this type. In 2001 the book was filmed as a notable chick flick, in which we find her living in the BOROUGH. The second instalment, *Bridget Jones: The Edge of Reason*, appeared in 1999 and was also made into a film, in 2004.

Jones, Inigo The SMITHFIELD-born, self-educated clothworker's son (1573–1652) who has been called the first British designer to fully merit the description of architect. Early in his career he created stage sets and costumes for masques held at the court of James I. Recognizing his talents, the king made Jones surveyor-general in 1615 and he retained the post under Charles I. Most of his architectural achievements have been lost but those that survive include the BANQUETING HOUSE, the Queen's House at GREENWICH and St Paul's, COVENT GARDEN (*see the* ACTORS' CHURCH).

boy Jones, the *See under* BOY.

Jack Jones *See under* JACK.

Peter Jones *See under* PETER.

josser An outsider, in POLARI, the slang of the gay London underworld in the mid-2oth century.

Jubilee A book compiled or commissioned by John de Northampton, LORD MAYOR OF LONDON in 1381–3, which was said to have laid down relatively advanced principles for the CITY's governance. Northampton's successor Nicholas Brembre made some changes to the regulations and his successor, Nicholas Exton, ordered the book to be publicly burned in the GUILDHALL yard.

> The cordwainers of London, staunch supporters of Northampton ... complained to parliament of Exton. The book, said they, 'comprised all the good articles pertaining to the good government of the City', which Exton and all the aldermen had sworn to maintain for ever, and now he and his accomplices had burnt it without consent of the commons, to the annihilation of many good liberties, franchises, and customs of the City.
>
> REGINALD R. SHARPE: *London and the Kingdom*, Volume 1 (1894)

Jubilee line The newest line on the LONDON UNDERGROUND network, although it incorporates some long-existing stations. It is coloured silvery grey on the map. Inaugurated in 1979, the Jubilee line linked new sections of tunnelling in central London with the former BAKERLOO LINE branch between BAKER STREET and STANMORE. An extension from GREEN PARK to STRATFORD opened in 1999. The line is notable for some impressively large and modernistic stations, especially the new structures at CANARY WHARF and North GREENWICH, and the reconstructed WESTMINSTER station. The Jubilee is the only line on the network to connect, at some point, with all other existing lines. *See also the* FLEET LINE.

juggins A fool or dupe. The term arose in the late 19th century, apparently as a variation on muggins, and its most celebrated recipient was one Henry Ernest Schlesinger Benzon, the son of a highly successful Birmingham UMBRELLA frame-maker. He inherited the then huge sum of £250,000, and managed to go through it (largely by means of slow horses) in under two years. By 1887, the year of Queen Victoria's Golden Jubilee, he was practically broke, and the wags of London's sporting fraternity dubbed him the 'Jubilee Juggins'.

Julius (Caesar) 'Geezer' or 'freezer' or even 'cheeser' (a type of flat cap) in COCKNEY RHYMING SLANG. Like most terms that have more than one rhyming meaning, it is not in common usage.

Jullien's Concerts Features of the LONDON SEASON in the 1840s and 50s. Louis Antoine Jullien (1812–60) came to London in 1838 from Paris and began a series of summer concerts at DRURY LANE, and later winter concerts, at which the best artists were engaged. He raised the level of musical appreciation and introduced the PROMENADE CONCERT. He went bankrupt in 1857, returned to France and died in a mental asylum.

> And must you leave us, Jullien? must we wander
> Through life's hard pathways tuneless and alone,
> Whilst you are gone your magic notes to squander
> 'Midst savages in regions little known?
> What shall we have to cheer us when November
> Oppresses us with fogs and spleen galore,
> Whilst you are playing tunes we well remember,
> On Timbuctoo's inhospitable shore?
>
> *Punch* (13 November 1858)

jumble A white British person in the London slang of west African immigrants of the 1950s, from a corruption of 'John Bull', the archetypal bombastic Englishman.

Jumbo The name of an exceptionally large African elephant, which, after giving rides to thousands of children at LONDON ZOO, was sold to P.T. Barnum's 'Greatest Show On Earth' in 1882. He weighed 6½ tons and was accidentally killed by a railway engine in 1885. He was not the original owner of the name – it had been applied in English to various large ungainly people or animals since the 1820s, and it now standardly designates an object large for its type, such as a jumbo jet or a jumbo-size packet of commercial goods – but it is now synonymous with elephants in many minds. The name may come from Swahili *jambe*, 'chief', or from mumbo jumbo.

Jump, the The nickname of the Old Black Jack, a pub in Portsmouth Street, HOLBORN, from an occasion when Jack SHEPPARD jumped out of its first-floor window to escape the agents of Jonathan Wild, the THIEF-TAKER GENERAL. A club known as the Honourable Society of Jackers used to meet at the pub until 1816. The Magpie and Stump in DICKENS's *Pickwick Papers* (1836–7) may have been modelled on the Old Black Jack, although other scholars favour the George the Fourth, which stood in the same street. Both were demolished in 1896.

Junta A name applied by Sidney and Beatrice Webb to a group of trade union general secretaries in London who became 'an informal cabinet of the trade union world' in the 1860s. Others called them 'the Clique'. The Junta's influence came to an end with the foundation of the Trades Union Congress in 1868.

justice is open to all; like the Ritz hotel The more money you have, the better access you have to the legal system. This oft-quoted remark, or words to the same effect, has been attributed to Lord Birkett, Mr Justice Mathew, Lord Bowen and others.

> Very few supposedly 'normal' people could afford to take a photographic agency to court ... thus reinforcing the truth of the old saying that 'justice is open to all – like the Ritz hotel'.
>
> RICHARD INGRAMS, in *The Independent* (10 May 2008)

K

kangaroo 'Jew' in COCKNEY RHYMING SLANG. It was often shortened to 'kanga' but is seldom heard nowadays. In prison slang it can mean a warder, from the rhyme with 'screw'.

Kangaroo Valley or **Alley** A former nickname for the EARLS COURT area on account of its popularity as a place of residence (usually in the form of a flatshare) for Australians spending a year or two working in London. The term was popular from the 1960s to 80s but faded from use as Earls Court became more heterogeneous and antipodeans colonized several other metropolitan districts.

Kaspar An art-deco-style wooden black cat that is made available at dinners held at the SAVOY HOTEL when it is desired to increase the number of guests from 13 to 14. The practice of avoiding tables of 13 at the Savoy dates from a dinner party held in 1898 that was attended by that number. The host was the diamond mining magnate Woolf Joel, who was the first to leave the table afterwards, dismissing the suggestion that bad luck would consequently befall him. A few weeks later he was shot dead by a blackmailer in his Johannesburg office. Thereafter a member of staff was provided to make up the numbers on such occasions but this proved unpopular when private matters were under discussion. The problem was solved in 1926, when the architect Basil Ionides (1884–1950) designed Kaspar, who was carved from a single piece of LONDON PLANE. When Kaspar is invited to dine a napkin is tied around his neck and he is served in the same way as other guests. Winston Churchill insisted that Kaspar should be present at every meeting of The OTHER CLUB.

Kate

Kate and Sidney 'Steak and kidney' in a vaguely spooneristic kind of rhyming slang.

Kate (Carney) 'Army' in COCKNEY RHYMING SLANG. Kate Carney (1869–1950), 'the COSTER Comedienne', was a SOUTHWARK-born MUSIC HALL performer.

Katerfelto A generic name for a quack or charlatan. Gustavus Katerfelto (d.1799) was a celebrated quack who gained fame during the influenza epidemic of 1782, when he exhibited his solar microscope in PICCADILLY and created immense excitement by showing the infusoria of muddy water. He was a tall man, dressed in a long black gown and square cap, who was accompanied by a black cat.

> And Katerfelto, with his hair on end,
> At his own wonders, wondering for his bread.
>
> WILLIAM COWPER: *The Task*, 'The Winter Evening' (1785)

Kelmscott

Kelmscott House A house located at 26 Upper Mall, HAMMERSMITH, which William Morris (1834–96) bought in 1878 from the novelist George MacDonald and renamed after his earlier home, Kelmscott Manor, near Faringdon, Berkshire (now Oxfordshire). The Hammersmith Socialist Choir regularly rehearsed in the house, with Gustav Holst conducting. It was here in 1896 that the composer met his future wife, Isobel Harrison, the choir's youngest soprano.

Kelmscott Press A private printing press founded in 1890 by William Morris in a cottage adjoining KELMSCOTT HOUSE. Assisted by Emery Walker (1851–1933), who initially gave Morris the inspiration, and Sidney Cockerell, the aim was to revive good printing as an art. Morris himself created the Kelmscott Press fonts and ornamental letters and borders. The press issued 52 books, many of them Morris's own, but also several medieval texts.

The delicately drawn frontispiece to the Kelmscott Press edition of Morris's *News from Nowhere* (1891) shows the gabled manor and its garden and has the following caption in capital lettering:

> This is the picture of the old house by the Thames to which the people of this story went. Hereafter follows the book itself which is called *News from Nowhere or an Epoch of Rest* & is written by William Morris.

Kenley A wealthy residential suburb situated in the southernmost part of GREATER LONDON, east of COULSDON. Kenley did not make its first recorded appearance until 1255 but the name is of Old English origin, probably meaning 'the woodland clearing of a man called Cēna'. Kenley was part of the medieval manor and parish of Waddington and was never a hamlet in its own right, but simply the name of a lane and a farm. Later it became part of the manor of Coulsdon. Around 1823 Kenley House was built on the site of Kenley Farm. When the Caterham Railway came through in 1856 Coulsdon station opened here but was soon renamed Kenley. From the 1950s many of the suburb's Victorian and Edwardian properties were converted to flats or nursing homes or replaced by smaller houses and bungalows.

Kenley Aerodrome An airfield that opened in 1917 and became an important fighter station during the Battle of Britain, as RAF Kenley. The base closed in 1959 but the airfield continues to be used for gliding. Flying scenes for the films *Angels One Five* (1953) and *Reach for the Sky* (1956) were shot at Kenley Aerodrome.

Kenna The fabled founder of KENSINGTON and its gardens. Her story was told by Thomas Tickell (1685–1740) in his long poem, 'Kensington Garden' (1722), which Dr Brewer summarized in the first edition of his *Dictionary of Phrase and Fable* (1870):

> Oberon, king of the fairies, held his royal seat in these gardens, which were fenced round with spells 'interdicted to human touch;' but not unfrequently his thievish elves would rob the human mother of her babe, and leave in its stead a sickly changeling of the elfin race. Once on a time it so fell out that one of the infants fostered in these gardens was Albion, the son of 'Albion's royal blood;' it was stolen by a fairy named Milkah. When the boy was nineteen, he fell in love with Kenna, daughter of King Oberon, and Kenna vowed that none

but Albion should ever be her chosen husband. Oberon heard her when she made this vow, and instantly drove the prince out of the garden, and married the fairy maid to Azuriel, a fairy of great beauty and large possessions, to whom Holland Park belonged. In the meantime, Albion prayed to Neptune for revenge, and the sea-god commanded the fairy Oriel, whose dominion lay along the banks of the Thames, to espouse the cause of his lineal offspring. Albion was slain in the battle by Azuriel, and Neptune in revenge crushed the whole empire of Oberon. Being immortal, the fairies could not be destroyed, but they fled from the angry sea-god, some to the hills and some to the dales, some to the caves and others to riverbanks. Kenna alone remained, and tried to revive her lover by means of the herb moly. No sooner did the juice of this wondrous herb touch the body than it turned into a snowdrop. When Henry Wise laid out the grounds for the Prince of Orange, Kenna planned it 'in a morning dream,' and gave her name to the town and garden.

Kennington An area of terraced houses and tower blocks east of VAUXHALL. First recorded in Domesday Book as Chenintune, the name probably meant 'the farm of a man called Cēna', although others have suggested 'place of the king'. In 1337 Kennington was given to Edward, the Black Prince, and a royal palace was built here. Though the palace has long gone, the manor has belonged to the eldest son of England's monarchs ever since, as part of the Duchy of Cornwall. Most of the modern layout of Kennington was set by 1799, although the southwestern part developed a little later. Tram and bus routes later converged here; Kennington was described in the 1920s as 'the CLAPHAM JUNCTION of the southern roads'. Kennington was the birthplace of Bernard Montgomery (1887–1976), later Field Marshal Viscount Montgomery of Alamein.

Kennington Common A former venue for fairs and executions; St Mark's Church stands on the site of the gallows. In 1848 a huge crowd assembled here intending to march on Parliament to present its Chartist petition. The march was banned and the crowd was persuaded by the Chartist leader Feargus O'Connor MP to disperse peacefully. In 1852 the common was converted to 'a pleasant place of recreation' and renamed Kennington Park.

Kennington Oval See the OVAL.

Kensals, the A collective name for the undermentioned places. The 13th-century name 'Kingisholt', of which 'Kensal' is a corruption, meant 'king's wood', but the king remains unidentified.

Kensal Green An increasingly fashionable residential quarter – more accurately, triangle – situated on the HARROW ROAD between West KILBURN and HARLESDEN. The green was first recorded in 1550, when it was surrounded by thick woodland. Surprisingly, it was the opening of the cemetery (see below) that first made this a popular residential area. From soon after the Second World War a West Indian community developed at Kensal Green, growing especially large in the 1960s and 1970s. The district has recently been undergoing a moderate level of GENTRIFICATION as an overspill zone from NOTTING HILL.

Kensal Green Cemetery A privately developed cemetery laid out in 1832 on 56 acres (23 hectares) of land between HARROW ROAD and the GRAND UNION CANAL, Kensal Green was the first of many suburban cemeteries created by joint-stock companies in response to the difficulties of finding burial space in central London churchyards. Father and son engineers Sir Marc and Isambard Brunel, the writers Thackeray and Trollope, and the French acrobat and tightrope walker BLONDIN are among those buried here.

> For there is good news yet to hear and fine
> things to be seen,
> Before we go to Paradise by way of Kensal Green.
>
> G.K. CHESTERTON: 'The Rolling English Road' (1914)

Kensal Rise As its name suggests, this late Victorian suburb occupies the slopes above KENSAL GREEN. The most distinctive properties are on Clifford Gardens, where an old HAMPSTEAD man was employed to decorate the gables with what BRENT council calls 'quaint and curious stucco scenes'. A national athletic ground was laid out in 1890 but never amounted to much and soon succumbed to the demand for building land. Kensal Rise gained one of the earliest free libraries in the area, opened in 1900 by Mark Twain. The locality has recently been losing its identity because many estate agents treat it as part of QUEEN'S PARK.

Kensal Town An infrequently used name for a heavily redeveloped part of north-east NORTH KENSINGTON, situated between the GRAND UNION CANAL and the main railway line into PADDINGTON. Kensal New Town, as it was originally called, was laid out from the mid-19th century following Kensal Green's successful development. From the start, however, it was poorer and less fashionable and it deteriorated into a notorious slum. In 1903 Charles BOOTH described it as 'an isolated district shaped like a shoe and just as full of children and poverty as was the old woman's dwelling in the nursery rhyme'. From the 1930s the council began a programme of slum clearance and estate building that accelerated after the Second World War and erased much of the original street pattern. The process culminated on the east side with TRELLICK TOWER in 1972.

Kensington An eminently salubrious residential and institutional district situated north-west of CHELSEA. The name was first recorded in Domesday Book and (notwithstanding the fairy tale of KENNA) probably derives from a Saxon farmer called Cynesige. Despite its exalted reputation, Kensington was a late developer. A few gentlemen's residences were built in the early 17th century, of which only two significant examples survive, in completely contrasting forms: Sir Walter Cope's mansion is now the bombed-out shell of Holland House (see HOLLAND PARK), while Sir George Coppin's house has grown several times over to become KENSINGTON PALACE. In 1685 the developer Thomas Young began to lay out Kensington Square but this long remained an isolated outpost of civilized London amid the fields and gravel pits that covered most of the parish. The establishment of the museums and colleges of ALBERTOPOLIS enhanced Kensington's reputation in the second half of the 19th century and the district quickly filled with high-class STUCCOED terraces and detached villas. Property developers made up the name 'West Kensington' for what had formerly been FULHAM's lowly North End; by contrast, NORTH KENSINGTON was a genuine part of the medieval parish but has never been a prestigious locality.

Kensington and Chelsea, Royal Borough of An INNER LONDON borough created in 1965 from the former metropolitan boroughs of the same names. The 'royal' element dates from a charter of 1901 that bestowed the honorific on

Kensington, as the borough in which Queen Victoria was born. Kensington and Chelsea has the second smallest population of London's boroughs. Among its districts are EARLS COURT, NOTTING HILL and HOLLAND PARK. The town hall is in Hornton Street, off KENSINGTON HIGH STREET, with some offices at CHELSEA's old town hall on the KING'S ROAD. The borough's elegant coat of arms was the work of Sir Anthony Wagner (1908–95) and features royal and religious references, as well as a flowering broom bush for BROMPTON. The civic motto is *quam bonum in unum habitare*; the words are adapted from the opening line of the 133rd psalm and mean 'what a good thing it is to dwell together in unity'.

Kensington Gardens A royal park adjoining the west side of HYDE PARK, of which it originally formed a part. The gardens were laid out from the 1690s by Henry Wise and from 1728 by his successor as royal gardener, Charles Bridgeman, under the direction of Queen Caroline, queen consort of George II, who was the last reigning monarch to live at KENSINGTON PALACE. Near the boundary with Hyde Park six pools formed by the River WESTBOURNE were connected to create the Long Water and the SERPENTINE. The future Queen Victoria was born at Kensington Palace in 1819 and she chose Kensington Gardens as the site for the fabulously ostentatious ALBERT MEMORIAL, erected in 1872 to commemorate her late husband's achievements. The gardens have inspired many artists and writers, including the poet Matthew Arnold and most famously J.M. Barrie, whose *Peter Pan in Kensington Gardens* (1906) introduced the little boy who refused to grow up. In 1912 Barrie commissioned the sculptor George Frampton to create a statue of Peter Pan, which stands by the Long Water. The gardens' status as 'the world capital of fairies, gnomes and elves' was buttressed by the addition in 1928 of the ELFIN OAK.

Kensington Gore A section of Kensington Road between Queen's Gate and Alexandra Gate on the southern edge of KENSINGTON GARDENS. A gore was a wedge-shaped plot of land and between the 13th and 17th centuries this was the King's Gore, but it is not known who the original royal owner was. William Wilberforce (1759–1833) lived at Gore House and held anti-slavery meetings there. The house stood on the site of the ALBERT HALL. *See also* HOT AND COLD CORNER.

In theatrical slang, Kensington Gore is a punning term for stage blood.

Kensington High Street A shopping street located 1 mile (1.6 km) west of KNIGHTSBRIDGE and widely referred to as 'High Street Ken'. From the late 19th century entrepreneurs opened shops here that grew to become department stores, the most successful of which was the now-defunct Barkers, which absorbed its main rival Derry and Toms in 1921. In the last quarter of the 20th century the street went into a decline but this had the benefit of allowing quirkier boutiques and indoor markets to flourish, offering better bargains and more 'urban' styles than could be found in Knightsbridge. However, a subsequent recovery in the street's mainstream popularity has forced out most of the independent retailers.

Kensingtonian (A native or inhabitant) of Kensington. The word often connotes snootiness or hauteur, especially as betrayed by speech:

> Superior Margery Seymour, with her Kensingtonian 'mothah and brothah'.
>
> *Times Literary Supplement* (27 June 1936)

Kensington Olympia An exhibition centre located at the western end of KENSINGTON HIGH STREET. Following the success of the AGRICULTURAL HALL in ISLINGTON, which held military tournaments as well as every kind of animal show, the public demanded a larger arena where mock battles could be played out on a grand scale. Olympia opened in 1886 and proceeded to stage a series of lavish entertainment spectaculars, although it struggled to turn a profit. Pleasure gardens were laid out in the grounds and some of the world's first motor shows were held in the hall in the early 20th century. The National Hall was added on the south-west side in 1922, followed in 1929 by the Empire Hall, later known as Olympia 2. London's first multi-storey car park was built for Olympia in 1937.

Kensington Palace A royal residence situated on the west side of KENSINGTON GARDENS. Around 1605 Sir George Coppin, clerk of the Crown to James I, built a house here with 36 acres (15 hectares) of grounds. Later known as Nottingham House, it was acquired by the joint monarchs William III and Mary II in 1689 and remodelled as Kensington Palace. The palace was further extended by George I and has not significantly changed since. It remained the official residence of British monarchs until

BUCKINGHAM PALACE supplanted it on the accession of Queen Victoria in 1837. Kensington Palace retains residential apartments and offices for several members of the royal family; it was home to Diana, Princess of Wales, until her death in 1997 (*see also* PRINCESS DIANA MEMORIAL FOUNTAIN). Visitors can tour the state apartments and view the royal ceremonial dress collection.

Kensington stitch A needlework stitch (called in full Kensington outline stitch) formed by putting the needle into the material from the front and returning it some way back while splitting the thread.

Kent House Border territory between BECKENHAM and PENGE, taking its name from a house that used to be the first building in the county of Kent on the local road from London via SURREY; it was in existence by 1240. The Russian banker and LLOYD's insurer John Julius ANGERSTEIN acquired Kent House in 1784. It became a farmhouse from around 1806, and later a nursing home and then a private hotel before being pulled down in 1957. W.M. Thackeray once stayed at Kent House and the author's notes for his unfinished novel *Denis Duval* (1864) suggest that it was intended to be the protagonist's home.

Kentish

Kentish Mess A junior category of membership of CLIFFORD'S INN; its links with Kent are lost in obscurity. The senior body was known as the Principal and Rules. On the death of a Rule, a member of the Kentish Mess would be elected to succeed him. The junior MESS would sit at their own table at dinnertime in the inn's hall, where a bizarre custom was observed:

At the conclusion of dinner, the chairman of the Kentish Mess, first bowing to the principal of the Inn, who is seated at the table at his right hand, takes from the hands of a servitor a batch of four small rolls or loaves of bread – neither more nor less than that number; and, without saying a word, he dashes them three times on the table; he then discharges them to the other end of the table, from whence the bread is removed by a servant in attendance. Solemn silence – broken only by the three impressive thumps upon the table – prevails during this strange ceremony, which takes the place of grace after meat in Clifford's Inn Hall; and

concerning which, not even the oldest member of the Society is able to give any explanation.
Notes and Queries (1856)

Kentish Town A tarnished but characterful district situated north of CAMDEN TOWN. The name is of obscure origin and is more likely to be related to a man called Kentish than to the county of Kent. The settlement evolved as a ribbon development on the road to HIGHGATE and there is some evidence that it moved northwards to its present location, having first begun near ST PANCRAS Church. William Bruges lavishly entertained the Emperor Sigismund at his country house in Kentish Town in 1416. As late as 1840 the village was still semi-rural, with a community of artists and engravers, but it was almost entirely built over during the following 30 years. Its popularity was aided by a London doctor who praised the healthy air and clean water, calling Kentish Town 'the MONTPELLIER OF ENGLAND', and came to live here himself. Mary Shelley, however, condemned the place as an 'odious swamp'. Plans for aggressive redevelopment were tabled after the Second World War but a milder version was implemented and by 1960 the middle classes were beginning to rediscover Kentish Town.

Men begin in Kentish Town with £80 a year, and end in Park Lane with a hundred thousand. They want to drop Kentish Town; but they give themselves away every time they open their mouths.
GEORGE BERNARD SHAW: *Pygmalion* (1913)

Shrew of Kentish Town *See* MOTHER RED CAP.

Kenton A flourishing multicultural community situated north-east of HARROW. Like several other London suburbs, its centre was shifted by the siting of its railway station. The old village lay in the immediate vicinity of Kenton Grange, now in Woodcock Park. The opening of a station on the London and Birmingham (later London and North Western) Railway three-quarters of a mile (1.2 km) to the west in 1912, and the expansion of KINGSBURY's territory, pushed the village's midpoint towards WEALDSTONE. In the ten years to 1931, when its development peaked, Kenton's population increased twenty-fold.

Kenwood A landscaped estate located to the north-east of HAMPSTEAD HEATH, south of Hampstead Lane. The park boasts a fine collection of trees and some of the most beautiful rhododendron gardens in London. Sir Arthur Crosfield led a successful campaign after the First World War to save the estate from housing development. Lakeside concerts, traditionally of classical music, are held at Kenwood in the summer. In recent years the programme has incorporated a wider range of musical genres.

Kenwood House An English Heritage property, remodelled in neo-classical style by Robert ADAM in 1764. It opened to the public in 1928, as the bequest of its final private owner, the brewing magnate Edward Cecil Guinness, 1st Earl of Iveagh, who also endowed its collection of old master paintings, including a Rembrandt self-portrait, one of only five Vermeers in Britain, Gainsborough's portrait of Countess Howe and works by Reynolds and Turner. Kenwood House has frequently served as a film location, including scenes in *101 Dalmatians* (1996) and *Notting Hill* (1999).

Keston A dispersed village situated south of BROMLEY. It is claimed that the name relates to Julius Caesar's presence in the area in 55 BC, although this is extremely improbable. However, it is likely that Romans settled here around AD 200 and relics of a Roman cemetery have been found. The old parish church, opposite the western end of DOWNE Road, was the centre of medieval Keston but after the GREAT PLAGUE development began anew 1½ miles (2.5 km) to the north, in a clearing between HAYES[1] and Keston Commons. Most of the recent construction is hidden from the main road, allowing Keston to maintain the impression – by London standards – of an unspoilt rural community. The surrounding farmland is littered with evidence of Neolithic as well as Roman occupation, and there is a weather-boarded windmill dated 1716, and restored in 1913, but most of these sites are inaccessible to the public.

Keston Common Open space bordering the east side of the village of Keston. It was one of the first pieces of common land to be protected by Act of Parliament from further encroachment (in 1865). It now has perhaps the most diverse range of habitats of any common in London, with the greatest number of rare species.

Keston Mark A largely 20th-century extension of Keston, this was once a hamlet on the northern perimeter of Keston parish; 'mark' means a boundary and was once common in

place names, though few examples survive in the London area.

Keston Ponds A small group of pools located near the private estate of HOLWOOD. They are fed from the fancifully named Caesar's Well, the source of the River RAVENSBOURNE.

kettle A wristwatch. It may have originated as 'kettle and hob', COCKNEY RHYMING SLANG for a fob watch. Apart from an episode of MINDER, in which Arthur DALEY referred to 'dodgy kettles' (and did not mean the electrical appliances), the term has rarely been heard in recent decades.

Kew An attractive village lying in a crook of the THAMES, opposite CHISWICK and BRENTFORD. The name is probably derived from *key-hough*, the wood or 'hough' by the quay, and was first mentioned in 1327. When the Tudors made RICHMOND UPON THAMES a regular seat of their court, Kew benefited as a home for their courtiers. The village had a chapel from the 16th century and St Anne's Church was built on Kew Green in 1714, when a public subscription raised the money and Queen Anne granted the plot of land. The landscape and portrait painter Thomas Gainsborough was buried in St Anne's churchyard in 1788. The massive archive repositories of the Public Record Office were built at the end of Ruskin Avenue in the mid-1970s, when the institution moved here from CHANCERY LANE.

Kew Bridge A river crossing and station located where the THAMES makes the first northward loop on its journey through London. The present bridge was designed by John Wolfe-Barry and opened in 1903 by Edward VII. The construction of the bridge, in concrete and granite, was a joint project by the county councils of SURREY and MIDDLESEX. Kew Bridge station, on the HOUNSLOW loop line, opened in 1850. In 1869 the London and South Western Railway Company built Kew railway bridge at STRAND ON THE GREEN to provide a shorter route for its line to RICHMOND.

Kew Bridge Steam Museum A former water pumping station that now hosts an exhibition on the story of London's water supply and the world's largest collection of steam pumping engines, several of which can be seen in action at weekends.

Kew Gardens The Royal Botanic Gardens occupy the north-western part of the Kew peninsula, across the THAMES from BRENTFORD. The gardens are a convergence of three 17th-century projects: the Dutch House (later Kew Palace) and the White House and their grounds, and the northward expansion of the royal gardens of RICHMOND UPON THAMES. An octagonal ten-storey pagoda was built in 1762 as a surprise for Princess Augusta, the Dowager Princess of Wales, and Capability BROWN remodelled the gardens of Richmond (formerly Ormonde) Lodge for George III and Queen Charlotte in 1765, but the lodge itself was demolished in the following decade. Queen Charlotte is said to have designed the cottage that was built at the edge of the Old Deer Park in the early 1770s. At this time, Joseph Banks (1743–1820) was made director of the gardens and set about importing, cultivating and then re-exporting consignments of exotic plants from Britain's colonies abroad. Banks set up satellite botanical gardens as far afield as St Vincent in the West Indies and Madras in India. The various gardens of Kew were united in 1802 and adopted as a national botanical garden in 1841. Its Victorian directors added magnificent new buildings for the cultivation of plants requiring different climatic conditions, including the Winter Garden (now the Temperate House) and the Palm House. Successive new buildings have subsequently entrenched Kew's status as a world-class centre of botanical research, as well as a breathtaking spectacle.

> Go down to Kew in lilac-time (it isn't far from London!)
> And you shall wander hand in hand with love in summer's wonderland.
>
> ALFRED NOYES: 'The Barrel-Organ' (1904)

key worker scheme A government-funded programme, formally entitled the Key Worker Living Programme, offering assistance with the cost of buying or renting a home to certain public sector workers. Qualifying professions include teaching, nursing and social work. The scheme is limited to London and those counties of southeast and eastern England where the LONDON EFFECT has pushed the price of housing beyond the reach of many on below-average incomes.

khazi A slang term for a lavatory, possibly from Italian *casa*, 'house'. It is also spelt with almost every possible variation imaginable.

Khyber (Pass) 'Arse' in COCKNEY RHYMING SLANG, or occasionally 'glass'. The Khyber Pass is a route through the mountains that separate Pakistan and Afghanistan and was a place of much bloodshed during the Anglo-Afghan Wars (1839–42; 1878–80; 1919), which were parodied in the 1968 film *Carry On up the Khyber* (*see* CARRY ON FILMS).

> I come back from three weeks in Nicosia, most of which I spent lying flat in the corridors of the Ledra Palace Hotel, waiting for some Turk to put a bullet up my Khyber ...
>
> CHRISTOPHER HAMPTON: *Treats* (1975)

kibosh In addition to its usage in the phrase below, the word meant one shilling and sixpence (7½p) in 19th-century London slang. It was also employed with reference to an 18-month prison sentence.

put the kibosh on, to To put a stop to; to prevent from continuing. The word is of unknown origin: suggestions have included the heraldic term 'caboshed', referring to the depiction of an animal's head, cut off behind the ears or horns, and the Hebrew or Yiddish *kabas*, *kabasten* 'to suppress'. All its early recorded appearances in print come in London publications, with various spellings, and some are suggestive of COCKNEY usage:

> 'Hooroar,' ejaculates a pot-boy in parenthesis, 'put the kye-bosk on her, Mary!'
>
> DICKENS: *Sketches by Boz* (1836)

kick Former slang for a sixpence, but usually only in compounds, as 'two-and-a-kick', otherwise two shillings and sixpence.

Kidbrooke A socially mixed residential district situated south of CHARLTON and east of BLACKHEATH. A watercourse called Kid Brook runs to the south-west, but this may have been named after the settlement, as the derivation is probably 'marshy ground with kites'. Most of the land was given over to pasture and arable use with a little market gardening until the 1860s, when housebuilding began to cut ribbons through the agricultural holdings and St James's Church was built. Kidbrooke School was the first purpose-built comprehensive school in the UK when it opened in 1954. GREENWICH council built the FERRIER estate in the 1970s and is now in the process of rebuilding it.

Kidd, Captain William Kidd (1645–1701), privateer and pirate, about whom many stories and legends have arisen. He was commissioned in 1696 to attack the French and seize pirates, but turned the expedition into one of piracy. He was eventually arrested at Boston, Massachusetts, and subsequently hanged at EXECUTION DOCK.

Kilburn The former heartland of London's Irish community, now more multicultural, located north-west of ST JOHN'S WOOD and MAIDA VALE. The name comes from a stream (which could have been 'cold bourne', 'cow's bourne' or 'King's bourne') that formerly constituted the upper part of the River WESTBOURNE. Kilburn Priory was founded in the 12th century on the site of a former hermitage and the Red Lion, which was said to date from 1444, may have begun life as the priory's guest house. A number of private schools opened in the mid-19th century, including one run by A.A. Milne's father, which the writer attended, as did H.G. Wells and the newspaper proprietor Alfred Harmsworth. The district became poorer later in the century, the schools closed, large houses were subdivided or took in lodgers, and a variety of immigrants began to move here, especially the Irish. Kilburn became a popular place for public entertainment and entrepreneurs established several variety theatres, all now closed. The Tricycle Theatre is the modern district's leading cultural venue.

Kilburn and the High Roads The band that gave singer/songwriter Ian Dury (1942–2000) his first break in the early 1970s.

king

King Bomba A former delicatessen on OLD COMPTON STREET, specializing in wines, salami, cheeses and dried herbs. King Bomba was a nickname given to Ferdinand II (1810–59), king of Naples (from 1830), for his heavy bombardment of Sicilian cities in 1848 to suppress a revolution. Run by the Italian anarchist Emidio Recchioni (1864–1933), the SOHO establishment was a focus for anti-fascist activities in the 1920s and 1930s, including a plot to kill Mussolini.

kingdom come 'Bum' in COCKNEY RHYMING SLANG, in the sense of the posterior. On the rare occasions the term is used the context is usually feminine.

Her scotches, long and slender,
Reached to her kingdom come …

RONNIE BARKER: *Fletcher's Book of Rhyming Slang* (1979)

King George V Dock See the ROYAL DOCKS.

King of Clowns See the CLOWNS' SERVICE.

king of cockneys A master of the revels formerly chosen by students at LINCOLN'S INN on Childermas Day (28 December). Given the antiquity of the office, the word 'COCKNEY' may have been used in an earlier sense than that of 'Londoner'.

Item, that the king of cockneys on Childermas Day should sit and have due service … and that the said king of cockneys … meddle neither in the buttery, nor in the steward of Christmas, his office, upon pain of forty shillings for every such meddling.

Black Book of Lincoln's Inn (1518)

King of Corsica Theodor Stephan von Neuhoff (1694–1756), also known as Stephen Theodore, a Prussian adventurer who briefly ruled Corsica in 1736. He spent his latter years in SOHO, trying to raise funds with which to recapture the island from the Genoese. Instead he was jailed for debt in the KING'S BENCH PRISON, where he continued to receive visitors with an attempt at ceremony. Afterwards he subsisted on the benefaction of Horace Walpole and others. On his death he was buried in the churchyard of St Anne's, Soho, and Walpole composed these lines for his epitaph:

The grave, great teacher, to a level brings
Heroes and beggars, galley slaves and kings.
But Theodore this moral learned ere dead:
Fate poured its lessons on his living head,
Bestowed a kingdom, and denied him bread.

Theodore's title was used during his lifetime for a brand of LONDON GIN, and was later recalled by the King of Corsica pub on BERWICK STREET, an establishment that now calls itself the Endurance.

king of hoteliers and hotelier to kings See the RITZ.

King of Misrule See LORD OF MISRULE.

king of quacks John St John Long (1798–1834), who in 1829 set up shop in HARLEY STREET, offering his cures by rubbing and inhalation, and causing traffic jams as his titled and wealthy clients thronged to attend. In 1830 a coroner's jury found him guilty of the manslaughter of a patient, Catherine Cashin, but he was later acquitted of the same charge at the OLD BAILEY.

'The primary cause of disease,' he said, 'consists of a morbid fluid inherent in the system, and incident to all of the human race.' To the quantity of this morbific humour, more or less, he attributed the common origin of all diseases.

London Medical and Surgical Journal (12 July 1834)

king of skiffle The sobriquet of Lonnie Donegan (1931–2002), who grew up in EAST HAM. He pioneered British skiffle, a style of jazz-influenced folk music, endowing the American genre with a COCKNEY flavour in recordings such as 'My Old Man's A Dustman' (1960).

king of skinkers A nickname given by Ben Jonson to Simon Wadloe (d.1627), the proprietor of the Devil Tavern, which stood near TEMPLE BAR until 1787. The tavern was named from its sign, which showed St Dunstan tweaking Satan's nose with a pair of hot tongs. A skinker was someone who draws or pours out liquor and Wadloe performed this task frequently for Jonson, who praised the Devil on more than one occasion in his writings and belonged to a convivial society that met in the tavern's Apollo room. *See also* GO TO THE DEVIL.

> No 'faith
> Dine in Apollo with Pecunia,
> At brave Duke Wadloe's, have your Friends about you,
> And make a day on't.
>
> BEN JONSON: *Staple of News*, II, v (1625)

King's or **Queen's beasts** A range of heraldic animals that have featured in the armorial bearings of the British monarch's forebears. Their best-known manifestation was the ten beasts whose images, modelled by James Woodford, stood guard over WESTMINSTER ABBEY during the Coronation of Elizabeth II in 1953: the Black Bull of Clarence, the Falcon of the Plantagenets, the White Greyhound of Richmond, the GRIFFIN of Edward III, the Lion of England, the Red Dragon of Wales, the Unicorn of Scotland, the White Horse of Hanover, the White Lion of Mortimer and the Yale of Beaufort. Stone replicas of them were placed in KEW GARDENS in 1956. There are several others besides these, however, including the Hind of Edward V, the Panther of Henry VI, the Unicorn of Edward III, the White Hart of Richard II and the White Swan of Bohun. The original figures of the beasts were used to adorn HAMPTON COURT PALACE in celebration of the marriage of Henry VIII to Jane Seymour in 1536. They were demolished in William III's reign, and replaced in 1909. The beasts that now line

the bridge across the moat in front of the palace date from 1950.

King's or **Queen's Bench Prison** Initially a prison that travelled with the royal household but from the 14th century permanently based near BOROUGH High Road. It was attacked in both the PEASANTS' REVOLT and the Jack CADE rebellion and burnt down in the GORDON RIOTS though it was soon rebuilt. The new building was renowned for the contrasting conditions in which rich and poor prisoners were kept. It later became a military prison before being closed in 1880. *See also the* ST GEORGE'S FIELDS MASSACRE.

King's College Hospital A teaching hospital established in 1840 in the vacant ST CLEMENT DANES workhouse, south of LINCOLN'S INN FIELDS. The workhouse was replaced by a purpose-built hospital in 1861. Joseph Lister (1827–1912) was invited onto the staff in 1877 and he performed the first ever major elective operation under strict antiseptic conditions on a patient at King's. Late in the 19th century the disruption caused by the development of KINGSWAY, the ALDWYCH and the ROYAL COURTS OF JUSTICE prompted the hospital to plan a move south of the THAMES and in 1913 it relocated to DENMARK HILL. In 1966 King's took over management responsibility for five south London hospitals known as the CAMBERWELL Group. The long-term aim is to consolidate all these hospitals onto one site.

King's College London A university college founded in 1829 by George IV and the Duke of Wellington (then prime minister), and named in honour of the former. It was established in the tradition of the Church of England, in response to the contrasting stance of London University, the GODLESS INSTITUTION OF GOWER STREET. King's has grown through mergers with several institutions, notably the United Medical and Dental Schools of Guy's and St Thomas' Hospitals; Chelsea College; Queen Elizabeth College and the Institute of Psychiatry. The college has five campuses, including its original home on the STRAND, next to SOMERSET HOUSE, and nowadays welcomes students of any faith, or none. Among King's notable alumni are John Keats, Thomas Hardy, Virginia Woolf, Arthur C. Clarke and Archbishop Desmond Tutu. *See also* DUEL DAY.

King's Cross A rapidly changing inner-city

district located south-west of ISLINGTON and formerly called BATTLE BRIDGE. The modern name comes from a statue of George IV that was erected at the junction of EUSTON ROAD, GRAY'S INN ROAD and PENTONVILLE Road in 1830. The statue was removed only 15 years later owing to its unpopularity with the local community. However, the name proved more resilient and was subsequently applied to an expanding neighbourhood to the north and south, much of which was previously known as ST PANCRAS. Following a long period of decline a massive regeneration programme is under way, which will take many years to complete. At the heart of the project is the redevelopment of 67 acres (27 hectares) of railway land as King's Cross Central, a mixed-use scheme that is planned to include 3 parks, 5 squares, 20 streets, up to 50 arts and music venues and a new campus for the UNIVERSITY OF THE ARTS LONDON.

King's Cross station The terminus of the Great Northern Railway opened in 1852 on the site of the former London Smallpox Hospital, and was at the time the largest station in England. The building, designed by Lewis Cubitt, has a plain brick facade composed of two impressive arches, at present partially obscured by excrescences perpetrated in the 1960s to accommodate a new booking hall and concourse. It is some- what overshadowed by the Gothic dignity of ST PANCRAS STATION and the Midland Grand Hotel just to the west. King's Cross station is now the London terminus for the east-coast main line to north-east England and eastern Scotland (in the days of steam, the FLYING SCOTSMAN left from here) and for some East Anglian services, and also for north-eastern suburban services. King's Cross station hides two secrets; legend has it that BOUDICCA, queen of the Iceni, is buried beneath platform 10 or 11, while Harry POTTER and his schoolmates board the Hogwarts Express at platform 9¾.

King's Cross St Pancras underground station opened in 1863. It originally served the Inner Circle (now the CIRCLE LINE), and was called simply King's Cross. It was given its present name in 1933, and six lines now use it (more than any other LONDON UNDERGROUND station). In November 1987 31 people were killed in a fire on the escalators and in the booking hall. One victim of the conflagration was not identified until 2004.

King's Jester or **Royal Jester** A nickname for Dan Leno, better known as the FUNNIEST MAN ON EARTH, from the command performance he gave for Edward VII at Sandringham in 1901.

King's mark See HALLMARK.

King's Privy Wardrobe See the JEWEL TOWER.

King's or **Queen's remembrancer** Originally an exchequer clerk sharing the work of establish- ing and collecting fixed revenues and debts with the Lord Treasurer's remembrancer. In 1877 the office was transferred to the Supreme Court and is now held by the senior master of the King's or Queen's Bench Division of the High Court. His or her duties are concerned with the selection of sheriffs, with the swearing-in of the LORD MAYOR OF LONDON and with revenue cases. See also QUIT RENT.

King's Road 'The longest catwalk in the world' runs south-westwards from SLOANE SQUARE to FULHAM, where it becomes the New King's Road. It originated as a private highway from London to HAMPTON COURT, created by Charles II. The royal highway became a public thoroughfare by degrees. In the mid-18th century passes were issued to suitable gentlemen but enterprising locals forged their own. The King's Road opened formally to the masses in 1830, by which time houses and inns were scattered along most of its length. Later in the 19th century shops appeared, especially towards the Sloane Square end, and James Whistler and friends founded the CHELSEA ARTS CLUB. Places of entertainment included the Palaseum and Gaumont cinemas, which still operate but under different names. Mary QUANT opened the King's Road's first boutique in 1955 and by the mid-1960s the street had become a fashion centre that was rivalled only by CARNABY STREET. Gandalf's Garden and the CHELSEA DRUG STORE were among the many hang-outs for hippies and curious onlookers. Punk clothing appeared at WORLD'S END in the early 1970s, a few years before its musical accompaniment (see PUNK ROCK). The street has become more straightforwardly commercial and less cutting- edge since those times, but remains immensely popular, as much for its bars and restaurants as its fashion retailers and antiques dealers.

> No finer honour can be bestowed on a man down the King's Road than to be called a together cat.
>
> *Daily Mirror* (27 August 1968)

King Street

1. A street linking Garrick Street with COVENT GARDEN. It was built in the 1630s and named in honour of Charles I. The composer Thomas Arne (1710–78) was born in King Street, and the GARRICK CLUB was founded here in 1831. The first permanent premises of Moses Moses, whose firm later became the outfitters and suit-hirers MOSS BROS, were in King Street, where they remain more than a century and a half later. Between 1920 and 1980 the headquarters of the Communist Party of Great Britain Executive Committee were at No.16, and for a while King Street became a metonym for the party or its leaders or members:

> One version of events is that 'King Street' had decided the miners wouldn't end the strike unless they were given 25 per cent.
>
> *The Observer* (8 October 1972)

2. A street in ST JAMES'S, first developed in the 1670s. There has been a Golden Lion public house at 25 King Street since at least 1732. The auctioneers Christie's moved to 8 King Street in 1823, still its London headquarters today. The St James's Theatre opened on King Street in 1835. Despite protest marches and an attempted intervention by Winston Churchill, the theatre was demolished in 1957 and replaced by St James's House, an office block. *See also* ALMACK'S.

3. The principal shopping street of HAMMERSMITH, extending from HAMMERSMITH BROADWAY westward to STAMFORD BROOK, where it meets CHISWICK High Road. The Lyric Theatre is a focal arts venue for west London. A gilt and velvet auditorium has been rebuilt inside this 1970s concrete structure. Latymer Upper School's performing arts centre, at 237 King Street, is a new building with a four-storey atrium serving as a theatre foyer and art gallery.

Kingsbury

A mixed METROLAND and municipally built suburb covering a large area north-east of WEMBLEY and west of HENDON. Known in ancient times as Tunworth, it was mentioned in Domesday Book as Chingesberie, which meant 'king's manor'. Kingsbury's most distinctive asset is a series of follies and cottage-style houses by the architect Ernest George Trobridge (1884–1942), some of which look more like little medieval castles than interwar suburban homes.

Kingsland A historically poor and densely populated locality situated immediately west of DALSTON, of which it is nowadays considered a part. Its name derives from the former royal ownership of parts of HACKNEY. Samuel PEPYS wrote in 1667 that he had boarded at Kingsland as a boy, 'and used to shoot with my bow and arrows in these fields. A very pretty place it is'. During the first quarter of the 19th century some terraces of very cramped houses were laid out, creating an increasingly sharp contrast with the early stages of respectable suburbanization in Dalston. Throughout the second half of the 20th century, council intervention nibbled away at Kingsland's already meagre heritage, but more recent City Challenge funding has produced some improvements.

Kingsland Waste The stretch of Kingsland Road between Forest Road and Middleton Road, with a long-established but faded Saturday market selling all kinds of goods.

kingsman An oversized, colourful handkerchief worn by COSTERMONGERS, probably emulating established practice among Gypsies. Women draped them over their shoulders, while men wore them around their necks, folded and crossed at the front. Kingsmen were usually woven from silk and fashionable colourways came and went with the seasons. One year it was the done thing to be seen in green and purple squares; the next, red and yellow stripes with blue spots and a green border. If ever two costers fought, they would first remove their kingsmen and tie them around their legs or waists or put them aside in a safe place.

> The only object she possessed of any value was a huge coloured silk neckerchief, what is called a 'kingsman', which she wore about her shoulders.
>
> CHARLES H.E. BROOKFIELD: *Random Reminiscences* (1902)

Kingston

Kingston Bridge

1. For nearly a thousand years the lowest THAMES crossing except for LONDON BRIDGE. A stone bridge replaced its wooden predecessor in 1828.

2. A card bent so that, when the pack is cut, it is cut at this card.

Kingston bypass One of Britain's earliest urban bypasses, now part of the A3. Planning of the bypass began in the 1920s, and the name came to encapsulate the mixed pleasures and frustrations of motoring in and around London.

> Give me the Kingston By-Pass
> And a thoroughly 'posh' machine
> Like a Healey three-litre
> All complete with heater
> Or a shiny grey Chevrolet Limousine.
>
> NOËL COWARD: *The Globe Revue*, 'Give Me the Kingston By-Pass' (1952)

Kingston Hill A tree-lined road running along the south-eastern edge of RICHMOND PARK. Just north of the park's Ladderstile Gate is Galsworthy House, formerly Parkfield, the birthplace of the novelist John Galsworthy (1867–1933).

Kingston University A 'new' university, created in 1992 as the successor to Kingston Polytechnic. It began as Kingston Technical Institute in 1899, becoming a college in 1926 and merging with Kingston College of Art in 1970 to form the polytechnic. In 1975 the poly absorbed GIPSY HILL College of Education, which had moved after the Second World War to Kingston Hill Place, a mansion that had supposedly belonged to Lillie Langtry, mistress of the Prince of Wales (later Edward VII). The university presently has around 20,000 students at four campuses in and around Kingston upon Thames.

Kingston upon Thames The coronation place of Saxon kings, hence 'king's town', situated just over 3 miles (5 km) south of RICHMOND UPON THAMES. In 838 it was chosen as the seat of the great council convened by King Egbert and presided over by Ceolnothus, the Archbishop of Canterbury. The town's long association with royalty continued in the 10th century with Edward the Elder, son of Alfred the Great, who was the first of seven Saxon kings to be crowned here. The Coronation Stone, probably the town's most notable possession, stands by the 12th-century Clattern Bridge over the River Hogsmill, outside the more recent Guildhall. There has been a market in Kingston since at least the 13th century, and pottery, fishing, tanning and the wool trade were key industries throughout the Middle Ages. Kingston was an important coaching town in the 18th century but the Druid's Head is the only contemporary survivor from the inns of that period. Civic resistance blocked the arrival of the railway until 1863, although Kingston-on-Railway opened at SURBITON in 1838. Kingston has become the prime retail location for south-west

London, yet retains one of the best medieval street plans outside the CITY. Its flagship store, Bentalls, opened in 1867 and was reconstructed at the end of the 1980s, when it met with competition from JOHN LEWIS.

Kingston upon Thames, Royal Borough of An OUTER LONDON borough from 1965, before which Kingston had been the county town of SURREY. Surrey County Council is still headquartered in Kingston. In addition to Kingston itself, the new borough incorporated the municipal boroughs of Malden and Coombe and SURBITON. The other main districts are TOLWORTH, HOOK and CHESSINGTON, which together form a long peninsula jutting into Surrey. Kingston is the oldest of Britain's four royal boroughs, the others being Windsor, Caernarvon and KENSINGTON AND CHELSEA. The council chambers and offices are at the Guildhall in Kingston High Street. The borough's coat of arms manages to work in all the heraldry of its constituent parts, with a shield from Kingston, a crest from Malden and Coombe and supporters from Surbiton. The shield has three salmon, symbolizing the town's ancient fisheries, which were mentioned in Domesday Book.

Kingston Vale A suburbanized village nestling between KINGSTON HILL and PUTNEY VALE, with RICHMOND PARK to the north-west and WIMBLEDON COMMON to the east. Formerly known as Kingston Bottom, the name was changed in deference to Victorian sensibilities. Dorich House, now part of Kingston University, has works by the Russian sculptress Dora Gordine and a collection of Russian art and artefacts assembled by her husband. The house was built to the couple's design and is occasionally opened to the public. *See also the* ROBIN HOOD DISTRICT.

Kingsway A road joining High HOLBORN in the north with the ALDWYCH in the south. It was named in honour of Edward VII, who performed the opening ceremony in 1905, and was a key component in a late Victorian traffic management scheme, intended to relieve the congestion that had been building up in the latter years of the 19th century. A collaterally beneficial effect was that its construction involved the demolition of some particularly noxious slums in the DRURY LANE area. A tram tunnel was opened beneath the road in 1906; its southern end is still in use as a traffic underpass. The LONDON

SCHOOL OF ECONOMICS is close to the southern end of Kingsway, on the east side.

Kingsway Hall A former place of worship at the northern end of the road, it was for many years a highly rated recording venue.

Kinks, the Formed in 1963, The Kinks were the quintessential London rock group of their time. The core members were the brothers Ray (b.1944) and Dave (b.1947) Davies, who grew up in FORTIS GREEN, attended what is now Fortismere School and first performed in public at their local, the Clissold Arms. Between 1964 and 1970, 14 of the band's singles entered the UK top ten. In addition to their best-remembered hit, 'Waterloo Sunset' (1967), the Kinks recorded songs about MUSWELL HILL, WILLESDEN GREEN, Berkeley Mews (in MARYLEBONE), HOLLOWAY PRISON, DENMARK STREET, CARNABY STREET and SOHO.

kipper

kipper season Among BLACK CAB drivers, any period when business is slow and one's earnings are low. The weeks immediately following the Christmas and New Year holidays typically fall into this category. The term is also used by market traders and the like and derives from the diet upon which one might have to subsist at such times.

kipper tie A very wide and brightly coloured tie popular in the 1960s, so named punningly because it was promoted by the MAYFAIR menswear designer Michael Fish. The width became fashionable again in the early 21st century.

giddy little kipper *See under* GIDDY.

Kishereware *See* MORTLAKE.

Kit-Cat Club A club formed about 1700 by the aristocratic whigs of the day who dined in the house of Christopher (Kit) Cat, a pastry cook of Shire Lane, near TEMPLE BAR. His mutton pies, called 'kitkats', always formed part of their meals. Among the distinguished noblemen and gentlemen were Jonathan Swift, Sir Richard Steele, Joseph Addison, William Congreve, Sir Samuel Garth, Sir John Vanbrugh, Sir Robert Walpole and the Duke of Somerset. Jacob Tonson (1656–1737), the publisher, was the secretary.

Sir Godfrey Kneller (*c.*1649–1723) painted 42 portraits (now in the NATIONAL PORTRAIT GALLERY) of the club members for Tonson, in whose villa at BARN ELMS the meetings were latterly held. The paintings were made three-quarter length (36 x 28 in/91 x 71 cm) in order to accommodate them to the size of the club's dining room. Hence a three-quarter length portrait came to be called a 'kitcat' (or 'kitkat'). The club closed *c.*1720.

Klondike In the late 19th century SEVEN KINGS was so nicknamed, because of its rapid growth and relative inaccessibility.

knees-up A boisterous and energetic dance, in which the dancers raise alternate knees. Hence any lively party or celebration. The dance gets its name from the song to which it is traditionally performed, 'Knees up, Mother Brown!'

> Ooh! Knees up Mother Brown!
> Well! Knees up Mother Brown!
> … knees up, knees up!
> Don't get the breeze up
> Knees up Mother Brown.
>
> HARRIS WESTON and BERT LEE (1939)

knight

Knight Bus A purple, triple-decker ROUTEMASTER bus mentioned in J.K. Rowling's 'Harry Potter' stories. The name is a punning reference to London's NIGHT BUSES. Driver Ernie Prang and conductor Stan Shunpike rescue stranded wizards and witches. The Knight Bus made a memorable journey through London in the film *Harry Potter and the Prisoner of Azkaban* (2004).

Knight's Hill A low-rent street that is part of the A215, rising from WEST NORWOOD to Norwood Heights, and named after a 16th-century family that owned a broad swathe of land in the area. The topographical feature called Knight's Hill lies east of TULSE HILL and its summit is around 220 feet (67m) above sea level, distinctly lower than the highest point of the road. The grandest local resident was Lord Thurlow, lord chancellor from 1778 to 1783, who went to live at Knight's Hill Farm in the 1780s. It is said that he chose this modest dwelling to spite the architect who had overspent in building his nearby residence, Thurlow Park.

Knights Hospitaller An order founded at Jerusalem (*c.*1048), also known as the Knights of St John of Jerusalem. They were called Hospitallers because they provide *hospitium* ('lodging and entertainment') for pilgrims. Benefactors granted them lands in several parts of the London area, including for a priory at CLERKENWELL that became their English headquarters. The order came to an end in England after the Reformation, but a branch was revived in 1831, which declared itself an independent order in 1858 and is now styled the Order of the Hospital of St John of Jerusalem. It founded the St John Ambulance Association in 1877.

Knights Templar A monastic order founded by nine French knights in 1119 and called the Templars because they had their headquarters in a building on the site of the old Temple of Solomon at Jerusalem. In England the order had its first house (*c*.1121) near HOLBORN BARS, but it later settled on the site still called the TEMPLE. Henry II granted the Knights Templar several manors in southern England, including a large area bordering the River LEA north of STRATFORD. The order was dissolved in the early 14th century, when much of the Templars' property passed to the KNIGHTS HOSPITALLER.

Knightenguild or **Knightengild** *See* PORT-SOKEN.

Knightsbridge A street extending westward from HYDE PARK CORNER along the edge of the park to its north, and the neighbouring prestigious locality. There are at least four explanations of how the former bridge (over the River WESTBOURNE) acquired its name, the quaintest and least likely being that two knights, on their way to seek the blessing of the bishop of London, quarrelled and fought to their deaths here. With the growth of KENSINGTON, CHELSEA and BELGRAVIA as high-class residential districts from the late 18th century, retailers began to locate in Knightsbridge. Benjamin Harvey opened a linen shop in 1813 (*see* HARVEY NICKS) and Charles Henry Harrod brought his grocery business from STEPNEY in 1849. Knightsbridge station opened in 1906, by which time stores had lined BROMPTON Road, Knightsbridge and SLOANE STREET and were specializing in increasingly exclusive ranges. Dressmakers, furriers and milliners replaced shops that had catered to the more everyday needs of a local customer base. Food shops either moved out or, like HARRODS, expanded into new lines. Over the course of the 20th century a more cosmopolitan mix of retailers and service outlets evolved; however, Knightsbridge retains a large number of stores catering to the very wealthy.

Knightsbridge Barracks A barracks (also known as Hyde Park Barracks) in Kensington Road that accommodates the Household Cavalry (*see* HOUSEHOLD TROOPS) and their horses. The government established the barracks after the GORDON RIOTS of 1780, in case of further insurrection. The present building was designed by Sir Basil Spence in 1960, but not completed until 1970. Two soldiers and seven horses from the barracks were killed when the IRA exploded a nail bomb in HYDE PARK on 20 July 1982.

Knightsbridge March The last of the three movements of the *London Suite* (1932) by Eric Coates. It was used as the signature tune of *In Town Tonight* (*see* CARRY ON, LONDON!).

knock, to In slang of former days, to create a great impression; to be irresistible, as in Albert Chevalier's song 'Knocked 'em in the OLD KENT ROAD' (1892), i.e. astonished the inhabitants or filled them with admiration. *See also* ALBERT THE GREAT.

In current colloquial usage the verb means 'to criticize adversely', 'to belittle', 'to disparage'.

knock three times and ask for Alice! Formerly a stock interruption made when someone was giving long-winded directions. Like many COCKNEY catchphrases it spread beyond London via servicemen's usage.

Knockturn Alley A dark and twisting passageway off DIAGON ALLEY in the Harry POTTER stories by J.K. Rowling. The name plays on the word 'nocturnally'. The alley's dark arts shops (notably Borgin & Burkes), street vendors and customers are collectively unwholesome.

> 'Skulkin' around Knockturn Alley, I dunno –
> dodgy place, Harry – don' want no one ter see
> yeh down there –'
>
> *Harry Potter and the Chamber of Secrets* (1998)

Knowledge, The The test that drivers of London BLACK CABS must pass to show that they know the name and location of every street and the shortest or quickest route to it. The Public Carriage Office (PCO), originally a branch of the METROPOLITAN POLICE, first established the standards for drivers of horse-drawn HACKNEY carriages in 1851. Then, as now, they were required to know the area within a 6-mile (9.65-km) radius of CHARING CROSS, which encompasses 113 square miles (293 sq km). Nowadays the PCO is part of Transport for London and issues candidates with a BLUE BOOK that lists 320 routes (called 'runs') to be learnt, together with all the places of interest and important landmarks (known as 'points') on and around these runs. It takes between two and four years to learn and pass the written and oral examinations of the 'All London Knowledge', after which drivers are issued with a GREEN BADGE, entitling them to work anywhere in GREATER LONDON. Less ambitious candidates can apply at a secondary level, whereby a driver must be able to demonstrate a full knowledge of routes within one of nine suburban sectors and a partial knowledge of adjoining sectors, including central London. Successful suburban candidates are licensed to ply for hire only within their designated sector. Despite the advent of in-car satellite navigation, there are no plans to alter the existing system, which ensures that drivers have a comprehensive understanding of the capital's geography and are immune from the risks of technological failure. It also serves to limit the number of black cab drivers, thus protecting their continuing income levels.

Acquiring the Knowledge has been shown to increase the size of part of the brain. In a study supported by the Wellcome Trust, the neuroscientist Dr Eleanor Maguire reported in 2000 that test subjects who had spent an average of two years learning the Knowledge had a larger right hippocampus than control subjects, and the longer they had thereafter worked as a black cab driver the larger their hippocampus was. By contrast, hippocampal enlargement was not observed in contestants at the World Memory Championships, who use techniques that avoid the necessity for large-scale learning of the kind that is essential to pass the Knowledge.

Knowledge Boy or **Girl** A student of the Knowledge, of whatever age. Drivers have typically prepared for the test by riding a scooter or moped around the streets while memorizing BLUE BOOK routes from a plan clipped to the handlebars. This particular method formed the subject of Jack Rosenthal's television play *The Knowledge* (1979), with Nigel Hawthorne as the sadistic examiner.

There in the road, pulled over to the kerb, was a Knowledge Boy on a scooter; or rather, a Knowledge Man, because when he pushed his full-face crash helmet up on his head to speak

to them Carl saw that he was older than Dave would have been – had he lived – for another decade.

WILL SELF: *The Book of Dave* (2006)

know one's onions, to To be knowledgeable in one's particular field. The expression is sometimes jokingly said to refer to the lexicographer C.T. Onions, co-editor of the *Oxford English Dictionary* and author of books on English, but it may actually derive from COCKNEY RHYMING SLANG, with 'onions' short for 'onion rings', meaning 'things'.

Korea Town A nickname for NEW MALDEN, a suburban district situated east of KINGSTON UPON THAMES. With around 10,000 Korean residents in the vicinity, it has the largest and most concentrated Korean population in Europe. No one is quite sure how this came about. One explanation is that 1970s Korean expatriates followed the example of their ambassador and settled in WIMBLEDON, but when prices there rose excessively they decamped to nearby New Malden. The community is served by its own shops, restaurants and other enterprises, and several local churches hold services in the Korean language.

KPG An initialism for Kensington Palace Gardens, a private road to the west of the palace where many embassies are located, sometimes called MILLIONAIRES' ROW.

Kray twins The murderers Ronnie (1933–95) and Reggie (1933–2000) Kray were born in BETHNAL GREEN, where they ran a criminal Mafia-style operation in the 1960s. Their 'firm' collected protection money, organized illegal gambling and drinking clubs, and participated in gang warfare. The dominant twin was Ronnie, who modelled himself on Chicago gangsters. In March 1966 he entered the Blind Beggar, a pub on the MILE END Road, and shot dead George Cornell, a member of a rival gang, and in October 1967 Reggie lured JACK 'THE HAT' McVitie to a STOKE NEWINGTON flat and stabbed him to death, with Ronnie's encouragement. The twins were tried at the OLD BAILEY in 1969 and given prison sentences of not less than 30 years. A campaign to free them failed, and Ronnie died in prison. In 1999 a further campaign to free Reggie was mounted on the grounds that he had now served the full prison term. Suffering from inoperable bladder cancer, he was released on compassionate grounds in August 2000, and died five weeks later. Both received lavish EAST END funerals. A memorable biopic, *The Krays*, appeared in 1990, directed by Peter Medak and starring Gary and Martin Kemp as the brothers.

Perhaps the most distinctive aspect of the Krays' story is that, despite their brutality, they were folk heroes to many EAST ENDERS. They were always polite, loved their mother and, allegedly, never harmed one of their own. They were seen as a late flourishing of the 'old-style' school of gangsterism, soon to be replaced by operators from abroad who had no respect for traditional villainy. This criminal culture clash is an enduring theme of books, films and computer games set in the London underworld.

They were very respectful, charming. If my mother was behind the counter and someone swore they would ask them to show some respect.

NEVIO PELLICCI, Bethnal Green café owner, quoted in *The Daily Telegraph* (8 March 2005)

L

Ladbroke Grove A lively, racially mixed district centred on the street of that name, which runs between HOLLAND PARK and KENSAL GREEN. Sir Richard Ladbroke, a banker, MP and LORD MAYOR OF LONDON in 1747, acquired four large parcels of land here in 1750. His heir planned an extravagant estate with Ladbroke Grove as the central boulevard but financial difficulties forced the project into abeyance. John Whyte opened the Hippodrome racecourse on the still-undeveloped farmland in 1837 but it closed after four unprofitable years and work slowly resumed on the Ladbroke Grove estate. The resultant luxury housing is now generally referred to as 'NOTTING HILL', while Ladbroke Grove's name has become associated with the vicinity of the station, which opened on the HAMMERSMITH AND CITY Railway in 1864. The station's environs were smashed apart by the construction in the 1960s of the WESTWAY, an urban motorway that now soars across the locality. Like much of NORTH KENSINGTON, Ladbroke Grove became a hang-out for rock, punk and reggae artists in the 1970s, including Hawkwind, The CLASH and Aswad, and it retains a musical community today. The central section of the street is a focal part of the NOTTING HILL CARNIVAL route and is further enlivened by links with PORTOBELLO ROAD to its east.

> Saw you walking down by Ladbroke Grove this morning
> Catching pebbles for some sunny beach –
> You're out of reach.
>
> VAN MORRISON: 'Slim Slow Slider' (song) (1968)

Ladbroke Grove rail crash A train disaster sometimes called the 'Paddington rail crash', in which 31 people were killed and more than 400 injured when a Thames Trains turbo hit a London-bound Great Western high-speed train near the Ladbroke Grove bridge on 5 October 1999.

Ladder A nickname for the streets lying immediately west of the HARRINGAY part of GREEN LANES, deriving from their rigidly gridded arrangement. The Ladder makes up most of the ward of Harringay, which has a high proportion of well-educated young adults.

lady

Ladies' Bridge A (rarely heard) nickname for WATERLOO BRIDGE, derived from the predominantly female labour force employed in its construction during the Second World War. The term is most often used by male guides on London riverboats, who exploit it as a springboard for various 'witty' remarks.

Ladies' Mile A stretch of the road on the north side of the SERPENTINE, much favoured in Victorian days by 'equestriennes'. The Coaching and Four-in-hand clubs held their meets there in the spring.

> We fall into line, and move up and down the space which only with ladies' accuracy is called the Ladies' Mile.
>
> *London Society* (magazine), 'From Albert Gate to Hyde Park Corner' (October 1868)

Ladies' University of Female Arts A 17th-century nickname for HACKNEY, derived from the large number of private girls' schools in the parish. Samuel PEPYS went on a gawping expedition under the pretence of desiring to attend a service at St Augustine's Church:

> That which we went chiefly to see was the young ladies of the schools, whereof there is great store, very pretty; and also the organ, which is handsome ...
>
> diary (21 April 1667)

Lady Godiva 'Fiver' (five pounds sterling) in COCKNEY RHYMING SLANG, from the famous patroness of Coventry who rode naked through the town to persuade her husband to reduce taxation on his tenants.

Ladykillers, The A sublime and enduring EALING COMEDY (1955) about a gang of criminals who base themselves in the quiet KING'S CROSS house of a little old lady, pretending for her benefit to be amateur classical musicians, while in fact planning and executing a security van robbery. The irony in the title lies in the fact that none of the criminals (Alec Guinness, Peter Sellers, Cecil Parker, Herbert Lom and Danny Green) turns out to be prepared to murder the old lady (Katie Johnson) after she discovers what they have really been up to, and they are instead obliged to kill each other. A pale and superfluous remake, transposed to the American South, appeared in 2004.

Lady of the Lamp or **Lady with the Lamp** A name given to Florence Nightingale (1820–1910), from her nightly rounds of the hospital wards at Scutari during the Crimean War (1854–6), carrying a lighted lamp. She founded a training school for nurses at ST THOMAS' HOSPITAL, where the Florence Nightingale Museum commemorates her work. Her Turkish lantern is among the exhibits.

lakes (of Killarney) 'Barmy' (crazy) in imperfect COCKNEY RHYMING SLANG, from the scenic attraction in south-west Ireland. The term is no longer heard, but it was once commonplace, so much so that it was occasionally extended to 'Lew Lakes', from the comedian who created the BLOOMSBURY BURGLARS.

lally A POLARI word for the leg, generally used in the plural, like legs themselves.

Lamb and Flag The Holy Lamb bearing a cross surmounted by a golden streamer is the armorial device of the MIDDLE TEMPLE. It derives from ancient tiles in TEMPLE CHURCH, said to have represented an emblem used by the KNIGHTS TEMPLAR. The FLEET STREET gateway to the inn has a sculpture of the Lamb and Flag on its keystone, dated 1684. The Middle Temple's adoption of the Lamb and Flag led to its once-common use as a London public house sign, including at the establishment nicknamed the BUCKET OF BLOOD.

Lambeth An ancient south London district bordering the THAMES opposite WESTMINSTER. The name probably meant that lambs were offloaded at a landing place here, although others suggest that it is a corruption of 'loamhithe', and thus refers to the muddy nature of the landing place. This was the spot from where archbishops of Canterbury took the ferry across to Westminster and thus made an ideal location for their London pied à terre (*see* LAMBETH PALACE). By the early 19th century, a warren of streets had surrounded the palace and filled the former Lambeth Marsh to its north (now the SOUTH BANK and WATERLOO areas). Residents worked at the wharves and boatyards on the waterfront, in small factories making whitewash or at Doulton's pottery. Soon afterwards the construction of the Albert EMBANKMENT erased many of the riverside yards, while helping to protect the area from flooding. Following the deterioration of the housing stock and severe bomb damage in the Second World War, the GREATER LONDON COUNCIL redeveloped the area south of Lambeth Road in the 1960s and its former character has been lost. Other streets made way for the expansion of ST THOMAS' HOSPITAL.

Lambeth, London Borough of An INNER LONDON borough formed in 1965 by merging the metropolitan borough of Lambeth with the eastern part of WANDSWORTH. Among its districts are KENNINGTON, VAUXHALL, BRIXTON, STOCKWELL, part of NORWOOD and most of CLAPHAM and STREATHAM. Its shape has been described as 'a slice of London's cake', with the tip pointing northwards. The town hall was built in 1908 at the corner of Acre Lane and Brixton Hill. Lambeth is one of London's poorest boroughs, scoring very highly on a number of depressing social indicators. Its coat of arms carries references to the archbishops of Canterbury and to the duchy of Cornwall – landlords of Kennington – with elements from the county arms of both London and SURREY. The crest is surmounted by a lamb. The civic motto is the widely used *spectemur agendo* – 'let us be judged by our deeds'.

Lambeth Articles A set of doctrinal statements promulgated in 1595 by the then archbishop of Canterbury, John Whitgift (*c.*1530–1604). They were strongly Calvinistic, upholding the view that each individual soul is predestined to salvation or damnation.

Lambeth books A name sometimes given to the symbolic poems that William Blake wrote and etched while living in Hercules Road, just east of LAMBETH PALACE, from 1790 to 1800. They include *America*, *Europe* and *The Song of Los*.

Lambeth Bridge A five-arch bridge across the THAMES, upstream from the PALACE OF WESTMINSTER. Although other bridges existed nearby, ferries continued to provide the most direct means of crossing the river here until 1862, when a suspension bridge connected Lambeth Road with Westminster's Horseferry Road. After a long period during which Lambeth Bridge was restricted to pedestrian use, it was rebuilt in 1932.

Lambeth Conference An assembly of the archbishops and bishops of the Anglican Church from around the world, held every ten years under the presidency of the archbishop of Canterbury. From 1867 to 1958 it was held in LAMBETH PALACE, in 1968 at Church House, WESTMINSTER and subsequently at the University of Kent. Divisions over the issue of homosexuality caused controversy at both the 1998 and 2008 conferences.

Lambeth degree A degree in divinity, arts, law, medicine, music or other subjects, conferred by the archbishop of Canterbury, who was empowered to do so by a statute of 1533.

Lambeth Palace The London residence of the archbishops of Canterbury since the 12th century. The oldest parts are the chapel built by Archbishop Boniface in 1245, and its undercroft. The buildings have been steadily added to and modified through the centuries; the most recent phase of major work was a refurnishing and enlargement carried out for Archbishop Langton in the early 1830s by Edward Blore. Originally called Lambeth House, it came to be called Lambeth Palace *c.*1658 owing to the decay of the palace at Canterbury. It is the archbishop's principal residence, but he now has another palace at Canterbury.

Lambeth pedlar *See* PEDLAR'S ACRE.

Lambeth Poisoner Thomas Neill Cream (1850–92), a Glasgow-born, Canadian-bred doctor who in 1891 killed four Lambeth prostitutes by lacing their drinks with strychnine. He also committed at least one murder in North America, while other intended victims declined his offers of pills or drinks:

To Violet Beverley he offered an 'American drink' but she was loyal to her British heritage and chose beer. Her patriotism was much to her advantage for the drink almost surely contained

a good quantity of the doctor's white powder. It also may be regarded as a tribute to her palate, considering what some London hotels and pubs still serve as an 'American cocktail'.

ORVILLE T. BAILEY: *Migration and Nemesis* (1977)

Charged with and convicted of one of the Lambeth poisonings, that of 27-year-old Matilda Clover, Cream was hanged at NEWGATE PRISON on 15 November 1892. With very little credibility, he has also been named as a possible suspect in the case of JACK THE RIPPER.

Lambeth quadrilateral The four points suggested by the LAMBETH CONFERENCE of 1888 as a basis for Christian reunion: the Bible, the Apostolic and Nicene Creeds, two Sacraments (baptism and the eucharist) and the historic Episcopate.

Lambeth Walk A thoroughfare in Lambeth leading from Black Prince Road to the Lambeth Road. It gave its name to a COCKNEY song and dance featured by Lupino Lane (from 1937) in the musical show *Me and My Gal* at the VICTORIA PALACE, and very popular during the Second World War:

Any time you're Lambeth way,
Any evening, any day,
You'll find us all
Doin' the Lambeth walk.

DOUGLAS FURBER and ARTHUR ROSE: 'Doin' the Lambeth Walk' (1937)

The dance has couples strutting forwards, arms linked, then strutting back and jerking their thumbs in the air to the exclamation 'Oi!' Many council estates now have a Lambeth Walk as a memento. The term has also been used in COCKNEY RHYMING SLANG for chalk (as used in billiards and snooker).

lame as St Giles' Cripplegate, as *See under* AS.

Lammas land The church festival of Lammas on 1 August each year celebrated the harvesting of the grain crops. The name derives from Old English *hlāfmœsse*, 'loaf mass'. Lammas land was land opened up to use by commoners, primarily to graze their livestock, after the harvest had been gathered in. Many of London's surviving open spaces were once Lammas lands, such as HACKNEY and WALTHAMSTOW marshes.

Lancaster

Lancaster Gate A densely built-up but wealthy

residential locality and hotel zone situated north-east of KENSINGTON GARDENS, halfway along BAYSWATER Road. It derives its identity from an entrance to the gardens, so called in honour of Queen Victoria in her guise as Duchess of Lancaster. The area was laid out with prestigious terraced houses from the 1840s. Lytton Strachey (1880–1932), the eminent biographer, lived for 25 years at 69 Lancaster Gate.

Lancaster House A grand government building in ST JAMES'S, managed by the Foreign & Commonwealth Office. Built in the late 1820s as York House, it was acquired in 1912 by Lord Leverhulme, who named it after his native county and presented it to the nation the following year. It has been the venue for meetings preparing for independence in several parts of the British empire, including the Kenyan conferences of the early 1960s.

Lancaster House Agreement An arrangement reached in September 1979 at LANCASTER HOUSE that resulted in Rhodesia becoming independent as Zimbabwe, with a black majority government, in 1980.

Lane, the Most often, a short form of WHITE HART LANE, PETTICOAT LANE or DRURY LANE.

Langbourn A CITY of London ward centred on LEADENHALL MARKET. In his classic *Survey of London* (1598 and several subsequent editions), John Stow wrote of a stream called the Langbourn, which had risen in FENCHURCH STREET, flowed along LOMBARD STREET and then turned south towards the THAMES, but its existence is strongly doubted, especially as the route would have taken the water uphill at points. It seems more likely that the ward's name is a corruption of the Old English words *lang bord*, 'long table(s)', which probably referred to market stalls.

Lansbury

Lansbury, George A radical politician (1859–1940) whose campaigns and improvement schemes had a lasting effect on London. He served as mayor of POPLAR and MP for BROMLEY and BOW. In 1913 he was jailed for his activities in support of the suffragette movement. While in parliament he was first commissioner of works in the Labour government of 1929–31 and led the Labour Party in opposition thereafter. The Poplar-born actress Angela Lansbury (b.1925) is his granddaughter. *See also* POPLARISM.

Lansbury estate A large council estate situated in the part of POPLAR once known as Poplar New Town and named in honour of George Lansbury (*see above*). Wartime bombing destroyed or damaged nearly a quarter of the buildings in this area, which was one of the first to be redeveloped by the LONDON COUNTY COUNCIL after 1945. In 1951 the barely finished Lansbury estate became the 'Live Architecture Exhibition' of the FESTIVAL OF BRITAIN.

Lansbury's lido An old nickname for the SERPENTINE lido in HYDE PARK, sponsored by George Lansbury (*see above*) when he was first commissioner of works in the second Labour government (1929–31).

Lapland mutton The jocular name for meat sold at the FROST FAIR of February 1814 at the exorbitant price of one shilling (5p) a slice. Even the privilege of watching the lamb being roasted whole (and warming oneself beside the fire) cost sixpence (2½p).

Lasso line A nickname for the extended CIRCLE LINE, on which trains start from HAMMERSMITH, join the 'true' Circle line at PADDINGTON and complete a full clockwise circuit, terminating at EDGWARE ROAD. They then reverse and return to Hammersmith via the same route, anticlockwise. The innovation, from December 2009, is designed to permit a speedier recovery of normal service if there is disruption on any of the lines that use the same tracks as the Circle, as well as almost doubling service frequency at stations formerly served only by the HAMMERSMITH AND CITY LINE.

Last Night of the Proms The final evening of the annual Promenade Concerts (*see the* PROMS) at the ALBERT HALL in September, popularly regarded as the apotheosis of the series. The standing members of the audience enthusiastically join in the traditional choruses of 'Land of Hope and Glory' and 'Rule, Britannia' while waving Union Jacks, bursting balloons, throwing streamers and evincing other manifestations of patriotic fervour and good humour.

> Little, it seems, is ever going to change at the Last Night of the Proms. So there is no point in worrying about the hopefully good-natured jingoism of those who believe that, once a year at least, Britannia still Rules the Waves.
>
> *The Times* (14 September 1998)

Events of the same name and featuring a similar repertoire are nowadays held elsewhere in the English-speaking world; they all derive from the London original.

Laughing Cavalier, The The name given to the portrait (1624) of an unknown gallant, by the Dutch painter Frans Hals, now in the WALLACE COLLECTION. The title is inaccurate, as the subject is smiling, not laughing.

Lavender Hill A street and locality in south BATTERSEA, with CLAPHAM JUNCTION station at its western end. Its name derives from the lavender that was once cultivated in market gardens to the north of the road. Charles BOOTH rated the 19th-century school board division of Lavender Hill one of London's most 'comfortable' quarters. Battersea town hall opened on Lavender Hill in 1893 and just under a century later the building became Battersea Arts Centre. BAC, as it likes to call itself, is highly regarded for its fringe theatre productions.

Lavender Hill Mob, The A sparkling EALING COMEDY (1951), written by T.E.B. Clarke and directed by Charles Crichton, about a mild-mannered civil servant who decides to use his inside knowledge of bullion transport to steal a million pounds' worth of gold and then spirit it out of the country after melting it down into miniature Eiffel Towers. The ludicrous notion that such a retiring, dull individual could pull off this breathtaking crime is underlined by the film's title, which cheekily conveys the unlikelihood of hardened criminals hailing from such a respectable part of London as Lavender Hill. The film stars Alec Guinness as the criminal mastermind, and Stanley Holloway as his right-hand man.

Law Courts *See the* ROYAL COURTS OF JUSTICE.

Lawn Road Flats *See* ISOKON.

LBC Radio London's first legal commercial radio station, launched a week before CAPITAL RADIO in October 1973. The acronym originally stood for the London Broadcasting Company, although the station has lately styled itself 'London's Biggest Conversation', alluding to the FM stream's emphasis on talk. The medium-wave stream carries more news.

LCC *See* LONDON COUNTY COUNCIL.

LDN An initialism for 'London', used in rap music lyrics, 'text speak' and the like. The definite article is occasionally attached, as in 'I come from the LDN'. It is arguably London's attempted counterpart to 'NYC' – for 'New York City' – but is considered by many to sound pretentious. In 2001 the BBC introduced 'LDN' as a unifying identity for its metropolitan television, radio and online services; it has since reverted to 'BBC London'. 'LDN' was also the title of a 2006 single by Lily Allen.

Lea or **Lee** (The alternative spelling is nowadays rarely applied to the river itself but continues to be used for its valley and the Navigation.) A river that rises in southern Bedfordshire and flows 46 miles (74 km) south-east and then south via the marshes of WALTHAMSTOW, HACKNEY and STRATFORD to join the River THAMES near CANNING TOWN. Its name probably comes from the Celtic root *lug-* meaning 'bright', 'light' but also forming the base of the name of the god Lugus, so it either meant 'bright river' or 'river dedicated to Lugus'. In former times the river constituted the boundary between MIDDLESEX and ESSEX. The Lea has been an important route since at least Roman times, and canalization schemes are almost as ancient. Today the River Lee Navigation runs from Hertford virtually to the Thames. Beside the river are several huge reservoirs, which furnish a sixth of London's water supply. In 1967 the Lee Valley Regional Park was constituted, which supervises the provision of a wide range of recreational facilities, from sailing and windsurfing on the lakes and reservoirs to fishing and bird-watching. The joys of fishing on the Lea were already familiar in the 17th century to Izaak Walton, and it figures prominently in *The Compleat Angler* (1653).

Without the Lea Valley, East London would be unendurable … The Lea is nicely arranged, walk as far as you like then travel back to Liverpool Street from any one of the rural halts that mark your journey. Railway shadowing river, a fantasy conjunction; together they define an Edwardian sense of excursion, pleasure, time out.

IAN SINCLAIR: *London Orbital* (2002)

In 19th-century COCKNEY RHYMING SLANG, 'River Lea' was used to mean both 'tea' and 'sea'.

Lea Bridge An industrial and working-class residential district straddling the River LEA east of CLAPTON. During the latter part of the

19th century filter-beds were constructed on both sides of the river and in the 1930s factories replaced agricultural smallholdings. Some of the old utilities and industries have since closed and the Middlesex Filter Beds have become a nature reserve within the Lee Valley Regional Park.

Leadenhall A lead-roofed mansion originally belonging to the 13th-century nobleman Hugh Neville. Subsequently there was a granary here and a market for all kinds of food, cloth and ironmongery (*see* LEADENHALL MARKET). Dick WHITTINGTON was granted the leasehold on the manor of Leadenhall in 1408. The mansion burned down in 1484.

Leadenhall blade One that would not cut.

Leadenhall Building *See the* CHEESEGRATER.

Leadenhaller *See* BAGMAN.

Leadenhall Market A covered Victorian market situated just south of BISHOPSGATE, with access from GRACECHURCH STREET. After the destruction of the LEADENHALL an open market was established on the site, dealing mainly in fish, meat, poultry and corn. Samuel PEPYS recorded that he bought a good leg of beef for sixpence in 1663, three years before much of the market burned down in the GREAT FIRE OF LONDON. Leadenhall Market continued to operate from a variety of buildings, and became especially noted for poultry and game. The COR-PORATION OF LONDON commissioned the present wrought-iron and glass-roofed buildings, which were completed in 1881, to the design of Sir Horace Jones (1819–87), who was also responsible for the Victorian market halls at SMITHFIELD and BILLINGSGATE. The buildings were restored on their centenary, bringing the luscious internal colour scheme back to life. Leadenhall Market has now been colonized by fashion and accessory retailers, coffee shops and restaurants.

> Wouldst thou with mighty beef augment thy meal,
>
> Seek Leadenhall; St James's sends thee veal;
>
> JOHN GAY: *Trivia*, II (1716)

Leadenhall Market sportsman An obsolete term for a landowner who sold his game to Leadenhall Market poulterers.

Leadenhall Street A street in the CITY of London, leading west to east from CORNHILL to ALDGATE. Between 1648 and 1861 it contained the headquarters of the EAST INDIA COMPANY, and

its name came to be used as a metonym for the company itself:

> It showed, how the elegant mothers of Leadenhall Street, might, with the greatest gentleness, strain their young ones to bosoms equally soft, while they themselves were nourished by the blood and sweat of the unhappy peasant of Bengal.
>
> J. BOADEN: *Life of Mrs Jordan* (1831)

Beau of Leadenhall Street *See* DIRTY DICK'S.

Leadville *See the* WESTERN AVENUE.

Leaky Cauldron A ramshackle old inn, built *c*.1500, and the entrance to DIAGON ALLEY in the Harry POTTER books by J.K. Rowling. It is 'hidden in plain sight' between a bookshop and a record shop on CHARING CROSS ROAD. Harry stays in room 11 for three weeks following an unfortunate incident involving his aunt Marge.

Leamouth An isolated pair of peninsulas formed by the meanderings of the River LEA (here called BOW Creek) as it reaches the THAMES. A close-knit (and allegedly inbred) residential population was dispersed by a slum clearance programme in the 1930s. Until recently a vegetable oil refinery covered nearly all of Goodluck Hope, the northern peninsula. Plans for the redevelopment of the site include a footbridge link to CANNING TOWN. Leamouth's most enduring employer was the Corporation of TRINITY HOUSE, which occupied the tip of the eastern peninsula from 1803 to 1988. Trinity Buoy Wharf is now used for arts and community projects while the restored chainstore and lighthouse host leisure and cultural events. *See also* CONTAINER CITY.

leather

Leather Apron The nickname of a suspect in the case of JACK THE RIPPER. At the time of the murders he was widely and sensationally reported as the likely culprit, especially in the American press. He was later identified as Jack Pizer, a man whom prostitutes claimed had extorted money from them, but there was no evidence that he was a killer.

Leather Lane A street leading south from Clerkenwell Road, parallel to and to the west of HATTON GARDEN. It was probably 'Lēofrūn's lane', from an Old English female personal name. It has long had its own market, selling food and general goods. It seems always to have had a reputation for low-quality wares, and in the early 19th century 'leather-lane' was slang for 'poorly made', 'shoddy' or 'second-rate'. 'Leather Lane' was also employed metaphorically for the vagina (the usage of 'leather' to mean vagina dates back to the mid-16th century).

Lee An aggregation of several formerly separate settlements situated south of BLACKHEATH and west of LEWISHAM. The name means 'woodland clearing'. The Manor House was built around 1771 and was sold in 1796 to Sir Francis Baring, co-founder of the Baring Brothers merchant bank. The house later became a military college and is now a public library. Lee acquired a certain trendiness in the 1960s and a hint of this remains today.

River Lee *See* LEA.

Leg of Mutton London has ponds of this name in BUSHY PARK and RICHMOND PARK and on HAMPSTEAD'S WEST HEATH(2), all so called because of their shape. On the CASTELNAU peninsula, the similarly shaped Lonsdale Road reservoir is the focus of the Leg o' Mutton nature reserve.

Legoland A nickname for the MI6 building at VAUXHALL CROSS, because it looks vaguely as though it has been assembled from large toy bricks.

Leicester Square 'The quintessence of the WEST END', according to WESTMINSTER council, linked to PICCADILLY CIRCUS by Coventry Street. Originally a square plot of LAMMAS LAND in the parish of ST MARTIN-IN-THE-FIELDS, the area acquired the name Leicester Fields when Robert Sidney, 2nd Earl of Leicester (1595-1677), built a residence here in 1636. From 1712 to 1760 Leicester House served as a palace for two princes of Wales (*see the* POUTING PLACE OF PRINCES) and the nascent square consequently became a fashionable resort. In 1771 Sir Ashton Lever converted Leicester House to a 'museum of curiosities' called the HOLOPHUSIKON, which attracted smaller crowds than the street entertainers and gambling dens that were present by this time. The house was demolished a few years later as part of a phase of rebuilding that brought traders and craftsmen to the square in place of private residences and created roughly its present lay-

out. The centre of Leicester Square was used for exhibitions (*see the* GREAT GLOBE) and public lectures until gardens were laid out in 1874, with a central fountain and statue of SHAKESPEARE and busts of notable former residents at each corner. Theatres, oyster rooms and Turkish baths were by then appearing and its MUSIC HALLS included the EMPIRE and the ALHAMBRA. A few Georgian and Victorian buildings have survived but most of the square now dates from the 1930s onwards and it is especially renowned for its cinemas, which regularly host film premieres. Nightclubs, bars and fast-food joints abound, and the square is a magnet for BUSKERS, flyer distributors and itinerant preachers.

Former residents of Leicester Square include the 18th-century artists William HOGARTH and Sir Joshua Reynolds.

Leighton House *See the* HOLLAND PARK CIRCLE.

lemon
lemon (flavour) 'Favour' in COCKNEY RHYMING SLANG. This is a fairly recent coinage and is heard most often in the phrase 'do me a lemon'.

> Six? Do me a lemon. That's a poor IQ for a glass of water!
>
> ROB GRANT and DOUG NAYLOR: *Red Dwarf,* 'Queeg' (TV comedy) (1988)

lemon (squeezer) *See* ICE CREAM (FREEZER).

leopard's head *See* HALLMARK.

Lesnes Abbey An Augustinian priory founded in 1178 near what is now ABBEY WOOD by Richard de Luci (or Lucy) as penance for his part in the murder of Thomas Becket in Canterbury Cathedral in 1170. After Henry VIII's dissolution of the monasteries (1536–9), Lesnes Abbey fell into disuse and its walls crumbled. The minimal remains, excavated in the 1950s and 1960s, lie at the foot of the gently sloping hill off Abbey Road. The ruins have been reconsecrated and services of worship are occasionally held on the site.

Lesnes Abbey Woods Ancient woodland covering 215 acres (87 hectares) south-east of ABBEY WOOD. The woods are noted for their oak and sweet chestnut trees and a spring carpet of 20 acres (8 ha) of wild daffodils. An exposed fossil bed contains the remains of shells, fish, reptiles and mammals. A memorial at the edge of the woods honours William Morris (1834–96), who used to pass the spot on his way from RED HOUSE to ABBEY WOOD station.

levee (French *lever*, 'to rise') A morning assembly or reception. In Britain the word is particularly associated with the royal levees formerly held at ST JAMES'S PALACE, official occasions when the sovereign received men only, most usually in the afternoon. Before the French Revolution it was customary for the French monarch to receive visitors (court physicians, nobles, messengers and the like) at the time of his levée, i.e. just after rising from bed.

Levellers In Cromwellian times a group of radical republicans who wanted the franchise for 'freeborn Englishmen' (not necessarily including servants and labourers) and who were prominent at London and in the ranks of the army until their power was broken by Cromwell, after the mutinies of 1647 and 1649. Their influence waned steadily, especially after the suppression in 1652–3 of their leader, John Lilburne (*see* FREEBORN JOHN).

Lewis, John *See under* JOHN.

Lewisham A large south-east London suburb and commercial centre, situated on the River RAVENSBOURNE, 1½ miles (2.5 km) south of GREENWICH. This was an ancient manor, granted by Elfrida, niece of King Alfred, to the Abbey of St Peter at Ghent. It was Lievesham at that time: probably the homestead of a man called Lēofsa. In the 18th century the 'healthy air' encouraged merchants to build some high-quality residences here. Many of these earliest properties had already been demolished and replaced by the end of the 19th century. With its growth as a transport hub, served by two railway lines, trams and buses, Lewisham became an important shopping centre. By the 1960s it was evolving into a multi-ethnic community, the largest minority being of black Caribbean origin.

Lewisham, London Borough of An INNER LONDON borough formed in 1965 by merging DEPTFORD and Lewisham metropolitan boroughs. NEW CROSS, FOREST HILL, SYDENHAM, LEE, CATFORD and BLACKHEATH are among the principal districts. Lewisham town hall is located at the corner of Catford Road and Rushey Green. The borough's coat of arms includes references to King Alfred and shipbuilding, and uses green,

purple and black in allusions to Lee Green, Hither (heather) Green and Blackheath. HITHER GREEN's name does not derive from 'heather'; this is merely a heraldic pun. Lewisham's motto is the same as HARROW's: *salus populi seprema lex* – 'the welfare of the people shall be the highest law'.

Leysian Mission A philanthropic project by the old boys of the Leys School, Cambridge, founded in 1886. The mission operated from two smaller sites before the construction in 1904 of a grand edifice in bright red brick at the corner of OLD STREET and CITY ROAD. The building was sold when the mission's work was merged with that of Wesley's chapel (*see the* CATHEDRAL OF WORLD METHODISM) in 1989 and has since been converted into flats.

Leyton A Victorian suburb separated from HACKNEY by the River LEA, from which it takes its name. The village was also known as Low Leyton, from its setting on the river's flood plain; a patch of Leyton Marsh survives near Lea Bridge. Walnut Tree House, on Leyton High Road, is probably the borough's oldest structure – though there is no record of precisely when it was built or for whom. Its timber-framed core dates from roughly 1500, with matching wings added later. Known until recently for the manufacture of neckties, Leyton has also been home to the factories of Aquascutum and Thermos, but manufacturing has declined in favour of service industries over the past few decades.

Leyton Orient FC A professional FOOTBALL club that began in 1881 as a winter activity for members of the Glyn Cricket Club, which had earlier been founded by staff and students of Homerton College, now part of Cambridge University but then located in HACKNEY. The footballers became CLAPTON Orient in 1898 and moved to Brisbane Road in 1937. The 'Orient' name had been the suggestion of a player who worked for the Orient Line shipping company, since it fitted the east London location. The club changed its name to Leyton Orient in 1946 and enjoyed its greatest period of success in the 1960s.

Leytonstone A multicultural district situated between WANSTEAD and LEYTON, taking its name from an old milestone, which is now topped by a 19th-century Portland stone obelisk known as the 'high stone'. The stone stands at the junction of New Wanstead and Hollybush Hill – and finds itself in the borough of REDBRIDGE, owing to boundary changes. Much of the district was rapidly built up with two-storey yellow-brick terraced houses in the 1880s, providing affordable accommodation (and season tickets) for city clerks. Leytonstone's greatest son was the film director Alfred Hitchcock (1899–1980), whose parents ran a modest grocery store in the High Road.

Leytonstonia A protest camp – or 'autonomous republic' – established in February 1994 by ecological activists seeking to prevent the construction of a link road to the M11 motorway. It centred on squatted houses in Fillebrook Road, Leytonstone, and on wood-framed shelters set up in a grove of nearby trees. The metropolitan authorities invaded and crushed Leytonstonia on 13 June 1994. *See also* WANSTONIA.

Liber Albus A rulebook compiled from every source available at the time and published in 1419 by John Carpenter, town clerk of the CITY of London. In what he called a 'repertory', Carpenter detailed in Latin and Anglo-Norman London's laws and customs, and the duties and privileges of both City officials and commoners. He went beyond the conventional remit of a 'custumal' by summarizing important legal precedents. Many of the customs listed in the book are those of the excise duty kind; the City at that time imposed thousands of different dues upon merchants. Building regulations, fixed prices for a wide variety of goods and trading standards legislation were also specified, as well as the penalties for transgression:

> And if any default shall be found in the bread of a baker of the City, the first time, let him be drawn upon a hurdle from the Guildhall to his own house, through the great streets where there may be most people assembled, and through the great streets that are most dirty, with the faulty loaf hanging from his neck. [A second offence warranted the pillory; a third offence meant no more baking in London.]

(translation by Henry Thomas Riley) (1861)

liberty

liberties In medieval England the word applied to areas that were to varying extents free from royal jurisdictions in whole or in part, such as the Liberty of HAVERING. The areas belonging to the CITY of London immediately outside the City walls were called liberties, and in the course of time these were attached to the nearest ward within the walls. *See also* TOWER LIBERTY.

Liberties of the Fleet The district immediately surrounding the FLEET PRISON, in which prisoners were sometimes allowed to reside but beyond which they were not permitted to go. They included the north side of LUDGATE HILL and the OLD BAILEY to Fleet Lane (a turning off the Old Bailey, parallel to Ludgate Hill), down the lane to the old Fleet Market (situated in what is now Farringdon Street), and on the east side along by the prison wall to the foot of Ludgate Hill.

Liberty of London A luxurious department store founded in 1875 (on a more modest scale) by Arthur Liberty (1843–1917) at 218a REGENT STREET. Liberty began by selling ornaments, fabric and objets d'art from the Orient, especially Japan. Within a decade he had added costume, carpeting and furniture departments and moved to larger premises a few doors away. In 1924 the business relocated to newly built Tudor-style premises in GREAT MARLBOROUGH STREET, with a facade constructed from the timbers of the navy's last two wooden warships, HMS *Impregnable* and HMS *Hindustan*. Liberty of London opened a second branch in 2008, a two-storey boutique on SLOANE STREET.

> [W.S.] Gilbert may also have used Japanese prints from Liberty's as source material. Liberty's employee Jessie Flood recalled a show for the press in Liberty's shop in 1882, at which she modelled a 'beautiful white and gold embroidered kimono, which was sold to Jessie Bond, the actress, to play in the Mikado'.

HUGH CORTAZZI (editor): *Britain and Japan*, Volume 4 (2002)

Liberty of the Clink *See* CLINK.

Liberty of the Mint From the 17th century the colloquial name for a collection of small tenements that lay within the estate of Suffolk Place, in the vicinity of BOROUGH High Street. A mint had been established at Suffolk Place around 1545. Persons taking refuge in the Liberty of the Mint were immune from arrest, in practice if not by the letter of the law, on the grounds that they were within the rules of the KING'S BENCH PRISON.

Liberty of the Tower *See* TOWER LIBERTY.

lickpenny *See* LONDON LICKPENNY.

Life with the Lyons A pioneering radio, cinema and television comedy series based on the real lives of American husband and wife Ben Lyon (1901–79) and Bebe Daniels (1901–71), and their children Richard and Barbara. It began in 1940 as a segment of the radio comedy *Hi Gang!* and gained its own radio series in 1951. Two spin-off movies appeared in 1954 and the TV series ran from 1955 to 1960, first on BBC and then ITV. The family also gave seven royal command performances. The radio series ended in 1962. The Lyons lived in a house near MARBLE ARCH, subsequently moving (both in real life and in the show) to HOLLAND PARK.

like

like London buses The opening words of a saying that continues in the following vein: 'you wait an hour (or 'all day' or 'an age' or 'forever') for one and then three turn up at once.' In the appropriate context, the short form of the adage is widely understood on its own. The perception is not erroneous. If a bus is delayed it will progressively find more would-be passengers waiting at each stop. The following service will then have fewer people to pick up and will narrow the gap. If it catches up with the first bus the two may begin to leapfrog each other, while yet another catches up. However, GPS devices and radio contact with controllers nowadays permit buses to be held back in such circumstances, to regulate the service.

> Ferdinand's goals are like London buses: You wait and wait and nothing comes, and then three come at once.
>
> *International Herald Tribune* (22 January 2006)

like Piccadilly Circus (in) here Said of a place that is very busy, especially with a lot of coming and going. The phrase is the British equivalent of the American 'like Grand Central station'.

like the ladies of Barking Creek Said of young women who decline sexual intercourse on the grounds of menstruation. The catchphrase came into vogue around 1910 and derived from a rhyme alleging that 'the ladies of Barking Creek / Have their periods three times a week'.

like the two kings of Brentford Formerly said of persons who were once rivals, but have become reconciled. The allusion is to Act II, scene ii of *The Rehearsal* (1672), by George Villiers, 2nd Duke of Buckingham, and others, in which the two kings of Brentford enter the stage hand in hand. The actors, to heighten the absurdity, used to portray them 'smelling at one nosegay'. The play satirized *The Conquest of Granada* (1670), in which John Dryden eulogized the male bonding of two sovereigns. Buckingham clearly chose BRENTFORD in deliberate contrast to the romance of Spain.

> And the two advocates, like the two kings of Brentford, march together, cheek-by-jowl, smelling at the same nosegay.
>
> JEREMY BENTHAM: letter to Étienne Dumont (9 December 1825)

Lillywhites A sports outfitters founded in the HAYMARKET in 1863 by James Lillywhite (1825–82), who came from a family of successful Sussex cricketers. The store relocated to its present address in PICCADILLY CIRCUS in 1925, where it offered a very wide range of sporting apparel and equipment. Although it retains its original name, Lillywhites is now part of a national chain and has shifted its marketing emphasis from quality and distinction towards mainstream lines and competitive pricing.

Lilywhites A secondary nickname for TOTTENHAM HOTSPUR FC, better known as Spurs.

lime

Lime Grove A street in SHEPHERD'S BUSH, perhaps named after a long-lost grove of lime trees. Film studios were opened here in 1915. They were the Gaumont-British company's centre of operations. In 1949 they were sold to the BBC, which used them as television studios until 1991, after which they were demolished and replaced by housing. *See also* NEIGHBOURS TO THE NATION.

Lime Street A CITY of London street and ward. The street runs between LEADENHALL STREET and FENCHURCH STREET and takes its name from a place where lime was burnt and sold. The ward covers an area to the east of BISHOPSGATE from Camomile Street in the north to Lime Street in the south; its predominant buildings are the premises of insurance companies and banks.

One Lime Street *See the* LLOYD'S BUILDING.

Limehouse[1] Part gentrified, part solidly working-class, this EAST END district forms the north-western gateway to the ISLE OF DOGS. It takes its name from the limekilns that operated from the mid-14th century, converting Kentish chalk into quicklime for the capital's building industry. From the late 16th century ships were built at Limehouse and traders supplied provisions for voyages. Wealthy merchants erected fine houses on Narrow Street, especially in the early decades of the 18th century, when Nicholas Hawksmoor built St Anne's Church, which is regarded as one of the architect's greatest achievements and has the highest church clock in London. With the growth of its docks, Limehouse acquired an immigrant population and became London's first CHINATOWN. The community was never very large but it gained a reputation for gambling and opium-smoking (*see also* FU MANCHU).

Limehouse Basin A canal basin in which the REGENT'S CANAL is joined by the LIMEHOUSE CUT before debouching into the THAMES. The basin is nowadays framed by upmarket apartment blocks.

Limehouse Blues

1. A song (1921) telling 'a story of old Chinatown', written by Philip Braham and Douglas Furber, made famous by Gertrude Lawrence and subsequently performed by Rosemary Clooney and Julie Andrews. It is now much better known as an instrumental and has been recorded in this form by Duke Ellington, Charlie Parker, Django Reinhardt and many others.

2. A film (1934) directed by Alexander Hall and starring George Raft as a part-Chinese American who takes over an illegal import business in Limehouse and runs a nightclub where Anna May Wong plays the principal attraction.

Limehouse Cut London's oldest canal, constructed around 1770 to link the River LEA at BOW with the THAMES at Limehouse, thus saving a journey around the ISLE OF DOGS. In the past its name has been used as COCKNEY RHYMING SLANG for gut, usually with reference to the size of someone's paunch.

Limehouse declaration A document setting out the founding principles of the Social Democratic Party, which was established by the Labour Party moderates Roy Jenkins, David Owen, Bill Rodgers and Shirley Williams at Owen's Narrow Street home in 1981. The SDP merged with the Liberal Party in 1988.

Limehouse Hole An old name for the riverside district centred on present-day Westferry Circus, on the ISLE OF DOGS. From the 17th century it was a plying place for WATERMEN and it later became densely filled with shipyards and other dock-related industries.

> I, Roger Riderhood, Lime'us Hole, Waterside character, tell you, Lawyer Lightwood, that the man Jesse Hexam … told me that he done the deed.
>
> DICKENS: *Our Mutual Friend* (1865)

Limehouse Nights A collection of short stories (1916) by the prolific POPLAR-bred author Thomas Burke (1886–1945). Set in London's original CHINATOWN, *Limehouse Nights* caused controversy for its sympathetic portrayal of aspects of the EAST END underworld and was banned for immorality by the national subscription libraries. Burke produced several more collections of Limehouse tales (and poetry), often featuring Quong Lee, an elderly Chinese character based on a man he had known in his childhood.

> I got a feeling from reading Thomas Burke's *Limehouse Nights* … There is beauty in the slums! – for those who can see it despite the dirt and sordidness. There are people reacting toward one another there – there is *life*, and that's the whole thing!
>
> CHARLIE CHAPLIN, interviewed in the *Los Angeles Herald* (2 December 1919)

Limehouse Reach The stretch of the River THAMES opposite Limehouse, extending down the western side of the ISLE OF DOGS.

Limehouse ware England's first soft-paste porcelain, produced in the 1740s by a short-lived pottery in Limehouse.

Lord Love-a-Duck of Limehouse *See under* LORD.

limehouse[2] In Britain in the early part of the 20th century, a verb meaning 'to use coarse abusive language, especially in a political speech'. The usage arose from a notably acerbic speech that the Liberal politician David Lloyd George made in Limehouse on 30 July 1909, in which he attacked the aristocracy, financial magnates, etc.

Lincoln's Inn One of the four INNS OF COURT, situated west of CHANCERY LANE. Opinions differ as to the origin of the name, but the Honourable Society of Lincoln's Inn believes it probably derives from the patronage of Henry de Lacy, 3rd Earl of Lincoln (d.1311). The inn's BLACK BOOKS constitute a record of its activities since 1422. The earliest buildings have not survived but the complex that evolved on the site has elements from every century since the 15th, including the Old Hall of 1492 and a chapel rebuilt in 1623, from an outline plan drawn up by Inigo JONES. The writer Anthony Trollope (1815–82) spent time in his father's chambers in Lincoln's Inn and it was the first London home of Eric Gill (1882–1940), who has been called 'perhaps the finest English artist-craftsman of the 20th century'.

Lincoln's Inn Fields The largest square in central London, situated south-east of HOLBORN station. Property developer William Newton acquired the 12 acres (5 hectares) of Lincoln's Inn Fields in two stages, in 1629 and 1638, and began to erect houses on each side except the east, which backed onto the buildings of LINCOLN'S INN. It is said that Newton employed Inigo JONES as the scheme's architect but this is doubted by some. The only survivor from Newton's project is Lindsey House, home of the Earl of Lindsey in the early 18th century. Much of the square was inappropriately redeveloped in the 19th century but more recent neo-Georgian replacements have attempted to match the earlier scale. Lincoln's Inn Fields has two museums: Sir John Soane's House (*see under* SOANE) and the HUNTERIAN MUSEUM, at the headquarters of the Royal College of Surgeons. The actress and royal mistress Nell GWYN lived in the square and her son, the Duke of St Albans, was born in her lodgings there. *See also the* DEVIL'S GAP.

lion

Lions The nickname of MILLWALL FC since a giant-killing FA Cup run of 1900, when the then Southern League team defeated reigning champions Aston Villa to reach the semi-finals. The club introduced a lion as its emblem and named its next ground the Den. Millwall had formerly been known as the Dockers.

Lion Sermon A sermon preached annually on 16 October at St Katharine Cree Church, LEADENHALL STREET, to commemorate 'the wonderful escape' of Sir John Gayer from a lion that he met in the desert while he was travelling in Turkish dominions. Sir John was LORD MAYOR OF LONDON in 1646. The sermon nowadays concerns an aspect of the challenges facing Christian faith and is given by an eminent guest speaker; in 2007 this was Canon Andrew White, 'the vicar of Baghdad', and in 2008 the botanist

and ecologist Sir Ghillean Prance. Members of the Gayer family attend and read lessons.

Lions' Tower A bulwark formerly sited at the western entrance to the TOWER OF LONDON. It was built for Edward IV and contained cages for the royal menagerie and lodging for the keeper.

Essex lion *See under* ESSEX.

see the lions, to *See under* SEE.

South Bank lion *See under* SOUTH.

Lisson In the place names below, Lisson is a corruption of Lilestone, a medieval manor that stretched north from MARYLEBONE to HAMPSTEAD. First recorded in Domesday Book, the name derived from the farmstead of a man called Lill. Lisson Green's Lilestone estate, begun before and finished after the Second World War, recalls the area's earlier identity.

Lisson Green The old name for the locality now more commonly known as LISSON GROVE, situated in north-west MARYLEBONE. Lisson Green was a 'little manor' that broke away from its parent as early as 1236, with its own manor house and one carue (*c.*100 acres, 40 hectares) of land. Among those who in the early 19th century moved here for the country air were several artists and writers, who later decamped to ST JOHN'S WOOD. Sir Edward Baker (who gave his name to BAKER STREET) acquired the southern part of Lisson Green in 1821 and built large blocks of flats as an extension of Marylebone, but further north the area began to decline as unscrupulous landlords put up shoddy houses and overfilled them with poor tenants, especially Irish labourers. Lisson Green became filthy, disease-ridden and, in parts, criminal. Philanthropists turned their attention to the locality and built artisans' cottages and airy tenements in place of the squalid slums. Municipal authorities took up the baton in the 20th century.

Lisson Grove A cosmopolitan street running south-eastwards from ST JOHN'S WOOD into MARYLEBONE, in parallel with EDGWARE ROAD. The neighbouring locality was known as Lisson Green until it became urbanized. The street was laid out in the late 18th century and was soon lined with STUCCOED houses towards its southern end, while a white lead manufactory operated further north. For a while it was a smart address but within a few decades Lisson Grove had become very rough. From the 1850s slum clearance projects slowly began to improve the quality of life in Lisson Grove, though it remained poor. Parts have since been gentrified. The historical painter Benjamin Haydon described a Lisson Grove dinner party with William Wordsworth, John Keats and Charles Lamb at which Lamb got drunk and berated the 'rascally Lake poet' for calling Voltaire a dull fellow.

little A prefix used in nicknames for several quarters of London presently or formerly characterized by an immigrant population of some particular nationality. 'Little' is followed either by the name of the migrants' country of origin or its capital. *See also* PETTY FRANCE.

Little Algiers Blackstock Road, a somewhat down-at-heel shopping street in FINSBURY PARK, has been thus called for the number of Algerian refugees who live in the vicinity.

little apples grow quickly please A mnemonic used by students of the KNOWLEDGE to remember the order of the theatres on SHAFTESBURY AVENUE, from west to east as far as CAMBRIDGE CIRCUS. They are the Lyric, Apollo, Gielgud (formerly Globe), Queen's and Palace.

Little Barbary An old nickname for WAPPING, probably deriving from the presence of north African immigrants in the 18th century.

Little Ben A cast iron clock tower in the style of a miniature BIG BEN. It was erected in VICTORIA in 1892, removed in 1964 to allow road widening, and reinstalled on a traffic island at the junction of Victoria Street, Wilton Road and Vauxhall Bridge Road in 1981.

Little Britain A street in SMITHFIELD, originally Bretton-Strete, which became Lyttell Bretton in late Elizabethan times. It is said to be named from a Duke of Brittany who had a residence here. It was once noted for its booksellers.

> Little Britain may truly be called the heart's core of the city, the stronghold of true John Bullism.
> WASHINGTON IRVING: *The Sketch Book*, 'Little Britain' (1819–20)

Just a few years after Irving wrote these words, others were characterizing the locality as a slum and a ROOKERY.

Little Chelsea

1. An isolated settlement that lay along the part of the FULHAM ROAD nowadays sometimes called the BEACH. The name was in use from the early 17th century to the 1850s, after which its separate identity was erased by the creation of

new streets in its hinterland, which connected it to nearby localities.

2. A name used by estate agents for the 'ever popular' set of streets on the MORTLAKE side of BARNES. It is said that the name was coined in the 1960s by the wife of a Polish property developer, who noted the similarity of cottages here to those in parts of CHELSEA.

Little Cork An early nickname for the Ford Motor Company's works at DAGENHAM, derived from its great number of Irish employees, many of whom had previously worked at the company's factory in Cork. *See also* DAGENHAM YANKS.

Little Dorrit *See the* CHILD OF THE MARSHALSEA.

Little Ealing Now the southernmost part of South EALING, the hamlet of Little Ealing was in existence by the mid-17th century. Rochester House was probably built in the 1710s for John Pearce, a London distiller; its present name honours Pearce's son Zachary, bishop of Rochester (1690–1774), who died here.

little gentleman in velvet or **black velvet** A favourite Jacobite toast in the reign of Queen Anne. The reference was to the mole that raised the molehill against which William III's horse Sorrel stumbled in HAMPTON COURT PARK (21 February 1702). The king broke his collar bone and died at KENSINGTON PALACE (8 March).

> He urged his horse to strike into a gallop just at a spot where a mole had been at work. Sorrel stumbled on the mole-hill, and went down on his knees. The king fell off and broke his collar bone.
> LORD MACAULAY: *History of England* (1849, 1855)

Little Ilford The half-forgotten north-eastern corner of EAST HAM, situated on the opposite side of the River RODING (and the NORTH CIRCULAR ROAD) from ILFORD itself. Domesday Book identifies this as the original location of Ilford and there was a wooden church here in Saxon times. From the 1880s the creation of cemeteries in the area led to a rush on the remaining available building land. By this time, however, the wider district was being called MANOR PARK and the parish was absorbed into East Ham. Little Ilford Park, formerly the grounds of Little Ilford manor house, is located at the eastern end of Church Road.

Little Italy A nickname applied to the western

side of CLERKENWELL because of its strong Italian connections, which go back at least two centuries. Also once known as Italian Hill, its boundaries are recognized as Clerkenwell Road, FARRINGDON ROAD and Rosebery Avenue. The Catholic church of St Peter was built in 1863 and the area's Italian population reached a peak in the late 19th century. Until then the SAFFRON HILL vicinity had been notorious for the pickpockets and fences portrayed in OLIVER TWIST and the authorities were glad to see these characters supplanted by the more respectable Italians. Giuseppe Mazzini (1805–72), the writer and political leader, lived in Laystall Street and founded an Italian language school in nearby HATTON GARDEN in 1841. London's Italians are now spread more thinly throughout the capital, but Sunday worship at St Peter's still provides a focal point. The Processione della Madonna del Carmine, held on the Sunday after 16 July, is Little Italy's most important event. Except during wartime it has taken place every year since 1896.

Little India The nickname has been applied to SOUTHALL, WEMBLEY and the Drummond Street area in west EUSTON, the latter because of its restaurants rather than the ethnicity of the residents, who are more likely to be of Bangladeshi origin.

Little Jerusalem A 19th-century nickname for the SPITALFIELDS area.

Little Moscow A nickname applied to parts of London that exhibited 'red' tendencies in the mid-20th century. The LONDON COUNTY COUNCIL's Watling estate, in southern EDGWARE, drew early residents from ISLINGTON and ST PANCRAS and for a while a quasi-COCKNEY community spirit prevailed. The shops and market on Watling Avenue had the flavour of CHAPEL MARKET and the campaigning *Watling Resident* newspaper sold 3,000 copies at its peak in 1929. Middle-class neighbours did not like what they saw and accordingly coined the 'Little Moscow' tag, although communist candidates received fewer than 100 votes in local elections. Assimilation and a broader variety of incomers had combined to dilute Watling's early character by the mid-1930s. Around that time, FINSBURY gained a reputation as a hotbed of socialism and during the Second World War a memorial was erected here to Lenin, who had lived and worked in the borough. It was designed by the modernist architect Berthold Lubetkin (*see* TECTON). Even

at the height of fraternal feelings with the Soviet Union the memorial was none too popular, and soon after the war it was quietly removed.

Little Nell The child companion and support of her feeble grandfather in DICKENS's *The Old Curiosity Shop* (1840–1). 'Nearly fourteen' and of angelic character, she is terrified by her grandfather's moneylender, Daniel Quilp, who lusts after her. When the old man loses his shop and all his property through gambling, the pair leave London to escape from Quilp and Nell's dissolute elder brother, Fred Trent, who believes their grandfather is hoarding money to give to her.

Little Paris A nickname for SOUTH KENSINGTON, which has francophone bookshops, doctors, dentists and other specialist services, as well as several French restaurants. The Institut français, in Queensberry Place, hosts cultural events and presents (mainly) French films at the Ciné lumière. The French Consulate is on Cromwell Road but the embassy is in KNIGHTSBRIDGE.

little season A minor sibling of the LONDON SEASON. For some while (notably during the Regency period) it was primarily autumnal; later it acquired a pre-Lenten aspect. It was less formal and consisted more of dinner parties and dances than attendance at grand balls or public events. And, whereas the London season was the province of royalty and the nobility, the little season principally attracted senior members of the professional classes. The only aristocrats to join the fun were either those who lacked a country estate or the younger generation, who quickly grew bored with rural life.

Little South India TOOTING has been so called for the size of its south Asian – notably Tamil – population and for its variety of affordable south Indian restaurants. The main streets have shops specializing in saris and Asian sweets, jewellery and films.

Little Stanmore A significant medieval parish lying west of EDGWARE, now almost lost within neighbouring suburbs, notably CANONS PARK. St Lawrence's Church was built in white stone during the 12th century, but the oldest surviving part of the present structure is its late 14th-century tower. The rest of the church was rebuilt in 1715, with a startlingly ornate interior that has woodcarvings attributed to Grinling Gibbons (1648–1721). It is probable that Handel performed the first of his *Chandos Anthems* at St Lawrence's.

Little Theatreland A designation applied by the Theatres Trust to the linear stretch of ISLINGTON that extends from SADLER'S WELLS to HIGHBURY CORNER. Its venues include the ALMEIDA and pub theatres at the King's Head, Old Red Lion and Hen and Chickens.

Little Tich The stage name of the MUSIC HALL star Harry Relph (1867–1928), the 15th child born to the landlord of the Blacksmith's Arms in Cudham, now in the London Borough of BROMLEY. In addition to his comedic talents, he was an accomplished dancer, even when wearing ridiculously oversized boots; the ballet dancer Nijinsky described him as 'un grand artiste'. Relph was called Little Tich because he bore a childhood resemblance to Arthur Orton, the man who claimed to be the missing heir to the English baronetcy, Sir Roger Tichbourne. Originally it was simply the 'Little' part of his stage name that related to his height (not much more than 4 feet or 1.2m), but as a consequence of his fame the word 'Tich' came to be inextricably linked with diminutive stature.

> I had been fascinated by the movements of Little Tich, whom I had seen in London in 1914, and ... by the art of this great clown.
>
> IGOR STRAVINSKY, with ROBERT CRAFT: *Memories and Commentaries* (1960)

Little Tramp The sobriquet of Charlie Chaplin (1889–1977), from the character he portrayed in some of his finest silent movies, notably *The Tramp* (1915), *The Gold Rush* (1925) and *Modern Times* (1936). Born in East Street, WALWORTH, he grew up at various addresses in KENNINGTON and LAMBETH. His parents divorced when he was young and his mother spent long periods in mental hospitals, so Chaplin boarded at the Central London District School, a paupers' institution in HANWELL. Following some early successes on the London stage he toured the United States with FRED KARNO's troupe and then made 35 short films for Mack Sennett's Keystone Studios in the space of a single year, 1914, when he originated the character of the awkwardly dignified tramp. Chaplin abandoned his alter ego after *Modern Times*, although it is echoed in his first dialogue film, *The Great Dictator* (1940). *See also* TRAMP.

Little Venice A canal intersection and its vicinity, located on the border of PADDINGTON and MAIDA VALE. A pool was created here in the 1810s at the meeting point of the REGENT'S CANAL and the Paddington arm of the GRAND JUNCTION CANAL, and was originally known as Paddington Broadwater. The neighbouring area was built up in a piecemeal but harmonious fashion from the second quarter of the 19th century, especially with terraces and pairs of three-storey STUCCOED houses. In her 1934 detective novel *Death of a Ghost*, Margery Allingham gave the name 'Little Venice' to a house overlooking the canal. The name caught on with estate agents after the Second World War and is still much used for the pricey properties in the locality. Artists' studios on the east side of the pool were demolished and replaced by a small park, named Rembrandt Gardens in 1975 to commemorate the 700th anniversary of the founding of the city of Amsterdam, the 'Venice of the North'. The poet Robert Browning, playwright Christopher Fry, novelist Elizabeth Jane Howard, artist Lucian Freud and Icelandic chanteuse Björk are among those who have had homes in Little Venice.

Little Woman of Peckham Lucy Wanmer, who was 32 inches (81cm) tall. She kept a school at PECKHAM and despite being shorter than the pupils was said to 'have proved herself an excellent disciplinarian'. She died in 1821, aged about 71.

Liverpool Street A short street in the city of London, a turning to the west off BISHOPSGATE, named in honour of Robert Banks Jenkinson, 2nd Earl of Liverpool (1770–1828), prime minister from 1812 to 1827. The first edition of the Communist Party Manifesto was printed at 46 Liverpool Street in February 1848, in German.

Liverpool Street station A main-line railway station located at the corner of Liverpool Street and BISHOPSGATE; the terminus for train services to the eastern and north-eastern suburbs, Stansted Airport and East Anglia. Although the London to East Anglia route first began to operate in the 1840s, it was not until 1874 that Liverpool Street station replaced Bishopsgate as the terminus. It is now London's third busiest main-line terminus, after WATERLOO and VICTORIA. Improvements made in the early 1990s combined the restoration of many original features with sensible modernization. Liverpool Street underground station, now on the CENTRAL, CIRCLE, HAMMERSMITH AND CITY and METROPOLITAN lines, opened in 1875 (originally under the name Bishopsgate).

livery companies The modern representatives in the CITY of London of the old craft guilds, which were originally associations for religious and social purposes and later trade organizations for fixing wages, standards of craftsmanship and the like. They also acted as friendly societies. Their members wore distinctive livery on special occasions, hence the name 'livery company'.

The 12 'great' companies in order of civic precedence, with the dates of their first royal charter, are the:

1. MERCERS (1394)
2. Grocers (1345)
3. Drapers (1364)
4. Fishmongers (1272)
5. Goldsmiths (1327)
6/7. Merchant Taylors (1327)
6/7. Skinners (1327)
8. Haberdashers (1448)
9. Salters (1559)
10. Ironmongers (1463)
11. Vintners (1363)
12. Clothworkers (1528)

The Pepperers and Spicers amalgamated in 1345 to become later known as the Grocers, and the Haberdashers were originally known as the Hurrers. Samuel PEPYS was Master (1677) of the Clothworkers, which was a 16th-century incorporation of the Shearmen and the Fullers.

Among the 100-odd lesser livery companies are the:

Apothecaries (1617)
Armourers and Brasiers (1453)
Blacksmiths (1571)
Butchers (1605)
Cordwainers (1439)
Dyers (1471)
Farmers (1952)
Furniture Makers (1963)
Glovers (1639)
Leathersellers (1444)
Plaisterers (1501)
Stationers and Newspaper Makers (1556)

The Weavers (1184) claim to be the oldest company. The specializations of some of the newer livery companies provide an insight into the City's changing character. They include:

Environmental Cleaners (1986)
Information Technologists (1992)
World Traders (2000)
Water Conservators (2000)
Management Consultants (2004)
International Bankers (2004)
Tax Advisers (2005)
Security Professionals (2008)

Only a handful of the longest-established companies (among them the Fishmongers) continue to regulate aspects of their trades, but many still have their halls in the City and contribute generously from their funds to charities, especially to sheltered accommodation and education. Merchant Taylors' School, the Haberdashers' schools, ST PAUL'S SCHOOL, GOLDSMITHS College and many other such institutions owe much to their benevolence. Most of the companies also function as fraternities, providing their members with what are nowadays called 'high-level networking opportunities'. *See also at* SIXES AND SEVENS.

liverymen The freemen of the London livery companies are so called because they are entitled to wear the livery of their respective companies.

Liza Formerly a generic term for a working-class London girl or young woman. The name was employed in two definitive portrayals of such characters: Maugham's LIZA OF LAMBETH and SHAW's Eliza DOOLITTLE.

Liza of Lambeth W. Somerset Maugham's first novel (1897). A portrait of a poor London streetgirl, it owes as much to Zola as to Maugham's experience of LAMBETH when a medical student at ST THOMAS' HOSPITAL, but is nonetheless a convincing portrait of a figure over-determined and burdened by her environment.

outside, Liza! *See under* OUTSIDE.

Lloyd's of London An international insurance market in the CITY of London and the world centre of shipping intelligence that began in the 17th-century COFFEE HOUSE of Edward Lloyd in LOMBARD STREET. It was originally a market for marine insurance only but now deals with nearly all forms of insurance. Lloyd's was incorporated by Act of Parliament in 1871. Insurance is accepted by individual underwriters, not by Lloyd's of London, which provides the premises, intelligence and other facilities. Lloyd's agents throughout the world send shipping information, which is published in Lloyd's List and Lloyd's Shipping Index. *See also the* BALTIC; *the* LUTINE BELL.

Lloyd's building The colloquial name for One LIME STREET, the headquarters of Lloyd's of London since 1986. Designed by the Richard Rogers Partnership, its distinctive characteristic is the externalization of structural details and utilities such as ducts and glass lifts. Combined with stainless steel cladding, and especially when illuminated at night, the effect at the time of its construction was ultra-modern.

Loadsamoney A character created by the British comedian Harry Enfield (b.1961), first appearing on Channel 4's *Saturday Live* in 1986–7. Loadsamoney was an obnoxious skilled or semi-skilled working-class type in his 20s, an archetypal ESSEX MAN, who had done well under Thatcherism and liked nothing better than to rub his wad in one's face. The catch-phrase 'Loadsamoney!' was seized on by journalists and taken up by the Labour leader Neil Kinnock, who in May 1988 accused Margaret Thatcher's Conservative administration of fostering an uncaring 'loadsamoney mentality'.

loaf (of bread) 'Head' in COCKNEY RHYMING SLANG, most often heard in the exhortation 'use your loaf'.

> When you talk to your master, take your hat off, oaf,
> And mind your manners. Time you learned to use your loaf!
>
> MOLIÈRE: *The School for Wives*, I, iii (1662) (translated by Maya Slater, 2001)

lock

Lock & Co. A headwear supplier founded by Robert Davis, a hatter from BISHOPSGATE, who in 1676 leased five houses on the west side of ST JAMES'S STREET and set up shop in one of these, drawing eminent customers from the local COFFEE SHOPS. James Lock entered into an apprenticeship at the hatters in 1747 and subsequently married into the Davis family. He inherited the business in 1759 and six years later acquired new premises across the road at No.6 St James's Street, where the firm remains today, and in which indirect descendants of Robert Davis and James Lock are still partners. *See also* BOWLER HAT; TWEED.

lock hospitals Hospitals specializing in the treatment of sexually transmitted diseases, pioneered in London from 1746. They evolved out of the medieval lazar houses – leprosy

isolation hospitals. Although some syphilitics were forcibly detained behind bolted doors and barred windows, the 'lock' name probably derives from the French *loques*, 'rags', referring to the bandages that were used to bind lepers' sores. The first London Lock Hospital stood at Grosvenor Place, near HYDE PARK CORNER, from 1746 to 1841, whereafter its successor opened on the HARROW ROAD, WESTBOURNE GREEN, with buildings designed by Lewis Vulliamy (1791–1871). The hospital accommodated women and later incorporated a 'rescue home' that had originally been set up in KNIGHTSBRIDGE for discharged patients. Men were treated as outpatients. A male clinic opened in 1862 in Dean Street, SOHO, and was soon enlarged with the aid of a government subsidy in return for treating military patients. The Harrow Road and Dean Street hospitals closed in 1952, when their functions were integrated into the National Health Service.

Lock, Stock and Two Smoking Barrels A critically and commercially successful film (1998) directed by Guy Ritchie (b.1968), set mainly in the criminal underworld of the EAST END. With its idiosyncratically nicknamed COCKNEYS, droll dialogue, high body count and numerous plot twists, it established a model for Ritchie's subsequent London-based gangster movies, such as *Snatch* (2000) and *RocknRolla* (2008).

Lockit

Lockit's (or Locket's) ordinary A dining and entertainment house that operated near the corner of the MALL and WHITEHALL at the beginning of the 18th century. An ordinary was a place where a good meal could be had at a fixed price. Mrs Lockit's French cuisine and gambling tables were popular with the gentry and aristocracy; W.M. Thackeray made her establishment the setting for an ultimately fatal dispute between Lords Mohun and Castlewood in his novel *The History of Henry Esmond* (1852):

> 'Faith,' says Westbury, 'the little scholar was the first to begin the quarrel – I mind me of it now – at Lockit's. I always hated that fellow Mohun. What was the real cause, of the quarrel betwixt him and poor Frank? I would wager 'twas a woman.'

Lockit, the Jailer A character in the BEGGAR'S OPERA who sees Captain MacHeath saunter in and out of his custody. He is father to Lucy Lockit, one of the captain's many lovers, and has a partnership in crime with Thomas Peachum the lawyer, which sways unstably due to their vanities and rivalry. Like Peachum, he stands for corrupt authority, no better than the criminals it condemns.

Lombard

1. A banker or moneylender in medieval London. Merchants from Lombardy in north Italy established financial operations in the CITY in the late 13th century and also flourished as pawnbrokers. The three golden balls of the pawnshop are said to be taken from the armorial bearings of the Medici of Florence.

> This merchant, who was wary and discreet,
> Soon managed to negotiate his loan;
> The bond that he had signed became his own
> For he paid down the money to a franc
> To certain Lombards at their Paris Bank.
>
> CHAUCER: 'The Shipman's Tale' (c.1387) (translated by Nevill Coghill, 1951)

2. An acronym for 'Loads of money but a right dickhead'. It dates from the rise of the yuppie, when such coinages were all the rage.

> Not since the arrival of Lombard ... in the
> Eighties have we seen an acronym that dares to
> co-opt a proper name, in the case of Lombard
> risking potential confusion between City boys
> in ill-fitting suits and a kingdom overthrown by
> Charlemagne in 773.
>
> TIM DOWLING, in The Independent (29 April 1999)

Lombard fever Indebtedness to a banker.
Lombard Street A street in the CITY of London, running south-eastwards from BANK to GRACECHURCH STREET. This was the place where the Lombard merchants set up most of their businesses. It remains a street of bankers (no longer particularly Italian), and in its time has hosted the head offices of Barclays Bank and of LLOYD'S. So strong is the financial connection that its name has become a virtual metonym for the City's banking sector:

> Trade then shall flourish, and ilk art
> A lively vigour shall impart
> To credit languishing and famisht,
> And Lombard-street shall be replenisht.
>
> ALLAN RAMSAY: Rise and Fall of Stocks (1721)

all Lombard Street to a China orange See under ALL.

Londinium

The Roman city that would become LONDON, established c.AD 47 in the area of modern CORNHILL and LUDGATE HILL. The first surviving reference to Londinium is found in Tacitus (Annals, xiv, written AD 115–117). Having quickly became an important trading centre, the settlement was sacked and burned by BOUDICCA in AD 60, but it was soon rebuilt and continued to grow in wealth and importance over the next 300 years. A permanent bridge over the THAMES had been built before the end of the 1st century AD, near the site of the present LONDON BRIDGE, and between about 190 and 225 a substantial wall was erected around the city. Londinium became the fifth-largest conurbation in the western world. It was the hub of Roman Britain's road system and its financial centre. The Romans withdrew in 410 (the most notable survival of their period is the TEMPLE OF MITHRAS), and London's political status and influence waned over the succeeding centuries.

London

The capital city of England and of the United Kingdom. It covers an area of 607 square miles (1,572 sq km) and had an estimated population of 7,557,000 in mid-2007. The name may have meant 'place at the navigable or unfordable river' (referring to a settlement downstream of the lowest fordable point on the River THAMES, at WESTMINSTER), from two pre-Celtic (pre-Indo-European) roots with added Celtic suffixes. The theory that the name was based on an Old Celtic male personal name Londinos, meaning literally 'the wild or bold one', is no longer generally accepted. The notion that it comes from King LUD is attractive but quite false.

London was founded on a naturally protected site at the lowest bridging point and highest navigable point for sea shipping on the Thames, the principal entry into England from mainland Europe. There is evidence (for example, the BATTERSEA SHIELD) of Celtic settlement in areas of what is now INNER LONDON, but the first to establish themselves in what would become the CITY of London were the Romans (see LONDINIUM). It remained a significant international port in the Anglo-Saxon period, and an important trading centre grew up to the west of the walled town, known as Lundenwic (see ALDWYCH). The old town itself – where Mellitus, Bishop of London, founded the church of ST PAUL'S in 604 – had become in anglicized form Lundene and also, with assorted Old English suffixes, Lundenburg 'fortified town of London',

Lundenceaster 'Roman town of London' and Lundentun 'village or estate of London'. It was sacked by the Viking Danes in 842 and 851, and had become their winter quarters by 871, but in 886 Alfred the Great recaptured the city and repaired its walls. The Danish Cnut, king of England from 1016 to 1040, made London his capital in preference to Winchester and, although Edward the Confessor subsequently moved the royal seat to Westminster, after the Norman Conquest William I designated London his joint capital with Winchester. He also built the WHITE TOWER of the TOWER OF LONDON to protect and dominate the city.

Over the course of the Middle Ages the importance of Winchester declined, and London became the sole capital of England. But increasingly the king and court came to prefer Westminster and its palace, leaving London and its administration in the hands of its powerful merchants (their autonomy is symbolically re-enacted today whenever the sovereign wishes to enter the City of London, and has to stop at TEMPLE BAR to receive official authorization). Trade associations known as 'guilds' began to flourish in London from the 12th century onwards, and they came to play a more and more central role in the government of the city – for example, in nominating civic officials. The most important of these was, and is, the LORD MAYOR OF LONDON. Many of the guilds still survive as LIVERY COMPANIES. Thanks to the feverish economic activity of these guilds' members, and of the merchants who did their business via its port, London grew and prospered during the Middle Ages.

During the Civil War the City of London was a centre of nonconformity and gave its backing to Parliament, its support being a large factor in the defeat of Charles I. Disenchantment with Oliver Cromwell's regime soon set in, however, and London too welcomed the Restoration of Charles II in 1660. It soon suffered two severe setbacks: the GREAT PLAGUE of 1665, which killed over one-sixth of its population; and the following year the GREAT FIRE OF LONDON. Many of the institutions that characterize the City as a financial centre had their beginnings during the phase of reconstruction that followed: Edwin Lloyd opened his coffee house, precursor of LLOYD'S OF LONDON and scores of other insurance houses, in 1688, and in 1694 the BANK OF ENGLAND was founded.

By 1700 London was the largest city in western Europe. During the 18th century the WEST END became the fashionable place to live, and elegant residential streets and squares were built here, while to the east of the City the need for labour for the rapidly developing docks sowed the seeds of the EAST END. To the north, London swallowed up more and more villages and hamlets in MIDDLESEX and ESSEX, establishing the pattern of GREATER LONDON as a mosaic of individual communities. Improved cross-Thames communication (the river was bridged four times in the London area in the 18th century) increasingly brought parts of SURREY and Kent within London's orbit too. A major factor from the 1830s onwards was the railways, which spawned a swathe of new suburbs, filled with modest dwellings for the growing lower middle class of clerks and shop assistants. This rapidly growing urban organism needed a higher degree of control and management than had hitherto sufficed: the METROPOLITAN POLICE force was established in 1829, and the fabric of local government was overhauled twice, with the creation in 1855 of the METROPOLITAN BOARD OF WORKS, and in 1888 of the LONDON COUNTY COUNCIL.

London got off relatively lightly in the First World War (870 people were killed by German bombs), but in the Second it suffered grievously, both in the BLITZ, which started on 7 September 1940, and later in the V1 and V2 rocket attacks. In some parts, such as the City and POPLAR, a third of the buildings were destroyed, and about 30,000 people were killed in the Greater London area. Postwar reconstruction saw communities, particularly from the East End, moved out wholesale to NEW TOWNS, and those that remained housed in tower blocks. Until well after the Second World War, London was still the UK's major port (*see the* PORT OF LONDON) but the docks had vanished by the early 1970s and were replaced from the 1980s by the new developments of DOCKLANDS.

London in the 21st century is a world city and a collection of villages, with a vibrant and bracing social and ethnic mix; a financial and commercial centre; seat of Britain's legislature and of England's highest courts of law; a richly endowed capital of culture; a magnet for tourists (whose spending provides a significant amount of its income); and a repository of the history and traditions of the English, and British, people.

London Airport The official name of HEATH-ROW AIRPORT until 1966. Eight major and minor airports nowadays prefix their name with the word London, of which the majority are situated well outside GREATER LONDON.

London Heathrow
LONDON CITY
London BIGGIN HILL
London Ashford, Kent
London Gatwick, West Sussex
London Luton, Bedfordshire
London Southend, Essex
London Stansted, Essex

London Apprentice A public house in ISLE-WORTH. It dates from 1731 and is said to have been named after the APPRENTICES who rowed all the way here from the CITY on their days off.

London Assembly A scrutinizing body containing 25 members, elected by the voters of GREATER LONDON at the same time as they vote for the MAYOR OF LONDON. It was established in 2000, and meets in CITY HALL. For electoral purposes, London is divided into 14 assembly constituencies, consisting of two or more boroughs:

BARNET and CAMDEN
BEXLEY and BROMLEY
BRENT and HARROW
City and East London (BARKING AND DAGENHAM, CITY of London, NEWHAM, TOWER HAMLETS)
CROYDON and SUTTON
EALING and HILLINGDON
ENFIELD and HARINGEY
GREENWICH and LEWISHAM
HAVERING and REDBRIDGE
LAMBETH and SOUTHWARK
MERTON and WANDSWORTH
North East (HACKNEY, ISLINGTON, WALTHAM FOREST)
South West (HOUNSLOW, KINGSTON UPON THAMES, RICHMOND UPON THAMES)
West Central (HAMMERSMITH AND FULHAM, KENSINGTON AND CHELSEA, WESTMINSTER)

London Assurance A play (1841) by the Irish dramatist Dion Boucicault. Hovering somewhere between Restoration-style comedy and Oscar Wilde, it recounts the triumphs and disasters of various interwoven amorous intrigues.

London Bach The sobriquet of Johann Christian Bach (1735–82), reflecting his 20-year residence in the British capital. Born in Leipzig, he was the eleventh and youngest son of J.S. Bach. In 1762 he settled permanently in London and was appointed composer to the London Italian opera. He became musician to Queen Charlotte Sophia (1763) and later collaborated with Karl Friedrich Abel (1723–87). The young Mozart on his London visit (1764) took to him and was influenced by his style. Bach developed symphonic form, and was twice painted by Thomas Gainsborough.

London Belongs to Me
1. A film (1948), directed by Sidney Gilliat, based on a book by Norman Collins (1945). It revolves around a young man (Richard Attenborough) charged with murder and the support he receives from his fellow lodgers in a KENNINGTON boarding house. Alastair Sim steals many scenes as a fraudulent medium.
2. A song by Saint Etienne, from the album *Foxbase Alpha* (1991). Notwithstanding their foreign name, inspired by a French football team, Saint Etienne have perhaps done more to celebrate London than any rock band since the CLASH, including making two films that document aspects of the metropolitan landscape. A 2009 compilation of their music was entitled *London Conversations*.

London Below A subterranean world created by the fantasy author Neil Gaiman (b.1960) for the BBC TV series and its subsequent novelization *Neverwhere* (both 1996). Features of this magical realm such as Night's Bridge have parallels in the 'London Above' with which it co-exists, and disused TUBE stations serve as gateways between the two. Character names include the Angel Islington, Serpentine, Ruislip and Hammersmith, and there are clans called the Crouch Enders, Seven Sisters and Black Friars. The low-budget television production was relatively unsuccessful but the book has been translated into more than a dozen other languages.

> Old Bailey pulled on his glasses. He took the object from de Carabas. It was cold to the touch. He sat down on an air-conditioning unit, then, turning the black obsidian statue over and over in his hand, he announced: 'It's the Great Beast of London.'

London Bridge
1. London's longest established THAMES crossing. The first bridge was built around AD 50 and, with its many successors, it was for nearly 1,700

years the CITY's only Thames bridge. Work on the construction of a stone bridge began in 1176. That bridge stood for more than six centuries and was possibly the most painted of all the capital's scenes; it is represented in almost every gallery in London. Houses, shops and a chapel were built on the bridge, mills operated beneath several of its arches and until 1660 the heads of traitors were mounted on spikes by the southern gatehouse. Old London Bridge was replaced in 1831 and London Bridge was replaced again in the early 1970s and its predecessor was sold for $1.8 million to the McCulloch Oil Corporation of the United States, which re-erected it at Lake Havasu City, Arizona. It was long rumoured that the Americans thought they were buying TOWER BRIDGE, a canard hotly denied by the company chairman, George McCulloch. *See also* THE BATTLE OF LONDON BRIDGE.

> Unreal City,
> Under the brown fog of a winter dawn,
> A crowd flowed over London Bridge, so many,
> I had not thought death had undone so many.

T.S. ELIOT: *The Waste Land* (1922)

2. A designation nowadays applied to the historic environs of the southern side of the bridge. The area became increasingly crowded in the early 19th century, with wharves at SHAD THAMES, industry on BANKSIDE and the slums of the BOROUGH. ST THOMAS' HOSPITAL moved to LAMBETH in 1871 but the neighbouring GUY'S HOSPITAL has remained and progressively expanded. The vicinity of LONDON BRIDGE STATION is a significant commercial centre. Among the area's tourist attractions are the LONDON DUNGEON, on TOOLEY STREET, and HMS BELFAST, a floating museum of naval history.

London Bridge is built upon woolpacks An old saying referring to the wool tax that provided funds for the construction of the medieval bridge.

London Bridge is falling down *See* BATTLE OF LONDON BRIDGE; MY FAIR LADY.

London Bridge station A busy (in fact, somewhat congested) main-line and underground station that opened in 1836 as the terminus for the first steam railway to run into London (from DEPTFORD). Its present building was begun in the 1840s. It carries lines from south-east London, Kent and the south coast. The TUBE station,

now on the NORTHERN and JUBILEE lines, opened in 1900.

London Bridge Tower *See the* SHARD (OF GLASS).

London Bridge was made for wise men to go over and fools to go under A saying dating from before the removal of the medieval London Bridge in 1832. Navigation through the arches of the old bridge was notoriously dangerous because of the swirling currents. *See also* SHOOTING THE BRIDGE.

London Broadcasting Company *See* LBC RADIO.

London broil An American dish, unknown to Londoners, consisting of a large beef steak grilled and then cut in thin slices for serving.

London Broncos *See* HARLEQUINS.

London burkers A gang that in the early 1830s murdered at least two boys and one woman and sold their bodies for dissection, in the manner of Edinburgh's Burke and Hare. They began in the 1820s as 'resurrection men', breaking open the coffins of the newly buried to supply the demands of the surgical and medical schools, but later decided that it would be less troublesome to obtain the bodies by more direct means. Their method was to force a cocktail of drink and drugs on the intended victims and then drown them after they had passed out. Their crimes came to light with the case of the 'Italian Boy' (later discovered to be a Lincolnshire cattle drover), whom John Bishop and Thomas Williams murdered at their home in Nova Scotia Gardens, BETHNAL GREEN, on 3 November 1831. Surgeons called in the police after their suspicions were aroused by the fresh state of the corpse and, within the space of a month, Bishop and Williams were arrested, tried, convicted, executed and publicly dissected. Other members of their resurrectionist gang successfully pleaded ignorance of the means by which Bishop and Williams had latterly been obtaining their merchandise. In a separate case that came to trial a month later, Edward Cook and Eliza Ross were hanged for murdering Catherine Walsh, an 84-year-old WHITECHAPEL lace seller, and selling her body to surgeons. Public outrage at these crimes contributed significantly to the passing of the Anatomy Act of 1832, which increased the legal supply of cadavers.

London-by-the-Sea A nickname for BRIGHTON since at least the early 19th century, and also sometimes for Southend, in ESSEX. The latter has been more specifically called 'East London-by-the-Sea'. For south-east Londoners, Margate has performed a similar role.

London calling A broadcasting identification first used in May 1922 for radio transmissions from Marconi House in the STRAND: 'This is London calling – 2LO calling.' The newly formed BBC took over the 2LO service soon afterwards (*see* SAVOY HILL). With radio's instant popularity, the phrase soon entered the metropolitan vocabulary and Noël Coward used it in September 1923 as the title of a musical revue at the Duke of York's Theatre. From 1930 the US journalist Cesar Saerchinger regularly opened his European reports on CBS radio with the words: 'Hello America, London calling.' In 1932 'London calling' became the identifying announcement of the BBC Empire Service, renamed the General Overseas Service in November 1939. The service's use of the identification throughout the Second World War gave the words an iconic resonance.

> This is London. London calling in the Home, Overseas and European services of the BBC and through United Nations Radio, Mediterranean, and this is John Snagge speaking. Supreme Headquarters of the Allied Expeditionary Force have just issued a communiqué and in a few seconds I will read it to you.
>
> preamble to an announcement of the D-Day landings (6 June 1944)

London Calling was the allusive title of a 1979 album and single by the CLASH. The band's frontman Joe Strummer subsequently presented a music show on the BBC World Service (the ultimate successor to the General Overseas Service), which he was persuaded to entitle *London Calling*.

London Canal Museum A museum of inland waterways, the ice trade and ice cream, located on New Wharf Road, KING'S CROSS. The museum occupies a former cold store, built in 1863 to preserve ice imported from Norway, and brought to the store via the REGENT'S CANAL. The business was the creation of Carlo Gatti (1817–78), a Swiss Italian who ran an ice empire in London, making ice cream, operating a café in HUNGERFORD MARKET and supplying ice to butchers and fishmongers. After conversion to a conventional warehouse, and then a period of

disuse, the building was taken on by the Canal Museum Trust in 1989.

London Central Mosque *See* REGENT'S PARK MOSQUE.

London Charivari *See* PUNCH.

London City Airport A short-take-off-and-landing airport located in eastern DOCKLANDS. It opened in 1987 on the quays between the former King George V and Royal Albert Docks, with a terminal building of almost cosy proportions. The King George V Dock office buildings are used as a transit office. Only low-noise, mid-range airliners can use the airport, which offers flights to UK and European destinations. Around three million passengers now pass through City Airport each year, with a target of eight million by 2030. A DOCKLANDS LIGHT RAILWAY connection opened in 2005.

London Clay A Lower Eocene (Ypresian) formation in south-eastern England. It is a marine deposit, laid down between 58 and 52 million years ago, mostly coloured dark brown, sometimes with a bluish tint. *See also* LONDON STOCK BRICK.

London Clinic A private hospital situated in Devonshire Place, MARYLEBONE. It opened in 1932. The Chilean former dictator Augusto Pinochet (1915–2006) was arrested here in 1998 while undergoing treatment for a bad back.

London Corresponding Society A pressure group founded in 1792 by Thomas Hardy (1752–1832), a PICCADILLY shoemaker, to agitate for universal manhood suffrage via debate, petitions and peaceful protest. The term 'corresponding' was a device to circumvent the law prohibiting the formation of a national political organization and the LCS formed informal alliances with societies in other major cities. It organized very large demonstrations in and around London and from 1793 the wars with France prompted the government to enact a series of increasingly restrictive statutes, culminating in the Corresponding Societies Act of 1799, which succeeded in snuffing out the movement. *See also the* POP-GUN PLOT.

London Coliseum *See the* COLISEUM.

London County Council In 1889 the metropolis of London (at that time covering 116 square miles (300 sq km) was officially designated a county, under the aegis of the London County Council (LCC), which absorbed the METROPOLITAN BOARD OF WORKS. COUNTY HALL became the council's headquarters in 1922. The GREATER LONDON COUNCIL, covering a far larger area, replaced the LCC in 1965.

London Cuckolds, The A farcical sub-Restoration-style comedy (1682) by Edward Ravenscroft, which used to be performed on LORD MAYOR'S DAY in the 18th century, and is occasionally revived today.

London Dock or **Docks** A former group of inland basins and wharves in WAPPING, first mooted in the late 18th century and granted parliamentary consent in 1800, despite some questioning the wisdom of such a scheme:

> In pure good-nature 'twas they plann'd the docks,
> They thought the town in want of laughing-stocks.
> Wapping a dock, forsooth! the man's a fool.
>
> ANON: 'The Story of Tom Cole, with Old Father Thames's Malediction of the Wapping Docks' (1796)

The dock opened in 1805 and its early specialities were tobacco, rice, wine and wool. Like the rest of DOCKLANDS, the London Dock's facilities were unable to cope with containerization and it closed in 1971. Most of the site was redeveloped with housing but some waterways and warehouses have been preserved.

London Docklands Development Corporation An urban regeneration body established by the government in 1981 to oversee the redevelopment of disused docks and neighbouring sites in the boroughs of SOUTHWARK, TOWER HAMLETS and NEWHAM. Using its powers of compulsory purchase, the LDDC acquired and resold 1,066 acres (431 hectares) of land and sponsored the construction of the DOCKLANDS LIGHT RAILWAY and other infrastructural improvements, spending almost £2 billion in the process. Depending on the radically contrasting viewpoints of various interested parties, the LDDC was either the saviour of a blighted wasteland or the destroyer of long-established working-class communities. The corporation began to withdraw from control of its designated areas in 1994 and was formally wound up in June 1998. Local authorities and specialist agencies have continued some aspects of the LDDC's work, notably in the vicinity of the ROYAL DOCKS, where much remains to be done.

London Dungeon A horror museum situated in the vaults beneath LONDON BRIDGE STATION. It opened in 1975 on TOOLEY STREET. Unsurpris-

ingly, JACK THE RIPPER and the DEMON BARBER OF FLEET STREET loom large, while other attractions include experiencing the 'burning reality' of the GREAT FIRE OF LONDON and observing 'the seeping sores and vomiting victims' of the GREAT PLAGUE.

London effect A term used to describe a variety of phenomena, in which events or trends in the capital have an impact on other parts of the UK, especially the London 'brain drain' and the long-term outward ripple of rising salaries and property prices. In the mid-1980s New Labour politicians warned of a London effect whereby so-called 'loony left' council policies harmed the party's electoral appeal nationwide. Also, the way in which uniquely metropolitan circumstances can misleadingly skew statistical data for the entire country:

> Stripping London out would reduce the national annual rate to 7.2 per cent. 'The London effect is getting greater over time, reflecting the fact that the market there is out of kilter with the rest of England and Wales. The London 'effect' is now over 2 percentage points,' said Mr Williams.
>
> *Financial Times* (7 September 2007)

Londoner A native or inhabitant of London. The word is first recorded in the 15th century.

> Maybe it's because I'm a Londoner
> That I love London so.
> Maybe it's because I'm a Londoner
> That I think of her wherever I go.
> I get a funny feeling inside of me
> Just walking up and down.
> Maybe it's because I'm a Londoner
> That I love London Town.
>
> HUBERT GREGG: 'Maybe It's Because I'm a Londoner' (song) (1947)

London Eye A big wheel (also known as the Millennium Wheel) erected on the SOUTH BANK adjacent to COUNTY HALL in 2000 to celebrate the Millennium. Designed by David Marks and Julia Barfield, it is, at 442 feet (135m) high, Europe's tallest observation wheel. Its 32 glass capsules complete one revolution every half an hour, giving their occupants (a maximum of 25 apiece) an unparalleled array of often surprising London vistas. Itself visible across the rooftops from many parts of the capital, it has quickly become a London landmark, and its originally brief life has been extended until at least 2031. During London's New Year's Eve fireworks display the Eye is nowadays transformed into a gigantic Catherine-wheel, a telegenic gimmick that ensures its appearance in news bulletin clips around the world.

London Fields

1. An area of former grazing land, about 27 acres (11 hectares), so called because it lay on the London side of HACKNEY. In the 19th century it acquired a poor reputation on account of it being the resort of various members of the criminal classes. It has recently been undergoing GENTRIFICATION.

2. A bleakly comic novel (1989) by Martin Amis (b.1949), in which the author conducts a sweeping examination of metropolitan mores in the late 20th century. The story is set in and around LADBROKE GROVE and NOTTING HILL.

London Film Festival A showcase for new films from around the world, held every October at the BFI Southbank (*see* BRITISH FILM INSTITUTE) and other London venues. It was founded in 1957 by Dilys Powell and Derek Prouse.

London Films A film production company formed in the mid-1930s by Alexander Korda (1893–1956). Its headquarters were at Denham Studios in Buckinghamshire.

London fog A smoke-laden fog, or SMOG, of the sort that enveloped and asphyxiated London from the early 19th century until the Clean Air Acts of the mid-20th century. It killed thousands of people, and entered popular folklore. It insinuated itself into songs ('A foggy day in London Town / Had me low and had me down', Ira Gershwin (1937)); was adopted in America as the name of a Hollywood nightclub, a gin and pastis cocktail and an outerwear company; and Australians even used its name for a manual worker who does not do his share of the work (i.e. like a London fog, he 'will not lift'). Canned London fog was a CARNABY STREET gimmick of the 1960s. *See also the* GREAT SMOG.

London Gateway

1. A new port planned to be built at the site of the former Shell Haven oil refinery in Thurrock, ESSEX. The first ships are expected to arrive in 2011 but the port will not be completed for at least another decade thereafter.

2. A blander and less disconcerting name latterly applied to the former Scratchwood Service Area on the M1 motorway. The original name may have meant 'Devil's Wood' in early Modern English, reflecting a reputation of the place as being haunted or unlucky.

London Gazette The official organ of the British government and the appointed medium for all official announcements of pensions, promotions, bankruptcies, dissolutions of partnerships and similar events. It appeared first as the *Oxford Gazette* in 1665, when the court was at Oxford, and Henry Muddiman (1629–92) started it as a daily newsletter or newspaper. It was transferred to London in 1666 and is now published five times a week, in print and online.

London General Omnibus Company *See* GENERAL.

London gin A variety of spirit first distilled in London in the mid-18th century. The word 'gin' derives from *genever*, Old Dutch for juniper, the berry that is the drink's principal source of flavour. Historically, drinkers have recognized two main types of gin: the original Dutch (or Holland) gin and the drier London gin. In its revised spirit drink regulations, ratified in February 2008, the European Union adopted a three-tier classification pyramid: 'gin', 'distilled gin' and 'London gin'. Unlike its lesser relations (and among other restrictions), London gin may contain no colourings or artificial flavourings, and its natural flavour must be imparted before distillation, with only an almost imperceptible amount of sweetening permitted to be added afterwards. The directive does not assign geographical protection, so London gin may be produced anywhere, unlike the only other English variant, Plymouth gin. *See also* BEEFEATER GIN; GIN LANE; TIPPLING ACT.

> London gin is a type of distilled gin ... whose flavour is introduced exclusively through the re-distillation in traditional stills of ethyl alcohol in the presence of all the natural plant materials used ... The term London gin may be supplemented by the term 'dry'.
>
> *Regulation (EC) No 110/2008 of the European Parliament and of the Council of the European Union*

London Group A still-surviving society of artists founded in 1913 by an amalgamation of the CAMDEN TOWN GROUP with various small groups and individuals. The first president was Harold Gilman (1876–1919) and apart from other former Camden Town Group artists there were those who would subsequently be associated with Vorticism, including David Bomberg

(1890–1957), Sir Jacob Epstein (1880–1959), C.R.W. Nevinson (1889–1946) and Edward Wadsworth (1889–1949). The group's aim was to break away from academic tradition and to draw inspiration from French Post-impressionism. Today, it is essentially an umbrella collective of visual artists with a catholic range of styles and themes. (For the poets' set sometimes known as the London Group, *see the* GROUP.)

London Guildhall University A former university in the CITY of London and EAST LONDON, founded as a polytechnic in 1970. In 2002 it was combined with the University of North London to form LONDON METROPOLITAN UNIVERSITY.

London Hospital *See the* ROYAL LONDON HOSPITAL.

London Idol A nickname for the MUSIC HALL star Vesta Tilley (born Matilda Alice Powles, 1864, died Lady de Frece, 1952), who was especially noted as a male impersonator. She made her first London appearance in 1874, at the age of 10, and continued performing and touring until 1920. The 'London Idol' tag was used more by Miss Tilley's publicists to promote her appearances in other cities than by Londoners themselves; nevertheless, she was enormously popular in the capital.

> Until I saw Vesta Tilley I did not know that a stage walk could express so much, could give such perfect point to vapid words and common place melody ... I would walk miles on the darkest night to hear her sing 'Jolly good luck to the girl who loves a soldier.'
>
> *The Play Pictorial*, Volume 15, issue 91 (1910)

London Institute *See the* UNIVERSITY OF THE ARTS LONDON.

London Irish RFC A rugby union club, founded in 1898 by a group of London-based Irish exiles. The club played at Sunbury-on-Thames, SURREY (with a short period at BLACKHEATH in the late 1940s and 1950s) from 1931 until 2001, when its home games moved to the Madejski Stadium in Reading, Berkshire. Its headquarters remains in Sunbury.

Londonistan A nickname given to London from the end of the 20th century by foreign intelligence agencies, who see it as a refuge for Islamist radicals plotting terrorist activities around the world. Those using the nickname believe that Britain has been too tolerant in providing asylum to such people. The city has also

been dubbed Beirut-on-Thames. The name came to prominence in the British press following the London bombings of July 2005 (*see* 7/7).

> The measures against what the police here call 'preachers of hate' follow years of taunts by foreign intelligence services that British tolerance of radical clerics and terror suspects wanted in other places had turned London into 'Londonistan' or 'Beirut-on-Thames'.
>
> *International Herald Tribune* (21 July 2005)

London ivy A late 19th-century slang term applied to both 'dust' and (more often) to 'fog' – in each case because it tends to obscure what it 'grows on'. The expression is first recorded in Charles DICKENS's *Bleak House* (1852–3), in which the fogs of London are a pervasive presence.

> A very severe cold caught by nine hours' contact with London ivy.
>
> *Sporting Life* (4 January 1889)

London jury hangs half and saves half, a A very old saying implying that busy Londoners had no time to carefully weigh up the arguments in a trial but simply consigned every other defendant to the gallows. It was also said of ESSEX and MIDDLESEX juries. The city's historians have been at pains to deny this, stressing that London jurors have almost always inclined 'to the merciful side in saving life, when they can find any cause or colour for the same', as Thomas Fuller put it, in his *History of the Worthies of England* (1662).

London Labour and the London Poor A group of articles by journalist Henry Mayhew (1812–87), collected under this title in 1851. It became a classic work of Victorian reportage, and, together with the work of DICKENS, has shaped modern conceptions of the urban poor in the mid-19th century.

London Library A subscription library based in ST JAMES'S SQUARE, with a collection of around a million books, centred on the humanities. Its special collections include the Higginson Collection of hunting and field sports, the Montefiore Collection of material of Jewish interest, and the Heron Allen Collection of the *Rubáiyát of Omar Khayyám*. The London Library was founded by Thomas Carlyle (1795–1881) in 1841 and has had many distinguished writers among its members.

London lickpenny A lickpenny was 'something that licks up, or is a drain upon, one's money'.

New arrivals in London would formerly refer to the city thus. (Nowadays they express the same thought in a different way.) The term was first recorded in a ballad of that title, sometimes attributed to John Lydgate, and probably written early in the 15th century. It concerns a man who comes up to London from Kent and discovers that everything he could wish for is available, but at prices he cannot afford. In particular, he finds that the city's lawyers have set the price of justice beyond his reach. He returns to Kent, where he resumes the life of a ploughman.

London Magazine, The A name given to several periodicals published in London over the past 300 years, of which the most distinguished include one that appeared 1820–9, edited by John Scott (essentially a literary miscellany that featured the work of new young writers and poets such as William Wordsworth, John Keats, William Hazlitt and Thomas Carlyle) and one founded in 1954 by John Lehmann, which covers a broad spectrum of the arts. The title has also been appropriated by a property magazine, published by a consortium of estate agents since 1991 and thrust through the letterboxes of what it claims are '85,000 of the wealthiest households in London' every month.

London Marathon An annual MARATHON race for elite and amateur runners and wheelchair users, founded by Chris Brasher and John Disley and first held in 1981. Up to 2009 it was sponsored by the margerine brand Flora, but from 2010 it will be sponsored by Virgin. The race starts in BLACKHEATH for the masses and GREENWICH PARK for elite runners and other special categories of entrants, heads east through CHARLTON and WOOLWICH, turns west and passes the CUTTY SARK on its way to crossing the THAMES at TOWER BRIDGE. The course then loops round the EAST END and the ISLE OF DOGS before heading back west via the EMBANKMENT to PARLIAMENT SQUARE, BIRDCAGE WALK and to the final corner in front of BUCKINGHAM PALACE. The first marathon ended on CONSTITUTION HILL, and from 1982 to 1993 the finish was on WESTMINSTER BRIDGE, but since then it has been in the MALL. 46,500 amateur runners take part each year, selected by ballot from around twice that number of applicants. More than 10,000 usually drop out en route. A notable feature of the marathon is the large number of charity runners dressed in outlandish costumes.

London Mechanics' Institution *See* BIRKBECK COLLEGE.

London Mela *See* MELA.

London Merchant, The *See* BARNWELL, GEORGE.

London Metal Exchange A commodity market in London for trade in metals, incorporated in 1881. With the Commodity Exchange of New York, it is the world's most important for copper, nickel and zinc. It also trades in futures, and organizes the storage of metals. It was originally established in LOMBARD STREET, and is presently based in LEADENHALL STREET.

London Metropolitan Archives A research facility located in Northampton Road, CLERKENWELL, just south of EXMOUTH MARKET. It is based in the former home of the Temple Press, built in the late 1930s. Previously the Greater London Record Office, it adopted its present name in 1997. The LMA is the archive repository for the records of many London-wide bodies, including the CORPORATION OF LONDON and the former GREATER LONDON COUNCIL, LONDON COUNTY COUNCIL, MIDDLESEX County Council and their predecessors, and numerous religious, public and commercial institutions. The majority of items held can be freely viewed by the public.

London Metropolitan University A university formed in 2002 from a merger of LONDON GUILDHALL UNIVERSITY and the University of North London. With over 34,000 students London Met is the city's largest unitary university. Its main campus, on HOLLOWAY ROAD, gained an iconic landmark in 2004 with the opening of the graduate school, the capital's first building by the US architect Daniel Libeskind, supplementing Rick Mather's curved white block of 2000 and a brutalist concrete tower from its polytechnic era.

London Museum A former museum of London's history. Housed in KENSINGTON PALACE, it was founded in 1911 and in 1975 was merged with the GUILDHALL Museum and relocated to form the MUSEUM OF LONDON.

London Necropolis Company A private company that in 1854 opened the world's largest cemetery, in Brookwood, SURREY. The company built the London Necropolis station, adjacent to WATERLOO STATION, from where special trains carried both the deceased and their mourners to the cemetery. The rail service was withdrawn when the station was bombed in 1941 and did not resume after the war. The cemetery remains in existence; more than a quarter of a million interments have taken place here.

London Nobody Knows, The A documentary film (1967), directed by Norman Cohen and loosely based on a book of the same name (1962) written and illustrated by Geoffrey Fletcher. Narrated by James Mason, the film explores a variety of unfamiliar locations and offbeat institutions shortly before many of them vanished or were transformed beyond recognition.

> Carnaby chicks and chaps, the 1967 we have been led to remember, are shockingly juxtaposed with feral meths drinkers, filthy shoeless kids, squalid Victoriana. Camden Town still resembles the world of Walter Sickert. There is romance and adventure, but mostly there is malnourishment.
>
> BOB STANLEY, in *The Guardian* (21 November 2003)

London nose A facetious name, modelled on the LONDON EYE, for a protuberance on the inside wall of the northernmost main archway of ADMIRALTY ARCH. It is approximately the size, shape and colour of a Caucasian human nose. There is no record of when or why it was placed there. Some say it represents Napoleon's proboscis, others the Duke of Wellington's, although both these great men flourished a century before Admiralty Arch was built. Cavalrymen riding through the arch have traditionally touched the nose for luck (it is at a convenient height for someone on horseback), and newly qualified BLACK CAB drivers have recently begun to do the same, as a post-KNOWLEDGE ritual.

London Open House *See* OPEN HOUSE.

London Oratory *See* BROMPTON ORATORY.

London ordinary Mid-19th-century slang for BRIGHTON beach. An ordinary was formerly a restaurant where meals could be had at a fixed price; in Brighton the 'eight-hours-at-the-seaside' excursionists dined in the open air.

London over the Border An old name for the CANNING TOWN area. The River LEA used to form the boundary between London and ESSEX.

London Overground A grouping of pre-existing railway services under new management. The Railways Act (2005) gave Transport for London control of the NORTH LONDON LINE and other main-line services that operate wholly within the same area as the LONDON UNDERGROUND network. These include local trains between EUSTON

and Watford Junction and the West London line from WILLESDEN JUNCTION to CLAPHAM JUNCTION. The EAST LONDON LINE will be integrated within the London Overground network when it reopens in extended form. The long-term aim is to create a fully orbital railway but funding has yet to be secured to complete the circuit between Clapham Junction and SURREY QUAYS.

London Overture, A A concert overture (1936) by John Ireland (1879–1962). Mainly perky and ebullient in mood, it incorporates a theme suggested by a bus conductor's cry of 'Dilly! Piccadilly!'

London Palladium A theatre in Argyll Street, a turning to the south off OXFORD STREET, just east of OXFORD CIRCUS. It opened in 1910 (as simply 'the Palladium') as a MUSIC HALL. It staged revues in the 1920s, and after the Second World War it became known for its variety shows and pantomimes. The variety programme *Sunday Night at the London Palladium* (1955–67), originally compered by Tommy Trinder, was a key ingredient in the early success of ITV. The Palladium has often hosted the annual Royal Variety Performance.

> Bright coloured lights, Palladium nights
> And a world that was always gay
>
> HAROLD PURCELL and GEORGE POSFORD: 'The London I Love' (song) (1941)

London Parade *See the* NEW YEAR'S DAY PARADE.

London particular A colloquial term used in the 19th and early 20th centuries for a LONDON FOG. The sulphurous coal smoke of the period gave London SMOG a yellowish tinge, and it may be that the term was inherited from a variety of Madeira wine of similar colour, so called because it was imported 'particularly' for London merchants.

> 'This is a London particular'. I had never heard of such a thing. 'A fog, miss', said the young gentleman.
>
> DICKENS: *Bleak House* (1852–3)

London Pavilion A place of entertainment on the north side of PICCADILLY CIRCUS. It opened in 1885 as a theatre and later became a cinema. It is now part of the TROCADERO, a dining, entertainment and shopping centre.

London Philharmonic Orchestra A symphony orchestra founded in London in 1932 by

Sir Thomas Beecham (1879–1961). It is based at the ROYAL FESTIVAL HALL.

London Pianoforte School A group of composer-pianists working in London at the turn of the 19th century. They pioneered the Romantic style of keyboard playing, based on a legato touch, and began to develop a more complex harmonic language that ultimately replaced the Classical style. The group included Muzio Clementi, Jan Dussek and John Field.

London pigeon *See the* ROCK PIGEON.

London plane *Platanus* x *hispanica* or *hybrida* or *acerifolia*, the most characteristic tree of central London streets. It is regarded as being a hybrid of the Oriental plane and the American plane (also called the American sycamore) and may have evolved naturally from two of the parent trees standing close to each other in Spain (hence x *hispanica*). It has been widely grown in England since the late 17th century and particularly caught on in Victorian London because its flaking bark helps it shrug off pollution. In addition it can tolerate inferior and impacted soil, regular pruning and conditions of dampness or drought. London planes have been plentifully planted in many temperate cities, including New York, Buenos Aires, Paris, Melbourne and Shanghai.

> Green is the plane-tree in the square,
> The other trees are brown;
> They droop and pine for the country air;
> The plane-tree loves the town.
>
> AMY LEVY: 'A London Plane-Tree' (1889)

London pride A name applied to various flowering plants. In the 17th century it chiefly denoted the SWEET WILLIAM, whose flowers were reportedly very much sought out by Londoners for their beauty, but nowadays it is the little pink-and-white flowering plant *Saxifraga* x *urbium*. It may be an Irish-Pyrenean hybrid. The precise origin of the name is uncertain. Bishop Walsham How (1823–97) once wrote a poem addressed to the flower, rebuking it for possessing the sinful attribute. A lady called his attention to the fact that the name did not mean that the plant was proud, but that London was proud of it, whereupon the bishop wrote a second poem apologizing to it. The literal meaning of the name was exploited by Noël Coward in his patriotic song 'London Pride' (1941), designed to boost Londoners' morale during the dark days of the Second World War:

> London Pride has been handed down to us.
> London Pride is a flower that's free.
> London Pride means our own dear town to us,
> And our pride it for ever will be.

The term is now also the proprietary name of a bitter beer produced by the CHISWICK brewer Fuller's.

London Regiment A regiment formerly consisting of two regular battalions of the City of London Regiment (Royal Fusiliers) and a number of Territorial battalions, including the London Rifle Brigade, Kensingtons, Artists' Rifles and London Scottish. It is now a wholly Territorial regiment.

London Residuary Body *See the* GREATER LONDON COUNCIL.

London Review of Books A cultural periodical, founded in 1979 and published twice a month. It was inspired in its look and coverage by the *New York Review of Books*, within which its very early editions appeared. Unapologetically high-brow, its contents tend to be more spikily provocative than the otherwise comparable *Times Literary Supplement*; some anti-American views expressed in it after the 11 September (2001) terrorist incidents prompted a high-profile intellectual spat, which spilled out into the popular press. Bucking populist trends, the London Review Bookshop was established in BLOOMSBURY in 2003 to sell serious books and host events.

> There aren't many magazines that can boast that half their readers have a higher degree.
>
> *The Guardian* (3 December 2001)

London rocket *Sisymbrium irio*, a relative of the leafy salad ingredient, with very small yellow flowers. It got its name when, according to the contemporary naturalist John Ray, it sprang up in profusion in waste places in the wake of the GREAT FIRE OF LONDON in 1666. It is actually a native of the Mediterranean area, but it is an enthusiastic colonizer of patches of devastation anywhere: the ruins around ST PAUL's Cathedral were covered with it after the BLITZ.

London's Burning A soap opera (1988–2002) about the firefighters of Blue Watch B25, BLACKWALL. It had its origin in a one-off television play of the same name by Jack Rosenthal (1931–2004), broadcast in 1986. For most of its run, the series dwelt as much on the fighters' heroics in the many spectacular conflagrations as on their domestic problems. The title comes from the old round about the GREAT FIRE OF LONDON:

London's burning,
Look yonder,
Fire, fire,
And we have no water.

London School of Economics A constituent college of the UNIVERSITY OF LONDON, founded in 1895. As its full name, the London School of Economics and Political Science, suggests, it specializes in economics and politics, but it also covers the broad spectrum of the social sciences and some other disciplines. Its first chairman was the economist and socialist Sidney Webb (1859–1947). Many influential figures in the political and economic establishments of Britain and other countries have studied here. It formerly had a reputation for radicalism, and many of its undergraduates took leading roles in the student unrest of the late 1960s, but in the 1980s it embraced Thatcherism.

London Scottish FC A rugby union club originally founded in 1878 by a group of London-based Scots exiles. Based in Richmond, the club enjoyed a distinguished history in rugby union's amateur period up until 1995, contributing numerous players to the Scottish national side. London Scottish failed to survive as a professional club, however, and was disbanded in 1999 (when it was nominally merged with LONDON IRISH). A resuscitated amateur club has since worked its way up several divisions from the bottom of the league pyramid and assumed semi-professional status.

London season Formerly the period from May to July when debutantes were presented at court and aristocratic and fashionable society resided in London, attending charity balls, dinner parties and a range of public or semi-public occasions, such as opening nights at the ballet or opera at COVENT GARDEN, private viewing day at the SUMMER EXHIBITION and several sporting fixtures, notably Royal Ascot. The first fund-raising event to constitute a recognized part of the season (at least with hindsight) was QUEEN CHARLOTTE'S BALL in 1780. Over the course of the 19th and early 20th centuries a succession of new events joined the calendar, including the Eton–Harrow cricket match at LORD'S, Henley

Regatta, WIMBLEDON fortnight and the CHELSEA FLOWER SHOW. The season traditionally finished with 'Glorious Goodwood', a Sussex race meeting held at the end of July.

> August is the month when exhausted Londoners are supposed to be recuperating amid the quietness of moor, fell and sea. London by tradition is 'empty'. Every night for ten weeks the pattern has remained the same … a whirl of receptions, theatres and dances. The non-stop party has now broken up.
> LOUIS STANLEY: *The London Season* (1956)

The abolition in 1958 of the annual presentations at court brought an end to the London season as a formal institution, although publications like *Burke's Peerage* and *Tatler* and organizers of events such as the BERKELEY DRESS SHOW have endeavoured to perpetuate aspects of the tradition.

London shrinking A conditioning and stabilizing process applied to cloth, in which it is heavily dampened and then laid flat and allowed to dry while it takes up its natural size and shape. Despite the simplicity of the method, modern science has not been able to improve upon it.

London's larder A nickname for the wharves and warehouses that lay on the south side of the THAMES east of LONDON BRIDGE, from their emphasis on foodstuffs. *See also* HAY'S WHARF; SHAD THAMES.

London smoke A late 19th-century high-society slang term for a yellowish colour, like the polluted London SMOG.

London South Bank University A university founded in 1992, based on the former SOUTH BANK Polytechnic, which had begun in 1892 as the BOROUGH Polytechnic Institute. Its main campus is in Borough Road.

London stock brick The definitive London building material, light in weight, usually yellowish in colour and coarsely textured. The bricks were originally hand-made in London itself, using LONDON CLAY mixed with ground chalk, together with ash, cinders or sometimes other refuse (known as 'Spanish'), to facilitate firing. Machine-made London stock bricks later came via the THAMES from Kent and ESSEX, and after the middle of the 19th century from MIDDLESEX, Bedfordshire and Buckinghamshire too, especially from brickworks near the GRAND UNION CANAL. Billions of these bricks were used during the massive expansion of Victorian London, when they were preferred to conventional red bricks because they were believed to be longer-lasting. However, they had a tendency to discolour easily in the filthy London air of the time.

London Stock Exchange *See the* STOCK EXCHANGE.

London Stone A block of oolitic limestone set into the wall of No.111 CANNON STREET. It is an ancient relic of uncertain history. The present stone is merely a chunk (perhaps the uppermost part) of the original, which was described as a 'pillar', set deep into the ground. There is no record of how or when it came to be fragmented or what happened to the rest of it, but the diminution must have happened several centuries ago; a woodcut of *c*.1700 shows a stone of the same size as it is today. London Stone has been the subject of various legends, including that BRUTUS brought it here, that it marked the site of Druidic sacrifices, and that London's prosperity depended on its safekeeping. The antiquary William Camden thought it to be the point from which the Romans measured distances; another theory is that it was an Anglo-Saxon ceremonial stone or a focus for judicial proceedings. Edward III made it the axis of the CITY's trade in 1328, when he granted Londoners the right to hold markets within a 7-mile (11-km) radius of London Stone, as it had by then come to be known. According to *Holinshed's Chronicles* (1577), the 15th-century rebel Jack CADE struck it with his sword when proclaiming himself master of the city, and the incident is mentioned in SHAKESPEARE's *Henry VI, Part 2*, IV, vi (early 1590s). The stone was placed against the wall of St Swithin's Church in 1798 as a safeguard against its destruction. When a bomb destroyed the church in 1940 the CORPORATION OF LONDON moved the stone to the GUILDHALL. In 1960 it was relocated to its present position, on the site of St Swithin's. It may be moved again, temporarily or permanently, if the building at 111 Cannon Street is demolished and replaced, as has been proposed.

The visionary artist and poet William Blake (1757–1827) regarded London Stone as the hidden centre of London and of the world, the modern equivalent of the Omphalos at Delphi, and he alluded to it repeatedly in *Jerusalem: The Emanation of the Giant Albion* (*c*.1821). Blake seemed

to believe that it should be the foundation stone upon which a new and divine city must be built.

London Suite An orchestral composition (1932) by Eric Coates (1886–1957), portraying three areas of the capital in a 'tarantelle' for COVENT GARDEN, a 'meditation' for WESTMINSTER and a 'march' for KNIGHTSBRIDGE. Its success prompted him to compose a *London Again Suite* (1935), consisting of a 'march' for OXFORD STREET, an 'elegy' for Langham Place (the home of All Souls Church, at the northern end of REGENT STREET) and a 'valse' for MAYFAIR.

London Symphonies The collective name for twelve compositions by Joseph Haydn, written between 1791 and 1795, when he was living in the city. He wrote them at the instigation of the London impresario Salomon, who commissioned them for his HANOVER SQUARE concerts (they are occasionally also called the 'Salomon symphonies'). They include many of Haydn's best-known symphonies, including the 'Surprise', the 'Military', the 'Clock' and the 'Drum Roll'. The last of the series, No.104 in D major, is often known simply as the 'London Symphony', which the musicologist Michael Steinberg calls 'one of the most pointless of musical nicknames' – given that the name might equally well apply to the other eleven. Haydn also wrote a string quartet in D minor (Opus 76, No.2) that is sometimes called the 'Bell' because its first four notes match the WESTMINSTER CHIMES.

London Symphony, A A symphony by Ralph Vaughan Williams, his second. It was completed in 1913, but Vaughan Williams subsequently made substantial revisions to it, and the standard version played today dates from the 1930s. The original version was not recorded until 2000. Although not programmatic (the composer himself preferred to refer to it as a 'Symphony by a Londoner'), it does incorporate some London sounds, such as the WESTMINSTER CHIMES and shipping on the THAMES.

London Symphony Orchestra A classical concert orchestra founded in London in 1904 by breakaway members of Henry Wood's Queen's Hall Orchestra. It is the oldest surviving orchestra in London. Elgar conducted it in many of his recordings of his own music. It is now based at the BARBICAN CENTRE and LOUSY ST LUKE'S.

London taxi Allegedly, COCKNEY RHYMING SLANG for 'jacksie' (or 'jacksy'), which in turn is slang for anus or buttocks, but the term is almost never heard. It is also, of course, an alternative description of a BLACK CAB.

London Terminal Aerodrome The earliest civil airport in the country, situated on HOUNS-LOW HEATH. The first commercial flight was from Bristol to Hounslow and the inaugural scheduled air service was from Hounslow to Paris. On 12 November 1919, the first flight to Australia left Hounslow, arriving 28 days later. Commercial aviation moved to CROYDON in 1920 and the airport closed. Its buildings were destroyed by fire in 1929 but a plaque in Staines Road marks the site.

London to a brick An expression of Australian origin, dating from the 1960s and meaning 'an absolute certainty'. The reference is to the speaker's willingness to wager the former on some predicted outcome against something of very little value. A 'brick' was a £10 note in pre-decimalization Australian slang.

London Transport The semi-official name for the body responsible for London's public transport system from 1933. The formal name – originally the London Passenger Transport Board – and the remit and structure of the organization changed several times during the remainder of the 20th century. Transport for London is the present successor to the mantle and has persuaded most Londoners to call it TfL rather than London Transport.

London Transport Suite See VICTORLOO.

London Underground A network of interconnecting rail lines and their frequent services, running both below and above ground and covering much of the GREATER LONDON area (especially north of the THAMES) and a little beyond. The inaugural section of CUT AND COVER line opened on 10 January 1863 between PADDINGTON (Bishop's Road) and FARRINGDON Street. The world's first deep-level railway (see the TUBE) opened in 1880, connecting STOCKWELL and the CITY. By the end of the 19th century seven of the eleven present-day lines were in full or partial existence. From 1902 all but one of the private companies that had built this original network embarked on a series of mergers that created the Underground Electric Railway Company of London, known as the Underground Group. Together with the still independent Metropolitan Railway, the Underground Group become part of the London Passenger Transport Board in 1933. The subsidiary organization, London Under-

ground Limited, was not formally established until 1985.

The London Underground lines are:

BAKERLOO
CENTRAL
CIRCLE
DISTRICT
HAMMERSMITH AND CITY
JUBILEE
METROPOLITAN
NORTHERN
PICCADILLY
VICTORIA
Waterloo and City (see the DRAIN)

A twelfth London Underground line, the EAST LONDON LINE, closed for upgrading and extension in 2007 and will form part of the LONDON OVERGROUND when it reopens.

London Underground map An icon of British design, created in the early 1930s by Harry Beck (1903–74). He was not the first draughtsman to render the underground network in diagrammatic form but his map introduced a new level of schematic rigidity, based on electrical circuit layouts. The emphasis was primarily on the connections between lines rather than on the geographical reality of the system. Routes were drawn only horizontally, vertically or at 45 degrees, and wherever possible the distances between stations were equalized. Beck had some difficulty in persuading his employers of the map's merits and then, once they had been convinced, in retaining control over his creation. However, almost all the key elements of his original design have been retained (or reinstated) in the present-day map, which is now acknowledged as a design classic and recognized the world over. The concept has been copied by many other transit systems and endlessly parodied, most famously in Simon Patterson's artwork *The Great Bear* (1992).

London University See the UNIVERSITY OF LONDON.

London Wall A street in the CITY of London that approximately follows the alignment of part of the former Roman wall that encircled the SQUARE MILE. The wall was built of alternate layers of broad, flat bricks and Kentish ragstone *c*.AD 200. It originally began near the present-day TOWER OF LONDON, running north via ALDGATE, BISHOPSGATE and HOUNDSDITCH, west to AL-

DERSGATE and then back down to the THAMES at BLACKFRIARS via LUDGATE. Shortly before they abandoned the city the Romans completed the circuit by adding another wall along the shore of the Thames. Even after the wall's obsolescence as a defensive structure it was retained and reinforced by medieval Londoners as a useful commercial barrier. The riverside wall fell victim to erosion, while most of the inland wall was dismantled piecemeal in the 17th and 18th centuries, together with its seven gates. The most vigorous period of demolition came in the early 1760s. Significant fragments survive at TOWER HILL and near the western end of the street called London Wall, which extends from Broad Street to Aldersgate Street, crossing MOORGATE. *See also the* SEVEN GATES OF THE CITY.

London Wasps *See* WASPS.

London Weekend Television An independent television company (abbreviation LWT, latterly its official name), which in 1967 won the ITV franchise for broadcasting to the London area at weekends. It first went on the air on 2 August 1968. Among its notable successes were the period drama series UPSTAIRS, DOWNSTAIRS, the arts magazine *The South Bank Show* and the firefighting soap opera LONDON'S BURNING. In 2002 it was swallowed up by ITV and subsequently lost its separate identity.

London weighting Additional pay attached to a job based in or near London to compensate for the higher cost of living.

London Welsh RFC A rugby union club founded in 1885 by a group of London-based Welsh exiles. London Welsh (or Clwb Rygbi Cymry Llundain) play their home games at the Old Deer Park, RICHMOND UPON THAMES.

London Wetland Centre A Wildfowl & Wetlands Trust nature reserve occupying the site of BARN ELMS reservoirs, which became redundant after the inauguration of the Thames Water Ring Main in the mid-1990s. Partially funded by the building of luxury housing nearby, the £16-million project covers 104 acres (42 hectares) of the CASTELNAU peninsula. The western side of the reserve is devoted to reconstructions of 14 wetland habitats, including Siberian tundra, tropical swamps and an Australian billabong. Walkways and hides help visitors get close to the waterfowl without disturbing them.

London Zoo A zoo in the northern part of REGENT'S PARK. It was established in 1828 under the aegis of the Zoological Society of London. Among its most famous and crowd-pulling animals have been Tommy the chimpanzee (1830s), JUMBO the elephant (1870s), the polar-bear cub Brumus (1950s) and the giant panda CHI CHI (1960s). Its architecture is almost as varied as its animal collection, ranging from the 'Raven's Cage' (1829), through the Mappin Terraces (1913), an artificial mountain-range for goats, bears, etc. (now disused), Lubetkin's futuristic penguin pool (1936) and the Snowdon Aviary (1963–4) to the Blackburn Pavilion (2008), a tropical birdhouse. A new children's zoo opened in 2009. Particular emphasis is nowadays placed on conservation and on the relationship between people and wildlife, and cages and bars have been removed where possible to create more natural forms of enclosure. Around one million people visit London Zoo every year.

> You can learn a great deal about the character of a country by going to its zoo and studying its arrangement and the behaviour of the animals. The London zoo is an animal microcosm of London, and even the lions, as a rule, behave as if they had been born in South Kensington.
> LEONARD WOOLF: *Downhill all the Way* (1967)

as sure as the devil is in London *See under* AS.

Battle of London *See under* BATTLE.

City of London *See under* CITY.

Corporation of London *See under* CORPORATION.

don't turn that side to London *See under* DO.

Great Fire of London *See under* GREAT.

like London buses *See under* LIKE.

lord mayor of London *See under* LORD.

mayor of London *See under* MAYOR.

Mother London *See under* MOTHER.

multicultural London English *See* JAFAIKAN.

Museum of London *See under* MUSEUM.

Nine Worthies of London *See under* NINE.

No.1 London *See under* NUMBER.

Pool of London *See under* POOL.

Seven Curses of London, The *See under* SEVEN.

seven sights of London *See under* SEVEN.

Streets of London *See under* STREET.

Tower of London *See under* TOWER.

Treaty of London *See under* TREATY.

Londrix An old slang term for London, probably from the French, *Londres*.

loneliest village in London A long out-dated nickname for NEASDEN. In the 1820s the village consisted of six cottages, four larger houses or farms, a public house and a smithy, grouped around the green. It may not have been quite the most isolated settlement in the London area but it certainly remained the most rural part of WILLESDEN until the arrival of the railway in 1880, by which time its housing stock had risen to around 50 and the Spotted Dog inn was attracting London day-trippers. Neasden was wholly transformed after the arrival of the NORTH CIRCULAR ROAD in 1923.

long

Long Acre The central thoroughfare of COVENT GARDEN, extending from CHARING CROSS ROAD to DRURY LANE. The narrow strip of pasture from which it takes its name was recorded as 'The Long Acurs, the baksyde of Charing Cross' in 1556. The street was formerly known as the Elms.

Long Good Friday, The A highly regarded film (1980), written by Barrie Keeffe and directed by John Mackenzie, about a London gangster boss who embarks on a mission to find out who is murdering his henchmen. Starring Bob Hoskins as crime boss Harold and Helen Mirren as his wife, Victoria, the film follows what happens in the course of a Good Friday in the early 1980s after Harold is given just 24 hours by his Mafia contacts to solve the mystery or risk a major deal with them falling through.

> For more than ten years there's been peace – everyone to his own patch. We've all had it sweet. I've done every single one of you favours in the past – I've put money in all your pockets. I've treated you well, even when you was out of order, right? Well now there's been an *eruption*.
>
> *The Long Good Friday*

long, lazy, lousy Lewisham After work began on building the first St Mary's Church at the end of the 15th century the village of LEWISHAM progressively stretched out in an elm-lined ribbon along what is now the High Street. Thus its length was undeniable, but the accusation of laziness and lousiness seems to have been added solely for the sake of alliteration. The extent and prettiness of the settlement was said (with some

credibility) to have so impressed James I that he declared: 'On my soul, I will be king of Lusen.'

Long Meg of Westminster A noted virago in the reign of Henry VIII, around whose exploits a comedy (since lost) was performed in London in 1594.

> Lord Proudly: What d'ye this afternoon?
> Lord Feesimple: Faith, I have a great mind to see Long Meg and The Ship at the Fortune.
>
> NATHAN FIELD: *Amends for Ladies*, II, i (1610)

Her name has been given to several articles of unusual size. Thus, the large blue-black marble in the south cloister of WESTMINSTER ABBEY, over the grave of Gervasius de Blois, is called 'Long Meg of Westminster'. Thomas Fuller says the term is applied to things 'of hop-pole height, wanting breadth proportionable thereunto', and refers to a great gun in the TOWER OF LONDON, so called, taken to Westminster in troublesome times. The *Edinburgh Antiquarian Magazine* (September 1769) tells of Peter Branan, aged 104, who was six foot six (1.9m) high and commonly called Long Meg of Westminster.

Long-town An old Irish nickname for London.

Long Walk to Finchley, The A BBC4 docu-drama (2008) portraying the early political career of Margaret Thatcher and her selection in 1958 as the Conservative party candidate for the FINCHLEY constituency. Thatcher won the seat in the following year's general election and subsequently represented Finchley throughout her time in the House of Commons. The title par-odied that of Nelson Mandela's autobiography, *Long Walk to Freedom* (1994).

Long Water *See* HAMPTON COURT PARK; *the* SERPENTINE.

Longford A village located at the north-western corner of HEATHROW AIRPORT, 1 mile (1.6 km) south-west of HARMONDSWORTH. The name comes from an oblique crossing over the River Colne. Longford grew up as a halt on the Bath Road and the White Horse inn was in existence by the 17th century; it survives today, together with a handful of houses and cottages from that period. The opening of the Colnbrook bypass in 1929 and subsequent traffic exclusion measures and conservation area status have helped preserve Longford's remarkably villagey character, despite some intrusions from the late 20th century.

Longford River An artificial watercourse that

Charles I had constructed to feed the lakes at HAMPTON COURT and BUSHY PARK. The course of the river was changed in the 1940s as a result of the creation of London (now Heathrow) Airport and has been changed again with the construction of the new fifth terminal (*see* T5).

Lonrho A multinational company run for many years by Tiny Rowland (born Roland Fuhrhop; 1917–98), who initiated a controversial diversification programme that included owning *The Observer* newspaper from 1981 to 1993, and attempting to acquire HARRODS. The name of the company derived from the London and Rhodesian Mining and Land Company, with which Rowland merged his own business interests in 1961. The company renamed itself Lonmin in 1999 and now focuses on platinum mining in South Africa.

lord

Lord love a duck! An expression of surprise, probably of COCKNEY origin. It may have begun as a jokey variation on 'Lord love us!'

> 'Well, Lord love a duck!' replied the butler, who in his moments of relaxation was addicted to homely expletives of the lower London type.
>
> P.G. WODEHOUSE: *The Coming of Bill* (1920)

Lord Love-a-Duck of Limehouse The title that Clement Attlee (1883–1967), Labour prime minister (1945–51), said he would take should he ever be elevated to the peerage. When Attlee resigned as Labour Party leader in 1955 he actually became 1st Earl Attlee of WALTHAMSTOW, Viscount Prestwood.

lord mayor of London The head of the CORPORATION OF LONDON, nowadays formally called the lord mayor of the City of London to avoid confusion with the MAYOR OF LONDON. The first known holder of the office was Henry Fitzailwyn, who was mayor from 1192 until his death in 1212 (the title 'lord mayor' was not formalized until the mid-16th century); the best known was undoubtedly Richard (Dick) WHITTINGTON, mayor four times at the turn of the 15th century. The lord mayor is elected on Michaelmas Day (or the next weekday) by the Court of Aldermen and must be a serving ALDERMAN who has previously held the office of sheriff. He or she (there has so far been only one 'she') nowadays holds the post for one year without possibility of re-election, and resides in the MANSION HOUSE.

The position is unpaid and non-party-political. The lord mayor's principal role today is as an ambassador for the financial and professional services of the city and of the UK as a whole. Among several other duties, the mayor serves as chief magistrate of the City, admiral of the PORT OF LONDON, chancellor of CITY UNIVERSITY and a trustee of ST PAUL'S Cathedral.

Lord Mayor's Banquet An annual dinner held at the GUILDHALL soon after the inauguration of the new lord mayor, in honour of the immediate past lord mayor. Traditionally, the prime minister attends and makes a major speech on world affairs.

Lord Mayor's Day The day on which the lord mayor of the City of London takes office. Originally the mayor was elected on the Feast of St Simon and St Jude (28 October), and although the election day was altered, admittance to office continued to take place on that day until 1751. From 1752, following the adoption of the Gregorian calendar, Lord Mayor's Day became 9 November. Since 1959 the lord mayor has been sworn in at the GUILDHALL on the second Friday in November, being presented to the lord chief justice on the following Saturday. The change was made to avoid traffic congestion. *See also the* SILENT CEREMONY.

Lord Mayor's Show The annual procession that accompanies the lord mayor through the CITY of London to the ROYAL COURTS OF JUSTICE on the second Saturday in November. It has developed in scale over the years, and from 1453 until 1856 a river pageant was part of the proceedings. The bill for the procession and the LORD MAYOR'S BANQUET is met by the lord mayor and the sheriffs. *See also* AFTER THE LORD MAYOR'S SHOW.

lord of the manor of Tyburn An old nickname for the common hangman.

Lord's The headquarters of the MARYLEBONE CRICKET CLUB (MCC), the MIDDLESEX COUNTY CRICKET CLUB and the England and Wales Cricket Board, in ST JOHN'S WOOD. The ground was opened by Thomas Lord (1757–1832) who was groundsman at the White Conduit Club, ISLINGTON, in 1780. In 1797 he started a cricket ground of his own on the site of what is now Dorset Square, MARYLEBONE, where he founded the MCC. In 1811 he moved the turf to a new site near the REGENT'S CANAL, and in 1814 he transferred to the present ground, the site of a former duck pond. The success of the venture prompted him to build a pavilion and a tavern. Lord retired in 1825, leaving behind a club that had become the country's leading cricket team and the game's recognized governing body. From 1838 lawn tennis was also played at Lord's and a sub-committee of the Marylebone club later formulated that game's first laws. In 1878 the MCC invited Middlesex County Cricket Club to make Lord's its home. The ground was extended with the acquisition of Henderson's nursery – hence the 'nursery end'. An underground station was built at Lord's in 1868 (originally named St John's Wood Road), but closed with the opening of the present St John's Wood station in 1939. As well as the home games of the Marylebone and Middlesex clubs, the venue also hosts international matches and the Eton v. HARROW and Oxford v. Cambridge fixtures. At the 2012 OLYMPIC GAMES, the archery competition is planned to be held at Lord's.

I doubt if there be any scene in the world more animating or delightful than a cricket-match – I do not mean a set match at Lord's ground for money, hard money, between a certain number of gentlemen and players, as they are called.

MISS MITFORD: *Our Village*, 'A Country Cricket-Match' (1832)

Lord's Taverners An association of cricket-lovers founded in 1950 by Martin Boddey. It stages matches and other events to raise funds for charity. There is a large 'stage-and-screen' element in its membership and its patron is the Duke of Edinburgh. Its name commemorates the Tavern at LORD'S cricket ground, a hostelry to the right of the pavilion which was demolished in the early 1960s (the Tavern Stand now occupies its site).

Lothbury A short CITY of London street running along the north side of the BANK OF ENGLAND. First recorded c.1190 as Lodebure, it takes its name from the manor of a man called Hlotha. Lothbury was also an old name for the city ward extending to the street's north-west, now called Broad Street.

lousy St Luke's An old nickname for ST LUKE'S Church, OLD STREET. It derived from the widespread (and not yet entirely eradicated) misconception that the golden dragon sitting atop its weather vane is really a plague flea. The church was completed in 1733 and is attributed

to Nicholas Hawksmoor and John James. Problems caused by settlement led to the church's closure in 1959, and the removal of its roof. It lay derelict until 2003, when an education centre and rehearsal hall for the LONDON SYMPHONY ORCHESTRA were built in its shell. The grade I listed exterior has been faithfully restored and a new extension added.

lovely

lovely jubbly! Good! Excellent! From the 1990s a general term of approval, popularized by the character 'DEL BOY' in the television sitcom ONLY FOOLS AND HORSES (set in PECKHAM), and subsequently given an extended life by the MOCKNEY chef Jamie Oliver. The phrase is more narrowly used as a slang term for money or wealth, and has its roots in an advertising slogan of the 1950s for an orange drink called 'Jubbly' (possibly a blend of 'juice' and 'bubbly', although the drink was not carbonated). The second word is not thus simply a meaningless rhyme on the first.

Lovely Rita A jolly song that appears on the Beatles album *Sgt. Pepper's Lonely Hearts Club Band* (1967), credited to John Lennon and Paul McCartney. The Rita (meter maid) of the title is based on a real-life encounter McCartney had with a traffic warden called Meta Davis outside ABBEY ROAD STUDIOS.

loving cup At the LORD MAYOR OF LONDON's or City LIVERY COMPANIES' banquets the loving cup is a silver bowl with two handles, a napkin being tied to one of them. Two people stand up, one to drink and the other to defend the drinker. Having taken his draught, the first wipes the cup with the napkin and passes it to his 'defender', when the next person rises up to defend the new drinker and so on.

lower

Lower Alsatia A term that was occasionally used to identify the LIBERTY OF THE MINT in SOUTHWARK, as opposed to the better-known ALSATIA of WHITEFRIARS.

Lower Tooting *See* TOOTING GRAVENEY.

loyal

Loyal Antediluvian Order of Buffaloes *See the* ROYAL ANTEDILUVIAN ORDER OF BUFFALOES.

loyal heart may be landed at Traitor's Gate, a A proverbial saying first quoted (as 'a loyal heart may be landed under Traytor's Bridge') in

Thomas Fuller's *History of the Worthies of England* (1662).

LSE An acronym for both the LONDON SCHOOL OF ECONOMICS (*see under* LONDON) and the London STOCK EXCHANGE.

L-Shaped Room, The A film (1962) directed by Bryan Forbes, based on the novel (1960) by Lynne Reid Banks. It stars Leslie Caron as a pregnant, unmarried French woman who comes to London to take stock of her life. The eponymous room is her home in a seedy WESTBOURNE PARK boarding house populated by social outsiders.

Lucan, Lord Richard John Bingham, 7th Earl of Lucan (b.1934), nicknamed 'Lucky' for his success at the gaming table, who in 1974 allegedly murdered the family nanny, Sandra Rivett, following an unsuccessful attack on his estranged wife. He then disappeared and was fruitlessly sought for many years. In 1999 his family was granted probate by the High Court and he was officially declared dead in a document stating: 'Be it known that the Right Honourable Richard John Bingham, Seventh Earl of Lucan, of 72a Elizabeth Street, London SW1, died on or since the 8th day of November 1974.'

Lucifer match or **Lucifer** A match. The friction match was invented by John Walker (*c.*1781–1859) in 1826 and at first called a 'friction light'. The invention was copied by Samuel Jones of the STRAND and sold as the 'Lucifer' (*c.*1829). The term 'match' was taken over from the name given to the spill used as secondary tinder in the days when the tinderbox was used for this purpose. *See also* CONGREVES.

Lucius A mythical British king of the second century, mentioned in Geoffrey of Monmouth's notoriously unreliable *Historia Regum Britanniae* (*History of the Kings of Britain*, *c.*1136). Lucius legendarily founded St Peter upon CORNHILL, as the first Christian church in London. It is said to have remained the metropolitan church of the kingdom until the coming of St Augustine, 400 years later.

Lud, **Ludd** or **Llud** A mythical king of Britain. According to Geoffrey of Monmouth, he was the beautifier of London, who in 66 BC built the gate that was later named in his honour. On his death

he was buried nearby. It is also suggested that the name Lud is that of a Celtic river-god.

Ludgate One of the former western gates of the CITY of London, built by the Romans *c.*AD 200 but not documented by name until the 12th century. Notwithstanding the legend of King Lud, the name probably derives from Old English *ludgeat*, 'postern', 'back gate'. Ludgate stood halfway up LUDGATE HILL, was rebuilt after extensive damage in 1586 and demolished in the early 1760s. From the time of Richard II there was a prison above the gateway, for debtors and petty criminals. The statues of LUD and his two sons that once adorned the gate are now in the porch of St Dunstan-in-the-West, a church on FLEET STREET.

Ludgate Circus The uninspiring junction of LUDGATE HILL, New Bridge Street, FLEET STREET and Farringdon Street. It was laid out in 1864. Ludgate Circus would have had a station on the FLEET LINE, had it been built as planned.

Ludgate Hill The hill upon which ST PAUL'S Cathedral stands, and also the name of the street leading up to the cathedral from LUDGATE CIRCUS. In the 18th and 19th centuries the London Coffee House, on the north side of Ludgate Hill, provided secure overnight accommodation for OLD BAILEY juries that had been unable to reach a verdict. In 1865 a railway viaduct was thrown across the street, providing access to the now vanished Ludgate Hill station and ruining the striking view of St Paul's from FLEET STREET. The viaduct was demolished in 1990, when the line was taken underground and City Thameslink station opened (originally as St Paul's Thameslink).

Ludgate West A new commercial development by British Land on the east side of Farringdon Street, near Ludgate Circus. For the site's history, *see the* FLEET PRISON *and* CONGREGATIONAL MEMORIAL HALL.

Lulu The central character in a duet of plays, *The Earth Spirit*, originally *Erdgeist* (1895), and *Pandora's Box*, originally *Die Büchse der Pandora* (1903), by the German playwright Frank Wedekind (1864–1918). The plays are about the sexual career of Lulu, a dancer, and although her uninhibited enjoyment of sex is essentially innocent, her character has gone down as a symbol of feminine guile and eroticism, whose licentiousness proves fatal to the men who fall for her. At the close of the second play she is reduced to working as a prostitute in London and meets her end at the hands of JACK THE RIPPER.

Lundenwic *See* ALDWYCH.

lush *See* ALDERMAN LUSHINGTON IS CONCERNED; *the* CITY OF LUSHINGTON.

    lush at Freeman's Quay, to A variation on DRINK AT FREEMAN'S QUAY.

Lutine bell A ship's bell rung at LLOYD'S before certain important announcements. The bell was carried originally on board the French frigate *La Lutine*, which surrendered to the British in 1793. Six years later, as HMS *Lutine*, carrying a cargo of gold and silver bullion, it sank off the Dutch coast. The cargo, valued then at around £1 million, was insured by Lloyd's underwriters who paid the claim in full. The bell, which for unknown reasons bears the inscription 'St Jean 1779', was salvaged in 1858 and hung in Lloyd's underwriting room in the ROYAL EXCHANGE from the 1890s to 1928, and thereafter in the underwriting room of successive incarnations of the LLOYD'S BUILDING. Traditionally the Lutine bell was struck once for bad news, usually that a ship had sunk, and twice for good news, such as the announcement that a missing vessel had been found safe. During the Second World War it was also sounded as an air-raid warning. Its use is nowadays restricted to ceremonial occasions, with rare exceptions such as the terrorist attacks of 11 September 2001.

Lyons' Corner Houses Cavernous WEST END eating houses that were operated by the HAMMERSMITH-based food processor, J. Lyons & Co. The company began its catering operations with a teashop on PICCADILLY in 1894, expanding to a chain of around 250 branches nationally, including seven along the length of OXFORD STREET. The first Corner House opened in 1909, at the corner of Rupert Street and Coventry Street, followed by two others, in the STRAND and TOTTENHAM COURT ROAD, and the very similar Maison Lyons Corner Houses at MARBLE ARCH and in SHAFTESBURY AVENUE. Each Corner House filled four or five floors, had numerous differently themed restaurants and employed several hundred staff, including permanent orchestras and most famously the 'Nippies', as Lyons' waitresses were called after 1926. The last Corner House closed in 1977. *See also* RAINBOW CORNER.

> Goldberg: Webber, you're a fake. When did you last wash up a cup?
> Stanley: The Christmas before last.
> Goldberg: Where?
> Stanley: Lyons Corner House.
> Goldberg: Which one?
> Stanley: Marble Arch.
> HAROLD PINTER: *The Birthday Party*, II (1958)

Lyon's Inn A former INN OF CHANCERY (and before that a conventional inn) that was attached to the INNER TEMPLE. The inn stood near present-day ALDWYCH and was demolished in 1863.

Macaroni A dandy who affected foreign manners and style. The word is derived from the Macaroni CLUB, instituted in London about 1760 by a set of flashy men who had travelled in Italy and who introduced at ALMACK'S subscription table the new-fangled Italian food, macaroni. The Macaronis were exquisite fops, vicious, insolent, fond of gambling, drinking and duelling, and they became the curse of VAUXHALL GARDENS. *See also* MOHOCKS.

Macaroni parson The Rev Dr William Dodd (1729–77) was so nicknamed from his expensive habits, which resulted in a well-known forgery. He graduated in mathematics at Cambridge in 1750 and was soon ordained, becoming chaplain of the recently opened Magdalen Hospital for Penitent Prostitutes, in ST GEORGE'S FIELDS, SOUTHWARK, where his sermons soon attracted a fashionable following. He was editor of *The Christian Magazine* (1760–7) and published numerous books during his lifetime. He became a royal chaplain in 1763, but his attempt to secure the rich living of St George's HANOVER SQUARE by improperly offering money through the lord chancellor's wife cost him his chaplaincy. He held various other preferments during his career but became deeply in debt and signed a cheque for £4,200 in the name of his former pupil, the 5th Lord Chesterfield. When the forgery was discovered he repaid much of the money but was confined in NEWGATE PRISON and sentenced to death. He received support from Dr JOHNSON and many others, but George III refused clemency to his one-time chaplain, who was hanged in July 1777.

Mackworth's Inn *See* BARNARD'S INN.

Madam Cyn The self-styled nickname of Cynthia Payne (b.1932), a STREATHAM brothel-keeper who was revealed in the 1970s as selling £25 luncheon vouchers to her clients by way of an entitlement to food, drink, a striptease and a spell upstairs with a girl of their choice. In 1987 she was cleared by an OLD BAILEY jury of technically running a brothel in the so-called 'sex on the stairs' case. Julie Walters played her in the biopic *Personal Services* (1986) as did Emily Lloyd in a more fictionalized prequel, *Wish You Were Here* (1987).

Madame Tussauds An exhibition of wax models of prominent as well as notorious people established in London by Marie Tussaud (née Grosholtz) in 1802. She was born in Strasbourg in 1761 and was taught the art of modelling in wax in Paris and in due course gave lessons to Louis XVI's sister, Madame Élisabeth. After a short imprisonment during the French Revolution she came to London where she died in 1850. The museum relocated from the BAKER STREET BAZAAR to its present site on MARYLEBONE ROAD in 1884 and is now the capital's most popular paid-for visitor attraction after the LONDON EYE (which is owned by the same parent company). The Chamber of Horrors is filled with figures of notorious murderers and instruments of torture and punishment, including the guillotine blade that beheaded Marie-Antoinette in 1793. A newer attraction, called the Spirit of London, takes the form of a time-travel taxi ride through 400 years of the capital's history, while the Stardome offers a film 'experience' projected inside the former London Planetarium.

Mad Tom of Bedlam *See* TOM O' BEDLAM.

Magic Circle A British society of magicians founded in 1905 at Pinoli's, a restaurant in WARDOUR STREET, with the first official meeting held at the Green Man, a pub in BERWICK STREET. The famous David Devant (real name David Wighton; 1868–1941) and Nevil Maskelyne (1839–1917) were the society's earliest presidents and Maskelyne edited the first edition of its journal, *The Magic Circular*, in June 1906. Members meet once a week at the society's headquarters in Stephenson Way, EUSTON, where there are libraries, a small theatre and a museum of historic conjuring apparatus. The highest distinction is to be a member of the Inner Magic Circle. The motto of the Circle is *indocilis privata loqui*, 'not apt to disclose secrets', and its symbol the circular sign of the zodiac, which appears on the floor of the club room. The name ultimately puns on the magic circle invented by Benjamin Franklin in 1749 as an arrangement of numbers in radially divided concentric circles with arithmetical properties similar to those of a magic square.

Magnificent Seven A collective name for the seven superior cemeteries established by private developers in a ring around central London in the ten years from 1832. They were created in response to the rapid growth of London's population at that time, and the insanitary overcrowding in its churchyards and burial grounds. The term seems to have been coined by Hugh Meller, in his book *London Cemeteries: An Illustrated Guide and Gazetteer* (1981). The seven, with their dates of opening, are:

KENSAL GREEN CEMETERY (1832)
WEST NORWOOD CEMETERY (1837)
HIGHGATE CEMETERY (1839)
NUNHEAD CEMETERY (1840)
ABNEY PARK (1840)
BROMPTON CEMETERY (1840)
TOWER HAMLETS CEMETERY (1841)

Maida

Maida Hill The lesser-known neighbour and precursor of MAIDA VALE. In the early 19th century villas were built on Hill House Fields, together with a public house named the Hero of Maida. The hero was Major-General Sir John Stuart (1759–1815), who in 1806 led British troops to victory over a larger French force on the plain of Maida in southern Italy. By 1810 the locality was being marked as 'Maida' on maps. The part of EDGWARE ROAD immediately north of the REGENT'S CANAL was originally called Maida Hill, and later Maida Hill East, while modern Maida Avenue was formerly Maida Hill West. In 1868 the whole stretch of the former Edgware Road north of the canal was united as Maida Vale and Maida Hill's name faded into obscurity

for a while. It was later revived to identify the area to the south-west of Shirland Road (well to the west of its point of origin), which had been called St Peter's Park when it was built up from the mid-1860s.

Maida Vale Mansion block territory located west of ST JOHN'S WOOD. A short stretch of the EDGWARE ROAD was called Maida Vale in 1828 although the name was not applied to the neighbouring locality until much later in the century. Maida Vale Hospital for nervous diseases opened in 1866 and staff there were later the first to identify and successfully operate on a brain tumour. From the 1880s the area's early villas began to be demolished and replaced by flats. The trend reached its peak in the early years of the 20th century when massive mansion blocks went up on the main road, with smaller blocks in the streets behind. Clarendon Court even boasted its own restaurant and booking office for theatres. Maida Vale maintains a reputation as an address for wealthy dowagers, but in fact it has fewer pensioners living alone than most parts of the City of WESTMINSTER and most residents have never been married.

Maida Vale Studios A capacious suite of recording studios built by the BBC on the site of a disused roller-skating rink on Delaware Road. From their inception in 1934 the studios became the home of the BBC Symphony Orchestra, and later of the BBC Radiophonic Workshop. Countless important classical and modern musical performances have been recorded here but the studios' future is uncertain. The name 'Maida Vale' is nowadays almost synonymous with rock session recordings, especially for Radio 1 shows presented by John Peel (1939–2004).

> ... through myriad catacombs of BBC Maida Vale Studios, where direction signs hold no grip on reality and where scruffy engineers dart to and fro, and sullen violinists lurk in the toilets, lost in musicianly reverie.
> MICK MIDDLES and MARK E. SMITH: *The Fall* (2003)

Mail Rail The semi-official nickname of the Post Office Railway, an underground service that carried letters and parcels between the central sorting office at MOUNT PLEASANT and district offices to its west and east. The line opened in 1927 and extended 6½ miles (10.5 km) from PADDINGTON to WHITECHAPEL, with six (later seven) intermediate stops. Owing to increased running costs and the progressive relocation of most of the sorting offices along its route, Mail Rail was shut down in 2003. No other use has been found for the line and a fleet of vans and lorries nowadays distributes the mail instead.

Malden

Malden Rushett A hamlet situated at a crossroads south of CHESSINGTON WORLD OF ADVENTURES, in the southernmost part of the 'tongue' of the Royal Borough of KINGSTON UPON THAMES that protrudes into the SURREY woodland. Eleventh-century Malden rambled across two manors, one of which has since become Malden Rushett, a reference to the rushes that grew here. Malden Rushett, also known as Lower Chessington or 'the Rushett', remained part of Malden parish until 1884 when it was transferred to Chessington. Before the transfer, residents of the hamlet's cottages had to go to (Old) Malden to be married, although they could be buried in Chessington.

New Malden See under NEW.
Old Malden See under OLD.

Mall, The A road leading from CHARING CROSS to BUCKINGHAM PALACE, bordered by ST JAMES'S PARK along most of its southern side. Charles II laid out the Mall in 1662 as a successor to the glorified croquet alley of PALL MALL. The boulevard grew in significance when ST JAMES'S PALACE became the monarch's principal home following the destruction by fire of the Palace of WHITEHALL in 1698. As the sport of *pallemaille* declined in popularity the Mall became a place of public promenade, later giving its name to the American cultural phenomenon the shopping mall, which was originally a store-lined street closed to vehicular traffic. With the accession of Victoria to the throne in 1837, Buckingham Palace became the new royal residence and the Mall's straight-line approach to the palace brought it even greater status. From the late 19th century the Mall served as the carriage drive for all royal processions and for the arrival of foreign heads of state. The construction of ADMIRALTY ARCH and the Victoria Memorial at opposite ends of the Mall in 1910 and 1911 brought greater formality to the ceremonial route.

> Noe persons shall after play carry their malls out of St James's Park without leave of the said keeper.
>
> *Order Book of the General Monk* (1662)

man

Man About the House An ITV sitcom that ran for six seasons between 1973 and 1976. Richard O'Sullivan, Paula Wilcox and Sally Thomsett starred as flatmates living in Myddleton Terrace, EARLS COURT. The show spawned two spin-offs: ROBIN'S NEST and GEORGE & MILDRED.

man about town A fashionable idler, especially in Regency times, such as BEAU BRUMMELL or POODLE BYNG.

Man from Aldersgate, The A sobriquet of John Wesley (1703–91), who at a religious meeting in ALDERSGATE on 24 May 1738 felt his heart 'strangely warmed' as he listened to a reading of Martin Luther's preface to the Epistle to the Romans. Wesley went on to found a network of evangelical societies, at first within the Church of England, that later formed the nucleus of the Methodist Church. Outside the entrance to the MUSEUM OF LONDON a bronze memorial in the shape of a flame marks the site of Wesley's conversion.

Man Loaded with Mischief A signboard said to have been painted by William HOGARTH for an alehouse on OXFORD STREET, subsequently copied and used by taverns elsewhere. It depicted a man carrying his drunken wife, a monkey and a magpie on his back. In his wife's hand is a glass of gin and around his neck is a padlocked chain.

man on the Clapham omnibus In legal parlance, 'the reasonable citizen'. Possibly the phrase was first used by Sir Charles Bowen, QC (later Lord Bowen). Nowadays 'person' is often substituted for 'man'.

> Listening to the lawyers, I think they have managed to obfuscate something which is not that difficult. The person on the Clapham omnibus would probably understand pretty well what Part 1 is trying to say. We seem to be going around the houses.
>
> THE EARL OF ERROLL, in *Lords Hansard* (20 December 2005)

Man who Built London Transport, The The title of a biography of Frank Pick (1878–1941) written by his former assistant Christian Barman in 1979. Pick began working for the newly created Underground Group in 1906 and soon became its publicity officer. He was managing director of the group from 1928 and chief executive of LONDON TRANSPORT from its inception in 1933 until 1940. Pick commissioned many of the most influential early features of the underground network, including its iconic posters, the JOHNSTON SANS typeface and the 'BULLSEYE' device, and later the classic station designs of Charles Holden and others. When buses and trams came within his purview he walked the length of each proposed new route, often suggesting deviations. Almost the only great innovation for which Pick could not claim maximum credit was Harry Beck's LONDON UNDERGROUND MAP, which he approved for a trial print run while remaining unconvinced of its merits.

Men Behaving Badly A television sitcom written by Simon Nye. It was first shown in 1991 and conceived as a slap in the face to political correctness in general and to the cult of the new man in particular. The story centres on the antics of Gary Strang, played by Martin Clunes, and Dermot, played by Harry Enfield (later Tony, played by Neil Morrissey), who share a chaotic London flat. They swig beer, talk out their fantasies and try to avoid work by opening another can or heading off to their private room for the pleasures of *Playboy*. Two women, Deborah, played by Leslie Ash, and Dorothy, played by Caroline Quentin, are embroiled in the goings-on. Location filming centred on EALING.

Manchu, Fu *See under* FU.

manor (Old French *manoir*, from Latin *manere*, 'to remain') A word introduced after the Norman Conquest and used of a dwelling of a man of substance but not necessarily a large holding; later it denoted a self-contained estate. In London (especially SOUTH OF THE RIVER) the word has come to mean one's home patch. In the context of criminal activity it refers to one's area of operations. The south London gangster Charlie Richardson (b.1937) chose the title *My Manor* for his 1991 autobiography.

> When asked how he felt about the [Olympic] Games potentially coming to his 'hood', Beckham replied: 'You mean my manor? It would be incredible for me if it was held there.'
>
> *The Times* (6 July 2005)

Manor House A PICCADILLY LINE station, and by extension its immediate vicinity, located at the eastern corner of FINSBURY PARK. Thomas Widdows of STOKE NEWINGTON Church Street, allegedly 'a most lascivious old fellow', built the Manor Tavern in 1832 and it was rebuilt exactly a

century later as the Manor House. The ROLLING STONES played weekly gigs at the pub in February and March 1963. It has since been converted to a supermarket.

Manor Park A network of Victorian terraces situated between FOREST GATE and ILFORD. Most of the area was part of the manor of LITTLE ILFORD until it gained a separate identity following the opening of its station. The new suburb took its name from the manor house built around 1810 for the lord of the manor of WEST HAM on his Hamfrith estate. The house still stands in Gladding Road but has been much altered and converted into flats. Manor Park station opened in 1872 and the Manor Park Cemetery Company bought the eastern part of Hamfrith Farm in the same year. Streets of terraced housing were laid out on the neighbouring fields from the 1880s. Little Ilford's Manor Farm was developed more cheaply as the Manor House estate after 1895. The actors Stanley Holloway (1890–1982) and Greer Garson (1904–96) were born in Manor Park.

Mansion House The official residence of the LORD MAYOR OF LONDON, situated at the western end of LOMBARD STREET, opposite the BANK OF ENGLAND. The STOCKS MARKET and the Church of St Mary Woolchurch Haw stood here until the GREAT FIRE OF LONDON. The idea of commissioning a grand house for the mayor was first discussed after the fire but nothing came of it and the Stocks Market was rebuilt in enlarged form instead. Only when other large cities started to build such mansions did London decide it was not to be outdone. The site was chosen in 1736 and seven architects submitted proposals. The City's clerk of works, George Dance the Elder (1695–1768), won the competition with a Palladian design featuring a large Corinthian portico. Completed in 1752, the structure made innovative use of hidden iron chains running through the brick interior walls. Mansion House originally had an internal courtyard at first-floor level, but this was covered over when Dance the Younger made several improvements to the house's capacity and safety in 1795.

Mansion House station An underground station on the CIRCLE LINE and DISTRICT LINE. It opened in 1871, originally as the eastern terminus of the Metropolitan District Railway, which was extended to WHITECHAPEL in 1884. The station is located some distance from Mansion House itself, at the junction of CANNON STREET and Queen Victoria Street, but was given the name of the nearest landmark building.

Mapesbury A Victorian estate and conservation area located on the BRONDESBURY/CRICKLEWOOD border. This area was part of the broad expanse of territory held by ST PAUL'S Cathedral from the end of the first millennium. Each of the cathedral's canons took responsibility for an individual manor, and Mapesbury derives its name from Walter Map, prebendary of the manor in the last quarter of the 12th century.

marathon In the modern OLYMPIC GAMES the marathon race was instituted in 1896, the distance being standardized at 26 miles 385 yards (42.195 km) from the 1924 Olympics onwards. This had been the length of the course at the 1908 games in London, when the race was run from Windsor Castle to WHITE CITY. *See also the* LONDON MARATHON.

marble

Marble Arch A road junction and monument at the north-eastern corner of HYDE PARK. John Nash designed the Marble Arch in 1828 as the main gateway to BUCKINGHAM PALACE. Fashioned from white Carrara marble, it was inspired by the Arch of Constantine in Rome. When the palace was extended in 1851 the Marble Arch was moved to its present site, where it formed an entrance to Hyde Park. Like its counterpart at HYDE PARK CORNER, the arch has been marooned on a traffic island as a result of traffic circulation improvements in the early 1960s. Noel Gay and Ralph Butler's 1932 composition 'Round the Marble Arch' was a hit for Henry Hall and his orchestra.

> The marble single arch in front of the Palace cost £100,000 and the gateway in Piccadilly cost £40,000. Can one be surprised at people becoming Radical with such specimens of royal prodigality before their eyes? to say nothing of the character of such royalties themselves.
>
> THOMAS CREEVEY: letter to Miss Ord (20 May 1835)

Marble Hill A riverside slope in TWICKENHAM, recorded in 1350 as Mardelhylle. The derivation is uncertain but had nothing to do with marble; the corruption to the present form (which was in use by 1650) is the result of folk etymology. George II had Marble Hill House built for his mistress

Henrietta Howard in the 1720s and the elegantly simple Palladian villa became a playground for the celebrities of the day. The LONDON COUNTY COUNCIL bought Marble Hill in 1902 and opened its parkland grounds to the public in the following year. The LCC's successor, the GREATER LONDON COUNCIL, restored the house beautifully in the mid-1960s.

march

Marching Watch The guard of civilians enrolled in medieval London to keep order in the streets on the Vigils of St Peter (29 June) and St John the Baptist (24 June) during the festivities. The phrase was used also of the festivities themselves, which were discontinued in the early 16th century after they became a threat to public order.

March to Finchley, The A painting (1749–50) by William HOGARTH, inspired by the 1745 Jacobite Rising. The scene depicts soldiers setting off from London to take on the rebels, while being distracted by all the temptations of city life (principally drink and whores). When the painting was shown to George II, the king was apparently immune to the anti-Jacobite subtleties of the work, as the following famous exchange indicates: 'Pray, who is this Hogarth?' 'A painter, my liege.' 'I hate bainting and boetry too! neither one nor the other ever did any good! Does the fellow mean to laugh at my guards?' 'The picture, may it please your Majesty, must undoubtedly be considered a burlesque.' – 'What, a bainter burlesque a soldier? He deserves to be picketed for his insolence! Take his trumpery out of my sight.'

Marchioness In DICKENS's *The Old Curiosity Shop* (1840–1) the nickname given by Dick Swiveller to the small, shrewd, servant girl employed and badly treated by Sampson Brass and Sally Brass. Swiveller secretly becomes her friend, and she runs away to nurse him when he falls ill. When the Brasses plot to have Kit Nubbles arrested, she overhears them, and her revelations lead to their downfall and Daniel Quilp's. Finally, Swiveller re-names her Sophronia Sphynx, pays for her to be educated as a lady, and marries her. The word was later used as a generic term for a maid-of-all-work.

Marchioness disaster A fatal accident on the THAMES on 20 August 1989 involving a pleasure boat, the *Marchioness*. On the night in question the boat had been hired for a birthday party by a young CITY businessman. In the early hours of the morning a Thames dredger, the *Bowbelle*, collided with the *Marchioness*, which rapidly sank, resulting in the deaths of 51 people.

Mardi Gra The codename of Edgar Pearce, a LEYTON-born former advertising employee, living in CHISWICK, who for five years from 1994 waged a campaign across London and the HOME COUNTIES in an attempt to extort millions of pounds from Barclays Bank and Sainsbury's supermarkets. He planted some 36 explosive devices, injuring six, and took his name because he began his campaign on a Tuesday, alluding to the French *Mardi Gras* or Shrove Tuesday festival. He omitted the final 's' so that the police would recognize the bombs as his work. He was finally arrested in April 1999 moments after withdrawing £700 from a cash machine in WHITTON. In some respects he was a paler version of the American Unabomber.

Marie Stopes International A leading provider of sexual and reproductive healthcare services, founded by Dr Marie Stopes (1880–1958). It began in 1921 as Britain's first birth control clinic, at 61 Marlborough Road, Upper HOLLOWAY. The Mother's Clinic for Constructive Birth Control was so successful that it soon moved to FITZROVIA, where the headquarters remains. The international organization was founded in 1976 and now operates around 500 clinics in 40 developing countries, partly funded by surplus funds from its UK work.

Marine Ices Probably London's best-known ice cream parlour (and also an Italian restaurant), located in CHALK FARM, just north-west of CAMDEN TOWN. Southern Italian immigrant Gaetano Mansi opened a grocery store in Drummond Street, EUSTON, in 1928. To avoid wasting over-ripe fruit he began to make sorbets, which soon became his bestselling line, prompting him to open Mansi's Café at the foot of HAVERSTOCK HILL in 1931. After the Second World War Mansi's eldest son rebuilt the café in 'marine' style, and renamed it accordingly. From the mid-1960s the business began supplying its frozen desserts to other London restaurants, and theatres and hotels, as it still does. Marine Ices is presently run by members of the fourth generation of the Mansi family.

I walk on, round a slight bend, and there before me glints the evidence: massive lights ranked on the pavement outside Marine Ices, where the first day's filming is taking place … a pivotal moment in a much-loved Italian restaurant where my three protagonists converge.

JOANNA BRISCOE, on the ITV production of her novel *Sleep With Me*, in *The Independent* (2 June 2008)

Mark Lane A street running south from FENCHURCH STREET, east of MINCING LANE. This was Marthe Lane *c.*1200, probably reflecting either a female personal name or the Old English *mearth*, 'marten' (the valuable fur of which may have been sold here in early times). The present form of the name is first recorded in 1481. Previously the haunt of wine importers, the lane was very badly damaged during the BLITZ. The former Mark Lane underground station was renamed TOWER HILL in 1946. When the station was relocated in 1967 the old building was demolished, but not before it had served as Hobbs End station in the sci-fi horror film QUATERMASS AND THE PIT (1967).

walk penniless in Mark Lane, to *See under* WALK.

Marks Gate A northern outpost of the London Borough of BARKING AND DAGENHAM, located a mile (1.6 km) north of CHADWELL HEATH, and still surrounded by the fields of wheat, oats, barley that were once its raison d'être. Around 600 BC a fortified hilltop village was established here, of which almost nothing remains but the hill itself. The medieval manor of Marks was one of BARKING's oldest free tenements (an estate held for life or longer), with its own manor court from the 14th century and special rights in HAINAULT Forest. Marks Hall, the 20-bedroom moated manor house, was built in the mid-15th century and demolished in 1808. The estate, which was much reduced over the centuries, was sold to the Crown in 1855. It is now part of Warren Hall Farm, where part of the moat survives, as does a 17th-century brick barn, which is still in use.

Marlborough

Marlborough House A mansion in PALL MALL, built for Sarah, Duchess of Marlborough (1660–1744) in 1709–11. In 1817 it reverted to the Crown, and its most famous resident thereafter was the Prince of Wales (later Edward VII). During his occupancy it became the centre of fashionable society and the Prince's inner circle became known as the Marlborough House Set. In 1959 it was given to the Government for use as a Commonwealth Centre.

Marlborough Street See GREAT MARLBOROUGH STREET.

Marquee Club Probably the most prestigious London music club of the 1960s and 70s, it was influential in popularizing several genres, including skiffle, rhythm and blues and PUNK ROCK. The Marquee began as a jazz club on OXFORD STREET in 1958, relocating in 1964 to 96 WARDOUR STREET, where it thrived until 1988, when the site was sold for redevelopment. A succession of owners attempted to revive the name and its distinctive stripy trademark at other locations, none with lasting success. Among the artists to have played some of their earliest or most significant gigs at the Marquee were the ROLLING STONES, the Yardbirds, Led Zeppelin, Pink Floyd, David Bowie and the SEX PISTOLS.

marrowbone stage See the MARYLEBONE STAGE.

Marshalsea Prison An old prison in BOROUGH High Street, SOUTHWARK, the prison of the Marshalsea Court, which was originally a court of the royal household, presided over by the Earl Marshal. The court, with the Knight Marshal for judge, existed until December 1849. From the 1430s the prison also received admiralty prisoners and debtors. It moved to newer premises in 1799 and was closed in 1842. In 1381 its marshal was beheaded by the rebels under Wat Tyler. Charles DICKENS's father was imprisoned there in 1824.

> Necessarily, he was going out again directly, because the Marshalsea lock never turned upon a debtor who was not.
>
> DICKENS: *Little Dorrit* (1855–7)

Mary
Black Mary's Hole See under BLACK.
Mary Poppins See under POPPINS.
Mary Quant See QUANT, MARY.
Queen Mary's Gardens See under QUEEN.
Queen Mary's Hospital See under QUEEN.
Queen Mary, University of London See under QUEEN.
St Mary-at-Lambeth See the GARDEN MUSEUM.
St Mary Axe See under SAINT.
St Mary-le-Bow See under SAINT.

St Mary Matfelon See under SAINT.
St Mary Overy See under SAINT.

Maryland A disadvantaged neighbourhood in north-east STRATFORD. In 1638 the ILFORD-based merchant Richard Lee (c.1613–1664) migrated to America, where he acquired an estate at Maryland Point on the Potomac River. After 20 years he returned to Ilford and bought land at Stratford, where he built a house that he called Maryland Point. After he died his family returned to America, apparently in fulfilment of the conditions of his will. The house was sold in 1678 and its subsequent fate is not known. Maryland Point first appeared as a London place name on a map of 1696 and Daniel DEFOE mentioned the existence of a 'new' settlement here in 1722. Richard Lee's grandson Thomas established a plantation in Virginia in the late 1730s, which he named Stratford Hall, and this was the birthplace in 1807 of Thomas's grandson Robert E. Lee, the most successful general of the Confederate forces during the American Civil War.

Marylebone or **St Marylebone** A 'high status, non-family area', as demographers call it, situated south and west of REGENT'S PARK. The village that grew up by the path to PRIMROSE HILL was originally called TYBURN but after the construction of a new church in 1400 it became known as St Mary-a-le-bourne. St Mary's stood on the present Marylebone High Street, as did an older manor house, later known as Marylebone Palace. The grounds of Marylebone Place became pleasure gardens in 1737, when the village remained sufficiently remote for its church to be 'much favoured for hasty or secret weddings'. The pleasure gardens closed in 1778 and Marylebone Palace was demolished in 1791. The present parish church of St Mary was built on MARYLEBONE ROAD in 1817.

Marylebone Cricket Club A cricket club (abbreviation MCC) founded in 1787 by members of the old White Conduit Club of ISLINGTON, with which it later merged. In 1814 it moved to LORD's cricket ground, which it bought in 1866 and which is still its headquarters. By the middle of the 19th century it was generally recognized as the premier club in the game, its decisions deferred to in matters of interpretation of the rules. By the 20th century it was virtually the ruling body of cricket in England (with wide influence on world cricket to boot), and until the

1970s the England team toured abroad under the banner of the MCC. By then, though, its image as an exclusive men's club was widely thought to be inappropriate to a ruling body of a national sport, and it devolved most of its powers to other organizations, of which the latest incarnations are the England and Wales Cricket Board (ECB) and the International Cricket Council. In 1998 it admitted female members for the first time in its 211-year history.

Marylebone Road An east–west highway driven across the parish of Marylebone in the 1750s as part of the NEW ROAD. Marylebone Road was transformed over the course of the 20th century, with the construction of mansion flats, curtain-walled office blocks, hotels and a new campus for what is now the UNIVERSITY OF WESTMINSTER.

Marylebone stage To take, go by or ride in the Marylebone stage (or Marylebone coach) was a 19th-century colloquialism for going on foot. There were many similar expressions in use at the time, of which the healthiest survivor is 'shanks's pony'. 'Marylebone' was formerly often written 'Marrowbone', including by PEPYS, while 'marrowbones' was slang for the knees. In fact, the term probably began as 'the marrowbone stage' but must always have been a pun on the place name.

> 'The cabmen are trying it on, anyhow, just now,' thought Mr Sheldon; 'but I don't think they'll try it on with me. And if they do, there's the Marylebone stage. I'm not afraid of a five-mile walk.'
>
> MARY ELIZABETH BRADDON: *Charlotte's Inheritance* (1868)

Marylebone station A railway terminus opened by the Great Central Railway Company in 1897. This was the last of the London railway termini and the least commercially successful, but its underuse has precluded the need for subsequent expansion, resulting in perhaps the capital's prettiest and most unspoilt main-line station building. Marylebone underground station, on the BAKERLOO line, opened in 1907, originally under the name 'Great Central'; it was changed to 'Marylebone' in 1917.

Massacre of St George's Fields *See the* ST GEORGE'S FIELDS MASSACRE.

master

Master of the Rolls The judge who presides over civil cases in the Court of Appeal, and as such the most important civil judge outside the House of Lords. His title goes back to the 16th century, when he was the keeper of CHANCERY records or rolls and legal assistant to the chancellor. In 1838 he was given control of the newly created Public Record Office (now part of the National Archives at KEW), a post that in 1958 was transferred to the lord chancellor. *See also the* CHAPEL OF THE ROLLS.

Master of the Temple The preacher of the TEMPLE church.

match girls The workers at Bryant and May's match factory, built in 1860 in Fairfield Road, BOW. In June 1888 *The Link* published an article by Annie Besant, entitled 'White Slavery in London', in which she drew attention to working conditions in the factory. Three employees who had provided information to Besant were sacked and a three-week strike began in July, which resulted in their reinstatement, small wage increases and concessions regarding terms and conditions. However, it was many years before the factory ceased using white phosphorous, which had caused illness (known as 'phossy jaw') and death among those exposed to it.

> Bryant and May have a rough set of girls. There are 2000 of them when they are busy. Rough and rowdy but not bad morally. They fight with their fists to settle their differences, not in the factory for that is forbidden, but in the streets when they leave work in the evening. A ring is formed, they fight like men and are not interfered with by the police.
>
> CHARLES BOOTH: notebook (1 June 1897)

Maundy Money Gifts in money given by the sovereign on Maundy Thursday, the day before Good Friday, to the number of aged poor men and women that corresponds with his or her age. Broadcloth, fish, bread and wine were given in the reign of Elizabeth I, later clothing and provisions. The clothing was replaced by money in 1725 and the provisions in 1837. In due course the ceremony was transferred from the chapel at WHITEHALL to WESTMINSTER ABBEY. Personal distribution of the doles ceased in 1688 until George V restarted it in 1932, as did Edward VIII in 1936. Queen Elizabeth II has made a personal distribution in most years since 1953, and the ceremony is nowadays held at a different

British cathedral or abbey every year, usually returning to Westminster Abbey in the first year of each decade. The money is specially struck in silver pennies, twopennies, threepences and fourpences and is unaffected by decimalization.

maupygernon *See* DILLIGROUT.

mausoleum The name was originally that of the tomb of Mausolus, King of Caria, to whom his wife Artemisia erected a splendid monument at Halicarnassus (353 BC). Parts of the sepulchre, one of the Seven Wonders of the Ancient World, are now in the BRITISH MUSEUM.

Mawney A half-forgotten mini-suburb situated between ROMFORD and COLLIER ROW, and traversed by the River Rom. During the 14th century the manor of Romford came into the possession of the celebrated soldier Sir Walter de Mauny (d.1372). Thereafter, the manor was called Mawneys, a form still used by local people and by the council but not by most cartographers.

May

May Day The first day of May was formerly the occasion of the London chimney-sweeps' festival.

May meetings The yearly gatherings of religious and charitable societies, formerly held in London in May or June to hear the annual reports and appeals for further support. *See also* EXETER HALL.

maypole Dancing around the maypole on May Day is an ancient relic of nature worship. In CORNHILL a great shaft or maypole was set up near the church of St Andrew. The annual dancing of people under the pole gave the church its present name of St Andrew Undershaft. The tradition was suspended after EVIL MAY DAY. St Andrew's now lies in the shadow of the GHERKIN's prodigious shaft.

Maypole in the Strand This once famous landmark was probably erected in the time of Elizabeth I (r.1558–1603), on a spot now occupied by the church of St Mary-le-Strand. It was destroyed by the Puritans in 1644. A replacement – 134 feet (41m) high – was set up in 1661, it is said, by the farrier John Clarges to celebrate the marriage of his daughter to General Monck. By 1713 this was decayed and another was erected, which was removed in 1718. It was bought by Sir Isaac Newton, who sent it to his friend James

Pound, the rector of WANSTEAD. Pound and his nephew James Bradley, the astronomer royal, used the maypole to support what was then the largest telescope in Europe.

What's not destroyed by Time's devouring hand?
Where's Troy, and where's the Maypole in the Strand?

JAMES BRAMSTON: *The Art of Politics* (1729)

Evil May Day *See under* EVIL.

Maybe It's Because I'm a Londoner *See* LONDONER.

Mayfair An elite residential and commercial quarter bounded by PARK LANE, OXFORD STREET, REGENT STREET and PICCADILLY. In 1686 a two-week fair transferred from HAYMARKET to Great Brook Field, where Curzon Street and SHEPHERD MARKET now stand. In common with almost every London fair it became notorious for its 'loose, idle and disorderly' crowds and the event was exiled to BOW in 1764. By this time, the neighbouring fields had been laid out with high-class residential streets and squares, notably GROSVENOR SQUARE and BERKELEY SQUARE, while BOND STREET had filled with fashionable shops. Some of Mayfair's most charming streets are the ones that its developers reserved for tradesmen and which were later distinctively rebuilt; the 1890s terracotta frontages of Mount Street and Arts and Crafts houses in Mount Row provide the best examples. Together with neighbouring ST JAMES'S, Mayfair has in recent years become a centre for hedge funds, asset managers, private equity firms and financial advisers. The twin districts have been described as London's 'third axis of financial power alongside the Square Mile and Canary Wharf'. However, some of these companies moved out or closed down during the economic downturn that began in 2008.

Benjamin Disraeli, prime minister in 1868 and from 1874 to 1880, died at 19 Curzon Street in 1881. Other Mayfair residents have included the writers R.B. Sheridan and Somerset Maugham. Queen Elizabeth II was born at 21 Bruton Street in 1926. The romantic comedy film *Maytime in Mayfair* (1949), starring Michael Wilding and Anna Neagle, was set in the world of Mayfair haute couture.

Mayfair marriages 'The Rev Alexander Keith's

Chapel' on Curzon Street was notorious for its traffic in private and secret weddings until the Marriage Act (1753) stopped the trade. On Valentine's Day 1752 James, 6th Duke of Hamilton, married the Irish beauty Elizabeth Gunning only weeks after meeting her at a masquerade. The ring was from a bed curtain and the ceremony took place half an hour after midnight. *See also* FLEET MARRIAGES.

Mayfair mercenary A young woman whose indeterminate social class is transcended by her beauty and her ambition to climb in society, often as the mistress of a successful wealthy man. The term originated in *Harpers and Queen* magazine around 1980.

mayor The Norman *maire* (mayor) was introduced by Henry II (r.1154–89) and it supplanted the old name of portreeve. The chair of a borough or town council in England and Wales has the right to the designation 'mayor'. The chair of a city council is a 'lord mayor'. He or she holds office for 12 months.

In 2000 the concept of directly elected mayors, based on the US model and functioning almost as the chief executive of a local authority, was introduced to England and Wales. He or she holds office for four years. The exercise of the option to create such an office is decided by referendum. Six London boroughs have held such referenda, with EALING, HARROW and SOUTHWARK voting against and HACKNEY, LEWISHAM and NEWHAM deciding in favour of having a directly elected mayor.

mayor of Garratt or **Garrat** The 'mayor' of Garratt, near WANDSWORTH, was really the chairman of an association of villagers formed to resist encroachments on the common in the 1740s. It became the practice to choose a new 'mayor' at the same time as the occurrence of a general election. These events became popular public occasions and at one such there were more than 80,000 people present, the candidates usually being lively characters who were chosen on the basis of their witty speech and sometimes their physical deformities. The elections became increasingly radicalized and died out around 1800. During one election a dead cat was thrown at the hustings and a bystander remarked that it stank 'worse than a fox'. 'That's no wonder,' replied Sir John Harper (one of the mayors), 'for you see, it's a poll-cat.'

Samuel Foote has a farce called *The Mayor of Garratt* (1764), and the place name still survives in Garratt Lane, which connects Wandsworth with TOOTING BROADWAY.

mayor of London A directly elected position introduced in 2000 following a referendum on the proposed creation of the GREATER LONDON AUTHORITY. The mayor is based at CITY HALL and holds office for four years, after which he or she may stand for election again. The mayor represents and promotes London at home and abroad, and sets the budget for the Greater London Authority and for functional bodies responsible for transport, economic development, policing, housing and fire and emergency planning. In consultation with the London boroughs and other interested parties, the mayor also devises London-wide strategies in matters such as culture, skills development, energy efficiency and waste management. For the first eight years the post was held by Ken Livingstone (*see* RED KEN), who was succeeded in 2008 by Boris Johnson (*see* BO-JO).

lord mayor of London *See under* LORD.

mazarine A former term for a common councilman of the CORPORATION OF LONDON, who wore a mazarine blue silk gown.

Maze Hill A hillside road forming the eastern boundary of GREENWICH PARK since the enclosure of the common in the 15th century, and probably a cart track from the THAMES to BLACKHEATH for many years before that. Despite evidence that the road once led to a turf maze in Blackheath, the name appears to come from a 16th-century resident, Sir Algernon May. Around 1720 the playwright and architect Sir John Vanbrugh (1664–1726) built Vanbrugh Castle, a fortress-like complex of mock-medieval buildings. Only its centrepiece survived a spate of redevelopment that followed the opening of Maze Hill station in 1876. The Blackheath Preservation Trust bought the site in 1976, restoring the castle and converting it into four dwellings.

MCC *See* MARYLEBONE CRICKET CLUB.

Meard Street A pedestrianized street in SOHO, running between WARDOUR STREET and Dean Street. Its name is often said to be a corruption of the French *merde*, 'shit', but it in fact derives from John Meard the Younger, a master carpenter whose yard lay here. Meard acquired and developed the neighbouring land from the early 1720s, and built for himself a six-storey terraced house that survives today.

meat

meat market An old nickname for the corner of Broad Street (now Broadwick Street) and Lexington Street, in SOHO. The 'meat' was of the human kind: unemployed members of the tailoring profession would formerly gather here, scanning noticeboards filled with job vacancies, usually for very low paid work in backstreet sweatshops.

> Fortune's victims jostle against the victims of drink and their own folly; the pinch of poverty afflicts them all; and at each the most saddening sight is that of young girls lounging about, waiting for something to turn up, indulging in coarse jokes, and coarser actions.
>
> ALFRED T. CAMDEN PRATT: *Unknown London: Its Romance and Tragedy* (1896)

meat rack A former nickname for PICCADILLY CIRCUS, from its reputation as a haunt of male prostitutes. The term was not current among the wider populace but was universally understood within the pre-decriminalization gay community.

> Instead, he joined the Piccadilly rent scene, 'which was much more open in those days, with geezers hanging over the railings of the old meat rack'.
>
> D.J. WEST and BUZ DE VILLIERS: *Male Prostitution* (1992)

megalopolis (Greek *mega*, 'big', and *polis*, 'city') The term has been used to encompass GREATER LONDON and the urban parts of the HOME COUNTIES, or beyond. Some social scientists consider the London megalopolis to extend up to 75 miles (120 km) from the city centre, even including parts of Dorset, Wiltshire, Northamptonshire and Cambridgeshire. However, the term 'megalopolis' is more often applied to the Washington–Boston corridor in the USA or the gigantic conurbations of the developing world, such as Mexico City, Cairo, Mumbai, São Paulo and Shanghai.

> The lower course of the Thames River in southeastern England collects most of the water draining the London megalopolis.
>
> HERVÉ CHAMLEY: *Geosciences, Environment and Man* (2003)

megaphone man *See* DON'T BE A SINNER, BE A WINNER.

mela A Sanskrit word meaning 'meeting' or 'gathering', used in several south Asian languages. The term has recently been applied to Asian-themed open-air festivals held throughout Britain, including at BARKING, CROYDON and PLUMSTEAD in London. By far the most successful is the GUNNERSBURY Mela, also known as the London Mela, which was first held in 2003 and has been nicknamed (perhaps by its organizers) 'the Asian Glastonbury'. Spread over 30 acres (12 hectares) of Gunnersbury Park, the event attracts up to 100,000 revellers on a Sunday in mid-August.

Melancholy Walk
A path that marked the northern edge of ST GEORGE'S FIELDS in SOUTHWARK. The name reflected the miserable character of the dwellings – and life in general – in the vicinity. Nearby thoroughfares were called Deadman's Place, Dirty Lane, Foul Lane and Labour-in-Vain Alley. Surrey Row now follows the route of Melancholy Walk.

Memorial Hall
See the CONGREGATIONAL MEMORIAL HALL.

mercer

Mercers' Company Originally an association of traders in fine fabrics, chartered in 1394 and ranking first in order of precedence among the CITY of London LIVERY COMPANIES. Based at Mercers' Hall on Ironmonger Lane, the company nowadays functions as a members' fraternity and a charitable institution. The latter is funded primarily from the income on a property portfolio that includes BARNARD'S INN, six blocks in COVENT GARDEN and shared ownership with the CORPORATION OF LONDON of the ROYAL EXCHANGE.

Mercers' Maiden The symbol of the Mercers' Company, and since 1911 its coat of arms. Of unknown origin, the maiden first appeared on a seal in 1425. Maiden 'property marks', usually crafted out of stone, can be seen on the exterior walls of buildings belonging to the company.

mermaid

Mermaid Tavern The meeting place in BREAD STREET of the wits, literary men and men about town in the early 17th century. Among those who met there at a sort of early CLUB were Ben Jonson, Sir Walter Raleigh, Francis Beaumont,

John Fletcher, John Selden and, in all probability, SHAKESPEARE.

> Souls of Poets dead and gone,
> What Elysium have ye known,
> Happy field or mossy cavern,
> Choicer than the Mermaid Tavern?

JOHN KEATS: 'Lines on the Mermaid Tavern' (1818)

Mermaid Theatre A theatre located at PUDDLE DOCK, in BLACKFRIARS, that developed from one created in 1951 by Sir Bernard Miles and his wife in the garden of their house in ST JOHN'S WOOD. They named it after the MERMAID TAVERN. The Mermaid now functions primarily as a conference and events centre and was granted a change of use certificate in 2008, removing its theatrical status and potentially paving the way for the site's redevelopment.

Merry Devil of Edmonton, The An anonymously authored play (c.1604) that was performed at Court and at the GLOBE THEATRE. Supposedly based on the true story of one Peter Fabell, it tells of a prankster who on one occasion fools the Devil himself. With its scenes of magic, deer poaching and abduction from a nunnery, the play was highly popular with Elizabethan audiences. Its earlier attribution to SHAKESPEARE has been wholly discredited.

Merton The compact remnant of a historic parish, situated midway between WIMBLEDON and MITCHAM, squeezed almost out of existence by newer suburbs with more marketable names. Merton remained a farming community, with textile-printing mills by the River WANDLE, until the East India merchant Richard Hotham bought Moat House Farm in 1764 and enlarged the farmhouse, renaming it Merton Place. Admiral Horatio Nelson (1758–1805) acquired Merton Place and its spacious grounds in 1802 and lived here in a ménage à trois with Sir William and Lady Hamilton until he left in September 1805 for Trafalgar, where he died the following month. Emma Hamilton sold 'Paradise Merton', as she had called it, in 1808 and the house was demolished and the estate broken up in 1823. The novelist Ford Madox Ford (1873–1939) was born in Merton. Shaun Hutson's novel *Slugs* (1982) describes the invasion of Merton by gigantic and voracious gastropods.

Merton, London Borough of An OUTER LONDON borough formed in 1965 by merging the municipal boroughs of MITCHAM and WIMBLEDON and the urban district of Merton and Morden. Merton is the only borough south of the THAMES that borders neither the river nor the GREATER LONDON boundary. The borough's coat of arms draws heavily on the arms of MERTON PRIORY, while the crest is topped by a sprig of lavender – for Mitcham – and a Cornish chough, taken from the arms of Thomas Cromwell, former lord of the manor of Wimbledon. The civic motto is 'stand fast in honour and strength'.

Merton Park A leafy suburb situated on the south-western side of MERTON. The businessman John Innes (1829–1904) acquired Manor Farm in 1867 with the intention of profiting from the growth of WIMBLEDON by developing an estate here. He rebuilt the manor house (a former farmhouse) and made it his own home, while laying out broad avenues across the fields. A horticultural institution established at Merton Park with funds bequeathed by John Innes developed the well-known compost that bears his name. Merton Park Studios made 130 B-movies between 1934 and 1976. Edna O'Brien wrote her trilogy *The Country Girls* while living in Merton Park in the 1960s.

Merton Priory or **Abbey** An Augustinian priory founded by Gilbert le Norman, Sheriff of Surrey, in 1115. In 1236 a group of leading barons held a Great Council here, forcing the Statutes of Merton onto the reluctant Henry III. The priory was pulled down in 1538 and its stones were taken away to build NONSUCH PALACE. John Leach established a riverside mill in 1802, at which his son-in-law later produced colourful handkerchiefs. Towards the end of the 19th century that mill produced all the fabrics for LIBERTY OF LONDON, which subsequently took ownership of the operation; Liberty's printworks continued to operate until 1972. The artist-craftsman William Morris leased a site at Merton in 1881, refurbishing existing buildings and setting up a manufacturing base. For almost 60 years Morris & Company produced a huge variety of decorative items here, including painted glass windows, tapestries, carpets and upholstery. Much of the site of Morris's works is now occupied by the shops and market stalls of Merton Abbey Mills, which specialize in arts and crafts. The Abbey Mills' working waterwheel is used as the symbol of the borough of MERTON.

mess The usual meaning today is 'a dirty, untidy state of things', 'a muddle', but the word originally signified 'a portion of food' (Latin *missum*, from *mittere*, 'to send'; compare with French *mets*, 'viands', Italian *messa*, 'a course of a meal'). Hence it came to mean 'mixed food, especially for an animal', and so 'a confusion, medley or jumble'. Another meaning was 'a small group of persons (usually four) who sat together at banquets and were served from the same dishes'. This gave rise to the army and navy 'mess', the place where meals are served and eaten, and to the Elizabethans using it in place of 'four' or 'a group of four'. Thus, SHAKESPEARE has Berowne say in *Love's Labour's Lost* (IV, iii (1594)), 'You three fools lack'd me fool to make up the mess.' Members of the INNS OF COURT still dine in groups of four at long tables that they share with several other messes. *See also the* KENTISH MESS.

> The person nearest the High Table on the left hand side of each Mess is the Captain. Traditionally, the Captain served each member of the Mess (with himself or herself last). This custom has disappeared since the food is now served individually, but a tradition remains of not conversing with members of the adjoining messes during the meal (although you are allowed to ask for the condiments).
>
> *Middle Temple, General Guide for Students* (September 2007)

Met A short form of the word 'Metropolitan', used in several past and present London contexts, including as the familiar name of the former Metropolitan Music Hall in EDGWARE ROAD. Nowadays the abbreviation usually identifies the METROPOLITAN POLICE or the METROPOLITAN LINE. 'London Met' is a colloquialism for the LONDON METROPOLITAN UNIVERSITY.

Metrocab A competitor of the classic FX4 taxi, first mass-produced in 1987. The cab's most distinctive characteristics were its glass-fibre body and the angular styling that some have compared with a hearse. Production stopped and restarted more than once before the Metrocab was finally discontinued in 2006. The marque's present owner mooted the introduction of a hybrid-powered successor in 2008.

metrocentric In a British context the term usually signifies a focus on London. It is often employed pejoratively, to suggest that the capital is receiving overweighted attention at the expense of other parts of the country, especially in relation to media coverage and expenditure.

> Broadcasting chiefs have condemned Channel 4 for being 'hideously metrocentric' and ordered the station to quadruple the amount of cash it spends north of the border.
>
> *Scotland on Sunday* (14 September 2008)

Metroland The term was coined by the Metropolitan Railway Company (*see* METROPOLITAN LINE) in 1915 to describe its catchment area north-west of London, as part of a marketing campaign that lasted for two decades. The arrival of the LONDON UNDERGROUND network transformed the appeal of numerous previously remote villages such as EASTCOTE, ICKENHAM and KINGSBURY. The railway company had much to gain from the success of new estates in these places; as well as acquiring tens of thousands of fare-paying commuters, it was able to sell plots of land alongside the railway lines and around the stations.

The scandalous Lady Metroland, née Margot Beste-Chetwynde, is the wife of Lord Metroland, né Humphrey Maltravers, minister of Transportation, in Evelyn Waugh's *Decline and Fall* (1928) and later novels and stories. John Betjeman made a BBC television documentary about Metroland in 1973 and a book followed. Julian Barnes's novel *Metroland* (1980) is the tale of a young man's coming of age in the 1960s, set in north-west London and Paris. The 1999 film version starred Christian Bale and Emily Watson.

metropolitan The adjective (from the Greek *mētēr*, 'mother', and *polis*, 'city') began to be widely applied to London's ever-expanding conurbation in the early 19th century, and was formally endorsed with the creation of the METROPOLITAN POLICE in 1829. In 1889 the Metropolis of London, at that time covering 116 square miles (300 sq km), officially became a county, under the aegis of the LONDON COUNTY COUNCIL.

Metropolitan Board of Works From 1855 to 1889 the body responsible for London's infrastructure and public amenities. Among its most significant achievements were the overhaul of the capital's sewerage system following the GREAT STINK OF LONDON, the acquisition of many open spaces for use as public parks and the construction of several THAMES bridges and important thoroughfares. Corruption scandals and public dissatisfaction with the board's lack of accountability contributed to its replacement by the LONDON COUNTY COUNCIL.

Metropolitan Free Drinking Fountain Association A philanthropic body established in 1859 to provide Londoners with free, sanitary drinking water. In 1867 it changed its name to the Metropolitan Drinking Fountain and Cattle Trough Association, bringing free water to animals too, especially cab drivers' horses. Around a hundred of the association's troughs and fountains survive, many of the former now serving as flowerbeds, while a number of the latter remain in working order. The charity continues its work to the present day, concentrating its efforts on the provision of clean water to poor communities in parts of Africa and Asia.

Metropolitan line A LONDON UNDERGROUND line (although only one-seventh of it is actually under ground) running from ALDGATE to BAKER STREET on the same tracks as the CIRCLE LINE, and then branching north-westwards to HARROW-ON-THE-HILL, where it divides and continues to UXBRIDGE, Amersham, Chesham and Watford. It is coloured burgundy (officially 'magenta') on the map. The Metropolitan Railway Company was the creator of London's first underground railway, which opened between PADDINGTON and FARRINGDON Street in January 1863. In 1868 the St John's Wood Railway Company opened a line from Baker Street to SWISS COTTAGE, and that company had amalgamated with the Metropolitan by 1879, when the line was extended to WILLESDEN GREEN. Further extensions spread tentacles throughout METROLAND, including in 1932 a branch to STANMORE that later became part of the BAKERLOO LINE and then the JUBILEE LINE.

Metropolitan Police The London-wide police force was established in 1829, when it took over the responsibilities of a variety of former official and semi-official law enforcement agencies, most of which had been staffed by volunteers. In 1839 the Met's most notable predecessors, the BOW STREET RUNNERS, were subsumed within the new service. The force initially had responsibility for policing within a 7-mile (11-km) radius of CHARING CROSS. Its area of operation progressively expanded until 2000, when it was reduced to align with the boroughs of GREATER LONDON, excluding the CITY, which retains its own force.

The Metropolitan Police Service's headquarters is New SCOTLAND YARD.

Metropolitan Police Dog Training Establishment See NASH.

Metropolitan Police Training School See HENDON POLICE COLLEGE.

Metropolitan Tabernacle A cavernous Baptist church established at the ELEPHANT AND CASTLE by Charles Spurgeon (*see the* PRINCE OF PREACHERS) in 1861. The tabernacle has since been twice rebuilt but its original portico survives.

London Metropolitan University See *under* LONDON.

mews Stables, but originally a cage for hawks when moulting (Old French *mue*, from Latin *mutare*, 'to change'). The word acquired its new meaning because the royal stables built in the 17th century occupied the site of the King's Mews where formerly the king's hawks were kept. It is now the site of the NATIONAL GALLERY. With the development of fashionable London in the 19th century, rows of stabling, with accommodation above for the coachman, were built and called mews. Since the 1920s these have been steadily converted into garages with flats or into fashionable maisonettes.

MI

MI5 The semi-official name for the Security Service, which is responsible for protecting the UK against threats to national security. It was organized by Captain Vernon Kell (1873–1942) when, in 1909, the Admiralty established the Secret Service Bureau to counter the threat posed by the expanding German fleet. Kell became responsible for counter-espionage within the British Isles, and in 1915 his service was incorporated in the Directorate of Military Intelligence as MI5. The number originally indicated Europe as its area of operations, as distinct from MI1, MI2, MI3 and MI4, which covered the other continents. It became the Security Service in 1931 but still uses the 'MI5' name informally, not least because this is preferable to 'the SS'. Its headquarters is at Thames House, on the corner of MILLBANK and Horseferry Road. The Security Service website (www.mi5.gov.uk) points out that 'the building that represents the exterior of Thames House in the TV series *Spooks* ... is actually Freemasons' Hall in Great Queen Street, COVENT GARDEN, and the interior depicted in the series is a studio set'. The website also has a list of 'myths' about the service that it seeks to dispel, including 'MI5 carries out assassinations' and 'MI5 does not recruit tall people'.

MI6 The colloquial name for the Secret Intelligence Service, which provides the government with 'a global covert capability to promote and defend the national security and economic well-being of the United Kingdom'. In its modern form it dates from 1909 when Captain Mansfield Cumming (1859–1923) was put in charge of overseas intelligence operations, with senior staff drawn from the Royal Navy. MI6 has been based at several locations in the London, notably 54 BROADWAY and now VAUXHALL CROSS. The SIS insists that the name MI6 was never more than a 'a flag of convenience' that helped distinguish it from MI5. However, it is primarily as MI6 rather than the SIS that it has achieved worldwide fame through the exploits of its agent 007, James Bond. *See also the* CIRCUS.

mickey-taking *See* TAKE THE MICKEY OUT OF SOMEONE, TO.

Middlesex The original territory of the Middle Saxons, which seems to have included the area of the later counties of Middlesex and Hertford, between ESSEX and Wessex. It became a shire in the 10th century, was much reduced in area by the Local Government Act of 1888, and its official existence was finally terminated in 1965, when most of it was absorbed into GREATER LONDON. The demise of the county was far from universally popular with its residents, and they at least have the consolation that it survives in the 'Middlesex station' (the option closer to the north bank of the River Thames for the crews in the Oxford and Cambridge BOAT RACE), in MIDDLESEX UNIVERSITY and as a participant in cricket's 'first-class' county structure.

The legacy of Middlesex is the suburbia of north-west London. Squire Bramble in Tobias Smollett's *Humphry Clinker* (1771) was already noting the creeping building blight ('If this infatuation continues for half a century I suppose the whole county of Middlesex will be covered with brick'), but until the early years of the 20th century large parts of the county were still essentially rural, little changed from the landscape that had inspired John Keats – if not quite the 'lost Elysium' celebrated by John Betjeman:

With a thousand Ta's and Pardon's

Daintily alights Elaine;
Hurries down the concrete station
With a frown of concentration,
Out into the outskirts' edges
Where a few surviving hedges
Keep alive our lost Elysium – rural Middlesex
again.

JOHN BETJEMAN: 'Middlesex' (1954)

Betjeman's poems contain a litany of former Middlesex villages and hamlets long since swallowed up by southern METROLAND.

Middlesex County Cricket Club Although other teams had earlier represented the county, the present-day club was founded in 1864 at the instigation of the Walker family of ARNOS GROVE, and played in ISLINGTON and FULHAM before being invited by the MARYLEBONE CRICKET CLUB to make LORD'S its home in 1878. Middlesex play some minor home games at a variety of other venues, including grounds in UXBRIDGE, EALING, SOUTHGATE and RICHMOND UPON THAMES. Its most famous players have included Denis Compton (*see the* BRYLCREEM BOY), Mike Brearley, Mike Gatting and Phil Tufnell.

Middlesex Hospital Formerly a hospital in Mortimer Street, FITZROVIA. It was founded in 1745 as the Middlesex Infirmary, and moved to its final location in the 1750s. It closed in 2005, when its facilities were merged within those of UNIVERSITY COLLEGE HOSPITAL. The site of the Middlesex Hospital will be redeveloped as housing and offices but the final form of the project was left uncertain following the property market turmoil that began in 2008. *See also* NOHO.

Middlesex Regiment *See the* DIEHARDS.

Middlesex Street A commercial thoroughfare leading south-eastwards off BISHOPSGATE towards ALDGATE. It received its name around 1830, because it formed the boundary between the CITY of London and the ancient county of Middlesex, replacing the earlier PETTICOAT LANE, which survives as the name of a market held here.

Middlesex University A North London university established in 1992, formerly Middlesex Polytechnic. Its ancestors were St Katherine's College in TOTTENHAM, HORNSEY School of Arts and Crafts, PONDERS END and HENDON Technical Institutes and Trent Park College of Education. From 1973 a series of mergers brought the polytechnic into being. Middlesex University has campuses at Hendon, the WHITTINGTON HOSPITAL in ARCHWAY, and at Cat Hill and Trent Park (both near COCKFOSTERS). A business school opened in Dubai in 2005. Future London developments will all be focused on the Hendon campus.

Middle Temple One of the four INNS OF COURT, sharing with the INNER TEMPLE the site of the former headquarters of the KNIGHTS TEMPLAR, south of the western end of FLEET STREET. There is some debate about when, why and even *if* the college for students of law divided itself into two separate inns of Court. The usual explanation is that at some time in the late 14th century the lawyers agreed on the split for administrative purposes. Another theory holds that there were always two societies, which later came to be called the 'Inner Temple' and 'Middle Temple' because the former lay nearer the CITY while the latter occupied the buildings in the middle of the complex. Middle Temple Hall, completed in 1574, has a double-hammer beam roof, an intricately carved screen, a minstrels' gallery and fine oak panelling. Elizabeth I dined in the hall on many occasions and SHAKESPEARE performed here in the first recorded production of *Twelfth Night* in 1602. *See also the* LAMB AND FLAG; TEMPLE.

Midtown A newish name for HOLBORN and south-east BLOOMSBURY. Although the name is the creation of property developers and letting agents, it is a useful designation for this resurgent area between the WEST END and the CITY of London, although some are overextending it to cover the entire southern part of the London Borough of CAMDEN.

Mi-krauliskey gav The Gypsy name for London, according to George Borrow in his *Romano Lavo-Lil*, or 'Word Book of the Romany' (1874). The words mean 'My king's town'. Borrow lists nearly 40 other Romany names for British places but only one of these is a settlement in what is now GREATER LONDON: Boro-rukeneskey gav, which is the 'Great tree town' of FAIRLOP.

Mildmay Park An increasingly cosmopolitan street and locality situated on the north-eastern edge of CANONBURY, north of BALLS POND ROAD. The estate was the property of the Halliday/Mildmay family from the early 17th century until the first half of the 19th century, when Lady St

John Mildmay began to sell off land in lots for building, although the main phase of activity did not come until a network of streets was laid out in the 1850s.

Mile End A contrasting district of 18th-century terraces and 1960s and 1970s tower blocks, situated west of BOW. The name derives from a hamlet, first recorded in 1288, that grew up 1 mile (1.6 km) from ALDGATE. Over the course of the 18th century the Mile End Road was lined with a disparate mix of merchants' houses and industrial buildings, including a brewery and a distillery. A blue plaque at 88 Mile End Road marks the site of the house where Captain James Cook (1728–79) once lived. Following an exodus of the mercantile population, the mostly poor Jewish community swelled. A large open space known as the Mile End Waste was used for political and religious meetings. Dr BARNARDO converted warehouses alongside the REGENT'S CANAL into Copperfield Road RAGGED SCHOOL (now a museum) in 1876, and colleges were established on the Mile End Road in the 1880s that became part of the UNIVERSITY OF LONDON in 1915. Conditions in the district deteriorated during the first half of the 20th century and after the Second World War the LONDON COUNTY COUNCIL and Stepney borough council cleared bomb sites and slums (including Captain Cook's house) and began a process of intensive rebuilding that continued into the 1970s. Pulp's song 'Mile End' (1995) bewails life in a tower block squat off Burdett Road:

Below the kids come out at night,
They kick a ball and have a fight
And maybe shoot somebody if they lose at pool.
Ooh, it's a mess all right,
Yes it's Mile End.

Miles's boy In the 19th century this young man was often adduced as a source of private information, as today one might say, 'a little bird told me'. He was also held responsible for tall tales and, when someone was sent on a fool's errand, the blame might be laid with Miles's boy. Conflicting attempts have been made to identify the original Miles, some suggesting he was a printer, others a tax collector, but usually agreeing that he lived in London. William Robins, in his *Paddington: Past and Present* (1853), is sure he was a coach driver who operated at the beginning of the 19th century:

> Mr Miles, his pair-horse coach, and his redoubtable Boy ... were for a long time the only appointed agents of communication between Paddington and the City ... Miles's Boy not only told tales, to the great amusement of his master's customers, but gave them some equally amusing variations on an old fiddle, which was his constant travelling companion, and which he carefully removed from its green-baize covering, to beguile the time at every resting-place on the road.

mill

Mill Hill A rambling, multi-focal village-cum-suburb situated between EDGWARE and FINCHLEY. Its self-explanatory name was first recorded in 1374. Quakers met at Rosebank, on the Ridgeway, from 1678 to 1719 and the weatherboarded building survives today. In 1807 a group of Nonconformist ministers and CITY merchants founded a Protestant Dissenters' grammar school in the former home of botanist Peter Collinson. By the end of the 19th century almost one-third of Mill Hill was covered by institutional buildings and their grounds – Mill Hill School alone covers 120 acres (49 hectares). As a result, most 20th-century development took place in what was virtually a fresh suburb, in the vicinity of MILL HILL BROADWAY. The National Institute for Medical Research moved to its imposing purpose-built home on the Ridgeway in 1950. The institute doubled as Arkham asylum in the film *Batman Begins* (2005).

> If you see her, tell her
> I'm standing at the Fiveways as the world spins round around me.

EDWARD BALL: 'The Mill Hill Self Hate Club' (song) (1996)

Mill Hill Broadway A main-line station and effectively Mill Hill's town centre, although it is located well to the west of the settlement's old heart. The station – first called Bunn's Lane – opened in 1868.The Broadway, which had formerly been the lower end of Lawrence Street, gained its present name when the Watford Way (A1) cut through the area in the 1920s. Over the following decade the Broadway became a major shopping centre and most of the surrounding fields were converted to middle-class housing estates as Mill Hill's centre of gravity shifted

away from the Ridgeway. Since 1965 the elevated section of the M1 motorway has soared over the district, with the station on one side and the Broadway itself on the other.

Mill Meads A nature reserve and historic industrial district situated among the creeks and channels of the River LEA, south of STRATFORD. A 'mead' was a meadow and the mills were mainly of the tidal variety, taking advantage of the twice-daily swell of the river where it becomes Bow Creek. Products milled here from the 16th century included corn, gunpowder and, later, grain for distilling gin. To the south of the Channelsea River lay Sir William Congreve's munitions works (*see* CONGREVE ROCKET).

Millbank A THAMES-side street extending from VAUXHALL BRIDGE to just short of the PALACE OF WESTMINSTER. This was land belonging to WESTMINSTER ABBEY when it was first recorded in 1546. The name referred to the presence of watermills on the embanked riverside. The last of these mills, which stood at the very northern end of Millbank, was pulled down early in the 18th century. Following the demolition of MILLBANK PENITENTIARY in 1892, the Royal Army Medical College and the Tate Gallery were built on its site. The former building is now home to the CHELSEA COLLEGE OF ART AND DESIGN; the latter has been rebranded TATE BRITAIN. Security service MI5 is headquartered at the forbidding-looking Thames House. One of J.M.W. Turner's first experiments in oil, *Moonlight, a Study at Millbank* (*c.*1797), hangs in Tate Britain.

Millbank Penitentiary A prison opened in 1816 (although construction was not completed until 1821) on a low-lying, marshy site beside the THAMES at Millbank. It embodied some of the philosopher Jeremy Bentham's ideas for a PANOPTICON, in which prisoners housed around the circumference of the building could be kept under constant observation by someone stationed in the centre. The resulting structure was shaped like a six-pointed star, surrounded by an octagonal wall. This was the largest prison in the country and became infamous for its harsh regime, although its founding principles were relatively enlightened by the standards of the time. The penitentiary closed in 1890.

Millbank Tendency A contemptuous nickname coined by adherents of 'Old Labour' for the New Labour apparatchiks whose tentacles spread over the Labour Party from their head-quarters in MILLBANK TOWER. The term was based on 'Militant Tendency', the name of the Trotskyite group that infiltrated the Labour Party in the 1980s.

Millbank Tower A 32-storey office block erected at 30 Millbank between 1960 and 1963. In 1997 the Labour Party relocated its headquarters here from working-class WALWORTH. In an era when New Labour spin ruled, the metonym 'Millbank' took on connotations of thought-control and amorality that sometimes verged on the sinister. In an imperfectly conceived cost-cutting exercise, Labour moved across WESTMINSTER to Old Queen Street in 2002, and then to VICTORIA STREET in 2005, the same year in which the Conservative Party moved its campaign headquarters into Millbank Tower.

millennium A thousand years (Latin *mille*, 'thousand', and *annus*, 'year'). What was technically the 'bimillennium' fell strictly speaking in 2001, but the appeal of a round figure easily drowned out the protests of the pedants, and special celebrations were held around the world to mark the arrival of the year 2000. In Britain the focus was on the Millennium Experience exhibition at the DOME.

Millennium Bridge See the WOBBLY BRIDGE.

Millennium Dome See the DOME.

Millennium Mills A vast granary built at the ROYAL DOCKS by Spiller's in the early 1930s, replacing earlier mills. The building has lain derelict since the closure of the docks. Neighbouring mills and storehouses have been demolished but this granary seems likely to be converted to apartments.

Millennium Quarter A regeneration zone located south of CANARY WHARF on the ISLE OF DOGS. It is dominated by two residential skyscrapers called the Pan Peninsula towers. *See also* SOUTH QUAY.

Millennium Village An urban village under development on the GREENWICH PENINSULA, south-east of the DOME. Built on the site of a former gasworks, the project has aimed for good standards of design and innovation in environmental sustainability. On balance, it is succeeding.

Millennium Wheel See the LONDON EYE.

Millionaires' Row The nickname has been applied to several exclusive London thoroughfares,

notably KENSINGTON Palace Gardens from the 19th century and the BISHOPS AVENUE since the 1930s. Upper Cheyne Row is the only candidate that already bears the name 'Row'. In the far north-west, Astons Road has recently been labelled 'London's Indian millionaires' row' – but it actually lies just beyond the capital's border, in Moor Park, Hertfordshire.

Mills, Bertram See BERTRAM MILLS.

Millwall A primarily residential district in the south-western part of the ISLE OF DOGS. Its name derives from the windmills that once lined the western embankment. Before the mills appeared this was Pomfret Manor, the base for the earliest recorded THAMES ferry east of the CITY of London, which plied between here and GREENWICH in the mid-15th century. Great Eastern pier was the site of the Scott Russell shipyard, where the steamship SS *Great Eastern* was built and launched in 1857, subsequently laying the first Atlantic telecommunications cable. In 1868 Millwall Docks opened to handle imports of timber and grain, and McDougall's flour works was established. Other industries included shipbuilding, engineering and chemicals, and an oil works owned by local resident Alexander Duckham. Millwall suffered heavily during the BLITZ and was afterwards redeveloped intensively, first with council housing and since the 1980s with upmarket apartment blocks.

Millwall Chainsaws A PUNK ROCK group formed in the late 1970s that developed into Pogue Mahone, later known as The Pogues, the hybrid punk-Irish folk band fronted by the singer and songwriter Shane MacGowan (b.1957).

Millwall FC An association FOOTBALL club founded in 1885 by workers at Morton's, a cannery specializing in preserves. The club played at several grounds on the ISLE OF DOGS before moving in 1910 to the Den, on Cold Blow Lane, NEW CROSS. In the latter part of the 20th century its supporters gained an above-average reputation for truculence and their motto became NO ONE LIKES US, WE DON'T CARE. In 1993 the LIONS moved a short distance to a new stadium at Senegal Fields, South BERMONDSEY.

Millwall Reserves A football-derived COCKNEY RHYMING SLANG term – also plain Millwalls – from the 1950s, meaning 'nerves' (as in 'get on someone's Millwalls').

Milton

Milton, John The English poet (1608–74) and author of, *inter alia*, *Comus* (1633), *Paradise Lost* (1667), *Paradise Regained* (1671) and *Samson Agonistes* (1671). He was born in BREAD STREET and educated at ST PAUL'S SCHOOL and Christ's College, Cambridge. He dwelt in the CITY for most of his adult life, spending his latter years in a house on Artillery Walk (now Bunhill Row), near BUNHILL FIELDS. Milton was buried in St Giles' CRIPPLEGATE.

> Milton is the deity of prescience; he stands
> ab extra, and drives a fiery chariot and four,
> making the horses feel the iron curb which
> holds them in.
>
> SAMUEL TAYLOR COLERIDGE: *Table Talk* (1835)

Milton Street
1. A short street located at the north-east corner of the BARBICAN. Formerly GRUB STREET, it was renamed in 1829 after the carpenter and builder who was the ground landlord. Milton Street was subsequently denuded of dwellings following an influx of businesses to the area and an exodus of residents, a process that was bolstered by the extension of the underground railway line from FARRINGDON to MOORGATE in 1865.
2. The former identity of BALCOMBE STREET.

mince pies 'Eyes' in COCKNEY RHYMING SLANG, sometimes abbreviated to 'minces'.

> Rafe and Timothy Spall as the Emersons père
> et fils, seemed to have come to Florence on a
> Pearly Kings' holiday. 'Why Miss Honeychurch,
> haven't you got a luvverly pair of mince pies?
> Let's have a bubble bath down Fiesole way.'
>
> *Independent on Sunday* (11 November 2007)

Mincing Lane A short street branching south from the middle of FENCHURCH STREET. It was called in the 13th century 'Menechinelane', 'Monechenlane', and the like, and in the time of Henry VIII (r.1509–47) 'Mynchyn Lane'. The name is from Old English *mynecen*, 'nun' (feminine of *munuc*, 'monk'), and the street is probably so called from the tenements held there by a house of nuns. Mincing Lane was the traditional centre of the TEA trade, for which its name was formerly often used as a generic term.

> Mincing Lane is pretty confident of higher
> prices for Africans [i.e. African teas] by the end
> of the first quarter of this year.
>
> *East African Standard* (Nairobi) (23 January 1970)

Minder An ITV comedy-drama series of 1979–94 about a well-meaning bodyguard or 'minder', Terry McCann, played by Dennis Waterman (later replaced by Gary Webster as Terry's cousin), and his boss, a shady second-hand car dealer, Arthur DALEY, played by George Cole. Set in WILLESDEN, the series began as a thriller but low ratings and critical disfavour caused a reduction in its violence and an increase in its humour, to the benefit of all concerned.

Channel Five revived *Minder* in 2009, without the original characters and backdrop. Instead, Shane Ritchie plays Daley's nephew Archie, Lex Shrapnel is his minder Jamie Cartwright, and the action takes place mainly in south-east London.

mind the gap The most famous recorded announcement on the LONDON UNDERGROUND network. The necessity for the warning arises when inevitably straight-carriaged trains arrive at stations with curving platforms, upon which the cautionary advice is often stencilled. The brevity of the phrase is said to derive from the limitations of solid-state digital recording technology when it was first introduced in the late 1960s. T-shirts and various gift items bearing the message have become popular tourist souvenirs.

> A voice came over the loudspeaker, that formal,
> disembodied male voice that warned 'Mind the
> Gap'. It was intended to keep unwary passengers
> from stepping into the space between the train
> and the platform. Richard, like most Londoners,
> barely heard it anymore – it was like aural
> wallpaper.
>
> NEIL GAIMAN: *Neverwhere* (1996)

Minerva Press A printing establishment in LEADENHALL STREET that was famous in the late 18th century for its trashy and sentimental novels, characterized by complicated plots.

ministry

Ministry of Magic *See* POTTER, HARRY.
Ministry of Sound A large nightclub situated on Gaunt Street, ELEPHANT AND CASTLE, opened in a converted bus garage in 1991. Despite its unglamorous location and an absence of alcohol, the operation was a success, spawning a record label, internet radio station and a range of youth-oriented 'lifestyle products'.

The group Future Bitch, for example, announcing its début at the Ministry of Sound – which is the heart of London's youth culture – declares its aim 'to disorientate its audience, pushing the current cultural scene to its limits and towards the millennium.'

ROGER SCRUTON: *Modern Culture* (2007)

Minories A street running southwards from ALDGATE to TOWER HILL. In 1294 a nunnery, the abbey of the Franciscan nuns or Minoresses of St Clare (Poor Clares) was established here, giving the street its name. It was dissolved in 1538. From the 16th to the 18th centuries the street was noted for its gunsmiths' shops.

mint A place where money is coined gets its name from Old English *mynet*, in turn from Latin *moneta*, 'money', itself from the temple of Juno Moneta, used as a mint in ancient Rome. The chief seat of the Mint was situated in the TOWER OF LONDON from its erection until 1810, when it moved to new premises upon TOWER HILL and was one of the earliest public buildings lighted with gas. The Mint was removed to Llantrisant, west of Cardiff, in 1968. There was also a Mint at SOUTHWARK (*see* LIBERTY OF THE MINT).

misers Among the most renowned are:

Baron Aguilar or Ephraim Lopes Pereira d'Aguilar (1740–1802): born in Vienna and died in ISLINGTON, worth £200,000 (*see also* STARVATION FARM)

Daniel Dancer (1716–94): lived at Waldo's Farm, HARROW WEALD, but refused to go to the expense of cultivating the land; in wintertime he defrosted food by sitting on it rather than light a fire, and knocked out his dog's teeth to avoid compensating neighbours if it attacked their livestock; his story was the subject of various popular accounts, including *The Strange and Unaccountable Life of the Penurious Daniel Dancer Esq., A Miserable Miser, Who died in a Sack* (1797)

Jemmy Taylor (*c*.1723–93): the SOUTHWARK USURER

Sir Hervey Elwes (d.1763): worth £250,000 but never spent more than £110 a year; his sister-in-law inherited £100,000, but actually starved herself to death, and her son John (1714–89), an MP and eminent brewer in SOUTHWARK, never bought any clothes, never allowed his shoes to be cleaned, and grudged every penny spent on food

Thomas Guy (*c*.1645–1724): founder of GUY'S HOSPITAL

misery line An enduring nickname for the NORTHERN LINE, first popularized at a time of particularly persistent delays in the 1980s. Problems with rolling stock breakdowns were exacerbated by the line's multiple bifurcations, which meant that even when a train did arrive it would often not be 'the right one'.

I recently read these lines, from Ariel's song in The Tempest, … as one of London Transport's series of posters Poems on the Underground. There I was, on what travellers know as the 'Misery Line', my body impacted with the suffering flesh of a thousand fellow-passengers. I looked up, read the poster, and for a moment the Misery Line suffered a sea change.

GRAHAM HOLDERNESS: *Cultural Shakespeare: Essays in the Shakespeare Myth* (2001)

The tag has also sometimes been applied to other railways in the London area, notably the main-line service out of FENCHURCH STREET.

Mitcham A sprawling south London suburb with an ancient village at its heart, situated south of TOOTING. Elizabeth I is said to have granted a charter for an annual fair after she had enjoyed watching the formerly unofficial festivities. CITY gentlemen established country retreats in the mid-17th century, attracted by the village's reputation for clean air at a time when London was frequently ravaged by epidemics. Mitcham can make a strong claim to have the country's oldest cricket ground in continual use, with good evidence that games were being played on the Cricket Green in 1685. From the mid-18th century large parts of Mitcham were given over to the cultivation of aromatic plants and shrubs, including camomile, poppies, liquorice and anise. Ephraim Potter and William Moore took advantage of Mitcham's rich black loam to grow lavender, setting up a distillery at Tamworth Farm. Others soon followed, and even after the physic gardens had been built over or converted to market gardens the finest extracts were still described as 'Mitcham lavender oil'.

The poet John Donne lived on Whitford Lane from 1605 to 1608.

Mitcham Common A 460-acre (186-hectare) expanse of open terrain, located south-east of the centre of Mitcham. The common was cleared of its oak trees in Neolithic times and extensive grazing kept the acidic soil infertile. Gravel extraction in the 19th century created depressions and ponds, of which Seven Islands Pond is the largest. In 1891 the Mitcham Common Conservators took the land under their wing and ended destructive practices such as gravel extraction and turf removal, while permitting golfing in a limited area. Postwar waste disposal created the common's low hills and destroyed some wetland habitats, but raised money for the conservators, who have more recently enhanced the acid grassland and heathland.

> ... the endless and verdant Mitcham Common, with her ponds ... a soft green golf-course, copses, unthreatening marshes, stands of poplars, cedars and ... pedestrian bridges of wood and iron spanning a railway, sandy bunkers and depressions.
>
> MICHAEL MOORCOCK: *Mother London* (1988)

Mitcham whisper An old term for a raised voice.

> ... for you can hear them outside the house; they generally speak four or five at a time, and every one in a Mitcham whisper, which is very like a shout.
>
> quoted in R.B. COOK: *The Wit and Wisdom of Rev Charles H. Spurgeon* (1892)

Mitre Tavern A tavern in FLEET STREET, first mentioned in 1603, but probably a good deal older. It was a frequent resort of Samuel JOHNSON and James Boswell and ceased to be a tavern in 1788. Another Mitre, mentioned by Ben Jonson and Samuel PEPYS, existed in Wood Street.

mockney (a blend of 'mock' and 'cockney') An affected imitation of COCKNEY speech or vocabulary, or a person who adopts such speech. Those accused of peddling the vernacular have included the musicians Damon Albarn and Nigel Kennedy, the actor Keith Allen and his singer/songwriter daughter Lily, the film director Guy Ritchie, the chef Jamie Oliver and even some younger members of the royal family. *See also* FROCKNEY.

> The original Mockney, Sir Michael Phillip 'Mick' Jagger discovered the blues, the music of oppressed Southern blacks, growing up in Kent.
>
> *The Times* (20 June 2008)

Mods A teenage cult (from 'modern') that developed in London in the early 1960s, initially putting emphasis on fastidiousness and extravagance in dress and fashion. The rise of CARNABY STREET as their dress centre was a consequence. Mods were distinguished by their fondness for the anoraks known as Parkas, patriotic insignia, motor scooters and the music of The Who, whose song 'My Generation' (1965, including the lyric 'Hope I die before I get old') became something of a Mod anthem. With the rise of the rival gangs of leather-jacketed Rockers, trouble began. Bank holiday clashes between Mods and Rockers, who arrived in their hordes on scooters and motorcycles, made some seaside resorts hazardous places.

mogadored EAST END slang, almost but not quite obsolete, meaning 'confused' or 'perplexed'. The word may have come into use as COCKNEY RHYMING SLANG for 'floored' but its deeper origins remain obscure. The *Oxford English Dictionary* (which prefers the spelling 'moggadored') dates its first appearance in print to 1936 but cannot help with an etymology. Irish, Romany, Moroccan and French roots have all been suggested. In the example below, the word seems to be employed as a euphemism for 'buggered':

> But she'd never seen Granny Weatherwax in rouge. All her normal expletives of shock and surprise fused instantly, and she found herself resorting to an ancient curse belonging to her grandmother. 'Well, I'll be mogadored!' she said.
>
> TERRY PRATCHETT: *Maskerade* (1995)

Mogden An old name for a part of south ISLEWORTH now dominated by Thames Water's Mogden sewage treatment works. Opened in 1936 on the site of Mogden Farm, it treats the waste water of a population of about 1.8 million people living in a 60-square mile (155-sq km) catchment area of north and west London.

Mogden formula A sewerage industry pricing structure that seeks to link charges to the volume and strength of trade effluent discharged.

Mohocks Ruffians (many of whom were said to be 'of the higher classes') who in the 18th century infested the streets of London. They were so called from the Mohawk nation, indigenous people of North America. According to John Gay, one of their 'new inventions' was to roll people down SNOW HILL in a tub. Another was to overturn coaches on rubbish heaps. However, Jonathan Swift thought that tales of the Mohocks' misdeeds were greatly exaggerated. *See* *also* HAWCUBITES; ROARING BOYS; SCOWERERS; TITYRE-TUS.

> ... they take care to drink themselves to a pitch, that is, beyond the possibility of attending to any motions of reason and humanity; then make a general sally, and attack all that are so unfortunate as to walk the streets through which they patrol. Some are knock'd down, others stabb'd, others cut and carbonado'd.
>
> 'PHILANTHROPOS', in *The Spectator*, No.324 (12 March 1712)

moke A COSTERMONGER's donkey.

> These donkeys – 'mokes' in the vernacular – are regarded by costers as their best and dearest friends. Consequently they are treated most unmercifully, but not quite so cruelly, perhaps, as their wives.
>
> *New York Times* (26 March 1893)

Mole Man The sobriquet of William Lyttle (b.1931), a retired electrical engineer of Mortimer Road, DE BEAUVOIR TOWN. Having inherited a 20-room Victorian house in the 1960s, Lyttle began digging downwards and then outwards in several directions. Over a 40-year period he removed an estimated 3,500 cubic feet (100 m³) of soil, almost causing the property to collapse and bringing the risk of subsidence to nearby roads. HACKNEY council evicted the Mole Man in August 2006 to allow work to stabilize the house and in April 2008 presented him with a repair bill for nearly £300,000.

> I first tried to dig a wine cellar, and then the cellar doubled, and so on. But the idea that I dug tunnels under other people's houses is rubbish. I just have a big basement. It's gone down deep enough to hit the water table – that's the lowest you can go.
>
> WILLIAM LYTTLE, quoted in *The Guardian* (8 August 2006)

monarch of the road An epithet applied to the ROUTEMASTER bus by the musical duo Flanders and Swann in their song 'Transport of Delight' (1960):

> When cabbies try to pass us, before they overtakes,
> My driver sticks his hand out and jams on all the brakes.
> Them jackal taxi drivers can only swear and cuss
> Behind that monarch of the road,

> Observer of the Highway Code,
> That big six-wheeler scarlet-painted London Transport diesel-engined 97-horsepower omnibus.

The Routemaster Association has published a photographic book entitled *Monarch of the Road: A Celebration of a London Icon*, recording a rally of more than a hundred Routemasters that took place in FINSBURY PARK and on the streets of London in 2004.

Monday Pops A contraction of 'Monday Populars', meaning popular concerts for classical music, introduced at St James's Hall, PICCADILLY, by Arthur Chappell in 1858. The series continued for 40 years. There were Saturday Pops also.

Mongrel Parliament The Parliament that Charles II summoned at Oxford in 1681 to deprive the Whigs of the support of the CITY of London in their struggle to alter the succession, i.e. to exclude the Duke of York, a Roman Catholic.

Monken Hadley Like neighbouring HIGH BARNET and Chipping Barnet, HADLEY and Monken Hadley are historically one and the same place but are now shown separately on maps. Monken Hadley, so called because the manor once belonged to the Benedictine monks of Walden Abbey in Essex, tends to be identified as the part to the north. The origin of this distinction is that a 27-acre (11-hectare) civil parish called Hadley was detached from the parish of Monken Hadley in 1894 and given to BARNET urban district council, while the remaining 668 acres (270 ha) became part of EAST BARNET Valley urban district. The two parts were reunited within the London Borough of Barnet in 1965, which created the conservation area of Monken Hadley in 1968.

monkey Slang for £500. Said to derive from the Indian 500 rupee note, which carried a picture of a monkey.

Monks Orchard An interwar middle-class housing development located on the borders of BECKENHAM and SHIRLEY. An ADDINGTON family called Monk owned a farm here sometime before the mid-17th century and Monksmead and Monks Orchard were the names given to their meadow and wood respectively. Lewis Lloyd acquired the estate in the early 1850s and and built a 19-bedroom mansion that he named after the wood. The CORPORATION OF LONDON acquired the property in 1924 for the relocation of the Bethlem Royal Hospital (*see* BEDLAM) from LAMBETH. Construction of the hospital began in 1928 and the mansion was demolished. The corporation did not require all the land it had bought so the remainder was sold off for housing and the present street plan was soon laid out.

Monmouth Street Now part of the COVENT GARDEN retail experience, this street was formerly famed for its sign-board painters, public houses that held fancy dog shows, and affordable retailers who specialized at various times in amateur theatrical properties, singing birds, laced and embroidered coats, and second-hand clothes and footwear, hence the old expression 'Monmouth Street finery' for tawdry, pretentious clothes.

> [At the Venetian carnival] you may put on whate'er
> You like by way of doublet, cape or cloak,
> Such as in Monmouth Street or in Rag Fair
> Would rig you out in seriousness or joke.
> LORD BYRON: 'Beppo' (1818)

Monopoly The popular board game, based on the acquisition of real estate, originated in the USA in about 1930 as the brainchild of Charles B. Darrow, a heating equipment engineer, who set the game in Atlantic City, New Jersey, as this was where the Darrows spent their holidays. In 1936 the Leeds-based printer John Waddington Ltd launched a British version of the game that was marketed in Europe and much of the English-speaking world, excluding North America. Waddington's version featured London streets (and the Angel, Islington) and KING'S CROSS, MARYLEBONE, FENCHURCH STREET and LIVER-POOL STREET stations (each valued at £200). The streets and their values are as follows:

OLD KENT ROAD (£60)
WHITECHAPEL Road (£60)
The ANGEL, ISLINGTON (£100)
EUSTON ROAD (£100)
PENTONVILLE Road (£120)
PALL MALL (£140)
WHITEHALL (£140)
NORTHUMBERLAND AVENUE (£160)
BOW STREET (£180)
(GREAT) MARLBOROUGH STREET (£180)
VINE STREET (£200)
STRAND (£220)
FLEET STREET (£220)
TRAFALGAR SQUARE (£240)
LEICESTER SQUARE (£260)
Coventry Street (£260)
PICCADILLY (£280)
REGENT STREET (£300)
OXFORD STREET (£300)
BOND STREET (£320)
PARK LANE (£350)
MAYFAIR (£400)

Monster A tavern and its adjacent tea gardens that stood at the corner of St George's Row and Buckingham Palace Road, PIMLICO. The name was said to have been a corruption (perhaps in deliberate jest) of 'Monastery', from an earlier inn sign commemorating the medieval possession of the site by the Abbot and Monastery of Westminster. The tavern was for some years the starting point for the Monster line of omnibuses. The Monster was destroyed during the BLITZ and a block of flats afterwards took its place.

Monster Soup The title of a memorable and much-reproduced etching (*c*.1828) by William Heath (1795–1840), depicting the state of London's drinking water. It shows a woman examining a droplet of THAMES water under a microscope and reacting in horrified disgust to the world of grotesque creatures she discovers therein.

monstrous carbuncle Prince Charles's description in May 1984 of a planned extension to the NATIONAL GALLERY. At a gala evening held at HAMPTON COURT PALACE to celebrate the 150th anniversary of the Royal Institute of British Architects, he likened the modernist design, by the architectural partnership Ahrends Burton Koralek, to a 'a kind of municipal fire station ... a monstrous carbuncle on the face of a much-loved and elegant friend'. The prince's controversial criticism influenced the cancellation of the commission and its replacement with a more complementary design by Robert Venturi and Denise Scott Brown. The Sainsbury Wing opened in July 1991. The term 'monstrous carbuncle' has since been employed to describe any proposed development that is perceived to be inappropriate to its setting.

> The language of popular judgement, with its 'monstrous carbuncles', 'wobbly bridges' and

'erotic gherkins', is intelligible and occasionally amusing, but it does not support serious, extended discussion of the merits of the buildings most people routinely use.

THOMAS A. MARKUS and DEBORAH CAMERON: *The Words Between the Spaces: Buildings and Language* (2002)

Montpellier or Montpelier of England

An epithet formerly applied to several salubrious places across the southern half of the country. In the London area, MITCHAM and CAMBER-WELL Grove have both been so called. Elizabeth Montagu, founder of the BLUE STOCKING Club, described PORTMAN SQUARE in the same words. Developers appropriated the French resort's name (which is nowadays always spelt 'Montpellier') for more than a dozen streets in the capital, as did the builders of a similar number of grand houses. The most handsome terrace bearing the name is Montpellier Row, built on the edge of MARBLE HILL Park in the early 1720s. The Montpelier Tea Gardens were established at WALWORTH around 1780, and the Montpelier Cricket Club played there from 1796 to 1844, when the land was acquired for development. The club found a new home in KENNINGTON, leasing a market garden to create a ground that became known as the OVAL.

Monument

A fluted Roman-Doric column of Portland stone standing at the junction of Monument Street and Fish Street Hill, just north of LONDON BRIDGE. Erected between 1671 and 1677 to the design of Sir Christopher Wren, the Monument commemorates the GREAT FIRE OF LONDON that had destroyed most of the CITY in 1666. It stands 202 feet (61.5m) high – its precise distance from the fire's source, a bakery in Pudding Lane – and is topped by a gilded flame. The pedestal originally carried an inscription blaming Roman Catholics for the fire. Referring to this, Alexander Pope wrote:

Where London's column pointing at the skies,
Like a tall bully, lifts its head and lies.

Moral Essays, Epistle iii (1731–5)

In 1831 the CORPORATION OF LONDON erased the offending words. Over 100,000 visitors a year climb the 311-step spiral staircase to the Monument's observation platform, now enclosed to prevent the suicides for which it was once notorious. The column was floodlit in 1994 and extensively restored the following year.

Monument station A LONDON UNDERGROUND station that opened in October 1884 on a section of track that completed what became the CIRCLE LINE. It was called EASTCHEAP for the first month of its existence.

Moorfields

Originally a large open space that stretched from the north side of the CITY wall towards HOXTON and ISLINGTON. From 1415 the Moor Gate opened onto Moorfields, newly acquired by the CORPORATION OF LONDON. At that time the fields were marshland – the origin of the Walbrook watercourse and 'full of noisome waters' – although the Corporation soon set to work improving the drainage. Moorfields frequently froze over in winter to form London's first skating rink, on which young men wearing 'shin-bone' ice skates played a game that involved tilting at their comrades with iron-tipped sticks. In 1675 the Bethlem Royal Hospital (*see* BEDLAM) moved from BISHOPSGATE to Moorfields, and then in 1815 to LAMBETH. George Dance the Younger (1741–1825) planned the redevelopment of Lower Moorfields in the late 18th century, creating FINSBURY Square, Finsbury Circus and the surrounding streets. The scheme included the City of London's finest Roman Catholic church, St Mary Moorfields. This was demolished at the end of the century, when the whole area was rebuilt, and replaced by the present, more recessive church on Eldon Street. A back street named Moorfields survives near LONDON WALL, by MOORGATE station. A nonsense nursery rhyme probably dating from the 17th century begins:

As I was walking o'er little Moorfields,
I saw St Paul's a-running on wheels,
With a fee, fo, fum.

Moorfields Eye Hospital The largest specialist eye hospital in the world, opened in 1805 in CHARTERHOUSE Square by John Cunningham Saunders (1773-1810), primarily in response to a severe outbreak of ophthalmia among troops returning from the Napoleonic Wars in Egypt. It began as the London Dispensary for the Relief of the Poor Afflicted with Diseases of the Eye and Ear, and in 1822 moved to purpose-built new premises at Finsbury Circus, Lower Moorfields, becoming the Royal London Ophthalmic Hospital in 1837. Because of its location it was generally known as 'Moorfields Eye Hospital' but this did not become its official name until 1956. The hospital moved to its present site on CITY ROAD in 1899, since when it has been much enlarged.

Moorgate A commercial street running from the north-west corner of the BANK OF ENGLAND northwards to the edge of the CITY of London. The Moor Gate was built in 1415 and demolished in 1761, when its stones were used to repair LONDON BRIDGE. Moorgate Street, as the thoroughfare was initially called, was constructed in the late 1830s as part of a new route to London Bridge. The underground station, also originally named Moorgate Street, opened in 1865, at the expense of several little alleys and courts. In the four decades before 1930 almost all of Moorgate was rebuilt with stone-faced office blocks, of which a handful of good examples survive. Much of the street has been rebuilt again over the past 25 years, with plentiful use of glass and steel. The poet John Keats (1795–1821) was born in a stable in Moorgate and lived at No.85 until he was 9 years old.

Moorgate disaster On 28 February 1975 a NORTHERN LINE train smashed into the tunnel end at Moorgate station almost at full speed, killing 43 people. The driver was among the dead, and whether he crashed the train deliberately or suffered some sudden mental incapacitation has never been satisfactorily determined. An automatic stopping system introduced to prevent such an event occurring again is known as 'Moorgate control'.

Morden A sea of 1930s suburbia graced by two islands of parkland, located south-west of MERTON and MITCHAM. Early Morden developed around twin nuclei: St Lawrence Church (and later Morden Park House) in the south-west and Morden Hall in the north-east. A snuff manufacturer and would-be country squire, Gilliat Hatfeild (1827–1906), bought Morden Hall in 1872 and protected the neighbourhood from early suburban development. The NORTHERN LINE (as it is now) was extended here from CLAPHAM COMMON in 1926. Fares were set low with the deliberate intention of stimulating a housing boom in Morden and the plan worked. Gilliat Hatfeild's son Gilliat Edward died in 1941 and left Morden Hall Park to the National Trust. The council bought Morden Park in 1945, preserving 90 acres (36 hectares) as open space and playing fields.

Walking down Cannon Hill Lane,
I saw the flowers lay where a car crash took place.
A drug dealer crashed into a chicane,
It sort of sums up where we live: in Morden.
GOOD SHOES: 'Morden' (song) (2007)

more

more front than Selfridges Said of someone who is perceived to be excessively pushy or self-assured. Other London establishments to have served similar duties include HARRODS, BUCKINGHAM PALACE and the ALBERT HALL. There are numerous international variations on the theme, from Australia's Myer department stores to assorted pleasure beaches and buxom actresses.

Mr Braithwaite called on Mr Treves to resign. 'Vanni Treves has more front than Selfridges and is continuing to tough it out,' he said. 'Anyone with a shred of honour would have fallen on his own sword.'
The Times (11 October 2005)

more rabbit than Sainsbury's *See* RABBIT (AND PORK).

Don't Have Any More, Mrs Moore *See under* DO.

Moriarty The arch-enemy of Sherlock HOLMES, said to have been partly modelled on the German-born criminal Adam Worth (1844–1902), who, like Moriarty, was nicknamed 'the NAPOLEON OF CRIME'. The character's full name is Professor James Moriarty and he came to London following rumours of nefarious deeds at an unnamed provincial university where he held the chair in mathematics. He was devised by Conan Doyle as a character who could effectively kill off Holmes. The two men finally meet in a 'clash of the titans' above the Reichenbach Falls in Switzerland. After a hand-to-hand struggle, they apparently fall to their deaths in the cataracts below. However, Conan Doyle subsequently resurrected Holmes, although the evil Moriarty remained dead.

Morningside Park The disguised identity of WORCESTER PARK in H.G. Wells's novel *Ann Veronica* (1909). Wells had lived for a while at 41 The Avenue, Worcester Park, and described it in the novel as 'a suburb that had not altogether, as people say, come off'.

Mornington Crescent A street and underground station located at the junction of Hampstead Road and CAMDEN High Street. The crescent was created in the 1820s and named in honour of Richard Wellesley (1760–1842), who became the 2nd Earl of Mornington in 1781. Greater London House is an imposing office block occupying the arc of the crescent; it was formerly the Carreras 'Black Cat' cigarette factory. Except for CHEYNE WALK, few streets have rivalled Mornington Crescent as a creative hotbed. Its former residents have included the artists Spencer Gore, Clarkson Stanfield and Walter Sickert, who was living here when he founded the post-Impressionist CAMDEN TOWN GROUP in 1911. The illustrator and political caricaturist George Cruikshank lived in Mornington Place.

> I acted so tragic the house rose like magic,
> The audience yelled 'You're sublime!'
> They made me a present of Mornington Crescent,
> They threw it a brick at a time.
> WILLIAM HARGREAVES: 'The Night I Appeared As Macbeth' (song) (1922)

The name 'Mornington Crescent' has been given to an improvised parlour game played by panel members on the BBC radio programme 'I'm Sorry, I Haven't a Clue' (from 1972). The ostensible 'aim' of the game is to move from station to station around the LONDON UNDERGROUND system according to a set of obscure and indeterminate rules and conventions (about which the players argue and on which they learnedly digress), and to be the first to get to Mornington Crescent station.

morocco men Men who, about the end of the 18th century, used to visit London public houses touting for illegal lottery insurances. They were so called because they tallied their accounts in notebooks bound in morocco leather. Their rendezvous was a tavern in Oxford Market, at the OXFORD STREET end of GREAT PORTLAND STREET.

Mortlake A THAMES-side settlement, lying opposite the tip of the CHISWICK peninsula. Its name probably derives from the Old English words *mort*, a young salmon, and *lacu*, a small stream (since lost). Around 1743 John Sanders founded his Mortlake pottery, becoming London's largest manufacturer of stoneware. Joseph Kishere, a former employee at Sanders' pottery, subsequently established his own pottery on the south side of the high street, making decorative pots known as Kishereware. During the latter part of the 18th century, when some fine houses were being erected by the river, James Weatherstone ran a successful brewery that he extended to the waterfront in 1807. The business went on to benefit from lucrative contracts to supply the British army in India with pale ale and was subsequently acquired by Watney's. Mortlake's entrepreneurial achievements continued when Richard Wesley Gale began bottling his prize honey here in 1919. The Stag brewery is the only significant industrial enterprise still operating in Mortlake, nowadays producing Budweiser lager for Anheuser-Busch, but the owners propose to close it in 2010.

Mortlake tapestries Highly detailed 17th-century wall-hangings, many depicting biblical or mythical scenes, woven for palaces and stately homes. The village of Mortlake consisted of just a few riverside houses on a single street in 1619, when James I provided financial backing for the establishment of a tapestry works employing Flemish weavers. Charles I bought out the enterprise in 1636 and it continued until 1703. KENSINGTON PALACE and HAMPTON COURT PALACE possess sets of Mortlake tapestries.

Moscow Hall The nickname of the lower level concourse of GANTS HILL station, built in 1947, from its resemblance to the station designs of the Moscow metro, though on a more modest scale.

Moss Bros The well-known firm of outfitters ultimately takes its name from Moses Moses, a Jewish bespoke tailor who set up shop in KING STREET, COVENT GARDEN, in 1860. The 'Bros' were two of his five sons, George and Alfred, who inherited the business on their father's death in 1894, anglicizing their surname to Moss. The Moss Bros Group, based at CLAPHAM JUNCTION, controls several brands and retail fascias, with Moss Bros stores specializing in hiring out dress suits.

most

most famous street in the world PICCADILLY has been thus exalted, as once was the STRAND, but so have thoroughfares in a dozen other great cities, notably the Avenue des Champs-Elysées in

Paris. In New York City, 42nd Street, Broadway, Fifth Avenue and Wall Street have all laid claim to the title.

> Night crowds, made up, not of lords and ladies, but of ordinary Londoners, filled the Strand, for years the most famous street in the world. It handed its supremacy to Piccadilly almost in our own times ...
>
> HENRY MORTON: *H.V. Morton's London* (1940)

most visible church *See the* VISIBLE CHURCH.

mother

Mother Clap's Molly House A place of entertainment in FIELD LANE, kept by one Margaret Clap in the 1720s. Up to 50 homosexual men would consort there every night, until the house was raided in February 1726. Mother Clap was tried at the OLD BAILEY, convicted of keeping a disorderly house and sentenced to be pilloried in SMITHFIELD and imprisoned for two years. One client, Gabriel Lawrence, was found guilty of sodomy and sentenced to death. The events have been the subject of an academic study by Rictor Norton (1992) and the inspiration for a play by Mark Ravenhill with songs by Matthew Scott (2001), both entitled *Mother Clap's Molly House*.

> Samuel Stevens thus depos'd ... Sometimes they'd sit in one another's Laps, use their Hands indecently Dance and make Curtsies and mimick the Language of Women – O Sir! – Pray Sir! – Dear Sir! Lord how can ye serve me so! – Ah ye little dear Toad! Then they'd go by Couples, into a Room on the same Floor to be marry'd as they call'd it.
>
> *Old Bailey Proceedings*, trial transcript (11 July 1726)

Mother London A socially panoramic history novel (1988) by Michael Moorcock. It moves around the capital from the BLITZ to the 1980s, allowing a wide range of voices to be heard via its conceit of giving its three central characters – all from a mental hospital – abilities to 'hear' conversations in their minds.

> I am familiar with every crack in every paving stone from here to Hornsey, to Harrow, to Hounslow, Hammersmith, Hayes, Ham (East and West), Harold Hill – London's encircled by more aitches than ditches.
>
> *Mother London*

Mother Red Cap An early 17th-century tavern in what was at that time part of KENTISH TOWN, now CAMDEN TOWN, said to have been the

frequent resort of Moll CUTPURSE. It was named after a former tenant of the premises, one Jinny Bingham, a woman of witch-like appearance who scraped a living from fortune-telling and curing obscure diseases. She habitually wore a 'grotesque' red cap, kept a huge black cat by her side and was also known as the Shrew of Kentish Town and Mother Damnable. When she died, the Devil was seen to enter her house, but not to re-emerge. However, some authorities disbelieve much of this narrative (and the many variations on it) and suspect that a colourful legend has been invented, based primarily on the distinctive pictorial signboard of a long-established public house.

Motspur Park An interwar suburban locality situated on the south-eastern side of NEW MALDEN, best known for its sports grounds. The Mot family lived in the area in the 14th century and gave their name to a farm that lay west of the present railway line. In 1627 the farm was called Motes Firs, a reference to the furze (gorse) that grew round about. It had become Motts Spur Farm by 1823.

Mottingham A residential locality situated east of GROVE PARK in the London Borough of LEWISHAM, dominated by an interwar council estate that was built in the direction of CHISLEHURST. An Anglo-Saxon charter of 862 identified the boundary of land belonging to Mōda's people. The name Mōda suggested someone who was proud, bold and hard-working.

Mount Pleasant

1. A densely built-up street and locality in west CLERKENWELL, rising from FARRINGDON ROAD to GRAY'S INN ROAD, behind Rosebery Avenue. The heaps of cinders and other refuse dumped at the end of what was originally a country track gave rise to the ironic name Mount Pleasant. In 1886 the Post Office acquired the former COLD BATH FIELDS Prison, rebuilding it as Mount Pleasant sorting office, which became the largest mail centre in Europe. Until 2003 the sorting office had its own subterranean rail link to PADDINGTON and WHITECHAPEL (*see* MAIL RAIL).
2. A mixed-use locality, also known as HAREFIELD WEST, situated on the extreme western edge of GREATER LONDON. The construction of the GRAND JUNCTION CANAL brought some noxious industries and their spoil heaps in the early 19th

century, and it is likely that the name Mount Pleasant was applied ironically. Limekilns, copper mills and ironworks were followed later by factories making printing inks and rubber products.

Mousetrap, The By far the longest-running stage show in London, and indeed the world. The country house murder mystery is an adaptation of Agatha Christie's radio play *Three Blind Mice* (1947). After a short pre-WEST END tour, *The Mousetrap* opened in November 1952 at the Ambassadors Theatre and in 1974 moved to the neighbouring St Martin's Theatre, where it seems likely to remain for the foreseeable future, assuming tourists continue to visit London. At the end of every performance the audience is asked not to reveal the *dénouement* to the uninitiated but it has become something of a naughty London tradition to spill the beans whenever the opportunity arises.

> Going to see *The Mousetrap*, as she [the Queen] was reminded by her 2002 visit, is very much like taking a trip in a time machine. The St Martin's Theatre is a very attractive panelled auditorium that looks more like an English country house than a West End theatre, and the play's setting, construction, plot and characters are all very 1950s.
>
> SHERIDAN MORLEY: *Theatre's Strangest Acts* (2006)

Moving Church In 1951 Major the Rev Vivian Symonds was appointed to the living of St Mark's, BIGGIN HILL, the church then being a 50-year-old iron building that had never been consecrated. In order to rebuild it he obtained permission to use material from a war-damaged church, All Saints, PECKHAM, 17 miles (27 km) away. Standing on a lorry facing the latter, he is said to have commanded in a loud voice: 'In the name of Jesus Christ be thou removed to Biggin Hill.' Working with volunteer labour, but often quite alone, he rebuilt St Mark's, the 'Moving Church', over a period of three years.

Several other churches in OUTER LONDON have been similarly reconstructed. For example, the newer of the two St Andrew's Churches that share the same churchyard in KINGSBURY was formerly an Anglo-Catholic church in MARYLEBONE. Conveniently already dedicated to St Andrew, it was transported to Kingsbury stone by stone in 1933.

Mr

Mr and Mrs Clark and Percy One of the best-known post-Pop, 'cool', naturalistic portraits by David Hockney (b.1937), painted in 1970–1 and now in TATE BRITAIN's collection. It is one of a series of double portraits of Hockney's friends and features the British fashion designer Ossie Clark (1942–96) and his wife, the fabric designer Celia Birtwell (b.1941), together with one of their cats. He painted the work from photographs and drawings, and simplified the interior of the Clarks' flat in Linden Gardens, NOTTING HILL GATE. Hockney made the portrait as a wedding present, but the marriage ended in 1974. Clark was subsequently killed by his Italian lover, Diego Cogolato.

Mr Plinge is waiting *See* PLINGE, WALTER.

Mr Punch *See* PUNCH AND JUDY.

Mr Sands *See* INSPECTOR SANDS.

Mrs

Mrs Dale's Diary A radio soap opera broadcast on the BBC between 1948 and 1969 depicting the placid, middle-class life of Mary Dale and her husband Jim, a doctor, in the fictional south London suburb of Parkwood Hill, said to have been based on SUTTON. The title was changed to *The Dales* in 1962 when the family moved to the expanding new town of Exton somewhere in the HOME COUNTIES. Despite the blandness of the action and the paleness of the characters, the programme was generally regarded with affection and attracted many regular listeners.

Mrs Henderson Presents *See the* WINDMILL THEATRE.

Don't Have Any More, Mrs Moore *See under* DO.

you must know Mrs Kelly? *See under* YOU.

M25 London's orbital motorway, at 117 miles (188 km) the second longest city ring road in Europe, after the Berliner Ring. It was completed in 1986 and by the end of that year was carrying 113,000 vehicles a day, rising to 186,000 in 1998 and peaking at almost 200,000 in 2003; already clogged by the extra traffic its multiple lanes had so predictably created, it had become a scorned exemplar of the stresses and frustrations of car travel. It has 33 junctions and there are 234 bridges and other crosses over and under the motorway.

Iain Sinclair's *London Orbital* (2002) describes a walk around the M25:

As soon as the M25 was opened, swans lifting from the Thames at Staines mistook the bright silver surface for water; there were several nasty accidents. A report in the *Evening Standard* ... described the trauma suffered by a man, on his way to visit a retired rock star in the Surrey stockbroker belt, when a large white bird crashed onto the bonnet of his car.

mud

Mudchute An urban farm and park on the ISLE OF DOGS. Its undulations and its name derive from silted mud dredged from the MILLWALL docks from the 1880s onwards. Huge quantities of sludge were pumped here and spewed out of a giant pneumatic tube. Following complaints that the mud heap was a health hazard, 'mud-chuting' ceased around 1910. The site was later considered for housing but in 1977 it became Mudchute Farm, a 32-acre (13-hectare) public park consisting of a working farm, designated wildlife areas, riding stables, wooded areas and open parkland.

Mud Island East London slang for Southend-on-Sea, ESSEX, in the days when it was almost the only seaside resort that COCKNEYS ever saw.

mudlark Originally an EAST END urchin who scrabbled around on the THAMES foreshore for items of value. They were often characterized as criminals by the police and magistrates, who named 'lumpers, scuffle-hunters, mud-larks, glut-men, scullers' and others as being prey to the temptation to plunder poorly guarded vessels. The word subsequently took on a less pejorative meaning, similar to 'beachcomber'.

muesli belt A general nickname for a middle-class district where people are or were likely to eat muesli and other 'health foods'. More specifically, MUSWELL HILL has been nicknamed 'Muesli Hill' by some. The term arose in the late 1970s.

Muffin Man, The A nursery rhyme about a character who lived in DRURY LANE. A muffin man was a seller of the buns now known internationally as 'English muffins'. Like many seemingly innocent children's rhymes, 'The Muffin Man' may have had its origins in a more adult theme. The rhyme was often sung as a duet between two young women, who found that they both knew the muffin man, perhaps carnally. His chosen place of residence was formerly well known

for its brothels. The performance of the rhyme as a two-parter was taken a step further in the animated feature film *Shrek* (2001), where it is played out as a quick-fire question-and-answer dialogue.

Muggletonian A follower of Lodowick(e) (or Lodovic) Muggleton (1609–98), a BISHOPSGATE-born journeyman tailor, who in about 1651 made himself out to be a prophet. He was eventually sentenced at the OLD BAILEY for blasphemous writings to stand in the pillory, and was fined £500. The members of the sect, which maintained some existence until *c*.1865, believed that their two founders, Muggleton and John Reeve, were the 'two witnesses' spoken of in Revelation 11:3.

> And as all Hereticks covet to be Authors and Ring-leaders to a Sect, so by divers printed Books and Corner conferences, he easily seduced divers weak and instable people (especially of the Female-Sex) to become his Proselytes, who from him call themselves Muggletonians ...
> *Old Bailey Proceedings*, trial summary (17 January 1677)

Mulberry Garden A fashionable resort that lay in the vicinity of what is now the MALL. Its mulberry trees were planted at the behest of James I, as part of a project to boost the national economy by establishing a home-grown silk industry. When the scheme proved a resounding failure the garden was opened to the public as a recreation ground. It was particularly popular in spring and summer, when the abundance of trees and bushes helped conceal various amorous encounters. John Dryden is said to have enjoyed eating mulberry tarts here, accompanied by his favourite actress, Mrs Reeve. Sir Charles Sedley wrote a successful comic play entitled *The Mulberry Garden* (1668), in which a young lady comments that, 'the air of this place is a great softener of men's hearts'. The garden was closed to the public in 1673.

> My Lady Gerrard treated us at Mulberry Garden, now the only place of refreshment about town for persons of quality to be exceedingly cheated at; Cromwell and his partisans having shut up and seized on Spring Garden, which, till now, had been the usual rendezvous for the ladies and gallants at this season.
> JOHN EVELYN: diary (10 April 1654)

multicultural London English *See* JA-FAIKAN.

murder mile A nickname for various stretches of road with a dangerous reputation. In 21st-century London these have included KENTISH TOWN Road and part of the HARROW ROAD, among several others. Following a spate of drug-related shootings in the early 2000s the tag was most often applied to the Lower CLAPTON Road and part of the Upper Clapton Road. Despite a subsequent abatement of the violence the nickname has endured, although it is nowadays heard less often.

> Ten days ago [Superintendent Leroy] Logan's officers closed a nightclub on murder mile, the Lower Clapton Road, to avert the threat of shootings, a decision that highlights the relationship between music and violence that Logan identifies as a major driver of murders in Hackney.
>
> *The Observer* (18 February 2007)

Muscadins Parisian exquisites who aped those of London about the time of the French Revolution. They wore top-boots with long tails, and a high stiff collar, and carried a thick cudgel called a 'constitution'. It was thought 'John Bullish' to assume a huskiness of voice, a discourtesy of manners and a swaggering vulgarity of speech and behaviour.

> Cockneys of London, Muscadins of Paris.
>
> LORD BYRON: *Don Juan*, Canto 8 (1819)

museum

Museumland A nickname for SOUTH KENSINGTON, and in particular for the area south of the ALBERT HALL where the VICTORIA AND ALBERT MUSEUM, the SCIENCE MUSEUM and the NATURAL HISTORY MUSEUM are located.

Museum of Childhood A subsidiary of the VICTORIA AND ALBERT MUSEUM, housing the national childhood collection. It is situated on Cambridge Heath Road, BETHNAL GREEN. Formerly located in SOUTH KENSINGTON and known as the BROMPTON BOILERS, the building became the Bethnal Green Museum in 1872, when it displayed a somewhat arbitrary selection of material from the GREAT EXHIBITION. From the 1920s the museum focused increasingly on exhibits that would be of interest to children and it adopted its present identity in 1974.

Museum of Garden History *See the* GARDEN MUSEUM.

Museum of London One of the world's largest urban history museums, with over two million objects in its collection. It was created in 1975 by an amalgamation of the former GUILDHALL Museum (Roman and medieval) and LONDON MUSEUM (Tudor and later) and is situated at the junction of LONDON WALL and ALDERSGATE STREET, adjacent to the BARBICAN. The museum's exhibits tell the story of London from prehistory to the 21st century, with emphases on archaeology and culture. 'London's Burning' is a permanent special exhibition devoted to the GREAT FIRE OF LONDON and its aftermath.

Museum of London Docklands Formerly the Museum in Docklands, this subsidiary of the MUSEUM OF LONDON is housed in a 200-year-old warehouse at WEST INDIA QUAY. Its exhibits chart the history of London as a port, through stories of trade, migration and commerce. The museum holds the archive of the PORT OF LONDON AUTHORITY and its predecessor dock companies and river conservancy bodies. The SAINSBURY Archive documents the history and development of the well-known food retailer from its foundation in London in 1869.

music

Musical Museum A museum in BRENTFORD that specializes in historic automatic musical instruments, from miniature musical boxes to a self-playing Wurlitzer organ. It also possesses the world's largest collection of musical rolls. Established in 1963 in the disused St George's Church, Brentford High Street, the Musical Museum reopened in 2007 in much larger purpose-built premises at the eastern end of the same street. Concerts are occasionally held in the 230-seat auditorium.

Musical Small-Coal Man Thomas Britton (*c.*1654–1714), a coal dealer of CLERKENWELL, who established a musical club over his shop in Aylesbury Street, in which all the musical celebrities of the day took part. The club met every Thursday night and was frequented by professional musicians such as Handel, talented amateurs such as Roger L'Estrange, and lovers of music generally. The musical invitation to his soirées ran thus:

> Upon Thursdays repair to my palace, and there
> Hobble up stair by stair, but I pray you take care

That you break not your shins by a stumble;
And without e'er a souse, paid to me or my
spouse,
Sit still as a mouse at the top of the house,
And there you shall hear how we fumble.

On his death (said to have been the consequence of a prank played by the TALKING SMITH) he left a collection of rare old books and manuscripts and 27 fine musical instruments.

music hall This essentially popular form of variety entertainment had its origins in the 'free and easy' of the public houses and in the song and supper rooms of early Victorian London. Food, drink and the singsong were its first ingredients, and its patrons came from the working classes. The first music hall proper, the Canterbury, was opened in 1852 by Charles Morton (1819–1905), 'the Father of the Halls', and a native of HACKNEY. It was specially built for the purpose, consequent upon the success of his musical evenings at the Canterbury Arms, LAMBETH, of which he became the landlord in 1849. Music halls eventually became more numerous in London and the provinces than the regular theatres, and such names as the Palladium, Palace, Alhambra, Coliseum, Empire, Hippodrome and so on proclaim their former glories. Their best days were before 1914, after which revue, the cinema, radio and, later, television, helped to bring about their eclipse. They have left a legacy of popular ballad and song, and memories of a host of great entertainers whose fame depended upon the intrinsic qualities of their individual acts. *See also* COLLINS'S MUSIC HALL; EVANS MUSIC-AND-SUPPER ROOMS.

Music Hall War The nickname given to strike action taken by London music hall artistes in 1907, which aimed to improve the pay and conditions of rank-and-file performers, musicians and stage-hands. They were supported on the picket lines by many stars of the day, such as LITTLE TICH and the QUEEN OF THE MUSIC HALL, Marie Lloyd. The dispute was settled at arbitration, although a number of music hall owners subsequently tried to evade compliance with the terms of the agreement.

Muswell Hill An Edwardian suburb situated north-west of HORNSEY. The topographic feature from which the district takes its name is now surmounted by the ALEXANDRA PALACE. Muswell is a corruption of 'mossy well' and there was a spring here that was reputed to have restored the health of Malcolm IV of Scotland. Neither the opening of Alexandra Palace nor a half-hearted railway connection (since closed) significantly disturbed the area's semi-rural serenity until the sale of several grand houses and their spacious grounds in the mid-1890s. This led to the comprehensive transformation of Muswell Hill over a 20-year period, with just two building firms responsible for almost all the work, which resulted in a particularly harmonious effect. Former residents have included Vivian Stanshall (1944–95), leader of the surreal and satirical 1960s Bonzo Dog Doo-Dah Band, who died in a fire at his home, and the Russian dissident Alexander Litvinenko (1962–2006), who died at UNIVERSITY COLLEGE HOSPITAL from the effects of polonium poisoning.

Muswell Hillbillies The title of an album (1971) by the KINKS, the band formed in the early 1960s by local resident siblings Ray and Dave Davies. The album's tracks include 'Holloway Jail' and 'Muswell Hillbilly'.

I'm a Muswell Hillbilly boy
But my heart lies in old West Virginia.
Though my hills are not green
I have seen them in my dreams.
'Muswell Hillbilly'

Mutt and Jeff or **mutton** 'Deaf' in rhyming slang, perhaps of theatrical rather than COCKNEY origin. The term derives from a pair of male cartoon characters introduced in the USA in 1907 by Harry C. 'Bud' Fisher (1885–1954), in what has been claimed as the first daily comic strip.

my

My Beautiful Laundrette A successful low-budget film (1985) written by Hanif Kureishi (b.1954) and directed by Stephen Frears (b.1941). Set mainly within London's Asian community and filmed in and around STOCKWELL and BATTERSEA, the central theme is the relationship between two young men, one a British Pakistani and the other a white racist, who together transform a run-down laundrette.

My Fair Lady A film musical (1964) based on a stage musical by Alan Lerner (1918–86) and Frederick Loewe (1901–88) depicting the transformation of roughly spoken COCKNEY flower girl Eliza DOOLITTLE into a well-groomed society lady through the efforts of the arrogant linguist

Professor Henry Higgins. Starring Audrey Hepburn and Rex Harrison, the film was derived ultimately from the play PYGMALION (1913) by George Bernard SHAW (1856–1950). The musical's title was extracted from a traditional rhyme:

> London Bridge is falling down, falling down,
> falling down,
> London Bridge is falling down, my fair lady.

my old Dutch See DUCH(ESS OF FIFE).

Myddelton House A house in Bulls Cross, ENFIELD, named in honour of Hugh Myddelton (*see* *the* NEW RIVER) and nowadays the headquarters of the Lee Valley Regional Park Authority (*see* *the River* LEA). Myddelton House was built in 1818 for Henry Carrington Bowles and his wife Anne, née Garnault. Henry came from a long line of publishers and print sellers and his father Carrington Bowles was one of the men behind the creation of the TOBY JUG. Ann was a member of a wealthy Huguenot family connected to the New River Company, and it was she who had inherited the Enfield estate, from her brother. The horticulturist E.A. Bowles (1865–1954) was born in the house and died there. He published books on its garden and on growing crocus, narcissus and colchicum. The grounds have been restored as an example of a 20th-century plantsman's garden.

N

naff 'Inferior' or 'worthless'. The word is now in widespread colloquial usage but it has been claimed, and not disproved, that it originated within the POLARI lexicon as an acronym for 'not available for fucking'.

Nag's Head A bustling commercial zone centred around the junction of Seven Sisters Road and HOLLOWAY ROAD, regarded by ISLINGTON council as one of the borough's two most important 'town centres'. It is named after a public house that was in existence from around 1800. At the end of the 19th century the vicinity became a hub for shops serving the expanding middle-class community of HOLLOWAY and the pub was rebuilt in Italianate style. It spent its latter years as an Irish theme bar and has recently been converted to retail use.

Nag's Head consecration An early 17th-century story designed to deride the validity of the apostolic succession in the Church of England and in particular the validity of Archbishop Parker's consecration. The story is that on the passing of the Act of Uniformity of 1559 in Queen Elizabeth's reign, 14 bishops vacated their sees, and all the other sees were vacant except that of Llandaff, whose bishop refused to officiate at Parker's consecration. He was, therefore, irregularly consecrated at the Nag's Head tavern in CHEAPSIDE by John Scory, who had been deprived of the see of Chichester under Mary. In fact, the consecration took place at LAMBETH PALACE on 17 December 1559 by four bishops (Barlow, Scory, Coverdale and Hodgkin) who had held sees under Edward VI. Those who took part in the consecration apparently dined at the Nag's Head afterwards. The story was first put into circulation by the Jesuit Christopher Holywood in *De Investigenda Vera ac Visibili Christi Ecclesia Libellus*, published in Antwerp in 1604.

naked

Naked Beauty The enduring nickname of Hurst House, WOODFORD GREEN, which was built *c.*1714 for the WAPPING brewer Henry Raine (1679–1738). The nickname is usually said to derive from a statue that once stood in its garden but others have suggested that it was prompted by the house's formerly isolated and exposed position on Salway Hill.

Naked Boy courts and **alleys** There were formerly several in and around the CITY of London, all of which were named from the public house sign of Cupid.

Naked Lady The colloquial name of *La Délivrance*, a bronze statue of a naked woman holding a sword aloft, located at Henly's Corner, on the NORTH CIRCULAR ROAD. The work of the French sculptor Émile Guillaume (1867–1942), it was inspired by the allied victory at the First Battle of the Marne, which delivered Paris from the threat of German seizure in 1914. The statue was exhibited at the 1920 Paris Salon, where it was bought by the newspaper magnate Lord Rothermere, who donated it to FINCHLEY council in honour of his mother, a resident of TOTTERIDGE. Lloyd George unveiled the statue in October 1927 before a crowd of 8,000.

Nancy A prostitute and thief who works for FAGIN in Charles DICKENS's *Oliver Twist* (1838). She is the mistress of Bill SIKES, to whom she remains loyal, despite his brutality. She befriends Oliver, proving that 'there was something of the woman's original nature left in her still'. When she reveals to Rose Maylie and Mr Brownlow what she knows about the plot to defraud Oliver, Fagin tells Bill Sikes, and Sikes murders her.

Miss Nancy *See* NARCISSA.

Napoleon

Napoleon of Crime The nickname bestowed by SCOTLAND YARD detective Robert Anderson on Adam Worth (1844–1902), a professional criminal of German-Jewish descent who grew up in New

York. His exploits in America, north-west Europe and South Africa included fraud, bank robbery and the operation of illegal gambling dens. From the mid-1870s Worth ran a 'web of crime' from a house on CLAPHAM COMMON and stole Gainsborough's portrait of *Georgiana, Duchess of Devonshire* from the MAYFAIR gallery of Thomas Agnew and Sons. He is said to have become obsessed with the painting, keeping it for 25 years before claiming the reward a few months before his death from the effects of alcoholism. Worth was buried in HIGHGATE CEMETERY under the alias of Henry Judson Raymond. Arthur Conan Doyle appropriated the 'Napoleon of Crime' nickname for Professor MORIARTY, the arch-enemy of Sherlock HOLMES.

Napoleon of Notting Hill, The A novel (1904) by G.K. Chesterton that was a kind of forerunner of the EALING COMEDY *Passport to Pimlico*. Considered a madman because of his visionary single-mindedness, Adam Wayne is the provost of NOTTING HILL. He clashes with Auberon Quin, king of London, who cannot take local patriotism seriously. Wayne's determination to preserve the independence of Notting Hill residents results in an eccentrically medieval war against all the other boroughs.

Nappy Valley A somewhat clichéd term – modelled on 'happy valley' – for a residential quarter popular with professional couples who have babies or young children. The nickname has been applied to several inner-suburban areas of London, perhaps most often to parts of CLAPHAM and its neighbouring localities, and also to CROUCH END.

Narcissa In Pope's *Moral Essays* (1731–5) 'Narcissa' represents the actress Anne Oldfield (1683–1730), who was also known as Miss Nancy or simply Nance. When she died, her remains lay in state attended by two noblemen. She was buried in WESTMINSTER ABBEY in a fine Brussels lace head-dress, a holland shift, with a tucker and double ruffles of the same lace, and new kid gloves.

> 'Odious! In woollen! 'twould a saint provoke'
> (Were the last words that poor Narcissa spoke).
>
> ALEXANDER POPE: *Moral Essays*, i (1731–5)

'In woollen' is an allusion to the old law enacted for the benefit of the wool trade, that all shrouds were to be made of wool.

nark or **copper's nark** An antiquated term for a police spy or informer, from a Romany word, *nāk*, 'nose'. The term was also applied to a policeman.

nark it A slang expression from the middle half of the 20th century, meaning 'stop it', 'pack it in'. The term entered the national vocabulary but was probably of COCKNEY origin.

> Clive shrugged himself into his storm coat. 'Nark it. You know we don't carry squabbles over to the next day. Clean slate each morning, right?'
>
> ALAN GARNER: *The Owl Service* (1967)

Nash A farming hamlet lying three-quarters of a mile (1.2 km) south-west of KESTON, in the London Borough of BROMLEY. Its name means 'place at the ash tree'. The METROPOLITAN POLICE Dog Training Establishment moved to Layhams Road in 1953. Its 15-acre (6-hectare) site has over a hundred kennels and a unique, purpose-built facility performing artificial insemination using frozen genetic material that has been taken from working police dogs.

Nathan Barley A Channel 4 sitcom (2005) set in the fictional district of Hosegate, satirizing the allegedly asinine and self-absorbed new media community of HOXTON and south SHOREDITCH. Describing himself as a 'self-facilitating media node', the eponymous TRUSTAFARIAN protagonist was played by Nicholas Burns and created by Charlie Brooker, who co-wrote the series with Chris Morris. The show was notable for its preposterous catchphrases, such as 'it's well Jackson', 'totally Mexico' and 'keep it foolish'.

> A satirical television series that mercilessly attacks London's trendier-than-thou, gadget-obsessed 'creative' community has outraged business and community leaders in the district where it is set.
>
> *The Sunday Times* (20 February 2005)

national

National Cruet-Stand An early nickname for the NATIONAL GALLERY, derived from what was perceived as the building's excess of petty architectural detail, and from the pepperpot-shaped cupolas with which it is crowned.

> This is Trafalgar Square and that is the National Cruet-Stand, and now you shall see another

British institution, who is quite as well known as they.

DICKENS: *Household Words*, Volume 18 (1858)

National Gallery A major museum of western European painting, including English portraits and landscapes, Italian religious and mythological scenes and a significant collection of Impressionist art. The government acquired its core collection in 1824 from John Julius ANGERSTEIN, and this was initially displayed in the banker's PALL MALL house. In 1837 the gallery moved to its present home on the site of the King's MEWS, on the north side of TRAFALGAR SQUARE. It shared the building with the ROYAL ACADEMY until the latter moved to BURLINGTON HOUSE in 1868. The building has been enlarged four times, most recently with the opening in 1991 of the Sainsbury Wing, put up after a previous design had been castigated by the Prince of Wales as a MONSTROUS CARBUNCLE. More than four million people visit the National Gallery every year.

National Maritime Museum The nation's naval and nautical museum, based in the Queen's House and its flanking wings (which house the Maritime galleries), in GREENWICH. Opened in 1937, the museum has over two million items in its collection, including tens of thousands of manuscripts and portraits, many on loan to museums elsewhere in Britain. The public galleries display a thematically arranged selection and the remainder are accessible for research in various ways. The museum's small-boat collection is on display at its new Cornish branch in Falmouth. GREENWICH OBSERVATORY was transferred to the National Maritime Museum's care in 1960 and the Queen's House was reorganized to showcase the Museum's fine-art collection in 2001.

National Physical Laboratory The UK's central institute for developing and applying the most accurate measurement standards for scientific and technological purposes, situated in TEDDINGTON. It was founded in 1900 to promote links between science and commerce, and Queen Victoria gave Bushy House, in BUSHY PARK, as its base. The laboratory remains on the same site, where it has vastly expanded the scale of its operations. It famously tested the bouncing bomb during the Second World War and the first working atomic clock was built here in 1955. Among its many present-day roles, the NPL is responsible for regulating GREENWICH MEAN TIME.

National Portrait Gallery A museum of biographical history as much as a collection of art, located in St Martin's Place, at the southern end of CHARING CROSS ROAD, around the corner from the adjoining NATIONAL GALLERY. It was founded by the government in 1856 following persistent pressure from Philip Henry Stanhope, 5th Earl Stanhope (1805–75), with the support of Thomas Babington Macaulay (1800–59) and Thomas Carlyle (1795–1881). Its first acquisition, the gift of Lord Ellesmere, was the so-called Chandos portrait of SHAKESPEARE. In the early years of its existence the gallery had no permanent base, spending time in SOUTH KENSINGTON and at what is now the MUSEUM OF CHILDHOOD, in BETHNAL GREEN, before moving in 1896 to its present home, which has since been enlarged and enhanced. The gallery's collection of paintings, sculpture, drawings, prints and photographs draws around one million visitors a year.

National Theatre A group of theatres situated east of the southern end of WATERLOO BRIDGE. The idea of a national theatre was first advocated in 1848 and plans were drawn up in 1903 but it was not until after the Second World War that politicians and leading cultural figures united to implement a proposal to bring such an institution to a bomb site on the SOUTH BANK after it was vacated by the FESTIVAL OF BRITAIN. The angular and layered concrete structure was the creation of the architect Denys Lasdun (1914–2001), who also designed a neighbouring opera house that was removed from the plan owing to budget constraints. Opened in 1976, the National contains three auditoriums: the open-staged Olivier, the Lyttelton, which has a proscenium format, and the Cottesloe studio theatre. By the end of the 20th century its design had become unpopular with many but it has recently come to be viewed more fondly and future changes are unlikely to radically alter its appearance, not least because the structure is grade II* listed. The National's repertoire ranges from SHAKESPEARE, through Broadway hits to fringe productions.

National Theatre of Brent A minimalist comedy theatre company created in the early 1980s by Patrick Barlow (b.1947). In the persona of Desmond 'Olivier' Dingle he stages productions notable chiefly for their economy of resources (as typified by the NTOB's first effort, a two-man version of the *Charge of the Light Brigade*; other highlights have included *Zulu* and a television series (1985) called *Mighty Moments from World History*). His best-known associate has been Wallace, played by Jim Broadbent.

National Valhalla In Scandinavian mythology Valhalla was the hall in the celestial regions where the souls of heroes slain in battle were carried by the Valkyries, to spend eternity in joy and feasting. Hence the name has sometimes been applied to buildings used as the last resting place of a nation's great men and women. In a British context the reference is almost always to WESTMINSTER ABBEY. *See also* VICTORIAN VALHALLA.

> There was also a leading article, in which it was made perfectly clear that England would stand ashamed among the nations, if she did not inter her greatest painter in Westminster Abbey. Only the article, instead of saying Westminster Abbey, said National Valhalla. It seemed to make a point of not mentioning Westminster Abbey by name, as though Westminster Abbey had been something not quite mentionable, such as a pair of trousers.
>
> ARNOLD BENNETT: *Buried Alive* (1908)

Natural History Museum The largest natural history collection in the world, with over 70 million specimens, based on the Cromwell Road in SOUTH KENSINGTON. It originated with the collection of natural curiosities left to the nation by Sir Hans SLOANE in 1753. This at first formed part of the BRITISH MUSEUM but as other collections were added the government agreed to fund a purpose-built home that was designed in German Romanesque style by Alfred Waterhouse (1830–1905) and opened in 1881. The neighbouring Geological Museum, on EXHIBITION ROAD, merged with the Natural History Museum in 1985 and is now referred to as the 'Red Zone'. A newly built extension to the NHM serves as a research centre and houses 20 million insect and plant specimens. The Darwin Centre's showpiece is a public viewing gallery that takes the form of an eight-storey cocoon in its atrium.

NatWest Tower A skyscraper located at 25 Old Broad Street, in the CITY of London. It was officially opened in 1981 as the new headquarters of the National Westminster Bank. Seen from above, the tower forms the shape of the bank's trademark device, a chopped-cornered triangle made from three chevrons. The NatWest Tower was badly damaged by a Provisional IRA truck bomb in 1993 and the bank did not reoccupy it after its renovation. Subsequently renamed Tower 42, in a reference to the number of floors, the building is now owned by a real estate consortium and occupied by a mix of tenants, including a top-floor restaurant.

Naughty Nineties The 1890s in London and beyond, when the puritanical Victorian code of behaviour and conduct gave way in certain wealthy and fashionable circles to growing laxity in sexual morals, a cult of hedonism, and a more light-hearted approach to life generally. MUSIC HALLS were at the height of their popularity, and the EMPIRE PROMENADE was in its heyday.

Navvies' Island A Victorian settlement that occupied the site of a former brickfield on HACKNEY DOWNS. It was the creation of the Great Eastern Railway Company, which built a branch line on the west side of the downs in 1867 and put up 150 houses for its construction workers. Local landowner Lord Amhurst wanted to upgrade the cottages of Navvies' Island in the late 1950s but HACKNEY council demurred, preferring to knock them down and build the Landfield estate.

Neasden A residential district sliced in two by the NORTH CIRCULAR ROAD and separated from WEMBLEY by the River BRENT. Its name may have meant 'nose hill', a reference to its location on a small promontory at the end of the DOLLIS HILL ridge. Neasden was satirically pictured as a typically faceless and formless London suburb by *Private Eye*, perhaps partly on account of its name, which suggests 'Nilsdon' or in US terms 'Nowheresville'. In 1995 Neasden became the unlikely home of the biggest Hindu temple outside India: the Shri Swaminarayan Mandir. *See also the* LONELIEST VILLAGE IN LONDON.

Neasden FC *See* BONKERS, SID AND DORIS.

Neckinger A 'lost river' that rose in the vicinity of ST GEORGE'S FIELDS, SOUTHWARK, looped through BERMONDSEY and joined the THAMES at St Saviour's Dock, SHAD THAMES. In the 16th century it was the Devills Neckercher (neckerchief), an old term for the hangman's noose. Popular myth has it that this was an allusion to the practice of hanging pirates from a gibbet set up at St Saviour's Dock, but in fact it probably referred to the stream's twisting course. The Neckinger has long been assimilated within the underground drainage system.

Necropolis Railway *See the* LONDON NECROPOLIS COMPANY.

Needle A ghost of Scottish origin in Muriel Spark's 'The Portobello Road', in *The Go-Away Bird and Other Stories* (1958). Her name derives from her literally finding a needle in a haystack in her youth. She always had a sense of being special and wanted to write about life, but was prevented by her perfectionism. She was thus irritated when people regarded her as lucky because of the ease with which she drifted along. A Catholic convert, she now haunts her murderer in the PORTOBELLO ROAD.

Cleopatra's Needle *See under* CLEOPATRA.

Neighbours to the Nation The BBC's tagline for *The Grove Family* (1954–7), widely regarded as Britain's first television soap opera for adults. Some TV historians prefer to call the programme a 'continuous serial' because plotlines were introduced and resolved in a single episode, so that new viewers could join at any stage. The show was set in HENDON and the family was named after the BBC's LIME GROVE Studios. A film spin-off, *It's a Great Day*, appeared in 1955. Few of the 138 twenty-minute episodes survive because most were broadcast live and went unrecorded. By today's standards, some of the scripts appear less than gripping:

> Police officer: Have you got a television set?
> Bob Grove: Certainly I have.
> Police officer: The criminal is a student of people's habits. Make sure your windows and doors are fastened before you start viewing ... and don't leave furs and valuables upstairs in the bedroom. It's much better to have them down beside you.

> quoted in JANET THUMIM: *Inventing Television Culture: Men, Women, and the Box* (2004)

Nell

Nell Gwyn *See* GWYN.

Nellie Duff *See* NOT ON YOUR NELLIE.

Nelson's Column or **the Nelson Column**

A Corinthian column of Devonshire granite on a square base in TRAFALGAR SQUARE, completed in 1843. The four lions, by Edwin Landseer (1802–73), were added in 1867. It stands 185 feet (56.4m) high overall. The column is a copy of one in the temple of Mars Ultor (the Avenger) at Rome. The statue of Horatio Nelson (1758–1805), by Edward Hodges Baily (1788–1867), is 17 feet (5.2m) high. The following bronze reliefs are on the sides of the pedestal: (north) the Battle of the Nile (1798), (south) Nelson's death at Trafalgar (1805), (east) the Battle of Copenhagen (1801), (west) the Battle of Cape St Vincent (1797).

Nephew of the Almighty One of the titles assumed by Richard Brothers (1757–1824), a Newfoundland-born prophet who began spreading his speculations in London in the late 18th century. Despite the craziness of most of his preaching, Brothers acquired numerous followers and his proposal that the Jewish Diaspora should return to Palestine may have had a genuine influence on the evolution of the Zionist movement in Britain. He also styled himself the Prince and Prophet of the Hebrews and planned to rule over Israel until the second coming of Jesus Christ. When Brothers predicted not only the destruction of London but the death of George III, the authorities feared a self-fulfilling prophecy and he was arrested and committed to the madhouse in 1795.

netball The sport was introduced to Britain at Martina Bergman Österberg's training college for teachers of physical education, at 1 Broadhurst Gardens, SOUTH HAMPSTEAD, where in 1895 a visiting American demonstrated a version of basketball that the girls played with wastepaper baskets at each end of the hall. The rules were at first imprecise, but were codified in 1901. Netball's association with girls' schools stems from this particular place of origin. From the mid-20th century the sport became familiar to Londoners and visitors to London from the lunchtime games played by office staff in LINCOLN'S INN FIELDS.

> The girls' netball team troops along to Lincoln's Inn Fields in lunch hours and there, in shorts and blouses, goes into battle with equally comely rivals.

> ROY F. BELL: *Gordon and Gotch, London* (1953)

never

never knowingly undersold The slogan of

JOHN LEWIS department stores since around 1930, warranting that the price of any item will always be as low as the lowest price in the neighbourhood.

Never Mind the Quality, Feel the Width A television sitcom broadcast from 1967 to 1971, centring on the unlikely business partnership formed in WHITECHAPEL between Patrick Kelly, an Irish Catholic trouser-maker, played by Joe Lynch (initially by Frank Finlay), and Emmanuel Cohen, a Jewish jacket-maker, played by John Bluthal. The humour largely devolves on the inability of each to understand the other's religious beliefs, patriotic loyalties or philosophy of life. Yet, although they are apparently incompatible, the two need each other to succeed in their enterprise, just as a jacket needs trousers. The title is said to have derived from a phrase that one of the scriptwriters, Vince Powell, had heard an Irish tailor use, presumably as a deliberate inversion of a cloth trade saying: 'Never mind the width, feel the quality.'

Neverwhere *See* LONDON BELOW.

new

New Addington A 20th-century creation located in the far east of the borough of CROYDON, set on a steep hillside rising into the North Downs. In 1935 the First National Housing Trust acquired 569 acres (230 hectares) of Fisher's Farm to lay out a 'garden village'. Croydon council supported the plan as a way of reducing the over-crowding in its semi-slum urban areas, and over a thousand homes had been built by the time that the outbreak of the Second World War halted construction. After the war the borough took over the housing trust's unused land and acquired a further 400 acres (160 ha), while the land west of Lodge Lane was designated as part of the GREEN BELT. Construction to the original plan was completed by 1963, but continuing housing need prompted another extension to New Addington five years later. This latter part is known as the Fieldway estate and has become the most disadvantaged part of the district.

New Barnet A Victorian township that sprang up between BARNET and EAST BARNET following the opening of a station on the new Great Northern Railway line in 1850.

New Cross A racially and socially diverse district located south-west of DEPTFORD. This was the site of a crossroads on the Kent/SURREY border and New Cross Heath was recorded in the 15th century, when the surrounding area was still heavily wooded. Two CITY guilds have had a defining influence on New Cross. The Worshipful Company of Haberdashers acquired much of the land in 1614 as an endowment for its charity. The company leased large houses to its members and other gentlemen in the 18th century and developed the land more intensively from the mid-19th century, after the coming of the railway. The Royal Naval School opened in 1843 and the building was taken over by the Goldsmiths' Company's Technical and Recreative Institute in 1891. It subsequently evolved into one of London's best-known university colleges (*see* GOLDSMITHS).

New Cross Gate The western part of NEW CROSS, taking its name from a tollgate erected in 1718 at the top of what is now Clifton Rise. The gate was relocated in 1813 to the junction of New Cross Road and Peckham Lane (now Queens Road).

New Cross scene or **NXS** A rock music scene that flourished briefly in early 21st-century New Cross, primarily because several pubs in the area regularly hosted live music performances by unsigned artists, which in turn related to the local presence of GOLDSMITHS college. Bloc Party and Art Brut were among the bands described as having emerged from the New Cross scene.

New End The north-eastern corner of central HAMPSTEAD, east of Heath Street. With the development of Hampstead as a spa at the beginning of the 18th century an ancillary quarter sprang up here with gambling dens and souvenir shops surrounded by new homes and lodging houses.

New End Theatre A theatre founded in 1974 in the former mortuary of HAMPSTEAD's New End Hospital, where Karl Marx was laid out before his burial in HIGHGATE CEMETERY.

New Jerusalem A mid-19th-century nickname for BELGRAVIA, which at that time was known for its sizeable population of wealthy Jews. For the same reason, the district was also called ASIA MINOR.

New London Theatre *See the* OLD MO.

New Malden A multicultural district situated south-east of NORBITON. New Malden began to develop as a separate township from KINGSTON UPON THAMES in the second half of the 19th century, boosted by the coming of the railway. Suburban development reached a peak in the

1930s, with modest terraced and semi-detached houses filling the area south of Kingston Road, and the town become a borough in 1936. New Malden has long had an industrial element and was subjected to bombing during the BLITZ, which had the effect of clearing the way for more housing after the war. Motor vehicle repair is the dominant surviving form of light industry. Two 16-storey office blocks were built near the station in the mid-1960s, and more offices appeared later on Kingston Road. The sculptor Anthony Caro (b.1924) and the folk violinist Dave Swarbrick (b.1941) were both born in New Malden. *See also* KOREA TOWN; OLD MALDEN.

New River An artificial waterway constructed in the early 17th century to bring water from Hertfordshire to London, a distance of 38 miles (61 km). It was built by Hugh Myddelton, a rich entrepreneur. Its London end was the New River Head at CLERKENWELL, from which clean water (or cleaner than that available from the THAMES or FLEET) was distributed to those willing to pay for it. The waterway was largely rebuilt in the 19th century. Until the late 20th century the New River Estate encompassed large areas of ISLINGTON.

New Road London's first (albeit partial) ring road, constructed around the northern perimeter of the capital in the mid-1750s. The MARYLEBONE, EUSTON and PENTONVILLE Roads nowadays follow its route. Soon after its completion it was extended from the ANGEL, ISLINGTON to MOORFIELDS, in the form of the CITY ROAD.

New Scotland Yard *See* SCOTLAND YARD.

New Southgate A residential district situated to the south of ARNOS GROVE STATION. The invention of the 'New Southgate' name was essentially a Victorian device designed to dissociate the settlement from the nearby mental hospital at COLNEY HATCH. Much of New Southgate was rebuilt after the Second World War.

New Southgate Cemetery An expansive burial ground opened in 1861 as the Great Northern Cemetery. It includes Caribbean, Greek Orthodox and Roman Catholic sections, and is the resting place of Shoghi Effendi (1897–1957), guardian of the Baha'i faith, who died while visiting London.

New Spring Gardens *See* VAUXHALL GARDENS.

new town Either a town established as an entirely new settlement or a substantial en-

largement of an existing town, with the aim of relocating populations away from large cities. The first new towns in Britain were inspired by the garden city concept formulated at the end of the 19th century by Ebenezer Howard (1850–1928). They were proposed in the New Towns Act of 1946, and 12 were designated in England and Wales over the next four years, with a further two in Scotland. Each had its own development corporation financed by the government. Further new towns were set up in the 1960s. Those designed, at least in part, to syphon residents out of London were:

Basildon (Essex), Bracknell (Berkshire), Corby (Northamptonshire), Crawley (West Sussex), Harlow (Essex), Hatfield (Hertfordshire), Hemel Hempstead (Hertfordshire), Milton Keynes (Buckinghamshire), Northampton, Peterborough (Cambridgeshire), Stevenage (Hertfordshire), Welwyn Garden City (Hertfordshire).

New Troy *See* TROYNOVANT.

New Year's Day Parade An American-style street parade, the largest of its kind in Europe, held annually from midday on 1 January. It began in 1987 as the Lord Mayor of Westminster's Big Parade and was renamed the London Parade in 1994. In recent years the 2.2-mile (3.5-km) route has begun at PARLIAMENT SQUARE and ended on PICCADILLY, by GREEN PARK station. Participants include marching bands (especially from the USA), dance troupes, vintage vehicles and carnival-style floats. The event draws a street-side audience of around 500,000 and is widely televised around the world.

Newyears Green or **New Years Green** A scattered collection of small farms and civic amenities situated north of ICKENHAM and west of RUISLIP, and surrounded on all sides by GREEN-BELT farmland. The origin of the name is uncertain. It is probably a corruption of a landowner's name but may refer to annual festivities – which would have been held on 'Lady Day', the feast of the Annunciation of the Blessed Virgin on 25 March, which was reckoned as the beginning of the year in England from the Middle Ages until 1752.

Newgate Originally built by the Romans around 200, it was the main entrance to the CITY from the west, and was referred to in Anglo-Saxon times as the 'West Gate'. Newgate, presumably alluding to a rebuilding of the gate in the late

Anglo-Saxon or early Norman period, is first recorded in the late 13th century. The gate, which stood at the northern end of the street called OLD BAILEY, was demolished in 1767. It was notorious as the site of NEWGATE PRISON.

Newgate bird A slang term between the 17th and 19th centuries for a prisoner, especially one who had been a confidence trickster.

Newgate Calendar A biographical record of the more notorious criminals confined at Newgate. It was begun in 1773 and continued at intervals for many years. In 1824–8 Andrew Knapp and William Baldwin published, in four volumes, *The Newgate Calendar, comprising Memoirs of Notorious Characters*, partly compiled by George Borrow, and in 1886 C. Pelham published his *Chronicles of Crime, or the New Newgate Calendar* (two volumes). Another such calendar was published in 1969. The term is often used as a comprehensive expression embracing crime of every sort.

Newgateer A 17th-century slang term for a prisoner in Newgate.

Newgate fashion Two by two. Prisoners used to be conveyed to Newgate coupled together in twos.

> Falstaff: must we all march?
> Bardolph: Yea, two and two, Newgate fashion.
>
> SHAKESPEARE: *Henry IV, Part 1*, III, iii (*c.*1596)

Newgate fringe A 19th-century term for a beard worn under the chin – so called because it occupied the position of the rope round the neck of a man about to be hanged. Contemporary synonyms were Newgate collar and Newgate frill.

Newgate gaol 'Tale' in 20th-century COCKNEY RHYMING SLANG, especially in the sense of 'hard-luck story'.

Newgate hornpipe An early 19th-century slang term for a hanging (victims would 'dance' as they jerked to death – gallows humour at its most literal).

Newgate knocker A lock of hair twisted into a curl, once worn by COSTERMONGERS and persons of similar status. It was so called because it resembled a knocker, and the wearers were often Newgate inmates. *See also* AS BLACK AS NEWGATE'S KNOCKER.

Newgate novel A somewhat dismissive term for a genre of 19th-century English fiction that features the lives of criminals in sensational-

ized and sentimentalized form, with the noose dangling balefully at the end. William Harrison Ainsworth's *Rookwood* (1824), featuring Dick TURPIN, and Jack SHEPPARD (1839) were typical examples, and the school also included Edward Bulwer-Lytton and Charles Whitehead. William Thackeray, who satirized the genre in his *Catherine* (1839–40), liked to include Charles DICKENS among their number.

Newgate Prison The first prison (over the gate) existed in the reign of King John (r.1199–1216). The last prison on the site (designed in 1770) was closed in 1880 and demolished in 1902, and it was for long the prison for the City of London and County of Middlesex. Many notorious criminals and state prisoners were confined there, as well as debtors. Condemned criminals were executed in the street outside, 'condemned sermons' being preached the preceding Sunday, to which the public were formerly admitted.

From its prominence, Newgate came to be applied as a general name for gaols, and Thomas Nashe, in *Pierce Pennilesse, his Supplication to the Divell* (1592), says it is 'a common name for all prisons, as homo is a common name for a man or woman'.

Newgate ring A tonsorial adornment from the mid-19th century, featuring a moustache and beard but no sidewhiskers. The motivation of the coinage was similar to that of NEWGATE FRINGE.

Newgate saint An 18th-century slang term for a prisoner under sentence of death.

Newgate seize me if I do, there now! 'An asseveration of the most binding nature', according to Jon Bee, in his *Dictionary of the Turf* (1823).

Newgate solicitor A term around the turn of the 18th and 19th centuries for a second-rate lawyer who hung around NEWGATE PRISON in the hope of picking up work.

Newham, London Borough of A London borough formed in 1965 by combining the former county boroughs of EAST HAM and WEST HAM, and including STRATFORD, BECKTON, CANNING TOWN, FOREST GATE, NORTH WOOLWICH, PLAISTOW and SILVERTOWN. Its shape is relatively square, skewed slightly to lean westward at Stratford. In Newham's early days it was earnestly hoped by officialdom that its invented name would be pronounced with full value given to each letter, and as if it were two separate words, but the 'h' has been decisively dropped. The new borough lay outside the old LONDON COUNTY COUNCIL boundary, and thus by definition constituted an OUTER LONDON borough at the time of its creation. However, it has since been reallocated to INNER LONDON for official statistical purposes. Newham's red and gold coat of arms has an unexpectedly classic appearance, but this is because it simply took over West Ham's arms of 1887, while using East Ham's motto: 'progress with the people'.

Newington The correct name for the southern part of SOUTHWARK, which is generally called ELEPHANT AND CASTLE to avoid confusion with STOKE NEWINGTON. It seems likely that Newington (which means 'new farmstead') grew up after about 1200, when the establishment of nearby LAMBETH PALACE brought increased traffic along the Kent road.

Newington Butts 'Guts' in COCKNEY RHYMING SLANG. The BUTTS at Newington were used for archery practice in the 16th and 17th centuries.

> I hate your guts, Newington Butts
> I'll put the black on you
> I'm the blackmail man.
>
> IAN DURY and STEVE NUGENT: 'Blackmail Man' (song by Ian Dury) (1977)

Niagara (Falls) 'Balls' (testicles) in COCKNEY RHYMING SLANG, usually rendered as 'Niagaras'. Unlike 'COBBLERS', the term is used solely in the literal sense. 'Orchestra stalls' is a less common, probably older, alternative.

> 'He's pretty bruised in the Niagaras so something has hit him,' said [David] Bassett.
>
> *The People* (30 December 2001)

nice

nice little earner See Arthur DALEY.

nice one! An exclamation of commendation of something well done (or often, ironically, of criticism of something badly done). It came to fame in Britain in the early 1970s in the phrase 'Nice one, Cyril!', which was used in a television advertisement for Wonderloaf. This was enthusiastically taken up by football fans as a chant aimed at the TOTTENHAM HOTSPUR player Cyril Knowles (1944–91). The Spurs team went on to record, under the name 'Cockerel Chorus', a song based on the phrase:

> Nice one, Cyril,

> Nice one, son!
> Nice one, Cyril,
> Let's have another one.
>
> SPIRO AND CLARKE: 'Nice One, Cyril' (1973)

Nichol, the See the JAGO.

nickers A band of early 18th-century London rioters who made a practice of smashing windows by throwing copper coins at them.

nick nick The catchphrase of the comedian Jim Davidson (b.1953), who grew up in Holburne Road, KIDBROOKE. He won ITV's *New Faces* in 1976, went on to host primetime TV shows and featured regularly in the tabloid newspapers as a consequence of his four marriages, alcohol problems and in 2006 his bankruptcy. Davidson's act was frequently criticized for its alleged misogyny and racism.

Nicks, Harvey See under HARVEY.

night buses London buses that begin running around midnight and continue until normal services resume in the morning. Most of the dedicated night routes are relatively lengthy and radiate from stops in or near TRAFALGAR SQUARE, using service numbers prefixed with the letter N. Given the overnight closure of the LONDON UNDERGROUND network, the buses are an asset both to clubgoers and shift workers. The long-standing premium fare for night travel was removed by Ken Livingstone when he was MAYOR OF LONDON. *See also the* KNIGHT BUS.

nine

Nine Elms A predominantly commercial riverside area situated between BATTERSEA PARK and VAUXHALL. In 1838 the London and Southampton Railway Company opened its terminus at Nine Elms. The line was extended to WATERLOO in 1848 and Nine Elms became the site of a goods yard and locomotive works. A gasworks was built and in 1865 this was the scene of the largest explosion in 19th-century London, which killed eleven men. In 1974 COVENT GARDEN's flower market and fruit and vegetable market moved to Nine Elms, taking over the site of the north and south railway goods depots. Waterside apartment complexes have since added an upmarket residential aspect to the district.

Nine Elms corridor A name used by planners and would-be developers for the strip of land beside the THAMES in Nine Elms, including BATTERSEA POWER STATION. Encompassing an area of 193 acres (78 hectares), the corridor is mostly occupied by disused industrial sites or by commercial tenants who could be persuaded to move elsewhere. It thus represents one of the largest regeneration opportunities in central London. The US Embassy and, reportedly, CHELSEA FC are among those considering a move here.

Nine Elms Settlement A pioneering charity established in 1914 by the Women's Freedom League. It served children with dinners of vegetarian soup and large slices of pudding, which they could either eat there or take home.

nine hairs and a bit of cotton A slang term of the early 20th century for a head of sparse or fine hair.

> I had large green eyes, a protuberant mouth, full of black teeth, and curly brown hair, this last evidently inherited from my father, since my mother had only what she called 'nine hairs and a bit of cotton'.
>
> ANGELA RODAWAY: *A London Childhood* (1960)

Nine Worthies of London, The A kind of chronicle history in mixed verse and prose of nine prominent citizens of London, published in 1592 by Richard Johnson, author of *The Seven Champions of Christendom*. His worthies are:

Sir William Walworth, who stabbed Wat Tyler the rebel and was twice LORD MAYOR OF LONDON (1374, 1381)

Sir Henry Picard (or Pritchard), who hosted the feast of the FIVE KINGS

Sir William Sevenoke, who fought with the Dauphin of France, was lord mayor in 1418 and endowed a grammar school

Sir Thomas White, a merchant taylor, who was lord mayor in 1553, founder of St John's College, Oxford, and a founder of Merchant Taylors' School

Sir John Bonham, entrusted with a valuable cargo for the Danish market and made commander of an army raised to stop the progress of the army of Suleiman the Magnificent (r.1520–66)

Christopher Croker, famous at the siege of Bordeaux and companion of the Black Prince (1330–76), when he helped Don Pedro to the throne of Castile

Sir John Hawkwood (d.1394), famous soldier and commander of the White Company in Italy, who

is known in Italian history as Giovanni Acuto, the latter an alteration of his surname

Sir Hugh Calveley (d.1393), soldier and commander of free companies; he fought under the Black Prince against the French and became governor of the Channel Islands, and was famous for ridding Poland of a monstrous bear

Sir Henry Maleverer, generally called Henry of CORNHILL, who lived in the reign of Henry IV (1399–1413); he was a crusader and became the guardian of 'Jacob's Well', in the Holy Land.

The above are essentially noted for their military rather than their civic achievements.

Nippies *See* LYONS' CORNER HOUSES.

nisi prius (Latin, 'unless previously') Originally a writ commanding a sheriff to empanel a jury that should be at the Court of WESTMINSTER on a certain day, unless the justices of assize have previously come to his county. The second Statute of Westminster (1285) instituted judges of *nisi prius*, who were appointed to travel through the shires three times a year to hear civil causes. A trial at *nisi prius* was later a trial by jury in a civil cause before a single judge.

Nitrate King The sobriquet of 'Colonel' John Thomas North (1842–96) of AVERY HILL, from the wealth he accumulated dealing in sodium nitrate from Chile. North devoted a large part of his fortune to building Avery Hill House in 1891, dismissing his architect for going 50% over budget in creating what was virtually a palace.

no

No Hope Square *See* NOHO SQUARE.

no, I'm with the Woolwich *See* I'M WITH THE WOOLWICH.

No Man's Land A play (1975) by Harold Pinter. A celebrated man of letters in his sixties, Hirst has one night either invited or been accompanied by Spooner, a shabby poet, to his impressive home in north-west London (presumably HAMPSTEAD). Powerful, arrogant and frequently befuddled by drink, he is a man of uncertain temper and memory – his recollections of his wife, whom Spooner also appears to have known, and of bucolic summers, are distinctly dubious. He is, it appears, tormented, incapable of salvation and retreating, as Spooner observes, into a 'no man's land ... which remains forever, icy and silent'.

no man's land Unclaimed or unused land,

especially that lying between the entrenched positions of opposing forces in wartime. The earliest recorded uses of the term came in the 1320s, referring to a patch of wasteland – *Nonesmanneslond extra Londonias* – in the vicinity of present-day CHARTERHOUSE, where convicted criminals were beheaded. According to John Stow's *Survey of London* (1598) the bishop of London bought the land from the KNIGHTS HOSPITALLER in 1348. Encircled by a brick wall, it was consecrated as a burial ground for victims of the Black Death. Thereafter known as PARDON CHURCHYARD, it remained in use for a further two centuries and 50,000 interments are said to have taken place here.

no one likes us, we don't care The unofficial motto of MILLWALL FC, much chanted by the club's fans to the approximate tune of 'Sailing' (Gavin Sutherland, 1972). Also the title of a book by Garry Robson, subtitled 'The Myth and Reality of Millwall Fandom' (2000). For much of the late 20th century, sections of the media portrayed Millwall supporters as football's worst HOOLIGANS, sometimes labelling them as white, working-class racists. The chant reflects the fans' attitude to being thus stigmatized.

> No one likes us, no one likes us,
> No one likes us, we don't care.
> We are Millwall, super Millwall,
> We are Millwall, from the Den.

no roads in the City of London The assertion that there are no roads in the CITY of London began as a quip and has since become the answer to a catch question. SHAKESPEARE's use of the word 'road' (or 'rode', as he spelt it) in *Henry IV, Part 1* (*c.*1596) was its first recorded appearance with the usual modern meaning and by that time all the streets, lanes and alleys in the City already had well-established designations. A few thoroughfares were created or renamed within the SQUARE MILE after the word came into being but still none was given a name ending in 'road'. However, the verity is spoilt by the encroachment of Goswell Road at the City's north-western corner.

Noak Hill A village perched amidst rolling farmland in the far north-eastern corner of GREATER LONDON. The name signified a place by an oak tree and was first recorded in 1490 but is certainly of considerably earlier origin. From the late 18th century until after the First World

War Noak Hill was very much the fiefdom of the extremely wealthy Neave family. Their nearby mansion, Dagnams, was demolished in 1950 during preparations for the creation of HAROLD HILL.

Noel Park A multi-ethnic locality situated to the south-east of WOOD GREEN underground station. Its streets were laid out by the Artisans', Labourers' and General Dwellings Company between 1883 and 1907, and the estate was named after the company's chairman, Ernest Noel (1831–1931).

Noho A neologism that property developers have recently attempted to apply to FITZROVIA, or at least its southern half. In particular, the name was championed by the would-be creators of NOHO SQUARE. The blend of 'north of SOHO' imitates New York nomenclature but without the same logic; that city's NoHo and SoHo are thus named because they lie north and south of Houston Street. The coinage has been resisted and ridiculed by many Fitzrovians but has been taken up by estate agents and a few journalists, mostly restaurant critics and the like. In 2009 one estate agent's website implausibly stated: 'We are located on Charlotte Street in fashionable Fitzrovia, better known as "Noho".'

Noho Square A commercial and residential complex planned for the site of the former MIDDLESEX HOSPITAL. The project was disrupted by the economic downturn that began in 2008 and subsequently nicknamed 'No Hope Square'. A new joint venture partnership was set up in July 2010, intending to draw up revised plans for the development, possibly under a different name.

None But the Lonely Heart A film (1944) adapted by US playwright Clifford Odets from a novel of the same title by the Welsh writer Richard Llewellyn (1906–83). It tells the story of a shiftless young COCKNEY who drifts into a life of crime. Starring Cary Grant and Ethel Barrymore, it took its title from a song of 1869 written by Tchaikovsky, which was itself based on 'Mignon's Song' in the novel *Wilhelm Meisters Lehrjahre* (1795–6) by Goethe. In Tchaikovsky's song the relevant lyric is usually translated as:

> None but the weary heart can understand how I
> have suffered and how I am tormented.

Nonsuch A palace that stood near the southern edge of what is now GREATER LONDON, near Ewell, SURREY. In 1538 Henry VIII acquired the manor of Cuddington, obliterated all the existing buildings and commissioned the construction of Nonsuch Palace. The lord of the manor received the priory of ISLEWORTH in compensation for his loss. Although primarily intended as a hunting lodge, Nonsuch was built and decorated to impressive standards of grandeur that were designed to rival Chambord, the Loire Valley palace of the French king Francis I. Work was close to completion when Henry died in 1547. Nonsuch remained in the possession of the Crown until Charles II gave it to his mistress Barbara Villiers, who demolished the palace in 1684 and sold off the materials. Nonsuch Park, which contains the site of the palace and some relics of its heyday, lies west of CHEAM.

Norbiton An eastern extension of KINGSTON UPON THAMES. The settlement was recorded in 1205 as Norberton, signifying a northern grange or an outlying farm, with its southern counterpart at SURBITON. In the mid-18th century Norbiton Hall was the residence of Sir John Phillips, whose Senegalese retainer Cesar Picton later became a respected coal merchant and gentleman of Kingston, in an early example of successful black entrepreneurship. The hall was swallowed by suburban London after the coming of the railways, and was later rebuilt as a mansion block. Other purpose-built apartment blocks have begun to change the residential landscape in recent years.

Norbiton Common A 320-acre (120-hectare) common that was enclosed in 1808 and soon filled with farms and smallholdings. After the railway reached Norbiton in the 1850s much of the agricultural land was sold off for development. Around Kingston Road the original dwellings have almost all been replaced with council houses.

Norbury A multi-ethnic district consisting mainly of former council houses, situated between THORNTON HEATH and STREATHAM. The existence of a manor house was first noted in 1229 and it was known by 1359 as Northbury, the 'northern manor house' of CROYDON. The manor extended across the London road (now a section of the A23) and included the common later

called Thornton Heath. It was in the possession of the Carews of BEDDINGTON for almost five centuries from 1385.

Sherlock HOLMES wanted Dr WATSON to whisper 'Norbury' in his ear whenever he became over-confident, on account of his misinterpretation of the evidence in 'The Adventure of the Yellow Face' (1894). Norbury was the home of Derek Bentley, controversially hanged for his part in the killing of a Croydon policeman in 1952.

north

north and south 'Mouth' in COCKNEY RHYMING SLANG.

> What a mouth! What a mouth! What a north and south!
> Blimey what a mouth he's got.
>
> R.P. WESTON: 'What a Mouth' (song) (1906)

North Castle An early slang term for HOLLOWAY PRISON, from its location in north London and the castellated architecture of its original gateway.

North Circular Road An orbital trunk road curving through outer north London, created in the 1920s and later repeatedly upgraded. It nowadays extends from junction 1 of the M4 motorway, at GUNNERSBURY, to BECKTON, where it meets the A13. Designated the A406, it is referred to as 'the North Circular' (sometimes colloquially abbreviated to 'North Circ') throughout its length, although some individual sections have their own names, especially towards each end. Unlike its half-hearted counterpart SOUTH OF THE RIVER, the North Circular is a cohesive route and ascribes an approximation of a genuine semi-circle. The arrival of the North Circular initially brought industry to parts of its hinterland, and later retail superstores, particularly near its junctions with major radial roads.

> A Sunday whizz around the North Circular. Sikhs aren't supposed to cop for religious pilgrimages. North Circular must be the exception. They've got IKEA while the Hindus paddle barefoot through their ice-cream temple in Neasden.
>
> IAIN SINCLAIR: *Landor's Tower* (2001)

North End A sparsely populated part of HAMPSTEAD HEATH, located at the apex of North End Way and Spaniards Road, and best known for two pubs: the OLD BULL AND BUSH and the early 17th-century (but much altered) Spaniards Inn, supposedly the residence of the Spanish ambassador to the court of James I. Another pub, JACK STRAW'S CASTLE, has been converted to residential use. North End has been the home of the statesman William Pitt the Elder, the Florentine engraver Francisco Bartolozzi, the dancer Anna Pavlova and Raymond Unwin, who planned HAMPSTEAD GARDEN SUBURB. Samuel Richardson wrote his mould-breaking novel *Pamela* in 1740 while living at The Grange, a house owned from 1867 by the artist Edward Burne-Jones. The Grange was controversially demolished in 1958.

North Finchley The primary commercial centre of FINCHLEY, linked to its CHURCH END by Ballards Lane. Finchley and North End (as it was earlier called) began to coalesce after the opening of stations at Finchley (now Finchley Central) in 1867 and Torrington Park (now Woodside Park) in 1872, whereafter the village came to be known by its present name. The introduction of trams in 1905 brought further growth and shops soon lined this section of the High Road in an unbroken continuum. Between the wars the Tally Ho public house replaced the Park Hotel, several major retailers built imposing stores and an Odeon (later Gaumont) cinema opened in 1939. Some of the biggest retailers have since moved away but BARNET council still rates North Finchley as one of its three major town centres. The Gaumont closed in 1979 and the Artsdepot has recently been built on its site. North Finchley has been home to a roll call of British comic talent: Spike Milligan lived in Holden Road, Eric Morecambe in Torrington Park and David Jason in Lodge Lane.

North Greenwich Nowadays this name is used for the northern part of the GREENWICH PENINSULA. However, in the late 19th century it was applied to the southern tip of the ISLE OF DOGS, where North Greenwich station opened in 1872. The railway company operated a ferry service across the Thames to what it called 'South Greenwich'. Island Gardens DOCKLANDS LIGHT RAILWAY station now occupies roughly the same site as the old North Greenwich station.

North Greenwich Arena Another name for the DOME.

North Harrow The north-western part of HARROW. Developers' preference for the cachet of the Harrow name snuffed out the hamlet of Hooking Green when suburban housebuilding began in the early 20th century. North Harrow

station opened in 1915 and the district filled with affordable homes between the world wars.

North Hyde A densely built-up residential and commercial locality tucked between the GRAND UNION CANAL and the M4 motorway, south of SOUTHALL and west of NORWOOD GREEN. North Hyde was the northernmost part of the parish of HESTON – and indeed of the whole of the ISLEWORTH hundred, an ancient subdivision of the county consisting of 100 HIDES. The name dates from the 13th century, when Heston became a separate parish from Isleworth.

North Kensington A multicultural district sometimes considered to constitute the area lying west of LADBROKE GROVE and north of the WESTWAY. A wider definition takes in neighbouring localities such as KENSAL TOWN, NOTTING DALE and beyond. Unlike 'West Kensington', a name invented by property developers to improve the image of north FULHAM, this area was genuinely part of the parish of KENSINGTON but was a poor district from the earliest days of its development. Conditions barely improved through the first half of the 20th century and in the late 1950s the notorious landlord Peter Rachman (*see* RACHMANISM) let out a number of run-down properties here, after which the council stepped up its slum clearance programme. Caribbeans arrived in the first wave of postwar immigration, often disembarking from boat trains at KENSINGTON OLYMPIA and finding this to be the nearest affordable district within walking distance. They were followed later by Moroccans, Filipinos and East Africans.

North London Central Mosque *See* FINSBURY PARK MOSQUE.

North Ockendon The only village in London that is outside the M25, and the most remote from the city centre, North Ockendon lies 2 miles (3 km) east of CORBETS TEY. It is a scattered farming community with labourers' cottages and the flint-faced church of St Mary Magdalene at its core. The village became part of HORNCHURCH urban district in 1935, hence its present inclusion within GREATER LONDON. The much larger settlement of South Ockendon falls within the district of Thurrock, in ESSEX.

north of Watford or **(the) Watford Gap** A reference to the supposition (often ascribed to those living in south-east England) that civilization does not extend very far north of London. The Watford Gap is a dip between the hills of Northamptonshire (and home of the UK's first motorway service station), lying some 50 miles (80 km) north of the Hertfordshire town of Watford, yet the two places are called upon almost interchangeably to the same effect. It is sometimes claimed that the Watford Gap was the original point of reference and that the use of 'Watford' is an ignorant abbreviation of the 'true' phrase, but there is no evidence to support this assertion.

> Now I come to the most extraordinary piece of casting in recent years: Mr Frank Pettingell, known to London audiences chiefly as the portrayer of the kind of clownish bumpkin with which the average Londoner imagines every town north of Watford is exclusively populated, will play the part of Wilde!
>
> STEPHEN WILLIAMS, in the *Evening Standard* (30 May 1935)

North Romford An umbrella term for COLLIER ROW and its neighbouring localities, namely MAWNEY, Havering Park, Chase Cross and Rise Park. Some definitions of the area extend as far as NOAK HILL. Although the name features as a bus destination, it is not favoured by residents.

North Weezy A contemporary urban slang term for north-west London, especially the NW2 (CRICKLEWOOD), NW6 (KILBURN) and NW10 (WILLESDEN) POSTAL DISTRICTS, but even heard in the heights of HAMPSTEAD. It is apparently a contraction of 'north-west easy'. Variant spellings range from 'Norf Wheezy' to 'North Weezie'. The latter was employed in 2009 by the Bishop of Willesden, the Rt Rev Pete Broadbent, as part of the graphic device identifying his 'micro-blog' on the social networking website Twitter.

North Woolwich A changing DOCKLANDS district lying between the King George V Dock and the THAMES, east of SILVERTOWN. Wool from ESSEX sheep may have been landed or traded here by the Saxons and there is speculation that this could have been the original WOOLWICH, later lending its name to the settlement that evolved on the opposite bank of the river.

Northern line A LONDON UNDERGROUND line running from MORDEN in the south to termini at EDGWARE, MILL HILL East and HIGH BARNET in the north. The Northern line is coloured black on the map. The line divides at the OVAL and recombines at CAMDEN TOWN, taking separate routes through central London, one via CHARING CROSS

and the other via BANK (with both branches passing through KENNINGTON and EUSTON). This complex structure derives from its origins as two separate railways: the City and South London Railway – the world's first electric deep-level TUBE line – which opened in 1890 and ran from King William Street in the CITY to STOCKWELL; and the Charing Cross, Euston and Hampstead Railway, which opened in 1907. Between 1922 and 1926 the City and South London Railway was rebuilt and linked with the Hampstead Railway at Camden Town. It was renamed the Northern line in 1937 and a series of extensions culminated in the present layout in 1941. *See also the* MISERY LINE.

Northfields The south-western corner of EALING. Great and Little Northfields were two large fields in the late Middle Ages. An orchard had been planted in Little Northfield by 1738 and in the 19th century the Steel family of market gardeners grew apples across the entire area on an almost industrial scale. With the coming of electric trams to Uxbridge Road in 1901, the Steels turned to property development and began to grub up the fruit trees and lay out streets; Julien Road, Wellington Road and Bramley Road, south of Northfields station, are named after cooking apples that the family cultivated. *See also* BLONDIN.

Northolt A large and unexciting set of housing estates, many of them council built, situated north-west of GREENFORD. This was originally Northall, the northern counterpart to SOUTHALL. A settlement has existed at Northolt since the 8th century, originally on higher ground to the north-east of the church. The manor house was thrice pulled down and twice rebuilt in the 14th century, and gained a moat, but was left in ruins after its last owner was hanged for treason. In the two decades after the Second World War EALING council built almost 3,500 homes in the area, more than half its total for the whole borough. Belvue Park and the old village centre retain some rural elements, and the moated site of the manor house is a scheduled ancient monument.

Northolt Aerodrome A military airfield that opened in 1915, when Royal Flying Corps patrols provided cover against Zeppelin raids over London. A series of allied and British Hurricane and Spitfire squadrons were based here during the

Second World War, including a complete Polish wing (*see the* POLISH WAR MEMORIAL). Because of its proximity to central London, RAF Northolt retains important strategic and ceremonial roles, especially as the home of No.32 (the Royal) Squadron, which, in addition to its military duties, provides air transport for the monarch, the prime minister and other high-ranking dignitaries.

Northolt Park A postwar municipal housing estate occupying the northern part of NORTHOLT. This was a patch of open farmland until Northolt Park racecourse opened in 1929, as the national centre for the new sport of pony racing. The sport was cheaper to run than horse racing and the track's excellent facilities attracted large crowds over the next decade. The film and MUSIC HALL star George Formby rode here in 1938 and returned the following year to make the EALING STUDIOS film *Come On, George*, performing all his own stunts. There was little racing after the outbreak of the Second World War and in 1940 the government requisitioned the site to intern Italian prisoners, later converting it to an army camp. Attempts to restart pony racing after the war were thwarted by Ealing council's determination to use the land to ease its housing shortage.

Northumberland

Northumberland Avenue A street running east from CHARING CROSS to the EMBANKMENT, on the edge of the WHITEHALL district. It was laid out in 1875, partly on the site of the former Northumberland House, the 17th-century London residence of the Percy family, dukes of Northumberland.

Northumberland Development Project A scheme to build a 58,000-seat arena and a club museum for TOTTENHAM HOTSPUR FC, on a site fractionally to the north of the present WHITE HART LANE stadium, which would then be replaced by 450 homes, a hotel and new public spaces. The project is provisionally scheduled for completion in 2014.

Northumberland Heath A residential district standing on high ground in south-west ERITH, known locally as North Heath. The name Northumberland Heath has been in use since the 13th century and has no connection with the county; it means 'the heathland north of the watercourse'.

Northumberland Park A multicultural, deprived satellite of TOTTENHAM, situated in the north-east corner of the borough of HARINGEY. A curving avenue was laid out in the late 1850s between Tottenham High Road and Marsh Lane (now Northumberland Park) station, on land behind the site of the Black House, a medieval mansion that had been owned by the dukes of Northumberland. The avenue was accordingly named Northumberland Park and was built up with villas for the upper middle classes. Over a 15-year period from the late 1950s a medieval farmhouse, disused industrial sites and most of Northumberland Park's villas were replaced by Tottenham council's expansive Northumberland estate of slab blocks and dull terraces.

Northwick Park A METROLAND suburb wedged between KENTON and HARROW. Development began here before the First World War, under the aegis of the established owners of the land, the Churchill-Rushout family. Northwick Park was their estate in Worcestershire and several of the new roads were given the names of places in its vicinity. Harrow Technical College, now part of the UNIVERSITY OF WESTMINSTER, was established here in 1959 and the substantial Northwick Park Hospital opened in 1969. The 120-acre (48-ha) open space called Northwick Park has extensive sports facilities.

Northwood A stockbroker-belt residential district located on the GREATER LONDON border, 4 miles (6.5 km) north-west of HARROW. From at least the 14th century there was a hamlet here, separated from RUISLIP and EASTCOTE by Park Wood, Copse Wood and Ruislip Common. Many of the houses built from the 1890s onwards were ostentatiously grand and some have since been replaced by flats. Those that survive encompass a wide range of styles, including neo-Georgian, mock-Tudor, hacienda and neo-English baroque. Infilling and 'garden grabbing' continue wherever developers can find a vacant space.

Northwood Hills The south-eastern end of Northwood, named to convey an impression of poshness. Its station opened in November 1933 and the construction of houses nearby began almost immediately afterwards and continued for two decades. During the 1960s the young Elton John (born Reginald Dwight, 1947) lived in Northwood Hills with his mother and stepfather-to-be. At the age of 16 he began performing at the

Northwood Hills Hotel every weekend, for £1 a night plus the proceeds of a whip-round.

Norton Folgate Now just a short section of road linking BISHOPSGATE with SHOREDITCH High Street, Norton Folgate was formerly a well-known mercantile neighbourhood. As Mr Burgess says in Shaw's play *Candida* (1898): 'I never met a man as didn't know Nortn Folgit before.' Until its merger with the parish of SPITALFIELDS in 1911, Norton Folgate was an extra-parochial liberty, which meant that it was outside the jurisdiction of the local parish church. The playwright Christopher Marlowe (1564–93) was living here in 1589. A century later, Spital Square and its surrounding streets began to fill with fine homes for silk merchants and master weavers, while artisans and journeymen occupied the diverging alleys and courts. Norton Folgate's residential population declined during the course of the 19th century as homes were converted into warehouses and business premises.

Norway spruce *See the* TRAFALGAR SQUARE CHRISTMAS TREE.

Norwood A sprawling south London suburb that begins south of TULSE HILL and extends almost as far south as CROYDON. The Great North Wood of SURREY covered the whole of modern Norwood until the 17th century. The woods provided timber for building ships (including the GOLDEN HIND) and houses, a livelihood for charcoal burners and pig-keepers, and a home for squatters and the NORWOOD GIPSIES. By the mid-18th century deforestation had created large areas of heathland. From 1799 the enclosure commissioners sold or allocated plots of land of varying sizes and entirely new settlements arose. Where groups of small plots were sold, as in Lower Norwood (later renamed WEST NORWOOD) and South Norwood, working-class housing frequently appeared. Elsewhere, for example on Beulah Hill and in other parts of Upper Norwood, substantial villas began to be built for CITY merchants, although the process did not accelerate until transport links improved. With the opening of BEULAH SPA in 1831, the JOLLY SAILOR station in 1839 and the relocation of the CRYSTAL PALACE to SYDENHAM Hill in 1854, Norwood rapidly filled with homes for the middle classes, while enclaves like Norwood New Town provided reservoirs of tradesmen. Despite the ravages of the 20th century, much of Norwood retains a Victorian air. James Thomson praised the rural seclusion of the Great North Wood in his 'Hymn on Solitude' (1729):

Perhaps from Norwood's oak-clad hill,
When meditation has her fill,
I just may cast my careless eyes
Where London's spiry turrets rise,
Think of its crimes, its cares, its pain,
Then shield me in the woods again.

Norwood Gipsies or **Gypsies** For more than two centuries the most entrenched minority community in the London area. Samuel PEPYS recorded his wife's visit to their camp in August 1668 to have her fortune told. The most famous of all the mystics was Margaret Finch, who lived in a tepee-like structure made from branches, at the foot of an ancient tree. Allegedly, she was 109 when she died in 1740 and had to be buried in a deep, square box because she had sat cross-legged for so long that her limbs could not be straightened. Finch's successors lived on at the timber-built Gipsy House until the early 19th century. A pantomime called *The Norwood Gipsies* was staged at COVENT GARDEN in 1777. *See also* GIPSY HILL.

Norwood Green A relatively upmarket part of SOUTHALL, situated to the north-west of OSTERLEY PARK. Originally just called Norwood, it was first mentioned in a will of 832, which bequeathed the manor to the archbishop of Canterbury. Several handsome villas were built here in the late 18th and early 19th centuries, most of which have since been lost to suburban development. The finest survivor is Sir John SOANE's Norwood Hall, which he designed for a friend in 1803. The house, which has original Soane drawings and a large walled garden, was modified and extended in the late 19th century. It became home to a Sikh faith school in 2009.

nose

nosey parker A prying person. The term is first recorded only in the early 20th century, and according to one account it was the nickname given to a man who spied on courting couples in HYDE PARK. An alteration of 'nose-poker' is a possibility. *See also Aloysius* PARKER.
London nose *See under* LONDON.

not

not a lot of people know that A catchphrase

personifying the actor Sir Michael Caine (b. Maurice Micklewhite, 1933). It originated in a remark made by Peter Sellers, interviewed by Michael Parkinson in 1972:

> Mike's always quoting from the *Guinness Book of Records*. At the drop of a hat he'll trot one out. 'Did you know that it takes a man in a tweed suit five and a half seconds to fall from the top of Big Ben to the ground? Now there's not many people know that!'

> quoted in NIGEL REES: *Brewer's Famous Quotations* (2006)

Caine was born in ROTHERHITHE, the son of a BILLINGSGATE MARKET porter, and grew up in CAMBERWELL (where he attended Wilson's grammar school) and the ELEPHANT AND CASTLE. He has played major parts in more than a hundred films, including ALFIE (1966), *Get Carter* (1971), *Mona Lisa* (1986), *Little Voice* (1998) and *Harry Brown* (2009). *See also* YOU'RE ONLY SUPPOSED TO BLOW THE BLOODY DOORS OFF.

not a sausage Nothing at all. The expression originally denoted a lack of money, and is said to derive from COCKNEY RHYMING SLANG, in which 'bangers and mash' (i.e. sausages and mash) represents 'cash'.

not bloody likely A line famously uttered by Eliza DOOLITTLE in Act 3 of George Bernard SHAW's PYGMALION (1913): 'Walk! Not bloody likely. I am going in a taxi.' It caused considerable outrage at the time and the mock-euphemistic 'not Pygmalion likely' was afterwards used in literate circles. Although the real-life usage of the phrase long ago lost its exclusivity to London, it retains some of its original associations:

> Jerry: Did she think she was gonna leave this incredibly erotic message on my tape and I was just gonna let it go? Not bloody likely.
> Kramer: What is that?
> Jerry: That's my cockney accent.

> LARRY DAVID, DON MCENERY and BOB SHAW: *Seinfeld*, 'The Tape' (TV comedy) (1991)

not half! A positive response to a question, usually regarding one's approval or appreciation of something or someone. The expression was in use throughout the 20th century and is still heard. Eric Partridge's *Dictionary of Catch Phrases* (2nd edition, edited by Paul Beale, 1985) calls it 'a good example of cockneys' ironic meiosis'.

Not Only ... But Also *See the* DAGENHAM DIALOGUES.

not on your Nellie or **Nelly** Not likely; not on any account; not on your life. Probably from COCKNEY RHYMING SLANG, 'Not on your Nellie Duff', 'Duff' rhyming with 'puff', which is old slang for 'breath' and thus life itself. The phrase was used as the title of a LONDON WEEKEND TELEVISION sitcom (1974–5), in which Hylda Baker played Nellie Pickersgill, the Lancastrian landlady of the Brown Cow, a public house in FULHAM.

Notting In NOTTING DALE and NOTTING HILL the name probably derives from a Saxon family called Cnottingas, sons of Cnotta.

Notting Dale A notoriously deprived enclave located to the west of the much better-known and better-off district of NOTTING HILL. From the 1860s Notting Dale was built up with cheap housing and the new residents scraped a living by taking in laundry or keeping pigs. Having started badly, conditions got worse and Charles BOOTH charted terrible hardship just a short distance from the wealth that radiated outwards from Lansdowne Crescent. Some of London's first housing associations began their work in Notting Dale.

Notting Hill

1. A district of social and ethnic contrasts, situated west of BAYSWATER. The southern and largest part of Notting Hill was built up from the second quarter of the 19th century with the Norland and Pembroke estates in the south-west and south-east and the Ladbroke Grove estate in the centre. Here, the grandest terraced houses rise to five storeys, with private communal gardens to the rear, yet the location made the properties affordable to the upper middle classes rather than the aristocracy of MAYFAIR and BELGRAVIA. Further north, Notting Hill blurs with what is now thought of as the LADBROKE GROVE locality. By the late 19th century this borderland area had suffered a decline, the middle classes moved away and properties were subdivided into flats between the wars, while the central and southern parts of the district remained well-to-do. Notting Hill's contrasts extend west and east too, to the much poorer and lesser known district of NOTTING DALE and the busy market on PORTOBELLO ROAD. London has many areas where rich and poor exist cheek by jowl but Notting Hill is perhaps the most remarkable, with rock stars and Hollywood actors living

just a few streets from a crowded, multi-ethnic neighbourhood to the north and west.

2. A film (1999), written by Richard Curtis and directed by Roger Michell, about a celebrated US film actress who falls for a humble British bookshop owner while on a visit to London. Anna Scott (Julia Roberts) and William Thacker (Hugh Grant) first meet in Thacker's bookshop on POR-TOBELLO ROAD, while other scenes were shot in Lansdowne Road, Golborne Road and NOTTING HILL GATE, and Thacker lives on Westbourne Park Road, in what was actually Curtis's home at the time. The sunny conceit, that despite numerous problems a transatlantic relationship could blossom between a global celebrity and a nonentity, had wide appeal.

Notting Hillbillies A country music band organized by Mark Knopfler as a sideline to his involvement with Dire Straits. The Notting Hillbillies released one album, *Missing ... Presumed Having A Good Time* (1990).

Notting Hillbilly A jocular name for a resident of Notting Hill. The expression dates from the end of the 20th century, when the already bohemian status of the area was altered by the influx of a trendy, creative crowd.

> Before her, Chloé was about as relevant in high fashion as Laura Ashley. [Stella] McCartney and her Notting Hillbilly posse gave the label a hip replacement.
>
> *Independent on Sunday* (6 March 2005)

Notting Hill Carnival Europe's largest street festival, held annually on the last (bank holiday) weekend of August as a celebration of the West Indian way of life. Partly in response to the NOTTING HILL RIOTS a multiracial carnival was organized in January 1959 at ST PANCRAS town hall. The carnival was held annually thereafter at a succession of halls before taking to the streets of Notting Hill from 1964, with steel bands providing the music, and food and drink provided by local traders. In due course the colour and extravagance of costumes, volume and variety of music, and originality and ingenuity of the floats rivalled the panache of New Orleans or Rio de Janeiro and a huge amount of trade was generated. The carnival was dogged by violence and disorder for many years, notably in 1976, when black youths clashed with police, but since the 1990s it has been mostly peaceful.

Notting Hill Gate A visually dull but culturally interesting stretch of road situated at the meeting point of Bayswater Road, Kensington Church Street, Holland Park Avenue and Pembridge Road. This was a lonely stretch of the 'way to UXBRIDGE' beside the KENSINGTON gravel pits with a few cottages until a tollgate was set up in the mid-18th century. The gate stood at the junction with what was then PORTOBELLO Lane, now Pembridge Road, and was rebuilt twice over the following 100 years. In the late 1950s Notting Hill Gate was brutally redeveloped in a road-widening programme, creating a monotonous streetscape out of what had formerly been a characterful if messy thoroughfare and combining two underground stations within a single concourse. The artist Damien Hirst ran the ultra-trendy Pharmacy restaurant here from 1997 to 2003, selling its fixtures and fittings for £11 million after its closure. Notting Hill Gate has four venues that are popular with the cultural cognoscenti: the Coronet opened as a theatre in 1898 and became a cinema after the First World War; the Gate was converted from a coffee palace into a cinema in 1911, originally as the Electric; the Gate Theatre was established in 1979 in a room above the Prince Albert pub on Pembridge Road; and the Nottinghill Arts Club aims to be at the cutting edge of trends in niche music and the visual arts.

> Things look great in Notting Hill Gate;
> We all sit around and meditate.
>
> RAJA RAM and SHIVA JONES: 'Notting Hill Gate' (song by Quintessence) (1969)

Notting Hill riots A series of violent demonstrations that took place in and around Notting Hill in late August and early September 1958. These were triggered by earlier clashes in Nottingham, after which organized activists whipped up racial hatred among white youths in London. The riots brought the issue of 'race relations' to prominence in Parliament and the media for the first time.

Notting Hill set A description in the summer of 2004 by the Conservative MP Derek Conway of certain younger members of the parliamentary party, whom he accused of mounting a whispering campaign against older Tory MPs and specifically of suggesting that the latter were preventing younger Tories from standing for parliament:

> This is what we call the Notting Hill Tory set.

They sit around in these curious little bistros in parts of London, drink themselves silly and wish they were doing what the rest of us are getting on with. They'll just have to be a little more patient.

DEREK CONWAY, quoted in *The Guardian* (27 July 2004)

The Napoleon of Notting Hill *See under* NAPOLEON.

now then, what's all this? The stock opening words of the London BOBBY of yesteryear when happening upon some incident. Variant second elements included 'what's going on 'ere?' and 'what 'ave we 'ere then?' As with the comparable 'hello hello hello', the phrase spread nationwide but primarily as a stereotype. No police officer today would use such words, except in a clichéd comedy show.

Jasper Gerard's Opinion piece headlined: 'Now then, what's all this nonsense about pay rises?' (last week) is a tongue-in-cheek sneer about police pay, but he has some of his facts wrong.

PHILIP CHAMBERS: letter to *The Observer* (23 December 2007)

nudge, nudge, wink, wink A phrase expressive of heavy-handed sexual innuendo, often quoted with ironic reference to its source, a 1969 sketch in the BBC television comedy show *Monty Python's Flying Circus* in which Eric Idle obscurely but salaciously quizzes a bemused Terry Jones about the sexual habits of his wife, who comes from PURLEY.

Say no more, Purley, say no more. Purley, eh? Know what I mean, know what I mean?

number

Number Eleven 11 DOWNING STREET, the official residence of the chancellor of the exchequer, next door to NUMBER TEN.

Number Nine A colloquialism in the early 19th century for the FLEET PRISON, which was located at 9 Fleet Market.

No.1 Croydon *See the* 50P BUILDING (*under* FIFTY).

No.1 London The nickname of Apsley House, HYDE PARK CORNER, because it was the first dwelling on the London side of the former KNIGHTSBRIDGE tollgate. It was built by Robert Adam in 1778 for the lord chancellor, Lord Apsley, and became the home of the Duke of Wellington in 1817. The duke made significant improvements

to the house and filled it with works of art that he had received as gifts. It is now a museum and gallery, largely unchanged from the time of Wellington's residence.

No.1 Strand A house that stood near the western end of the STRAND, on the south side. In the 17th century it was the official residence of the secretary of state (the chief government minister). It was one of the earliest addresses in London to be numbered, possibly the first ever. Like the neighbouring Northumberland House, it was demolished in 1874 to make way for NORTHUMBERLAND AVENUE.

Number Ten Media shorthand for 10 DOWNING STREET, the official residence of the prime minister, and a metonym for the office of the prime minister.

The Chancellor, who is said to have resisted pressure from Number Ten to introduce an even bolder fiscal stimulus on Monday, denied having had rows with Gordon Brown.

The Observer (30 November 2008)

Nunhead A run-down district with a handful of highlights – especially the almshouses at Nunhead Green – situated east of PECKHAM RYE. The name was first mentioned in 1583, when Edgar Scot sold Thomas and William Patching certain estates 'lying at None-Head'. The name may relate to ownership of land here by the SHOREDITCH nunnery of St John the Baptist in the late 12th century. Others have suggested that it originates from a pub sign, but the sign itself could have derived from the same root. Brock's firework factory (*see also* BROCK'S BENEFIT) operated at Nunhead and in 1870 contracted to make two million cartridge tubes for the French army during the Franco-Prussian War. The district was developed in the 1870s and 1880s by a variety of speculative builders. Before and after the Second World War, the London County Council built numerous blocks of flats in the area, notably on the Nunhead estate in the 1950s, although some pockets of Victorian housing remain. Charles Peace, the murderous Victorian burglar, made Evelina Road his London home.

Nunhead Cemetery Nunhead was a market gardening hamlet when 58 acres (23 hectares) were taken for All Saints' Cemetery in the late 1830s. The main entrance lodge was built on Linden Grove, where Charles DICKENS later set up an apartment for his mistress. Among those buried here is Thomas Tilling, the operator of the fleet nicknamed TIMES BUSES. The cemetery is now an attractive wilderness, although parts have recently been restored.

nun of Syon with the friar of Sheen, the An old expression usually said to equate to 'birds of a feather'. However, some sources add a second element: 'went under the water to play the quean' – which meant 'to play the whore'. SYON ABBEY and the Carthusian monastery at Sheen (modern RICHMOND UPON THAMES) lay on opposite sides of the THAMES and it was popularly supposed that the two establishments were connected by a secret tunnel.

NW Twee A nickname for the NW3 POSTAL DISTRICT, which is centred on HAMPSTEAD.

How easy it is for Guardian readers, safely tucked away in the enchanted kingdom known to my colleague Julie Burchill as NW Twee, to dismiss as dimwits those brave and resourceful men and women who keep this country safe for decent folk.

MATTHEW NORMAN, in *The Guardian* (2 January 2001)

nylon A synthetic polymer first produced by the Du Pont Company in the USA in the 1930s. There is no evidence to support the assertion that the name is a blend of 'New York' and 'London'.

Nyp Shop According to Francis Grose's *Classical Dictionary of the Vulgar Tongue* (1796 edition), this was a nickname for the Peacock, a public house in what is now GRAY'S INN ROAD (then Lane), which sold strong Burton ale by the half-pint.

Oak Apple Day or **Royal Oak Day** This falls on 29 May, the birthday of Charles II (1630–85) and the day on which he entered London at the Restoration in 1660. It was commanded by Act of Parliament in 1664 to be observed as a day of thanksgiving. A special service (expunged in 1859) was inserted in the Book of Common Prayer, and people wore sprigs of oak with gilded oak-apples on that day. It commemorates Charles II's concealment with Major Careless in the 'Royal Oak' at Boscobel, near Shifnal, Shropshire, after his defeat at Worcester (3 September 1651). The occasion is still celebrated by CHELSEA PENSIONERS.

Oakleigh Park A pricey residential locality situated east of WHETSTONE and south of EAST BARNET. Oakleigh Road is an old route, called Avernstreet in 1499 and by a number of other names in subsequent centuries, but its present identity dates from the Whetstone Freehold Estate Company's invention of the Oakleigh Park name after it acquired land here in 1869. Until then this had been Matthews Farm, the property of the Haughton Clarke family, who had made their money from the slave trade. When the station opened here in 1873 the estate company ensured that it too was named Oakleigh Park.

Oaks, The One of the classic races of the turf, it is for three-year-old fillies and is run at Epsom the day before the Derby. It was instituted in 1779 and so called from the Earl of Derby's estate, situated south of CARSHALTON, in what is now the London Borough of SUTTON. Much of the estate is now a park, sports centre and public golf course. *See also* EPSOM RACES.

Oakwood A park and PICCADILLY LINE station in the far north of SOUTHGATE that have given their name to the disparate private and municipal estates clustered around them. In 1870 Samuel Sugden, a homeopathic chemist, bought land here, renovated a farmhouse and renamed it Oak Lodge, and added a walled garden and an orchard. Oak Lodge was demolished around 1920. Southgate council acquired the lodge's 64 acres (26 hectares) of grounds and invented the name 'Oakwood' for the park it opened in 1927.

Oates, Titus *See the* POPISH PLOT.

Oatmeals A little-used 17th-century nickname given to profligate bands in the streets of London. The term may have been related to a satirical pamphlet (1595) entitled 'A Quest of Enquirie by Women to know Whether the Tripewife were trimmed by Doll, yea or no: gathered by Oliver Oat-meale'.

> Swagger in my pot-meals:
> Damn-me's rank with,
> Do mad prank with
> Roaring boys and Oatmeals.
>
> JOHN FORD and THOMAS DEKKER: *The Sun's Darling*, I, i (1656)

October Club In the reign of Queen Anne, a group of High Tory MPs who met at a tavern near the PALACE OF WESTMINSTER to drink October ale and to abuse the Whigs. It became a politically prominent gathering about 1710 although it had probably existed from the end of William III's reign.

odd

Oddfellows A friendly society first recorded in 1730 in the form of the Loyal Aristarcus Lodge. It met in the Oakley Arms in SOUTHWARK, the Globe Tavern in HATTON GARDEN and the Boar's Head in SMITHFIELD. During the period of the French Revolutionary Wars many lodges were prosecuted for alleged 'seditious' activities, as were many harmless organizations. In 1813 the Independent Order of Odd Fellows was formed at Manchester and it became the most influential in England.

Sette of Odd Volumes A literary dining society founded in 1878 by the antiquarian bookseller Bernard Quaritch (1819–99). It usually convened at Limmer's Hotel, in MAYFAIR.

oh

oh, my Sunday helmet Probably the best-known catchphrase and strongest language used by Constable Archibald Berkeley-Willoughby in *The Adventures of PC 49* (*see* PC 49).

oh, Pollaky! *See* PADDINGTON POLLAKY.

Oh, What a Lovely War! A musical (1963) created by Joan Littlewood's Theatre Workshop at the Theatre Royal, STRATFORD East, as a satirical commentary on the huge losses suffered in the First World War. The show featured lampoons of popular songs of the day, as sung by soldiers in the trenches.

oily (rag) 'Fag' in COCKNEY RHYMING SLANG, usually meaning a cigarette.

OK Yardie A nickname invented in the 1990s for a SLOANE RANGER living in a multicultural and supposedly 'edgy' area such as LADBROKE GROVE. The term, which is not widely used, is a blend of 'ok, yah' and 'yardie'. *See also* TRUSTAFARIAN.

> ... the real voice of choice here is OK Yardie, an unlikely coupling of the area's upper middle-class dropouts with the black roots they aspire to.
> *The Independent* (25 May 1997)

old

Old Admiralty *See the* ADMIRALTY.

Old Alleynian A former pupil of DULWICH COLLEGE.

Old Bailey A street in the CITY of London, running north–south between NEWGATE Street and LUDGATE HILL. It follows the line of the old city wall between Ludgate and Newgate and the name referred to an outwork or defensive rampart on the outside of that wall.

The Old Bailey, with the definite article, is an informal name for the Central Criminal Court, which is situated at the northern end of Old Bailey, on the site formerly occupied by NEWGATE PRISON. It has jurisdiction over the City and (approximately) the GREATER LONDON area. The first courthouse in the street was built in 1539, next to Newgate Prison (it is recorded in 1555 as

'le Justice Hall in le Olde Bailie'). It was replaced by a new building in 1774. The present court building was opened, by Edward VII, in 1907. The statue of Justice on its dome, blindfolded and holding a sword and a pair of scales, has become an icon not only of the building but of the impartial administration of the legal process. Almost as famous is the motto above the main door: 'Defend the children of the poor and punish the wrongdoer.' An extension was added to the building in 1972.

In exceptional circumstances, cases from outside its London jurisdiction are tried at the Old Bailey. Among the more notorious murderers to have stood trial at the Old Bailey are Dr CRIPPEN (1910), George 'BRIDES IN THE BATH' Smith (1915), John Christie, of the 10 RILLINGTON PLACE murders (1953) and Peter Sutcliffe, the 'Yorkshire Ripper' (1981).

Old Bexley Also known as Bexley Village, this is the historic heart of BEXLEY, situated at the south-eastern corner of the modern suburb. The 'Old' prefix helped distinguish the village from Bexley New Town, as BEXLEYHEATH was called in the second half of the 19th century. Among the surviving older properties are the King's Head public house, the former parish workhouse, Styleman's almshouses, High Street House and Cray House.

Old Bill A nickname for the police, and the METROPOLITAN POLICE in particular. It probably derives from a walrus-moustached, disillusioned old COCKNEY soldier in the First World War, created by Captain Bruce Bairnsfather (1887–1959), artist and journalist, in his publications *Old Bill* and *The Better 'Ole*. Cowering in a wet and muddy shell hole in the midst of a withering bombardment, he says to his grousing pal Bert, 'If you knows of a better 'ole, go to it.' The joke and Old Bill struck the public fancy, and Old Bill became the embodiment of a familiar type of simple, cynical, long-suffering, honest old grumbler. The precise connection between the character and the police is uncertain; it may be that many ex-servicemen took employment with the Metropolitan Police after the war, or that such servicemen were recruited by posters showing Bairnsfather's Old Bill in a special constable's uniform, or that policemen between the wars often wore walrus moustaches.

Old Brentford The south-eastern corner of BRENTFORD, located at the mouth of the River

BRENT, and nowadays more commonly known as Brentford Dock. Medieval Brentford was divided between the parishes of HANWELL and EALING and the two halves were later distinguished as New and Old Brentford. New Brentford, which is no longer shown on maps, was associated with the manor of Bordeston, which came to be called BOSTON MANOR. *See also* AS DIRTY AS OLD BRENTFORD AT CHRISTMAS.

Old Bull and Bush A public house located on NORTH END Way, between HAMPSTEAD and GOLDERS GREEN. A haunt of the artists HOGARTH, Reynolds and Gainsborough, it gave its name to a famous MUSIC HALL song:

Come, come, come and make eyes at me
Down at the Old Bull and Bush,
Come, come, have some port wine with me,
Down at the Old Bull and Bush.

HUNTING, KRONE, STIRLING and VON TILZER: 'Down at the Old Bull and Bush' (song popularized by Florrie Forde) (1903)

Old Clem A nickname of St Clement and the title given to the chief celebrant of St Clement's Day (23 November) festivities formerly held by blacksmiths' apprentices in WOOLWICH. The chosen personage was dressed in a greatcoat, given a face mask, a flaxen wig and a long white beard, and seated on a wooden throne. A procession then carried Old Clem around the town, accompanied by attendants bearing banners, torches and weapons and playing on the fife and drum. After they had called at nearly every public house on the route, Old Clem would then deliver the following speech:

I am the real St Clement, the first founder of brass, iron, and steel, from the ore. I have been to Mount Etna, where the god Vulcan first built his forge, and forged the armour and thunderbolts for the god Jupiter. I have been through the deserts of Arabia; through Asia, Africa, and America; through the city of Pongrove; through the town of Tipmingo, and all the northern parts of Scotland. I arrived in London on the 23rd of November, and came down to His Majesty's dockyard, at Woolwich, to see how all the gentlemen Vulcans came on there. I found them all hard at work, and wish to leave them well on the 24th.

A similar ceremony was held at Chatham Dockyard, in Kent.

Old Compton Street SOHO's gay heartland, situated north of SHAFTESBURY AVENUE, running parallel with its middle section. It was named after landowner Spencer Compton, the Earl of Northampton, who died at the Battle of Hopton Heath in 1643. Compton's son Henry became bishop of London and commissioned the building of St Anne's Church. New Compton Street, across CHARING CROSS ROAD, is named after him. The street is nowadays famed for its gay bars and specialist retail outlets. The bombing of the Admiral Duncan pub by a right-wing fanatic in 1999 killed three people and injured more than 80.

Old Court Suburb A nickname for KENSINGTON, from the royal court formerly held at its palace. It was coined by Leigh Hunt as the title of a set of historical vignettes begun in the weekly magazine *Household Words* in 1853–4 and then completed and published in two volumes (1855).

Old Curiosity Shop, The A novel (1840–1) by Charles DICKENS, it tells the story of LITTLE NELL, whose grandfather owns the titular establishment. A curiosity shop was formerly a dealer in antiques and the trade was especially associated with WARDOUR STREET. Dickens was said to have modelled his shop on one in Portsmouth Street, LINCOLN'S INN FIELDS, a claim that is doubted by many, notwithstanding the building's undeniable antiquity. Nevertheless, that shop was renamed accordingly after the novel was published. *See also the* MARCHIONESS.

Old Father Thames *See* FATHER THAMES.

Old Ford Situated in the far north of BOW, this was an early crossing point of the River LEA on what was the main road from London into ESSEX in the early Middle Ages. There is archaeological evidence of active commercial traffic from the middle of the 1st century into the 4th century. Old Ford's waterworks were responsible for London's last cholera epidemic in 1866, although they were not shut down until 1891. Sylvia Pankhurst (1882–1960) ran the militant East London branch of the suffragette movement from rooms on Old Ford Road. On the same road she also opened a mother-and-baby clinic in a former pub (which she renamed the Mother's Arms) and a 'cost price restaurant'.

Old Grog The sobriquet of Admiral Edward Vernon (1684–1757), because he habitually wore a cloak made from grogram (a kind of coarse cloth of silk and mohair). Born in WESTMINSTER and educated at WESTMINSTER SCHOOL, Vernon led a famous naval victory at PORTOBELLO in 1789. The word 'grog' derives from Vernon's nickname, because he provided his men with rations of rum mixed with water.

Old Harrovian A former pupil of HARROW SCHOOL.

Old Holborn The brand name of a type of loose tobacco for roll-your-own cigarettes, nowadays manufactured by Gallaher. The half-timbered frontage of STAPLE INN that used to be pictured on the label is still in existence. It was formerly home to a branch of the tobacconist John Brumfit.

Old Jewry A street in the CITY of London, running north to south from Gresham Street to POULTRY. It lay within an area in which many Jews lived in the 12th and 13th centuries, but they were expelled from it on the orders of Edward I in 1290 – hence its name.

Old Kent Road A downmarket commercial thoroughfare extending from east NEWINGTON to NEW CROSS GATE. The road closely follows the line of the medieval route to Canterbury and formerly crossed the River NECKINGER, which now runs underground. It was at that ford that the pilgrims watered their horses in Chaucer's *Canterbury Tales*. Once known for its shops selling JELLIED EELS and PIE AND MASH, the Old Kent Road is now increasingly popular for its clubs and other forms of nightlife. Albert Chevalier's MUSIC HALL song 'Knocked 'em in the Old Kent Road' (1892) was performed by Shirley Temple in the 1939 movie *The Little Princess*:

Wot cher! all the neighbours cried
Who yer gonna meet, Bill?
Have yer bought the street, Bill?
Laugh! I thought I should've died
Knocked 'em in the Old Kent Road.

Old Lady of Threadneedle Street A synonym for the BANK OF ENGLAND, which stands in this street. The term dates from the late 18th century, and there is a caricature by James Gillray, dated 22 May 1797, depicting the bank as an old lady with a dress made of paper money, seated firmly on the bank's gold and ignoring the advances of the then prime minister, William Pitt the Younger. It was entitled *Political Ravishment; or the Old Lady of Thread-needle Street in Danger*, and it referred to Pitt's instruction that the bank should not redeem its notes in gold and that it should issue £1 notes instead.

Old Malden A well-to-do suburb separated from TOLWORTH by the Hogsmill River. The manor was recorded in Domesday Book as Meldune, which meant 'the hill with a cross'. At 93 feet (28m) above sea level, the hill is not especially prominent. In 1264 Walter de MERTON made Malden manor house the base for the educational foundation that subsequently became the University of Oxford's Merton College. This was perhaps the greatest advance in the development of higher education in the London area until the creation of the UNIVERSITY OF LONDON. The village began to grow slowly after the opening of Old Malden and Worcester Park station (later WORCESTER PARK) in 1859. Old Malden today is very much a product of the 20th century, especially the period between the wars, when Malden Manor station opened. The St John's and Plough Green conservation areas preserve a fine collection of older buildings and a fragment of the medieval landscape.

Old Mo The Middlesex Music Hall, DRURY LANE, was so called after the Mogul Tavern (named for the Mogul of Hindustan), which was incorporated into the premises. After rebuilding in 1911 it became the New Middlesex Theatre of Varieties and in 1919 the Winter Garden Theatre, which survived for a further 40 years. Following a period of dereliction the building was replaced in 1973 by the New London Theatre.

Old Operating Theatre A small museum located in the roof space of the former St Thomas's Church, SOUTHWARK. From 1822 to the early 1860s it was used as an auditorium, in which ST THOMAS' HOSPITAL medical students could observe surgical procedures.

Old Parr The nickname of Thomas Parr (c.1483–1635), who, if his claimed date of birth is to be believed, was Britain's oldest ever man. At the supposed age of 152 he was brought from Shropshire to London by Thomas Howard, Earl of Arundel, and stayed at Arundel House, in the STRAND. He was presented to Charles I, had his portrait painted by Rubens and Van Dyck and dined at many of the highest tables in town. All this proved too much for the 'old, old, very old man', as John Taylor, the WATER POET, called him, and he soon expired. On the instructions of the king he was buried in WESTMINSTER ABBEY.

Black jealousies of Mr Toots arise, and Briggs is of opinion that he ain't so very old after all. But this disparaging insinuation is speedily made nought by Mr Toots saying aloud to Mr Feeder, BA, 'How are you, Feeder?' and asking him to come and dine with him today at the Bedford; in right of which feats he might set up as Old Parr, if he chose, unquestioned.

DICKENS: *Dombey and Son* (1847–8)

old pot and pan *See* POT AND PAN.

Old Price riots or **the O.P. riots** A series of commotions that took place at the Covent Garden Theatre (now the ROYAL OPERA HOUSE) in 1809. After its predecessor had been destroyed by fire a new incarnation of the theatre opened on 18 September, charging higher prices to help cover the cost of the rebuilding. As soon as the national anthem had been sung the audience began to shout 'old prices, old prices', and the chant continued throughout much of the performance of *Macbeth*. A posse of BOW STREET officers was called and magistrates read the Riot Act but the crowd did not disperse until after midnight. Similar disturbances took place for more than two months, after which John Philip Kemble (1757–1823), the theatre's owner-manager, relented.

> It was a noble sight to see so much just indignation in the public mind; and we could not help thinking, as Mr Kemble and Mrs Siddons stood on the stage, carrying each £500 in clothes upon their backs, that it was to feed this vanity, and to pay an Italian singer, that the public were screwed.
>
> *The Times* (19 September 1809)

Old Q The nickname of William Douglas, 3rd Earl of March and 4th Duke of Queensberry (1724–1810), who was also known as the Star or Rake of Piccadilly. He was immensely wealthy and notoriously dissipated, fathering numerous illegitimate children. In his latter years he would sit for hours on the balcony of his house at what is now 138 PICCADILLY, ogling female passers-by and making suggestive remarks. *See also* RUNNING FOOTMEN.

> Thank heav'n he's gone! exclaimed Miss Prue,
> My mother, and grandmother, too
> May now walk safe from that Old Q,
> The Star of Piccadilly.
>
> ALEXANDER BOSWELL: 'Verses on a report of the Duke of Q——'s Death' (1810)

Old Spitalfields Market *See* SPITALFIELDS MARKET.

Old Street An ancient route connecting CLERKENWELL with SHOREDITCH, bisected by the CITY ROAD. This was one of the earliest ribbon developments outside the CITY walls and was *eald* (old) when its name was first recorded as Ealdestrate around 1200. Houses began to extend westward from Shoreditch High Street in the late Middle Ages and development intensified when HOXTON became a fashionable resort towards the end of the 17th century. Nearer the western end of the street, the growth of ST LUKE's had a similar effect in the 18th century. Old Street was heavily built up in the mid-19th century but few of its early Victorian buildings remain, as a result of road widening in the 1870s and later slum clearance and bomb damage.

Old Timber A punning nickname of the London-born conductor Sir Henry Wood (1869–1944), who founded the Promenade Concerts ('the PROMS') in 1895 and continued to conduct them until his death. He was knighted in 1911.

Old Tom

1. A specially potent gin. The story goes that a Thomas Norris, employed in Messrs Hodges' distillery, opened a gin palace in Great Russell Street, COVENT GARDEN, in the late 18th century, and called the gin concocted by Thomas Chamberlain, one of the firm of Hodges, 'Old Tom', as a compliment to his former master.

2. A gander that evaded slaughter at LEADENHALL, became a market favourite and was fed at local pubs. He allegedly survived to the age of 38. On his death in 1835 he lay in state at the market and was buried there.

Old Vic A theatre situated in The Cut, in WATERLOO. It opened in 1818 as the Royal Coburg Theatre, taking its name from its founding patrons, Prince Leopold of Saxe-Coburg (1790–1865), the future King Leopold I of Belgium, and his recently deceased wife Princess Charlotte (1796–1817). In 1833 it was renamed the Royal Victoria in honour of 14-year-old Princess Victoria, later Queen Victoria. It was soon popularly known as the 'Vic', but by the start of the 20th century this name had been expanded to 'Old Vic', partly in reference to Victoria's age and reign (she died aged 81 after 64 years on the throne, longer than any other British monarch), but mainly as a token of affection. It became famous for its Shakespearean productions under the management of Lilian Baylis (1874–1937), who took over from her aunt, Emma Cons, in 1912. It was the temporary home of the National Theatre from 1963 to 1976. In 1977 the Prospect Theatre moved in but it failed in 1981. In 1982 the Old Vic was bought by a Canadian businessman, Edwin Mirvish, and after extensive renovations reopened in 1983. Having failed to make any money from the project, Mirvish sold the theatre in 1998 to the Old Vic Theatre Trust 2000, a registered charity set up by the impresario Sally Greene. The US actor Kevin Spacey became its artistic director in 2003. *See also* SADLER'S WELLS; YOUNG VIC.

Oliver

Oliver's Island A small island in the THAMES, lying off STRAND ON THE GREEN. Its name derives from a story that Oliver Cromwell once took refuge on the island but there is almost certainly no truth in this. The island was called Strand Ayt until a century after the Civil War, by which time the myth had arisen that Cromwell had used the Bull's Head in Strand on the Green as an intermittent headquarters. The story was further embellished with suggestions of a secret tunnel connecting the inn and the island, allegedly constructed to help Catholic priests escape Protestant persecutors.

Oliver Twist A novel (1838) by Charles DICKENS. The eponymous hero is an orphan, born in the workhouse where his mother dies. He is farmed out to a branch workhouse and removed at the age of 9 by Mr Bumble to be apprenticed to Mr Sowerberry, from whom he runs away and becomes enmeshed in FAGIN's den of child pickpockets. Jack Dawkins (the ARTFUL DODGER) teaches him the trade, NANCY treats him kindly and Bill SIKES tries to make him a criminal. Proved innocent after his false arrest for thieving, he is rescued from the world of crime and vice by Mr Brownlow, Mrs Maylie and Rose Maylie. The story formed the basis of Lionel Bart's stage musical *Oliver!* (1960), which was made into a film in 1968, directed by Carol Reed.

Olympia *See* KENSINGTON OLYMPIA.

Olympic Games The modern games, a revival of the ancient Greek festival held every four years at Olympia, were organized in 1896 as international sporting contests. The Summer Olympics were held in London in 1908 and 1948, at WHITE CITY and WEMBLEY STADIUM respectively. The 2012 Olympic Games and Paralympic Games will take place at a newly created Olympic Park north-west of STRATFORD. In addition to the main stadium, the park will encompass an aquatics centre, basketball arena, handball arena, hockey centre and velopark. With the exception of mountain biking, sailing, rowing, canoeing, kayaking and most football matches, all other Olympic events will take place within GREATER LONDON, at the following venues:

The DOME (gymnastics and basketball)
EARLS COURT (volleyball)
EXCEL (boxing, fencing, judo, table tennis, taekwondo, weightlifting and wrestling)
GREENWICH PARK (equestrian and modern pentathlon events)
HORSE GUARDS PARADE (beach volleyball)
HYDE PARK and the SERPENTINE (triathlon and 10 km open water swim)
LORD'S (archery)
REGENT'S PARK (road cycling)
ROYAL ARTILLERY BARRACKS (shooting)
WEMBLEY ARENA (badminton and rhythmic gymnastics)
WEMBLEY STADIUM (football)
WIMBLEDON (tennis)

omi or **omee** A POLARI word for a man, from the Italian *uomo*. An omi-paloni (literally manwoman) was a homosexual man, a contrivance that could have been considered offensive had it not been invented by gay men themselves.

omnibus *See* SHILLIBEER'S OMNIBUS.

Omnibus row or **the Tamburini riot** An incident of May 1840, in which occupants of the omnibus boxes (proscenium boxes at stage level) at Her Majesty's Theatre, in the HAYMARKET, aggressively barracked the Italian baritone Filippo Coletti (1811–94), who had replaced his countryman Antonio Tamburini (1800–76). The crowd then stormed the stage and the curtain fell to their cries of 'Victory!' What made the episode remarkable was that the HOOLIGANS were mostly aristocrats, and their ringleader was the soprano Giulia Grisi (1811–69). The theatre manager afterwards re-engaged the services of Tamburini.

Folks of all sorts and of every degree,
Snob, and snip, and haughty grandee,
Duchesses, countesses, fresh from their tea,
And shopmen, who'd only come there for a spree,
Halloo'd, and hooted, and roar'd with glee.

R.H. BARHAM: *Ingoldsby Legends*, 'A Row in an Omnibus (Box): A Legend of the Haymarket' (1840)

man on the Clapham omnibus *See under* MAN.

on

On the Buses A popular ITV sitcom that ran for seven series between 1969 and 1973 and spawned three spin-off feature films. The COCKNEY character actor Reg Varney (1916–2008) starred as Stan Butler, driver of the number 11 bus to the Cemetery Gates in the fictional HOME COUNTIES district of Luxton. The TV show was filmed at studios and external locations in London, including WOOD GREEN bus garage and the entrance to ENFIELD's Lavender Hill cemetery.

on the cotton *See* COTTON.

one

one and a peppermint drop London street slang for a one-eyed person, in the late 19th and early 20th centuries.

One Canada Square *See* CANARY WHARF.

One Hyde Park A 'super-prime' KNIGHTSBRIDGE apartment complex due for completion in 2010, replacing Bowater House, a 1950s office block. Despite the state of the property market at the time, most of the 86 flats were sold in advance, at an average of more than £20 million each. Four penthouses were reportedly priced at £100 million each, potentially making them the most expensive flats in the world.

One Lime Street *See the* LLOYD'S BUILDING.

one never knows The motto of the PEARLY KINGS AND QUEENS.

one–nil to the Arsenal In the mid-1990s this became the most frequently heard refrain at HIGHBURY, sung to the tune of 'Go West' (Morali/Belolo/Willis, 1979). The chant reflected well on the solidity of ARSENAL's defence but poorly on what was widely perceived at the time as a 'boring' style of play, unlikely to result in a flood of goals. It is still sung at the EMIRATES STADIUM but not quite so often.

'One-nil to the Arsenal' has rarely sounded sweeter to the Londoners' ears as they became the first English club to win at the Bernabeu.

The Daily Telegraph (23 February 2006)

one of our own Said of someone who is, or is considered to be, part of one's close community. The expression is not exclusive to London but is firmly rooted in the language of the EAST END.

One of Our Own is the title of a 1973 story of East End life by the author and playwright Frank Norman.

When it [The LONG GOOD FRIDAY] finally came out, [Bob] Hoskins was hailed by those that he portrayed. 'I met some top gangsters after filming, who said "I've seen the film and I'm glad to say we're so proud one of our own is doing so well."'

The Independent (22 September 2006)

ones and twos 'Shoes' in COCKNEY RHYMING SLANG.

One Square Mile *See the* SQUARE MILE.

one stop short of Barking A fairly recent coinage that makes use of the terminology of TUBE travel to question someone's sanity. The idiom upon which it puns – 'barking mad' – has no etymological connection with the east London district.

One Tree Hill *See* HONOR OAK.

one under A term employed by LONDON UNDERGROUND staff and fire service rescue crews (and increasingly by regular travellers) to describe the situation formally known as a 'person under a train'. Usage of the expression is spreading across the whole British railway network but it is still most often heard in London, because of the frequency with which such incidents occur here.

No.1 London *See under* NUMBER.

Only Fools and Horses A long-running
BBC television sitcom, written by John Sullivan (b.1946), who also sang the theme tune. It was first screened from 1981 to 1991, with several Christmas specials thereafter. The title referenced an old COCKNEY expression suggesting that 'only fools and horses work [for a living]'. The lead characters are the wheeler-dealing Derek 'DEL BOY' Trotter and his gormless younger brother Rodney, played by David Jason and Nicholas Lyndhurst. Plots often revolve around Del Boy's flawed get-rich-quick schemes, usually involving 'hooky' goods. The series is memorable for its colourful writing, and the dialogues of the two are peppered with slang words such as 'dipstick' and 'PLONKER' for an idiot and 'LOVELY JUBBLY!' as a term of approval. *Only Fools and Horses* is set in PECKHAM, where the brothers reside in the fictional Nelson Mandela House. Exterior shots featured a tower block in South ACTON in the

show's early years but later switched to Bristol, as did most other location filming.

Open House An architectural showcase held annually in London since 1992, on the third weekend of September, in which several hundred significant structures are freely opened to the public. Some are buildings that are regularly accessible at a price but where the admission charge is waived. Many others are private premises, such as corporate headquarters, domestic residences or parts of public buildings that are normally off limits. In certain places guided tours are arranged; in others visitors may wander freely. Related special events, walks and talks are also held. Numerous companies, institutions and individual homeowners participate, as well as all the London boroughs, with just one recalcitrant exception. More than a quarter of a million people are nowadays estimated to take part each year.

> Mr Architect opens the door, distractedly running his fingers down the front of his pale grey alpaca sweater. 'Could everyone take off their shoes, please,' he says, without making eye contact. It is raining and I am standing on the doorstep of a self-consciously modern house in Hampstead, removing my footwear. Along with seven other adults. Architecture makes us do crazy things. This is the essence of London Open House, next weekend, when not just public but some very, very private dwellings are made accessible to the prying hordes.
>
> CAROLINE ROUX, in *The Guardian* (14 September 2002)

opera
Opera Holland Park An opera company that stages summer festivals in HOLLAND PARK, under the aegis of the Royal Borough of Kensington and Chelsea and with the support of commercial sponsors. For several decades various arts events have been held in and around the bombed-out shell of Holland House, especially from 1988, when a canopy was installed. The events' organizers pursued an increasingly operatic direction in response to complaints from nearby residents about noise, and Opera Holland Park was established in 1996. Six operas are nowadays staged each season, between the beginning of June and mid-August, with around 45 performances in total. The City of London Sinfonia is the resident orchestra. The company staged its first produc-

tion outside Holland Park in February 2009: Puccini's *Tosca* at RICHMOND Theatre.
English National Opera *See under* ENGLISH.
Royal Opera House *See under* ROYAL.

Operation Trident *See* TRIDENT.

opinicus A fabulous monster in heraldry, compounded from dragon, camel and lion. It forms the badge of the Worshipful Company of Barbers and features in a stained-glass window at Barber-Surgeons' Hall, installed to mark the new millennium. The name seems to be an alteration of 'Ophiucus', the classical name of the constellation the Serpent-Holder (Greek *ophis*, 'snake').

Oranges and Lemons A nursery rhyme dating from at least the mid-18th century, and later a children's singing game, based on the sounds of the bells of several churches in and around the CITY of London. Alternative versions feature a wider range of churches, but the best known runs thus:

> 'Oranges and lemons', say the bells of St. Clement's
> 'You owe me five farthings', say the bells of St. Martin's
> 'When will you pay me?' say the bells of Old Bailey
> 'When I grow rich', say the bells of Shoreditch
> 'When will that be?' say the bells of Stepney
> 'I do not know', says the great bell of Bow
> Here comes a candle to light you to bed
> And here comes a chopper to chop off your head!
> Chip chop, chip chop – the last man's dead.

There is some dispute as to which St Clement's is referred to in the rhyme. The stronger case is for the church in St Clements Lane, EASTCHEAP, which lies near former wharves where citrus fruit was unloaded. However, the church of ST CLEMENT DANES, on the STRAND, has usurped the claim by introducing the tune of the rhyme to its bell peal. The other churches mentioned are St Martin Orgar, most of which was destroyed in the GREAT FIRE OF LONDON; St Sepulchre-without-Newgate, by the OLD BAILEY; St Leonard's SHOREDITCH; St Dunstan's STEPNEY and ST MARY-LE-BOW. There is disagreement too on the original meaning, if any, of the last lines. They may refer to the execution of Charles I in 1649 or of prisoners held in the TOWER OF LONDON.

Oranges and Lemons service A children's service held annually at ST CLEMENT DANES on or near 31 March, at which pupils of St Clement Danes primary school are presented with oranges and lemons.

Orators' Corner An old name for SPEAKERS' CORNER.

Order of St John See the KNIGHTS HOSPITALLER.

Orfling A dark-complexioned orphan girl, otherwise known as Clickett, in Charles DICKENS's *David Copperfield* (1849–50). Brought up in ST LUKE's workhouse, she is the maid-of-all-work for Mr and Mrs Micawber. DAVID COPPERFIELD entertains her with 'some astonishing fictions respecting the wharves and the Tower; of which I can say no more than that I hope I believed them myself.'

Oriel A fairy whose dominion lay along the banks of the THAMES. See also KENNA.

Orpington An extensive dormitory town situated 4 miles (6.5 km) south-east of BROMLEY. The place was first recorded in 1032 as Orpedingtun – the farmstead of a man called Orped, a name which meant 'active' or 'bold'. All Saints' Church is of Saxon origin and has a sundial inscribed in runes. The church was remodelled around 1200 and a priory was built nearby before 1270. The priory was enlarged and improved in the following two centuries and served both as a residence for the rector and chaplains and as an overnight stop for the priors of Canterbury Cathedral. Except on its far eastern side, Orpington is the epitome of comfortable suburbia, and its prime attraction is the museum and gardens of the priory.

Orpington Buff A breed of chicken first presented in 1894 by local poultry breeder William Cook at the annual fair held on White Hart Meadow. Orpington Buffs rapidly gained popularity as an excellent meat bird but lost out as the commercial roaster market developed, partly because of their excessively pale skin. Bugs Bunny's friend Miss Prissy is allegedly an Orpington Buff.

Orpington man A term that enjoyed a currency in the 1960s following the Liberal victory in the Orpington by-election of 1962, when Eric Lubbock took the seat with a then-sensational 27 per cent swing. 'Orpington man' was the typical home-county commuter who abandoned the habits of a lifetime to vote Liberal rather than Conservative. See also ESSEX MAN; ISLINGTON MAN; SELSDON MAN.

Osidge A comfortable 1930s suburban locality lying on a westerly slope beside the Pymmes Brook west of SOUTHGATE. Its name comes from Old English, meaning 'hedge belonging to a man named Osa'. Hugh Davies, the developer of the Osidge estate in the 1930s, advertised the proximity of Southgate station with a paraphrase of a popular song: 'Home, James, and don't spare the horses, it's a home on the Tube for me.' The singer/songwriter Amy Winehouse (b.1983) grew up on Osidge Lane.

Ossulstone Hundred See OSWULF'S STONE.

Osterley A compact residential locality situated 1½ miles (2.5 km) west of BRENTFORD. Osterley was first recorded in 1274, and the name derives from Old English words meaning 'sheepfold clearing'. Suburban development began here after the construction of the GREAT WEST ROAD. The present station, a classic Charles Holden design, opened in 1934.

Osterley Park An estate and its stately home of the same name, located north of OSTERLEY station. The banker Sir Francis Child acquired the house in 1713 and around 1760 his grandson commissioned Robert ADAM (and probably others) to remodel the exterior and create lavishly furnished and decorated new rooms inside, while the grounds were landscaped and endowed with a chain of lakes. In 1939 the Earl of Jersey opened the house to the public and ten years later gave it to the National Trust. It has been a popular location for filming country house dramas, including the 1999 version of *Mansfield Park*. The park, now split in two by the M4 motorway, includes woods, farms and sporting facilities.

Oswulf's Stone or **Oswald's Stone** A Roman or possibly pre-Roman monolith that stood at TYBURN. It probably served as a boundary marker and acquired its name from an Anglo-Saxon settler. In the corrupted form of Ossulstone it gave its name to an early settlement and later to the MIDDLESEX hundred (administrative division) that encompassed most of modern INNER LONDON north of the THAMES, including CHELSEA, WESTMINSTER, HAMPSTEAD and STEPNEY. The stone's fate is a mystery: it is said to have leant for a while against the MARBLE ARCH after that structure was moved to its present site in 1851, but it has not been seen since 1869.

Other Club, The A dining club founded in 1911 by Sir Winston Churchill and F.E. Smith (Lord Birkenhead) and said to be so called because they were not wanted at an existing fraternity known as The Club. It still meets at the SAVOY, and membership is not confined to Tories or politicians. *See also* KASPAR.

O2 *See the* DOME.

out-county A term used by the LONDON COUNTY COUNCIL with reference to the housing estates that it built beyond the border of the county of London as it existed at the time. The projects included BECONTREE, NORBURY and Watling (*see* LITTLE MOSCOW), all of which now lie within GREATER LONDON.

Outer London A collective term for the suburban parts of London, broadly corresponding with the areas that were added to the capital in 1965 to form GREATER LONDON, consisting of the following boroughs:

BARKING AND DAGENHAM	HAVERING
BARNET	HILLINGDON
BEXLEY	HOUNSLOW
BRENT	KINGSTON UPON THAMES
BROMLEY	MERTON
CROYDON	NEWHAM
EALING	REDBRIDGE
ENFIELD	RICHMOND UPON THAMES
HARINGEY	SUTTON
HARROW	WALTHAM FOREST

Subsequently, compilers of official statistics introduced a revised definition of Outer London that excluded Haringey and Newham and included GREENWICH. *See also* INNER LONDON.

outrooper (Dutch *uitroepen*, 'to cry out', 'to proclaim') In the 17th century the publicly appointed town crier of the CITY of London.

outside, Eliza! or **Liza!** Be off with you! The expression apparently derived from a court case in which a barman stated that he said to the accused over and over again, 'Outside, Eliza.' But she would not go, and finally smashed a plate-glass window. For the same reason, a drunken woman was sometimes called an 'outside Eliza'.

He glanced first at the clock and then at his engagement tablet, and saw with satisfaction that in a quarter of an hour he would have an excuse for saying 'Outside, Eliza!' which was his vulgar way of dismissing friends and semi-friends.

EDGAR WALLACE: *The Lady of Ascot* (1930)

Oval, The or **Kennington Oval** A cricket ground in KENNINGTON that takes its name from a street layout devised in 1790, although the plan was never fully realized. It has a spectator capacity of over 23,000. In 1844 the Montpelier Cricket Club leased 10 acres (4 hectares) of the Oval's market gardens after it had been ejected from its ground at WALWORTH. Cabbage patches were buried under turf brought from TOOTING Common and an embankment was raised using soil excavated during the enclosure of the River Effra at VAUXHALL Creek. Shortly after the ground opened a group of aficionados founded SURREY COUNTY CRICKET CLUB at a meeting in the neighbouring Horns Tavern; Surrey played its first county cricket match against Kent in 1846. The first test match in England was staged here, in 1880 (between England and Australia – England won by five wickets). It was after Australia's victory at the Oval in 1882 that the ASHES came into being. In the past the Oval has been associated with various other activities, sporting and otherwise. Most FA Cup finals between 1872 and 1892 were played here, as were England's first rugby union matches against Scotland and Wales. During the Second World War it was a prisoner-of-war camp and in 1971 it hosted its first pop concert but nowadays the playing area is reserved largely for cricket. At 558 feet (170m) by 492 feet (150m) it has the largest area of any cricket ground and the gasholders on its north-eastern side have become an Oval icon. It is presently known as the Brit Oval, owing to the sponsorship of a BISHOPSGATE-based insurance company. The Oval has given its name to cricket grounds in several former British colonies, including Sri Lanka and Barbados. *See also* LORD'S.

Overy, Mary *See* ST MARY OVERY (*under* SAINT).

Oxford

Oxford Circus The crossroads of OXFORD STREET and REGENT STREET. The junction was created in the early 1820s by the construction of

Regent Street and was originally named Regent Circus North. Its southern counterpart – now called PICCADILLY CIRCUS – was a grander affair; there was never a circular arrangement to the buildings at the northern crossroads, just a rounding of corners. The Corinthian arcades of the circus itself were probably by John Nash (1752–1835), the architect of Regent Street, while the surroundings were developed by a local speculative builder, Samuel Baxter. By the 1890s the general public had started to refer to the junction as Oxford Circus, and it had become a notorious traffic blackspot, crowded with horse-drawn carriages from dawn until dusk. During this decade the linen draper Peter Robinson relocated here, operating premises at both the north-western and north-eastern corners, while Dickens and Jones took up residence at the south-eastern corner. Oxford Circus was rebuilt over an eleven-year period from 1912 as part of the reconstruction of Regent Street.

Oxford Street London's busiest shopping street, running east–west from ST GILES CIRCUS to MARBLE ARCH. This was a medieval track, part of 'the way to UXBRIDGE', and was formerly known as TYBURN Road. The change to Oxford Street took place gradually between about 1718 and 1729 and the modern name probably derives from former landowners the earls of Oxford. The commercial development of the street began in earnest in the 1820s with the creation of REGENT STREET, which formed a crossroads at what is now OXFORD CIRCUS. Thereafter, small shops such as booksellers, shoemakers and goldsmiths spread outwards from this focal point and the street became increasingly congested in the latter part of the century. Grand emporiums made their appearance in the 1890s and the opening of four CENTRAL LINE stations on the street in 1900 allowed customers to come from further afield. In 1902 the Bourne and Hollingsworth brothers-in-law moved their store to Oxford Street from WESTBOURNE GROVE, which had been a rival for shoppers' attentions. Thereafter the street became single-mindedly devoted to retailing and the last private houses disappeared in 1930, to be replaced by a Gamage's department store. Marks and Spencer opened its Marble Arch store in 1930 and the PANTHEON store in 1938. The first display of Christmas lights on Oxford Street was turned on in 1959 and the event is now a heavily publicized part of the promotional calendar, usually

involving celebrities who appeal to an audience of parents and children. See also DEBENHAMS; JOHN LEWIS; SELFRIDGES.

Oxo Tower A SOUTH BANK landmark surmounting a former cold store and meat products factory, built in the late 1920s by the Liebig Company and then known as Stamford Wharf. To circumvent a prohibition on riverfront advertising, the company had the tower's windows framed and glazed in a way that spelt out the name of its leading brand of meat extract. After a period of dereliction the building was restored in the mid-1990s and renamed Oxo Tower Wharf. Its units include flats, retail design studios, specialist shops, galleries and places to eat and drink.

oyster

Oyster card A 'smart card' issued by Transport for London since 2003. The name was created by a marketing consultancy and has no special significance, notwithstanding Londoners' historical fondness for oysters. The card can function as a season ticket or as a cashless payment method for individual journeys and may be used on buses, the TUBE, trams, the DOCKLANDS LIGHT RAILWAY, LONDON OVERGROUND and some National Rail services in London. Pay-as-you-go users are generally charged less than the equivalent single fare for any given journey. In many cases the discounts appear extremely generous, although this is mainly because prices of regular tickets have been increased exorbitantly, primarily in a (successful) attempt to persuade most travellers to use the card. For the most part, the system works efficiently but civil liberties campaigners have expressed concerns regarding data privacy.

Oyster Street A COSTERMONGERS' nickname for the long row of oyster boats that used to moor alongside the wharf at BILLINGSGATE.

> On looking down the line of tangled ropes and masts, it seems as though the little boats would sink with the crowds of men and women thronged together on their decks. It is as busy a scene as one can well behold ... 'Who's for Baker's?' 'Who's for Archer's?' 'Who'll have Alston's?' shout the oyster-merchants, and the red cap of the man in the hold bobs up and down as he rattles the shells about with his spade.
>
> HENRY MAYHEW: *London Labour and the London Poor,* Volume 1 (1851)

P

padded cells The nickname of the City & South London Railway's passenger cars, from their cramped accommodation, floor-to-ceiling upholstery, high-backed seats and very small windows. The C&SLR opened in 1890 and its routes now form part of the NORTHERN LINE.

Padder An old abbreviation for PADDINGTON STATION, formerly used by Londoners studying at Oxford University.

Paddington Once a parish and metropolitan borough stretching as far as West KILBURN, but now a compact, densely built-up commercial locality surrounding the station that bears its name. This 'farmstead associated with a man called Padda' was first recorded in 998. The landscape gained a predictable smattering of gentlemen's seats in the 18th century but was also much disfigured by gravel workings. From the start of the 19th century the village became the focus of a series of transportation initiatives that hastened its urban development. PADDINGTON BASIN opened for business in 1801, London's first OMNIBUS service began operating from PADDINGTON GREEN in 1829 and the railway arrived at PADDINGTON STATION in 1838. By the 1850s the village had become a crowded, semi-industrial suburb, while the south-eastern part of the parish had meanwhile been built up as fashionable TYBURNIA. Piecemeal rebuilding from the late 19th century to the present day has left central Paddington with a streetscape that ranges from fine Georgian terraced houses to seedy flats. The MARYLEBONE flyover and the elevated section of the WESTWAY were built in the second half of the 1960s, dividing the station and its environs from the settlement that had grown up around the green.

Paddington Basin A narrow inland dock constructed at the eastern end of the Paddington branch of the GRAND JUNCTION CANAL and opened in 1801. The canal company also sponsored the construction of Grand Junction Street (now Sussex Gardens) and PRAED STREET. The basin, which lies north-east of PADDINGTON STATION, now forms the focal attraction of PADDINGTON WATERSIDE.

Paddington Bear An anthropomorphic character created in 1958 by the children's author Michael Bond (b.1926). Originally from Peru – *Darkest* Peru – the bear was found by the Brown family at Paddington station, and named accordingly, and went to live with them at 32 Windsor Gardens, NOTTING HILL. Paddington has an excellent command of English, is partial to marmalade sandwiches and usually wears a blue duffel coat, an old bush hat and wellington boots. The Paddington books have been translated into more than 40 languages, including Latin. Bond ceased writing the stories in 1979 but the bear made a one-off return in *Paddington Here and Now* (2008) to mark his 50th anniversary.

Paddington Express The nickname of Terry Downes, former world middleweight boxing champion, who was born in Paddington in 1936.

Paddington fair day Eighteenth-century slang for an execution day at TYBURN, which lay in the parish of Paddington. Similarly, to 'dance the Paddington frisk' was to be hanged at Tyburn.

Paddington Green A messy locality separated by the HARROW ROAD and the end of the WESTWAY from the rest of Paddington, but formerly the focus of the medieval village. The parish church of St Mary was built in the 17th century and rebuilt in 1791, when the village had become popular as a rural retreat. During the 19th century Paddington Green lost its refined air as urbanization took hold and by the 1850s the surrounding area was densely built up, mostly with working-class terraced housing. Slum housing was cleared away from 1937 onwards, usually to be replaced by blocks of council flats. The large amount of bed and breakfast accommodation in the area has led to the placement here of many refugees and asylum-seekers.

The green provided the setting for scenes in the stage show *Oliver!* (*see* OLIVER TWIST). Paddington Green – and the surrounding 4 square miles (10.6 sq km) – was the subject of a BBC television 'docu-soap' of that name that ran for six series from the end of 1998. The shows examined the lives of some of the area's colourful characters – including a transsexual prostitute and a safe-cracker. *See also* PRETTY POLLY PERKINS OF PADDINGTON GREEN.

Paddington Green police station A fortress-like structure best known as the location to which suspected terrorists are usually taken for questioning in London. It was built on the site of the Metropolitan Music Hall, which had been demolished in 1962 as a consequence of construction work on the MARYLEBONE flyover. The IRA exploded a bomb outside the police station in 1992.

Paddington omnibus *See* OMNIBUS.

Paddington Pollaky or **Pollacky** The so-briquet of Ignatius Paul Pollaky (1827–1918), London's first eminent private detective (unless one counts the THIEF-TAKER GENERAL). He maintained an office at PADDINGTON GREEN from 1865 until his retirement in 1882 and for a while worked as a special constable with X DIVISION. Like his fictional successor Sherlock HOLMES, he placed cryptic advertisements in the agony column of *The Times* in pursuit of his enquiries. In the late 19th century the exclamation 'oh, Pollaky!' was employed in response to excessive questioning.

> A smack of Lord Waterford, reckless and
> rollicky –
> Swagger of Roderick, heading his clan –
> The keen penetration of Paddington Pollaky –
> Grace of an Odalisque on a divan –
>
> W.S. GILBERT: *Patience*, I (1881)

Paddington spectacles The cap drawn down over the eyes of one about to be hanged at TYBURN. *See also* PADDINGTON FAIR DAY.

Paddington station A Great Western Railway terminus that opened in 1838, initially in a temporary building that later became the site of a goods depot. Queen Victoria alighted here in 1842 after her first-ever train journey, which had begun in Slough, Berkshire. A permanent station opened in 1854, designed by the railway's chief engineer, Isambard Kingdom Brunel. In 1863 Paddington (Bishop's Road) station became the western terminus of the world's first underground railway line. In 2000 Michael Bond unveiled a 'life-size' bronze statue of his creation PADDINGTON BEAR in the main-line station's new retail and eating area.

Paddington Waterside A 21st-century mixed-use development situated in the vicinity of PADDINGTON STATION and PADDINGTON BASIN. This is one of the largest such schemes the capital has seen since the regeneration of DOCKLANDS. The first phase of the Sheldon Square office complex at Paddington Central was opened in 2002 and Marks and Spencer moved its headquarters from BAKER STREET to Waterside House in 2004.

painted

Painted Chamber The king's private apartment in the medieval PALACE OF WESTMINSTER. In its earliest days the House of Commons sometimes convened in the chamber and state openings of Parliament were held there from the 14th century until the devastating fire of 1512.

Painted Hall A lavishly decorated dining hall, divided into three parts, in King William Court at the Old Royal Naval College, originally GREENWICH HOSPITAL. Christopher Wren designed the building and James Thornhill (1675/6–1734) devoted 19 years to painting its walls and ceilings. The body of Admiral Nelson lay in state here in January 1806.

> With its carved detail by Nicholas Hawksmoor
> and flowing figure paintings by Sir James
> Thornhill with their complicated royal
> iconography, this magnificent spatial sequence
> is one of the finest Baroque ensembles in
> Europe.
>
> DAVID WATKIN: *A History of Western Architecture* (4th
> edition, 2005)

Painted Tavern *See* THREE CRANES IN THE VINTRY.

painter

Painter of the Suburbs The sobriquet of the 'plein-air' artist Harry Bush (1883–1957), who painted many scenes in the immediate vicinity of his home in Queensland Avenue, MERTON, from the 1920s. His wife Noel Laura Nisbet

(1887–1956) was also an artist but preferred more classical subjects.

Peter the Painter *See under* PETER.

pair of compasses London slang for a man's legs, dating from the late 19th and early 20th centuries, when tighter trousers were coming into fashion.

Palace Without the definite article, 'Palace' is generally a reference to CRYSTAL PALACE FC. 'The Palace' (or 'the palace') usually means BUCKINGHAM PALACE, often as a metonym for the royal household.

> A terse statement from the palace said: 'This is a serious matter which was resolved within the family and is now in the past and closed.'
>
> *The Guardian* (14 January 2002)

Palace of Westminster A residence of English kings from the mid-11th century but now the seat of government, also known as the Houses of Parliament. Parliament emerged in the late 13th century as an extension of the King's Council. From the end of the 14th century the Lords sat regularly at the Palace of Westminster, as did the Commons intermittently. It ceased to be a royal residence after a serious fire in 1512, when the king moved to WHITEHALL PALACE. By 1550 the House of Commons was meeting regularly in ST STEPHEN'S CHAPEL. The palace was destroyed by a devastating fire in 1834, London's biggest conflagration since the GREAT FIRE OF LONDON. WESTMINSTER HALL, the crypt of St Stephen's Chapel and the JEWEL TOWER survived and a new, purpose-built structure was erected around these by Charles Barry and Augustus Pugin and brought into service in 1867. The chamber of the House of Commons was destroyed in a 1941 air raid. It was sensitively rebuilt by Sir Giles Gilbert Scott and reopened in 1950.

Palace of Whitehall *See* WHITEHALL PALACE.

palare *See* POLARI.

Palladium *See the* LONDON PALLADIUM.

Pall Mall A prestigious thoroughfare in ST JAMES'S, connecting the southern end of ST JAMES'S STREET with TRAFALGAR SQUARE. The name is now usually pronounced as in 'pallet' and 'mallet' but was earlier delivered as 'pell mell', as indicated in John Gay's poem 'Fair Pall Mall' (1716):

> O bear to me the paths of fair Pall Mall
> Safe are thy pavements, grateful is thy smell!

Pall Mall and then the MALL developed in the mid-17th century as boulevards where the well-to-do of WESTMINSTER played the imported sport of *pallemaille*, a cross between croquet and polo, but without the horses. Pall Mall later became a fashionable meeting place, famed for its coffee and chocolate houses. Members of the nobility built houses on the south side of Pall Mall, with gardens backing onto St James's Park. In the 19th century numerous gentlemen's clubs were established on Pall Mall; several remain here today, including the ATHENAEUM, the Reform Club and the Travellers' Club. In the second half of the 19th century Pall Mall's name became synonymous with the War Office, which stood here until 1906. In addition to its clubs, Pall Mall is now home to serviced offices, the Institute of Directors and the Royal British Legion.

The artist Thomas Gainsborough lived at Schomberg House in Pall Mall between 1774 and 1788. The cigarette brand Pall Mall took its name from the street in 1899.

Pall Mall Gazette An evening newspaper founded in 1865, it aimed to add human interest to its political coverage. It was absorbed by the *Evening Standard* in 1923.

Palmers Green 'A poor man's MUSWELL HILL', as architectural historian Nikolaus Pevsner called it, consisting of an Edwardian core surrounded by interwar estates on the southern borders of SOUTHGATE and WINCHMORE HILL. The sale of several large estates after the death of their owners and a rush of interest from builders resulted in the development of almost all the land near the railway between 1900 and 1918. The poet and novelist Stevie Smith (1902–71) lived at 1 Avondale Road from the age of 5 until her death. Her writings contain many thinly disguised allusions to Palmers Green and its residents, including an unpleasant caricature of her bank manager.

paloni or **palone** A POLARI word for a woman or a girl, possibly from Italian *pollone*, 'big chicken'.

Pan

Pan, Peter *See under* PETER.

Pan, the A Victorian slang term for ST PANCRAS workhouse.

Pancake Greaze or **Scrimmage** *See the* GREAZE.

Pancridge An old corruption of ST PANCRAS. The name acquired connotations of mockery: the victor in a local archery contest was dubbed the Earl of Pancridge (*see also the* DUKE OF SHOREDITCH) and a pompous character was consequently sometimes called a Pancridge earl. An 'old Pancridge' was a term of contempt.

> Turfe: My daughter is to be married: I'll but go
> To Pancridge-Church, hard by, and return instantly,
> And all my neighbourhood shall go about it.
> Hilts: Tut, Pancridge, me no Pancridge; if you let it
> Slip, you will answer it, and your cap be of wool;
> Therefore take heed, you'll feel the smart else,
> Constable.
>
> BEN JONSON: *A Tale of a Tub* (produced 1633)

panjandrum A pretentious or pompous of-ficial, a local 'potentate'. The word occurs in the farrago of nonsense composed in 1755 by Samuel Foote (1720–77) to test Charles Macklin (*c.*1697–1797), the Irish actor who staged an entertainment at the Covent Garden Theatre (now the ROYAL OPERA HOUSE) that he called the British Inquisition. Macklin claimed to have brought his memory to such perfection that he could remember anything after reading it over once. There is more than one version of the following test passage:

> So she went into the garden to cut a cabbage-leaf to make an apple-pie, and at the same time a great she-bear came running up the street and popped its head into the shop. 'What! no soap?' So he died, and she – very imprudently – married the barber. And there were present the Picninnies, and the Joblillies, and the Garyulies, and the Grand Panjandrum himself, with the little round button at top, and they all fell to playing the game of catch-as-catch-can till the gunpowder ran out at the heels of their boots.

It is said that Macklin was so outraged at this nonsense that he refused to repeat a word of it.

Panopticon (Greek *pan*, 'all', and *optikos*, 'of sight')

1. The name given by Jeremy Bentham (1748–1832) to his proposed circular prison with a warder's well in the centre from which convicts could be inspected. MILLBANK PENITENTIARY adopted some of its principles.

2. The Royal Panopticon of Science and Art, in LEICESTER SQUARE, was opened in 1854 as a place of popular instruction and a home for the sciences and music. It was built in the Moorish style but failed in its original intention. It was renamed the Alhambra in 1858 and became a theatre in 1871. It was burnt down in 1882, rebuilt the following year and demolished in 1936. The Odeon cinema stands on the site.

Panorama (Greek *pan*, 'all', and *horāma*, 'a view', from *horaein*, 'to see') An exhibition mounted in 1792 by Robert Barker (1739–1806) at 28 Castle Street, which then lay south-east of LEICESTER SQUARE. It was a canvas-mounted painting of London in the round, of a kind that Barker had earlier produced in Edinburgh. Its success spawned a rash of imitators, such as that at the COLOSSEUM.

Pantechnicon (Greek, 'belonging to all the arts') The name was originally coined for a bazaar for the sale of artistic work built *c.*1830 in Motcomb Street, BELGRAVIA. As this was unsuccessful, the building was converted into a warehouse for storing furniture and the name retained. It is now still sometimes used to mean a furniture removal van.

Pantheon A palace of entertainment opened in OXFORD STREET in 1772. Designed in the neo-classical style by James Wyatt (1746–1813) it was ornamented with Grecian reliefs, and statues of classical deities, and of Britannia, George III and Queen Charlotte. The Pantheon was used for mu-sical promenades and was much patronized by those of rank and fashion. It was converted into a theatre for Italian opera in 1791 and the orchestra included Johann Baptist Cramer, La Motte and Cervetto. It was burned down in 1792, rebuilt as a theatre in 1795 and eventually became a bazaar in 1835. Marks and Spencer's Pantheon branch opened on its site in 1938.

Panyer stone A stone relief bearing what Dr Brewer called 'a rude representation of a boy sitting on a pannier'. It was originally let into a building on Panyer Alley, a narrow passage that led off NEWGATE Street, and commemorated the Panyer Boy, an inn burnt down in the GREAT FIRE OF LONDON. In the Middle Ages the alley was a popular standing place for boys selling bread from baskets. The stone, which is dated 1688, has been moved more than once because of rebuilding and is presently embedded in a wall beside the southern entrance to ST PAUL'S station. An inscription claiming that the ground is the highest point in the CITY has never been quite true of any of its locations.

> A remarkable conspiracy was detected by the authorities of the City a few days ago, when an attempt was made to steal the celebrated Panyer stone ... It appears that a rich American bribed one of the workmen, engaged in pulling down the old warehouse in which the stone is fixed, asking him to exchange the old relic for a modern stone, and promising to pay £50 for the deception. The workman conveyed notice of this to the City authorities, and a guard has now been placed upon the original stone, which is a cherished heirloom of the City.
>
> *The Echo* (21 January 1893)

paradise

Paradise at Tooting, The An essay (20 January 1849) by Charles DICKENS describing the wrongdoings at Surrey Hall, a farming establishment for pauper children, situated on TOOTING BROADWAY. Set in 7 acres (3 hectares) of grounds, this was a sizeable and profitable operation for its owner, Peter Drouet, until disgraceful sanitary conditions contributed to an outbreak of cholera in 1848 in which more than a hundred children died. Drouet was put on trial for felonious killing but found not guilty. He sold up soon afterwards and the tragic episode prompted major municipal improvements to the area's drainage.

Paradise Merton *See* MERTON.

cockney paradise *See under* COCKNEY.

paraffin (lamp) 'Tramp' in COCKNEY RHYMING SLANG, either in the sense of a gentleman of the road or as a pejorative term for a sexually promiscuous woman.

Pardon churchyard The name of two churchyards in medieval London. The better known of the pair lay within the precinct of ST PAUL'S and contained a chapel and a cloister painted with the DANCE OF DEATH. It continued to be known as Pardon churchyard after its conversion to a garden following the destruction of the cloister in 1549. It was built over *c.*1650. The other was a burial ground near the present-day junction of

St John Street and CLERKENWELL Road, a site earlier known as NO MAN'S LAND. It too retained the name Pardon churchyard after a garden was laid out here in the mid-16th century.

park

Park Lane A prestigious avenue that began as TYBURN Lane, a rough track on the eastern border of HYDE PARK, created when Henry VIII enclosed the park in the early 16th century. As MAYFAIR grew, titled gentlemen erected mansions on the east side of the lane, especially from the 1820s onwards. With such fine views across the park, the high values of these mansions did not deter property speculators from redeveloping the road between the wars, mostly with luxury hotels. When the art deco Park Lane Hotel opened in 1927 it was the first British hotel with a bathroom for every bedroom. GROSVENOR HOUSE and the DORCHESTER HOTEL followed soon afterwards. In 1962 part of Hyde Park was taken to allow Park Lane to be made into a dual carriageway and the road was diverted at the south end to enter HYDE PARK CORNER by the side of Apsley House (*see* NO.1 LONDON). A cavernous underground car park was built beneath Hyde Park, with single-storey space for 1,100 cars and innovative automatic entry barriers. The 28-storey Hilton became a new London landmark on its completion in 1963. In addition to its hotels, Park Lane also has prestige offices and showrooms for exclusive car marques. Only near its northern end is there any semblance of conventional retailing at street level.

> A group of new age squatters has taken over two mansions worth £30 million in one of London's most exclusive addresses ... 20-year-old Daniel Moreira, from Portugal, admitted: 'It feels pretty good, it's the dream of everyone in London to live for a little bit in Park Lane.'
>
> *The Daily Telegraph* (23 January 2009)

Park Lane residences signify high social status for Frederick Augustus Bullock in Thackeray's *Vanity Fair* (1848) and for the Honourable Ronald Adair in Conan Doyle's 'Adventure of the Empty House' (1903).

Park Royal An extensive industrial and commercial estate in the far north of ACTON, between the WESTERN AVENUE and the GRAND UNION CANAL. Formerly the village of Twyford, the present name derives from the Royal Agricultural Society exhibitions held here from 1903 to 1905.

Munitions factories were built on the site during the First World War. Park Royal developed as an important industrial estate after hostilities ended and there were stadiums for greyhound racing and football. Following the departure of all its early tenants, including the Guinness brewery in 2005, the area has recently been a focus of regeneration efforts, led by the Park Royal Partnership.

Park Village A delightful pair of streets situated on the south-western edge of CAMDEN TOWN, created in the 1820s by John Nash (1752–1835) as part of his masterplan for REGENT'S PARK. Park Village West, which survives intact, is a crescent located just north of Regent's Park barracks, off Albany Street. Park Village East meanders gently south as an extension of Prince Albert Road. Nash and his protégé James Pennethorne combined STUCCOED villas and terraced houses of sharply differing proportions and styles, including Gothic, Italianate and Tudor, on either side of an arm of the REGENT'S CANAL that was later filled in. The village was a model for subsequent Victorian estates and has even been identified as the first modern suburb, albeit in miniature – but there are many other contenders for the title, which is so hard to define, from CLAPHAM to Cambridge, Massachusetts. Just a generation after its completion, half of Park Village East was torn down to make way for the London and Birmingham Railway.

parker

Parker, Aloysius The COCKNEY retainer to Lady Penelope Creighton-Ward in the children's TV series *Thunderbirds*, which first aired in the mid-1960s. Nicknamed 'Nosey' or 'the Nose', he is a reformed criminal who specialized in safe-breaking. His distinctive style of hypercorrected speech involves dropping every legitimate aitch while adding an illegitimate one wherever possible. For example: 'Some hinterlopers 'ave gained haccess to the 'ouse, milady.'

nosey parker See under NOSE.

Parkwood Hill See MRS DALE'S DIARY.

Parliament

Parliament Hill A hill located near the south-eastern corner of HAMPSTEAD HEATH. It rises to 319 feet (97m) above mean sea level. The name was not recorded until around 1875, and despite its recentness is of uncertain origin. The obvious

explanation is that the hill provides superb views of WESTMINSTER. A more specific and legendary reason is that Guy FAWKES and his co-conspirators intended to watch the blowing up of the Houses of Parliament from here and this story is echoed in an earlier name, Traitors' Hill.

The poet John Betjeman was born in the 'red brick gloom' of Parliament Hill Mansions in Lissenden Gardens in 1906. George Orwell lived on the road named Parliament Hill, at No.77.

Parliament Hill Fields 267 acres (108 hectares) of fields now constituting the south-eastern part of HAMPSTEAD HEATH. The Hampstead Heath Enlargement Act formally joined the hill and its fields to the heath in 1889, ensuring their permanent preservation. Parliament Hill Fields are regarded as north London's premier kite-flying spot. The fields' athletics track is the base for Highgate Harriers and London Heathside athletics clubs.

Parliament Hill or **Hampstead Heath Lido** An open-air, unheated swimming pool built in the late 1930s. This grade II listed amenity is run by the London Borough of CAMDEN and owned by the CORPORATION OF LONDON.

Parliament Square A square at the southern end of Parliament Street (an extension of WHITEHALL) and the western end of WESTMINSTER BRIDGE. It was laid out in 1868, after the completion of the new Houses of Parliament. It is dominated by BIG BEN and other parliamentary buildings, and contains many statues of national leaders (including Robert Peel, Benjamin Disraeli and Winston Churchill). Of late it has been liberally obstacled with concrete blocks to deter terrorist attacks.

Houses of Parliament See the PALACE OF WESTMINSTER.

Parr, Thomas See OLD PARR.

Parsons Green A highly gentrified locality in central FULHAM, arranged around a triangular green and the larger Eel Brook Common, which lies to its north-east. The green's name derives from the former presence of Fulham rectory, which stood on the site of St Dionis' Church from the 14th century. A clump of trees on the west side of the green was known as Parson's Grove by 1424. The Midland District Railway opened a station in 1880 and within a decade an irregular grid of terraced houses had filled the entire vicinity. St Dionis' Church and the White Horse (*see* *the* SLOANY PONY) were rebuilt and the village pond, known as Colepitts, was drained.

parvis (Old French, from Late Latin *paradisus*, 'church close') The term was originally applied to the court in front of St Peter's at Rome in the Middle Ages, and hence came to denote the court before the main entrance of a cathedral. In the parvis of ST PAUL'S Cathedral, lawyers used to meet for consultation as brokers did at the ROYAL EXCHANGE. The word is now applied to the room above a church porch.

Passport to Pimlico A film comedy (1948) in which PIMLICO declares itself to be an independent state after the discovery of an ancient charter identifying the area as part of Burgundy. Directed by Henry Cornelius and starring Stanley Holloway and Margaret Rutherford among the citizens of the breakaway republic, it was the first of the EALING COMEDIES, and its title is still commonly quoted whenever a British village, town or city threatens to exert political independence in some form or other.

Paternoster

Paternoster Row A street in the CITY of London, north of ST PAUL'S Cathedral. It was probably so named from the rosary or paternoster makers who lived and worked here from the Middle Ages. There is mention as early as 1374 of a Richard Russell, a 'paternosterer', who dwelt there, and archives tell of 'one Robert Nikke, a paternoster maker and citizen', in the reign of Henry IV. Another suggestion is that it was so called because funeral processions on their way to St Paul's Cathedral began their *Pater noster* (chanting of the Lord's Prayer) at the beginning of the row. By the end of the 16th century it was also the home of booksellers and publishers, and it remained a centre of the publishing business for over 300 years, until it was devastated in an air raid on 28 December 1940. About 6 million books were destroyed. *See also* AMEN CORNER; AVE MARIA LANE; CREED LANE.

Paternoster Square An area just to the northwest of ST PAUL'S Cathedral and within its precincts. From the 17th century until 1889 it was the site of a meat market, but this closed down when SMITHFIELD market opened. The area was very badly damaged in the air raid that destroyed much of PATERNOSTER ROW. In the 1960s it was redeveloped as a pedestrian precinct with shops

and office blocks. This never found favour, however, with either the critics or the public and in the 1990s it was demolished and replaced by a new, more harmonious development that is, at least, an improvement on its predecessor. Its frontage on to St Paul's is Juxon House, an office block tricked out with mock-classical features. The TEMPLE BAR has been transferred to Paternoster Square.

Patriarch, the Derived from his benevolent appearance, this is the deceptive nickname of Christopher Casby in Charles DICKENS's *Little Dorrit* (1855–7). He is the hard, avaricious landlord of BLEEDING HEART YARD and conceals his extortionate practices by using his agent, Mr Pancks, to collect his rents.

patron saint of Willesden Properly St Mary but the title has been jocularly applied to the writer Zadie Smith (b.1975), who comes from the district. She has used WILLESDEN as the backdrop for much of her writing, notably in the bestselling novel *White Teeth* (2000).

Paul

Pauline In a London context, the word usually refers to an alumnus of ST PAUL'S SCHOOL. A Paulina is an alumna of ST PAUL'S GIRLS' SCHOOL.

Paul's The name by which old ST PAUL'S Cathedral was familiarly known and which stuck for a while to its replacement, especially in poetry:

'Twas on a holy Thursday, their innocent faces clean,
The children walking to and fro, in red, and blue, and green,
Grey-headed beadles walked before, with wands as white as snow,
Till into the high dome of Paul's they like Thames waters flow.

WILLIAM BLAKE: *Songs of Innocence*, 'Holy Thursday' (1789)

Paul's or **St Paul's Cross** A pulpit in the open air situated on the north side of old ST PAUL'S Cathedral, in which, from 1259 to 1643, eminent divines preached in the presence of the LORD MAYOR OF LONDON and ALDERMEN every Sunday. Heretics were forced to recant here and Protestant books were burned. It was demolished in 1643 by order of Parliament. A memorial, erected in 1910, is surmounted by a gilded statue of St Paul holding a cross. *See also* POL'S STUMP.

The inscription on it [the present monument] says that the new cross has been raised to commemorate the ancient cross 'whereat amid such scenes of good and evil as make up human affairs the conscience of Church and Nation through five centuries found public utterance'. That conscience which there found utterance was a stumbling and groping thing.

WALTER RUSSELL BOWIE: *The Renewing Gospel* (1935)

Paul's man A braggart; a captain out of service, with a long rapier; so called because the walk down the centre of the old ST PAUL'S was at one time the haunt of such characters, who were also known as Paul's walkers. Ben Jonson called Captain Bobadil a Paul's man in the dramatis personae of *Every Man in His Humour* (1598).
as old as Paul's See *under* AS.

PC 49 A dated nickname for a policeman, especially a 'bobby on the beat'. It derives from the central character of the radio series *The Adventures of PC 49*, created by Alan Stranks and broadcast from 1947 to 1953, in which the improbably upper-class METROPOLITAN POLICE constable so numbered was actually named Archibald Berkeley-Willoughby. Two films based on the series were released in 1949 and 1951 and his adventures appeared in a strip cartoon in the *Eagle* comic (1950–7). 'PC 49' was earlier the title of a popular song by W.F. Hargreaves (1846–1919), author of 'Burlington Bertie from Bow' (*see* BURLINGTON BERTIE).

PDC See POVERTY DRIVEN CHILDREN.

Peabody Buildings A series of London tenements endowed by George Peabody (1795–1869), an American financier, born in South Parish, Danvers, Massachusetts, a district now renamed Peabody. In 1837 he established himself in London as a merchant and banker, raising loans for US causes. He amassed a fortune of $20 million and spent much of it on philanthropic works in America, also donating $2.5 million for the development of low-rent housing in London. Beginning with a block in SPITALFIELDS in 1864, the Peabody Donation Fund built homes in localities throughout the inner city, including BETHNAL GREEN, BLOOMSBURY, CLERKENWELL, NORTH KENSINGTON, SHADWELL, SHOREDITCH and SOUTHWARK. He died in London and was interred with full funeral honours at WESTMINSTER ABBEY for 30 days, after which, in accordance with his deathbed wish, his embalmed body was taken to Massachusetts for permanent burial. At the personal behest of Queen Victoria, Britain's newest and largest warship, HMS *Monarch*, transported the coffin in a specially built mortuary chapel. William Story's statue of this remarkable philanthropist, seated in an armchair, was unveiled in THREADNEEDLE STREET in 1871. Now called simply Peabody, his charity has evolved into a housing association, providing homes for almost 50,000 people.

> You will know that I refer to the death of Mr Peabody, a man whose splendid benefactions ... taught us in this commercial age ... the most noble and needful of all lessons – ... how a man can be the master of his wealth instead of its slave.
>
> WILLIAM GLADSTONE, quoted in *The Times* (10 November 1869)

peace
Peace Descending on the Quadriga of War See QUADRIGA.
Peace Pledge Union A body pledged to renounce war, founded in 1935 at a meeting in the ALBERT HALL organized by Canon Dick Sheppard (1880–1937), formerly vicar of ST MARTIN-IN-THE-FIELDS. The PPU is based at 1 Peace Passage, KENTISH TOWN. The present wording of the pledge is:

> War is a crime against humanity. I renounce war, and am therefore determined not to support any kind of war. I am also determined to work for the removal of all causes of war.

peacock
Peacock, The See the NYP SHOP.
Peacocks The nickname of Bedfont Green FC, from the BEDFONT PEACOCKS.

pearly kings and queens
The COSTER 'kings' and 'queens', 'princes' and 'princesses' of the districts of London are so named from their black suits studded with innumerable mother-of-pearl buttons, many of which are arranged as representational symbols, including:

anchor (hope)
bell (ST MARY-LE-BOW)
cross (Christian faith)
daisy (flower seller)
dove (peace)
heart (charity)
horseshoe (luck)

semi-circle (scallop, representing a fish stall)

wheel (coster's barrow or the boroughs of London)

Their attire is an elaboration on the decorative use of such buttons by Victorian costermongers and FLASH BOYS, and was pioneered in the early 1880s by Henry Croft (1862–1930), a SOMERS TOWN rat-catcher and road sweeper. Croft may have sifted the buttons from his sweepings or obtained a share of the salvage from an incident when a boat spilled its cargo of Japanese pearl buttons after foundering in the THAMES. According to some, pearly kings were originally elected by street traders to safeguard their rights from interlopers and bullies, but they have always collected for charities and such work is nowadays their sole focus. There was formerly a pearly king for each of the boroughs that comprised the LONDON COUNTY COUNCIL (and a pearly king of London was enthroned for the FESTIVAL OF BRITAIN) but the definition of a 'pearly kingdom' has been less clear-cut since the creation of GREATER LONDON in 1965. Furthermore, with the disintegration of traditional COCKNEY communities many pearlies have moved away from the areas they represent and their numbers are in long-term decline. To make matters worse, inter-regal disputes have split the remaining pearlies into rival groupings that adhere to conflicting beliefs regarding the story of Henry Croft and hold separate HARVEST FESTIVAL services and other charity fund-raising events.

Peasants' Revolt The name given to the English peasant risings of 1381, which were immediately occasioned by an unpopular poll tax at a time when there was a growing spirit of social revolt. Its chief centre was south-eastern England, especially Kent and ESSEX. Wat Tyler's men beheaded the archbishop of Canterbury (Sudbury) and temporarily held London; and John Ball (d.1381), an excommunicated priest, joined the Kentish rebels. Richard II (1377–99), still only 14 years old, promised free pardon and redress of grievances (including the abolition of villeinage). On 15 June 1381 Wat Tyler was slain by William Walworth, the LORD MAYOR OF LONDON. Severe retribution was meted out to the rebels, and the boy king's promises were not kept.

pea-souper A 19th-century phrase for a particularly dense smog, and particularly that associated with London before the Clean Air Acts of the 1950s. The reference is to the colour and dense consistency of soup made from yellow split peas.

> Upon sallying out this morning encountered the old-fashioned pea soup London fog – of a gamboge color. It was lifted, however, from the ground & floated in mid air. When lower, it is worse.
>
> HERMAN MELVILLE: *Journal of a Tour to London and the Continent in 1849–50* (24 November 1849)

Peckham A steadily recovering but still deprived district situated east of CAMBERWELL. Peckham appears in Domesday Book as Pecheham, meaning a 'homestead by a hill' – probably a reference to what is now called Telegraph Hill. It remained a rural area until the Industrial Revolution, growing crops for the London market. In the early 19th century Peckham became a desirable middle-class suburb but it subsequently began a long decline and, by the time of 10-year-old Damilola Taylor's violent death on a North Peckham estate in 2000, the area had become a byword for inner-city crime and desolation. Change was already in hand, however, with the regeneration of its grimmest estates and the opening of Will Alsop's landmark library in 2000. Over a third of all residents are of black African descent, by far the highest proportion in London. The neighbourhood featured in the television comedies ONLY FOOLS AND HORSES and DESMOND'S.

Peckham Frolic, The A play (1799) by Edward Jerningham, alternatively titled *Nell Gwyn*.

Peckham Rye A triangular common and its adjoining public park, located on the south side of Peckham. 'Rye' is a corruption of Old English *rith*, a small stream. Legend has it that BOUDICCA died of poisoning here and William Blake (1757–1827) had his first 'vision of angels' on Peckham Rye in the mid-1760s. Peckham Rye station opened in 1866, some way to the north but close enough to stimulate suburban development. In 1868 CAMBERWELL vestry bought out the lord of the manor's rights to the common, permanently preserving it as public open space. The LONDON COUNTY COUNCIL acquired the neighbouring Homestall Farm in 1892 and laid it out as Peckham Rye Park.

Peckham (Rye) 'Tie' in COCKNEY RHYMING SLANG, in the sense of the item of neckwear.

Put on your dicky dirt and your Peckham Rye,
'Cause time's soon hurrying by.

QUINCY JONES and DON BLACK: 'Get A Bloomin' Move On!'
(song from the film *The Italian Job*) (1969)

all (a) holiday at Peckham *See under* ALL.
Ballad of Peckham Rye, The *See under* BAL-
LAD.
Fat Boy of Peckham *See under* FAT.
go to Peckham, to *See under* GO.
Little Woman of Peckham *See under* LITTLE.

peculiar A parish or group of parishes exempt
from the jurisdiction of the ordinary of the
diocese. There were many such in medieval
England, e.g. monastic peculiars, royal peculiars,
archiepiscopal and diocesan peculiars, peculiars
belonging to orders and cathedral peculiars. In
1832 there were still over 300 peculiars, which
were abolished between 1838 and 1850, the
exceptions being cathedral peculiars, WESTMIN-
STER ABBEY and those of the royal residences
including the CHAPEL ROYAL of the SAVOY. *See
also the* DEAN OF THE ARCHES.
Peculiar People *See the* PLUMSTEAD PECU-
LIARS.

Pedlar's Acre A portion of LAMBETH Marsh
bequeathed to the parish church of St Mary,
and possibly originally a 'squatting place' of
pedlars. In the church is a window containing
a representation of a pedlar and his dog, and
the story is that a pedlar bequeathed 'his acre'
to the church on the condition that he and his
dog were commemorated in a window. It has
been suggested that it is a rebus on Chapman,
the name of a benefactor – a chapman was a
hawker of books or pamphlets of popular stories.
The deconsecrated church is now home to the
GARDEN MUSEUM.

Pedro Jonez Seldom used SLOANE RANGER
slang for PETER JONES.

peel
Peel, Emma The neat and nimble black-dressed
heroine of the television series *The* AVENGERS
(1961–8), who was for several seasons the assistant of the dapper secret agent John Steed. Her
name is meant to suggest 'M appeal', i.e. 'man
appeal'. She was played by Diana Rigg (b.1938) in
the TV series and by Uma Thurman (b.1970) in
the film *The Avengers* (1998).
Peel Centre *See* HENDON POLICE COLLEGE.

Peeler Old slang for a policeman, first applied to
the Irish constabulary founded by Sir Robert Peel
when he was chief secretary for Ireland (1812–18),
and later to the METROPOLITAN POLICE, which he
established in 1829 when he was home secretary.
See also BOBBY.

In the 16th century the word was applied to
robbers, from 'peel' (later 'pill'), to plunder, strip
of possessions or rob. *See also* POVERTY DRIVEN
CHILDREN.

Peep Show A critically acclaimed, London-
based sitcom broadcast on Channel 4 since 2003.
Peep Show is so called because the viewer observes events through the eyes of the characters
and hears their thoughts. The two protagonists
are an odd-couple pairing, played by David
Mitchell and Robert Webb. Although the title
sequence features CROUCH END Broadway, most
of the location scenes are filmed in the CROYDON
area.

Peerless Street A street branching westward
from the CITY ROAD, south of MOORFIELDS EYE
HOSPITAL. Neighbouring Baldwin Street was
formerly the site of the Peerless Pool, an open-air
swimming bath (*see the* PERILOUS POND).

Pegasus The winged horse is used by the INNER
TEMPLE as its armorial device, specifically: Azure
a pegasus salient argent. It is first mentioned in
Gerard Legh's account of the Christmas revels of
1561, when Robert Dudley, 1st Earl of Leicester
(c.1532–88), acted the principal part of Prince
Pallaphilos, constable-marshal of the Inner
Temple, and patron of the Honourable Order of
Pegasus. It has been suggested that the choice
of Pegasus reflected Dudley's real-life office of
Master of the Horse. Alternatively, it may have
resulted from a misinterpretation of ancient
tiles in TEMPLE CHURCH showing the profile of a
knight on horseback with a horizontally barred
shield that could have been mistaken for a wing.
Representations of the flying horse were thereafter widely used on the inn's property, sometimes
as a badge or crest, sometimes borne on a shield.
In 1709 Sir James Thornhill painted an allegorical
scene at the east end of the Inner Temple Hall
showing Pegasus rising from Mount Helicon.

Pelmanism A system of mind and memory
training. It takes its name from Christopher
Louis Pelman, who, with William Joseph En-

never, founded the Pelman Institute for the Scientific Development of Mind, Memory and Personality around 1898. The institute functioned until 1940 and was based for most of its existence in BLOOMSBURY Street. Because of the extensive advertising, the verb 'to pelmanize', meaning to obtain good results by training the memory, was coined. It also gave its name to a card game, formerly popular with children, which largely depends on mental concentration and memory.

Penge A less favoured corner of the London Borough of BROMLEY, lying on the south-eastern side of CRYSTAL PALACE Park. The name derives from Celtic words meaning 'head of the wood'; Pencoed in Wales has exactly the same origin. This is one of the few Celtic place names in London and suggests the survival of a native British contingent after Anglo-Saxon colonization. In 957 King Eadwig (or Edwy All-Fair) granted the manor of BATTERSEA to 'Lyfing, his faithful minister', together with swine pasture at Penge, which remained a detached portion of Battersea parish for more than a thousand years.

> Now, Penge is a town in size and population, in appearance a waste of modern tenements, mean, monotonous and wearisome.
>
> JAMES THORNE: *Handbook to the Environs of London* (1876)

Penge bungalow murders A case regarded by John Mortimer's irascible barrister RUMPOLE OF THE BAILEY as his greatest triumph, and mentioned teasingly throughout the canon. The full story of a young man accused of killing his father and his father's friend was finally revealed in the novel *Rumpole and the Penge Bungalow Murders* (2004).

Penge Papers A collection (1985) of gloomily humorous reflections on suburban life by Brian Wright, characterized as 'the confessions of an unwaged metropolitan househusband'.

Penguin Books The paperbacks so called take their name from the publishing firm founded in 1935 by Allen Lane (1902–70), the name itself being one suggested by his secretary, Joan Coles. Earlier considered names were 'Dolphin' and 'Porpoise', but another publisher, Faber and Faber, already owned the latter. The company began operating in the crypt of Holy Trinity Church, opposite GREAT PORTLAND STREET station, and moved to purpose-built premises in HARMONDSWORTH in 1937. Since the return of the editorial offices to central London they have led a peripatetic existence that most recently took them to 80 STRAND, in 2001.

penny

penny chute A century-old means of making small charitable donations to the HOUSE OF ST BARNABAS, through a slotted plate mounted in the building's SOHO SQUARE railings. Coins tinkle across the void between the pavement and the house via an iron pipe, and thence into a collection box in the basement.

penny plain, twopence coloured A phrase originating in Pollock's toy theatre shop, formerly in HOXTON, now in Scala Street, FITZROVIA, where it functions primarily as a museum. The scenery and characters for the plays to be 'acted' were printed on sheets of thick paper ready to be cut out, these being sold at 1d if plain, 2d if coloured.

> I own I like a definite form in what my eyes are to rest upon; and if landscapes were sold, like the sheets of characters of my boyhood, one penny plain and twopence coloured, I should go to the length of twopence every day of my life.
>
> R.L. STEVENSON: *Travels with a Donkey*, 'Father Apollinaris' (1879)

pension The annual payment made by the members of the INNS OF COURT for the upkeep of the inn. The officer who collected the payments used to be called the pensioner. Also, a collective formal meeting of BENCHERS at GRAY'S INN is called a pension.

Pensioners *See the* BLUES.

Chelsea Pensioner *See under* CHELSEA.

Pentonville An underprivileged inner-city district situated between KING'S CROSS and the ANGEL, ISLINGTON. The NEW ROAD brought access to the land west of Islington in 1756 and the development opportunity was seized by Captain Henry Penton (1736–1812), MP for Winchester, who began to lay out what has been called London's first planned suburb during the latter years of the 18th century. A few of the original houses survive in CHAPEL MARKET, which, as Chapel Street, marked the Penton estate's eastern boundary. By the late 19th century parts of Pentonville had degenerated into slums, which were cleared in stages from the 1930s. The district is now dominated by postwar council housing.

Pentonville Prison A prison situated on the

CALEDONIAN ROAD (some way to the north of Pentonville proper), built in 1842 to a radical radial plan. Its designers, Joshua Jebb (1793–1863) and Charles Barry (1795–1860), created what was literally a model institution, since it has been called 'the most copied prison in the world'. Although much refurbishment has taken place, the original four cellblocks are as they were when the prison opened. It is a local prison, accepting all suitable male prisoners over the age of 21 from courts in its catchment area.

People's Palace The short name of the People's Palace of Delights for the Eastenders, now part of the MILE END campus of QUEEN MARY, UNIVERSITY OF LONDON. It was built in 1886 to the design of Edward Robert Robson (1836–1917) for the 'recreation and cultivation' of EAST ENDERS and housed one of the first public libraries in EAST LONDON. The palace burned down in 1931 and its replacement opened in 1937. That building now houses the Skeel lecture theatre and the Great Hall where college ceremonies, including graduation, take place.
People's Palace Projects An arts organization based at QUEEN MARY, UNIVERSITY OF LONDON.

Pepys, Samuel London's most celebrated diarist (1633–1703). He was born above his father's tailoring shop in Salisbury Court, off FLEET STREET, and attended ST PAUL'S SCHOOL and Magdalene College, Cambridge. Taking advantage of opportunities that opened up under the the Cromwellian Protectorate he became a civil servant, achieving great success as a naval administrator. Pepys began keeping a shorthand diary in 1658, ceasing in 1669 because he feared he was losing his sight. In addition to its eye-witness accounts of momentous events such as the GREAT FIRE OF LONDON, the diary is remarkable for its vivid portrayal of everyday life in the city and for Pepys' candid and often self-effacing admissions regarding his private thoughts and deeds. Long after he discontinued the diary Pepys remained a colourful figure in London; he was imprisoned in the TOWER OF LONDON in 1679 on a charge of treason, which was later dropped, and became president of the ROYAL SOCIETY in 1684. He died at home in CLAPHAM and was buried in St Olave Hart Street (see ST GHASTLY GRIM).

This day died Mr. Sam Pepys, a very worthy,

industrious, and curious person, none in England exceeding him in knowledge of the navy … He was universally belov'd, hospitable, generous, learned in many things, skill'd in music, a very greate cherisher of learned men of whom he had the conversation.

JOHN EVELYN: diary (26 May 1703)

Percy's Reliques The collection of old ballads and poems published as *Reliques of Ancient English Poetry* by Thomas Percy (1729–1811) in 1765. He was encouraged in his project by William Shenstone, Samuel JOHNSON, David GARRICK and others. The collection includes the following London poems and ballads:

The Beggar's Daughter of Bednall Green (*see the* BLIND BEGGAR OF BEDNALL GREEN)

Jane Shore (whose death in a ditch legendarily gave SHOREDITCH its name)

The Downfall of CHARING CROSS (on the removal of the original ELEANOR CROSS there)

Old Tom of Bedlam (*see* TOM O' BEDLAM)

George BARNWELL

The TOURNAMENT OF TOTTENHAM

Performance An avant-garde film (1970) depicting the seamier side of SWINGING LONDON, directed by Donald Cammell and Nicolas Roeg. It stars James Fox as a gangster who hides out in the basement flat of a semi-retired rock star, played by Mick Jagger, and becomes enmeshed in his hedonistic lifestyle. The flat is in Powis Square, a somewhat run-down corner of NOTTING HILL that has since undergone profound GENTRIFICATION.

Perilous Pond A large, deep and dangerous pond in MOORFIELDS that augmented London's water supply before the arrival of the NEW RIVER. Also known as the Parlous Pond, it was the scene of many drownings, especially of wintertime skaters who fell through the ice. In 1743 local jeweller William Kemp converted it into the open-air Peerless Pool, which was said to have been 'the completest swimming bath in the whole world'. It was 170 feet (52m) long, with a marble entrance pavilion and an adjacent fish pond for anglers. An embankment, plentiful trees and shrubbery and a high wall protected the modesty of the 'gentlemen lovers of swimming and bathing'. It was filled in and built over in 1869. Deryn Lake's novel *Death in the Peerless*

Pool (1999) is a Georgian detective story featuring his recurring character John Rawlings, apothecary and amateur sleuth, and Sir John Fielding, the BLIND BEAK OF BOW STREET.

Perivale An industrial and residential area in east GREENFORD, bounded by the River BRENT and the PADDINGTON branch of the GRAND UNION CANAL. Perivale was originally Greenford Parva, or Little Greenford, and the present name may be a corruption of Parva. Alternatively it may derive from 'pure vale' or 'pear vale'. The availability of open land and the coming of the WESTERN AVENUE brought industry after 1930, including Sanderson's wallpaper factory and the HOOVER BUILDING.

Perivale Mill *See the* DEVIL'S PLAT.

Perivale Wood A patch of ancient woodland formerly known as Braddish Wood, privately owned by the Selborne Society. This is the second oldest nature reserve in the country but is not generally open to the public.

Peter

Peter Jones A flagship branch of the JOHN LEWIS chain of department stores, situated at the corner of SLOANE SQUARE and the KING'S ROAD. Peter Jones (1843–1905) came to London from Wales in 1864 and took a job at a draper's in NEWINGTON. After running some smaller shops of his own he acquired premises at the present site in 1877 and the business quickly grew to occupy a series of disconnected buildings. The store was unified into a single grand emporium during the redevelopment of HANS TOWN in the late 1880s. On Jones's death the store was acquired by the elder John Lewis and from 1914 was managed by his son John Spedan Lewis, who transformed the fortunes of what had been a failing enterprise. The present Peter Jones store opened in 1937 to widespread architectural acclaim for its pioneering use of curtain-walling; it has recently been extensively modernized.

Peter Pan The little boy who never grew up, the central character of J.M. Barrie's play of this name (1904). One night Peter enters the nursery window of the BLOOMSBURY house of the Darling family to recover his shadow. He flies back to Never Never Land accompanied by the Darling children, to rejoin the Lost Boys. Eventually all are captured by pirates, except Peter, who secures their release and the defeat of the pirates. The children, by now homesick, fly back to the

nursery with their new friends, but Peter refuses to stay as he does not wish to grow up. The story has been adapted for numerous stage and film productions, including Walt Disney's animated cartoon version (1953) and the live-action film *Peter Pan* (2003).

The name of Barrie's hero resulted from a combination of those of the Greek god Pan and of Peter Llewelyn Davies, one of the five young sons of Barrie's friends Arthur and Sylvia Llewelyn Davies, of Campden Hill Square, HOLLAND PARK (who became Mr and Mrs Darling in the play). Barrie explained to the boys that he made Peter Pan 'by rubbing the five of you violently together, as savages with two sticks produce a flame', but it was Peter Llewelyn Davies who came to be most closely associated with the character. He was named Peter after the title character in his grandfather George Du Maurier's novel *Peter Ibbetson* (1891). The five brothers generally met unhappy fates: one (George) died fighting in the First World War; another (Michael) drowned while at Oxford; and Peter himself (by then a publisher) committed suicide in 1960 by throwing himself under a train at SLOANE SQUARE station.

The statue of Peter Pan by Sir George James Frampton (1860–1928) was placed in KENSINGTON GARDENS by Barrie in 1912. It was modelled not on Peter Llewelyn Davies, but on his brother Michael.

Peter Pan Cup The prize in an annual 100-yard (91m) swimming race held on the SERPENTINE on Christmas morning. The water temperature is usually below 4°C.

Peter the Painter The nickname of a Latvian anarchist, a sign painter by trade, whose real name may have been Peter Piatkow. He was said to have been the leader of a gang that killed three policemen during a bungled raid on a HOUNDSDITCH jeweller's in December 1910. The gang was cornered in the SIEGE OF SIDNEY STREET but Peter the Painter (if, as was popularly supposed, he was there) escaped. He became an anti-hero of EAST END folklore and for a decade after the events the catchphrase 'here's Peter the Painter' was used as a bantering form of greeting. IRA fighters nicknamed the Mauser C96 a 'Peter the Painter' because he allegedly used that pistol. When Tower Hamlets Community Housing built two blocks of flats at the southern end of Sidney Street in 2006 it named them Peter House and

Painter House, to the disgust of some who felt it inappropriate to honour such a figure.

> Sarah Drury, of the [Metropolitan Police] federation, said: 'It's disappointing the local housing association has chosen to honour the anarchists in this manner when once again terrorism is at the forefront of people's minds.'
>
> *Daily Mail* (26 September 2008)

In his song 'Peter the Painter' (co-written with Michael McEvoy, 1984), Ian Dury applied the nickname to the London-based Pop artist Peter Blake (b.1932).

St Peter *See under* SAINT.

St Peter ad Vincula *See under* SAINT.

Peterborough The name at the head of a diary column that appeared in *The Daily Telegraph* until February 2003. It derived from Peterborough Court, a small alleyway beside the old Telegraph building in FLEET STREET, which was so called because between the 14th and 19th centuries the site was owned by the bishops of Peterborough.

Petersham A prosperous village almost surrounded by green spaces, situated south of RICHMOND UPON THAMES. The land belonged to St Peter's Abbey in Chertsey, SURREY, from the 7th century, although its name refers to the homestead of a man called Peohtrīc rather than to the saint. In the Middle Ages it was a place of sanctuary where no one could be arrested. Petersham's later role as a refuge for the London rich has left it with a legacy of fine Stuart and Georgian houses and it has been called the most elegant village in England. Petersham Park, Common and Meadows are extensions of RICHMOND PARK. The meadows form the tranquil foreground of the famous vista of south-west London from RICHMOND HILL.

Pete Tong 'Wrong' in modern rhyming slang. Peter Tong (b.1960) is a club and radio DJ, specializing in electronic dance music. The term is said to have been coined by another DJ, Marc 'Lard' Riley, and gained additional currency with the release of the film *It's All Gone Pete Tong* in 2004.

Pet Shop Boys A pop-rock duo (Neil Tennant (b.1954) and Chris Lowe (b.1959)) formed in London in 1981, originally as West End. Tennant is said to have suggested that three friends working in an EALING pet shop should start their own band and call themselves the Pet Shop Boys. When they failed to follow his advice Tennant and Lowe appropriated the name for their own act. The lyrics of several Pet Shop Boys songs concern aspects of life in the capital, including 'West End Girls' (1984), 'King's Cross' (1987) and 'London' (2002).

Petticoat Lane A historic market street located north of ALDGATE. In 1373 this was the muddy Berwardes Lane. In 1500 it had become an elm-lined avenue called Hog Lane. By 1603 it was known as Petticoat Lane, probably because dealers in old clothes operated here. The word 'petticoat' formerly embraced a wider variety of skirts than it does now. Dutch, French and British traders had established a major street market by the mid-18th century. In 1830 the lane's name was prudishly changed to Middlesex Street but this has never entered popular usage. At the end of the 19th century the road was widened and lined with shops, which were intended to replace the old barrows. Most retailers dealt in clothes but others offered takeaway foods such as hokey-pokey (an inferior type of ice cream) and wally wallies (gherkins). When more and more street traders returned to set up stalls here the CORPORATION OF LONDON at first tried to expel them but relented in 1927 and introduced a regulation scheme for stallholders' pitches. Sunday trading was legalized in 1936, in response to the wishes of the EAST END's large Jewish community. Nowadays, Wentworth Street has a weekday market and this spreads into Middlesex Street and its offshoots on Sundays, when over 1,000 stalls operate.

Petts Wood The acme of Kentish suburbia, situated midway between CHISLEHURST and ORPINGTON, and previously divided between those two parishes. The wood is believed to have been planted in the last quarter of the 16th century by the Pett family, who were leading shipwrights for 200 years and are mentioned in PEPYS's diaries.

petty
Petty France
1. A street in WESTMINSTER, just to the south of ST JAMES'S PARK, linking Buckingham Gate with Tothill Street. It is perhaps so called because it was in an area once occupied by French

merchants. John MILTON lived here while he was writing his epic poem *Paradise Lost* in the 1650s. For many years the only occasion most people had to be aware of it was when they applied for a passport – it housed the headquarters of the Passport Office.

2. An 18th-century nickname for the SPITAL-FIELDS area, because of its predominantly Huguenot population.

Petty Italia An alternative name for LITTLE ITALY.

Petty Wales A lost street in the Tower Street (now TOWER) ward of the CITY of London. The origin of the name is uncertain; it does not appear to derive from a past contingent of Welsh residents and there seems to have been little foundation for John Stow's hypothesis regarding the presence of a lodging house for the princes of Wales.

Phantom Raspberry Blower of Old London Town

A character in the mould of JACK THE RIPPER who menaced Londoners in the late 19th century, dispatching them by means of a deafening RASPBERRY. The creation of Spike Milligan, he first appeared in an episode of *Six Dates with Barker* (1971) and returned in 1976 for a longer run in the *The Two Ronnies*, with scripts by Ronnie Barker and raspberries blown by David Jason.

Philadelphians

A religious sect emphasizing brotherly love, founded in London in 1652 by followers of the German mystic Jakob Boehme (1575–1624). Some of the prominent members were Anglican clergymen; others were Lutherans, Catholics and even Calvinists.

Philadelphians' Prophetess Jane Leade (1624–1704), a visionary who led the Philadelphians after 1681. Some writers have portrayed her as a kind of proto-feminist, while others have detected an erotic quality in her visions.

> Her concern was directed particularly towards the inhabitants of the capital, 'O City of London! A Mighty Angel doth fly, with this Thundering Cry, saying, Do not despise Prophesy, neither decry down the Ark of the Living testimony; from which the Spirit, as a flowing Stream, must renew Paradise upon the earth.'
>
> JULIE HIRST: *Jane Leade* (2006)

Phoenix

An independent cinema in EAST FINCH-LEY. Dating from 1910, when it began life as the Picturedrome, the Phoenix is one of the oldest working cinemas in the country. It featured in the film *Interview with the Vampire* (1994).

Piccadilly

The road that now runs from HYDE PARK CORNER to PICCADILLY CIRCUS was part of an ancient route known as 'the way to Colnbrook' or 'the way to Reading'. The western and eastern halves were later called Hyde Park Road and Portugal Street, the latter in honour of Catherine of Braganza, queen of Charles II. In the early 1610s a house was built here by Robert Baker (d.1623), a tailor who had got rich by selling a kind of starched collar called a piccadill. The house was playfully nicknamed 'Piccadilly Hall' and although other residences soon followed, the locality acquired the name of the first. By the end of the 19th century Piccadilly had become fashionable as both a shopping and a residential area for the rich and famous but, from 1905 to 1910, many of the earliest buildings were swept away in a road-widening project.

Piccadilly Butchers A somewhat exaggerated nickname applied to the Life Guards in 1810 after they charged a stone-throwing mob. The cause of the riot was the government's attempt to arrest the radical politician Sir Francis Burdett (1770–1844) at his home in Piccadilly, a mission that succeeded after three days of resistance, whereupon he became the last state prisoner to be held in the TOWER OF LONDON.

Piccadilly Circus The focus of the WEST END, located at the point where MAYFAIR, SOHO and ST JAMES'S meet. Regent Circus South, as it was first named, was created by John Nash in 1819 as a crossroads on REGENT STREET. There was no roundabout but the buildings at the corners were given curved frontages. The layout was disrupted in the late 1880s by the addition of SHAFTESBURY AVENUE on the north-east side. As the result of continual road alterations the circus has now become triangular in shape and EROS has been relocated. Almost throughout its history Piccadilly Circus has served as a meeting place for various subcultures, including prostitutes and their clients, gay men – especially before the legalization of homosexuality – and 'drop-outs' and drug dealers in the 1960s and 1970s. Recent initiatives have ensured that its attractions are now more family-oriented. Research conducted in 2004 by the owners of the PICCADILLY LIGHTS indicated that an average of 160,000 people pass through Piccadilly Circus every day.

Piccadilly Circus station A LONDON UNDERGROUND station that opened on the BAKERLOO LINE in March 1906 and on the PICCADILLY LINE the following December. The station was rebuilt in 1928 to provide increased capacity.

Piccadilly cramp An 18th-century slang expression for venereal disease.

Piccadilly crawl An affected style of walking adopted by fashionable society during the 1880s.

Piccadilly daisy A slang term in the first half of the 20th century for a prostitute. The allusion is to Piccadilly and PICCADILLY CIRCUS as notorious pick-up points in the era of street prostitution. In Second World War army slang, prostitutes were Piccadilly commandos.

Piccadilly fringe A women's hairstyle, popular in the late 19th century, in which the hair was cut short into a fringe and curled over the forehead.

Piccadilly Johnny with the Little Glass Eye, The or **Algy** A MUSIC HALL song (1895) written by Harry B. Norris and famously performed by Vesta Tilley (*see the* LONDON IDOL). She sang the song (and played the eponymous role) at the first Royal Variety Performance in 1912.

Piccadilly lights The electronic billboards at PICCADILLY CIRCUS, mounted on the building now called One Piccadilly Lights, home to a flagship branch of Barclays bank. The first illuminated signs appeared in the early 1890s, initially above the existing rooflines, but these were removed at the insistence of the LONDON COUNTY COUNCIL. The LCC decreed that advertisements must appear only on the facades of the buildings, which they did from the first decade of the 20th century. Early advertisers included Bovril and Schweppes. Coca-Cola has had a famous presence since 1954 and introduced its present fully programmable LED display in 2003.

Piccadilly line A deep-level line on the LONDON UNDERGROUND system, running between COCKFOSTERS in the north-east and HEATHROW and UXBRIDGE in the west. It opened in 1906 and is coloured dark blue on the map. It is known to those who work on the TUBE as 'the Pic'. The distance between LEICESTER SQUARE and COVENT GARDEN (0.16 miles, 0.25 km) is the shortest between any two stations on the underground.

Piccadilly Percy 'Mercy' in COCKNEY RHYMING SLANG of the 1970s.

Piccadilly polari or **palare** See POLARI.

Piccadilly weepers In the more elaborate and formal funeral ceremonial of the 19th century, undertakers attending (called 'mutes') and the principal male mourners wore long black streamers hanging from the hatband. These were commonly known as weepers, as was also the widow's long black veil. In humorous allusion to the former, the long side whiskers in fashion in the 1860s were called 'Piccadilly weepers'.

Piccadilly window A late 19th- and early 20th-century slang term for a monocle, as affected by the fashionable men promenading in Piccadilly.

> And to fink last week that I was poor!
> But nah I'm goin' to be a reg'lar toff ...
> A Piccadilly winder in my eye.
>
> GEORGE LE BRUNN and E. GRAHAM: 'The Golden Dustman' (song) (1897)

like Piccadilly Circus (in) here See under LIKE.

Star or **Rake of Piccadilly** See OLD Q.

Pickett's Lock A 125-acre (50-hectare) leisure zone situated in north-east EDMONTON, named after a lock on the River LEA Navigation, rebuilt in 1855. In 2000 Pickett's Lock was selected as the new home for British athletics, the proposed site for the 2005 world athletics championships and the focus of a planned bid for the OLYMPIC GAMES. However, the Millennium DOME debacle and difficulties with the WEMBLEY STADIUM project prompted the government to reconsider its involvement and the scheme was abandoned. The fiasco briefly made Pickett's Lock something of a byword for unfulfilled aspirations in athletics funding.

Pickled Egg Walk A former name of Crawford Passage in CLERKENWELL, derived from the presence of a small public house called the Pickled Egg. The pub gained its name from a 17th-century landlord who came from Dorset or Hampshire and brought with him the recipe for the eponymous delicacy, which was at that time unknown in London. Charles I is said to have stopped here to taste a pickled egg.

Pickwick Papers The familiar title of a novel by Charles DICKENS, originally published in instalments as the *The Posthumous Papers of the Pickwick Club* (1836–7). A retired man of business and confirmed bachelor, 'the very personation of kindness and humanity', Samuel Pickwick is the genial founder and chairman of the Pickwick Club. With three other members, Tracy Tupman, Augustus Snodgrass, Nathaniel Winkle and his servant, Sam Weller, he sets out on two years of travel and adventures, intending to record his observations. They are initially involved in merely comic incidents, but the innocent Pickwick's encounters with the law and imprisonment for debt in the FLEET PRISON introduce him to the darker side of life and 'scenes of which I had no previous conception'. On his discharge from the Fleet, he resigns from the club, it is dissolved, and he settles down in DULWICH, contented to see his young friends happily married, including Sam Weller, whose wife he makes his housekeeper.

pie

pie and mash A traditional dish among working-class Londoners, especially those in the EAST END and inner south-east London. Minced beef is the customary filling for the pie, which is accompanied by a scoop or two of mashed potato and a parsley sauce known as 'liquor'. Authentic pie and mash cafés (which are always called 'shops') usually also serve both stewed and JELLIED EELS. London's longest established purveyors of pie and mash – each in business for more than a century – are F. Cooke of HOXTON; Goddard's, founded in DEPTFORD in 1890; and the Manze family, whose best-known shop is in PECKHAM.

pie (and mash) 'Cash' in COCKNEY RHYMING SLANG. Occasionally it can alternatively mean a 'slash', in the sense of the act of urination.

Pie & Mash Club A convivial society founded in 1994, it seeks to encourage appreciation of the dish by organizing regular outings to London's surviving pie and mash shops.

Pie Corner See PYE CORNER.

Pield Heath A partially developed locality lying south of BRUNEL UNIVERSITY and north-west of HILLINGDON Hospital, either side of the River Pinn. Its 16th-century name is pronounced 'peeled', which is what it means: a piece of heathland stripped bare of vegetation.

Pierpoint's Refuge The nickname of London's first traffic island, placed at the top of ST JAMES'S STREET in 1864 at the personal expense of a Colonel Pierpoint, who feared being run over on his way to WHITE'S. According to an oft-told story, Pierpoint was knocked down and killed by a cab while admiring his creation on its completion. The refuge appears to have been removed c.1887.

pig

Piggery Junction A nickname for Latimer Road station at the time of its opening in 1868 on what is now the HAMMERSMITH AND CITY LINE. Many of the area's impoverished inhabitants subsisted by taking in laundry or keeping pigs.

pig's ear 'Beer' in COCKNEY RHYMING SLANG, sometimes shortened simply to 'pig'. To make a pig's ear of something, however, is to botch it. The ear of a slaughtered pig is its most worthless part, no good for anything.

Bartholomew pig See under BARTHOLOMEW.

pigeon See ROCK PIGEON.

Pill Avenue BLACK CAB drivers' slang for HARLEY STREET.

Pimlico A STUCCOED residential enclave situated south-east of VICTORIA STATION. It probably borrowed its name from a well-known public house in HOXTON, owned by one Ben Pimlico, who also brewed Pimlico ale in the early 17th century. The earliest incarnation of Pimlico here was a group of taverns and coffee houses clustered south of Buckingham House. These were squeezed out when the mansion became BUCKINGHAM PALACE in 1825 and the name drifted further south to a new residential area under development by Thomas CUBITT, which had at first been called South BELGRAVIA. Cubitt died in 1855 and is commemorated by a statue on Denbigh Street. Pimlico soon became popular with artists and writers and a literary institute was founded in 1861, next door to the busy MONSTER tavern. The south-western part of Pimlico gained a reputation as a red-light district in the latter part of the 19th century, allegedly aided by its proximity to the PALACE OF WESTMINSTER. Pimlico was very badly damaged by bombing in the Second World War, suffering some of the worst destruction outside the EAST END, and large parts were rebuilt with municipal housing after hostilities ended. The rest of Pimlico had slipped from genteel to shabby by this time, but it staged an impressive recovery in the last quarter of the 20th century.

The writers George Eliot and Joseph Conrad both lodged in Pimlico, and the artist Aubrey Beardsley and composer Sir Arthur Sullivan had homes here. *See also* PASSPORT TO PIMLICO.

Pimm's The proprietary cocktail takes its name from James Pimm (*c.*1798–1866), who invented it *c.*1840. Pimm was a BILLINGSGATE shellfish dealer who in 1823 established an oyster bar in POULTRY and later opened four more CITY branches. The best known cocktail is Pimm's No.1, which is gin-based. For many years there were five other varieties based on other spirits. Pimm's No.2 had a base of whisky, Pimm's No.3 of brandy, Pimm's No.4 of rum, Pimm's No.5 of rye, and Pimm's No.6 of vodka.

pinchbeck A yellow alloy of copper with much less zinc than ordinary brass, developed by the CLERKENWELL-born clockmaker Christopher Pinchbeck (*c.*1670–1732), who owned a shop in FLEET STREET, where he sold trinkets, timepieces and jewellery. The purpose of the alloy was to affordably simulate gold and, although Pinchbeck was honest about its use, many jewellers who copied his formula were not, so the word came to signify a sham, or something tawdry.

> When I was even younger than you are still, I read some of that book-wright's romances and became enduringly convinced that he [Edward Bulwer-Lytton] was one of the most thorough and hollow humbugs of his age; false and flashy in everything; with pinchbeck poetry, pinchbeck philosophy, pinchbeck learning, pinchbeck sentiment; stealing whatever good thing he could lay his hands on, and making it a bad thing as he uttered it.
>
> HENRY STEPHENS SALT: *The Life of James Thomson* (1898)

Pinner An ancient village surrounded by an affluent 20th-century suburb, north-west of HARROW. The name is probably of Saxon origin, meaning 'place by a peg-shaped ridge'. From the 1230s this ridge had a church and a street of houses leading down to a brook that was later called the River Pinn. The Church of St John the Baptist was rebuilt in 1321 and the saint's feast day was celebrated at a midsummer fair from 1336. The fair is still held every June. By the 16th century the village had a butcher, a baker, a candlestick-maker and several other cottage tradesmen. The arrival of the Metropolitan Railway in 1885 brought significant suburban growth, mostly of a

superior form. In the early years of the 20th century the suburb expanded eastwards, meeting the even faster-growing Harrow at HEADSTONE and NORTH HARROW. Large projects between the wars included an estate at Pinnerwood Park in the north. Townhouses and blocks of flats completed the picture in the 1960s and 1970s. The old village is relatively well preserved, with a profusion of timber-framed buildings.

Among Pinner's many notable residents have been the illustrator W. Heath Robinson, the Nazi diplomat Joachim von Ribbentrop, the astronomer Patrick Moore, the actor Ronnie Barker and the singer Simon Le Bon. In the late 1930s the novelist Howard Spring contributed to *The Villager*, the journal of the Pinner Association.

> Early Electric! Sit you down and see,
> 'Mid this fine woodwork and a smell of dinner,
> A stained-glass windmill and a pot of tea,
> And sepia views of leafy lanes in Pinner, –
> Then visualize, far down the shining lines,
> Your parents' homestead set in murmuring pines.
>
> JOHN BETJEMAN: 'The Metropolitan Railway' (1958)

Pip The narrator and hero of Charles DICKENS's *Great Expectations* (1860–1). He is known as Pip from his infant inability to pronounce his full name. When very young, he helps an escaped convict, Abel Magwitch, who remembers his kindness years later, having made good in Australia. Told that he has a secret benefactor, he goes to London to be educated as a gentleman.

> My father's family name being Pirrip, and my Christian name Philip, my infant tongue could make of both names nothing longer or more explicit than Pip. So I called myself Pip, and came to be called Pip.

pipe rolls or **great rolls of the pipe** The name given to a class of Exchequer records on account of their being kept in rolls in the form of a pipe. They began in 1131 and continued until 1831, and contain the annual accounts of sheriffs with the Exchequer, county by county. They are now in the National Archives at KEW.

Pippin Woman *See* DOLL THE PIPPIN WOMAN.

pips The term for the time signal on BBC radio, consisting of five short pips and one longer one on the hour, the exact hour beginning at the start of the latter. The pips were first broadcast in

1924 and until 1990 were officially known as the GREENWICH Time Signal. An additional short pip is inserted when an adjustment (called a 'leap second') is needed to maintain the correlation between Coordinated Universal Time, formerly known as GREENWICH MEAN TIME, and the earth's rotational period.

Pirate Castle A mock castle built in 1977 at Gilbeys Wharf, which is named after a former gin warehouse in CHALK FARM. It is home to a boating club and youth activities centre founded by Viscount St Davids, who lived nearby.

piss

Pissing Conduit A vulgar name for a small conduit that was located near the ROYAL EXCHANGE. Such conduits were London's principal source of relatively clean water until the arrival of the NEW RIVER. SHAKESPEARE had Jack CADE make reference to it:

> Now is Mortimer lord of this city. And here, sitting upon London Stone, I charge and command that, of the city's cost, the pissing conduit run nothing but claret wine this first year of our reign.

Henry VI, Part 2, IV, vi (early 1590s)

Piss Pot Hall The nickname of a five-bay house that stood in Lower CLAPTON, built in the late 1710s for a manufacturer of novelty chamber pots. The most successful item in his range bore the image of Dr Sacheverell inside the bowl (*See the* SACHEVERELL RIOTS). Piss Pot Hall later became the British Asylum for Deaf and Dumb Females.

Pitshanger A former manor in EALING that once covered an area stretching from HANGER HILL to Mattock Lane. The name was first recorded in 1493 and may refer to a wooded slope frequented by hawks or kites. Pitshanger Farm (for a while called Pitch Hanger Farm) lay in the north of the manor in the 18th and 19th centuries.

Pitshanger or **Pitzhanger Manor House** A municipal cultural venue in Walpole Park, EALING. The house was acquired in 1800 by Sir John SOANE, who had most of it demolished and rebuilt to his own design. It served as his weekend country retreat until he sold it in 1810. A later extension is now a repertory gallery of contemporary art, while the main house is hired out for weddings and other functions. Ealing

council has rebranded this double act the PM Gallery and House.

Pitshanger Village An estate agents' name for one of the most advantaged parts of north EALING, centred on Pitshanger Lane and sometimes taken to include the garden suburb of Brentham.

Placentia *See* GREENWICH.

Plague of London *See the* GREAT PLAGUE OF LONDON.

Plaistow[1] (London Borough of Newham) A traditionally working-class district situated on the south-east side of WEST HAM. It has now acquired the COCKNEY pronunciation 'plarstow' but the name probably derives from 'play-stow', a place of recreation, although a link has been suggested with a former lord of the manor, Hugh de Plaiz. In the 18th century Plaistow was a popular retreat for 'sedate merchants and citizens of credit and renown'. Like many villages at this distance from the capital, the intrusion of the railway drove the gentry away during the 19th century and the old mansions were demolished and their grounds were replaced with constricted streets of shabby tenements and unsanitary conditions. Perhaps it was more than coincidence that John Jeyes began to make his patented germicidal fluid in Plaistow in 1885. Extensive municipal rebuilding after the Second World War replaced bomb sites.

Plaistow Patricia A degraded woman imagined by Ian Dury in his song of that name (co-written with Steve Nugent), which appeared on the album *New Boots and Panties!!* (1977).

Plaistow[2] (London Borough of Bromley) An area of mixed socio-economic character situated at the northern end of BROMLEY. Here the name is usually pronounced 'playstow'. Peter THELLUSSON bought the Plaistow estate in 1777 and built Plaistow Lodge, which is now home to a primary school. Plaistow station opened in 1878 on the new line to Bromley North. The station was rebuilt in 1896 and renamed SUNDRIDGE PARK to avoid confusion with the Plaistow in EAST LONDON. The rock star David Bowie (b.1947) lived in Plaistow Grove as a child.

plates (of meat) 'Feet' in COCKNEY RHYMING SLANG.

> 'I rise to my plates of meat,' I riposted, 'as a fully

paid-up member of the Cockney Language Bleeding Preservation Society all ready for a bull and a cow with any fascist swine as tries to put the mockers on our hallowed way of ball and chalking.'

Punch (18 February 1970)

Platform for Art The more imaginative and still the better-known name for the cultural programme now called Art on the Underground, which is run by LONDON UNDERGROUND. Its prime showcase is the unused fourth platform on the Circle and District Line level at GLOUCESTER ROAD station, which is regularly filled with works by artists of international stature, sometimes publicizing temporary exhibitions at London galleries.

Platt's Eyot The westernmost and one of the largest of London's THAMES islets. The words 'eyot' and 'ait' are used interchangeably to denote the small islands of the Thames and the two are pronounced identically (as 'eight'). Platt's Eyot owes its hilly topography to the dumping of soil excavated during the creation of additional filter beds at HAMPTON waterworks at the end of the 19th century. It was home to the Thorneycroft boatyard, which built torpedo boats in both world wars.

Please Sir! One of the top ITV sitcoms of its day (1968–71), centring on the experiences of a newly qualified teacher at Fenn Street School, a tough south London secondary modern (in an unidentified borough). His lofty idealism is predictably blunted, not least by the ineducable Class 5C, whose form teacher he is. The hapless hero, Bernard Hedges, nicknamed 'Privet' by his pupils, was played by John Alderton. *Please Sir!* was the creation of John Esmonde and Bob Larbey, who also scripted the 1971 film of the same name and *The Fenn Street Gang* (1971–3), a TV spin-off following some of the pupils' lives after leaving school.

Plinge, Walter A pseudonym used in London theatre when a part has not been cast, an actor is playing two parts or an actor does not want his or her real name to appear in the programme. There are two stories to account for the name. The first derives it from the landlord of a public house near the stage door of the Lyceum Theatre, *c.*1900, who was honoured by a group of

actors with the borrowing of his name because he had consistently allowed them to put their drinks on the slate. The second takes it from a phrase 'Mr Plinge is waiting', used by an actor for a supposedly convivial acquaintance who has invited him out for a drink. The first to use the name on a playbill may have been the actor and producer Oscar Asche (1871–1936), who took over the management of His Majesty's Theatre in 1907. For unknown reasons, 2 December has been designated Walter Plinge Day. The US equivalent of Walter Plinge is George Spelvin.

plonker Originally, in mid-19th-century slang, anything large or substantial. By the 1960s the term was being applied to the penis, and soon, as commonly happens with 'penis'-words, it was being used to mean 'fool'. This last usage was widely popularized in the 1980s by the BBC television sitcom ONLY FOOLS AND HORSES.

Plumstead A Victorian outgrowth of WOOL-WICH, which lies to its west. This place where the plum trees grew was first recorded around 970 as Plumstede. It is possible that the Romans planted orchards here on an agricultural scale.
Plumstead Common A wiggling chain of open spaces covering an undulating plateau in south Plumstead, linking to Winn's Common in the east.
Plumstead Peculiars A religious sect (more generally known as 'the Peculiar People') founded in 1838, and one of the more exotic forms of nonconformism that characterized the area. Its adherents refused medical aid, but not surgical, and relied on the efficacy of prayer and on anointing with oil by the elders. The sect's name was based on Titus 2:14: 'Who gave himself for us, that he might ... purify unto himself a peculiar people' (*peculiar* in this context means 'belonging particularly to himself', not 'odd'). Their chapel closed in 1934.
Plumstead Potter See ROMFORD SLIM.

Poems on the Underground A long-running series of TUBE CARDS featuring short poems or verses from longer works. The scheme was conceived in 1986 by the London-based American writer Judith Chernaik, together with Gerard Benson and Cicely Herbert, with the aim of disseminating poetry beyond those who regularly read it, and it has probably succeeded better than any other such vehicle in modern Britain.

Similar programmes have since been adopted on a dozen other subway systems worldwide. Funding comes from the British Council, London Arts, the Poetry Society and the Arts Council of England. Poets from ancient to modern are showcased; the summer 2008 batch, for example, included works by John MILTON (1608–74) and Frances Leviston (b.1982). New sets of poems generally appear three times a year. Collections of the poems are published regularly in book form, reaching the eleventh edition in 2009. Sales of all the editions, including various spin-offs, have exceeded a quarter of a million copies.

Poets' Corner

1. The southern end of the south transept of WESTMINSTER ABBEY, first so called by Oliver Goldsmith because it contained the tomb of Chaucer. Joseph Addison had previously alluded to it in *The Spectator* (No.26, 1711) as the 'poetical quarter', in which he says:

> I found there were Poets who had no Monuments, and Monuments which had no poets.

Among writers buried here are Edmund Spenser, John Dryden, Samuel JOHNSON, Richard Brinsley Sheridan, Charles DICKENS, Robert Browning, Alfred, Lord Tennyson, Lord Macaulay, Thomas Hardy and Rudyard Kipling. There are also many monuments to writers not buried here. Ben Jonson was buried in the north aisle of the Abbey, and Joseph Addison in Henry VII's Chapel.

2. An estate agents' term for any collection of vaguely attractive streets named after poets. These include parts of ACTON, HANWELL and HERNE HILL. In the TV sitcom *The* FALL AND RISE OF REGINALD PERRIN, the eponymous hero lived in Coleridge Close, on the 'Poets' Estate' in the fictional suburb of Climthorpe.

point In the vocabulary of the KNOWLEDGE, a point is a place within 6 miles (9.65 km) of CHARING CROSS that a BLACK CAB driver must know. Defined points include:

civil, criminal and coroners' courts	places of interest to tourists
clubs	places of worship
diplomatic premises	police stations
financial and commercial centres	prisons
government offices and departments	register offices
hospitals	schools, colleges and universities
hotels	societies, associations and institutions
housing estates	sports stadiums
leisure centres	stations
museums and art galleries	theatres and cinemas
parks and open spaces	town halls

Point Counter Point A satirical novel (1928) by Aldous Huxley (1894–1963), often epigrammatic in style and cynical in tone, portraying 'modern' London life in the 1920s. It is also a *roman à clef*, featuring a large number of mostly unsympathetic characters drawn from the British upper classes and intelligentsia: there are thinly disguised portraits of, among others, D.H. and Frieda Lawrence, Augustus John, Sir Oswald Mosley, John Middleton Murry, Katherine Mansfield and Huxley himself. The title's reference to musical counterpoint (in which two or more melodic lines occur simultaneously, complementing one another) is reflected in some of the structural features of the novel, for example, the relationships between and among the various couples, and the fact that the novel planned by the Huxley character, Philip Quarles, parallels the real life going on around him; indeed, the overall structure of the book is said to be based on J.S. Bach's Suite No.2 in B minor.

polari or **palare** A slang lexicon popular in the 1950s and 60s among members of London's gay underworld, notably male prostitutes operating in the vicinity of the MEAT RACK at PICCADILLY CIRCUS. Its name derives from the Italian *parlare*, 'to talk'. Like most such argots, polari fostered a sense of community among its users and aimed to baffle and exclude non-members of that community, especially the police. The vocabulary was never extensive, with just two or three dozen words and phrases in regular usage and a few hundred in total. Many of the terms related to one's appearance, to parts of the body, and to practices of specific interest to its users. Paul Baker, author of *Fantabulosa: A Dictionary of Polari and Gay Slang* (2002), has pointed out that it was ideal for gossip. Polari derived from a mixture of sources, including BACK-SLANG, thieves' cant, Italian, Romany and Yiddish, with words often borrowed from the slang of the theatrical and circus worlds. It was famously brought into the public domain in the mid-1960s by the characters Julian and Sandy in the BBC radio comedy series *Round the Horne*. This publicity was a factor in its decline – because it let the secret out, as was the partial decriminalization of homosexuality in 1967 and a subsequent attitude among some gay activists that polari's connotations of effeminacy made its use self-demeaning. Certain polari words regained a degree of fashionability in the 1990s and a few of the most popular are included in this dictionary in their respective alphabetical locations, including those that appear in these lines:

The Piccadilly palare was just silly slang
Between me and the boys in my gang
So bona to vada (oh) you!
Your lovely eek and your lovely riah.

MORRISSEY: 'Piccadilly Palare' (song) (1990)

Polish

Polish corridor A nickname for EARLS COURT, or specifically the Earls Court Road, in the years after the Second World War, when many Polish exiles settled here. Over the course of the 20th century the area probably had more nicknames than any other part of London, as a consequence of its shifting popularity with various minority groups.

Polish War Memorial A monument located at the intersection of the WESTERN AVENUE and West End Road, in South RUISLIP, nowadays best known as a traffic report landmark. The neighbouring NORTHOLT AERODROME was the main base for the Polish Air Force during the early part of the Second World War. The memorial, surmounted by an eagle, was unveiled in 1948 and is engraved with the names of the 14 squadrons of the PAF. Behind is a wall with the names of almost two thousand members of PAF crews who died on operational flights. The memorial was repaired and rededicated in the mid-1990s.

Pollards Hill A somewhat disadvantaged district lying on the eastern edge of MITCHAM, south-west of NORBURY. Pollards are trees that have been cut back to promote the growth of new, short branches. The 'physic gardener' James Arthur grew aromatic herbs here in the mid-19th century.

Pollock

Jackson Pollocks See under JACKSON.

Pollock's Toy Shop See PENNY PLAIN, TWO-PENCE COLOURED.

Polly

Polly Cleanstairs A long-standing nickname for the Royal Oak public house in BEXLEYHEATH. The alternative name is sufficiently well established to merit its own sign outside the building and may derive from a house-proud 19th-century landlady, Mary Ann Elms.

Polly Perkins of Paddington Green See PRETTY POLLY PERKINS OF PADDINGTON GREEN.

Pol's Stump An alternative name for the original PAUL'S CROSS. Some have suggested that 'Pol' was not a corruption of Paul but of Apollo or the Nordic sun god Balder, or some blend of the latter two, and that the stone stump was a place of pagan worship before early Christians mounted a cross upon it.

Polytechnic Institution A former institute of learning founded at 309 REGENT STREET in 1838, originally for the exhibition of objects connected with the industrial arts, the name itself deriving from the Greek for 'many arts'. Under the patronage of Prince ALBERT it became the Royal Polytechnic Institution in 1841 and played a significant role in demonstrating new technologies and inventions to the public, as something of a forerunner to the SCIENCE MUSEUM. The Royal Polytechnic closed in 1881 and in the following year its building became home to the Young Men's Christian Institute, founded by Quintin Hogg (1845–1903). This soon became known as the Polytechnic and, when it gained public funding in 1891, was officially renamed the Regent Street Polytechnic. The Polytechnic progressively expanded its range of day and evening courses in technical and commercial subjects, evolving into a broad-based college with a special emphasis on sporting activities. The Polytechnic ultimately became the core institution of what is now the UNIVERSITY OF WESTMINSTER.

Ponders End An industrial and residential district situated on the eastern edge of ENFIELD. The name was first recorded in the late 16th century and probably derives from one John Ponder, who was living here in 1373.

I had thought in a green old age (O green thought!) to have retired to Ponders End, emblematic name, how beautiful!

CHARLES LAMB: letter to William Wordsworth (20 March 1822)

Pontoon Dock A former repair facility, originally called the Victoria Graving Dock, built in the late 1850s on the south side of what became the Royal Victoria Dock (*see the* ROYAL DOCKS). Using an innovative system of hydraulic jacks, vessels were raised out of the water on pontoons, which were then drained of their ballast water and shunted into a finger dock for repair or overhaul. There were four of these splayed fingers at each end of the dock but most have now been filled with concrete.

Pont Street A street in BROMPTON, running from the eastern end of BEAUCHAMP PLACE eastwards across SLOANE STREET towards Belgrave Square (*see* BELGRAVIA). Pont Street was laid out around 1830 and its name probably referred to a bridge crossing the WESTBOURNE stream. Oscar Wilde was arrested on charges of homosexual practices in 1895 at the Cadogan Hotel, on the corner of Pont Street and Sloane Street.

To the right and before him Pont Street
Did tower in her new built red,
As hard as the morning gaslight
That shone on his unmade bed.

JOHN BETJEMAN: 'The Arrest of Oscar Wilde at the Cadogan Hotel' (1937)

Pont Street Dutch A term coined by the cartoonist and architectural writer Osbert Lancaster (1908–86) for a 19th-century architectural style typified by the large gabled redbrick mansions that line Pont Street and nearby streets.

Pseudish. This style which attained great popularity both in this country and in America (where it was generally known as Spanish-colonial), is actually our old friend Pont Street Dutch with a few Stockholm trimmings and a more daring use of colour.

OSBERT LANCASTER: *Pillar to Post* (1938)

pony The sum of £25. The term is of uncertain origin, with several conflicting derivations proposed, including the former cost of hiring a pony-drawn wedding carriage. To 'pony up' is to pay up.

pony (and trap) 'Crap' in COCKNEY RHYMING SLANG.

But the real tragedy is that the original working-class East Enders – or Cockneys, born within earshot of Bow Bells – have been pushed out by soaring property prices and the wealthier 'Mockneys' (those try-hards who affect an East End accent). To that, they probably retort, 'What a load of pony and trap.'

FLEUR BRITTEN: *A Hedonist's Guide to London* (2006)

Poodle Byng The sobriquet of Frederick Byng (*c*.1784–1871), from his head of thick curly hair when young. He was a noted MAN ABOUT TOWN of the Regency era, member of BROOKS'S and frequenter of ALMACK'S. He lived for 60 years in ST JAMES'S.

If he [Beau Brummell] was ever witty, then the remark he made to 'Poodle' Byng may be regarded as a slender proof of it, for, meeting Byng driving with a *caniche* by his side, he called out: 'Ah, how d'ye do, Byng! – a family vehicle I see.'

E. BERESFORD CHANCELLOR: *Memorials of St. James's Street* (1922)

Pool An abbreviated term for the POOL OF LONDON.

Pool of London A reach of the River THAMES that extends eastwards from LONDON BRIDGE to CUCKOLD'S POINT and LIMEHOUSE. It is divided into a western section (the Upper Pool) and an eastern section (the Lower Pool). It is the farthest point up-river that large ships can find sufficient depth, and from Roman times until the 19th century, when enclosed docks began to be built further downstream, it was London's main port, and this stretch of the river was always crowded with masts (or, latterly, funnels), its banks a seamless succession of wharves and cranes. As recently as 1894 TOWER BRIDGE was built with raisable sections to allow shipping free passage, but today commerce has gone elsewhere, and they are seldom lifted.

She had a gentle voice and that kind of London accent which is like the waters of the Thames at the Pool, by no means unpleasant but the least bit thick.

MARGERY ALLINGHAM: *The Tiger in the Smoke* (1952)

Pool price In the days of London's docks, the wholesale price of coal at the POOL OF LONDON.

poor

Poor Cow A novel (1963) by Nell Dunn. Living in London with a small baby, little money and a husband who haunts the edges of the criminal underworld, Joy finds life full of pain and disappointment. Enriched by theft the couple move to a luxury flat in RUISLIP. After her husband goes to prison Joy returns to FULHAM with her baby to live with an aunt. Unable to function well in relationships with men, and supported only by the well-meaning affection of a feckless friend, she stumbles from miserable situation to crisis and feels control slipping through her fingers as she finds herself wading through the shabbiness of a lifestyle that has few moments of happiness or hope. Ken Loach directed a film version in 1967.

poor man's Carlton An early nickname for Bruce House, a homeless men's shelter in COVENT GARDEN, built by the LONDON COUNTY COUNCIL in 1906. The reference to César Ritz's CARLTON HOTEL, which then stood in the HAYMARKET, was not wholly ironic since the hostel's accommodation was the best and most expensive of its kind in London. The housing and regeneration trust Peabody (*see* PEABODY BUILDINGS) now runs a community centre and training facility at Bruce House.

> To see the aristocrats of the underworld one should go to Bruce House ... The spacious rooms, scrupulously clean, decorated with plaques of red tiles, engravings of well-known pictures or Cecil Aldin's sporting prints; the bearing and speech and manners of many of the inmates; the bill of fare which begins with cold salmon and cucumber for 3d, and goes on through a long list of appetizing dishes at prices varying from 1d to 3d, all combine to give it much more the atmosphere of a hotel than of a municipal lodging-house.
>
> *The Times* (10 June 1914)

Pooter A comically self-important person who is overly concerned with the minutiae of life. The usage was inspired by Charles Pooter, the fictional lower-middle-class clerk with modest but determined (yet constantly undermined) aspirations whose mundane and accident-prone existence forms the substance of George and Weedon Grossmith's *Diary of a Nobody* (1892). He lives at 'The Laurels, Brickfield Terrace', an address that has been linked with the real-life 1 Pemberton Gardens, Upper HOLLOWAY.

pop

Pop Goes the Weasel Now regarded as a children's song, the original was obviously intended for their parents:

> Up and down the City Road,
> In and out the Eagle.
> That's the way the money goes,
> Pop goes the weasel.

The Eagle was a tavern and old-time MUSIC HALL in the CITY ROAD and a popular rendezvous for singing and Saturday night drinking, which explains the need to 'pop' or pawn the 'weasel'. What the 'weasel' was is not clear, but it may have been COCKNEY RHYMING SLANG for a coat, from 'weasel and stoat'. Alternative theories propose that it was either a tailor's iron or a weaver's shuttle. *See also the* EAGLE (1).

Pop-Gun Plot An alleged conspiracy to assassinate George III in 1794 using a hollow walking stick capable of discharging a poison dart. The plot was the figment of the imagination of Thomas Upton, a watchmaker who forged letters to implicate several members of the LONDON CORRESPONDING SOCIETY. Another member of the society, the physician Dr James Parkinson (of Parkinson's Disease fame), was a key witness for the defence at the Privy Council investigation into the affair. After spending a considerable period in jail, where some may have been tortured, all the accused were eventually acquitted or freed without trial.

Pope

Pope, Alexander *See the* BARD OF TWICKENHAM.

Popish Plot A fictitious Jesuit plot (1678) to murder Charles II and others, enthrone the Duke of York and set fire to the CITY of London, after which, with the aid of French and Irish troops, a massacre of Protestants was to ensue. The plot was invented by the scoundrelly Titus Oates (1649–1705). Before the anti-Catholic panic abated in 1681, some 35 Catholics were judicially murdered, including the Roman Catholic Primate of Ireland. Oates was eventually pilloried, whipped and imprisoned when James II became king. He was set free in the Glorious Revolution of 1688–9. *See also* GREEN, BERRY AND HILL.

Poplar An EAST END district situated immediately north of the ISLE OF DOGS and taking its name from the native trees (*Populus canescens* and *Populus nigra*) that once thrived on the moist alluvial soil beside the marshes. From the 17th century Poplar provided homes for workers at the docks that lined the riverfront from LIME-HOUSE around the Isle of Dogs to BLACKWALL. It became one of London's first multi-ethnic districts, with inhabitants of Indian, Chinese and 'Nubian' origin. Poplar Fields, the area north of East India Dock Road, was built up as Poplar New Town from the 1830s to the mid-1850s. Joseph Stalin, leader of the Soviet Union from 1924 to 1953, lived in Poplar in the early 1900s as a political refugee. Nowadays the district consists almost entirely of council flats and houses dating from the 1950s to 1970s, although DOCKLANDS regeneration has brought some private residential and commercial properties. Only a few structures, mainly churches, pubs and public buildings, pre-date the Second World War.

Poplar gaol A nickname applied to Poplar baths after they opened in 1934, derived from the brutish appearance of the building's East India Dock Road frontage.

Poplarism A nickname coined in 1922 by the *Glasgow Herald* for POPLAR council's militant campaign to relieve the suffering of its poor, especially its demand that London's wealth should be distributed more evenly among its constituent parts. George LANSBURY, later leader of the Labour Party, was imprisoned for supporting a rates strike. The term became generic for allegedly spendthrift Labour councils.

> Those … will demand increased subsidies, allowances, and 'Poplarised' social services, to be paid for out of the proceeds of very high taxation.
>
> *The Daily Telegraph* (6 November 1928)

Poppins

Poppins, Mary The children's nanny who possesses magical powers in the books by P.L. Travers, beginning with the one named after her (1934). She can not only slide up the banisters but walk into a picture, understand what dogs are saying and travel round the world in seconds. She was played by Julie Andrews in the film of 1964, also named after her, which is notable for Dick Van Dyke's alarming attempt at a COCKNEY accent.

Poppins Court A narrow thoroughfare running between FLEET STREET and St Bride Street. This was formerly Poppingay Alley, from an inn sign

depicting a popinjay, or parrot. The author P.L. Travers (1899–1996) once worked nearby and it has been suggested that she took the name of her most famous creation, Mary Poppins (*see above*), from this place. That the magical nanny carried a parrot-headed umbrella may however be pure coincidence.

> Poppin's Court (No. 109) marks the site of the ancient hostel (hotel) of the Abbots of Cirencester – though what they did there, when they ought to have been on their knees in their own far-away Gloucestershire abbey, history does not choose to record.
>
> WALTER THORNBURY: *Old and New London*, Volume 1 (1878)

pork

Pork Halfacre A medieval parcel of land in HARLINGTON, probably bequeathed by the rector of St Peter and St Paul's Church. The land was traditionally used to rear pigs, and some of their meat provided an annual dinner of pork for the bellringers. After the half-acre (0.2 hectares) was sold in 1879 the income from the proceeds continued to be put to the same use.

porky 'Lie' in COCKNEY RHYMING SLANG, from 'pork pie', also sometimes rendered as 'porky pie'. Often used in the plural, the term suddenly became popular from the 1970s, when policemen in television programmes always seemed to be questioning suspects with lines such as, 'You wouldn't be telling me porkies, would you, son?' It usually connotes a relatively minor falsehood.

> Finally, questionnaires may give rise to 'social desirability' effects, with respondents telling porkies about their income or sexual practices to look good to the experimenter.
>
> ANDY FIELD and GRAHAM HOLE: *How to Design and Report Experiments* (2003)

porridge A colloquial term for imprisonment, punning on earlier 'stir' as a slang word of Romany origin for prison while also referring to a supposedly typical prison breakfast. The expression, dating from the 1940s, was brought before a wider public as the title of a television sitcom series of 1973–7 starring Ronnie Barker as the wily old London lag Norman Stanley Fletcher. *See also* GOING STRAIGHT (*under* GO).

Porridge Island The derisive nickname of a paved alley that used to lead from the churchyard of ST MARTIN-IN-THE-FIELDS to Round

Court. It was chiefly inhabited by cooks who sold soup and cheap cuts of meat. Porridge Island was swept away during the wholesale clearance of the area's slums in 1829.

> Hundreds of your fellow-creatures, dear lady, turn another way, that they may not be tempted by the luxuries of Porridge Island to wish for gratifications they are not able to obtain. You are certainly not better than all of *them*; give God thanks that you are happier.
>
> SAMUEL JOHNSON, quoted in JAMES BOSWELL: *Life of Samuel Johnson* (1791)

portcullis (Old French *porte coleïce*, 'sliding gate') The badge of Henry VII and Henry VIII, used in their honour as decoration in the PALACE OF WESTMINSTER when it was rebuilt following a fire in 1512. When Charles Barry submitted his designs for the new palace after the devastating fire of 1834, which according to the rules of the competition had to be submitted pseudonymously, he adopted the portcullis as his identifying mark. On winning the competition Barry and his collaborator Augustus Pugin chose to use the emblem liberally throughout the new building. It was carved in the woodwork, stamped on the furnishings and on the books in the library and even cast in the metal of the great bell known as BIG BEN. As a consequence the portcullis became the unofficial symbol of both Houses of Parliament. Her Majesty the Queen formally authorized its use for that purpose in 1996.

The City of WESTMINSTER has also employed the portcullis as its symbol since Tudor times and many Westminster institutions have followed this example, notably London's seminal insurance company, the Westminster Fire Office, from its incorporation in 1717. The Westminster firemark – a plaque bearing a portcullis surmounted by the three feathers of the Prince of Wales – served to identify a company-insured building to private fire brigades.

The portcullis first appeared on coinage during the reign of Henry VIII, identifying coins minted at the TOWER OF LONDON. The presence of the device on the silver halfpenny issued under Elizabeth I led to that coin being nicknamed a 'portcullis'. A crowned portcullis graced the reverse of the British one penny coin from decimalization in 1971 until 2008.

Portcullis House A parliamentary office block situated at the corner of Bridge Street and Victoria EMBANKMENT, immediately north of the PALACE OF WESTMINSTER and in the shadow of BIG BEN. Completed in 2001, it sits above the void of WESTMINSTER station's ticket hall, supported inside its perimeter on just six columns. The requirement that the building should be bomb-proof, combined with a desire to make architectural references to its Gothic neighbour, has resulted in a somewhat fortress-like appearance. However, criticism in the press focused less on aesthetics and more on the building's cost of around £235 million, which represented more than £1 million for each MP's office here.

porter A dark-brown malt liquor, probably so called from its popularity with porters at London markets.

Portland

Portland Place A street running from Park Crescent (at the southern end of REGENT'S PARK) in the north to Langham Place in the south. It was named in honour of the 2nd Duke of Portland, who owned land in the area. Laid out around 1778 by the ADAM BROTHERS, Portland Place is unusually wide, an undertaking having been given at the time of building to Lord Foley, who lived at the southern end, that his view northwards would never be blocked. The buildings along either side now house embassies, legations and the offices of learned societies, but the street's most famous occupant is the BBC. Its former headquarters, the curvilinear BROADCASTING HOUSE, was constructed at the southern end in the late 1920s. 'Portland Place' was almost synonymous with the BBC until most of its departments and senior managers decamped to WHITE CITY.

Portland spies Two clerks, Harry Houghton and Ethel ('Bunty') Gee, at the Underwater Weapons Establishment in Portland, Dorset, who were discovered in 1961 to have been taking secret documents up to London and handing them to a man called Gordon Lonsdale near the OLD VIC. Lonsdale (in reality a Russian named Konon Trofimovich Modoly) passed the material to Peter and Helen Kroger of 45 Cranley Drive, RUISLIP, where the documents were reduced to microdots that were then sent to Russia pasted over full stops in second-hand books. Houghton and Gee got 15 years in prison, Lonsdale 15 years and the Krogers 20 years. Lonsdale was in the end exchanged for Greville Wynne in 1964 (Wynne was a British businessman jailed by the Russians for bringing out material from a Soviet double agent called Oleg Penkovsky).

Portland vase A cinerary urn of the 1st century AD made of dark blue glass decorated with white figures, the finest surviving Roman example of cameo glass. It was found in a tomb near Rome in the 17th century and in 1770 was purchased from the Barberini Palace by Sir William Hamilton for 1,000 guineas. In 1787 it came into the possession of the Duke of Portland, one of the trustees of the BRITISH MUSEUM, who placed it in that institution for exhibition. In 1845 a deranged person named Lloyd dashed it to pieces, but it was so skilfully repaired that the damage is barely visible. It is 10in (25cm) high and 6in (15cm) in diameter at the broadest part.

Portman Square A square in south MARYLEBONE, at the southern end of BAKER STREET. It was laid out in 1764 by the landowner Henry William Portman (1738–96) and built up over the following two decades. Houses by Robert ADAM and ATHENIAN STUART made the square the jewel in the crown of the Portman Estate. Elizabeth Montagu, whose BLUE STOCKING Club met here in the square's earliest days, called it 'the MONTPELLIER OF ENGLAND'. She held an annual MAY DAY party for young chimney-sweeps in Montagu House and its garden.

> How did the party go in Portman Square?
> I cannot tell you; Juliet was not there.
> And how did Lady Gaster's party go?
> Juliet was next to me and I do not know.
>
> HILAIRE BELLOC: 'Juliet' (1916)

Portobello A colloquialism for both PORTOBELLO ROAD and (more often) its market. It originated in a former farm that was renamed in honour of Vice-Admiral Edward Vernon's (*see* OLD GROG) defeat of the Spanish fleet at Porto Bello (now Portobelo in Panama) in 1739. The country track that traversed its fields was later called Portobello Lane.

Portobello Market One of the most distinctive street markets in London. Over the second half of the 20th century the shops and stalls of PORTOBELLO ROAD increasingly specialized in antiques and bric-à-brac. The market has stalls every weekday and is especially big on Saturdays, when it claims to become the world's largest

antiques market. Its popularity may prove to be its downfall; traders have sought the council's help in preventing generic outlets like coffee bars from squeezing out the traditional shops that have made Portobello what it is. A plaque on the wall of 115 Portobello Road commemorates June Aylward, who established the street's first antiques shop.

> Street where the riches of ages are stowed.
> Anything and everything a chap can unload
> Is sold off the barrow in Portobello Road.
> You'll find what you want in the Portobello
> Road.
>
> RICHARD M. SHERMAN and ROBERT B. SHERMAN: 'Portobello Road' (song from the film *Bedknobs and Broomsticks*) (1971)

Portobello Road A street winding in a north-north-westerly direction from NOTTING HILL GATE, where it branches off Pembridge Road. In 1801 the GRAND JUNCTION CANAL cut across the northern part of Portobello Lane, which was subsequently further truncated by the railway and the redevelopment of KENSAL TOWN. From the mid-19th century the LADBROKE GROVE estate progressively filled the territory to the south-west and the owners of Portobello Farm began to sell off their land for housing. In 1864 the Portobello farmhouse was sold to the Little Sisters of the Poor, who built St Joseph's Convent on the site of its orchard. As development slowly moved northwards (and socially downwards) over the remainder of the century, terraces of working-class housing lined the rest of what had become Portobello Road. A music scene evolved from the late 1960s, when Island Records moved to nearby Basing Street. Live music venues and specialist record shops appeared on Portobello Road and PUNK ROCK, reggae and later rap and hip-hop artists performed and recorded here, often renting homes – or squatting – in the vicinity.

Port of London Authority A statutory body set up in 1908 to take charge of the tidal part of the River THAMES (from TEDDINGTON to its mouth) and the docking activities along its banks. Since the closure of the docks within London its main responsibilities have been ensuring navigational safety, promoting use of the river and safeguarding the environment.

Portsoken The most easterly of the ancient wards of the CITY of London. The name meant 'district outside a city over which jurisdiction is extended', ulimately derived from Old English *port*, 'town', and *sōcn*, 'franchise'. It was the soke of the old Knightenguild outside the city wall in the parish of St Botolph, ALDGATE. In the 10th century Edgar the Peaceful (some say King Cnut, in the following century) granted the Knightenguild to 13 of his most trusted knights. According to legend each of them had first to prove victorious in three combats, one above ground, one underground and one in the water, and they afterwards had to joust against all comers at East Smithfield.

posh This colloquialism for 'grand', 'swell' or 'first rate' is traditionally said to have originated in the old days of constant steamship travel between England and India, when passengers might have booked their return passage with the arrangement 'Port Outward Starboard Homeward', thus ensuring cabins on the cooler side of the ship. However, this explanation is almost certainly fictitious and the likeliest source for the usage is actually 19th-century London street slang, where 'posh' meant money (probably from Romany *posh* 'half, halfpenny'), which could easily have evolved semantically via wealthy to upper-class or grand.

post

postal districts Rowland Hill (1795–1879) introduced the division of London addresses by points of the compass in 1857–8. The system initially covered the area within 12 miles (19.3 km) of the General Post Office in St Martin's le Grand, and mail was thenceforth sorted for local delivery at an office based in each district. The immediate vicinity of the General Post Office was divided into the EC (east central) and WC (west central) districts. In his capacity as a Post Office surveyor, the novelist Anthony Trollope recommended changes in 1866, including the merger of the north-east district within the east. Two years later the southern district was split into south-west and south-east parts. The districts were subdivided numerically in 1917, to assist inexperienced women who had been recruited to do the job of postmen who had gone to fight in the war. In each compass-point area, the head district (nearest central London) was numbered '1', while the remaining districts were numbered in alphabetical order. Thus, for example, in the south-east, the SE1 head district covers the

SOUTHWARK area, while SE2 is centred on ABBEY WOOD, SE3 on BLACKHEATH, SE4 on BROCKLEY, and so on. Because the system was created before the inception of London as a county, and refined before the creation of GREATER LONDON and its boroughs, there is no correlation between the capital's administrative boundaries and the division or extent of the London postal districts. Many parts of OUTER LONDON did not gain alphanumeric designations (such as BR1 for central BROMLEY, TW1 for central TWICKENHAM, etc.) until the nationwide introduction of the postcode system in the late 1960s, a process that began in CROYDON.

> I thought of London spread out in the sun,
> Its postal districts packed like squares of wheat
> ...
> PHILIP LARKIN: 'The Whitsun Weddings' (1964)

postcode wars Territorial hostility between rival gangs based on the POSTAL DISTRICTS in which members live or operate. Similar turf battles occur in provincial cities such as Sheffield, but they are especially virulent in the capital. In parts of INNER LONDON some young people risk being attacked if they stray across the invisible barrier that divides one postal district from another. Several murders have been attributed to breaches of these demarcation lines and to violations of related but more tightly defined 'road codes'.

> Their trial heard that the Cathall Street Bois were a notorious force on their home turf – the Cathall Estate – engaged in a 'postcode war' against anyone living outside their patch of E11.
> *Daily Mail* (10 April 2008)

Postman's Park A small park located off St Martin's le Grand in the CITY of London. The name refers to its former role as a place of relaxation for workers at the nearby General Post Office. The park has a permanent display of commemorative tiles dedicated to ordinary people who heroically gave their lives in order to save others.

Post Office Railway *See* MAIL RAIL.

Post Office Tower *See the* BT TOWER.

pot and pan 'Man' in COCKNEY RHYMING SLANG, heard almost exclusively in the phrase 'my old pot and pan', meaning one's husband or father, usually the latter.

This book is dedicated to my old pot and pan Joe Peterson: a Real Legend.

CHARLES BRONSON (né MICHAEL PETERSON): *Legends* (2000)

Potato Pete A human figure in the form of a potato publicized in posters by the Ministry of Food in the Second World War with the aim of encouraging people to make the most of available vegetables. He had a companion in Doctor Carrot. JOHN LEWIS held a 'Potato Christmas Fair' sponsored by Potato Pete in its bombed-out premises in OXFORD STREET. Children received hot baked potatoes as they pledged: 'I promise as my Christmas gift to the sailors who have to bring us our bread that I will do all I can to eat home-grown potatoes instead.'

potter

Potter, Harry A boy-wizard whose adventures are chronicled in an award-winning and commercially very successful sequence of children's novels by J.K. Rowling (b.1965). Rowling makes London the home of several institutions of the magical world, but generally gives few hints to their precise location. The Ministry of Magic's headquarters is entirely underground and visitors must gain access via a disused red telephone box on an unidentified street. St Mungo's Hospital for Magical Maladies and Injuries is concealed behind the frontage of Purge and Dowse, an abandoned department store. Even fewer clues are offered regarding the whereabouts of the Museum of Quidditch or the offices of the Society for Tolerance of Vampires. Other magical places in London include DIAGON ALLEY, KNOCKTURN ALLEY and the LEAKY CAULDRON, which are all near CHARING CROSS ROAD, and No.12 GRIMMAULD PLACE. The books also mention real London places, notably KING'S CROSS STATION but also BETHNAL GREEN, CLAPHAM, VAUXHALL and the ELEPHANT AND CASTLE. *See also the* WOBBLY BRIDGE.

Potters Fields A public park located immediately east of CITY HALL and north of TOOLEY STREET. It was landscaped in 2007 and is one of the few green open spaces along the riverside. The name 'potter's field' was traditionally applied to a burial ground reserved for strangers and the friendless poor, in an allusion to the field bought by the chief priests with the 30 pieces of silver returned to them by the repentant Judas Iscariot. However, in this case, the park's identity seems to derive from the presence of potteries operated hereabouts by Dutch immigrants in the late 16th and early 17th centuries. To mark this association a long stone bench has been inlaid with English Delftware patterns.

In September/October 2003 an estimated 250,000 people visited Potters Fields over a 44-day period to watch (and in some cases abuse) the American illusionist and endurance artist David Blaine as he dangled in the air inside a transparent case.

Poultry An eastward continuation of CHEAPSIDE to BANK. It had acquired its name, from the poultry market held here, by the end of the 13th century. As might be expected in a market street there were plenty of taverns (including one appropriately called the Red Cock) and by the time of the GREAT FIRE OF LONDON they were the street's main claim to fame. The redevelopment of the site at No.1 Poultry was much argued over in the latter part of the 20th century, a proposed design by the modernist architect Mies van der Rohe causing particular controversy. It was finally filled by a postmodern polychrome office block (1998) by Sir James Stirling.

The poet Thomas Hood (1799–1845) was born in a house in Poultry, and alludes to it in his famous lines in 'I Remember' (1802):

I remember, I remember,
The house where I was born,
The little window where the sun
Came peeping in at morn.

Poultry Compter A sheriff's prison that stood in Poultry until 1817. The inmates of the Compter were felons and debtors jailed by the LORD MAYOR OF LONDON and conditions were relatively good, with prisoners often dining on leftovers from the mayor's banquets. It was the only prison in the country that had a ward reserved exclusively for Jews.

pouting place of princes LEICESTER SQUARE was so called by Thomas Pennant in *Some Account of London* (1813), because George II, when Prince of Wales, having quarrelled with his father, retired to Leicester House; and his son Frederick, Prince of Wales, did the same, for the very same reason.

poverty

Poverty Corner The corner of Waterloo Road and York Road, by WATERLOO STATION, was formerly so called. Unemployed actors, singers and musicians would congregate here every morning, awaiting appointments with theatrical agents based in York Road or Stamford Street, or hoping to be picked out of the crowd. Many also took lodgings in the vicinity. The impresario Fred Karno (1866–1941) was among those who found work at Poverty Corner, when he was starting out as a stage acrobat.

> I thought we might as well try the saloon bar of the York Hotel, which abuts on the famous 'Poverty Corner', so much frequented by ladies and gentlemen of the 'halls', when, sorely against their inclinations, they are 'resting'.
>
> ERNEST ALFRED VIZETELLY: *With Zola In England* (1899)

Poverty Driven Children or **PDC** A street gang based in BRIXTON. They were formerly the Peel (or Pil) Dem Crew, a name that derived from the Jamaican slang term 'peel dem', meaning to 'steal from them'. Some members of the PDC have claimed Islamic affiliation (calling themselves the Muslim Boys) while others have recently attempted to establish a new reputation as legitimate entrepreneurs, primarily in the music business. However, the gang continues to be associated with robberies and other acts of violence. In the 2008 season of the Channel 4 reality show *Big Brother*, one participant was evicted after she warned rival housemates of potential retribution from her 'gangster friends' – reported to have been a reference to PDC members.

> He didn't want to be like his dad had been. He was already trying to think beyond gangs. *True stories*. It was a phrase the PDC used a lot. It meant 'for real'.
>
> TIM PRITCHARD: *Street Boys* (2008)

Praed Street A road linking the EDGWARE ROAD in the east with PADDINGTON STATION in the west. It was laid out by the GRAND JUNCTION CANAL Company in the 1820s to serve PADDINGTON BASIN and named after the first company's chairman, William Praed. It contains St Mary's Hospital, where in 1928 Alexander Fleming discovered penicillin.

Pratts Bottom An expanded village situated on the London/Kent border, a mile (1.6 km) south of CHELSFIELD. The 14th-century name derives from the family of Stephen Prat and the low-lying location of the settlement, nestling in a valley at the foot of Rushmore Hill. With its terraces of weatherboarded and flint cottages and its ancient inn, Pratts Bottom has been called 'almost the archetype of English villages' but unsympathetic late 20th-century housebuilding has undermined its charm.

preach

preach at Tyburn cross, to Slang in the 16th century for 'to be hanged'. The allusion is to the last words permitted to the prospective suspendee at TYBURN. 'To preach on TOWER HILL' was a more exalted version of the same gallows humour.

Black Preacher, the See under BLACK.

Prince of Preachers See under PRINCE.

Pre-Raphaelite Brotherhood

A group of artists formed in London in 1848 consisting of William Holman Hunt, John Everett Millais, Dante Gabriel Rossetti and the sculptor Thomas Woolner. It was later joined by James Collinson, Walter Howell Deverell, Frederick Stephens and William Michael Rossetti. Ford Madox Brown and John Ruskin supported their movement, which espoused a closer study of nature than was practised by those tied to academical rules, and the study of the method and spirit of the artists before ('pre') Raphael (1483–1520). Hence the name. Nevertheless, their works contained much artificiality of literary origins. The group was attacked by many artists and critics, especially by Charles DICKENS in *Household Words* (1850). From this date Rossetti ceased to exhibit publicly. Their works are characterized by exaggerated attention to detail and a high degree of finish, and their earlier lives, at least, by bohemian activities. *See also* CLEVELAND STREET.

Press Yard An enclosed space that lay between NEWGATE PRISON and the OLD BAILEY, in which alleged criminals were pressed to death if they refused to enter a plea at their trial. The prisoner would be spread-eagled on the bare earth with increasingly heavy weights of iron or stone laid upon his body and left there until he answered the charge or died. The principal reason for submitting to the torture of *peine forte et dure* was to prevent one's property being forfeited to the Crown, as it would be if a defendant charged with a hanging offence entered a guilty plea or was found guilty. The practice continued into the 18th century, but was by then used very rarely.

The yard was also used for other punishments, such as whipping, and as an exercise ground for the condemned.

> In days gone by, sir, this is where the prisoners was pressed. They was squashed, sir. Weighed down by stones, sir, to persuade them to tell the truth. We don't do it any longer, sir, more's the pity, and as a consequence they lies like India rugs, sir, like India rugs.
>
> BERNARD CORNWELL: *Gallows Thief* (2001)

Preston A comfortable, multi-ethnic corner of North WEMBLEY, south-east of KENTON. The name, which meant 'priest's farmstead', is not widely used locally. Domesday Book recorded the presence of a landowning priest in the district. John Lyon, the yeoman who founded HARROW SCHOOL, lived at Preston in the 16th century and bequeathed his farm to provide funds for the upkeep of the school.

pretty

Pretty Bessee and the London Merchant An alternative title of the ballad better known as the BLIND BEGGAR OF BEDNALL GREEN.

Pretty Polly Perkins of Paddington Green A Victorian MUSIC HALL song (1864) that became a big hit before the First World War. Harry Clifton (1832–72) is said to have been inspired to write the song by a real girl called Annette Perkins, who may have lived in Albert (later Consort) Street, a former cul-de-sac off the HARROW ROAD south of the green.

> She was as beautiful as a butterfly and proud as a queen,
> Was pretty little Polly Perkins of Paddington Green.

Pride of North London An honorary footballing accolade claimed for their clubs by supporters of both TOTTENHAM HOTSPUR FC and ARSENAL FC. Bob Goodwin's book *The Pride of North London* (1997) chronicles the pair's derby matches. The term has also been applied to the statue better known as the NAKED LADY.

prime

Prime Meridian *See* GREENWICH MERIDIAN.

Prime Minister of Mirth The billboard byname of the entertainer George Robey (originally George Edward Wade) (1869–1954), given when he was well established in his career. The analogy is perhaps not so much with a political prime minister as with a person supremely skilled in ministering (i.e. providing) laughter. Robey was born in HERNE HILL and got his first break at the Royal Aquarium (*see the* AQ). Unlike many stars of the London MUSIC HALLS, his stage persona was decidedly middle class rather than COCKNEY. He was knighted in the year of his death.

Prime Suspect A groundbreaking ITV crime drama created by Lynda La Plante (b.1946) that ran for six short series between 1991 and 2006. It starred CHISWICK-born Helen Mirren (b.1945) as Jane Tennison, a METROPOLITAN POLICE CID officer leading a team of murder detectives who often manifested resistance to her authority. The series was acclaimed for its scripts, realism and acting, especially that of Mirren, whose multifaceted performances won her several BAFTA and Emmy awards.

Primrose Hill A delightful vantage point and its expensive residential surroundings, situated immediately north of REGENT'S PARK. The woodland here was granted to Eton College by Henry VI (r.1422–61) at a time when the name Primrose Hill was first coming into use. The hill was cleared of trees in the mid-17th century and remained as farmland until the arrival of the railway, when both the college and the neighbouring landowner, Lord Southampton, seized the opportunity to sell building plots. St Mark's Church was begun in 1851, and a station opened in the same year, under the name Hampstead Road (later CHALK FARM, and ultimately Primrose Hill). Shortly afterwards Chalcot Square was laid out with STUCCOED Italianate villas, while its central garden was planted with acacia trees. The Crown acquired the summit of the hill for public use, granting the college some land near Windsor in exchange. Primrose Hill Road was built in the 1870s to improve access to the college estate. By 1900 the present built environment was almost complete. The sightlines from Primrose Hill towards ST PAUL'S Cathedral and the PALACE OF WESTMINSTER are among a handful of officially designated strategic views that are safeguarded from inappropriate development. Primrose Hill station closed in 1992.

Sylvia Plath wrote her autobiographical novel *The Bell Jar* (1963) while living in Chalcot Square. The poet W.B. Yeats and writers Alan Bennett,

Kingsley Amis and Martin Amis are among other literati who have lived locally.

> The fields from Islington to Marybone,
> To Primrose Hill and Saint John's Wood
> Were builded over with pillars of gold;
> And there Jerusalem's pillars stood.
>
> WILLIAM BLAKE: 'Jerusalem' (1815)

prince

Prince and Prophet of the Hebrews *See* NEPHEW OF THE ALMIGHTY.

Prince of Perfumers A nickname bestowed upon the French cosmetician Eugène Rimmel (1820–87). Having served an apprenticeship in the BOND STREET perfumery managed by his father, he began his own business in 1834, at the age of 14. Among his innovations in fragrances, healthcare and cosmetics, Rimmel's mascara gained such fame that the brand name became synonymous with that eyelash adornment in some countries. The House of Rimmel is now part of the German-owned, American-based group Coty Inc. However, the company continues to place great emphasis on Rimmel's London origins and claims that the city remains 'a constant source of inspiration' for its range.

> And sweet the perfumes breathed from
> Rimmel's shop,
> And sweet the mushroom on manurèd leas;
> And sweet the turnip-lantern on a mop,
> And sweet the cheerful sign of the 'Cross Keys;'
>
> *Punch* (29 October 1881)

Prince of Preachers The sobriquet of Charles Spurgeon (1834–92), London's greatest preacher of his day, noted for the good-humoured eloquence with which he proclaimed the Baptist faith. At the age of 20 he became pastor of New Park Street Chapel, in SOUTHWARK, where he reversed a decline in its fortunes to the extent that services had to be switched to EXETER HALL and Surrey Music Hall, where the congregations were said to number in excess of 10,000. One of his sermons, concerning baptismal regeneration, sold 200,000 copies. In 1861 Spurgeon's ministry moved permanently to the newly constructed METROPOLITAN TABERNACLE. The Baptist educational institution that he established was renamed Spurgeon's College on its relocation to South NORWOOD in 1923. He also founded an orphanage in STOCKWELL that has since evolved

into the Northamptonshire-based international childcare charity Spurgeons.

Prince of Purpoole The sovereign of an imaginary kingdom within GRAY'S INN, who intermittently reigned over Christmas festivities held there in the late 16th and early 17th centuries. Gray's Inn occupies the approximate site of the ancient manor house of Purpoole. An account of the revels of 1594/5 was published in 1688 with the following lengthy title, probably reprinted from the original programme:

> Gesta Grayorum; or the History of the high
> and mighty Prince Henry, Prince of Purpoole,
> Archduke of Stapulia and Bernardia [Staple
> and Barnard's Inns], Duke of High and Nether
> Holborn, Marquess of St Giles and Tottenham,
> Count Palatine of Bloomsbury and Clerkenwell,
> Great Lord of the Cantons of Islington, Kentish
> Town, Paddington and Knightsbridge, Knight
> and Sovereign of the most heroical order of the
> Helmet, who reigned and died A.D. 1594.

During that season the Prince and his retinue also performed before Elizabeth I at GREENWICH. On one of the nights at Gray's Inn an organizational failure forced the students to call in a company of 'common players' and it seems that their play may have been *The Comedy of Errors*, with SHAKESPEARE among the cast.

Prince Regent A DOCKLANDS LIGHT RAILWAY station situated east of the EXCEL exhibition centre. Unlike the other royally associated stations in the area, Prince Regent is not named after a dock but after the road that runs northward from here to PLAISTOW[1]. The route was in existence from the late Middle Ages and was formerly Trinity Marsh Lane, then Prince Regent's Lane in the 19th and early 20th centuries and is now Prince Regent Lane.

Princes in the Tower The boy king Edward V and his younger brother Richard, Duke of York, who were lodged in the TOWER OF LONDON (May and June 1483), after which their uncle Richard, Duke of Gloucester, assumed the crown as Richard III. The princes disappeared at this time and are generally presumed to have been murdered by their uncle, but there is no conclusive evidence. Bones found during excavations near the WHITE TOWER in 1674 were transferred to WESTMINSTER ABBEY. In 1933 experts proclaimed them to be bones of children of 12 or 13, the very ages of the princes.

princess

Princess Alice A pleasure steamer named in honour of Queen Victoria's second daughter (1843–78). Following an excursion to Gravesend on the evening of 3 September 1878 the boat collided with a Newcastle collier, the *Bywell Castle*, at GALLIONS REACH. The *Princess Alice* sank and more than 600 died, the greatest loss of life in a single event in London's recorded history. A memorial was erected in WOOLWICH cemetery, funded with the proceeds of a national appeal.

> Oh! weep for the fate that befell the gay,
> For the young who too early died,
> For manhood and beauty swept away
> By that cold, unpitying tide!
>
> WILLIAM DIGBY SEYMOUR: 'The Foundering of The Princess Alice' (1878)

Princess Diana memorial fountain An oval water feature in the south-west corner of HYDE PARK, commemorating the life of Diana, Princess of Wales (1961–97). Designed by Kathryn Gustafson (b.1951) and constructed from Cornish granite, it was opened by Her Majesty the Queen in 2004. The fountain attracts around one million visitors every year. A playground in KENSINGTON GARDENS is also dedicated to the princess's memory, as is a 7-mile (11-km) memorial walk through Kensington Gardens, Hyde Park, GREEN PARK and ST JAMES'S PARK.

Princess of Kensington, A A light opera (1903) by Sir Edward German, with a libretto by Basil Hood, based on Thomas Tickell's poem 'Kensington Garden' (1722). It failed to live up to the considerable success of its predecessor, *Merrie England* (1902). *See also* KENNA.

Princess Puffer An old hag and opium addict who runs the EAST END opium den frequented by Mr John Jasper in Charles DICKENS's *The Mystery of Edwin Drood* (1870).

Printer's Devil A pub in FETTER LANE that closed in 2008. It was formerly the Black Horse and 'Printer's Devil' (slang for a printer's apprentice) was originally a nickname bestowed upon it owing to its popularity with FLEET STREET printworkers and subeditors.

Printing House Square Often used as synonymous with *The Times* newspaper, which was produced there from its inception until 1974. The paper began in 1785 as the *Daily Universal Register*, which became *The Times* in 1788. Print-

ing House Square was at BLACKFRIARS and was earlier the site of the King's Printing House.

Priory, The London's oldest private psychiatric hospital and the UK's best-known celebrity rehabilitation clinic, situated on Priory Lane, ROEHAMPTON. The Priory was built in 1811 as a private home and converted into a hospital in 1872. It was acquired in 1980 by a US healthcare company that went on to build a network of similar hospitals, all branded 'Priory', as well as secure units and specialist education facilities. The Priory Group has two other hospitals in London, at SOUTHGATE and HAYES[1]. The Royal Bank of Scotland is presently the group's main shareholder.

Profumo Affair Perhaps the most extensive political scandal in Britain in the postwar years takes its name from the Conservative politician John Profumo (1915–2006), secretary of state for war under Harold Macmillan. Rumours began circulating that he was consorting with the UXBRIDGE-born model and SOHO showgirl, Christine Keeler (b.1942), mistress of the Soviet assistant naval attaché, Yevgeny Ivanov (1926–94). In March 1963 Profumo assured the House of Commons that there was no truth in the allegation, but three months later he confessed that he had lied and resigned his seat. The doubts cast upon the efficiency of the security service almost resulted in the downfall of the government. However, in July 1963 Macmillan commented:

> I was determined that no British government should be brought down by the action of two tarts.
>
> quoted in ANTHONY SAMPSON: *Macmillan* (1967)

The other 'tart' was Keeler's colleague, Mandy Rice-Davies (b.1944). Profumo retired from public life, and became a voluntary worker at Toynbee Hall, a social-outreach centre in Commercial Street, SPITALFIELDS.

Promiscuity Hill A modern nickname for PRIMROSE HILL, prompted by rumours of wife-swapping among its A-list celebrity residents, not including the racing pundit John McCririck, who complained to the HAM AND HIGH in July 2006 that he did not know where the alleged orgies were taking place.

It is said you are never more than ten feet away

from a swinger in London, and in Primrose Hill it seems they are within even easier grasp. If the gossip columns are to be believed (and I believe very little else), all the celebrities in 'Promiscuity Hill' have been at it.

ANNALISA BARBIERI, in the *New Statesman* (7 February 2005)

Proms A summer season of concerts organized and broadcast by the BBC. The name derives from 'promenade concerts', at which some of the audience stand in an open area of the concert room floor. They date back to the days of pleasure gardens such as VAUXHALL and RANELAGH. JULLIEN'S CONCERTS were the first such entertainments to be held in the WEST END. In 1895 Sir Henry Wood (1869–1944) began the Promenade Concerts at the Queen's Hall, Langham Place, which he conducted for over half a century and which became a regular feature of London life. In 1927 the BBC took over the Proms' management from Chappell's. The destruction of the hall by enemy action in 1941 caused a break in the concerts but they were renewed at the ALBERT HALL. The popular high point of the annual series is the LAST NIGHT OF THE PROMS.

Prospect of Whitby An antiquated public house situated on Wapping Wall in SHADWELL. Its predecessor, the Devil's Tavern, dated from the early 16th century. The pub was rebuilt in the late 18th century following a fire in which only the original stone floor survived and its present name derives from the *Prospect*, a Whitby-registered collier that used regularly to moor nearby. Antique fixtures and fittings have been imported from other sites in a (highly successful) bid to enhance the Prospect of Whitby's tourist appeal.

Protein Man The sobriquet of Stanley Green (1915–93), of NORTHOLT, who for much of the late 20th century daily walked the streets of the WEST END, especially OXFORD STREET, purveying 'protein wisdom'. His particular concern was the supposed role of surplus protein in intensifying carnal desire. He carried a placard advising 'Less passion from less protein' and retailed a hand-printed leaflet entitled 'Eight Passion Proteins with Care'. On his death, the MUSEUM OF LONDON acquired his placards and a set of all the editions of his pamphlet (of which he is said to have printed 87,000) for its 'Londoners' collection.

For twenty-five years, crowds swirled about him, almost oblivious of his presence, engaged only in their usual uproar.

PETER ACKROYD: *London: The Biography* (2000)

public

public house signs Among those with specific relevance to London are:

BAG OF NAILS

Bell Savage: *see* BELLE SAUVAGE

Bolt in Tun: the punning heraldic badge of Prior Bolton, last of the clerical rulers of St Bartholomew's before the reformation

CASE IS ALTERED

Devil: *see* GO TO THE DEVIL

DIRTY DICK'S

King LUD

LAMB AND FLAG

MAN WITH A LOAD OF MISCHIEF

Moon under Water: The name chosen by George Orwell for his ideal English pub, in an article published in the *Evening Standard* in 1947

Only Running Footman: from the liveried servant who used to run before the nobleman's carriage to clear people from its path

Queen Victoria: *see* EASTENDERS

Royal Oak: a reference to Charles II, who hid in an oak tree after his defeat at the Battle of Worcester in 1651; *see also* OAK APPLE DAY

Swan and Harp: *see* GOOSE AND GRIDIRON

SWAN WITH TWO NECKS

TABARD

Three Horseshoes: the arms of the Worshipful Company of Farriers

Three Tuns: a reference to the arms of both the Worshipful Company of Vintners and the Worshipful Company of Brewers

Two Chairmen: found in the neighbourhood of fashionable quarters when sedan chairs were in vogue

Wheatsheaf: found in many coats of arms, including that of the Brewers' Company

White Horse: a widespread heraldic symbol, occurring in many coats of arms, including those of many London guilds; *see also the* SLOANY PONY

public school The schools so designated are in fact private (fee-paying) and independent. They came to be so called in the 18th century when the reputation of grammar schools spread beyond their immediate neighbourhood and they began taking resident students from elsewhere.

They were thus public, or open to all, and not simply local.

Among the oldest public schools founded in London, with their years of foundation, are:

ST PAUL'S SCHOOL (1509)

WESTMINSTER SCHOOL (1560)

Merchant Taylors' School, now in Hertfordshire (1560)

HIGHGATE SCHOOL (1565)

HARROW SCHOOL (1571)

Charterhouse School, now in Surrey (1611)

DULWICH COLLEGE (1619)

Most public schools, although originally founded as boys' schools, are now co-educational, or at least take girls in the sixth form. London's oldest girls' public schools include:

Lady Eleanor Holles School (1711)

James Allen's Girls' School (1741)

St Margaret's School, now in Hertfordshire (1749)

Royal Masonic School, now in Hertfordshire (1788)

pudding

Pudding Lane A street in the CITY of London, just to the east of LONDON BRIDGE, running from EASTCHEAP in the north towards Lower Thames Street in the south (in former times it led right down to the THAMES). In Middle English 'pudding' meant 'bowels, entrails, guts' and the lane's name probably arose because it was the route along which the butchers of Eastcheap meat market transported unwanted offal down to the river for loading on to the dung barges. Alternatively, hogs' puddings may have been made at butchers' scalding houses here. The GREAT FIRE OF LONDON began in Farryner's baking shop in Pudding Lane on 2 September 1666.

Pudding Mill River One of the BOW back rivers, which are minor tributaries of the River LEA. The mill that gave its name to the river and to Pudding Mill Lane was wind-driven, unlike its many water-powered neighbours. The history of the mills in this area is somewhat uncertain but the Pudding Mill was probably named because of its shape and was demolished during the first half of the 19th century.

Puddle Dock A street in the CITY of London, just to the east of BLACKFRIARS BRIDGE, running from Queen Victoria Street in the north to Upper Thames Street in the south. The 'puddle' was a former small inlet on the site with wharfage facilities. *See also the* MERMAID THEATRE.

On the Banks of the River Thames, are the Wharfs of Puddle Dock, used for a Laystall for the Soil of the Streets; and much frequented by Barges and Lighters, for taking the same away.

JOHN STRYPE: *Stow's Survey of London* (1720)

Punch

Punch or **The London Charivari** A satirical humorous weekly paper, named after Mr Punch, who naturally featured prominently on the cover design for very many issues. It first appeared in July 1841 under the editorship of Mark Lemon (1809–70) and Henry Mayhew (1812–87). A falling circulation led to its closure in 1992. It was relaunched in 1996 by the owner of HARRODS, Mohamed Fayed, but it folded again in 2002.

Punch and Judy The children's entertainment seems to have been introduced into England c.1666, when an Italian puppeteer set up a booth at CHARING CROSS. He paid a small rent to the overseers of the parish of ST MARTIN-IN-THE-FIELDS, and was referred to as 'Punchinello' in their records.

punk rock

punk rock This rebellious musical genre of the second half of the 1970s was as focused on London as the beat music of the early 1960s was on Liverpool. It was influenced musically by New York's Ramones and aesthetically by a handful of iconoclastic fashion boutiques on the KING'S ROAD, especially Sex (later Seditionaries), a shop run by the entrepreneur Malcolm McLaren (1946–2010) and the designer Vivienne Westwood (b.1941). McLaren became manager of the SEX PISTOLS on their foundation in 1975 and that band's crude musicianship, anti-establishment lyrics and belligerent attitude proved inspirational to many who attended their early performances on the London art-school circuit, notably members of the CLASH and the Damned. The acceptable breadth of the term 'punk rock' has long been a matter of debate but others influenced by, if not encompassed within, the punk movement included Elvis Costello and the Attractions, the Jam and the Stranglers. The latter two bands were formed in SURREY but soon adopted London as their spiritual home. Only Manchester's Buzzcocks significantly intruded on London's dominance of the emerging scene. Other London-based punk bands included the Vibrators, the Ruts, Chelsea (which evolved into Generation X), the Slits, X-Ray Spex, Siouxsie and the Banshees (*see the* BROMLEY CONTINGENT), COCKNEY REJECTS and – at the outset of their career – ADAM AND THE ANTS.

Purley A moneyed 20th-century suburb located on the southern outskirts of CROYDON. In 1200 this was Pirlee, which most authorities suggest was 'the woodland clearing where the pear trees grow'. However, it has been credibly argued that the name may have been brought by an immigrant from Purley Magna, near Reading, who owned an estate in SANDERSTEAD. Until the 19th century this remained an inconsequential settlement consisting of Purley House (later Purley Bury) and a scattering of farmsteads. A waterworks was built on Brighton Road in 1901, when suburban growth was beginning in the hinterland of the railway lines. Purley expanded rapidly between the world wars, especially after the construction of Croydon's bypass, Purley Way, in 1928. From the 1960s office blocks were built on the arterial routes.

The politician John Horne Tooke (1736–1812) established his reputation with *The Diversions of Purley* (1782), his medley of etymology, grammar and politics, and Peter Ackroyd gave the same title to a book of poems (1987).

put

put on a Tyburn piccadill, to *See* TYBURN PICCADILL.

put the kibosh on, to *See* KIBOSH.

Putney FULHAM's counterpart on the south side of the THAMES, lying west of WANDSWORTH. Putney – the landing place of either the hawk (Old English *pyttel*) or a man called Putta – was Putelei in Domesday Book and Puttenhuthe in 1279. Its position on the Thames was the making of Putney as an early place of recreation and some commerce, with a busy ferry trade until the construction of the first PUTNEY BRIDGE. The railway arrived in 1844 and large estates soon began to be sold for building and market gardens and orchards were erased as Gothic and Italianate villas spread out from the High Street and up Putney Hill. Between the world wars, middle-class suburban expansion filled the remaining gaps between Putney and its neighbours, especially to the west. Putney's riverside does not have the industrial history of downstream districts, so there has been less opportunity for the construction of modern apartment blocks

and developers have instead turned their attentions inland. *See also the* BOAT RACE.

Putney Bridge A busy river crossing linking Putney and FULHAM, and the name of the station on its north side. In 1729 local master carpenter Thomas Philips completed the first permanent structure, to the design of Sir Jacob Ackworth, providing the only dry crossing of the THAMES between the CITY and KINGSTON. Sir Joseph Bazalgette built a new bridge in 1886 and this was widened in the 1930s. Putney Bridge station (originally Putney Bridge and Fulham) opened in 1880 as the terminus of the Metropolitan District Railway's newly extended WEST BROMPTON branch.

The writer Mary Wollstonecraft (1759–97) tried to drown herself by leaping from Putney Bridge one night in October 1795. WATERMEN pulled her unconscious from the river.

Putney Debates A series of debates held in St Mary's Church by the Parliamentarian Army Council in October 1647, during the Civil War, to discuss the 'Agreement of the People'. This was a document presented by the radical reformist LEVELLERS seeking a new social contract. The debates ended in deadlock.

Putney Heath The northern continuation of WIMBLEDON COMMON and, as a residential area, the southernmost part of Putney. It is said that when the Swedish botanist Linnaeus saw the golden bloom of the furze on Putney Heath, he fell on his knees thanking God for its beauty. The scientist David Hartley (1732–1813) built himself a house called Wildcroft in 1776, employing experimental techniques he had devised to prevent the spread of fire. His work is commemorated by an obelisk on the heath. Duels were fought on Putney Heath in the 18th and 19th centuries, including several between eminent politicians. The heath has woods, wilderness, grassland and five ponds.

The actress Sarah Siddons lived in a 'little nutshell' on Putney Heath in the late 18th century, possibly a cottage next to Bowling Green House, where William Pitt the Younger died in 1806. A more obscure former prime minister, Frederick Robinson, Viscount Goderich, died at his home in Putney Heath in 1859.

Putney Vale A micro-locality separating WIMBLEDON COMMON from RICHMOND PARK. The first significant structure in Putney Vale was the Halfway House, later the Bald Faced Stag, a public house established around 1650. The notorious highwayman Jerry ABERSHAW made the tavern the base for his operations from 1790 until 1795, when he was hanged. In 1912, working in the cellar of the disused Bald Faced Stag, racing car driver Kenelm Lee Guinness (1887–1937) developed a spark plug that could withstand very high engine temperatures. Its applicability to fast cars, motor cycles and aeroplanes made the invention an immediate success and KLG became the largest employer in the area, with over 1,400 workers in 1918. As well as making spark plugs and special engines, Kenelm Guinness built two world record-breaking cars at his ROBIN HOOD engineering works in Putney Vale. Malcolm Campbell reached 175 mph (282 kph) driving *Bluebird* on Pendine Sands in 1927. Two years later Henry Segrave achieved 231 mph (372 kph) with *Golden Arrow* at Daytona, Florida. Smith's Industries bought the company in 1927 and built a new factory just in time for the outbreak of the Second World War. That factory was demolished in 1989 and replaced by a supermarket, a burger bar and a petrol station.

P.W. Abney The nickname of a funereal style of hat that was fashionable in the closing years of the 19th century. It featured three black, upright ostrich feathers, reminiscent of the three feathers of the Prince of Wales's crest. *See also* ABNEY PARK.

Pye Corner or **Pie Corner** A former name for the junction of COCK LANE and GILTSPUR STREET, in SMITHFIELD. It may have derived from an inn sign depicting a magpie. This was the place where the authorities blew up houses in a successful bid to halt the GREAT FIRE OF LONDON. In SHAKESPEARE's *Henry IV, Part 2*, II, iv (*c.*1597), Falstaff is accused of continually going to Pye Corner 'to buy a saddle'. This could mean that he regularly purchased saddles of mutton or pork, or horses' saddles, which were readily available in the vicinity, but it probably refers to his patronage of the brothels for which Pye Corner and Cock Lane were once well known.

Pye Corner law An unwritten rule among certain men in Jacobean London. It decreed that, in the case of rivalry for a young woman's affections, the first to possess her carnally (possibly in return for a monetary consideration) should have the right to marry her.

> Two wooers for a wench were each at strife,
> Which should enjoy her to his wedded wife:
> Quoth th' one, she's mine, because I first her saw,
> She's mine, quoth th' other, by Pye Corner law;
> Where, sticking once a Prick on what you buy
> It's then your own, which no man must deny.
>
> HENRY PARROT: *Laquei ridiculosi*, 'Consuetudo, lex' (1613)

Pye Corner muse An old term for a writer of doggerel, who was inspired by little more than the odours of the cooks' stalls at that location.

Golden Boy of Pye Corner *See under* GOLDEN.

Pygmalion A play (1913) by George Bernard SHAW about a phonetician's campaign to transform Eliza DOOLITTLE, a roughly spoken COCKNEY flower girl, into a sophisticated society lady. She wants to improve her speech to work in a florist's; he accepts a wager from Colonel Pickering that he can thereby infiltrate her into polite society. Eliza later resents being remodelled into an automaton and having her feelings disregarded. She does not want Higgins's love but his respect. Her eventual rebellion is so devastating that by the end of the play she has asserted her right to live her own life and state the terms of any relationship. The play was the basis of the popular musical MY FAIR LADY (1956; film 1964). The title refers to Ovid's story of Pygmalion, the sculptor whose statue of a beautiful woman comes to life so that he can marry her. The inclusion of the word 'bloody' in the script, the first time it had been heard on the English stage, caused a sensation (*see* NOT BLOODY LIKELY).

Pyx *See* TRIAL OF THE PYX.

Quadrant, The The name given to the curved southern end of REGENT STREET, which describes a quarter-circle. It was designed by John Nash (1752–1835) in 1813, and when built had two Doric colonnades, the cast iron columns being made at the Carron ironworks, near Falkirk, Scotland. These were removed in 1848. The original buildings were demolished in 1928. Except for its listed structures, much of the Quadrant is presently undergoing redevelopment, which will continue until at least 2012.

quadriga A contraction of *quadrijugae* (Latin *quadri-*, 'four', and *jugum*, 'yoke'). In classical antiquity, a two-wheeled chariot drawn by four horses harnessed abreast. The WELLINGTON ARCH at HYDE PARK CORNER is surmounted by a fine bronze group, *Peace Descending on the Quadriga of War*, executed by Adrian Jones in 1912. The cost of the sculpture was met by Herbert Stern, 1st Baron Michelham (1851–1919), whose 11-year-old son Herman served as a model for the boy who pulls at the reins of the four horses harnessed to the quadriga as a huge figure of Peace descends upon them from heaven.

Quant, Mary An innovative and influential fashion designer (b.1934), especially during the 1960s. She was born in BLACKHEATH and studied illustration at GOLDSMITHS. In 1955 she opened a pioneering boutique, Bazaar, on the KING'S ROAD and added a second branch in KNIGHTSBRIDGE in 1957. Her bohemian, classless designs attracted a new generation who wanted to dress distinctively differently from their parents. In the mid-1960s she popularized the mini-skirt – the definitive fashion statement of SWINGING LONDON – and later in the decade invented hot pants. Quant built an international fashion business that from the 1980s focused on cosmetics and was acquired by her Japanese licensees in 2000. That company now also mar-

kets a clothing and accessories range in Japan called Mary Quant London. In 2009 the Royal Mail featured Quant's 'banana split' dress on a postage stamp, one of a set celebrating British design classics that also included PENGUIN BOOKS, the ROUTEMASTER bus and the LONDON UNDERGROUND MAP.

quarter flash and three parts foolish Formerly said of one whose showy appearance and urbane demeanour barely concealed his naivety. Later popular in Australia as a description of new immigrants, the phrase originated on the streets of London in the early 19th century.

> ... to use a current expression among the knowing ones, do not let it be said of you, sneeringly, that you are quarter flash, and three parts foolish! ... In flattering yourself that you are knowing, whisper into your own ear, and make an allowance that there are to be found in company persons as knowing as yourself, if not more knowing!
> PIERCE EGAN: *Life in London* (1821)

Quatermass and the Pit A BBC television series (1958–9) and a HAMMER FILM (1967), one of a sequence of sci-fi dramas written by Nigel Kneale (1922–2006) and featuring the scientist Professor Bernard Quatermass. The plot concerns the menacing presence of a buried alien spacecraft discovered during construction work in the fictional Hobbs Lane (in KNIGHTSBRIDGE in the TV series and NORTH KENSINGTON in the film).

queen
Queen Anne Churches *See* FIFTY NEW CHURCHES.
Queen Anne's footstool A name given to St John's Church, SMITH SQUARE, a fine specimen of baroque architecture by Thomas Archer, completed in 1728. There is an apocryphal story that

Queen Anne, when interviewing the architect, kicked over her footstool and said 'Make it like that', the four upturned legs representing the towers. In reality, the building began to settle during construction and to stabilize it a tower and lantern turret were added at each corner. Lord Chesterfield likened the church to an elephant thrown on its back with its four feet erect. It was burned out in 1742 and again in 1941, after which it was reopened in 1969 as a concert and lecture hall.

Queen Charlotte's Ball A royal ball first held in 1780 to raise funds for Queen Charlotte's Lying-in Hospital (now Queen Charlotte's and Chelsea Hospital). *See also the* LONDON SEASON.

Queen Mary's Gardens Formal gardens laid out within the Inner Circle of REGENT'S PARK in 1932 and named in honour of the queen consort of George V (r.1910–36). There are over 100 rose beds in Queen Mary's Gardens, each with between 150 and 225 rose bushes of many varieties and colours.

Queen Mary's Hospital Now a large community hospital, it was founded in ROEHAMPTON in 1915 to treat war casualties. The hospital pioneered the development of modern artificial limbs and the Battle of Britain pilot Douglas Bader had his legs fitted here. An entirely new hospital was built in the grounds of the old one in 2006 and maintains Queen Mary's reputation as a specialist centre for amputee rehabilitation.

Queen Mary, University of London A multifaculty college of the UNIVERSITY OF LONDON, based primarily in the EAST END. Its main campus at MILE END has evolved from the Victorian PEOPLE'S PALACE, a philanthropic scheme for the enlightenment and entertainment of EAST ENDERS. Queen Mary's medical and scientific departments are divided between WHITECHAPEL and the SMITHFIELD area, close to the ROYAL LONDON HOSPITAL and BART'S respectively. The college's law faculties are at LINCOLN'S INN FIELDS. In 1989 Queen Mary absorbed Westfield College, which had been founded in HAMPSTEAD in 1882 as a higher education institution for women.

Queen of Bohemia Formerly a disreputable public house on DRURY LANE, occupying part of Craven House, which had been the London home of William Craven, 1st Earl of Craven (1608–97). The pub was named after Elizabeth of Bohemia (1596–1662), Craven's mistress. She was also known as the Queen of Hearts, 'from her amiable character and engaging manners, even in her lowest estate', as Dr Brewer put it.

Queen of the Blues Elizabeth Montagu, née Robinson (1720–1800), was so called by Samuel JOHNSON from her leadership of the BLUE STOCKINGS.

Queen of the Costermongers A title arrogated by Mary Robinson (d.1884) of SOMERS TOWN. She began as a vendor of cats' meat and later made a fortune from loaning money to other COSTERMONGERS at 12.5 per cent weekly interest. In accordance with the conditions of her will, she was buried with sumptuous style in FINCHLEY cemetery.

> For the funeral she had arranged that the coffin should be carried by four men wearing white smocks, followed by twenty-four women wearing violet dresses and white aprons with feathers.
>
> JOHN RICHARDSON: *London & Its People* (1995)

Queen of the Forest The sobriquet given by Norwegian foresters to the spruce they select each year to become the TRAFALGAR SQUARE CHRISTMAS TREE.

Queen of the Music Hall or **Queen of the Halls** The sobriquet of the HOXTON-born singer Marie Lloyd (née Matilda Wood, 1870–1922). She first appeared at the EAGLE (1) tavern in the CITY ROAD and went on to achieve triumphant success in the London MUSIC HALLS, and later in the USA. Her act included many songs laced with double entendres, which she magnified with a repertoire of winks and naughty gestures that earned her the opprobrium of the moral guardians of the era. She collapsed on stage during a show at the EDMONTON Empire in October 1922 and died three days later. It has been estimated that 50–100,000 people lined the route of her funeral procession to HAMPSTEAD Cemetery. Jessie Wallace starred in a BBC dramatization of her turbulent life in 2007.

> The working man who went to the music hall and saw Marie Lloyd and joined in the chorus was himself performing part of the work of acting; he was engaged in that collaboration of the audience with the artist which is necessary in all art and most obviously in dramatic art.
>
> T.S. ELIOT, in *The Dial* (magazine) (December 1922)

Queen of the Suburbs EALING was at one time so called from the social status or genteel lifestyle of its residents. The sobriquet has also been applied to the equally salubrious SURBITON.

Queen's Club A private members' sports club situated on Palliser Road, BARONS COURT. Established in 1886, the Queen's Club claims to have been the first multi-purpose sports complex anywhere in the world. It is now best known for the pre-WIMBLEDON tennis championships held here every June, for many years sponsored by Stella Artois and from 2009 by the life insurance and pensions group Aegon. Queen's Club is the national headquarters for real tennis and rackets.

Queen's garden party See BUCKINGHAM PALACE GARDEN PARTY.

Queen's House See GREENWICH; NATIONAL MARITIME MUSEUM.

Queen's Park A residential district situated south-west of KILBURN. Its southern part was laid out from 1873 as the Queen's Park estate by the Artisans', Labourers' and General Dwellings Company on land acquired from All Souls College, Oxford. Queen Victoria opened the International Exhibition of the Royal Agricultural Society on land north of the railway line in 1879. The greensward that survives north of Harvist Road was a section of the showground and was opened to the public as Queen's Park in 1887. The park's immediate vicinity was built up over the following 25 years, much of it with generously proportioned detached and semi-detached houses.

Queens Park Rangers FC An association FOOTBALL club formed in 1882 by the old boys of Droop Street Board School. Originally called St Jude's, the club took its present name after a merger with Christchurch Rangers in 1886. QPR has played outside the QUEEN'S PARK neighbourhood for the majority of its existence, mostly at its present ground in Loftus Road, WHITE CITY. The club was in and out of top-flight football from the late 1960s to the mid-1990s, but was afterwards adversely affected by persistent financial problems. In 2007 three billionaires collectively assumed ownership of Queens Park Rangers, opening the way for a potential (but hitherto unrealized) foray into the upper echelons of the national game.

Queen Square Hermit Jeremy Bentham (1748–1832), the philosopher and father of Utilitarianism, who lived at No.1 Queen Square, BLOOMSBURY. His embalmed figure, seated and

fully dressed, is preserved at UNIVERSITY COLLEGE LONDON.

Queen's tobacco pipe A kiln at LONDON DOCKS for burning contraband goods. It functioned until 1891.

Queenhithe A small street in the CITY of London, leading down from Upper Thames Street to the north bank of the THAMES, upstream of SOUTHWARK BRIDGE. There was a harbourage here in Anglo-Saxon times (a charter of Alfred the Great (898) refers to it as *Ætheredes hyd*, 'Æthelred's harbour', probably from Alfred's son-in-law, who controlled London at that time), and up to the 15th century it was the most important dock in London, mainly handling corn and fish. By the early 12th century its name was Queenhithe, literally 'queen's wharf', signifying that it was the property of Queen Matilda (1100–35), first wife of Henry I, and in the later Middle Ages queens of England continued to exercise the right to charge tolls here. By the middle of the 16th century its name had been transferred to the street leading off it. The inlet where the harbour was can still be seen but the dock itself was demolished in 1971 and a hotel was built on the site, which was subsequently converted into an apartment block. *See also the* SINKING OF QUEEN ELEANOR.

In P.D. James's *Adam Dalgleish Mysteries* (1962 onwards), the eponymous SCOTLAND YARD detective lives in a Queenhithe flat.

Queensberry

Queensberry Rules The regulations governing boxing matches in which gloves were worn, formulated in 1867 by John G. Chambers (1843–83), founder of the FULHAM-based Amateur Athletic Club, and sponsored by the club's patron, John Sholto Douglas, 8th Marquess of Queensberry (1844–1900). They superseded the earlier London Prize Ring Rules.

William Douglas, 4th Duke of Queensberry *See* OLD Q.

Queensbury An interwar suburban creation situated south of LITTLE STANMORE. Although the Metropolitan Railway had begun its service to STANMORE at the end of 1932, it was two years before a station was added here, not just to encourage housebuilding but because so much growth had already taken place. The railway company ran a newspaper competition to devise a name for the station, and the winning entry played on the new town's proximity to KINGSBURY.

Queensway A central north-south axis of the BAYSWATER district, consisting mostly of 20th-century apartment blocks with shops and restaurants at street level. This was formerly Black Lion Lane, which ran from KENSINGTON to WESTBOURNE GREEN; an entrance to the north-western corner of KENSINGTON GARDENS is still called Black Lion Gate. The lane was a favourite ride of the young Princess Victoria and after her coronation it was renamed Queen's Road. This was changed to Queensway a century later to distinguish it from the many other Queen's Roads. By the 1890s a cosmopolitan variety of shops had lined the street and WHITELEY'S department store moved here from WESTBOURNE GROVE in 1911; it has since closed but the building survives. From the mid-1980s, an influx of wealthy Arabs to Bayswater brought a change in Queensway's character. With its Palestinian grocers, Egyptian newsagents, Persian cafés and Lebanese restaurants, modern Queensway has been called 'an oasis for London's Arab diaspora'.

queer

Queer Street The imaginary place where debtors, etc. live. It was first recorded in *Lexicon Balatronicum* (1811), an updated version of Francis Grose's *Dictionary of the Vulgar Tongue*, in which it was defined as 'Wrong. Improper. Contrary to one's wish.' There is no foundation for the claim that the term is a corruption of CAREY STREET, since the bankruptcy court was not established there until 1840. However, it is possible that the assonance of the real and fictitious street names contributed to the primary connotation of financial adversity that being in Queer Street later acquired.

> 'But,' resumed Darvil, helping himself to another slice of beef, 'you are in the wrong box – planted in Queer Street, as we say in London.'
>
> EDWARD BULWER-LYTTON: *Ernest Maltravers* (1837)

as queer as a clockwork orange *See under* AS.

quid Nowadays an almost universally understood informal word for a pound sterling, but formerly signifying a guinea. It is of obscure etymology but very probably originated among the London underclasses. It may ultimately come from Latin *quid*, 'what'.

> Ah, my pretty rogue! Pox o' the country, I say! Captain, captain, here! let me equip thee with a quid!
>
> THOMAS SHADWELL: *The Squire of Alsatia*, III, i (1688)

Quins The shortened name of HARLEQUINS Rugby Union and Harlequins Rugby League. Both clubs play at the Twickenham STOOP.

quit rent A rent formerly paid to the lord of a manor by freeholders and copyholders that was an acquittal of all other services. It is nowadays a token or nominal rent. The ancient ceremony of rendering the quit rent service due to the Crown by the CORPORATION OF LONDON is still held before the KING'S or QUEEN'S REMEMBRANCER every October at the ROYAL COURTS OF JUSTICE. The services are rendered for two holdings, one in Shropshire and the other a forge that formerly lay south of ST CLEMENT DANES. The latter service is performed by the CITY comptroller, who produces to the remembrancer 6 large horseshoes and 61 nails, which must be counted out in court before the remembrancer pronounces 'Good service'. The horseshoes date from 1361, when the tenant of the forge was permitted to pay 18 pence per year provided she had these shoes made for use each year. They may be the oldest set of horseshoes in existence. The remembrancer also receives the newly elected sheriffs of the City of London at the quit rents ceremony and gives each of them their warrant of approbation from the Queen.

Quo Vadis A restaurant in Dean Street, SOHO, founded in 1926 by Peppino Leoni in premises formerly occupied by Karl Marx. It began as a seven-table Italian restaurant in one room, and expanded to fill four adjacent townhouses, now all knocked together. Over the decades it became a notable fixture on the Soho scene. After changing hands a number of times the establishment was acquired in 2007 by the brothers Sam and Eddie Hart, who reinvented it as a traditional British restaurant and a private members' club. Marx's attic rooms comprise the Harts' offices.

> While the food was Italian, it was a somewhat anglicized version. 'He was a shameless self-publicist and always entertaining Lord and Lady Muck,' Eddie Hart says. 'Leoni would have

had no qualms about serving shepherd's pie if someone had wanted it.'

Caterer and Hotelkeeper (5 June 2008)

quoz! A one-word catchphrase that was on every common Londoner's lips in the late 18th and early 19th centuries. The *Oxford English Dictionary* says it was 'used as ejaculation or retort, to express incredulity, contempt, etc.' Its appeal has been compared with that of the recently popular exclamation 'not!' – although 'quoz!' was usually directed at another speaker, rather than jokily cancelling one's own false words.

> Many years ago the favourite phrase (for, though but a monosyllable, it was a phrase in itself) was Quoz.

CHARLES MACKAY: *Memoirs of Extraordinary Popular Delusions and the Madness of Crowds* (1841)

Q-Whitehall A secret government communications facility in tunnels 100 feet (30m) beneath WHITEHALL, extending, according to some reports, as far north as HOLBORN. Its size and scope have long fascinated investigative journalists and conspiracy theorists, and surface evidence is keenly sought: particular favourites are an extractor fan outside the INSTITUTE OF CONTEMPORARY ARTS in the MALL, with no obvious internal connection, and a mysterious doorway at the foot of the nearby Duke of York's Steps, both of which have been linked with a purported tunnel extension from Whitehall to BUCKINGHAM PALACE.

R

rabbit

rabbit (and pork) 'Talk' in COCKNEY RHYMING SLANG, used either as a verb or noun. A relatively modern 'classic' of the argot, it was first recorded in 1941. The prepositional verb 'to rabbit on about [something]' is especially familiar, well beyond the confines of the metropolis.

You won't stop talking,
Why don't you give it a rest?
You got more rabbit than Sainsbury's,
It's time you got it off your chest.

CHARLES HODGES and DAVID PEACOCK: 'Rabbit' (song by Chas & Dave) (1979)

rabbit pie shifter From around 1870 to 1920 the term was used to refer to an officer of the MET-ROPOLITAN POLICE. A rabbit pie was a prostitute, which in turn derived from an earlier sense of the word 'rabbit': the male member. Policemen were dismissively characterized as having little better to do than move harlots along.

Rachmanism The exploitation and intimidation of tenants by unscrupulous landlords. The name comes from that of Peter Rachman (1919–62), a Polish immigrant who bought his first house in the early 1950s, on St Stephen's Gardens, WESTBOURNE PARK. He went on to acquire a portfolio of properties throughout PADDINGTON, NOTTING HILL and NORTH KENSINGTON, forcing out sitting tenants and instead targeting newly arrived immigrants from the Caribbean, whose difficulties in finding accommodation made them easier to exploit. His activities came to light in the early 1960s and his name was brought to public attention after his death, from a former connection with the women in the PROFUMO AFFAIR.

RADA The Royal Academy of Dramatic Art, Britain's leading drama school. It was founded in 1904 by the actor Sir Herbert Beerbohm Tree (1852–1917) in the dome of His Majesty's Theatre in the HAYMARKET, but later that year was transferred to the Georgian house in GOWER STREET that it has occupied ever since. It was granted a royal charter by George V in 1920 and for many years was run by Sir Kenneth Barnes (1878–1957), under whom its theatre, the Vanbrugh, named after his sisters, the actresses Irene (1872–1949) and Violet (1867–1942) Vanbrugh, was built to replace an earlier one, destroyed in the BLITZ. Now called the Jerwood Vanbrugh Theatre, it was rebuilt again in 2000.

raddie A slang term for an Italian living in London, first recorded in 1938. According to the *Concise New Partridge Dictionary of Slang and Unconventional English* (2008) it derives from 'the raddled-seeming complexion of some Italians compared to that of a pale Londoner' and was originally used of Italian families living in CLERKENWELL. The word has declined as much in familiarity as has the Italian population of Clerkenwell.

RAF

RAF Chessington *See* CHESSINGTON.
RAF Church *See* ST CLEMENT DANES.
RAF Hendon *See the* ROYAL AIR FORCE MUSEUM.
RAF Hornchurch *See* HORNCHURCH.
RAF Kenley *See* KENLEY AERODROME.
RAF Northolt See NORTHOLT AERODROME.

rag

Rag, The The nickname of the Army and Navy CLUB, in PALL MALL. It is said to have originated in the remark of a dissatisfied member, one Captain William Duff of the 23rd Fusiliers, who grumpily described the refreshment available there as 'rag and famish'. Another suggestion is that the 'rag' is the flag.

Rag Fair A sprawling marketplace for cheap and second-hand clothes that operated in and around what is now Royal Mint Street, formerly Rosemary Lane, a western extension of CABLE STREET near the TOWER OF LONDON. It was at its height in the 18th century but continued until railway depots and warehouses annexed its territory following the creation of ST KATHARINE DOCKS.

> ... we bought each of us a pair of Rag-Fair stockings in the first place for 5d. Not 5d a pair, but 5d together, and good stockings they were too, much above our wear I assure you.
>
> DANIEL DEFOE: *Colonel Jack* (1722)

Ragged School Museum A museum of Victorian childhood, located on Copperfield Road in MILE END. Originally a lime juice storage facility beside the REGENT'S CANAL, Dr Thomas BARNARDO transformed it in 1868 to become the largest RAGGED SCHOOL in London. It closed in 1908 and reopened as a museum in 1990.

ragged schools Charitably funded schools (often of a Christian character) for the education of destitute children, originated by John Pounds (1766–1839), a Portsmouth shoemaker, about 1818. London's first ragged school was founded in 1839 in the DEVIL'S ACRE. Another opened in FIELD LANE in the early 1840s. Ragged Sunday schools, day schools and evening schools made an important contribution to the welfare of the homeless young of 19th-century London and elsewhere. The philanthropic 7th Earl of Shaftesbury was a notable benefactor.

Railway Cuttings *See* HANCOCK'S HALF HOUR.

rainbow

Rainbow Corner In the Second World War the LYONS' CORNER HOUSE in SHAFTESBURY AVENUE (opposite the rear of the TROCADERO) was taken over and turned into a large café and lounge for American servicemen under this name, and it became a general meeting place for Americans in London. The name was in reference to the 42nd Infantry Division of the US Army, nicknamed the Rainbow, and the rainbow in the insignia of SHAEF (Supreme Headquarters Allied Expeditionary Forces).

Rainbow Theatre *See the* FINSBURY PARK ASTORIA.

Rainham An industrial and residential district situated 3 miles (5 km) south of HORNCHURCH. The name may be a corruption of Old English

Reoginga-ham, possibly meaning 'settlement of the ruling people'. Rainham's medieval wharf was improved in the late 1710s by its owner, Captain John Harle, who went on to build Rainham Hall a decade later. This compact, elegant house is now a National Trust property.

rake

Rake of Piccadilly *See* OLD Q.

Rake's Progress, A A 'moral narrative' painted in 1733–5 by William HOGARTH (1697–1764), and subsequently made into popular engravings. The original canvases are on display in the SOANE MUSEUM. The narrative formed the basis of a 'neoclassical' opera (1951) by Igor Stravinsky (1882–1971), with a libretto by W.H. Auden and Chester Kallmann. The story concerns the decline and fall of one Tom Rakewell, who deserts Anne Trulove for the delights of London in the company of Nick Shadow, who turns out to be the Devil. Tom ends up in BEDLAM, and the moral of the tale is: 'For idle hearts and hands and minds the Devil finds a work to do.'

Ralph Roister Doister The name of the earliest English comedy on classical lines, so called from its chief character. It probably appeared in 1552 or 1553 and was written by Nicholas Udall, headmaster of Eton (1534–41) and headmaster of WESTMINSTER SCHOOL (1555–6). The play is presumed to be set in London.

Rambert Dance Company The oldest existing British ballet company arose from the dance studio opened in 1920 by Marie Rambert (1888–1982), a Polish-born dancer whose original name was Cyvia Rambam. By 1931 regular Saturday matinée performances were being given under the name of the Ballet Club, and in 1934 this became the Ballet Rambert. Its base was the minute Mercury Theatre in NOTTING HILL, a former Victorian school building, and this remained its home until the 1960s. Early choreographers were Frederick Ashton (1904–88) and Antony Tudor (1908–87). Rambert herself remained director until 1966. The company adopted its present name in 1987, after Richard Alston became director. Of all the established London dance companies the Rambert has consistently enjoyed a progressive and young-minded public. The company plans to move from its present base in CHISWICK to Doon Street, SOUTH BANK, when sufficient funds have been raised for the construction of new studios.

Ranelagh An old place of amusement on the site that now forms part of the grounds of CHELSEA ROYAL HOSPITAL. It was named after Richard Jones, 1st Earl of Ranelagh (1641–1712), who built a house and laid out gardens there in 1690. From 1742 to 1803 Ranelagh rivalled VAUXHALL GARDENS for concerts, masquerades and the like. A notable feature was the Rotunda, which was built in 1742 and was not unlike the ALBERT HALL in design. It was 185 feet (56m) across with numerous boxes in which refreshments were served, while the brightly lit floor formed a thronged promenade. There was also a Venetian pavilion in the centre of a lake. Unlike many such places of amusement, Ranelagh managed to keep out hoi polloi and remained a playground of the rich and titled until the Napoleonic Wars.

The Ranelagh Club was established in 1894 at BARN ELMS to provide facilities for polo, tennis, golf and other sports.

ranger
Ranger's House *See* GREENWICH PARK.
Sloane ranger *See under* SLOANE.

Raquel Welch 'Belch' in modern rhyming slang, from the American film star (b.1940). The term is used both as a verb and noun and was probably coined soon after the release of Hammer Films' *One Million Years BC* (1966), in which the actress played a memorable leading role as a cavewoman.

Rare Ben The inscription on the tomb of Ben Jonson (1573–1637), the dramatist, in the north nave aisle of WESTMINSTER ABBEY. 'O rare Ben Jonson', was, says John Aubrey, 'done at the charge of Jack Young (afterwards knighted), who, walking there when the grave was covering, gave the fellow eighteen pence to cut it.' 'Rare' here is Latin *rarus*, 'uncommon', 'remarkable'.

raspberry Nowadays a term for what *The Chambers Dictionary* calls 'a noise produced by blowing hard with the tongue between the lips' – a type of bilabial trill. This derives from its original COCKNEY RHYMING SLANG meaning: a fart, via 'raspberry tart'. *See also the* PHANTOM RASPBERRY BLOWER OF OLD LONDON TOWN.
raspberry ripple 'Cripple' in modern rhyming slang, from the ice cream flavour. As 'cripple' is

now considered an insensitive term for someone with a physical impairment, the same must be concluded of the rhyming slang equivalent. However, in the latter half of the 1990s disability campaigners organized the Raspberry Ripple Awards to highlight good and bad portrayals of disabled people in the media in a light-hearted way.

'Raspberry ripple' has also been used to mean 'nipple'.

rat
rat and mouse 'House' in COCKNEY RHYMING SLANG, but the plural means 'dice'. The Rat and Mouse is a blog-style website devoted to London's domestic property market, online at www.theratandmouse.co.uk since 2004.
rat, cat and dog

The Cat, the Rat, and Lovell our dog,
Rule all England under a hog.

These lines were affixed to the door of ST PAUL'S and other places in the CITY of London in 1484 at the instigation of William Collingbourne (or Colyngbourne), a Wiltshire gentleman of Edward IV's household, who may have been an agent for Henry Tudor (later Henry VII). For this deed, according to the *Great Chronicle of London*, 'he was drawn unto the Tower Hill and there full cruelly put to death, at first hanged and straight cut down and ripped, and his bowels cast into the fire'. The rhyme implied that the kingdom was ruled by Francis, Viscount Lovell, whose crest was a dog, Sir Richard Ratcliffe, the Rat, and Sir William Catesby, Speaker of the House of Commons, the Cat. The Hog was the white boar or cognizance of Richard III.

Ratcliff or **Ratcliffe** Although the name is still shown on some maps, this historic locality has become lost in LIMEHOUSE. It was situated at the point where, today, DOCKLANDS-bound traffic disappears below ground into the Limehouse Link tunnel. The hamlet first developed around the junction of two Roman roads as they converged on LONDINIUM. Ratcliff had a dock as early as the 14th century and there are records of timber deliveries from SURREY and the conscription of craftsmen from East Anglia to build ships for the king in the 1350s. Sir Hugh Willoughby sailed from Ratcliff in 1553 on an expedition that opened the trade route to Moscow. In 1576 Martin Frobisher departed on the first of his voyages in search of the north-west passage to Asia.

Ratcliff Highway The road that led from Ratcliff toward the CITY, now simply called the Highway. It was a notorious haunt for London's low life in the 18th and 19th centuries. 'Ratcliff Highway' is the title of a much-recorded shanty-style folk song that tells of a seaman's adventures ashore. In some versions the young doxies of Ratcliff relieve him of all his money; in others his conduct is the more perfidious.

> So come all you bold young sailors,
> That ramble down Ratcliff Highway,
> If you chance to pop into a gin-shop,
> Beware, lads, how long you do stay.

Ratcliff Highway murders A notorious case in which two entire households were brutally slain within the space of a few days in December 1811. The prime suspect hanged himself while awaiting trial.

raven

Ravenmaster or **Raven Master** The keeper of the RAVENS OF THE TOWER.

Raven's Ait A narrow islet in the THAMES lying between HAMPTON COURT PARK and south-west KINGSTON UPON THAMES. The Kingston Rowing Club, founded in 1858, was based here and held annual regattas. The AIT continues to be used as a base for sailing, canoeing and rowing. Kingston council acquired Raven's Ait in 1996 and leases it to a conference and banqueting business that attracts a regular stream of wedding parties.

ravens of the Tower The resident corvids of the TOWER OF LONDON. According to a legend of obscure provenance, the Tower and the kingdom will fall if they ever leave. One version has it that the head of the medieval Celtic warrior Brân (a name that means 'crow' or 'raven') lies buried beneath the WHITE TOWER and that the ravens embody his spirit. Charles II (r.1660–85) is said to have been the first monarch to decree that six ravens of the Tower should be protected, despite the complaints of his astronomer, John Flamsteed, that they impeded the business of his observatory in the White Tower. However, historians have struggled to find proof that ravens were routinely conserved at the Tower before the latter part of 19th century and prophecies of calamitous consequences in the event of their departure may be of even more recent origin. A history written in 1866 by the Tower's

lieutenant governor, Lord de Ros, has nothing to say about ravens. In *Birds in London* (1898), W.H. Hudson merely imparts that 'for many years past two or three ravens have usually been kept at the Tower of London', and adds that a raven named Jenny was the sole tenant from 1890 until the authorities got around to finding her a mate in 1897. Nevertheless, much play is nowadays made of the ravens' presence. At least seven are almost always in residence, occupying lodgings next to the Wakefield Tower and presiding over four different territories within the Tower precincts during daytime. Each bird has the lifting feathers of one wing clipped, thus unbalancing its flight and deterring it from straying far. BEEFEATERS are at pains to insist that the procedure does not harm the ravens in any way.

Ravensbourne A river that rises near KESTON PONDS and flows north to join the THAMES at DEPTFORD, where its tidal part is called Deptford Creek. Legend has it that Julius Caesar encamped his troops at KESTON and observed a raven frequently alighting nearby. He guessed that the bird might be quenching its thirst and ordered that its landing spot be examined, whereupon a little spring was found, which was then used to supply water for the legion. However, in the 14th century the river was called Rendesburne, which probably derived from Old English words meaning 'boundary stream'. The present version of the name is an example of folk etymology.

Ravenscourt Park A public park and its neighbouring residential locality, situated at the western end of HAMMERSMITH. From at least the 14th century this was the manor of Pallingswick or Paddenswick. In 1746 secretary to the Admiralty Thomas Corbett bought the estate and rebuilt the manor house, naming it Ravenscourt after the bird on his family's coat of arms (a reference to the derivation of the family name from the French *corbeau*). In 1887 the METROPOLITAN BOARD OF WORKS acquired Ravenscourt and converted its 32 acres (13 hectare) of grounds into a park. Ravenscourt served as a public library in its later years but was destroyed in an air raid in 1941.

> To my mind this indeed is the most beautiful park in London, or perhaps I should say that it would be the most beautiful if the buildings round it were not so near and conspicuous.
>
> W.H. HUDSON: *Birds in London* (1898)

raw lobsters *See* REDBREASTS.

Rayners Lane A suburban conglomeration situated to the west of HARROW, taking its identity from the tube station, which was itself named after the long and winding road that runs through here on its way from South Harrow to PINNER. It was originally called Bourne Lane, because it crossed several streams. The Rayner family, who lived here in the first half of the 19th century, were not property owners but working tenants of the farmer who had acquired the neighbouring land.

Raynes Park A southern satellite of WIMBLE-DON, named after Edward Rayne, who owned and managed Park House Farm from 1822. After Rayne's sudden death in 1847 his widow retained the farm until her son's financial mismanagement forced her to sell to the lord of the manor of MORDEN, Richard Garth, in 1867. Garth laid out Grand Drive and in 1871 funded the construction of a station. Raymond Briggs, creator of *The Snowman* and *Fungus the Bogeyman*, was educated at Raynes Park county school for boys.

RCA An acronym for the ROYAL COLLEGE OF ART.

RCA Secret A one-week exhibition and one-day sale held every November at the ROYAL COLLEGE OF ART since 1994. Famous artists and young art students are invited to submit an original piece of art that must be completed on a postcard and signed on the reverse. All the cards are sold at the same price and the buyer does not discover the artist's identity until after making the purchase. More than 1,000 artworks are donated each year and the proceeds fund student bursaries. Past contributing artists and designers have included David Hockney, Damien Hirst, Sam Taylor-Wood, Grayson Perry, Peter Blake, Paul and Stella McCartney, Manolo Blahnik, Giorgio Armani, David Bowie and Yoko Ono.

red

redbreasts or **robin redbreasts** A nickname for the BOW STREET RUNNERS. It derived from the scarlet waistcoat introduced in 1805 as part of the armed horse patrol's uniform. The colour scheme influenced the uniform of the early MET-ROPOLITAN POLICE officers, who were sometimes called 'raw lobsters'.

The police, thieves and thieves' attorneys were in those days upon the most friendly terms with one another ... This amiable union was destroyed by the introduction of the New Police Bill, by which raw lobsters were introduced in place of robin-red-breasts.

JOSEPH HEWLETT: *The Parish Clerk* (1841)

Red House A red-brick house built in the village of Upton, now part of BEXLEYHEATH, by Philip Webb (1831–1915) and William Morris (1834–96). The pair had conceived the notion while rowing down the River Seine in the summer of 1858 and put their plan into action the following year. With its informal, asymmetric design, Red House represents one of the earliest expressions of Arts and Crafts principles. Morris lived here from 1860 to 1865. The architect Edward Hollamby bought Red House in 1952 and restored it, living here until his death in 1999. The National Trust acquired the grade I listed property in 2003 for around £2 million.

It is the first private house of the new artistic culture, the first house to be conceived as a whole inside and out, the very first example in the history of the modern house.

HERMANN MUTHESIUS: *The English House* (1904)

Red Ken A fairly obvious media nickname for Ken Livingstone (b.1945), Labour leader of the GREATER LONDON COUNCIL from 1981 to its dissolution in 1986. He transformed the GLC from a mainly administrative body into an instrument of left-wing policies and a key tool in Labour's consistent criticism of the Conservative national programme. The right-wing press, in conjunction with Margaret Thatcher's government, launched a concerted campaign against him, portraying him and his policies as the epitome of the 'loony left'. However, Thatcher's decision to abolish the GLC in 1983 (implemented in 1986), together with Livingstone's self-deprecatory wit and GLC policies such as cutting fares on LONDON TRANSPORT, made him popular with Londoners, even with some Tory voters. In 1987 Livingstone became Labour MP for BRENT. In 2000 he stood in Labour's contest to select its candidate for MAYOR OF LONDON but narrowly lost to Frank Dobson, then secretary of state for health. He then stood as an independent, easily defeating his (official) Labour, Conservative and Liberal Democrat rivals to become London's first elected mayor. In January 2004 Livingstone was readmitted to the party and stood as the official

Labour Party candidate for mayor in the June 2004 election, which he won. While his policies as mayor had relatively little in common with those of the Red Ken of GLC days, his verbal forthrightness still ensured regular headlines. He was defeated in the 2008 mayoral election by Boris Johnson (*see* BO-JO).

red routes London roads marked with double red lines, signifying particularly stringent stopping and parking restrictions. They were instituted in the 1990s to reduce traffic congestion; HOLLOWAY ROAD was the first to be so designated.

Redbridge A well-connected suburban locality in north ILFORD, situated at the junction of the Eastern Avenue, the NORTH CIRCULAR ROAD and the southern end of the M11 motorway. There have been four bridges across the River RODING here. The earliest, known as Hockley's Bridge after a medieval landowner, was standing in the 16th century. A red-brick bridge was built in 1642 and survived for two centuries, after which an iron bridge was erected in its place. Red-brick terraced houses, now mostly pebble-dashed, were built here at the beginning of the 20th century using materials from the Ilford brickfields. Another spate of housebuilding followed the arrival of the Eastern Avenue in the mid-1920s, when the iron bridge was replaced by the present crossing. The CENTRAL LINE station opened in 1947.

Redbridge, London Borough of An OUTER LONDON borough created in 1965 by uniting the leafy borough of WANSTEAD and WOODFORD with the densely built-up borough of ILFORD, together with parts of DAGENHAM and Chigwell, ESSEX. The two main constituents had formerly been separated by the River RODING and the new borough's name was chosen because the bridge symbolized their linkage. Redbridge's coat of arms features a multiplicity of historical references, of which the most significant are the FAIRLOP OAK, a HAINAULT forester and Adeliza, who founded Ilford chapel. The civic motto is 'in unity progress'.

Redriff or **Redriffe** A 17th-century spelling of ROTHERHITHE, derived from a debased pronunciation of the name.

So walked to Redriffe, where I hear the sickness

is, and indeed is scattered almost everywhere – there dying 1089 of the plague this week.

SAMUEL PEPYS: diary (20 July 1665)

The historical spelling has long since reasserted its sway over the pronunciation, but a reminder of the intermediate form survives in Redriff Road, at SURREY QUAYS.

Regent London places with the word 'Regent' in their name are almost all so called in honour of George, Prince of Wales, afterwards George IV, who acted as regent during the illness of his father, George III. The style of the Regency period (1811–20) is characterized by its imitation of classical architecture, especially that of ancient Greece, and a restrained simplicity.

Regent's Bridge See VAUXHALL BRIDGE.

Regent's Canal A north London canal that runs 8½ miles (14 km) from LITTLE VENICE eastwards via CAMDEN TOWN, ISLINGTON and HACKNEY to LIMEHOUSE BASIN. Part of its course passes along the northern edge of Regent's Park. It was opened in 1820. It forms a branch of the GRAND UNION CANAL.

Regent's Canaletto A nickname for the HAMPSTEAD-born artist Algernon Newton (1880–1968), prompted by his work *The Regent's Canal, Paddington* (1930). He also painted *Paddington Basin* (1925), *The Surrey Canal, Camberwell* (1935) and *Canal Scene, Maida Vale* (1947). In 1947 he became a vice-president of the Inland Waterways Association, a position he held for the rest of his life.

Regent's Park A royal park and the neighbouring residential area lying north of MARYLEBONE ROAD. Formerly known as Marylebone Park, this was a royal hunting ground leased to the dukes of Portland. When the Portland lease expired in 1811 the Prince Regent commissioned architect John Nash to devise a masterplan for a large part of London's WEST END, with Regent's Park (originally, and still formally, *the* Regent's Park) as its crowning glory in the north. Nash envisaged a palace for the prince, surrounded by a private royal park, which would in turn be encircled by fine houses. The park was landscaped but only the grand STUCCOED terraced houses on the perimeter and a handful of villas were built and George IV (as the prince became) later chose to live at BUCKINGHAM PALACE. QUEEN MARY'S GARDENS were laid out in the early 1930s. The park has some of London's most extensive sporting grounds, with tennis courts, football, cricket, softball and rugby pitches and capacious changing facilities, notably at the Hub, a stylish circular building opened in 2005. An open-air theatre operates in the summer months and concerts are staged on the bandstands.

> Life itself, every moment of it, every drop of it, here, this instant, now, in the sun, in Regent's Park, was enough. Too much, indeed.
>
> VIRGINIA WOOLF: *Mrs Dalloway* (1925)

The neighbouring Regent's Park locality takes in radically contrasting housing stock, ranging from fine Georgian villas to CAMDEN council's deprived Regent's Park estate.

Regent's Park bomb An IRA bomb (20 July 1982) that exploded under Regent's Park bandstand while the Royal Green Jackets were giving a lunchtime concert. Six soldiers died. The Household Cavalry were targeted in HYDE PARK on the same day by a car bomb.

Regent's Park disaster One of London's worst calamities, it occurred on Regent's Park lake on 15 January 1867, when ice gave way beneath hundreds of skaters and 40 young men died. One causal factor, as *The Times* reported, was that park-keepers, 'paying more regard to the necessities of the waterfowl than to the security of the skating public, broke the ice for some distance along the edges, thereby destroying the connexion of the central field with the shore'. The lake at that time was 12 feet (nearly 4m) deep in places; it was subsequently made shallower. Henry Disley, ST GILES'S answer to William McGonagall, versified thus upon the tragedy:

> 'Twas near four o'clock, how dreadful to relate,
> The ice broke up in every quarter,
> Two hundred then fell in, oh what a sad fate,
> All struggled for their lives in the water.
>
> 'Terrible Accident on the Ice in Regent's Park, and Loss of 40 Lives' (1867)

Regent's Park explosion *See* BLOW-UP BRIDGE.

Regent's Park mosque The informal name of the London Central Mosque. With the support of the British government, George VI gave land on the west side of the park for the creation of an Islamic centre, in memory of Muslim soldiers who had died fighting for the British Empire. The mosque opened on the same site in 1977.

Regent's Park Zoo *See* LONDON ZOO.

Regent Street A prestigious WEST END shopping street, extending southwards and finally curving eastwards from PORTLAND PLACE to PICCADILLY CIRCUS (which was originally called Regent Circus South). Lower Regent Street continues south to Waterloo Place. In 1811 the architect John Nash planned the street for the Prince Regent as the central thoroughfare of a scheme linking his home at CARLTON HOUSE with the proposed site of a palace in REGENT'S PARK. Regent Street was completed in 1825 to widespread acclaim but flaws later became apparent in its commercial practicality. Colonnades had to be removed because streetwalkers had taken to lurking in their shadows and by the end of the century the intimate scale of the shops had become inappropriate to retailers' needs. A protracted rebuilding programme began in 1902, resulting in the present streetscape. Only All Souls' Church survives from the original project, at the street's far northern end. Regent Street remains the property of the Crown Estate, which oversees a continuous programme of investment designed to keep it at the forefront of the West End shopping experience.

Regent Street Polytechnic *See the* POLYTECHNIC INSTITUTION.

remembrancer *See the* KING'S or QUEEN'S REMEMBRANCER.

rep your ends 'Represent your neighbourhood' in modern urban slang, often spelt 'rep ur endz'. The term is primarily used in the context of rivalry between GRIME musicians from different parts of the capital. *See also* ENDS.

> According to a former employee of one of these small-scale urban cable stations, the more explicit the lyrics, the more likely it would be aired. She said: 'If they aren't talking about popping your gun and repping your ends the station didn't want to know.' ... White and Asian boys are 'repping their ends' too – in fact, many gangs are mixed.
>
> *The Observer* (11 February 2007)

resort of kings and princes Claridge's was so called by *The Times* in 1898. The BROOK STREET hotel was founded *c*.1812 by James Edward Mivart (1781–1856) and acquired in 1854 by William Claridge (*c*.1814–82). Richard D'OYLY CARTE bought the business in 1893 and commissioned the construction of the present building. Claridge's innumerable royal guests have included Crown

Prince Alexander of Yugoslavia, who was born in suite 212 on 17 July 1945. Winston Churchill declared the suite Yugoslav territory for the day so that the heir to the throne would be born in his own country, although it is doubtful whether this had any legal effect. In 2001, again in suite 212, the exiled prince had his citizenship formally restored by the Yugoslav government after the fall of Slobodan Milošević.

Reuters A leading international news agency, reputed for its integrity and impartiality, founded by Paul Julius Reuter (1816–99), a native of Kassel, Germany. He was of Jewish parentage and originally named Israel Beer Josaphat, but became a Christian and adopted the name of Reuter on his baptism in 1845 at St George's German Lutheran chapel, in WHITECHAPEL. The agency was established in two rooms at 1 Royal Exchange Buildings (next to the ROYAL EXCHANGE) in 1851, taking full advantage of the developing telegraph service, although links had to be completed by railway and pigeon post. Reuter developed a worldwide service in the ensuing years, and in 1871 he was made Baron de Reuter. Just before the outbreak of war in 1939 the agency moved to 85 FLEET STREET and in 2005 became the last major news organization to leave that street, when it transferred to CANARY WHARF. In 2008 Reuters Group PLC merged with the Thomson Corporation to form Thomson Reuters.

rhyming slang *See* COCKNEY RHYMING SLANG.

riah A BACK-SLANG and POLARI word meaning 'hair'. A riah zhoosher – or shusher – is (or was) a hairdresser.

Richard

Richard Jury mysteries A series of crime novels begun in 1981 by the US author Martha Grimes (b.1931). Jury is a SCOTLAND YARD inspector (ultimately superintendent) and many of the books are named after past or present London pub signs, including *The Man With a Load of Mischief* (1981), *I Am the Only Running Footman* (1986), *The Case Has Altered* (1997), *The Grave Maurice* (2002) and *The Old Wine Shades* (2006).
Richard the Third Originally 'bird' in COCKNEY RHYMING SLANG. The term was first used in the feathered sense of the word 'bird' and later for a young woman and, in theatrical circles, for *the*

bird – an audience's expression of disapproval. Nowadays, it is mostly used to mean 'turd'.

Richmond

Richmond Hill A superior road and its vicinity, located south of Richmond town centre. Charles I used to ride up the hill to hunt in RICHMOND PARK and the view from the summit has attracted artists and poets since the 17th century, including J.M.W. Turner, Philip Wilson Steer, John Ruskin, James Thomson and William Wordsworth. Grand houses lined the hill at well-spaced intervals during the late 18th century, including Downe House, which has been home to the dramatist Richard Sheridan, the actor John Mills and the rock star Mick Jagger, and Wick House, which was built for Sir Joshua Reynolds. The view from the hill was protected by act of Parliament in 1902 after developers had proposed to build on PETERSHAM Meadows and MARBLE HILL. *See also the* STAR AND GARTER.

> Heavens! what a goodly prospect spreads around,
> Of hills, and dales, and woods, and lawns, and spires.
> And glittering towns, and gilded streams, till all
> The stretching landscape into smoke decays!
> JAMES THOMSON: *The Seasons*, 'Summer' (1727)

Richmond Park London's greatest royal park, covering more than 2,500 acres (1,000 hectares) south-east of Richmond town centre. Charles I created the park in 1637, ordering it to be enclosed within a brick wall so that he might hunt deer. The enclosure was highly unpopular with local people, even though the king allowed them to walk and to gather firewood here – a right that still exists. When Charles was beheaded Parliament granted the park to the CITY of London, which prudently restored it to Charles II at the Restoration. In his role as Deputy Ranger, Viscount Sidmouth introduced a series of plantations from 1819 onwards and there are now more than a dozen woods, the most beautiful of which is the Isabella Plantation. As a result of public pressure, Edward VII disbanded the Royal Hunt and opened the park to the public in 1904. George V granted permission for the park's eastern section to be turned into a golf course, on the understanding that it was for 'artisans' who could not afford membership of a private club. The course opened in 1923 and was followed by another two years later. Richmond Park has several hundred fallow and red deer, and a wide variety of woodland wildlife, including badgers and foxes, although the official mole-catcher has been made redundant.

Richmond University The principal home of the American International University in London. The campus is centred on an impressive neo-Gothic structure that was originally the Wesleyan Theological Institution.

Richmond upon Thames An agreeable riverside town, situated 9 miles (14.5 km) south-west of central London. This was Sheen (or Shene or West Sheen) in the Middle Ages. Royal courts were held at the manor house from the end of the 13th century and Edward III died in 1377 at what had become Sheen Palace. Henry VII rebuilt the palace after a fire in 1497 and named it Richmond after his earldom in Yorkshire. Richmond Palace was the birthplace of Henry VIII, and Elizabeth I spent many summers here, maintaining a wardrobe of 2,000 dresses. After her death in 1603 the Stuarts allowed this stately collection of buildings to fall into decay and the palace was demolished in 1650. All that now remains are the Wardrobe and the gateway, beside Maids of Honour Row. A horse-drawn omnibus connected London and Richmond from 1830 but this was overtaken by the arrival of the railway in 1846. By the end of the 19th century suburban development had left little land available for building and only a few surviving mansions with grounds. Of those that remain, two have become hotels. The riverside between the bridge and Water Lane was redeveloped, incorporating and restoring some of the existing buildings, in the late 1980s. With its beautiful green, mall-free shopping streets and plenitude of places to eat and drink, Richmond draws numerous visitors and can become crowded in summer.

Richmond upon Thames, London Borough of An OUTER LONDON borough formed in 1965 by merging the boroughs of BARNES, Richmond and TWICKENHAM. It is the only London borough to straddle the THAMES, which winds erratically through it so that the river defines both the northern border at Barnes and KEW and its southern limit at HAMPTON. Richmond is just one of a dozen or so towns and villages that make up the borough; each has a distinct identity, with several of the shopping streets retaining a village character and charm. Although many residents work in the CITY and the WEST END, the borough

also boasts a thriving commercial life, with traditional retail and publishing businesses flourishing alongside new high-tech and light industrial developments. Its imposing coat of arms is dominated by Richmond's royal connections, with the addition of a swan representing Twickenham and two GRIFFINS for Barnes. Dark and light blue blades celebrate the BOAT RACE, which finishes at MORTLAKE.

Riddlesdown Chalk downland in north KENLEY, and its neighbouring residential locality. The name was first recorded in 1277 and derives from Old English and Middle English words meaning 'cleared woodland on a hill'. Part of the area contains Neolithic remains and is designated a scheduled ancient monument. The CORPORATION OF LONDON acquired the majority of Riddlesdown in 1883, preserving it as open space.

ride

ride backwards up Holborn Hill, to An 18th-century term meaning to travel from NEWGATE to be hanged at TYBURN. Condemned men were transported facing backwards, probably to prevent them panicking as the cart approached the gallows.

ride to Romford, to To get a new pair of breeches, or to get a new bottom put in an old pair. An expression dating from the late 18th and early 19th centuries, when ROMFORD was known for selling high-quality breeches, made from HORNCHURCH leather. Applied to a knife or similar implement, 'you may ride to Romford on it' indicated bluntness.

Rillington Place A former cul-de-sac behind LADBROKE GROVE station, where No.10, a shabby terraced house, was the location of the murders of at least eight women over the period 1943–53. John Christie had moved into the ground-floor flat with his wife in 1938 and ten years later Timothy Evans took the second-floor flat with his pregnant wife. In 1949 Evans, who was mentally retarded, confessed to the murder of his wife and baby girl and was hanged. In 1953 the mouldering bodies of three young women were found in Christie's kitchen cupboard by a new tenant. His wife's body was then discovered under the kitchen floorboards and the skeletons of two women buried some ten years earlier in the garden. Christie, a necrophiliac, confessed to these murders and to that of Mrs Evans, and was hanged. Evans was granted a posthumous pardon in 1966. The notoriety of the case led to Rillington Place being renamed, as Ruston Close, although it still attracted unwelcome sightseers. The terraces were demolished in the early 1970s and replaced by Bartle Road and Ruston Mews. The film *10 Rillington Place* (1971), based on a book by Ludovic Kennedy, offered a realistically sordid reconstruction of the cause célèbre, with Richard Attenborough in the role of the murderer and John Hurt as Evans.

ring

Ring, The A tree-lined circuit in the north part of HYDE PARK created by Charles I. It was described as being 'two or three hundred paces in diameter' and was favoured by the beau monde for riding in ostentatious coaches, sometimes in the hundreds. The enclosure formed by the Ring was often the site of duels. Today, the Ring is another name for the Carriage Drive, which runs around the park's perimeter.

> They take their rides in a coach in an open field where there is a circle, not very large, enclosed by rails. There the coaches drive slowly round, some in one direction, others the opposite way, which, seen from a distance, produces a rather pretty effect, and proves clearly that they only come there in order to see and to be seen.
>
> BÉAT DE MURALT: *Lettres sur les Anglais et les Français* (1727)

Ring of Edward the Confessor *See* I HAVE A RING.

Ring of Steel The protective cordon thrown up around the CITY of London after a series of IRA bombings in the 1980s and early 1990s. The number of roads via which vehicles could enter the City was reduced to seven, and checkpoints were set up. At first these were frequently manned by City of London police but, as the threat diminished, CCTV monitoring was usually deemed sufficient. At times of heightened security concerns, no longer nowadays from Irish republican extremists, manning is reintroduced.

Ripperologist One who studies, and speculates at length upon, the case of JACK THE RIPPER.

> Orthodox Ripperologists use terms like 'absolute rubbish' and 'sheer baloney' to dismiss Mr Wickes's claim that he has unearthed new documentary evidence that solves the case.
>
> *New York Times* (4 June 1988)

Ritz A prestigious hotel in PICCADILLY, built in 1905–6 on the site of the Walsingham House Hotel. The French chateau-style architecture, by Charles Mewès and Arthur Davis, conceals a steel frame that was an innovation at the time. The business was the creation of César Ritz (1850–1918), the 'king of hoteliers and hotelier to kings', who had earlier established his London reputation at the CARLTON HOTEL. The Ritz's Palm Court is a famed setting for afternoon TEA in the WEST END. Reclusive businessmen the Barclay brothers acquired the hotel in 1995.

The adjective 'ritzy' derives from the ostentatiously luxurious quality of the Ritz hotels in London, Paris and Madrid.

justice is open to all; like the Ritz hotel *See under* JUSTICE.

river

River Lea 'Tea' in early COCKNEY RHYMING SLANG, since replaced by the enduringly successful 'ROSIE (LEE)'. For the river itself, *see under* LEA.

River Ouse 'Booze' in COCKNEY RHYMING SLANG, i.e. alcoholic drink. There are three major rivers of this name in England. First recorded in the 1930s, and sometimes spelt 'River Ooze', the term is no longer much used.

road

Road, the The name by which CHARING CROSS ROAD, in its heyday as the centre of the second-hand book trade in London, was known to booksellers and bibliophiles.

no roads in the City of London *See under* NO.

roaring boys The riotous blades of Ben Jonson's time, whose delight it was to annoy quiet folk. At one time their pranks in London were carried on to an alarming extent. Thomas Dekker and Thomas Middleton wrote a play about Moll CUTPURSE called *The Roaring Girl* (*c.*1611). *See also* HAWCUBITES; MOHOCKS; SCOWERERS; TITYRE-TUS.

Robert A name sometimes formerly applied to a policeman, 'the man in blue', in allusion to Sir Robert Peel (1788–1850), who founded the METROPOLITAN POLICE force in 1829. *See also* BOBBY; PEELER.

Robert E. Lee 'Quay' in the old rhyming slang of London dockworkers, derived from the Confederate army general whose family, coincidentally, had emigrated to America from EAST LONDON. *See also* MARYLAND.

robin

Robin Hood district An old term for what is now the vicinity of KINGSTON VALE (*see under* KINGSTON UPON THAMES). The legendary outlaw is not supposed to have visited these parts but his name features widely throughout the locality. From the 15th century, travelling troupes of players dressed up as the merry men, performed little plays and put on displays of archery. Henry VIII is said to have watched such entertainments in RICHMOND PARK and their popularity was reflected in the naming of a nearby farm, an inn, a park gate and then other local places.

robin redbreasts See REDBREASTS.

Robin's Nest An ITV sitcom that ran for six seasons in 1977–81. The show was a spin-off from MAN ABOUT THE HOUSE. Richard O'Sullivan starred as Robin Tripp, the owner and chef of a FULHAM bistro.

rob Peter to pay Paul, to To take away from one person in order to give to another; to pay off one debt only to incur another. The expression is said to allude to the fact that on 17 December 1540 the abbey church of St Peter, WESTMINSTER, was advanced to the dignity of a cathedral by letters patent, but ten years later was joined to the diocese of London, and many of its estates appropriated to the repairs of ST PAUL'S Cathedral. But it was a common saying long before this and was used by Wycliffe about 1380:

> How should God approve that you rob Peter, and give this robbery to Paul in the name of Christ.

> *Select Works,* Volume 3

rock

rock of ages 'Wages' in COCKNEY RHYMING SLANG. The term is little used.

rock pigeon or **dove** *Columba livia,* the feral bird sometimes known as the 'London pigeon'. Its original habitat was coastal cliffs and it has adapted readily to the urban environment. Most London pigeons are descended from domesticated birds that escaped or were released from captivity. Although the SPARROW is often considered the classic London bird, feral pigeons have been a familiar sight in the city for centuries. During the GREAT FIRE OF LONDON Samuel PEPYS recorded with sadness that they would not leave their nests until it was too late, and they fell to the ground with their wings burnt. Until the clampdown on the sale of bird food in 2003, TRAFALGAR SQUARE was world-famous for its especially dense pigeon population.

Rock Pit See ELMSTEAD WOODS.

rockney A style of COCKNEY pub-rock music popularized by the north London duo Chas & Dave (Charles Hodges and David Peacock). *Rockney* (1978) was the title of their second album and later became the name of their record label. The term has been less convincingly extended by some to encompass the work of bands such as Squeeze and Ian Dury and the Blockheads. *See also* GERTCHA.

Roding A river that rises near Stansted Airport, ESSEX, and flows 30 miles (48 km) south to join the THAMES as BARKING CREEK. It was formerly the Hyle (*see* ILFORD). The present name was first recorded in the 16th century and derives (indirectly, via a group of Essex villages) from the followers of a man called Hrōth. Some purists pronounce the river's name 'roothing'.

Rods HARRODS, in the vernacular of the SLOANE RANGER.

Roehampton Originally a country village and later a select suburb, now augmented by assorted institutions and a pioneering council estate, lying on the western side of PUTNEY. The settlement gained an identity in the 14th century, at first as East Hampton and then Rokehampton. The 'roke' element may have referred to the presence of rooks, rocks or oaks. In the 18th century handsome villas peppered the locality's hills and vales, occupied by a succession of eminent figures. By the late 19th century, high-class suburban homes were increasingly in evidence and the aristocracy began to move away. Institutions and colleges took over some of the mansions but most were demolished during the 20th century. Private and council estates filled their former grounds, notably the ALTON ESTATE, built in the 1950s.

Benjamin Disraeli created an Earl and Countess of Roehampton in his semi-autobiographical novel *Endymion* (1880). The poet Gerard Manley

Hopkins studied at the Jesuit seminary in what is now a ROEHAMPTON UNIVERSITY building named Parkstead House. In sharp contrast, the risqué writer Frank Harris twice lived in Roehampton with his extremely young wife-to-be, Nellie O'Hara.

> His favourite places in the world, he once said, were the green strip of Roehampton, lying between Kingston and Putney, and the Riviera ...
>
> PHILIPPA PULLAR: *Frank Harris* (1975)

Roehampton Club A private members' sports club, originally established in 1901 as an officers' polo club. It has extensive sporting facilities, including a golf course and 29 tennis courts.

Roehampton Priory *See the* PRIORY.

Roehampton University A small, independent university based in south-west Roehampton, in the vicinity of the ALTON ESTATE. It was part of the University of Surrey until 2004. As the Roehampton Institute it united four former colleges, the oldest of which (Whitelands) began in CHELSEA in 1841 as a teacher training college for women.

Rokeby Venus The popular name for *The Toilet of Venus* (otherwise known as *Venus and Cupid*) by Velázquez (1599–1660), a rear view of a reclining nude painted *c*.1651 and now in the NATIONAL GALLERY. The popular name derives from the fact that until 1905 it hung in Rokeby Hall, County Durham, as part of the collection of the Morritt family. The postcard of the painting is apparently one of the most popular in the National Gallery shop (with male customers at least). On 10 March 1914 the painting itself was slashed with a meat chopper by a suffragette protesting at the re-arrest of Emmeline Pankhurst, but the damage was successfully repaired.

Rolling Stones, The The rock group so named was formed in 1962 with Mick Jagger (b.1943) as lead singer and Keith Richards (b.1943) as guitarist. The other early members were Brian Jones (guitarist, 1942–69), and the Londoners Charlie Watts (drummer, b.1941) and Bill Wyman (bassist, b.1941). They took their name from Muddy Waters's song 'Rollin' Stone' (1950), and their format was initially influenced by the American blues musician's electrically amplified band. They first performed as the Rollin' Stones at the MARQUEE CLUB in July 1962 with a line-up that did not include Watts or Wyman. With those two on board they were hired early in 1963 for residencies at venues that included the MANOR HOUSE, the Crawdaddy Club in RICHMOND and the EEL PIE ISLAND Hotel. They vied with the Beatles for pre-eminence in the rock music aristocracy until the latter disbanded leaving them free to claim the crown. Jones, who famously drowned in his swimming pool, was replaced by Mick Taylor (from 1969 to 1974) and then by Ronnie Wood.

Roman

Roman London *See* LONDINIUM.

Roman Road An EAST END market street extending between north BOW and east BETHNAL GREEN. Evidence of Roman transit has been discovered here but the road is thought unlikely to have been in significant use at that time. It was called Green Street from about 1790 and a section was earlier known as Driftway. The development of GLOBE TOWN from the late 18th century brought commerce to the road and a market began to operate here in 1843. The invention of the road's present name seems to have been a kind of mid-19th-century marketing ploy, inspired by the discovery of Roman remains at OLD FORD. The surrounding area was extensively rebuilt in the mid-20th century.

Rome

Romeland The name of four open spaces in the medieval CITY of London: near the TOWER OF LONDON, in DOWGATE ward, at BILLINGSGATE and at QUEENHITHE. Each of these Romelands was located near a wharf and at least two were the sites of markets for goods discharged there. Some have speculated that rents might once have been paid to the See of Rome, but the word's origin is more likely to be linked to that of 'room', i.e. available space.

Romeville An 18th-century slang term for London. Some Londoners felt a (largely unreciprocated) sense of rivalry with Rome, on account of its status as the first great city of Western civilization. This was also evident in the invention of legends surrounding the foundation of London, which tended to echo Roman myths as well as those of ancient Greece.

> LONDON ... the Metropolis of Great Britain, founded before the City of Rome, walled by

Constantine the Great, no ways inferior to the greatest in Europe for riches and greatness.

NATHAN BAILEY: *An Universal Etymological English Dictionary* (1721)

Romford The 'capital' of HAVERING since the Middle Ages, situated 5 miles (8 km) east of ILFORD. The name was first recorded in the mid-12th century and probably referred to a broad (or 'roomy') ford across the BEAM river, which was later called the River Rom locally. The settlement initially evolved to the south-west of the modern centre, around a chapel dedicated to St Andrew that was in existence by 1177. Henry III granted Romford the right to hold a market in 1247 and added permission for a Whitsun fair three years later. The focus of the village shifted to the new marketplace, whereupon it is said that the chapel was swallowed up by an earthquake, although its bells could still be heard on St Andrew's Day. By the 15th century the market was well known for the sale of leather goods made in nearby HORNCHURCH. From the 17th century it became a very large agricultural market, selling farm tools, livestock, fruit and vegetables. As a coaching halt on the London to Colchester road the town gained a plethora of inns and hotels. In 1799 Edward Ind bought a small brewery and later joined forces with Octavius and George Coope to form a partnership that became one of the largest brewers in the country. The town was still small and its environs almost entirely agricultural when the Eastern Counties Railway arrived in 1839, boosting both the market and the brewing industry. Landowners began to sell off their estates for suburban development in a protracted process that continued well into the 20th century. The town centre was redeveloped after the construction of the ring road in the late 1960s. The former Ind Coope brewery lay unoccupied for over a decade at the end of the century before its reconstruction as apartments, with additional houses and a retail and leisure development.

Romford lion Eighteenth-century slang for a calf – also called an ESSEX lion – in a reference to the area's reputation for breeding calves and supplying them to the London meat markets.

Romford Road A busy thoroughfare in MANOR PARK, linking STRATFORD and ILFORD. It is lined with a wide variety of shops, most of which are independent and cater to a very local catchment area. Towards the Ilford end, the road is noted for its many used-car dealers.

Romford Slim The snooker player Steve Davis (b.1957) was thus nicknamed by the pool commentator Sid Waddell, after the town where he began his career. Less kindly, he has been called 'the Romford Robot'. Davis has also been dubbed 'the PLUMSTEAD Potter', from his place of birth.

> More recently, as Davis has found richer pickings and easier pottings on the pool circuit, the Americans have taken to calling him 'Romford Slim' and although this would have been perfect for the figure that was once so wiry we imagined him snuggling up in his cue case at bedtime, even the briefest of glances at his middle-aged spread renders this wholly unsuitable.
>
> *The Independent on Sunday* (15 December 2002)

ride to Romford, to See under RIDE.

Ronan Point A residential tower that partially collapsed after a gas explosion in May 1968, killing five people. It was one of the nine newly built blocks of the Freemasons estate in CANNING TOWN. The disaster has been called 'modern architecture's Titanic' and it marked the start of a withdrawal from high-rise solutions to accommodation needs throughout the UK, as well as having a pivotal influence on subsequent designs for TALL BUILDINGS. It has been suggested that the effects of the terrorist attack on New York's World Trade Center in 2001 might have been less catastrophic had lessons from Ronan Point been incorporated into the twin towers' construction. The Admiral's Reach development, completed in 1993 by Barratt, occupies the site of the Freemasons estate.

Ronnie Scott's London's best-known jazz venue. Club Eleven, the first club set up in 1958 by the saxophonist Ronnie Scott (original name Ronald Schatt; 1927–97), closed after a few months following a drugs raid. In 1959 Scott opened a second club in Gerrard Street, SOHO, where he and his fellow jazz musicians could play. It attracted major figures from the world of jazz, and its heyday was in the latter half of the 1960s, following its move to larger premises in Frith Street. It remains a centre of British jazz today.

rookery A low, densely populated neighbourhood, especially one frequented by thieves and vagabonds. The allusion is to the way in which rooks build their nests closely together. Rookeries formerly peppered the fringes of the WEST END and CITY of London. The DEVIL'S ACRE, ST GILES, SAFFRON HILL and ST LUKE'S were among the most notorious. Some residents scraped an honest living, many others survived on the meagre proceeds of petty crime, making felonious forays into wealthier quarters and fleeing back to their maze of alleys, knowing they would not be pursued. Very often, new thoroughfares were driven through such areas from the mid-19th century onwards, partly to ease traffic congestion, but also to give the authorities an excuse to smash down the properties and exile the inhabitants. New Oxford Street, FARRINGDON ROAD, VICTORIA STREET and KINGSWAY were among the many roads that served such a purpose. Thereafter, slum clearance and rehousing programmes completed their extinction.

> The tenants of these Rookeries, like the birds from whom they take their names, have much in common – want, with its offspring, recklessness; they the pariahs, so to speak, of the body social, a distinct caste ...
>
> THOMAS BEAMES: *The Rookeries of London* (1850)

room

Room of One's Own, A A long essay by Virginia Woolf (1882–1941), published in 1929. The essay grew out of two lectures that Woolf had delivered to female students at Newnham College, Cambridge, the previous year, in which she addressed the difficulties that women writers would continue to face until they had the freedom and security of 'a room of one's own' and 'five hundred a year'. For Woolf herself the 'room of one's own' was the attic room of J.M. Keynes's house at 46 Gordon Square in BLOOMSBURY.

> A room of one's own can be a womb, but it can also be an ivory tower, a prison and a grave. Its dangers and promise are inherent in all Virginia Woolf's work.
>
> STEPHEN COOTE: *The Penguin Short History of English Literature* (1993)

Room 101 An office in BROADCASTING HOUSE, widely held to have been the inspiration for the room of that number in George Orwell's novel *1984*. Orwell worked at the BBC during the 1940s and called Broadcasting House: 'A cross between a girls' school and a lunatic asylum.' However,

it has been argued that Room 101 of the BBC's nearby PORTLAND PLACE building was the more likely prototype, as Orwell would have attended meetings there. In 1992 the BBC appropriated *Room 101* as the title of a Radio 4 programme in which celebrities proclaimed their pet hates. The show transferred to television in 1994 and continues to the present day. The original Room 101 at Broadcasting House was demolished during reconstruction work in 2003, but not before the artist Rachel Whiteread had made a plaster cast of it.

ropewalk Former barristers' slang for an OLD BAILEY practice. Thus 'gone into the ropewalk' means that the barrister concerned has taken up practice in the Old Bailey. The allusion is to the murder trials there, and to the convicted murderer 'getting the rope'.

Rory (O'More) 'Floor' in COCKNEY RHYMING SLANG, or occasionally 'door'. The term was first recorded in 1857 but is no longer in common usage. Colonel Rory O'More (or Moore) was a 17th-century Irish rebel.

rose

Rose, Richard Cook to Bishop John Fisher (*see* FISHER FC) at his LAMBETH townhouse. In 1531 Rose is said to have prepared a vat of poisoned soup for the episcopal household and the poor of Lambeth. The bishop was feeling unwell and did not partake but 16 other diners died. Rose was found guilty of treason and, in a punishment fitting the crime, he was publicly boiled alive at SMITHFIELD. Almost all the details of the story vary from source to source: the cook's name may have been Rouse or even Cook, only two or three victims may have died, the events may have taken place in the late 1520s and the dish may have been oatmeal porridge, not vegetable pottage. Some Londoners believed that Henry VIII was behind the attempt on the bishop's life.

Rose Alley Ambuscade The attack on John Dryden by masked ruffians, probably in the employ of John Wilmot, 2nd Earl of Rochester (1647–80), and the Duchess of Portsmouth (1649–1734), the mistress of Charles II, on 18 December 1679, in revenge for an anonymous *Essay on Satire* attacking Charles II, Rochester, and the duchesses of Cleveland and Portsmouth. The essay was erroneously attributed to Dryden but actually written by John Sheffield, 3rd Earl of Mulgrave, and later 1st Duke of Buckingham and Normanby (1648–1721). The attack took place in Rose Alley, now Rose Street, COVENT GARDEN, where Dryden had been on his way home from WILL'S COFFEE HOUSE.

Rose Coffee House An establishment that stood at the north-western corner of Russell Street and BOW STREET, in COVENT GARDEN, from about 1651. Also known as the Three Roses, it was formerly the Red Cow tavern and later WILL'S COFFEE HOUSE. It should not be confused with the nearby ROSE TAVERN.

Rose Tavern A famously rowdy COVENT GAR-DEN inn, it stood at the corner of Russell Street and Brydges Street, now Catherine Street. A scene in William Hogarth's RAKE'S PROGRESS depicts the kind of drunkenness and debauchery for which the tavern was notorious. The building was demolished in 1791 to make way for an extension to the THEATRE ROYAL, DRURY LANE.

Rose Theatre The first purpose-built theatre on BANKSIDE. Built in 1587, it premiered many plays by SHAKESPEARE and Christopher Marlowe and was managed by Edward ALLEYN from around 1592. Its well-preserved archaeology was uncovered in 1989 during a routine exploratory excavation held in the interval between site clearance and the construction of a new office block at the corner of Park Street and SOUTHWARK BRIDGE ROAD. Following a well-supported campaign, the office block (now the headquarters of the Health and Safety Executive) was redesigned to preserve the theatre's site in its basement. Regular tours are conducted here and the Rose Theatre Trust hopes to open the site to the public on a permanent basis if funds permit.

Rosetta Stone A stone found in 1799 by a French officer of engineers named Bouchard or Boussard in an excavation made near Rosetta (Rashid), in the Nile delta north-east of Alexandria. It has an inscription in two languages, Egyptian and Greek, and in three writing systems: hieroglyphics, demotic script and the Greek alphabet. It was erected (195 BC) in commemoration of the accession to the throne of Ptolemy Epiphanes. The great value of the stone is that it provided a key to the translation of Egyptian hieroglyphic writing. It is now in the BRITISH MUSEUM.

Rosie or **Rosy (Lee)** 'TEA' in rhyming slang. Although quickly adopted by COCKNEYS, the term probably began as army slang during the First World War and its earliest appearance in print was in Edward Fraser and John Gibbons's *Soldier and Sailor Words and Phrases* (1925). This discredits persistent suggestions of a derivation from the American burlesque artiste Gipsy Rose Lee (1911–70), who did not achieve fame until the 1930s.

> 'Best leave her be,' whispered Floss to her sister. 'Let's make her a nice cup of Rosie Lee. Three sugars. Settle her nerves.'
>
> JAMES RIORDAN: *War Song* (2001)

Rosslyn Park FC A rugby union club founded in HAMPSTEAD in 1879 and based in ROEHAMPTON since 1956.

Rota A short-lived political CLUB founded in 1659 by James Harrington (1611–77). Its republican principles are outlined in his *Oceana* (1656) and it advocated rotation of government offices and voting by ballot. It met at the Turk's Head, otherwise known as Miles' COFFEE HOUSE, in New Palace Yard, WESTMINSTER, and did not survive the Restoration.

Rotherhithe A broad THAMES peninsula formerly dominated by its docks, situated between BERMONDSEY and DEPTFORD. The name is probably a corruption of Old English *hrȳther hȳth*, 'cattle harbour', from which cattle may have been shipped across the river for the market at SMITHFIELD. Rotherhithe's moated manor house passed into Edward III's ownership in the mid-14th century and Henry IV visited in 1412 for a rest cure for leprosy. The site of the house lies opposite one of Rotherhithe's two most famous pubs, the Angel, from where Judge Jeffreys (*see the* HANGING JUDGE) reputedly watched executions on the far bank at WAPPING. The Mayflower dates from the 16th century but acquired its name when the Pilgrim Fathers' ship of the same name stopped there in 1620 before setting off for the New World. The ship's captain, Christopher Jones, is buried in St Mary's Church, which may have Saxon origins. Rotherhithe both built and broke up ships, notably the Trafalgar veteran *Temeraire*, immortalized by J.M.W. Turner on its last voyage. Rotherhithe built some of the first steamships and the first iron ship, the *Aaron Manby*. *See also* REDRIFF.

The actor Michael Caine was born in the charity wing of the now demolished St Olave's Hospital in 1933. 70 years later he unveiled a council plaque at the hospital's surviving gatehouse, on Ann Moss Way, off Lower Road. *See also* NOT A LOT OF PEOPLE KNOW THAT.

Rothschild The name is associated with the great wealth of the international banking family of Rothschild, whose name derives from the red shield by which their parent house at Frankfurt was known. The family banking business really stems from the activities of Mayer Amschel Rothschild (1744–1812), who made a fortune during the Napoleonic Wars. His five sons separated, extending the business throughout Europe. Nathan Mayer Rothschild (1777–1836) established himself at the ROYAL EXCHANGE in 1798 and staged a financial coup by his advance knowledge of the defeat of Napoleon at Waterloo in 1815 (*see the* ROTHSCHILD PILLAR). His son Lionel Nathan (1808–79) was best known for his work for Jewish emancipation in Great Britain. Lionel's son Nathan Mayer (1840–1915) was made a baron in 1885 and was the first Jew to be admitted to the House of Lords. Nathan's son Lionel Walter (1868–1937), the 2nd Baron Rothschild, was a noted collector and taxonomist. The 3rd baron, Nathan's grandson, was Nathaniel Mayer Victor Rothschild (1910–90), a zoologist and administrator. His own son, Nathaniel Charles Jacob (b.1936), 4th Baron Rothschild, largely assumed his father's administrative mantle. Nathaniel Charles Jacob's heir is Nathaniel Philip Victor James Rothschild (b.1971).

Rothschild Buildings A pair of SPITALFIELDS tenement blocks built in 1887 by the FOUR PER CENT INDUSTRIAL DWELLINGS COMPANY and named in honour of Baroness Charlotte de Rothschild (1819–84), mother of the charity's founder, the younger Nathan Mayer Rothschild (1840–1915). The buildings were demolished in 1972 and replaced by low-rise housing. Jerry White's book *Rothschild Buildings* (1980) examines the lives of those who lived there up until 1920. Their conflicting perceptions of the place are illustrated by quotes that the author uses as section headings: 'More like warehouses than homes'; 'We had it very nice'; 'Not much of a kit-chen there at all'; 'I don't know where our mother put us'; 'Rothschilds was luxury'.

Rothschild pillar A vantage point in the ROYAL EXCHANGE beside which Nathan Mayer Rothschild customarily stood, hands in pockets, awaiting approaches from those with privileged information or proposals of business. It was from this spot, on 18 June 1815, that Rothschild gave signals to his agents to begin selling government bonds (known as 'consuls'). Other traders assumed that Napoleon had won the Battle of Waterloo and dumped their holdings in a frenzy of selling that rendered the bonds almost worthless. In fact, a courier had brought Rothschild advance news of Wellington's victory, and he soon made a subtle change to his signals, perceptible only to his agents, who then began to buy up every available consul. It is said that he multiplied his wealth twenty times as a result of this subterfuge.

> On Tuesdays and Fridays you would always find him at 'Rothschild Pillar' on the stock exchange. A broker by the name of Rose was the only man that was bold enough to occupy the stand of the Money King, and he disputed the right but an hour.
>
> *Hunt's Merchants' Magazine and Commercial Review,*
> 'European Commercial Correspondence' (June 1857)

Rothschild Row A nickname (modelled on ROTTEN ROW) given in the late 19th and early 20th centuries to the western end of PICCADILLY, opposite GREEN PARK, on account of the large number of members of the Rothschild banking family who lived here then.

N.M. Rothschild & Sons Ltd An investment bank founded by Nathan Mayer Rothschild in 1811. Throughout its history the firm has been based at New Court, St Swithin's Lane.

rotten

Rotten, Johnny *See the* SEX PISTOLS.

Rotten Row A riding and carriage road in HYDE PARK, leading westwards from HYDE PARK CORNER to KENSINGTON GARDENS. The origin of the name is uncertain: it is recorded as a medieval street name elsewhere in England, the first element apparently from Middle English *ratoun* 'rat', and denoting a rat-infested street; it may have been re-applied facetiously here, with a play on 'rotten' alluding to the softness or looseness of the soil, suitable for horses and carriages. It is unlikely to be, as is often claimed, a direct alteration of *Route du Roi*, although that may have played some part in the pun; it *was* a 'route of the king' in the late 17th century, when William III used to ride this way from ST JAMES'S to KENSINGTON PALACE. He had 300 oil lamps hung from the adjacent trees, creating the first road in England to be lit at night.

There is a similar riding path in the north-western part of HAMPSTEAD HEATH called Rotten Row, after the one in Hyde Park.

In its time 'Rotten Row' has served as COCKNEY RHYMING SLANG for both 'bow' and 'blow'.

round

Roundheads Puritans of the time of the Civil War (1642–51), especially Oliver Cromwell's soldiers. They were so called from their close-cropped hair, as contrasted with the long hair fashionable among the Royalists. The name was first used in 1641 in the affrays at WESTMINSTER when APPRENTICES were demonstrating against the power of the bishops.

Roundhouse An arts venue in CHALK FARM that was originally a locomotive shed with tracks radiating from a central turntable. For a century it languished as a warehouse until Arnold Wesker set up the CENTRE 42 theatrical project here in the early 1960s. The Roundhouse name was appropriate for the theatre-in-the-round productions subsequently staged here, such as Peter Brook's experimental version of SHAKESPEARE's *The Tempest* in 1968. In the same year it also hosted a 'dialectics of liberation' conference organized by the psychiatrist R.D. Laing. Jimi Hendrix, the Doors and the Ramones were among those to play influential rock gigs here. After falling into disuse the Roundhouse reopened in 2006 as an impressively remodelled creative centre and performance space.

round the houses 'Trousers' in rhyming slang, with the appropriate COCKNEY pronunciation. Short forms include 'rounds' and 'rounders'. The term was first recorded in the mid-19th century.

roundel Transport for London's name for the registered trademark that was earlier called the BULLSEYE.

Routemaster The classic double-decker London bus with access via an open platform at the rear. The Routemaster was designed by LONDON TRANSPORT and built from 1954 by the SOUTHALL-based Associated Equipment Com-

pany and its sister business PARK ROYAL Vehicles. Production ceased in 1968, primarily because the bus was unsuitable for the more cost-effective system of one-person operation. For several decades the Routemaster was rivalled only by the BLACK CAB as a mobile emblem of the capital and was considered a vital prop in depictions of the city on postcards and in films. The ageing nature of the fleet and concerns regarding the safety of the open platform and its accessibility to disabled users were major factors in its progressive removal from service in the late 20th and early 21st centuries. The Routemaster was officially withdrawn from regular service on 9 December 2005, although it continues to ply two 'heritage routes' that take in many of the capital's best-known tourist destinations. BENDY BUSES controversially replaced the Routemaster on several of its former routes. *See also* MONARCH OF THE ROAD.

On his election as MAYOR OF LONDON in 2008 Boris Johnson launched a design competition for a new Routemaster that would be environmentally sensitive and accessible to all travellers. Joint first prize was awarded to the automotive designers Capoco and a collaborative effort by the architects Foster + Partners and car maker Aston Martin. Bus manufacturers were then invited to develop the ideas into a final design and submit tenders to build it. Transport for London hopes that the first of the new Routemasters will be on the streets of London by 2011.

> I want the people of London to have restored to them the Routemaster bus that was so brutally taken away from them.
>
> BORIS JOHNSON, interviewed in *The Times* (6 December 2008)

Row, the The name by which PATERNOSTER ROW was known to its former community of booksellers and publishers and by which the haut monde of 19th-century London knew ROTTEN ROW.

Roxburghe

Roxburghe binding A style of bookbinding, usually quarter leather with plain sides, used by the ROXBURGHE CLUB and imitated by similar publishers.

Roxburghe Club An association founded in 1812 for the purpose of printing rare works or manuscripts. It came into existence when a group of bibliophiles dined together on the eve

of the sale of the library of historically significant works amassed by John Ker, 3rd Duke of
Roxburghe (1740–1804), at his house in HANOVER
SQUARE. The club owns a complete set of its own
and its members' publications, kept by the Society of Antiquaries in BURLINGTON HOUSE.

royal

Royal Academicians The 80 governing artists
of the ROYAL ACADEMY, of whom there must
always be at least 14 sculptors, 12 architects and
8 printmakers, with the balance being drawn
from the painters' category. All members are
required to bestow an example of work to the
Royal Academy and these works form part of its
permanent collection. Past and present Royal
Academicians have included John Constable,
Thomas Gainsborough, J.M.W. Turner, David
Hockney and Tracey Emin.

Royal Academy The first institution in Great
Britain devoted solely to the promotion of the
visual arts and to raising the standing of art,
artists and architecture. The Royal Academy of
Arts was founded by George III in 1768, with Sir
Joshua Reynolds (1723–92) as the first president.
It was based briefly in PALL MALL and then at
SOMERSET HOUSE until 1837, when it relocated
to the the east wing of the newly completed
NATIONAL GALLERY. In 1868 the RA moved to its
present home at BURLINGTON HOUSE. *See also
the* SUMMER EXHIBITION.

Royal Academy of Dramatic Art *See* RADA.

Royal Agricultural Hall *See the* AGRICULTURAL
HALL.

Royal Air Force Museum A museum of aviation opened in 1972 on Grahame Park Way,
COLINDALE. The pioneering British aviator
Claude Grahame-White (1879–1959) founded
the London Aerodrome on the site in 1911.
During the First World War the airfield served
as a base for the Royal Naval Air Service and
the Royal Flying Corps, becoming RAF HENDON
in 1927. Aircraft were manufactured and flown
from Hendon for another ten years, after which
its enclosure by suburban housing made aviation
increasingly impractical, although it operated
briefly as a fighter station during the Battle
of Britain. From 1940 RAF Hendon became a
transport, communications and training base.
Over a hundred aeroplanes are on show at the
museum and there is a special emphasis on the
Battle of Britain.

Royal Albert Hall *See under* ALBERT.

Royal Antediluvian Order of Buffaloes An
international fraternity that claims to have 16th-
century roots but seems in fact to date from the
founding of its first lodge, at the Harp Tavern on
Russell Street, COVENT GARDEN, in 1822. The Harp
had for some while been the meeting place of the
CITY OF LUSHINGTON, a club for men of the theatrical world. When that club decided to restrict
membership to actors, disgruntled stagehands
and other behind-the-scenes workers formed the
Loyal Antediluvian Order of Buffaloes. The name
had no ostensible significance and was probably
intended simply to sound humorously grand.
Travelling theatrical workers subsequently founded lodges far and wide, and changed the 'Loyal'
to 'Royal', without any form of regal consent. The
order is organized along Masonic lines but has
no formal connection with FREEMASONRY. The
cartoon character Fred Flintstone belonged to
the Loyal Order of Water Buffaloes.

Royal Aquarium *See the* AQ.

Royal Artillery Barracks The former headquarters of the Royal Regiment of Artillery,
established on WOOLWICH COMMON in 1776.
Shooting events will take place at the barracks
in the 2012 OLYMPIC GAMES and Paralympic
Games.

Royal Arsenal *See* WOOLWICH ARSENAL.

Royal Arsenal Co-operative Society London's most successful consumer co-operative,
founded by workers at WOOLWICH ARSENAL in
1868, operating at first from members' houses
in PLUMSTEAD and then from 147 Powis Street,
Woolwich. In addition to running shops of almost all kinds, the society built a large housing
estate at BOSTALL HEATH from the end of the
19th century. The Co-operative Wholesale Society absorbed the enterprise in 1985.

Royal Borough A name sometimes applied
(perhaps most often by the borough itself) to
KENSINGTON AND CHELSEA. Royal status was
granted to KENSINGTON in 1901 by Edward VII
in honour of Queen Victoria, who died that
year and who had been born at KENSINGTON
PALACE, and when the boroughs of Kensington
and Chelsea merged in 1965 the honorific title
passed to them jointly. KINGSTON UPON THAMES
is London's other royal borough.

Royal Botanic Gardens *See* KEW GARDENS.

Royal Caledonian Ball A traditional curtain
raiser to the LONDON SEASON, first organized on

a charitable basis by the Duke and Duchess of Atholl in 1849. Since 1930 it has been held in the GREAT ROOM at GROSVENOR HOUSE.

Royal College of Art A postgraduate university of art and design based at KENSINGTON GORE. It began at SOMERSET HOUSE in 1837 as the Government School of Design. Following the GREAT EXHIBITION of 1851 it added art to the curriculum, moved to SOUTH KENSINGTON and was renamed the National Art Training School. In 1896 it became the Royal College of Art. It achieved independent university status with the grant of its royal charter in 1967. RCA alumni include Barbara Hepworth, Henry Moore, James Dyson, David Hockney, Tracey Emin and Ridley Scott. *See also* RCA SECRET.

Royal Courts of Justice The permanent home of the High Court of Justice (which deals mainly with important civil disputes) and the Court of Appeal, situated at the eastern end of the STRAND. The complex was built in Gothic style to the designs of G.E. Street between 1874 and 1882, before which the courts had been held in WESTMINSTER HALL, LINCOLN'S INN and various other buildings around London. It was reported that 4,175 people lived in the 450 houses that were demolished to make way for the new buildings. Subsequent extensions have included the West Green Building (1912), the Queen's Building (1968) and an additional twelve courts for the CHANCERY Division, named the Thomas More Courts (1990).

Royal Court Theatre A two-auditorium theatre in SLOANE SQUARE, regarded as England's foremost home for new playwrights. It has staged works by Bertolt Brecht, Eugene Ionesco, Samuel Beckett, Jean-Paul Sartre, Arnold Wesker and, perhaps most influentially of all, John Osborne's *Look Back in Anger* in 1956, the year in which the theatre became the home of the English Stage Company. The fabric of the building dates from 1888; the interior was radically remodelled at the end of the 20th century.

Royal Docks The collective name for the Royal Victoria, Royal Albert and King George V docks, located between BECKTON and CANNING TOWN and the riverside districts of SILVERTOWN and NORTH WOOLWICH. The three docks opened in 1855, 1880 and 1921 respectively, each designed to handle the ever-increasing size of ocean-going vessels. The docks progressively adapted to changes in the nature of trade, with lineal quays

replacing jetties and transit sheds replacing warehouses. The Royals suffered devastating bomb damage in the Second World War. They were subsequently repaired and reopened but soon began to decline as a result of the increasing use of containers and the consequent rise of the docks downstream at Tilbury in ESSEX. The Royal Docks were closed in the early 1980s and are now used for sailing and rowing, while their quays have been redeveloped primarily for commercial purposes. LONDON CITY AIRPORT was laid out between the Royal Albert and King George V docks. The recently created ward of Royal Docks is at present by far the smallest in NEWHAM, but this will change within a few decades as more housing is constructed as part of the THAMES GATEWAY plan.

Royal Exchange The original exchange, situated at the apex formed by CORNHILL and THREADNEEDLE STREET, was founded by Sir Thomas Gresham, whose crest was a GRASSHOPPER, was opened by Elizabeth I in 1568 and was modelled on the Bourse at Antwerp as a place for London merchants to transact their business. It burnt down in the GREAT FIRE OF LONDON and a new exchange was opened in 1670, but this was again destroyed by fire in 1838. It is said that before the bells fell they had chimed: 'There's nae luck aboot the hoose.' The third building was opened by Queen Victoria in 1844. In 1939 the Exchange ceased its original function and the building was taken over by the Royal Exchange Assurance Corporation, which had occupied offices there since 1720. The London International Financial Futures Exchange (now NYSE Liffe) was based at the Royal Exchange from its inception in 1982 until its move to Cannon Bridge House in 1991. The Royal Exchange was remodelled as a luxury shopping mall in 2001. Jewellers, watchmakers and fashion accessory boutiques predominate and there are five cafés and restaurants.

There is no place in the town which I so much love to frequent as the Royal Exchange. It gives me a secret satisfaction, and in some measure gratifies my vanity, as I am an Englishman, to see so rich an assembly of countrymen and foreigners consulting together upon the private business of mankind, and making this metropolis a kind of emporium for the whole earth.

JOSEPH ADDISON, in *The Spectator* (19 May 1711)

Royal Festival Hall A concert venue on the SOUTH BANK. It opened in May 1951 for the FESTIVAL OF BRITAIN and its facilities have since been much enhanced, including a two-year refurbishment that was completed in 2007. The Arts Council's Saison poetry library moved into level 5 of the building in 1988, the year in which the structure achieved grade I listed status. The London Philharmonic Orchestra became the hall's resident symphony orchestra in 1992.

Royal Holloway *See* BEDFORD COLLEGE; UNIVERSITY OF LONDON.

Royal Horse Guards *See the* HORSE GUARDS.

Royal Institution An independent charity supporting scientific research and encouraging public involvement with the world of science. Soon after its foundation in 1799 the RI moved to 21 Albemarle Street, MAYFAIR, where it has remained ever since. The building was radically refurbished in 2008, to a design by Sir Terry Farrell, and its Faraday exhibition is open to the public every weekday.

Royal London Hospital One of London's major teaching hospitals, founded in 1740 as the London Hospital. It moved to its present site in WHITECHAPEL in the late 1750s. It was able to add 'Royal' to its name in 1990, and in 1994 it was combined with St Bartholomew's Hospital (*see* BART'S) to form the Barts and The London NHS Trust. Joseph Merrick, the ELEPHANT MAN, was a long-term in-patient at the hospital.

Royal Military School of Music *See* WHITTON.

Royal Oak Day *See* OAK APPLE DAY.

Royal Observatory *See* GREEENWICH OBSERVATORY.

Royal Opera House A theatre for opera and ballet in COVENT GARDEN, situated to the immediate north of the piazza. There has been a theatre on the site since the 1730s, and the first opera house opened here in 1809. It burnt down in 1857, and the present-day Royal Opera House (known to devotees as 'Covent Garden' or 'the Garden' and to insiders as 'the House') replaced it in 1858. It was extensively redesigned and modernized in the 1980s and 1990s, but it retains its classical entrance portico in BOW STREET. Despite the tribulations of underfunding and recurrent criticism of its artistic standards it remains one of Britain's flagship cultural venues, home to the Royal Opera and the Royal Ballet.

Royal Small Arms Factory A munitions works established at ENFIELD LOCK *c.*1804, soon after which it began to assemble muskets. The first Enfield rifle was made here in 1853 and construction of a much larger factory began in the following year. Arms manufacture reached a peak in the Second World War and so did the area that the factory occupied. With its testing ranges, the site covered around 100 acres (40 hectares). Production declined after the war, although the enterprise still employed over a thousand workers in the 1970s. The factory closed in 1988 and most of the site is now occupied by ENFIELD ISLAND VILLAGE. A few of the old buildings have been preserved.

Royal Society The premier scientific society in Britain. It was established in 1660 and incorporated as the Royal Society in 1662, but its origins can be traced to the meetings of philosophers and scientists held at Gresham College in 1645. It met at the college until 1710 and then moved to Crane Court, FLEET STREET. In 1780 it transferred to SOMERSET HOUSE, in 1857 to BURLINGTON HOUSE and most recently to CARLTON HOUSE TERRACE in 1967. Fellowship of the Royal Society is the most coveted honour among scientists; past fellows have included Isaac Newton, Benjamin Franklin, Charles Babbage, Charles Darwin and Sigmund FREUD.

Royal Society of Arts The abbreviated name of the Royal Society for the Encouragement of Arts, Manufactures and Commerce, an institution that seeks to stimulate enlightened thinking and socially beneficial innovation. The society was founded in 1754 at Rawthmell's COFFEE HOUSE in Henrietta Street, COVENT GARDEN, admitting men and women on an equal basis from the outset. As part of their ADELPHI scheme, the ADAM BROTHERS built a permanent home for the RSA in the early 1770s, on what is now John Adam Street. RSA members (called 'fellows' since 1914) have included Benjamin Franklin, Elizabeth Montagu (*see* BLUE STOCKING), Michael Faraday, Isambard Kingdom Brunel, Karl Marx, MARIE STOPES, Stephen Hawking and Nelson Mandela.

Royal Star and Garter Home *See the* STAR AND GARTER.

Royal Victoria Patriotic Asylum An imposing Gothic edifice built on part of WANDSWORTH COMMON in the late 1850s for the 'education and training of three hundred orphan daughters of soldiers, seamen and marines who perished in the Russian War, and for those who hereafter may require like succour'. In the Second World War it served as a detention centre, holding the Nazi defector Rudolf Hess, among others. In the mid-1980s it was converted to apartments, studios and workshops.

Royal Zoological Society Gardens *See* LONDON ZOO.

rub-a-dub(-dub) 'Pub' in COCKNEY RHYMING SLANG, with various abbreviations, such as 'rubbidy' and 'rubber'. The term is also popular in Australia. It derives from the nursery rhyme that begins 'Rub-a-dub-dub, three men [or maids] in a tub'.

Ruby (Murray) 'Curry' in one of the most widely used and understood modern additions to the lexicon of COCKNEY RHYMING SLANG. Ruby Murray (1935–96) was a Belfast-born popular singer who had a string of hits and a television show in the mid-1950s.

> I love a Ruby and the Coriander is the only Indian restaurant on Lordship Lane I haven't tried yet. Must rectify this soon. Thanks for the tip.
>
> forum post at www.eastdulwichforum.co.uk (26 March 2007)

Rudge, Barnaby *See* BARNABY RUDGE.

Ruffians' Hall A very old nickname for SMITHFIELD, especially the part that was later the site of a horse market. Amateur swordsmen used to come here to practise their swashbuckling skills but the place degenerated into a venue for brawling. 'He is only fit for Ruffians' Hall' was a catchphrase applied to 'quarrelsome people', especially if their manner of dress disguised their true nature.

> And this field, commonly called West Smithfield, was for many years called Ruffians Hall, by reason it was the usual place of Frayes and common fighting, during the Time that Sword-and-Bucklers were in use.
>
> *Howe's continuation of Stowe's 'Annals'* (1631)

Ruislip An archetypal METROLAND suburb, strung along the outer edge of built-up London north of NORTHOLT AERODROME. The first element of its name refers to the rushes that grew on the marshy banks of the River Pinn; the second part may be corrupted from Old English *slæp*, 'a wet slippery place', or *hylpe*, 'a

leap'. The medieval manor of Ruislip covered all of what became Ruislip (originally Westcote), NORTHWOOD and EASTCOTE. From the 15th century the manor was in the hands of King's College, Cambridge, which leased the land for farming until the arrival of the railway at the start of the 20th century. After briefly flourishing as a resort for day-trippers, Ruislip was built up with low-density housing, with spacious gardens and landscaped streets – an appealing prospect for city dwellers who hankered after a life in the country. Leslie Thomas's novel *Tropic of Ruislip* (1974) examines the fears, frustrations and lusts of a group of well-heeled executives on a luxury housing estate as they contemplate the approach of middle age.

> Gaily into Ruislip Gardens
> Runs the red electric train,
> With a thousand Ta's and Pardon's
> Daintily alights Elaine.
>
> JOHN BETJEMAN: 'Middlesex' (1954)

Ruislip Lido Originally a reservoir created in 1811 as a feeder for the GRAND JUNCTION CANAL. It was never particularly successful at performing this task so the owners redeveloped it as a lido in the mid-1930s and Ruislip–Northwood urban district council took it over in 1951. The main lido building was demolished in 1994, after a fire the previous year. With its woodland setting, sandy beach, pub and miniature railway, Ruislip Lido attracts thousands of local people each summer. The *Titanic* sank at Ruislip Lido in the film *A Night to Remember* (1958), and scenes for the *The Young Ones* (1961), starring Cliff Richard, were filmed on the beach, with local teenagers appearing as extras.

Ruislip spies *See the* PORTLAND SPIES.

Rumpole of the Bailey An eccentric barrister who stars in a series of stories by John Mortimer (1923–2009) and was memorably played on television by Leo McKern (1920–2002). After a mediocre start at a minor public school and armed with a third-class degree in law from Oxford, Rumpole made a dazzling entry to his legal career, achieving some astonishing acquittals, as in the case of the PENGE BUNGALOW MURDERS. Ever unlucky in love, he was proposed to by Hilda, daughter of his Head of Chambers, who took his silence for assent. Grubbily resplendent in his tattered court garb, endlessly puffing at small cigars, Rumpole stalks the corridors of the

OLD BAILEY and the cells of BRIXTON and makes occasional forays to Pommeroy's Wine Bar for a large dose of Château Thames Embankment. He is kept going by the faint hope that his actions will keep some young lad from following in his father's criminal footsteps.

running footmen Men servants in the early part of the 18th century whose duty it was to run beside the slow-moving coach horses and advise the innkeeper of his approaching guests, bear torches, pay turnpikes and so on. The pole that they carried was to help the cumbrous coach out of the numerous sloughs. The 4th Duke of Queensberry (*see* OLD Q) was said to have been the last to employ them.

> The duke was in the habit of trying the pace of candidates for his service by seeing how they could run up and down Piccadilly, watching and timing them from his balcony. They put on a livery before the trial. On one occasion, a candidate presented himself, dressed, and ran. At the conclusion of his performance he stood before the balcony. 'You will do very well for me,' said the duke. 'And your livery will do very well for me,' replied the man, and gave the duke a last proof of his ability as a runner by then running away with it.
>
> EDWARD WALFORD: *Old and New London*, Volume 4 (1878)

The last of the breed is commemorated in the name of a pub-cum-restaurant on Charles Street in MAYFAIR. Formerly called 'I Am the Only Running Footman' it is now simply 'The Only Running Footman'.

Russell Square Central London's second largest square, located to the north-east of the BRITISH MUSEUM in BLOOMSBURY. The Russell family, earls of Bedford from 1550, gained possession of Bloomsbury by marriage into the Southampton family in 1669. The area remained mostly open fields until the mid-18th century. The square was laid out in 1801 by Humphry Repton on land first called Southampton Fields and subsequently Long Fields. James Burton (1761–1837) was the designer of the square's original buildings, only a few of which now remain. Built at the turn of the 20th century, the Russell Hotel is a chateau-style terracotta extravagance, regarded as the finest work of the architect Charles Fitzroy Doll (1851–1929). Russell Square Gardens were relaid in 2002, returning them to something like their appearance in the early 1800s by reproducing the original twisting paths and planting a new lime walk.

Russell Square is the main setting for the events of William Thackeray's 'novel without a hero', *Vanity Fair* (1848). The poet T.S. Eliot worked for nearly 40 years for the publishers Faber & Faber at 24 Russell Square, a building now occupied by the School of Oriental and African Studies, a constituent college of the UNIVERSITY OF LONDON.

S

Saatchi Gallery A contemporary art gallery established in 1985 by the advertising mogul Charles Saatchi (b.1943). Its first premises were in Boundary Road, ST JOHN'S WOOD. In 2003 it reopened at COUNTY HALL and in 2008 moved to the Duke of York's HQ, in the KING'S ROAD. The gallery is to be presented to the nation, becoming the Museum of Contemporary Art for London..

Sacheverell Affair On 5 November 1709, on the anniversary of William III's landing at Torbay in 1688, Dr Henry Sacheverell (*c.*1674–1724) preached a sermon in ST PAUL'S before the LORD MAYOR OF LONDON reasserting the doctrine of non-resistance and by implication attacking the principles of the Glorious Revolution and the Dissenters. The sermon, *The Perils of False Brethren*, was subsequently printed, and the Whig ministry ill-advisedly impeached him (1710). The affair aroused great excitement. Queen Anne attended WESTMINSTER HALL daily, and the London mob burned Dissenters' chapels. Sacheverell was declared guilty by 69 votes to 52 and sentenced to abstain from preaching for three years and to have his sermon burned by the common hangman. It was substantially a moral victory for Sacheverell and his Tory adherents.

saddling the spit A disgraceful custom formerly observed in certain London parishes, notably that of ST CLEMENT DANES. On the occasion of an annual lump sum being paid to parish officers to meet the needs of abandoned infants, the recipients would treat themselves to a 'hilarious and bacchanalian' feast. Such parties were in theory held in the children's honour but the foundlings were afterwards handed over to 'nurses', in whose 'care' they frequently met an early death. The practice of saddling the spit was stamped out following the publication of a damning parliamentary report in 1716:

That a great many poor infants and exposed bastard children are inhumanly suffered to die by the barbarity of nurses, who are a sort of people void of commiseration or religion, hired by the churchwardens to take off a burthen from the parish at the cheapest and easiest rates they can, and these know the manner of doing it effectually, as by the burial books may evidently appear.

House of Commons Journals (8 March 1716)

Sadler's Wells 'London's dance house', as it now styles itself, situated on Rosebery Avenue, at the southern edge of ISLINGTON. There was once a holy well at this place belonging to St John's Priory, CLERKENWELL. It was blocked up at the Reformation but rediscovered by Thomas Sadler in 1683 when workmen were digging for gravel. The waters were pronounced to contain salts of iron, and the discovery was turned to immediate profit. However, when attendance at the well declined, MUSIC HALL entertainment was provided, and from the 1690s this became the chief attraction under James Miles. In 1765 a builder named Rosoman erected a proper theatre, which became famous for burlettas, musical interludes and pantomimes (it features in Tobias Smollett's *Humphry Clinker* (1771)). Edmund Kean, Charles Dibdin and Joseph Grimaldi all appeared there. In 1844 Samuel Phelps took over and produced SHAKESPEARE, but after his retirement the boom in WEST END theatres cast the Wells into the shade and it eventually became a cinema, which closed in 1916.

A new theatre, built with the help of the Carnegie United Kingdom Trust, opened in 1931 under Lilian Baylis of the OLD VIC and it became one of the leading houses in London for the production of ballet and opera. In 1946 the ballet transferred to the ROYAL OPERA HOUSE; it retained its named link with the Wells, though, and in due course became the Sadler's Wells

Royal Ballet. The Sadler's Wells Opera Company relocated to the London COLISEUM in 1969 and in 1974 became known as ENGLISH NATIONAL OPERA. In 1996 the old Sadler's Wells theatre was effectively rebuilt; it reopened in 1998.

saffron

Saffron Hill A street extending southwards from CLERKENWELL Road, parallel with FARRINGDON ROAD. This was once part of the gardens of ELY PLACE, and takes its name from the flowers that grew there. By the early 18th century Saffron Hill had become the principal thoroughfare of a notorious ROOKERY. The area was sanitized in the 1840s and 50s.

Saffron Park The disguised identity of BEDFORD PARK in G.K. Chesterton's tale of suburban anarchism *The Man Who Was Thursday* (1908).

Sage of Chelsea

Thomas Carlyle (1795–1881), essayist and historian, was so called. He and his wife Jane moved from Dumfriesshire to No.5 (now 24) Cheyne Row, CHELSEA, in 1834, where they lived for the remainder of their lives. It was here that they played host to many of the cultural figures of the Victorian age, including Tennyson, DICKENS, Ruskin and Darwin.

Sainsbury's

A national supermarket chain founded by John James Sainsbury (1844–1928) and his wife Mary Ann (1849–1927). John James was born in LAMBETH and Mary Ann Staples came from ST PANCRAS, and they met while working at businesses in Strutton Ground, off VICTORIA STREET. They opened their first shop at 173 DRURY LANE in 1869 and their second at 159 Queen's Crescent, KENTISH TOWN, in 1876. The couple lived above the Queen's Crescent store until 1886, by which time they had opened additional branches in the ISLINGTON area and could afford a villa in HIGHGATE. Sainsbury's now has around 800 stores nationwide. Its headquarters at HOLBORN Circus occupies the former site of the Mirror Building. A move to KING'S CROSS is planned for around 2012. The MUSEUM OF LONDON DOCKLANDS holds the company's historical archive.

> Keep the shops well lit.
>
> JOHN JAMES SAINSBURY: attributed last words (1928)

Sainsbury Wing *See* MONSTROUS CARBUNCLE.

saint

St Agnes Well A well or pool that formerly lay near the PERILOUS POND, in MOORFIELDS. It was earlier called Dame Annis the Clear and, corruptly, Anniseed Cleer. Dame Annis was said to have been a rich widow who was seduced, impoverished and deserted by a 'riotous courtier' of Edward I (r.1272–1307) and who then drowned herself in a ditch. In 1547 a conduit was constructed to carry the well water to LOTHBURY. St Agnes Well is nowadays the name of the underpass complex and sunken shopping area at OLD STREET station.

St Benet Fink A THREADNEEDLE STREET church named after St Benedict and one Robert Fink, or Finch, who paid for its construction (or reconstruction) in the 13th century. The writer Samuel Clarke (1599–1682), author of *A General Martyrology* (1651), was the church's pastor until his ejection in 1662. St Benet Fink was destroyed in the GREAT FIRE OF LONDON, rebuilt by Christopher Wren and demolished in the 1840s to allow the expansion of the ROYAL EXCHANGE. St Benet Fink, TOTTENHAM, was built with the proceeds of the sale.

St Bride's, Fleet Street *See the* WEDDING CAKE CHURCH.

St Clement Danes The central church of the Royal Air Force, situated on an island site in the STRAND, just east of the ALDWYCH. According to tradition the first church of St Clement's was built by Danes expelled from the CITY of London by King Alfred in the 9th century. It is said to be the burial place of the half-Danish Harold I (Harefoot), who ruled England from 1035 to 1040, first as regent for his half-brother and then as king. The church escaped damage in the GREAT FIRE OF LONDON but was rebuilt in 1681 by Christopher Wren and a steeple was added to the tower by James Gibbs in 1719. Incendiary bombs gutted the building in May 1941 and it was rebuilt in the mid-1950s. St Clement Danes was re-consecrated in 1958 as a shrine of remembrance to those killed on active service and those of the Allied Air Forces who gave their lives during the Second World War. *See also* ORANGES AND LEMONS.

St George in the East A parish in north WAPPING, created in 1729, the year of the church's completion on Cannon Street Road. St George in the East was one of three EAST END churches designed by Nicholas Hawksmoor, the others being at SPITALFIELDS and LIMEHOUSE. With the construction of the COMMERCIAL ROAD and the coming of railways, inland docks and heavy industry to the East End, St George in the East became a solidly urban and extremely poor parish over the course of the 19th century.

St George's Fields

1. Former meadows in SOUTHWARK, named after the adjacent church of St George the Martyr. From the late Middle Ages open-air preachers, banned from London, would frequently hold forth there. The fields survived until the beginning of the 19th century (although in an increasingly contaminated state), after which they were rapidly built over.

> Saint George's Fields are fields no more.
> The trowel supersedes the plough;
> Huge inundated swamps of yore,
> Are changed to civic villas now.
>
> HORACE and JAMES SMITH: 'New Buildings' (1812)

2. A green and gated estate built in the early 1970s to the north of BAYSWATER Road, a quarter of a mile (0.4 km) west of MARBLE ARCH. This was a burial ground from 1763, later used for archery, games and as allotments. The land was owned by the church of St George's, HANOVER SQUARE, which sold it to developers in 1967.

St George's Fields Massacre The name sometimes given to the events of 10 May 1768, when 15,000 protesters assembled on St George's Fields, SOUTHWARK, demanding the release of the radical MP John Wilkes (1725–97) from the nearby KING'S BENCH PRISON. Soldiers shot into the crowd, killing seven, including two bystanders. Public outrage at the bloodshed prompted disturbances across London.

St Ghastly Grim A nickname coined by Charles DICKENS for the church of St Olave Hart Street, in the CITY of London, from the macabre ornamentation on the churchyard gateway, erected in 1658. Among those buried here are Samuel PEPYS and, so it is said, the woman who inspired the pantomime character Mother Goose.

> It is a small small churchyard, with a ferocious, strong, spiked iron gate, like a jail. This gate is ornamented with skulls and cross-bones, larger than the life, wrought in stone; but it likewise came into the mind of Saint Ghastly Grim, that to stick iron spikes a-top of the stone skulls, as though they were impaled, would be a pleasant device. Therefore the skulls grin aloft horribly, thrust through and through with iron spears. Hence, there is attraction of repulsion

for me in Saint Ghastly Grim and, having often contemplated it in the daylight and the dark, I once felt drawn towards it in a thunderstorm at midnight.

> DICKENS: *The Uncommercial Traveller* (1860)

St Giles or **St Giles's** Formerly London's most notorious neighbourhood, situated south-east of present-day TOTTENHAM COURT ROAD underground station. St Giles came into existence in the year 1101, when Henry I's wife Matilda founded a hospital for lepers here. There have been three churches of St Giles-in-the-Fields; the present one dates from 1734. Until the mid-19th century the St Giles district was a ROOKERY that provided refuge from the officers of the law, who would seldom venture into the warren of slums in pursuit of a fleeing criminal. The turning point came in 1840, when the police defeated a gang of counterfeiters after a battle lasting several hours. Within a year the authorities were planning to force New Oxford Street through the district in a deliberate act of decontamination by demolition. By the autumn of 1849 only 95 houses remained, which, it is claimed, had a total of 2,850 inhabitants. The creation of SHAFTESBURY AVENUE and CHARING CROSS ROAD completed the area's sanitization. During the course of the 20th century the area was rebuilt with a mix of offices (notably at CENTRE POINT), light industrial premises, shops and council flats.

St Giles blackbirds An 18th-century nickname for the Afro-Caribbean community of St Giles, including those who did not live in the locality but found it a relatively tolerant place to socialize with their kin.

St Giles Greek The thieves' slang used by the denizens of that quarter from the early 17th century to the 19th.

St Helier An extensive housing estate, separated from MITCHAM by the River WANDLE. It was built between the wars by the LONDON COUNTY COUNCIL and named in honour of Lady St Helier (1845–1931), a prominent philanthropist who had been an LCC alderman. The other St Helier, chief town of Jersey, objected to the choice of name and vainly advocated 'Jeuneville', because Lady St Helier was known as Lady Jeune before her husband was given a peerage. Many of the roads were given the names of religious centres (arranged alphabetically to help newcomers orient themselves), marking the former ecclesiastical ownership of lands hereabouts, notably by MERTON PRIORY.

St James's One of the WEST END's most prestigious quarters, St James's lies south of PICCADILLY and west of WHITEHALL. Most of the district was laid out and developed from 1662 onwards by Henry Jermyn, Earl of St Albans (c.1604–84). In 1685 St James's was made a separate parish (from ST MARTIN-IN-THE-FIELDS) and Christopher Wren built St James's Church, with interior carvings by Grinling Gibbons. Much of the district was rebuilt from the mid-1850s and the residential character of St James's shifted from the aristocratic to the merely upper middle class, accompanied by art galleries, restaurants and gentlemen's outfitters. Together with neighbouring MAYFAIR, the district is nowadays notable for its concentration of specialist financial businesses, especially hedge funds and private equity firms.

St James's Palace A royal palace occupying the site of a hospital for 'leprous maidens' founded around 1117 by Queen Matilda, the consort of Henry I, and dedicated to St James the Less. With the progressive eradication of leprosy in Britain, the house had been turned into a convent by the mid-15th century. The palace was begun by Henry VIII in 1531 and served as a military prison during the Civil War. After WHITEHALL PALACE burned down in 1698 St James's Palace succeeded it as the royal seat. It ceased to be the sovereign's residence in 1837, but was used for LEVEES and other official functions. Today it is the London residence of the Princess Royal and Princess Alexandra, and houses the offices of several departments of the royal household. Its main surviving Tudor portions are the imposing gatehouse and the CHAPEL ROYAL.

St James's Park The oldest of London's royal parks, situated to the south of St James's Palace, on marshy land which had previously been pasturage for pigs. About 90 acres (36 hectares) in extent, it is bounded to the north by the MALL, to the east by HORSE GUARDS Road and to the south by BIRDCAGE WALK. BUCKINGHAM PALACE is at its western end. It was landscaped in the style of Versailles after the Restoration, with its long lake, known as the Canal. John Nash was responsible for the present appearance of the park in the late 1820s.

William Wycherley's first play (1671) was *Love in a Wood, or, St James's Park*, a comedy of intrigue.

St James's Square An imposing square with a pleasing garden, situated centrally in the St James's district. It was created in the late 1660s and the 1670s by Henry Jermyn as part of his planned development of the wider district. The square's tenants include the Naval and Military Club (*see the* IN AND OUT) at No.4, once the home of Nancy Astor, the first woman to sit in Parliament, CHATHAM HOUSE at No.10, the former home of three prime ministers, including Gladstone, and the LONDON LIBRARY at No.14.

St James's Street A street in west St James's, extending south from PICCADILLY towards St James's Palace. It marked the western boundary of the estate developed by Henry Jermyn and from the end of the 17th century became a popular location for COFFEE HOUSES, several of which subsequently evolved into gentlemen's CLUBS.

> The street is still a lively tomb
> For rich, and gay, and clever;
> The crops of dandies bud, and bloom,
> And die as fast as ever.

FREDERICK LOCKER: *London Lyrics*, 'St James's Street' (1867)

St John's Wood A plush 19th-century suburb with interwar augmentation, situated on the north-west side of REGENT'S PARK. The name was recorded in Latin form at the end of the 13th century, when the land came into the possession of the Order of the Hospital of St John of Jerusalem (*see the* KNIGHTS HOSPITALLER). The English name was first mentioned in 1524. The Eyre family laid roads across the estate they owned here in the 1820s and agreed building contracts with a number of small firms, who did most of their work in the 1840s. Standards were kept high and the new inhabitants were bankers, merchants and gentlemen of independent means. Later phases of building, especially towards the west, were less exclusive. Blocks of private flats replaced many of the early Victorian houses during the 1930s. After the Second World War the municipal authorities rebuilt so extensively in the north and west that some parts of the former Eyre estate are no longer thought of as being in St John's Wood. However, the surviving Victorian properties and the classiest of the flats and mansion blocks form a prestigious enclave that reaches its acme on Avenue Road.

The Hungarian film producer Alexander Korda lived on Avenue Road from 1933 to 1939 and the composer Benjamin Britten lived on St John's Wood High Street in the mid-1940s.

> Your mother, she's an heiress,
> Owns a block in St John's Wood.
> And your father'd be there with her,
> If he only could.
>
> MICK JAGGER and KEITH RICHARDS: 'Play With Fire' (song by the Rolling Stones) (1965)

St John's Wood Clique A group of artists who lived in the St John's Wood area in the late 19th century and influenced each other's styles. Their work became highly fashionable around the turn of the 20th century, but now few of their names ring bells. The principal members included G.D. Leslie, H. Stacey Marks, G.A. Storey, W.F. Yeames and P.H. Calderon. Probably the clique's best-known painting is Yeames's *And When Did You Last See Your Father?* (1878), a genre picture featuring a small Royalist boy being interrogated by Cromwellian soldiers.

St Katharine Docks A revitalized part of the former London docks, located between WAPPING and the TOWER. In 1147 Queen Matilda established a church-cum-hospital dedicated to St Katharine, which adapted and survived until the coming of the docks. The surrounding marshes were drained in the early 16th century but the busy settlement that grew up here was torn apart after Parliament passed the St Katharine Docks Act in 1825. Over 11,000 people were displaced by the works, which swept away slums like Dark Entry, Cat's Hole and Pillory Lane. Construction was led by the great railway builder Thomas Telford, in his only major project in London. With its tight security, St Katharine's specialized in high-value exotic goods such as ivory, indigo powder, shells and feathers, as well as handling staples like TEA and wool. The docks were wrecked by wartime bombs but limped on until their final closure in the late 1960s. In the 1970s and 1980s St Katharine's was redeveloped in a pioneering mixed-use project that created private and public housing, offices and leisure facilities.

St Luke's Now a little-used name for the area surrounding the western half of OLD STREET. From medieval times until the slum clearance programme of the 1870s its position on the edge of the CITY of London made St Luke's a haven for all kinds of prohibited activities, from astrology and wizardry to bear-baiting and prostitution.

Thieves and pickpockets could make regular forays into the City and then lose any pursuer in the maze of courts and alleyways around WHITECROSS STREET. The reputation of St Luke's as a ROOKERY reached a peak in the first half of the 19th century, when FLASH HOUSES were more numerous here than anywhere else in London. By 1900 southern St Luke's had become a district of workshops and warehouses, with new tenement blocks providing homes for law-abiding citizens. However, many of the worst elements simply decamped to the other side of Old Street and this part remained disreputable until the 1930s. *See also* LOUSY ST LUKE'S.

St Luke's Club or **Vandyke's Club** A cultural association that met in various London taverns to discuss matters of artistic taste and judgement in a convivial atmosphere. They held an annual dinner on 18 October to celebrate the festival of St Luke, the patron saint of painters, and were also known as the Society of the Virtuosi of St Luke. Founded around 1689, the club was perhaps the first organized set of artists in Britain. In addition to leading painters, the membership included all the most important collectors of the time and in some respects the club was the forerunner of the ROYAL ACADEMY. The Virtuosi held their last meeting in 1743.

St Margaret's, Westminster *See* WESTMINSTER.

St Martin-in-the-Fields A church located at the north-east corner of TRAFALGAR SQUARE. The first documented reference to a church on the site dates from a dispute of 1222, between the abbot of WESTMINSTER and the bishop of London, regarding the bishop's authority over the church. The archbishop of Canterbury decided in favour of the abbot. Henry VIII built a new church *c.*1542 and this was enlarged in 1607 and replaced in 1726 by the present structure, designed by James Gibbs. Since Dick Sheppard's time as vicar (1914–26) St Martin's has been conspicuously involved in several charitable and humanitarian movements, especially those connected with homelessness. The church nowadays holds regular services in English, Cantonese and Mandarin.

The Academy of St Martin in the Fields, a renowned chamber orchestra, gave its first performance in the church in 1959. The Academy of St Martin in the Fields Chorus was founded in 1975.

St Martin's beads Cheap counterfeit beads, jewellery, lace, rings and so on were so called. When the old collegiate church of ST MARTIN'S LE GRAND was demolished, hucksters established themselves on the site and carried on a considerable trade in artificial jewellery and cheap wares generally. Hence the use of the saint's name in this connection.

St Martin's le Grand A street connecting ST PAUL'S with the southern end of ALDERSGATE STREET. It takes its name from a church and college that stood here from 1056 until the late 1540s. The church's precincts were a place of sanctuary. In 1829 the General Post Office moved its headquarters and main sorting office from LOMBARD STREET to an imposing new building occupying the church's former site, designed by Sir Robert Smirke. The operation subsequently expanded to fill much of both sides of St Martin's le Grand and the street's name was often used as a metonym for the postal authorities. Letter sorting moved to MOUNT PLEASANT in 1900, while administrative offices and public counters progressively relocated to King Edward Street. Smirke's grand edifice in St Martin's le Grand was demolished in 1913.

In COCKNEY RHYMING SLANG, 'St Martin's le Grand' means 'hand'. Often abbreviated to 'martin', the term was in use as early as the mid-19th century but is almost never heard now. *See also* GERMAN (BAND).

St Martin's, Ludgate A Wren church on LUDGATE HILL. According to the 13th-century chronicler Robert of Gloucester, the first church on the site was founded by the 7th-century king of the Britons Cadwallo, also known as Cadwallon ap Cadfan, who is said (even more dubiously) to have been buried here.

St Mary Axe A street in the CITY of London, running from HOUNDSDITCH in the north to LEADENHALL STREET in the south, named after the former 12th-century church of St Mary Axe, which closed in 1560. The church acquired its name from its claim to possess one of the three axes used by henchmen of Attila the Hun to behead the 11,000 virgins said to have accompanied St Ursula on a 5th-century mission to convert the heathen. The Victorian BALTIC Exchange building was situated here, but was very badly damaged by an IRA bomb in 1992, and subsequently demolished to make way for the GHERKIN.

St Marylebone *See* MARYLEBONE.

St Mary-le-Bow London's most famous parish church, situated near the midpoint of CHEAPSIDE, on the south side of the road. The first St Mary-le-Bow was built *c.*1080 by Archbishop Lanfranc, and may have replaced a church of Saxon origin. Its name probably refers to the bowed shape of the arches supporting its undercroft, which were a novelty at that time. St Mary-le-Bow was substantially rebuilt after a fire in 1196 and that building was demolished and rebuilt by Christopher Wren after the GREAT FIRE OF LONDON. Wren's church was almost completely destroyed by a German bomb in May 1941. The church was eventually rebuilt under the direction of Laurence King and was re-consecrated by the bishop of London in 1964. *See also* BORN WITHIN (THE) SOUND OF BOW BELLS.

St Mary Matfelon A chapel (later a church) built among the cornfields west of STEPNEY between 1250 and 1286. Its white stone fabric gave WHITECHAPEL its name. St Mary's was rebuilt after a great storm in 1362, rebuilt again in 1673, and yet again in 1880 after a disastrous fire. St Mary's underground station opened in 1884. Later renamed St Mary's (Whitechapel Road), it closed in 1938 when ALDGATE East station was relocated eastwards, reducing the distance between the two. The station building was destroyed by bombing in 1940 and so was the church, which this time was not rebuilt. The neighbouring district has long been renowned for its poverty and still scores highly on indices of deprivation.

St Mary Overy or **Overie** (Old English *ofer ea*, 'over the river') The priory church of St Mary Overy, renamed St Saviour's in 1540 and which became SOUTHWARK CATHEDRAL in 1905. It is said in legend to have been founded by a ferryman's daughter called Mary Overs. Her miserly father, Awdrey, feigned death in the hope that sorrow would restrain his household's consumption of victuals. Instead they rejoiced and made merry, whereupon Awdrey rose up in anger, only to be slain as a ghost. Mary, now possessed of his fortune, sent for her lover, but he was thrown from his horse and was killed. In sorrow she founded the nunnery, which she entered.

St Mary Undercroft *See* ST STEPHEN'S CHAPEL.

Saint Monday Monday was so called by some

of the London mechanics, who often made that day a holiday.

St Mungo's London's largest charity for the homeless, headquartered in HAMMERSMITH. It began in BATTERSEA in 1969 with the opening of a house for rough sleepers, with a soup run operating from the kitchen. Although not a religious organization, its Glaswegian founder named the charity in honour of the patron saint of his native city. St Mungo's nowadays runs residential care homes, specialist hostels, day centres and other services.

St Mungo's Hospital for Magical Maladies and Injuries *See* POTTER, HARRY.

St Pancras Nowadays the identity of the district situated to the north-east of BLOOMSBURY and formerly a metropolitan borough extending as far north as HIGHGATE. The saint's name is an anglicization of the Latin *St Pancratius*, a 3rd-century martyr who was beheaded at the age of 14. The old church that was dedicated to St Pancras may be of 7th-century origin and was probably rebuilt in the 12th century. However, its parishioners migrated northwards to KENTISH TOWN and the church was left isolated in the fields. St Pancras Old Church survives on Pancras Road but a neo-Grecian church of the same name was built in 1822 on the corner of present-day EUSTON ROAD and Upper Woburn Place to serve the streets that were spilling out of Bloomsbury at this time. This was never an area of the highest class and it deteriorated with the arrival of the railway termini, the first of which was EUSTON in 1837. North of the Euston Road conditions became particularly bad in the parts of SOMERS TOWN that were not taken for station buildings or goods yards.

St Pancras station A railway terminus built, together with the Midland Grand Hotel, from 1865 to 1874 by Sir George Gilbert Scott (1811–78) for the Midland Railway Company. Scott was a builder of churches and a restorer of great cathedrals and this experience shows in his work here. The hotel's interior is, if anything, even more opulent than its facade but it was converted to office use after 1935 and renamed St Pancras Chambers. The offices too were closed in the mid-1980s when the building failed to pass fire regulations. British Rail tried in vain to gain permission to demolish the hotel building and it long remained empty, while the platforms behind were underused. Finally, an additional use was found for the station and from 2007, as St Pancras International, it became the London terminus for EUROSTAR services. The Manhattan Loft Corporation is restoring St Pancras Chambers as apartments and a hotel, a project due for completion early in 2011.

St Paul's The cathedral of the diocese of London, crowning LUDGATE HILL. Its site has long been used for worship: there was a Roman temple here and the first St Paul's Cathedral was founded in 604, probably by Mellitus, Bishop of London, at the request of King Ethelbert of Kent. It was rebuilt in 962 following Viking raids. In 1087 'old' St Paul's was begun in grand Norman style; its completion took over 200 years. Old St Paul's burned down in the GREAT FIRE OF LONDON, after which Christopher Wren (1632–1723) was commissioned to produce a design for a new cathedral, which was completed in 1710. The cathedral is built of Portland stone and surmounted by a dome inspired by St Peter's Basilica in Rome.

> It is true, St Peter's, besides its beauty in ornament and imagery, is beyond St Paul's in its dimensions, is every way larger; but it is the only church in the world that is so; and it was a merry hyperbole of Sir Christopher Wren's, who, when some gentlemen in discourse compared the two churches, and in compliment to him, pretended to prefer St Paul's, and when they came to speak of the dimensions, suggested, that St Paul's was the biggest: I tell you, says Sir Christopher, you might set it in St Peter's, and look for it a good while, before you could find it.
>
> DANIEL DEFOE: *Tour Through the Whole Island of Great Britain*, Volume 2 (1725)

St Paul's famously survived bombing raids during the BLITZ, thanks to good fortune and the valiant efforts of firefighters, and it became a symbol of London's wartime resistance. *See also* PAUL'S.

Many distinguished Britons are buried in St Paul's capacious crypt (believed to be the longest in Europe), most notably national heroes Nelson and Wellington. It is also the last resting place of the cathedral's architect, above whose tomb is the inscription (composed by his son) *Lector, si monumentum requiris, circumspice* ('Reader, if you seek his monument, look around you'). St Paul's is used for great national occasions, such as thanksgivings for victory and monarchs' jubilee services. The state funeral of Sir Winston

Churchill took place at the cathedral in 1965 and Prince Charles married Lady Diana Spencer here in 1981.

St Paul's Churchyard A street that surrounds the western end of St Paul's Cathedral. In the days of Old St Paul's, when it was still an actual churchyard, it was the centre of the London book trade (at that time churchyards were not used as graveyards). All the major printers and booksellers of the 16th and early 17th centuries had premises there, including most notably Wynkyn de Worde (*see also* FLEET STREET).

St Paul's, Covent Garden *See the* ACTORS' CHURCH.

St Paul's Girls' School A sister institution to ST PAUL'S SCHOOL, founded in 1904 in BROOK GREEN, where it remains today. Its first high mistress was Frances Gray, a leading figure in the women's education movement, and she appointed Gustav Holst as director of music. The school's alumnae include the writers Monica Dickens, Dodie Smith and Marghanita Laski, the actresses Natasha Richardson and Rachel Weisz and the politicians Shirley Williams and Harriet Harman.

St Paul's School A school for boys established by Dean Colet in ST PAUL'S CHURCHYARD in 1509. Colet's generous endowment helped make it the largest school in England, with 153 scholars – a biblical reference to the 'miraculous draught of fishes' (John 21:11) – who were all taught in one large room, sometimes divided by curtains. The school was free, though pupils were required to bring their own wax candles, an expensive rule that was enforced until 1820. The first building was destroyed in the GREAT FIRE OF LONDON but the school was soon rebuilt on the same site and rebuilt again in 1824. St Paul's School moved to BROOK GREEN in 1884, and then across the THAMES to the CASTELNAU peninsula in 1968. St Paul's alumni include Samuel PEPYS, Edmund Halley, G.K. Chesterton and Field Marshal Bernard Montgomery.

St Paul's Stump *See* POL'S STUMP.

St Peter Some time in the early 7th century, according to legend, the first apostle showed himself to a fisherman on the SURREY side of the THAMES on the night before the dedication of a church built by Sebert, king of the East Saxons, on THORNEY ISLAND (now WESTMINSTER). At Peter's behest, the fisherman rowed him across the river and the saint entered the church, which suddenly seemed bathed in a fiery light. The

saint performed the rites of consecration, wrote upon the pavement in Greek and Hebrew and anointed the walls with holy oil, while celestial choirs scattered sound and fragrance. The fisherman (who was rewarded with a generous catch of salmon) told the news to the bishop of London, who collected the relics of the apostolic consecration and placed them in a shrine, where they were last seen in the 14th century.

St Peter ad Vincula (Latin, 'St Peter in Chains') The CHAPEL ROYAL of the TOWER OF LONDON, founded in the 12th century for the use of prisoners. Its name refers to the miraculous release of St Peter from his prison chains by an angel (Acts 12:7). It was incorporated into the walls of the fortress during its expansion under Henry III (r.1216–72) and has been rebuilt at least twice, once in the late 13th century and then in its present form during the reign of Henry VIII (1509–47). Two of Henry's wives are buried here: Anne Boleyn and Catherine Howard, as are Lady Jane Grey and two saints of the Roman Catholic Church, Sir Thomas More and Bishop John Fisher. The chapel remains a place of worship for the Tower's resident community.

St Reatham A mildly amusing word play on STREATHAM, pretending to try to make the place sound more genteel. It was popular among upwardly mobile house-buying twenty- and thirty-somethings in the 1980s and 1990s.

St Stephen's Parliament was sometimes so called, because for nearly 300 years prior to the destructive fire of 1834, the House of Commons used to sit in ST STEPHEN'S CHAPEL.

St Stephen's Chapel A chapel in the PALACE OF WESTMINSTER, said to have been founded by King Stephen (r.1135–41). It was rebuilt over a prolonged period from 1290 and ostentatiously ornamented with gold and silver. When in residence at Westminster, the king worshipped in St Stephen's, while his courtiers did likewise in the crypt below, which is now known as the Chapel of St Mary Undercroft. The Canons of St Stephen's, the religious order that had held the services for the royal family, were dismissed in 1547 and soon afterwards the chapel became the first permanent home of the House of Commons. During its life as a debating chamber, the chapel was progressively remodelled (by Christopher Wren, among others) until almost no trace remained of its original incarnation. The upper part of St Stephen's was destroyed in the fire of

1834 but the undercroft survived and is nowadays used by MPs and peers and their offspring for weddings and christenings.

St Thomas' Hospital A major London teaching hospital situated on the opposite bank of the THAMES from the PALACE OF WESTMINSTER. It was founded some time in the 12th century as the infirmary of the Augustinian priory of St Thomas, in SOUTHWARK, with 40 beds for the poor including the 'sick and the merely needy'. It was originally located near the present-day GUY'S HOSPITAL and was re-established after a fire in 1212 on the east side of BOROUGH High Street. In 1871, following the building of the railway, the hospital relocated to its present site north of LAMBETH PALACE. St Thomas' formed a combined NHS trust with Guy's in 2004. *See also* DREADNOUGHT; LADY OF THE LAMP; OLD OPERATING THEATRE.

House of St Barnabas *See under* HOUSE.

Salvation Army A religious organization founded by William Booth (1829–1912), originally a Methodist minister. It developed from his Christian Mission, founded in WHITECHAPEL in 1865, and the movement took its present name in 1878. Booth himself became the 'General' and the 'Army' was planned on semi-military lines. The motto adopted was 'Through Blood and Fire', and the activities were directed towards the poor, outcast and destitute. Though Booth was often imprisoned for preaching in the open air, his men and women waged war on such evils as sweated labour and child prostitution, and a worldwide network of social and regenerative agencies was established. Opinion changed, and Booth was made a freeman of the CITY of London and was a guest at Edward VII's coronation. The Salvation Army established a college at DENMARK HILL in 1929; the campus is now also home to the organization's international headquarters.

Samaritans A support group for those experiencing feelings of distress or despair, including those which could lead to suicide. The organization is named after the biblical story of the Good Samaritan (Luke 10:30–7) and is now based in Ewell, SURREY. Samaritans was founded by the Lincolnshire-born clergyman Chad Varah (1911–2007), who conceived the idea for a telephone helpline when he was serving as vicar of St Paul's, CLAPHAM. In 1953 he found time to implement the initiative when he became rector of St Stephen Walbrook in the CITY of London, a post he retained for 50 years. He set up the first telephone in the crypt of the church, and recruited a handful of volunteers to take the calls. The organization now has over 200 branches nationally, and around 17,000 trained volunteers.

Sanger's Circus One of the most spectacular entertainments of Victorian England. In 1845 the brothers John (1816–89) and George (1825–1911) Sanger began a conjuring exhibition at Birmingham and from this they ventured into a travelling circus business. Their success was such that they were eventually able to lease the AGRICULTURAL HALL and in 1871 purchased ASTLEY'S. Their mammoth shows were a distinctive feature of the entertainment world, but they subsequently dissolved the partnership and after John's death only 'Lord' George's circus continued on the road.

Sapphire A METROPOLITAN POLICE project specializing in the investigation of rape and sexual assault cases, and seeking to improve standards of victim care and support. Each borough has a dedicated Sapphire team. *See also the* HAVENS.

Saracens FC A rugby union FOOTBALL club nowadays based at Watford FC's Vicarage Road stadium, in Hertfordshire. Saracens was founded in 1876 by the Old Boys of the Philological School, later MARYLEBONE Grammar School, and its first fixture was at PRIMROSE HILL playing fields. The club merged with the neighbouring Crusaders in 1878, retaining the Saracens name, and played at a variety of grounds in north London before moving to Watford in 1997.

Sarf London A facetious spelling of SOUTH LONDON, imitating the supposed pronunciation of those who live there, although, when spoken, the word 'south' is more likely to be delivered as something like 'saahf'.

> However, come the 19th-century railway age, and we find sarf London transforming itself within the popular imagination.
>
> WILL SELF, in *The Independent* (10 March 2007)

Sassoon, Vidal Probably the most influential figure in the history of modern hairdressing. Vidal Sassoon (b.1928) grew up in a tenement on PETTICOAT LANE, where he was apprenticed to Adolph Cohen, a hairdresser nicknamed 'the professor'. In the face of the blackshirted anti-Semitism troubling the EAST END at that time, Sassoon became active in a Jewish paramilitary group while working in a MAYFAIR salon and would explain away his scratches and bruises by telling his refined clients, with tongue in cheek, that he had tripped over a hairpin. He left the country in 1948 to fight for Israeli independence. Following his return, Sassoon created a short, asymmetrical hairstyle that became part of the defining imagery of SWINGING LONDON. He went on to build a network of salons and endorsed numerous haircare products. Sassoon presently resides in Beverly Hills, California.

saucepan (lid) 'Yid' (offensive), 'kid' or 'quid' in COCKNEY RHYMING SLANG. One is left to guess from the context which meaning is intended.

> I can talk cock-er-nee. 'How's yer saucepans?'
>
> IAN HOLLOWAY, at news.bbc.co.uk/sport (31 August 2007)

sausage The word has been recorded in several rhyming slang coinages; so many, in fact, as to render it almost useless because the intended sense is often unclear. The meanings include: 'cash', 'crash' and 'smash', from 'sausage and mash'; and 'dole' and 'pole', from 'sausage roll'.
not a sausage See under NOT.

Saveloy An old COCKNEY nickname for the SAVOY HOTEL.

Savile Row A street that runs parallel with REGENT STREET, to its west, south of Conduit Street. In order to alleviate his financial difficulties, Richard Boyle, 3rd Earl of Burlington (1695–1753), offered developers the land behind BURLINGTON HOUSE in 1717. Savile Row was laid out in the early 1730s and named after Boyle's wife, Lady Dorothy Savile. Tailors began to set up shop in the streets of the Burlington estate in the late 18th century, making a first appearance on Savile Row by 1806. BEAU BRUMMELL was an early patron of this fashionable new quarter. By 1838 the street was teeming with tailors, and when Henry Poole inherited his father's Old Burlington Street business in 1846 he enlarged the premises and created a new entrance on Savile Row. Poole became the street's foremost tailor, fitting out monarchs and, later, Hollywood stars. Hawkes & Company, later to become Gieves & Hawkes, moved to Savile Row in 1912.

Successful apprentices of the leading firms have often started their own businesses on the street, as have several cloth merchants. Recent arrivals have included some of the leading names in contemporary male couture. The street has become an international byword for gentlemen's tailoring; the Japanese word for a suit, *sebiro*, is a direct transliteration of 'Savile Row'.

The playwright Richard Sheridan died in Savile Row in 1816. The headquarters of the Beatles' Apple Corporation were at 3 Savile Row, previously the home of the Albany club and of Lord Nelson and Lady Hamilton. The band's famous rooftop concert, its final performance, took place here in January 1969.

Savoy A precinct situated off the STRAND, centred on the former Savoy Palace, encompassing a narrow area either side of what is now Lancaster Place. In 1245 Henry III granted it to his wife's uncle, Peter, Count of Savoy (whence its name). After he left, in 1263, it became the residence of Eleanor of Castile, wife of Prince Edward (afterwards Edward I). It was later given to Queen Eleanor's second son, Edmund of Lancaster. In the latter part of the 14th century it was the residence of John of Gaunt. On the accession of Henry IV in 1399, it was annexed to the Crown as part of the estates of the Duchy of Lancaster. Most of the original buildings had been destroyed by Wat Tyler's followers during the Peasants' Revolt in 1381, but Henry VII bequeathed funds for the reconstruction of the palace as a hospital for the poor under the name of St John's Hospital. It became a military hospital, then a barracks under Charles II, but this was demolished with the construction of John Rennie's WATERLOO BRIDGE, which was completed in 1831. In the late 17th century, the Savoy precinct became a notorious ROOKERY for evil-doers claiming rights of sanctuary. See also ALSATIA.

Savoyard A term for a denizen or habitué of the Savoy, adapted from its original application to a native of Savoy in France. In the 17th and 18th centuries it denoted the desperadoes and outlaws who hid out in the Savoy at that time, and more recently it has been used for a performer in, or devotee of, the SAVOY OPERAS.

Savoy Chapel A chapel in Savoy Street, originally within the precincts of the Savoy Palace (*see* SAVOY). It was built in 1505 and, after the destruction of St Mary le Strand by Edward Seymour, 1st Duke of Somerset (Lord Protector of England during Edward VI's minority), became known as St Mary le Savoy. It was repaired and restored several times in the 18th century and again by Queen Victoria in 1843 and 1864. In 1890 it became the first place of worship to be lit by electricity. In 1939 it was further refurbished, and designated the King's Chapel of the Savoy.

Savoy Conference A conference held at the Savoy in 1661, after the Restoration of Charles II, between the bishops and the Presbyterian clergy to review the Book of Common Prayer. It resulted in only minor changes, which were included in the revised book of 1662. Most of the Presbyterian demands were rejected.

Savoy Hill A street leading down from the STRAND to the Victoria EMBANKMENT. It was the site of the first studios of the BBC in 1922, and until 1932 its headquarters, the original BBC call sign being 2LO (i.e. No.2, London). The building is now known as Savoy Hill House. *See also* LONDON CALLING.

Savoy hotel A luxury hotel on the site of the old Savoy Palace (*see* SAVOY), between the STRAND and the north bank of the THAMES. Richard D'OYLY CARTE had it built in the mid-1880s. It was one of the first hotels in London to be equipped with electric lifts and electric lighting. Its first manager was César Ritz (who went on to found the RITZ HOTEL) and its first chef Auguste Escoffier, who created the Peach Melba here in honour of Dame Nellie Melba's visit in 1892. Its main restaurants, the Savoy Grill and the River Restaurant, are world-renowned. Its forecourt is the only street in the British Isles where traffic must keep to the right.

Arnold Bennett's *Imperial Palace* (1930), his last and longest novel, is set in the Savoy. The Savoy features as the place of punishment of 'Godolphin Horne', the subject of one of Hilaire Belloc's *Cautionary Tales for Children* (1907) and a well-born child who is beset by the sin of pride:

So now Godolphin is the Boy
Who blacks the boots at the Savoy.

Savoy Operas The comic operas with words by W.S. Gilbert (1836–1911) and music by Arthur Sullivan (1842–1900), produced by Richard D'OYLY CARTE. Most of the operettas, from *Iolanthe* (1882) onwards, were first produced at the SAVOY THEATRE.

Savoy Orpheans A dance orchestra that regu-larly broadcast on the BBC from the Savoy hotel between the First and Second World Wars. It made its debut in 1923, under Debroy Somers, but its most famous years were under the lead-ership of the pianist Carroll Gibbons.

Savoy Theatre A theatre built by Richard D'OYLY CARTE in the STRAND to stage his productions of the Gilbert and Sullivan operettas. It opened in 1881, with *Patience* (transferred from another theatre). The first original production here was *Iolanthe* (1882) and the last – *The Grand Duke* (1896) – a flop. At the beginning of the 20th century D'Oyly Carte sold the lease, and it turned into a general theatre. It became known for its Christmas productions of J.M. Barrie's PETER PAN.

scarper To make a quick exit. The word probably entered the English language via an early form of POLARI, from Italian *scappare*, to escape or run away. The meaning may have been strengthened by the COCKNEY RHYMING SLANG term 'Scapa Flow', to go. Scapa Flow was the site of a naval base in the Orkney Islands.

Scavenger's daughter An instrument of tor-ture whose invention has been attributed to Sir Leonard Skevington or Skeffington, Lieutenant of the TOWER OF LONDON in the reign of Henry VIII (1509–47). It was also known as Skeffington's gyves, and consisted of a large iron hoop hinged in two halves. Victims were made to kneel on the lower half. The upper half was then closed on them with a screw. As this was tightened, the body was pressed ever closer together, chest against knees, belly against thighs, and thighs against legs. The spine was thus gradually dislo-cated and the breastbone and ribs fractured.

Science Museum The principal institution of the National Museum of Science and Industry, located on EXHIBITION ROAD in SOUTH KENSING-TON. It had its origins in the South Kensington Museum (*see the* BROMPTON BOILERS), which included machinery and some miscellaneous sci-entific items among its exhibits. From 1862 part of the growing science and technology collection was moved into the building on the west side of Exhibition Road that had housed that year's International Exhibition. The collection gained an officially distinct identity as the Science Mu-seum when the VICTORIA AND ALBERT MUSEUM replaced the South Kensington Museum in

1909. The museum's permanent, purpose-built home was opened in 1928 and enlarged in the 1950s and again in 2000, with the opening of the Wellcome Wing. The Science Museum presently has an IMAX 3D cinema, numerous interactive exhibits and major galleries devoted to space exploration, power generation and the making of the modern world. The museum focuses its efforts on 'bringing science to life, and life to science' – an approach exemplified in a six-month exhibition in 2009 entitled 'Wallace & Gromit present a World of Cracking Ideas'.

Scoop, The A sunken amphitheatre with stepped limestone seating for 800, located beside the THAMES to the west of CITY HALL. A programme of free, open-air arts events has been held at the Scoop every summer since 2003.

Scope, The A nature reserve at the southern end of WANDSWORTH COMMON. It was here in 1852 that the Rev John Craig (1805–77) set up the largest (but not best) refracting telescope in the world, in a brick tower 60 feet (18m) high. The project was not a success, partly because air pollution impaired visibility, and the 'leviathan' was dismantled c.1880.

Scotch

Scotch Corner At the junction of KNIGHTS-BRIDGE and the BROMPTON Road; the Scotch House tartan shop opened here in 1900. In 2002 the Scotch House was converted to a branch of Burberry by Great Universal Stores, which at that time owned both brands.

Scotch (peg) 'Leg' in COCKNEY RHYMING SLANG, first recorded in 1859 and still in use today in the truncated form. Modern users have adopted 'Scotch egg' as the long form.

Scotland Yard Originally – and still – a short street (in full, Great Scotland Yard), branching from the eastern side of WHITEHALL, towards its northern end. Its name derives from its being the approximate site of the London residence of the kings of Scotland from the 12th century. The street's connection with the police began in 1829, when part of the precincts became the headquarters of the newly formed METROPOL-ITAN POLICE. The link with law enforcement was firmly established by the end of the century, and when in 1890 the Met moved to new premises at the southern end of Victoria EMBANKMENT

it named them New Scotland Yard. Designed by Norman Shaw in somewhat baronial style, this was the building that became familiar in film and television police dramas in the middle part of the 20th century. The granite with which it was faced was quarried by convicts on Dartmoor. An adjacent second building, initially known as Scotland House, provided much needed additional space from 1906. In 1967 the Metropolitan Police moved yet again, to a modern 20-storey headquarters at the corner of BROADWAY and VICTORIA STREET, taking the name 'New Scotland Yard' with it. A revolving three-sided sign in front of the building is a frequently used television image. The old premises were renamed the Norman Shaw Buildings and are now used as parliamentary offices.

'Scotland Yard' (or often simply 'the Yard') has long been used as a metonym for the Metropolitan Police, and more particularly for its CID: if London's detectives were having difficulty with a case, the tabloid headline was sure to be 'Yard baffled'. High-profile detectives would have the sobriquet 'of the Yard' after their name – real ones, fictional ones and even combinations of the two (as in the case of *Fabian of the Yard*, a BBC police drama of the mid-1950s based on the real-life career of Detective Inspector Robert Fabian). *Private Eye* magazine styled its all-purpose bungling detective INSPECTOR KNACKER OF THE YARD.

Scouts *See* BOY SCOUTS.

scrap

Scrap Iron Park A 19th-century nickname for what is now Island Gardens, a small riverside park located at the tip of the ISLE OF DOGS. The developer William Cubitt had leased land from the Admiralty to put up a handful of grand villas along the waterfront, and to accompany these he commissioned a plantation, with dozens of varieties of trees and shrubs. The ground was planted but the villa scheme was a failure; the plantation fell into neglect and by the 1880s it was a derelict dumping ground. In 1895 the LONDON COUNTY COUNCIL created a park with walks, a play area, bandstand and a terrace offering a superb view across the THAMES to GREENWICH.

Scrapyard Meadow The nickname of a field on the outskirts of BOW that was added to TOWER HAMLETS CEMETERY in the mid-1890s.

scratch

Scratching Fanny The nickname given to the deceased Fanny Kent, in her supposed guise as the abrasive COCK LANE GHOST.

Scratchwood See LONDON GATEWAY (2).

Screaming Lord Sutch The assumed name of David Edward Sutch, a rock musician and political activist born at NEW END Hospital, HAMPSTEAD, in 1940. Styling himself Screaming Lord Sutch, 3rd Earl of HARROW, he founded the Monster Raving Loony Party and stood unsuccessfully for parliament in 41 elections and by-elections. He was found dead at his South Harrow home in 1999; a post-mortem later confirmed that he had hanged himself after a long battle with depression. His sobriquet has been used to mean 'crotch' in rhyming slang.

Screw Plot The story is that before Queen Anne went to ST PAUL'S in 1708 to offer thanksgiving for the victory at the Battle of Oudenaarde, conspirators removed certain screw-bolts from the roof beams of the cathedral so that the fabric might fall on the queen and her entourage and kill them. In fact, it appears that some iron fastenings were omitted by one of the workmen because he thought the timbers were already sufficiently secured.

Scrooge, Ebenezer The miserly, misanthropic moneylender and surviving partner in the firm of Scrooge and Marley in DICKENS's *A Christmas Carol* (1843). Once a 'good-hearted lad', he has become 'a squeezing, wrenching, grasping, scraping, clutching, covetous old sinner'. But after a vivid dream on Christmas Eve, in which he is visited by a series of ghosts, the pity and terror he feels teach him a lesson, and he becomes a kind and generous benefactor to the Cratchit family. Dickens may have come up with the character's name while on a visit to SIPSON House. However, opinions are divided as to whether the inspiration came from nearby Scroogeall Cottages or from a local shepherd who assured the author that his sheep would be able to 'scrooge' through a narrow gate.

Scrubs, the A nickname for WORMWOOD SCRUBS PRISON.

Sir Hannibal Grunt-Gobbinette is threatening, between spasms of yellow bile foaming out his nose, to bring the matter up in Parliament. 'I'll see you two in the Scrubs if it kills me!'

THOMAS PYNCHON: *Gravity's Rainbow* (1973)

season, the See the LONDON SEASON.

Second Fire of London A collective name for the 1,500 fires that broke out across the capital following a two-hour German air raid on the night of 29 December 1940, in which 163 people died. The attack was timed to coincide with a low THAMES tide, making it difficult to draw sufficient water to extinguish the fires, but over the following 24 hours around 100 million gallons (455 million litres) were pumped. Most of the bombs fell on the CITY, where numerous churches and livery halls were destroyed, along with several entire streets and most of CHEAPSIDE. Herbert Mason's photograph of a smoke-wreathed ST PAUL'S Cathedral, taken from the roof of the *Daily Mail's* Northcliffe House on the night of the Second Fire, is widely regarded as the most evocative image of London during the BLITZ.

secret

Secret Agent, The A novel by Joseph Conrad (1857–1924), published in 1907. The setting is London, and the 'secret agent' is Verloc, an agent provocateur for a foreign power anxious to discredit anarchist groups, and also an informer for the Home Office. Stevie, the younger brother of Verloc's wife, ends up being blown up while carrying a bomb. This part of the plot was based on an incident that took place on 18 February 1894, when Marcel Boudin, an anarchist, blew himself up in error near GREENWICH OBSERVATORY.

RCA Secret See under RCA.

Securicor The security services company began its career in 1935 as Night Watch Services, a small private business specializing in guarding the homes of wealthy Londoners. Contracts were at first hard to come by, and at the outbreak of the Second World War it had just 12 patrol guards. After the war its luck changed following a move into industrial security and the return into the jobs market of hundreds of soldiers. It changed its name to Security Corps and then, in response to Home Office concerns that this sounded too military, to Securicor in the early 1950s, by which time it employed nearly 200 guards. It subsequently entered the 'cash-in-transit' business, as well as parcels delivery and detective work. In 2004 Securicor merged with Group 4, another security firm.

Security Service *See* MI5.

see the lions, to To see the sights, an expression that first came into use in the late 16th century. It derived from the lions formerly kept at the TOWER OF LONDON, which were once *the* sight to see. Similarly, 'to show someone the lions' was to take a visitor on a sightseeing tour.

> He ... has been in London too, and seeing all the lions under my escort.
>
> DICKENS: letter to Professor Felton (2 March 1843)

seething

Seething Lane A street in the CITY of London, north-west of the TOWER. The name derives from Old English *sifetha*, 'siftings', probably indicating that cereal crops were threshed and winnowed here, leaving the lane full of chaff. The church that DICKENS called ST GHASTLY GRIM stands at the corner of Seething Lane and Hart Street.

Seething Wells A locality in west SURBITON, on the bank of the THAMES. It takes its name from a spring that was said to 'bubble up' from the ground beside the Portsmouth Road. Following several outbreaks of cholera in London the Metropolis Water Act of 1852 legislated that drinking water should not be extracted from the Thames below TEDDINGTON. This immediately prompted the LAMBETH Water Company to relocate its reservoir and works to Seething Wells. Shortly afterwards the CHELSEA Water Company established its works next door. The two waterworks eventually descended into the hands of Thames Water, which closed most of the operations in the early 1990s and sold the land for housing. A Victorian pump house has been converted into a health and leisure club and KINGSTON UNIVERSITY has built halls of residence nearby. The waterworks' former filter beds have been designated as metropolitan open land and are rich in wildlife.

The ranting punk poet Steven Wells (1960–2009) adopted the pseudonym Seething Wells in the late 1970s. He later became a mainstream journalist.

Selfridges The OXFORD STREET store of this name was opened on 15 March 1909 as the creation of the US entrepreneur Harry Gordon Selfridge (1858–1947), the son of the owner of a dry goods business. It was Britain's first 'democratic' department store, where customers could walk around as they pleased rather than being shown from counter to counter. The grandiose emporium originally had 130 departments and a wide range of facilities for its customers, including its own library, a post office, rooms for foreign visitors, an American soda room, a department for the clergy and a 'silence room' with a notice reading 'Ladies Will Refrain From Conversation'. Miss Selfridge, providing for teenage fashions, opened as a spin-off in 1966. Selfridges, which now also has stores in Birmingham and Manchester, was acquired by the Canadian businessman Galen Weston in 2003. *See also* SHOPPING DAYS TO CHRISTMAS (*under* SHOP).

more front than Selfridges *See under* MORE.

Selhurst A socially deprived part of north CROYDON. Selhurst was first recorded in 1225 and its name may have meant either 'dwelling where the sallow willows grow' or 'dwelling in a wood'. Selhurst (later Heaver's) Farm was in existence by the early 19th century, when the Croydon Canal skirted its southern and eastern edges. Following the closure of the canal in 1836 a railway track was laid along its route. Croydon races were held at Heaver's Farm from 1858 until the mid-1860s. Selhurst station opened in 1865, followed by churches and schools as the village evolved into a suburb of Croydon.

Selhurst Park Formerly a gated estate of high-class housing, tentatively begun in the late 1850s between Upper Grove and Oliver Grove on the north side of Selhurst. The project soon foundered and the land went through several changes of hands and at least one bankruptcy. Parts of Selhurst Park remained undeveloped at the end of the First World War, when CRYSTAL PALACE FC leased a ground known as the Nest, near Selhurst station. The Nest held 25,000 spectators but views were poor, especially when smoke from shunting engines drifted across the pitch, so the club acquired a disused brickworks in Selhurst Park in 1922. The team played its first game at the new ground in 1924, when there was just one stand, with open terraces on the other three sides. The stadium was completely modernized in the 1990s, a period when it was also home to WIMBLEDON FC.

Selsdon A prosperous southerly outpost of CROYDON, situated in an elevated position to the north-east of Sanderstead. Most of Selsdon used to be a single farm covering more than one square mile (2.5 sq km), and its woodland was used for pheasant shooting in the 19th century, with clearings and rides that can still be seen. In 1923 the farm was sold off and split up. The early 19th-century farmhouse-cum-mansion became Selsdon Park Hotel and was much extended, and its parkland was laid out as a golf course in 1929.

Selsdon Group A right-wing Conservative pressure group formed at a meeting held at the Selsdon Park Hotel in September 1973. Its aims were outlined in the Selsdon Declaration, which upheld the SELSDON MAN principles that its members believed were at that time being abandoned by prime minister Edward Heath.

Selsdon Man A nickname coined by Harold Wilson (1916–1995) for the figuratively Neanderthal creator of the policy of tax cuts and free market economics outlined at a Conservative shadow cabinet conference held at the Selsdon Park Hotel at the beginning of February 1970.

> Selsdon Man is not just a lurch to the right. It is an atavistic desire to reverse the course of 25 years of social revolution. What they are planning is a wanton, calculated and deliberate return to greater inequality.
>
> HAROLD WILSON: speech (6 February 1970)

Semi-Detached An installation by Michael Landy (b.1963), exhibited at TATE BRITAIN in 2004. It was a full-size replica of his parents' house at 62 Kingswood Road, SEVEN KINGS. The house was demolished after the six-month show. Landy, a GOLDSMITHS graduate, is probably best known for a performance piece entitled 'Break Down' (2001). Having gathered together and catalogued all his worldly possessions from his car to his birth certificate, he transferred them to a disused C&A clothing store on OXFORD STREET and, with the help of nine assistants and a conveyor belt, systematically dismantled and then shredded everything except his cat.

Semolina Pilchard Allegedly, a nickname coined by John Lennon for Detective Sergeant Norman 'Nobby' Pilcher (b.1936), of SCOTLAND YARD's drugs squad. The words 'semolina pilchard' appear in the Beatles' song 'I Am the Walrus' (1967). Pilcher is also said to have been caricatured as 'Spiny Norman' in Monty Python's 'Piranha Brothers' sketch (1970). The detective made a name for himself by pursuing high-profile rock stars on suspicion of possessing illegal drugs, including Donovan and members of the Beatles and ROLLING STONES. Some of those he arrested, notably Lennon, claimed that drugs had been planted in their homes. In 1972 Pilcher was extradited from Australia and subsequently convicted of conspiracy to pervert the course of justice. He was sentenced to four years' imprisonment. The American rock band Primus made his rise and fall the subject of a song, 'Pilcher's Squad' (2003).

Senior, the The nickname of the United Services Club, founded in 1815. Its original membership consisted mainly of senior military and naval officers. The club closed in 1976 and its former home at 116 PALL MALL is now occupied by the Institute of Directors.

Senrab FC A multi-team amateur FOOTBALL club for boys and girls, established in 1961 and named after Senrab Street, STEPNEY, where its founder lived. ('Senrab' is a reverse spelling of Barnes, the name of the street's builder.) Senrab presently fields 20 teams, ranging from under 7s to under 17s, playing their home games on WANSTEAD FLATS. Past club members could almost assemble a creditable England team on their own; they include John Terry, Sol Campbell, Jermain Defoe, Ledley King and Bobby Zamora, as well as several illustrious coaches.

septic (tank) 'Yank' (an American) in COCKNEY RHYMING SLANG. Some have taken this to have derogatory implications. The term is widely used in Australia too, where the abbreviation 'seppo' is commonplace. 'Sherman (tank)' is also heard. Minor alternatives for 'yanks' include 'ham shanks', 'petrol tanks' and 'Tom Hanks'.

Serjeants-at-law A superior order of barristers superseded by King's Counsel in 1877. Their title comes from Medieval Latin *servientes ad legem*, 'those who serve the king in matters of law'. They formed an Inn called Serjeants' Inn which was in FLEET STREET and later in CHANCERY LANE. The best-known literary example of the species is DICKENS's Mr Serjeant Buzfuz in PICKWICK PAPERS.

Serpentine A long lake in HYDE PARK and KEN-SINGTON GARDENS, named for its twisting shape. Strictly speaking, the part in Kensington Gardens is the Long Water and only the part in Hyde Park is the Serpentine, but the name is commonly applied to the entire lake. It was created when the small River WESTBOURNE was dammed in 1730, the idea originating with Caroline of Anspach (1683–1737), consort of George II. It has long been popular for swimming (the Serpentine Lido opened in the early 20th century) and boating in summer, and has a less fortunate claim to fame as a chosen spot for suicides. It may have been in the Serpentine that Harriet Westbrook, deserted and pregnant wife of the poet Shelley, drowned in 1816. In the mid-20th century its name was often shortened colloquially to 'the Serps'.

> I am hoping for a row … on the Serpentine, which is really almost as good as a lake.
>
> GEORGE ELIOT: letter (22 October 1853)

Serpentine Gallery An art gallery situated a little to the south-west of the Serpentine, built as a tea house in 1934. It was converted into a contemporary art gallery in 1970 and has since staged a remarkable number of influential exhibitions for such a diminutive space.

set

Sette of Odd Volumes *See under* ODD.

set the Thames on fire, to Usually used in such expressions as 'he'll never set the Thames on fire', meaning 'he'll never make a name for himself', 'he'll never do anything memorable'. The popular explanation is that the word 'Thames' is a pun on the word 'temse', a 'corn sieve', and that the parallel French locution 'he will never set the Seine on fire' is a pun on 'seine', a 'dragnet'. But these solutions are not tenable. There is a Latin saw, *Tiberim accendere nequaquam potest* (He can in no wise set the Tiber on fire), which is probably the source of other parallel sayings. The Germans had *den Rhein anzünden* (to set the Rhine on fire) as early as 1630.

> His second novel was successful, but not so successful as to arouse the umbrageous susceptibilities of his competitors. In fact it confirmed them in their suspicions that he would never set the Thames on fire.
>
> W. SOMERSET MAUGHAM: *Cakes and Ale* (1930)

The phrase has occasionally been taken more literally, though: at a friend's stag party the writer Robert Byron (1905–41) poured 20 gallons (90 litres) of petrol on to the river, and ended up setting fire to the party hotel.

Settles' Folly The nickname of a cavernous Congregationalist church built in Grove Crescent Road, STRATFORD in 1867. William Settles was a CITY merchant living in what is now ROMFORD ROAD and he lent most of the money for the project, interest free. The church had a 115-foot (35m) spire and could seat 1,600. The project was at first more successful than the nickname implies but membership declined steeply during the first half of the 20th century and the building ended its days as a furniture factory before it was gutted by fire in 1952 and later demolished.

seven

Seven Curses of London, The A book (1869) written by the social investigator James Greenwood under the pseudonym the 'Amateur Casual'. According to Greenwood, the seven curses were: neglected children, professional thieves, professional beggars, fallen women, drunkenness, 'betting gamblers' and waste of charity.

Seven Dials Originally, a seven-road junction in the vicinity of COVENT GARDEN (the roads were Great Earl Street, Little Earl Street, Great White Lion Street, Little White Lion Street, Great St Andrew's Street, Little St Andrew's Street and Queen Street). In the reign of Charles II (1660–85) a Doric pillar was placed in the centre, topped with a set of sundials pointing down each of the streets. One pair of streets had to make do with a single sundial, but this slight anomaly was brushed under the carpet when the dials came to give their name to the junction. The column and dials were removed in 1773. In 1989 a new pillar with dials was erected on the original site and ceremonially unveiled by Queen Beatrix of the Netherlands. The four roads that meet here now are Earlham Street, Mercer Street, Monmouth Street and Shorts Gardens. Meanwhile, the name of the crossroads had passed to the district around it, which came to be notorious for squalor, vice, crime and general degradation. It was long the headquarters of the ballad printers and balladmongers. Most of the slums were cleared away when the area was redeveloped in the 1870s and 1880s. Seven Dials is now a thriving locality with a mix of small traditional shops, boutiques and New Age-ish establishments.

Nineteenth-century authors and poets seeking to contrast London's high society with its low life would often choose Seven Dials to exemplify the latter. W.S. Gilbert did so in *Iolanthe* (1882), as did Henry S. Leigh in *Carols of Cockayne* (1868):

> The Fates, you see, have will'd it so
> That even folks in Rotten Row
> Are not without their trials;
> Whilst only those that know the ways
> Of stony London's waifs and strays
> Can fancy how the seven days
> Pass o'er the Seven Dials.
>
> 'A Very Common Child'

Seven Dials raker Late 19th- and early 20th-century slang for a prostitute whose home is in SEVEN DIALS and who plies her trade elsewhere. As J. Redding Ware reported in his *Passing English of the Victorian Era* (1908), she 'never smiles out of the Dials'.

seven gates of the City The main gates in the Roman wall that encircled the SQUARE MILE, mentioned in literature and statutes from the 12th century onwards. They were later considered to be: LUDGATE, NEWGATE, ALDERSGATE, CRIPPLEGATE, MOORGATE, BISHOPSGATE and ALDGATE. However, as Moorgate was a relatively late creation, the original seventh may have been either the Postern gate, near the TOWER OF LONDON, or LONDON BRIDGE. The list included only the gates through which roads passed, not the watergates on the riverfront. In his poem celebrating 'The First Anniversary of the Government under His Highness the Lord Protector' (1655), Andrew Marvell calls London: 'Th'harmonious city of the seven gates'.

Seven Kings A 'people's suburb', as its developer described it, in eastern ILFORD. Legend has it that in Saxon times seven royal huntsmen met here by a stream at a clearing in the HAINAULT Forest, pausing while their horses drank. Sadly, a less romantic explanation has a greater ring of truth: that the name is a corruption of Seofecingas, which meant 'settlement of Seofeca's people'. Seven Kings, or at least the part with the street plan that looks like an egg slicer, has been called 'the town built in a year'. This was 1898–9, when Archibald Cameron Corbett, later 1st Baron Rowallan (1856–1933), laid out an estate of good quality houses that clerks and lower grade civil servants could afford.

Seven Million Londoners A campaign launched after the 7/7 bombings (*see below*), stressing London's multiculturalism and aiming to foster a spirit of unity. It was led by the MAYOR OF LONDON, with the support of commercial sponsors. A similarly themed successor was entitled 'We are Londoners, We are One'. Rounded to the nearest million, London's estimated population reached eight million in 2007.

7/7 The designation given by the press to the London bombings of 7 July 2005, on the model of 9/11. During the morning rush hour, four young British-born Islamist suicide bombers detonated their explosives on three LONDON UNDERGROUND trains and a bus, killing 52 people (plus the perpetrators) and injuring 700. The bombings, in which Al-Qaida claimed to have had a hand, came the day after the announcement that London was to host the 2012 OLYMPIC GAMES. Two weeks later, on 21 July, four more Islamist terrorists attempted a repeat attack on London's transport system (three underground trains and a bus), but, although the detonators went off, the main devices failed to explode. The perpetrators fled, but were later arrested. *See also the* STOCKWELL SHOOTING.

seven sights of London An unguessable list of London spectacles compiled in verse form by Richard Brathwaite in 1638.

> Seven hills there were in Rome, and so there be
> Seven sights in New Troy crave our memory:
> Tombs, Guildhall giants, stage plays, Bedlam poor.
> Ostrich, bear garden, lions in the Tower.
>
> *Drunken Barnaby's Four Journeys to the North of England*

The tombs were those of WESTMINSTER ABBEY, the giants were GOG AND MAGOG, the ostrich remains unidentified and the bear garden was at BANKSIDE.

Seven Sisters A poor, multi-ethnic neighbourhood encircling the junction of Seven Sisters Road and the High Road in South TOTTENHAM. It is said that sometime around 1350 seven elm trees were planted in a ring around a walnut tree by the roadside at Page Green by seven sisters when they were about to go their separate ways. A Protestant martyr was later supposed to have been burnt here, after which the walnut tree flourished without growing bigger. Although parts of the story are almost certainly mythical, the trees definitely existed in the 17th and 18th centuries. The walnut had died by 1790 but the elms lasted long enough to give their name to a turnpike road built in 1833 to provide improved access from Tottenham to WESTMINSTER. The elms were removed around 1840; the seven daughters of a Tottenham butcher later planted a new set, which has not survived. Seven Sisters station opened on the Great Eastern Railway in 1872 and it became a VICTORIA LINE interchange in 1968.

Severndroog Castle A Gothic folly in Castle Wood, SHOOTERS HILL, commissioned in 1784 by Lady James of Eltham to commemorate her late husband's capture of the fortress of Suvarnadurg on India's Malabar coast in 1755.

Sex Pistols The most famous of all PUNK ROCK acts, founded in 1975 at Sex, the KING'S ROAD fashion boutique run by Vivienne Westwood and the group's manager-to-be, Malcolm McLaren. The original line-up was Johnny Rotten (b.1956, as John Lydon), who grew up in FINSBURY PARK, and Steve Jones (b.1955), Glen Matlock (b.1956) and Paul Cook (b.1956), all west Londoners. Despite a lack of technical ability, the Pistols' powerful on-stage presence, nihilistic attitude and headline-grabbing truculence quickly established them as flag-bearers of the punk movement. Most of the other major artists of the early phase of punk rock cited their attendance at a Sex Pistols gig as a prime influence on their musical direction, or even on their decision to become musicians at all. In November 1976 the Pistols released their first single: 'Anarchy in the UK', which set the tone for their subsequent lyrical output:

I am an Antichrist,
I am an anarchist.
Don't know what I want
But I know how to get it.

In 1977 Sid Vicious (1957–79, real name Simon Ritchie) replaced Glen Matlock and the group released three more singles, including the widely banned 'God Save the Queen', and the provocatively titled album *Never Mind the Bollocks, Here's the Sex Pistols*. They broke up in 1978, although the original members have since played some lucrative reunion gigs.

Sexton Blake *See* BLAKE, SEXTON.

Shacklewell A multiracial neighbourhood with some light industry, almost squeezed out of existence by HACKNEY and STOKE NEWINGTON, which lie on either side. The name may refer to a wellspring in a sunken place or where animals could be shackled (tethered), but was not recorded until 1490 despite its probable Old English origin. In the early 16th century Sir John Heron, reputedly the richest man in Hackney, owned a large estate centred on a manor house here; its site is now covered by shops. Shacklewell remained an isolated settlement until Hackney expanded outwards to meet it in the mid-19th century. Parts became a slum and several streets were cleared in the 1930s to make way for municipal and philanthropic housing projects.

shades Originally a vault where barrels of wine or beer were stored, and where the merchandise could be sampled at an adjacent bar. The term was subsequently extended to encompass other kinds of subterranean taverns and those sheltered by an arcade.

> The Shades at London Bridge are under Fishmongers' Hall. Sound wine out of the barrel, reasonable and tolerably good, are characteristics of this establishment. The Shades at Spring Gardens is a subterranean ale-shop.
>
> JOHN BEE: *Dictionary of the Turf* (1823)

Shad Thames A riverside street, and by extension the surrounding area, located on the south bank of the THAMES, east of TOWER BRIDGE. The name is a corruption of 'St John at Thames', a reference to the Knights of St John (*see* KNIGHTS HOSPITALLER), the former landowners. The parish church of HORSELYDOWN was dedicated to St John when it was built in 1728. This stretch of the shoreline later became part of LONDON'S LARDER, dominated by the TEA, coffee, spice and dried fruit warehouses of Butler's Wharf, which were completed in 1873. A century later the last warehouses closed and the area was redeveloped from the mid-1980s, with offices, shops, cafés, bars and restaurants. Shad Thames is still criss-crossed by the overhead goods gantries that linked the warehouses, many of which retain interior fitments too. *See also the* DESIGN MUSEUM.

Shadwell Now the north-eastern part of WAPPING, but once a separate Tower hamlet (*see* TOWER HAMLETS). Shadwell's Old English name means 'shallow spring, or stream'. Archaeological excavations have revealed evidence of a Roman quarry here, subsequently used as a cemetery, with a mausoleum tower. By the 3rd century the area had been divided into plots, on which homes were built. Maritime industries brought growth from the 1630s and Shadwell became a parish in 1669, when its 8,000 residents included many seafarers. By the early 19th century much of the district had become overcrowded and insanitary and its character did not fundamentally alter until after the Second World War, when council blocks sprouted in all corners.

> The shape and soul of Shadwell are reflected in its name. Shadwell! Cold, grey, stony syllables, without lustre or savour; flat to the eye and the palate.
>
> THOMAS BURKE: *More Limehouse Nights*, 'The Yellow Scarf' (1921)

Shaftesbury Avenue The central thoroughfare of London's THEATRELAND, connecting PICCADILLY CIRCUS with the eastern end of New Oxford Street. The road-building project was planned from 1877 by the METROPOLITAN BOARD OF WORKS' architect George Vulliamy and the celebrated engineer Sir Joseph Bazalgette. The avenue opened in 1886 and was named after the campaigning philanthropist Anthony Ashley Cooper, 7th Earl of Shaftesbury, who had died in the previous year. The first theatres to open were the Shaftesbury and the Lyric in 1888. The Lyric survives but the original Shaftesbury was destroyed during the Second World War. The Royal English Opera House opened in 1891, flopped, and became the Palace Theatre the following year. Shaftesbury Avenue's heavy architecture came in for some early criticism but progressive rebuilding on the north side improved its status, especially with the construction of a string of theatres in the first decade of the 20th century, namely the Apollo, Hicks (renamed Globe, now Gielgud), Queen's and, at the far north-eastern end, the New Princes Theatre (now Shaftesbury). The last theatre to open on the avenue was the Savile in 1931, which has spent most of its life as a cinema, currently named the Odeon COVENT GARDEN. The Curzon cinema opened in 1959 as the Columbia, in the basement of an office development. *See also* LITTLE APPLES GROW QUICKLY PLEASE.

Shakespeare, William Widely regarded as

the greatest English poetic dramatist (1564–1616), he is usually associated with his birthplace, Stratford-upon-Avon, but spent most of his adult life in the capital. Despite exhaustive detective work, Shakespearean scholars have been unable to track his movements with full continuity but it appears that he was working in SHOREDITCH by the early 1590s, often performing in plays he had written himself, and was probably living in a rented room in the parish of St Helen's, BISHOPSGATE. He next moved to BANKSIDE, which was fast becoming the new centre of the London theatrical scene and offered the added benefit of sanctuary from those who were pursuing him for non-payment of taxes in Bishopsgate. Shakespeare's time on Bankside was a period of considerable success for him, as a poet and playwright, as an actor with the Lord Chamberlain's Men, later the King's Men, and as an investor in theatrical enterprises, notably at the GLOBE. Nevertheless, it seems he could not yet afford a house of his own, for in 1604 he was lodging in Silver Street, CRIPPLEGATE, in the home of a Huguenot wig-maker (and possibly theatrical costumier) who was apparently a notorious skinflint.

> You can see the house quite clearly in the woodcut map of Elizabethan London ... known as the 'Agas' map. It has steeply pitched gables, and a projection suggestive of a 'pentice' or penthouse above a shop front, and then those four tantalizing windows upstairs – but here the map fails us, for the windows are only little blocks of printer's ink which the magnifying-glass cannot pry into.
>
> CHARLES NICHOLL: *The Lodger: Shakespeare on Silver Street* (2007)

In 1608 Shakespeare was a partner in the resumption of activities at BLACKFRIARS Theatre and in March 1613 he paid £140 for a property nearby, in what is now Ireland Yard. The building was the former Blackfriars Priory gatehouse, to which he made improvements, according to a legal document of 1615. However, by that date he seems to have been spending much of his time back in Stratford, where he died the following year.

Shakespeare's Globe *See the* GLOBE THEATRE.

Shard (of Glass) The alternative name of LONDON BRIDGE Tower, a skyscraper under construction at 32 London Bridge Street, designed by the Italian architect Renzo Piano (b.1937). The main part of the building will be a soaring glass-clad spire with a jagged tip. The epithet 'shard of glass' was first used with disparaging intent by English Heritage, which opposed the project, but it has since been adopted by the developers. If, as seems likely, the Shard is completed as planned (although behind the original schedule, in 2012) it will be by far London's highest structure, at 1,017 feet (310m). Most of the tower will be office space but the upper floors will include a hotel and luxury apartments from which, promotional material claims, one will be able to see France.

Shaw

Shaw, George Bernard London's greatest dramatist since SHAKESPEARE and a campaigning socialist (1856–1950). He grew up in Dublin and came to England at the age of 20, living mostly with his mother and sister in FITZROVIA until his marriage to the Irish heiress Charlotte Payne-Townshend in 1898. The couple shared her home in ADELPHI Terrace until 1906, when they moved to Hertfordshire. They retained a London pied-à-terre, at first at the Adelphi and then at Whitehall Court, on the EMBANKMENT, until Charlotte's death in 1943. Many of Shaw's plays vividly evoke the London of his time, including *Mrs Warren's Profession* (1893), *Candida* (1898), *Major Barbara* (1905) and, most famously of all, PYGMALION (1913). He was awarded the Nobel Prize for Literature in 1925.

Shaw served as a ST PANCRAS vestryman and councillor from 1897 to 1903, during which time he worked to establish the first free ladies' public lavatory in the borough. He was made a freeman of St Pancras on his 90th birthday.

Shaw Library A secondary library at the LONDON SCHOOL OF ECONOMICS, containing its collection of general fiction and other literature for leisure and entertainment. Meetings and concerts are also held here. George Bernard Shaw was instrumental in the LSE's foundation and early development.

Shaw Theatre A theatre on EUSTON ROAD, just west of the BRITISH LIBRARY. Named in honour of George Bernard Shaw, it opened in 1971. The theatre stages mostly modern plays and also hosts concerts and stand-up comedy shows.

shay (informal form of 'chaise') Formerly a light cart. The term was not exclusive to London but was much used by cockney COSTERMONGERS.

You ain't forgotten how we drove that day,
Dahn to the Welsh 'Arp in my donkey shay ...
Me in my pearlies felt a toff that day,
Dahn at the Welsh 'Arp, which is 'Endon way.
ALBERT CHEVALIER and JOHN CROOK: 'The Coster's Serenade' (song) (1894)

Shed End or **the Shed** The official (originally unofficial) nickname for the south stand at STAMFORD BRIDGE, the stadium of CHELSEA FC. It dates from the erection in 1930 of a tin roof covering the south terrace, an area that later became the home of the team's most zealous supporters. When the old stand was demolished in 1994 the 'Sheddites' moved to the north stand (now the Matthew Harding Stand). The club and supporters' groups launched a 'back to the Shed' campaign in 2007 in an attempt to augment the atmosphere at home games.

Sheen or **Shene** The old name for what is now RICHMOND UPON THAMES, recalled in the outlying localities of EAST SHEEN and North Sheen.
the nun of Syon with the friar of Sheen *See under* NUN.

shepherd

Shepherd Market An area of small, narrow streets (including one itself named Shepherd Market), situated just to the north of PICCADILLY at its south-western end. It is on the site of the original 'May Fair' (*see* MAYFAIR), which was suppressed more than once in the early 18th century for its licentiousness. Edward Shepherd built a two-storey market house here in the early 1730s, in which an entirely respectable meat market operated, but the area never lost its population of commercial ladies. It has always been the 'village' at the heart of Mayfair, and in the latter part of the 20th century it developed into a more family-friendly area of restaurants, food shops, etc.

Shepherd's Bush A lively residential district and minor cultural zone situated north of HAMMERSMITH. It probably derives its name from shepherds who used to rest their flocks on the triangular green on their way to market in London. The vicinity remained entirely rural until the late 18th century, when ribbons of housing appeared along the main roads, followed by terraces to the north. By 1830 semi-detached houses were going up on the west side of the green but fields lay to the south for several more decades.

Stations have opened and closed at Shepherd's Bush since 1844 but the first really useful halt was built on the Hammersmith & City Railway in 1864. Shepherd's Bush was almost wholly built up by the time the Central Railway's TUBE reached here in 1900. By the 1930s much of the area had become very run down and the council cleared slums and built flats during the third quarter of the 20th century.

Shepherd's Bush has a long-standing association with the BBC. It owned the Empire Theatre (*see the* COLISEUM OF WEST LONDON) and television studios in LIME GROVE, and in the 1950s constructed the BBC Television Centre on a site acquired from the WHITE CITY.

> 'There are *no* shepherds in Shepherd's Bush. I've been there. It's just houses and stores and roads and the BBC. That's all,' pointed out Richard, flatly. 'There are shepherds,' said Hunter, from the darkness just next to Richard's ear. 'Pray you never meet them.' She sounded perfectly serious.
>
> NEIL GAIMAN: *Neverwhere* (1996)

'Shepherd's Bush' has been used in modern rhyming slang to signify both 'the push', in the sense of dismissal from employment, and one's 'mush' – face.

Sheppard, Jack

A notorious thief, the son of a carpenter in SMITHFIELD and brought up in BISHOPSGATE workhouse. Sheppard (1702–24) was known for his prison escapes, especially when he broke out of 'the Castle' of NEWGATE via the chimney. He was soon afterwards taken and hanged at TYBURN, allegedly in sight of 200,000 spectators.

> 'I say, master, did you ever hear tell of Mr Wood's famous 'prentice?'
> 'What apprentice?' asked the stranger, in surprise.
> 'Why, Jack Sheppard, the notorious housebreaker – him as has robbed half Lunnon to be sure.'
>
> W.H. AINSWORTH: *Jack Sheppard* (1839)

sherbet (dab)

'Cab' in COCKNEY RHYMING SLANG, from the confectionery pairing of tangy powdered sugar and a lollipop. This is proving one of the more popular coinages of the past two decades and is widely understood in abbreviated form, especially among younger Londoners. However, it is not yet on a par with the classics in terms of usage and for some of the older generation 'a sherbet' is still a colloquial term for an alcoholic drink.

Sherborne Lane

A narrow street in the CITY of London, running south from King William Street towards CANNON STREET. It was first recorded in 1273, as Shitterborwelane. Despite the more polite explanations proposed by some writers, it appears that the name is probably corrupted from Middle English *shite burgh*, a jocular term that was the equivalent of the modern 'shithouse'.

Sherlockian

Pertaining to Sherlock HOLMES. As a noun, the word signifies a student of all things Sherlockian (or HOLMESIAN).

> In short, I was a Sherlockian. I consumed the corpus, ardently wishing that Sir Arthur Conan Doyle had written more Holmes stories. Then, to my parents' relief, the fever passed.
>
> CHRISTOPHER HIRST, in *The Independent* (21 December 2004)

Sherman (tank)

See SEPTIC (TANK).

She Was Poor But She Was Honest

See IT'S THE POOR WHAT GETS THE BLAME.

Shillibeer's omnibus

The first London bus, colloquially called a 'Shillibeer'. In 1829 George Shillibeer (1797–1866) borrowed both the idea and the name from a new kind of horse-drawn carriage that had been introduced in Paris, an innovation with which he had been involved as a coachbuilder. The omnibus differed from its forerunner the stagecoach in that it was larger, better sprung and more stable. All the passengers rode inside and the fares were more affordable, at least to the middle classes. His first route ran from the Yorkshire Stingo public house in PADDINGTON to the BANK, via the NEW ROAD. Shillibeer's omnibuses were initially barred from plying within the CITY of London but permission was granted in 1832, despite opposition from HACKNEY carriage drivers.

ship (in full sail)

'Ale' in 19th-century COCKNEY RHYMING SLANG.

Shirley

A relatively (in parts very) affluent neighbourhood situated between Addiscombe and ADDINGTON. The name was first recorded in 1314 and could have meant 'shire clearing', in reference to its location near the border between

SURREY and Kent, or 'bright clearing'. In the 17th century it was a hamlet beside a common on the old road from CROYDON to WEST WICKHAM. Much of present-day Shirley was built up in the 1930s with semi-detached houses, though a few Victorian buildings survive. Later developments to the south in Upper Shirley and in the north at Shirley Oaks are of contrasting characters.

Shirley poppy *Papaver rhoeas Shirley*, a poppy distinctively lacking the black blotch that is present at the base of each petal in its common-or-garden relatives. In the summer of 1880 the Rev William Wilks (1843–1923) found a lone poppy with a white border to its red petals. He carefully marked the flower and returned in the autumn to collect its seed. Next spring he planted out several hundred seedlings in his garden at the vicarage in Shirley Church Road and bred progressively paler plants, including an all-white variety. Wilks later became secretary of the Royal Horticultural Society and was instrumental in the inception of the CHELSEA FLOWER SHOW.

Shoe Lane A road linking FLEET STREET with HOLBORN Circus to the north. It was probably originally Shoeland, that is, 'land given so that shoes may be bought'. In this case the land was given to the canons of ST PAUL'S, so that they might buy footwear with the income accruing from it. It was a rough locality in the late Middle Ages, when the only respectable dwelling was the London residence of the bishop of Bangor. The poet Richard Lovelace (*see* ALTHEA) died at his squalid lodgings in an alley off Shoe Lane in 1657. At that time the lane was known for its signwriters and authors of broadsheets, and later for its coppersmiths. Until 1989 the offices of the EVENING STANDARD were in Shoe Lane.

shoot
Shoot, the
1. A nickname in the early 1880s for Walworth Road station, from the immense number of persons 'shot' out there. The station closed in 1916 and did not reopen after the war.
2. A pejorative slang term for WALTHAMSTOW in the early 20th century (from rubbish-shoot), because, unlike nearby CHINGFORD and WOODFORD, its population was predominantly working class.

shooting the bridge Navigation of a boat through the arches of medieval LONDON BRIDGE.

The breadth and profusion of the starlings (pilings protecting the bridge's piers) created treacherous currents, and the fall of water at the ebb tide could be as great as 6 feet (2m). For some Londoners shooting the bridge was a thrill, for others a risk not worth taking. Registers of local burials often showed 'drowned at the bridge' as the cause of death. The old bridge was removed in 1832, whereupon the hazard subsided.

> 'Shoot we the bridge!' – the venturous boatmen cry –
> 'Shoot we the bridge!' – the exulting fare reply.
> – Down the steep fall the headlong waters go.
> Curls the white foam, the breakers roar below.
> The veering helm the dexterous steersman stops.
> Shifts the thin oar, the fluttering canvas drops;
> Then with closed eyes, clenched hands, and quick-drawn breath,
> Darts at the central arch, nor heeds the gulf beneath.
>
> GEORGE CANNING: *The Loves of the Triangles*, Canto 1 (1798)

Shooters Hill Ancient woodland and its accompanying residential locality, lying between PLUMSTEAD and ELTHAM. The road of the same name was part of WATLING STREET, the Roman road to Dover. At 432 feet (132m), the summit is one of the highest points in GREATER LONDON. The name was first recorded in 1226 and probably derives from the use of the slopes for archery practice, although other sources suggest a link with highwaymen. Henry IV ordered the clearance of trees bordering the road in an unsuccessful bid to protect travellers from 'violent practices'. DICKENS's novel *A Tale of Two Cities* (1859) opens on Shooters Hill. *See also* SEVERNDROOG CASTLE.

> Don Juan had got out on Shooters Hill;
> Sunset the time, the place the same declivity
> Which looks along that vale of good and ill
> Where London streets ferment in full activity ...
>
> LORD BYRON: *Don Juan*, Canto 11 (1823)

'Shooters Hill' was a jocular 19th-century term for the female genitalia and mons pubis.

shop
Shop, the In military slang, the former Royal Military Academy at WOOLWICH. The academy taught every branch of military science, as well as French and Latin, writing, fencing and draw-

ing. It closed at the outbreak of the Second World War and afterwards became part of the Royal Military Academy at Sandhurst, Berkshire.

shopping days to Christmas Preceded by a figure, such as 50, the phrase is an irritating reminder of the decreasing opportunities to buy Christmas presents. The commercial countdown was first promoted by SELFRIDGES department store, and its US founder, Gordon Selfridge (1856–1947; *see also the* CUSTOMER IS ALWAYS RIGHT), when still in his native Chicago, is said to have sent out an instruction to Marshall Field's heads of departments and assistants reading: 'The Christmas season has begun and twenty-three more shopping days remain in which to make our holiday sales record.' As virtually every day of the week is now a shopping day, the figure is essentially the number of days to 25 December. The countdown usually begins in earnest from October, and there are 85 shopping days from the 1st of that month.

Shoreditch A high-density employment area situated north of LIVERPOOL STREET STATION. The former parish and borough of Shoreditch embraced HOXTON and Haggerston; the vicinity of the medieval village is now sometimes called South Shoreditch (or occasionally SOSHO). The name is of Old English origin and refers to a dyke by a steep bank but the more romantic explanation, espoused in PERCY'S RELIQUES, is that Jane Shore, mistress of Edward IV, died in a ditch here in 1527:

> Thus, weary of my life, at length
> I yielded up my vital strength
> Within a ditch of loathsome scent,
> Where carrion dogs did much frequent:
> The which now since my dying day
> Is Shoreditch called, as writers say.

Augustinian nuns founded a priory in Shoreditch in the 12th century but significant development did not begin in the area until the 16th century, when building extended northward from BISHOPSGATE. In 1576 James Burbage opened a playhouse here called 'the Theatre'. It was the first of its type in the country, and survived until 1598, when it was moved south of the THAMES and reopened as the GLOBE. Another theatre, the Curtain, opened here in 1577, and many actors lived in the vicinity. Shoreditch was one of the first 'outer London' districts to fuse with the CITY and the parish had around 10,000 inhabitants

by 1750, together with 15 almshouses and St Leonard's Church. Within a hundred years the population had increased tenfold, with many residents working in local industries, especially the furniture, upholstery and timber trades. In the early 1990s Shoreditch became popular with a wide spectrum of the arts and media communities, ranging from sculptors to website designers. The trend stuttered as a result of rising rents, and perhaps an excess of hype, but the phenomenon is far from dead.

Shoreditch fury A 19th-century slang term for an aggressive woman.

Shoreditch Toff, The A MUSIC HALL song composed and sung in the late 1860s by Arthur Lloyd (1839–1904). In it he took on the persona of 'Immensikoff', and wore a voluminous fur coat; these became fashionable garments among men about town in the late 19th century, and were known as Immensikoffs.

Shoreditch Tw*t A 2002 Channel 4 television production based on the content of a long-running fanzine (which did not use an asterisk) that lampooned the lifestyle of local media trendies. *See also* NATHAN BARLEY.

duke of Shoreditch *See under* DUKE.

shrimp

Shrimp, the A media nickname for the model Jean Shrimpton (b.1942), who introduced the miniskirt to a delighted or dismayed public and was at the centre of the SWINGING LONDON scene. Her boyfriends included the photographer David Bailey and the actor Terence Stamp. She retired from modelling at the age of 28 and became a virtual recluse, telling one interviewer: 'The trouble is I really hate clothes.'

Shrimp Girl, The A painting (*c*.1745) by William HOGARTH showing a vivacious vendor of shellfish from BILLINGSGATE. It hangs in the NATIONAL GALLERY.

Sidcup A primarily 1930s suburb situated between CHISLEHURST and BEXLEY. The name was first recorded in 1254 and is derived from Old English words meaning either a 'fold in a hill' or a 'flat hilltop'. This was essentially a field name and there is no record of a hamlet existing here until 1675. Sidcup House (now Sidcup Place) was said to have been built in 1743 by an officer in the army engineers as a star-shaped fort. If this is true, the house was soon remodelled on more conventional lines and has since been much extended. After the First World War, and especially in the ten years from 1929, a building boom carried Sidcup across the railway line and south to the new bypass to fill roughly its present sprawling extent, while a denser network of streets encircled the old village.

In Harold Pinter's influential play *The* CARE-TAKER, the tramp Davies insists repeatedly but implausibly that everything will be all right if he can only get down to Sidcup.

siege

Siege of Sidney Street An incident on 3 January 1911 when police and soldiers, on the orders of the home secretary Winston Churchill who personally (and somewhat ostentatiously) attended the siege, surrounded 100 Sidney Street in west STEPNEY. Inside the house were three Latvian anarchists who had killed three policemen during a raid on a HOUNDSDITCH jeweller's on 16 December 1910. A lengthy gun battle ensued and the house eventually caught fire. Two of the gang died but, if he was ever there, PETER THE PAINTER escaped. The siege has also been called 'the Battle of Stepney'.

Balcombe Street siege *See under* BALCOMBE STREET.

Sikes, Bill A villainous housebreaker with no redeeming qualities in Charles DICKENS's *Oliver Twist* (1838), he terrorizes everyone he meets, including his 'fence', FAGIN. He fails in helping Fagin to turn OLIVER TWIST into a thief and brutally murders NANCY when Fagin reveals she has informed on them. He makes a terrified dash to escape arrest on JACOB'S ISLAND but dies by accidentally hanging himself as he falls from a roof. After the appearance of the novel, Sikes's name was for a while used as a generic term for a ruffianly housebreaker.

Silent Ceremony The procedure by which the LORD MAYOR OF LONDON is formally admitted to office in November. It takes place on the day before the LORD MAYOR'S SHOW and is known as the Silent Ceremony because, apart from a short declaration of office by the incoming lord mayor, no words are spoken. The outgoing lord mayor ceremonially hands the CITY insignia to his successor.

Silvertown A steadily regenerating DOCKLANDS district situated between the THAMES and the

ROYAL DOCKS. It takes its name from one of the first manufacturers, Samuel Winkworth Silver's India-rubber, Gutta-percha, and Telegraph Company, which opened in 1852 and grew to employ 3,000 workers. Henry TATE set up his sugar-cube factory in Silvertown in 1877 (*see also the* SUGAR MILE). London's largest-ever explosion occurred in 1917 at the Brunner Mond munitions factory; 73 people were killed and most of the town was destroyed, only to be rebuilt after the First World War along the same lines as before. During the Second World War Silvertown was a prime target for German bombing. On one occasion a ring of fire forced the WOOLWICH ferries to mount a Dunkirk-style evacuation of the inhabitants. Tate and Lyle's sugar refinery was rebuilt from the 1950s and is the district's leading present-day employer. Silver's rubber factory was demolished in the 1960s and many other industries have also moved away, leaving sites for new housing.

> On Silvertown Way, the cranes stand high,
> Quiet and grey against the still of the sky.
> They won't quit and lay down, though the action has died,
> They watch the new game in town on the Blackwall side.
>
> MARK KNOPFLER: 'Silvertown Blues' (song) (2000)

Simpson's-in-the-Strand London's best-known restaurant for traditional British fare, especially a roast beef dinner. John Simpson opened a chess club and COFFEE HOUSE on the STRAND in 1828. He next added a refreshment room with smoking facilities, which he called the Grand Cigar Divan, and followed this in 1848 with a 'Restauratum'. Large joints of meat were placed on silver-domed trolleys and wheeled to guests' tables to avoid disturbing the chess games; the practice continues at Simpson's today, although the chess games are long gone. The original buildings were demolished when the Strand was widened in 1903 and Simpson's was rebuilt as part of the complex linked to the SAVOY HOTEL, which had acquired the business in 1898. Famous diners at the restaurant have included Sherlock HOLMES, in 'The Adventure of the Illustrious Client' (1924), and Vincent Van Gogh.

singing bus driver Matt Monro (1930–85) was thus nicknamed for his day job at the time of his early recordings for Decca in the mid-1950s.

The SHOREDITCH-born crooner later gained international fame for his live performances and chart successes, notably his rendition of the main theme for the James Bond film *From Russia with Love* in 1963.

> When he was discovered and turned into a star, Matt Monro was a bus driver on the number 27 route between Teddington and Highgate.
>
> PETE FRAME: *Rockin' Around Britain* (1999)

Sinister Street A novel (1913–14) by Compton Mackenzie (born Edward Montague Compton; 1883–1972), originally published in two volumes. It is divided into four books: 'The Prison House' (Michael's childhood), 'Classical Education' (school), 'Dreaming Spires' (Oxford) and 'Romantic Education'. The last book largely concerns Michael's ultimately fruitless efforts to find and redeem a former girlfriend who has become a prostitute in London, in the course of which he takes lodgings in ALBANY and traverses streets that are the haunts of the city's lowest life. In a dedication, the author states: 'Sinister Street is a symbolic title which bears no reference to an heraldic euphemism.' Some critics complained that the novel has too much flowery description and not enough character development but it was both successful and influential.

> The existence of the Seven Sisters Road had probably not occurred to Michael since in the hazel-coppices of Clere Abbey he had first made of it at Brother Aloysius' behest the archetype of Avernus, and yet his choice of it now for the entrance to the underworld was swift as instinct. The quest of Lily was already beginning to assume the character of a deliberate withdrawal from the world in which he familiarly moved.
>
> 'Romantic Education'

sink

sinking of Queen Eleanor According to legend, Eleanor of Castile, queen consort of Edward I, sank at CHARING CROSS and rose again at QUEENHITHE. The story seems to have begun with a vituperative ballad that suggests, among much anti-Spanish derision, that Eleanor murdered the LORD MAYOR OF LONDON's wife by thrusting venomous snakes into her bosom. When Edward accused his queen of the deed she denied it and wished the ground might swallow her up if she lied:

> With that, at Charing Cross she sunk
> Into the ground alive;
> And after rose with life again,
> In London, at Queenhithe.

Thereafter she languished 20 days in pain, and confessed to the crime and also to bearing a child by a friar. The choice of location for the sinking is curious (but presumably deliberate), as the cross was placed at Charing after Eleanor's death by the grieving king. The anonymous ballad-maker was said to have composed the piece during the reign of Mary I and the story was taken up by George Peele in his dramatic chronicle *Edward the First* (*c.*1590). Thomas Middleton and John Webster jokily transposed the direction of subterranean travel in their play *Anything for a Quiet Life* (1662):

> If lords may be trusted no better than thus, I will go home and cut my wife's nose off. I will turn over a new leaf and hang up the page. Lastly, I will put on a large pair of wet-leather boots and drown myself; I will sink at Queenhithe and rise again at Charing Cross, contrary to the statute in Edwardo primo.

sink of Surrey WANDSWORTH was formerly so dubbed, not for its degeneracy but for its liability to flooding, owing to its low-lying situation on the bank of the THAMES at the mouth of the River WANDLE.

sinner

Sinner from Pinner A name bestowed by the British media on the PINNER-bred teenager Jane March (b.1973) when she appeared in *The Lover* (1992), a film adaptation of a novel by the French writer Marguerite Duras. Such was the 'erotic authenticity' of March's love scenes with her co-star Tony Leung that rumours began to circulate that there was no 'acting' involved.

Sinner/Winner Man *See* DON'T BE A SINNER, BE A WINNER (*under* DO).

Sipson A linear village stretching three-quarters of a mile (1.2 km) along Sipson Road, most of which lies just west of the M4 HEATHROW spur road. Gravel excavations have revealed Neanderthal hand-axes and Bronze Age loom-weights, the latter providing the earliest known evidence of weaving in the London area. A small cremation cemetery from the middle Bronze Age has also been discovered. Sipson was first mentioned by name in 1214, as Sibwineston – 'Sibwine's farmstead'. The village grew slowly from the late 18th century, when Sipson House was built. Over the second half of the 20th century Sipson's character was greatly affected by the growth of Heathrow. Sipson House has been converted to office use by the British Airports Authority and renamed Sipson Court, with only its original facade surviving. The entire village will be demolished if construction of the third runway at Heathrow proceeds as planned, and Terminal 6 will fill most of its former site.

siren suit A one-piece lined and warm garment, similar to a boiler suit, sometimes worn in London in air-raid shelters during the bombing raids of the Second World War. It was famously worn by Winston Churchill, who referred to his blue siren suit as his 'rompers', and was so named from its being slipped on over nightclothes at the first wail of the air-raid siren.

Sir John Soane's Museum *See under* SOANE.

sisters of the Bank An old term for prostitutes. The reference was to BANKSIDE, which was once notorious for its brothels.

> Come, I will send for a whole coach or two of Bankside ladies, and we will be jovial.
>
> THOMAS RANDOLPH: *The Muses' Looking Glass*, II, iv (*c*.1630)

six

at sixes and sevens Higgledy-piggledy; in a state of confusion; or, of persons, unable to come to an agreement, at loggerheads. The phrase probably comes from an old dicing game called hazard, and may have arisen as a mistranslation of Old French *cinque et sice*, 'five and six'. Nicholas Udall, in *Erasmus' Apothegmes* (1542) says: 'There is a proverb *Omnem jacere aleam*, to cast all dice by which is signified to set all on six and seven ... assaying the wild chance of fortune, be it good, be it bad.'

However, it is also traditionally held that the expression arose out of a dispute between two of the great LIVERY COMPANIES, the Merchant Taylors and the Skinners, as to which would go sixth and which would go seventh in processions held in the CITY of London, both companies having been chartered in 1327 within a few days of each other. In 1484 they submitted the matter to the judgement of the then LORD MAYOR OF LON-

DON, Sir Robert Billesden, and the ALDERMEN. The award was that the master and wardens of both companies entertain each other to dinner annually and that the Skinners were to precede the Taylors in that year's procession. The next year the Taylors were to take the sixth place and this alternation was to continue 'ever more'. The story is colourful and apparently true but chronologically it holds no water as the derivation of the phrase.

> Lat not this wreched wo thyne herte gnawe,
> But manly, set the world on six and sevene,
> And if thou deye a martyr, to go hevene.
>
> CHAUCER: *Troilus and Criseyde*, iv (*c*.1386)

Six Pillars A grade II* listed Modernist house situated on Crescent Wood Road, SYDENHAM Hill, built for the headmaster of DULWICH COLLEGE Preparatory School by the TECTON partnership in 1935. It was primarily the work of Valentine Harding, a young architect who was killed on active service in the Second World War. Six Pillars was refurbished in 2003 and is occasionally opened to the public.

Sixteen-String Jack John Rann (*c*.1750–74), a highwayman who usually operated in the vicinity of HOUNSLOW HEATH and was noted for his foppery. He wore 16 tags, eight at each knee. Convicted at the OLD BAILEY of robbing Dr William Bell, chaplain to Princess Amelia, he was hanged at TYBURN.

skin and blister 'Sister' in COCKNEY RHYMING SLANG. The term is almost always used in full, because referring to one's sister as a 'skin' could sound disrespectful.

> 'Hey, that's my skin and blister, Pete – as we say in London. But I suppose she is sort of, well ... formidable looking.' Again she dissolved into laughter.
>
> PAT BOOTH: *The Sisters* (1987)

sky

Skylon A futuristic sculpture consisting of a large streamlined spindle-shaped object pointed at each end, somewhat reminiscent of a space projectile, held upright in the air by wires. It was made for the SOUTH BANK exhibition as part of the 1951 FESTIVAL OF BRITAIN. A year after the festival closed the sculpture was dismantled and sold to a scrap merchant. A bar and grill called Skylon opened at the ROYAL FESTIVAL HALL in 2007.

sky (rocket) 'Pocket' in slightly dated COCKNEY RHYMING SLANG.

> 'That's enough, Reverend. You must have been born in a harem, the way you roll a fag. Put a hand full in your sky rocket, and count out tens over here, will you? Then we'll be finished for the night and we can shift out of it.'
>
> RICHARD LLEWELLYN: *None but the Lonely Heart* (1943)

Slade School of Fine Art The art school of UNIVERSITY COLLEGE LONDON. It was founded in 1871 with a bequest from the English art collector and philanthropist Felix Slade (1788–1868) and is concerned with contemporary art and the practice, history and theories that inform it. Past members of the teaching staff include Henry Tonks, Lucian Freud and Roger Fry. Slade School alumni include Spencer Gore, Richard Hamilton, Augustus John, Wyndham Lewis and Rachel Whiteread.

Slasher Jack An approving sobriquet for Jack Cohen (1898–1979), the WHITECHAPEL-born founder of TESCO, derived from his 'pile 'em high, sell 'em cheap' style of cut-price grocery retailing.

Sloane or **Sloanie** Colloquial abbreviations of SLOANE RANGER.

> 'A Sloanie has a pony' is ... ingrained in the Sloane mind.
>
> PETER YORK and ANN BARR: *Official Sloane Ranger Handbook* (1982)

Sloane, Hans An eminent physician, naturalist and public benefactor (1660–1753). His employment as chief physician to the West Indian Fleet, while he was still in his late twenties, was reasonably lucrative and gave him the opportunity to greatly augment his existing collection of European botanical specimens. He was personal physician to Queen Anne and George I, for which service he was knighted in 1716. He succeeded Sir Isaac Newton as president of the ROYAL SOCIETY in 1727 and held the post until 1741. Sloane moved to CHELSEA in 1742 and subsequently endowed the CHELSEA PHYSIC GARDEN. His scientific and literary collection became the nucleus of the BRITISH MUSEUM after his death.

Sloane Ranger A British social stereotype of the late 1970s to early 1990s: a young upper-class or upper-middle-class person who is disciplined, well mannered and speaks educated English.

Sloane Rangers are conservative in dress, the women having no freakish hair styles and the men being clean shaven. The women wear expensive but informal country clothes and the men the attire of a city gentleman or country squire, with those in London living around SLOANE SQUARE, HOLLAND PARK and KENSINGTON.

The term, which puns on the Lone Ranger, the cowboy hero of western stories and films, was reputedly coined by Martina Margetts, a subeditor on *Harpers & Queen*, and introduced to a wider public by the style writer Peter York in an article in the magazine in October 1975. He and Ann Barr elaborated the concept in the *Official Sloane Ranger Handbook* in 1982.

Sloane Square Now seen as the 'gateway to the KING'S ROAD', Sloane Square was laid out in the late 1780s as part of the HANS TOWN development. It was formerly known as Great Bloody Field, presumably after a battle here. Both the town and the square were named after Sir Hans Sloane (*see above*). The square functioned as a service provider for the new district, with stables, sheds, workshops, bakehouses and some accommodation for staff. In 1868 the Metropolitan District Railway Company opened Sloane Square station and in 1877 PETER JONES took over a drapery establishment at the corner of the King's Road. Jones unified the store's disparate parts in the late 1880s, a period which also saw the construction of the ROYAL COURT THEATRE on the site of the former Court Theatre. These changes to the square's perimeter resulted in roughly the current layout, except that the roads then met at a central crossroads. In the early years of the 20th century many of the surviving houses from the first phase of the square's existence were demolished and replaced. A circulatory traffic system was introduced in 1929 and the centre of the square was paved over. In 2007 KENSINGTON AND CHELSEA council withdrew a plan to restore the crossroads arrangement.

Sloane Street A street leading north from Sloane Square by way of Cadogan Square towards KNIGHTSBRIDGE. Especially in its upper reaches it is liberally populated with celebrated and expensive couture houses, and HARVEY NICKS is on its top right-hand corner. LIBERTY OF LONDON opened a boutique on the street in 2008.

Sloany Pony A nickname frequently applied to

the White Horse public house in PARSONS GREEN on account of its perceived popularity with SLOANE RANGERS. In existence as a coaching inn by 1688, the White Horse was rebuilt in the early 1890s.

Sloper's Island A semi-generic nickname in the 19th century for a London locality crowded with cheap tenements for rent. One meaning of the verb 'to slope' was to leave one's lodgings without paying.

smith

Smith, James *See* UMBRELLA.

Smith of Smiths The Rev Sydney Smith (1771–1845), a Whig clergyman and canon of ST PAUL'S, was so called by Thomas Macaulay. He was renowned as a conversationalist for his drollery and brilliance of wit as well as for the incisive quality of his writings.

Smith of the alleyways The nickname of the protagonist in Leon Garfield's children's novel *Smith* (1967). He is 12 years old, a 'dirty, weaselish, villainous-looking remnant', a pipe-smoking gin-swigging survivor of the treacherously dark alleys around 18th-century ST PAUL'S.

Smiths of Surbiton, The A middle-class 'comedy without a plot' (1906) by Keble Howard, pseudonym of John Keble Bell (1875–1928). It was followed by *The Smiths of Valley View* (1909) and *The Smiths in Wartime* (1917). The original novel (which D.H. Lawrence called 'drivel') was adapted for the stage in 1922.

> It is just as easy to make acquaintants in Surbiton as it is difficult to make friends.
>
> *The Smiths of Surbiton*

Smith Square A square leading off the western side of MILLBANK, just to the south of the PALACE OF WESTMINSTER. It was laid out around 1726 and probably named after Henry Smith, former owner of the land on which it was built. It long had contrasting political associations, and at one time held the headquarters of the Conservative, Labour and Liberal parties. Until 1980 the Labour Party was at TRANSPORT HOUSE; the Conservatives occupied red-brick neo-Georgian premises at No.32 from 1958 to 2004; the Liberals were based at 36 Smith Square from 1965 to 1968. *See also* QUEEN ANNE'S FOOTSTOOL.

Battle of Mr Smith's club *See under* BATTLE.

Talking Smith, the *See under* TALKING.

Smithfield Properly known as West Smithfield,

this is the home of London's main wholesale meat market, located just west of the BARBICAN. The Romans used this 'smooth field' as a cemetery in the 3rd and 4th centuries and it was later the site of public executions, including the burning of witches and martyrs, though probably not as many as folklore suggests. Oxen were sold here from 1305 and the CORPORATION OF LONDON gained the right to collect market tolls from 1400, although it was not until 1638 that a formal charter was granted. The scale of operations at the livestock market created an increasingly hazardous public nuisance but self-interested parties long resisted relocation to a more suitable site. Finally, the Smithfield Market Removal Act of 1852 transferred the trade in live animals to COPENHAGEN FIELDS. In the mid-19th century Smithfield's street pattern was reconfigured, focused on new central buildings for the market. These have since been refurbished to bring them up to European Union hygiene standards. Smithfield is the only significant wholesale market that has not relocated outside central London and the possibility remains that the butchers will be displaced so that more profitable use can be made of the site. *See also* BARTHOLOMEW FAIR; CHARTERHOUSE; *The* ELMS; RUFFIANS' HALL.

Smithfield bargain The expression originally referred to a deal in which the purchaser was deceived or exploited, but it later came to signify a marriage of convenience, especially financial convenience on the part of the groom, in which as Frances Grose put it: 'the fair sex are bought and sold like cattle at Smithfield.' Both the term and the phenomenon were especially common in the 18th and early 19th centuries. A 'Smithfield match' was the same thing.

> Why, is it not provoking? When I thought we were coming to the prettiest distress imaginable, to find myself made a mere Smithfield bargain of at last! There, had I projected one of the most sentimental elopements! So becoming a disguise! So amiable a ladder of ropes! Conscious moon – four horses – Scotch parson – with such surprise to Mrs Malaprop – and such paragraphs in the newspapers! Oh, I shall die with disappointment!
>
> R.B. SHERIDAN: *The Rivals*, V, i (1775)

The term was further extended to other improper dealings, such as an MP who allowed his parliamentary vote to be bought.

Smithfield races A nickname for the old horse market. Horse racing did take place in Smithfield several centuries ago but the tag stuck to the marketplace long after there was no room left for an animal to trot even a short distance.

smog Both the word and the phenomenon are a blend of fog and smoke. The term was popularized by Dr Harold Antoine des Voeux, honorary treasurer of the Coal Smoke Abatement Society, who in 1905 proposed that London should be renamed Smog, so endemic was the problem. He advocated the use of the underground railway system to 'tube' fresh air from the countryside to crowded city districts. *See also the* GREAT SMOG.

> These visitations, which a witty English writer once designated by the name 'smog', represent a condition of the atmosphere when it is saturated with moisture and charged with soot and the fumes of sulfur and carbonic acid gas from the chimneys and smokestacks of the great city [London].
>
> *Los Angeles Times* (18 January 1893)

Smoke, the or the Big Smoke One of the

nicknames of London. It appears to have had its beginnings in the English used by Australian Aborigines in the first half of the 19th century, applied to any large city, and it continues to be a characteristically Australian English usage, but it was well established in Britain too by the end of the century:

> Till that last awful winter! ... when the farmers had been mostly ruined, and half the able-bodied men of Mellor had tramped 'up into the smoke', as the village put it, in search of London work.
>
> MRS HUMPHRY WARD: *Marcella* (1894)

The capital has suffered little from coal smoke since the Clean Air Acts of the 1950s, yet the term is as widely used as ever. *Smoke: A London Peculiar* is a magazine of 'words and images inspired by the city', published three times a year.

Snaresbrook An elegant and well-preserved residential locality in north-west WANSTEAD. The name was first recorded in its present form in 1599; its first part is of uncertain origin, although it could be connected with the use of snares for trapping animals or birds in EPPING FOREST. The stream that gave the village its name is no longer visible above ground. In 1843 Leopold I,

King of the Belgians, opened an infant orphan asylum that subsequently became the Royal Wanstead School and is now Snaresbrook Crown Court. Snaresbrook station opened in 1856 on the Loughton branch of the Eastern Counties Railway. The line was electrified in 1947, when it became part of the CENTRAL LINE.

snow

snowdrop A flower that first grew in KENSINGTON, according to the fairy tale of KENNA, transformed from the lifeless body of her lover Albion.

> When lo! the little shape by magic power
> Grew less and less, contracted to a flower;
> A flower, that first in this sweet garden smil'd,
> To virgins sacred, and the Snowdrop styl'd.
> The new-born plant with sweet regret she view'd,
> Warm'd with her sighs, and with her tears bedew'd,
> Its ripen'd seeds from bank to bank convey'd,
> And with her lover whiten'd half the shade.
>
> THOMAS TICKELL: 'Kensington Garden' (1722)

Snow Hill A street in south-west SMITHFIELD, connecting FARRINGDON ROAD and HOLBORN Viaduct. Its name derives from Old English *snōr*, 'road that curves across a gradient'. The MOHOCKS were said to have lurked here, amusing themselves by grabbing the occasional passer by, stuffing him into a tub and rolling him down the hill.

Soane

Sir John Soane An architect and antiquarian (1753–1837), born near Reading, Berkshire. He trained under George Dance the Younger, for whom he had first worked as an errand boy, and won ROYAL ACADEMY medals for his architectural drawings. In 1777 he travelled to Italy and spent three years studying classical architecture. On his return he designed numerous public buildings, churches and country houses. In 1788 he was appointed architect to the BANK OF ENGLAND and he later served as clerk of works at ST JAMES'S PALACE, the PALACE OF WESTMINSTER and CHELSEA ROYAL HOSPITAL. Surviving Soane buildings in London include BENTLEY PRIORY, DULWICH PICTURE GALLERY, HOLWOOD HOUSE, Norwood Hall (*see* NORWOOD GREEN), PITSHANGER MANOR HOUSE and a set of houses in LINCOLN'S INN FIELDS, now the home of the SOANE MUSEUM.

Soane Museum or **Sir John Soane's House** An extraordinary collection of books and manuscripts, works of art, classical artefacts and casts and models of the remains of antiquity assembled by Sir John Soane as an 'academy of architecture' in the connecting houses that he designed in LINCOLN'S INN FIELDS. He bequeathed the buildings and the collection to the nation because his wife and one of his sons predeceased him and he intensely disliked his surviving son.

> Few people know of it, and fewer visit it, which is much to be regretted, since, though, as Dr Waagen says, the overcrowded and labyrinthine house leaves an impression as of a feverish dream, it contains, together with much rubbish, several most interesting pictures.
>
> AUGUSTUS HARE: *Walks in London* (1878)

Soapsuds Island A nickname formerly applied to more than one part of west London with a high concentration of laundries. Such 'islands' tended to develop at the edge of the capital's urban sprawl, where land and labour were cheap and the air was a little cleaner, allowing laundered items to be hung out to dry without getting dirty again. NORTH KENSINGTON fitted the bill for a while in the mid-19th century but it soon became too densely built up and much of the industry relocated to South ACTON.

> Fulham, Hammersmith and particularly Acton in the western suburbs became centres where, by the end of the [19th] century, there were concentrations of large and small factory laundries so prominent that the term 'Soapsuds Island' became their identifying sobriquet ...
>
> PATRICIA E. MALCOLMSON: *English Laundresses: A Social History, 1850–1930* (1986)

society

Society of Dilettanti See the DILETTANTI SOCIETY.

Society of the Virtuosi of St Luke's See ST LUKE'S CLUB.

Sodomites' Walk The 18th-century nickname of a path across MOORFIELDS, roughly aligned with what is now the south side of Finsbury Square. The path ran beside a wall separating two gardens and was well known as a place of

homosexual solicitation, where men might stand pretending to 'make water' while in fact signalling their availability to others. However, the walk was also frequented by agents provocateurs employed by the police, and those entrapped could expect a lengthy prison sentence as well as time in the pillory.

soft-roed 'Wet behind the ears', or of a too-gentle disposition, in 19th-century COCKNEY slang.

> This ere one we're talking about is what I call a soft-roed un. He takes after his mother, and he ain't got the pluck of a tame rabbit.
>
> JAMES GREENWOOD: *Toilers in London* (1883)

Soho A compact commercial quarter bounded on the west, north and east by REGENT STREET, OXFORD STREET and CHARING CROSS ROAD respectively. In the south, CHINATOWN forms a less well-defined border. Soho now encompasses the entire area once known as Kempsfield, of which it was originally just a part. Its name is said to derive from a cry similar to 'tally-ho', for this was a hunting ground in the 16th century. Built up after 1679 by the speculative builder Richard Frith, Soho at first attracted aristocrats but soon provided a haven for Greek Christians and Huguenots fleeing religious persecution. German, Italian and Hungarian radicals came to Soho after the failed revolutions of 1848. Some of these migrants opened restaurants specializing in their national cuisine, attracting London's bohemian community from the early part of the 20th century and especially in the 1930s and 1940s. After the Second World War Soho became notorious as the WEST END's red-light district but in this respect it is now a shadow of its former self. An unintended consequence of WESTMINSTER council's suppression of the sex industry was the rise of Soho's gay community, which is focused on OLD COMPTON STREET. Soho is also home to advertising, media and film distribution companies (especially on WARDOUR STREET and in SOHO SQUARE) and it is famed for its pubs and clubs, a declining proportion of which are colourfully seedy.

Soho's residents have included Canaletto, Casanova, William Blake, William Hazlitt, John Constable and Karl Marx.

Soho Academy In 1717 Martin Clare established in SOHO SQUARE a boys' school that later became known as the Soho Academy. Until the end of the 18th century the academy enjoyed one of the best reputations of London's private boarding schools. It was noted for its Shakespearean theatrical productions, which helped several scholars become noted actors, while its art classes were of benefit to the pupils Thomas Rowlandson and J.M.W. Turner.

Soho Nailbomber The epithet attached to the now-imprisoned David Copeland, who in 1999 planted nail bombs in the Admiral Duncan, a Soho public house with a mainly gay clientele, killing three people. He also caused explosions in BRIXTON and BRICK LANE. He was motivated by hatred of homosexuals and non-whites.

Soho Square The only formal square in Soho, situated near the district's north-east corner. Constructed in the 1680s, it was first called King Square (the original stone statue of Charles II, now rather the worse for wear, still graces the square, albeit no longer in its central position). Originally the site of aristocratic townhouses (almost all now gone), and later of embassies, today it is home to media groups, a French Protestant church and St Patrick's Roman Catholic Church. The gardens remain popular with the lunchtime al fresco sandwich-eaters and summer sunbathers.

Soho tapestry A type of tapestry produced in and around Soho in the late 17th and 18th centuries. Many of the weavers were of Flemish origin and had previously been employed at the tapestry works in MORTLAKE.

Soldier's Well A well by which 'wonderful cures' were said to have been effected, both on the blind and the lame. It was discovered in 1649 near Southampton House, HOLBORN, and named for the profession of its finder.

so long as the stone of Brutus is safe, so long shall London flourish An old saying referring to the supposed Trojan origin of LONDON STONE and its mythical significance to the City. *See also* BRUTUS.

Somerset House A cultural centre and government office building situated between STRAND and the THAMES, immediately east of WATERLOO BRIDGE. It occupies the site of the former mansion of Edward Seymour, 1st Duke of Somerset, brother of Jane Seymour and uncle of Edward VI. The building became Crown property after Somerset's execution (1552) and was later renamed Denmark House by James I, in honour of his queen, Anne of Denmark. It was occupied in turn by two other queens, Henrietta Maria of France and Catherine of Braganza. The present neoclassical structure was built (1776–86) by Sir William Chambers. It has been put to several uses by the government, most famously as the central record office for births, marriages and deaths. The principal present-day occupants are HM Revenue & Customs and the art galleries of the Courtauld Institute. The central Fountain Court hosts open-air concerts and film shows in summer and is converted to an ice rink in winter.

Somers Town Sandwiched between EUSTON and ST PANCRAS, Somers Town has been transformed several times in its 200-year existence. At the end of the 17th century Sir John Somers, appointed lord chancellor and created Baron Somers of Evesham in 1697, acquired the local freehold. The arrival of the NEW ROAD (now EUSTON ROAD) improved access to the area and in 1793 a Frenchman, Jacob Leroux, leased land from the Somers family for building. His scheme was not as profitable as he had hoped and the neighbourhood soon acquired a 'shabby genteel' status. No.29 Johnson Street, now Cranleigh Street, was the home of the young Charles DICKENS when it was newly built in 1824. Many residents were displaced by the creation of ST PANCRAS STATION and the subsequent establishment of a goods depot in 1875. The depot's site is now occupied by the BRITISH LIBRARY. Most of the streets behind the library are filled with late 20th-century council housing and the residential mix is multi-ethnic, with an especially strong Bangladeshi presence, contrary to the impression given in Shane Meadows's monochrome film *Somers Town* (2008).

sorrowful tale 'Jail', usually three months' incarceration therein, in early COCKNEY RHYMING SLANG.

Sosho or **SoSho** South SHOREDITCH, in the parlance of the area's restaurateurs, publicans and nightclub owners. Some of the establishments' patrons also use the term but generally with tongue in cheek.

> Located in south Shoreditch, where the
> City begins – an area known to the property

developers as SoSho, revoltingly enough – the new restaurant is a big, confident project, obviously designed to appeal as much to bankers as to website designers.

The Independent (15 September 2001)

Sotheby's An auction house that began as an antiquarian book saleroom in COVENT GARDEN in 1744. Its founder, 'honest' Sam Baker (1712–78), bequeathed a half-share in the business to his nephew, John Sotheby, and he and his descendants specialized increasingly in the art market. Sotheby's opened its premises in New BOND STREET in 1917 and now operates globally.

south

South Bank A THAMES-side cultural quarter situated opposite the Victoria EMBANKMENT. After the marshes were drained at the beginning of the 18th century, the area was successively home to a pleasure garden, LAMBETH waterworks and the Lion Brewery. Work on the construction of COUNTY HALL began in 1912 and it was opened in 1922. Later in the 1920s the OXO TOWER was built at the opposite end of the South Bank. Between these two landmarks lay a derelict industrial wasteland that was developed on a monumental scale over a prolonged period following the Second World War. The ROYAL FESTIVAL HALL was built for the FESTIVAL OF BRITAIN, together with an array of attractions like the DOME OF DISCOVERY and the SKYLON. The temporary structures were replaced by the Shell buildings and a series of arts venues, which included the NATIONAL THEATRE, National Film Theatre (now BFI Southbank), and the Queen Elizabeth Hall. South-west of the arts complex the Jubilee Gardens were laid out in 1977 and now possess the capital's most successful recent tourist attraction, the LONDON EYE.

Southbank Centre The collective name for the ROYAL FESTIVAL HALL, the Queen Elizabeth Hall and the Hayward, a contemporary art gallery. Several ancillary amenities and event spaces are contained within the three main buildings, including the Saison poetry library at the Festival Hall, the Purcell Room at the QEH and the Waterloo Sunset pavilion at the Hayward.

South Bank lion A 13-ton COADE STONE lion that from 1837 stood on a parapet of the Lion Brewery on the South Bank. It is the work of the sculptor W.F. Woodington (1806–93). The

brewery was demolished in 1950 to make way for the construction of the ROYAL FESTIVAL HALL but the lion was saved, reportedly at the request of George VI, painted gloss red and mounted on a plinth outside the WATERLOO STATION gate to the FESTIVAL OF BRITAIN site. When the station was enlarged in 1966 the lion was relocated to its present prominent position near the eastern end of WESTMINSTER BRIDGE, and stripped to the bare stone.

South Bank religion A journalistic label for the religious activities in the diocese of SOUTHWARK. It was associated with Mervyn Stockwood, Bishop of Southwark (1959–80), John Robinson, Suffragan Bishop of Woolwich (1959–69), author of *Honest to God* (1963), and some of their diocesan clergy. Characterized by outspokenness on moral and political issues, often from a socialist angle, and energetic attempts to bring the Church into closer relation with contemporary society and its problems, South Bank religion was not without its critics and the label was often applied disparagingly.

That is rather the new idea inside the Church. I should definitely say you were a South Banker.

AUBERON WAUGH: *Consider the Lilies* (1968)

South Bank Show, The A television arts programme, presented from its inception in 1978 to its proposed termination in 2010 by Melvyn Bragg. The headquarters of LONDON WEEKEND TELEVISION, which originally produced it, were on the South Bank and the show continued to be made here, at what became the main studios of ITV.

South Bank University *See the* LONDON SOUTH BANK UNIVERSITY.

South Circular Road A route rather than a cohesive road, it runs in a roughly semicircular 20-mile (32-km) loop through the built-up areas of SOUTH LONDON and together with the NORTH CIRCULAR ROAD forms an annular traffic artery through the inner suburbs of the capital. It extends from KEW BRIDGE in the west to WOOLWICH in the east.

South City Estate agents' hyperbole for ELEPHANT AND CASTLE.

South Croydon A relatively expensive residential part of Croydon with ill-defined borders. The medieval manor of Haling Park covered 400 acres (160 hectares) of the western side of the district. Elizabeth I granted the manor to Lord Howard of Effingham in 1592. The Haling

Park estate was sold for building in 1850 and its northern part was laid out with winding avenues lined at discreet intervals with Italianate villas. The great majority of these have been replaced, often by flats, but those that survive comprise the Waldrons conservation area. South Croydon station opened in 1865 and the subsequent growth of the district brought the destruction of most of its older buildings. The Whitgift School moved to Haling Park in 1931 and has since been progressively extended. Away from the school grounds, terraced and semi-detached houses filled the surviving open spaces or replaced Victorian mansions.

The journalist and moralist Malcolm Muggeridge (1903–90), actress Dame Peggy Ashcroft (1907–91) and film director Sir David Lean (1908–91) all grew up in South Croydon.

South Hampstead The vicinity of SWISS COTTAGE. The term 'South Hampstead' is not widely used and might have faded from use altogether were it not for the presence of its station and the will of local estate agents. South Hampstead was built up in the late 19th century, on lands that had belonged to KILBURN Priory and the Maryon Wilsons, lords of the manor of HAMPSTEAD. South Hampstead should not be confused with Hampstead's South End, which is the locality abutting HAMPSTEAD HEATH station. *See also* NETBALL.

South Ken A familiar name for SOUTH KENSINGTON.

South Ken Dutch A little-used alternative for PONT STREET DUTCH.

South Kensington South-west London's museum and academic quarter. The efforts of Sir Henry Cole (*see* COLEVILLE) and the influence of Prince ALBERT drove the creation here of the Victorian age's finest expression of intellectual achievement. Using proceeds from the 1851 GREAT EXHIBITION, an 88-acre (36-hectare) site was acquired on the edge of BROMPTON, streets were laid out and the South Kensington Museum opened in 1857 as an exhibition of industrial and decorative arts, nicknamed the BROMPTON BOILERS. Albert died in 1861 and the ALBERT HALL was built in his memory, opposite KENSINGTON GARDENS. The hall's neighbours on KENSINGTON GORE include colleges and scientific institutions. The NATURAL HISTORY MUSEUM brought the BRITISH MUSEUM's rocks, fossils and skeletons to Cromwell Road in 1881. The VICTORIA AND ALBERT MUSEUM – originally a museum of manufacturing – was opened in its present form by Edward VII in 1909, on the site of the former South Kensington Museum. The SCIENCE MUSEUM (in its present form) followed in 1928. The residential streets of South Kensington are lined with four- and five-storey STUCCO houses, many of which have been converted to flats. Most of the properties are part of the Wellcome Trust and Thurloe estates.

South Lambeth A densely built-up locality, separated from its parent district by KENNINGTON. South Lambeth was an extensive manor in the Middle Ages, stretching almost as far as MITCHAM. The manor was probably in the possession of the Crown for much of its existence, until it was absorbed within VAUXHALL at the end of the 13th century. Several grand houses were built here during the 18th century, but only a few fragments of their walls remain today. The construction of Vauxhall Bridge in 1816 linked South Lambeth Road with WESTMINSTER. Two decades later the Southampton Railway established its London terminus at NINE ELMS, and that area's subsequent industrialization stimulated a requirement for workers' housing nearby. Interwar and postwar municipal estates have since replaced many of the early dwellings, and most of the surviving 19th-century terraced houses are now in conservation areas. *See also the* ARK (1).

South London That part of London to the south of the River THAMES. In its broadest interpretation the term can be all-encompassing – so WIMBLEDON, for example, is in South London, and so is CROYDON. But it tends to have a particular connotation: of those modest inner suburbs that mushroomed with the spread of the railways in the second half of the 19th century, covering the fields of SURREY and Kent with serried ranks of scarcely distinguishable terraces – BALHAM, CAMBERWELL, CATFORD, KENNINGTON, LEWISHAM, STREATHAM and their ilk. In many parts of South London (BRIXTON and PECKHAM, for instance), the make-up of the community has been radically altered since the Second World War by immigration.

south of the river A seemingly straightforward THAMES-related descriptor but one that is redolent with the suggestion of a divided city. Like SOUTH LONDON, the term is mainly employed in the context of the inner suburbs that evolved over the latter part of the 19th century, when the nickname GEORGIUM SIDUS was coined with disparaging intent. Some north Londoners continue to insinuate that to cross south of the river is to enter a region that is less cultured, more dangerous and not quite the 'real London'. The most stereotypical manifestation of the divide is the pervasive (although rarely vindicated) expectation that a BLACK CAB hailed in the WEST END, especially late at night, will refuse to take a passenger south of the river.

> The Seine in Paris and the Tiber in Rome
> pull their respective capitals together, but
> the muddy waters of the Thames are an
> impenetrable psychological barrier.
>
> *Time Out* (6 September 1995)

Blake Morrison's novel *South of the River* (2007) follows five characters through the early years of the Blair era, celebrating South London 'in all its tawdry glory', according to *The Times*.

South Quay A DOCKLANDS development zone located on the southern side of the former WEST INDIA DOCKS. Until regeneration began in the 1980s the quayside was occupied by warehouses storing produce from the Far East. Despite favourable indications that initially encouraged developers' ambitions, South Quay has had a chequered history. Receivers were called in during an early phase of development after lack of interest from potential tenants, and floor space was offered at less than a quarter of CITY of London prices but uptake was still slow. In February 1996 the Provisional IRA broke its 18-month ceasefire with a massive truck bomb at Marsh Wall, causing two deaths and up to a £100 million-worth of damage to property. Much of the bomb site lay dormant until work began in 2001 on the MILLENNIUM QUARTER.

Southall A primarily Asian residential and commercial district, separated from HAYES[2] to the west by the GRAND UNION CANAL and from HANWELL to the east by the River BRENT. Southall was first mentioned in 1198 and the early hamlet seems to have grown up around SOUTHALL GREEN. Widespread development did not begin here until the 1890s, with factories flanking the railway line. The arrival of affordable and convenient electric trams in the early years of the 20th century brought a surge in suburban housebuilding and by 1944 overcrowding was said to have reached 'acute' proportions but

recommendations that industrial development should cease were not followed. From the late 1950s onwards Asian immigrants began to settle in Southall. Its proximity to HEATHROW and the availability of work in local factories were both influential factors, but the subsequent escalation has been a snowball phenomenon that could have happened almost anywhere. Punjabis are the main ethnic sub-group and the principal religion is Sikhism, but there are also many Hindus and Muslims, from East Africa, Pakistan and Bangladesh. The Sri Guru Singh Sabha Gurdwara, on Havelock Road, is the largest Sikh temple outside India.

Southall Green The core of the early village of Southall, flanking the road now called King Street to the south and the Green to the north. The manor house was built (or rebuilt) in 1587 and although it has since been altered and restored, it remains the most authentic survival of its kind in London. The council acquired the house in 1913, eventually restoring the building and using it as offices. The grounds are open to the public in daylight hours and have yew trees and a mulberry tree said to have been planted by Henry VIII.

Southcottians The followers of Joanna Southcott (1750–1814), one-time domestic servant at Exeter. Starting as a Methodist, she became a prophetess and declared herself to be the 'woman clothed with the sun, and the moon under her feet, and upon her head a crown of twelve stars' (Revelation 12:1). She came to London in 1802 and at the age of 64 she announced that she was to be delivered of a son. 19 October 1814 was the date fixed for the birth, which did not take place, but the prophetess died in a trance soon afterwards and was buried in ST JOHN'S WOOD burial ground, where her weathered gravestone may still be seen. She left a locked wooden box usually known as Joanna Southcott's Box, which was not to be opened until a time of national crisis, and then only in the presence of all the bishops in England. Attempts were made to persuade the episcopate to open it during the Crimean War (1854–6) and again in the First World War. It was opened in 1927 at Church House, WESTMINSTER, in the presence of one reluctant prelate, and found to contain a few oddments and papers, among which were a lottery ticket and a copy of John

Cleland's *The Romance of a Day, or An Adventure in Greenwich Park, last Easter* (1764). It is claimed by some that the box opened was not the authentic one.

Southgate A 1930s suburb located 2 miles (3 km) south-west of ENFIELD. The hamlet that grew up by the southern gate to ENFIELD CHASE was first mentioned in 1370. After the chase was enclosed in 1777 the area was divided up among wealthy knights and gentlemen and Southgate became known for its elegant mansions. This state of affairs persisted well into the 19th century, because of the absence of main roads, the hilly terrain that kept away the early railway builders, and the disinclination of several of the larger estates' owners to sell their land. At the outbreak of the First World War Southgate was still essentially rural. After the war improvements in bus services brought some ripples of interest from potential commuters but it was the arrival of the PICCADILLY LINE in 1933 that turned the tide. In the space of six years the area was almost entirely built up with houses and shopping parades, except for chunks of parkland that the enlightened council had acquired earlier.

Southwark SOUTH LONDON's most ancient town, situated directly across the THAMES from the CITY of London. Its Old English name, Sudwerca, meant 'southern defensive work or fort'. Southwark can lay claim to the longest history of any part of London, since it was here that the Romans chose to build the first bridge across the Thames following the invasion of AD 43 (*see* LONDON BRIDGE). The settlement was an integral part of Roman LONDINIUM, with public, industrial and domestic buildings on islands and reclaimed marshland. Its fortunes were always tied to those of the City on the opposite bank as it benefited from the flow of trade and transport across the river and also acted as a place of refuge and retreat. There were travellers' needs to be met, and Southwark became famous for its inns: notably the TABARD, where Chaucer's pilgrims met, the White Hart and the GEORGE INN. It had a reputation for entertainment: Southwark (and in particular BANKSIDE) was the place to go for theatres, brothels, bear-baiting, dog-fighting, etc. Not surprisingly, it also had several prisons, including the CLINK and the MARSHALSEA. It possessed two mints, and between the early 15th century and 1763 the annual Southwark Fair

was held here. In 1550 most of Southwark was bought from the king by the City of London. It was officially constituted as a City ward (named 'Bridge Ward Without'), and came to be known as 'Southwark borough' (connoting a suburb, outside the City). Over four centuries later, the heart of Southwark is still 'the BOROUGH'. Southwark became an independent borough in 1899.

Southwark, London Borough of An INNER LONDON borough formed in 1965 from the metropolitan boroughs of BERMONDSEY, CAMBERWELL and Southwark. The borough stretches 5 miles (8 km) to the south in a roughly triangular shape to the site of the CRYSTAL PALACE and has some of the most diverse townscapes anywhere in London. These range from the very urban north with its mixture of new and old, residential and industrial, commercial and recreational through areas of largely intact 19th-century suburban development to its leafy spacious south. Southwark's coat of arms is almost a pictogram of the borough's history, with allusions to *The Canterbury Tales*, SHAKESPEARE's *Hamlet*, Edward ALLEYN and the SURREY DOCKS. The civic motto is 'united to serve'.

Southwark Bridge The first Southwark Bridge was privately built in 1815, a quarter of a mile (0.4 km) west of LONDON BRIDGE. It was subsequently bought by the CORPORATION OF LONDON using rent money from the tenants of London Bridge. The present bridge, designed by the Scottish engineer John Rennie, was completed in 1921.

Southwark Bridge Road The southern approach road to Southwark Bridge, constructed in the early 1820s. The road's alignment is far from straight because the neighbourhood was already heavily developed by the time it was built and extensive demolition would have proved costly and time consuming for the promoters. The Evelina children's hospital (now situated on the ST THOMAS' HOSPITAL campus) was founded on Southwark Bridge Road in 1869.

Southwark Cathedral A church was built on the site of the present-day Southwark Cathedral in around 607 and dedicated to ST MARY OVERY. It came under the jurisdiction of the bishops of Winchester, who built their palace on a site to the west. The church was rebuilt in the 12th century and again in 1207 following a fire. Its resident Augustinian friary was dissolved in 1540 and it was rededicated to St Saviour, the nave being rebuilt in the late Victorian era after a period of decline and disrepair. The diocese of Southwark, covering SOUTH LONDON and part of SURREY, was created in 1905 (its territory was formerly part of Rochester diocese) and St Saviour's was designated its cathedral. *See also* SOUTH BANK RELIGION.

Famous members of the congregation include John Harvard (1607–38), who was born in Southwark and after whom Harvard University is named. The cathedral contains monuments to the medieval poet John Gower and to William SHAKESPEARE, whose youngest brother Edmund is buried here.

Southwark Cross *See the* BRIDGE MARK.

Southwark delftware A type of tin-glazed earthenware made in Southwark during the 17th and 18th centuries.

Southwark Usurer or **Miser** Jemmy Taylor (*c.*1723–93), a Leicestershire-born weaver who made a fortune from money-lending and stock-broking, the latter primarily by spreading false rumours. He lived in apparent penury and was a friend of Daniel Dancer (*see* MISERS).

> He sent for the parish officers, the parson, and the curate [when on his deathbed], and, entreating their prayers, he paid them down twelve hundred pounds; but it is said that he would not conclude his bequest until they consented to return him a twelvemonths' interest, by way of discount for prompt payment!

> F.S. MERRYWEATHER: *Lives and Anecdotes of Misers* (1850)

Spaced A Channel 4 sitcom written by and starring Simon Pegg (b.1970) and Jessica Stevenson (now Jessica Hynes, b.1972). It was set at 23 Meteor Street (actually Carleton Road), TUFNELL PARK. *Spaced* ran for two series in 1999 and 2001 and its acutely observed portrayal of twenty-something flat-sharing life made it a cult hit.

Spa Fields An open space – long since covered over – in CLERKENWELL, named after a chalybeate spring discovered in the fields in the 17th century, and developed later for medicinal purposes. Spafield Street is a surviving reminder.

Spa Fields riots An insurrection that developed out of a mass meeting organized at Spa Fields on 2 December 1816 to call for universal suffrage and reform of Parliament. Radical agitators led the crowd on the CITY of London, where they were confronted by the lord mayor at the head of a force of police. The ensuing disorder was eventually quelled by troops.

sparrow While ROCK PIGEONS have long been more visibly prevalent, the sparrow remains the definitive London bird, though its brazen scavenging formerly led some to regard it with distaste:

> ... what would she say of London sparrows! of the true cockney-breed, who are seen in their monstrous perfection (at the West End, and the suburbs, they are comparatively gentlemanly birds) in Holborn and Fleet Street, in the avenues of Fetter Lane and Shoe Lane, and the 'bosky dells' between Saffron Hill and Mutton Hill? Your true cockney-sparrow is the very chimney-sweeper and blackguard of birds – there is nothing like him on earth, or in air, in any other part of the world.

> *The Metropolitan* (December 1837)

From the 17th century to call a woman a 'sparrow' was to imply lustfulness, from the belief that the birds were especially highly sexed. However, the later term 'cockney sparrow' (or 'sparrer', with phonetic spelling) merely connoted a native Londoner of either sex, especially a 'chirpy' or diminutive one with a strong accent. Various notables have been nicknamed the Cockney Sparrow, including the politician Sir Kingsley Wood (1881–1943) and the actress Barbara Windsor (b.1937).

Speakers' Corner A small area near MARBLE ARCH in the north-east corner of HYDE PARK, where a motley band of speakers holds forth every Sunday. The name is relatively recent but the practice dates from 1855, when a large crowd gathered here to protest against Lord Robert Grosvenor's Sunday Trading Bill. There was no right of assembly then, but it was granted in 1872 and anyone may now indulge in soapbox oratory on any subject they choose, so long as it is not obscene or blasphemous, or does not constitute an incitement to a breach of the peace. Nowadays most of the speakers are religious extremists, with a few enjoyable exceptions.

> It [Speakers' Corner] is a communication system organized in a specific way. The physical layer of this communication system (the park) is a commons; the logical layer (the language used) is also a commons. And the content layer (what these nuts say) is their own creation. It

too is unowned. All three layers in this context are free; no one can exercise control over the kinds of communications that might happen here.

LAWRENCE LESSIG: 'The Architecture of Innovation', lecture published in *Duke Law Journal*, Volume 51 (2002)

Spencean philanthropists Followers of Thomas Spence (1750–1814), who ran a bookshop called the Hive of Liberty, in Little Turnstile, HOLBORN. They formed the Society of Spencean Philanthropists in 1812 and thought that their plan heralded the millennium. Spence denounced the landed aristocracy and was constantly in trouble for his views and pamphlets. It was the Spenceans who advocated seizing power by force. They addressed the meeting that preceded the SPA FIELDS RIOTS and they were prominent in the CATO STREET CONSPIRACY of 1820.

Spencer House An aristocratic townhouse situated at 27 St James's Place, overlooking GREEN PARK. It was built in 1756–66 for John, 1st Earl Spencer. The exterior was designed by the Palladian architect John Vardy, while the neoclassical interior was mostly the work of ATHENIAN STUART. Other eminent architects later remodelled parts of Spencer House, notably Henry Holland in the mid-1780s and Philip Hardwick in the 1840s. The Spencer family lived at the house until 1895, and again from 1910 to 1927. Subsequent tenants have included the Ladies' Army and Navy Club, the auctioneers Christie's, the Economist Intelligence Unit and the present leaseholders, RIT Capital Partners. Parts of the house are open to the public at limited times.

Spike An engaging COCKNEY vampire, played by James Marsters (b.1962), who regularly appeared in the cult US television series *Buffy the Vampire Slayer* between 1997 and 2003, and in the spin-off series *Angel* (1999–2004). Said to have been born in London sometime in the 19th century, he seems later to have modelled his appearance on that of the STANMORE-born rock star Billy Idol, an erstwhile member of the BROMLEY CONTINGENT, although it was suggested in one episode of *Buffy* that Idol had borrowed his look from Spike.

spike Slang for the workhouse, so that 'to go on the spike' was to become a workhouse inmate.

The origin of the term remains unclear; it may have derived from the implement used by residents to break rocks to earn their keep or from a device to which drunks were strapped to hold them upright. London's best-known spike was in Gordon Road, PECKHAM, and was known as 'HEADQUARTERS'.

spike hotel In the early to mid-19th century a generic nickname for a prison, from the spiked railings that surrounded it. The term was especially applied to the KING'S BENCH (*see also* SPIKE PARK) and FLEET prisons.

Spike Island The former nickname of common land at North Heath, in ERITH, from the workhouse built there in 1806, with the permission of the lord of the manor, William Wheatley.

Spike Park or **the Spikes** 19th-century nicknames for the KING'S BENCH PRISON (or the Queen's Bench Prison, as it became after 1838).

Spiny Norman *See* SEMOLINA PILCHARD.

spital or **spittle** Contractions of 'hospital'. Walter and Rose Brown (or Brune) founded the hospital and priory known as St Mary Spital in 1197 and it gave its name to the district of SPITALFIELDS.

Spitalfields A historically deprived, multicultural district situated between SHOREDITCH and ALDGATE. The hospital of St Mary Spital was closed in 1538 and its buildings were adapted as homes and workshops in the first of a series of changes of use that came to characterize the district. Suburban expansion began after the GREAT FIRE OF LONDON and from the late 17th century French Huguenot refugees settled here in their thousands, greatly expanding the area's existing silk-weaving industry. By the early 19th century that industry was declining in the face of cheap foreign imports and the increasingly anglicized Huguenots dispersed around London. They were replaced by poor Jews from Amsterdam, whose specialist trade was the manufacture of cigars and cigarettes. After 1845 Spitalfields' cheap accommodation attracted Irish immigrants fleeing their country's potato famine, many of whom helped to build London's docks. Jewish refugees from the pogroms in Russia formed the next wave of newcomers after the 1880s, bringing skills in tailoring and cabinet-making, and strengthening the area's role as a trading district. By the mid-20th century Spitalfields' Jews were moving away to suburbs in north and east London. A Bengali community established itself in the 1960s – although Muslims from the Sylhet district of Assam had been settling here since the late 19th century. In recent years surviving weavers' houses have been renovated and warehouses have been converted to apartment blocks with galleries and cafés at street level, but behind these conspicuous developments this is still a district of run-down tenements, where overcrowding is high and incomes are low.

Dominating the entire area is the austere form of Nicholas Hawksmoor's Christ Church, Spitalfields, built between 1714 and 1729. It is a brooding presence in Peter Ackroyd's novel *Hawksmoor* (1985).

Spitalfields breakfast Nineteenth-century slang for no breakfast at all – i.e. going hungry. The contemporary lexicographer J.C. Hotten defined it laconically as 'a tight necktie and a short pipe'. The reference is, of course, to the area's poverty and deprivation.

Spitalfields Festival A music festival held annually in June. From a single event held at Christ Church in 1976 it has grown to become an established item on the classical music calendar. A spin-off organization, Spitalfields Music, encourages emerging talent in the EAST END.

Spitalfields Market A market situated on the west side of Commercial Street, established in the 1680s. New buildings for the fruit, vegetable and flower market were erected in 1893 and extended in 1928. Spitalfields wholesale market moved to a purpose-built site in LEYTON in 1991 and its buildings have since become home to the only retail market in London that can even vaguely rival CAMDEN TOWN for its youth appeal. However, the value of the site leaves its future in almost continuous doubt.

Spital Sermons Sermons originally preached on Good Friday and on the following Monday, Tuesday and Wednesday from the Pulpit Cross (or Spital Cross), Spitalfields, which were attended by the LORD MAYOR OF LONDON and ALDERMEN and the boys of Christ's Hospital (*see the* BLUECOAT SCHOOL). The pulpit was destroyed in the Civil War (1642–51) and at the Restoration the Spital Sermons were revived at St Bride's, FLEET STREET. From 1797 they were delivered at Christ Church, NEWGATE STREET, and reduced to two. This church was destroyed by incendiary bombs in 1941. The one Spital Sermon is now

given in the CORPORATION OF LONDON's church of St Lawrence Jewry.

spring

Spring Gardens or **The Spring Garden** From the 16th century a place of public resort near CHARING CROSS. The gardens took their name from a device that shot a jet of water into the air when an unwary visitor stepped on a concealed mechanism, a popular source of Elizabethan amusement. Various forms of entertainment were laid on and the gardens were periodically suppressed and then permitted to reopen before they were built over at the end of the 17th century. Part of the site was subsequently occupied by LOCKIT'S (OR LOCKET'S) ORDINARY and later by the short street called Spring Gardens.

> For Locket's stands where gardens once did spring.
>
> WILLIAM KING: *The Art of Cookery* (1709)

Other pleasure resorts afterwards appropriated the name 'Spring Gardens', notably VAUXHALL GARDENS.

Spring Grove A well-preserved, and in parts grand, suburb situated south-east of OSTERLEY, and known until the late 19th century as Smallbury Green. The settlement grew up on common land that once lay between ISLEWORTH and HESTON and takes its modern name from a house built during the Civil War for Sir John Offley. Within the grounds was a spring, providing water that was piped to the house. Another mansion replaced the original Spring Grove just over a century later. Sir Joseph Banks, the botanist and pioneering developer of KEW GARDENS, lived at this house for 40 years and laid out the gardens with a lake and springs and a magnificent variety of plants. He died here in 1820. The London and South Western Railway branch line arrived in 1849, with a station at Isleworth, originally called Spring Grove. In 1886 Spring Grove House was sold to Andrew Pears, great-grandson of the creator of the famous translucent soap. Pears rebuilt Banks's house as the mansion that is now home to West Thames College.

Spring-Heeled Jack An almost certainly imaginary character who was sighted in various locations throughout Victorian England. In contrast with the axe murderers of modern urban myths, Jack behaved primarily as a prankster, scaring travellers by appearing out of nowhere and then bounding away in great leaps, often sideways. He was also said to possess devilish physical characteristics and to wear skin-tight apparel. Most of the early sightings were in the London area, including an appearance on CLAPHAM COMMON in October 1837. As stories of his deeds spread, eye-witness reports increased, with embellishments such as the molestation of terrified servant girls, sometimes with added fire-breathing. Spring-Heeled Jack was spotted in an arc of London suburbs in 1838, from EALING in the west, through all the major districts of inner south London, to BOW and LIMEHOUSE in the east. After a few months of mass hysteria London sightings abated but similar stories were reported from the provinces and in November 1845 he was held responsible for the death of a young prostitute in the FOLLY DITCH, in BERMONDSEY. He made a minor comeback in the 1870s, mostly keeping well away from London, except for an excursion into Streatham Lane (now Road) on Figge's Marsh, where a local posse was got up in a vain attempt to catch him.

Spring in Park Lane A romantic comedy film (1948) directed by Herbert Wilcox and starring Michael Wilding and Anna Neagle.

Tom Spring One of the great pugilists of the English prize ring, Spring (1795–1851) claimed the title of English champion on the retirement of Tom Cribb (1781–1848). His real name was Winter, and on retiring (1828) he became landlord of the Castle Tavern, HOLBORN.

Shall I name thee last? ay, why not? I believe that thou art the last of all that strong family still above the sod, where mayest thou long continue – true piece of English stuff, Tom of Bedford – sharp as winter, kind as spring. Hail to thee, Tom of Bedford, or by whatever name it may please thee to be called, Spring or Winter … 'Tis a treat to see thee, Tom of Bedford, in thy 'public' in Holborn way, whither thou hast retired with thy well-earned bays.

GEORGE BORROW: *Lavengro* (1851)

Spurs The primary nickname of TOTTENHAM HOTSPUR FC.

square

Square, the Contemporary tabloid shorthand for ALBERT SQUARE or for the world of EASTENDERS in general.

Square Mile An epithet applied to the CITY of London, on account of its area (rather than

any regularity in its shape), which as a result of boundary changes has progressively increased from almost exactly a square mile to 1.12 square miles (2.9 sq km) today. The measurement has long been employed to emphasize the compactness of the district into which so much has been crammed:

The Corporation of the City of London represents the greatest and most important community in the world. You talk of your square mile. It may be a square mile, but what a square mile it is!

EDWARD CLARKE: speech to the House of Commons (23 March 1899)

Increasingly, the term was used as a synonym for the City as a place (at first often as 'the one square mile') and by the 1930s it was regularly being spelt with initial capitals:

The City Corporation has the Lord Mayor and the ceremonial traditions, the annual banquet and the trappings of tinsel and gold – to say nothing of the enormous wealth of the Square Mile.

WILLIAM A. ROBSON: *The Development of Local Government* (1932)

In 1953 Alec Guinness narrated a documentary film 'essay' on the lord mayoralty of London and the City Corporation entitled *The Square Mile*. With the long-term decline in its artisan trades, traditional merchants and residential population, the City became ever more single-mindedly devoted to the world of finance, and the term 'the Square Mile' (synonymously with 'the City') came to signify this world:

Thus the 'Square Mile of Finance' is invited to continue in its role of equipping the East to undercut the West (and Britain in particular) as it did in the case of Japan between the wars.

ROBERT ROW, in *The European*, 'The Industrial Attack on Britain' (July 1957)

square mile of piety See STAMFORD HILL.

squire

Squire of Alsatia, The A very popular comic play (1688) by Thomas Shadwell (c.1641–92). Shadwell drew heavily on Terence's *Adelphoe* (*The Brothers*, 160 BC), tranposing the action to the precincts of the former WHITEFRIARS Monastery, where the lowest of London's low life try to strip a gullible country gentleman of his inheritance. The term 'a squire of ALSATIA' consequently came to mean a rich fool, one who could easily be persuaded to pay the whole bill at the end of a night's drinking.

Squire of the Bears The supervisor of the royal bears, bulls and mastiffs in Jacobean London. The holder of the office had the very profitable power to licence various cruel sports, such as dog fights and the whipping of blind bears. The actor-manager Edward ALLEYN is said to have made a considerable sum of money during his time as squire.

Stab in the Back The nickname of the White Hart, a pub that stood on New FETTER LANE. 'The Stab', as it was often known, was said by some to have gained its sobriquet from one or more acts of treachery at the Mirror Group, which provided a large proportion of the pub's clientele; however, the nickname could have been a clever pun, as 'stab' was printers' shorthand for 'establishment' and this establishment was situated at the back of the Mirror Building. Many stories are told of newsmen's drunken excesses at the pub, especially in its heyday of the 1960s and 70s, and bar staff allegedly charged a pound to deny the presence of a journalist to a caller from the Mirror newsdesk and double that sum to tell the same lie to wives. After the demise of the FLEET STREET newspaper industry and the demolition of the Mirror Building the pub closed and was replaced by a pizza restaurant.

Stamford

Stamford Bridge Now the home of CHELSEA FC, Stamford Bridge stadium opened in 1877. It is named after a 15th-century crossing (a sandy ford) at Counters Creek, which formed the boundary between FULHAM and CHELSEA. In its early years the stadium was used primarily by the London Athletic Club and also hosted grey-hound racing and baseball. In 1904 the ground was bought by the building contractor Gus Mears, who had already acquired a neighbouring market garden. Resisting a tempting offer for the site from the Great Western Railway, Mears and his brother set out to create London's premier footballing venue, commissioning the east stand from the great stadium builder Archibald Leitch. The remainder was terraced with spoil from construction work on the LONDON UNDERGROUND. Chelsea FC began playing at Stamford Bridge on the club's inception in 1905 and has remained here ever since. The erection of a tin roof over the south terrace in 1930 gave rise to the nickname

'the SHED' and this end of the ground became the home of the team's most zealous supporters. From 1994 to 2001 the stadium was completely redeveloped, with associated leisure and hotel facilities.

Stamford Brook A compact locality squeezed between HAMMERSMITH and CHISWICK and centred on Stamford Brook Common (also known as the Green). It is named after a stream that ran through the area, which in turn took its name from a 'stony ford' at the GREAT WEST ROAD. A hamlet of 'seven cottages or tenements' was recorded in 1699, amidst strips of arable farmland and pasture. A century later, when there were 168 dwellings at nearby TURNHAM GREEN, Stamford Brook had only four houses. One of these was The Brook, which was bought in 1878 by Thomas Hussey, a builder who had leased meadows at Stamford Brook for brickmaking. Hussey supplied tens of millions of bricks for Jonathan Carr's development at neighbouring BEDFORD PARK and soon began to put up his own houses on what became Stamford Brook Avenue. In 1902 he leased The Brook to the artist Lucien Pissarro (1863–1944) and his wife Esther (1870–1951), who spent the rest of their days here. The early years of the 20th century saw the last of Stamford Brook's market gardens and orchards disappear as the village became a suburb.

Stamford Hill Located north of STOKE NEW-INGTON, Stamford Hill is one of London's most distinctive quarters, with a highly independent community of about 15,000 Hasidic Jews. In the 13th century this was Sanford, where a sandy ford crossed a tributary of the River LEA. In the late 18th and early 19th centuries its elevated situation attracted wealthy merchants, notably Moses Vita Montefiore, an Italian Jew who died here in 1789. From the late 19th century, and particularly after the 1920s, upwardly mobile Jews moved here from the EAST END, as they did to DALSTON and Stoke Newington. Several synagogues were relocated or founded here and some larger old houses were converted for use as Jewish schools or other institutions. In the mid-20th century Hasidic Jewish immigrants from eastern Europe (most fleeing Nazi persecution or its aftermath) created a 'square mile of piety' at Stamford Hill. The Hasidim have their own schools, conventicles and kosher food shops. Outside Israel, only New York has a larger community of Hasidic Jews and they are the sole British Jewish group still to speak Yiddish. Stamford Hill also has residents of black African, black Caribbean, Turkish and Kurdish descent.

Because of Stamford Hill's special character, it has featured in several television documentaries and dramas. Programmes have included a Channel 4 documentary, VOLVO CITY (1991), and the BBC play *Wall of Silence* (1993). The latter caused controversy with its portrayal of a psychopathic Hasidic murderer, played by Warren Mitchell. Stamford Hill was the home of Marcus, the young prodigy in Bernice Rubens's novel *Madame Sousatzka* (1962).

Stamford Hill cowboy A male Hasidic resident of Stamford Hill or its environs.

> From the wide-brimmed hat that is conventionally worn and the consequent image created by a group with the sun behind them.
>
> TOM DALZELL and TERRY VICTOR (editors): *The Concise New Partridge Dictionary of Slang and Unconventional English* (2008)

stammer and stutter 'Butter' in COCKNEY RHYMING SLANG, but seldom heard. The same applies to 'stutter and stammer' for 'hammer'.

stand

stand on the right A rule of etiquette that applies on escalators within the LONDON UNDERGROUND network, allowing those who wish to walk to pass on the left. With its formative role in the development of underground railways, London was the first city to adopt the convention, which has since been introduced on many other metro systems around the world. There are signs on most escalators stating the rule but these are not always highly visible and breaches of observance can sometimes be a cause of frustration.

> It was a distinguished French visitor to England, the Baron de Montesquieu, who was moved to note about 250 years ago ... 'The English are even ruder than the French.' It would help, of course, if foreigners would learn to stand on the right side of the escalator.
>
> DAVID ATKINSON, addressing the Council of Europe (29 September 1990)

(it) stands to reason, dunnit? A COCKNEY expression emphasizing the logical force of some statement. 'Dunnit' is a corruption of 'doesn't it'.

> 'Well, it stands to reason, dunnit, I mean,' said a man at the factory where 316 Brick Lane had

once stood. 'You couldn't call it like Bethnal Green Furniture, now could you? I mean, who'd buy it?'
>
> JOHN BOWEN: *The Birdcage* (1962)

Stane Street A Roman road that led southwestwards from LONDON BRIDGE through the North Downs and on to Chichester, Sussex. The name derives from Old English *stan*, 'stone', signifying a paved road. The northernmost part of its course is represented today by BOROUGH High Street.

Stanmore An expansive suburb running into open countryside east of HARROW WEALD. The name was first recorded in Domesday Book as Stanmere, a stony pool. It was later known as Great Stanmore, to distinguish it from the separate settlement of LITTLE STANMORE, which lay to the south-east. Over the course of the 18th century several very grand houses were either newly built or greatly enlarged from existing properties, including STANMORE PARK and BENTLEY PRIORY. Modern suburban development began after the construction of the Metropolitan Railway (later the BAKERLOO and now the JUBILEE LINE) terminus in 1932.

Stanmore Common A 120-acre (49-hectare) common situated just inside the GREATER LONDON boundary, north of Stanmore. It has more rare plant species than any other open space in London except KESTON COMMON and HAMPSTEAD HEATH, and some scarce moths, flies and beetles.

Stanmore Park An RAF station established in 1938 on the site of an early 18th-century mansion that was demolished in the process. The station closed in 1997 and has been replaced by housing.

Staple Inn The most intact survivor of the INNS OF CHANCERY, situated immediately south of CHANCERY LANE underground station. First recorded in the 13th century as 'le Stapled Halle', the name probably signified a covered hall built with pillars (from Old English *stapel*, 'column' or 'tree trunk'). Originally a wool market, it became *c*.1415 the home of the Society of Staple Inn, an association of lawyers and legal students. In 1580 the society built a new and magnificent hall, followed in 1586 by buildings facing High Holborn. The latter remain almost unaltered but the hall was hit by a flying bomb in 1944. It was afterwards rebuilt to the original plan, retaining materials that had been salvaged from the wreckage or, like the stained-glass windows, had been earlier placed in storage. Since 1887 Staple Inn has been the headquarters of the Institute of Actuaries.

Staples Corner A road intersection located between CRICKLEWOOD and West HENDON, formed when the NORTH CIRCULAR ROAD cut across the EDGWARE ROAD in the mid-1920s. The junction is named after the Staples mattress factory, which was located on the south-west corner and was the first of more than 50 factories built here between the wars, erasing the hamlet of Oxgate. In the early 1970s the junction's character was effaced by the building of the Edgware Road flyover and the termination of the M1 motorway just to the east. The former industries of Staples Corner have been replaced by car dealers, a multiplex cinema and retail warehouses, including a Staples stationery superstore.

star

Star and Garter The Star and Garter inn was built at the top of RICHMOND HILL in 1738, and named after the royal insignia of the Order of the Garter. The establishment was progressively enlarged by a series of ambitious owners, at least one of whom went bankrupt in the process, and largely rebuilt in 1864 as a chateau-like hotel. In its early days it played host to exiled crowned heads of Europe but two serious fires and a gradual decline in business prompted its sale in 1915 to the Auctioneers and Estate Agents' Institute for presentation to Queen Mary, as patron of the British Red Cross Society. The old buildings were demolished and replaced by the Royal Star and Garter Home for Disabled Sailors, Soldiers and Airmen, which opened in 1924. The charity is now in the process of relocating the residents to purpose-built care homes elsewhere and the Star and Garter is likely to be converted to apartments or a hotel.

Star Chamber A court of medieval origin, composed of the King's Council, reinforced by judges, which developed criminal jurisdiction. It was so named from its meeting place, the Star Chamber in the PALACE OF WESTMINSTER, the ceiling or roof of which was decorated with stars. The reputation it acquired for harshness (which survives to this day in the metaphorical application of its name to a severe and capri-

cious tribunal) was largely unjustified, and it was frequently attacked by the Common Lawyers who resented its jurisdiction. It was abolished by the Long Parliament in 1641.

Star, News and Standard The familiar London newsvendors' cry of the mid-20th century, followed (at least in the movies) by 'read all abaht it' and then some momentous or scandalous headline of the day. *The Star* merged with the *Evening News* in 1960, and the EVENING STANDARD absorbed the *News* in 1980.

> Above all, coarse, chesty tone – the newspaper boy's 'Star, News and Standard' voice – must be looked out for and must be avoided at all costs.
>
> HAROLD SMETHURST: *Opera Production for Amateurs* (1951)

Star of Piccadilly *See* OLD Q.

Starvation Farm or **Farmyard** The nickname of a small farm that stood on Colebrooke Row, ISLINGTON. It belonged to Baron Aguilar (1740–1802), a notorious MISER. Despite having acquired a fortune via two marriages to heiresses, Aguilar deserted his second wife, shut up his properties in BETHNAL GREEN, TWICKENHAM and SYDENHAM and set himself up as a smallholder. He kept a variety of underfed livestock in atrocious conditions, to the outrage of nearby residents, who regularly jeered him and threw things at him. Nevertheless he is said to have made 'manifold and secret' donations to the poor.

steel

Steel, the *See* BASTILLE.

Steelyard The London depot of the Hanseatic League from 1320 to 1597, occupying premises between Upper Thames Street and the THAMES. The buildings were ultimately sold in 1853 and demolished ten years later to make way for CANNON STREET STATION. The name is a mistranslation of German *Stalhof*, 'a sample yard or hall'.

Steinbock ('ibex') The codename for the German bombing campaign in January–May 1944 against London and various British ports, also known as the 'baby BLITZ'.

Stepney Once the unofficial capital of the EAST END, Stepney is now reduced in extent and significance to a collection of terraced streets and blocks of flats wedged between the COMMERCIAL

ROAD and the MILE END Road. The name is a corruption of Stibenhede – Stibba's haven. It was first recorded in the 11th century, when the principal landowner was the bishop of London. By the 16th century the episcopal manor of Stepney covered almost all of what became known as the East End. Following the growth of the Tudor navy and the mercantile marine, Stepney became a popular place of residence for seamen and retired naval officers. From the late 17th century, and especially in the early 18th, speculative developers built small groups of houses here, which included some short rows of terraced houses, a ground-breaking innovation at that time. Over the course of the 19th century Stepney's character was transformed as London expanded to absorb it. After the Second World War old neighbourhoods were erased as the borough and county councils erected some of the East End's most colourless and ungainly estates. From the 1980s immigrants from the New Commonwealth became the dominant ethnic groups, especially those from the Sylhet district of Bangladesh. Council signage in Stepney is generally written in both English and Bengali script.

The actor Terence Stamp (b.1939) and the playwright Arnold Wesker (b.1932) were both born in Stepney.

Stepney Green A station, road and park located in north-central Stepney. Although Stepney is one of east London's most ancient settlements, Stepney Green is a 19th-century invention. Both the road and its neighbouring common land were formerly called MILE END Green. There are earlier mentions of a green at Stepney but these do not necessarily identify the present locality. The green was flanked by fine houses in the 17th and 18th centuries and some of these survive today. Tenement blocks were built from the late 19th century, of which the most distinctive was the FOUR PER CENT INDUSTRIAL DWELLINGS COMPANY's Stepney Green Court. Like the rest of Stepney, the vicinity of the green was heavily redeveloped with municipal housing from the 1930s to the 1970s.

In 1905 the ringleader of the mutiny aboard the Russian battleship *Potemkin*, torpedo quartermaster Afanasy Matushenko, sought refuge at an anarchist and socialist meeting place in Dunstan House on Stepney Green. Matushenko soon returned to Russia, where he was caught and hanged in 1907.

born in Stepney *See under* BORN.
Hamlet of Stepney Green, The *See under* HAMLET.

stepney or **stepony** A now-forgotten sweet beverage made of lemon and raisins boiled in spring water. Some lexicographers believe it was associated with the district of STEPNEY but other (perhaps more credible) explanations abound, and the spelling 'stepney' may have been folk etymology.

> Among other events are the following ... Since Old Noll's lady sold stepony (a cooling drink for hot weather): 2 years. Since Hugh Peter's wife caught him in bed with a Dutch woman: 5 years.
> WILLIAM GODWIN: *Lives of Edward and John Philips* (1815)

A stepney was also a type of spare wheel for early motor cars. The name derived from Stepney Street, Llanelli, where the wheels were first made. However, that street took its name from a family of landowners who originated from London's Stepney.

Steptoe and Son A classic BBC television sitcom (1962–5; 1970–4), centring on the relationship between a father and son in the rag-and-bone trade, living at 24 Oil Drum Lane, SHEPHERD'S BUSH. The wilful, manipulative and eccentric old father, Albert Steptoe, played by Wilfrid Brambell (1912–85), and the perpetually exasperated son, Harold, struggling for independence, played by Harry H. Corbett (1925–82), invariably end up by thwarting each other's dearest aspirations. The genius of the series lay in its finely balanced blend of humour and pathos.

stew

stewed prune 'Tune' in 19th-century COCKNEY RHYMING SLANG.

> Not in the sense 'that is a pretty stewed prune', but, to the man with the mouth-organ, 'give us a stewed prune.' The term is now dead because it is usual to say 'turn on the wireless'.
> JULIAN FRANKLYN: *A Dictionary of Rhyming Slang* (1960)

stews An old name for brothels or a prostitutes' quarter, probably derived from the steaming hot baths provided at such places. In late medieval London the term was especially applied to the BANKSIDE area of SOUTHWARK, where the brothels were closed by royal proclamation in 1546.

stick it, Jerry! A British war cry of 1914–18. It

originated in the antics of Nobbler and Jerry, characters in the MUSIC HALL routine 'The BLOOMSBURY BURGLARS'. Jerry would hurl missiles at a policeman while Nobbler urged him on by shouting the catchphrase.

Stiff Records A pioneering independent record label founded in WESTBOURNE PARK in 1976. In October that year Stiff released what is generally accepted as having been the UK's first PUNK ROCK single, the Damned's 'New Rose', and it went on to launch the careers of Ian Dury, Madness and Elvis Costello. Noted for its guerrilla marketing techniques and wacky slogans, the company later merged with Island Records.

stock

stockbroker belt A term for the area outside a city, and especially London, as the stereotypical abode of stockbrokers and other wealthy people.

> Henk Huffener's house, off the Guildford–Dorking road, is not merely in the Surrey stockbroker belt – it is at its very buckle.
>
> *The Times* (1 March 1999)

Stock Exchange The market in which stocks and shares are bought and sold. Such markets had long existed in London (and elsewhere) and in the 18th century speculators and dealers met at JONATHAN'S and various other premises. In 1773 they formed an association, meeting in Sweeting's Alley in what came to be known as the Stock Exchange COFFEE HOUSE or tavern. In 1801 it was decided that a more suitable building was needed, and the Stock Exchange in CAPEL COURT was opened in 1802, being considerably enlarged in 1853–4 and subsequently. The exchange received its own coat of arms in 1923, with the motto *dictum meum pactum*, 'my word is my bond'. In 1972 the Stock Exchange relocated to a purpose-built tower block at 125 Old Broad Street, on the corner of THROGMORTON STREET. Historically, the activities of the market had been focused on a single trading floor but that aspect of the institution withered away following the deregulation project known as the BIG BANG. In 1991 the exchange became a private limited company named the London Stock Exchange. The company went public in 2000, since when it has faced, and so far resisted, periodic takeover approaches and bids from foreign exchanges, and has itself taken over the Borsa Italiana. In

2004 the Stock Exchange moved to its present home, at 10 PATERNOSTER SQUARE.

Stocks Market A food market that formerly operated at the western end of LOMBARD STREET. The market was established *c*.1282 and perhaps named after a fixed pair of stocks (a pillory) that had earlier stood here. After the GREAT FIRE OF LONDON the Stocks Market was rebuilt in enlarged form, covering the neighbouring site of St Mary Woolchurch Haw, a church that was lost in the fire and never rebuilt. In 1736 the CITY authorities decided to build the MANSION HOUSE here and the market was demolished the following year and relocated to what is now Farringdon Street, where it was called the Fleet Market.

It has been claimed that the flowers known as stocks (genus *Matthiola*) are so called because they were first sold at the Stocks Market.

Brompton stock *See under* BROMPTON.

Stockwell An ethnically and socially mixed neighbourhood, often regarded as the northernmost part of BRIXTON. The name, which referred to a wellspring by a tree trunk or stump, was first recorded in 1197. The medieval manor house was demolished around 1755 and a new mansion was built which survived for less than a century – a period in which Stockwell changed from a collection of nurseries with the usual scattering of grand houses into a nascent 'villa land'. William Cox of KENNINGTON began to develop Stockwell Park as a high-class estate after 1838, whereupon several other builders pitched in with variations on his theme. Many of the villas were terraced or otherwise tightly packed, which has helped ensure their survival to the present day. Stockwell became the southern terminus of London's first deep TUBE line in 1890 but it was not until after the Second World War that the landscape was again transformed, this time by the construction of several large municipal estates. A third of Stockwell's residents are black or black British and nearly 15 per cent are non-British white, including a strong Portuguese community.

Stockwell ghost A supposed ghost that created a great sensation in Stockwell in 1772. The author of the strange noises turned out to be Anne Robinson, a maidservant.

Stockwell shooting The fatal police action taken against Jean Charles de Menezes, a Brazilian electrician, at Stockwell station on 22 July 2005. He had been wrongly identified as a suspect in the previous day's failed attempts to set off bombs on three TUBE trains and a bus, which paralleled the London bombings of 7/7 (*see under* SEVEN). Police followed Menezes from his home in TULSE HILL and, when he boarded a train at Stockwell, shot him seven times at close range without warning. In December 2008 an inquest jury returned an open verdict, after the coroner had ruled out unlawful killing as an option.

Stockwell Strangler The nickname of Kenneth Erskine (b.1962), who in 1986 murdered seven elderly people, most of whom lived in or near Stockwell. He was convicted in 1988 and sentenced to life imprisonment, with a recommendation that he serve at least 40 years.

Stoke

Stoke Newington A traditionally nonconformist community, in every sense, situated north-west of HACKNEY. The medieval village grew up around the twin nuclei of Newington Green and the junction of Church Street with what is now Stoke Newington High Street. Outsiders of all kinds were recorded here from the 15th century. In 1709 the parish built four houses to accommodate Protestant refugees from the Rhine Palatinate. Among the wealthy Quakers living in the townhouses on Church Street was John Wilmer, who in 1764 was buried in a vault in his garden with a bell attached to his wrist in case he was not dead. The beautiful ABNEY PARK Cemetery was laid out in 1840 on unconsecrated ground, which made it popular with Nonconformists. Quaker resident Joseph Beck helped establish CLISSOLD PARK in 1889. From around that time poor Jewish immigrants from Russia, Poland and Germany began arriving in the south of Stoke Newington. In the 1930s wealthier Jews came to the northern part of the borough and they were subsequently supplemented by Hasidic Jews from eastern Europe, especially in the STAMFORD HILL area. From the 1960s West Indians, Greek Cypriots and Turks further enhanced the diversity of the community. During the 1980s Stoke Newington became something of a 'new ISLINGTON', a working-class district increasingly colonized by the young middle classes, many of them politically radical and working in arts-related professions. A host of shops and wine bars sprang up to serve these 'Stokeys',

whose lifestyle was satirized by comedians such as Alexei Sayle. *See also* COKEY STOKEY.

The writer and religious Nonconformist Daniel Defoe married a girl from Newington Green in 1684 and tried to raise civet cats here to make perfume. The philosopher John Stuart Mill and the author (and Quaker) Anna Sewell lived here in the 1810s and 1820s respectively, when they were both young children. Other residents have included the Nonconformist hymn-writer Isaac Watts, the writers Joseph Conrad and Edgar Allen Poe and the glam-rock star Marc Bolan, who spent his childhood at 25 Stoke Newington Common (*see also* EAST SHEEN).

Stoke Newington Eight Alleged members of the ANGRY BRIGADE who in May 1972 were tried for conspiracy to cause explosions. The eight began as the 'Amhurst Four' – John Barker, Hilary Creek, James Greenfield and Anna Mendleson – who shared an upstairs flat at 359 Amhurst Road, Stoke Newington. A police raid on the flat had uncovered an 'arsenal' of weapons, together with equipment that had been used to produce Angry Brigade communiqués; the defendants claimed that the evidence had been planted. Four associates of the flat's occupants were also subsequently charged. At the conclusion of the trial in December 1972 the Amhurst Four were found guilty and each sentenced to ten years' imprisonment. The other four were acquitted.

Stoke-on-Trent 'Bent' in COCKNEY RHYMING SLANG, in either the criminal sense or as a derogatory epithet for a homosexual. *Compare* BURTON (-ON-TRENT).

> So this is your first night down in the Big Smoke, is it? ... And where are you from, young boy? ... Stoke-on-Trent? Well, you know what they say? Stoke-on-Trent: bent.
>
> ROB NEWMAN, in *Newman and Baddiel in Pieces* (TV comedy) (1993)

Stompie A non-functional Soviet T-34 battle tank that since 1995 has stood on a small piece of waste ground at the corner of Mandela Way and Pages Walk, BERMONDSEY. It was named Stompie by its owner, a local resident, in memory of James 'Stompie' Moeketsi (1975–89), who was kidnapped and murdered by members of Winnie Mandela's bodyguard. The tank has been artistically repainted on several occasions (and then adorned with graffiti). As of March 2009 it was camouflaged in swirling black and white.

The authorities, for their part, were interested in Stompie. For a while a 'remove for disposal' sticker adorned its green-grey sides. The spectre of planning permission was raised. Finally, the MoD wondered if it had been properly decommissioned, and suggested it might be a security risk.

JONATHAN GIBBS, in *The Independent on Sunday* (2 November 2003)

Stonebridge A troubled but improving council-built estate and its vicinity, situated north-west of HARLESDEN. The name derives from the stone bridge of 1745 that carried the HARROW ROAD over the River BRENT. Until very late in the 19th century this was the site of Stonebridge Farm and of WILLESDEN's first sewage works but it was then rapidly built over, although some earlier large houses survived for a while. After the First World War Willesden council built houses west of Brentfield Road as part of its response to Lloyd George's call for 'homes for heroes'. During the 1950s the council planned a massive redevelopment and more than 2,000 units were built, mostly in high-rise blocks, the first of which opened in 1967. These have recently been the focus of extensive regeneration efforts. Stonebridge has the second highest proportion of black residents of any ward in London, after PECKHAM. The boxer Audley Harrison (b.1971) grew up on the Stonebridge estate.

Stone of Scone The great coronation stone, the Stone of Destiny, on which the Scottish kings were formerly crowned at Scone, near Perth. It was removed by Edward I in 1296 and brought to WESTMINSTER ABBEY, where it was housed under the Chair of St Edward. It was stolen on the night of 24–25 December 1950 (a tale related in the 2008 film *Stone of Destiny*), but restored to its place in February 1952. Since 1996 the stone has been kept at Edinburgh Castle but it is expected to be temporarily returned to Westminster Abbey for future coronations.

Stoop, the The informal name of the Twickenham Stoop, formerly the Stoop Memorial Ground, which is situated on Langhorn Drive in north-west TWICKENHAM. The Harlequin (rugby union) Football Club acquired the pitch for training purposes in 1963, subsequently playing its home matches here. Since 2005 HARLEQUINS' sister rugby league club has shared

the ground, which is named after Adrian Dura Stoop (1883–1957), a London-born rugby union player of Dutch descent. Stoop played 182 times for Harlequins, serving as team captain for eight years and later becoming the club's honorary secretary and then president. Quite separately, 'the stoop' was formerly a slang term for the pillory.

Stow, the The colloquial short form of WALTHAMSTOW Stadium, once London's most famous and popular greyhound racing venue. Despite the efforts of 'Save Our Stow' campaigners, the stadium closed in August 2008.

Since the closure was announced, the Stow has been packed like the old days, with Saturday crowds nearing 5,000. Many are saying goodbye to an old friend. Others have turned up for a belated gawp, like anthropologists exploring 'the lost world of the dog men'.

MICK HUME, in *The Times* (16 August 2008)

Straits of St Clement's A cant name for Butcher's Row, an alley of run-down buildings that formerly stood near ST CLEMENT DANES Church. Also nicknamed 'the Pass', it took its formal name from an earlier role as a shambles. A 'chamber' in the vicinity was one of the places in which the GUNPOWDER PLOT was said to have been concocted. The alley was swept away in a slum clearance project in 1813.

strand Both the STRAND and STRAND ON THE GREEN take their names from this Old English word, meaning 'bank' or 'shore'.

Strand, The A commercial and institutional thoroughfare running eastward from CHARING CROSS and meeting FLEET STREET just west of the junction with CHANCERY LANE, where TEMPLE BAR once stood. The name was first recorded in 1185, when the road ran close to the THAMES, but it now lies inland as a result of the construction of the Victoria EMBANKMENT. Forming part of the connection between the early twin centres of WESTMINSTER and the CITY of London, the Strand has been a place of settlement for centuries. John of Gaunt's Savoy Palace was destroyed in the Peasants' Revolt of 1381; it lay a little to the east of the present SAVOY HOTEL. Edward Seymour, 1st Duke of Somerset, built a riverside mansion on the Strand in 1547, which later served as a royal residence (*see* SOMERSET HOUSE). In the late 1820s KING'S COLLEGE was founded on a site next to Somerset House, and SIMPSON'S-IN-THE-STRAND opened. The temple-like buildings of the ROYAL COURTS OF JUSTICE were erected east of the ALDWYCH in the 1870s. In the late 19th and early 20th centuries the Strand was pre-eminently an entertainment zone: it had more theatres than any other street in London (including the Gaiety and the Adelphi), several notable restaurants (such as Romano's and the Tivoli) and large numbers of MUSIC HALLS and pubs. It was the place where Londoners of all classes went for a good night out:

Let's all go down the Strand (Have a banana!)
Oh! What a happy land!
That's the place for fun and noise,
Come with me, and see what we can find
All among the girls and boys.
So let's all go down the Strand.

HARRY CASTLING and C.W. MURPHY: 'Let's All Go Down the Strand!' (1904)

Much of the Strand was lined with offices over the course of the 20th century, of which the most imposing is the Shell-Mex building of 1931 at 80 Strand (*see also* PENGUIN BOOKS).

Strand Magazine, The A monthly magazine founded in 1890 by George Newnes (1851–1910) and published until 1950. It contained a mixture of factual articles, short stories and serials. *The Strand Magazine's* early success was driven by the appearance of Arthur Conan Doyle's Sherlock HOLMES stories, which appeared in almost every issue until 1927. Other famous contributors included Kipling, Chesterton, Tolstoy and Simenon.

Strand on the Green A riverside village situated just east of KEW BRIDGE. From the 13th century to the 17th century it was simply Strand. In its early days there was no path along the riverbank, just a series of interconnecting wharves. During the 18th century the village attracted wealthy residents who built some grand homes here; and the Ship, Bull's Head, Bell and Crown, and City Barge public houses all came into existence. The opening of the first Kew Bridge in 1759 improved accessibility, increased land values and drew some of George III's courtiers when the king was living at Kew Palace. By 1800 a continuous footpath ran along the bank. The whole locality was built up by the 1930s.

The German-born painter Johann Zoffany (1733–1810) lived at 65 Strand on the Green from 1790 until his death. Zoffany sometimes used local fishermen as his models; for example, as Christ's disciples. The author Margaret Kennedy lived for a while at Strand Green House and made it the setting for her bestseller *The Constant Nymph* (1924). Other village residents have included press baron Hugh Cudlipp, poet Dylan Thomas, writer Nancy Mitford and actor Donald Pleasence.

Maypole in the Strand *See under* MAY.

Stratford An important commercial and industrial centre situated north-west of WEST HAM, of which it was once a part. Cistercian monks founded Langthorne Abbey in the marshes near the River LEA in 1135 and it grew to become one of the richest religious houses in England. The village was originally known as Stratford Langthorne – 'street ford near Langthorne Abbey' – to distinguish it from Stratford-atte-BOW, on the other side of the river. The village was a centre for the slaughter of livestock brought from East Anglia and for baking bread, using corn ground at the riverside mills on Stratford Marsh. In 1844 (the year that the poet Gerard Manley Hopkins was born here) Stratford began to be transformed as a result of the Metropolitan Building Act. This forced noxious industries to move outside London, and Stratford was the first place across the border in ESSEX, with good road and water connections into the city. The well-established mills, distilleries and breweries were joined by engineering works, printers, ink and dye works and every kind of processor of coal, oil, manure and animal bones. The town centre was built up with shops, public houses, places of entertainment and municipal institutions in the late 19th and early 20th centuries. Relatively sympathetic regeneration around the turn of the 21st century has brought an almost metropolitan style to parts of the town centre. To the north-west a former industrial wasteland is being transformed as the home of the 2012 OLYMPIC GAMES.

strawberry

Strawberry Fayre An annual fair held in June in ELY PLACE to raise money for charity. It celebrates the strawberries for which the bishop of Ely's garden was once famous.

My lord of Ely, when I was last in Holborn,
I saw good strawberries in your garden there:
I do beseech you send for some of them.

SHAKESPEARE: *Richard III*, III, iv (c.1592)

Strawberry Hill A sumptuous mansion situated between TWICKENHAM and TEDDINGTON, and by extension the neighbouring locality. In 1698 the Earl of Bradford's retired coachman built or bought a house here, which was acquired in 1747 by the politician and man of letters Horace Walpole (1717–97).

> ... it is the prettiest bauble you ever saw. It is set in enamelled meadows with filigree hedges ... but, thank God! the Thames is between me and the duchess of Queensbury.
>
> HORACE WALPOLE: letter to Henry Seymour Conway (8 June 1747)

Walpole renamed the house Strawberry Hill, after a field in the grounds, although there is no real hill here, merely a slight elevation of the terrain. He spent much of his life adding extra rooms and features to the 'little cottage', creating a Gothic fantasy that became famous throughout Europe, set in a landscaped garden. After Walpole's death the property passed to his relatives, the Waldegrave family. Frances, widow of the 7th Earl of Waldegrave, added a new wing of her own design in 1862. In the following year the railway passed to the west of the house but it was ten years before a station opened in Strawberry Hill. Some have suggested that the station was built at the behest of the countess, for the convenience of her house guests, but it is more probable that property speculators pressurized the railway company into providing the facility. One of these developers was Chichester Fortescue, Frances's fourth husband, who laid out streets of villas on the edge of the family estate. St Mary's College moved from BROOK GREEN to Strawberry Hill in 1925, and the mansion was further extended.

Strawberry Hill Gothic The style of early Gothic Revivalist architecture inspired and epitomized by STRAWBERRY HILL.

strawberry (tart) 'Heart' in COCKNEY RHYMING SLANG, perhaps inspired by the vague resemblance of the fruit to that bodily organ. 'Don't do that or you'll give me a dickey strawberry' was a postwar catchphrase. *See also* TREACLE (TART).

streaking The act of running naked in a public place by way of a stunt, sometimes under the influence of a stimulant other than a bet or the buzz of bravado. The feat is usually staged out of doors, typically at a sporting venue, but may also be enacted in a public building such as a restaurant. In Britain the activity caught the attention of the public in 1974, when the Australian Michael O'Brien was escorted off the pitch at TWICKENHAM during an England v. France rugby match, a policeman using his helmet to restore the culprit's modesty. The following year, during the ASHES series, Michael Angelow jumped over the stumps at LORD'S cricket ground, wearing only his plimsolls. According to John Ballard and Paul Suff's *Dictionary of Football* (1999) the first female streaker at a major FOOTBALL match was Variana Scotney, who ran on to the pitch at HIGHBURY when ARSENAL were playing TOTTENHAM HOTSPUR in 1981. *See also the* TWICKENHAM STREAKER.

Streatham An extensive south London suburb stretching southwards from BRIXTON to NORBURY. Streatham was first recorded in Domesday Book as Estreham, but this is likely to have been a transcription error, since the name simply means 'street ham', a reference to a small settlement beside a Roman road. After the Reformation and as the woodland was cleared the district was broken up into several farms and some of the landowners began to sell these off in the 18th century. Full suburbanization began after the opening of railway stations in the mid-19th century and the process reached a peak between 1880 and 1914, when the parish's cottages, mansions and fields were erased by a series of estates. In the latter decades of the 20th century Streatham gained a multi-ethnic population; the largest minorities are of Caribbean and African origin.

Streatham Common A butterfly-shaped open space and its surrounding housing, situated at the south-eastern corner of Streatham's sprawl. The METROPOLITAN BOARD OF WORKS acquired the common from the Ecclesiastical Commissioners in 1884, preserving it as public open space.

Streatham Hill Not quite 'the Regent Street of south London' that its creator intended but a significant leisure zone on the Streatham/BRIXTON border. When leases on villas south of Telford Avenue began to expire in the 1920s, they were progressively acquired by Hugh Sewell Kingdon, whose project to create an entertainment centre involved a restaurant, dance hall, theatre, cinema and shops. In 1962, Streatham Hill Theatre was converted into a bingo hall and the Gaumont

Palace cinema became the largest bowling alley in Europe. The Locarno has remained a dance venue, under a variety of names including the Cat's Whiskers and Caesars.

Streatham Park Originally a substantial villa built in the 1730s by the SOUTHWARK brewer, Ralph Thrale, who had obtained a lease on 100 acres (40 hectares) of TOOTING COMMON from the Duke of Bedford, allegedly in return for a constant supply of ale and PORTER at the duke's principal seat, Woburn Abbey. In 1767 Hester Salusbury married Ralph's son Henry at St Anne's Church in SOHO and went to live with him at Streatham Park. Henry Thrale was MP for Southwark in the 1770s and his vivacious wife was a socialite who kept a revealing diary of her early years here. Dr JOHNSON was a close friend of the family and such a regular guest that he had his own apartment at Streatham Park. From the 1870s the estate was developed for high-class suburban housing, a process that took 60 years to complete. Dixcote, at 8 North Drive, is the largest house in London by the renowned architect C.F.A. Voysey, built in 1897. Most of the late Victorian villas have since been replaced by council housing.

street

street markets London's earliest markets were set up in the streets and many of the capital's 100-odd modern markets continue to operate in the same manner. Most remain on the sites where they first flourished more than a century ago. Among the best-known locations are:

BERMONDSEY Square
BERWICK STREET
BRICK LANE
CHAPEL MARKET
Club Row, north of Brick Lane
COLUMBIA ROAD
East Street, WALWORTH
LEATHER LANE
Lower Marsh, WATERLOO
PECKHAM (several streets off Rye Lane)
PETTICOAT LANE
PORTOBELLO ROAD
Queen's Crescent, KENTISH TOWN
Queens Market, GREEN STREET
Ridley Road, DALSTON
ROMAN ROAD
SHEPHERD'S BUSH Market
Strutton Ground, off VICTORIA STREET
WALTHAMSTOW High Street

In addition, many stalls are set up outdoors at CAMDEN MARKET, notably on Inverness Street, and a long stretch of BAYSWATER Road serves as an open-air art market on Sundays. Except on event days, a Sunday market is held in WEMBLEY STADIUM car park; with over 500 stalls it claims to be the largest market of its kind in England.

Street of Shame A nickname for FLEET STREET in the days when it was the home of newspapers. Popularized by the magazine *Private Eye*, the nickname alluded both to the lurid exposés published by the papers and to the drunken excesses of many journalists. Fleet Street has also been called the Street of Ink, of Fame, of Adventure and of Dreams.

Streets of London Possibly the most famous song about London since the MUSIC HALL era. Written in 1969 by Ralph McTell (b.1944), who grew up in CROYDON, it became a hit for him in 1974 and subsequently served as the title for his 1980s television series and his 'greatest hits' album. The song recommends sympathetic observation of the lifestyles of London's down-and-outs as an antidote to feelings of loneliness or dissatisfaction. According to McTell's official website there are 212 known recorded versions of the song.

> So how can you tell me you're lonely,
> And say for you that the sun don't shine?
> Let me take you by the hand and lead you
> through the streets of London,
> I'll show you something to make you change
> your mind.
>
> 'Streets of London' (chorus)

strike (me dead) 'Bread' in almost obsolete COCKNEY RHYMING SLANG. Gerald Kersh, in *Sergeant Nelson of the Guards* (1945), writes of 'a you 'n' a strike', meaning a cup of YOU AND ME and a slice of bread and butter.

Stringfellows A COVENT GARDEN nightclub opened in 1980 by the self-proclaimed 'world's greatest disco owner' Peter Stringfellow (b.1940). It is brash and garish by comparison with AN-NABEL'S or TRAMP, but it has several celebrities among its mostly middle-aged businessmen members.

Strong Man of Islington The sobriquet of Thomas Topham (1710–49), landlord of the Duke's Head and other establishments in the ISLINGTON area. The former carpenter could break thick ropes, pull a horse lying on its back and lift an oak table with his teeth. For a while, the BRITISH MUSEUM exhibited among its curiosities a sturdy pewter dish that Topham had rolled up with his bare hands. He could also bend a kitchen poker nearly to right angles by striking it against his arm or his neck, and then straighten it out again. That feat is echoed in the Sherlock HOLMES story 'The Adventure of the Speckled Band' (1892), in which the threatening Dr Grimesby Roylott bends a poker and Holmes unbends it. Topham is said to have found a watchman asleep in his box one night, whereupon he carried the box and sleeping man on his shoulders and dumped them over the wall of BUNHILL FIELDS Cemetery. In 1741 he put on a show in COLD BATH FIELDS, in commemoration of Vice-Admiral Vernon's victory at PORTOBELLO. In Vernon's presence he picked up three hogshead casks filled with water in a harness-style lift. However, he lost a bet with some FINSBURY archers when he failed to draw an arrow two-thirds of its length and was obliged to stand them a bowl of punch. Also called the British Samson, Thomas Topham died of self-inflicted wounds after beating and stabbing his unfaithful wife.

struggle

struggle and grunt *See* GRUMBLE (AND GRUNT).

struggle (and strife) 'Wife' in COCKNEY RHYM-ING SLANG, but 'TROUBLE (AND STRIFE)' is usually preferred.

stucco (Italian; from Old High German *stucchi* 'crust', 'coating') Any kind of plaster or cement used to coat exterior walls or make architectural mouldings, or the decorative work on a building done in stucco, generally afterwards painted white or cream. The builders of Georgian London made great use of stucco, especially on the facades of high-class villas and terraced houses.

stuccoed Faced or overlaid with stucco.

Stucconia An invention of Charles DICKENS, on the model of TYBURNIA, signifying some prestigious district, probably not far from the WEST END.

> Also, how the fair bride was married from the house of Hamilton Veneering, Esquire, of Stucconia, and was given away by Melvin Twemlow, Esquire, of Duke Street, St James's ...
>
> DICKENS: *Our Mutual Friend* (1865)

Stuccovia A similar invention to STUCCONIA, coined at the beginning of the 20th century.

> Here, as the conversation begins to soar dangerously high, we Stuccovians turn hastily to less exalted but safer themes.
>
> G.W.E. RUSSELL: *A Londoner's Log-Book* (1902)

subtopia A word coined (from 'suburb' and 'Utopia') by the WEMBLEY-born architectural journalist Ian Nairn (1930–83) to denote the sprawling suburban housing estates built to satisfy the urban workers' yearning for country surroundings while clinging to the amenities of the town. The term includes all the paraphernalia of concrete posts, lamp standards, chain link fencing and other uglinesses associated with a disfigured landscape.

> There will be no real distinction between town and country. Both will consist of a limbo of shacks, bogus rusticities, wire and aerodromes, set in some fir-poled fields ... Upon this new Britain the Review bestows a name in the hope that it will stick – Subtopia.
>
> IAN NAIRN: *Architectural Review*, 'Outrage' (1955)

Sudbury A peaceful residential backwater situated west of WEMBLEY. The name was first recorded in the late 13th century as Suthbery: the southern manor house. Its northern counterpart may have been the manor house of HARROW. Sudbury Court was the principal MIDDLESEX residence of the archbishops of Canterbury until the end of the 14th century. This was the first part of the Wembley area to undergo suburban development and when present-day Wembley Central station opened in 1842 it was initially called Sudbury. In the first decade of the 20th century Sudbury gained two electric train services as well as electric trams. Day-trippers visited the Swan's tea garden and a racecourse operated for a while. Many Victorian villas were quickly demolished and their grounds were developed with housing. Outlying farms suffered the same fate after the First World War.

Sudbury box A simple, elegantly efficient architectural style introduced to surface-level station buildings on the PICCADILLY LINE by Charles Holden (1875–1960). Opened in 1931, Sudbury Town was the first station to employ the technique, which Holden over-modestly characterized as 'a brick box with a concrete lid'. Other architects commissioned by LONDON

TRANSPORT soon began to copy the format. Usage of the term 'Sudbury box' is sometimes limited to rectangular structures but can encompass other shapes, such as those at ARNOS GROVE (circular) and Bounds Green (octagonal).

> When his client Francis Russell, Earl of Bedford, asked [Inigo] Jones to add a chapel 'as cheap as a barn' to his smart residential development built around the new Covent Garden piazza, the architect replied 'then you shall have the handsomest barn in England'. Sudbury Town station is surely transport design's equivalent of St Paul's, Covent Garden.
>
> JONATHAN GLANCEY, in *The Guardian* (16 October 2007)

Sugar Mile A former nickname for the industrialized highway running through SILVERTOWN, derived from the presence of treacle refineries, jam-makers, Henry TATE's sugar-cube factory and Abram Lyle's GOLDEN SYRUP works at nearby PLAISTOW Wharf. Much of the Sugar Mile was devastated by bombing during the BLITZ.

> ... and Gibb from Beckton says, the Sugar Mile is burning, boys and girls, the world's aglow
> this Gibb from Beckton says
> with Tate and Lyle's
> finest dark selection ...
>
> GLYN MAXWELL: *The Sugar Mile*, 'Home Guard Man Breathless' (2005)

suicide bridge *See* ARCHWAY; BRIDGE OF SIGHS.

summer

Summer Exhibition A selling exhibition held at the ROYAL ACADEMY every year without interruption since 1769. It nowadays attracts around 10,000 submissions by both established and unknown living artists, of which around 1,200 are selected for inclusion, making this the world's largest open contemporary art exhibition. It takes place at BURLINGTON HOUSE from early June to mid-August.

Summer Time *See* DAYLIGHT SAVING TIME.

Sundridge Park A mansion, its parkland and the neighbouring residential area in north BROMLEY. Sundridge Park was created in the late 1790s for Sir Claude Scott (1742–1830). The STUCCOED mansion was designed by John Nash and the work was completed under the direction of Samuel Wyatt. The surrounding farmland was transformed into parkland to a plan by Humphry

Repton. Towards the end of the 19th century Sir Edward Scott began to sell off the estate for housing development and a rebuilt station opened to the public as Sundridge Park in 1896. The park became a golf course, with a new clubhouse opened in 1903 by the prime minister, A.J. Balfour. What began as a nine-hole course has since grown into a pair of what architectural historian Nikolaus Pevsner called 'unusually umbrageous' 18-hole courses. The mansion functioned as a luxury hotel until after the Second World War and became a management centre in 1956.

Sun Hill *See the* BILL.

sup with Sir Thomas Gresham, to *See to* DINE WITH DUKE HUMPHREY.

Surbiton The embodiment of London suburbia, partly because it sounds like a contraction of 'suburban town', Surbiton originated in the 12th century as a farm located south of KINGSTON UPON THAMES – and 'southern homestead' is the real meaning of the name. In the early 19th century the hamlet consisted of around 40 dwellings and the Waggon and Horses public house, but because Kingston brushed the railway aside Surbiton acquired a station very early. This opened as Kingston-on-Railway in 1838, and over the following half-century high-class housing spread across the new suburb. By the end of the 19th century its fashionability had begun to decline, although growth continued in more modest form. The opening of the KINGSTON BYPASS in 1927 helped stimulate a building boom that filled the former farmland of TOLWORTH, Southborough and Berrylands.

The town's stereotypical reputation was fostered by literary works, such as Barry Pain's ELIZA series (1900–13) and Keble Howard's *The* SMITHS OF SURBITON (1906), and later by the setting here of the television comedy series *The* GOOD LIFE.

sure as the devil is in London, as *See under* AS.

Surrey The county bordering most of SOUTH LONDON. It originally extended to the SOUTH BANK (still sometimes called the Surrey side) of the THAMES, including SOUTHWARK, but over the centuries it has steadily lost its territory to London, the last major readjustment being in

1965. Its administrative headquarters remain in KINGSTON UPON THAMES, despite this now being in GREATER LONDON.

Surrey County Cricket Club Traditionally one of the strongest 'first-class' county cricket clubs, founded in 1845. Since its inception, the club's home ground has been the OVAL. In 1915 the future Edward VIII, then Prince of Wales and Duke of Cornwall (and in the latter capacity the Oval's landlord), granted the club the right to use the Prince of Wales feathers as its insignia. Surrey also plays some home games at SUTTON, PURLEY and the Whitgift School in SOUTH CROYDON. The club's most famous players have included Jack Hobbs, Peter May, Alec Bedser, Ken Barrington, Alec Stewart and Graham Thorpe.

Surrey Docks The former docks of ROTHER-HITHE. In 1695 Wriothesley Russell (later 2nd Duke of Bedford) married Elizabeth Howland and the Russell family thus gained control of the potentially valuable Rotherhithe peninsula. He was 14 at the time and she was 11. Excavation of the Howland Great Wet Dock (later GREENLAND DOCK) began the following year and work was completed by 1700. In the 1790s theft and congestion caused chaos in the POOL OF LONDON, creating an intense demand for additional inland facilities, and over the following century several rival companies filled the peninsula with a series of new docks. Ruinous competition between the companies prompted their merger in 1865 as the Surrey Commercial Docks Company. The East London Railway traversed the docks in 1869 and Deptford Road (later Surrey Docks) station opened in 1884. The PORT OF LONDON AUTHORITY assumed control of the docks after its establishment in 1908. With the decline of the whole of the London DOCKLANDS, the Surrey Docks were progressively shut down in the 1960s and closed completely in 1970.

> She used to do a topless down at the Surrey Docks,
> With tassels on her whatsits she did a t'riffic job
> Of raising all the eyebrows of every lunchtime mob.
>
> CHRIS DIFFORD and GLENN TILBROOK: 'It's Not Cricket' (song by Squeeze) (1978)

In common with several other 'docks', Surrey Docks has proved admirably appropriate, both phonologically and semantically, as COCKNEY RHYMING SLANG for 'pox'.

Surrey Quays The post-regeneration name for the vicinity of the former Surrey Docks. The renaming of Surrey Docks station as Surrey Quays in 1989 caused some resentment at the time, as it seemed to embody a denial of the area's working-class history and presage its wholesale GENTRIFICATION. Most of the docks were filled in, unlike those across the river, and the LONDON DOCKLANDS DEVELOPMENT CORPORATION oversaw the construction of mixed-tenure housing, together with shopping and leisure facilities at CANADA WATER.

Surrey Row *See* MELANCHOLY WALK.

Surreyside theatres *See* TRANSPONTINE THEATRES.

Sutton A busy town since the Victorian era, situated 4 miles (6.5 km) west of CROYDON. Domesday Book provided the first reliable mention of the estate, as Sudtone. The name means 'south farmstead' and may have referred to its position in relation to MORDEN or MITCHAM. Little is known of medieval Sutton, which may not even have existed as a focused settlement until much later. By the mid-18th century the village consisted of a loose ribbon of houses along the High Street. An increase in coaching traffic on the BRIGHTON road and the subsequent arrival of the railway in 1847 brought early growth and the town continued to expand after trams came from Croydon in 1906. West Sutton and Sutton Common filled with compact housing in the 1930s, following the construction of the Sutton bypass and the railway loop line to WIMBLEDON. After the Second World War, and especially in the 1960s, much of the old town centre was redeveloped with shops and offices, although not on the scale witnessed in Croydon. Initiatives since the mid-1970s have included the pedestrianization of the High Street and the opening of the multi-use civic centre and two shopping malls.

Sutton, London Borough of An OUTER LONDON borough created in 1965 by merging the borough of Sutton and CHEAM, the borough of BEDDINGTON and WALLINGTON and CARSHALTON urban district. In general, Sutton's more deprived wards are in the north of the borough, while the southern half is distinctly STOCKBROKER BELT. Its coat of arms has coded references to former lords of the borough's manors, surmounted by a popinjay from the arms of the Lumley family of Cheam. A tiny Hannibal airliner symbolizes CROYDON AIRPORT, part of which lay in the borough. The civic motto manages to amalgamate elements from those of its three predecessors: *per ardua in fide servite Deo* means 'through difficulties serve God in faith'.

Sutton, Thomas *See* CROESUS.

Sutton for mutton The opening words of an old rhyme that continued: CARSHALTON for beeves, Epsom for whores and Ewell for thieves. Sheep were reared on the North Downs near Sutton, while cattle were better suited to Carshalton's meadows. When the ditty was written it was Epsom's mineral waters, not races, that had made the place into a pleasure resort and attracted ladies of easy virtue. Ewell (which, like Epsom, lies beyond the GREATER LONDON border) was a poor relation, offering cheaper lodgings that attracted 'inferior sharpers and other idle retainers'. Another version ran:

Sutton for good mutton,
Cheam for juicy beef,
Croydon for a pretty girl,
And Mitcham for a thief.

The rhyme was adapted for different Suttons in other parts of the country; the third town was sometimes damned, sometimes praised, but the fourth was always identified with thieves, which was the verse's main purpose.

Sutton Hoo Treasure An Anglo-Saxon ship burial of the early 7th century, discovered at Sutton Hoo near Woodbridge, Suffolk, in 1939. It is one of the richest ever found and the treasure, consisting of a sword and sheath, helmet, bowls and other objects in precious metals, is now in the BRITISH MUSEUM.

Sutton House A National Trust property situated on HOMERTON High Street, built in 1535 (as Brick Place) for Sir Ralph Sadleir (1507–87), principal secretary of state to Henry VIII. Its present name derives from the Victorians' belief that it was at one time a residence of Thomas Sutton (*see* CROESUS) but it has since been established that he owned a neighbouring property, Tan House, which has not survived. Despite centuries of alterations and additions, this rare example of a Tudor red-brick house retains many early details, even in rooms of later periods, including original linenfold panelling and 17th-century wall paintings.

Sutton's Hospital See CHARTERHOUSE.

Sven from Swiss Cottage A caller to Clive Bull's late-night phone-in show on LBC RADIO. Sven rang in several times between 1988 and 1992, mostly to discuss the subjects of fish and lost love. The Norwegian fisherman was the creation of the comedian Peter Cook (1937–95) but Bull did not at first know this. After discovering the deception, he continued to play along. Transcripts of the calls are included in *Tragically I Was an Only Twin* (2002), an anthology of Cook's work.

> The point, surely Clive, is if the woman you love wants to go off with the fish, then why not? It's not for me to interfere.

swan

Swan Feast An annual dinner held by the Vintners' Company on the last Thursday of November. In former years roast swan was the main dish on the menu, stuffed with herbs and pork fat and sealed in a paste of flour and water, but more conventional meats are nowadays prepared.

swan upping Traditionally, a taking up of swans and placing of the marks of ownership on their beaks, especially annual expeditions for this purpose up the River THAMES. Since the 15th century the Crown's ownership of swans on the Thames has been shared with the Vintners' and Dyers' Companies (*see* LIVERY COMPANIES). Royal swans were marked with five nicks, two lengthways and three across the bill, the Vintners' birds were marked with two nicks and those of the Dyers' with one nick. Bill marking ceased in 1997 but the expedition still takes place in the third week of July, with an emphasis on conservation and educational activities involving local schoolchildren. The birds are ringed on the right leg with individual identification numbers, unless they are sick or injured, in which case they are taken to a swan sanctuary for treatment. A ring bearing the crest of the relevant company is placed on the left leg of each swan belonging to Dyers or Vintners. As the parent swans should already have been identified in previous years, only cygnets are usually ringed. Ownership descends through the generations; in the case of mixed parentage, ownership of the cygnets is divided accordingly. If there is an odd number of cygnets, the extra bird is allotted the same ownership as the male parent (cob). The ceremonial trip upriver used to begin in London but the boats nowadays set off from Sunbury, SURREY.

Swan with Two Necks An old tavern sign, said to be an alteration of the 'two nicks' with which the Vintners' Company marked the beaks of its swans. In coaching days The Swan with Two Necks in Lad Lane (now Gresham Street) was the chief London departure point for the north. *See also* SWAN UPPING.

swear

swear (and cuss) 'Bus' in old-fashioned COCK-NEY RHYMING SLANG, perhaps coined while waiting for one.

swearing on the horns In public houses at HIGHGATE it was once customary to administer an oath to travellers who called. A pair of horns mounted on a pole was brought in, the person to be sworn placed his right hand on one of the horns, and after a call for 'Silence!' the landlord proceeded to deliver his charge: 'You must not eat brown bread while you can get white, except you like brown the best. You must not drink small beer while you can get strong, except [etc.]. You must not kiss the maid while you can kiss the mistress, except you like the maid best, or have the chance to kiss them both.' Then finally: 'And now, my son, kiss the horns, or a pretty girl if you see one here, and so be free of Highgate.' One estimate suggests that in the early 19th century around 250 people a day took the oath. However, by 1832 'the ceremony had been abandoned by all respectable members of society'.

Many to the steep of Highgate hie;
Ask, ye Bæotian shades! the reason why?
Grasped in the holy hand of Mystery,
In whose dread name both men and maids are sworn,
And consecrate the oath with draught and dance till morn.

LORD BYRON: *Childe Harold's Pilgrimage*, Canto 1 (1809)

sweaty (sock) 'Jock', i.e. a Scot, in mildly offensive COCKNEY RHYMING SLANG. The following example of usage (which also includes another cockney coinage: TEA-LEAF) puns on the literal and slang meanings of the term:

The players don't necessarily need the money, but you could probably say the same about the tennis tealeaf who has nicked so many wallets out of locker rooms at Wimbledon that players will soon go on court, like Sunday League

footballers, with a valuables bag, their cash and jewellery wrapped in a sweaty sock (so long as Andy Murray isn't otherwise engaged).

Daily Mirror (3 July 2007)

Sweeney A shortening of 'Sweeney Todd', COCK-NEY RHYMING SLANG for FLYING SQUAD. The name is that of the DEMON BARBER OF FLEET STREET. The character's grim persona and grisly deeds presumably appealed to the coiners of the term, which dates from the 1930s. It was brought before a wide public by the television crime drama series *The Sweeney* (1975–82), centring on Detective Inspector Jack Regan, played by John Thaw, and his sidekick George Carter, played by Dennis Waterman. Both characters regularly ignored the rule book, associated with villains, swore and drank to excess and generally presented an unflattering portrait of their templates in their pursuit of various villains and 'bad boys'. *See also* GET YOUR TROUSERS ON, YOU'RE NICKED.

The Sweeney was the antithesis of *Dixon* and heralded the heyday of an overtly macho, controlling image of policing that captured the mood of 1970s Britain and was echoed in other programmes like *The Professionals*.

FRANK LEISHMAN and PAUL MASON: *Policing and the Media* (2003)

Sweet Thames A novel (1992) by Matthew Kneale set in London in 1849 against the backdrop of the threat of a cholera epidemic, concerning the efforts of a civil engineer to improve the sewerage system. Its name is an ironic allusion to Edmund Spenser's characterization of the river in 'Prothalamion' (1596):

Sweet Thames, run softly, till I end my song.

swell An old term for a dandy, a fashionable or finely dressed person. In the 19th and early 20th centuries it was especially applied to a working-class Londoner who put on airs, a COCKNEY toff.

They are not like the trees of the country – no more than a Cockney swell, who does not know the difference between grass and gorse, is like a man!

JAMES HOGG (editor): *Hogg's Instructor*, Volume 3 (1849)

Swinging London A phase that London went through in the mid-1960s, when it presented itself as the last word in fashionability, uninhibitedness, unconventionality, liveliness and hipness. It was the era of CARNABY STREET, the KING'S ROAD, the Beatles, the ROLLING STONES, the KINKS, the films of Dick Lester and Clive Donner, Vidal SASSOON's asymmetric bob, Mary QUANT, BIBA and the contraceptive pill. Hitherto grey, stuffy London suddenly found itself, much to its surprise, fixed in the world's gaze at the centre of the youth-culture revolution. The expression 'swinging London' seems to have originated with Diana Vreeland, editor of the fashion magazine *Vogue*, and it was popularized by *Time* magazine in 1966.

Swiss

Swiss banker 'Wanker' in COCKNEY RHYMING SLANG.

Swiss Cottage A locality in SOUTH HAMPSTEAD, with amenities serving a wide catchment area north of ST JOHN'S WOOD. FINCHLEY ROAD and Avenue Road converged here in the 1820s and Adelaide Road cut across Eton College's land in 1830. By 1841 the Swiss Cottage tavern stood on the island formed at the junction of the three roads. It has since been rebuilt and enlarged while retaining its chalet style. In the late 1930s a bulky Odeon cinema and the flats of Regency Lodge filled out the tavern's island site. A library and swimming pool and a new home for HAMPSTEAD Theatre opened in the early 1960s. When these needed renewing at the beginning of the 21st century, Camden council invested in Swiss Cottage on a scale not seen since the days of Victorian municipal largesse. An £85 million project includes a leisure centre, community centre, social and private housing and a park.

Swiss Cottage slickster A greased-back hairstyle that flourished briefly in the early 2000s.

Swiss Light A set of luminous panels that surmounted the chimney of TATE MODERN from the gallery's opening in 2000. The work of Michael Craig-Martin (b.1941) and funded by the government of Switzerland, the Swiss Light was damaged by high winds in 2008 and dismantled.

Swiss Re Tower *See the* GHERKIN.

Sven from Swiss Cottage *See under* SVEN.

Swone-one Society slang (pronounced 'swun-wun') in the 1970s and 1980s for BATTERSEA, an area to which SLOANE RANGERS had recourse if they could not afford to live on the opposite side of the THAMES. A verbalization of SW11, the

locality's POSTAL DISTRICT, it made it sound a little like SW1, which encompasses ST JAMES'S, WESTMINSTER, PIMLICO and BELGRAVIA. Battersea is sometimes jokily pronounced 'Battersia' to make it sound more like Belgravia. It has also been referred to as South CHELSEA, a nod to the diaspora from the more chic address.

Sydenham A formerly grand Victorian suburb situated south of DULWICH and FOREST HILL. This was Chipeham in 1206, probably the farmstead of a man called Cippa, and the name evolved in stages over several centuries. The last change, when the 'p' became a 'd', did not occur until the late 17th century. In 1854 the CRYSTAL PALACE was brought from HYDE PARK and rebuilt on the southern ridge of Sydenham Hill in the south-west corner of the district. This event transmuted the fortunes of the extended village, with hotels and every kind of amenity catering to the needs of the tens of thousands of tourists. Imposing houses were built for the new residents, including Crystal Palace managers and directors, with attendant accommodation for those who provided their services or laboured less lucratively at the palace. The appeal of the Crystal Palace declined in the 20th century but its destruction by fire in 1936 was still a tremendous blow. Many of Sydenham's grandest houses were replaced by homes for the new breed of commuter, while municipal estates were built in several corners. Despite the changes, the hilly terrain and surviving vestiges of its Victorian heyday continue to endow Sydenham with a distinctive character.

Sykes A BBC television sitcom screened from 1960 to 1965 and 1971 to 1979, featuring the self-improving Sykes, played by Eric Sykes (b.1923), and his twin sister Hattie, played by Hattie Jacques (1922–80), the two sharing a house at 24 Sebastopol Terrace, EAST ACTON. Early episodes opened with the arrival of some new gadget or new goods, but later plots centred on a series of domestic crises. Deryck Guyler played Corky, a pompous police constable, to add to the gentle humour.

Hell-and-Fury Sykes The sobriquet of James Sykes, an agent of Jonathan Wild, the THIEF-TAKER GENERAL. A former RUNNING FOOTMAN for Philip, 1st Duke of Wharton, Sykes captured Jack SHEPPARD in April 1724, but the famous criminal soon escaped from prison.

Symphony by a Londoner *See A* LONDON SYMPHONY.

Syon

Syon Abbey In 1431 the English followers of the teachings of St Bridget of Sweden moved their headquarters from TWICKENHAM to a site south of BRENTFORD and built Syon Abbey, which took its name from the biblical Mount Zion. There are few remnants of the abbey but archaeological surveys have located the sites of some former outbuildings and determined that the main structure may have been almost as large as Salisbury Cathedral. When Henry VIII dissolved the monastic establishments in the 1530s, he gave the estate to Edward Seymour, the uncle of his son, the future Edward VI (*see also* SAVOY CHAPEL; SOMERSET HOUSE).

Syon House The London seat of the dukes of Northumberland. An admirer of Italian Renaissance architecture, Edward Seymour, 1st Duke of Somerset, built Syon House in that style over the foundations of the west end of Syon Abbey's church between 1547 and his death by execution in 1552. Sir Hugh Smithson, later 1st Duke of Northumberland, acquired the estate through his marriage to Elizabeth Seymour in 1740. The couple employed Robert ADAM to remodel the interior of the house, which is nowadays open to the public three days a week in summer.

Syon Park The grounds of Syon House, occupying a long stretch of the THAMES riverside between BRENTFORD and ISLEWORTH. The northeastern part of the park was the scene of the battles of Brentford in 1016 and 1642. Capability BROWN landscaped the grounds for Sir Hugh Smithson and Elizabeth Seymour in 1760. The park's Great Conservatory made pioneering use of glass and metal when it was built in the 1820s.

the nun of Syon with the friar of Sheen *See under* NUN.

syrup (of fig) 'Wig' in COCKNEY RHYMING SLANG. The term is probably in more common usage than the laxative from which it derives. 'Irish jig' is the best known of several alternatives, none of which comes close to the familiarity of 'syrup'.

> Cynically perhaps, you leap to the assumption that the people of Milton Keynes are suspicious types who drowned out the jingly balalaika magic of Eurovision with debate about whether the presenter wears a syrup.
>
> VICTORIA COREN, in *The Observer* (28 May 2006)

T

T

T5 The colloquial short form of HEATHROW AIR-PORT Terminal 5. The terminal cost £4.3 billion to build, is exclusively used by British Airways and at full capacity it is designed to handle 35 million passengers a year. T5 was planned from the late 1980s and more than 80,000 artefacts were uncovered during archaeological excavations prior to the commencement of construction in 2002. When the terminal opened in March 2008 system faults and problems with 'staff familiarization' caused baggage delays, tem-porary suspensions of check-in facilities and the cancellation of more than 500 flights over a ten-day period. A House of Commons Transport Committee report later called this a 'national embarrassment'. For the most part, T5 has since functioned smoothly.

TM2 *See* TATE MODERN.

TX series *See* FX4.

Tabard The inn from which pilgrims from London used to set out on their journey to Canterbury. It was on the London estate of the abbots of Hyde (near Winchester) and lay in SOUTHWARK (now BOROUGH) High Street, a little to the south of LONDON BRIDGE. The Tabard was rebuilt as the Talbot after a fire in 1676 – the change of name apparently being the result of a misunderstanding by the signwriter. The Talbot was pulled down in 1875, despite protests, and its site is marked by a commemorative plaque. The inn and its host Harry Baily are immortalized in *The Canterbury Tales*. Nearby Pilgrimage Street, Manciple Street and Pardoner Street all com-memorate Chaucer's tale tellers.

> It happened in that season that one day
> In Southwark, at The Tabard, as I lay
> Ready to go on pilgrimage and start
> For Canterbury, most devout at heart,
> At night there came into that hostelry

> Some nine and twenty in a company.
>
> CHAUCER: *The Canterbury Tales*, 'The Prologue' (*c.*1387) (modern translation by Nevill Coghill, 1951)

Taggs Island A populous THAMES atoll for-merly called Walnut Tree Island or Garrick's Upper Eyot, located between HAMPTON and HAMPTON COURT. From the 1850s the convenient nearby presence of Hampton Court station drew day-trippers to the island's shabby pub and skittle alley, the Angler's Retreat. Thomas Tagg set up both a home and a boat-building business here in 1868 and soon acquired the lease on the Angler's Retreat and rebuilt it as a hotel. Poor summers and unfavourable economic conditions forced Tagg's son to sell up in 1903. The centre of the island was excavated in 1983 to create a la-goon that increased the capacity for houseboats and a bridge capable of carrying cars was built. The island's community is entirely based on houseboats; there are no longer any permanent structures here.

tailor

devil among the tailors, the *See under* DEVIL.

three tailors of Tooley Street *See under* THREE.

take

take a turn in Bushy Park, to *See* BUSHY PARK.

take the mickey out of someone, to To tease them. 'Mickey' probably represents 'Mickey Bliss', COCKNEY RHYMING SLANG for 'piss', so that the expression is a euphemism for 'to take the piss'. This in turn alludes to the deflating of a person, as a bladder deflates when emptying.

talk

Talking Smith, the The sobriquet of Samuel Honeyman, a blacksmith who in the early 18th century lived in Bear Street, near LEICESTER

SQUARE. A skilful ventriloquist and notorious prankster, he was said to have used his powers to terrify Dr SACHEVERELL, among others, but took his trickery too far with Thomas Britton, the MUSICAL SMALL-COAL MAN:

> Honeyman, without moving his lips, or seeming to speak, announced, as from afar off, the death of poor Britton within a few hours, with an intimation that the only way to avert his doom was for him to fall on his knees immediately and say the Lord's Prayer. The poor man did as he was bid, went home and took to his bed, and in a few days died ...
>
> JOHN HAWKINS: *General History of the Science and Practice of Music*, Volume 2 (1776)

Talk of the Town A dinner-dance venue that operated from 1958 to 1982 at the corner of Cranbourn Street and CHARING CROSS ROAD, just off LEICESTER SQUARE. In its heyday the Talk of the Town attracted all the leading stars, including Frank Sinatra, Sammy Davis Jr, Eartha Kitt and Tom Jones. Judy Garland's five-week comeback engagement in 1968–9 broke box office records. The building was originally the London Hippodrome, built by Frank Matcham for Edward Moss in 1900 as a circus variety theatre. It is now the Hippodrome again, and seems likely to be redeveloped as a casino in 2010, with a cabaret area and restaurant on the first floor.

tall buildings A euphemism for skyscrapers or tower blocks, popularized during the mayoralty of Ken Livingstone (*see* RED KEN). Before the decline in property values that began in 2008 developers were proposing new office (and occasionally residential) towers in numerous parts of the capital. Many Londoners considered the proliferation of such structures to be inappropriate to the city's character and rival politicians adopted competing stances on where they should and should not be permitted. A widely advocated view was that the tallest tall buildings should only be permitted in the vicinities of CANARY WHARF, BISHOPSGATE, LONDON BRIDGE STATION and central CROYDON.

Since 1098 the following buildings have at some stage been London's tallest (excluding transmitter masts):

WHITE TOWER (1098–1310)

Old St Paul's Cathedral (1310–1666)

St Saviour's Church (now SOUTHWARK CATHEDRAL) (1666–77)

The MONUMENT (1677–83)

ST MARY-LE-BOW Church (1683–1710)

ST PAUL'S Cathedral (1710–1939)

BATTERSEA POWER STATION (1939–62)

BT TOWER (1962–80)

NATWEST TOWER (1980–91)

One Canada Square, CANARY WHARF (1991–2012)

SHARD (OF GLASS) (from 2012)

All but one of these structures (Old St Paul's) survives today.

Tamburini riot *See the* OMNIBUS ROW.

Tamesis The Latin name for the River THAMES, first recorded in the writings of Julius Caesar in 51 BC.

> I send, I send here my supremest kiss
> To thee, my silver-footed Thamasis;
> No more shall I reiterate thy strand,
> Whereon so many stately structures stand ...
>
> ROBERT HERRICK: *Hesperides*, 'His Tears to Thamasis' (1648)

Tangier A large, gloomy cell in which debtors were confined at NEWGATE PRISON. Located in the centre of the building, at street level, it was said to be the second worst place in the gaol, after the Lower Ward. The inmates were called Tangerines.

tank
Bermondsey tank *See* STOMPIE.
septic (tank) *See under* SEPTIC.
Tank, the *See the* AQ.

tankard bearer One who delivered tankards of water drawn from conduits. For Londoners who could afford such a service this was the standard means of obtaining water until the creation of the NEW RIVER. A tankard held about 3 gallons (14 litres). Ben Jonson alludes several times to tankard bearers in his plays, each time connoting someone of lowly status.

Ta-ra-ra-boom-de-ay! This song, with a refrain redolent of the Victorian MUSIC HALL, was the hallmark of the comedienne Lottie Collins (1866–1910), a blackface minstrel's daughter, who first performed it at the Tivoli Music Hall in the STRAND in 1891 and who could never subsequently appear without singing it. It was of US origin and had words by Richard Morton. The song was all the rage in London and soon became popular in continental Europe, where

Anton Chekhov heard it and incorporated it in his play *The Three Sisters* (1901).

Tardis A nickname for the Blind Beggar public house on WHITECHAPEL Road. The original Tardis is the time-travelling vehicle of Dr Who in the long-running BBC TV series of that name; a contraption that is far larger inside than is suggested by its external appearance as a police call box. The import of the Blind Beggar's nickname is that the pub would have required similar elasticity to accommodate the many thousands of EAST ENDERS who later claimed to have been there on the night that Ronnie Kray shot George Cornell (*see the* KRAY TWINS).

tart See RASPBERRY; STRAWBERRY (TART); TREACLE (TART).

Tate

Tate, Henry A Lancashire-born industrialist and philanthropist (1819–99) whose name is now inextricably linked with art. Having first built a sugar refining business in Liverpool he established the Thames Refinery at SILVERTOWN in 1877 and four years later set up home in STREATHAM. Tate's acquisition of the British rights to a French method of purifying sugar and a German process for cutting the sugar into cubes made him a fortune, much of which he used to endow colleges, hospitals and free libraries. He was a voracious collector of contemporary art, especially the works of the PRE-RAPHAELITE BROTHERHOOD, and he displayed the paintings in a gallery at his home, to which he admitted the public on Sundays. When the collection grew too large he offered to donate most of it to the nation and, on being told that the NATIONAL GALLERY lacked the space to display all 60 canvases, proposed to finance the construction of a new gallery dedicated to British art on condition the government provided the site (*see* TATE BRITAIN).

Tate bricks The name by which the installation entitled *Equivalent VIII*, by the US sculptor and poet Carl Andre (b.1935), has become popularly known. The installation, consisting of 120 firebricks arranged in a rectangle two bricks deep, was first created in 1966 and purchased by the Tate Gallery in 1972. The work was vandalized in 1976 when a visitor threw dye over it in protest at what he considered to be a waste of public money.

Tate Britain A prominent museum of art overlooking the THAMES east of PIMLICO, occupying most of the former site of MILLBANK PENITENTIARY. The building was designed by Sydney R.J. Smith and opened in 1897 as the National Gallery of British Art, soon becoming better known as the Tate Gallery, after its benefactor Sir Henry Tate (*see above*). That name was officially adopted in 1932, by which time the gallery's remit had expanded to embrace international modern art. A series of extensions to the building culminated in 1987 with the construction of the Clore Gallery, which is dedicated to the work of J.M.W. Turner. With the creation of TATE MODERN the gallery assumed its present name and reverted to displaying exclusively British art, from 1500 to the present day.

Tate Modern The national gallery of international modern art, situated in a converted power station on BANKSIDE, opposite ST PAUL'S Cathedral. The building was designed by Sir Giles Gilbert Scott and constructed in two phases, beginning in 1947. It ceased generating electricity in 1982 and reopened as a museum of art in 2000, with the TURBINE HALL forming the entrance area and the boiler house divided into galleries. Tate Modern's collection includes important paintings by the leading surrealists, abstract expressionists, minimalists and Pop artists of the 20th century as well as more recent conceptual works. The runaway success of Tate Modern has prompted plans for an entirely new building connected to the south side of the present one and the conversion of the power station's ancillary facilities: a switch station and underground oil tanks. Tate Modern 2 (also known as TM2) is scheduled for completion in 2012.

taters (in the mould) 'Cold' in COCKNEY RHYMING SLANG, usually in the context of ambient temperature. 'Taters' is short for 'potatoes'. Some users of the term do not realize it is rhyming slang, a sure sign of its entrenchment in the wider language.

> Mr Dick Lucas: A bit taters in here this morning, innit?
>
> Captain Peacock: You needn't concern yourself with the heat, Mr Lucas. Mr Rumbold is going to make an announcement about that in a few moments.
>
> DAVID CROFT and JEREMY LLOYD *Are You Being Served?* (TV comedy) (1972)

Tattersalls A name synonymous with horse racing and betting. It is that of the horseman Richard Tattersall (1724–95), who founded a firm of racehorse auctioneers at HYDE PARK CORNER in 1766. When the 99-year lease on 'The Corner' expired the business moved to Albert Gate, KNIGHTSBRIDGE, where it remained until the Second World War. Tattersalls is now based in Newmarket, Suffolk.

> Oh, yes; I stopped at Tattersall's, as I came by, and there I found Lord James Jessamy, Sir William Wilding and Mr —. But, now I think on't, you shan't know a syllable of the matter; for I have been informed you never believe above one half of what I say.
>
> HANNAH COWLEY: *The Belle's Stratagem*, I, iv (1780)

Tattycoram A character in Charles DICKENS's *Little Dorrit* (1855–7). As Harriet Beadle, she is taken in as a maid by Mr and Mrs Meagles, who rename her Tattycoram after Thomas Coram's Hospital, in BLOOMSBURY, where she had been a foundling.

Tavistock

Tavistock Clinic A mental health clinic established in TAVISTOCK SQUARE in 1920. In its early years much of the clinic's work centred on helping ex-servicemen who had been traumatized by their experiences in the First World War. The Tavistock later did pioneering work with families and its best-known practitioner was the psychiatrist R.D. Laing (1927–89). Since 2006 the clinic has been part of the Tavistock and Portman NHS Foundation Trust. It is based at the corner of Belsize Lane and FITZJOHN'S AVENUE, in SWISS COTTAGE.

Tavistock Institute An independent social science research, advisory and training organization headquartered in Tabernacle Street, near the southern end of CITY ROAD. It was founded in 1947 as a charitable sister company of the TAVISTOCK CLINIC.

Tavistock Square A square in north BLOOMSBURY, taking its name from the marquesses of Tavistock, a subsidiary title of the Russell family, owners of the BEDFORD ESTATE. It is the home of the British Medical Association, and the HOGARTH PRESS was based in the square from 1921 to 1939. The north-east corner of Tavistock Square was the scene of the bus bombing in the 7/7 terrorist attacks (*see under* SEVEN).

taxi *See* BLACK CAB.

taxi-cabs or **taxis** 'Crabs' in COCKNEY RHYMING SLANG, in the sense of pubic lice. In the singular, the term has occasionally been used to mean the more appetizing kind of crab.

taxi (rank) 'Wank' in COCKNEY RHYMING SLANG, or very occasionally 'bank'. *See also* J. ARTHUR (RANK); JODRELL (BANK).

TBH A POLARI initialism meaning 'to be had', i.e. sexually available.

TCR An increasingly popular initialism – both spoken and informally written – for TOTTENHAM COURT ROAD.

> Just saw Chandra spinning down TCR, doing the courier thing on a piece of red steel. What happened to the Dolan?
>
> forum post at www.londonfgss.com (20 March 2008)

tea The beverage was introduced to London by Amsterdam merchants in the mid-17th century. Thomas Garraway began selling tea at his COFFEE HOUSE in Change Alley (*see the* ALLEY) in 1657, and he wrote a pamphlet entitled 'An exact description of the growth, quality, and vertues of the leaf tee' (1660) to explain its origins and benefits to his perplexed customers. Samuel PEPYS gave it a try but recorded no opinion on its merits.

> And afterwards I did send for a Cupp of Tee (a China drink) of which I never had drank before, and went away.
>
> diary (25 September 1660)

The EAST INDIA COMPANY ordered its first shipment of China tea in 1669 and the product became one of its staples in the 18th century. Clippers like the CUTTY SARK later raced to bring consignments to SHAD THAMES and ST KATHARINE DOCKS. The custom of taking afternoon tea, in the sense of a light snack accompanied by a pot of tea, was popularized *c.*1840 by Anna Maria, Duchess of Bedford, although she is unlikely to have invented the idea. As prices came down, the brew's popularity spread far beyond the upper classes: tea gardens sprang up all around Victorian London, while retailers encouraged home consumption with marketing devices such as framed prints GIVEN AWAY WITH A POUND OF TEA. In the latter part of the 19th century it was estimated that 95 per cent of all British tea was sold at trade auctions in MINCING LANE, and London-based merchants like Frederick Horniman (who founded the HORNIMAN MUSEUM), Joseph Tetley and Thomas Lipton made their fortunes from the leaf. Just before the outbreak of the First World War London's grand hotels began hosting tea dances, as did William WHITELEY'S department store in 1919. Among the most prestigious places to take tea in 21st-century London are FORTNUM & MASON, the Lanesborough Hotel at HYDE PARK CORNER and the Palm Court at the RITZ HOTEL.

tea-leaf or **tealeaf** 'Thief' in long-lasting COCK-NEY RHYMING SLANG, originally restricted to pickpockets and the like, but now used more widely and often in light-hearted contexts. Although it is not abbreviated, the term has become so commonplace that many users do not realise it is rhyming slang.

> Tea-leaf: Thief. Different from a snatcher, who is a bloody hooligan. A tea-leaf treats his victim very kindly. Doesn't let him know he has been robbed. Wherever a tea-leaf goes he finds something to take.
>
> RAPHAEL SAMUEL: *East End Underworld: Chapters in the Life of Arthur Harding* (1981)

teapot (lid) 'Kid' in COCKNEY RHYMING SLANG, both as a noun meaning a child and occasionally as a verb meaning to fool (about with) someone. Like 'saucepan lid', it is also used to mean 'Yid', a derogatory word for a Jew, and 'quid', one pound sterling. And like most rhyming slang with multiple meanings, the term is not widely used.

Tecton (Greek *tektōn*, 'builder') A pioneering architectural practice founded in London in 1932. The left-leaning group was brought together by the Russian émigré Berthold Lubetkin (1901–90), in collaboration with six British architects, of whom the most distinguished was Denys Lasdun (1914–2001). During the 1930s Tecton designed the gorilla house and penguin pool for LONDON ZOO, Highpoint One and Two in HIGHGATE for the copier king Sigmund Gestetner, a health centre for the progressive Metropolitan Borough of FINSBURY and several housing schemes. The group re-formed after the Second World War but its modernist style did not suit the conservative political climate and the partnership dissolved in 1948. Lubetkin went into semi-retirement, while Lasdun continued to produce important works, notably the NATIONAL THEATRE.

Teddington A large and comfortable Victorian suburb located south of TWICKENHAM. It was first documented in the 11th century, although it is not mentioned in Domesday Book, and its name probably derives from words meaning 'farmstead of a man called Tuda'. The popular theory that the name means 'tide end town', referring to its position on the THAMES, is neat but untrue. In the Middle Ages the village grew near the river, around St Mary's Church and the manor house. There was a fishing weir on the thames at Teddington between 1345 and *c.*1535. Teddington Lock was constructed in 1811 and marks the end of the tidal reach of the Thames. It was rebuilt with an additional side-lock in 1857. In that same year the author R.D. Blackmore (1825–1900) bought Gomer House, now demolished. He established a peach orchard there and wrote numerous novels, including the romantic adventure story *Lorna Doone* (1869). The actor and dramatist Noël Coward (1899–1973) was born in Teddington. *See also the* NATIONAL PHYSICAL LABORATORY.

Teddington Hockey Club A field hockey club based at Teddington School. It began in 1871 as a winter activity for members of Teddington Cricket Club, playing its early games in BUSHY PARK, and is the world's oldest hockey club with a continuous history.

Teddington Studios A television production facility situated between Broom Road and the THAMES in north-east Teddington. The studios began making silent films before the First World War and boomed after Warner Bros leased and then bought the operation in the 1930s, when it was said to have produced 10 per cent of British films. The complex was substantially rebuilt after being bombed during the Second World War and began making television shows in 1958. TV comedy series produced at Teddington have included MAN ABOUT THE HOUSE, GEORGE AND MILDRED, MEN BEHAVING BADLY and BLACK BOOKS.

Templar A student or lawyer, living or with chambers, in the TEMPLE. *See also the* KNIGHTS TEMPLAR.

Temple An autonomous district of the CITY of London, composed of two of the four INNS OF COURT, situated south of the western half of FLEET STREET. The KNIGHTS TEMPLAR established a church and residential quarters by the river around 1160. Temple Church was built in two phases and completed in 1240. The order's clergy occupied a consecrated precinct on the east side of the church and the knights, squires and various lay brothers lived to the south and west. The order was suppressed in 1312 and Parliament voted its buildings to the KNIGHTS HOSPITALLER, who leased them to students of law. By the late 14th century the lawyers had organized themselves into two societies, known as the INNER TEMPLE and MIDDLE TEMPLE. Most of the medieval buildings were destroyed in the GREAT FIRE OF LONDON and in three subsequent fires in the second half of the 17th century and the Temple was rebuilt to a more collegiate plan. The grounds were extended southwards with the construction of the Victoria EMBANKMENT in 1870, when Temple station opened (originally as The Temple). The Temple and its church were badly bomb-damaged during the Second World War but sensitive restoration has preserved the other-worldly intimacy of this enclave. Law is no longer taught here and barristers' chambers occupy most of the buildings.

> ... those bricky towers
> The which on Thames' broad aged back do ride,
> Where now the studious lawyers have their bowers,
> There whilom wont the Templar Knights to bide,
> Till they decay'd through pride ...
>
> EDMUND SPENSER: 'Prothalamion' (1596)

Temple Bar A location at the point where FLEET STREET becomes the STRAND, marking the western limit of the CITY of London. A barrier is first recorded here in the late 13th century (*barram Novi Templi*). This seems to have been nothing more than a chain between two posts, but by the middle of the 14th century there was an arched gateway here, with a prison on top. This survived the GREAT FIRE OF LONDON, but was nevertheless demolished, and a new one was erected in the 1670s to a design by Christopher Wren. In the late 17th century it became the practice to display the heads of traitors impaled on spikes on top of the gate (it was quite a high gate, and those who wanted to get a better view could hire a telescope for a halfpenny). The last shrivelled head apparently fell off *c*.1772. By the middle of the 19th century Temple Bar's central arch was becoming too much of an

impediment to traffic, and in 1878 it was re-moved. It was later re-erected in Theobalds Park, Hertfordshire, where it remained for more than a hundred years. In 2004 it was returned to the City, incorporated into the PATERNOSTER SQUARE redevelopment. While the arch itself has gone, its location retains its symbolic significance: a sovereign who wishes to enter the City via Fleet Street, typically on his or her processional way to ST PAUL's Cathedral, must stop here and ask permission of the LORD MAYOR OF LONDON. The line is marked by a memorial in the centre of the road, erected in 1880, and surmounted by a DRAGON that is frequently misidentified as a GRIFFIN.

Temple Mills A regenerated area beside the River LEA in west LEYTON, formerly dominated by industry, commerce and railway yards. A crossing point on the river brought early human activity and evidence has been found of a Roman camp nearby. In 1185 William of Hastings, steward to Henry II, granted land here to the KNIGHTS TEMPLAR, who later built wooden watermills. After the dissolution of the order in the 14th century their property passed through a variety of hands (including the Crown's) and milling and related agricultural industries continued to grow. In the latter part of the 19th century the mills were demolished and the Great Eastern wagon works were moved northwards from STRATFORD, with marshalling yards spreading inexorably. In the late 1950s the works were the largest in Britain. Temple Mills is presently being transformed for the 2012 OLYMPIC GAMES.

Temple of Apollo A place of Roman worship said to have occupied the site of WESTMINSTER ABBEY, and to have been aligned with the TEMPLE OF DIANA on LUDGATE HILL.

Temple of Diana According to an old legend, the Romans built a temple dedicated to their goddess Diana on the site now occupied by ST PAUL's Cathedral, probably at the time of the Diocletian persecution of Christians in the early 4th century. Excavations in the mid-14th century revealed an enormous quantity of animal bones, together with 'instruments and vessels', possibly remnants from sacrifices to the goddess. One or more effigies of Diana are said to have been found in the vicinity. Christopher Wren found no evidence of either the temple or the sacrifices during his own deep excavations for the construction of the present cathedral and contemptuously dismissed the fable.

Temple of Health or **Hymen** An exclusive resort established in 1781 at Schomberg House, 81 PALL MALL, by James Graham (1745–94), a quack doctor. The admission fee was a startling two guineas. The air was filled with music and perfume, Graham lectured on health and sold 'medicines', while scantily clad young women posed among statues. One of these models was Emma Lyon, later Horatio Nelson's mistress Lady Hamilton. For £50, a patron and his partner could spend the night in the Celestial Bed, which was about four times the size of a normal double bed and was said by Graham to guarantee fruitfulness of the loins. The mattress was filled with sweet new wheat, rose leaves, lavender flowers and hair from the tails of fine English stallions. Behind the lovers, magnetically induced electricity crackled across the headboard of the bed, allegedly giving the necessary degree of strength and exertion to the nerves. Although successful, the Temple of Health was not sufficiently profitable to eradicate Graham's debts and in 1784 he closed it down and moved to Edinburgh.

Temple of Mithras A Roman ruin discovered on the bank of the WALBROOK stream during rebuilding work in 1954. Erected sometime in the mid-3rd century AD, the temple appears to have been dedicated to Mithras, the god of light of the ancient Persians, and possibly to other gods too. Mithras is represented as a young man wearing a Phrygian cap and plunging daggers into the neck of a bull that lies upon the ground. In order to permit the postwar construction work to proceed, the ruins were uplifted and reassembled at an open-air site on Queen Victoria Street, just east of its junction with Queen Street. There are plans to relocate the temple closer to its original site, as part of a mixed-use scheme called Walbrook Square, should that project proceed.

temple-pickling An underworld slang term from the late 17th century to the early 19th for the ducking of court officials beneath a pump; in the 17th century any bailiff caught within the precincts of the TEMPLE was automatically punished in this way.

Temple Street The nickname of a temporary 'street' created on the frozen THAMES during the great frost of 1683/4. Temple Street consisted of a double row of tents stretching across the river from Temple Stairs and was the main centre of activity for that winter's FROST FAIR.

> 'Blanket-fair, or, The history of Temple Street being a relation of the merry pranks plaid on the River Thames during the great frost'
>
> title of a ballad printed and sold on the ice (1684)

ten

10 Downing Street See DOWNING STREET; NUMBER TEN.

10 Rillington Place See RILLINGTON PLACE.

Terry and June An undemanding BBC TV sitcom that ran for nine seasons between 1979 and 1987. Terry Scott and June Whitfield played a middle-aged couple living in PURLEY.

Tesco The third largest grocery retailer in the world. The business began in Well Street market, South HACKNEY, where WHITECHAPEL-born Jack Cohen (1898–1979) made his first sales from a hired barrow in 1919. His opening day's profit was £1, on sales of £4. In 1924 he launched an 'own label' product, Tesco tea, creating the brand name from the initials of his supplier, T.E. Stockwell, and the first two letters of his own surname. Cohen opened the inaugural Tesco store in 1929, in BURNT OAK. The company's first headquarters was in Angel Road, EDMONTON; it subsequently moved north to Cheshunt, Hertfordshire. Tesco floated on the STOCK EXCHANGE in 1947 and nowadays operates more than 2,000 stores in the UK and almost as many again overseas, with total annual sales in excess of £50 billion. *See also* SLASHER JACK.

Testicle, the (Glass) See EGG, THE (GLASS).

Thames (Old English *Temese*, from Latin *Tamesa*, *Tamesis*; ultimately perhaps from an Indo-European river name, from a word meaning 'to flow turbidly') The longest river entirely in England (and the second-longest in the United Kingdom, after the Severn), it rises at Thames Head, at the foot of the Cotswolds, flows 210 miles (338 km) in a broadly south-easterly direction through Lechlade (where its headstreams unite), Oxford and Windsor, and then flows eastward through London, beyond which it widens into the Thames Estuary, and enters the North Sea at the Nore. The Thames is tidal as far as TEDDINGTON and there are 20 road and 10 rail bridges between HAMPTON COURT and the TOWER OF LONDON.

From its mouth upstream as far as KEW the river is divided into 28 sections known as 'reaches' (*see, for example,* GALLIONS REACH).

London grew because it was the first place up-river that could be bridged and the highest point to which large cargo vessels could be brought. The Thames has always played a key role in the capital's – and hence the country's – life: the conduit for vital exports and imports; the gateway to a wider world (including a far-flung empire); a daily thoroughfare for all, from the lowest to the highest; and witness to many of Britain's most significant moments of the past two millennia; the Romans bridged it during their period of occupation and it provided the water to put out the fires of the BLITZ. The Thames in London has performed other less noble but no less important functions too: it was once the ultimate dumping ground for most of the capital's sewage, until the noisome years leading up to the GREAT STINK OF LONDON galvanized Parliament into having a modern sewerage system built.

Until the 1960s the Thames was still busy with coal barges, and cranes still bent over riverside wharves in the heart of the capital. Then, almost in the blink of an eye, it was over. The river's work evaporated, the docks closed and the Thames became, it seemed, the forgotten river – little more than an obstacle to be traversed in getting from one side to the other. Londoners appeared to have averted their eyes from their river: certainly, sporadic attempts to set up river-based transport links met with tepid support. Yet the sinuous looping Thames remains central to the idea of London – unmistakable alike to those who fly along its course on their way to HEATHROW and to those who see it in the opening and closing credits of EASTENDERS. So iconic is it that it is frequently used in graphic devices representing the capital, sometimes without the need for any embellishment whatsoever.

Thames & Hudson A still-independent publishing house famous for its art books. It was founded in 1949 with offices in London and New York, hoping to attract an English-speaking readership on both sides of the Atlantic – hence its name, from the rivers on which London and New York respectively stand. The origin is also pictorially represented in its colophon of two dolphins, the upper one facing left or west, the lower right or east.

Thames barge A type of round-bowed, flat-bottomed, massively strong sailing barge used on the Thames in the 19th and early 20th centuries. Its most distinctive rig is a 'spritsail', a huge tarred canvas mainsail stretched diagonally by a spar. Thames barges are still kept and sailed recreationally by enthusiasts.

Thames Barrier A movable barrier across the River Thames at WOOLWICH Reach that forms part of London's flood defences. A GREATER LONDON COUNCIL project, it became operational in October 1982, was first used in February 1983 and was officially opened by HM the Queen on 8 May 1984. The width of the barrier from the south bank at New CHARLTON to the north bank at SILVERTOWN is about 1,700 feet (520m). Its central section consists of two large and four massive floodgates that can be raised when dangerously high tides are expected. When not in use these gates rest out of sight in curved recesses in the riverbed. The engine houses of the piers to which the gates are attached are roofed with helmet-like stainless steel shells that give the barrier its distinctive appearance.

Thamesbeat A south-west London music scene that has surfaced intermittently since the late 1970s. Like the TOTTENHAM SOUND, an earlier 'answer' to Liverpool's Merseybeat, the genre has existed more in the minds of rock journalists than as a cohesively identifiable reality. Artists associated with Thamesbeat in recent years have included the Mystery Jets (a band formed on EEL PIE ISLAND), Larrikin Love and Jamie T.

> He'll probably hate me for saying it, but rising punk-pop star Jamie T is the Jamie Oliver of the new Thamesbeat scene, bursting out all over with infectious nice-guy-getting-stuck-in, estuary-English enthusiasms.
>
> HELEN BROWN, in *The Daily Telegraph* (12 April 2007)

Thames butter Late 19th-century slang for totally rancid butter. The term seems to have arisen out of a garbled contemporary press report to the effect that a French chemist was making butter out of Thames mud at BATTERSEA. In fact he was extracting yellow grease from Thames mud-worms.

Thames Conservancy A body set up by Act of Parliament in 1857 to be responsible for all aspects of the administration and control of the River Thames. It replaced the former Thames Commissioners. Powers relating to the tidal part of the river (downstream of TEDDINGTON) passed in 1909 to the PORT OF LONDON AUTHORITY, and its jurisdiction over the rest of the river was transferred in 1974 to the Thames Water Authority.

Thames Embankment *See the* EMBANKMENT.

Thames Gateway A planners' designation for a corridor extending either side of the Thames in outer east London and beyond. The Thames Gateway is the proposed site for a raft of projects that will create mixed residential communities by attracting people on a range of incomes, as well as providing employment areas and shopping and leisure facilities. Most of the building in GREATER LONDON will take place on former industrial land, some of which is at risk from flooding. Up to 120,000 new homes may be built by 2016.

Thames House The headquarters since 1995 of MI5, situated on MILLBANK, near the PALACE OF WESTMINSTER. The building was originally owned by Imperial Chemical Industries, the chemical and paint manufacturer, and its design is similar to that of Nobel House on the other side of Horseferry Road, which was also built for ICI at the same time. Thames House is nowhere near as flamboyant as the headquarters of MI5's sister service, MI6, at VAUXHALL CROSS.

Thames Ironworks The leading shipbuilders of Victorian London. Shipwright Thomas J. Ditchburn (1801–70) and engineer and naval architect Charles Mare (1815–98) founded the business in DEPTFORD in 1837 and in the following year relocated to LEAMOUTH. Ditchburn and Mare graduated from building paddle steamers to warships, and expanded to the ESSEX side of Bow Creek at CANNING TOWN, eventually occupying a 30-acre (12-hectare) site. After a period of insolvency the business was reborn under new ownership in 1857 as the Thames Ironworks and Shipbuilding and Engineering Company, building mail steamers and warships that successively broke tonnage records. It also cast the ironwork for bridges (including WESTMINSTER BRIDGE), railway stations and exhibition halls and built more than 200 lifeboats for the RNLI. Thirty-eight spectators died at the ironworks when the slipway collapsed at the launch of the warship HMS *Albion* in 1898. In the early 20th century the company found itself constrained by limitations in the size of ships it could build beside the Thames and faced increasingly aggressive competition from northern shipyards, especially on the Tyne and Clyde. After completing one last big contract – HMS *Thunderer* – Thames Ironworks closed in 1912.

The company's patriarchal chairman, Arnold Hills (1857–1927), encouraged a wide range of sporting activities among his employees, most notably in the form of Thames Ironworks FC, formed in 1895 and relaunched as WEST HAM UNITED FC in 1900.

Thameslink A railway service linking Bedford and BRIGHTON via London. It was started in 1989 following the reopening of the SNOW HILL Tunnel beneath central London. Expansion of the service in the early 21st century was planned under the title Thameslink 2000 but that project did not get properly under way until 2009.

Thamesmead Once dubbed the 'town of the 21st century', Thamesmead is a vast agglomeration of municipal and private housing estates, with some peripheral industry, situated on former marshland between WOOLWICH and ERITH. Its name was the winning entry in a newspaper competition. After the land was vacated by the military, the GREATER LONDON COUNCIL developed Thamesmead spasmodically from the mid-1960s to the early 1980s. The topography is dominated by a series of lakes and canals that drain surface water and relieve the starkness of the built environment. The founders' vision of a futuristic community was later discarded in favour of traditional British suburban housebuilding and, because of the switch from tower blocks to conventional houses, forecasts of Thamesmead's final population have halved from the original target of 100,000.

Thames Path A national trail that runs alongside the Thames from its source to the THAMES BARRIER, a distance of about 180 miles (288 km).

Thames Television A television broadcaster that between 1968 and 1991 held the ITV weekday franchise for the London region. Amongst its biggest hits were *The* SWEENEY and MINDER. Its studios were at TEDDINGTON. As half of Talkback Thames (ultimately part of the RTL Group), it continues as a television production company, with studios in MERTON.

Thames Tideway *See* TIDEWAY.

Thames Tunnel

1. A tunnel beneath the River Thames linking ROTHERHITHE with WAPPING. It was the first underwater tunnel in the world. Plans for it were produced at the beginning of the 19th

century, but work did not get under way until the mid-1820s, under the direction of Marc Isambard Brunel. There were many delays due to flooding, and work was suspended altogether between 1828 and 1835 when the money ran out, but it was finally finished in 1843. At first it was used only by pedestrians, but in the 1860s it was converted into a railway tunnel. It now carries the EAST LONDON LINE.

2. The main tunnel planned for construction as part of the TIDEWAY TUNNELS project. It is provisionally scheduled for completion around 2020.

Father Thames *See under* FATHER.

Great Thames Disaster *See the* PRINCESS ALICE.

set the Thames on fire, to *See under* SET.

Thavies Inn or **Davies Inn** An INN OF CHANCERY that stood near present-day HOLBORN Circus. The poet John Donne read law at Thavies Inn. It was founded in the mid-14th century and named after John Thavie (or various other spellings), an 'honest and liberal-minded' armourer who was the original landlord. Thavie was of Welsh origin and it appears that many of the inn's early law students were his fellow countrymen. Thavies Inn belonged to LINCOLN'S INN from some time before 1422 until 1771. The dilapidated college buildings were thereafter replaced by a group of tall houses collectively known as Thavies Inn, which was occupied by 'various classes of persons' and, for a while, an 'anatomical theatre' of dubious repute. The houses were bombed in the BLITZ and an office building called Thavies Inn House now fills part of their site.

> The house in Thavies Inn had bills in the windows announcing that it was to let, and it looked dirtier and gloomier and ghastlier than ever.
>
> DICKENS: *Bleak House* (1852–3)

theatre

Theatre, The London's first purpose-built playhouse, built in 1576 by James Burbage at what is now New Inn Broadway, SHOREDITCH. Excavations beneath a disused warehouse, conducted by MUSEUM OF LONDON archaeologists in 2008–9, appear to indicate that it was a timber-framed polygonal structure on a masonry foundation. Many historians believe that William SHAKESPEARE's first plays were performed here,

with the author himself among the cast. Following a disagreement between Burbage and his landlord in 1598, the Theatre was dismantled and its timbers were taken to BANKSIDE, where they were used to construct the GLOBE. The Tower Theatre Company, a non-professional theatre organization, plans to build a 21st-century equivalent of the Theatre on the Shoreditch site, opening in 2012.

Theatreland A media and tourist industry term for the quarter in which most of the WEST END's playhouses are to be found, centred on CAMBRIDGE CIRCUS and SHAFTESBURY AVENUE. The theatres are mostly of Victorian construction and the term was introduced by the *Daily Chronicle* in its issue of 28 December 1905. There is no agreed definition of the extent of Theatreland but it is widely considered to extend south as far as the HAYMARKET and east to the ALDWYCH. The City of WESTMINSTER captions selected street signs with a Theatreland logo.

Theatre Royal, Covent Garden The identity until 1892 of what then became the ROYAL OPERA HOUSE.

Theatre Royal, Drury Lane A COVENT GARDEN theatre located at the corner of DRURY LANE and Catherine Street. It is the fourth on the site; the first was built by the dramatist Thomas Killigrew under charter from Charles II and opened in 1663. The Theatre Royal burned down in the early 1670s and was rebuilt with almost three times its original capacity. The actor David GARRICK and writer Richard Brinsley Sheridan managed the theatre in the second half of the 18th century and it was rebuilt again in 1794 and finally in 1812. It later became renowned for its Victorian melodramas but since the 1920s has mostly hosted musicals, notably MY FAIR LADY, *Miss Saigon* and *Oliver!*

Theatre Royal, Haymarket A theatre situated near the southern end of the HAYMARKET, on the east side. It was established in 1720 on a site a little to the north of the present-day structure and was earlier known as the New or Little Theatre, and as the Haymarket Theatre. The present theatre was designed by John Nash and opened in 1821.

Thellusson

Thellusson, Peter An exceptionally wealthy French-Swiss banker (1737–97) who ran a finance house in Philpot Lane, near the MONUMENT, and in 1777 acquired the PLAISTOW[2] estate, BROMLEY. He wrote the most complex will in English history, which forced an immediate change in testamentary law (*see below*) and may have provided inspiration for the Jarndyce and Jarndyce CHANCERY case in Charles DICKENS's novel *Bleak House* (1852–3). Thellusson's eldest son was made 1st Baron Rendlesham in 1806.

Thellusson Act An Act (1800) to prevent testators from leaving their property to accumulate for more than 21 years. It was passed in reference to the will of Peter Thellusson (*see above*), who left £600,000 and £4,500 a year to accumulate for the benefit of his eldest great-grandson after the death of all his sons and grandsons. The last grandson died in 1856, and the expense of the legal actions that followed swallowed up all the accumulated interest, so that Thellusson's eldest son's eldest grandson received barely the amount of the original legacy. It was better known as the Accumulations Act and was replaced by the Law of Property Act 1925.

they

They Came from SW19 A comic novel (1992) by Nigel Williams. It revolves around events at the fictional First Church of Christ the Spiritualist, South WIMBLEDON. The locality at one time had more Nonconformist adherents than Anglicans, though few of a spiritualist persuasion.

they had no choice The closing words of the main inscription on the wall of *Animals In War*, a memorial located near HYDE PARK's Brook Gate, on PARK LANE. Designed by the sculptor David Backhouse (b.1941), it is carved from Portland stone and accompanied by bronze statues of two mules, a horse and a dog. A national appeal raised the £2 million required to fund the memorial, which was unveiled by the Princess Royal in 2004.

> This monument is dedicated to all the animals that served and died alongside British and allied forces in wars and campaigns throughout time. They had no choice.

they shall not pass The slogan of anti-fascist protesters at the BATTLE OF CABLE STREET (4 October 1936). It was borrowed from the cry of the Republicans in the Spanish Civil War: *no pasarán*.

thief

Thiefrow A rhyming nickname (first recorded in

1973) for HEATHROW AIRPORT, from its reputation at the time for lax security and lost or purloined luggage. The cargo area in particular has often been the target of thieves and London's biggest ever robbery took place here in 1983, when £26 million worth of gold bullion and diamonds was stolen from the Brinks-Mat high security vault; most of the gold was never recovered. Security is nowadays a little better.

Thief-Taker General The self-styled title of Jonathan Wild (*c*.1683–1725), a Wolverhampton-born buckle-maker who settled in London *c*.1709. After serving time as a debtor in Wood Street Compter he moved to COVENT GARDEN and set himself up as an agent who could recover stolen property in return for a fractional fee, and apprehend the thieves. His success enabled him to establish a national network of operatives, and his men famously captured Jack SHEPPARD on several occasions in 1724. Wild at first enjoyed great acclaim for his deeds but the public turned against him, initially because of the brutality of his methods, and then because it was discovered that he had commissioned many of the crimes he purported to have solved, and had run a clearing house for ill-gotten goods. In May 1725 he was found guilty at the OLD BAILEY of taking £10 for returning a length of stolen lace to its owner when he had in fact instigated the theft. Wild was hanged at TYBURN and his body was afterwards dissected. His skeleton is kept on display at the HUNTERIAN MUSEUM.

thieves' kitchen A generic name for a squalid hideout in which thieves cook up their schemes, especially applied to FAGIN's den in OLIVER TWIST. Also, BLACK CAB drivers' slang for the STOCK EXCHANGE, dating from a period when fraudulent trading was particularly widespread.

Thieves' Market A nickname for the old CALEDONIAN MARKET. It operated under the medieval law of 'market overt' (or *marché ouvert*), which guaranteed a buyer title of ownership provided an item was bought in good faith, even if it later turned out to have been stolen. The same law subsequently applied to the New Caledonian Market in BERMONDSEY; it was abolished by the Sale of Goods (Amendment) Act 1994. Some have suggested that Bermondsey market suffered a damaging drop in business as a result of the law's abolition.

> The Bill has one simple, but important, aim – to

outlaw the practice of market overt. Members on both sides of the House will know that if goods in Bermondsey market, which is the one that is almost always quoted, are bought between sunrise and sunset, the title of the goods purchased passes to the purchaser, regardless of the origin of the goods. The market has been castigated as a thieves' den for that reason.

PATRICK CORMACK, addressing the House of Commons (15 July 1994)

thirteen houses, fourteen cuckolds and never a house between STRAND ON THE GREEN at one time, allegedly. The extra cuckold was a son who lived with his parents, or perhaps just with his father. The saying was first recorded in 1602 and subsequently appeared in several dictionaries of proverbs.

Thomas

Thomas More 'Whore' in old COCKNEY RHYMING SLANG. However, this is unlikely to be the origin of the same sense of the word 'tom'.

Thomas Tilling 'Shilling' in pre-decimalization COCKNEY RHYMING SLANG. *See also* TIMES BUSES.

St Thomas' Hospital *See under* SAINT.

Thorney Island A former area of low-lying marshy land on the north bank of the THAMES, where WESTMINSTER ABBEY now stands. 'Thorney' is a corruption of 'thorn tree'. It appears to have been characterized as an 'island' on account of the ditches that surrounded and defined it, but its precise outline is no longer clear. It was an open, desolate area in Anglo-Saxon times (it is described in an 8th-century charter as *loco terribili*, 'at the terrible place'), but after the 1060s, when Edward the Confessor re-established the abbey here and built himself a royal palace, it was gradually reclaimed and it came to be filled with smallholdings and market gardens. There were still open fields here in the 18th century, but since then the buildings of Westminster have obliterated all trace of Thorney Island.

Thornton Heath A sprawling SOUTH LONDON suburb extending from the edge of SELHURST PARK in the east to POLLARDS HILL in the west. The heath was originally common land covering 36 acres (15 hectares) and stretching northwards towards NORBURY, with a pond used for watering horses and cattle. Charcoal burners carried water from the pond along what is now Colliers Water Lane. The road across the heath was infested with highwaymen in the 17th and 18th centuries, and Dick TURPIN is said to have operated here. Despite progressive rebuilding throughout the 20th century, much of late Victorian Thornton Heath survives, although the area has not succumbed to significant GENTRIFICATION.

Thousand Pound church A nickname for the former Christ Church, LANCASTER GATE, from the handsome sums collected from the wealthy congregation every Sunday. Dry rot led to the demolition of the body of the church in 1978 and the spire now finds itself attached to an ecclesiastical-looking block of flats.

Threadneedle Street A street in the CITY of London, connecting the junction at BANK with BISHOPSGATE to the east. The name probably relates to the street's early role as a centre of the tailoring trade; the Merchant Taylors' Company's hall has been here since the 14th century. However, contrary to a much-repeated fallacy, neither a thread nor a needle appear in the Merchant Taylors' coat of arms. The name first appears in 1598 as Three Needle Street and if this spelling is reliable there may be a link with the arms of the Needlemakers' Company, in which three needles appear, or with a signboard depicting three needles that hung outside the Merchant Taylors' hall. A less likely possibility is that it derives from the children's game of thread-the-needle having been played here. Threadneedle Street seems previously to have been called Broad Street, forming part of what is now Old Broad Street. It is sometimes claimed that the street was earlier called Gropecuntelane, from the presence of medieval brothels. However, although there was indeed such a lane in the vicinity of CHEAP in the 13th and 14th centuries, its precise location has not been confirmed and its alignment may not have corresponded with that of any present-day street. The BANK OF ENGLAND has occupied much of the northern side of Threadneedle Street since 1734.

Old Lady of Threadneedle Street *See under* OLD.

three

three blind mice 'Rice' in very dated COCKNEY RHYMING SLANG.

three-card trick A game, also known as 'find the lady' or 'three-card monte', in which bets are placed on which is the queen of three cards lying face downwards. The gullible punter never wins. The swindle was traditionally worked by grafters on OXFORD STREET but is rarely seen there nowadays.

Three Cranes in the Vintry An ancient CITY inn that stood on what is now Queen Street, in the ward of VINTRY. The hostelry was earlier called the Painted Tavern, from the 'circumstance of its outer walls being fancifully coloured and adorned with Bacchanalian devices'. The Painted Tavern was said to have been a haunt of the future Henry IV in the late 14th century. There is some dispute regarding its next name – possibly the Crane, or the Crown or Three Crowns – but it later became the Three Cranes, with a signboard showing three long-necked birds, each with a golden fish in its bill. Most authorities claim that this was a punning allusion to the three wooden cranes installed at Vintry wharf for offloading butts and hogsheads of wine. The Three Cranes had a rough reputation in certain respects but, unsurprisingly, was said to have kept very good wine.

'Less than superlative?' said Giles Gosling, drinking off the cup, and smacking his lips with an air of ineffable relish, – 'I know nothing of superlative, nor is there such a wine at the Three Cranes, in the Vintry, to my knowledge; but if you find better sack than that in the Sheres, or in the Canaries either, I would I may never touch either pot or penny more.'

SIR WALTER SCOTT: *Kenilworth* (1821)

three devils of St Peter See the CORNHILL DEVILS.

three golden balls The once familiar pawnbroker's sign is said to have been taken from the coat of arms of the Medici family and first introduced to London by the LOMBARD bankers and moneylenders. The positioning of the balls was popularly explained in that there were two chances to one that what was brought to 'uncle' would be redeemed.

I say to myself each day
In definitely Marble Halls,
Today it may be three white feathers,
But yesterday it was three brass balls.

NOËL COWARD: *Set to Music* (1938)

Three Mills An industrial island formed by the dividing and recombining tributaries and channels of the River LEA, situated in MILL MEADS between BROMLEY-BY-BOW and WEST HAM. Three Mills' name was in use from the 16th century but none of the structures from that period have survived and only two mills have stood here for much of the time since then. House Mill, which dates from 1776, is the largest watermill in Britain and its milled grain was a source of much of London's flour – and gin. The more picturesque Clock Mill was rebuilt in 1817 from an earlier mill.

Three Mills Studios Film and television studios owned by the London Development Agency. Productions here have included the television series *Footballers' Wives* (see EARLS PARK) and *Bad Girls* and the feature films *28 Days Later*, LOCK, STOCK AND TWO SMOKING BARRELS and *Tim Burton's Corpse Bride*. This was also the site of the *Big Brother* house, used for the first two series of the Channel 4 reality show before its relocation to Elstree in Hertfordshire.

Three Needle Street See THREADNEEDLE STREET.

threepenny bit building See the 50P BUILDING (*under* FIFTY).

threepenny bits 'Tits' (breasts) in COCKNEY RHYMING SLANG, often abbreviated to 'thrupennies'. The reference is to a pre-decimalization coin. Like the word it signifies, 'thrupennies' is employed figuratively as well as anatomically, for example in expressions such as 'he/she gets on my thrupennies', signifying irritation with someone. 'Bristols' (*see* BRISTOL (CITY)) has become a more popular alternative in literal usage.

The whole point about Abi Titmuss is that she seemed different from the rest. She wasn't a hanger-on, she wasn't a vacuous dolly bird who needed to get her thrupennies out to make men notice her.

Sunday Mirror (10 August 2003)

threepenny-bus In Bunthorne and Grosvenor's duet in *Patience* (1881) W.S. Gilbert uses the epithet to signify conventionality:

A Chancery Lane young man,
A Somerset House young man,
A very delectable, highly respectable,
Threepenny-bus young man!

Competition between London bus operators had brought formerly disparate fares down to a standard 3d at the time. For the 1900 revival of

Patience, Gilbert changed 'threepenny-bus' to 'TWOPENNY-TUBE'.

Threepenny Opera *See the* BEGGAR'S OPERA.

Three 'R's, The Reading, writing and arithmetic. The phrase is said to have been originated by Sir William Curtis (1752–1829), an illiterate ALDERMAN and LORD MAYOR OF LONDON, who gave this as a toast, i.e. 'Riting, Reading and Rithmetic'.

three stops down from Plaistow A contemporary expression meaning 'mad', in reference to PLAISTOW underground station's separation from BARKING (as in 'barking mad') on the DISTRICT LINE. This is not a widely used expression because it is too obtuse. The more direct 'ONE STOP SHORT OF BARKING' is heard more often.

three tailors of Tooley Street The statesman George Canning (1770–1827) recounted that three tailors of TOOLEY STREET once addressed a petition of grievances to the House of Commons, beginning: 'We, the people of England'. Hence the phrase came to be used of any pettifogging coterie that fancied it represented the nation.

> It is at such lecturing and debating work, and on squalid little committees and ridiculous little delegations to conferences of the three tailors of Tooley Street, with perhaps a deputation to the Mayor thrown in once in a blue moon or so, that the ordinary Fabian workman or clerk must qualify for his future seat on the Town Council, the School Board, or perhaps in the Cabinet.
>
> GEORGE BERNARD SHAW, addressing the Conference of Fabian Societies (6 February 1892)

three Yahoos of Twickenham Henry Bolingbroke's nickname for the writers Alexander Pope, John Gay and Jonathan Swift. Pope lived at TWICKENHAM, in a house he called 'my TUSCULUM', and Gay and Swift were frequently among his guests.

Tottenham Three *See under* TOTTENHAM.

Throgmorton Street A street in the CITY of London, running to the north of and parallel to THREADNEEDLE STREET, named after Sir Nicholas Throckmorton (1515–71), Elizabeth I's ambassador to France and Scotland. The south side was occupied by the STOCK EXCHANGE until 2004, and the name of the street was formerly employed as a metonym for the Stock Exchange or for the financial world of the City of London in general (the City column of *The Observer* was called 'Throg Street').

Tiara Triangle A nickname for the high-class shopping streets of BROMPTON and KNIGHTSBRIDGE. The nodes of the triangle lie in the vicinity of HARVEY NICKS, SLOANE SQUARE and the Michelin building at the top of the FULHAM ROAD. A narrower definition focuses on Brompton Cross, the confluence of streets around the Michelin building, where 'bespoke design outlets' predominate.

tich or **titch** *See* LITTLE TICH.

Tiddy Doll The sobriquet of John Ford (d.1752), 'the king of itinerant tradesmen', a flamboyant baker and hawker of gingerbread. He gained the name from his repetitious renditions of a popular ballad that ended with those words as a kind of 'fol-de-rol'. William HOGARTH depicted him, gingerbread in hand, at the TYBURN execution of the 'Idle Prentice' (1747). When Tiddy Doll once went missing from his regular spot in the HAYMARKET, because he was visiting a country fair, an account of his alleged murder was quickly printed and sold in the thousands. He was an annual presence at the event that gave MAYFAIR its name and attended the FROST FAIR of 1739/40, where it was rumoured that he had died in the manner of DOLL THE PIPPIN WOMAN. James Gillray drew a famous caricature (1806) of Napoleon as Tiddy Doll, baking a new batch of kings. Richard Grenville-Temple, 2nd Earl Temple (1711–79), was nicknamed Tiddy Doll for his cavalier manners.

> He is quite the Tiddy Doll! This saying originated from a celebrated vendor of gingerbread, who frequented the fairs in and about London, during the last century, and who affected the fine gentleman by an extravagance of dress.
>
> WILLIAM PULLEYN: *The Etymological Compendium* (1830)

Tideway The tidal stretch of the THAMES that extends from TEDDINGTON Lock through central London to the North Sea, a distance of almost 100 miles (160 km).

Tideway Tunnels A major capital project designed to capture storm sewage and reduce the quantity discharged into the THAMES. Two separate, deep-level tunnels are planned, costing a total of more than £2 billion. The Lee Tunnel (as the planners have chosen to spell it) will run 4 miles (6.5 km) underground (not under the River LEA) from ABBEY MILLS to BECKTON, where the capacity of the existing sewage works will be enhanced. The Thames Tunnel will be much larger, extending approximately 20 miles (32 km) from the vicinity of HAMMERSMITH to Beckton, broadly following the path of the river. Construction of the Lee Tunnel is scheduled for completion in 2014; the Thames Tunnel may be completed by 2020.

Tilbury A once fashionable well-sprung, two-wheeled horse carriage or gig, without top or cover, designed by John Tilbury, of Dove House Farm, HATCH END, in the early 19th century. Napoleon III of France visited Dove House and copied its stables for those that he built for his palace at Chantilly.

Tilbury Docks 'Pox' in outdated COCKNEY RHYMING SLANG, in the sense of a sexually transmitted disease, usually abbreviated to 'the Tilburys'. SURREY DOCKS and others have been used to the same effect. 'Tilbury Docks' was also formerly used to mean 'socks'.

Till Death Us Do Part *See* GARNETT, ALF.

times

times buses The nickname of Thomas Tilling's buses. HENDON-born Thomas Tilling (1825–93) founded his omnibus service in 1851, initially operating between Rye Lane in PECKHAM and OXFORD CIRCUS. An emphasis on predetermined stopping points and strict adherence to a timetable prompted the 'times buses' tag, which Tilling later used as the name for his fleet. Especially in SOUTH LONDON, Tilling's business was for decades the only serious rival of the London GENERAL Omnibus Company but the latter's predominance eventually forced his heirs to diversify into provincial services. The company's London buses and routes were compulsorily acquired by LONDON TRANSPORT in 1933.

Times Square When the site of the original offices of *The Times* at Printing House Square, BLACKFRIARS, was redeveloped in the 1990s the location was renamed Times Square, partly to commemorate the newspaper but partly also to attract US corporate clients.

tin

Tin House A nickname for the stylish family residence built in 2003 by and for the architect

William Russell at 23 Bacon Street, just off BRICK LANE. The 'tin' is actually galvanized steel.

Tin Pan Alley A colloquial name (probably derived from late 19th-century US musicians' slang for a cheap, tinny piano) for a street inhabited by publishers of popular music, and hence applied metonymically to the pop-music industry in general. The original reference was to the area of Broadway and 14th Street in New York City, but the nickname was soon adopted on the other side of the Atlantic for DENMARK STREET.

Tiny Tim The disabled youngest son of Bob Cratchit and his wife, in Charles DICKENS's *A Christmas Carol* (1843). He 'bore a little crutch, and had his limbs supported by an iron frame', but does not allow his misfortune to dampen his spirits. He joins in the family's toast to Christmas with the words: 'God bless us, every one!' When Ebenezer SCROOGE is given a vision of the scene, he is particularly moved by the plight of Tiny Tim. The Ghost of Christmas Present foresees that Tiny Tim will die unless Scrooge learns the lessons of charity and benevolence.

Tippling Act The colloquial name of a statute of 1751 that effectively prevented retailers from selling small quantities of 'spirituous liquors' on credit. Previous legislation having failed to control London's epidemic of 'gin madness' (*see* GIN LANE), the Tippling Act tried a different approach, making it harder for independent gin shops to operate profitably, and thus concentrating production and distribution in the hands of larger enterprises. This ultimately brought about the demise of the cheap, syrupy hooch that had become an addictive favourite of the London poor and its replacement by a drier, more subtly flavoured spirit that became known as LONDON GIN.

titfer 'Hat' in COCKNEY RHYMING SLANG, from 'tit for tat'.

'Oi!' said the nasty voice from behind again. 'Ow about taking your titfer off?'
Paddington turned round and stared in the direction of the speaker. 'My titfer?' he exclaimed. 'Take my titfer off?'
'That's right,' said the voice. 'Your tit for tat.'
'I think he means your hat, dear,' explained Mrs Brown. 'It's probably getting in the way of the screen.'

MICHAEL BOND: *Paddington Helps Out* (1960)

Toby jug A small jug in the form of a squat old man in 18th-century dress, wearing a three-cornered hat, one corner of which forms the lip. The name comes from a poem (1761) about one 'Toby Philpot', adapted from the Latin by Francis Fawkes (1720–77), and the design of the jug from a print sold by Carrington Bowles, a CORNHILL print seller (later of ST PAUL'S CHURCHYARD), to Ralph Wood, a Staffordshire potter, who turned out a great number of Toby jugs.

Toc H The old telegraphy code for the letter T and H, as the initials of Talbot House. The term was used in the First World War, when the first Talbot House was founded in December 1915 at Poperinghe, Belgium, in memory of Gilbert Talbot, third son of Edward Stuart Talbot (1844–1934), Bishop of Winchester, who had been killed at Hooge earlier that year. The Rev P.T.B. 'Tubby' Clayton (1885–1972) made it a rest and recreation centre. From 1919 he founded a succession of similar centres in London, notably at 23 Queen's Gate Gardens, off GLOUCESTER ROAD, and then in towns and cities around the country. Toc H later evolved into an interdenominational association for Christian social service. Clayton was vicar of All Hallows by the Tower, on Byward Street, TOWER HILL, from 1922 to 1962.

Tod (Sloan) 'Alone' in COCKNEY RHYMING SLANG, often used in the phrase 'on your tod', i.e. on your own. James 'Tod' Sloan was a hugely popular and flamboyant American jockey who earned (and then squandered) a fortune from riding winners on both sides of the Atlantic, mostly in the 1890s. He died, alone, of cirrhosis in 1933. *See also* JACK JONES.

Todd, Sweeney *See the* DEMON BARBER OF FLEET STREET.

Todgers's Commercial Boarding House

An establishment located in a paved yard beneath the shadow of the MONUMENT in Charles DICKENS's *Martin Chuzzlewit* (1844). The interior is 'very black, begrimed, and mouldy' and smells of cabbage, 'as if all the greens that had ever been boiled there were evergreens, and flourished in immortal strength'. Mrs Todgers, however, is a kind-hearted landlady. Seth Pecksniff stays at the house with his daughters Charity and Mercy.

> Mr Pecksniff looked about him for a moment, and then knocked at the door of a very dingy

edifice, even among the choice collection of dingy edifices at hand; on the front of which was a little oval board like a tea-tray, with this inscription – 'Commercial Boarding House: M. Todgers.'

Tolmers Village An urban community in West EUSTON, with Tolmers Square in its south-west corner. The square was laid out with housing from 1861 to 1864 on land belonging to the NEW RIVER Company, and named after a Hertfordshire hamlet near the river's source. From the late 1950s, the neighbourhood attracted the interest of property developers and residents began a long campaign of resistance. In the early 1970s the struggle to save Tolmers Village, as it was dubbed at the time, became a cause célèbre with the Left, and students from nearby UNIVERSITY COLLEGE LONDON joined with squatters and trade unionists in resisting evictions. The activists failed to prevent the destruction of much of the original housing, but succeeded in persuading CAMDEN council to compulsorily purchase the site and Tolmers Square was rebuilt with council flats and a pub.

Tolworth An unprepossessing district situated south-east of SURBITON. Tolworth was recorded as 'Taleorde' in Domesday Book (after a man called Tala) and mutated through 'Talworth' before the present version of the name became fixed in the late 19th century. With the opening of the KINGSTON BYPASS in 1927 a massive programme of expansion began, with houses and amenities replacing farms. In the late 1960s the creation of an underpass helped relieve congestion at Tolworth Junction. Like other parts of the borough of KINGSTON UPON THAMES, Tolworth has a sizeable Korean community.

Tolworth Tower An office block designed by Richard Seifert and built in 1964 on the site of a former Odeon cinema. It was the tallest building in OUTER LONDON until Croydon's 50P BUILDING (also by Seifert) exceeded it by a fraction in 1970. Its 22 storeys reach 265 feet (81m) and the supermarket at ground level was the largest in southern England when it opened.

Tom

Tom-all-Alone's The colloquial name of a tumbledown street in Charles Dickens's *Bleak House* (1852–3). It is the home of Jo, an orphaned, illiterate young crossing-sweeper. The street's closest real-life counterparts lay in the vicinity of ST GILES and SEVEN DIALS. Before he began writing *Bleak House*, Dickens considered several alternative titles for the book, most of which included the name Tom-all-Alone's, indicating that he originally planned to make the slum a more significant setting.

> Jo lives – that is to say, Jo has not yet died – in a ruinous place known to the like of him by the name of Tom-all-Alone's. It is a black, dilapidated street, avoided by all decent people, where the crazy houses were seized upon, when their decay was far advanced, by some bold vagrants who after establishing their own possession took to letting them out in lodgings. Now, these tumbling tenements contain, by night, a swarm of misery.

Tom and Dick 'Sick' in COCKNEY RHYMING SLANG.

> So annoyed that I missed this, I was a bit Tom and Dick this past weekend so didn't want to go too far from my bed.
>
> forum post at www.efestivals.co.uk (8 February 2007)

Tom and Jerry Corinthian Tom and Jerry Hawthorn, the two chief characters in *Life in London* (1821 onwards), a Rabelaisian part-work by Pierce Egan the Elder (1772–1849), illustrated by George Cruikshank (1792–1878). This was the first but by no means last use of the names for a pair of comical characters. 'Tom-and-Jerryism' became a term for riotous behaviour, while a 'Tom and Jerry shop' was a low beer-house.

Tom o' Bedlam An anonymously written ballad telling the first-person story of an ABRAHAM MAN, probably dating from the beginning of the 17th century. The work exists in several forms; the 'mad song' entitled 'Old Tom of Bedlam', reproduced in PERCY'S RELIQUES, bears only a passing resemblance to versions that are nowadays better known. Although it provides some biographical glimpses, much of the ballad consists of 'strokes of sublime imagination', as Isaac D'Israeli put it, 'mixed with familiar comic humour'.

> With a heart of furious fancies,
> Whereof I am commander,
> With a burning spear
> And a horse of air
> To the wilderness I wander;
> With a knight of ghosts and shadows,
> I summoned am to Tourney,

> Ten leagues beyond
> The wide world's end,
> Methinks it is no journey.

Tom's A noted COFFEE HOUSE of the late 18th century that was in existence in Russell Street, COVENT GARDEN, as late as 1865. It was owned and named after Thomas West, and here in 1764 was founded Tom's Club, which included most of the literary and social notables of the day.

Tom Spring *See under* SPRING.

Tom (tit) 'Shit' in COCKNEY RHYMING SLANG, usually in the sense of the act of defecation rather than as an expletive.

> Going for a Tom Tit (on work time, natch). Best thing ever. Performing a necessary body function whilst racking up some clocked-in time is one of the truly great things in life.
>
> forum post at www.beexcellenttoeachother.com (17 April 2008)

tomfoolery 'Jewellery' in COCKNEY RHYMING SLANG, sometimes abbreviated to 'tom' when the context makes this intended meaning clear.

tonic sol-fa A system of musical notation and sight singing in which diatonic scales are written always in one way (the keynote being indicated), the tones being represented by syllables or initials, and time and accents by dashes and colons. It was developed in the 1840s by the Rev John Curwen (1816–60), a Congregationalist minister who made use of the earlier work of Miss Sarah Anna Glover (1786–1867). Curwen established the Tonic Sol-Fa Press (later the Curwen Press) in PLAISTOW[1] and the Tonic Sol-Fa College in FOREST GATE, where he taught the method. His son John S. Curwen (1847–1916) founded a music festival in STRATFORD.

tontine A form of annuity shared by several subscribers, in which the shares of those who die are added to the holdings of the survivors until the last survivor inherits all. It is so named from Lorenzo Tonti (1620–90), a Neapolitan banker who introduced the system into France in 1653. In 1765 the House of Commons raised £300,000 by way of tontine annuities at 3 per cent, and as late as 1871 the *Daily News* announced a proposed tontine to raise £650,000 to purchase the ALEXANDRA PALACE and 100 acres (40.5 hectares) of land.

Tooley Street A street in SOUTHWARK, running

parallel with the THAMES to the north and the arches beneath the approach to LONDON BRIDGE STATION to the south. It was earlier St Olave's Street, from the former church here dedicated to St Olave (demolished in 1928). The much eroded form Tooley Street (via St Tooley's Street) is first recorded in the 17th century. In the days when the POOL OF LONDON was still a working port most of the street's northern side was taken up with wharfside warehouses. Tooley Street is nowadays best known as the home of Hay's Galleria (*see* HAY'S WHARF), the LONDON DUNGEON and the UNICORN THEATRE.

Tooley Street Fire A disastrous conflagration that broke out at Cotton's Wharf on 22 June 1861 and rapidly spread to HAY'S WHARF. The London Fire Engine Establishment arrived promptly but a low tide restricted the volume of water that could be pumped. It was more than a month before the last embers had died down and insurance claims exceeded £2 million. Among those who lost their lives in the fire was the chief of the fire service, James Braidwood. The human and financial costs of the Tooley Street Fire contributed significantly to the formation of the Metropolitan Fire Brigade in 1865.

three tailors of Tooley Street *See under* THREE.

Tooting

1. A densely populated multiracial district situated west of STREATHAM. The name is of uncertain Anglo-Saxon origin and may have referred to 'the people of the lookout place'. The two manors of Tooting (subsequently TOOTING GRAVENEY and TOOTING BEC) were in existence by the time of Domesday Book and each became the centre of a farming village over the course of the Middle Ages. Tooting's transformation from a pair of villages into a London suburb was completed following the arrival of fwhat is now the NORTHERN LINE in 1926. Later residential development has mostly involved the replacement of former institutional buildings, including hospitals – although St George's remains; it moved here from HYDE PARK CORNER in 1980 and is one of the biggest hospitals in the country. Perhaps because it has a silly sounding name, Tooting has been the setting for several television comedies, including *Hugh and I* (1962–7) and CITIZEN SMITH (1977–80), which used the Castle public house for location scenes.

2. A crater located in the eastern Amazonis Planitia on Mars. Possibly the planet's youngest large meteorite crater, it was named in 2005 by Pete Mouginis-Mark, director of the Hawaii Institute of Geophysics and Planetology, who grew up in Trinity Road, Tooting.

Tooting Bec The names Tooting Bec and Upper Tooting are interchangeable. Most maps show the area as Upper Tooting but residents usually call it Tooting Bec because of the name of the station. Tooting's northern manor was given by William the Conqueror to Richard of Tonbridge, who in turn endowed it to the abbey of Notre Dame du Bec in Normandy. There is speculation that the monks of Bec may have established a priory here, around which a settlement coalesced in the 12th century, but if this is the case its site has not been located. Tooting Bec station opened in 1926, originally as Trinity Road.

Tooting (Bec) 'Peck' in COCKNEY RHYMING SLANG, usually in the sense of a light kiss but sometimes meaning a bite to eat.

Tooting Bec Lido An impressive open-air swimming pool opened on Tooting Bec Road in 1906. The South London Swimming Club was formed here in the same year. It is said to be the largest freshwater pool in England and the widest in Europe.

Tooting Broadway A shopping parade and NORTHERN LINE station located at the crossroads where Garratt Lane and Mitcham Road meet Tooting High Street, which was known in the past as Tooting Corner. A statue of Edward VII attired as commander-in-chief of the army was erected on the corner in 1911. The independent shops and stalls of Broadway Market and the nearby streets reflect the neighbourhood's wide ethnic diversity: Tamil, Konkani, Ibo, Tagalog and Creole French are among the most common languages spoken at local schools. *See also the* PARADISE AT TOOTING.

Tooting Common or **Commons** The unified identity of the historically distinct TOOTING BEC and TOOTING GRAVENEY commons, which formerly lay in separate parishes, with an avenue of trees marking the boundary. The METROPOLITAN BOARD OF WORKS bought the two commons in 1873 and 1875 respectively, preserving them for the public benefit.

Tooting Granada A cinema (now a bingo hall) built in 1931 at 50 Mitcham Road. Its magnificent interior, by the Russian set designer Theodore

Komisarjevsky (1882–1954), was modelled on the lavish American picture palaces of the era. The Granada was described by John Betjeman as 'a Spanish-Moorish-Gothic cathedral for the people of Tooting'; the architectural critic Ian Nairn (*see* SUBTOPIA) said: 'Miss the Tower of London if you have to but don't miss this.' It was the first British cinema to be granted Grade I listed status.

Tooting Graveney The more southerly of the two manors into which Tooting was divided at the time of Domesday Book. The manor was owned by Chertsey Abbey and was leased in the 12th and 13th centuries to the Graveney (or Gravenel) family, who may have taken their name from the village of Graveney in north Kent. The village of Tooting Graveney (also known as Lower Tooting) was consumed by suburban housing over the latter years of the 19th century.

Tooting Tragedy The killing in March 1895 of eight members of one family living at 12 Fountain Road, Tooting. Frank Taylor cut the throats of his wife, six of his children and then himself, after he had been laid off as a plasterer and had failed to find an alternative source of income. Only the eldest son escaped with his life. A very religious man, Taylor left notes affirming his confident belief that the family would be reunited in heaven.

tosher A man who in the 19th century stole copper from the hulls of ships moored in the THAMES. Also someone who searched the London sewers for items of value. What these scavengers found was known as 'tosh'.

Tottenham A densely built-up, multiracial district situated about 6 miles (10 km) north of the TOWER OF LONDON. 'Toteham' (the farmstead of a man called Totta) was first recorded in Domesday Book, as was a weir at present-day TOTTENHAM HALE. From the 12th century Tottenham's accessibility to London attracted wealthy merchants and religious institutions to its wooded slopes, although the main village consisted only of a cluster of dwellings at Tottenham Green. Tottenham manor house (now BRUCE CASTLE) lay almost a mile (1.6 km) to the north of the green. Over the course of the next two centuries mansions, private schools, groups of almshouses and other charitable institutions were built near the High Road, while extensive woodland survived to the west and the marshy meadows lay undisturbed to the east. Only in the late 18th century did development begin

to branch away from the High Road along old tracks like WHITE HART LANE. Tottenham remained suburban rather than urban until the coming of the railways to the east side of the parish in the 1840s, to the west side in the 1850s and through the middle in the 1870s. The last pockets of farmland disappeared in the 1920s, when municipal housebuilding began in earnest. After the Second World War council flats dominated the construction programme, with massive projects in the 1960s – notably at NORTHUMBERLAND PARK and BROADWATER FARM – and smaller, low-rise estates in the 1970s, for example at SEVEN SISTERS. This was a period of significant change in Tottenham's residential profile, with the arrival of immigrants first from the Caribbean and later from Turkey and Africa.

Tottenham Court Road A commercial thoroughfare running along the western edge of BLOOMSBURY. This was the route from ST GILES to the manor house of Tottenhall (on what is now EUSTON ROAD), a name that had become corrupted to Tottenham by the time of the house's demolition in the early 18th century. The change was influenced by public familiarity with the north London district of TOTTENHAM, although the manor had no connection with that place. From the late 18th century and especially in the 19th century, Tottenham Court Road was known for the manufacture of furniture, especially cabinets. Some of the workshops later turned to piano-making. Furniture retailing grew in tandem with the manufacturing industry and several grand stores opened in the 1910s and 1920s. The finest of these was – and still is – Heal's, a store that had opened in 1854 and was magnificently rebuilt in 1917. To the present day, the street's main specialism north of GOODGE STREET is furniture retailing. Further south, Tottenham Court Road is famed for its retailers of computers and audiovisual and photographic equipment.

Tottenham Hale The south-eastern part of Tottenham, nowadays dominated by municipally built housing. Residents of 'the Hale' (Old English *halh*, 'secluded spot') were recorded from the late 13th century, although the first mention of Tottenham Hale did not come until 1754. By this time the settlement was Tottenham's largest satellite, with an inn and several dozen dwellings. The village had more than 600 inhabitants in 1840, when the railway arrived and Tottenham (now Tottenham Hale) station was built. From the early 1860s suburban development began to connect Tottenham Hale with its parent district and its separate existence had been wholly lost by the 1890s.

Tottenham Hotspur FC An eminent professional FOOTBALL club, formed (originally as Hotspur FC) from an older cricket club in 1882. Its home ground is WHITE HART LANE. Most of the club's founders were old boys of St John's Presbyterian School and Tottenham Grammar School. The 'Hotspur' name was inspired by the area's connection with the dukes of Northumberland: in the 18th century a Tottenham man, Hugh Smithson, married into the Percy family, eventually becoming 1st Duke; and Henry Percy (1364–1403), son of the 1st Earl of Northumberland (who features in SHAKESPEARE's *Henry IV, Part I*), acquired through his impulsiveness the nickname 'Hotspur'. Spurs' greatest achievements of recent decades came in the 1960s, most notably the winning of the League and FA Cup double in 1960–1. The club is noted for its loyal fan base among north London's Jewish community.

Tottenham Outrage On 23 January 1909 two Latvian anarchists stole wages from a factory on Tottenham High Road. They were chased by police and local tradesmen, and responded by firing pistols wildly in their pursuers' direction, killing PC William Frederick Tyler and a 10-year-old delivery boy. The robbers hijacked a tram, a horse-drawn milk cart and a greengrocer's van in their attempt to escape but they were cornered in Hale End, north of WALTHAMSTOW, where they shot themselves dead rather than surrender. A commemorative plaque was unveiled at Tottenham police station in 2009, to mark the centenary of the outrage.

Tottenham pudding A feed for pigs or poultry, consisting of sterilized kitchen waste. It was developed in Tottenham during the Second World War.

Tottenham shall turn French Most lexicographers assert that this was an ironic old saying of the 'pigs might fly' variety, referring to something that would never happen. However, Francis Grose, in his *Provincial Glossary* (1787), renders the proverb as 'Tottenham is turned French', and explains it thus:

> After the beginning of the reign of Henry VIII a vast number of French mechanics came over

to England, filling not only the outskirts of the town, but also the neighbouring villages ... This proverb is used in ridicule of persons affecting foreign fashions and manners, in preference to those of their own country.

Tottenham sound Supposedly, London's answer to Liverpool's Merseybeat in the early to mid-1960s. In reality, the 'Tottenham sound' emanated from only one significant act, the Dave Clark Five, who played their first gig at a SEVEN SISTERS youth club in January 1962 and took their name from their Tottenham-born drummer. Nevertheless, the term achieved media exposure on both sides of the Atlantic.

> Music reaches the soul. The Dave Clark Five lifted ours with a concussive beat and a reverb tremolo echo chamber of a sound – the Tottenham sound – from Lansdowne Studios in Holland Park, London, that commanded you ... to yell at your dad: 'Turn it up!'
>
> TOM HANKS: speech at the DC5's induction into the Rock and Roll Hall of Fame (10 March 2008)

Tottenham Three The collective name given to Winston Silcott, Engin Raghip and Mark Braithwaite, who were sentenced to life imprisonment in 1987 for 'having common cause' with the mob who murdered PC Keith Blakelock during the October 1985 BROADWATER FARM RIOT. Their convictions were quashed in 1991 after tests revealed that Silcott's confession had been tampered with. Braithwaite and Raghip were released, though Silcott remained in jail until 2003 as he was serving a sentence for another murder as well.

Tournament of Tottenham *See under* TOURNAMENT.

Totterdown The first COTTAGE ESTATE to be built by the LONDON COUNTY COUNCIL. In 1901 the council acquired Totterdown Fields, TOOTING, and erected 1,229 houses here over the following ten years. All Saints' Church was built as the centrepiece of the new estate, in imposing Gothic style. While Totterdown itself had only four shops, its presence wrought a transformation of the amenities at TOOTING BROADWAY.

Totteridge A ribbon village strung along the road from WHETSTONE to HIGHWOOD HILL. Opinions differ on the derivation of the first part of its name, which was first recorded as Taderege in the 12th century. Most experts now propose an association with a man called Tāta, but others have suggested that 'tot' meant either a height or a place of worship. The 'ridge' part is undisputed: Totteridge sits on a crest that rises well above 400 feet (123m). Several structures survive from the late 17th and early 18th centuries, mostly farm outbuildings. The oldest mansion is Totteridge Park, built in 1750 but remodelled in the early 20th century. Totteridge's other grand houses are mostly recent creations, as the village has become a haven for business and media moguls who wish to retreat behind high walls and security gates.

Tour, the Another name for the RING in HYDE PARK.

Tournament of Tottenham, The A mock-heroic metrical romance written around 1425. It was probably intended as a satire on the dangers and costs of the jousting events that were popular at the time. A number of clowns are introduced, practising warlike games and making vows like knights of high degree. They tilt on carthorses, fight with ploughshares and flails, and wear wooden bowls and saucepan lids for armour. The poem was republished in PERCY'S RELIQUES (1765).

> It befell in Tottenham on a deare day
> There was made a shurting [feast] by the highway.
> Thither came all the men of the country
> Of Hyssyltoun, of Hygate, and of Hakenay ...

Tower

1. In a London context, and accompanied by the definite article, the word usually refers to the TOWER OF LONDON.

2. An irregularly shaped ward at the south-east corner of the CITY of London. Formerly called Tower Street ward, it takes in the MINORIES and CRUTCHED FRIARS, but not the TOWER OF LONDON, which is in TOWER HAMLETS. In addition to the predictable predominance of office buildings, the ward possesses a smattering of hotels and apartment blocks, as well as TRINITY HOUSE and the church known as ST GHASTLY GRIM.

Tower Bridge London's most iconic bridge, built from 1886 under the direction of the engineer Sir John Wolfe Barry and the architect Sir Horace Jones. As the furthest THAMES bridge downstream at that time it was necessary to construct the roadway in the form of two coun-terbalanced see-saws, or bascules, which could be tipped using hydraulic engines. The advanced engineering was clothed in Gothic towers to harmonize with the neighbouring fortress. The bridge was opened (literally) by the Prince of Wales in 1894. The bascule-raising machinery was converted to electric power in 1976, allowing many internal areas to be opened up to visitors.

Tower 42 *See the* NATWEST TOWER.

Tower Gateway A station opened in 1987 as the original western terminus of the DOCKLANDS LIGHT RAILWAY system. It has been relatively little used since the completion of the extension to BANK in 1991.

Tower Green An open space immediately to the west of the WHITE TOWER, where highly placed traitors were executed to spare them the indignity of public beheading on TOWER HILL. Victims include Anne Boleyn, Catherine Howard and Lady Jane Grey. It is the site of the church of ST PETER AD VINCULA, founded in the 12th century for the use of Tower prisoners. Many of them (including the above three) are buried here.

Tower Hamlets, London Borough of A borough of EAST LONDON, immediately to the east of the CITY of London and bounded to the north by HACKNEY, to the east by NEWHAM and to the south by the River THAMES. It was created in 1965 by the amalgamation of the metropolitan boroughs of BETHNAL GREEN, POPLAR and STEPNEY. The name chosen for it is a revival of a term originally applied in the 16th century to the large area of East London from which the Lieutenant of the TOWER OF LONDON had the right to call men up for guard duty. By the 18th century it was the name of an administrative district covering 21 hamlets (including some in the eastern part of the City). This formed the basis of the parliamentary constituency of Tower Hamlets, created in 1832. In 1918 that was broken up into Bethnal Green, HACKNEY and SHOREDITCH, and the name 'Tower Hamlets' went out of use until its resurrection in 1965. The borough's coat of arms is very similar to that of the Metropolitan Borough of Stepney, with references to silk weaving, metalworking and seafaring. The crest is surmounted by a representation of the WHITE TOWER and supported by a seahorse and a talbot, the latter (a large-eared hound) symbolizing the ISLE OF DOGS. The civic motto is 'from great things to greater' – an English translation of the former Stepney motto.

Tower Hamlets Cemetery or **Bow Cemetery** One of the so-called MAGNIFICENT SEVEN London cemeteries, situated between MILE END and BROMLEY-BY-BOW. It opened in 1841 and was enlarged in the mid-1890s. The heavily wooded cemetery closed to burials in 1966 and is now a 33-acre (13-hectare) public park and nature reserve.

Tower Hill A street on rising ground immediately to the north and west of the TOWER OF LONDON. It occupies the site of what was formerly the principal place of execution of traitors held in the Tower. Among the 125 to have met their end here were Sir Thomas More, Thomas Cromwell, Archbishop Laud, the Duke of Monmouth and (in 1747) Lord Lovat, the last person to be executed by beheading in England. Up until the 1780s there was still a gallows here where criminals were hanged. The execution site is marked by a memorial plaque in Trinity Square Gardens.

Tower Hill play 18th-century slang for giving someone a slap around the face or a kick up the backside, such eventualities once being frequent in the rough-housing environs of TOWER HILL.

Tower Hill station A LONDON UNDERGROUND station, on the CIRCLE LINE and DISTRICT LINE, opened in 1967 on the site of what had been TOWER OF LONDON underground station (1882–4). It replaced the previous Tower Hill station (1946–67), originally named MARK LANE (1884–1946).

Tower Horn A silver-plated unicorn's horn said to have been kept with the CROWN JEWELS in the early 1640s. It seems to have been spirited away during the Civil War and its subsequent fate is not known. As the item is unlikely to have been a real unicorn's horn, historians have suggested that it was probably a narwhal tusk.

Tower Liberty The TOWER OF LONDON with the fortifications and TOWER HILL. This formed part of the ancient demesne of the Crown, with jurisdiction and privileges distinct from and independent of the CITY of London. Its bounds are still beaten triennially by choirboys and children after a service in the CHAPEL ROYAL of ST PETER AD VINCULA. Governor, chaplain, BEEFEATERS and residents accompany them and at each of the 31 boundary stones the chaplain exclaims: 'Cursed is he who removeth his neighbours' landmark.' The chief warder then says: 'Whack it, boys, whack it.'

Tower of London A fortress located on the north bank of the River THAMES, at the western extreme of the borough of TOWER HAMLETS, on a site said once to have been occupied by Julius Caesar's fort. Its nucleus is a massive stone keep built in the latter part of the 11th century and later known as the WHITE TOWER. Further fortifications were added to it over the centuries, and its great outer wall was completed in the reign of Edward I (1272–1307). Amongst its other features the most notable are the BLOODY TOWER, the chapel of ST PETER AD VINCULA, the Byward Tower (built in the 1270s – a 'byward' is a subsidiary guard) and TRAITOR'S GATE. As well as being a fortress, the Tower has a special place in English history, both as a royal residence down to the time of James I (r.1603–25) and as a state prison. It has also housed the Royal Mint (until 1810), a menagerie, a notable collection of arms and armour (now removed to the Royal Armouries Museum in Leeds) and the Public Records; and it is still the home of the CROWN JEWELS. State prisoners confined here range from the turbulent Norman cleric Ranulf Flambard to Sir Thomas More, Sir Walter Raleigh, Guy FAWKES, Sir Roger Casement and Rudolf Hess. During both world wars several German spies were executed here by firing squad. The Tower is one of London's leading tourist sites, not the least of the attractions being the BEEFEATERS and the RAVENS OF THE TOWER. The Tower of London was declared a UNESCO world heritage site in 1988.

Tower of London, The A novel (1840) by William Harrison Ainsworth, based loosely on the story of Lady Jane Grey.

Tower Pier A jetty on the north bank of the River THAMES, at the western end of the TOWER OF LONDON. It was a stopping-off point on the hydrofoil service introduced between CHARING CROSS and GREENWICH in the 1970s, and in former times paddle steamers plied between here and Southend-on-Sea, taking Londoners on their seaside outings. The launch *Havengore* bore Sir Winston Churchill's body from here to the Festival Pier and WATERLOO STATION after his funeral in 1965.

Tower pound The legal pound of 5400 grains (11¼ ounces troy weight, 350 grams), used in England until the adoption of the troy pound in 1526. It was so called from the standard pound kept in the TOWER OF LONDON.

Tower Subway A tunnel running 1,350 feet (412m) beneath the River THAMES linking the TOWER OF LONDON on the north bank with TOOLEY STREET on the south bank. Opened in 1870, it was the first tube tunnel under the Thames. At first traversed by a steam-powered tramcar, it was later converted to pedestrian use. After TOWER BRIDGE opened in 1894 it was closed down (although it still carries cables and water mains). Its northern entrance is marked by a kiosk at the foot of TOWER HILL.

Tower Theatre Company See the THEATRE.

Tower weight Weight expressed in terms of TOWER POUNDS.

Bloody Tower See under BLOOD.

fool will not part with his bauble for the Tower of London, a See under FOOL.

Lions' Tower See under LION.

Princes in the Tower See under PRINCE.

ravens of the Tower See under RAVEN.

White Tower See under WHITE.

town Central London, in casual parlance. The City is just the SQUARE MILE but 'town' encompasses a wider area.

> London is 'Town' without the article, and is in fact, three towns, viz. London (the city proper), Westminster and the borough of Southwark, or Tripoli – without taking into estimate the outlying parishes. This is the district for seeing life in its varieties, as the present work attests. A man 'in town', is in cash – 'out of town', without blunt.
>
> JON BEE: A Dictionary of the Turf (1823)

Trabb's boy The impudent shop-boy of Trabb, the tailor and undertaker, in Charles DICKENS's Great Expectations (1860–1). He habitually embarrasses PIP in public after he has come into his 'great expectations': 'Words cannot state the amount of aggravation and injury wreaked upon me by Trabb's boy.' Performing a variety of extravagant antics in the street as Pip passes by, he is fondest of yelling: 'Don't know yah, don't know yah, 'pon my soul don't know yah!'

Tradescant

Tradescant, Evelyn The protagonist of A.N. Wilson's novel The Sweets of Pimlico (1977). Left vulnerable after the ending of a shaky love affair, she consoles herself with a lifelong enthusiasm for nature study. In KENSINGTON GARDENS she meets Theo Gormann, who refuses to conform to any of the taxonomic pigeonholes she has created for men.

Tradescant, John See the ARK (1).

Trafalgar An operational command unit within the METROPOLITAN POLICE dealing with non-TRIDENT, non-fatal shootings in distinct communities across London and targeting illegal firearms suppliers and converters.

Trafalgar Square London's best-known square, located immediately north of CHARING CROSS. The church of ST MARTIN-IN-THE-FIELDS has stood to the north-east of what is now the square since the 13th century and has been twice rebuilt. From the 14th to the 19th centuries the locality was the site of the royal MEWS, where Geoffrey Chaucer once toiled as a clerk of works. The square was laid out in 1830 and named after the battle (1805) at which Vice-admiral Horatio Nelson died. Seven years later the NATIONAL GALLERY was erected on the north side. This was followed in 1843 by Edward Baily's statue of Nelson, erected in celebration of his naval victories at Cape St Vincent, the Nile, Copenhagen and Trafalgar and mounted on a granite column 151 feet (46m) high (see NELSON'S COLUMN). In the same year an equestrian statue of George IV was placed on a plinth in the north-east corner of the square, with statues of imperial generals Charles James Napier and Henry Havelock later added in the south-west and south-east corners (see also the FOURTH PLINTH). It was not until 1867 that Nelson's memorial was finally completed by the installation of Sir Edwin Landseer's four bronze lions. Canada House and South Africa House, the high commissions of their respective countries, overlook the east and west sides of the square. In 2003 MAYOR OF LONDON Ken Livingstone (see RED KEN) oversaw the pedestrianization of the area in front of the National Gallery and the virtual eradication of the square's infamous ROCK PIGEON population.

Almost from the beginning Trafalgar Square has been a venue for political demonstrations, including the Chartist rally of 1848, the so-called BLOODY SUNDAY encounter in 1887, the rallies of the Aldermaston Marches in the late 1950s and early 1960s, followed by decades of anti-apartheid demonstrations, directed towards South Africa House, and the poll tax riots of 1990. The square has hosted numerous national celebrations too, and until recently was the traditional place for New Year revellers to gather, until they were lured away to the riverside by fireworks displays.

> I live in Trafalgar Square, with four lions to guard me.
> Fountains and statues all over the place,
> And the Metropole staring me right in the face.
>
> C.W. MURPHY: 'I Live in Trafalgar Square' (song) (1902)

Trafalgar (Square) 'Chair' in COCKNEY RHYMING SLANG of the late 20th century.

Trafalgar Square Christmas tree A Norwegian spruce (*Picea abies*) erected in Trafalgar Square every Christmas since 1947. It is donated by the city of Oslo, in recognition of Britain's assistance to Norway during the Second World War. The tree is usually over 65 feet (20m) tall and 50–60 years old. It is selected from the forests surrounding Oslo several months in advance and felled in November in a ceremony attended by the lord mayor of WESTMINSTER, the British ambassador to Norway and the mayor of Oslo. In the middle weeks of December the tree provides a focus for a programme of carol-singing events, to raise money for charities.

Trafalgar Square Freeze A FLASH MOB event of 16 February 2008, wherein several hundred people – including PEARLY KINGS AND QUEENS – converged on the square, adopted various stances and then stood motionless for five minutes from 3.30pm. Video clips of the event have been viewed more than three million times on YouTube. Similar events have taken place elsewhere, including at WATERLOO STATION.

Traffic Light Tree A sculpture installed at HERONS QUAYS roundabout in 1998, funded by the Public Art Commissions Agency. It was created from 75 working traffic signal heads by the Paris-born artist Pierre Vivant (b.1952).

trainbands Local bodies of citizen soldiers or militia of little military value, with the exception of those of London. They derived from an order of Elizabeth I (1573) that a 'convenient number' in every county were to be organized in bands and trained. They were not willing to leave their districts and were seldom suitably trained.

> John Gilpin was a citizen
> Of credit and renown,
> A train-band captain eke [also] was he

> Of famous London town.
>
> WILLIAM COWPER: 'The Diverting History of John Gilpin' (1782)

Traitor's Gate or **Bridge** A watergate beneath St Thomas's Tower through which prisoners were delivered to the TOWER OF LONDON.

> On through that gate misnamed, through which
> Went Sidney, Russell, Raleigh, Cranmer, More,
> On into twilight within walls of stone,
> Then to the place of trial; and alone ...
>
> SAMUEL ROGERS: *Human Life* (1819)

Tramp A private members' nightclub located at 40 JERMYN STREET. It was opened in 1969 by Johnny Gold, who took its name from a television documentary describing Charlie Chaplin as 'the greatest tramp of them all'. Its members include many celebrities.

Little Tramp See under LITTLE.

transpontine theatres (Latin *trāns*, 'across', and *pōns, pontis*, 'a bridge') The playhouses of SOUTHWARK and LAMBETH, which from earliest times were characterized by freer attitudes than their counterparts north of the THAMES. The term, or the equivalent 'Surreyside theatres', was much used in the 19th century, when sensationalism, melodrama and low comedy dominated the bills of the transpontine theatres and the audiences were of a distinctly lower class than in the WEST END. The transpontine phenomenon has acquired a new face in the 21st century, whereby nightclubs south of the Thames have tended to benefit from a more permissive municipal stance on opening hours. *See also* GONE! AND NEVER CALLED ME 'MOTHER' (*under* GO).

> Can I forget those hearts of oak.
> Those model British tars;
> Who crack'd a skull or crack'd a joke,
> Like true transpontine stars;
> Who hornpip'd *à la* T. P. Cooke,
> And sang – at least they tried –
> Until the pit and gallery shook,
> Upon the Surrey side?
>
> HENRY S. LEIGH: *Carols of Cockayne*, 'Over the Water' (1868)

transport
Transport for London See LONDON TRANSPORT.

Transport House A former name for the leadership of the Labour Party, from its headquarters in SMITH SQUARE. The building was also the head office of the Transport and General Workers' Union, hence its name. The Labour Party moved from Smith Square to Walworth Road in 1980 and is now in VICTORIA STREET. The TGWU (also known as T&G, and now a section of the Unite super-union) later moved to a new Transport House in Theobalds Road, HOLBORN. *See also the* MILLBANK TENDENCY.

treacle (tart) 'Sweetheart' in COCKNEY RHYMING SLANG. In recent decades the term was most famously employed by the character Pete Beale (played by Peter Dean) in EASTENDERS, who would greet female acquaintances with the enquiry: 'All right, treacle?' The Radio 1 DJ Scott Mills later borrowed the salutation. 'Jam tart' is also sometimes used to mean 'sweetheart', but not abbreviated. The use of the word 'tart' in reference to a young woman (nowadays, in London, disparagingly) may derive from this slang, although a direct contraction of 'sweetheart' is more likely. 'RASPBERRY (tart)' has quite a different meaning. *See also* STRAWBERRY (TART).

treaty
Treaty of Greenwich
1. A pair of treaties signed by Henry VIII and James Hamilton, 2nd Earl of Arran, on 1 July 1543. They provided for 'eternal peace' between England and Scotland and for the future marriage of Edward VI of England and Mary, Queen of Scots. Almost immediately after the signing, Henry attempted to vary the terms of the agreement and the Scottish parliament repudiated it on 11 December.
2. An agreement signed in May 1596 by which Elizabeth I agreed to provide troops to support Henry of Navarre in his war against the Spanish-backed Catholic League.
Treaty of Lambeth or **Kingston** An agreement of 1217 by which Prince Louis (later Louis VIII) of France agreed to cease his support for the barons' campaign against Henry III. The alternative names for the treaty reflect uncertainty regarding the place where it was signed, which may in fact have been Staines, then in MIDDLESEX. The archbishop of Canterbury is said to have journeyed from LAMBETH PALACE to play a part in the preliminary negotiations, which took place at HOUNSLOW.
Treaty of London Any of a wide range of international agreements concluded in London,

dating back to the 14th century. Among the more notable have been the treaty of 1518, forming an alliance with France (cemented at the Field of the Cloth of Gold in 1520); the treaty of 1604, in which James I made peace with Spain; the treaty of 1831, in which the independence and neutrality of the newly formed Belgium were guaranteed; and the secret treaty of 1915, in which Italy agreed to come into the First World War on the side of the Triple Entente (Britain, France and Russia). *See also the* TREATY OF WESTMINSTER.

Treaty of Uxbridge The misleading name for an abortive conference held between Royalist and Parliamentary representatives from 29 January to 22 February 1645 in an attempt to end the Civil War. The negotiations took place at a mansion called The Place, which was later reduced in size and renamed the Treaty House. It is now the Crown and Treaty public house, on Oxford Road, UXBRIDGE.

Treaty of Westminster Either of two treaties signed at WESTMINSTER. The first (1462; also known as the TREATY OF LONDON) was an underhand and abortive attempt by Edward IV to gain control of the Scottish throne. The second (5–15 April 1654) concluded the first Anglo-Dutch War.

tree of heaven *Ailanthus altissima*, a tree frequently planted in the streets, squares and parks of central London because, like the LONDON PLANE, it thrives well in a temperate urban environment. Introduced from northern China in the mid-18th century, it has a smooth, grey bark and pointed leaf tips. The exceptionally large tree of heaven in RAVENSCOURT PARK has been selected as one of the GREAT TREES OF LONDON.

Trelawney of the Wells A play (1898) by the comic dramatist and farceur Arthur Wing Pinero. It revolves around the travails of actress Rose Trelawney, contrasting thespian life at SADLER'S WELLS with the 'respectable' gentility of marriage. It is regularly revived by amateur groups, and has been produced at the NATIONAL THEATRE on two occasions.

Trellick Tower A 31-storey residential block with a distinctive free-standing service tower, situated at the northern end of Golborne Road, on the east side of KENSAL TOWN. Designed by Ernö GOLDFINGER as a *unité d'habitation* in the style of Le Corbusier, it was completed in 1972.

Built to high standards and visible for miles, Trellick Tower is now grade II listed as a relic of a bygone age of monumental municipal building.

Trial of the Pyx (Latin *pyxis*, 'small box', originally made of boxwood) An annual trial to establish that British coins produced at the Royal Mint are within the statutory limits for metallic composition, weight and size. It was initiated in the reign of Edward I (r.1272–1307) and formerly took place in the Chapel of the Pyx in WESTMINSTER ABBEY. Since 1870 the trial has been held at Goldsmiths' Hall. One coin is nowadays put aside for testing from every batch of each denomination minted, amounting to several thousand coins in total. The Trial of the Pyx is conducted in February, in the presence of the KING'S or QUEEN'S REMEMBRANCER and a jury of goldsmiths. Some two months later, once the Assay Office has verified the coins, the verdict is delivered to the chancellor of the exchequer or his or her representative.

Trico strike A labour dispute at the Trico-Folberth windscreen-wiper factory at BRENTFORD in 1976. As a result of their action, the company's women workers achieved equal pay under the terms of the Equal Pay Act (earlier strikes and tribunals elsewhere had failed). It was celebrated in a song called 'The Trico Strike' (1977) by Sam Richards. Very much in the standard mould of the genre, it begins:

> Now stop what you're doing and listen,
> Here's a story I know you will like,
> Three hundred women at Brentford,
> They spent a long summer on strike.

Trident An operational command unit within the METROPOLITAN POLICE dealing with gun-related activity in London's black communities. The unit began in 1998 as Operation Trident, an intelligence-based initiative in the boroughs of LAMBETH and BRENT. It was set up in response to a spate of shootings and murders, often committed with semi-automatic weapons, that were made harder to investigate by the unwillingness of witnesses to come forward through fear of reprisals. Trident was later implemented on a London-wide scale and co-operates with government agencies such as immigration, customs and excise and the Serious Organised Crime Agency, as well as with the Jamaican Constabulary. *See also* TRAFALGAR.

Ten years ago, the Metropolitan police set up Operation Trident in an attempt to reduce gang violence, much of it drug-related, in the black community. Since then there have been numerous prosecutions with jail sentences totalling 852 years handed out in 2005–6 to criminals convicted under Trident. But the killings have continued.

The Sunday Times (30 March 2008)

Trilby Trilby O'Ferrall, the heroine of George du Maurier's novel *Trilby* (1894), which is set in Paris and London. She is an artist's model with pretty feet who cannot sing unless hypnotized by Svengali, her sinister manager. She becomes a famous performer under his influence but loses her voice when he dies. In 1895 Herbert Beerbohm Tree produced Paul Potter's stage version of *Trilby* at the THEATRE ROYAL, HAYMARKET. So great was its success that Tree (who played Svengali) was able to build the present incarnation of Her Majesty's Theatre out of the profits. In that stage adaptation Trilby (played by Dorothea Baird) wore a soft felt hat with an indented crown; enterprising London hatters made replica hats that they named after her.

trilby (hat) 'Prat' in COCKNEY RHYMING SLANG, i.e. a fool.

trinity

Trinity Buoy Wharf *See* LEAMOUTH.

Trinity House, Corporation of The chief lighthouse and pilotage authority of the United Kingdom, which controls the lighting and marking of British coastal waters and certain maritime charities. Its headquarters are at TOWER HILL and its work is controlled by Elder Brethren, consisting of master mariners who have had long experience of command in the Royal Navy or merchant navy, together with individuals from the world of commerce. It developed from the Guild of Mariners and Lodesmen of DEPTFORD (also known as the Fraternity of the Holy Trinity), who obtained a charter from Henry VIII in 1514, and it acquired the Lord High Admiral's rights of buoyage and beaconage in 1594. Private lighthouses were acquired under an Act of 1836.

Trivia John Gay's name for his invented goddess of streets and ways (Latin *trivius*, 'of three roads'). His burlesque in three books entitled *Trivia, or the Art of Walking the Streets of London* (1716) is a mine of information on the outdoor life of Queen Anne's time.

Trocadero or **the Troc** Originally a theatre that opened in 1829 at what is now the junction of SHAFTESBURY AVENUE and PICCADILLY CIRCUS. It took its glamorous name from a Spanish island that had been the scene of a French military victory in 1823. Over the course of its existence and under several different names, the building has been much altered and put to a variety of purposes, of which only its period as an opulent J. Lyons restaurant (from 1896 to 1965) proved a lasting success. There are plans for the Trocadero to be radically redeveloped yet again, perhaps from 2010, as a hotel and apartment complex with associated shopping and leisure facilities.

Trojan A CO19 armed response vehicle, around a dozen of which patrol the streets of London at any given time. Most of the vehicles are high-performance cars, crewed by a driver, communications operator and observer/navigator.

troop

Troop, the The official nickname of the King's Troop Royal Horse Artillery, the sovereign's ceremonial saluting battery, stationed in ST JOHN'S WOOD. A mounted unit noted for its equestrian skills, the Troop is an integral part of the HOUSEHOLD TROOPS. Its duties include the firing of salutes in HYDE PARK on royal anniversaries and state occasions and providing a gun carriage and team of black horses for state and military funerals. Members of the Troop also serve abroad as fighting soldiers.

Trooping the Colour The annual ceremony on HORSE GUARDS PARADE, in which the colour or regimental flag is carried between files of troops and received by the sovereign. The ceremony dates from the early 18th century and was originally a guard-mounting parade, with the flag of that day's royal guard being carried along its ranks. In 1748 it was ordered that this parade would mark the official birthday of the sovereign.

trouble (and strife) 'Wife' in COCKNEY RHYMING SLANG, infrequently doubled up to 'froth and bubble'.

Besides, it's nothing unusual for me because I'm

a man of the people, a *homo novus*, not from a hereditary line, like my trouble and strife ...

IVAN TURGENEV: *Fathers and Sons* (1862) (translated by Richard Freeborn, 1991)

Rather stupidly, given the familiarity of its primary meaning, the term has occasionally been used more recently to mean 'life'.

Troynovant or **Troy Novant** A name given by early chroniclers to London. It was an alteration of Trinovant, denoting the 'town of the Trinovantes', a British tribe inhabiting the area of Essex and southern Suffolk. This came to be interpreted as if it meant 'New Troy' (Troy Novant), in line with the legend, originally promulgated by Geoffrey of Monmouth in his *Historia Regum Britanniae* (*c.*1136) and widely accepted in the Middle Ages, that London had been founded by a Trojan called BRUTUS. The Scottish poet William Dunbar made reference to 'thou lusty Troynovant' in 'To the City of London' (1501), and the epithet was later taken up by writers such as Thomas Dekker and Edmund Spenser.

For noble *Britons* sprong from *Troians* bold,
And *Troynouant* was built of old *Troyes* ashes cold.

EDMUND SPENSER: *The Faerie Queene*, III, ix (1590)

trustafarian A young, usually white, person who enjoys a bohemian lifestyle financed by a trust fund or other unearned income. The term is an American coinage, with particular applicability to New York, but it was successfully imported to London in the mid-1990s. Early differences between the American and British understandings of the word have diminished but the London species seems more inclined towards unadulterated hedonism. It has been suggested that if Bertie WOOSTER were alive today he would be a trustafarian. NOTTING HILL has been called 'London's trustafarian suburb'.

The common stereotype is that anyone who lives in Notting Hill or Ladbroke Grove is a try-hard trustafarian whose home was bought by daddy and who floats through life on a combination of drugs and privilege; in short a nauseatingly irritating type.

SARFRAZ MANZOOR, in *The Guardian* (24 August 2007)

tube or **Tube** The informal name for the LONDON UNDERGROUND. From almost the inaugural days of Britain's railways the word 'tube' was used as an occasional alternative for 'tunnel', as it was for other kinds of underground conduits, such as those carrying telegraph wires. London's (and the world's) first deep-level railway was the electrically powered City and South London (now part of the NORTHERN LINE), which opened in 1890, and its twin tunnels were often spoken of as 'tubes'.

> For, of course, there is no smoke, and the tiled walls are immaculately clean; as up and down lines each have a separate tube or tunnel, there is a platform but to one side ...
>
> *Harper's New Monthly Magazine* (January 1896)

However, it was the TWOPENNY TUBE that launched the term into the popular vocabulary when what is now the CENTRAL LINE opened in 1900. Usage of the word 'tube' soon evolved to encompass all London's underground railways, whether constructed by the CUT AND COVER method or deep-level boring.

> ... a large number of passengers who are not pressed for time will prefer a ride in the fresh air on the outside of a 'bus to one in the tube, no matter how well ventilated it may be ...
>
> *New York Times* (22 December 1901)

tube cards The colloquial term for 'tube car panels', the advertisements inside LONDON UNDERGROUND train carriages. Advertisers like them because they are inexpensive (around £10 per card per week in 2009) and members of the captive audience spend an average of 13 minutes' 'dwell time' within view of them. Travellers like them because, as the market research company TNS pointed out in 2007: 'They provide the traditionally reserved British public somewhere to direct one's gaze, so as not to risk catching the eye of a fellow passenger.' Historically memorable users of tube cards have included BROOK STREET BUREAU, the KING'S ROAD hardware retailer Knobs & Knockers and POEMS ON THE UNDERGROUND.

tube map *See the* LONDON UNDERGROUND MAP.

Tufnell Park A distinctive 19th-century residential scheme, characterized by wide, tree-lined streets and individually styled housing, situated north-east of KENTISH TOWN. From early times this was part of the manor of BARNSBURY, which William Tufnell inherited in 1754. Tufnell's heirs sought permission to grant building leases in 1822 and created Tufnell Park Road two years later. Other roads were named after branches of the extended family. Most of the terraced houses were built in the 1850s and 1860s, often with separate gabled roofs to make them look like semi-detached houses. Only two architects were employed throughout the project but they built adventurously, differentiating each street and sometimes every villa within a street. Less elegant dwellings filled out the area later in the 19th century.

Tulse Hill A socially disadvantaged locality situated on the south-eastern edge of BRIXTON. Three estates, Bodley, Upgrove and Scarlettes, were united in 1352 under the ownership of the Hospital of St Thomas the Martyr, an Augustinian priory then located in SOUTHWARK. Henry VIII seized the property at the dissolution of the monasteries and in 1656 the estate was in the hands of the Tulse family. Sir Henry Tulse was LORD MAYOR OF LONDON in 1683–4 and made a fortune from the West African slave trade. In 1856 the astronomer Sir William Huggins built a private observatory at Tulse Hill, where he conducted pioneering research into the spectra of stars, nebulae and comets. Huggins continued his work until 1908, dying here two years later. In 1939 the LONDON COUNTY COUNCIL began the construction of the large Tulse Hill estate, where the former MAYOR OF LONDON Ken Livingstone (*see* RED KEN), grew up. The locality has frequently been the subject of jokey references. Carter USM's 1991 album *101 Damnations* includes a track called '24 Minutes from Tulse Hill'. Wendy Cope created a Tulse Hill-based character called Jason Strugnell, whose verses parodied the work of well-known poets:

> If men deride and sneer, I shall defy them
> And soar above Tulse Hill on poet's wings –
> A brother to the thrush in Brockwell Park ...
>
> *Making Cocoa for Kingsley Amis*, 'Strugnell's Sonnets', VI (1986)

tumbler A member of a gang of London ruffians in the early 1710s who set women on their heads and committed 'various indecencies and barbarities' upon their exposed limbs, according to the 19th-century historian William Lecky.

Turbine Hall The cavernous entrance area of TATE MODERN, so called because it housed the steam turbine when the building was an electricity generating station. The hall is nowadays used as a temporary display space for very large sculptural projects.

Turkey

Turkey Brook A tributary of the River Lee Navigation (*see* LEA) that rises near Potters Bar, Hertfordshire, and intertwines with the eastern section of TURKEY STREET, from which it takes its name. It was formerly called the Maiden's Brook.

Turkey Street A road linking ENFIELD WASH with Bulls Cross. It seems likely that the name derives from a former resident called something like Tuckey, and that the 19th-century corruption to 'Turkey' was the result of folk etymology. ENFIELD's first almshouses were built in Turkey Street by Ann Crowe. In her will of 1763 she left money to repair them and to buy coal for the inmates. The original almshouses were replaced by the present group in the early 1890s, when a station was opened nearby. This closed in 1909 and did not reopen until 1961.

turn

Turnagain Lane A yard branching east from FARRINGDON Street, just south of HOLBORN Viaduct. It was first recorded in 1293 as Wendageyneslane, later Windagain Lane. The lane originally ran down to the FLEET river, 'from whence men must turn again the same way they came, for there it stopped', as John Stow put it in his *Survey of London* (1598). *See also* HE MUST TAKE A HOUSE IN TURNAGAIN LANE.

turn the best side to London, to To make the best of things, to put on a good show. *See also* DON'T TURN THAT SIDE TO LONDON.

> They love pomp and greatness, and they are ever trying, as men say, to turn the best side to London.
>
> E.J. SILVERTON: *The Humorous Parson* (1874)

Turnham Green

Turnham Green The commercial centre of CHISWICK since the mid-19th century, straddling Chiswick High Road. By 1630 a hamlet separate from the riverside settlement at Chiswick was firmly established around the green, with 60 ratepayers. Several noble families established country retreats hereabouts in the 18th century, while the village grew in significance as a coaching halt on the road to Bath. In 1821 the Horticultural Society of London began to lay out a garden that extended from the south of the green towards Chiswick. The society organized an annual fête that was a forerunner of the modern CHELSEA FLOWER SHOW. Turnham Green gained its church in 1843 and a station in 1877. By the end of the 19th century the substantial villas that had lined Chiswick High Road at discrete intervals were being replaced by a ribbon of terraces with shops at street level, while the hinterland filled with a mix of properties, generally getting smaller the later they were built. John Heath-Stubbs's poem 'Turnham Green' (1968) commemorates the Italian poet Ugo Foscolo, who died here in 1827.

Battle of Turnham Green *See under* BATTLE.

Turnmill

Turnmill Brook An early name for the FLEET river, or at least the section that ran where FARRINGDON ROAD and Farringdon Street now stand. The name derived from the profusion of medieval watermills along its course.

Turnmills A former nightclub located at the corner of Turnmill Street and CLERKENWELL Road. It was the first in the UK to obtain a 24-hour dance licence and at one time ranked alongside the MINISTRY OF SOUND as one of the most popular clubs in London. Turnmills closed in 2008 as a consequence of dwindling crowds.

Turnpike Lane

Turnpike Lane A road connecting HORNSEY with the southern tip of WOOD GREEN, where the Turnpike Lane PICCADILLY LINE station opened in 1932. In the early 18th century the road through Wood Green became increasingly busy as travellers sought a route that avoided the WHETSTONE turnpike on the GREAT NORTH ROAD. The STAMFORD HILL and GREEN LANES Turnpike Trust erected a gate here in 1765. For the next 27 years this was the only tollgate on Green Lanes, which at that time extended much further north. The highwayman Dick TURPIN allegedly leapt the spike-topped gate on his horse Black Bess on one occasion, when pursued by a posse led by the chief constable of WESTMINSTER.

Turpentine, the

Turpentine, the A rhyming nickname for the SERPENTINE, occasionally abbreviated to 'the Turps', from the oil or spirit distilled from the resin of the terebinth tree.

> In the midst is a winding lake called the Serpentine, a corruption of Turpentine, with which fluid it was originally filled in the old days

before gas and other modern improvements. Now, however, there is water there ...

Punch (24 October 1906)

Turpin, Dick The 'King of the Road' (1705–39) was born at the Bell Inn, Hempstead, Essex, and apprenticed to a butcher at WHITECHAPEL at the age of 16. He soon became a footpad to supplement his earnings and, after his marriage in 1728, set up as a butcher in Essex. He took to stocking his shop with stolen cattle and sheep and, on discovery, joined a gang of smugglers near Canvey Island and there turned to housebreaking with Gregory's Gang in EPPING FOREST. In 1735 he became a highwayman, working around the south of London, and in 1736 began his partnership with Tom King. His boldness became a public legend, as did his activities in Epping Forest and on HOUNSLOW HEATH. After the death of King in 1737, he shifted to Lincolnshire and thence to Yorkshire, where he was finally apprehended and hanged at the Mount, outside the walls of York. The legend of his horse Black Bess and the ride to York derives from Harrison Ainsworth's *Rookwood* (1834).

turtle dove 'Love' or 'glove' in somewhat dated COCKNEY RHYMING SLANG. With the latter sense, the plural may be abbreviated to 'turtles'.

Tusculum A nickname applied by Alexander Pope (1688–1744) to his retreat in TWICKENHAM, after Cicero's villa outside Rome. The poet moved to a riverside house on the southern side of Twickenham in 1719. He laid out gardens on the other side of Cross Deep (a road named after the neighbouring stretch of the THAMES), which were connected with the house via a tunnel. Pope expounded his seminal thinking on the 'Genius of the Place' – the need for harmony with nature in landscape design – while writing in this garden. When Baroness Howe bought the property in 1807 she commissioned the construction of Ryan House next door and then demolished Pope's former home. The TEA merchant Thomas Young put up a grand new house on the site in 1842, naming it Pope's Villa. St Catherine's Convent School moved to Pope's Villa in 1919. It is now home to St James Independent School for Senior Boys.

tweed The origin of this name of a woollen cloth used for garments is to be found in a blunder. It should have been 'tweel', the Scots form of 'twill', but when the Scottish manufacturer sent a consignment to LOCK & CO., of ST JAMES'S STREET, in 1826, the name was badly written and misread, and as the cloth was made on the banks of the Tweed, 'tweed' was accordingly adopted.

Twelve Apostles A once-popular nickname for the dozen parallel streets that were laid out in Bushey Mead when this extension of WIMBLEDON first took shape in the early years of the 20th century. The name was said to have been invented by the local district nurses.

Twickenham A pleasant riverside residential district, situated south-west of RICHMOND. There is mention made of a settlement at Tuicanhom – probably meaning 'river-bend land of a man called Twicca' – on the ground by EEL PIE ISLAND, in AD 704. The village grew during the Middle Ages along Church Street and King Street and in alleys from them to the river, and was surrounded by stretches of open field and meadows. In the early 16th century Richmond and HAMPTON COURT both became royal palaces; Twickenham lay between them and members of the royal households began to build homes in the area. A small number of the best houses, including Orleans House, MARBLE HILL House and York House, occupied the riverside and in the 18th century the village's grassy riverfront contributed to the famous view from Richmond Hill. In the latter part of the 19th century increased traffic and easier access by railway made Twickenham less of a riverside retreat than it had been and the large estates started to be broken up and sold off for plots for smaller houses. By the 1950s most of the large houses that had characterized the district had submitted to the spread of more affordable housing.

Amongst those who lived in Twickenham, either permanently or temporarily, were Colly Cibber, Horace Walpole (*see* STRAWBERRY HILL), Alfred Tennyson, Walter de la Mare and J.M.W. Turner. The exiled Louis-Philippe of France (1773–1850) also stayed here on several occasions and four generations of his descendants lived in Twickenham or its neighbourhood at various times.

Twickenham Nightingale A nickname given by Lord Byron to Alexander Pope and also by Twickenham residents to Nöel Coward's aunt Hilda, who sang very high.

Twickenham Stadium A rugby ground opened in Twickenham in 1909 on land beside the Duke of Northumberland's River, bought in 1907 by William Williams (*see* BILLY WILLIAMS' CABBAGE PATCH). The stadium, often known affectionately as 'Twickers', has undergone continual expansion and updating since the 1920s. It was extensively rebuilt in the 1990s and now has a capacity of 75,000. It is the venue for all of England's home matches (its first international match was staged in 1910), and is the headquarters of the English Rugby Football Union and the home of the World Rugby Museum.

Twickenham Stoop *See the* STOOP.

Twickenham Streaker A nickname applied both to Michael O'Brien, who introduced STREAKING to Britain when he sprinted naked across the Twickenham pitch during an England v. France rugby game in 1974, and to Erica Roe, who in 1982 ran topless across the same pitch at half-time during a match between England and Australia.

Bard of Twickenham *See under* BARD.

three Yahoos of Twickenham *See under* THREE.

Twiggy The internationally known identity of the model and actress Lesley Lawson, née Hornby, who was born in NEASDEN in 1949. 'Twiggy' was a childhood nickname that her manager suggested she use professionally. In the mid-1960s she personified the look of SWINGING LONDON, arguably becoming the world's first 'supermodel', and her skinny proportions and androgynous, waiflike appearance, which were novel at the time, influenced subsequent trends in modelling on both sides of the Atlantic. Twiggy turned to acting with a starring role in Ken Russell's *The Boyfriend* (1971). In 2005–7 she was a judge on the TV show *America's Next Top Model* and around the same time appeared in a high-visibility advertising campaign for Marks & Spencer.

Twin Towers In London, the name referred to the iconically distinctive pair of towers that adorned WEMBLEY STADIUM before it was demolished to make way for a new stadium at the beginning of the 21st century.

twirly A nickname applied by transport staff in London to a FREEDOM PASS holder or someone who attempts to buy or use an off-peak travelcard or other discounted ticket before the permitted time. Such persons will often disingenuously enquire: 'Am I too early?'

> Are you a twirly? I'm a twirly, I've been one for a month now. You must be 59 or younger if you're not. Us twirlies are people in possession of concessionary bus passes, passes that we're not allowed to use before 9am Monday to Friday (though we can at weekends and on public holidays).
>
> MICHAEL WHITE, in *The Guardian* (30 November 2005)

Twist, Oliver *See* OLIVER TWIST.

two

two and a kick Half a crown (two shillings and sixpence), in pre-decimalization London slang. The term was in use from the early 18th century.

> When he was out of work my mother used to give him two and a kick and tell him to go out and not come home until he'd drunk himself cheerful and loving like.
>
> G.B. SHAW: *Pygmalion* (film version) (1938)

two-and-eight 'State' in COCKNEY RHYMING SLANG, usually in the sense of a state of mind, often one of nervous agitation, but alternatively a mess of some kind, such as a state of untidiness or dishevelment. The term derived from a sum of pre-decimal currency and is still in widespread use. It is frequently prefixed with the emphatic adjective 'right' and heard in phrases such as 'he was in a right two-and-eight about something' or 'your bedroom's in a right two-and-eight'.

> EastEnders star Lucy Speed looks a right two-and-eight … as she steps out for the soap's Christmas bash.
>
> *Sunday Mirror* (12 December 2000)

2i's An OLD COMPTON STREET café with a basement bar that in the late 1950s became a wellspring of British rock 'n' roll, rivalled only by the Gyre and Gimble in John Adam Street. Run by a former professional wrestler, the 2i's showcased jazz, blues, skiffle and calypso, attracting both talent and customers from around the country. Tommy Steele, Cliff Richard and Adam Faith were among the young hopefuls who performed there.

Two Peacocks of Bedfont *See the* BEDFONT PEACOCKS.

Twopenny (or Tuppenny) Tube A nickname for the Central London Railway, now the CENTRAL LINE, which opened in 1900. The fare was originally 2d but the name lingered on for several years after it was raised to 3d in 1907. *See also the* TUBE.

Tyburn (Old English *teo*, 'boundary', and *burna*, 'stream', referring to the boundary between the manors of EBURY and WESTMINSTER)

1. A tributary of the River THAMES, now contained within an underground conduit. It rises at HAMPSTEAD and flows beneath REGENT'S PARK, GREEN PARK and BUCKINGHAM PALACE and into the Thames to the west of VAUXHALL BRIDGE. Huge metal pipes carry it through the LONDON UNDERGROUND stations at BAKER STREET and VICTORIA. The Tyburn gave its name to the village that was later called MARYLEBONE.

2. The historic place of execution in London, located at the corner of the EDGWARE ROAD and BAYSWATER Road, close to where the MARBLE ARCH now stands. The first hanging took place here in 1388 and a permanent gallows was set up in 1571. This was replaced by a movable gallows in 1759. Among those to meet their fate here were Perkin Warbeck, pretender to the English throne (1499), Oliver Plunket, the last Catholic martyr to die in the British Isles (1681) and Jack SHEPPARD, highwayman (1714, in front of a crowd of 200,000). After the Restoration of Charles II the body of Oliver Cromwell was dug up, set on a gibbet at Tyburn and later buried in a pit at the foot of the gallows. The last criminal to be hanged here was John Austin in 1783. After that, executions were carried out at NEWGATE until its demolition. The site of the gallows is marked by three brass triangles let into the pavement here, recalling Tyburn's 'Triple Tree', a three-cornered gallows that could dangle 21 persons at a time.

Tyburn blossom A budding criminal.

> A young thief or pickpocket, who in time will ripen into fruit borne by the deadly never-green [i.e. TYBURN TREE].
>
> FRANCIS GROSE: *A Classical Dictionary of the Vulgar Tongue* (1796 edition)

Tyburn check Slang in the late 18th and early 19th centuries for a hangman's noose, and by extension a length of rope generically.

Tyburn collar A mid-19th-century term for a fringe of beard worn under the chin. *See also* NEWGATE FRINGE.

Tyburn face A late 17th-century colloquialism for a miserable, down-in-the-mouth look, as if expecting the worst.

Tyburn foretop A term around the turn of the 19th century for a wig (also called simply a Tyburn top) with the lock of hair at the front combed forwards over the eyes. Such wigs were especially popular among the underworld fraternity.

Tyburnia A somewhat literary name used in the second half of the 19th century for the high-class residential district that had recently been built along the Bayswater Road from MARBLE ARCH (site of the former Tyburn gallows) to LANCASTER GATE and northwards. The area is now generally regarded as the south-east corner of BAYSWATER.

Tyburn Lane A former name for PARK LANE.

Tyburn piccadill Slang in the 17th century for a hangman's noose; hence to 'put on a Tyburn piccadill' was to be hanged – a piccadill was a type of lace-trimmed collar fashionable at that time (*see* PICCADILLY).

Tyburn Road A former name for OXFORD STREET.

Tyburn stretch Slang from the late 17th to the early 19th centuries for a hanging.

Tyburn string Late 18th-century slang for a hangman's noose.

Tyburn ticket A certificate that, under a statute of William III (1698), was granted to prosecutors who had secured a capital conviction against a criminal, exempting them from all parish and ward offices within the parish in which the felony had been committed. This, with the privilege it conferred, might be sold once, and once only, and the *Stamford Mercury* for 27 March 1818 announced the sale of one for £280. The Act was repealed in 1818, but as late as 1856 a Mr Pratt of BOND STREET claimed exemption from sitting on an OLD BAILEY jury on the strength of the possession of a Tyburn ticket and was successful.

Tyburn tiffany Slang in the 17th century for a hangman's noose. A tiffany was a garment, especially a head- or neckscarf, made of sheer gauze muslin.

Tyburn tippet Slang from the 16th to the 19th centuries for a hangman's noose.

> And how many of our Popish Martyrs ... have worne the Tiburn-tippet, as Father Latimer phraseth it?
>
> JOHN TRAPP: *Commentary upon 1 Corinthians* (1647)

Tyburn tree Slang from the mid-18th century to

the early 19th century for the gallows at Tyburn, and in particular for the permanent gallows that had been erected in 1571 (*see above*). A large triangular structure capable of 'turning off' 21 malefactors simultaneously, its first victim was the 'Romish Canonical Doctor' John Story.

Since laws were made for ev'ry degree,
To curb vice in others, as well as me,
I wonder we han't better Company,
Upon Tyburn Tree!

JOHN GAY: *The Beggar's Opera*, I, xiii (1728)

U

umbrella (Latin *umbra*, 'shade') The device was used in ancient China, Babylon, Egypt and elsewhere, but it was not commonly found in England until the early 18th century, when it was considered suitable only for women.

> The tucked-up sempstress walks with hasty strides,
> While streams run down her oiled umbrella's sides.
>
> JONATHAN SWIFT: 'City Shower' (1710)

Jonas Hanway (1712–86), the philanthropist, publicized masculine usage from about 1750 by carrying one regularly in the streets of London. He incurred a good deal of ridicule in the process. In 1830 James Smith opened London's first umbrella shop and in 1857 his son, also James, moved the business to New Oxford Street, where it remains today. The umbrella became an essential accoutrement of the traditional CITY businessman and the stereotypical image still resonates internationally:

> In the [Travelers' insurance] ad, a British-looking fellow in a bowler hat and vested suit uses his 35-foot red umbrella to shield children from the rain, to be a ferry boat for stranded circus workers and, Mary Poppins-style, to fly home a boy and girl whose bicycle broke down.
>
> USA Today (4 July 2008)

Uncle Willy 'Silly' or, occasionally, 'chilly' in COCKNEY RHYMING SLANG. Numerous other uncles have rhyming slang associations, including Bert for 'shirt' (and Bertie for 'shirty'), Dick for 'sick', Fred for 'bread', Gus for 'bus', Ned or Ted for 'bed' or 'head' and Reg for 'veg'. The ever-growing family has recently admitted Lester or Fester, a 'child molester', and Toby, a 'moby' (mobile phone).

unclubable or **unclubbable** 'A very unclubable man' is one who is very unsocial; one lacking in urbanity. A word coined by Dr Johnson and applied by him to Sir John Hawkins (1719–89), one of the original members of the Literary CLUB founded in 1763, which met at the Turk's Head, Gerrard Street, now the main thoroughfare of CHINATOWN.

uncrowned king of Limehouse The nickname of Charlie Brown, landlord of the Railway Tavern in WEST INDIA DOCK Road from the mid-1890s. He used his wealth, which was of uncertain origin, to amass a large and valuable collection of antiquities, including Ming vases, which he kept in the upper rooms of the pub. Lesser curiosities were displayed in the bars. He frequently helped out customers who were in financial difficulties and donated generously in support of striking dockworkers in 1912, after which he was made an honorary member of the stevedores' union. Charlie Brown died in 1932 and his funeral procession was said to have been London's best attended until that of Winston Churchill, with crowds five or six deep lining the entire route to TOWER HAMLETS CEMETERY. The Railway Tavern was demolished in 1989 during the construction of the DOCKLANDS LIGHT RAILWAY. *See also* CHARLIE BROWN'S ROUNDABOUT.

Underground Ernie A computer-animated TV series and eponymous character created for the BBC in 2006 and aimed at three- to eight-year-olds. Ernie is a station supervisor on the 'International Underground', which bears a close resemblance to the LONDON UNDERGROUND, especially in its branding. The trains have human characteristics, in the style of *Thomas the Tank Engine*, and are named after foreign cities and London Underground lines. An extensive variety of themed merchandise has been marketed.

Underhill A mixed area of rented and privately owned housing lying 'under' BARNET Hill.

Underhill Stadium The home ground of Barnet FC since 1907. Underhill also hosts home games for ARSENAL reserves and the Arsenal first team plays a traditional pre-season friendly here against Barnet. The Bees have long wanted to move to a new home but every proposed site has been dogged by controversy and their eventual future may lie outside the borough.

Underneath the Arches A poignant little song about urban vagrancy (1932), written by the WHITECHAPEL-born Bud Flanagan, a member of the CRAZY GANG, with 'additional American lyric' by Joseph McCarthy.

unicorn

unicorn's horn See the TOWER HORN.

Unicorn Theatre A theatre for young people, based in TOOLEY STREET since 2008. It evolved from a mobile theatre founded in 1947 by Caryl Jenner (1917–73), which operated at first in the northern HOME COUNTIES and then nationwide. As the English Children's Theatre, the company produced its first season at the Arts Theatre, Great Newport Street, in 1961 and the following year changed its name to the Unicorn Theatre Club for Children. The company remained at the Arts Theatre until 1999, after which it performed at various theatres while a purpose-built home was designed and constructed. The Unicorn stages its own productions and those by other British and international theatre companies, as well as hosting workshops and related theatrical activities.

Universal Provider, The William WHITELEY, the department store magnate, claimed this title for himself, boasting that he could supply 'anything from a pin to an elephant at short notice'. He is said to have proved his credentials by delivering a large specimen of the latter to a previously sceptical Church of England clergyman at 4pm on the day the order was placed.

university

University Boat Race See the BOAT RACE.

University College Hospital The largest constituent institution of the UNIVERSITY COLLEGE LONDON HOSPITALS group. It began in 1834 as the North London Hospital but soon became known by its present name because its primary role was to provide clinical training for medical students at what is now UNIVERSITY COLLEGE LONDON. The hospital was rebuilt in flamboyantly baroque style by Sir Alfred Waterhouse and his son Paul over the ten years to 1906. Now known as the Cruciform, this building became part of UCL's teaching facilities in 1996. The hospital moved into a spectacular pair of new buildings on EUSTON ROAD in 2005.

University College London An institution of higher education founded as London University in 1826; it admitted its first students two years later. Most of the leading figures in the university's creation were Scotsmen, notably James Mill (1773–1836), father of the utilitarian philosopher John Stuart Mill, the statesman Henry Brougham (1778–1868) and the poet Thomas Campbell (1777–1844). In 1836 it was renamed University College and began awarding UNIVERSITY OF LONDON degrees, in common with its rival, KING'S COLLEGE. The college's first home was the Wilkins Building, erected on land that had been intended for yet another BLOOMSBURY square. It has since progressively expanded to consume most of the east side of GOWER STREET and the land behind it. Among the college's departments are the Institute of Archaeology, the Jill Dando Institute of Crime Science, the SLADE SCHOOL OF FINE ART and the School of Slavonic and East European Studies. UCL alumni include Walter Bagehot, Joseph Lister, Alexander Graham Bell, Mohandas Gandhi, G.K. Chesterton, MARIE STOPES and Ricky Gervais.

University College London Hospitals An NHS foundation trust established in 1994. It encompasses the following extant institutions:

Eastman Dental Hospital
The Heart Hospital
Hospital for Tropical Diseases
National Hospital for Neurology and Neurosurgery
Royal London Homoeopathic Hospital
UNIVERSITY COLLEGE HOSPITAL

In addition, UCLH has absorbed the former Elizabeth Garrett Anderson Hospital and MIDDLESEX HOSPITAL within the facilities at UCH.

University of East London A university formed in 1992 from the Polytechnic of East London. It evolved from the WEST HAM Technical Institute (founded in 1892) and technical colleges in WALTHAMSTOW and BARKING, which all amalgamated as the North East London Polytechnic in 1970. UEL has campuses at STRATFORD and at CYPRUS, where the most distinctive feature is a waterside row of drum-shaped halls of residence.

University of London A federal university, the

oldest in England after Oxford and Cambridge, and the largest for full-time students in the UK. Its original institutions were UNIVERSITY COLLEGE LONDON and KING'S COLLEGE. These, together with some hospital medical schools, were combined as the University of London in 1836. Its other constituents now include:

BIRKBECK COLLEGE

The Central School of Speech and Drama

Courtauld Institute of Art

GOLDSMITHS

Heythrop College

The Institute of Cancer Research

Institute of Education

London Business School

LONDON SCHOOL OF ECONOMICS

London School of Hygiene and Tropical Medicine

QUEEN MARY, UNIVERSITY OF LONDON

Royal Academy of Music

Royal Holloway, University of London

The Royal Veterinary College

St George's, University of London

The School of Oriental and African Studies

The School of Pharmacy

Additionally, an array of postgraduate-level research institutes are administered as the School of Advanced Study, including the Warburg Institute and the Institute of Historical Research. It opened all its degrees to women in 1878, the first British university to do so (Royal Holloway and Westfield colleges, although originally outside the university, were founded as women's colleges). Its administrative headquarters, the imposing Senate House in BLOOMSBURY, which also contains its central library, were built in the 1930s.

University of North London *See* LONDON METROPOLITAN UNIVERSITY.

University of Ponders End A students' nickname for what is now MIDDLESEX UNIVERSITY, dating from the days when it was a polytechnic.

University of the Arts London Europe's largest university for art, design, fashion, communication and the performing arts. Its constituent colleges are:

CAMBERWELL COLLEGE OF ARTS

CENTRAL SAINT MARTINS

CHELSEA COLLEGE OF ART AND DESIGN

London College of Communication

London College of Fashion

WIMBLEDON College of Art

The amalgamation project began in 1989, in the

form of the London Institute, and adopted its present identity in 2004. From September 2011 the university's largest campus will be at KING'S CROSS, where a new home is under construction for Central Saint Martins College of Art and Design.

University of the Ghetto A former Jewish nickname for WHITECHAPEL library. Among those who studied at the 'university' were the poet and artist Isaac Rosenberg, the writer Jacob Bronowski and the playwrights Arnold Wesker and Bernard Kops.

University of Westminster A university focused on 'educating for professional life', based at three campuses in central London and one in NORTHWICK PARK. It had its genesis in the Regent Street Polytechnic (*see the* POLYTECHNIC INSTITUTION), on which all other British polytechnics were originally modelled. In the 1960s the Polytechnic acquired new sites in MARYLEBONE ROAD to accommodate a college of architecture (where the rock bank Pink Floyd came together in 1965) and in New Cavendish Street to house engineering and science. It merged with the HOLBORN College of Law, Language and Commerce to form the Polytechnic of Central London in 1966. HARROW College of Higher Education merged with PCL in 1990 and two years later the combined institution became the University of Westminster. The university now has more than 22,000 students (including those taking short or part-time courses), 5,000 of whom come from overseas.

University Stone A small obelisk located upstream of PUTNEY BRIDGE on the SURREY side, marking the starting point of the BOAT RACE. It bears the inscription 'UBR', for University Boat Race. A similar stone marks the race's finishing point, just short of CHISWICK Bridge.

Unknown Warrior The body of an unknown British soldier of the First World War brought home from one of the battlefields of the Western Front and 'buried among the kings' in WESTMINSTER ABBEY (11 November 1920). The inscription, in capital letters, begins: 'Beneath this stone rests the body of a British warrior unknown by name or rank brought from France to lie among the most illustrious of the land and buried here on Armistice Day.'

up

Up the Junction

1. A collection of interwoven short stories (1963) by Nell Dunn, depicting aspects of life in BATTERSEA

in the era preceding its partial GENTRIFICATION. Ken Loach directed a gritty TV adaptation for *The Wednesday Play* (1965), which generated a record number of complaints for its bad language and non-judgmental portrayal of sexual promiscuity. Peter Collinson's film version (which premiered at the CLAPHAM JUNCTION Granada in 1968) focused on one of the book's storylines, the relationship between the upper-middle-class Polly (played by Suzy Kendall) and working-class Peter (played by Dennis Waterman).

2. A single by the SOUTH LONDON band Squeeze, written by Chris Difford and Glenn Tilbrook and taken from the album *Cool for Cats* (1979). The lyrics succinctly chart the course of a CLAPHAM-based relationship from optimistic beginnings to a sad end, three years and one baby later.

up west or **West** A colloquialism for the WEST END. One does not have to be travelling from the east to use the term but it originated in the EAST END, where it has (or had) connotations of a special trip, for a day's shopping or a night's entertainment. Residents of ALBERT SQUARE still speak excitedly of 'going up west'.

Round London: Down East and Up West
MONTAGU STEPHEN WILLIAMS (book title) (1893)

Upminster A predominantly white, home-owning dormitory suburb situated east of HORNCHURCH, enriched by a handful of important old buildings. Upminster's name derives from its parish church, said to have been founded in the 7th century by St Cedd, bishop of the East Saxons. The present church, dedicated to St Laurence, was built facing the village green in the early 13th century and its original tower survives intact, as does a 15th-century thatched barn near Hall Lane, which now accommodates an agricultural and folk museum, and an attractive smock mill near St Mary's Lane, built in 1803. In 1906 the ILFORD developer Peter Griggs began to create a 'new town on an American plan', covering 700 acres (283 hectares) of the Upminster Hall estate. The hall itself has survived as a clubhouse for Upminster golf course.

The rock singer Ian Dury (1942–2000) grew up in the suburb, and entitled his 1981 album *Lord Upminster*.

upper In place names, the prefix 'Upper' refers of course to the part of an area that stands on relatively high ground. Many towns or districts would be divided into roughly equal halves and named

accordingly. However, not only did the upper part of a locality often benefit from cleaner air and more sanitary drainage, the name simply *sounded* better. Consequently, an 'upper' locality might sometimes be invented where there was no concomitant 'lower' part. Elsewhere, the inhabitants (or developers) of a lower part might start calling their area something else; Lower STREATHAM, for example, became Streatham Vale, while Lower Norwood became WEST NORWOOD. Something similar happened with Upper and Lower Streets in ISLINGTON. The former proudly retained its name, while the latter became ESSEX ROAD.

Upper Alsatia A term sometimes used to distinguish the ALSATIA of WHITEFRIARS from the LIBERTY OF THE MINT in SOUTHWARK, which was occasionally called Lower Alsatia.

Upper Edmonton The densely populated southern part of EDMONTON, focused on Silver Street, Angel Road and Fore Street, which form the arms of the crossroads at the ANGEL, EDMONTON. From the late Middle Ages ribbon development along the coaching road to Hertford created a hamlet at Fore Street, with several well-known inns, most famously of all, the Bell (*see* GILPIN, JOHN). Upper Edmonton was aggressively built up from the 1880s and municipal housing projects again transformed large parts of the area after the Second World War.

Upper Street The central thoroughfare of ISLINGTON, extending for 1 mile (1.6 km) between HIGHBURY CORNER and the junction with Liverpool Road at its southern end. Upper Street was part of the cattle-droving route to Smithfield and a King's Head tavern is supposed to have existed from about 1543. Sir John Miller's house, which stood near Theberton Street, had become the Pied Bull by 1725. An unsubstantiated story persists that this had earlier been the residence of Sir Walter Raleigh. During the 19th century Upper Street's rows of houses were rebuilt as commercial premises, at first catering for the growing local population and later attracting customers from further afield. The street's non-stop commerce prompted the rector of St Mary's Church to found the Lord's Day Observance Society in 1831.

Despite Islington's ever-diminishing status as a residential district from the latter part of the 19th century, Upper Street's outfitters and drapers grew in prestige, and their trousseaux and underclothes were especially highly prized. Between the wars the big stores lost the battle with their rivals UP WEST and Upper Street went into a slow decline that lasted until an increasingly young and well-educated population presented new opportunities after the 1960s. Sisterwrite was Britain's first feminist bookshop when it opened on Upper Street in 1978, the King's Head began to stage theatrical performances and the Hope and Anchor became a leading pub venue for the burgeoning PUNK ROCK scene. Upper Street's variety of restaurants is now almost unrivalled outside the WEST END and the street forms the spine of LITTLE THEATRELAND.

Upper Tooting *See* TOOTING BEC.

Upper Woodcote A garden village situated on the western side of PURLEY. In 1859 James Watney bought 800 acres (324 hectares) of the Carew family's BEDDINGTON estate and his grandson sold about a third of the land to chartered surveyor William Webb in 1888. Webb planted trees, flowers and hedgerows that were allowed to mature before homes were built and offered for sale. He filled Rose Walk with 6,000 rose bushes, the South Border with herbaceous plants and Silver Lane with a double row of silver birch and a host of bulbs and wild flowers. The Promenade de Verdun came last, lined with an avenue of Lombardy poplars with their roots in soil brought from Armentières, sifted to remove shrapnel. At the end of the avenue is a granite obelisk dedicated to the memory of French soldiers who died in the First World War. Webb expounded his landscaping theories in *Garden First in Land Development* (1919).

Upstairs, Downstairs A LONDON WEEKEND TELEVISION drama (1971–5), set in a five-storey townhouse at 165 Eaton Place, BELGRAVIA. Over the course of five series, spanning the years 1903 to 1930, *Upstairs, Downstairs* observed the lives of the aristocratic Bellamy family upstairs and their domestic servants 'below stairs', especi-ally Rose Buck, the first parlour-maid (played by Jean Marsh, who co-created the show), Mr Hudson, the snooty butler (played by Gordon Jackson), and Mrs Bridges, the warm-hearted cook (said to have been HM the Queen's favour-ite TV character, played by Angela Baddeley). It has been estimated that more than a billion people in over 70 countries have viewed *Up-stairs, Downstairs*.

Upton Park A densely built-up district situated between WEST HAM and EAST HAM. The station opened on the London, Tilbury and Southend Railway in 1877 and the Upton Park estate was built following the sale of Plashet House and its grounds in 1883. District Railway trains began serving the station in 1902 and the old hamlets of Plashet, Upton and GREEN STREET gradually dissolved within the new district of Upton Park. During the first half of the 20th century Upton Park possessed a large Jewish community, which has now been replaced by an even larger south Asian population. WEST HAM UNITED FC moved to Green Street's BOLEYN GROUND in 1904, nine years after their formation as THAMES IRON-WORKS FC and four years after they had changed their name to attract broader support.

Ursa Major A nickname given to Dr JOHNSON by James Boswell's father, Lord Auchinleck.

use your loaf *See* LOAF (OF BREAD).

Uxbridge The administrative and commercial centre of the London Borough of HILLINGDON, situated on the western edge of GREATER LON-DON, south of the WESTERN AVENUE. The name almost certainly derives from the Wixan tribe who settled various parts of MIDDLESEX in the 7th century. Their bridge would have crossed the River Colne. However, no document recorded the existence of the village until the mid-12th century, when it was called Wixebrug. During the 18th century Uxbridge flourished as a coaching halt, with shops and inns on the High Street, and the present market house was built in 1788. The construction of the GRAND JUNCTION CANAL in the 1790s helped confirm Uxbridge's supremacy over Hillingdon as a market town, particularly for corn. Coach traffic continued to increase and the town had 54 licensed premises in 1853. Three years later the first railway station opened and road travel began to wane, with many inns and their stables converting to private dwellings. Two retail centres now dominate the High Street: the Pavilions and the Chimes. To the south-east of the shopping area stands Hillingdon civic centre, built in the mid-1970s in an original and influential style that avoided the grandly monu-mental approach taken by most town halls. *See also* BRUNEL UNIVERSITY.

Treaty of Uxbridge *See under* TREATY.

vada or **varda** A POLARI term meaning to look, probably derived from Venetian *vardar*, which has the same meaning.

Valence House A historic house located on what is now the north side of BECONTREE. Agnes de Valence, whose name derived from the French abbey of Valence, retired to DAGENHAM following the death of her third husband in 1291. On Agnes's demise in 1309 her brother Aylmer, later Earl of Pembroke, took possession of the estate and held it until his death in 1342, when he was buried in WESTMINSTER ABBEY. Valence House may have been built in the 14th century but was subsequently enlarged, then reduced and then enlarged again, as well as being remodelled on other occasions. At its heart, the present house is of late 17th-century origin. The LONDON COUNTY COUNCIL bought Valence House in 1901 and sold it to Dagenham council in 1926. It subsequently served as council offices and a library and is now partly a museum.

Valentines Park A public park and neighbouring Edwardian estate situated on the north side of central ILFORD. The name probably derives from a 16th-century landowner. A house was built here in the late 1690s for Elizabeth Tillotson, widow of John Tillotson, Archbishop of Canterbury (1630-94), but successive enlargements and improvements have erased almost every trace of this building. The mansion that stands today dates primarily from phases of work in 1769 and 1811. The council acquired most of the grounds and opened them in 1899 (originally as Central Park) and acquired Valentines mansion in 1912. It later served as a home for wartime refugees, a hospital, a public health centre and a council housing department. After standing empty for 15 years, Valentines was restored and reopened in 2009 as a multi-use community venue.

Vale of Health A mini-village in north-west HAMPSTEAD. This boggy part of HAMPSTEAD HEATH was originally known as Gangmoor, and later as Hatches (or Hatchett's) Bottom, after an early 18th-century cottager. The Hampstead Water Company created a pond here in 1777, which drained enough of the marsh to allow houses to be built. For much of its early existence, Hatches Bottom was not regarded as a picturesque village but as an intrusive presence on the heath. With the opening of the Hampstead Junction Railway in 1860 day-trippers began to swarm here in summertime and the Hampstead Heath Hotel and Vale of Health tavern were built, neither of which has survived. Those who wished to attract visitors invented and propagated the 'Vale of Health' name, although this did not fully supplant the older identity until the mid-20th century. Former residents include the artist Stanley Spencer, the writers Leigh Hunt, D.H. Lawrence, Stella Gibbons, Compton Mackenzie and Edgar Wallace, and the Nobel prize-winning Indian poet Rabindranath Tagore.

Valhalla *See* NATIONAL VALHALLA; VICTORIAN VALHALLA.

valley
Valley, The The home of CHARLTON ATHLETIC FC from 1919, located on Floyd Road, east of the station. It was formerly the site of a large sandpit. The club left the Valley in 1985 and returned in 1992, after fans had waged a vigorous campaign for the stadium to be rebuilt, in the face of council opposition. Their activities included the creation of a single-issue political party, the Valley Party, which attracted nearly 11 per cent of the vote in the 1990 borough council elections.
Valley Fields The disguised identity of DULWICH in the stories of P.G. Wodehouse, who went to school there. His characters return again and again to this 'fragrant backwater', with its 'purl-

ing brooks', tree-lined roads, neat little gardens and rustic front gates, to visit young friends who unfortunately have to work for a living, retired nannies and (relatively) impecunious aristocrats, living at addresses like Mon Repos, The Nook and Nasturtium Villas.

vampire

Vampire of London A nickname of John George Haigh (1909–49), also known as the Acid Bath Murderer, from his claim to have drunk the blood of his victims before dissolving their bodies in drums of concentrated sulphuric acid. He was convicted of six killings (and admitted three more) and hanged at WANDSWORTH PRISON.

Cripplegate 'vampire' *See under* CRIPPLE-GATE.

Society for Tolerance of Vampires See POT-TER, HARRY.

Vanbrugh

Vanbrugh Castle *See* MAZE HILL.
Vanbrugh Theatre *See* RADA.

Vandyke's Club *See* ST LUKE'S CLUB.

Vauxhall A THAMES-side locality and transport interchange in south-west LAMBETH, and formerly the site of famous pleasure gardens (*see below*). The Gascon mercenary Falkes de Bréauté gained possession of the manor in 1233 through his marriage to wealthy widow Margaret de Redvers and built Falkes' Hall, later called Fox Hall. Industry and commerce flourished along Vauxhall's riverside for more than three centuries, and still does at NINE ELMS. Much of Vauxhall was rebuilt with blocks of low-rise flats in the 1930s and parts had become very run down by the early 1990s, since when the area has been transformed in a variety of ways. Much of the riverside has filled with luxury apartment blocks that have proved popular with senior politicians, surviving Georgian and Victorian terraced houses have been gentrified, and huge sums have been spent on the regeneration of council housing. Vauxhall's Portuguese community has opened cafés and restaurants, while a 'village' of gay bars and nightclubs has also evolved.

Vauxhall and I A critically acclaimed album (1994) by the Mancunian singer/songwriter Morrissey (b.1959), who lived in the Vauxhall area for a while.

Vauxhall Bridge A road bridge linking LAM-BETH and PIMLICO, opened in 1816. Originally called the 'Regent's Bridge', it was the first iron bridge across the THAMES in London. It was replaced by the present structure in 1906.

Vauxhall Cross A traffic junction located at the south-western end of the Albert EMBANK-MENT. In 1994 the Secret Intelligence Service (MI6) moved to a purpose-built headquarters here, designed by Terry Farrell, which it named Vauxhall Cross. According to the James Bond film *Die Another Day* (2002), the basement of the building contains a disused underground station named Vauxhall Cross, but this is a fiction. Transport for London completed London's most distinctive bus station at Vauxhall Cross in 2004, with 'ski-ramp' solar panels that power most of the station's lighting.

Vauxhall End The name by which the northern end of the OVAL cricket ground is known.

Vauxhall Gardens London's longest-lasting pleasure gardens. Jane Vaux, possibly a descendant of Falkes de Bréauté (*see* VAUXHALL), owned a house at Vauxhall in 1615 with 11 acres (4.5 hectares) of grounds that were laid out as a pleasure park called New SPRING GARDENS *c*.1660. Samuel PEPYS recorded later in the decade that he went 'by water to Fox-hall, and there walked in Spring Garden'. The park's attractions were greatly enhanced in 1732 and the construction of WESTMINSTER BRIDGE in 1750 improved its accessibility. The gardens provided refreshments, musical entertainments, fireworks, displays of pictures and statuary and the like, and at night were lit by over 1,000 lamps. They also gave ample opportunity for amorous assignations, both amateur and professional. Such was the prestige of Vauxhall Gardens, as they were formally called from 1785, that similar parks were laid out in several cities, several of which borrowed the Vauxhall name (*see also* VOKZAL). The gardens closed in 1859 after two decades of financial difficulties but a small remnant, Spring Gardens, survives opposite the northern end of South Lambeth Road.

The gardens crop up frequently in English literature down the centuries – for example, in Vanbrugh's play *The Provok'd Wife* (1697), Swift's *Journal to Stella* (1710–13), DICKENS's *Sketches by Boz* (1836–7) and Thackeray's *Vanity Fair* (1847–8), although that novel's Captain Dobbin finds 'the Vauxhall amusements not particularly lively'. One of Thomas Rowlandson's most famous paintings is *Vauxhall Gardens* (1784); it was rediscovered in 1945, having for a long time been known only from an aquatint engraving.

Vauxhall Motors A company that began life as Vauxhall Iron Works and made its first car in 1903, badged with Falkes de Bréauté's heraldic GRIFFIN. The company relocated to Luton, Bedfordshire, in 1905 and became Vauxhall Motors two years later. A plaque at SAINSBURY'S petrol station on Wandsworth Road marks the site of the original factory.

Venice of Drains A nickname given to JACOB'S ISLAND by Henry Mayhew in an account published in the *Morning Chronicle* (24 September 1849).

Vera (Lynn) Originally 'gin' in COCKNEY RHYMING SLANG but nowadays more often used to mean 'skin', in the sense of a sheet of cigarette paper, probably to be used for rolling a joint. Vera Lynn (née Vera Welch, b.1917) grew up in EAST HAM and began singing in EAST END working men's clubs at the age of seven. She became 'the forces' sweetheart' during the Second World War and published an autobiography, *Some Sunny Day*, in 2009.

Vicky Park The local nickname of VICTORIA PARK.

Victoria The vicinity of VICTORIA STATION, located half a mile (800m) south of BUCKINGHAM PALACE. It is an area largely of offices, shops and mansion blocks. The first use of the queen's name in this area came one year after her accession in 1837 with the creation of Victoria Square, just south of the royal MEWS. This was followed in 1851 by the opening of VICTORIA STREET. In 1860 Grosvenor (or Victoria) railway bridge began to carry trains across the river to a new station under construction on a site vacated by the Chelsea Water Company following its relocation to SEETHING WELLS. Until then services had terminated south of the river at NINE ELMS.

Victoria and Albert Museum A splendid museum of art and design, situated at the eastern corner of EXHIBITION ROAD and Cromwell Road, SOUTH KENSINGTON. It was founded in 1852 as the Museum of Manufactures and became the South Kensington Museum when it moved into the BROMPTON BOILERS in 1857. It set out to ac-

quire the best examples of metalwork, furniture, textiles and all other forms of decorative art from all periods and many countries, while its scientific and technological objects were progressively displaced to form the core collection of what became the SCIENCE MUSEUM. Over the ten years from 1899 the Victoria and Albert Museum (as it was newly named) was enlarged and embellished to such a degree as to wholly eradicate its formerly utilitarian appearance. Since that time, the V&A has continued to expand its historical collections, especially of British silver, ceramics, textiles and furniture, while also promoting excellence in contemporary design.

Victoria coach station London's principal terminus for this mode of travel, built on Buckingham Palace Road in 1932, in art deco style. It was the responsibility of various private, then nationalized, then deregulated coach companies until it was transferred to LONDON TRANSPORT in 1988, passing to Transport for London in 2000.

Victoria Embankment *See the* EMBANKMENT.

Victoria line A LONDON UNDERGROUND line running north–south from WALTHAMSTOW to BRIXTON, opened in stages between 1968 and 1971. It is coloured light blue on the LONDON UNDERGROUND MAP. Except for the DRAIN, it is the only line on the network to run entirely underground. The Victoria line is also distinctive in having only one station, PIMLICO, that does not provide an interchange with another underground line or a main line.

Victoria Memorial *See the* WEDDING CAKE.

Victorian Valhalla John Betjeman's much-repeated description of HIGHGATE CEMETERY. *See also* NATIONAL VALHALLA.

Victoria Palace A theatre in VICTORIA STREET, built on the site of the Royal Standard Music Hall and opened in 1911. Among the long-running shows it has been associated with are the CRAZY GANG's comical extravaganzas (1947–62), the *Black and White Minstrel Show* (1962–70), the Buddy Holly bio-musical *Buddy* (1989–95) and *Billy Elliot the Musical* (2005–10, and possibly beyond).

Victoria Park A 213-acre (86-hectare) park with lakes and many amenities situated between South HACKNEY and OLD FORD. It was created to beautify the EAST END, provide recreational space and improve public health. Victoria Park opened unofficially in 1845, while landscaping was still in progress and before the lakes had been created.

Numerous ornamental structures were added in subsequent decades but most have been lost as a result of wartime bombing or neglect. Victoria Park has hosted political gatherings throughout its history, including Chartist rallies soon after it opened, striking dockworkers' meetings in the late 19th century and a Rock against Racism carnival in 1978 that was attended by more than 80,000 people.

Victoria station A main-line railway terminus opened in 1860, with services to Kent running from its eastern 'Chatham' side, while the larger 'Brighton' half mainly served destinations in Sussex. The two halves of the station were rebuilt and given their present facades between 1906 and 1909. It handles huge numbers of commuters during the week, and has long been a holidaymakers' departure point for the south coast, including Dover; in the days of boat-trains it was the home of the Golden Arrow express, and known as the 'Gateway to the Continent':

> My foreign policy is to be able to take a ticket at Victoria station and go anywhere I damn well please.
>
> ERNEST BEVIN, Foreign Secretary, in *The Spectator* (20 April 1951)

In Oscar Wilde's *The Importance of Being Earnest* (1895), Jack Worthing describes how he had been found as a baby in a handbag in the left-luggage office at Victoria Station (the Brighton line).

Victoria Street A commercial thoroughfare extending from the north side of VICTORIA STATION towards PARLIAMENT SQUARE. Victoria Street was planned from 1844 and officially opened in 1851, but not completed until the 1880s. It cut through Westminster's worst slum district, the DEVIL'S ACRE, displacing 5,000 poor, some of whom moved as short a distance away as they could, while others decamped south of the THAMES. The street was soon lined with innovative premises that included 'chambers' (suites of offices) and 'French flats' (fashionable apartment buildings). The Army & Navy department store opened in 1872 and traded under that name until 2005, when it became House of Fraser Victoria. *See also* WESTMINSTER CATHEDRAL.

Victoria Theatre *See the* OLD VIC.

Victorloo A notional amalgam of the railway termini at VICTORIA and WATERLOO, as featured in 'The 5.52 from Victorloo', a musical tribute to Southern Electric which formed the third movement of the *London Transport Suite* (1958), an orchestral suite by Sidney Torch.

Victory Square The guise in which TRAFALGAR SQUARE appears in George Orwell's *Nineteen Eighty-Four* (1949). Traitors and prisoners of war are executed there.

Village, the A 19th-century slang term for London, used among the sporting fraternity.

Ville, the An informal abbreviation for PENTONVILLE PRISON, mostly used by former inmates. *Voice of the Ville* is an 'in-house' magazine produced by prisoners at Pentonville.

> I remember a group of us young workers meeting in London. Someone said, 'They're in the 'Ville – let's go down there!' So we went and established a picket outside the jail.
>
> EDDIE PREVOST: in *Socialist Worker* (7 December 2002)

Vine Street The most obscure location on the British MONOPOLY board, branching off Swallow Street in the apex formed by PICCADILLY and REGENT STREET. Its name seems to derive from the Vine public house, which existed in the 18th century, and probably earlier, when the street was longer than it is now; the section that remains today was originally Little Vine Street. It was formerly best known for its police station, which came into existence with the creation of the METROPOLITAN POLICE in 1829 and remained (in rebuilt form) until the opening of West End Central police station on SAVILE ROW in 1940. Shortly after this Vine Street's name was changed to Piccadilly Place. Owing to a shortage of space at West End Central, the old police station reopened in 1971 and WESTMINSTER council agreed to resurrect the street's original identity, so that the station could retain the Vine Street name (Piccadilly Place is now merely a narrow alley connecting Vine Street with Piccadilly). The police station has recently been replaced by a mixed-use development and the streetscape has been enhanced.

It was to Vine Street police station, said to have been the busiest in the world, that the Marquess of Queensberry was taken in March 1895 to be charged with criminal libel against Oscar Wilde, thus setting in train the series of events that eventually led to Wilde's imprisonment. In the stories of P.G. Wodehouse, delinquent toffs are usually carted off to Vine Street police station.

> A bewildered man sat in a cell at Vine Street, his aching head between his large, grimy hands. He was trying, in his dull brutish way, to piece together the events of the previous night and of that morning.
>
> EDGAR WALLACE: *The Man who Bought London* (1915)

Vinopolis A 'wine tour' and corporate events venue filling a remarkably large area beneath railway arches at Bank End, near BOROUGH MARKET. It opened in 1999.

Vintry A CITY of London ward so called, according to John Stow's *Survey of London* (1598), from the site occupied by the wine merchants from Bordeaux, who settled on this part of the bank of the THAMES around QUEENHITHE. The Vintners built large houses with vaults, and the great house built by Sir John Stodie (LORD MAYOR OF LONDON in 1357) was called the Vintry. The local church of St Martin Vintry was destroyed in the GREAT FIRE OF LONDON. *See also* THREE CRANES IN THE VINTRY.

visible church In Christian terminology, the 'visible church' consists of all ostensible Christians, or those who profess to be Christians, or those who have been baptized and admitted into the communion of the church. According to an old story, several senior clerics were once discussing that subject in the presence of Charles II (r.1660–85). The king's contribution to their debate was to suggest that the most visible church was St Mary's, HARROW-ON-THE-HILL, which he said he could see wherever he went. That church has ever since been known as 'the visible church'.

vokzal An old-fashioned Russian word for 'railway station', derived from London's VAUXHALL. Because of Vauxhall's association with pleasure gardens and musical entertainments, its name was given to the grand station pavilion (where concerts were held) at the resort town of Pavlovsk, the destination of the first Russian railway line, which arrived there from St Petersburg in 1837.

Volvo City A nickname for STAMFORD HILL, derived from the (receding) popularity of this car marque with the locality's strong Hasidic Jewish community. Some have speculated that the tank-like construction of many older Volvos helped endow the occupants with a sense of insulation from undesirable aspects of the modern world. However, the simple truth of the marque's former predominance was that Volvos were the speciality of a local Hasidic second-hand car dealer. Channel 4 used *Volvo City* as the title of a 1991 documentary about the Hasidim of Stamford Hill.

waiter Formerly, a uniformed attendant at the London STOCK EXCHANGE.

Walbrook (Old English *Wala broc*, 'brook of the Celts or Britons')
1. A stream that rose in MOORFIELDS and flowed into the THAMES a short distance upstream of LONDON BRIDGE. The Romans built their settlement around it. It was covered over around the middle of the 16th century and today it functions as a sewer (the London Bridge Sewer). The Roman TEMPLE OF MITHRAS was discovered on its subterranean banks in 1954.
2. A street running southwards from BANK to CANNON STREET. It is about 150 feet (45m) east of the former stream from which it got its name. The Wren church of St Stephen Walbrook is on its eastern side: the SAMARITANS were founded here in 1953, and the dramatist and architect Sir John Vanbrugh (1664–1726) is buried here.
3. A CITY of London ward centrally located in the SQUARE MILE. Walbrook possesses a number of high-profile premises, including the BANK OF ENGLAND, but an extremely low residential population, usually in single figures, including the LORD MAYOR OF LONDON, at the MANSION HOUSE.

Walford The fictional EAST LONDON borough in which the BBC television soap opera EASTENDERS (1985–) is set. Its name is one of the most credible of all such inventions (much more so than, say, Climthorpe in *The* FALL AND RISE OF REGINALD PERRIN), combining the 'Wal-' element that often indicated a settlement belonging to Celts or Britons (as in places such as WALWORTH) with the common London affix 'ford'. Intentionally or not, it also calls to mind Edward Walford (1823–97), the author of such important works as three volumes of *Old and New London* (1878), *Londoniana* (1879) and *Greater London: A Narrative of Its History, Its People, and Its Places* (1884).

walk
Walkie Talkie The nickname for the proposed office tower at 20 FENCHURCH STREET, from its bulging and curving top-heavy shape, which resembles a two-way radio. The project was put on hold in 2008, owing to the downturn in the commercial property market.
walk penniless in Mark Lane, to To have been swindled. This ancient expression punned on a slang meaning of 'mark': one who is easily duped.

> When the prigger had smoked the game, and perceived he was bitten of all the bite in his bung, and turned to walk penniless in Mark Lane, as the proverb is, he began to chafe, and to swear ...
>
> ROBERT GREENE: *The Second Part of Cony-Catching* (1591)

walk the Round, to Lawyers frequently used to give interviews to their clients in the Round Church in the TEMPLE; and 'walking the Round' meant loitering about the church in the hope of being hired as a witness.

Wallace Collection A museum based at Hertford House in Manchester Square, MARYLEBONE, best known for its paintings by Titian, Rembrandt, Hals (*The* LAUGHING CAVALIER) and Velázquez and for its collections of 18th-century French paintings, porcelain, furniture and gold boxes. Hertford House was the main London townhouse of its former owners and the works were collected in the 18th and 19th centuries by the first four marquesses of Hertford and Sir Richard Wallace (1818–90), the illegitimate son of the 4th Marquess and Mrs Agnes Jackson, and bequeathed to the nation by Sir Richard's widow, Lady Wallace, in 1897.

Wallington An extensive commuter suburb situated east of SUTTON. The name derives from the same root as 'Wales' and almost certainly denoted an early Celtic settlement. Wallington's status as a hundred – an extensive administrative area – indicates its medieval importance, as did the size of its Norman manor, but the village had become BEDDINGTON's inferior by the late Middle Ages. The construction of the CROYDON to Epsom railway in 1847 triggered lasting changes. The owner of the Carshalton Park estate forbade the building of a station on his land, so CARSHALTON station (now Wallington) was sited here, to the south of the village. Development did not follow rapidly but by the 1910s the growing town was expanding across the former lavender fields and a new centre had taken shape along Woodcote Road to the south of the station. Wallington was the larger partner in its 1915 pairing with Beddington as an urban district and from the early 1960s the area around the station became a significant strategic centre, with several office blocks.

The writer and artist Mervyn Peake (1911–68) lived at 55 Woodcote Road as a young man in the 1920s and again in the 1950s, after his father died and left him the house. Wallington resident Craig Shergold (b.1979) achieved the world record in get-well cards, with over a hundred million. Despite a successful brain tumour operation in 1991, internet appeals for cards continued to circulate for many years afterwards, to the increasing desperation of Craig's family.

Waltham Forest, London Borough of

An OUTER LONDON borough formed in 1965 by merging the municipal boroughs of CHINGFORD, LEYTON and WALTHAMSTOW. It is mainly residential in character, and most of the housing stock is of Victorian origin, but there are belts of industry, particularly along the River LEA. EPPING FOREST was earlier called Waltham Forest and the borough's predominantly green and brown coat of arms contains several arboreal references. The civic motto is 'fellowship is life'; the words are those of the Walthamstow-born writer, designer and social critic William Morris, in *A Dream of John Ball* (1888).

Walthamstow The commercial and administrative centre of the borough of WALTHAM FOREST, situated to the east of the River LEA between LEYTON and CHINGFORD. Its name is often said to have begun as Wilcumestowe, possibly a 'holy place where guests are welcome'. However, an alternative theory suggests that this was a fanciful corruption of an earlier name that derived from three words: 'weald' (forest), 'ham' (a plot of land) and 'stow' (a place), and that the superfluous final syllable was added to distinguish it from Waltham Cross, Hertfordshire. Walthamstow began to develop relatively early for a village this far from the CITY of London. In the 18th century it was a collection of hamlets providing a popular country retreat for the wealthy, but enclosure in 1850 started the spread of terraced housing northwards across the parish and the bankers and merchants soon retreated still further. The railway arrived in 1872 and most of the district was built up by the end of the 19th century. In 1968 the VICTORIA LINE arrived at Hoe Street station, which was renamed Walthamstow Central. From Monday to Saturday the High Street hosts what is regularly touted as being 'Europe's longest street market', at 1,093 yards (1 km).

Walthamstow Marshes An area of semi-natural wetland lying in the south-western corner of Walthamstow. Alliott Verdon Roe (1877–1958) assembled his Avro No.1 triplane under a railway arch on Walthamstow Marshes and made the first all-British powered flight from here in 1909. The Lee Valley Regional Park Authority acquired the marshes in 1971 and is now responsible for their care and preservation. Much of the surviving marshland is designated a nature reserve and a site of special scientific interest.

Walthamstow Village A conservation area centred on St Mary's Church. The timber-framed Ancient House (formerly the White House) dates from the 15th century, with a west wing rebuilt in the 16th. Sir George Monoux founded almshouses on Vinegar Alley in 1527, together with a school (now Sir George Monoux College) that later relocated to Chingford Road. The Vestry House, which began life in 1730 as the parish workhouse, is now a local history museum and borough archive. Most of the village was built up in the 20 years following the enclosure of Church Common in 1850 and the village was saved from subsequent disfigurement by the opening of the station at Hoe Street, which drew commercial development away to the west.

Walworth A crowded and socially disadvantaged district situated east of NEWINGTON. Walworth – 'the enclosed settlement of the Britons' – was long a rural area producing fruit and vegetables in abundance (one local nurseryman had a list of 320 varieties of gooseberries) but over the course of the 19th century its population increased eightfold, reaching 122,200 in 1901. Much of the district was rebuilt after the Second World War, primarily in the form of massive council blocks, many of which are now being replaced as part of the regeneration of the ELEPHANT AND CASTLE area. The Labour Party had its headquarters here between 1980 and 1997, and 'Walworth Road' became a metonym for the party machine.

The mathematician and astronomer Charles Babbage (1791–1871), inventor of a forerunner of the computer, was born in Crosby Row (now Larcom Street). Charlie Chaplin (*see the* LITTLE TRAMP) was born in East Street in 1889, the son of MUSIC HALL entertainers.

Wandle A river that rises near CROYDON and flows 9 miles (14 km) northwards through MERTON and TOOTING into the THAMES to the west of WANDSWORTH BRIDGE. Its name was not recorded in English until the early 17th century, so it was probably an artificial reconstruction from Wandlesworth, an earlier form of WANDSWORTH; the medieval name of the river was Lidburn (or variations thereupon), perhaps 'stream called the loud one'.

Wandsworth A prominent riverside district flanked by PUTNEY to its west and BATTERSEA and CLAPHAM to the east. There is evidence that a Saxon named Wendel had established a fishery here by 693. Farming and market gardening constituted the principal inland occupations until the late Middle Ages. Thereafter Wandsworth supported several thriving industries, from dyeing and bleaching, fur-making and hatting (Wandsworth hats became famous throughout Europe) to munitions-making and brewing, notably at the Ram brewery from 1581. At Sword House (now the site of Wandsworth police station) Sir Everard Fawkener played host to Voltaire during his two years' exile from France in the late 1720s. Transport improvements in the 19th century made Wandsworth a viable place of residence for CITY workers and during Victoria's reign the district filled with housing, together with new public buildings and parks. Bomb damage in the early 1940s was the spur to an extensive programme of postwar reconstruction. Since the 1970s apartment complexes have replaced disused industrial premises along the riverside and in the town centre. The Ram brewery closed in 2006 and it is now the site of a proposed £1 billion redevelopment project.

Wandsworth, London Borough of An INNER LONDON borough formed in 1965 from the metropolitan borough of BATTERSEA and most of the metropolitan borough of Wandsworth. PUTNEY, BALHAM and TOOTING are among the major districts encompassed. The more interesting elements of the borough's coat of arms are a Viking longship, said to have sailed up the THAMES as far as Putney in the 9th century; a sprig of lavender, for LAVENDER HILL; and a set of silver droplets representing the tears of Huguenot exiles, many of whom settled by the banks of the WANDLE. The civic motto is 'we serve'.

Wandsworth Bridge A road bridge across the THAMES, linking Wandsworth with FULHAM. The original was built in the early 1870s; its replacement opened in 1940.

Wandsworth Common A wide strip of open land stretching from the east side of Wandsworth to the edges of TOOTING and BALHAM. Following a campaign to preserve the open space, John Spencer, 5th Earl Spencer and lord of the manor, agreed to transfer the common to public ownership in 1871. The elected group of conservators failed to prevent its deterioration into a large mud patch and the METROPOLITAN BOARD OF WORKS took it over in 1887. *See also the* ROYAL VICTORIA PATRIOTIC ASYLUM; *The* SCOPE.

Wandsworth Prison The most populous prison in the UK, opened in 1851 as the Surrey House of Correction. In 1895 Oscar Wilde spent the first six months of his sentence for homosexual offences here. The train robber Ronald Biggs escaped from Wandsworth Prison in 1965 and fled first to Australia and later to Brazil. He voluntarily returned to Britain in 2001.

Wanstead A pleasant suburban village situated north-east of LEYTONSTONE. Its name was first recorded in 824 and may have meant 'white house' or 'house on the wen-shaped hill' or 'place where wagons are kept'. Early settlement was confined to the vicinity of the manor house at what became WANSTEAD PARK, with its nearby church. When St Mary's was rebuilt in its present form in 1790 there were 120 houses here, four-fifths of which were gentry-owned. Suburban development began to the north around 1860 and steadily spread and intensified over the following century. The High Street was redeveloped from the early 1970s, when many of its older buildings were demolished. The rerouting of the A12 to provide a better link to the M11 necessitated some demolition and tree-felling in the mid-1990s, in the face of active resistance by conservationists (*see* WANSTONIA).

Former Wanstead residents include the dramatist R.B. Sheridan, the politician George Canning and the poet Thomas Hood – who all lived at a variety of addresses in the London area – and William Penn, the founder of Pennsylvania.

Wanstead Flats A large and featureless open space constituting the southernmost part of EPPING FOREST, although most of its trees were cleared several centuries ago. The terrain is now mainly acidic grassland with some playing fields, and is popular with horse riders. In former times 'Wanstead Flats' was COCKNEY RHYMING SLANG for 'spats'.

Wanstead Park A public park and a name used by estate agents for the neighbouring residential locality, situated to the south-east of Wanstead CENTRAL LINE station. The park was formed by enclosing part of EPPING FOREST in the mid-16th century. In 1717 the Astronomer Royal James Bradley and his uncle James Pound set up one of the world's largest telescopes in Wanstead Park, mounted on a maypole brought from the STRAND. The CORPORATION OF LONDON acquired the grounds of Wanstead House (which had been demolished in 1834) in 1880 and opened them to the public two years later. Wanstead golf course was laid out on and around the site of the mansion in 1893.

Wanstonia The 'Autonomous Area of Wanstonia' was a protest camp set up in September 1993 by activists seeking to prevent the construction of a link road through WANSTEAD to the M11 motorway. Although ultimately unsuccessful the campaign continued for several months, causing significant delays and additional expenses for the contractors. *See also* LEYTONSTONIA.

Wapping A recolonized waterfront neighbourhood situated midway between the CITY of London and DOCKLANDS. Its Old English name meant 'the settlement of Wæppa's people'. The modern heart of Wapping lies on the strip of alluvial plain once known as Wapping Marsh, but the original settlement stood on a higher gravel terrace, around what became the Highway. Construction of a wharf in 1395 sowed the seeds of a 15th-century riverside hamlet called Wapping-on-the-Woze (mud). Full-scale waterfront development with storehouses and tenements followed the draining of Wapping Marsh around 1540 and the newer village outgrew its predecessor, ultimately appropriating its name. In the century following the construction of LONDON DOCK in 1805 the neighbourhood became increasingly overcrowded and was allowed to deteriorate until the LONDON COUNTY COUNCIL implemented a comprehensive slum clearance scheme in 1926. The dock closed in 1971 and during the last two decades of the 20th century housebuilders squeezed the maximum possible number of flats, townhouses and warehouse conversions into Wapping's winding streets, targeting most of these at young professionals. Away from the riverside, Wapping is also home to a significant proportion of the EAST END's Bangladeshi community. *See also* EXECUTION DOCK.

Wapping was the setting for Johnny Speight's BBC television sitcom *Till Death Us Do Part* (*see* GARNETT, ALF).

Wapping dispute An industrial dispute that began in January 1986 when Rupert Murdoch's News International, publishers of *The Times* and *The Sun*, dismissed striking employees and simultaneously opened a new printworks in Pennington Street, Wapping, staffed by members of a different union. The sacked workers and their supporters picketed so-called Fortress Wapping for just over a year, frequently clashing with police, but failed to prevent the newspapers' publication and distribution and did not regain their jobs. Although they took place on a much smaller scale, the events at Wapping – and the underlying issues and consequences – mirrored those of the miners' strike of 1984–5 and the strikers' defeat signalled the end of the working practices that had formerly characterized FLEET STREET newspaper publishing.

News International moved its printing operation to Broxbourne, Hertfordshire, in 2008 but Wapping remains its editorial base, and the UK headquarters of the parent company, News Corporation.

Wardour Street A street in SOHO, running north to south from OXFORD STREET via SHAFTESBURY AVENUE to LEICESTER SQUARE. It was originally laid out in the 1680s and gained its name from Henry Arundell, 3rd Baron Arundell of Wardour (*c.*1608–94), who owned the land. The Arundells took their (now extinct) title from Wardour Castle in Wiltshire. In the latter part of the 19th century Wardour Street became known for its furniture shops, which specialized mainly in reproduction antiques of dubious quality and taste. In the early 20th century the furniture dealers were replaced by music publishers, and then after the First World War the film companies moved in, and Wardour Street became the centre of, and synonymous with, the British film industry.

> It amazes me how few films we manage to make in a year here: Wardour Street seems to have accepted defeat.

> *The Times* (20 December 1975)

The nuclear destruction of the street was playfully considered by the Jam in their 1978 song ""A" Bomb in Wardour Street'.

Wardour Street English The affected use of archaic words and phrases, as typically found in historical romances. The term was first applied by William Morris (1834–96) in 1888 to a translation of the *Odyssey* couched in language that reminded him of the pseudo-antique furniture that was in those days sold in Wardour Street.

warren

Warren, The The site on which the Royal Laboratory, later known as WOOLWICH ARSENAL, was established in 1695. Named for its large rabbit population, it is remembered now in Warren Lane.

Warren of Staines See HOUNSLOW HEATH.

Warren Street A Georgian street running westwards off the northern end of TOTTENHAM COURT ROAD. It was laid out with three-storey terraced houses in 1799 by Charles Fitzroy, first Baron Southampton, who named it after his wife, Anne Warren (1737–1807). Anne was the daughter of Admiral Sir Peter Warren, who founded New York's Greenwich Village and gave his name to more than one Warren Street in America. The new street was at first a popular place of residence for artists, especially engravers. Much later, used-car dealers set up showrooms here. Warren Street now possesses a diverse mixture of retailers and small businesses.

Warwick Avenue A broad, stuccoed street in

southern MAIDA VALE, running north-westwards from the HARROW ROAD at LITTLE VENICE. This was originally a track called Green Lane and was named Warwick Road (later changed to Avenue) on the street plan produced in 1827 by George Gutch, surveyor to the bishop of London. Gutch named the road after Jane Warwick, of Warwick Hall near Carlisle, who had married into a landowning family here in 1778. St Saviour's Church was consecrated in 1856 and its section of the road was widened to create a grand approach. Warwick Avenue station, originally to have been called Warrington Crescent, opened in 1915 as an intermediate stop on the Bakerloo Line's new extension from PADDINGTON to QUEEN'S PARK. St Saviour's was rebuilt in 1973–6.

wasp

Wasp of Twickenham *See the* BARD OF TWICKENHAM.

Wasps The short name of London Wasps and Wasps FC, both of which are rugby union clubs. Their mutual antecedent was formed in 1867 as a breakaway from Hampstead FC (*see also* HARLEQUINS) and played its early games at a ground on FINCHLEY ROAD. Wasps aspired to be founder members of the Rugby Football Union but failed to attend that body's inaugural meeting in January 1871. As the club's historian explains: 'In true rugby fashion the team turned up at the wrong pub, on the wrong day, at the wrong time.' Wasps rented several grounds around London before settling at SUDBURY in 1923. The club split into professional and amateur halves in 1996, the former subsequently adding 'London' to its name, although its home games are now played outside the capital at Adams Park in High Wycombe, Buckinghamshire. The club has contributed many players to the England national side, including Roger Uttley, Nigel Melville, Rob Andrew and Lawrence Dallaglio. Wasps FC plays at Twyford Avenue sports ground in ACTON, where the professional club trains and has its offices.

waste

Waste, the A short form of MILE END Waste.

wasteman A JAFAIKAN term for a worthless male, often used as an insult among young Londoners from minority ethnic groups. 'Waste' is something of an all-purpose word for anything deemed substandard. The female equivalents are 'wastewoman' or, unpleasantly, 'wastegash'.

watch (and chain) 'Brain' in COCKNEY RHYM-ING SLANG. The term is little used.

watcha or **watcher** Alternative spellings of WOTCHER.

water

waterman

1. One who ferries passengers, as opposed to a lighterman, who carries goods on the river. THAMES watermen were the river's equivalent of cab drivers from the Middle Ages to the mid-19th century. Parliament first regulated the fares they could charge in 1514 and the Company of Watermen was established by an Act of 1555 to oversee their practices, and to introduce apprenticeships (at first lasting one year, but increased to seven years in 1603). It became the Company of Watermen and Lightermen in 1700. Much of the watermen's trade came from ferrying passengers from one side of the river to the other, often for a night out. Others rowed private barges owned by wealthy individuals or City LIVERY COMPANIES, as well as the ceremonial royal barges. By the late 17th century there were 10,000 licensed watermen on the tidal Thames, plying from 100 sets of stairs down to the river. Competition from new bridges, and improved road and rail transport brought about their eventual demise, abetted by the dangers of the heavy wash caused by Thames steamers. *See also* DOGGETT'S COAT AND BADGE.

2. A licensed operative at HACKNEY coach stands, whose duty it was to water the cab horses, among other things.

waterpad A river thief, the THAMES equivalent of a footpad. The term was not in common usage but was recorded in James Caulfield's *Blackguardiana, or A Dictionary of Rogues* (1793) and a handful of other works.

Water Poet The sobriquet of John Taylor (1580–1653), a Thames WATERMAN, who churned out numerous works of poetry and prose, mostly of a satirical nature. He was notable more for his powers of wit and observation than for the quality of his verse, though he was admired in his lifetime by Ben Jonson, and Alexander Pope called him 'sweet bird of Thames'. Taylor escorted Queen Henrietta Maria out of London to escape the plague of 1625 and also gained fame as an adventurer, travelling throughout Britain and the continent. He once rowed 40 miles (64 km)

down the Thames in a paper boat, a record that stood until 2003. In his closing days he kept an alehouse in LONG ACRE.

> I was commanded with the Water Baylie
> To see the Rivers clensed both nights and dayly.
> Dead Hogges, Dogges, Cats, and well flayd
> Carryon Horses
> Their noysom Corpses soyld the dunge, Beasts guts and Garbage,
> Street durt, with Gardners weeds and Rotten Herbage.
> And from those Waters filthy putrifaction,
> Our meat and drink were made, which bred Infection.
>
> *All the Works of John Taylor the Water-Poet* (1630)

Water Rats A public house situated near the northern end of GRAY'S INN ROAD, long noted as a venue for live music. It was previously called the Pindar of Wakefield, after a traditional English ballad, and takes its present name from the foundation here in 1889 of the Grand Order of Water Rats, an entertainment industry charity. Dan Leno, the FUNNIEST MAN ON EARTH, was elected 'King Rat' in 1891, 1892 and 1897. The charity is still based at the pub.

Waterloo A railway terminus (*see* WATERLOO STATION) and its immediate environs, situated in the far north of LAMBETH, close to the SOUTH BANK CENTRE. Residential settlement and the provision of amenities increased on Lambeth Marsh following the opening in 1817 of the first WATERLOO BRIDGE. Goods yards and other railway facilities replaced several streets in the latter part of the 19th century, while many of the surviving properties were converted to cheap lodging houses for railway workers. Many of the remaining streets behind Waterloo station were torn down in the 1960s and replaced with council flats. Lower Marsh gives the best indication of the area's earlier character, and retains a busy street market. Located immediately north of the station, the BFI IMAX is a 485-seat cinema with a screen ten storeys high. *See also the* OLD VIC.

It has been speculated – and neither proved nor disproved – that 'loo', meaning 'lavatory', may be derived from the name of this area or the station.

Waterloo and City line *See the* DRAIN.

Waterloo Bridge

1. A road bridge across the THAMES linking the area of the STRAND and ALDWYCH with the

SOUTH BANK and the northern part of LAMBETH. The original bridge, designed by the Scottish engineer John Rennie (1761–1821) and described by the sculptor Antonio Canova (1757–1822) as the finest in Europe, was opened by the Prince Regent (later George IV) in 1817. At first it was to be called the Strand Bridge, but before its opening it had been patriotically decided to link it with Wellington's recent glorious victory at Waterloo. Until 1877 it was a toll bridge: the toll was a halfpenny, which led to that sum becoming known in 19th-century London slang as a 'waterloo'. As a result of subsidence, the bridge was controversially demolished in 1936. Its replacement, designed by Giles Gilbert Scott, was opened in 1942, after construction work had continued throughout the BLITZ. (*see also the* LADIES' BRIDGE).

2. A sentimental film melodrama (1931) starring Mae Clarke as a ballerina who marries an army officer (Kent Douglass) who is reported missing in action. Neglected by his family, she resorts to prostitution, offering her services on Waterloo Bridge. The superior 1940 remake stars Vivien Leigh and Robert Taylor.

Waterloo City Square A proposed scheme that would remodel the complex labyrinth of streets, squares, subways and raised walkways in the vicinity of the northern part of WATERLOO ROAD, creating a 'unified, high quality urban realm' that will make the area more welcoming and attract inward investment. The WALWORTH-based architects DSDHA were selected as the design team for the project in March 2009.

Waterloo churches A name applied in the 19th century to churches built (many of them in Greek Revival style) with funds provided under an Act of 1821, to mark victory at the Battle of Waterloo and the nation's deliverance from invasion during the Napoleonic Wars. The term was sometimes used specifically to refer to any of four churches dedicated to the evangelists in the old parish of LAMBETH: St John, Waterloo Bridge Road; St Luke, NORWOOD; St Mark, KENNINGTON; St Matthew, BRIXTON.

Waterloo Road A somewhat dingy thoroughfare running south-eastwards from WATERLOO BRIDGE. The WATERLOO CITY SQUARE project may transform the character of the northern part of the road. Sidney Gilliat's film *Waterloo Road* (1944), starred John Mills as a squaddie with doubts about his wife's faithfulness.

Waterloo Station London's busiest railway station in terms of passenger arrivals and departures, situated at the southern end of WATERLOO BRIDGE. It is the terminus for suburban services to and from south-west London and SURREY, and for main-line services to and from southern and south-western England. It began as the terminus of the London and South Western Railway Company in 1848. Six years later the LONDON NECROPOLIS COMPANY added a separate station to carry coffins and mourners on a dedicated line to Brookwood Cemetery. Waterloo Junction (now Waterloo East) station opened on the South Eastern Railway in 1869. The DRAIN opened in 1898 and Waterloo underground station, now on the BAKERLOO, JUBILEE and NORTHERN lines, followed in 1906. In 1922 the whole complex, with the exception of Waterloo East, became housed in a single brand-new building.

> The city overwhelmed our expectations. The Kiplingesque grandeur of Waterloo Station, the Eliotic despondency of the brick row in Chelsea where we spent the night in the flat of a vague friend …
>
> JOHN UPDIKE: 'A Madman', published in *The New Yorker* (22 December 1962)

In 1993 the station's north-western side, sumptuously re-roofed to the design of Nicholas Grimshaw and renamed Waterloo International, became the London terminus for EUROSTAR trains. The Eurostar service transferred to ST PANCRAS STATION in 2007 and the future use of the abandoned part of Waterloo station has yet to be determined. Waterloo has always been a stereotypically busy commuter station, the one sure landmark for rendezvous on its vast concourse being 'under the clock'.

Waterloo Sunset A song (1967) by the KINKS about loneliness, isolation and the consolations of the London scenes invoked by its lyrics. It was written by Ray Davies, who had originally intended it to be about the decline of the Merseybeat sound, and entitled 'Liverpool Sunset', but he chose instead to celebrate the beauty of his home town. It appeared on the album *Something Else* and reached No.2 in the UK charts as a single.

> Dirty old river, must you keep rolling, flowing into the night?
> People so busy, make me feel dizzy, taxi lights shine so bright,
> But I don't need no friends;

As long as I gaze on Waterloo sunset, I am in paradise.

Waterloo Vase A monumental urn (1820–7) executed by Richard Westmacott (1775–1856) to mark the British victory at Waterloo. Standing 15 feet (4.6m) high and weighing more than 15 tons, it was sculpted from a single piece of Carrera marble that Napoleon had seen on his way through Tuscany and had earmarked for a trophy. Following the emperor's defeat the Grand Duke of Tuscany presented the marble to the Prince Regent. Formerly exhibited at the NATIONAL GALLERY the vase was set up in the garden at BUCKINGHAM PALACE in 1906.

Watier's *See the* DANDIES' CLUB.

Watkin's Folly The nickname of the Great Tower, which was partially built at WEMBLEY PARK in the early 1890s as the centrepiece of a pleasure garden. Its design bore a striking resemblance to that of the Eiffel Tower and it was the brainchild of Sir Edward Watkin (1819–1901), chairman of the Metropolitan Railway Company, which owned the land. The tower had reached a height of only 155 feet (47m) when problems of finance and subsidence caused its abandonment. It was pulled down in 1907 and WEMBLEY STADIUM was later built on its site.

Watling
Watling estate *See* LITTLE MOSCOW.
Watling Street
1. A Roman road that ran from Dover via Canterbury, London, and St Albans to Wroxeter in Shropshire. It was the street (a word that generally signified a paved – and thus probably Roman – road in Old English usage) of Wacol's people. The Anglo-Saxons' name for it, which is first recorded in the 9th century, appears to be based on the same folk-name as Wæclingaceaster, an early name for St Albans. It could well be, therefore, that Watling Street was originally just the road from London to St Albans, and that the name was only later applied to the rest of the Roman road. It is not clear whether the sections north and south of the River THAMES formed a single continuous road in early Roman times, but if they did they may well have been linked by a ford in the WESTMINSTER area. Following the completion of LONDON BRIDGE its route may have been diverted through the CITY of London. The northern section left London along the line

of what is now the A5, past MARBLE ARCH and on up the EDGWARE ROAD.
2. A street in the CITY of London, running east–west between CHEAPSIDE to the north and CANNON STREET to the south. Its name is an alteration (no doubt under the influence of the original Watling Street, *above*) of the earlier Athelingstreet, 'street of the prince or princes'.
3. A jokey name used in the 17th century for the Milky Way.

Watson, Dr John The reader's representative in Arthur Conan Doyle's Sherlock HOLMES stories. A former British army surgeon, wounded at the Battle of Maiwand (1880), Watson is searching for rooms in London when a friend introduces him to Holmes, himself looking for accommodation. Watson thereby becomes Holmes's faithful and trusted associate, a companionship that never falters, even though Watson marries and temporarily leaves 221B BAKER STREET. He is stalwart, stoic, credulous, and narrates all but two of the adventures (Holmes foolishly tried his own hand twice). Watson though, is no fool, and reveals a mischievous humour, while living for the times when 'I found myself seated beside him in a hansom, my revolver in my pocket, and the thrill of adventure in my heart'.

Wealdstone A north-eastern extension of HARROW, taking its name from a stone, first recorded in the 16th century, marking the division between Harrow and HARROW WEALD. A station, on the London–Birmingham railway, opened in 1837 and was originally called Harrow; its name was changed to Harrow and Wealdstone in 1897. The area around the station was among the first in outer London to undergo railway-stimulated suburban development. Terraced housing spread in all directions, and several major factories were established here in the late 19th century, most notably that of Kodak Ltd. *See also the* HARROW RAIL DISASTER.

weasel (and stoat) 'Coat' in COCKNEY RHYMING SLANG. Lesser-used alternative terms for 'coat' include 'nanny (goat)', 'billy (goat)' and 'Quaker (oat)'. *See also* POP GOES THE WEASEL.

Wedding Cake A nickname (from its tiered arrangement) for the Imperial Memorial to Queen Victoria, which stands at the western end of the MALL, opposite the front gates of BUCKINGHAM

PALACE. Built in 1911, it was designed by Sir Aston Webb (1849–1930), with sculptures by Sir Thomas Brock (1847–1922).

Wedding Cake Church The nickname of St Bride's Church, which has also been called 'the cathedral of FLEET STREET'. A church was first built on this site in the 6th century and dedicated to St Bridgit or St Bride of Kildare. It was rebuilt in the 12th century and again in the 15th. Following its destruction in the GREAT FIRE OF LONDON the church was rebuilt yet again (1672–4), this time by Christopher Wren, who in 1701–3 added a steeple. Its shape does not merely resemble a very sharply pointed wedding cake, it is said to have inspired its invention. St Bride's was bombed to a shell during the night of the SECOND FIRE OF LONDON but the steeple survived. The church was restored with the financial support of the Fleet Street newspaper industry and rededicated in 1957.

weepers *See* PICCADILLY WEEPERS.

Well Hall The northernmost part of ELTHAM, containing the grounds of the former Tudor building of that name. Well Hall was recorded as early as the 13th century and its great house was built for Sir William Roper (*c.*1498–1578) and his wife Margaret, daughter of Sir Thomas More, after their marriage in 1521. Sir Gregory Page (*c.*1695–1775) bought the property in the 1730s and demolished the house, but its inner moat and barn have survived, the latter as a pub. Following the outbreak of the First World War, the government acquired farmland on either side of Well Hall Road to build an estate for munitions workers at WOOLWICH. Construction workers were drafted in from all parts of London to build 1,300 homes on 'garden city' lines and the project was completed by December 1915. The streets were named after men with historical associations with Woolwich. The house that Sir Gregory Page built to replace Well Hall (which was later given the same name) was pulled down in 1931 and the gardens of Well Hall Pleasaunce were laid out in its place.

The writer Edith Nesbit lived at Well Hall from 1899 to 1922, the politician Herbert Morrison lived with his family in Well Hall Road from 1923 to 1929, and the actress Sylvia Syms grew up in Maudsley Road in the 1930s.

Welling The second largest district in the Lon- don Borough of BEXLEY after BEXLEYHEATH, which lies to its east. Welling was first mentioned in 1362 as Wellyngs and its name may have indicated the presence of a well or spring, or may derive from Ralph Willing, who held land in Bexley earlier in the century; it is rarely clear in such cases whether the place name or the personal name came first. Welling evolved as a coaching halt on the route to Dover. It remained predominantly rural until the 1920s, when a welter of large and small developers descended on the village and its outlying farms, building low-cost houses for the lower middle classes and skilled working classes. Welling achieved notoriety in the early 1990s as the home of the British National Party, which was blamed for an increase in racialist violence in this overwhelmingly white area.

Wellington

Wellington Arch Also known as Constitution Arch, this is 'England's answer to the Arc de Triomphe', although it is somewhat smaller than its Parisian counterpart. It was erected in the late 1820s to the design of Decimus Burton (1800–81), and originally faced NO.1 LONDON. An oversized statue of the Duke of Wellington on horseback was perched on the monument in 1846. When the Wellington Arch was dismantled as part of a road-widening scheme and moved to its present position in 1882, the Iron Duke's statue was removed and taken to Aldershot, Hampshire. Its position atop the arch was taken in 1912 by Captain Adrian Jones's bronze statue of Peace Descending on the QUADRIGA of War. In 1960 the former crossroads at HYDE PARK CORNER became a roundabout, marooning the arch in its centre. A unit of cavalry parades through the arch each morning.

Wellington Museum *See* NO.1 LONDON (*under* NUMBER).

Welsh

Welsh Ambassador, His Excellency the The self-applied accreditation of one James Howell when he was the sub-lessee of Belsize House (*see* BELSIZE PARK). In 1720 Howell turned the stately home and its extensive grounds into a fashionable pleasure resort, laying on all sorts of entertainments and sporting challenges, from footmen's races to mud-wrestling. The gates opened at six o'clock each morning and a team of armed guards patrolled the road to London to protect the hundreds of daily visitors from highwaymen. The Prince and Princess of Wales attended in 1721. A year later an anonymous critic published a satirical volume exposing:

1. The Fops and Beaux who daily frequent that academy.
2. The characters of the women who make this an exchange for assignations.
3. The buffoonery of the Welsh ambassador.

Soon afterwards Howell was arrested and charged with operating an illegal gaming house but he continued to run the resort until 1740, while its reputation progressively declined. Belsize House was demolished in 1753.

Welsh Harp A nature reserve centred on the BRENT reservoir, situated between KINGSBURY and West HENDON. The Harp and Horn inn stood on the Edgware Road near Brent Bridge from the mid-18th century and had been renamed the Welsh Harp by 1803. It came to be known as the Old Welsh Harp after another inn named the Upper Welsh Harp was built further north. In the mid-1830s the confluence of the River Brent and the Silk Stream was dammed to create the Brent (or Kingsbury) reservoir, in order to supply the PADDINGTON branch of what is now the GRAND UNION CANAL. The Welsh Harp reservoir, as it became known, was enlarged in the early 1850s and the Old Welsh Harp gained enormous popularity as a destination for day-trippers. So great was the appeal of the pub and the reservoir that the Midland Railway opened Welsh Harp station in 1870 to cater for excursion traffic. The station closed in 1903 and the reservoir's appeal declined with the urbanization of the surrounding area, especially after the creation of the NORTH CIRCULAR ROAD, which had the benefit of allowing wildlife habitats to form. The Old Welsh Harp was rebuilt in 1937 but was later demolished to make way for the STAPLES CORNER flyover. In the 1948 OLYMPIC GAMES rowing competitions were held on the reservoir, which remains much used by rowers, sailors and canoeists.

Wembley A commercial and residential district with a significant Indian community, situated 9 miles (14.5 km) north-west of central London. It was recorded as Wembalea – 'Wemba's clearing' – in a charter of 825. It was not until the end of the 19th century that a sudden rush of building activity erased the old village and created a populous suburb. The arrival of Asian immigrants from India and east Africa began to transform the district in the late 1960s and Ealing Road is now one of London's four leading shopping areas for Asian goods, along with SOUTHALL, TOOTING and GREEN STREET, in UPTON PARK. At the 2001 census the Wembley Central ward had London's highest percentage of people born outside the European Union and Hinduism was the most common religion.

A satirical version of the successful, well-educated Indian families who characterize METROLAND Wembley appeared in the hit BBC television series *The Kumars at Number 42* (2001–6).

Wembley Arena Originally a swimming pool built for the 1934 British Empire Games, and used for the same purpose during the 1948 OLYMPIC GAMES. The Empire Pool was afterwards converted into an auditorium and used for entertainments as diverse as ice shows, sports promotions and musical extravaganzas. By the early 21st century the arena had become somewhat dilapidated. It was impressively refurbished in 2005–6.

Wembley Park The north-eastern quadrant of Wembley, named after and built on the site of a country estate that had a mansion at its centre and grounds laid out by Humphry Repton. The estate was sold in 1881 and part was acquired by the Metropolitan Railway Company. Wembley Park station opened in 1894, followed two years later by adjacent pleasure gardens (see WATKIN'S FOLLY). The gardens were replaced by the pavilions and palaces of the British Empire Exhibition of 1924–5, together with its sports arena the Empire Stadium (later WEMBLEY STADIUM). The remainder of Wembley Park was fully developed as a mixed residential and industrial area before the outbreak of the Second World War.

Wembley Stadium The home of English FOOTBALL. The original Wembley Stadium was built in 1922–3 as the Empire Stadium and within days of its completion hosted the WHITE HORSE FINAL. The opening ceremony of the Empire Exhibition was held here on 23 April 1923. Greyhound racing began at Wembley in 1927, a year after the craze had been initiated at Belle Vue in Manchester, and from 1929 it became the venue for the Rugby League Cup Final. It staged the OLYMPIC GAMES in 1948 and the World Cup Final in 1966. In addition to its sporting role, the stadium hosted many live music events, most famously the Live Aid concert of 1985. By the end of the 20th century its age was beginning to show, but plans for its refurbishment or complete redevelopment became so mired in political and financial difficulties that it was not until 2002 that the old stadium, with its celebrated TWIN TOWERS, was pulled down and rebuilding began, on a different axis. The new Wembley Stadium opened in March 2007. It has a capacity of 90,000 and its design features include a retractable roof and a landmark lattice arch. The football finals of the 2012 Olympics will be played here.

Wembley Way The informal name for the straight road leading from WEMBLEY PARK station to WEMBLEY STADIUM, which on match days is a seething mass of fans. Its official designation is Olympic Way.

Wen, the *See the* GREAT WEN.

we never closed The boast of Vivian van Damm (*c*.1889–1960), manager of the WINDMILL THEATRE during the Second World War. Even when a bomb landed next door, killing an electrician and injuring one of the performers, the show went ahead. Among the theatre's morale-boosting specialities were groups of unclothed women arranged in 'artistic' tableaux, with strict instructions not to move as much as an eyelid. When the doors opened for each performance there was a stampede of men to the front six rows, where the seats had constantly to be repaired. The theatre's motto was said to have been interpreted by one showgirl with a lisp as 'We never clothe.'

west

West Brompton Squeezed almost out of existence by FULHAM, CHELSEA and EARLS COURT, between which it lies, West Brompton was an area of fields and market gardens until the late 18th century. Much of the land was acquired from 1801 by the Gunter family, confectioners of BERKELEY SQUARE. Over the course of the 19th century the Gunters and their lessees built thousands of houses on newly created streets, named after a variety of family associations. Edith Grove, for example, honours Captain Robert Gunter's daughter, who died of scarlet fever at the age of eight. *See also* BROMPTON CEMETERY.

west central A mid-19th-century colloquialism

for a lavatory, from the concordance of the initials of the POSTAL DISTRICT and a water closet.

West Drayton An airport satellite district situated north-west of HEATHROW. The name is a corruption of Drægton – a place where small boats could be dragged across the marshes from the River Colne, perhaps to avoid a bend – and the manor was known as West Drayton by the 15th century, distinguishing it from Drayton Green in EALING. West Drayton Green is a conservation area, with 18th-century properties that include Southlands, now an arts centre, but the remainder of the district is almost entirely characterless. West Drayton was home to the UK's air traffic control centre until the operation moved to Swanwick, Hampshire, in 2002.

West End The UK's leading leisure destination. The term 'West End' has been in regular use since the early 19th century but there is no agreement on its ambit, although it undoubtedly takes in the entertainment area around LEICESTER SQUARE, PICCADILLY CIRCUS and SHAFTESBURY AVENUE, and the shopping district of OXFORD STREET, REGENT STREET and BOND STREET. Streets such as the HAYMARKET have long been famous for their theatres and after the creation of Regent Street in 1825 shops in the West End slowly began to cater for the many rather than the privileged few. In the late 19th and early 20th centuries a succession of MUSIC HALLS and new theatres, followed by cinemas and dance halls, progressively established the district's supremacy as London's entertainment centre, at the expense of the STRAND and the TRANSPONTINE THEATRES. Collective improvements in personal wealth from the late 1950s encouraged more day-trippers and short-stay visitors from around the country and an ever-growing number of foreign tourists. About one million people visit the West End every day.

West Ham Formerly an important industrial district situated south-east of STRATFORD. Its location to the east of the River LEA gave West Ham a strategic 'gateway' position in relation to the capital and also allowed the siting of noxious industries that were not permitted nearer the CITY. From the 1840s, chemical works, textile factories and distilleries all located here, and cheap workers' housing replaced former mansions. The greatest growth came during the latter half of the 19th century, when it gained the sobriquet 'the factory centre of the south of England'.

West Ham was ravaged during the BLITZ and its fortunes waned after the Second World War as the industries departed, the nearby docks closed and many east Londoners sought homes in ESSEX or in the NEW TOWNS of the HOME COUNTIES. Modern West Ham is a truly multiracial community, with significant numbers from all the main ethnic groups.

West Hampstead An area popular with upwardly mobile young professionals, situated to the south-west of its HAMPSTEAD parent between the FINCHLEY ROAD and KILBURN High Road. Lacking its own supply of spring water and situated away from the main roads, West End (as West Hampstead was earlier called) long remained an exceptionally quiet hamlet – so much so that its inhabitants claimed to have heard the cannon fire at the Battle of Waterloo. Following the arrival of three railways between 1857 and 1879 the district was rapidly built over with housing of widely varying quality and density.

West Ham reserves 'Nerves' in COCKNEY RHYMING SLANG, usually abbreviated to 'West Hams'. MILLWALL's second team is also called upon to the same effect.

West Ham United FC East London's pre-eminent FOOTBALL club, formed in 1900, five years after the inception of its forerunner, THAMES IRONWORKS FC. In 1904 the club moved to its present home, the BOLEYN GROUND in UPTON PARK. While never matching the achievements of London rivals ARSENAL, CHELSEA and TOTTENHAM HOTSPUR, the Hammers have won the FA Cup three times, in 1964, 1975 and 1980, and the European Cup Winners' Cup in 1965. West Ham's greatest player was undoubtedly Bobby Moore (1941–93), who played for the club from 1958 to 1974. *See also* I'M FOREVER BLOWING BUBBLES.

West Heath

1. (London Borough of Bexley) A part-Victorian, part-interwar locality that many residents consider to be part of BOSTALL HEATH. The first incarnation of West Heath House was built in the early 19th century for Sir Samuel Hulse, who was aide-de-camp to the Prince Regent, later George IV. The king visited West Heath House after Hulse had risen to become a field marshal and treasurer of the royal household.

2. (London Borough of Camden) An extension of HAMPSTEAD HEATH lying west of North End Way and south of Golders Hill Park. West Heath was

the site of an important Stone Age encampment, dating from the era when man first began to abandon a nomadic lifestyle and establish settlements. Excavations have uncovered over 100,000 flints. Horse races were held on West Heath from the 1730s. On the heath's west side Sandy Road and the LEG OF MUTTON Pond were created in the early 19th century as part of a poor relief scheme. West Heath has acquired a reputation as London's prime cruising ground for gay men, especially after dark.

> Under the oaks by West Heath Road
> the soil is fertile and sweet
> and loathsome as mechanically recovered meat.
>
> TOBIAS HILL: *A Year in London*, 'February' (2006)

West India Docks An inland docks complex that formerly occupied much of the northern part of the ISLE OF DOGS. The West India Docks opened in 1802, divided into separate import and export docks – setting a precedent in dock construction. South of the export dock the City Canal traversed the Isle of Dogs. The canal proved a commercial failure and was subsequently enlarged to become the South Dock. Sugar, rum, teak, mahogany and coffee made up the docks' principal imports. The following century saw alternating phases of enlargement, increased competition, financial difficulty and mergers with other London docks. Perhaps the most significant event, with hindsight, was the company's decision in 1881 to build a new dock at Tilbury, ESSEX, rather than further enlarging the West India Docks. Additional expansion did eventually come, especially after the creation of the PORT OF LONDON AUTHORITY in 1908, but the docks' long-term fate had by then been sealed. Most of the West India Docks were wrecked during the Second World War, after which the facility slowly declined until its closure in 1980. The docks have since been redeveloped as WEST INDIA QUAY, CANARY WHARF, HERON QUAYS and SOUTH QUAY.

West India Quay A DOCKLANDS LIGHT RAILWAY station and its immediate vicinity, situated in the north-western corner of the ISLE OF DOGS. The locality was formerly the North Quay of the WEST INDIA DOCKS and its surviving warehouses now provide amenities for local workers and residents. The MUSEUM OF LONDON DOCKLANDS is based in the former No.1 Warehouse. West

India Quay also has new apartment blocks and a 10-screen cinema.

West Kensington This was FULHAM's North End until the latter part of the 19th century, when speculative builders appropriated KENSINGTON's name to lend an upmarket cachet to their development here. The district became popular with artists and writers in the early years of the 20th century but after the Second World War gained a slightly seedy reputation, which has receded in recent times with the arrival of a stream of young professionals.

West Norwood Despite its name, this is the northern part of NORWOOD. Lower Norwood, as it was earlier called, began to grow early in the 19th century as small parcels of former common land were sold off for building, mostly for the middle classes. The name 'West Norwood' was adopted in 1885 in response to residents' sensitivities. Since that time the district has declined in prestige and gained a multi-ethnic community.

Camille Pissarro's painting *Lower Norwood, Londres, Effet de Neige* (1870) hangs in the NATIONAL GALLERY.

West Norwood Cemetery An early example of a non-denominational, landscaped public cemetery, opened in 1837. Among those buried here are Sir Henry TATE, the household management writer Mrs Beeton and the potter Sir Henry Doulton.

West Wickham A relatively uniform interwar suburb situated west of Hayes[1]. The name is of early Anglo-Saxon origin and denoted a homestead that was associated with a *vicus*, i.e. a former Romano-British settlement. The 'West' prefix was added in the 13th century to distinguish it from EAST WICKHAM, which lies some 10 miles (16 km) to the north-east. In 1469 the manor was sold to the Norfolk lawyer Henry Heydon, who rebuilt the Church of St John the Baptist and the manor house, Wickham Court. Both the church and Wickham Court were remodelled in the 19th century. The latter's castle-like appearance was augmented by the addition of battlements and other modifications. It is now an independent school.

Westbourne A minor river that rises in HAMPSTEAD and flows 12 miles (19 km) southwards into the THAMES at CHELSEA. Most of it had been covered over by the middle of the 19th century,

but a portion of it can still be seen above ground in the form of the SERPENTINE in HYDE PARK, which was created by damming the Westbourne. The Westbourne crosses above the tracks and trains at SLOANE SQUARE underground station inside a huge iron conduit.

Westbourne Green Definitions vary, but Westbourne Green is now generally considered to constitute the very mixed locality midway between BAYSWATER and MAIDA VALE, north of the WESTWAY. In the 13th century this was the 'place west of the stream (or bourne)' and it gave its name to the River Westbourne (*see above*). The whole of the western half of PADDINGTON parish was known as Westbourne Green by the 17th century, when the area had just a few mansions and the green was a popular beauty spot. Following the arrival of the GRAND JUNCTION CANAL in 1801 and of the railway in the 1830s the district expanded until it had met its neighbours on all sides by the 1880s. On its fringes the newly enlarged district mostly abutted well-to-do places and the quality of building here was suitably high. But more compact dwellings were built along the HARROW ROAD and this central part of Westbourne Green soon went into a decline from which it has never properly recovered. The county and borough councils replaced the most run-down housing with blocks of flats from the 1950s onwards, while the Westway disfigured the area in the mid-1960s.

Westbourne Grove A revived commercial thoroughfare running westward from QUEENSWAY into NOTTING HILL. This is the smallest of the Westbourne localities, consisting of a single street and its offshoots, but it was the commercial heart of BAYSWATER in the latter half of the 19th century. The road was created in the late 1830s and soon extended. From the mid-1850s shops began to replace houses. Many of these ventures failed and the road was nicknamed 'bankruptcy row' when William WHITELEY opened his first little shop here in 1863. In recent years antique dealers and upmarket boutiques have recolonized the street, which also has a growing number of restaurants with an exotic variety of cuisines.

Westbourne Park A fashionable residential locality occupying a crescent of land made by the elevated section of the WESTWAY, north-east of NOTTING HILL. A mansion called Westbourne Place (later Westbourne Park) stood north of here in the 1640s, with grounds stretching in this direction. In the mid-1850s the house was demolished and its grounds were covered by the generously proportioned semi-detached villas of Westbourne Park Road and Westbourne Park Villas, where the writer Thomas Hardy lived in the 1860s. Later in the century Westbourne Park Road was extended westwards by the simple device of renaming Cornwall Road. Like much of the surrounding area, Westbourne Park had declined by the middle of the 20th century and many houses had been subdivided. The locality was popular with hippies in the 1960s. It has since attracted wealthy figures from the worlds of fashion and music, with chic eateries and organic grocers that draw celebrity customers.

Westbournia An early name for the locality nowadays known as WESTBOURNE PARK. The 'ia' suffix, modelled on BELGRAVIA, was much used by the developers of upmarket estates in the mid-19th century.

Western Avenue An arterial road (A40) built in the 1920s, 1930s and early 1940s as a straighter and wider replacement for the initial section of the existing London-to-Oxford road. Starting north of SHEPHERD'S BUSH, it runs more or less directly westwards to just west of UXBRIDGE, where it now links up with the M40. In its early days it proved irresistible to ribbon-developers, who lined it with not only houses but also factories, most notably the HOOVER BUILDING. In the late 1960s its route was extended by the WESTWAY into Central London.

The stretch of the road from HANGER LANE to WHITE CITY was appropriately dubbed 'Leadville' by Edward Platt in his eponymous history of the Western Avenue and the unfortunates who have lived along its length from its construction to its partial demolition in the 1990s:

> The worst times are the summer afternoons, when the flood of traffic on Western Avenue thickens and congeals into a fetid stew of metal which clogs the road and gums up the air.
>
> EDWARD PLATT: *Leadville* (2000)

Westfield

Westfield College *See* QUEEN MARY, UNIVERSITY OF LONDON.

Westfield London A 'mega-mall', situated on WOOD LANE, on the north side of SHEPHERD'S BUSH. Among the indicators of its magnitude are its 96 escalators, 270 shops and 50 restaurants. In the first five months following its opening in October 2008 the centre attracted ten million visitors, resulting in congestion both on the surrounding streets and at the TUBE station that exists primarily to serve it.

Westminster The seat of Britain's government and home of some of its most important religious institutions. It lies across the THAMES from LAMBETH, from where it was once possible to cross the river at low tide to a marshy island of thorn trees, THORNEY ISLAND. A place called Westmunster is referred to in an Anglo-Saxon charter dated 785, but the trustworthiness of that document is questionable, and the first reliable evidence we have of Westminster is from the late 10th century as the site of a Benedictine monastic foundation, which Edward the Confessor re-endowed and to which he added a large, stone abbey church, consecrated in 1065; this was referred to as the 'west minster' to distinguish it from the 'east minster': ST PAUL'S Cathedral.

Edward decided to move his main royal residence from the CITY of London to Westminster to oversee personally the construction of his abbey, and since then Westminster has been a key seat of political power in England, Britain and the United Kingdom. The Lords, meeting as a parliament, from the first sat in the PALACE OF WESTMINSTER. The Commons met in the CHAPTER HOUSE of the abbey, and then in the abbey's refectory until 1547, when they moved into ST STEPHEN'S CHAPEL in the palace, and ever since the palace has been the home of both houses of Parliament.

St Margaret's, Westminster, Parliament's church, stands in the shadow of Westminster Abbey. It was founded in the mid-12th century. Samuel PEPYS and later Winston Churchill were married here; the printer William Caxton and the courtier, navigator and poet Sir Walter Raleigh are buried here. In 1987 Westminster Abbey, the Palace of Westminster and St Margaret's Church collectively became a UNESCO world heritage site.

Westminster, City of An INNER LONDON borough created in 1965 from the metropolitan boroughs of Westminster (officially designated a city in 1900), PADDINGTON and St MARYLEBONE. Its borders extend north as far as ST JOHN'S

WOOD, west to WESTBOURNE PARK and east to TEMPLE BAR, with the THAMES forming the southern boundary. In the city's coat of arms the crest is surmounted by a Parliamentary PORT- CULLIS and supported by the ermine lions of the Cecil family; William Cecil, 1st Baron Burghley (1520–98), was the first high steward of Westmin- ster and two of his descendants held the same position. The Cecils also acquired a substantial estate in the parish of ST MARTIN-IN-THE-FIELDS (*see also* CECIL COURT). The civic motto is *custodi civitatem Domine* – 'guard the city, O Lord'.

Westminster Abbey The Collegiate Church of St Peter, Westminster, the principal Anglican cathedral of London. In the 1040s the pious king Edward the Confessor, unable to make a pilgrim- age to Rome, vowed instead to found an abbey dedicated to St Peter. It was built on THORNEY ISLAND and consecrated on 28 December 1065. Eight days later Edward died; he was buried in front of the high altar. Within the year William the Conqueror had been crowned here. In the mid-13th century Henry III instigated the re- construction of the church in the Gothic style, and the building grew to its present form over the following three centuries, with two western towers added later by Wren and Hawksmoor. Since the Norman Conquest the coronation of every English (and then British) monarch except Edward V and Edward VIII has taken place in Westminster Abbey, and between the reigns of Henry III and George II most were buried here too. The abbey remains a royal PECULIAR – that is to say, it is directly under the jurisdiction of the sovereign, who appoints its dean and clergy. *See also* CHAPTER HOUSE; NATIONAL VALHALLA; POETS' CORNER; UNKNOWN WARRIOR.

In the 20th century 'Westminster Abbey' was used as COCKNEY RHYMING SLANG for 'cabbie' (taxi driver) and also (usually shortened to simply 'Westminster') for 'shabby'.

Westminster Abbey or victory! The re- ported words of Commodore Horatio Nelson (1758–1805) before the Battle of Cape St Vincent (1798), at which he was victorious. A year later, as rear-admiral commanding the British fleet at the Battle of the Nile, he is supposed to have said: 'Before this time tomorrow I shall have gained a peerage, or Westminster Abbey.' He was afterwards made Baron Nelson of the Nile. Vice- Admiral the Viscount Nelson died at the Battle of Trafalgar and was buried with unprecedented

pomp in ST PAUL's Cathedral in January 1806. *See also* TRAFALGAR SQUARE.

Westminster Assembly An assembly set up in 1643 by the Long Parliament to reform the English church. It consisted of 30 laymen and 121 clergy (of varying shades of opinion), and met in the precincts of WESTMINSTER ABBEY for ten years. Dominated by Presbyterians, it produced a directory of public worship to replace the Book of Common Prayer, and the WESTMINSTER CONFESSION. Its influence declined when the power of the army, which favoured toleration, increased after 1648.

Westminster Bank A former English clearing bank, founded in the CITY of London in 1834 as the London and Westminster Bank. In 1968 it merged with the National Provincial Bank and the District Bank to form the National Westmin- ster Bank, now known by the abbreviated name NatWest. Since 2000 it has been a member of the Royal Bank of Scotland Group. *See also the* NATWEST TOWER.

Westminster Bridge A road bridge across the THAMES linking PARLIAMENT SQUARE with LAMBETH. The original was opened in 1750. It was this bridge that inspired William Wordsworth to write these celebrated lines after he and his sister Dorothy had crossed at dawn on 3 Sep- tember 1802:

> Earth has not anything to show more fair:
> Dull would he be of soul who could pass by
> A sight so touching in its majesty:
> This City now doth like a garment wear
> The beauty of the morning; silent, bare,
> Ships, towers, domes, theatres, and to the sky;
> All bright and glittering in the smokeless air.

'Composed upon Westminster Bridge'

The old bridge was replaced by the present struc- ture in 1854–62. At its Lambeth end is the SOUTH BANK LION, on the Westminster side a statue of BOUDICCA by Thomas Thornycroft.

Westminster Cathedral A brick-built Roman Catholic cathedral set back from VICTORIA STREET, a little to the east of VICTORIA STATION. It was erected between 1895 and 1903 in neo- Byzantine style to the designs of J.F. Bentley. The cathedral is the seat of the archbishops of WEST- MINSTER, a post first held by Cardinal Wiseman (1850–65). The Most Rev Vincent Nichols (b.1945) became the eleventh archbishop in May 2009.

Westminster Chimes The pattern of chimes

struck at successive quarters by BIG BEN, and used for other clocks and now also for door chimes, mobile phone ringtones, etc. The tune was devised by Joseph Jowett and William Crotch and first employed in 1793 at the Church of St Mary the Great, Cambridge, and originally known as the 'Cambridge Chimes'. It uses four bells struck in five different four-note sequences, each of which occurs twice in the course of an hour. It is also known as Westminster quarters.

Westminster Confession The Presbyterian Confession of Faith adopted by the WESTMINSTER ASSEMBLY in 1646 and approved by Parliament in 1648. It became a standard definition of Presbyterian doctrine.

Westminster firemark See PORTCULLIS.

Westminster Hall The only major part of the ancient PALACE OF WESTMINSTER that survives in its original form. It was built by William II at the end of the 11th century and was originally used for feasting and entertaining. In 1399 Richard II commissioned a hammer-beam roof to arch across the entire span of the hall. Now reinforced by concealed steelwork it is the largest medieval timber roof in the country. From the 13th century Westminster Hall housed the law courts: the GUNPOWDER PLOT conspirators (1606) and Charles I (1649) were tried here. It survived the fire that destroyed the rest of the Palace of Westminster in 1834 and the ROYAL COURTS OF JUSTICE continued to sit here until 1882. The hall now serves as a venue for grand parliamentary occasions, and also for the lying-in-state of British kings and queens and of distinguished statesmen, including Gladstone and Churchill.

Westminster Hospital A former leading London hospital, the first in the capital to be founded by voluntary contributions. It was established in 1720 as Westminster Infirmary, and became Westminster Hospital in 1760. The hospital moved into its most famous premises, in Broad Sanctuary, near WESTMINSTER ABBEY, in 1834; it was there that Dr John Snow pioneered the use of anaesthesia. It transferred to a new building at the corner of Horseferry Road and Marsham Street just before the Second World War, and the old one was demolished in 1950 (the site is now occupied by the Queen Elizabeth II Conference Centre). In 1994 it was amalgamated with other hospitals to form the Chelsea and Westminster Hospital, which is situated in the FULHAM ROAD.

Westminster Palace See the PALACE OF WESTMINSTER.

Westminster Pit A dog-fighting establishment that flourished on Duck Lane (now St Matthew Street) from about 1800 to 1835. Bears were also baited and a bull terrier named Billy killed 100 rats in under 12 minutes at the pit in May 1821. The pit held around 300 spectators, most of whom attended for the purpose of wagering. In a jocular allusion, Parliament was later caricatured as the 'Westminster Pit'. See also JACKO MACACCO.

Westminster School A PUBLIC SCHOOL situated close to WESTMINSTER ABBEY. It had its origins in an abbey school founded in 1179 and was granted a charter by Elizabeth I in 1560. It was created as the Abbey's school, the Royal College of St Peter at Westminster, but the formal connection was severed in 1864. Since 1973 it has admitted girls to the sixth form. King's scholars (the holders of special scholarships) have the privilege of acclaiming sovereigns at their coronation with the cry 'Vivat rex!' or 'Vivat regina!' The school's alumni include the poets William Cowper (1731–1800), John Dryden (1631–1700) and Robert Southey (1774–1843), the philosopher John Locke (1632–1704), the historian Edward Gibbon (1737–94), the dramatists Ben Jonson (1572–1637) and Simon Gray (1936–2008), the actor Peter Ustinov (1921–2004) and the architect Sir Christopher Wren (1632–1723). Former pupils are known as Old Westminsters. See also the GREAZE.

Westminster wedding A marriage of two equally low characters. An anonymous ballad of that name was written about the hanging judge, George Jeffreys, after his hurried second marriage (and appointment as Recorder of London) in 1678.

> As for the business of friendship you mentioned, 'tis not to be had at a Westminster Wedding ... Where virtue is not made the measure of a correspondence, 'tis no better than that of thieves and pirates.
>
> JEREMY COLLIER: *Essays Upon Several Moral Subjects*, Part 3, 'Of Whoredom' (1709)

Cock of Westminster See under COCK.

Long Meg of Westminster See under LONG.

Treaty of Westminster See under TREATY.

University of Westminster See under UNIVERSITY.

westward ho! An old cry of London WATERMEN travelling westwards.

Westway The part of the A40 dual carriageway stretching from EAST ACTON to PADDINGTON. Its name is most often used with reference to the elevated section that connects WHITE CITY with the MARYLEBONE ROAD. Begun in 1964, the Westway was conceived as a solution to congestion caused by the absence of a link between central London and the WESTERN AVENUE. The GREATER LONDON COUNCIL forced this state-of-the-art highway through the NORTH KENSINGTON area amidst allegations of Soviet-style disregard for the effects on the local population. Angry protests greeted its opening in July 1970 and the GLC was forced to rehouse some residents living adjacent to the road. The Westway's bleak underbelly has frequently featured as a film location, and punk rockers the CLASH and the Jam employed Westway imagery.

> Corbusier remarked that a city built for speed is a city built for success, but the Westway, like Angkor Wat, the ancient temple city in Cambodia, is a stone dream that will never awake. As you hurtle along this concrete deck you become a citizen of a virtual city-state borne on a rush of radial tyres.
>
> J.G. BALLARD, in *The Observer* (4 November 2001)

Whetstone An enlarged village situated on high ground between BARNET and NORTH FINCHLEY. It was first recorded as 'Weston' in the late 14th century, disproving the myth that the name derives from a large whetstone used to sharpen blades before the BATTLE OF BARNET, and referring instead to the settlement's location west of FRIERN BARNET, its parochial parent. Whetstone grew up as a ribbon village on the GREAT NORTH ROAD, which was flanked by houses and inns here by 1677. Most of its inhabitants were employed in woodland-related industries like charcoal burning, or provided services to passing travellers. A few smart villas were built on the outskirts in the mid-19th century but the village itself had a reputation for drunkenness and brawling – and for outbreaks of typhoid – and remained solidly working-class until the 1920s. The character of the modern High Road reflects the increasingly affluent nature of its catchment area.

Whetstone or **Whetstone's Park** A lane that formerly ran between HOLBORN and LINCOLN'S INN FIELDS, connecting the Great and Little Turnstiles, which prevented cattle from straying. John MILTON is said to have lived in Whetstone Park for a short while. Until its sanitization in the early 18th century the thoroughfare was well known as a resort for 'women of the town', and was attacked by the London APPRENTICES in 1602. Many of the original houses spent their latter days as stables.

> Aldo: It is very well, sir; I find you have been searching for your relations, then, in Whetstone's Park!
>
> Woodall [his son]: No, sir; I made some scruple of going to the foresaid place, for fear of meeting my own father there.
>
> JOHN DRYDEN: *Limberham, or the Kind Keeper*, V, i (1678)

Whipps Cross A road junction and its vicinity, separating the eastern edge of WALTHAMSTOW from the northern tip of LEYTONSTONE. It is said that persons found stealing sheep or deer from adjacent parts of EPPING FOREST were whipped all the way from here to Walthamstow, but a more likely explanation of the name is that it is a corruption of Phippe's Cross, after late 14th-century resident John Phippe. Several Georgian properties, built around 1767, survive along Whipps Cross Road, which is now a conservation area. The stately Whipps Cross Hospital (nowadays known simply as 'Whipps' by its staff) was built in the grounds of Forest House in 1903. The footballer David Beckham was born at the hospital's maternity unit in 1975.

Whirlwind The nickname of the TOOTING-born snooker player Jimmy White (b.1962), from the rapidity of his playing style.
Whitechapel Whirlwind *See under* WHITECHAPEL.

Whispering Gallery An acoustically conductive platform located under the cupola of ST PAUL'S Cathedral, 99 feet (30m) above the floor. However, its ability to transmit a whisper from one side to the other is usually impaired by the sound of the crowd.

whistle (and flute) 'Suit' in COCKNEY RHYMING SLANG. The term has also occasionally been used to mean 'loot' (money) and more recently 'toot' (cocaine).

white

White Book *See* LIBER ALBUS.

White City A 200-acre (81-hectare) complex built in 1907–8 on both sides of WOOD LANE, north of SHEPHERD'S BUSH, with more than 100 exhibition halls, most covered in white STUCCO, a network of Venetian-style canals and a 150,000-capacity stadium. The Jewish-Hungarian émigré Imre Kiralfy (1848–1919) was the driving force behind the project and appropriated its name from the White City at the Chicago Columbian exhibition, which he had visited in 1893. In its inaugural year of 1908 the venue hosted the Franco-British Exhibition and the OLYMPIC GAMES. Its last show, the Anglo-American Exposition, came just six years later and was closed prematurely because of the outbreak of the First World War. By the early 1930s the exhibition halls had fallen into dereliction but the stadium was used by QUEENS PARK RANGERS FC for two seasons. Finding this unprofitable, the club returned to its earlier home in Loftus Road. The LONDON COUNTY COUNCIL demolished the beautiful but crumbling exhibition buildings and began to erect the 52-acre (21-hectare) White City housing estate, which was completed after the Second World War. Much of the rest of the exhibition site became home to BBC Television in the late 1950s. The BBC has progressively expanded the complex, building its corporate headquarters on the site of the old stadium in 1990.

White City's most famous resident was The Who's guitarist Pete Townshend (b.1945). His 1985 solo album was entitled *White City*, which he describes as 'a joke of a name' in the track 'White City Fighting'. Tim Lott's novel *White City Blue* (1991) explores a number of male friendships forged in the W12 POSTAL DISTRICT.

White Cube A pair of contemporary art galleries situated in HOXTON Square and Mason's Yard, ST JAMES'S.

white flight The term was coined in the USA in the 1960s. In a London context it generally refers to the supposed exodus of white, primarily working-class residents from areas of INNER LONDON to boroughs in OUTER LONDON or beyond. In particular, the phenomenon has been identified with those formerly living in inner east and south-east London who relocated to HAVERING, BEXLEY and BROMLEY, and to parts of ESSEX and Kent.

White Hart Lane A long and winding thoroughfare connecting the High Roads of TOTTENHAM and WOOD GREEN. The road was in existence by 1619, when its western part was called Apeland Street. The White Hart inn stood on the east side of Tottenham High Road and was used for court sessions in the 1650s. The newly professional TOTTENHAM HOTSPUR FC moved from NORTHUMBERLAND PARK in 1899 to a site behind the White Hart. Over the course of the 20th century the stadium was wholly remodelled in a series of projects and presently has an all-seater capacity of 36,310. *See also the* NORTHUMBERLAND DEVELOPMENT PROJECT.

White Horse Bridge A landmark footbridge crossing the railway line on one of the approaches to WEMBLEY STADIUM. Its name was chosen in an online poll in 2005 and commemorates the WHITE HORSE FINAL of 1923.

White Horse Final In footballing history, a nickname for the FA Cup Final of 28 April 1923 between Bolton Wanderers and WEST HAM UNITED at WEMBLEY. Thousands of fans spilled on to the pitch before the start of the game, and it required mounted police, and in particular Constable George Scorey on his 13-year-old white horse, Billy, to clear it before the match could begin. Although Scorey was only one of several mounted policemen on duty that day, his conspicuous horse gave the name by which the final has always been referred to since. Bolton won the match 2–0.

White Milliner The sobriquet, allegedly, of Frances Talbot, née Jennings, Duchess of Tyrconnel (*c*.1647–1730), who fell on hard times after the death of her husband in 1691 and was said to have resorted briefly to selling ribbons, lace and 'French gew-gaws' from a booth at the New Exchange (*see* BRITAIN'S BOURSE). The story goes that she always wore white clothes and disguised herself with a white mask. A further embellishment suggested that the business was really a cover for her political intrigues, which were fuelled by the gossip she picked up from well-connected customers. Douglas Jerrold made her story the subject of a two-act comedy of manners, *The White Milliner*, which was staged at the Covent Garden Theatre in 1841.

White's A chocolate house and later a fashionable CLUB, first opened by Francis White (d.1711) on the east side of ST JAMES'S STREET in 1693, moving across the street to larger premises in 1697. The fashionable fraternity soon congregated upstairs to avoid the general company of the chocolate house, which, after 1711, was in the hands of the Arthur family. Early on it earned notoriety as a gaming house. It also gained fame for the exclusiveness of its upstairs clientele, from which in due course White's Club developed. The transition was virtually complete by the mid-18th century, and it can with some justification be regarded as the first of the London clubs, moving to larger premises in 1755. Gambling and gaming excesses continued until the accession of George III (1760), when they were reduced to more modest proportions in keeping with the changed tone of the court. At this juncture a group of the more extravagant younger men from White's became the patrons of ALMACK'S.

White Tower The approximately square keep of the TOWER OF LONDON, constituting the oldest part of the fortress. It was built of stone by Gundulf, Bishop of Rochester, in the reigns of William the Conqueror and William II, with a view to intimidating the local populace and making it clear that the Normans were here to stay (most castles in that period were made of wood). In the *Anglo-Saxon Chronicle* for 1097 this is referred to as *thone tur* 'the tower'. There is a turret at each corner and the sides are over 100 feet (30m) wide, the walls being 15 feet (4.5m) thick in the lower parts and 11 feet (3.4m) thick in the upper storey. On its second floor is the Chapel of St John, the oldest intact church building in London, completed in 1080. Around 1240 the tower was whitewashed, and ever since has been called the 'White Tower'. It has housed many notable prisoners, most famously the PRINCES IN THE TOWER.

whitebait Formerly a popular London dish for special occasions, especially caught and served at BLACKWALL and GREENWICH. Numerous societies and institutions (including the Cabinet) used to organize trips down the THAMES for an annual whitebait dinner.

> We feasted full on every famous dish,
> Dress'd many ways, of sea and river fish –
> Perch, mullet, eels, and salmon, all were there,
> And whitebait, daintiest of our fishy fare ...
>
> THOMAS LOVE PEACOCK: 'A Whitebait Dinner at Lovegrove's at Blackwall' (1812)

Whitechapel A historic EAST END melting-pot situated east of ALDGATE. Some time in the 13th century ST MARY MATFELON was founded and became known as *alba capella* or the 'white chapel'. Around 1350 St Mary's became a parish church – although it survived only a few decades more before being rebuilt – and Whitechapel was the name given to the parish. The process of industrialization began locally in the late 15th century with the establishment of construction trades: brick- and tile-making, lime-burning and woodworking, accompanied by what John Stow later called the 'building of filthy cottages'. Jewish immigrants from Spain and Portugal settled here in the late 17th century, forming the nucleus of a community that would become known as 'the Jewish East End'. Over the course of the 19th century its housing became ever more overcrowded, especially after an influx of Ashkenazi Jews. One street of 176 houses had 2,516 inhabitants in 1881. Increasing hardship bred crime and prostitution, and the latter brought the district its enduring notoriety with JACK THE RIPPER's murders in 1888. Philanthropists worked hard to alleviate conditions, establishing every kind of life-improving institution, from soup kitchens to the WHITECHAPEL ART GALLERY. As Whitechapel's Jews moved to outer north and east London, their place was taken by south Asian immigrants, especially from the 1970s, and the majority of the population is now of Bangladeshi origin.

In the middle of the 19th century a 'Whitechapel' was (for reasons unknown) a score of two out of three wins in the game of coin-tossing; in late 19th-century slang a 'Whitechapel' was a sex murder (for very obvious reasons) and in the 20th century it was (inferior) COCKNEY RHYMING SLANG for 'apple'. For many outsiders, Whitechapel personified the East End in all its roughness, hence some of the pejorative slang terms below.

Whitechapel beau In late 18th-century slang, a man 'who dresses with a needle and thread, and undresses with a knife' (Francis Grose, *A Classical Dictionary of the Vulgar Tongue*, 1785).

Whitechapel Bell Foundry Britain's oldest manufacturing company, established in 1570, although its antecedents have been traced back as far as 1420. The firm moved from HOUNDSDITCH to its present address, 32/34 Whitechapel Road, in 1738. It was here that the hour bell of the Great Clock of Westminster (known as BIG BEN) and Philadelphia's Liberty Bell were cast. Most of the foundry's bells are made for church towers and after the Second World War it provided replacements for two of London's most famous sets, those of ST MARY-LE-BOW and ST CLEMENT DANES.

Name an important chimer from Western history and chances are Whitechapel Bell Foundry cast it.

JASON COCHRAN: *Pauline Frommer's London* (2007)

Whitechapel Boys The name given to a group of Anglo-Jewish writers and artists of the early 20th century. The group's members, not all of whom came from Whitechapel, included the poets Isaac Rosenberg and John Rodker, the painters David Bomberg and Mark Gertler, the critic and translator Joseph Leftwich, and the biographer Stephen Winsten and his wife, the artist Clare Winsten (née Clara Birnberg).

Whitechapel breed In late 18th-century slang, a woman who is 'fat, ragged and saucy' (Francis Grose, *A Classical Dictionary of the Vulgar Tongue*, 1785).

Whitechapel brougham An ironic 19th-century colloquialism for a donkey, often one pulling a COSTERMONGER's barrow, the horse-drawn brougham being well beyond the means of most Whitechapel residents.

Whitechapel cart A type of light two-wheeled horsedrawn spring cart, with panelled sides. In the 19th century they were generally known colloquially as simply 'Whitechapels'.

Whitechapel fashion Either one of various modes of (usually flashy) dress favoured by common Londoners, or some unrefined type of behaviour, such as speaking bluntly.

Whitechapel Gallery An art gallery located at the western end of the Whitechapel Road, in a *fin-de-siècle* Art Nouveau building designed by C.H. Townsend. The Whitechapel reopened in April 2009 following a two-year lottery-funded refit that has almost doubled its exhibition space. It specializes in exhibitions of contemporary art.

Whitechapel needles or **sharps** The district was long a centre for the production of sewing needles, or at least for their finishing, as the raw materials were often imported from Sweden. The name, sometimes shortened to 'chapel needles', was later used by manufacturers in the Midlands.

... for the sharpest needle, best Whitechapel,

warranted not to cut in the eye, was not sharper than Scrooge; blunt as he took it in his head to be.

CHARLES DICKENS: *A Christmas Carol* (1843)

Whitechapel oner Late 19th-century slang for an EAST END dandy.

Whitechapel play A condescending term implying that EAST ENDERS lack the skill and subtlety to play sophisticated middle-class games. From the 18th century it was applied in whist to techniques such as leading with all one's best cards, with no attempt to finesse one's opponent, or leading from a one-card suit in order to trump. From the 19th century a 'Whitechapel' meant the intentional potting of an opponent's ball in billiards.

Whitechapel portion or **fortune** A 19th-century slang term for a paltry inheritance, said to consist of 'a clean gown and a pair of pattens [wooden shoes]' or 'a clean apron and an umbrella'.

Whitechapel shave In mid-19th-century slang, whitening applied to the face to lighten the 'five o'clock shadow' (the poor of Whitechapel could not afford to pay a barber to shave them).

Whitechapel warriors A late 19th-century facetious colloquial name for the Aldgate militia (local part-time soldiers; ALDGATE is at the western end of Whitechapel).

Whitechapel Whirlwind The sobriquet of Daniel Mendoza (1764–1836), one of Britain's most illustrious boxers. He pioneered the use of defensive tactics, rather than simply punching and being punched, and used his skills to defeat bigger and stronger opponents. His fame was so great that he became the first Jew to be permitted to address George III.

Whitechapel Windmill The sobriquet of the boxer Judah Bergman, known as Jackie Kid Berg (1909–91). Born in CABLE STREET, he was world light welterweight champion in the early 1930s.

Whitecross Street A commercial thoroughfare (but not a vibrant one) situated north of the BARBICAN. It was so named for a white stone cross mentioned in the 13th century. Whitecross Street was best known for its debtors' prison in the 19th century, when the vicinity formed part of the ROOKERY of ST LUKE'S. The street has a small daily market.

Whitefriars The former name for the narrow

area between Whitefriars Street (earlier Water Lane) and the TEMPLE, south of FLEET STREET. A Carmelite monastery was founded here in 1241 and the monks were known as White Friars from the white mantle worn over a brown habit. In the 17th and 18th centuries it became an area of ill repute, known as ALSATIA.

Whitehall A street extending from the south side of TRAFALGAR SQUARE towards PARLIAMENT SQUARE. South of the CENOTAPH it becomes Parliament Street but this section is frequently considered part of Whitehall in colloquial usage. After fire destroyed WHITEHALL PALACE the street was progressively rebuilt with offices of state. The Treasury was completed in 1736 and by the end of the 18th century most of the key government offices were based in its vicinity. During the 19th century Whitehall became the administrative centre of the British Empire, and further building work by John SOANE and Charles Barry brought architectural cohesion to the assortment of buildings. On the eastern side are the BANQUETING HOUSE (1), the Department for Environment, Food and Rural Affairs, the Ministry of Defence, the Department of Health and the Department for Work and Pensions; on the western side, HORSE GUARDS, the Cabinet Office, the Foreign and Commonwealth Office and, at the northern end, the ADMIRALTY BUILDINGS. From its being the site of these major government offices, Whitehall has come to symbolize the executive branch of British government and the Civil Service.

> For in the case of nutrition and health, just
> as in the case of education, the gentleman in
> Whitehall really does know better what is good
> for people than the people know themselves.
>
> DOUGLAS JAY: *The Socialist Case* (1947 edition)

DOWNING STREET is a turning off the western side. *See also* Q-WHITEHALL; SCOTLAND YARD.

In the mid-18th century, Whitehall provided the setting for a plethora of works by the Venetian artist Canaletto (1697–1768), most of which are now in private collections.

Whitehallese A derogatory term for the sort of jargon regarded as typical of the Civil Service.

Whitehall farce A name given to any of a series of bedroom farces produced at the Whitehall Theatre, at the top end of Whitehall, in the middle years of the 20th century, and in particular

to the ones presented by Brian Rix between 1950 and 1967.

Whitehall Palace A royal palace that was situated on the eastern side of Whitehall. Walter de Grey, Archbishop of York, bought a property in the area soon after 1240 and called it York Place. In 1529 the house was confiscated by Henry VIII and the name Whitehall first appeared soon afterwards; it may have been inspired by the pale-coloured stone of the Great Hall that was added to the original house in 1528 by Cardinal Wolsey, who was archbishop of York at that time; alternatively it may have been a reappropriation of the name of the PALACE OF WESTMINSTER's White Hall, which lay south of WESTMINSTER HALL.

> You must no more call it York-place, that's past:
> For, since the cardinal fell, that title's lost:
> 'Tis now the king's, and call'd Whitehall.
>
> SHAKESPEARE: *Henry VIII*, IV, i (1612)

Henry rebuilt and extended the house to create a palace, with amenities that included tennis courts, a bowling alley, a cockpit, formal gardens and orchards. During subsequent reigns, Whitehall became more a place of accommodation than recreation. In 1649 Charles I was executed outside the BANQUETING HOUSE, which is the only part of the palace that now survives, the rest having been destroyed by fire in 1698.

Whitehall warrior A somewhat derisive colloquialism, dating from the 1960s, either for a civil servant, or more specifically for an officer in the armed forces employed as a civil servant, typically on retirement, rather than on active service – his 'battle' is thus with administrative matters rather than military ones.

Whiteley, William London's UNIVERSAL PROVIDER (1831–1907). He came to London from the West Riding of Yorkshire in the mid-1850s and by 1863 had saved enough money to establish his own business in WESTBOURNE GROVE, selling ribbons, laces, trimmings and fancy goods. Whiteley proved to be a very astute merchant and by 1876 he had acquired 15 adjacent shops, creating London's first 'great emporium'. This did not please smaller local traders and there was an outcry each time he branched into a new line of business. His buildings were always mysteriously catching fire but were soon rebuilt. To provide fresh produce for his shops, he established an extensive agricultural estate beside the River

Crane in HANWORTH, and spent much of his time living in a small bungalow there, despite his enormous wealth. On 24 January 1907 Whiteley was shot dead in his own office by a young man who claimed to be his bastard son. His legitimate sons relocated the business to an imposing new building on Queen's Road (now QUEENSWAY) in 1911. Later owners, the United Drapery Stores Group, closed the store in 1981 and the building has since been converted to a shopping and leisure centre.

Whittington

Whittington, Dick According to the popular legend and pantomime story, a poor boy who made his way to London when he heard that the streets were paved with gold and silver. He found shelter as a scullion in the house of a rich merchant who permitted each of his servants to partake in sending a cargo of merchandise to Barbary, and Dick sent his cat. He subsequently ran away because of the ill-treatment meted out to him by the merchant's cook. Resting upon HIGHGATE Hill he was recalled by Bow Bells seeming to say:

> Turn again Whittington
> Thrice Lord Mayor of London.

He returned to the house to find that his cat had been purchased for a vast sum by the king of Barbary, who was much plagued by rats and mice. He married his master's daughter Alice, prospered exceedingly, and became LORD MAYOR OF LONDON three times.

Richard Whittington (c.1358–1423) was, in fact, the youngest son of Sir William Whittington of Pauntley in Gloucestershire and duly became a mercer of London, having married Alice, the daughter of Sir Ivo Fitzwaryn. He became very wealthy, the richest merchant of his day, and was made lord mayor of London in 1397–8, 1406–7 and 1419–20. When he died he left his vast wealth for charitable and public purposes.

The part of the cat in the story has been explained as follows: he traded in coals brought to London in 'cats' (a type of sailing vessel), or that the word is a confusion with French *achat*, 'purchase' (a term then used for trading at a profit). Whatever the case, Dick Whittington and his cat are now inseparable and form the subject of many Christmas pantomimes.

Whittington Hospital An acute general teaching hospital situated in ARCHWAY, near the foot of HIGHGATE Hill. The first institution on the site was the Highgate Spytell, a leper hospital founded in 1473 on land given by Edward IV. By the late 16th century it had become a house for the poor. The present hospital was created following the foundation of the National Health Service in 1946, bringing together St Mary's Hospital (1848), Archway Hospital (1877) and Highgate Hill Infirmary (1900).

Whittington's College A nickname for NEWGATE PRISON, which was rebuilt soon after Sir Richard Whittington's death with money he had bequeathed. To have 'studied at Whittington's College' was to have been incarcerated in Newgate.

Whittington Stone An upright stone located near the foot of HIGHGATE Hill, supposedly marking the spot where Dick Whittington turned again. In fact, the first stone on the site was associated with the nearby leper hospital (*see the* WHITTINGTON HOSPITAL) but a successor was engraved with a dedication to the semi-legendary LORD MAYOR OF LONDON. The present stone (the third or fourth to have stood here) dates from 1821. A bronze cat was mounted atop the Whittington Stone in 1964.

Whitton A residential suburb situated on the south-eastern edge of HOUNSLOW and separated from TWICKENHAM by the Duke of Northumberland's River. Its name means 'white farm'. The German artist Sir Godfrey Kneller (1646 –1723) was the leading portrait painter of his day and founded the English Academy of Painting in 1711, the same year that he moved into his new house here, later called Kneller Hall. The house was demolished in 1847 and replaced by the present building, where in 1857 the Duke of Cambridge founded the Royal Military School of Music, which is still based at the hall. The singer/songwriter Elvis Costello (b.1954) grew up in Whitton, where his father had developed his own musical talents at the Royal Military School of Music.

Widmore A suburbanized hamlet located on the east side of BROMLEY. The name was first recorded as Withmere in 1226, and probably derives from Old English words meaning 'the pool where the willows grow'. According to an old story, Widmore would have been the site of Bromley's medieval church but for divine intervention:

Bromley old Church was attempted to be built at Wigmore [sic] but what was built by the men by day was carried away by night, and the stones placed where it now stands, so that the architect was at length obliged to acquiesce, and then the building regularly proceeded!

EDWARD STRONG: *A History of Bromley in Kent* (1858)

widow

widow's chamber The clothes and bedroom furniture of the widow of a London freeman, to which she was entitled.

Widow's Son, The A public house in Devons Road, BROMLEY-BY-BOW, taking its name from a sailor who is said to have lived with his mother in a house that occupied the site. One year, when the young man was due back from a voyage, the widow baked hot cross buns for him but he never returned. She continued to bake the buns for her lost son every year until her death. When a pub was later built on the site the tradition continued and to this day a navy seaman or Wren hangs a bun from the ceiling in an annual Good Friday ceremony.

Wigmore An old form of WIDMORE, unconnected with WIGMORE STREET.

Wigmore Hall An intimately proportioned concert hall located on the north side of WIGMORE STREET, just east of the junction with Welbeck Street. Built by the piano firm Bechstein next to its showrooms, it opened in 1901 as the Bechstein Hall. Because the business was German-owned it was seized by the government during the First World War and the building and its contents were sold to DEBENHAMS for a fraction of their true value. It reopened as Wigmore Hall in 1917 and nowadays aims to be the national concert hall for chamber music and song.

Wigmore Street A street in southern MARYLE-BONE, extending from PORTMAN SQUARE eastward to CAVENDISH SQUARE. Edward Harley (*see* HARLEY STREET), who owned and developed this area, was Earl of Oxford and Mortimer and Baron Harley of Wigmore Castle (in Herefordshire). The Italian poet and patriot Ugo Foscolo (1778–1827) lived in humble lodgings in Wigmore Street in 1821–2. *See also* JOHN BELL & CROYDEN.

Wilbur (Wright) 'Flight' in COCKNEY RHYMING SLANG, from the pioneering aviator. The best rhyming slang can be shortened without risking confusion with some other term and bears a

relationship to its paired word, and Wilbur qualifies on both counts. Regrettably, however, it has never been widely used.

Wilkite Riots *See the* ST GEORGE'S FIELDS MASSACRE.

Willesden A densely developed district separated from WEMBLEY to its west by the River BRENT. The name referred to a hill by a spring or stream and its first confirmed appearance was in Domesday Book in 1086, when the manor was owned by the dean and chapter of ST PAUL'S Cathedral. From the middle of the 19th century substantial houses were built for CITY merchants and professionals but Willesden's character began to change after the coming of the railways. Willesden Junction station opened in 1866, prompting the growth of HARLESDEN as a separate district. The Metropolitan Railway had a more direct effect on the growth of Willesden itself, with a station opening at WILLESDEN GREEN in 1879 and at NEASDEN the following year, prompting the rapid spread of working-class housing. Willesden became a municipal borough in 1933 and the incoming Labour council immediately set about building estates in the outlying areas not yet covered by housing. So keen was the council to reduce overcrowding that it left few open spaces, with the notable exception of GLADSTONE PARK.

Willesden formed the backdrop for ITV's long-running series MINDER, but its greatest modern claim to fame is as the setting for Zadie Smith's story of interracial relationships, *White Teeth* (2000).

Willesden Green

1. The east end of Willesden, now seen as more desirable than other parts of the district because it escaped wholesale redevelopment with highrise council estates after the Second World War. This was the geographical centre of Willesden parish from the late Anglo-Saxon period, when a hamlet grew up in a forest clearing beside a tributary of the River Brent.

2. The title of a mock-country song by the KINKS, recorded for the film *Percy* (1971).

Will's Coffee House A famous resort in the time of John Dryden (1631–1700), who added much to its popularity. It stood on the corner of BOW STREET and Russell Street, COVENT GARDEN. Originally called the Red Cow, then the ROSE, it took its name from Will Urwin, who was its proprietor at the time of the Restoration in 1660. Known as the 'Wits' Coffee House', it was the headquarters of Tory men of letters but from 1714 was rivalled by Button's coffee house, the home of the Whig literati. In his diary for 3 February 1664 Samuel PEPYS notes meeting 'Dryden, the poet I knew at Cambridge, and all the wits of the town'. Confusion sometimes arises from the coexistence of five or more coffee houses of this name, but this is undoubtedly the Will's associated with *The Spectator*. It closed some time before the middle years of the 18th century.

Willy G A modern colloquialism for WILLESDEN GREEN.

Wilton's Music Hall The oldest MUSIC HALL in London to survive in its original form, situated in Graces Alley, south of the western end of CABLE STREET. It was built in 1859 by John Wilton (1820–80), behind his Prince of Denmark public house. In its heyday Wilton's attracted crowds of up to 1,500 to variety shows that sometimes featured artistes from COVENT GARDEN, who arrived still in full costume to sing late-night arias. The building continued to function as a music hall for a few years after John Wilton's death and was then acquired by the Methodist Church for use as a mission hall. It was saved from demolition in the mid-1960s following a campaign led by John Betjeman, but remains in a precarious state structurally, in constant need of funds for its preservation and renovation.

Wimbledon

1. The home of British tennis (*see the* WIMBLEDON CHAMPIONSHIPS) and a Victorian and Edwardian suburb, situated 2 miles (3 km) south of PUTNEY. The name derives from Old English words meaning 'the hill of a man called Wynnman (or Wymbald)'. Around the 13th century, a collection of cottages and farmsteads was established on the heights of WIMBLEDON COMMON, which functioned as a grazing and hunting ground and a source of wood and water, but a settlement did not begin to coalesce around the present-day High Street for another 400 years. The first station opened in 1838, augmented by a link with CROYDON in 1855. From then onwards the parkland started to be sold off for redevelopment and Wimbledon grew rapidly as a desirable suburb, especially at the top of Wimbledon Hill,

in what is known as Wimbledon Village, which nowadays has appealing boutiques, bars and restaurants. Cultural amenities on the Broadway include the Polka Theatre, which specializes in productions for young audiences, and the New Wimbledon Theatre. In recent years Wimbledon has witnessed a remarkable influx of white South African immigrants, who tend to work in finance, health, education or social work and speak English rather than Afrikaans.

The poet and novelist Robert Graves (1895–1985), the painter John Bratby (1928–92) and the actor Oliver Reed (1938–99) were all born in Wimbledon, as was the fictional adventurer Lara CROFT.

2. A romantic film comedy (2004) starring Paul Bettany and Kirsten Dunst in which an ageing British tennis player, inspired by his ongoing relationship with a successful US woman player, achieves a highly implausible victory in the Wimbledon men's singles final. The real-life US tennis player Serena Williams, twice a Wimbledon ladies' singles champion, remarked a little ungenerously: 'It must be a comedy if a British player is winning at Wimbledon.'

Wimbledon Championships A tennis tournament held in Wimbledon since 1877. Men's and ladies' singles and doubles and mixed doubles titles are fought for in what is the only Grand Slam tournament still played on grass. It is run by the All England Lawn Tennis and Croquet Club (founded in 1877 as the All England Croquet and Lawn Tennis Club) and was first played at their Worple Road ground. It moved to its present site in Church Road in 1922. The tournament is firmly part of the LONDON SEASON and is rich with associations: the Virginia-creeper-covered Centre Court, the overpriced strawberries and cream, the Robinson's Barley Water, the rain breaks (though no longer on Centre Court, which had a retractable roof installed in 2009) and the voice of former BBC commentator Dan Maskell ('Oh, I say!'). The club has also hosted British home Davis Cup ties and will be the tennis venue for the 2012 OLYMPIC GAMES. The outside courts are available to members when not in use for the championships. Wimbledon is also the headquarters of the Lawn Tennis Association. *See also* HENMAN HILL.

Wimbledon Common A plateau of bogs and heathland stretching from RICHMOND PARK to Wimbledon town. Its most ancient feature is

Bensbury Camp, popularly though misleadingly known as CAESAR'S CAMP, a hill-fort that probably dates from around the 7th century BC. The common was for centuries part of the manor of MORTLAKE, owned by the archbishops of Canterbury, with rights of hunting and grazing granted to local tenants. It acquired a reputation as a duelling ground: the politicians Pitt the Younger, Castlereagh and Canning were among those who fought here. Earl Spencer gained legal authority to enclose the common in 1803, but backed down in the face of local protests. The best-known landmark on Wimbledon Common is the windmill, built in 1817 to grind corn and now a museum devoted to windmills and woodworking. The common has been in public ownership since 1871, but only when the National Rifle Association left for Bisley, Surrey, in 1889 did full freedom of movement become possible. Large parts of it are now given over to golf, but there is more than enough left for the horse-rider and dog-walker. *See also the* WOMBLES.

Wimbledon FC An association FOOTBALL club, nicknamed the Dons, founded in 1889 and elevated to the Football League in 1977. In a remarkable rise-and-fall story its finest hour came in 1988, when it beat Liverpool to win the FA Cup. Thereafter its fortunes went into a sharp decline, as it slid down the league and went into financial administration. The club relocated to Milton Keynes, Buckinghamshire, in 2003, as the renamed Milton Keynes Dons, and afterwards disconnected itself from its history. Aggrieved former supporters founded a new local club, AFC Wimbledon, owned by the fans.

Wimbledon Park A Victorian and interwar conservation area covering the extensive former grounds of Wimbledon Park House. George Eliot (Mary Anne Evans) lived at Holly Lodge, 31 Wimbledon Park Road, where she completed *The Mill on the Floss* (1860). The children's storyteller and illustrator Raymond Briggs was born in Wimbledon Park in 1934.

Wimbledon Poisoner, The A comic novel (1990) by Nigel Williams recounting the chaotic travails of a would-be suburban murderer. Williams returned to the same Wimbledon locale for THEY CAME FROM SW19 (1992) and *Scenes from a Poisoner's Life* (1994).

Wimpole Street A 'long unlovely street', according to Tennyson's *In Memoriam* (1849),

running north–south through central MARYLEBONE. Wimpole Hall is a palatial house in Cambridgeshire that belonged to the Harley family, developers of the Cavendish estate. Begun around 1724, Wimpole Street had just seven houses by the end of the decade. The Irish statesman and philosopher Edmund Burke was living here in 1759, at a time when the street was beginning to fill with substantial, if uninspiring, terraced houses. Upper Wimpole Street was created after the closure of Marylebone Gardens in 1778. Like Harley Street and the rest of the immediate area, Wimpole Street soon attracted the cream of London's fashionable society, before being colonized by doctors, mainly from the 1820s. Later still, the street gained popularity with opticians and dentists; Arthur Conan Doyle opened his ophthalmic practice in Upper Wimpole Street in 1891. The Royal Society of Medicine came to No.1 Wimpole Street in 1912. The British Dental Association and the General Dental Council are both based in the street and private dental consultants still abound here.

Elizabeth Barrett was kept a virtual prisoner at 50 Wimpole Street by her tyrannical father before eloping to Italy with fellow poet Robert Browning in 1846. The story of *The Barretts of Wimpole Street* became the subject of a play and a 1934 film, remade in 1957 with John Gielgud as the patriarch. Professor Henry Higgins lives at 27A Wimpole Street in George Bernard Shaw's play PYGMALION.

Winchester
Winchester goose
1. A prostitute who worked in the STEWS on BANKSIDE was so called, because of the tolerance extended by the bishops of Winchester, who owned the properties and benefited from the tax revenues.
2. A slang term from the 16th to the 18th century for venereal disease.

Winchester House or **Palace** The SOUTHWARK residence of the bishops of Winchester from about 1150 until the bishopric's suppression by the Puritans in 1642, when it was converted into a prison. The foundations and a 14th-century rose window may still be seen on CLINK STREET.

Winchmore Hill A superior Edwardian and interwar suburb focused on an agreeable village green, separated since the 15th century from SOUTHGATE to its west by the Grovelands estate.

The origin of the name is uncertain but it is probably a corruption of a personal name (Wynsige) plus 'mere', which could have meant a boundary or a pond. The poet and humorist Thomas Hood (1799–1845) came to live in Rose Cottage on Vicars Moor Lane in 1829 and his wife bore their third child here. Although the Hoods were not wealthy, their home was a grander affair than its quaint name suggests. The family moved to WANSTEAD in 1832.

Windmill Theatre A theatre in Great Windmill Street, SOHO, that was famous in the 1930s and the Second World War for its shows with nude women, who were allowed to appear so long as they remained still. The logic behind this was that movement would have given them a sexual import, whereas if they posed stationary they were regarded as artistic displays. The Windmill remained open right through the war, leading it to boast the proud slogan, 'WE NEVER CLOSED'. It closed in 1964, but has since periodically reopened under a succession of new owners, usually offering contemporary forms of 'nude entertainment'.

> Windmill: always nude but never rude
>
> *The Daily Telegraph*, headline (24 November 2005)

In 2005 the film *Mrs Henderson Presents* offered a version of the history of the shows' beginnings, concentrating on Laura Henderson (played by Judi Dench), who first organized the performances in 1932.

Winfield House The palatial residence of the ambassador of the United States of America to the COURT OF ST JAMES'S, situated at the western extremity of REGENT'S PARK in 12½ acres (5 hectares) of grounds. After inheriting $40 million from her grandfather, Frank Winfield Woolworth, Barbara Hutton built Winfield House in 1937 and donated it as a home for the American ambassador after the Second World War. Visiting US presidents often stay here.

Winnie-the-Pooh The 'Bear of Very Little Brain' who appears in the nursery verses and children's stories by A.A. Milne (1882–1956). He made his bow in 1924 and had his genesis in an actual teddy bear of the name owned by Milne's young son, Christopher Robin Milne, who also appears in the various narratives. The original Winnie was an American black bear, the mascot of a Canadian regiment. When the regiment was sent to France in 1914, Winnie was left in the care of the Zoological Society and lived in LONDON ZOO until her death in 1934.

wirewalkers Not funambulists, but boys employed by the Post Office during the BLITZ to walk around the CITY of London as roving post offices. They could take telegrams ('wires'), charge customers and give change, and to announce their services they wore signs saying 'Telegrams Accepted'. The general aim was to maintain a semblance of normality with 'business as usual'.

Wiseacres' Hall An old nickname for Gresham College, which was founded in 1597 by Sir Thomas Gresham (*see* GRASSHOPPER). The college does not award degrees or teach courses but instead provides free public lectures by its eight professors. Since 1991 it has been based at BARNARD'S INN, which is situated on the south side of HOLBORN, just west of its junction with FETTER LANE.

witch

Witch of Edmonton Elizabeth Sawyer, who in 1621 was accused of having witched her neighbour's children to death. She had the misfortune of being a deformed old spinster and was hanged at TYBURN after the devil's mark was found above the base of her spine.

> Elizabeth Sawyer: If every poor old woman be trod on thus by slaves, reviled, kicked, beaten, as I am daily, she, to be revenged, had need to turn witch.
>
> Sir Arthur: And you, to be revenged, have sold your soul to th' devil.
>
> WILLIAM ROWLEY, THOMAS DEKKER and JOHN FORD: *The Witch of Edmonton*, IV, i (1658)

Witch of Wapping Joan Peterson, who, until her downfall, was said to have been a physician of good repute in WAPPING and SHADWELL. She was hanged at TYBURN in 1652 after being found guilty of a catalogue of crimes that included bewitching a child, 'rocking a cradle in the likeness of a cat' and frightening a baker.

Wobbly Bridge or **Wibbly-Wobbly Bridge** A nickname for the London Millennium Footbridge, which crosses the THAMES between ST PAUL'S and TATE MODERN. Its architect, Lord Foster, likened the styling to a 'blade of light'. The structure exhibited unexpectedly strong oscillations when subjected for the first time to heavy usage after it opened in June 2000. The effect was amplified when pedestrians subconsciously (and in some cases deliberately, after the 'wobble' was discovered) responded to the movement by swaying as they walked, a phenomenon known as synchronous lateral excitation. The bridge was closed while £5 million was spent on retro-fitting shock-absorbing dampers. This successfully eliminated the problem but has failed to entirely expunge the nickname.

> The bridge became a tourist hot spot. I can tell you that my mother wanted nothing more that summer than a trip to the Wobbly Bridge. At last London had something to rival the Leaning Tower of Pisa. Then, of course, killjoy engineers closed the thing for a year and reopened it wobble-free.
>
> ALAN COOPER: *Bridges, Law and Power in Medieval England, 700–1400* (2006)

The bridge exhibits an extreme degree of wobbliness in the film *Harry Potter and the Half-Blood Prince* (2009), in which it is attacked by Lord Voldemort's Death Eaters.

Wombles Small, hairy, bear-like creatures that live underground, originally beneath WIMBLE-DON COMMON. Their name is said to have been derived from 'Wombledon', a fanciful variation on 'Wimbledon'. Individually the Wombles are Great Uncle Bulgaria, Orinoco, Wellington, Bungo, Tomsk, Madame Cholet, Miss Adelaide and the eccentric inventor Tobermory. They were the creation of Elisabeth Beresford, and after taking their bow in the children's book *The Wombles* (1968) they went on to be popular in animated form on television. They are dedicated conservationists and make ingenious use of the litter left by humans. The cult of the cuddly creatures was raised to greater heights by a pop group of the same name who dressed the part and took the charts by storm in 1974 with hits such as 'The Wombling Song' and 'Remember You're a Womble'.

> Underground, overground, wombling free,
> The Wombles of Wimbledon Common are we.
> Making good use of the things that we find,
> Things that the everyday folks leave behind.
>
> MIKE BATT: 'The Wombling Song' (1974)

'Wonderful' Radio London *See* BIG L.

wood

Wood Green A strategic shopping centre situated 2 miles (3 km) west of TOTTENHAM. Wood Green was first recorded in 1502 as a clearing on the edge of Tottenham Wood. Until its rapid growth after the arrival of the railway in the mid-19th century it remained an outlying hamlet in Tottenham parish, of much less significance than neighbouring HORNSEY. Wood Green gained municipal independence from Tottenham in 1894 and has had a local government headquarters ever since, now in the form of HARINGEY's civic centre. After the Second World War the retailers on the High Road began to outperform all their nearby rivals and Wood Green became north London's most important shopping destination until the creation of BRENT CROSS. The first true self-service supermarket in Britain, in the food department of Marks & Spencer, opened in Wood Green in 1948. In the mid-1970s the defunct Palace Gates station and many neighbouring buildings were demolished to make way for Wood Green Shopping City, a mall straddling the High Road, which elsewhere is flanked by a very mixed range of outlets. Cinemas and affordable restaurants have since broadened Wood Green's leisure appeal.

Wood Green Cultural Quarter An arts- and media-based regeneration scheme focused on the former factory of Barratts, the confectioners, which moved out in 1980 as part of a general trend for offices and shops to replace manufacturing as the district's principal employers. Several of the projects based here function as production facilities for the creative industry, rather than attractions for the general public, and this has resulted in widespread misunderstanding of the quarter's purpose and derision of its well-signposted and perhaps unduly pretentious name.

Wood Lane A road running northwards from SHEPHERD'S BUSH to the eastern side of WORMWOOD SCRUBS, where it becomes Scrubs Lane. It is best known as the address of BBC Television Centre. Wood Lane station opened in 2008 on the HAMMERSMITH AND CITY LINE, primarily to serve the new WESTFIELD LONDON shopping centre.

Woodford 'The geographical and social high point of east London', according to Simon Jenkins in his *Companion Guide to Outer London*

(1981), situated to the north-east of WALTHAM-STOW, from which it is separated by a sliver of EPPING FOREST. Like CHINGFORD to the west, the district was for centuries a collection of separate hamlets in forest clearings. Even before the Restoration, wealthy Londoners had begun to build grand houses here, and others later rented rooms for the summer. In the mid-18th century these rooms were said to be more expensive than in the capital itself. The coming of the railway brought suburban development, but not of the densely terraced kind so common elsewhere, because the railway company did not offer cheap fares for workmen. The council also conspired to keep out the lower classes by refusing entry to trams. The British Land Company bought the Woodford Hall estate in 1869 and laid out new roads west of the church. A series of similar developments in the grounds of old houses followed over the next 60 years and almost the whole of modern Woodford was built up by the outbreak of the Second World War. More affordable properties were built in South Woodford and east of the railway line.

Woodford Bridge A pleasant residential enclave divided from the rest of Woodford by the M11 motorway and spreading over the ESSEX border into the Epping Forest district. Before the first bridge was built in the 13th century, there was a woodland ford across the River RODING on the road to Abridge. The medieval village that grew up by the river was the first settlement in the area and the origin of the name 'Woodford'.

Woodford Green The west-central part of Woodford, and for centuries its most fashionable hamlet. The wide village green stretches along the eastern side of the High Road for almost a mile (1.6 km) and is claimed to have the oldest village cricket field still in use. A statue of Winston Churchill, the local MP for 40 years, was erected on the green in 1959. Woodford County High School for Girls is based at Highams, a mansion built to the west of the green in 1768, with gardens that were later landscaped by Humphry Repton. *See also the* NAKED BEAUTY.

Woodford Wells The northernmost of the ribbon of hamlets that has coalesced to form the modern district of Woodford. Despite claims for the medicinal properties of its waters, an 18th-century spa was never a commercial success but the name has stuck.

Woolwich A historic naval and military town, now much altered, situated 3 miles (5 km) east of GREENWICH. A community has existed by the river at Woolwich since at least the Iron Age, and the Romans built a fort here. Its Old English name probably means 'trading place for wool', but no evidence has been found of a wool market. The progressive expansion of WOOLWICH DOCKYARD and then WOOLWICH ARSENAL filled almost the entire waterfront, while pottery, glass, bricks and tiles were produced inshore. The run-down and eventual closure of the docks and arsenal brought a period of decline to Woolwich from which it is only now recovering. In 1975 Woolwich acquired the UK's first McDonald's hamburger restaurant, which took the place of a branch of Burton's, the tailors.

Of the suffragan bishops of Woolwich the best known have been John Robinson (1919–83), whose controversial *Honest to God* (1963) galvanized radical theological discussion in the 1960s, and the former England cricket captain David Sheppard (1929–2005).

Woolwich (and Greenwich) 'Spinach' in COCKNEY RHYMING SLANG. The term is not widely used but is noteworthy for indicating Londoners' pronunciation of 'Greenwich'.

Woolwich Arsenal The everyday name of the Royal Arsenal, an armaments factory formerly located on the eastern side of Woolwich. It began life in 1695 as the Royal Laboratory, manufacturing explosives, fuses and shot, and in the early 18th century the main government weapons factory moved here from MOORFIELDS. A burst of activity from 1716 to 1720 saw the construction of a brass foundry, the barracks of the Royal Regiment of Artillery, a new mansion house and the 'great pile' of buildings at Dial Square, which was probably the work of Nicholas Hawksmoor. The Royal Military Academy was founded here in 1741 (*see the* SHOP). In 1805 the Royal Arsenal was officially established and no expense was spared in making this the world's foremost munitions works. Arsenal workers set up a buyers' co-operative in 1868, which became the ROYAL ARSENAL CO-OPERATIVE SOCIETY. In 1886 another group of workers established a FOOTBALL club, known initially as Dial Square, and then Royal Arsenal. On moving to HIGHBURY in 1913 the club shortened its name to ARSENAL. By the early 20th century the Royal Arsenal covered 1,285 acres (520 hectares). Including its testing ranges, the site extended for 3 miles (5 km), and had three separate internal railway systems. At the outbreak of the First World War the Royal Arsenal employed over 70,000 workers. After the Second World War declining demand for armaments prompted diversification into manufacturing for civilian purposes, from railway trucks to automated equipment for the silk-weaving industry. The Royal Ordnance factory closed in 1967, although many of the buildings continued to be used for testing and storage. Much of the new town of THAMESMEAD covers the arsenal's eastern testing ranges. The final military withdrawal came in 1994 and the buildings were taken over by English Partnerships for the development of housing, light industry and leisure facilities. Royal Arsenal West has become Firepower – The Royal Artillery Museum. A new Greenwich Heritage Centre opened at Building 41 in 2003.

Woolwich Arsenal station opened in 1849 on the London to Dartford line. Constructed on the site of a former sandpit, the station has since been rebuilt twice.

Woolwich Common An elongated open space at the southern extremity of Woolwich, and its neighbouring residential area. The common formerly covered a much wider area, extending into CHARLTON, but was gradually encroached upon for the construction of army quarters. At the height of Britain's empire building in the 18th century and the first half of the 19th century, much of the British Army would regularly camp on Woolwich Common until called forward to WOOLWICH ARSENAL to collect stores and ammunition before embarking on ships moored in the THAMES. Between 1776 and 1802 new barracks were built here for the Royal Regiment of Artillery. In 1808 the Royal Military Academy (*see the* SHOP) moved to the east side of the common. Among the magnificent military buildings on the common is the Rotunda, designed by John Nash for an exhibition in ST JAMES'S PARK in 1814 and moved here six years later, when it became the first military museum. The common continued to be used as an artillery firing range until 1860. The ROYAL ARTILLERY BARRACKS remained home to the 16th Regiment Royal Artillery until 2007 and will be used for shooting events in the 2012 OLYMPIC GAMES.

Woolwich Dockyard A royal dockyard founded by Henry VIII in 1512 to build the ship *Henri Grace à Dieu*, popularly known as the *Great Harry*. Subsequent expansion brought a rope yard, ordnance storage and a gun battery to the waterfront, which at that time may have lain as much as 200 feet (60m) south of the present shoreline. Elizabeth I came to Woolwich in 1559 to mark the launch of her ship *Elizabeth Jonas*. During the 17th and 18th centuries the docks were progressively extended westwards. The yard was extended in 1833 and again in the 1840s, when modern docks were built. It closed in 1869, when the site was handed over to the War Department for use as an annexe of WOOLWICH ARSENAL.

Woolwich Dockyard station opened in 1849 on the South Eastern Railway's new line from London Bridge to Dartford, Gravesend and Strood.

Woolwich Ferry A free service operating between WOOLWICH and NORTH WOOLWICH, linking the NORTH CIRCULAR and SOUTH CIRCULAR roads across the THAMES. Although there are records of a ferry in the early 14th century there is no evidence that the service operated after the Middle Ages and the army found it necessary to establish its own ferry to serve WOOLWICH ARSENAL in 1810. A year later an Act of Parliament authorized the establishment of a commercial service that became known as the western ferry, run by the Woolwich Ferry Company. The western ferry operated until 1844, when the company was dissolved after a history of inept management. The free Woolwich Ferry was established in 1889, funded by the METROPOLITAN BOARD OF WORKS and afterwards by the board's successors. Its paddle steamers were replaced by motor ships in 1963.

In the 20th century 'Woolwich Ferry' enjoyed some currency as COCKNEY RHYMING SLANG for 'sherry'.

Woolwich infant A facetious 19th-century slang name for a type of heavy artillery piece.

Woolwich Wanderers A deprecating nickname for ARSENAL FC, questioning the depth of the club's north London roots. The term is used mainly by SPURS supporters.

I'm with the Woolwich *See under* I.

Wooster, Bertie The amiable young MAN ABOUT TOWN who, with his manservant Jeeves, has various comic and amorous adventures in the stories and novels by P.G. Wodehouse (1881–1975), of which he is the narrator. He is a member of the DRONES CLUB and lives in a flat on HALF MOON STREET. He is as dull-witted as Jeeves is clever, and his speech is a goldmine of fashionable pre-First World War slang. His indolent existence is marred chiefly by his fearsome aunts and his well-meaning attempts to assist friends of even lesser intelligence than himself are invariably inept, but Jeeves always saves the day.

Worcester Park One of few districts that blithely straddle the London border as though it were not there, Worcester Park falls partly in the SURREY district of Epsom and Ewell, and merges with OLD MALDEN to its north-west. The suburb takes its name from Worcester House, built by Edward Somerset, 4th Earl of Worcester (1553–1628), who in 1606 was appointed the keeper of NONSUCH Great Park. The house stood on high ground near the southern end of present-day Royal Avenue. The station opened in 1859 on the edge of Malden Green, but high-class suburban development did not begin here until the 1890s.

In 1851 the PRE-RAPHAELITE artists Sir John Millais and William Holman Hunt spent the summer at Worcester Park Farm. It was here that Hunt executed the first version of his famous painting *The Light of the World*, with Millais as the model for Christ. Millais probably painted the landscape background for his celebrated work *Ophelia* (1852), now in TATE BRITAIN, from a meadow beside the Hogsmill River, although the precise spot is still the subject of debate.

World's End The less expensive but still trendy part of CHELSEA, located towards the western end of the KING'S ROAD, where it dog-legs from the SW3 into the SW10 postal district. A 17th-century tavern and tea gardens bestowed their name on the hamlet that stood in this once-remote spot. As central Chelsea grew ever more fashionable in the 19th century, its working population was forced to move west and many settled here, in jerry-built and overcrowded tenements. Larger houses were soon subdivided for multiple occupation. In 1969, despite opposition from preservationists, the council demolished 11 acres (4.5 hectares) of two-storey houses and put up the tower blocks of the World's End estate. The PUNK ROCK phenomenon of the late 1970s can take some credit for the renaissance of this stretch of King's Road. Boutiques at World's End pioneered early punk fashion and their

successors still confer a distinctive personality on the quarter.

Worm, the A nickname for the interlinked stations at BANK and MONUMENT, from the intricacy of the network of pedestrian tunnels.

Wormwood Scrubs An open space with neighbouring institutional facilities, located to the north-east of EAST ACTON. It was first recorded in the 12th century as Wormeholte, an alteration of Old English *wyrmholt*, 'thicket or wood of snakes'. After the trees were felled it became a wasteland, with poor soil that was suitable only for grazing. The scrubs formerly stretched north as far as the HARROW ROAD. In 1801 the PADDINGTON branch of the GRAND JUNCTION CANAL cut off the northern section, which by that time had been mostly enclosed. From the late 1830s railway lines detached other parts of the common, which were later built on except for an area to the east, known as the Little Scrubs. Hammersmith Hospital was built next to WORMWOOD SCRUBS PRISON in 1905 and was later joined on the site by what is now Queen Charlotte's and Chelsea Hospital (*see also* QUEEN CHARLOTTE'S BALL). South of the WESTWAY, HAMMERSMITH council laid out the Wormholt estate in the early 1920s. The West London stadium opened in 1967 at the end of Artillery Lane. It was renamed in 1993 after the most famous member of host club Thames Valley Harriers, Linford Christie. It is also home to the London Blitz American Football Club and the London Nigerian RUFC.

Wormwood Scrubs Prison A very large local prison for adult males, situated on Du Cane Road at the southern edge of WORMWOOD SCRUBS. It was built using convict labour to the designs of penal reformer Sir Edmund du Cane (1830–1903) and opened in stages from 1874, replacing MILLBANK PENITENTIARY. A model institution at the time of its creation, it subsequently gained a reputation for low standards of sanitation and poor prisoner–staff relations, exacerbated by problems of overcrowding.

In October 1966 the British spy and Soviet double-agent George Blake (b.1922) escaped over the wall of Wormwood Scrubs Prison and fled to Moscow. He had served just over five years of a 42-year sentence for passing on secrets to the Russians – the longest jail term ever imposed by a British court.

worst

worst pies in London *See the* DEMON BARBER OF FLEET STREET.

worst street in London Historically, this label has been applied to various London thoroughfares including Flower and Dean Street in SPITALFIELDS, Vincent Street in CANNING TOWN and even Soho's GREEK STREET, which in its way is now one of the best. However, the description has stuck most firmly to Dorset Street in Spitalfields, the scene of the murder of Mary Kelly, the last of JACK THE RIPPER's victims. Jack London may have been the first to describe Dorset Street in such condemnatory terms but the lasting damage was done by the *Daily Mail*, which claimed in a 1901 article headlined 'The Worst Street in London' that the best of its residents were 'down on their luck' while the rest constituted a conclave of violent petty criminals. Furious locals held a packed protest meeting and published a pamphlet refuting the allegations, which repeated the *Mail's* headline on its cover. 'The Worst Street in London' is also the title of a chronicle of Dorset Street, written by Fiona Rule and published in 2008. The now-vanished street lay between White's Row and Brushfield Street.

> Of course, the aristocrats of crime – the forger, the counterfeiter, and the like do not come here. In Dorset Street we find more largely the common thief, the pickpocket ... the man who robs with violence, and the unconvicted murderer. The police have a theory, it seems, that it is better to let these people congregate together in one mass where they can easily be found than to scatter them abroad.
>
> *Daily Mail* (16 July 1901)

wotcher The definitive COCKNEY salutation, especially in the phrase 'wotcher cock!' It is a corruption of the much earlier interrogative greeting, 'what cheer?' One of the first recorded appearances of its modern form was in Albert Chevalier's MUSIC HALL song 'Knocked 'em in the OLD KENT ROAD' (1892). Despite its familiarity in London, the word remains unknown in much of the English-speaking world.

> What does 'wotcher' mean? One of the characters in the new Harry Potter book keeps saying it. I am reading the American translation, but they did not translate that word.
>
> forum post at www.phrases.org.uk (21 July 2003)

Wrekin, The One of the best-known theatrical taverns in COVENT GARDEN, it stood in the middle of Broad Court. An 18th-century proprietor of the rustic-looking establishment named it after the famous hill in his native Shropshire. Charles II and Nell GWYN were earlier said to have trysted at the Wrekin, among a hundred other places. Several CLUBS convened here, for dramatists, critics, actors and others, including the Catamarans, the Rationals and Douglas Jerrold's the Mulberries. When Edmund Kean collapsed while playing Othello at the Covent Garden Theatre on 25 March 1833 he was taken to the Wrekin to recover, but died two months later. The Wrekin was demolished in 1871.

Wren's Lantern St James GARLICKHYTHE, a church rebuilt by Christopher Wren in 1676–82. The tower was completed in 1717. Its nickname derived from the powerful illumination of its interior by natural light admitted through its many high windows, though their number was later reduced.

X Division Originally a temporary METRO-POLITAN POLICE division set up to patrol the International Exhibition of 1862 in SOUTH KENSINGTON. With the continuing expansion of policing in London a regular X Division was formed in 1865, headquartered at PADDINGTON and with a remit extending as far west as UXBRIDGE. (Y Division was created at the same time, based at HIGHGATE.) PADDINGTON POLLAKY joined X Division as a special constable in 1867. Letter codes I, O and U were never used and the alphabetical designation of territories culminated in the creation of Z Division for CROYDON in 1921, and has since been replaced by a system of borough-based command units. The symbolic value of the letter X prompted some writers to call upon the division – especially before the real thing existed – as a generic embodiment of the police on the streets.

> … if Demosthenes or Cicero, disguised as
> Chartist orators, mounting a tub at Deptford,
> were to Philippicize, or entertain this motley
> auditory with speeches against Catiline or
> Verres, straightway the Superintendent of the X
> division, with a *posse* of constables at his heels,
> dismounts the patriot orator from his tub, and
> hands him over to a plain-spoken businesslike
> justice of the peace, who regards an itinerant
> Cicero in the same unsympathizing point of
> view with any other vagabond.
> *Blackwood's Edinburgh Magazine*, 'The World of
> London' (March 1843)

X-Files *See* CHALFONTS.

X's Hall A 19th-century slang corruption of Hicks' Hall, the formal name of the sessions house (chief courthouse) of the county of MIDDLESEX from 1612 to 1782, and the informal name of its successor. The original hall was built by Sir Baptist Hicks, 1st Viscount Campden (1551–1629), near the southern end of St John Street, in SMITHFIELD. Its location was considered the starting point of the GREAT NORTH ROAD and all the distances shown on that road's milestones were measured from Hicks' Hall. It was superseded by what is now called the Old Sessions House, which stands on the west side of CLERKENWELL Green. Once the busiest court in England it closed in 1920.

yapp A type of limp binding in which the cover overlaps the edges of the book. William Yapp was a 19th-century bookseller whose shop was located on Old Cavendish Street, off OXFORD STREET. Something of a religious zealot, he carried a bible in his pocket at all times and became dissatisfied with how quickly it got tatty. Around 1860 he devised the extended flaps, originally made of leather, to overcome the problem.

Yard, the *See* SCOTLAND YARD.

Yeading A fast-growing residential district situated north-east of HAYES², from which it is separated by the Yeading Brook. In 757 Aethelbald, King of Mercia, made a grant of land that mentioned Geddinges, 'the settlement of Geddi's people'. A temporary smallpox hospital was built at this isolated spot in 1903 and the village had only 20 dwellings in 1938. After the Second World War housing estates, first municipal and then private, spread across to the GRAND UNION CANAL. Housebuilding continued into the 21st century wherever space permitted. Sikhs constitute the largest religious minority and Springfield Road has the country's first state-funded Sikh primary and secondary schools, the Guru Nanak.

Yellow Badge The badge issued to BLACK CAB drivers who have passed the Suburban London KNOWLEDGE examination. Unlike holders of the GREEN BADGE, Yellow Badge drivers are licensed to ply for hire only in the specific part of OUTER LONDON for which they are qualified.

Yid or **Yiddo** In most contexts this is a derogatory term for a Jew. However, to many supporters of TOTTENHAM HOTSPUR FC it is a badge of honour. It derives from the club's traditional popularity among north London's Jewish community. Although originally used disparagingly by some supporters of opposing teams, the term was taken up from the 1960s or 70s by home fans, who nowadays – whether Jewish or not – often refer to themselves as the 'Yid army'. The club has voiced concern about the phenomenon but, as one Jewish supporter has argued on a fans' message board: 'The more the word "Yid" is used in the context of the mighty Spurs then the less power it has as an insult.'

Yidsbury A mid-20th-century nickname for the FINSBURY PARK area, on account of its significant Jewish population. Not only was the term potentially offensive (although it may have been coined self-mockingly by Jews themselves) but it reinforced the misconception that FINSBURY and Finsbury Park are one and the same place. The latter locality is nowadays highly multicultural, and is more likely to be associated with Algiers than Jerusalem.

Yiewsley The northern half of the 'composite suburb' of Yiewsley and WEST DRAYTON. It was first recorded in 1235 as Wiuesleg, probably 'the woodland clearing of a man name Wifel'. Yiewsley's earliest links were with UXBRIDGE but by the 1910s these had been lost as the fusion with West Drayton took hold. After the formation of Yiewsley and West Drayton Urban District in 1930 much of the Victorian housing was cleared to make way for municipal estates. Yiewsley is the more commercial half of the district and a high-tech business park has been laid out to the east, at Stockley Park.

The rock guitarist Ronnie Wood (b.1947) grew up in a council house in Yiewsley and formed the Birds here in 1964. He went on to play with the Jeff Beck Group, the Faces and the ROLLING STONES.

yoof An informal term for young people, derived from the stereotypical COCKNEY pronunciation of the word 'youth'. It is frequently employed with derogatory intent, often in mockery of broadcasters, publishers or advertisers targeting a teenage audience. The concept of 'yoof culture' was originally associated in particular with the allegedly MOCKNEY speech of the FULHAM-bred television producer and presenter Janet Street-Porter (b.1946), who was the BBC's commissioning editor for youth television from 1988 to 1994.

> Unbowed, the Beeb's middle-aged 'yoof' telly executives are keen to commission a second series.
>
> KEVIN O'SULLIVAN, in the *Sunday Mirror* (5 April 2009)

York Column *See the* DUKE OF YORK'S COLUMN.

you

you and me 'Tea' in COCKNEY RHYMING SLANG. The term was once quite widely used but 'ROSIE LEE' is nowadays almost always preferred.

> Will you step up the apples and pears and have a cup of you and me? Freddy was a great boy for rhyming slang and taught me a lot ...
>
> STEVIE SMITH: *Novel on Yellow Paper* (1936)

you couldn't run a whelk stall A traditional COCKNEY insult suggesting stupidity or inexperience or both; a whelk stall was the most basic of London's retail institutions in the 19th and early 20th centuries.

> 'Some people develop ambition only when they realise that nothing seems to be getting in their way,' says one senior Tory who knows Johnson well. 'Despite all the evidence that he couldn't run a whelk stall, Boris is now in charge of the best city in the world.'
>
> *The Observer* (24 August 2008)

you couldn't throw your hat over the workhouse wall A COCKNEY catchphrase of the early 20th century, implying that the addressee had fathered several illegitimate children whom he had then abandoned. The suggestion was that one of these offspring might recognize him if he went to retrieve his hat.

you could ride bare-arsed to Romford on it! Said in the 18th century of a blunt blade.

Outside the capital, London itself was the destination employed.

you must go into the country to hear what news at London This 17th-century proverb was not intended to cast particular aspersions on Londoners' awareness of events in their own city, but rather to suggest that one may often apprehend the most accurate news of home when one goes abroad.

you must go to Battersea to get your simples cut *See under* GO.

you must know Mrs Kelly? A COCKNEY catchphrase popularized by the FUNNIEST MAN ON EARTH, Dan Leno. It was employed to various ends, or none, but particularly in order to cut short a long-winded speaker.

> I then addressed myself to him with the well-known query, 'Do you know Mrs Kelly? Oh, my word, you must know Mrs Kelly!' Dan [Leno] in a very serious tone replied, 'No!' ... Suddenly he slipped out of the box, and very soon returned with half a dozen boxes of chocolate, with which he pelted me as a present from Mrs. Kelly.'
>
> BRANSBY WILLIAMS: *An Actor's Story* (1909)

you're only supposed to blow the bloody doors off Probably the most famous COCKNEY-accented movie line of all time. It was written by Troy Kennedy-Martin (1932–2009) and delivered by Michael Caine (*see* NOT A LOT OF PEOPLE KNOW THAT), playing Charlie Croker in *The Italian Job* (1969), when his explosives 'expert' destroys an entire truck during a trial run of their planned heist.

Young Vic A theatre specializing in experimental works, often produced by a young team and aimed at young audiences. It opened in 1970 in a temporary structure on The Cut, a street near the OLD VIC, of which it was an offshoot. The theatre was rebuilt in 2004–6.

yours and ours 'Flowers' in COCKNEY RHYMING SLANG. The term was never in widespread general use but was once common among COVENT GARDEN market porters.

Z

Zazel The stage name of the 'exotic and beautiful' acrobat Rosa Matilda Richter, the London-born daughter of a circus and dramatic agent. A contender for the title 'the world's first human cannonball', she was propelled high into the air at the Royal Aquarium (*see the* AQ) on 2 April 1877, shortly before her 15th birthday, and in numerous repeat performances. In 1880 she began touring America with P.T. Barnum's circus and was advertised as 'the original Zazel' after imitators began using her name. Zazel retired in 1891 following a high-wire fall; she later made a minor comeback.

zhoosh A POLARI term meaning to fix, style, arrange or tidy, especially used in matters relating to one's appearance.

Zoological Society of London *See* LONDON ZOO.

Zorba (the Greek) 'Leak' (the act of urination) in COCKNEY RHYMING SLANG. The term acquired brief popularity following the release of the 1964 film of that name.

Zoroastrian Centre A former cinema on RAYNERS LANE, now London's principal place of worship for Zoroastrians. Designed in art deco style by Frederick E. Bromige, it opened as the Grosvenor in 1936.